P9-CDM-321

Calculus Volume 3

SENIOR CONTRIBUTING AUTHORS

EDWIN "JED" HERMAN, UNIVERSITY OF WISCONSIN-STEVENS POINT

GILBERT STRANG, MASSACHUSETTS INSTITUTE OF TECHNOLOGY

ISBN: 978-1-938168-07-9

OpenStax
Rice University
6100 Main Street MS-375
Houston, Texas 77005

To learn more about OpenStax, visit https://openstax.org.
Individual print copies and bulk orders can be purchased through our website.

HARDCOVER BOOK ISBN-13	**978-1-938168-07-9**
PAPERBACK BOOK ISBN-13	**978-1-947172-83-8**
B&W PAPERBACK BOOK ISBN-13	**978-1-50669-805-2**
DIGITAL VERSION ISBN-13	**978-1-947172-16-6**
Revision Number	**C3-2016-003(03/18)-MJ**
Original Publication Year	**2016**

Printed by
XanEdu
4750 Venture Drive, Suite 400
Ann Arbor, MI 48108
800-562-2147
www.xanedu.com

OpenStax

OpenStax provides free, peer-reviewed, openly licensed textbooks for introductory college and Advanced Placement® courses and low-cost, personalized courseware that helps students learn. A nonprofit ed tech initiative based at Rice University, we're committed to helping students access the tools they need to complete their courses and meet their educational goals.

Rice University

OpenStax, OpenStax CNX, and OpenStax Tutor are initiatives of Rice University. As a leading research university with a distinctive commitment to undergraduate education, Rice University aspires to path-breaking research, unsurpassed teaching, and contributions to the betterment of our world. It seeks to fulfill this mission by cultivating a diverse community of learning and discovery that produces leaders across the spectrum of human endeavor.

Foundation Support

OpenStax is grateful for the tremendous support of our sponsors. Without their strong engagement, the goal of free access to high-quality textbooks would remain just a dream.

Laura and John Arnold Foundation (LJAF) actively seeks opportunities to invest in organizations and thought leaders that have a sincere interest in implementing fundamental changes that not only yield immediate gains, but also repair broken systems for future generations. LJAF currently focuses its strategic investments on education, criminal justice, research integrity, and public accountability.

The William and Flora Hewlett Foundation has been making grants since 1967 to help solve social and environmental problems at home and around the world. The Foundation concentrates its resources on activities in education, the environment, global development and population, performing arts, and philanthropy, and makes grants to support disadvantaged communities in the San Francisco Bay Area.

Calvin K. Kazanjian was the founder and president of Peter Paul (Almond Joy), Inc. He firmly believed that the more people understood about basic economics the happier and more prosperous they would be. Accordingly, he established the Calvin K. Kazanjian Economics Foundation Inc, in 1949 as a philanthropic, nonpolitical educational organization to support efforts that enhanced economic understanding.

Guided by the belief that every life has equal value, the Bill & Melinda Gates Foundation works to help all people lead healthy, productive lives. In developing countries, it focuses on improving people's health with vaccines and other life-saving tools and giving them the chance to lift themselves out of hunger and extreme poverty. In the United States, it seeks to significantly improve education so that all young people have the opportunity to reach their full potential. Based in Seattle, Washington, the foundation is led by CEO Jeff Raikes and Co-chair William H. Gates Sr., under the direction of Bill and Melinda Gates and Warren Buffett.

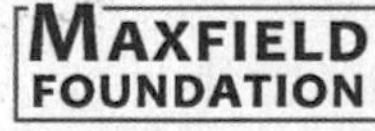

The Maxfield Foundation supports projects with potential for high impact in science, education, sustainability, and other areas of social importance.

Our mission at The Michelson 20MM Foundation is to grow access and success by eliminating unnecessary hurdles to affordability. We support the creation, sharing, and proliferation of more effective, more affordable educational content by leveraging disruptive technologies, open educational resources, and new models for collaboration between for-profit, nonprofit, and public entities.

The Bill and Stephanie Sick Fund supports innovative projects in the areas of Education, Art, Science and Engineering.

Table of Contents

PREFACE

Welcome to *Calculus Volume 3*, an OpenStax resource. This textbook was written to increase student access to high-quality learning materials, maintaining highest standards of academic rigor at little to no cost.

About OpenStax

OpenStax is a nonprofit based at Rice University, and it's our mission to improve student access to education. Our first openly licensed college textbook was published in 2012, and our library has since scaled to over 25 books for college and AP® courses used by hundreds of thousands of students. OpenStax Tutor, our low-cost personalized learning tool, is being used in college courses throughout the country. Through our partnerships with philanthropic foundations and our alliance with other educational resource organizations, OpenStax is breaking down the most common barriers to learning and empowering students and instructors to succeed.

About OpenStax's resources

Customization

Calculus Volume 3 is licensed under a Creative Commons Attribution 4.0 International (CC BY) license, which means that you can distribute, remix, and build upon the content, as long as you provide attribution to OpenStax and its content contributors.

Because our books are openly licensed, you are free to use the entire book or pick and choose the sections that are most relevant to the needs of your course. Feel free to remix the content by assigning your students certain chapters and sections in your syllabus, in the order that you prefer. You can even provide a direct link in your syllabus to the sections in the web view of your book.

Instructors also have the option of creating a customized version of their OpenStax book. The custom version can be made available to students in low-cost print or digital form through their campus bookstore. Visit your book page on OpenStax.org for more information.

Errata

All OpenStax textbooks undergo a rigorous review process. However, like any professional-grade textbook, errors sometimes occur. Since our books are web based, we can make updates periodically when deemed pedagogically necessary. If you have a correction to suggest, submit it through the link on your book page on OpenStax.org. Subject matter experts review all errata suggestions. OpenStax is committed to remaining transparent about all updates, so you will also find a list of past errata changes on your book page on OpenStax.org.

Format

You can access this textbook for free in web view or PDF through OpenStax.org, and for a low cost in print.

About *Calculus Volume 3*

Calculus is designed for the typical two- or three-semester general calculus course, incorporating innovative features to enhance student learning. The book guides students through the core concepts of calculus and helps them understand how those concepts apply to their lives and the world around them. Due to the comprehensive nature of the material, we are offering the book in three volumes for flexibility and efficiency. Volume 3 covers parametric equations and polar coordinates, vectors, functions of several variables, multiple integration, and second-order differential equations.

Coverage and scope

Our *Calculus Volume 3* textbook adheres to the scope and sequence of most general calculus courses nationwide. We have worked to make calculus interesting and accessible to students while maintaining the mathematical rigor inherent in the subject. With this objective in mind, the content of the three volumes of *Calculus* have been developed and arranged to provide a logical progression from fundamental to more advanced concepts, building upon what students have already learned and emphasizing connections between topics and between theory and applications. The goal of each section is to enable students not just to recognize concepts, but work with them in ways that will be useful in later courses and future careers. The organization and pedagogical features were developed and vetted with feedback from mathematics educators dedicated to the project.

Volume 1

Chapter 1: Functions and Graphs

Chapter 2: Limits

Chapter 3: Derivatives

Chapter 4: Applications of Derivatives

Chapter 5: Integration

Chapter 6: Applications of Integration

Volume 2

Chapter 1: Integration

Chapter 2: Applications of Integration

Chapter 3: Techniques of Integration

Chapter 4: Introduction to Differential Equations

Chapter 5: Sequences and Series

Chapter 6: Power Series

Chapter 7: Parametric Equations and Polar Coordinates

Volume 3

Chapter 1: Parametric Equations and Polar Coordinates

Chapter 2: Vectors in Space

Chapter 3: Vector-Valued Functions

Chapter 4: Differentiation of Functions of Several Variables

Chapter 5: Multiple Integration

Chapter 6: Vector Calculus

Chapter 7: Second-Order Differential Equations

Pedagogical foundation

Throughout *Calculus Volume 3* you will find examples and exercises that present classical ideas and techniques as well as modern applications and methods. Derivations and explanations are based on years of classroom experience on the part of long-time calculus professors, striving for a balance of clarity and rigor that has proven successful with their students. Motivational applications cover important topics in probability, biology, ecology, business, and economics, as well as areas of physics, chemistry, engineering, and computer science. **Student Projects** in each chapter give students opportunities to explore interesting sidelights in pure and applied mathematics, from navigating a banked turn to adapting a moon landing vehicle for a new mission to Mars. **Chapter Opening Applications** pose problems that are solved later in the chapter, using the ideas covered in that chapter. Problems include the average distance of Halley's Comment from the Sun, and the vector field of a hurricane. **Definitions, Rules,** and **Theorems** are highlighted throughout the text, including over 60 **Proofs** of theorems.

Assessments that reinforce key concepts

In-chapter **Examples** walk students through problems by posing a question, stepping out a solution, and then asking students to practice the skill with a “Checkpoint” question. The book also includes assessments at the end of each chapter so students can apply what they’ve learned through practice problems. Many exercises are marked with a **[T]** to indicate they are suitable for solution by technology, including calculators or Computer Algebra Systems (CAS). Answers for selected exercises are available in the **Answer Key** at the back of the book. The book also includes assessments at the end of each chapter so students can apply what they’ve learned through practice problems.

Early or late transcendentals

The three volumes of *Calculus* are designed to accommodate both Early and Late Transcendental approaches to calculus. Exponential and logarithmic functions are introduced informally in Chapter 1 of Volume 1 and presented in more rigorous terms in Chapter 6 in Volume 1 and Chapter 2 in Volume 2. Differentiation and integration of these functions is covered in Chapters 3–5 in Volume 1 and Chapter 1 in Volume 2 for instructors who want to include them with other types of functions. These discussions, however, are in separate sections that can be skipped for instructors who prefer to wait until the integral definitions are given before teaching the calculus derivations of exponentials and logarithms.

Comprehensive art program

Our art program is designed to enhance students' understanding of concepts through clear and effective illustrations, diagrams, and photographs.

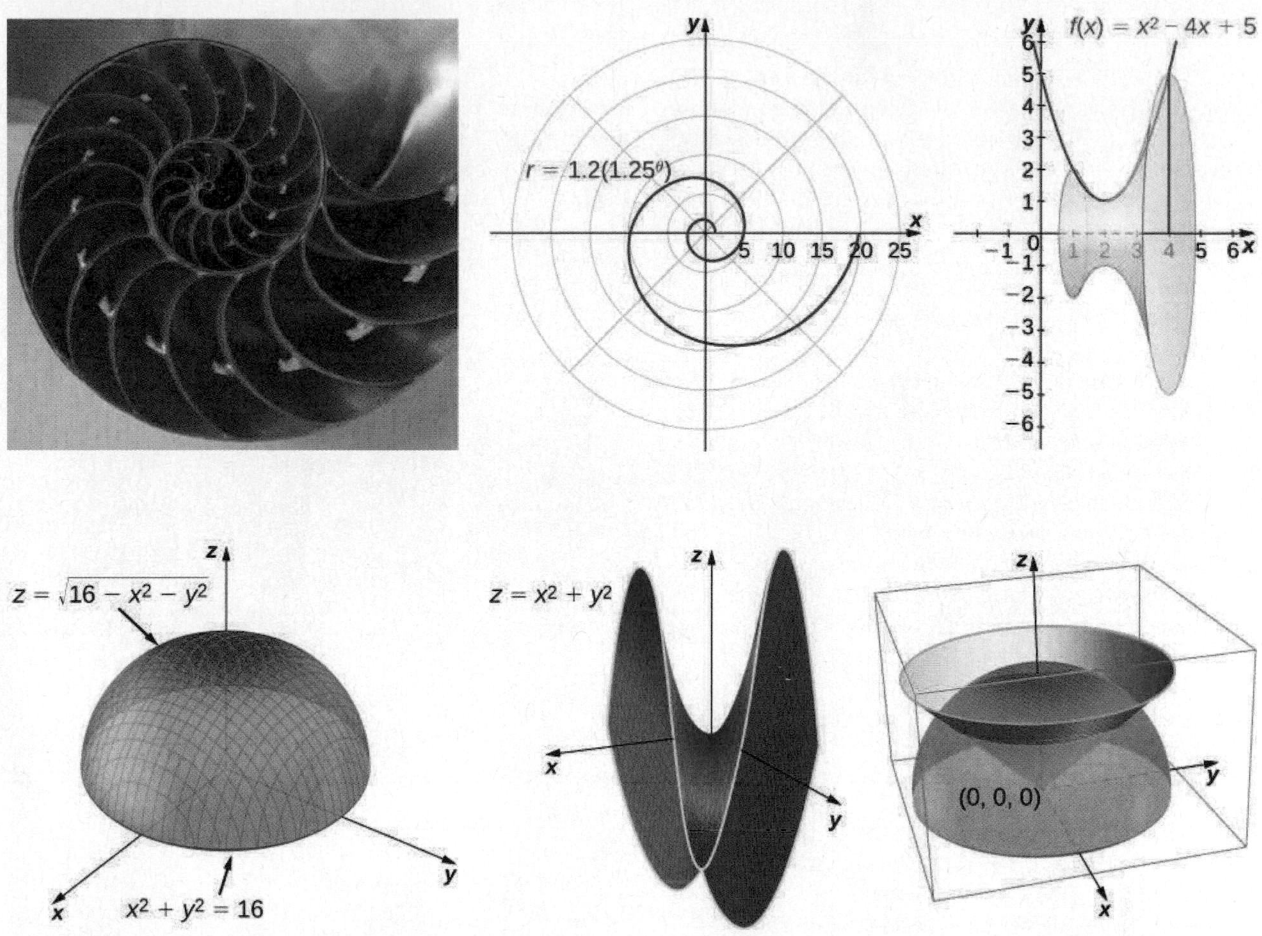

Additional resources

Student and instructor resources

We've compiled additional resources for both students and instructors, including Getting Started Guides, an instructor solution manual, and PowerPoint slides. Instructor resources require a verified instructor account, which you can apply for when you log in or create your account on OpenStax.org. Take advantage of these resources to supplement your OpenStax book.

Community Hubs

OpenStax partners with the Institute for the Study of Knowledge Management in Education (ISKME) to offer Community Hubs on OER Commons – a platform for instructors to share community-created resources that support OpenStax books, free of charge. Through our Community Hubs, instructors can upload their own materials or download resources to use in their own courses, including additional ancillaries, teaching material, multimedia, and relevant course content. We encourage instructors to join the hubs for the subjects most relevant to your teaching and research as an opportunity both to enrich your courses and to engage with other faculty.

To reach the Community Hubs, visit **www.oercommons.org/hubs/OpenStax**.

Partner resources

OpenStax Partners are our allies in the mission to make high-quality learning materials affordable and accessible to students and instructors everywhere. Their tools integrate seamlessly with our OpenStax titles at a low cost. To access the partner resources for your text, visit your book page on OpenStax.org.

About the authors

Senior contributing authors

Gilbert Strang, Massachusetts Institute of Technology
Dr. Strang received his PhD from UCLA in 1959 and has been teaching mathematics at MIT ever since. His Calculus online textbook is one of eleven that he has published and is the basis from which our final product has been derived and updated for today's student. Strang is a decorated mathematician and past Rhodes Scholar at Oxford University.

Edwin "Jed" Herman, University of Wisconsin-Stevens Point
Dr. Herman earned a BS in Mathematics from Harvey Mudd College in 1985, an MA in Mathematics from UCLA in 1987, and a PhD in Mathematics from the University of Oregon in 1997. He is currently a Professor at the University of Wisconsin-Stevens Point. He has more than 20 years of experience teaching college mathematics, is a student research mentor, is experienced in course development/design, and is also an avid board game designer and player.

Contributing authors

Catherine Abbott, Keuka College
Nicoleta Virginia Bila, Fayetteville State University
Sheri J. Boyd, Rollins College
Joyati Debnath, Winona State University
Valeree Falduto, Palm Beach State College
Joseph Lakey, New Mexico State University
Julie Levandosky, Framingham State University
David McCune, William Jewell College
Michelle Merriweather, Bronxville High School
Kirsten R. Messer, Colorado State University - Pueblo
Alfred K. Mulzet, Florida State College at Jacksonville
William Radulovich (retired), Florida State College at Jacksonville
Erica M. Rutter, Arizona State University
David Smith, University of the Virgin Islands
Elaine A. Terry, Saint Joseph's University
David Torain, Hampton University

Reviewers

Marwan A. Abu-Sawwa, Florida State College at Jacksonville
Kenneth J. Bernard, Virginia State University
John Beyers, University of Maryland
Charles Buehrle, Franklin & Marshall College
Matthew Cathey, Wofford College
Michael Cohen, Hofstra University
William DeSalazar, Broward County School System
Murray Eisenberg, University of Massachusetts Amherst
Kristyanna Erickson, Cecil College
Tiernan Fogarty, Oregon Institute of Technology
David French, Tidewater Community College
Marilyn Gloyer, Virginia Commonwealth University
Shawna Haider, Salt Lake Community College
Lance Hemlow, Raritan Valley Community College
Jerry Jared, The Blue Ridge School
Peter Jipsen, Chapman University
David Johnson, Lehigh University
M.R. Khadivi, Jackson State University
Robert J. Krueger, Concordia University
Tor A. Kwembe, Jackson State University
Jean-Marie Magnier, Springfield Technical Community College
Cheryl Chute Miller, SUNY Potsdam
Bagisa Mukherjee, Penn State University, Worthington Scranton Campus
Kasso Okoudjou, University of Maryland College Park
Peter Olszewski, Penn State Erie, The Behrend College
Steven Purtee, Valencia College
Alice Ramos, Bethel College

Doug Shaw, University of Northern Iowa
Hussain Elalaoui-Talibi, Tuskegee University
Jeffrey Taub, Maine Maritime Academy
William Thistleton, SUNY Polytechnic Institute
A. David Trubatch, Montclair State University
Carmen Wright, Jackson State University
Zhenbu Zhang, Jackson State University

1 | PARAMETRIC EQUATIONS AND POLAR COORDINATES

Figure 1.1 The chambered nautilus is a marine animal that lives in the tropical Pacific Ocean. Scientists think they have existed mostly unchanged for about 500 million years.(credit: modification of work by Jitze Couperus, Flickr)

Chapter Outline

Introduction

The chambered nautilus is a fascinating creature. This animal feeds on hermit crabs, fish, and other crustaceans. It has a hard outer shell with many chambers connected in a spiral fashion, and it can retract into its shell to avoid predators. When part of the shell is cut away, a perfect spiral is revealed, with chambers inside that are somewhat similar to growth rings in a tree.

The mathematical function that describes a spiral can be expressed using rectangular (or Cartesian) coordinates. However, if we change our coordinate system to something that works a bit better with circular patterns, the function becomes much simpler to describe. The polar coordinate system is well suited for describing curves of this type. How can we use this coordinate system to describe spirals and other radial figures? (See **Example 1.14**.)

In this chapter we also study parametric equations, which give us a convenient way to describe curves, or to study the position of a particle or object in two dimensions as a function of time. We will use parametric equations and polar coordinates for describing many topics later in this text.

1.1 | Parametric Equations

Learning Objectives

1.1.1 Plot a curve described by parametric equations.
1.1.2 Convert the parametric equations of a curve into the form $y = f(x)$.
1.1.3 Recognize the parametric equations of basic curves, such as a line and a circle.
1.1.4 Recognize the parametric equations of a cycloid.

In this section we examine parametric equations and their graphs. In the two-dimensional coordinate system, parametric equations are useful for describing curves that are not necessarily functions. The parameter is an independent variable that both x and y depend on, and as the parameter increases, the values of x and y trace out a path along a plane curve. For example, if the parameter is t (a common choice), then t might represent time. Then x and y are defined as functions of time, and $(x(t),\ y(t))$ can describe the position in the plane of a given object as it moves along a curved path.

Parametric Equations and Their Graphs

Consider the orbit of Earth around the Sun. Our year lasts approximately 365.25 days, but for this discussion we will use 365 days. On January 1 of each year, the physical location of Earth with respect to the Sun is nearly the same, except for leap years, when the lag introduced by the extra $\frac{1}{4}$ day of orbiting time is built into the calendar. We call January 1 “day 1” of the year. Then, for example, day 31 is January 31, day 59 is February 28, and so on.

The number of the day in a year can be considered a variable that determines Earth’s position in its orbit. As Earth revolves around the Sun, its physical location changes relative to the Sun. After one full year, we are back where we started, and a new year begins. According to Kepler’s laws of planetary motion, the shape of the orbit is elliptical, with the Sun at one focus of the ellipse. We study this idea in more detail in **Conic Sections**.

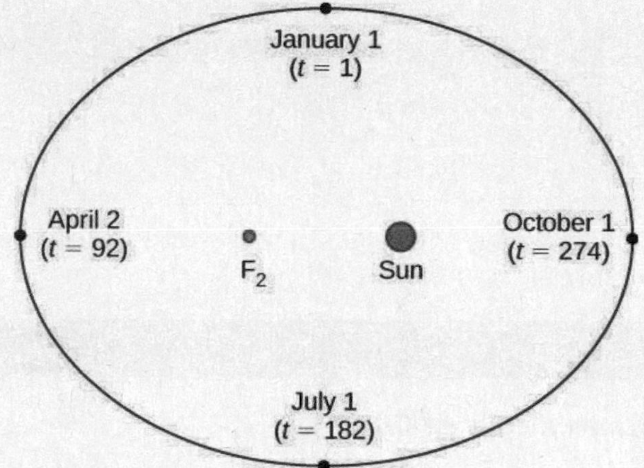

Figure 1.2 Earth's orbit around the Sun in one year.

Figure 1.2 depicts Earth's orbit around the Sun during one year. The point labeled F_2 is one of the foci of the ellipse; the other focus is occupied by the Sun. If we superimpose coordinate axes over this graph, then we can assign ordered pairs to each point on the ellipse (**Figure 1.3**). Then each x value on the graph is a value of position as a function of time, and each y value is also a value of position as a function of time. Therefore, each point on the graph corresponds to a value of Earth's position as a function of time.

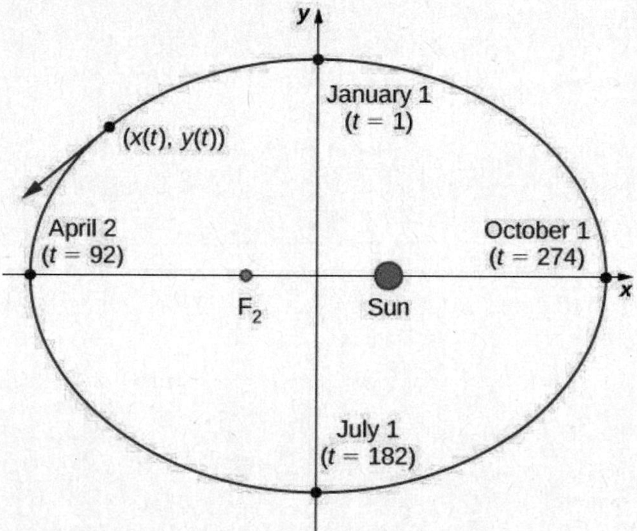

Figure 1.3 Coordinate axes superimposed on the orbit of Earth.

We can determine the functions for $x(t)$ and $y(t)$, thereby parameterizing the orbit of Earth around the Sun. The variable t is called an independent parameter and, in this context, represents time relative to the beginning of each year.

A curve in the (x, y) plane can be represented parametrically. The equations that are used to define the curve are called **parametric equations**.

Definition

If x and y are continuous functions of t on an interval I, then the equations

$$x = x(t) \text{ and } y = y(t)$$

are called parametric equations and t is called the **parameter**. The set of points (x, y) obtained as t varies over the interval I is called the graph of the parametric equations. The graph of parametric equations is called a **parametric curve** or *plane curve*, and is denoted by C.

Notice in this definition that x and y are used in two ways. The first is as functions of the independent variable t. As t varies over the interval I, the functions $x(t)$ and $y(t)$ generate a set of ordered pairs (x, y). This set of ordered pairs generates the graph of the parametric equations. In this second usage, to designate the ordered pairs, x and y are variables. It is important to distinguish the variables x and y from the functions $x(t)$ and $y(t)$.

Example 1.1

Graphing a Parametrically Defined Curve

Sketch the curves described by the following parametric equations:

a. $x(t) = t - 1, \quad y(t) = 2t + 4, \quad -3 \leq t \leq 2$

b. $x(t) = t^2 - 3, \quad y(t) = 2t + 1, \quad -2 \leq t \leq 3$

c. $x(t) = 4 \cos t, \quad y(t) = 4 \sin t, \quad 0 \leq t \leq 2\pi$

Solution

a. To create a graph of this curve, first set up a table of values. Since the independent variable in both $x(t)$ and $y(t)$ is t, let t appear in the first column. Then $x(t)$ and $y(t)$ will appear in the second and third columns of the table.

t	$x(t)$	$y(t)$
−3	−4	−2
−2	−3	0
−1	−2	2
0	−1	4
1	0	6
2	1	8

The second and third columns in this table provide a set of points to be plotted. The graph of these points appears in **Figure 1.4**. The arrows on the graph indicate the **orientation** of the graph, that is, the direction that a point moves on the graph as t varies from −3 to 2.

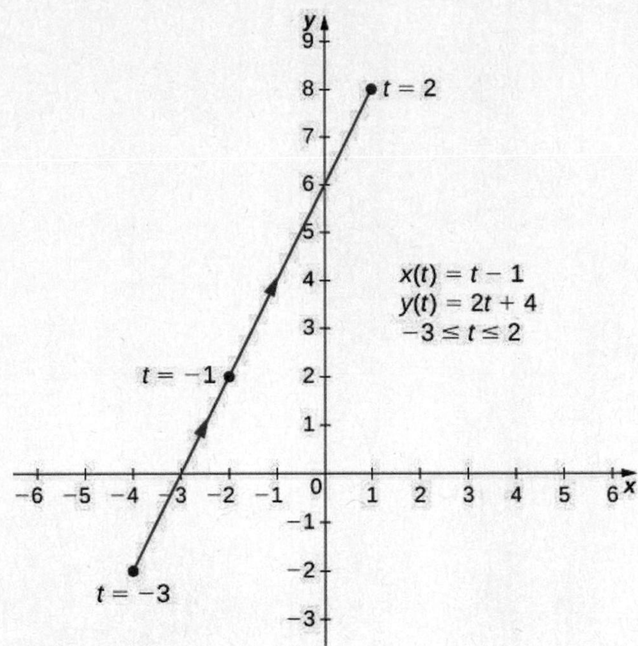

Figure 1.4 Graph of the plane curve described by the parametric equations in part a.

b. To create a graph of this curve, again set up a table of values.

t	$x(t)$	$y(t)$
−2	1	−3
−1	−2	−1
0	−3	1
1	−2	3
2	1	5
3	6	7

The second and third columns in this table give a set of points to be plotted (**Figure 1.5**). The first point on the graph (corresponding to $t = -2$) has coordinates $(1, -3)$, and the last point (corresponding to $t = 3$) has coordinates $(6, 7)$. As t progresses from −2 to 3, the point on the curve travels along a parabola. The direction the point moves is again called the orientation and is indicated on the graph.

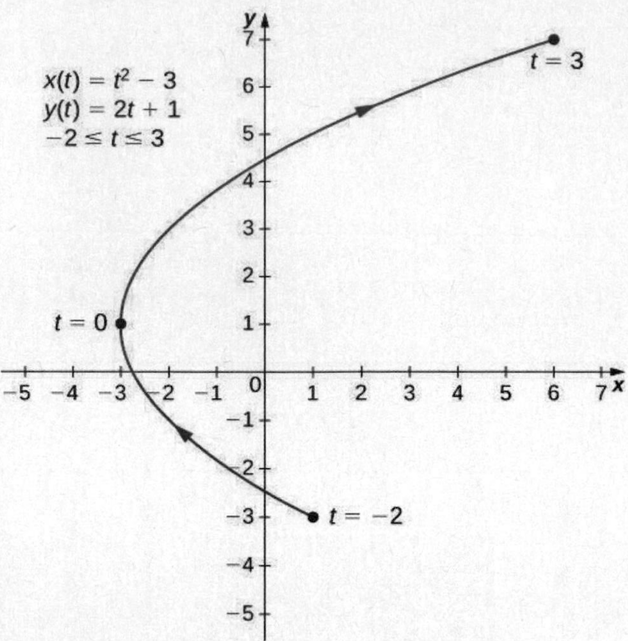

Figure 1.5 Graph of the plane curve described by the parametric equations in part b.

c. In this case, use multiples of $\pi/6$ for t and create another table of values:

t	$x(t)$	$y(t)$	t	$x(t)$	$y(t)$
0	4	0	$\frac{7\pi}{6}$	$-2\sqrt{3} \approx -3.5$	2
$\frac{\pi}{6}$	$2\sqrt{3} \approx 3.5$	2	$\frac{4\pi}{3}$	−2	$-2\sqrt{3} \approx -3.5$
$\frac{\pi}{3}$	2	$2\sqrt{3} \approx 3.5$	$\frac{3\pi}{2}$	0	−4
$\frac{\pi}{2}$	0	4	$\frac{5\pi}{3}$	2	$-2\sqrt{3} \approx -3.5$
$\frac{2\pi}{3}$	−2	$2\sqrt{3} \approx 3.5$	$\frac{11\pi}{6}$	$2\sqrt{3} \approx 3.5$	2
$\frac{5\pi}{6}$	$-2\sqrt{3} \approx -3.5$	2	2π	4	0
π	−4	0			

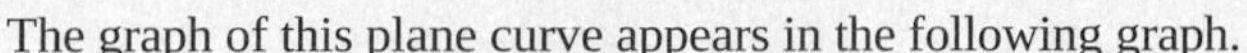

The graph of this plane curve appears in the following graph.

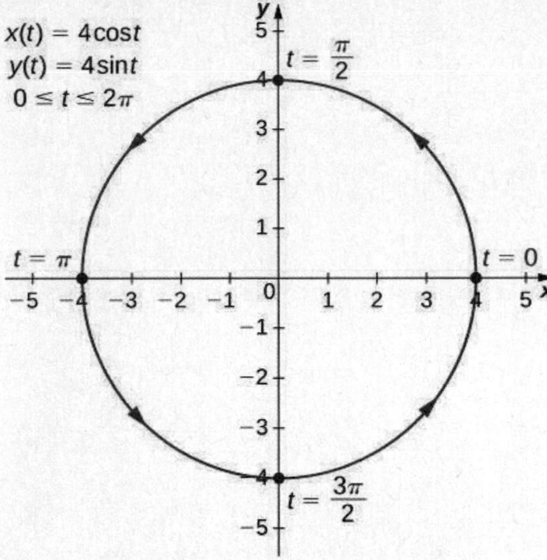

Figure 1.6 Graph of the plane curve described by the parametric equations in part c.

This is the graph of a circle with radius 4 centered at the origin, with a counterclockwise orientation. The starting point and ending points of the curve both have coordinates $(4, 0)$.

1.1 Sketch the curve described by the parametric equations

$$x(t) = 3t + 2, \quad y(t) = t^2 - 1, \quad -3 \le t \le 2.$$

Eliminating the Parameter

To better understand the graph of a curve represented parametrically, it is useful to rewrite the two equations as a single equation relating the variables x and y. Then we can apply any previous knowledge of equations of curves in the plane to identify the curve. For example, the equations describing the plane curve in **Example 1.1**b. are

$$x(t) = t^2 - 3, \quad y(t) = 2t + 1, \quad -2 \le t \le 3.$$

Solving the second equation for t gives

$$t = \frac{y - 1}{2}.$$

This can be substituted into the first equation:

$$x = \left(\frac{y - 1}{2}\right)^2 - 3 = \frac{y^2 - 2y + 1}{4} - 3 = \frac{y^2 - 2y - 11}{4}.$$

This equation describes x as a function of y. These steps give an example of *eliminating the parameter*. The graph of this function is a parabola opening to the right. Recall that the plane curve started at $(1, -3)$ and ended at $(6, 7)$. These terminations were due to the restriction on the parameter t.

Example 1.2

Eliminating the Parameter

Eliminate the parameter for each of the plane curves described by the following parametric equations and describe the resulting graph.

a. $x(t) = \sqrt{2t+4}, \quad y(t) = 2t + 1, \quad -2 \le t \le 6$

b. $x(t) = 4\cos t, \quad y(t) = 3\sin t, \quad 0 \le t \le 2\pi$

Solution

a. To eliminate the parameter, we can solve either of the equations for t. For example, solving the first equation for t gives

$$\begin{aligned} x &= \sqrt{2t+4} \\ x^2 &= 2t+4 \\ x^2 - 4 &= 2t \\ t &= \frac{x^2-4}{2}. \end{aligned}$$

Note that when we square both sides it is important to observe that $x \ge 0$. Substituting $t = \frac{x^2-4}{2}$ this into $y(t)$ yields

$$\begin{aligned} y(t) &= 2t+1 \\ y &= 2\left(\frac{x^2-4}{2}\right)+1 \\ y &= x^2-4+1 \\ y &= x^2-3. \end{aligned}$$

This is the equation of a parabola opening upward. There is, however, a domain restriction because of the limits on the parameter t. When $t = -2$, $x = \sqrt{2(-2)+4} = 0$, and when $t = 6$, $x = \sqrt{2(6)+4} = 4$. The graph of this plane curve follows.

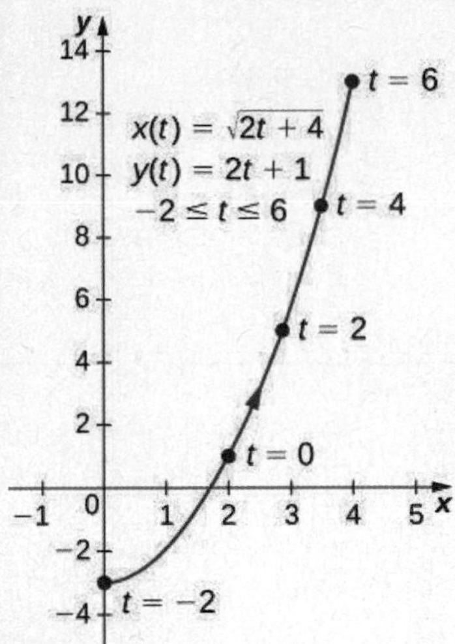

Figure 1.7 Graph of the plane curve described by the parametric equations in part a.

b. Sometimes it is necessary to be a bit creative in eliminating the parameter. The parametric equations for this example are

$$x(t) = 4\cos t \text{ and } y(t) = 3\sin t.$$

Solving either equation for t directly is not advisable because sine and cosine are not one-to-one functions. However, dividing the first equation by 4 and the second equation by 3 (and suppressing the t) gives us

$$\cos t = \frac{x}{4} \text{ and } \sin t = \frac{y}{3}.$$

Now use the Pythagorean identity $\cos^2 t + \sin^2 t = 1$ and replace the expressions for $\sin t$ and $\cos t$ with the equivalent expressions in terms of x and y. This gives

$$\begin{aligned} \left(\frac{x}{4}\right)^2 + \left(\frac{y}{3}\right)^2 &= 1 \\ \frac{x^2}{16} + \frac{y^2}{9} &= 1. \end{aligned}$$

This is the equation of a horizontal ellipse centered at the origin, with semimajor axis 4 and semiminor axis 3 as shown in the following graph.

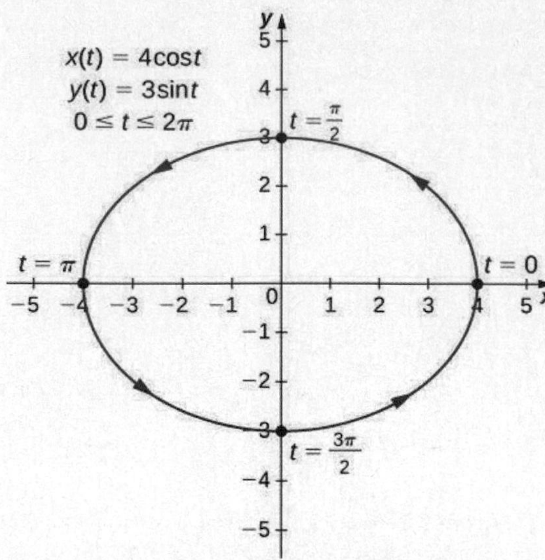

Figure 1.8 Graph of the plane curve described by the parametric equations in part b.

As t progresses from 0 to $2\pi,$ a point on the curve traverses the ellipse once, in a counterclockwise direction. Recall from the section opener that the orbit of Earth around the Sun is also elliptical. This is a perfect example of using parameterized curves to model a real-world phenomenon.

1.2 Eliminate the parameter for the plane curve defined by the following parametric equations and describe the resulting graph.

$$x(t) = 2 + \frac{3}{t}, \quad y(t) = t - 1, \quad 2 \le t \le 6$$

So far we have seen the method of eliminating the parameter, assuming we know a set of parametric equations that describe a plane curve. What if we would like to start with the equation of a curve and determine a pair of parametric equations for that curve? This is certainly possible, and in fact it is possible to do so in many different ways for a given curve. The process is known as **parameterization of a curve**.

Example 1.3

Parameterizing a Curve

Find two different pairs of parametric equations to represent the graph of $y = 2x^2 - 3.$

Solution

First, it is always possible to parameterize a curve by defining $x(t) = t,$ then replacing x with t in the equation for $y(t).$ This gives the parameterization

$$x(t) = t, \quad y(t) = 2t^2 - 3.$$

Since there is no restriction on the domain in the original graph, there is no restriction on the values of t.

We have complete freedom in the choice for the second parameterization. For example, we can choose $x(t) = 3t - 2$. The only thing we need to check is that there are no restrictions imposed on x; that is, the range of $x(t)$ is all real numbers. This is the case for $x(t) = 3t - 2$. Now since $y = 2x^2 - 3$, we can substitute $x(t) = 3t - 2$ for x. This gives

$$\begin{aligned} y(t) &= 2(3t-2)^2 - 2 \\ &= 2\left(9t^2 - 12t + 4\right) - 2 \\ &= 18t^2 - 24t + 8 - 2 \\ &= 18t^2 - 24t + 6. \end{aligned}$$

Therefore, a second parameterization of the curve can be written as

$$x(t) = 3t - 2 \text{ and } y(t) = 18t^2 - 24t + 6.$$

1.3 Find two different sets of parametric equations to represent the graph of $y = x^2 + 2x$.

Cycloids and Other Parametric Curves

Imagine going on a bicycle ride through the country. The tires stay in contact with the road and rotate in a predictable pattern. Now suppose a very determined ant is tired after a long day and wants to get home. So he hangs onto the side of the tire and gets a free ride. The path that this ant travels down a straight road is called a **cycloid** (**Figure 1.9**). A cycloid generated by a circle (or bicycle wheel) of radius a is given by the parametric equations

$$x(t) = a(t - \sin t), \quad y(t) = a(1 - \cos t).$$

To see why this is true, consider the path that the center of the wheel takes. The center moves along the x-axis at a constant height equal to the radius of the wheel. If the radius is a, then the coordinates of the center can be given by the equations

$$x(t) = at, \quad y(t) = a$$

for any value of t. Next, consider the ant, which rotates around the center along a circular path. If the bicycle is moving from left to right then the wheels are rotating in a clockwise direction. A possible parameterization of the circular motion of the ant (relative to the center of the wheel) is given by

$$x(t) = -a \sin t, \quad y(t) = -a \cos t.$$

(The negative sign is needed to reverse the orientation of the curve. If the negative sign were not there, we would have to imagine the wheel rotating counterclockwise.) Adding these equations together gives the equations for the cycloid.

$$x(t) = a(t - \sin t), \quad y(t) = a(1 - \cos t).$$

Figure 1.9 A wheel traveling along a road without slipping; the point on the edge of the wheel traces out a cycloid.

Now suppose that the bicycle wheel doesn't travel along a straight road but instead moves along the inside of a larger wheel, as in **Figure 1.10**. In this graph, the green circle is traveling around the blue circle in a counterclockwise direction. A point on the edge of the green circle traces out the red graph, which is called a hypocycloid.

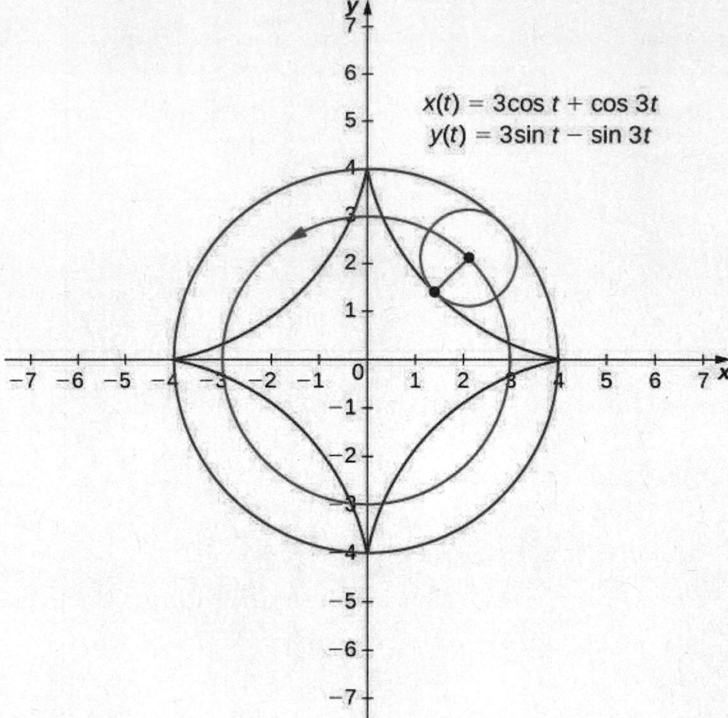

Figure 1.10 Graph of the hypocycloid described by the parametric equations shown.

The general parametric equations for a hypocycloid are

$$x(t) = (a - b)\cos t + b\cos\left(\frac{a - b}{b}\right)t$$
$$y(t) = (a - b)\sin t - b\sin\left(\frac{a - b}{b}\right)t.$$

These equations are a bit more complicated, but the derivation is somewhat similar to the equations for the cycloid. In this case we assume the radius of the larger circle is a and the radius of the smaller circle is b. Then the center of the wheel travels along a circle of radius $a - b$. This fact explains the first term in each equation above. The period of the second trigonometric function in both $x(t)$ and $y(t)$ is equal to $\frac{2\pi b}{a - b}$.

The ratio $\frac{a}{b}$ is related to the number of **cusps** on the graph (cusps are the corners or pointed ends of the graph), as illustrated in **Figure 1.11**. This ratio can lead to some very interesting graphs, depending on whether or not the ratio is rational. **Figure 1.10** corresponds to $a = 4$ and $b = 1$. The result is a hypocycloid with four cusps. **Figure 1.11** shows some other possibilities. The last two hypocycloids have irrational values for $\frac{a}{b}$. In these cases the hypocycloids have an infinite number of cusps, so they never return to their starting point. These are examples of what are known as *space-filling curves*.

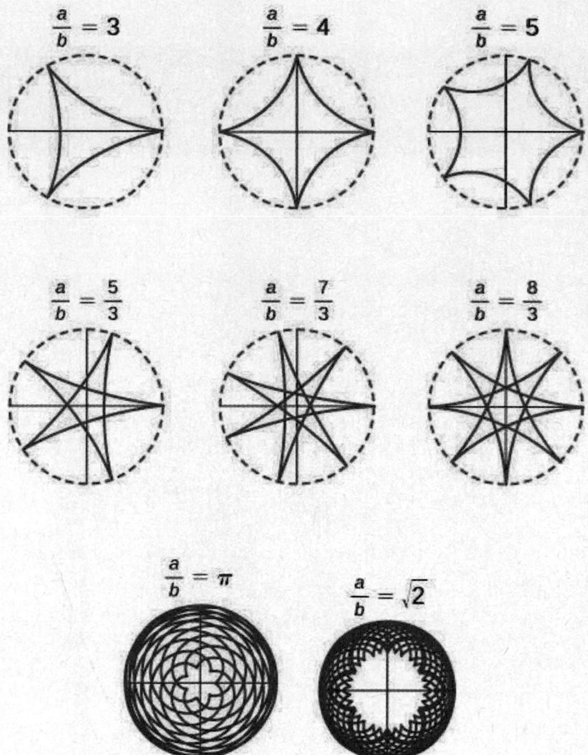

Figure 1.11 Graph of various hypocycloids corresponding to different values of a/b.

Student PROJECT

The Witch of Agnesi

Many plane curves in mathematics are named after the people who first investigated them, like the folium of Descartes or the spiral of Archimedes. However, perhaps the strangest name for a curve is the witch of Agnesi. Why a witch?

Maria Gaetana Agnesi (1718–1799) was one of the few recognized women mathematicians of eighteenth-century Italy. She wrote a popular book on analytic geometry, published in 1748, which included an interesting curve that had been studied by Fermat in 1630. The mathematician Guido Grandi showed in 1703 how to construct this curve, which he later called the "versoria," a Latin term for a rope used in sailing. Agnesi used the Italian term for this rope, "versiera," but in Latin, this same word means a "female goblin." When Agnesi's book was translated into English in 1801, the translator used the term "witch" for the curve, instead of rope. The name "witch of Agnesi" has stuck ever since.

The witch of Agnesi is a curve defined as follows: Start with a circle of radius a so that the points $(0, 0)$ and $(0, 2a)$ are points on the circle (**Figure 1.12**). Let O denote the origin. Choose any other point A on the circle, and draw the secant line OA. Let B denote the point at which the line OA intersects the horizontal line through $(0, 2a)$. The vertical line through B intersects the horizontal line through A at the point P. As the point A varies, the path that the point P travels is the witch of Agnesi curve for the given circle.

Witch of Agnesi curves have applications in physics, including modeling water waves and distributions of spectral lines. In probability theory, the curve describes the probability density function of the Cauchy distribution. In this project you will parameterize these curves.

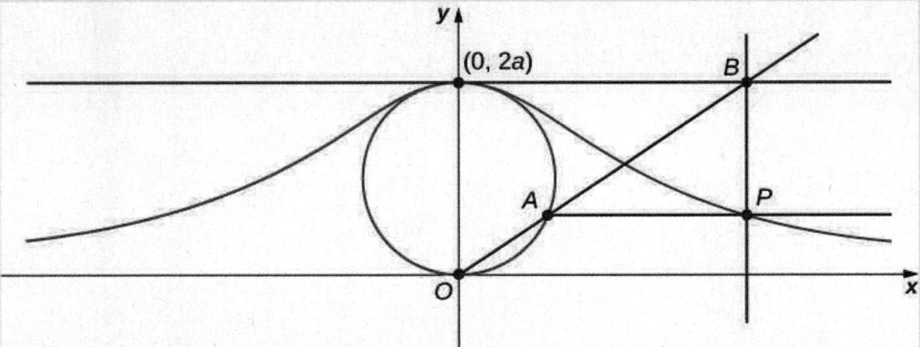

Figure 1.12 As the point A moves around the circle, the point P traces out the witch of Agnesi curve for the given circle.

1. On the figure, label the following points, lengths, and angle:
   a. C is the point on the x-axis with the same x-coordinate as A.
   b. x is the x-coordinate of P, and y is the y-coordinate of P.
   c. E is the point $(0, a)$.
   d. F is the point on the line segment OA such that the line segment EF is perpendicular to the line segment OA.
   e. b is the distance from O to F.
   f. c is the distance from F to A.
   g. d is the distance from O to B.
   h. θ is the measure of angle $\angle COA$.

The goal of this project is to parameterize the witch using θ as a parameter. To do this, write equations for x and y in terms of only θ.

2. Show that $d = \frac{2a}{\sin\theta}$.
3. Note that $x = d\cos\theta$. Show that $x = 2a\cot\theta$. When you do this, you will have parameterized the x-coordinate of the curve with respect to θ. If you can get a similar equation for y, you will have parameterized the curve.
4. In terms of θ, what is the angle $\angle EOA$?
5. Show that $b + c = 2a\cos\left(\frac{\pi}{2} - \theta\right)$.
6. Show that $y = 2a\cos\left(\frac{\pi}{2} - \theta\right)\sin\theta$.
7. Show that $y = 2a\sin^2\theta$. You have now parameterized the y-coordinate of the curve with respect to θ.
8. Conclude that a parameterization of the given witch curve is
$$x = 2a\cot\theta,\ y = 2a\sin^2\theta,\ -\infty < \theta < \infty.$$
9. Use your parameterization to show that the given witch curve is the graph of the function $f(x) = \frac{8a^3}{x^2 + 4a^2}$.

Student PROJECT

Travels with My Ant: The Curtate and Prolate Cycloids

Earlier in this section, we looked at the parametric equations for a cycloid, which is the path a point on the edge of a wheel traces as the wheel rolls along a straight path. In this project we look at two different variations of the cycloid, called the curtate and prolate cycloids.

First, let's revisit the derivation of the parametric equations for a cycloid. Recall that we considered a tenacious ant trying to get home by hanging onto the edge of a bicycle tire. We have assumed the ant climbed onto the tire at the very edge, where the tire touches the ground. As the wheel rolls, the ant moves with the edge of the tire (**Figure 1.13**).

As we have discussed, we have a lot of flexibility when parameterizing a curve. In this case we let our parameter t represent the angle the tire has rotated through. Looking at **Figure 1.13**, we see that after the tire has rotated through an angle of t, the position of the center of the wheel, $C = (x_C, y_C)$, is given by

$$x_C = at \text{ and } y_C = a.$$

Furthermore, letting $A = (x_A, y_A)$ denote the position of the ant, we note that

$$x_C - x_A = a \sin t \text{ and } y_C - y_A = a \cos t.$$

Then

$$\begin{aligned} x_A &= x_C - a \sin t = at - a \sin t = a(t - \sin t) \\ y_A &= y_C - a \cos t = a - a \cos t = a(1 - \cos t). \end{aligned}$$

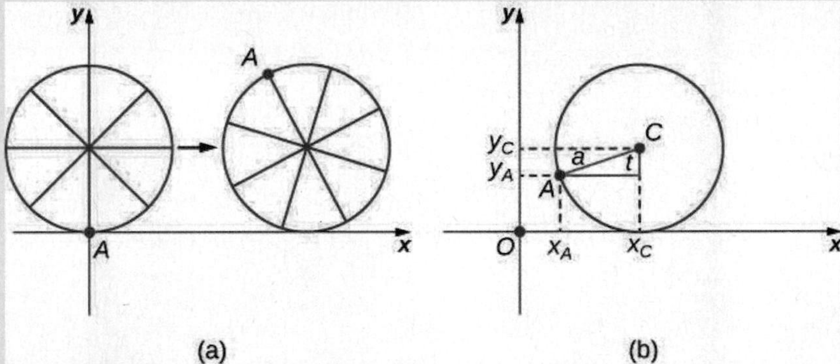

Figure 1.13 (a) The ant clings to the edge of the bicycle tire as the tire rolls along the ground. (b) Using geometry to determine the position of the ant after the tire has rotated through an angle of t.

Note that these are the same parametric representations we had before, but we have now assigned a physical meaning to the parametric variable t.

After a while the ant is getting dizzy from going round and round on the edge of the tire. So he climbs up one of the spokes toward the center of the wheel. By climbing toward the center of the wheel, the ant has changed his path of motion. The new path has less up-and-down motion and is called a curtate cycloid (**Figure 1.14**). As shown in the figure, we let b denote the distance along the spoke from the center of the wheel to the ant. As before, we let t represent the angle the tire has rotated through. Additionally, we let $C = (x_C, y_C)$ represent the position of the center of the wheel and $A = (x_A, y_A)$ represent the position of the ant.

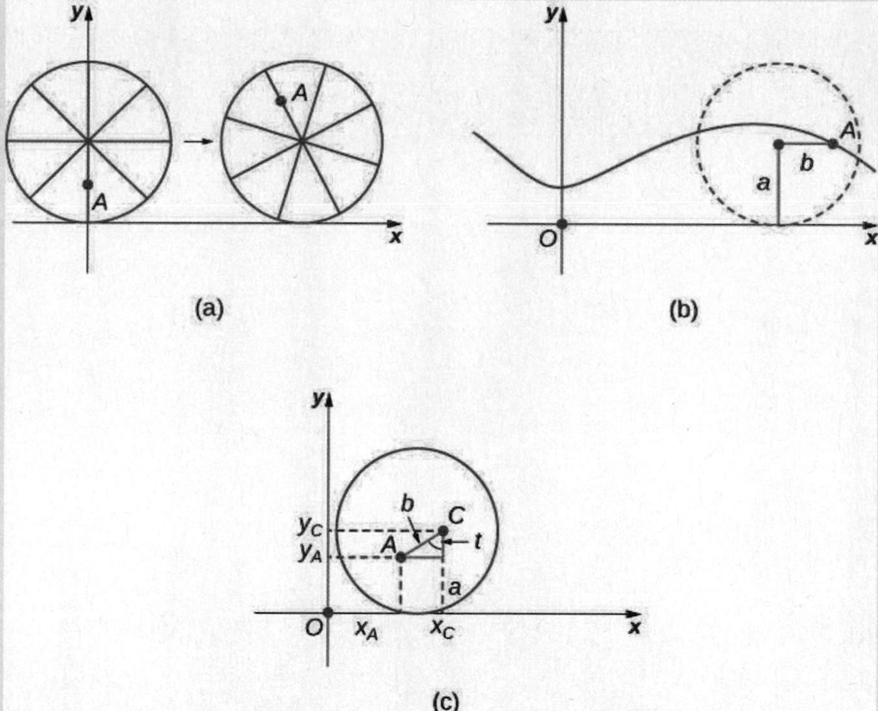

Figure 1.14 (a) The ant climbs up one of the spokes toward the center of the wheel. (b) The ant's path of motion after he climbs closer to the center of the wheel. This is called a curtate cycloid. (c) The new setup, now that the ant has moved closer to the center of the wheel.

1. What is the position of the center of the wheel after the tire has rotated through an angle of t?
2. Use geometry to find expressions for $x_C - x_A$ and for $y_C - y_A$.
3. On the basis of your answers to parts 1 and 2, what are the parametric equations representing the curtate cycloid?
   Once the ant's head clears, he realizes that the bicyclist has made a turn, and is now traveling away from his home. So he drops off the bicycle tire and looks around. Fortunately, there is a set of train tracks nearby, headed back in the right direction. So the ant heads over to the train tracks to wait. After a while, a train goes by, heading in the right direction, and he manages to jump up and just catch the edge of the train wheel (without getting squished!).
   The ant is still worried about getting dizzy, but the train wheel is slippery and has no spokes to climb, so he decides to just hang on to the edge of the wheel and hope for the best. Now, train wheels have a flange to keep the wheel running on the tracks. So, in this case, since the ant is hanging on to the very edge of the flange, the distance from the center of the wheel to the ant is actually greater than the radius of the wheel (**Figure 1.15**).
   The setup here is essentially the same as when the ant climbed up the spoke on the bicycle wheel. We let b denote the distance from the center of the wheel to the ant, and we let t represent the angle the tire has rotated through. Additionally, we let $C = (x_C, y_C)$ represent the position of the center of the wheel and $A = (x_A, y_A)$ represent the position of the ant (**Figure 1.15**).

   When the distance from the center of the wheel to the ant is greater than the radius of the wheel, his path of motion is called a prolate cycloid. A graph of a prolate cycloid is shown in the figure.

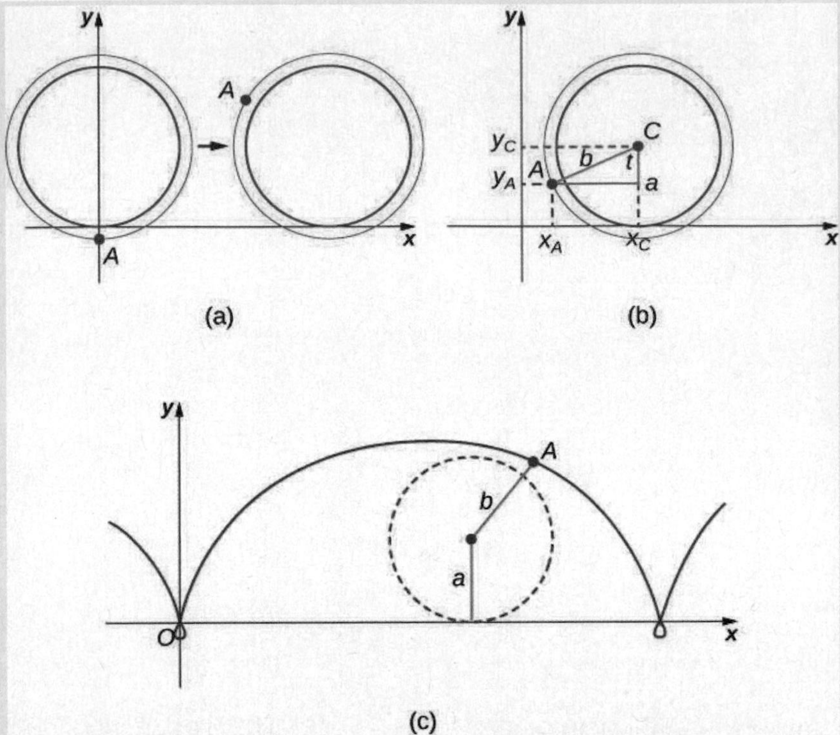

Figure 1.15 (a) The ant is hanging onto the flange of the train wheel. (b) The new setup, now that the ant has jumped onto the train wheel. (c) The ant travels along a prolate cycloid.

4. Using the same approach you used in parts 1– 3, find the parametric equations for the path of motion of the ant.
5. What do you notice about your answer to part 3 and your answer to part 4?
   Notice that the ant is actually traveling backward at times (the "loops" in the graph), even though the train continues to move forward. He is probably going to be *really* dizzy by the time he gets home!

1.1 EXERCISES

For the following exercises, sketch the curves below by eliminating the parameter t. Give the orientation of the curve.

1. $x = t^2 + 2t, \quad y = t + 1$

2. $x = \cos(t),\ y = \sin(t),\ (0,\ 2\pi]$

3. $x = 2t + 4,\ y = t - 1$

4. $x = 3 - t,\ y = 2t - 3,\ 1.5 \le t \le 3$

For the following exercises, eliminate the parameter and sketch the graphs.

5. $x = 2t^2, \quad y = t^4 + 1$

For the following exercises, use technology (CAS or calculator) to sketch the parametric equations.

6. **[T]** $x = t^2 + t, \quad y = t^2 - 1$

7. **[T]** $x = e^{-t}, \quad y = e^{2t} - 1$

8. **[T]** $x = 3\cos t, \quad y = 4\sin t$

9. **[T]** $x = \sec t, \quad y = \cos t$

For the following exercises, sketch the parametric equations by eliminating the parameter. Indicate any asymptotes of the graph.

10. $x = e^t, \quad y = e^{2t} + 1$

11. $x = 6\sin(2\theta),\ y = 4\cos(2\theta)$

12. $x = \cos\theta, \quad y = 2\sin(2\theta)$

13. $x = 3 - 2\cos\theta, \quad y = -5 + 3\sin\theta$

14. $x = 4 + 2\cos\theta, \quad y = -1 + \sin\theta$

15. $x = \sec t, \quad y = \tan t$

16. $x = \ln(2t), \quad y = t^2$

17. $x = e^t, \quad y = e^{2t}$

18. $x = e^{-2t}, \quad y = e^{3t}$

19. $x = t^3, \quad y = 3\ln t$

20. $x = 4\sec\theta, \quad y = 3\tan\theta$

For the following exercises, convert the parametric equations of a curve into rectangular form. No sketch is necessary. State the domain of the rectangular form.

21. $x = t^2 - 1, \quad y = \frac{t}{2}$

22. $x = \frac{1}{\sqrt{t+1}}, \quad y = \frac{t}{1+t},\ t > -1$

23. $x = 4\cos\theta,\ y = 3\sin\theta,\ t \in (0,\ 2\pi]$

24. $x = \cosh t, \quad y = \sinh t$

25. $x = 2t - 3, \quad y = 6t - 7$

26. $x = t^2, \quad y = t^3$

27. $x = 1 + \cos t, \quad y = 3 - \sin t$

28. $x = \sqrt{t}, \quad y = 2t + 4$

29. $x = \sec t, \quad y = \tan t,\ \pi \le t < \frac{3\pi}{2}$

30. $x = 2\cosh t, \quad y = 4\sinh t$

31. $x = \cos(2t), \quad y = \sin t$

32. $x = 4t + 3,\ y = 16t^2 - 9$

33. $x = t^2, \quad y = 2\ln t,\ t \ge 1$

34. $x = t^3, \quad y = 3\ln t,\ t \ge 1$

35. $x = t^n, \quad y = n\ln t,\ t \ge 1,$ where n is a natural number

36. $\begin{array}{l} x = \ln(5t) \\ y = \ln(t^2) \end{array}$ where $1 \le t \le e$

37. $\begin{array}{l} x = 2\sin(8t) \\ y = 2\cos(8t) \end{array}$

38. $\begin{array}{l} x = \tan t \\ y = \sec^2 t - 1 \end{array}$

For the following exercises, the pairs of parametric equations represent lines, parabolas, circles, ellipses, or hyperbolas. Name the type of basic curve that each pair of equations represents.

39. $x = 3t + 4$
$y = 5t - 2$

40. $x - 4 = 5t$
$y + 2 = t$

41. $x = 2t + 1$
$y = t^2 - 3$

42. $x = 3\cos t$
$y = 3\sin t$

43. $x = 2\cos(3t)$
$y = 2\sin(3t)$

44. $x = \cosh t$
$y = \sinh t$

45. $x = 3\cos t$
$y = 4\sin t$

46. $x = 2\cos(3t)$
$y = 5\sin(3t)$

47. $x = 3\cosh(4t)$
$y = 4\sinh(4t)$

48. $x = 2\cosh t$
$y = 2\sinh t$

49. Show that $\begin{matrix} x = h + r\cos\theta \\ y = k + r\sin\theta \end{matrix}$ represents the equation of a circle.

50. Use the equations in the preceding problem to find a set of parametric equations for a circle whose radius is 5 and whose center is $(-2, 3)$.

For the following exercises, use a graphing utility to graph the curve represented by the parametric equations and identify the curve from its equation.

51. **[T]** $x = \theta + \sin\theta$
$y = 1 - \cos\theta$

52. **[T]** $x = 2t - 2\sin t$
$y = 2 - 2\cos t$

53. **[T]** $x = t - 0.5\sin t$
$y = 1 - 1.5\cos t$

54. An airplane traveling horizontally at 100 m/s over flat ground at an elevation of 4000 meters must drop an emergency package on a target on the ground. The trajectory of the package is given by $x = 100t,\ y = -4.9t^2 + 4000,\ t \geq 0$ where the origin is the point on the ground directly beneath the plane at the moment of release. How many horizontal meters before the target should the package be released in order to hit the target?

55. The trajectory of a bullet is given by $x = v_0(\cos\alpha)\,t y = v_0(\sin\alpha)\,t - \frac{1}{2}gt^2$ where $v_0 = 500$ m/s, $g = 9.8 = 9.8\ \text{m/s}^2$, and $\alpha = 30$ degrees. When will the bullet hit the ground? How far from the gun will the bullet hit the ground?

56. **[T]** Use technology to sketch the curve represented by $x = \sin(4t),\ y = \sin(3t),\ 0 \leq t \leq 2\pi$.

57. **[T]** Use technology to sketch $x = 2\tan(t),\ y = 3\sec(t),\ -\pi < t < \pi$.

58. Sketch the curve known as an *epitrochoid*, which gives the path of a point on a circle of radius b as it rolls on the outside of a circle of radius a. The equations are
$$x = (a + b)\cos t - c\cdot\cos\left[\frac{(a + b)t}{b}\right]$$
$$y = (a + b)\sin t - c\cdot\sin\left[\frac{(a + b)t}{b}\right].$$

Let $a = 1,\ b = 2,\ c = 1$.

59. **[T]** Use technology to sketch the spiral curve given by $x = t\cos(t),\ y = t\sin(t)$ from $-2\pi \leq t \leq 2\pi$.

60. **[T]** Use technology to graph the curve given by the parametric equations $x = 2\cot(t),\ y = 1 - \cos(2t),\ -\pi/2 \leq t \leq \pi/2$. This curve is known as the witch of Agnesi.

61. **[T]** Sketch the curve given by parametric equations $\begin{matrix} x = \cosh(t) \\ y = \sinh(t), \end{matrix}$ where $-2 \leq t \leq 2$.

1.2 | Calculus of Parametric Curves

Learning Objectives

- **1.2.1** Determine derivatives and equations of tangents for parametric curves.
- **1.2.2** Find the area under a parametric curve.
- **1.2.3** Use the equation for arc length of a parametric curve.
- **1.2.4** Apply the formula for surface area to a volume generated by a parametric curve.

Now that we have introduced the concept of a parameterized curve, our next step is to learn how to work with this concept in the context of calculus. For example, if we know a parameterization of a given curve, is it possible to calculate the slope of a tangent line to the curve? How about the arc length of the curve? Or the area under the curve?

Another scenario: Suppose we would like to represent the location of a baseball after the ball leaves a pitcher's hand. If the position of the baseball is represented by the plane curve $(x(t), y(t))$, then we should be able to use calculus to find the speed of the ball at any given time. Furthermore, we should be able to calculate just how far that ball has traveled as a function of time.

Derivatives of Parametric Equations

We start by asking how to calculate the slope of a line tangent to a parametric curve at a point. Consider the plane curve defined by the parametric equations

$$x(t) = 2t + 3, \quad y(t) = 3t - 4, \quad -2 \leq t \leq 3.$$

The graph of this curve appears in **Figure 1.16**. It is a line segment starting at $(-1, -10)$ and ending at $(9, 5)$.

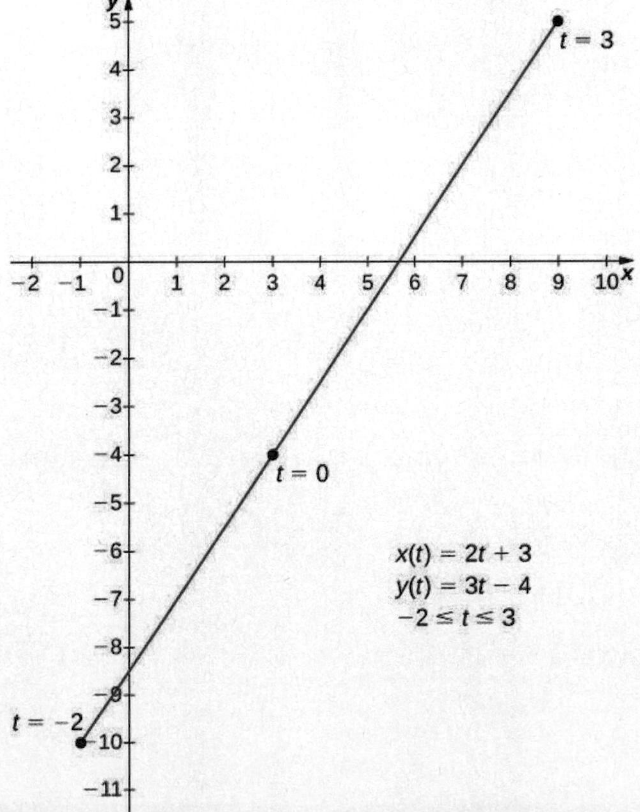

Figure 1.16 Graph of the line segment described by the given parametric equations.

We can eliminate the parameter by first solving the equation $x(t) = 2t + 3$ for t:

$$\begin{aligned} x(t) &= 2t + 3 \\ x - 3 &= 2t \\ t &= \frac{x - 3}{2}. \end{aligned}$$

Substituting this into $y(t),$ we obtain

$$\begin{aligned} y(t) &= 3t - 4 \\ y &= 3\left(\frac{x - 3}{2}\right) - 4 \\ y &= \frac{3x}{2} - \frac{9}{2} - 4 \\ y &= \frac{3x}{2} - \frac{17}{2}. \end{aligned}$$

The slope of this line is given by $\frac{dy}{dx} = \frac{3}{2}.$ Next we calculate $x'(t)$ and $y'(t).$ This gives $x'(t) = 2$ and $y'(t) = 3.$ Notice that $\frac{dy}{dx} = \frac{dy/dt}{dx/dt} = \frac{3}{2}.$ This is no coincidence, as outlined in the following theorem.

Theorem 1.1: Derivative of Parametric Equations

Consider the plane curve defined by the parametric equations $x = x(t)$ and $y = y(t).$ Suppose that $x'(t)$ and $y'(t)$ exist, and assume that $x'(t) \neq 0.$ Then the derivative $\frac{dy}{dx}$ is given by

$$\frac{dy}{dx} = \frac{dy/dt}{dx/dt} = \frac{y'(t)}{x'(t)}. \tag{1.1}$$

Proof

This theorem can be proven using the Chain Rule. In particular, assume that the parameter t can be eliminated, yielding a differentiable function $y = F(x).$ Then $y(t) = F(x(t)).$ Differentiating both sides of this equation using the Chain Rule yields

$$y'(t) = F'(x(t))x'(t),$$

so

$$F'(x(t)) = \frac{y'(t)}{x'(t)}.$$

But $F'(x(t)) = \frac{dy}{dx},$ which proves the theorem.

□

Equation 1.1 can be used to calculate derivatives of plane curves, as well as critical points. Recall that a critical point of a differentiable function $y = f(x)$ is any point $x = x_0$ such that either $f'(x_0) = 0$ or $f'(x_0)$ does not exist. **Equation 1.1** gives a formula for the slope of a tangent line to a curve defined parametrically regardless of whether the curve can be described by a function $y = f(x)$ or not.

Example 1.4

Finding the Derivative of a Parametric Curve

Calculate the derivative $\frac{dy}{dx}$ for each of the following parametrically defined plane curves, and locate any critical points on their respective graphs.

a. $x(t) = t^2 - 3, \quad y(t) = 2t - 1, \quad -3 \le t \le 4$

b. $x(t) = 2t + 1, \quad y(t) = t^3 - 3t + 4, \quad -2 \le t \le 5$

c. $x(t) = 5\cos t, \quad y(t) = 5\sin t, \quad 0 \le t \le 2\pi$

Solution

a. To apply **Equation 1.1**, first calculate $x'(t)$ and $y'(t)$:

$$x'(t) = 2t$$
$$y'(t) = 2.$$

Next substitute these into the equation:

$$\frac{dy}{dx} = \frac{dy/dt}{dx/dt}$$
$$\frac{dy}{dx} = \frac{2}{2t}$$
$$\frac{dy}{dx} = \frac{1}{t}.$$

This derivative is undefined when $t = 0$. Calculating $x(0)$ and $y(0)$ gives $x(0) = (0)^2 - 3 = -3$ and $y(0) = 2(0) - 1 = -1,$ which corresponds to the point $(-3, -1)$ on the graph. The graph of this curve is a parabola opening to the right, and the point $(-3, -1)$ is its vertex as shown.

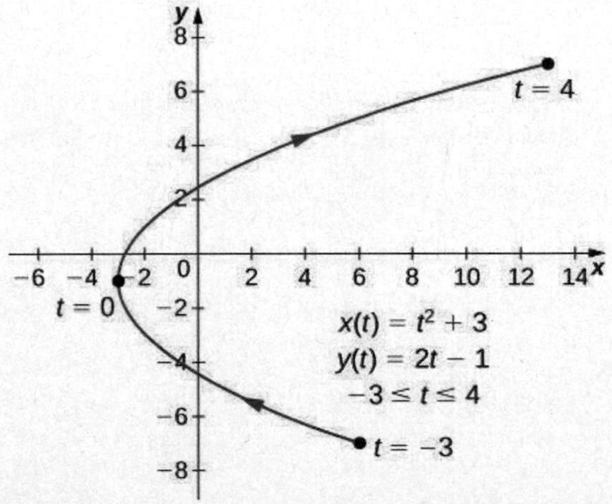

Figure 1.17 Graph of the parabola described by parametric equations in part a.

b. To apply **Equation 1.1**, first calculate $x'(t)$ and $y'(t)$:

$$x'(t) = 2$$
$$y'(t) = 3t^2 - 3.$$

Next substitute these into the equation:

$$\frac{dy}{dx} = \frac{dy/dt}{dx/dt}$$
$$\frac{dy}{dx} = \frac{3t^2 - 3}{2}.$$

This derivative is zero when $t = \pm 1$. When $t = -1$ we have

$$x(-1) = 2(-1) + 1 = -1 \text{ and } y(-1) = (-1)^3 - 3(-1) + 4 = -1 + 3 + 4 = 6,$$

which corresponds to the point $(-1, 6)$ on the graph. When $t = 1$ we have

$$x(1) = 2(1) + 1 = 3 \text{ and } y(1) = (1)^3 - 3(1) + 4 = 1 - 3 + 4 = 2,$$

which corresponds to the point $(3, 2)$ on the graph. The point $(3, 2)$ is a relative minimum and the point $(-1, 6)$ is a relative maximum, as seen in the following graph.

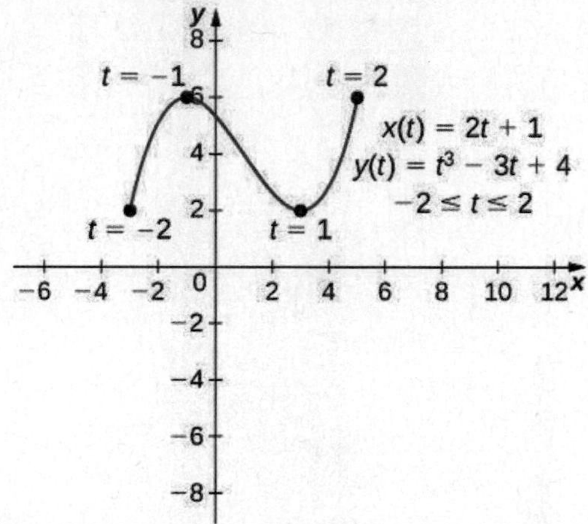

Figure 1.18 Graph of the curve described by parametric equations in part b.

c. To apply **Equation 1.1**, first calculate $x'(t)$ and $y'(t)$:

$$x'(t) = -5 \sin t$$
$$y'(t) = 5 \cos t.$$

Next substitute these into the equation:

$$\frac{dy}{dx} = \frac{dy/dt}{dx/dt}$$
$$\frac{dy}{dx} = \frac{5 \cos t}{-5 \sin t}$$
$$\frac{dy}{dx} = -\cot t.$$

This derivative is zero when $\cos t = 0$ and is undefined when $\sin t = 0$. This gives $t = 0, \frac{\pi}{2}, \pi, \frac{3\pi}{2},$ and 2π as critical points for t. Substituting each of these into $x(t)$ and $y(t)$, we obtain

t	$x(t)$	$y(t)$
0	5	0
$\frac{\pi}{2}$	0	5
π	−5	0
$\frac{3\pi}{2}$	0	−5
2π	5	0

These points correspond to the sides, top, and bottom of the circle that is represented by the parametric equations (**Figure 1.19**). On the left and right edges of the circle, the derivative is undefined, and on the top and bottom, the derivative equals zero.

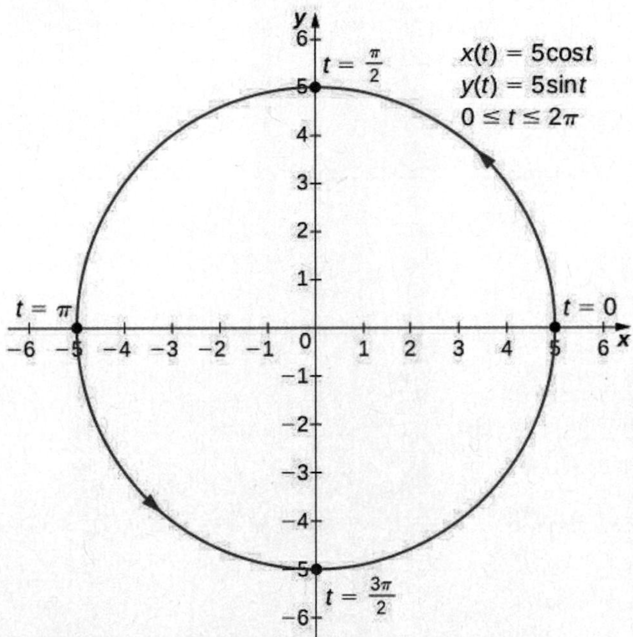

Figure 1.19 Graph of the curve described by parametric equations in part c.

 **1.4** Calculate the derivative dy/dx for the plane curve defined by the equations

$$x(t) = t^2 - 4t, \quad y(t) = 2t^3 - 6t, \quad -2 \le t \le 3$$

and locate any critical points on its graph.

Example 1.5

Finding a Tangent Line

Find the equation of the tangent line to the curve defined by the equations

$$x(t) = t^2 - 3, \quad y(t) = 2t - 1, \quad -3 \le t \le 4 \text{ when } t = 2.$$

Solution

First find the slope of the tangent line using **Equation 1.1**, which means calculating $x'(t)$ and $y'(t)$:

$$x'(t) = 2t$$
$$y'(t) = 2.$$

Next substitute these into the equation:

$$\frac{dy}{dx} = \frac{dy/dt}{dx/dt}$$
$$\frac{dy}{dx} = \frac{2}{2t}$$
$$\frac{dy}{dx} = \frac{1}{t}.$$

When $t = 2$, $\frac{dy}{dx} = \frac{1}{2}$, so this is the slope of the tangent line. Calculating $x(2)$ and $y(2)$ gives

$$x(2) = (2)^2 - 3 = 1 \text{ and } y(2) = 2(2) - 1 = 3,$$

which corresponds to the point $(1, 3)$ on the graph (**Figure 1.20**). Now use the point-slope form of the equation of a line to find the equation of the tangent line:

$$\begin{aligned} y - y_0 &= m(x - x_0) \\ y - 3 &= \frac{1}{2}(x - 1) \\ y - 3 &= \frac{1}{2}x - \frac{1}{2} \\ y &= \frac{1}{2}x + \frac{5}{2}. \end{aligned}$$

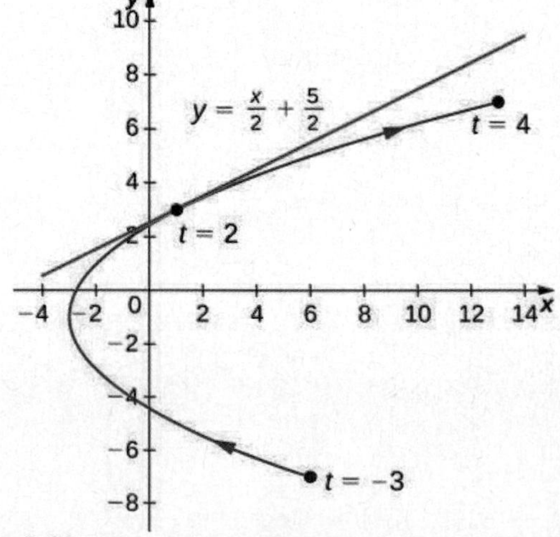

Figure 1.20 Tangent line to the parabola described by the given parametric equations when $t = 2$.

1.5 Find the equation of the tangent line to the curve defined by the equations

$$x(t) = t^2 - 4t, \quad y(t) = 2t^3 - 6t, \quad -2 \le t \le 3 \text{ when } t = 5.$$

Second-Order Derivatives

Our next goal is to see how to take the second derivative of a function defined parametrically. The second derivative of a function $y = f(x)$ is defined to be the derivative of the first derivative; that is,

$$\frac{d^2y}{dx^2} = \frac{d}{dx}\left[\frac{dy}{dx}\right].$$

Since $\frac{dy}{dx} = \frac{dy/dt}{dx/dt}$, we can replace the y on both sides of this equation with $\frac{dy}{dx}$. This gives us

$$\frac{d^2y}{dx^2} = \frac{d}{dx}\left(\frac{dy}{dx}\right) = \frac{(d/dt)(dy/dx)}{dx/dt}. \tag{1.2}$$

If we know dy/dx as a function of t, then this formula is straightforward to apply.

Example 1.6

Finding a Second Derivative

Calculate the second derivative d^2y/dx^2 for the plane curve defined by the parametric equations $x(t) = t^2 - 3,\ y(t) = 2t - 1,\ -3 \le t \le 4.$

Solution

From **Example 1.4** we know that $\frac{dy}{dx} = \frac{2}{2t} = \frac{1}{t}$. Using **Equation 1.2**, we obtain

$$\frac{d^2y}{dx^2} = \frac{(d/dt)(dy/dx)}{dx/dt} = \frac{(d/dt)(1/t)}{2t} = \frac{-t^{-2}}{2t} = -\frac{1}{2t^3}.$$

1.6 Calculate the second derivative d^2y/dx^2 for the plane curve defined by the equations

$$x(t) = t^2 - 4t, \quad y(t) = 2t^3 - 6t, \quad -2 \le t \le 3$$

and locate any critical points on its graph.

Integrals Involving Parametric Equations

Now that we have seen how to calculate the derivative of a plane curve, the next question is this: How do we find the area under a curve defined parametrically? Recall the cycloid defined by the equations $x(t) = t - \sin t, \quad y(t) = 1 - \cos t.$ Suppose we want to find the area of the shaded region in the following graph.

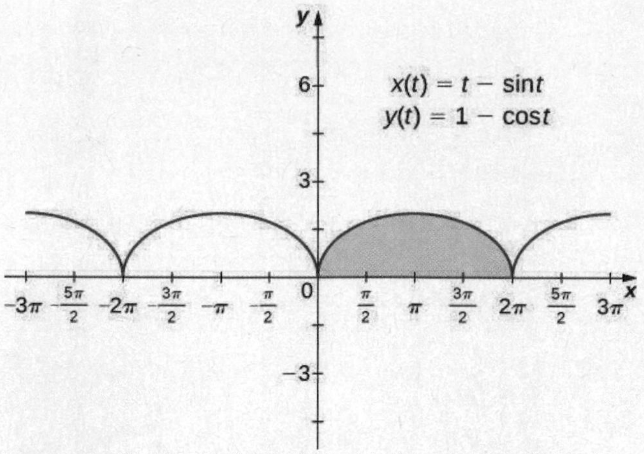

Figure 1.21 Graph of a cycloid with the arch over $[0, 2\pi]$ highlighted.

To derive a formula for the area under the curve defined by the functions

$$x = x(t), \quad y = y(t), \quad a \le t \le b,$$

we assume that $x(t)$ is differentiable and start with an equal partition of the interval $a \le t \le b$. Suppose $t_0 = a < t_1 < t_2 < \cdots < t_n = b$ and consider the following graph.

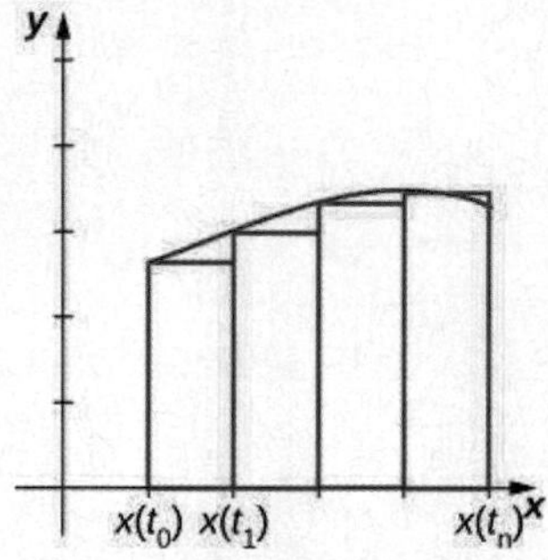

Figure 1.22 Approximating the area under a parametrically defined curve.

We use rectangles to approximate the area under the curve. The height of a typical rectangle in this parametrization is $y(x(\bar{t}_i))$ for some value $\bar{t}_i$ in the ith subinterval, and the width can be calculated as $x(t_i) - x(t_{i-1})$. Thus the area of the ith rectangle is given by

$$A_i = y(x(\bar{t}_i))(x(t_i) - x(t_{i-1})).$$

Then a Riemann sum for the area is

$$A_n = \sum_{i=1}^{n} y(x(\bar{t}_i))(x(t_i) - x(t_{i-1})).$$

Multiplying and dividing each area by $t_i - t_{i-1}$ gives

$$A_n = \sum_{i=1}^{n} y(x(\bar{t}_i))\left(\frac{x(t_i) - x(t_{i-1})}{t_i - t_{i-1}}\right)(t_i - t_{i-1}) = \sum_{i=1}^{n} y(x(\bar{t}_i))\left(\frac{x(t_i) - x(t_{i-1})}{\Delta t}\right)\Delta t.$$

Taking the limit as n approaches infinity gives

$$A = \lim_{n \to \infty} A_n = \int_a^b y(t)x'(t)\,dt.$$

This leads to the following theorem.

Theorem 1.2: Area under a Parametric Curve

Consider the non-self-intersecting plane curve defined by the parametric equations

$$x = x(t), \quad y = y(t), \quad a \le t \le b$$

and assume that $x(t)$ is differentiable. The area under this curve is given by

$$A = \int_a^b y(t)x'(t)\,dt. \tag{1.3}$$

Example 1.7

Finding the Area under a Parametric Curve

Find the area under the curve of the cycloid defined by the equations

$$x(t) = t - \sin t, \quad y(t) = 1 - \cos t, \quad 0 \le t \le 2\pi.$$

Solution

Using **Equation 1.3**, we have

$$\begin{aligned} A &= \int_a^b y(t)x'(t)\,dt \\ &= \int_0^{2\pi} (1 - \cos t)(1 - \cos t)\,dt \\ &= \int_0^{2\pi} (1 - 2\cos t + \cos^2 t)dt \\ &= \int_0^{2\pi} \left(1 - 2\cos t + \frac{1 + \cos 2t}{2}\right) dt \\ &= \int_0^{2\pi} \left(\frac{3}{2} - 2\cos t + \frac{\cos 2t}{2}\right) dt \\ &= \frac{3t}{2} - 2\sin t + \frac{\sin 2t}{4}\Big|_0^{2\pi} \\ &= 3\pi. \end{aligned}$$

1.7 Find the area under the curve of the hypocycloid defined by the equations

$$x(t) = 3\cos t + \cos 3t, \quad y(t) = 3\sin t - \sin 3t, \quad 0 \le t \le \pi.$$

Arc Length of a Parametric Curve

In addition to finding the area under a parametric curve, we sometimes need to find the arc length of a parametric curve. In the case of a line segment, arc length is the same as the distance between the endpoints. If a particle travels from point A to point B along a curve, then the distance that particle travels is the arc length. To develop a formula for arc length, we start with an approximation by line segments as shown in the following graph.

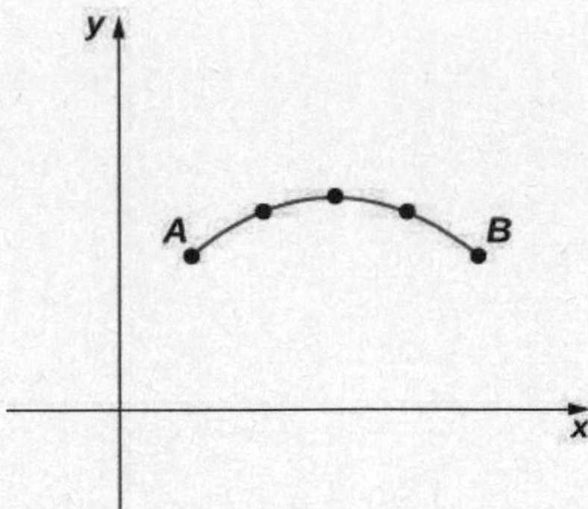

Figure 1.23 Approximation of a curve by line segments.

Given a plane curve defined by the functions $x = x(t), \ y = y(t), \ a \le t \le b,$ we start by partitioning the interval $[a, b]$ into n equal subintervals: $t_0 = a < t_1 < t_2 < \cdots < t_n = b.$ The width of each subinterval is given by $\Delta t = (b - a)/n.$ We can calculate the length of each line segment:

$$d_1 = \sqrt{(x(t_1) - x(t_0))^2 + (y(t_1) - y(t_0))^2}$$
$$d_2 = \sqrt{(x(t_2) - x(t_1))^2 + (y(t_2) - y(t_1))^2} \text{ etc.}$$

Then add these up. We let s denote the exact arc length and s_n denote the approximation by n line segments:

$$s \approx \sum_{k=1}^{n} s_k = \sum_{k=1}^{n} \sqrt{(x(t_k) - x(t_{k-1}))^2 + (y(t_k) - y(t_{k-1}))^2}. \tag{1.4}$$

If we assume that $x(t)$ and $y(t)$ are differentiable functions of t, then the Mean Value Theorem (**Introduction to the Applications of Derivatives (http://cnx.org/content/m53602/latest/)**) applies, so in each subinterval $[t_{k-1}, t_k]$ there exist $\hat{t}_k$ and $\tilde{t}_k$ such that

$$x(t_k) - x(t_{k-1}) = x'\left(\hat{t}_k\right)(t_k - t_{k-1}) = x'\left(\hat{t}_k\right)\Delta t$$
$$y(t_k) - y(t_{k-1}) = y'\left(\tilde{t}_k\right)(t_k - t_{k-1}) = y'\left(\tilde{t}_k\right)\Delta t.$$

Therefore **Equation 1.4** becomes

$$\begin{aligned} s &\approx \sum_{k=1}^{n} s_k \\ &= \sum_{k=1}^{n} \sqrt{\left(x'\left(\hat{t}_k\right)\Delta t\right)^2 + \left(y'\left(\tilde{t}_k\right)\Delta t\right)^2} \\ &= \sum_{k=1}^{n} \sqrt{\left(x'\left(\hat{t}_k\right)\right)^2 (\Delta t)^2 + \left(y'\left(\tilde{t}_k\right)\right)^2 (\Delta t)^2} \\ &= \left(\sum_{k=1}^{n} \sqrt{\left(x'\left(\hat{t}_k\right)\right)^2 + \left(y'\left(\tilde{t}_k\right)\right)^2}\right)\Delta t. \end{aligned}$$

This is a Riemann sum that approximates the arc length over a partition of the interval $[a, b]$. If we further assume that the derivatives are continuous and let the number of points in the partition increase without bound, the approximation approaches the exact arc length. This gives

$$\begin{aligned} s &= \lim_{n \to \infty} \sum_{k=1}^{n} s_k \\ &= \lim_{n \to \infty} \left(\sum_{k=1}^{n} \sqrt{\left(x'\left(\hat{t}_k\right)\right)^2 + \left(y'\left(\tilde{t}_k\right)\right)^2} \right) \Delta t \\ &= \int_a^b \sqrt{(x'(t))^2 + (y'(t))^2} dt. \end{aligned}$$

When taking the limit, the values of $\hat{t}_k$ and $\tilde{t}_k$ are both contained within the same ever-shrinking interval of width Δt, so they must converge to the same value.

We can summarize this method in the following theorem.

Theorem 1.3: Arc Length of a Parametric Curve

Consider the plane curve defined by the parametric equations

$$x = x(t), \quad y = y(t), \quad t_1 \le t \le t_2$$

and assume that $x(t)$ and $y(t)$ are differentiable functions of t. Then the arc length of this curve is given by

$$s = \int_{t_1}^{t_2} \sqrt{\left(\frac{dx}{dt}\right)^2 + \left(\frac{dy}{dt}\right)^2} dt. \qquad \textbf{(1.5)}$$

At this point a side derivation leads to a previous formula for arc length. In particular, suppose the parameter can be eliminated, leading to a function $y = F(x)$. Then $y(t) = F(x(t))$ and the Chain Rule gives $y'(t) = F'(x(t))x'(t)$. Substituting this into **Equation 1.5** gives

$$\begin{aligned} s &= \int_{t_1}^{t_2} \sqrt{\left(\frac{dx}{dt}\right)^2 + \left(\frac{dy}{dt}\right)^2} dt \\ &= \int_{t_1}^{t_2} \sqrt{\left(\frac{dx}{dt}\right)^2 + \left(F'(x)\frac{dx}{dt}\right)^2} dt \\ &= \int_{t_1}^{t_2} \sqrt{\left(\frac{dx}{dt}\right)^2 \left(1 + (F'(x))^2\right)} dt \\ &= \int_{t_1}^{t_2} x'(t) \sqrt{1 + \left(\frac{dy}{dx}\right)^2} dt. \end{aligned}$$

Here we have assumed that $x'(t) > 0,$ which is a reasonable assumption. The Chain Rule gives $dx = x'(t)\,dt,$ and letting $a = x(t_1)$ and $b = x(t_2)$ we obtain the formula

$$s = \int_a^b \sqrt{1 + \left(\frac{dy}{dx}\right)^2} dx,$$

which is the formula for arc length obtained in the **Introduction to the Applications of Integration (http://cnx.org/content/m53638/latest/)** .

Example 1.8

Finding the Arc Length of a Parametric Curve

Find the arc length of the semicircle defined by the equations

$$x(t) = 3\cos t, \quad y(t) = 3\sin t, \quad 0 \le t \le \pi.$$

Solution

The values $t = 0$ to $t = \pi$ trace out the red curve in **Figure 1.23**. To determine its length, use **Equation 1.5**:

$$\begin{aligned} s &= \int_{t_1}^{t_2} \sqrt{\left(\frac{dx}{dt}\right)^2 + \left(\frac{dy}{dt}\right)^2}\, dt \\ &= \int_0^{\pi} \sqrt{(-3\sin t)^2 + (3\cos t)^2}\, dt \\ &= \int_0^{\pi} \sqrt{9\sin^2 t + 9\cos^2 t}\, dt \\ &= \int_0^{\pi} \sqrt{9\left(\sin^2 t + \cos^2 t\right)}\, dt \\ &= \int_0^{\pi} 3dt = 3t|_0^{\pi} = 3\pi. \end{aligned}$$

Note that the formula for the arc length of a semicircle is πr and the radius of this circle is 3. This is a great example of using calculus to derive a known formula of a geometric quantity.

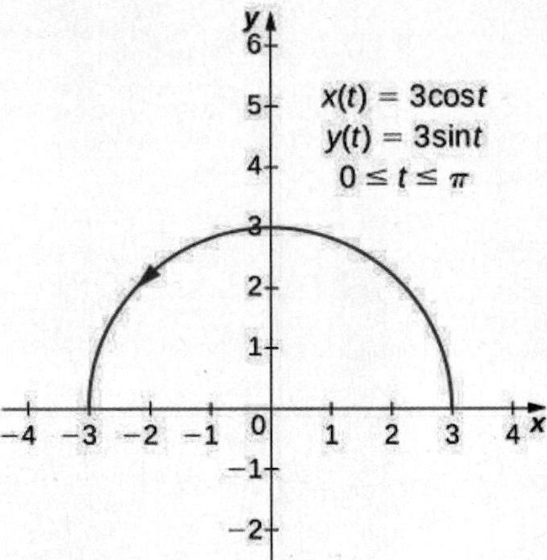

Figure 1.24 The arc length of the semicircle is equal to its radius times π.

1.8 Find the arc length of the curve defined by the equations

$$x(t) = 3t^2, \quad y(t) = 2t^3, \quad 1 \le t \le 3.$$

We now return to the problem posed at the beginning of the section about a baseball leaving a pitcher's hand. Ignoring the effect of air resistance (unless it is a curve ball!), the ball travels a parabolic path. Assuming the pitcher's hand is at the origin and the ball travels left to right in the direction of the positive x-axis, the parametric equations for this curve can be written as

$$x(t) = 140t, \quad y(t) = -16t^2 + 2t$$

where t represents time. We first calculate the distance the ball travels as a function of time. This distance is represented by the arc length. We can modify the arc length formula slightly. First rewrite the functions $x(t)$ and $y(t)$ using v as an independent variable, so as to eliminate any confusion with the parameter t:

$$x(v) = 140v, \quad y(v) = -16v^2 + 2v.$$

Then we write the arc length formula as follows:

$$\begin{aligned} s(t) &= \int_0^t \sqrt{\left(\frac{dx}{dv}\right)^2 + \left(\frac{dy}{dv}\right)^2}\,dv \\ &= \int_0^t \sqrt{140^2 + (-32v+2)^2}\,dv. \end{aligned}$$

The variable v acts as a dummy variable that disappears after integration, leaving the arc length as a function of time t. To integrate this expression we can use a formula from **Appendix A**,

$$\int \sqrt{a^2 + u^2}\,du = \frac{u}{2}\sqrt{a^2 + u^2} + \frac{a^2}{2}\ln\left|u + \sqrt{a^2 + u^2}\right| + C.$$

We set $a = 140$ and $u = -32v + 2$. This gives $du = -32dv$, so $dv = -\frac{1}{32}du$. Therefore

$$\begin{aligned} \int \sqrt{140^2 + (-32v+2)^2}\,dv &= -\frac{1}{32}\int \sqrt{a^2 + u^2}\,du \\ &= -\frac{1}{32}\left[\begin{array}{l} \frac{(-32v+2)}{2}\sqrt{140^2 + (-32v+2)^2} \\ +\frac{140^2}{2}\ln\left|(-32v+2) + \sqrt{140^2 + (-32v+2)^2}\right| \end{array}\right] + C \end{aligned}$$

and

$$\begin{aligned} s(t) &= -\frac{1}{32}\left[\frac{(-32t+2)}{2}\sqrt{140^2 + (-32t+2)^2} + \frac{140^2}{2}\ln\left|(-32t+2) + \sqrt{140^2 + (-32t+2)^2}\right|\right] \\ &\quad + \frac{1}{32}\left[\sqrt{140^2 + 2^2} + \frac{140^2}{2}\ln\left|2 + \sqrt{140^2 + 2^2}\right|\right] \\ &= \left(\frac{t}{2} - \frac{1}{32}\right)\sqrt{1024t^2 - 128t + 19604} - \frac{1225}{4}\ln\left|(-32t+2) + \sqrt{1024t^2 - 128t + 19604}\right| \\ &\quad + \frac{\sqrt{19604}}{32} + \frac{1225}{4}\ln\left(2 + \sqrt{19604}\right). \end{aligned}$$

This function represents the distance traveled by the ball as a function of time. To calculate the speed, take the derivative of this function with respect to t. While this may seem like a daunting task, it is possible to obtain the answer directly from the Fundamental Theorem of Calculus:

$$\frac{d}{dx}\int_a^x f(u)\,du = f(x).$$

Therefore

$$\begin{aligned} s'(t) &= \frac{d}{dt}[s(t)] \\ &= \frac{d}{dt}\left[\int_0^t \sqrt{140^2 + (-32v+2)^2}\,dv\right] \\ &= \sqrt{140^2 + (-32t+2)^2} \\ &= \sqrt{1024t^2 - 128t + 19604} \\ &= 2\sqrt{256t^2 - 32t + 4901}. \end{aligned}$$

One third of a second after the ball leaves the pitcher's hand, the distance it travels is equal to

$$\begin{aligned} s\left(\frac{1}{3}\right) &= \left(\frac{1/3}{2} - \frac{1}{32}\right)\sqrt{1024\left(\frac{1}{3}\right)^2 - 128\left(\frac{1}{3}\right) + 19604} \\ &\quad - \frac{1225}{4}\ln\left|\left(-32\left(\frac{1}{3}\right) + 2\right) + \sqrt{1024\left(\frac{1}{3}\right)^2 - 128\left(\frac{1}{3}\right) + 19604}\right| \\ &\quad + \frac{\sqrt{19604}}{32} + \frac{1225}{4}\ln\left(2 + \sqrt{19604}\right) \\ &\approx 46.69 \text{ feet.} \end{aligned}$$

This value is just over three quarters of the way to home plate. The speed of the ball is

$$s'\left(\frac{1}{3}\right) = 2\sqrt{256\left(\frac{1}{3}\right)^2 - 16\left(\frac{1}{3}\right) + 4901} \approx 140.34 \text{ ft/s.}$$

This speed translates to approximately 95 mph—a major-league fastball.

Surface Area Generated by a Parametric Curve

Recall the problem of finding the surface area of a volume of revolution. In **Curve Length and Surface Area (http://cnx.org/content/m53644/latest/)** , we derived a formula for finding the surface area of a volume generated by a function $y = f(x)$ from $x = a$ to $x = b,$ revolved around the *x*-axis:

$$S = 2\pi \int_a^b f(x)\sqrt{1 + \left(f'(x)\right)^2}dx.$$

We now consider a volume of revolution generated by revolving a parametrically defined curve $x = x(t),\ y = y(t),\ a \le t \le b$ around the *x*-axis as shown in the following figure.

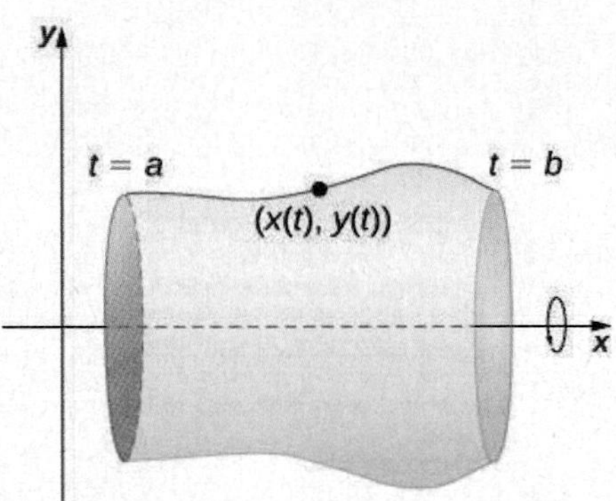

Figure 1.25 A surface of revolution generated by a parametrically defined curve.

The analogous formula for a parametrically defined curve is

$$S = 2\pi \int_a^b y(t)\sqrt{\left(x'(t)\right)^2 + \left(y'(t)\right)^2}dt \tag{1.6}$$

provided that $y(t)$ is not negative on $[a, b]$.

Example 1.9

Finding Surface Area

Find the surface area of a sphere of radius *r* centered at the origin.

Solution

We start with the curve defined by the equations

$$x(t) = r\cos t, \quad y(t) = r\sin t, \quad 0 \le t \le \pi.$$

This generates an upper semicircle of radius r centered at the origin as shown in the following graph.

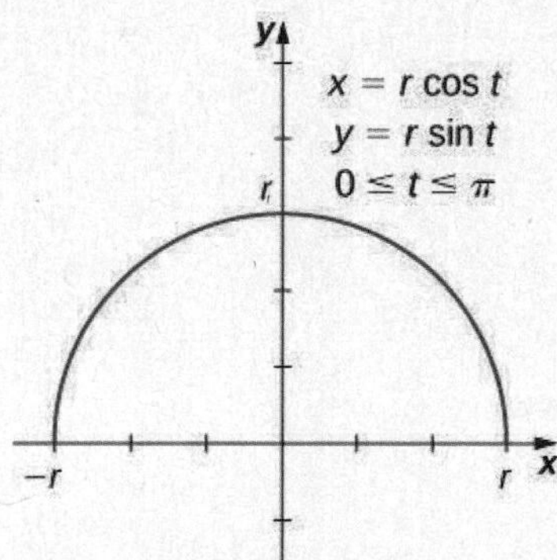

Figure 1.26 A semicircle generated by parametric equations.

When this curve is revolved around the x-axis, it generates a sphere of radius r. To calculate the surface area of the sphere, we use **Equation 1.6**:

$$\begin{aligned} S &= 2\pi \int_a^b y(t)\sqrt{(x'(t))^2 + (y'(t))^2}\,dt \\ &= 2\pi \int_0^{\pi} r\sin t\sqrt{(-r\sin t)^2 + (r\cos t)^2}\,dt \\ &= 2\pi \int_0^{\pi} r\sin t\sqrt{r^2\sin^2 t + r^2\cos^2 t}\,dt \\ &= 2\pi \int_0^{\pi} r\sin t\sqrt{r^2\left(\sin^2 t + \cos^2 t\right)}\,dt \\ &= 2\pi \int_0^{\pi} r^2 \sin t\,dt \\ &= 2\pi r^2 (-\cos t|_0^{\pi}) \\ &= 2\pi r^2(-\cos\pi + \cos 0) \\ &= 4\pi r^2. \end{aligned}$$

This is, in fact, the formula for the surface area of a sphere.

1.9 Find the surface area generated when the plane curve defined by the equations

$$x(t) = t^3, \quad y(t) = t^2, \quad 0 \le t \le 1$$

is revolved around the x-axis.

1.2 EXERCISES

For the following exercises, each set of parametric equations represents a line. Without eliminating the parameter, find the slope of each line.

62. $x = 3 + t, \quad y = 1 - t$

63. $x = 8 + 2t, \quad y = 1$

64. $x = 4 - 3t, \quad y = -2 + 6t$

65. $x = -5t + 7, \quad y = 3t - 1$

For the following exercises, determine the slope of the tangent line, then find the equation of the tangent line at the given value of the parameter.

66. $x = 3 \sin t, \quad y = 3 \cos t, \quad t = \frac{\pi}{4}$

67. $x = \cos t, \quad y = 8 \sin t, \; t = \frac{\pi}{2}$

68. $x = 2t, \quad y = t^3, \quad t = -1$

69. $x = t + \frac{1}{t}, \; y = t - \frac{1}{t}, \quad t = 1$

70. $x = \sqrt{t}, \quad y = 2t, \quad t = 4$

For the following exercises, find all points on the curve that have the given slope.

71. $x = 4 \cos t, \quad y = 4 \sin t, \quad$ slope = 0.5

72. $x = 2 \cos t, \quad y = 8 \sin t, \;$ slope $= -1$

73. $x = t + \frac{1}{t}, \; y = t - \frac{1}{t}, \;$ slope = 1

74. $x = 2 + \sqrt{t}, \quad y = 2 - 4t, \;$ slope = 0

For the following exercises, write the equation of the tangent line in Cartesian coordinates for the given parameter t.

75. $x = e^{\sqrt{t}}, \quad y = 1 - \ln t^2, \quad t = 1$

76. $x = t \ln t, \quad y = \sin^2 t, \; t = \frac{\pi}{4}$

77. $x = e^t, \quad y = (t - 1)^2, \quad$ at(1, 1)

78. For $x = \sin(2t), \; y = 2 \sin t$ where $0 \le t < 2\pi$. Find all values of t at which a horizontal tangent line exists.

79. For $x = \sin(2t), \; y = 2 \sin t$ where $0 \le t < 2\pi$. Find all values of t at which a vertical tangent line exists.

80. Find all points on the curve $x = 4 \cos(t), \; y = 4 \sin(t)$ that have the slope of $\frac{1}{2}$.

81. Find $\frac{dy}{dx}$ for $x = \sin(t), \; y = \cos(t)$.

82. Find the equation of the tangent line to $x = \sin(t), \; y = \cos(t)$ at $t = \frac{\pi}{4}$.

83. For the curve $x = 4t, \; y = 3t - 2,$ find the slope and concavity of the curve at $t = 3$.

84. For the parametric curve whose equation is $x = 4 \cos \theta, \; y = 4 \sin \theta,$ find the slope and concavity of the curve at $\theta = \frac{\pi}{4}$.

85. Find the slope and concavity for the curve whose equation is $x = 2 + \sec \theta, \; y = 1 + 2 \tan \theta$ at $\theta = \frac{\pi}{6}$.

86. Find all points on the curve $x = t + 4, \; y = t^3 - 3t$ at which there are vertical and horizontal tangents.

87. Find all points on the curve $x = \sec \theta, \; y = \tan \theta$ at which horizontal and vertical tangents exist.

For the following exercises, find d^2y/dx^2.

88. $x = t^4 - 1, \quad y = t - t^2$

89. $x = \sin(\pi t), \quad y = \cos(\pi t)$

90. $x = e^{-t}, \quad y = te^{2t}$

For the following exercises, find points on the curve at which tangent line is horizontal or vertical.

91. $x = t(t^2 - 3), \quad y = 3(t^2 - 3)$

92. $x = \frac{3t}{1 + t^3}, \quad y = \frac{3t^2}{1 + t^3}$

For the following exercises, find dy/dx at the value of the parameter.

93. $x = \cos t, \quad y = \sin t, \quad t = \frac{3\pi}{4}$

94. $x = \sqrt{t}, \quad y = 2t + 4, \qquad t = 9$

95. $x = 4\cos(2\pi s), \quad y = 3\sin(2\pi s), \qquad s = -\frac{1}{4}$

For the following exercises, find d^2y/dx^2 at the given point without eliminating the parameter.

96. $x = \frac{1}{2}t^2, \quad y = \frac{1}{3}t^3, \quad t = 2$

97. $x = \sqrt{t}, \quad y = 2t + 4, \quad t = 1$

98. Find t intervals on which the curve $x = 3t^2,\ y = t^3 - t$ is concave up as well as concave down.

99. Determine the concavity of the curve $x = 2t + \ln t,\ y = 2t - \ln t$.

100. Sketch and find the area under one arch of the cycloid $x = r(\theta - \sin\theta),\ y = r(1 - \cos\theta)$.

101. Find the area bounded by the curve $x = \cos t,\ y = e^t,\ 0 \le t \le \frac{\pi}{2}$ and the lines $y = 1$ and $x = 0$.

102. Find the area enclosed by the ellipse $x = a\cos\theta,\ y = b\sin\theta,\ 0 \le \theta < 2\pi$.

103. Find the area of the region bounded by $x = 2\sin^2\theta,\ y = 2\sin^2\theta\tan\theta$, for $0 \le \theta \le \frac{\pi}{2}$.

For the following exercises, find the area of the regions bounded by the parametric curves and the indicated values of the parameter.

104. $x = 2\cot\theta,\ y = 2\sin^2\theta,\ 0 \le \theta \le \pi$

105. **[T]** $x = 2a\cos t - a\cos(2t),\ y = 2a\sin t - a\sin(2t),\ 0 \le t < 2\pi$

106. **[T]** $x = a\sin(2t),\ y = b\sin(t),\ 0 \le t < 2\pi$ (the “hourglass”)

107. **[T]** $x = 2a\cos t - a\sin(2t),\ y = b\sin t,\ 0 \le t < 2\pi$ (the “teardrop”)

For the following exercises, find the arc length of the curve on the indicated interval of the parameter.

108. $x = 4t + 3, \quad y = 3t - 2, \quad 0 \le t \le 2$

109. $x = \frac{1}{3}t^3, \quad y = \frac{1}{2}t^2, \quad 0 \le t \le 1$

110. $x = \cos(2t), \quad y = \sin(2t), \quad 0 \le t \le \frac{\pi}{2}$

111. $x = 1 + t^2, \quad y = (1 + t)^3, \quad 0 \le t \le 1$

112. $x = e^t\cos t, \quad y = e^t\sin t, \quad 0 \le t \le \frac{\pi}{2}$ (express answer as a decimal rounded to three places)

113. $x = a\cos^3\theta,\ y = a\sin^3\theta$ on the interval $[0, 2\pi)$ (the hypocycloid)

114. Find the length of one arch of the cycloid $x = 4(t - \sin t),\ y = 4(1 - \cos t)$.

115. Find the distance traveled by a particle with position (x, y) as t varies in the given time interval: $x = \sin^2 t, \quad y = \cos^2 t, \quad 0 \le t \le 3\pi$.

116. Find the length of one arch of the cycloid $x = \theta - \sin\theta,\ y = 1 - \cos\theta$.

117. Show that the total length of the ellipse $x = 4\sin\theta,\ y = 3\cos\theta$ is $L = 16\int_0^{\pi/2}\sqrt{1 - e^2\sin^2\theta}\,d\theta$, where $e = \frac{c}{a}$ and $c = \sqrt{a^2 - b^2}$.

118. Find the length of the curve $x = e^t - t,\ y = 4e^{t/2},\ -8 \le t \le 3$.

For the following exercises, find the area of the surface obtained by rotating the given curve about the x-axis.

119. $x = t^3, \quad y = t^2, \quad 0 \le t \le 1$

120. $x = a\cos^3\theta, \quad y = a\sin^3\theta, \quad 0 \le \theta \le \frac{\pi}{2}$

121. **[T]** Use a CAS to find the area of the surface generated by rotating $x = t + t^3,\ y = t - \frac{1}{t^2},\ 1 \le t \le 2$ about the x-axis. (Answer to three decimal places.)

122. Find the surface area obtained by rotating $x = 3t^2,\ y = 2t^3,\ 0 \le t \le 5$ about the y-axis.

123. Find the area of the surface generated by revolving $x = t^2,\ y = 2t,\ 0 \le t \le 4$ about the x-axis.

124. Find the surface area generated by revolving $x = t^2,\ y = 2t^2,\ 0 \le t \le 1$ about the y-axis.

1.3 | Polar Coordinates

Learning Objectives

- **1.3.1** Locate points in a plane by using polar coordinates.
- **1.3.2** Convert points between rectangular and polar coordinates.
- **1.3.3** Sketch polar curves from given equations.
- **1.3.4** Convert equations between rectangular and polar coordinates.
- **1.3.5** Identify symmetry in polar curves and equations.

The rectangular coordinate system (or Cartesian plane) provides a means of mapping points to ordered pairs and ordered pairs to points. This is called a *one-to-one mapping* from points in the plane to ordered pairs. The polar coordinate system provides an alternative method of mapping points to ordered pairs. In this section we see that in some circumstances, polar coordinates can be more useful than rectangular coordinates.

Defining Polar Coordinates

To find the coordinates of a point in the polar coordinate system, consider **Figure 1.27**. The point P has Cartesian coordinates (x, y). The line segment connecting the origin to the point P measures the distance from the origin to P and has length r. The angle between the positive x-axis and the line segment has measure θ. This observation suggests a natural correspondence between the coordinate pair (x, y) and the values r and θ. This correspondence is the basis of the **polar coordinate system**. Note that every point in the Cartesian plane has two values (hence the term *ordered pair*) associated with it. In the polar coordinate system, each point also two values associated with it: r and θ.

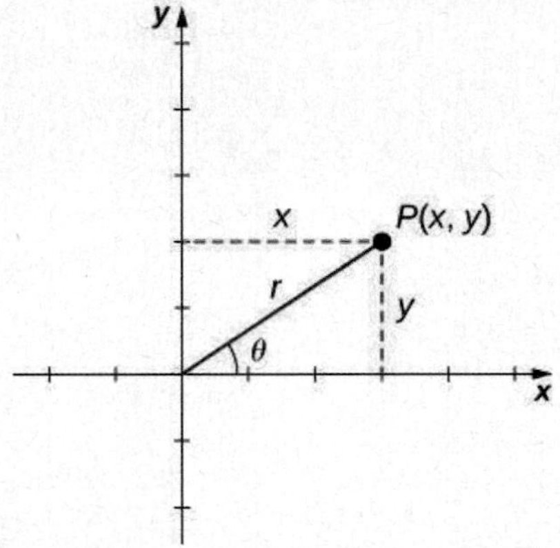

Figure 1.27 An arbitrary point in the Cartesian plane.

Using right-triangle trigonometry, the following equations are true for the point P:

$$\cos\theta = \frac{x}{r} \text{ so } x = r\cos\theta$$
$$\sin\theta = \frac{y}{r} \text{ so } y = r\sin\theta.$$

Furthermore,

$$r^2 = x^2 + y^2 \text{ and } \tan\theta = \frac{y}{x}.$$

Each point (x, y) in the Cartesian coordinate system can therefore be represented as an ordered pair (r, θ) in the polar coordinate system. The first coordinate is called the **radial coordinate** and the second coordinate is called the **angular coordinate**. Every point in the plane can be represented in this form.

Note that the equation $\tan\theta = y/x$ has an infinite number of solutions for any ordered pair (x, y). However, if we restrict the solutions to values between 0 and 2π then we can assign a unique solution to the quadrant in which the original point (x, y) is located. Then the corresponding value of r is positive, so $r^2 = x^2 + y^2$.

Theorem 1.4: Converting Points between Coordinate Systems

Given a point P in the plane with Cartesian coordinates (x, y) and polar coordinates (r, θ), the following conversion formulas hold true:

$$x = r\cos\theta \text{ and } y = r\sin\theta, \tag{1.7}$$

$$r^2 = x^2 + y^2 \text{ and } \tan\theta = \frac{y}{x}. \tag{1.8}$$

These formulas can be used to convert from rectangular to polar or from polar to rectangular coordinates.

Example 1.10

Converting between Rectangular and Polar Coordinates

Convert each of the following points into polar coordinates.

a. $(1, 1)$

b. $(-3, 4)$

c. $(0, 3)$

d. $(5\sqrt{3}, -5)$

Convert each of the following points into rectangular coordinates.

e. $(3, \pi/3)$

f. $(2, 3\pi/2)$

g. $(6, -5\pi/6)$

Solution

a. Use $x = 1$ and $y = 1$ in **Equation 1.8**:

$$\begin{aligned} r^2 &= x^2 + y^2 \\ &= 1^2 + 1^2 \\ r &= \sqrt{2} \end{aligned} \quad \text{and} \quad \begin{aligned} \tan\theta &= \frac{y}{x} \\ &= \frac{1}{1} = 1 \\ \theta &= \frac{\pi}{4}. \end{aligned}$$

Therefore this point can be represented as $\left(\sqrt{2}, \frac{\pi}{4}\right)$ in polar coordinates.

b. Use $x = -3$ and $y = 4$ in **Equation 1.8**:

$$\begin{aligned} r^2 &= x^2 + y^2 \\ &= (-3)^2 + (4)^2 \\ r &= 5 \end{aligned} \quad \text{and} \quad \begin{aligned} \tan\theta &= \frac{y}{x} \\ &= -\frac{4}{3} \\ \theta &= -\arctan\left(\frac{4}{3}\right) \\ &\approx 2.21. \end{aligned}$$

Therefore this point can be represented as $(5, 2.21)$ in polar coordinates.

c. Use $x = 0$ and $y = 3$ in **Equation 1.8**:

$$\begin{aligned} r^2 &= x^2 + y^2 \\ &= (3)^2 + (0)^2 \\ &= 9 + 0 \\ r &= 3 \end{aligned} \quad \text{and} \quad \begin{aligned} \tan\theta &= \frac{y}{x} \\ &= \frac{3}{0}. \end{aligned}$$

Direct application of the second equation leads to division by zero. Graphing the point $(0, 3)$ on the rectangular coordinate system reveals that the point is located on the positive *y*-axis. The angle between the positive *x*-axis and the positive *y*-axis is $\frac{\pi}{2}$. Therefore this point can be represented as $\left(3, \frac{\pi}{2}\right)$ in polar coordinates.

d. Use $x = 5\sqrt{3}$ and $y = -5$ in **Equation 1.8**:

$$\begin{aligned} r^2 &= x^2 + y^2 \\ &= \left(5\sqrt{3}\right)^2 + (-5)^2 \\ &= 75 + 25 \\ r &= 10 \end{aligned} \quad \text{and} \quad \begin{aligned} \tan\theta &= \frac{y}{x} \\ &= \frac{-5}{5\sqrt{3}} = -\frac{\sqrt{3}}{3} \\ \theta &= -\frac{\pi}{6}. \end{aligned}$$

Therefore this point can be represented as $\left(10, -\frac{\pi}{6}\right)$ in polar coordinates.

e. Use $r = 3$ and $\theta = \frac{\pi}{3}$ in **Equation 1.7**:

$$\begin{aligned} x &= r\cos\theta \\ &= 3\cos\left(\frac{\pi}{3}\right) \\ &= 3\left(\frac{1}{2}\right) = \frac{3}{2} \end{aligned} \quad \text{and} \quad \begin{aligned} y &= r\sin\theta \\ &= 3\sin\left(\frac{\pi}{3}\right) \\ &= 3\left(\frac{\sqrt{3}}{2}\right) = \frac{3\sqrt{3}}{2}. \end{aligned}$$

Therefore this point can be represented as $\left(\frac{3}{2}, \frac{3\sqrt{3}}{2}\right)$ in rectangular coordinates.

f. Use $r = 2$ and $\theta = \frac{3\pi}{2}$ in **Equation 1.7**:

$$\begin{aligned} x &= r\cos\theta \\ &= 2\cos\left(\frac{3\pi}{2}\right) \\ &= 2(0) = 0 \end{aligned} \quad \text{and} \quad \begin{aligned} y &= r\sin\theta \\ &= 2\sin\left(\frac{3\pi}{2}\right) \\ &= 2(-1) = -2. \end{aligned}$$

Therefore this point can be represented as $(0, -2)$ in rectangular coordinates.

g. Use $r = 6$ and $\theta = -\frac{5\pi}{6}$ in **Equation 1.7**:

$$\begin{aligned} x &= r\cos\theta \\ &= 6\cos\left(-\frac{5\pi}{6}\right) \\ &= 6\left(-\frac{\sqrt{3}}{2}\right) \\ &= -3\sqrt{3} \end{aligned} \quad \text{and} \quad \begin{aligned} y &= r\sin\theta \\ &= 6\sin\left(-\frac{5\pi}{6}\right) \\ &= 6\left(-\frac{1}{2}\right) \\ &= -3. \end{aligned}$$

Therefore this point can be represented as $(-3\sqrt{3}, -3)$ in rectangular coordinates.

1.10 Convert $(-8, -8)$ into polar coordinates and $\left(4, \frac{2\pi}{3}\right)$ into rectangular coordinates.

The polar representation of a point is not unique. For example, the polar coordinates $\left(2, \frac{\pi}{3}\right)$ and $\left(2, \frac{7\pi}{3}\right)$ both represent the point $(1, \sqrt{3})$ in the rectangular system. Also, the value of r can be negative. Therefore, the point with polar coordinates $\left(-2, \frac{4\pi}{3}\right)$ also represents the point $(1, \sqrt{3})$ in the rectangular system, as we can see by using **Equation 1.8**:

$$\begin{aligned} x &= r\cos\theta \\ &= -2\cos\left(\frac{4\pi}{3}\right) \\ &= -2\left(-\frac{1}{2}\right) = 1 \end{aligned} \quad \text{and} \quad \begin{aligned} y &= r\sin\theta \\ &= -2\sin\left(\frac{4\pi}{3}\right) \\ &= -2\left(-\frac{\sqrt{3}}{2}\right) = \sqrt{3}. \end{aligned}$$

Every point in the plane has an infinite number of representations in polar coordinates. However, each point in the plane has only one representation in the rectangular coordinate system.

Note that the polar representation of a point in the plane also has a visual interpretation. In particular, r is the directed distance that the point lies from the origin, and θ measures the angle that the line segment from the origin to the point makes with the positive x-axis. Positive angles are measured in a counterclockwise direction and negative angles are measured in a clockwise direction. The polar coordinate system appears in the following figure.

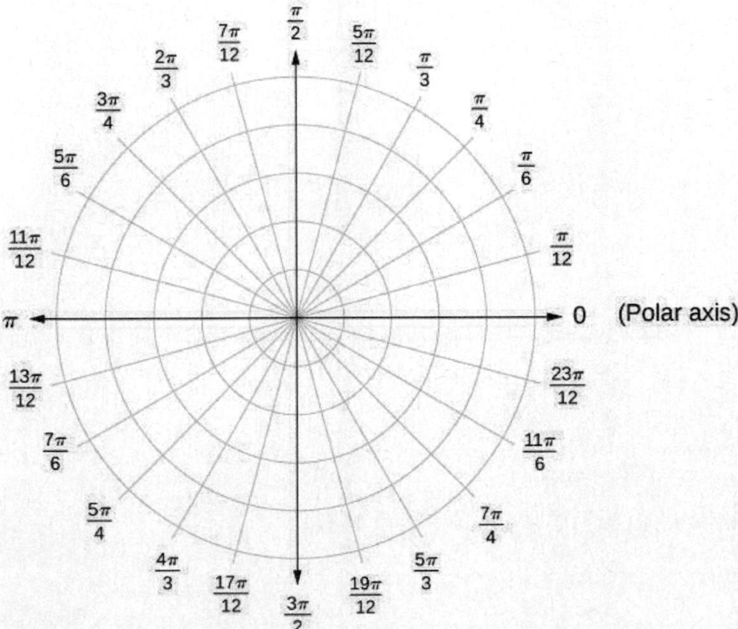

Figure 1.28 The polar coordinate system.

The line segment starting from the center of the graph going to the right (called the positive x-axis in the Cartesian system) is the **polar axis**. The center point is the **pole**, or origin, of the coordinate system, and corresponds to $r = 0$. The innermost circle shown in **Figure 1.28** contains all points a distance of 1 unit from the pole, and is represented by the equation $r = 1$.

Then $r = 2$ is the set of points 2 units from the pole, and so on. The line segments emanating from the pole correspond to fixed angles. To plot a point in the polar coordinate system, start with the angle. If the angle is positive, then measure the angle from the polar axis in a counterclockwise direction. If it is negative, then measure it clockwise. If the value of r is positive, move that distance along the terminal ray of the angle. If it is negative, move along the ray that is opposite the terminal ray of the given angle.

Example 1.11

Plotting Points in the Polar Plane

Plot each of the following points on the polar plane.

a. $\left(2, \frac{\pi}{4}\right)$

b. $\left(-3, \frac{2\pi}{3}\right)$

c. $\left(4, \frac{5\pi}{4}\right)$

Solution

The three points are plotted in the following figure.

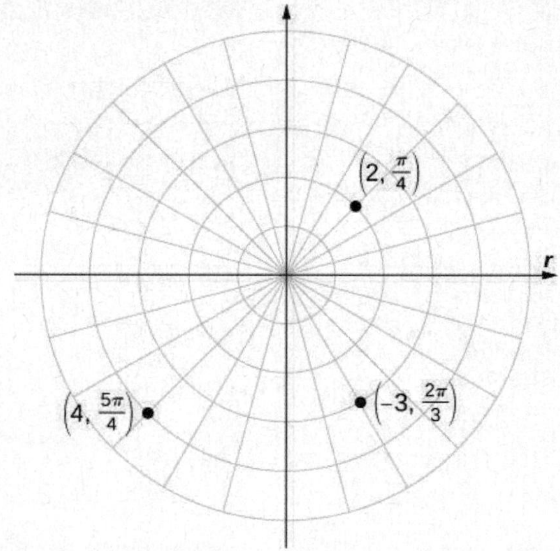

Figure 1.29 Three points plotted in the polar coordinate system.

1.11 Plot $\left(4, \frac{5\pi}{3}\right)$ and $\left(-3, -\frac{7\pi}{2}\right)$ on the polar plane.

Polar Curves

Now that we know how to plot points in the polar coordinate system, we can discuss how to plot curves. In the rectangular coordinate system, we can graph a function $y = f(x)$ and create a curve in the Cartesian plane. In a similar fashion, we can graph a curve that is generated by a function $r = f(\theta)$.

The general idea behind graphing a function in polar coordinates is the same as graphing a function in rectangular coordinates. Start with a list of values for the independent variable (θ in this case) and calculate the corresponding values of the dependent variable r. This process generates a list of ordered pairs, which can be plotted in the polar coordinate system. Finally, connect the points, and take advantage of any patterns that may appear. The function may be periodic, for example, which indicates that only a limited number of values for the independent variable are needed.

Problem-Solving Strategy: Plotting a Curve in Polar Coordinates

1. Create a table with two columns. The first column is for θ, and the second column is for r.
2. Create a list of values for θ.
3. Calculate the corresponding r values for each θ.
4. Plot each ordered pair (r, θ) on the coordinate axes.
5. Connect the points and look for a pattern.

Watch this **video (http://www.openstaxcollege.org/l/20_polarcurves)** for more information on sketching polar curves.

Example 1.12

Graphing a Function in Polar Coordinates

Graph the curve defined by the function $r = 4 \sin \theta$. Identify the curve and rewrite the equation in rectangular coordinates.

Solution

Because the function is a multiple of a sine function, it is periodic with period 2π, so use values for θ between 0 and 2π. The result of steps 1–3 appear in the following table. **Figure 1.30** shows the graph based on this table.

θ	$r = 4\sin\theta$		θ	$r = 4\sin\theta$
0	0		π	0
$\frac{\pi}{6}$	2		$\frac{7\pi}{6}$	-2
$\frac{\pi}{4}$	$2\sqrt{2} \approx 2.8$		$\frac{5\pi}{4}$	$-2\sqrt{2} \approx -2.8$
$\frac{\pi}{3}$	$2\sqrt{3} \approx 3.4$		$\frac{4\pi}{3}$	$-2\sqrt{3} \approx -3.4$
$\frac{\pi}{2}$	4		$\frac{3\pi}{2}$	4
$\frac{2\pi}{3}$	$2\sqrt{3} \approx 3.4$		$\frac{5\pi}{3}$	$-2\sqrt{3} \approx -3.4$
$\frac{3\pi}{4}$	$2\sqrt{2} \approx 2.8$		$\frac{7\pi}{4}$	$-2\sqrt{2} \approx -2.8$
$\frac{5\pi}{6}$	2		$\frac{11\pi}{6}$	-2
			2π	0

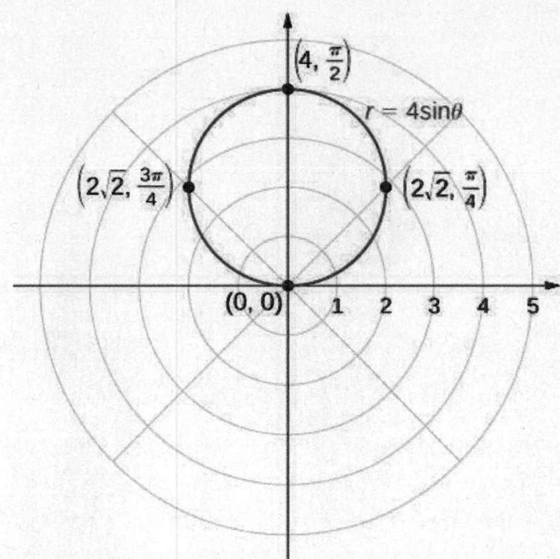

Figure 1.30 The graph of the function $r = 4 \sin \theta$ is a circle.

This is the graph of a circle. The equation $r = 4 \sin \theta$ can be converted into rectangular coordinates by first multiplying both sides by r. This gives the equation $r^2 = 4r \sin \theta$. Next use the facts that $r^2 = x^2 + y^2$ and $y = r \sin \theta$. This gives $x^2 + y^2 = 4y$. To put this equation into standard form, subtract $4y$ from both sides of the equation and complete the square:

$$\begin{aligned} x^2 + y^2 - 4y &= 0 \\ x^2 + \left(y^2 - 4y\right) &= 0 \\ x^2 + \left(y^2 - 4y + 4\right) &= 0 + 4 \\ x^2 + (y - 2)^2 &= 4. \end{aligned}$$

This is the equation of a circle with radius 2 and center $(0, 2)$ in the rectangular coordinate system.

 **1.12** Create a graph of the curve defined by the function $r = 4 + 4 \cos \theta$.

The graph in **Example 1.12** was that of a circle. The equation of the circle can be transformed into rectangular coordinates using the coordinate transformation formulas in **Equation 1.8**. **Example 1.14** gives some more examples of functions for transforming from polar to rectangular coordinates.

Example 1.13

Transforming Polar Equations to Rectangular Coordinates

Rewrite each of the following equations in rectangular coordinates and identify the graph.

a. $\theta = \frac{\pi}{3}$

b. $r = 3$

c. $r = 6\cos\theta - 8\sin\theta$

Solution

a. Take the tangent of both sides. This gives $\tan\theta = \tan(\pi/3) = \sqrt{3}$. Since $\tan\theta = y/x$ we can replace the left-hand side of this equation by y/x. This gives $y/x = \sqrt{3}$, which can be rewritten as $y = x\sqrt{3}$. This is the equation of a straight line passing through the origin with slope $\sqrt{3}$. In general, any polar equation of the form $\theta = K$ represents a straight line through the pole with slope equal to $\tan K$.

b. First, square both sides of the equation. This gives $r^2 = 9$. Next replace r^2 with $x^2 + y^2$. This gives the equation $x^2 + y^2 = 9$, which is the equation of a circle centered at the origin with radius 3. In general, any polar equation of the form $r = k$ where k is a positive constant represents a circle of radius k centered at the origin. (*Note*: when squaring both sides of an equation it is possible to introduce new points unintentionally. This should always be taken into consideration. However, in this case we do not introduce new points. For example, $\left(-3, \frac{\pi}{3}\right)$ is the same point as $\left(3, \frac{4\pi}{3}\right)$.)

c. Multiply both sides of the equation by r. This leads to $r^2 = 6r\cos\theta - 8r\sin\theta$. Next use the formulas

$$r^2 = x^2 + y^2, \quad x = r\cos\theta, \quad y = r\sin\theta.$$

This gives

$$\begin{aligned} r^2 &= 6(r\cos\theta) - 8(r\sin\theta) \\ x^2 + y^2 &= 6x - 8y. \end{aligned}$$

To put this equation into standard form, first move the variables from the right-hand side of the equation to the left-hand side, then complete the square.

$$\begin{aligned} x^2 + y^2 &= 6x - 8y \\ x^2 - 6x + y^2 + 8y &= 0 \\ \left(x^2 - 6x\right) + \left(y^2 + 8y\right) &= 0 \\ \left(x^2 - 6x + 9\right) + \left(y^2 + 8y + 16\right) &= 9 + 16 \\ (x-3)^2 + (y+4)^2 &= 25. \end{aligned}$$

This is the equation of a circle with center at $(3, -4)$ and radius 5. Notice that the circle passes through the origin since the center is 5 units away.

1.13 Rewrite the equation $r = \sec\theta\tan\theta$ in rectangular coordinates and identify its graph.

We have now seen several examples of drawing graphs of curves defined by **polar equations**. A summary of some common curves is given in the tables below. In each equation, a and b are arbitrary constants.

Name	Equation	Example
Line passing through the pole with slope tan K	$\theta = K$	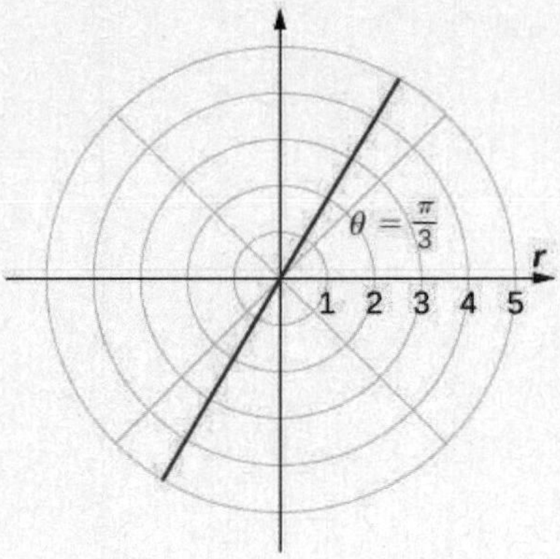 $\theta = \frac{\pi}{3}$
Circle	$r = a\cos\theta + b\sin\theta$	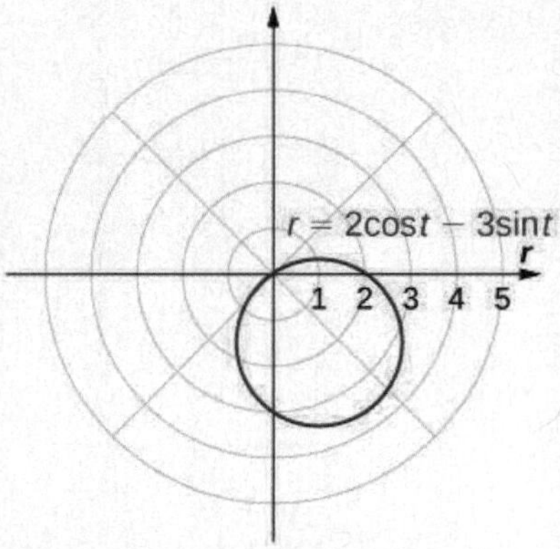 $r = 2\cos t - 3\sin t$
Spiral	$r = a + b\theta$	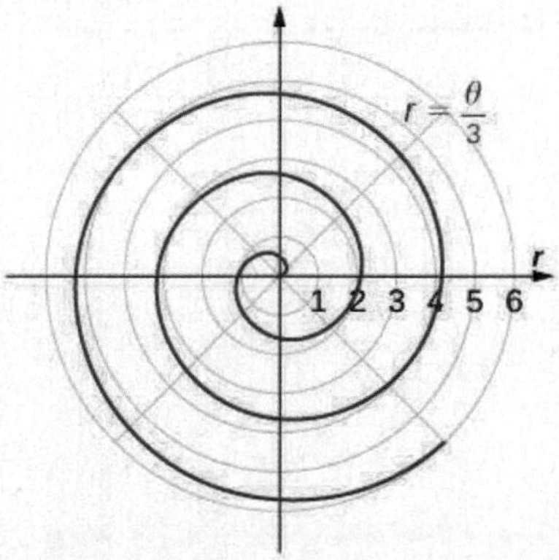 $r = \frac{\theta}{3}$

Figure 1.31

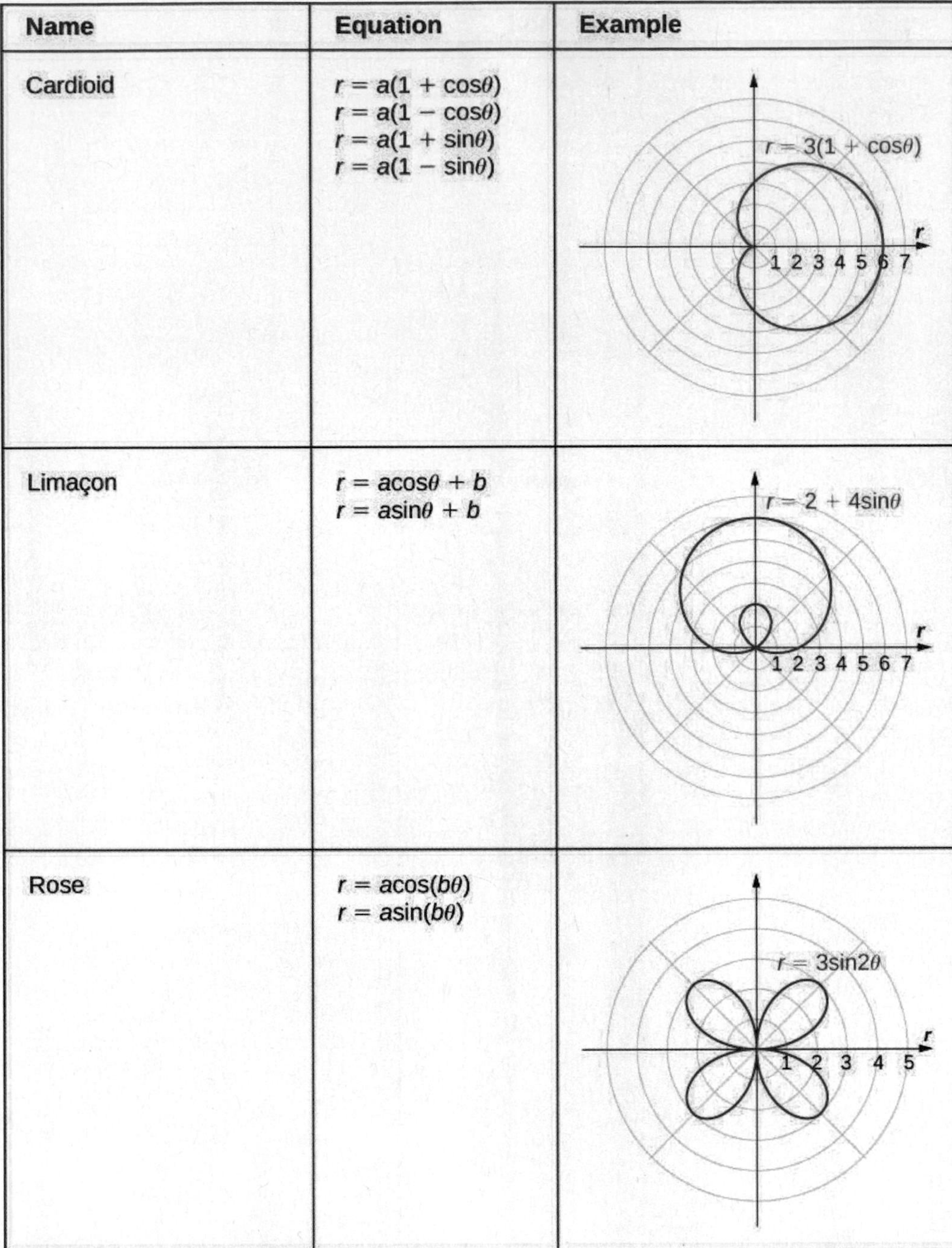

Name	Equation	Example
Cardioid	$r = a(1 + \cos\theta)$ $r = a(1 - \cos\theta)$ $r = a(1 + \sin\theta)$ $r = a(1 - \sin\theta)$	$r = 3(1 + \cos\theta)$
Limaçon	$r = a\cos\theta + b$ $r = a\sin\theta + b$	$r = 2 + 4\sin\theta$
Rose	$r = a\cos(b\theta)$ $r = a\sin(b\theta)$	$r = 3\sin 2\theta$

Figure 1.32

A **cardioid** is a special case of a **limaçon** (pronounced “lee-mah-son”), in which $a = b$ or $a = -b$. The **rose** is a very interesting curve. Notice that the graph of $r = 3\sin 2\theta$ has four petals. However, the graph of $r = 3\sin 3\theta$ has three petals as shown.

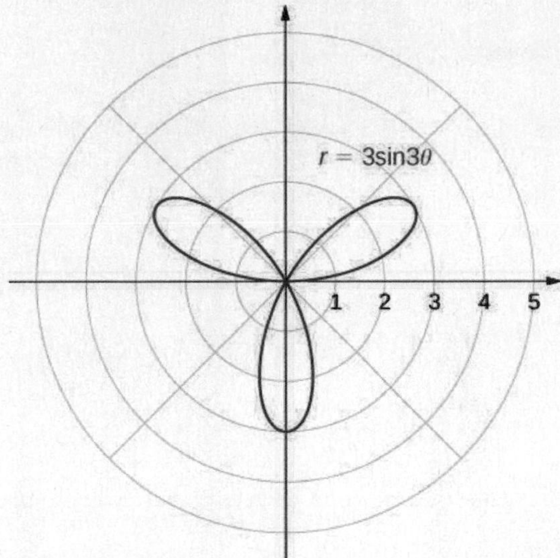

Figure 1.33 Graph of $r = 3\sin 3\theta$.

If the coefficient of θ is even, the graph has twice as many petals as the coefficient. If the coefficient of θ is odd, then the number of petals equals the coefficient. You are encouraged to explore why this happens. Even more interesting graphs emerge when the coefficient of θ is not an integer. For example, if it is rational, then the curve is closed; that is, it eventually ends where it started (**Figure 1.34**(a)). However, if the coefficient is irrational, then the curve never closes (**Figure 1.34**(b)). Although it may appear that the curve is closed, a closer examination reveals that the petals just above the positive x axis are slightly thicker. This is because the petal does not quite match up with the starting point.

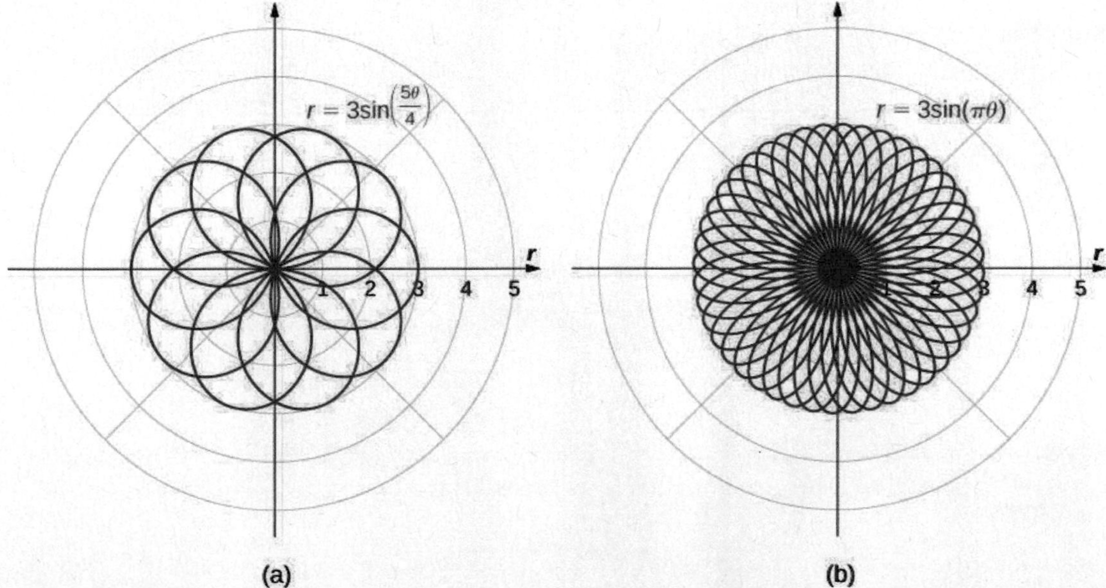

Figure 1.34 Polar rose graphs of functions with (a) rational coefficient and (b) irrational coefficient. Note that the rose in part (b) would actually fill the entire circle if plotted in full.

Since the curve defined by the graph of $r = 3\sin(\pi\theta)$ never closes, the curve depicted in **Figure 1.34**(b) is only a partial depiction. In fact, this is an example of a **space-filling curve**. A space-filling curve is one that in fact occupies a two-dimensional subset of the real plane. In this case the curve occupies the circle of radius 3 centered at the origin.

Example 1.14

Chapter Opener: Describing a Spiral

Recall the chambered nautilus introduced in the chapter opener. This creature displays a spiral when half the outer shell is cut away. It is possible to describe a spiral using rectangular coordinates. **Figure 1.35** shows a spiral in rectangular coordinates. How can we describe this curve mathematically?

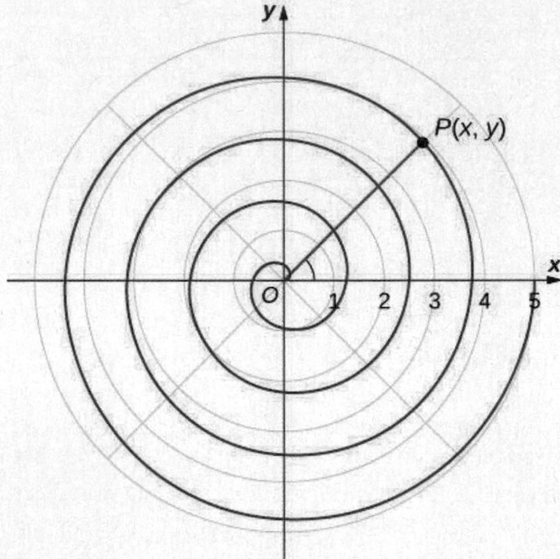

Figure 1.35 How can we describe a spiral graph mathematically?

Solution

As the point P travels around the spiral in a counterclockwise direction, its distance d from the origin increases. Assume that the distance d is a constant multiple k of the angle θ that the line segment OP makes with the positive x-axis. Therefore $d(P, O) = k\theta,$ where O is the origin. Now use the distance formula and some trigonometry:

$$\begin{aligned} d(P, O) &= k\theta \\ \sqrt{(x-0)^2 + (y-0)^2} &= k \arctan\left(\frac{y}{x}\right) \\ \sqrt{x^2 + y^2} &= k \arctan\left(\frac{y}{x}\right) \\ \arctan\left(\frac{y}{x}\right) &= \frac{\sqrt{x^2 + y^2}}{k} \\ y &= x \tan\left(\frac{\sqrt{x^2 + y^2}}{k}\right). \end{aligned}$$

Although this equation describes the spiral, it is not possible to solve it directly for either x or y. However, if we use polar coordinates, the equation becomes much simpler. In particular, $d(P, O) = r,$ and θ is the second coordinate. Therefore the equation for the spiral becomes $r = k\theta.$ Note that when $\theta = 0$ we also have $r = 0,$ so the spiral emanates from the origin. We can remove this restriction by adding a constant to the equation. Then the equation for the spiral becomes $r = a + k\theta$ for arbitrary constants a and $k.$ This is referred to as an Archimedean spiral, after the Greek mathematician Archimedes.

Another type of spiral is the logarithmic spiral, described by the function $r = a \cdot b^{\theta}.$ A graph of the function $r = 1.2\left(1.25^{\theta}\right)$ is given in **Figure 1.36**. This spiral describes the shell shape of the chambered nautilus.

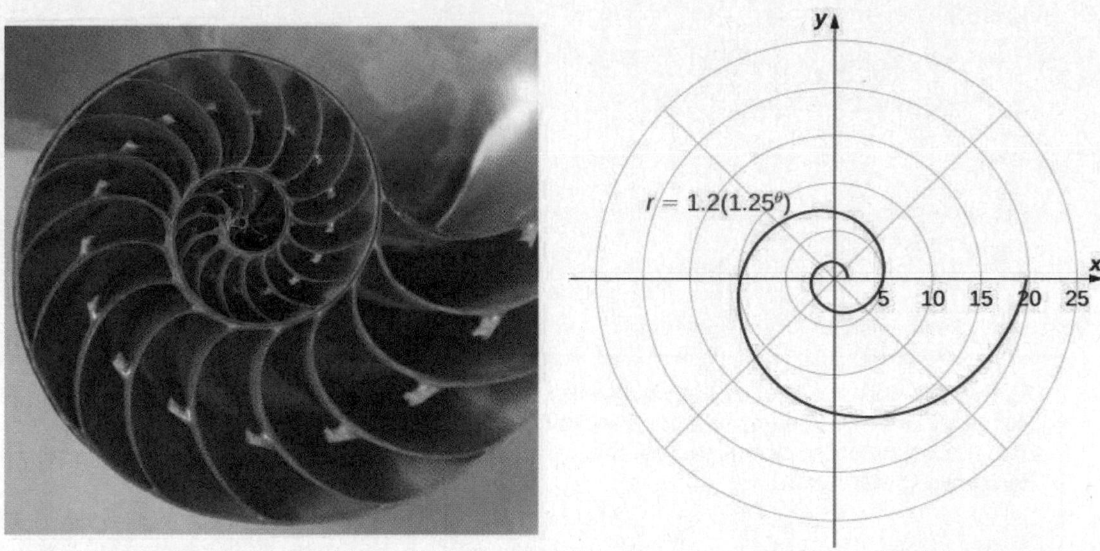

Figure 1.36 A logarithmic spiral is similar to the shape of the chambered nautilus shell. (credit: modification of work by Jitze Couperus, Flickr)

Suppose a curve is described in the polar coordinate system via the function $r = f(\theta)$. Since we have conversion formulas from polar to rectangular coordinates given by

$$x = r\cos\theta$$
$$y = r\sin\theta,$$

it is possible to rewrite these formulas using the function

$$x = f(\theta)\cos\theta$$
$$y = f(\theta)\sin\theta.$$

This step gives a parameterization of the curve in rectangular coordinates using θ as the parameter. For example, the spiral formula $r = a + b\theta$ from **Figure 1.31** becomes

$$x = (a + b\theta)\cos\theta$$
$$y = (a + b\theta)\sin\theta.$$

Letting θ range from $-\infty$ to ∞ generates the entire spiral.

Symmetry in Polar Coordinates

When studying symmetry of functions in rectangular coordinates (i.e., in the form $y = f(x)$), we talk about symmetry with respect to the *y*-axis and symmetry with respect to the origin. In particular, if $f(-x) = f(x)$ for all x in the domain of f, then f is an even function and its graph is symmetric with respect to the *y*-axis. If $f(-x) = -f(x)$ for all x in the domain of f, then f is an odd function and its graph is symmetric with respect to the origin. By determining which types of symmetry a graph exhibits, we can learn more about the shape and appearance of the graph. Symmetry can also reveal other properties of the function that generates the graph. Symmetry in polar curves works in a similar fashion.

Theorem 1.5: Symmetry in Polar Curves and Equations

Consider a curve generated by the function $r = f(\theta)$ in polar coordinates.

i. The curve is symmetric about the polar axis if for every point (r, θ) on the graph, the point $(r, -\theta)$ is also on the graph. Similarly, the equation $r = f(\theta)$ is unchanged by replacing θ with $-\theta$.

ii. The curve is symmetric about the pole if for every point (r, θ) on the graph, the point $(r, \pi + \theta)$ is also on the graph. Similarly, the equation $r = f(\theta)$ is unchanged when replacing r with $-r$, or θ with $\pi + \theta$.

iii. The curve is symmetric about the vertical line $\theta = \frac{\pi}{2}$ if for every point (r, θ) on the graph, the point $(r, \pi - \theta)$ is also on the graph. Similarly, the equation $r = f(\theta)$ is unchanged when θ is replaced by $\pi - \theta$.

The following table shows examples of each type of symmetry.

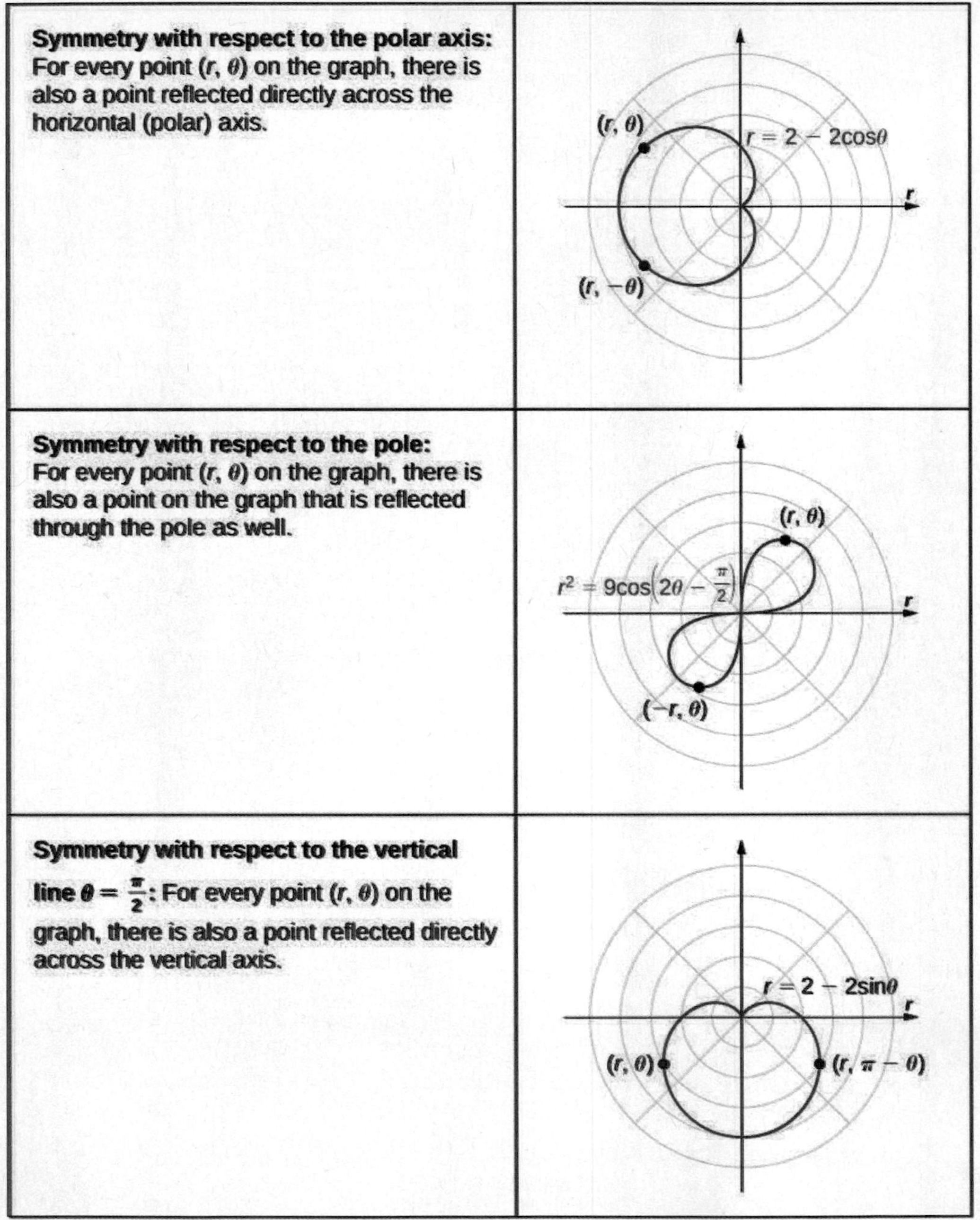
Symmetry with respect to the polar axis: For every point (r, θ) on the graph, there is also a point reflected directly across the horizontal (polar) axis.
(r, θ)
r = 2 − 2cosθ
r
(r, −θ)
Symmetry with respect to the pole: For every point (r, θ) on the graph, there is also a point on the graph that is reflected through the pole as well.
(r, θ)
r² = 9cos(2θ − π/2)
r
(−r, θ)
Symmetry with respect to the vertical line θ = π/2: For every point (r, θ) on the graph, there is also a point reflected directly across the vertical axis.
r = 2 − 2sinθ
r
(r, θ)
(r, π − θ)

Example 1.15

Using Symmetry to Graph a Polar Equation

Find the symmetry of the rose defined by the equation $r = 3\sin(2\theta)$ and create a graph.

Solution

Suppose the point (r, θ) is on the graph of $r = 3\sin(2\theta)$.

i. To test for symmetry about the polar axis, first try replacing θ with $-\theta$. This gives $r = 3\sin(2(-\theta)) = -3\sin(2\theta)$. Since this changes the original equation, this test is not satisfied. However, returning to the original equation and replacing r with $-r$ and θ with $\pi - \theta$ yields

$$\begin{aligned} -r &= 3\sin(2(\pi - \theta)) \\ -r &= 3\sin(2\pi - 2\theta) \\ -r &= 3\sin(-2\theta) \\ -r &= -3\sin 2\theta. \end{aligned}$$

Multiplying both sides of this equation by -1 gives $r = 3\sin 2\theta$, which is the original equation. This demonstrates that the graph is symmetric with respect to the polar axis.

ii. To test for symmetry with respect to the pole, first replace r with $-r$, which yields $-r = 3\sin(2\theta)$. Multiplying both sides by -1 gives $r = -3\sin(2\theta)$, which does not agree with the original equation. Therefore the equation does not pass the test for this symmetry. However, returning to the original equation and replacing θ with $\theta + \pi$ gives

$$\begin{aligned} r &= 3\sin(2(\theta + \pi)) \\ &= 3\sin(2\theta + 2\pi) \\ &= 3(\sin 2\theta \cos 2\pi + \cos 2\theta \sin 2\pi) \\ &= 3\sin 2\theta. \end{aligned}$$

Since this agrees with the original equation, the graph is symmetric about the pole.

iii. To test for symmetry with respect to the vertical line $\theta = \frac{\pi}{2}$, first replace both r with $-r$ and θ with $-\theta$.

$$\begin{aligned} -r &= 3\sin(2(-\theta)) \\ -r &= 3\sin(-2\theta) \\ -r &= -3\sin 2\theta. \end{aligned}$$

Multiplying both sides of this equation by -1 gives $r = 3\sin 2\theta$, which is the original equation. Therefore the graph is symmetric about the vertical line $\theta = \frac{\pi}{2}$.

This graph has symmetry with respect to the polar axis, the origin, and the vertical line going through the pole. To graph the function, tabulate values of θ between 0 and $\pi/2$ and then reflect the resulting graph.

θ	r
0	0
$\frac{\pi}{6}$	$\frac{3\sqrt{3}}{2} \approx 2.6$
$\frac{\pi}{4}$	3
$\frac{\pi}{3}$	$\frac{3\sqrt{3}}{2} \approx 2.6$
$\frac{\pi}{2}$	0

This gives one petal of the rose, as shown in the following graph.

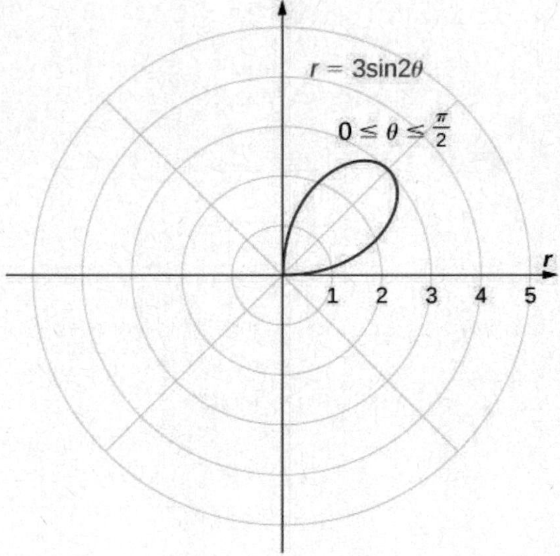

Figure 1.37 The graph of the equation between $\theta = 0$ and $\theta = \pi/2$.

Reflecting this image into the other three quadrants gives the entire graph as shown.

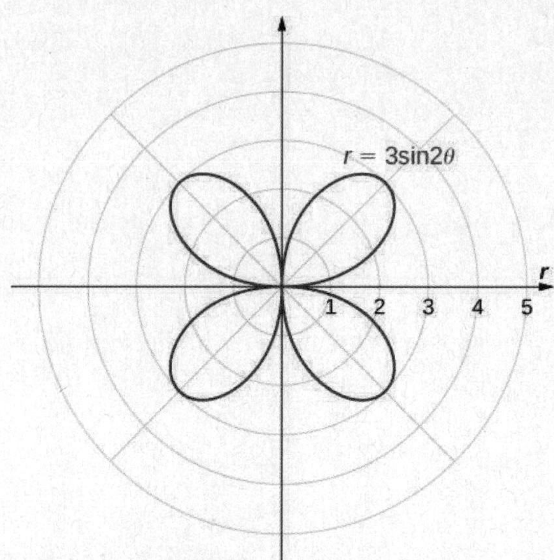

Figure 1.38 The entire graph of the equation is called a four-petaled rose.

1.14 Determine the symmetry of the graph determined by the equation $r = 2\cos(3\theta)$ and create a graph.

1.3 EXERCISES

In the following exercises, plot the point whose polar coordinates are given by first constructing the angle θ and then marking off the distance r along the ray.

125. $\left(3, \frac{\pi}{6}\right)$

126. $\left(-2, \frac{5\pi}{3}\right)$

127. $\left(0, \frac{7\pi}{6}\right)$

128. $\left(-4, \frac{3\pi}{4}\right)$

129. $\left(1, \frac{\pi}{4}\right)$

130. $\left(2, \frac{5\pi}{6}\right)$

131. $\left(1, \frac{\pi}{2}\right)$

For the following exercises, consider the polar graph below. Give two sets of polar coordinates for each point.

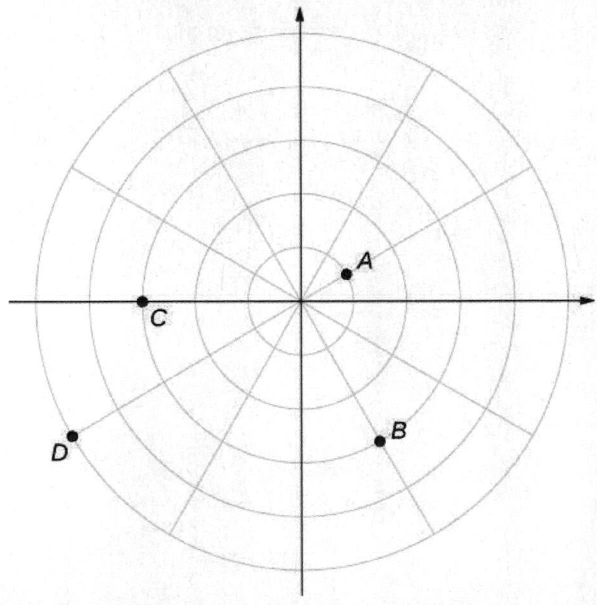

132. Coordinates of point *A*.

133. Coordinates of point *B*.

134. Coordinates of point *C*.

135. Coordinates of point *D*.

For the following exercises, the rectangular coordinates of a point are given. Find two sets of polar coordinates for the point in $(0, 2\pi]$. Round to three decimal places.

136. $(2, 2)$

137. $(3, -4)$ $(3, -4)$

138. $(8, 15)$

139. $(-6, 8)$

140. $(4, 3)$

141. $\left(3, -\sqrt{3}\right)$

For the following exercises, find rectangular coordinates for the given point in polar coordinates.

142. $\left(2, \frac{5\pi}{4}\right)$

143. $\left(-2, \frac{\pi}{6}\right)$

144. $\left(5, \frac{\pi}{3}\right)$

145. $\left(1, \frac{7\pi}{6}\right)$

146. $\left(-3, \frac{3\pi}{4}\right)$

147. $\left(0, \frac{\pi}{2}\right)$

148. $(-4.5, 6.5)$

For the following exercises, determine whether the graphs of the polar equation are symmetric with respect to the x -axis, the y -axis, or the origin.

149. $r = 3\sin(2\theta)$

150. $r^2 = 9\cos\theta$

151. $r = \cos\left(\frac{\theta}{5}\right)$

152. $r = 2\sec\theta$

153. $r = 1 + \cos\theta$

For the following exercises, describe the graph of each polar equation. Confirm each description by converting into a rectangular equation.

154. $r = 3$

155. $\theta = \frac{\pi}{4}$

156. $r = \sec\theta$

157. $r = \csc\theta$

For the following exercises, convert the rectangular equation to polar form and sketch its graph.

158. $x^2 + y^2 = 16$

159. $x^2 - y^2 = 16$

160. $x = 8$

For the following exercises, convert the rectangular equation to polar form and sketch its graph.

161. $3x - y = 2$

162. $y^2 = 4x$

For the following exercises, convert the polar equation to rectangular form and sketch its graph.

163. $r = 4\sin\theta$

164. $r = 6\cos\theta$

165. $r = \theta$

166. $r = \cot\theta\csc\theta$

For the following exercises, sketch a graph of the polar equation and identify any symmetry.

167. $r = 1 + \sin\theta$

168. $r = 3 - 2\cos\theta$

169. $r = 2 - 2\sin\theta$

170. $r = 5 - 4\sin\theta$

171. $r = 3\cos(2\theta)$

172. $r = 3\sin(2\theta)$

173. $r = 2\cos(3\theta)$

174. $r = 3\cos\left(\frac{\theta}{2}\right)$

175. $r^2 = 4\cos(2\theta)$

176. $r^2 = 4\sin\theta$

177. $r = 2\theta$

178. **[T]** The graph of $r = 2\cos(2\theta)\sec(\theta).$ is called a *strophoid*. Use a graphing utility to sketch the graph, and, from the graph, determine the asymptote.

179. **[T]** Use a graphing utility and sketch the graph of $r = \frac{6}{2\sin\theta - 3\cos\theta}.$

180. **[T]** Use a graphing utility to graph $r = \frac{1}{1 - \cos\theta}.$

181. **[T]** Use technology to graph $r = e^{\sin(\theta)} - 2\cos(4\theta).$

182. **[T]** Use technology to plot $r = \sin\left(\frac{3\theta}{7}\right)$ (use the interval $0 \le \theta \le 14\pi$).

183. Without using technology, sketch the polar curve $\theta = \frac{2\pi}{3}.$

184. **[T]** Use a graphing utility to plot $r = \theta\sin\theta$ for $-\pi \le \theta \le \pi.$

185. **[T]** Use technology to plot $r = e^{-0.1\theta}$ for $-10 \le \theta \le 10.$

186. **[T]** There is a curve known as the "*Black Hole*." Use technology to plot $r = e^{-0.01\theta}$ for $-100 \le \theta \le 100.$

187. **[T]** Use the results of the preceding two problems to explore the graphs of $r = e^{-0.001\theta}$ and $r = e^{-0.0001\theta}$ for $|\theta| > 100.$

1.4 | Area and Arc Length in Polar Coordinates

Learning Objectives

1.4.1 Apply the formula for area of a region in polar coordinates.
1.4.2 Determine the arc length of a polar curve.

In the rectangular coordinate system, the definite integral provides a way to calculate the area under a curve. In particular, if we have a function $y = f(x)$ defined from $x = a$ to $x = b$ where $f(x) > 0$ on this interval, the area between the curve and the *x*-axis is given by $A = \int_a^b f(x)\,dx$. This fact, along with the formula for evaluating this integral, is summarized in the Fundamental Theorem of Calculus. Similarly, the arc length of this curve is given by $L = \int_a^b \sqrt{1 + (f'(x))^2}\,dx$. In this section, we study analogous formulas for area and arc length in the polar coordinate system.

Areas of Regions Bounded by Polar Curves

We have studied the formulas for area under a curve defined in rectangular coordinates and parametrically defined curves. Now we turn our attention to deriving a formula for the area of a region bounded by a polar curve. Recall that the proof of the Fundamental Theorem of Calculus used the concept of a Riemann sum to approximate the area under a curve by using rectangles. For polar curves we use the Riemann sum again, but the rectangles are replaced by sectors of a circle.

Consider a curve defined by the function $r = f(\theta)$, where $\alpha \le \theta \le \beta$. Our first step is to partition the interval $[\alpha, \beta]$ into n equal-width subintervals. The width of each subinterval is given by the formula $\Delta\theta = (\beta - \alpha)/n$, and the ith partition point θ_i is given by the formula $\theta_i = \alpha + i\Delta\theta$. Each partition point $\theta = \theta_i$ defines a line with slope $\tan\theta_i$ passing through the pole as shown in the following graph.

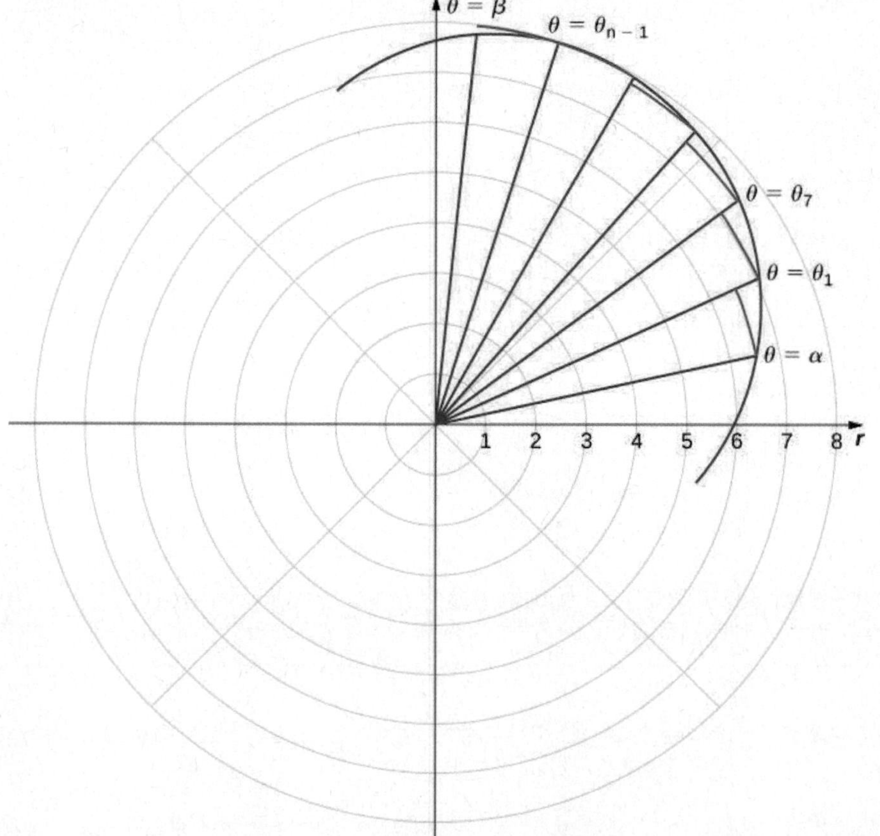

Figure 1.39 A partition of a typical curve in polar coordinates.

The line segments are connected by arcs of constant radius. This defines sectors whose areas can be calculated by using a geometric formula. The area of each sector is then used to approximate the area between successive line segments. We then sum the areas of the sectors to approximate the total area. This approach gives a Riemann sum approximation for the total area. The formula for the area of a sector of a circle is illustrated in the following figure.

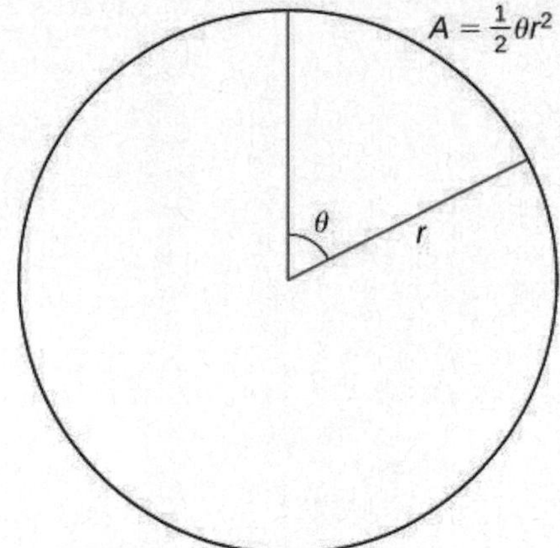

Figure 1.40 The area of a sector of a circle is given by $A = \frac{1}{2}\theta r^2$.

Recall that the area of a circle is $A = \pi r^2$. When measuring angles in radians, 360 degrees is equal to 2π radians. Therefore a fraction of a circle can be measured by the central angle θ. The fraction of the circle is given by $\frac{\theta}{2\pi}$, so the area of the sector is this fraction multiplied by the total area:

$$A = \left(\frac{\theta}{2\pi}\right)\pi r^2 = \frac{1}{2}\theta r^2.$$

Since the radius of a typical sector in **Figure 1.39** is given by $r_i = f(\theta_i)$, the area of the ith sector is given by

$$A_i = \frac{1}{2}(\Delta\theta)(f(\theta_i))^2.$$

Therefore a Riemann sum that approximates the area is given by

$$A_n = \sum_{i=1}^{n} A_i \approx \sum_{i=1}^{n} \frac{1}{2}(\Delta\theta)(f(\theta_i))^2.$$

We take the limit as $n \to \infty$ to get the exact area:

$$A = \lim_{n \to \infty} A_n = \frac{1}{2}\int_{\alpha}^{\beta} (f(\theta))^2\, d\theta.$$

This gives the following theorem.

Theorem 1.6: Area of a Region Bounded by a Polar Curve

Suppose f is continuous and nonnegative on the interval $\alpha \le \theta \le \beta$ with $0 < \beta - \alpha \le 2\pi$. The area of the region bounded by the graph of $r = f(\theta)$ between the radial lines $\theta = \alpha$ and $\theta = \beta$ is

$$A = \frac{1}{2}\int_{\alpha}^{\beta} [f(\theta)]^2\, d\theta = \frac{1}{2}\int_{\alpha}^{\beta} r^2\, d\theta. \quad (1.9)$$

Example 1.16

Finding an Area of a Polar Region

Find the area of one petal of the rose defined by the equation $r = 3\sin(2\theta)$.

Solution

The graph of $r = 3\sin(2\theta)$ follows.

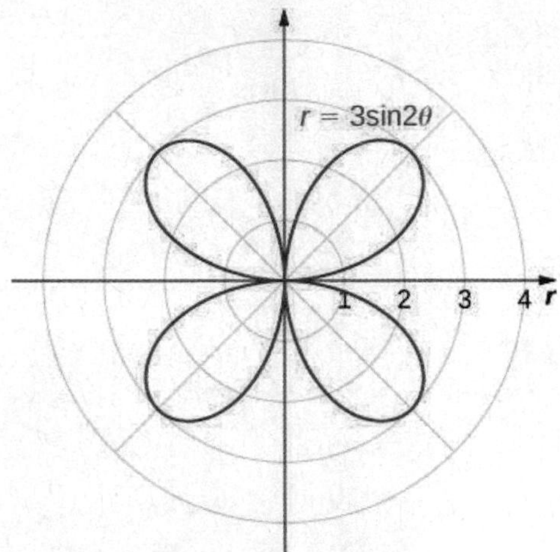

Figure 1.41 The graph of $r = 3\sin(2\theta)$.

When $\theta = 0$ we have $r = 3\sin(2(0)) = 0$. The next value for which $r = 0$ is $\theta = \pi/2$. This can be seen by solving the equation $3\sin(2\theta) = 0$ for θ. Therefore the values $\theta = 0$ to $\theta = \pi/2$ trace out the first petal of the rose. To find the area inside this petal, use **Equation 1.9** with $f(\theta) = 3\sin(2\theta)$, $\alpha = 0$, and $\beta = \pi/2$:

$$\begin{aligned} A &= \frac{1}{2}\int_{\alpha}^{\beta} [f(\theta)]^2 \, d\theta \\ &= \frac{1}{2}\int_{0}^{\pi/2} [3\sin(2\theta)]^2 \, d\theta \\ &= \frac{1}{2}\int_{0}^{\pi/2} 9\sin^2(2\theta) \, d\theta. \end{aligned}$$

To evaluate this integral, use the formula $\sin^2\alpha = (1 - \cos(2\alpha))/2$ with $\alpha = 2\theta$:

$$\begin{aligned} A &= \frac{1}{2}\int_0^{\pi/2} 9\sin^2(2\theta)\,d\theta \\ &= \frac{9}{2}\int_0^{\pi/2} \frac{(1-\cos(4\theta))}{2}\,d\theta \\ &= \frac{9}{4}\left(\int_0^{\pi/2} 1-\cos(4\theta)\,d\theta\right) \\ &= \frac{9}{4}\left(\theta - \frac{\sin(4\theta)}{4}\right)\Big|_0^{\pi/2} \\ &= \frac{9}{4}\left(\frac{\pi}{2} - \frac{\sin 2\pi}{4}\right) - \frac{9}{4}\left(0 - \frac{\sin 4(0)}{4}\right) \\ &= \frac{9\pi}{8}. \end{aligned}$$

 **1.15** Find the area inside the cardioid defined by the equation $r = 1 - \cos\theta$.

Example 1.16 involved finding the area inside one curve. We can also use **Area of a Region Bounded by a Polar Curve** to find the area between two polar curves. However, we often need to find the points of intersection of the curves and determine which function defines the outer curve or the inner curve between these two points.

Example 1.17

Finding the Area between Two Polar Curves

Find the area outside the cardioid $r = 2 + 2\sin\theta$ and inside the circle $r = 6\sin\theta$.

Solution

First draw a graph containing both curves as shown.

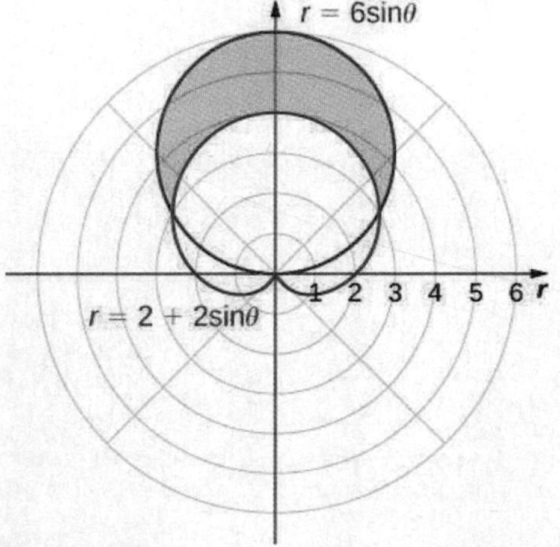

Figure 1.42 The region between the curves $r = 2 + 2\sin\theta$ and $r = 6\sin\theta$.

To determine the limits of integration, first find the points of intersection by setting the two functions equal to each other and solving for θ:

$$\begin{aligned}6\sin\theta &= 2+2\sin\theta\\ 4\sin\theta &= 2\\ \sin\theta &= \frac{1}{2}.\end{aligned}$$

This gives the solutions $\theta = \frac{\pi}{6}$ and $\theta = \frac{5\pi}{6}$, which are the limits of integration. The circle $r = 3\sin\theta$ is the red graph, which is the outer function, and the cardioid $r = 2+2\sin\theta$ is the blue graph, which is the inner function. To calculate the area between the curves, start with the area inside the circle between $\theta = \frac{\pi}{6}$ and $\theta = \frac{5\pi}{6}$, then subtract the area inside the cardioid between $\theta = \frac{\pi}{6}$ and $\theta = \frac{5\pi}{6}$:

$$\begin{aligned}A &= \text{circle} - \text{cardioid}\\ &= \frac{1}{2}\int_{\pi/6}^{5\pi/6}[6\sin\theta]^2\,d\theta - \frac{1}{2}\int_{\pi/6}^{5\pi/6}[2+2\sin\theta]^2\,d\theta\\ &= \frac{1}{2}\int_{\pi/6}^{5\pi/6}36\sin^2\theta\,d\theta - \frac{1}{2}\int_{\pi/6}^{5\pi/6}4+8\sin\theta+4\sin^2\theta\,d\theta\\ &= 18\int_{\pi/6}^{5\pi/6}\frac{1-\cos(2\theta)}{2}d\theta - 2\int_{\pi/6}^{5\pi/6}1+2\sin\theta+\frac{1-\cos(2\theta)}{2}d\theta\\ &= 9\left[\theta - \frac{\sin(2\theta)}{2}\right]_{\pi/6}^{5\pi/6} - 2\left[\frac{3\theta}{2} - 2\cos\theta - \frac{\sin(2\theta)}{4}\right]_{\pi/6}^{5\pi/6}\\ &= 9\left(\frac{5\pi}{6} - \frac{\sin 2(5\pi/6)}{2}\right) - 9\left(\frac{\pi}{6} - \frac{\sin 2(\pi/6)}{2}\right)\\ &\quad -\left(3\left(\frac{5\pi}{6}\right) - 4\cos\frac{5\pi}{6} - \frac{\sin 2(5\pi/6)}{2}\right) + \left(3\left(\frac{\pi}{6}\right) - 4\cos\frac{\pi}{6} - \frac{\sin 2(\pi/6)}{2}\right)\\ &= 4\pi.\end{aligned}$$

1.16 Find the area inside the circle $r = 4\cos\theta$ and outside the circle $r = 2$.

In **Example 1.17** we found the area inside the circle and outside the cardioid by first finding their intersection points. Notice that solving the equation directly for θ yielded two solutions: $\theta = \frac{\pi}{6}$ and $\theta = \frac{5\pi}{6}$. However, in the graph there are three intersection points. The third intersection point is the origin. The reason why this point did not show up as a solution is because the origin is on both graphs but for different values of θ. For example, for the cardioid we get

$$\begin{aligned}2+2\sin\theta &= 0\\ \sin\theta &= -1,\end{aligned}$$

so the values for θ that solve this equation are $\theta = \frac{3\pi}{2} + 2n\pi$, where n is any integer. For the circle we get

$$6\sin\theta = 0.$$

The solutions to this equation are of the form $\theta = n\pi$ for any integer value of n. These two solution sets have no points in common. Regardless of this fact, the curves intersect at the origin. This case must always be taken into consideration.

Arc Length in Polar Curves

Here we derive a formula for the arc length of a curve defined in polar coordinates.

In rectangular coordinates, the arc length of a parameterized curve $(x(t), y(t))$ for $a \le t \le b$ is given by

$$L = \int_a^b \sqrt{\left(\frac{dx}{dt}\right)^2 + \left(\frac{dy}{dt}\right)^2}\, dt.$$

In polar coordinates we define the curve by the equation $r = f(\theta)$, where $\alpha \le \theta \le \beta$. In order to adapt the arc length formula for a polar curve, we use the equations

$$x = r\cos\theta = f(\theta)\cos\theta \text{ and } y = r\sin\theta = f(\theta)\sin\theta,$$

and we replace the parameter t by θ. Then

$$\frac{dx}{d\theta} = f'(\theta)\cos\theta - f(\theta)\sin\theta$$
$$\frac{dy}{d\theta} = f'(\theta)\sin\theta + f(\theta)\cos\theta.$$

We replace dt by $d\theta$, and the lower and upper limits of integration are α and β, respectively. Then the arc length formula becomes

$$\begin{aligned} L &= \int_a^b \sqrt{\left(\frac{dx}{dt}\right)^2 + \left(\frac{dy}{dt}\right)^2}\, dt \\ &= \int_\alpha^\beta \sqrt{\left(\frac{dx}{d\theta}\right)^2 + \left(\frac{dy}{d\theta}\right)^2}\, d\theta \\ &= \int_\alpha^\beta \sqrt{\left(f'(\theta)\cos\theta - f(\theta)\sin\theta\right)^2 + \left(f'(\theta)\sin\theta + f(\theta)\cos\theta\right)^2}\, d\theta \\ &= \int_\alpha^\beta \sqrt{\left(f'(\theta)\right)^2\left(\cos^2\theta + \sin^2\theta\right) + \left(f(\theta)\right)^2\left(\cos^2\theta + \sin^2\theta\right)}\, d\theta \\ &= \int_\alpha^\beta \sqrt{\left(f'(\theta)\right)^2 + \left(f(\theta)\right)^2}\, d\theta \\ &= \int_\alpha^\beta \sqrt{r^2 + \left(\frac{dr}{d\theta}\right)^2}\, d\theta. \end{aligned}$$

This gives us the following theorem.

Theorem 1.7: Arc Length of a Curve Defined by a Polar Function

Let f be a function whose derivative is continuous on an interval $\alpha \le \theta \le \beta$. The length of the graph of $r = f(\theta)$ from $\theta = \alpha$ to $\theta = \beta$ is

$$L = \int_\alpha^\beta \sqrt{[f(\theta)]^2 + [f'(\theta)]^2}\, d\theta = \int_\alpha^\beta \sqrt{r^2 + \left(\frac{dr}{d\theta}\right)^2}\, d\theta. \qquad \textbf{(1.10)}$$

Example 1.18

Finding the Arc Length of a Polar Curve

Find the arc length of the cardioid $r = 2 + 2\cos\theta$.

Solution

When $\theta = 0$, $r = 2 + 2\cos 0 = 4$. Furthermore, as θ goes from 0 to 2π, the cardioid is traced out exactly once. Therefore these are the limits of integration. Using $f(\theta) = 2 + 2\cos\theta$, $\alpha = 0$, and $\beta = 2\pi$, **Equation 1.10** becomes

$$\begin{aligned} L &= \int_{\alpha}^{\beta} \sqrt{[f(\theta)]^2 + [f'(\theta)]^2}\, d\theta \\ &= \int_{0}^{2\pi} \sqrt{[2 + 2\cos\theta]^2 + [-2\sin\theta]^2}\, d\theta \\ &= \int_{0}^{2\pi} \sqrt{4 + 8\cos\theta + 4\cos^2\theta + 4\sin^2\theta}\, d\theta \\ &= \int_{0}^{2\pi} \sqrt{4 + 8\cos\theta + 4\left(\cos^2\theta + \sin^2\theta\right)}\, d\theta \\ &= \int_{0}^{2\pi} \sqrt{8 + 8\cos\theta}\, d\theta \\ &= 2\int_{0}^{2\pi} \sqrt{2 + 2\cos\theta}\, d\theta. \end{aligned}$$

Next, using the identity $\cos(2\alpha) = 2\cos^2\alpha - 1$, add 1 to both sides and multiply by 2. This gives $2 + 2\cos(2\alpha) = 4\cos^2\alpha$. Substituting $\alpha = \theta/2$ gives $2 + 2\cos\theta = 4\cos^2(\theta/2)$, so the integral becomes

$$\begin{aligned} L &= 2\int_{0}^{2\pi} \sqrt{2 + 2\cos\theta}\, d\theta \\ &= 2\int_{0}^{2\pi} \sqrt{4\cos^2\left(\frac{\theta}{2}\right)}\, d\theta \\ &= 2\int_{0}^{2\pi} 2\left|\cos\left(\frac{\theta}{2}\right)\right| d\theta. \end{aligned}$$

The absolute value is necessary because the cosine is negative for some values in its domain. To resolve this issue, change the limits from 0 to π and double the answer. This strategy works because cosine is positive between 0 and $\frac{\pi}{2}$. Thus,

$$\begin{aligned} L &= 4\int_{0}^{2\pi} \left|\cos\left(\frac{\theta}{2}\right)\right| d\theta \\ &= 8\int_{0}^{\pi} \cos\left(\frac{\theta}{2}\right) d\theta \\ &= 8\left(2\sin\left(\frac{\theta}{2}\right)\right)_{0}^{\pi} \\ &= 16. \end{aligned}$$

1.17 Find the total arc length of $r = 3\sin\theta$.

1.4 EXERCISES

For the following exercises, determine a definite integral that represents the area.

188. Region enclosed by $r = 4$

189. Region enclosed by $r = 3 \sin \theta$

190. Region in the first quadrant within the cardioid $r = 1 + \sin \theta$

191. Region enclosed by one petal of $r = 8 \sin(2\theta)$

192. Region enclosed by one petal of $r = \cos(3\theta)$

193. Region below the polar axis and enclosed by $r = 1 - \sin \theta$

194. Region in the first quadrant enclosed by $r = 2 - \cos \theta$

195. Region enclosed by the inner loop of $r = 2 - 3 \sin \theta$

196. Region enclosed by the inner loop of $r = 3 - 4 \cos \theta$

197. Region enclosed by $r = 1 - 2 \cos \theta$ and outside the inner loop

198. Region common to $r = 3 \sin \theta$ and $r = 2 - \sin \theta$

199. Region common to $r = 2$ and $r = 4 \cos \theta$

200. Region common to $r = 3 \cos \theta$ and $r = 3 \sin \theta$

For the following exercises, find the area of the described region.

201. Enclosed by $r = 6 \sin \theta$

202. Above the polar axis enclosed by $r = 2 + \sin \theta$

203. Below the polar axis and enclosed by $r = 2 - \cos \theta$

204. Enclosed by one petal of $r = 4 \cos(3\theta)$

205. Enclosed by one petal of $r = 3 \cos(2\theta)$

206. Enclosed by $r = 1 + \sin \theta$

207. Enclosed by the inner loop of $r = 3 + 6 \cos \theta$

208. Enclosed by $r = 2 + 4 \cos \theta$ and outside the inner loop

209. Common interior of $r = 4 \sin(2\theta)$ and $r = 2$

210. Common interior of $r = 3 - 2 \sin \theta$ and $r = -3 + 2 \sin \theta$

211. Common interior of $r = 6 \sin \theta$ and $r = 3$

212. Inside $r = 1 + \cos \theta$ and outside $r = \cos \theta$

213. Common interior of $r = 2 + 2 \cos \theta$ and $r = 2 \sin \theta$

For the following exercises, find a definite integral that represents the arc length.

214. $r = 4 \cos \theta$ on the interval $0 \le \theta \le \frac{\pi}{2}$

215. $r = 1 + \sin \theta$ on the interval $0 \le \theta \le 2\pi$

216. $r = 2 \sec \theta$ on the interval $0 \le \theta \le \frac{\pi}{3}$

217. $r = e^{\theta}$ on the interval $0 \le \theta \le 1$

For the following exercises, find the length of the curve over the given interval.

218. $r = 6$ on the interval $0 \le \theta \le \frac{\pi}{2}$

219. $r = e^{3\theta}$ on the interval $0 \le \theta \le 2$

220. $r = 6 \cos \theta$ on the interval $0 \le \theta \le \frac{\pi}{2}$

221. $r = 8 + 8 \cos \theta$ on the interval $0 \le \theta \le \pi$

222. $r = 1 - \sin \theta$ on the interval $0 \le \theta \le 2\pi$

For the following exercises, use the integration capabilities of a calculator to approximate the length of the curve.

223. **[T]** $r = 3\theta$ on the interval $0 \le \theta \le \frac{\pi}{2}$

224. **[T]** $r = \frac{2}{\theta}$ on the interval $\pi \le \theta \le 2\pi$

225. **[T]** $r = \sin^2\left(\frac{\theta}{2}\right)$ on the interval $0 \le \theta \le \pi$

226. **[T]** $r = 2\theta^2$ on the interval $0 \le \theta \le \pi$

227. **[T]** $r = \sin(3 \cos \theta)$ on the interval $0 \le \theta \le \pi$

For the following exercises, use the familiar formula from

geometry to find the area of the region described and then confirm by using the definite integral.

228. $r = 3\sin\theta$ on the interval $0 \le \theta \le \pi$

229. $r = \sin\theta + \cos\theta$ on the interval $0 \le \theta \le \pi$

230. $r = 6\sin\theta + 8\cos\theta$ on the interval $0 \le \theta \le \pi$

For the following exercises, use the familiar formula from geometry to find the length of the curve and then confirm using the definite integral.

231. $r = 3\sin\theta$ on the interval $0 \le \theta \le \pi$

232. $r = \sin\theta + \cos\theta$ on the interval $0 \le \theta \le \pi$

233. $r = 6\sin\theta + 8\cos\theta$ on the interval $0 \le \theta \le \pi$

234. Verify that if $y = r\sin\theta = f(\theta)\sin\theta$ then $\frac{dy}{d\theta} = f'(\theta)\sin\theta + f(\theta)\cos\theta.$

For the following exercises, find the slope of a tangent line to a polar curve $r = f(\theta)$. Let $x = r\cos\theta = f(\theta)\cos\theta$ and $y = r\sin\theta = f(\theta)\sin\theta,$ so the polar equation $r = f(\theta)$ is now written in parametric form.

235. Use the definition of the derivative $\frac{dy}{dx} = \frac{dy/d\theta}{dx/d\theta}$ and the product rule to derive the derivative of a polar equation.

236. $r = 1 - \sin\theta;\ \left(\frac{1}{2}, \frac{\pi}{6}\right)$

237. $r = 4\cos\theta;\ \left(2, \frac{\pi}{3}\right)$

238. $r = 8\sin\theta;\ \left(4, \frac{5\pi}{6}\right)$

239. $r = 4 + \sin\theta;\ \left(3, \frac{3\pi}{2}\right)$

240. $r = 6 + 3\cos\theta;\ (3, \pi)$

241. $r = 4\cos(2\theta)$; tips of the leaves

242. $r = 2\sin(3\theta)$; tips of the leaves

243. $r = 2\theta;\ \left(\frac{\pi}{2}, \frac{\pi}{4}\right)$

244. Find the points on the interval $-\pi \le \theta \le \pi$ at which the cardioid $r = 1 - \cos\theta$ has a vertical or horizontal tangent line.

245. For the cardioid $r = 1 + \sin\theta,$ find the slope of the tangent line when $\theta = \frac{\pi}{3}$.

For the following exercises, find the slope of the tangent line to the given polar curve at the point given by the value of θ.

246. $r = 3\cos\theta,\ \theta = \frac{\pi}{3}$

247. $r = \theta,\quad \theta = \frac{\pi}{2}$

248. $r = \ln\theta,\quad \theta = e$

249. **[T]** Use technology: $r = 2 + 4\cos\theta$ at $\theta = \frac{\pi}{6}$

For the following exercises, find the points at which the following polar curves have a horizontal or vertical tangent line.

250. $r = 4\cos\theta$

251. $r^2 = 4\cos(2\theta)$

252. $r = 2\sin(2\theta)$

253. The cardioid $r = 1 + \sin\theta$

254. Show that the curve $r = \sin\theta\tan\theta$ (called a *cissoid of Diocles*) has the line $x = 1$ as a vertical asymptote.

1.5 | Conic Sections

Learning Objectives

1.5.1 Identify the equation of a parabola in standard form with given focus and directrix.
1.5.2 Identify the equation of an ellipse in standard form with given foci.
1.5.3 Identify the equation of a hyperbola in standard form with given foci.
1.5.4 Recognize a parabola, ellipse, or hyperbola from its eccentricity value.
1.5.5 Write the polar equation of a conic section with eccentricity e .
1.5.6 Identify when a general equation of degree two is a parabola, ellipse, or hyperbola.

Conic sections have been studied since the time of the ancient Greeks, and were considered to be an important mathematical concept. As early as 320 BCE, such Greek mathematicians as Menaechmus, Appollonius, and Archimedes were fascinated by these curves. Appollonius wrote an entire eight-volume treatise on conic sections in which he was, for example, able to derive a specific method for identifying a conic section through the use of geometry. Since then, important applications of conic sections have arisen (for example, in astronomy), and the properties of conic sections are used in radio telescopes, satellite dish receivers, and even architecture. In this section we discuss the three basic conic sections, some of their properties, and their equations.

Conic sections get their name because they can be generated by intersecting a plane with a cone. A cone has two identically shaped parts called **nappes**. One nappe is what most people mean by "cone," having the shape of a party hat. A right circular cone can be generated by revolving a line passing through the origin around the *y*-axis as shown.

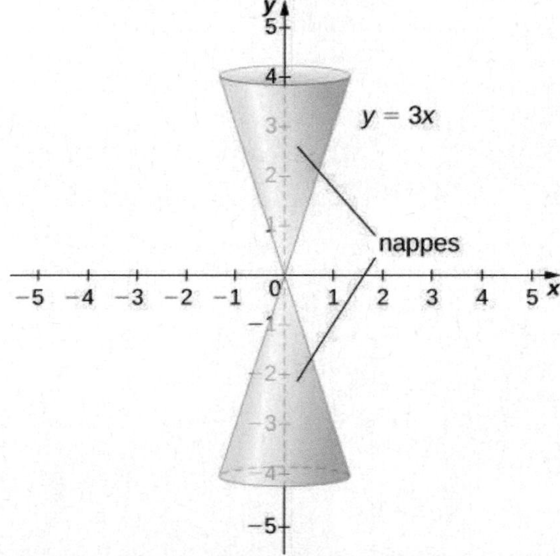

Figure 1.43 A cone generated by revolving the line $y = 3x$ around the y -axis.

Conic sections are generated by the intersection of a plane with a cone (**Figure 1.44**). If the plane is parallel to the axis of revolution (the *y*-axis), then the **conic section** is a hyperbola. If the plane is parallel to the generating line, the conic section is a parabola. If the plane is perpendicular to the axis of revolution, the conic section is a circle. If the plane intersects one nappe at an angle to the axis (other than $90°$), then the conic section is an ellipse.

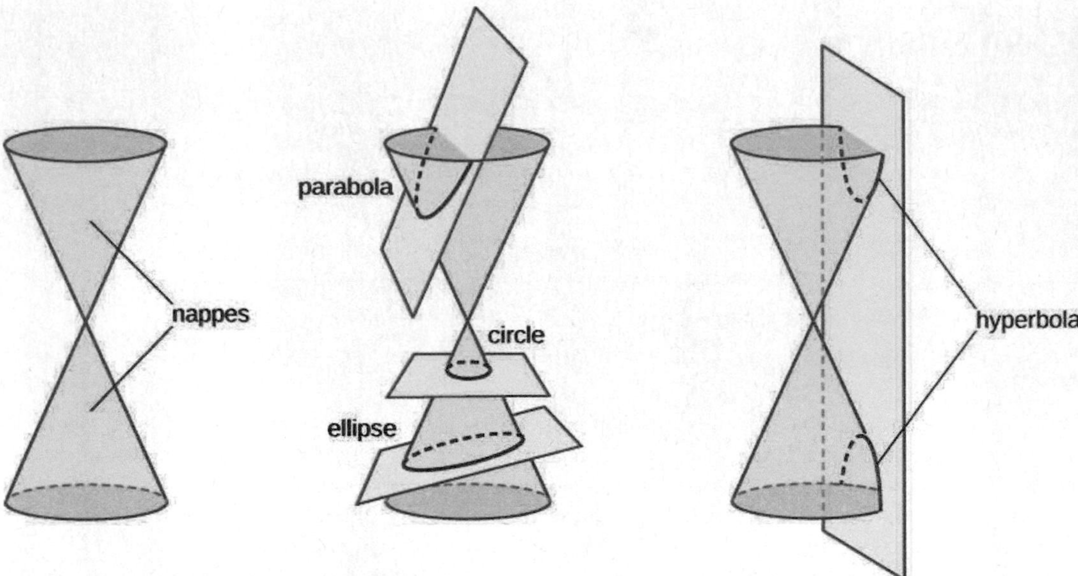

Figure 1.44 The four conic sections. Each conic is determined by the angle the plane makes with the axis of the cone.

Parabolas

A parabola is generated when a plane intersects a cone parallel to the generating line. In this case, the plane intersects only one of the nappes. A parabola can also be defined in terms of distances.

Definition

A parabola is the set of all points whose distance from a fixed point, called the **focus**, is equal to the distance from a fixed line, called the **directrix**. The point halfway between the focus and the directrix is called the **vertex** of the parabola.

A graph of a typical parabola appears in **Figure 1.45**. Using this diagram in conjunction with the distance formula, we can derive an equation for a parabola. Recall the distance formula: Given point P with coordinates (x_1, y_1) and point Q with coordinates (x_2, y_2), the distance between them is given by the formula

$$d(P, Q) = \sqrt{(x_2 - x_1)^2 + (y_2 - y_1)^2}.$$

Then from the definition of a parabola and **Figure 1.45**, we get

$$\begin{aligned} d(F, P) &= d(P, Q) \\ \sqrt{(0 - x)^2 + (p - y)^2} &= \sqrt{(x - x)^2 + (-p - y)^2}. \end{aligned}$$

Squaring both sides and simplifying yields

$$\begin{aligned} x^2 + (p - y)^2 &= 0^2 + (-p - y)^2 \\ x^2 + p^2 - 2py + y^2 &= p^2 + 2py + y^2 \\ x^2 - 2py &= 2py \\ x^2 &= 4py. \end{aligned}$$

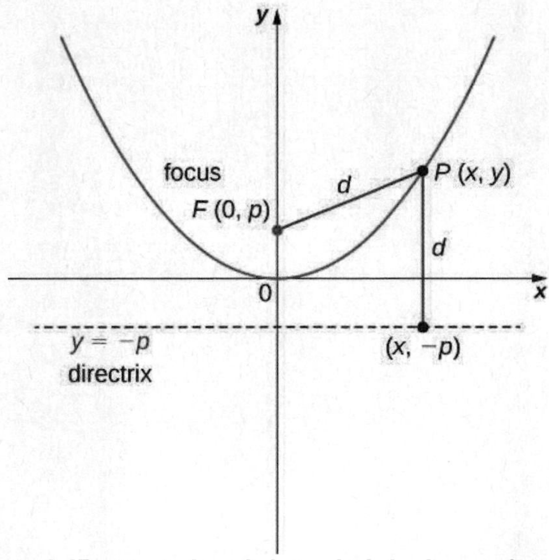

Figure 1.45 A typical parabola in which the distance from the focus to the vertex is represented by the variable p.

Now suppose we want to relocate the vertex. We use the variables (h, k) to denote the coordinates of the vertex. Then if the focus is directly above the vertex, it has coordinates $(h, k + p)$ and the directrix has the equation $y = k - p$. Going through the same derivation yields the formula $(x - h)^2 = 4p(y - k)$. Solving this equation for y leads to the following theorem.

Theorem 1.8: Equations for Parabolas

Given a parabola opening upward with vertex located at (h, k) and focus located at $(h, k + p)$, where p is a constant, the equation for the parabola is given by

$$y = \frac{1}{4p}(x - h)^2 + k. \tag{1.11}$$

This is the **standard form** of a parabola.

We can also study the cases when the parabola opens down or to the left or the right. The equation for each of these cases can also be written in standard form as shown in the following graphs.

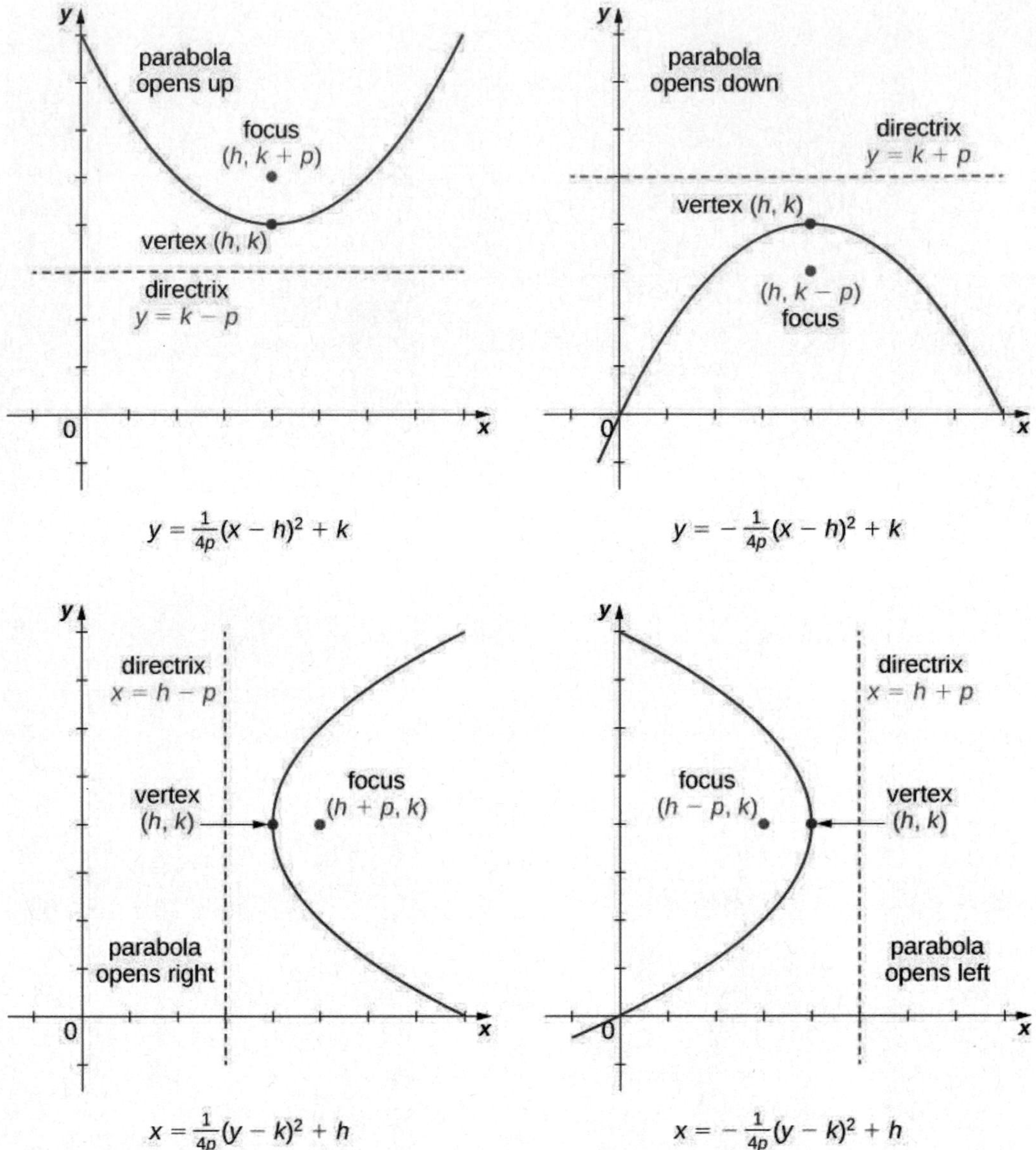

Figure 1.46 Four parabolas, opening in various directions, along with their equations in standard form.

In addition, the equation of a parabola can be written in the **general form**, though in this form the values of h, k, and p are not immediately recognizable. The general form of a parabola is written as

$$ax^2 + bx + cy + d = 0 \quad \text{or} \quad ay^2 + bx + cy + d = 0.$$

The first equation represents a parabola that opens either up or down. The second equation represents a parabola that opens either to the left or to the right. To put the equation into standard form, use the method of completing the square.

Example 1.19

Converting the Equation of a Parabola from General into Standard Form

Put the equation $x^2 - 4x - 8y + 12 = 0$ into standard form and graph the resulting parabola.

Solution

Since y is not squared in this equation, we know that the parabola opens either upward or downward. Therefore we need to solve this equation for y, which will put the equation into standard form. To do that, first add $8y$ to both sides of the equation:

$$8y = x^2 - 4x + 12.$$

The next step is to complete the square on the right-hand side. Start by grouping the first two terms on the right-hand side using parentheses:

$$8y = \left(x^2 - 4x\right) + 12.$$

Next determine the constant that, when added inside the parentheses, makes the quantity inside the parentheses a perfect square trinomial. To do this, take half the coefficient of x and square it. This gives $\left(\frac{-4}{2}\right)^2 = 4.$ Add 4 inside the parentheses and subtract 4 outside the parentheses, so the value of the equation is not changed:

$$8y = \left(x^2 - 4x + 4\right) + 12 - 4.$$

Now combine like terms and factor the quantity inside the parentheses:

$$8y = (x - 2)^2 + 8.$$

Finally, divide by 8:

$$y = \frac{1}{8}(x - 2)^2 + 1.$$

This equation is now in standard form. Comparing this to **Equation 1.11** gives $h = 2,\quad k = 1,\quad$ and $p = 2.$ The parabola opens up, with vertex at $(2,\ 1),\quad$ focus at $(2,\ 3),\quad$ and directrix $y = -1.$ The graph of this parabola appears as follows.

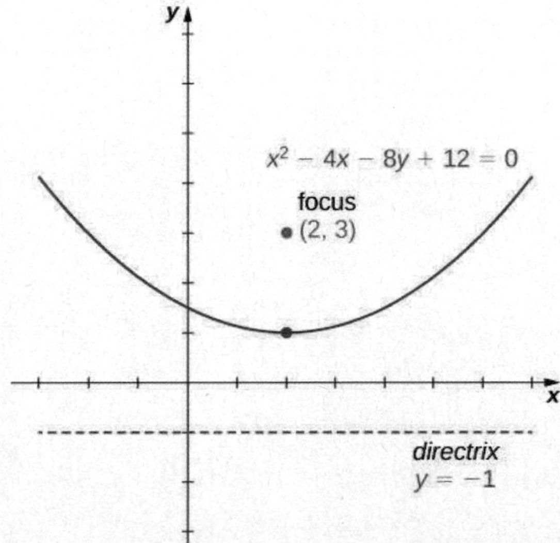

Figure 1.47 The parabola in **Example 1.19**.

1.18 Put the equation $2y^2 - x + 12y + 16 = 0$ into standard form and graph the resulting parabola.

The axis of symmetry of a vertical (opening up or down) parabola is a vertical line passing through the vertex. The parabola has an interesting reflective property. Suppose we have a satellite dish with a parabolic cross section. If a beam of electromagnetic waves, such as light or radio waves, comes into the dish in a straight line from a satellite (parallel to the axis of symmetry), then the waves reflect off the dish and collect at the focus of the parabola as shown.

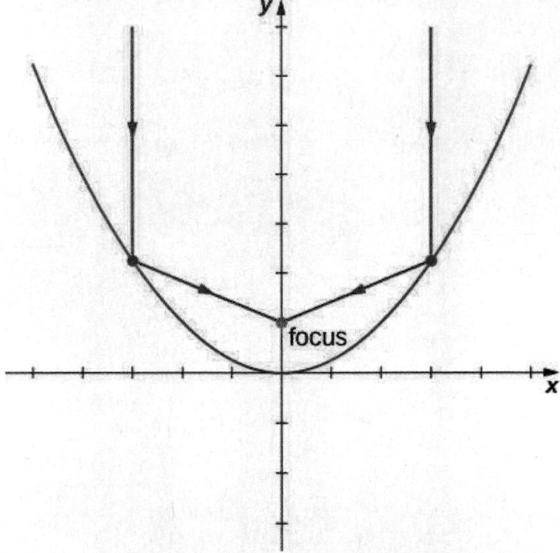

Consider a parabolic dish designed to collect signals from a satellite in space. The dish is aimed directly at the satellite, and a receiver is located at the focus of the parabola. Radio waves coming in from the satellite are reflected off the surface of the parabola to the receiver, which collects and decodes the digital signals. This allows a small receiver to gather signals from a wide angle of sky. Flashlights and headlights in a car work on the same principle, but in reverse: the source of the light (that is, the light bulb) is located at the focus and the reflecting surface on the parabolic mirror focuses the beam straight ahead. This allows a small light bulb to illuminate a wide angle of space in front of the flashlight or car.

Ellipses

An ellipse can also be defined in terms of distances. In the case of an ellipse, there are two foci (plural of focus), and two directrices (plural of directrix). We look at the directrices in more detail later in this section.

Definition

An *ellipse* is the set of all points for which the sum of their distances from two fixed points (the foci) is constant.

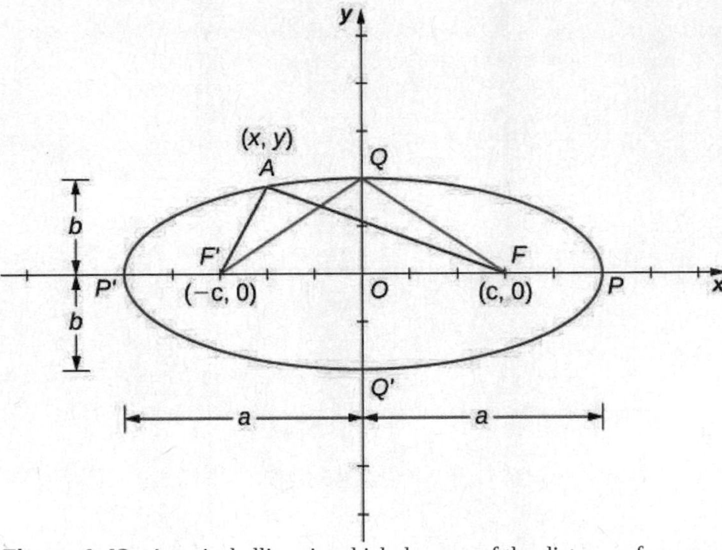

Figure 1.48 A typical ellipse in which the sum of the distances from any point on the ellipse to the foci is constant.

A graph of a typical ellipse is shown in **Figure 1.48**. In this figure the foci are labeled as F and F'. Both are the same fixed distance from the origin, and this distance is represented by the variable c. Therefore the coordinates of F are $(c, 0)$ and the coordinates of F' are $(-c, 0)$. The points P and P' are located at the ends of the **major axis** of the ellipse, and have coordinates $(a, 0)$ and $(-a, 0)$, respectively. The major axis is always the longest distance across the ellipse, and can be horizontal or vertical. Thus, the length of the major axis in this ellipse is $2a$. Furthermore, P and P' are called the vertices of the ellipse. The points Q and Q' are located at the ends of the **minor axis** of the ellipse, and have coordinates $(0, b)$ and $(0, -b)$, respectively. The minor axis is the shortest distance across the ellipse. The minor axis is perpendicular to the major axis.

According to the definition of the ellipse, we can choose any point on the ellipse and the sum of the distances from this point to the two foci is constant. Suppose we choose the point P. Since the coordinates of point P are $(a, 0)$, the sum of the distances is

$$d(P, F) + d(P, F') = (a - c) + (a + c) = 2a.$$

Therefore the sum of the distances from an arbitrary point A with coordinates (x, y) is also equal to $2a$. Using the distance formula, we get

$$\begin{aligned} d(A, F) + d(A, F') &= 2a \\ \sqrt{(x - c)^2 + y^2} + \sqrt{(x + c)^2 + y^2} &= 2a. \end{aligned}$$

Subtract the second radical from both sides and square both sides:

$$\begin{aligned} \sqrt{(x - c)^2 + y^2} &= 2a - \sqrt{(x + c)^2 + y^2} \\ (x - c)^2 + y^2 &= 4a^2 - 4a\sqrt{(x + c)^2 + y^2} + (x + c)^2 + y^2 \\ x^2 - 2cx + c^2 + y^2 &= 4a^2 - 4a\sqrt{(x + c)^2 + y^2} + x^2 + 2cx + c^2 + y^2 \\ -2cx &= 4a^2 - 4a\sqrt{(x + c)^2 + y^2} + 2cx. \end{aligned}$$

Now isolate the radical on the right-hand side and square again:

$$\begin{aligned} -2cx &= 4a^2 - 4a\sqrt{(x+c)^2+y^2} + 2cx \\ 4a\sqrt{(x+c)^2+y^2} &= 4a^2 + 4cx \\ \sqrt{(x+c)^2+y^2} &= a + \frac{cx}{a} \\ (x+c)^2 + y^2 &= a^2 + 2cx + \frac{c^2x^2}{a^2} \\ x^2 + 2cx + c^2 + y^2 &= a^2 + 2cx + \frac{c^2x^2}{a^2} \\ x^2 + c^2 + y^2 &= a^2 + \frac{c^2x^2}{a^2}. \end{aligned}$$

Isolate the variables on the left-hand side of the equation and the constants on the right-hand side:

$$\begin{aligned} x^2 - \frac{c^2x^2}{a^2} + y^2 &= a^2 - c^2 \\ \frac{(a^2-c^2)x^2}{a^2} + y^2 &= a^2 - c^2. \end{aligned}$$

Divide both sides by $a^2 - c^2$. This gives the equation

$$\frac{x^2}{a^2} + \frac{y^2}{a^2 - c^2} = 1.$$

If we refer back to **Figure 1.48**, then the length of each of the two green line segments is equal to a. This is true because the sum of the distances from the point Q to the foci F and F' is equal to $2a$, and the lengths of these two line segments are equal. This line segment forms a right triangle with hypotenuse length a and leg lengths b and c. From the Pythagorean theorem, $a^2 + b^2 = c^2$ and $b^2 = a^2 - c^2$. Therefore the equation of the ellipse becomes

$$\frac{x^2}{a^2} + \frac{y^2}{b^2} = 1.$$

Finally, if the center of the ellipse is moved from the origin to a point (h, k), we have the following standard form of an ellipse.

Theorem 1.9: Equation of an Ellipse in Standard Form

Consider the ellipse with center (h, k), a horizontal major axis with length $2a$, and a vertical minor axis with length $2b$. Then the equation of this ellipse in standard form is

$$\frac{(x-h)^2}{a^2} + \frac{(y-k)^2}{b^2} = 1 \tag{1.12}$$

and the foci are located at $(h \pm c, k)$, where $c^2 = a^2 - b^2$. The equations of the directrices are $x = h \pm \frac{a^2}{c}$.

If the major axis is vertical, then the equation of the ellipse becomes

$$\frac{(x-h)^2}{b^2} + \frac{(y-k)^2}{a^2} = 1 \tag{1.13}$$

and the foci are located at $(h, k \pm c)$, where $c^2 = a^2 - b^2$. The equations of the directrices in this case are $y = k \pm \frac{a^2}{c}$.

If the major axis is horizontal, then the ellipse is called horizontal, and if the major axis is vertical, then the ellipse is called vertical. The equation of an ellipse is in general form if it is in the form $Ax^2 + By^2 + Cx + Dy + E = 0,$ where A and B are either both positive or both negative. To convert the equation from general to standard form, use the method of completing the square.

Example 1.20

Finding the Standard Form of an Ellipse

Put the equation $9x^2 + 4y^2 - 36x + 24y + 36 = 0$ into standard form and graph the resulting ellipse.

Solution

First subtract 36 from both sides of the equation:

$$9x^2 + 4y^2 - 36x + 24y = -36.$$

Next group the x terms together and the y terms together, and factor out the common factor:

$$\begin{aligned}(9x^2 - 36x) + (4y^2 + 24y) &= -36\\ 9(x^2 - 4x) + 4(y^2 + 6y) &= -36.\end{aligned}$$

We need to determine the constant that, when added inside each set of parentheses, results in a perfect square. In the first set of parentheses, take half the coefficient of x and square it. This gives $\left(\frac{-4}{2}\right)^2 = 4.$ In the second set of parentheses, take half the coefficient of y and square it. This gives $\left(\frac{6}{2}\right)^2 = 9.$ Add these inside each pair of parentheses. Since the first set of parentheses has a 9 in front, we are actually adding 36 to the left-hand side. Similarly, we are adding 36 to the second set as well. Therefore the equation becomes

$$\begin{aligned}9(x^2 - 4x + 4) + 4(y^2 + 6y + 9) &= -36 + 36 + 36\\ 9(x^2 - 4x + 4) + 4(y^2 + 6y + 9) &= 36.\end{aligned}$$

Now factor both sets of parentheses and divide by 36:

$$\begin{aligned}9(x-2)^2 + 4(y+3)^2 &= 36\\ \frac{9(x-2)^2}{36} + \frac{4(y+3)^2}{36} &= 1\\ \frac{(x-2)^2}{4} + \frac{(y+3)^2}{9} &= 1.\end{aligned}$$

The equation is now in standard form. Comparing this to **Equation 1.14** gives $h = 2,$ $k = -3,$ $a = 3,$ and $b = 2.$ This is a vertical ellipse with center at $(2, -3),$ major axis 6, and minor axis 4. The graph of this ellipse appears as follows.

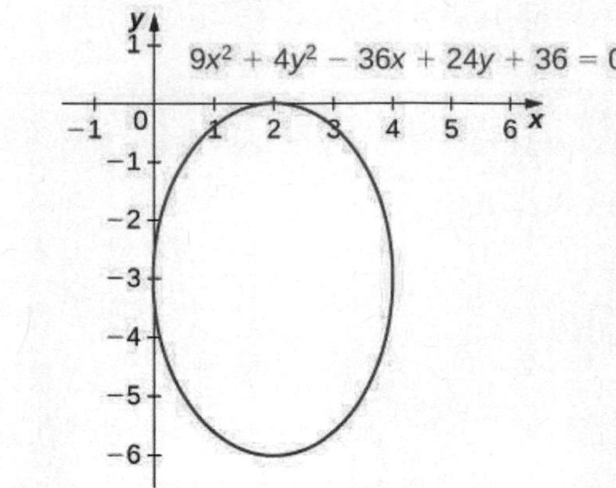

Figure 1.49 The ellipse in **Example 1.20**.

1.19 Put the equation $9x^2 + 16y^2 + 18x - 64y - 71 = 0$ into standard form and graph the resulting ellipse.

According to Kepler's first law of planetary motion, the orbit of a planet around the Sun is an ellipse with the Sun at one of the foci as shown in **Figure 1.50**(a). Because Earth's orbit is an ellipse, the distance from the Sun varies throughout the year. A commonly held misconception is that Earth is closer to the Sun in the summer. In fact, in summer for the northern hemisphere, Earth is farther from the Sun than during winter. The difference in season is caused by the tilt of Earth's axis in the orbital plane. Comets that orbit the Sun, such as Halley's Comet, also have elliptical orbits, as do moons orbiting the planets and satellites orbiting Earth.

Ellipses also have interesting reflective properties: A light ray emanating from one focus passes through the other focus after mirror reflection in the ellipse. The same thing occurs with a sound wave as well. The National Statuary Hall in the U.S. Capitol in Washington, DC, is a famous room in an elliptical shape as shown in **Figure 1.50**(b). This hall served as the meeting place for the U.S. House of Representatives for almost fifty years. The location of the two foci of this semi-elliptical room are clearly identified by marks on the floor, and even if the room is full of visitors, when two people stand on these spots and speak to each other, they can hear each other much more clearly than they can hear someone standing close by. Legend has it that John Quincy Adams had his desk located on one of the foci and was able to eavesdrop on everyone else in the House without ever needing to stand. Although this makes a good story, it is unlikely to be true, because the original ceiling produced so many echoes that the entire room had to be hung with carpets to dampen the noise. The ceiling was rebuilt in 1902 and only then did the now-famous whispering effect emerge. Another famous whispering gallery—the site of many marriage proposals—is in Grand Central Station in New York City.

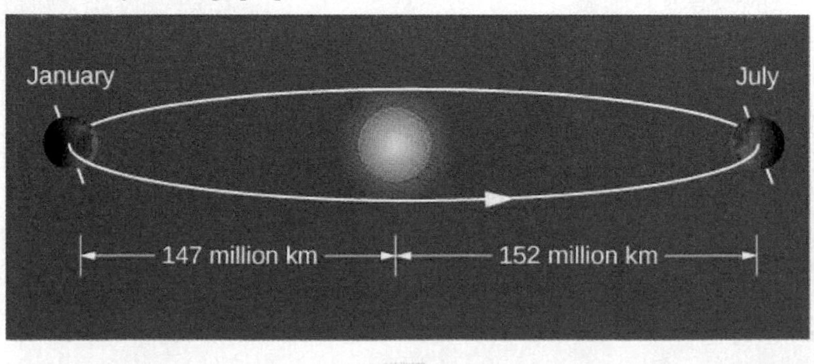

(a) (b)

Figure 1.50 (a) Earth's orbit around the Sun is an ellipse with the Sun at one focus. (b) Statuary Hall in the U.S. Capitol is a whispering gallery with an elliptical cross section.

Hyperbolas

A hyperbola can also be defined in terms of distances. In the case of a hyperbola, there are two foci and two directrices. Hyperbolas also have two asymptotes.

Definition

A hyperbola is the set of all points where the difference between their distances from two fixed points (the foci) is constant.

A graph of a typical hyperbola appears as follows.

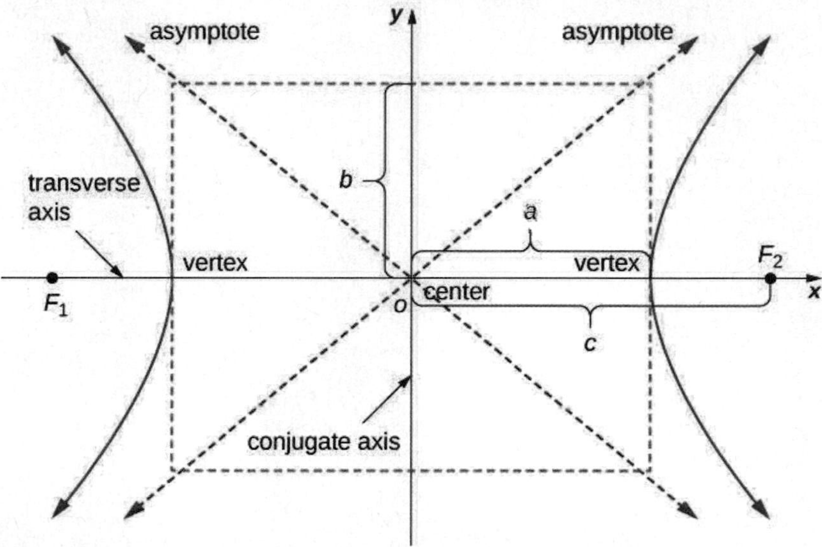

Figure 1.51 A typical hyperbola in which the difference of the distances from any point on the ellipse to the foci is constant. The transverse axis is also called the major axis, and the conjugate axis is also called the minor axis.

The derivation of the equation of a hyperbola in standard form is virtually identical to that of an ellipse. One slight hitch lies in the definition: The difference between two numbers is always positive. Let P be a point on the hyperbola with coordinates (x, y). Then the definition of the hyperbola gives $|d(P, F_1) - d(P, F_2)| = \text{constant}$. To simplify the derivation, assume that P is on the right branch of the hyperbola, so the absolute value bars drop. If it is on the left branch, then the subtraction is reversed. The vertex of the right branch has coordinates $(a, 0)$, so

$$d(P, F_1) - d(P, F_2) = (c + a) - (c - a) = 2a.$$

This equation is therefore true for any point on the hyperbola. Returning to the coordinates (x, y) for P:

$$\begin{aligned} d(P, F_1) - d(P, F_2) &= 2a \\ \sqrt{(x + c)^2 + y^2} - \sqrt{(x - c)^2 + y^2} &= 2a. \end{aligned}$$

Add the second radical from both sides and square both sides:

$$\begin{aligned} \sqrt{(x - c)^2 + y^2} &= 2a + \sqrt{(x + c)^2 + y^2} \\ (x - c)^2 + y^2 &= 4a^2 + 4a\sqrt{(x + c)^2 + y^2} + (x + c)^2 + y^2 \\ x^2 - 2cx + c^2 + y^2 &= 4a^2 + 4a\sqrt{(x + c)^2 + y^2} + x^2 + 2cx + c^2 + y^2 \\ -2cx &= 4a^2 + 4a\sqrt{(x + c)^2 + y^2} + 2cx. \end{aligned}$$

Now isolate the radical on the right-hand side and square again:

$$\begin{aligned}
-2cx &= 4a^2 + 4a\sqrt{(x+c)^2+y^2} + 2cx \\
4a\sqrt{(x+c)^2+y^2} &= -4a^2 - 4cx \\
\sqrt{(x+c)^2+y^2} &= -a - \tfrac{cx}{a} \\
(x+c)^2+y^2 &= a^2 + 2cx + \frac{c^2x^2}{a^2} \\
x^2+2cx+c^2+y^2 &= a^2 + 2cx + \frac{c^2x^2}{a^2} \\
x^2+c^2+y^2 &= a^2 + \frac{c^2x^2}{a^2}.
\end{aligned}$$

Isolate the variables on the left-hand side of the equation and the constants on the right-hand side:

$$\begin{aligned}
x^2 - \frac{c^2x^2}{a^2} + y^2 &= a^2 - c^2 \\
\frac{\left(a^2-c^2\right)x^2}{a^2} + y^2 &= a^2 - c^2.
\end{aligned}$$

Finally, divide both sides by $a^2 - c^2$. This gives the equation

$$\frac{x^2}{a^2} + \frac{y^2}{a^2-c^2} = 1.$$

We now define b so that $b^2 = c^2 - a^2$. This is possible because $c > a$. Therefore the equation of the ellipse becomes

$$\frac{x^2}{a^2} - \frac{y^2}{b^2} = 1.$$

Finally, if the center of the hyperbola is moved from the origin to the point (h, k), we have the following standard form of a hyperbola.

Theorem 1.10: Equation of a Hyperbola in Standard Form

Consider the hyperbola with center (h, k), a horizontal major axis, and a vertical minor axis. Then the equation of this ellipse is

$$\frac{(x-h)^2}{a^2} - \frac{(y-k)^2}{b^2} = 1 \qquad \textbf{(1.14)}$$

and the foci are located at $(h \pm c, k)$, where $c^2 = a^2 + b^2$. The equations of the asymptotes are given by $y = k \pm \frac{b}{a}(x-h)$. The equations of the directrices are

$$x = k \pm \frac{a^2}{\sqrt{a^2+b^2}} = h \pm \frac{a^2}{c}.$$

If the major axis is vertical, then the equation of the hyperbola becomes

$$\frac{(y-k)^2}{a^2} - \frac{(x-h)^2}{b^2} = 1 \qquad \textbf{(1.15)}$$

and the foci are located at $(h, k \pm c)$, where $c^2 = a^2 + b^2$. The equations of the asymptotes are given by $y = k \pm \frac{a}{b}(x-h)$. The equations of the directrices are

$$y = k \pm \frac{a^2}{\sqrt{a^2 + b^2}} = k \pm \frac{a^2}{c}.$$

If the major axis (transverse axis) is horizontal, then the hyperbola is called horizontal, and if the major axis is vertical then the hyperbola is called vertical. The equation of a hyperbola is in general form if it is in the form $Ax^2 + By^2 + Cx + Dy + E = 0,$ where A and B have opposite signs. In order to convert the equation from general to standard form, use the method of completing the square.

Example 1.21

Finding the Standard Form of a Hyperbola

Put the equation $9x^2 - 16y^2 + 36x + 32y - 124 = 0$ into standard form and graph the resulting hyperbola. What are the equations of the asymptotes?

Solution

First add 124 to both sides of the equation:

$$9x^2 - 16y^2 + 36x + 32y = 124.$$

Next group the x terms together and the y terms together, then factor out the common factors:

$$\begin{aligned}\left(9x^2 + 36x\right) - \left(16y^2 - 32y\right) &= 124 \\ 9\left(x^2 + 4x\right) - 16\left(y^2 - 2y\right) &= 124.\end{aligned}$$

We need to determine the constant that, when added inside each set of parentheses, results in a perfect square. In the first set of parentheses, take half the coefficient of x and square it. This gives $\left(\frac{4}{2}\right)^2 = 4.$ In the second set of parentheses, take half the coefficient of y and square it. This gives $\left(\frac{-2}{2}\right)^2 = 1.$ Add these inside each pair of parentheses. Since the first set of parentheses has a 9 in front, we are actually adding 36 to the left-hand side. Similarly, we are subtracting 16 from the second set of parentheses. Therefore the equation becomes

$$\begin{aligned}9\left(x^2 + 4x + 4\right) - 16\left(y^2 - 2y + 1\right) &= 124 + 36 - 16 \\ 9\left(x^2 + 4x + 4\right) - 16\left(y^2 - 2y + 1\right) &= 144.\end{aligned}$$

Next factor both sets of parentheses and divide by 144:

$$\begin{aligned}9(x + 2)^2 - 16(y - 1)^2 &= 144 \\ \frac{9(x + 2)^2}{144} - \frac{16(y - 1)^2}{144} &= 1 \\ \frac{(x + 2)^2}{16} - \frac{(y - 1)^2}{9} &= 1.\end{aligned}$$

The equation is now in standard form. Comparing this to **Equation 1.15** gives $h = -2,$ $k = 1,$ $a = 4,$ and $b = 3.$ This is a horizontal hyperbola with center at $(-2, 1)$ and asymptotes given by the equations $y = 1 \pm \frac{3}{4}(x + 2).$ The graph of this hyperbola appears in the following figure.

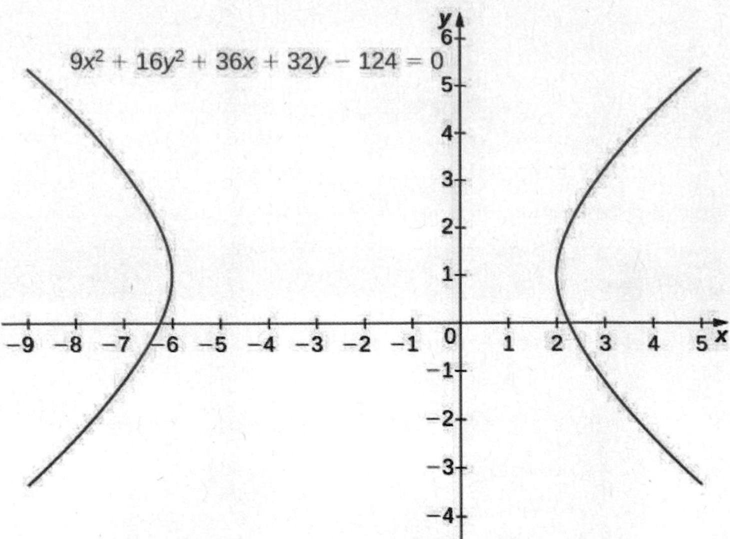

Figure 1.52 Graph of the hyperbola in **Example 1.21**.

1.20 Put the equation $4y^2 - 9x^2 + 16y + 18x - 29 = 0$ into standard form and graph the resulting hyperbola. What are the equations of the asymptotes?

Hyperbolas also have interesting reflective properties. A ray directed toward one focus of a hyperbola is reflected by a hyperbolic mirror toward the other focus. This concept is illustrated in the following figure.

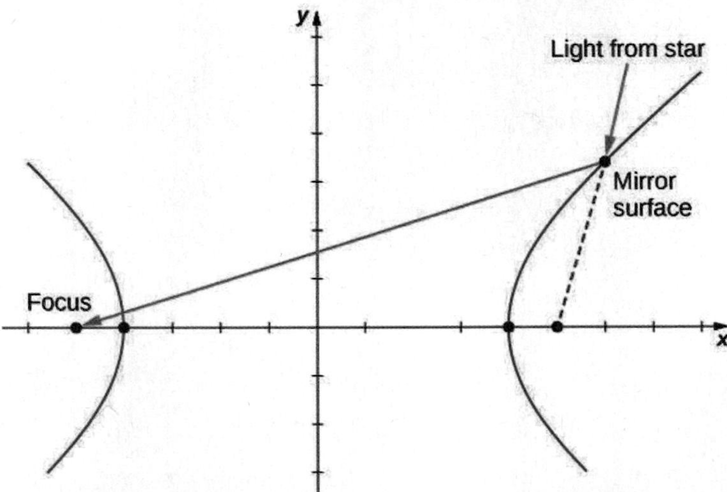

Figure 1.53 A hyperbolic mirror used to collect light from distant stars.

This property of the hyperbola has important applications. It is used in radio direction finding (since the difference in signals from two towers is constant along hyperbolas), and in the construction of mirrors inside telescopes (to reflect light coming from the parabolic mirror to the eyepiece). Another interesting fact about hyperbolas is that for a comet entering the solar system, if the speed is great enough to escape the Sun's gravitational pull, then the path that the comet takes as it passes through the solar system is hyperbolic.

Eccentricity and Directrix

An alternative way to describe a conic section involves the directrices, the foci, and a new property called eccentricity. We will see that the value of the eccentricity of a conic section can uniquely define that conic.

Definition

The **eccentricity** e of a conic section is defined to be the distance from any point on the conic section to its focus, divided by the perpendicular distance from that point to the nearest directrix. This value is constant for any conic section, and can define the conic section as well:

1. If $e = 1,$ the conic is a parabola.
2. If $e < 1,$ it is an ellipse.
3. If $e > 1,$ it is a hyperbola.

The eccentricity of a circle is zero. The directrix of a conic section is the line that, together with the point known as the focus, serves to define a conic section. Hyperbolas and noncircular ellipses have two foci and two associated directrices. Parabolas have one focus and one directrix.

The three conic sections with their directrices appear in the following figure.

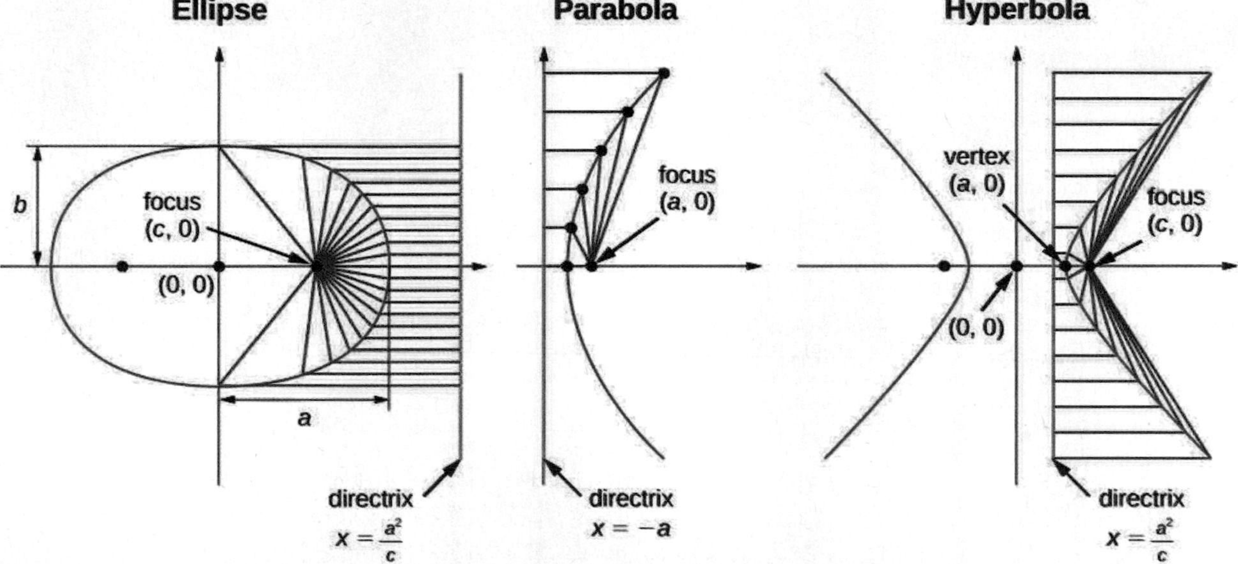

Figure 1.54 The three conic sections with their foci and directrices.

Recall from the definition of a parabola that the distance from any point on the parabola to the focus is equal to the distance from that same point to the directrix. Therefore, by definition, the eccentricity of a parabola must be 1. The equations of the directrices of a horizontal ellipse are $x = \pm\frac{a^2}{c}.$ The right vertex of the ellipse is located at $(a, 0)$ and the right focus is $(c, 0).$ Therefore the distance from the vertex to the focus is $a - c$ and the distance from the vertex to the right directrix is $\frac{a^2}{c} - c.$ This gives the eccentricity as

$$e = \frac{a - c}{\frac{a^2}{c} - a} = \frac{c(a - c)}{a^2 - ac} = \frac{c(a - c)}{a(a - c)} = \frac{c}{a}.$$

Since $c < a,$ this step proves that the eccentricity of an ellipse is less than 1. The directrices of a horizontal hyperbola are also located at $x = \pm\frac{a^2}{c},$ and a similar calculation shows that the eccentricity of a hyperbola is also $e = \frac{c}{a}.$ However in this case we have $c > a,$ so the eccentricity of a hyperbola is greater than 1.

Example 1.22

Determining Eccentricity of a Conic Section

Determine the eccentricity of the ellipse described by the equation

$$\frac{(x-3)^2}{16}+\frac{(y+2)^2}{25}=1.$$

Solution

From the equation we see that $a=5$ and $b=4$. The value of c can be calculated using the equation $a^2=b^2+c^2$ for an ellipse. Substituting the values of a and b and solving for c gives $c=3$. Therefore the eccentricity of the ellipse is $e=\frac{c}{a}=\frac{3}{5}=0.6$.

1.21 Determine the eccentricity of the hyperbola described by the equation

$$\frac{(y-3)^2}{49}-\frac{(x+2)^2}{25}=1.$$

Polar Equations of Conic Sections

Sometimes it is useful to write or identify the equation of a conic section in polar form. To do this, we need the concept of the focal parameter. The **focal parameter** of a conic section p is defined as the distance from a focus to the nearest directrix. The following table gives the focal parameters for the different types of conics, where a is the length of the semi-major axis (i.e., half the length of the major axis), c is the distance from the origin to the focus, and e is the eccentricity. In the case of a parabola, a represents the distance from the vertex to the focus.

Conic	e	p
Ellipse	$0<e<1$	$\frac{a^2-c^2}{c}=\frac{a(1-e^2)}{c}$
Parabola	$e=1$	$2a$
Hyperbola	$e>1$	$\frac{c^2-a^2}{c}=\frac{a(e^2-1)}{e}$

Table 1.7 Eccentricities and Focal Parameters of the Conic Sections

Using the definitions of the focal parameter and eccentricity of the conic section, we can derive an equation for any conic section in polar coordinates. In particular, we assume that one of the foci of a given conic section lies at the pole. Then using the definition of the various conic sections in terms of distances, it is possible to prove the following theorem.

Theorem 1.11: Polar Equation of Conic Sections

The polar equation of a conic section with focal parameter p is given by

$$r=\frac{ep}{1\pm e\cos\theta}\text{ or }r=\frac{ep}{1\pm e\sin\theta}.$$

In the equation on the left, the major axis of the conic section is horizontal, and in the equation on the right, the major axis is vertical. To work with a conic section written in polar form, first make the constant term in the denominator equal to 1. This can be done by dividing both the numerator and the denominator of the fraction by the constant that appears in front of the plus or minus in the denominator. Then the coefficient of the sine or cosine in the denominator is the eccentricity. This value identifies the conic. If cosine appears in the denominator, then the conic is horizontal. If sine appears, then the conic is vertical. If both appear then the axes are rotated. The center of the conic is not necessarily at the origin. The center is at the origin only if the conic is a circle (i.e., $e = 0$).

Example 1.23

Graphing a Conic Section in Polar Coordinates

Identify and create a graph of the conic section described by the equation

$$r = \frac{3}{1 + 2\cos\theta}.$$

Solution

The constant term in the denominator is 1, so the eccentricity of the conic is 2. This is a hyperbola. The focal parameter p can be calculated by using the equation $ep = 3$. Since $e = 2$, this gives $p = \frac{3}{2}$. The cosine function appears in the denominator, so the hyperbola is horizontal. Pick a few values for θ and create a table of values. Then we can graph the hyperbola (**Figure 1.55**).

θ	r	θ	r
0	1	π	−3
$\frac{\pi}{4}$	$\frac{3}{1+\sqrt{2}} \approx 1.2426$	$\frac{5\pi}{4}$	$\frac{3}{1-\sqrt{2}} \approx -7.2426$
$\frac{\pi}{2}$	3	$\frac{3\pi}{2}$	3
$\frac{3\pi}{4}$	$\frac{3}{1-\sqrt{2}} \approx -7.2426$	$\frac{7\pi}{4}$	$\frac{3}{1+\sqrt{2}} \approx 1.2426$

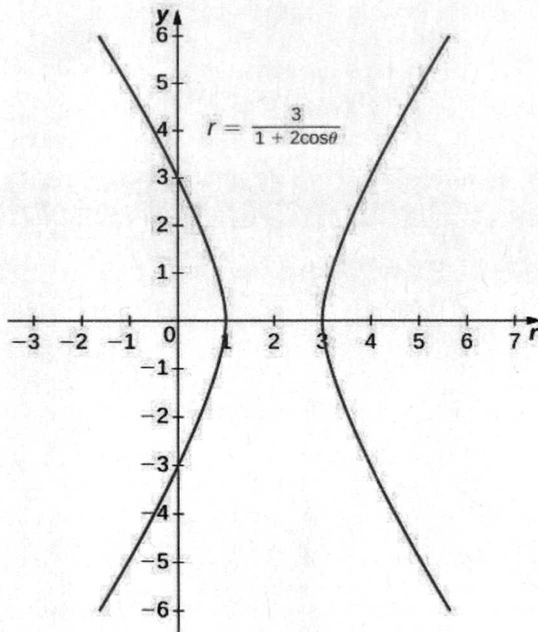

Figure 1.55 Graph of the hyperbola described in **Example 1.23**.

1.22 Identify and create a graph of the conic section described by the equation

$$r = \frac{4}{1 - 0.8 \sin \theta}.$$

General Equations of Degree Two

A general equation of degree two can be written in the form

$$Ax^2 + Bxy + Cy^2 + Dx + Ey + F = 0.$$

The graph of an equation of this form is a conic section. If $B \neq 0$ then the coordinate axes are rotated. To identify the conic section, we use the **discriminant** of the conic section $4AC - B^2$. One of the following cases must be true:

1. $4AC - B^2 > 0$. If so, the graph is an ellipse.
2. $4AC - B^2 = 0$. If so, the graph is a parabola.
3. $4AC - B^2 < 0$. If so, the graph is a hyperbola.

The simplest example of a second-degree equation involving a cross term is $xy = 1$. This equation can be solved for y to obtain $y = \frac{1}{x}$. The graph of this function is called a *rectangular hyperbola* as shown.

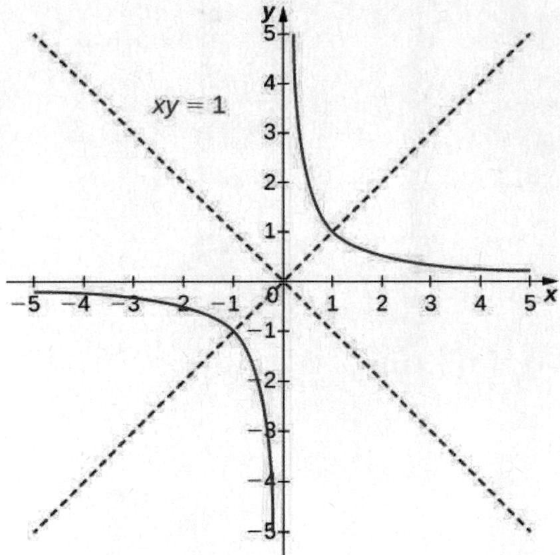

Figure 1.56 Graph of the equation $xy = 1$; The red lines indicate the rotated axes.

The asymptotes of this hyperbola are the x and y coordinate axes. To determine the angle θ of rotation of the conic section, we use the formula $\cot 2\theta = \frac{A - C}{B}$. In this case $A = C = 0$ and $B = 1$, so $\cot 2\theta = (0 - 0)/1 = 0$ and $\theta = 45°$. The method for graphing a conic section with rotated axes involves determining the coefficients of the conic in the rotated coordinate system. The new coefficients are labeled $A', B', C', D', E',$ and F', and are given by the formulas

$$\begin{aligned} A' &= A\cos^2\theta + B\cos\theta\sin\theta + C\sin^2\theta \\ B' &= 0 \\ C' &= A\sin^2\theta - B\sin\theta\cos\theta + C\cos^2\theta \\ D' &= D\cos\theta + E\sin\theta \\ E' &= -D\sin\theta + E\cos\theta \\ F' &= F. \end{aligned}$$

The procedure for graphing a rotated conic is the following:

1. Identify the conic section using the discriminant $4AC - B^2$.
2. Determine θ using the formula $\cot 2\theta = \frac{A - C}{B}$.
3. Calculate $A', B', C', D', E',$ and F'.
4. Rewrite the original equation using $A', B', C', D', E',$ and F'.
5. Draw a graph using the rotated equation.

Example 1.24

Identifying a Rotated Conic

Identify the conic and calculate the angle of rotation of axes for the curve described by the equation

$$13x^2 - 6\sqrt{3}xy + 7y^2 - 256 = 0.$$

Solution

In this equation, $A = 13, B = -6\sqrt{3}, C = 7, D = 0, E = 0,$ and $F = -256.$ The discriminant of this equation is $4AC - B^2 = 4(13)(7) - (-6\sqrt{3})^2 = 364 - 108 = 256.$ Therefore this conic is an ellipse. To calculate the angle of rotation of the axes, use $\cot 2\theta = \frac{A - C}{B}.$ This gives

$$\begin{aligned} \cot 2\theta &= \frac{A - C}{B} \\ &= \frac{13 - 7}{-6\sqrt{3}} \\ &= -\frac{\sqrt{3}}{3}. \end{aligned}$$

Therefore $2\theta = 120^{\text{o}}$ and $\theta = 60^{\text{o}},$ which is the angle of the rotation of the axes.

To determine the rotated coefficients, use the formulas given above:

$$\begin{aligned} A' &= A\cos^2\theta + B\cos\theta\sin\theta + C\sin^2\theta \\ &= 13\cos^2 60 + (-6\sqrt{3})\cos 60\sin 60 + 7\sin^2 60 \\ &= 13\left(\frac{1}{2}\right)^2 - 6\sqrt{3}\left(\frac{1}{2}\right)\left(\frac{\sqrt{3}}{2}\right) + 7\left(\frac{\sqrt{3}}{2}\right)^2 \\ &= 4, \\ B' &= 0, \\ C' &= A\sin^2\theta - B\sin\theta\cos\theta + C\cos^2\theta \\ &= 13\sin^2 60 + (-6\sqrt{3})\sin 60\cos 60 = 7\cos^2 60 \\ &= \left(\frac{\sqrt{3}}{2}\right)^2 + 6\sqrt{3}\left(\frac{\sqrt{3}}{2}\right)\left(\frac{1}{2}\right) + 7\left(\frac{1}{2}\right)^2 \\ &= 16, \\ D' &= D\cos\theta + E\sin\theta \\ &= (0)\cos 60 + (0)\sin 60 \\ &= 0, \\ E' &= -D\sin\theta + E\cos\theta \\ &= -(0)\sin 60 + (0)\cos 60 \\ &= 0, \\ F' &= F \\ &= -256. \end{aligned}$$

The equation of the conic in the rotated coordinate system becomes

$$\begin{aligned} 4(x')^2 + 16(y')^2 &= 256 \\ \frac{(x')^2}{64} + \frac{(y')^2}{16} &= 1. \end{aligned}$$

A graph of this conic section appears as follows.

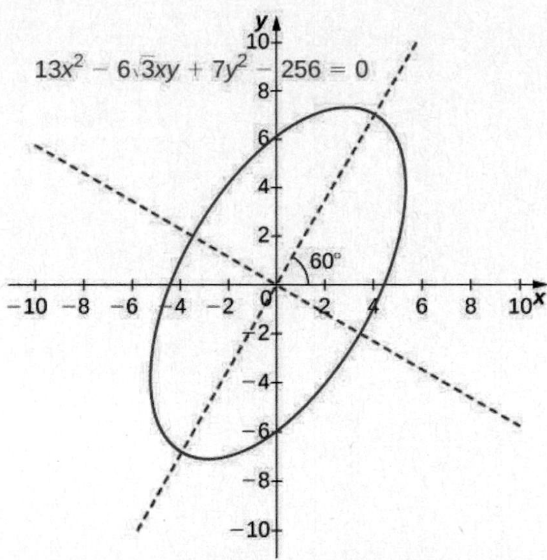

Figure 1.57 Graph of the ellipse described by the equation $13x^2 - 6\sqrt{3}xy + 7y^2 - 256 = 0$. The axes are rotated $60°$. The red dashed lines indicate the rotated axes.

1.23 Identify the conic and calculate the angle of rotation of axes for the curve described by the equation

$$3x^2 + 5xy - 2y^2 - 125 = 0.$$

1.5 EXERCISES

For the following exercises, determine the equation of the parabola using the information given.

255. Focus $(4, 0)$ and directrix $x = -4$

256. Focus $(0, -3)$ and directrix $y = 3$

257. Focus $(0, 0.5)$ and directrix $y = -0.5$

258. Focus $(2, 3)$ and directrix $x = -2$

259. Focus $(0, 2)$ and directrix $y = 4$

260. Focus $(-1, 4)$ and directrix $x = 5$

261. Focus $(-3, 5)$ and directrix $y = 1$

262. Focus $\left(\frac{5}{2}, -4\right)$ and directrix $x = \frac{7}{2}$

For the following exercises, determine the equation of the ellipse using the information given.

263. Endpoints of major axis at $(4, 0), (-4, 0)$ and foci located at $(2, 0), (-2, 0)$

264. Endpoints of major axis at $(0, 5), (0, -5)$ and foci located at $(0, 3), (0, -3)$

265. Endpoints of major axis at $(0, 2), (0, -2)$ and foci located at $(3, 0), (-3, 0)$

266. Endpoints of major axis at $(-3, 3), (7, 3)$ and foci located at $(-2, 3), (6, 3)$

267. Endpoints of major axis at $(-3, 5), (-3, -3)$ and foci located at $(-3, 3), (-3, -1)$

268. Endpoints of major axis at $(0, 0), (0, 4)$ and foci located at $(5, 2), (-5, 2)$

269. Foci located at $(2, 0), (-2, 0)$ and eccentricity of $\frac{1}{2}$

270. Foci located at $(0, -3), (0, 3)$ and eccentricity of $\frac{3}{4}$

For the following exercises, determine the equation of the hyperbola using the information given.

271. Vertices located at $(5, 0), (-5, 0)$ and foci located at $(6, 0), (-6, 0)$

272. Vertices located at $(0, 2), (0, -2)$ and foci located at $(0, 3), (0, -3)$

273. Endpoints of the conjugate axis located at $(0, 3), (0, -3)$ and foci located $(4, 0), (-4, 0)$

274. Vertices located at $(0, 1), (6, 1)$ and focus located at $(8, 1)$

275. Vertices located at $(-2, 0), (-2, -4)$ and focus located at $(-2, -8)$

276. Endpoints of the conjugate axis located at $(3, 2), (3, 4)$ and focus located at $(3, 7)$

277. Foci located at $(6, -0), (6, 0)$ and eccentricity of 3

278. $(0, 10), (0, -10)$ and eccentricity of 2.5

For the following exercises, consider the following polar equations of conics. Determine the eccentricity and identify the conic.

279. $r = \frac{-1}{1 + \cos\theta}$

280. $r = \frac{8}{2 - \sin\theta}$

281. $r = \frac{5}{2 + \sin\theta}$

282. $r = \frac{5}{-1 + 2\sin\theta}$

283. $r = \frac{3}{2 - 6\sin\theta}$

284. $r = \frac{3}{-4 + 3\sin\theta}$

For the following exercises, find a polar equation of the conic with focus at the origin and eccentricity and directrix as given.

285. Directrix: $x = 4$; $e = \frac{1}{5}$

286. Directrix: $x = -4$; $e = 5$

287. Directrix: $y = 2$; $e = 2$

288. Directrix: $y = -2$; $e = \frac{1}{2}$

For the following exercises, sketch the graph of each conic.

289. $r = \frac{1}{1 + \sin\theta}$

290. $r = \frac{1}{1 - \cos\theta}$

291. $r = \frac{4}{1 + \cos\theta}$

292. $r = \frac{10}{5 + 4\sin\theta}$

293. $r = \frac{15}{3 - 2\cos\theta}$

294. $r = \frac{32}{3 + 5\sin\theta}$

295. $r(2 + \sin\theta) = 4$

296. $r = \frac{3}{2 + 6\sin\theta}$

297. $r = \frac{3}{-4 + 2\sin\theta}$

298. $\frac{x^2}{9} + \frac{y^2}{4} = 1$

299. $\frac{x^2}{4} + \frac{y^2}{16} = 1$

300. $4x^2 + 9y^2 = 36$

301. $25x^2 - 4y^2 = 100$

302. $\frac{x^2}{16} - \frac{y^2}{9} = 1$

303. $x^2 = 12y$

304. $y^2 = 20x$

305. $12x = 5y^2$

For the following equations, determine which of the conic sections is described.

306. $xy = 4$

307. $x^2 + 4xy - 2y^2 - 6 = 0$

308. $x^2 + 2\sqrt{3}xy + 3y^2 - 6 = 0$

309. $x^2 - xy + y^2 - 2 = 0$

310. $34x^2 - 24xy + 41y^2 - 25 = 0$

311. $52x^2 - 72xy + 73y^2 + 40x + 30y - 75 = 0$

312. The mirror in an automobile headlight has a parabolic cross section, with the lightbulb at the focus. On a schematic, the equation of the parabola is given as $x^2 = 4y$. At what coordinates should you place the lightbulb?

313. A satellite dish is shaped like a paraboloid of revolution. The receiver is to be located at the focus. If the dish is 12 feet across at its opening and 4 feet deep at its center, where should the receiver be placed?

314. Consider the satellite dish of the preceding problem. If the dish is 8 feet across at the opening and 2 feet deep, where should we place the receiver?

315. A searchlight is shaped like a paraboloid of revolution. A light source is located 1 foot from the base along the axis of symmetry. If the opening of the searchlight is 3 feet across, find the depth.

316. Whispering galleries are rooms designed with elliptical ceilings. A person standing at one focus can whisper and be heard by a person standing at the other focus because all the sound waves that reach the ceiling are reflected to the other person. If a whispering gallery has a length of 120 feet and the foci are located 30 feet from the center, find the height of the ceiling at the center.

317. A person is standing 8 feet from the nearest wall in a whispering gallery. If that person is at one focus and the other focus is 80 feet away, what is the length and the height at the center of the gallery?

For the following exercises, determine the polar equation form of the orbit given the length of the major axis and eccentricity for the orbits of the comets or planets. Distance is given in astronomical units (AU).

318. Halley's Comet: length of major axis = 35.88, eccentricity = 0.967

319. Hale-Bopp Comet: length of major axis = 525.91, eccentricity = 0.995

320. Mars: length of major axis = 3.049, eccentricity = 0.0934

321. Jupiter: length of major axis = 10.408, eccentricity = 0.0484

CHAPTER 1 REVIEW

KEY TERMS

angular coordinate θ the angle formed by a line segment connecting the origin to a point in the polar coordinate system with the positive radial (x) axis, measured counterclockwise

cardioid a plane curve traced by a point on the perimeter of a circle that is rolling around a fixed circle of the same radius; the equation of a cardioid is $r = a(1 + \sin \theta)$ or $r = a(1 + \cos \theta)$

conic section a conic section is any curve formed by the intersection of a plane with a cone of two nappes

cusp a pointed end or part where two curves meet

cycloid the curve traced by a point on the rim of a circular wheel as the wheel rolls along a straight line without slippage

directrix a directrix (plural: directrices) is a line used to construct and define a conic section; a parabola has one directrix; ellipses and hyperbolas have two

discriminant the value $4AC - B^2$, which is used to identify a conic when the equation contains a term involving xy, is called a discriminant

eccentricity the eccentricity is defined as the distance from any point on the conic section to its focus divided by the perpendicular distance from that point to the nearest directrix

focal parameter the focal parameter is the distance from a focus of a conic section to the nearest directrix

focus a focus (plural: foci) is a point used to construct and define a conic section; a parabola has one focus; an ellipse and a hyperbola have two

general form an equation of a conic section written as a general second-degree equation

limaçon the graph of the equation $r = a + b \sin \theta$ or $r = a + b \cos \theta$. If $a = b$ then the graph is a cardioid

major axis the major axis of a conic section passes through the vertex in the case of a parabola or through the two vertices in the case of an ellipse or hyperbola; it is also an axis of symmetry of the conic; also called the transverse axis

minor axis the minor axis is perpendicular to the major axis and intersects the major axis at the center of the conic, or at the vertex in the case of the parabola; also called the conjugate axis

nappe a nappe is one half of a double cone

orientation the direction that a point moves on a graph as the parameter increases

parameter an independent variable that both x and y depend on in a parametric curve; usually represented by the variable t

parameterization of a curve rewriting the equation of a curve defined by a function $y = f(x)$ as parametric equations

parametric curve the graph of the parametric equations $x(t)$ and $y(t)$ over an interval $a \le t \le b$ combined with the equations

parametric equations the equations $x = x(t)$ and $y = y(t)$ that define a parametric curve

polar axis the horizontal axis in the polar coordinate system corresponding to $r \ge 0$

polar coordinate system a system for locating points in the plane. The coordinates are r, the radial coordinate, and θ, the angular coordinate

polar equation an equation or function relating the radial coordinate to the angular coordinate in the polar coordinate system

pole the central point of the polar coordinate system, equivalent to the origin of a Cartesian system

radial coordinate r the coordinate in the polar coordinate system that measures the distance from a point in the plane to the pole

rose graph of the polar equation $r = a\cos 2\theta$ or $r = a\sin 2\theta$ for a positive constant a

space-filling curve a curve that completely occupies a two-dimensional subset of the real plane

standard form an equation of a conic section showing its properties, such as location of the vertex or lengths of major and minor axes

vertex a vertex is an extreme point on a conic section; a parabola has one vertex at its turning point. An ellipse has two vertices, one at each end of the major axis; a hyperbola has two vertices, one at the turning point of each branch

KEY EQUATIONS

- **Derivative of parametric equations**
  $$\frac{dy}{dx} = \frac{dy/dt}{dx/dt} = \frac{y'(t)}{x'(t)}$$
- **Second-order derivative of parametric equations**
  $$\frac{d^2y}{dx^2} = \frac{d}{dx}\left(\frac{dy}{dx}\right) = \frac{(d/dt)(dy/dx)}{dx/dt}$$
- **Area under a parametric curve**
  $$A = \int_a^b y(t)x'(t)\,dt$$
- **Arc length of a parametric curve**
  $$s = \int_{t_1}^{t_2} \sqrt{\left(\frac{dx}{dt}\right)^2 + \left(\frac{dy}{dt}\right)^2}\,dt$$
- **Surface area generated by a parametric curve**
  $$S = 2\pi\int_a^b y(t)\sqrt{(x'(t))^2 + (y'(t))^2}\,dt$$
- **Area of a region bounded by a polar curve**
  $$A = \frac{1}{2}\int_\alpha^\beta [f(\theta)]^2\,d\theta = \frac{1}{2}\int_\alpha^\beta r^2\,d\theta$$
- **Arc length of a polar curve**
  $$L = \int_\alpha^\beta \sqrt{[f(\theta)]^2 + [f'(\theta)]^2}\,d\theta = \int_\alpha^\beta \sqrt{r^2 + \left(\frac{dr}{d\theta}\right)^2}\,d\theta$$

KEY CONCEPTS

1.1 Parametric Equations

- Parametric equations provide a convenient way to describe a curve. A parameter can represent time or some other meaningful quantity.
- It is often possible to eliminate the parameter in a parameterized curve to obtain a function or relation describing that curve.
- There is always more than one way to parameterize a curve.
- Parametric equations can describe complicated curves that are difficult or perhaps impossible to describe using rectangular coordinates.

1.2 Calculus of Parametric Curves

- The derivative of the parametrically defined curve $x = x(t)$ and $y = y(t)$ can be calculated using the formula $\frac{dy}{dx} = \frac{y'(t)}{x'(t)}$. Using the derivative, we can find the equation of a tangent line to a parametric curve.
- The area between a parametric curve and the x-axis can be determined by using the formula $A = \int_{t_1}^{t_2} y(t)x'(t)\,dt$.
- The arc length of a parametric curve can be calculated by using the formula $s = \int_{t_1}^{t_2} \sqrt{\left(\frac{dx}{dt}\right)^2 + \left(\frac{dy}{dt}\right)^2}\,dt$.
- The surface area of a volume of revolution revolved around the x-axis is given by $S = 2\pi \int_a^b y(t)\sqrt{(x'(t))^2 + (y'(t))^2}\,dt$. If the curve is revolved around the y-axis, then the formula is $S = 2\pi \int_a^b x(t)\sqrt{(x'(t))^2 + (y'(t))^2}\,dt$.

1.3 Polar Coordinates

- The polar coordinate system provides an alternative way to locate points in the plane.
- Convert points between rectangular and polar coordinates using the formulas

$$x = r\cos\theta \text{ and } y = r\sin\theta$$

and

$$r = \sqrt{x^2 + y^2} \text{ and } \tan\theta = \frac{y}{x}.$$

- To sketch a polar curve from a given polar function, make a table of values and take advantage of periodic properties.
- Use the conversion formulas to convert equations between rectangular and polar coordinates.
- Identify symmetry in polar curves, which can occur through the pole, the horizontal axis, or the vertical axis.

1.4 Area and Arc Length in Polar Coordinates

- The area of a region in polar coordinates defined by the equation $r = f(\theta)$ with $\alpha \le \theta \le \beta$ is given by the integral $A = \frac{1}{2}\int_\alpha^\beta [f(\theta)]^2\,d\theta$.
- To find the area between two curves in the polar coordinate system, first find the points of intersection, then subtract the corresponding areas.
- The arc length of a polar curve defined by the equation $r = f(\theta)$ with $\alpha \le \theta \le \beta$ is given by the integral $L = \int_\alpha^\beta \sqrt{[f(\theta)]^2 + [f'(\theta)]^2}\,d\theta = \int_\alpha^\beta \sqrt{r^2 + \left(\frac{dr}{d\theta}\right)^2}\,d\theta$.

1.5 Conic Sections

- The equation of a vertical parabola in standard form with given focus and directrix is $y = \frac{1}{4p}(x - h)^2 + k$ where p is the distance from the vertex to the focus and (h, k) are the coordinates of the vertex.

- The equation of a horizontal ellipse in standard form is $\frac{(x-h)^2}{a^2}+\frac{(y-k)^2}{b^2}=1$ where the center has coordinates (h, k), the major axis has length $2a$, the minor axis has length $2b$, and the coordinates of the foci are $(h \pm c, k)$, where $c^2 = a^2 - b^2$.
- The equation of a horizontal hyperbola in standard form is $\frac{(x-h)^2}{a^2}-\frac{(y-k)^2}{b^2}=1$ where the center has coordinates (h, k), the vertices are located at $(h \pm a, k)$, and the coordinates of the foci are $(h \pm c, k)$, where $c^2 = a^2 + b^2$.
- The eccentricity of an ellipse is less than 1, the eccentricity of a parabola is equal to 1, and the eccentricity of a hyperbola is greater than 1. The eccentricity of a circle is 0.
- The polar equation of a conic section with eccentricity e is $r=\frac{ep}{1 \pm e\cos\theta}$ or $r=\frac{ep}{1 \pm e\sin\theta}$, where p represents the focal parameter.
- To identify a conic generated by the equation $Ax^2 + Bxy + Cy^2 + Dx + Ey + F = 0$, first calculate the discriminant $D = 4AC - B^2$. If $D > 0$ then the conic is an ellipse, if $D = 0$ then the conic is a parabola, and if $D < 0$ then the conic is a hyperbola.

CHAPTER 1 REVIEW EXERCISES

True or False? Justify your answer with a proof or a counterexample.

322. The rectangular coordinates of the point $\left(4, \frac{5\pi}{6}\right)$ are $\left(2\sqrt{3}, -2\right)$.

323. The equations $x = \cosh(3t)$, $y = 2\sinh(3t)$ represent a hyperbola.

324. The arc length of the spiral given by $r = \frac{\theta}{2}$ for $0 \le \theta \le 3\pi$ is $\frac{9}{4}\pi^3$.

325. Given $x = f(t)$ and $y = g(t)$, if $\frac{dx}{dy} = \frac{dy}{dx}$, then $f(t) = g(t) + \text{C}$, where C is a constant.

For the following exercises, sketch the parametric curve and eliminate the parameter to find the Cartesian equation of the curve.

326. $x = 1 + t, \quad y = t^2 - 1, \quad -1 \le t \le 1$

327. $x = e^t, \quad y = 1 - e^{3t}, \quad 0 \le t \le 1$

328. $x = \sin\theta, \quad y = 1 - \csc\theta, \quad 0 \le \theta \le 2\pi$

329. $x = 4\cos\phi, \quad y = 1 - \sin\phi, \quad 0 \le \phi \le 2\pi$

For the following exercises, sketch the polar curve and determine what type of symmetry exists, if any.

330. $r = 4\sin\left(\frac{\theta}{3}\right)$

331. $r = 5\cos(5\theta)$

For the following exercises, find the polar equation for the curve given as a Cartesian equation.

332. $x + y = 5$

333. $y^2 = 4 + x^2$

For the following exercises, find the equation of the tangent line to the given curve. Graph both the function and its tangent line.

334. $x = \ln(t), \quad y = t^2 - 1, \quad t = 1$

335. $r = 3 + \cos(2\theta), \quad \theta = \frac{3\pi}{4}$

336. Find $\frac{dy}{dx}$, $\frac{dx}{dy}$, and $\frac{d^2x}{dy^2}$ of $y = \left(2 + e^{-t}\right)$, $x = 1 - \sin(t)$

For the following exercises, find the area of the region.

337. $x = t^2, \quad y = \ln(t), \quad 0 \le t \le e$

338. $r = 1 - \sin\theta$ in the first quadrant

For the following exercises, find the arc length of the curve over the given interval.

339. $x = 3t + 4, \quad y = 9t - 2, \quad 0 \le t \le 3$

340. $r = 6\cos\theta, \quad 0 \le \theta \le 2\pi.$ Check your answer by geometry.

For the following exercises, find the Cartesian equation describing the given shapes.

341. A parabola with focus $(2, -5)$ and directrix $x = 6$

342. An ellipse with a major axis length of 10 and foci at $(-7, 2)$ and $(1, 2)$

343. A hyperbola with vertices at $(3, -2)$ and $(-5, -2)$ and foci at $(-2, -6)$ and $(-2, 4)$

For the following exercises, determine the eccentricity and identify the conic. Sketch the conic.

344. $r = \dfrac{6}{1 + 3\cos(\theta)}$

345. $r = \dfrac{4}{3 - 2\cos\theta}$

346. $r = \dfrac{7}{5 - 5\cos\theta}$

347. Determine the Cartesian equation describing the orbit of Pluto, the most eccentric orbit around the Sun. The length of the major axis is 39.26 AU and minor axis is 38.07 AU. What is the eccentricity?

348. The C/1980 E1 comet was observed in 1980. Given an eccentricity of 1.057 and a perihelion (point of closest approach to the Sun) of 3.364 AU, find the Cartesian equations describing the comet's trajectory. Are we guaranteed to see this comet again? (*Hint*: Consider the Sun at point $(0, 0)$.)

2 | VECTORS IN SPACE

Figure 2.1 The Karl G. Jansky Very Large Array, located in Socorro, New Mexico, consists of a large number of radio telescopes that can collect radio waves and collate them as if they were gathering waves over a huge area with no gaps in coverage. (credit: modification of work by CGP Grey, Wikimedia Commons)

Chapter Outline

Introduction

Modern astronomical observatories often consist of a large number of parabolic reflectors, connected by computers, used to analyze radio waves. Each dish focuses the incoming parallel beams of radio waves to a precise focal point, where they can be synchronized by computer. If the surface of one of the parabolic reflectors is described by the equation $\frac{x^2}{100} + \frac{y^2}{100} = \frac{z}{4},$ where is the focal point of the reflector? (See **Example 2.58**.)

We are now about to begin a new part of the calculus course, when we study functions of two or three independent variables in multidimensional space. Many of the computations are similar to those in the study of single-variable functions, but there are also a lot of differences. In this first chapter, we examine coordinate systems for working in three-dimensional space, along with vectors, which are a key mathematical tool for dealing with quantities in more than one dimension. Let's start here with the basic ideas and work our way up to the more general and powerful tools of mathematics in later chapters.

2.1 | Vectors in the Plane

Learning Objectives

- **2.1.1** Describe a plane vector, using correct notation.
- **2.1.2** Perform basic vector operations (scalar multiplication, addition, subtraction).
- **2.1.3** Express a vector in component form.
- **2.1.4** Explain the formula for the magnitude of a vector.
- **2.1.5** Express a vector in terms of unit vectors.
- **2.1.6** Give two examples of vector quantities.

When describing the movement of an airplane in flight, it is important to communicate two pieces of information: the direction in which the plane is traveling and the plane's speed. When measuring a force, such as the thrust of the plane's engines, it is important to describe not only the strength of that force, but also the direction in which it is applied. Some quantities, such as or force, are defined in terms of both size (also called *magnitude*) and direction. A quantity that has magnitude and direction is called a **vector**. In this text, we denote vectors by boldface letters, such as **v**.

Definition

A vector is a quantity that has both magnitude and direction.

Vector Representation

A vector in a plane is represented by a directed line segment (an arrow). The endpoints of the segment are called the **initial point** and the **terminal point** of the vector. An arrow from the initial point to the terminal point indicates the direction of the vector. The length of the line segment represents its **magnitude**. We use the notation $\|\mathbf{v}\|$ to denote the magnitude of the vector $\mathbf{v}$. A vector with an initial point and terminal point that are the same is called the **zero vector**, denoted $\mathbf{0}$. The zero vector is the only vector without a direction, and by convention can be considered to have any direction convenient to the problem at hand.

Vectors with the same magnitude and direction are called equivalent vectors. We treat equivalent vectors as equal, even if they have different initial points. Thus, if $\mathbf{v}$ and $\mathbf{w}$ are equivalent, we write

$$\mathbf{v} = \mathbf{w}.$$

Definition

Vectors are said to be **equivalent vectors** if they have the same magnitude and direction.

The arrows in **Figure 2.2**(b) are equivalent. Each arrow has the same length and direction. A closely related concept is the idea of parallel vectors. Two vectors are said to be parallel if they have the same or opposite directions. We explore this idea in more detail later in the chapter. A vector is defined by its magnitude and direction, regardless of where its initial point is located.

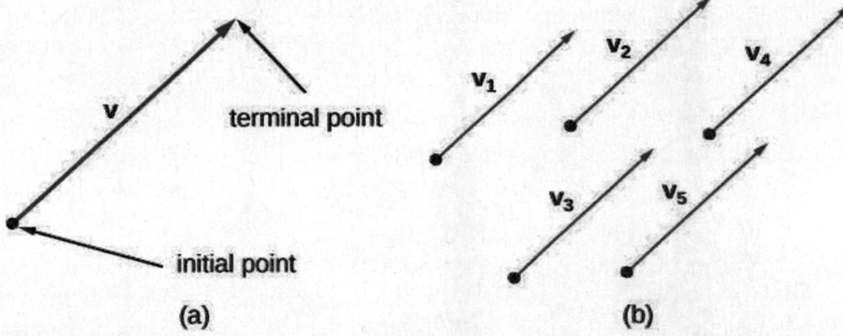

Figure 2.2 (a) A vector is represented by a directed line segment from its initial point to its terminal point. (b) Vectors $\mathbf{v}_1$ through $\mathbf{v}_5$ are equivalent.

The use of boldface, lowercase letters to name vectors is a common representation in print, but there are alternative notations. When writing the name of a vector by hand, for example, it is easier to sketch an arrow over the variable than to simulate boldface type: $\vec{v}$. When a vector has initial point P and terminal point Q, the notation $\overrightarrow{PQ}$ is useful because it indicates the direction and location of the vector.

Example 2.1

Sketching Vectors

Sketch a vector in the plane from initial point $P(1, 1)$ to terminal point $Q(8, 5)$.

Solution

See **Figure 2.3**. Because the vector goes from point P to point Q, we name it $\overrightarrow{PQ}$.

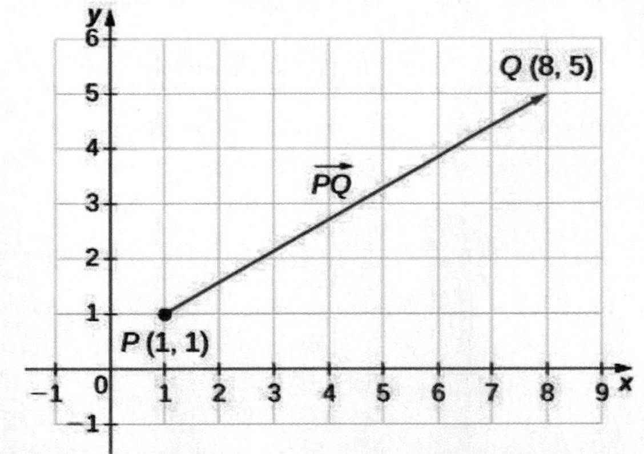

Figure 2.3 The vector with initial point $(1, 1)$ and terminal point $(8, 5)$ is named $\overrightarrow{PQ}$.

2.1 Sketch the vector $\overrightarrow{ST}$ where S is point $(3, -1)$ and T is point $(-2, 3)$.

Combining Vectors

Vectors have many real-life applications, including situations involving force or velocity. For example, consider the forces acting on a boat crossing a river. The boat's motor generates a force in one direction, and the current of the river generates a force in another direction. Both forces are vectors. We must take both the magnitude and direction of each force into account if we want to know where the boat will go.

A second example that involves vectors is a quarterback throwing a football. The quarterback does not throw the ball parallel to the ground; instead, he aims up into the air. The velocity of his throw can be represented by a vector. If we know how hard he throws the ball (magnitude—in this case, speed), and the angle (direction), we can tell how far the ball will travel down the field.

A real number is often called a **scalar** in mathematics and physics. Unlike vectors, scalars are generally considered to have a magnitude only, but no direction. Multiplying a vector by a scalar changes the vector's magnitude. This is called scalar multiplication. Note that changing the magnitude of a vector does not indicate a change in its direction. For example, wind blowing from north to south might increase or decrease in speed while maintaining its direction from north to south.

Definition

The product $k\mathbf{v}$ of a vector $\mathbf{v}$ and a scalar k is a vector with a magnitude that is $|k|$ times the magnitude of $\mathbf{v},$ and with a direction that is the same as the direction of $\mathbf{v}$ if $k > 0,$ and opposite the direction of $\mathbf{v}$ if $k < 0.$ This is called **scalar multiplication**. If $k = 0$ or $\mathbf{v} = \mathbf{0},$ then $k\mathbf{v} = \mathbf{0}.$

As you might expect, if $k = -1,$ we denote the product $k\mathbf{v}$ as

$$k\mathbf{v} = (-1)\mathbf{v} = -\mathbf{v}.$$

Note that $-\mathbf{v}$ has the same magnitude as $\mathbf{v},$ but has the opposite direction (**Figure 2.4**).

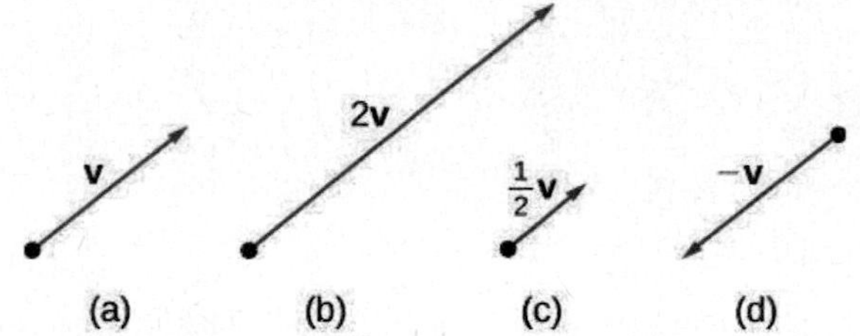

Figure 2.4 (a) The original vector **v** has length *n* units. (b) The length of $2\mathbf{v}$ equals $2n$ units. (c) The length of $\mathbf{v}/2$ is $n/2$ units. (d) The vectors $\mathbf{v}$ and $-\mathbf{v}$ have the same length but opposite directions.

Another operation we can perform on vectors is to add them together in vector addition, but because each vector may have its own direction, the process is different from adding two numbers. The most common graphical method for adding two vectors is to place the initial point of the second vector at the terminal point of the first, as in **Figure 2.5**(a). To see why this makes sense, suppose, for example, that both vectors represent displacement. If an object moves first from the initial point to the terminal point of vector $\mathbf{v},$ then from the initial point to the terminal point of vector $\mathbf{w},$ the overall displacement is the same as if the object had made just one movement from the initial point to the terminal point of the vector $\mathbf{v} + \mathbf{w}.$ For obvious reasons, this approach is called the **triangle method**. Notice that if we had switched the order, so that $\mathbf{w}$ was our first vector and **v** was our second vector, we would have ended up in the same place. (Again, see **Figure 2.5**(a).) Thus, $\mathbf{v} + \mathbf{w} = \mathbf{w} + \mathbf{v}.$

A second method for adding vectors is called the **parallelogram method**. With this method, we place the two vectors so they have the same initial point, and then we draw a parallelogram with the vectors as two adjacent sides, as in **Figure 2.5**(b). The length of the diagonal of the parallelogram is the sum. Comparing **Figure 2.5**(b) and **Figure 2.5**(a), we can see that we get the same answer using either method. The vector $\mathbf{v} + \mathbf{w}$ is called the **vector sum**.

Definition

The sum of two vectors $\mathbf{v}$ and $\mathbf{w}$ can be constructed graphically by placing the initial point of $\mathbf{w}$ at the terminal point of $\mathbf{v}$. Then, the vector sum, $\mathbf{v} + \mathbf{w}$, is the vector with an initial point that coincides with the initial point of $\mathbf{v}$ and has a terminal point that coincides with the terminal point of $\mathbf{w}$. This operation is known as **vector addition**.

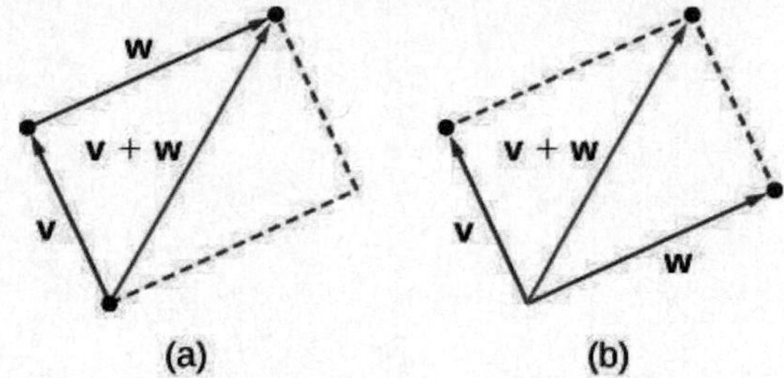

Figure 2.5 (a) When adding vectors by the triangle method, the initial point of $\mathbf{w}$ is the terminal point of $\mathbf{v}$. (b) When adding vectors by the parallelogram method, the vectors $\mathbf{v}$ and $\mathbf{w}$ have the same initial point.

It is also appropriate here to discuss vector subtraction. We define $\mathbf{v} - \mathbf{w}$ as $\mathbf{v} + (-\mathbf{w}) = \mathbf{v} + (-1)\mathbf{w}$. The vector $\mathbf{v} - \mathbf{w}$ is called the **vector difference**. Graphically, the vector $\mathbf{v} - \mathbf{w}$ is depicted by drawing a vector from the terminal point of $\mathbf{w}$ to the terminal point of $\mathbf{v}$ (**Figure 2.6**).

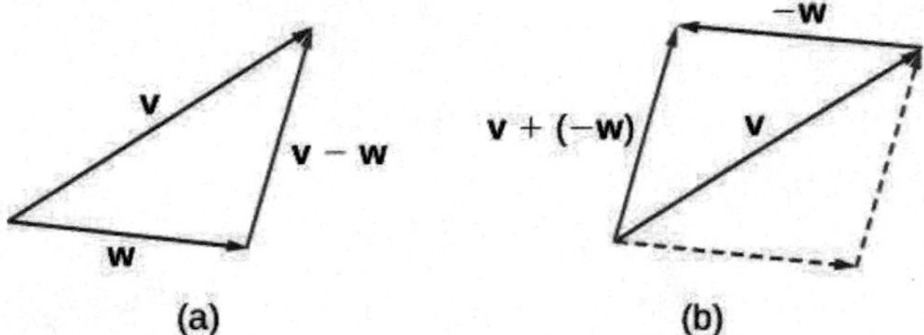

Figure 2.6 (a) The vector difference $\mathbf{v} - \mathbf{w}$ is depicted by drawing a vector from the terminal point of $\mathbf{w}$ to the terminal point of $\mathbf{v}$. (b) The vector $\mathbf{v} - \mathbf{w}$ is equivalent to the vector $\mathbf{v} + (-\mathbf{w})$.

In **Figure 2.5**(a), the initial point of $\mathbf{v} + \mathbf{w}$ is the initial point of $\mathbf{v}$. The terminal point of $\mathbf{v} + \mathbf{w}$ is the terminal point of $\mathbf{w}$. These three vectors form the sides of a triangle. It follows that the length of any one side is less than the sum of the lengths of the remaining sides. So we have

$$\| \mathbf{v} + \mathbf{w} \| \leq \| \mathbf{v} \| + \| \mathbf{w} \| .$$

This is known more generally as the **triangle inequality**. There is one case, however, when the resultant vector $\mathbf{u} + \mathbf{v}$ has the same magnitude as the sum of the magnitudes of $\mathbf{u}$ and $\mathbf{v}$. This happens only when $\mathbf{u}$ and $\mathbf{v}$ have the same direction.

Example 2.2

Combining Vectors

Given the vectors $\mathbf{v}$ and $\mathbf{w}$ shown in **Figure 2.7**, sketch the vectors

a. $3\mathbf{w}$

b. $\mathbf{v} + \mathbf{w}$

c. $2\mathbf{v} - \mathbf{w}$

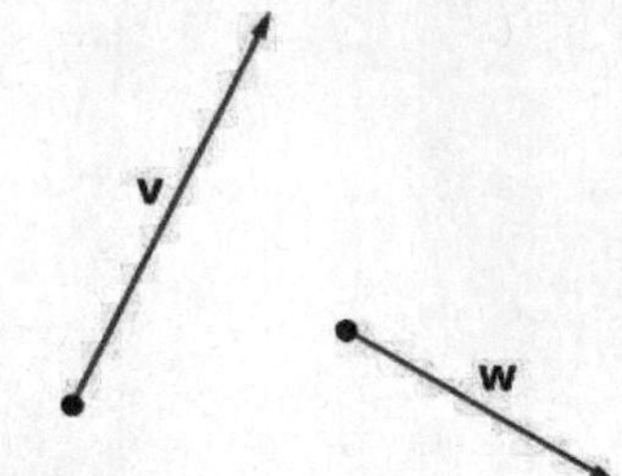

Figure 2.7 Vectors $\mathbf{v}$ and $\mathbf{w}$ lie in the same plane.

Solution

a. The vector $3\mathbf{w}$ has the same direction as $\mathbf{w}$; it is three times as long as $\mathbf{w}$.

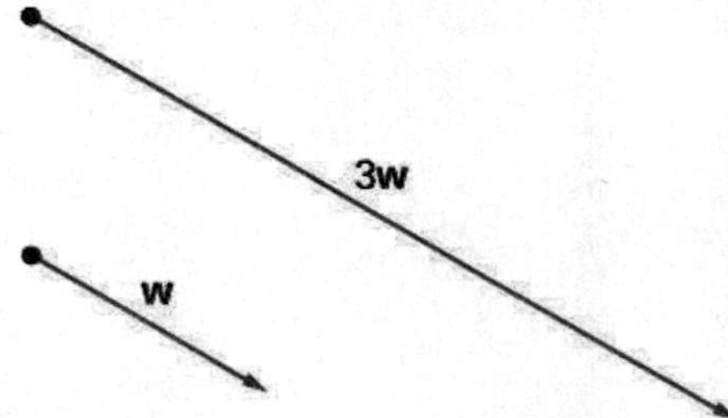

Vector $3\mathbf{w}$ has the same direction as $\mathbf{w}$ and is three times as long.

b. Use either addition method to find $\mathbf{v} + \mathbf{w}$.

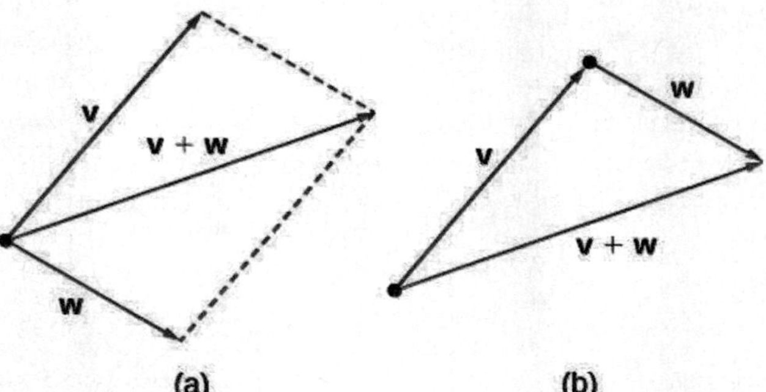

Figure 2.8 To find $\mathbf{v} + \mathbf{w}$, align the vectors at their initial points or place the initial point of one vector at the terminal point of the other. (a) The vector $\mathbf{v} + \mathbf{w}$ is the diagonal of the parallelogram with sides $\mathbf{v}$ and $\mathbf{w}$ (b) The vector $\mathbf{v} + \mathbf{w}$ is the third side of a triangle formed with $\mathbf{w}$ placed at the terminal point of $\mathbf{v}$.

c. To find $2\mathbf{v} - \mathbf{w}$, we can first rewrite the expression as $2\mathbf{v} + (-\mathbf{w})$. Then we can draw the vector $-\mathbf{w}$, then add it to the vector $2\mathbf{v}$.

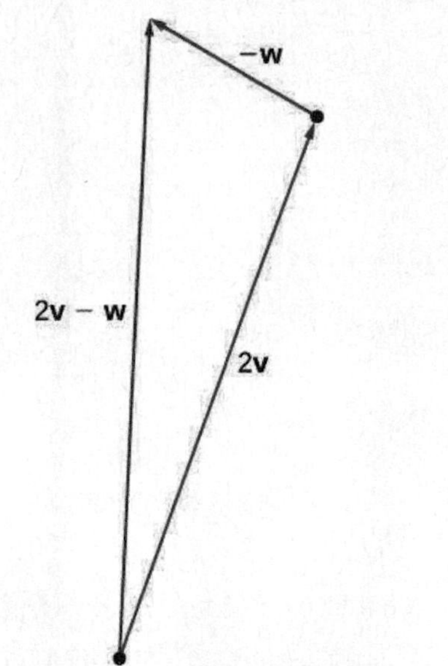

Figure 2.9 To find $2\mathbf{v} - \mathbf{w},$ simply add $2\mathbf{v} + (-\mathbf{w}).$

2.2 Using vectors $\mathbf{v}$ and $\mathbf{w}$ from **Example 2.2**, sketch the vector $2\mathbf{w} - \mathbf{v}.$

Vector Components

Working with vectors in a plane is easier when we are working in a coordinate system. When the initial points and terminal points of vectors are given in Cartesian coordinates, computations become straightforward.

Example 2.3

Comparing Vectors

Are $\mathbf{v}$ and $\mathbf{w}$ equivalent vectors?

a. $\mathbf{v}$ has initial point $(3, 2)$ and terminal point $(7, 2)$
   $\mathbf{w}$ has initial point $(1, -4)$ and terminal point $(1, 0)$

b. $\mathbf{v}$ has initial point $(0, 0)$ and terminal point $(1, 1)$
   $\mathbf{w}$ has initial point $(-2, 2)$ and terminal point $(-1, 3)$

Solution

a. The vectors are each 4 units long, but they are oriented in different directions. So $\mathbf{v}$ and $\mathbf{w}$ are not equivalent (**Figure 2.10**).

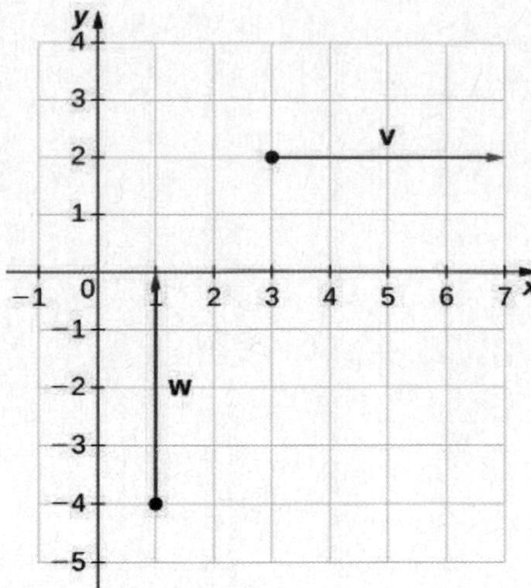

Figure 2.10 These vectors are not equivalent.

b. Based on **Figure 2.11**, and using a bit of geometry, it is clear these vectors have the same length and the same direction, so **v** and **w** are equivalent.

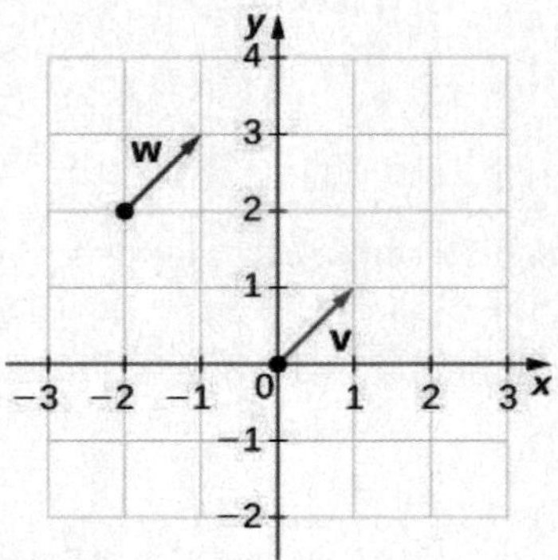

Figure 2.11 These vectors are equivalent.

2.3 Which of the following vectors are equivalent?

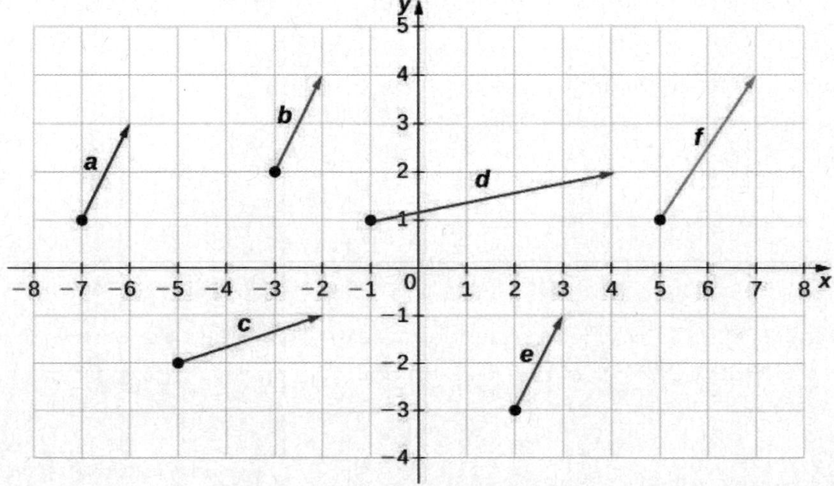

We have seen how to plot a vector when we are given an initial point and a terminal point. However, because a vector can be placed anywhere in a plane, it may be easier to perform calculations with a vector when its initial point coincides with the origin. We call a vector with its initial point at the origin a **standard-position vector**. Because the initial point of any vector in standard position is known to be $(0, 0)$, we can describe the vector by looking at the coordinates of its terminal point. Thus, if vector **v** has its initial point at the origin and its terminal point at (x, y), we write the vector in component form as

$$\mathbf{v} = \langle x, y \rangle .$$

When a vector is written in component form like this, the scalars *x* and *y* are called the **components** of **v**.

Definition

The vector with initial point $(0, 0)$ and terminal point (x, y) can be written in component form as

$$\mathbf{v} = \langle x, y \rangle .$$

The scalars x and y are called the components of **v**.

Recall that vectors are named with lowercase letters in bold type or by drawing an arrow over their name. We have also learned that we can name a vector by its component form, with the coordinates of its terminal point in angle brackets. However, when writing the component form of a vector, it is important to distinguish between $\langle x, y \rangle$ and (x, y). The first ordered pair uses angle brackets to describe a vector, whereas the second uses parentheses to describe a point in a plane. The initial point of $\langle x, y \rangle$ is $(0, 0)$; the terminal point of $\langle x, y \rangle$ is (x, y).

When we have a vector not already in standard position, we can determine its component form in one of two ways. We can use a geometric approach, in which we sketch the vector in the coordinate plane, and then sketch an equivalent standard-position vector. Alternatively, we can find it algebraically, using the coordinates of the initial point and the terminal point. To find it algebraically, we subtract the *x*-coordinate of the initial point from the *x*-coordinate of the terminal point to get the *x* component, and we subtract the *y*-coordinate of the initial point from the *y*-coordinate of the terminal point to get the *y* component.

Rule: Component Form of a Vector

Let **v** be a vector with initial point (x_i, y_i) and terminal point (x_t, y_t). Then we can express **v** in component form as $\mathbf{v} = \langle x_t - x_i, y_t - y_i \rangle$.

Example 2.4

Expressing Vectors in Component Form

Express vector **v** with initial point $(-3, 4)$ and terminal point $(1, 2)$ in component form.

Solution

a. Geometric

1. Sketch the vector in the coordinate plane (**Figure 2.12**).
2. The terminal point is 4 units to the right and 2 units down from the initial point.
3. Find the point that is 4 units to the right and 2 units down from the origin.
4. In standard position, this vector has initial point $(0, 0)$ and terminal point $(4, -2)$:

$$\mathbf{v} = \langle 4, -2 \rangle .$$

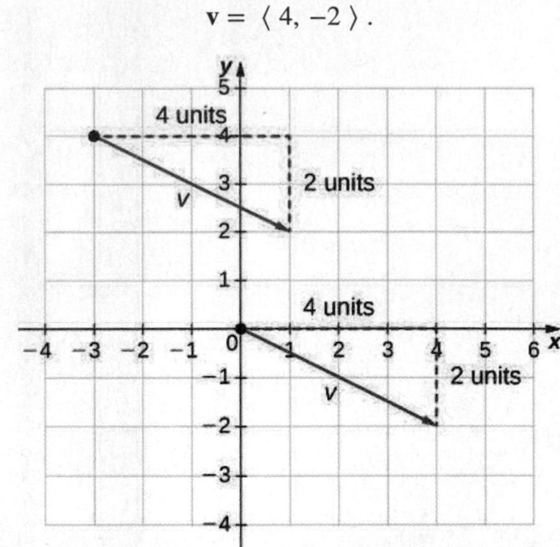

Figure 2.12 These vectors are equivalent.

b. Algebraic
In the first solution, we used a sketch of the vector to see that the terminal point lies 4 units to the right. We can accomplish this algebraically by finding the difference of the x-coordinates:

$$x_t - x_i = 1 - (-3) = 4.$$

Similarly, the difference of the y-coordinates shows the vertical length of the vector.

$$y_t - y_i = 2 - 4 = -2.$$

So, in component form,

$$\begin{aligned} \mathbf{v} &= \langle x_t - x_i, y_t - y_i \rangle \\ &= \langle 1 - (-3), 2 - 4 \rangle \\ &= \langle 4, -2 \rangle . \end{aligned}$$

2.4 Vector $\mathbf{w}$ has initial point $(-4, -5)$ and terminal point $(-1, 2)$. Express $\mathbf{w}$ in component form.

To find the magnitude of a vector, we calculate the distance between its initial point and its terminal point. The magnitude of vector $\mathbf{v} = \langle x, y \rangle$ is denoted $\| \mathbf{v} \|$, or $|\mathbf{v}|$, and can be computed using the formula

$$\| \mathbf{v} \| = \sqrt{x^2 + y^2}.$$

Note that because this vector is written in component form, it is equivalent to a vector in standard position, with its initial point at the origin and terminal point (x, y). Thus, it suffices to calculate the magnitude of the vector in standard position. Using the distance formula to calculate the distance between initial point $(0, 0)$ and terminal point (x, y), we have

$$\begin{aligned} \| \mathbf{v} \| &= \sqrt{(x - 0)^2 + (y - 0)^2} \\ &= \sqrt{x^2 + y^2}. \end{aligned}$$

Based on this formula, it is clear that for any vector $\mathbf{v}$, $\| \mathbf{v} \| \geq 0$, and $\| \mathbf{v} \| = 0$ if and only if $\mathbf{v} = \mathbf{0}$.

The magnitude of a vector can also be derived using the Pythagorean theorem, as in the following figure.

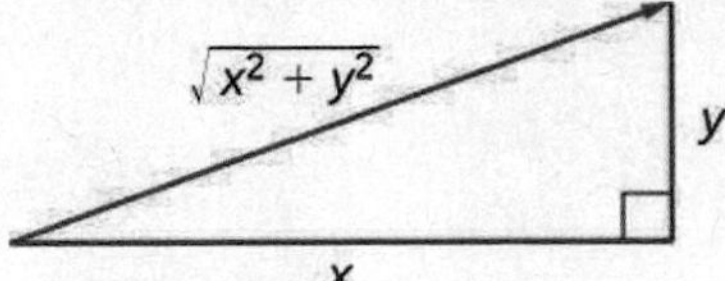

Figure 2.13 If you use the components of a vector to define a right triangle, the magnitude of the vector is the length of the triangle's hypotenuse.

We have defined scalar multiplication and vector addition geometrically. Expressing vectors in component form allows us to perform these same operations algebraically.

Definition

Let $\mathbf{v} = \langle x_1, y_1 \rangle$ and $\mathbf{w} = \langle x_2, y_2 \rangle$ be vectors, and let k be a scalar.

Scalar multiplication: $k\mathbf{v} = \langle kx_1, ky_1 \rangle$

Vector addition: $\mathbf{v} + \mathbf{w} = \langle x_1, y_1 \rangle + \langle x_2, y_2 \rangle = \langle x_1 + x_2, y_1 + y_2 \rangle$

Example 2.5

Performing Operations in Component Form

Let $\mathbf{v}$ be the vector with initial point $(2, 5)$ and terminal point $(8, 13)$, and let $\mathbf{w} = \langle -2, 4 \rangle$.

a. Express $\mathbf{v}$ in component form and find $\| \mathbf{v} \|$. Then, using algebra, find

b. $\mathbf{v} + \mathbf{w}$,

c. $3\mathbf{v}$, and

d. $\mathbf{v} - 2\mathbf{w}$.

Solution

a. To place the initial point of $\mathbf{v}$ at the origin, we must translate the vector 2 units to the left and 5 units down (**Figure 2.15**). Using the algebraic method, we can express $\mathbf{v}$ as $\mathbf{v} = \langle 8 - 2, 13 - 5 \rangle = \langle 6, 8 \rangle$:

$$\| \mathbf{v} \| = \sqrt{6^2 + 8^2} = \sqrt{36 + 64} = \sqrt{100} = 10.$$

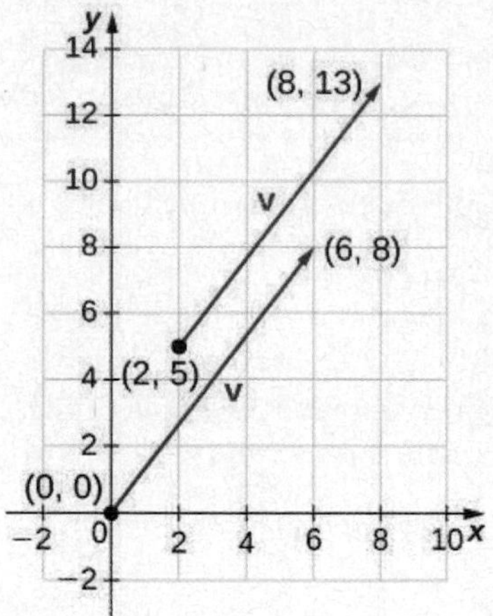

Figure 2.14 In component form, $\mathbf{v} = \langle 6, 8 \rangle$.

b. To find $\mathbf{v} + \mathbf{w}$, add the x-components and the y-components separately:

$$\mathbf{v} + \mathbf{w} = \langle 6, 8 \rangle + \langle -2, 4 \rangle = \langle 4, 12 \rangle.$$

c. To find $3\mathbf{v}$, multiply $\mathbf{v}$ by the scalar $k = 3$:

$$3\mathbf{v} = 3 \cdot \langle 6, 8 \rangle = \langle 3 \cdot 6, 3 \cdot 8 \rangle = \langle 18, 24 \rangle.$$

d. To find $\mathbf{v} - 2\mathbf{w}$, find $-2\mathbf{w}$ and add it to $\mathbf{v}$:

$$\mathbf{v} - 2\mathbf{w} = \langle 6, 8 \rangle - 2 \cdot \langle -2, 4 \rangle = \langle 6, 8 \rangle + \langle 4, -8 \rangle = \langle 10, 0 \rangle.$$

2.5 Let $\mathbf{a} = \langle 7, 1 \rangle$ and let $\mathbf{b}$ be the vector with initial point $(3, 2)$ and terminal point $(-1, -1)$.

a. Find $\|\mathbf{a}\|$.

b. Express $\mathbf{b}$ in component form.

c. Find $3\mathbf{a} - 4\mathbf{b}$.

Now that we have established the basic rules of vector arithmetic, we can state the properties of vector operations. We will prove two of these properties. The others can be proved in a similar manner.

Theorem 2.1: Properties of Vector Operations

Let $\mathbf{u}$, $\mathbf{v}$, and $\mathbf{w}$ be vectors in a plane. Let r and s be scalars.

i.	$\mathbf{u} + \mathbf{v}$	=	$\mathbf{v} + \mathbf{u}$	Commutative property
ii.	$(\mathbf{u} + \mathbf{v}) + \mathbf{w}$	=	$\mathbf{u} + (\mathbf{v} + \mathbf{w})$	Associative property
iii.	$\mathbf{u} + \mathbf{0}$	=	$\mathbf{u}$	Additive identity property
iv.	$\mathbf{u} + (-\mathbf{u})$	=	$\mathbf{0}$	Additive inverse property
v.	$r(s\mathbf{u})$	=	$(rs)\mathbf{u}$	Associativity of scalar multiplication
vi.	$(r + s)\mathbf{u}$	=	$r\mathbf{u} + s\mathbf{u}$	Distributive property
vii.	$r(\mathbf{u} + \mathbf{v})$	=	$r\mathbf{u} + r\mathbf{v}$	Distributive property
viii.	$1\mathbf{u}$	=	$\mathbf{u},\ 0\mathbf{u} = \mathbf{0}$	Identity and zero properties

Proof of Commutative Property

Let $\mathbf{u} = \langle x_1, y_1 \rangle$ and $\mathbf{v} = \langle x_2, y_2 \rangle$. Apply the commutative property for real numbers:

$$\mathbf{u} + \mathbf{v} = \langle x_1 + x_2, y_1 + y_2 \rangle = \langle x_2 + x_1, y_2 + y_1 \rangle = \mathbf{v} + \mathbf{u}.$$

□

Proof of Distributive Property

Apply the distributive property for real numbers:

$$\begin{aligned} r(\mathbf{u} + \mathbf{v}) &= r \cdot \langle x_1 + x_2, y_1 + y_2 \rangle \\ &= \langle r(x_1 + x_2), r(y_1 + y_2) \rangle \\ &= \langle rx_1 + rx_2, ry_1 + ry_2 \rangle \\ &= \langle rx_1, ry_1 \rangle + \langle rx_2, ry_2 \rangle \\ &= r\mathbf{u} + r\mathbf{v}. \end{aligned}$$

□

2.6 Prove the additive inverse property.

We have found the components of a vector given its initial and terminal points. In some cases, we may only have the magnitude and direction of a vector, not the points. For these vectors, we can identify the horizontal and vertical components using trigonometry (**Figure 2.15**).

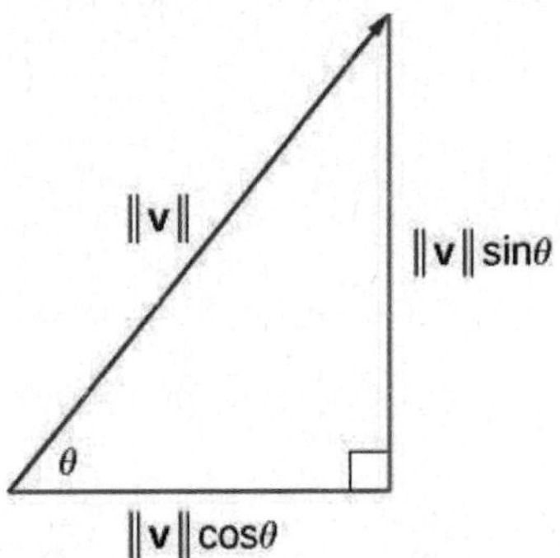

Figure 2.15 The components of a vector form the legs of a right triangle, with the vector as the hypotenuse.

Consider the angle θ formed by the vector $\mathbf{v}$ and the positive x-axis. We can see from the triangle that the components of vector $\mathbf{v}$ are $\langle \|\mathbf{v}\| \cos\theta, \|\mathbf{v}\| \sin\theta \rangle$. Therefore, given an angle and the magnitude of a vector, we can use the cosine and sine of the angle to find the components of the vector.

Example 2.6

Finding the Component Form of a Vector Using Trigonometry

Find the component form of a vector with magnitude 4 that forms an angle of $-45°$ with the x-axis.

Solution

Let x and y represent the components of the vector (**Figure 2.16**). Then $x = 4\cos(-45°) = 2\sqrt{2}$ and $y = 4\sin(-45°) = -2\sqrt{2}$. The component form of the vector is $\langle 2\sqrt{2}, -2\sqrt{2} \rangle$.

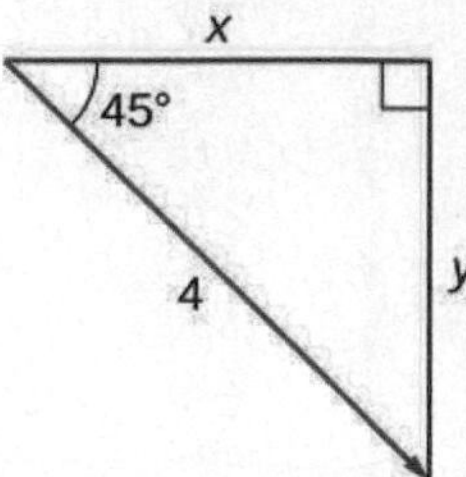

Figure 2.16 Use trigonometric ratios, $x = \| \mathbf{v} \| \cos \theta$ and $y = \| \mathbf{v} \| \sin \theta,$ to identify the components of the vector.

2.7 Find the component form of vector $\mathbf{v}$ with magnitude 10 that forms an angle of $120°$ with the positive x-axis.

Unit Vectors

A **unit vector** is a vector with magnitude $1.$ For any nonzero vector $\mathbf{v},$ we can use scalar multiplication to find a unit vector $\mathbf{u}$ that has the same direction as $\mathbf{v}.$ To do this, we multiply the vector by the reciprocal of its magnitude:

$$\mathbf{u} = \frac{1}{\| \mathbf{v} \|}\mathbf{v}.$$

Recall that when we defined scalar multiplication, we noted that $\| k\mathbf{v} \| = |k| \cdot \| \mathbf{v} \|.$ For $\mathbf{u} = \frac{1}{\| \mathbf{v} \|}\mathbf{v},$ it follows that $\| \mathbf{u} \| = \frac{1}{\| \mathbf{v} \|}(\| \mathbf{v} \|) = 1.$ We say that $\mathbf{u}$ is the *unit vector in the direction of* $\mathbf{v}$ (**Figure 2.17**). The process of using scalar multiplication to find a unit vector with a given direction is called **normalization**.

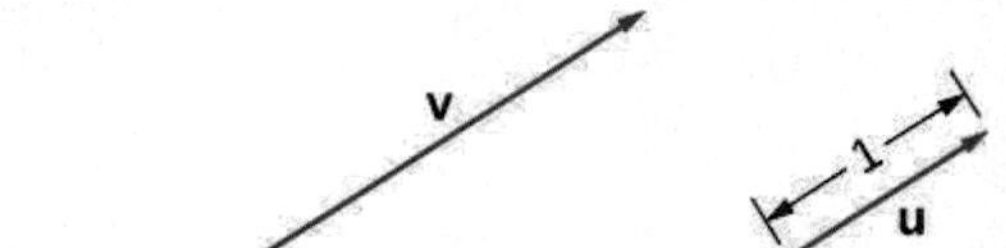

Figure 2.17 The vector $\mathbf{v}$ and associated unit vector $\mathbf{u} = \frac{1}{\| \mathbf{v} \|}\mathbf{v}.$ In this case, $\| \mathbf{v} \| > 1.$

Example 2.7

Finding a Unit Vector

Let $\mathbf{v} = \langle 1, 2 \rangle.$

a. Find a unit vector with the same direction as $\mathbf{v}.$

b. Find a vector $\mathbf{w}$ with the same direction as $\mathbf{v}$ such that $\| \mathbf{w} \| = 7.$

Solution

a. First, find the magnitude of $\mathbf{v}$, then divide the components of $\mathbf{v}$ by the magnitude:

$$\| \mathbf{v} \| = \sqrt{1^2 + 2^2} = \sqrt{1 + 4} = \sqrt{5}$$

$$\mathbf{u} = \frac{1}{\| \mathbf{v} \|}\mathbf{v} = \frac{1}{\sqrt{5}} \langle 1, 2 \rangle = \langle \frac{1}{\sqrt{5}}, \frac{2}{\sqrt{5}} \rangle.$$

b. The vector $\mathbf{u}$ is in the same direction as $\mathbf{v}$ and $\| \mathbf{u} \| = 1$. Use scalar multiplication to increase the length of $\mathbf{u}$ without changing direction:

$$\mathbf{w} = 7\mathbf{u} = 7 \langle \frac{1}{\sqrt{5}}, \frac{2}{\sqrt{5}} \rangle = \langle \frac{7}{\sqrt{5}}, \frac{14}{\sqrt{5}} \rangle.$$

2.8 Let $\mathbf{v} = \langle 9, 2 \rangle$. Find a vector with magnitude 5 in the opposite direction as $\mathbf{v}$.

We have seen how convenient it can be to write a vector in component form. Sometimes, though, it is more convenient to write a vector as a sum of a horizontal vector and a vertical vector. To make this easier, let's look at standard unit vectors. The **standard unit vectors** are the vectors $\mathbf{i} = \langle 1, 0 \rangle$ and $\mathbf{j} = \langle 0, 1 \rangle$ (**Figure 2.18**).

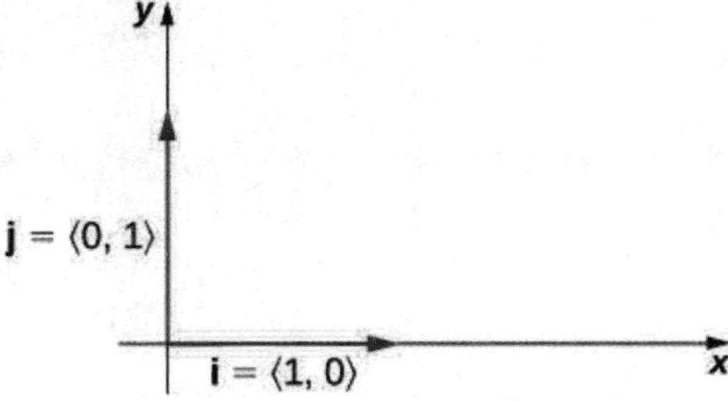

Figure 2.18 The standard unit vectors $\mathbf{i}$ and $\mathbf{j}$.

By applying the properties of vectors, it is possible to express any vector in terms of $\mathbf{i}$ and $\mathbf{j}$ in what we call a *linear combination*:

$$\mathbf{v} = \langle x, y \rangle = \langle x, 0 \rangle + \langle 0, y \rangle = x \langle 1, 0 \rangle + y \langle 0, 1 \rangle = x\mathbf{i} + y\mathbf{j}.$$

Thus, $\mathbf{v}$ is the sum of a horizontal vector with magnitude x, and a vertical vector with magnitude y, as in the following figure.

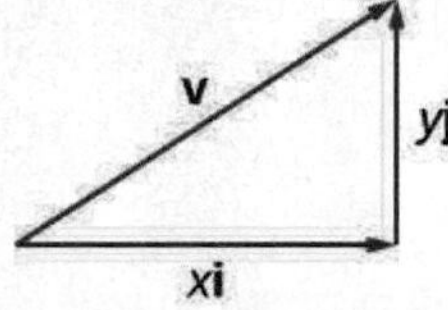

Figure 2.19 The vector $\mathbf{v}$ is the sum of $x\mathbf{i}$ and $y\mathbf{j}$.

Example 2.8

Using Standard Unit Vectors

a. Express the vector $\mathbf{w} = \langle 3, -4 \rangle$ in terms of standard unit vectors.

b. Vector $\mathbf{u}$ is a unit vector that forms an angle of $60°$ with the positive x-axis. Use standard unit vectors to describe $\mathbf{u}$.

Solution

a. Resolve vector $\mathbf{w}$ into a vector with a zero y-component and a vector with a zero x-component:

$$\mathbf{w} = \langle 3, -4 \rangle = 3\mathbf{i} - 4\mathbf{j}.$$

b. Because $\mathbf{u}$ is a unit vector, the terminal point lies on the unit circle when the vector is placed in standard position (**Figure 2.20**).

$$\begin{aligned} u &= \langle \cos 60°, \sin 60° \rangle \\ &= \langle \frac{1}{2}, \frac{\sqrt{3}}{2} \rangle \\ &= \frac{1}{2}\mathbf{i} + \frac{\sqrt{3}}{2}\mathbf{j}. \end{aligned}$$

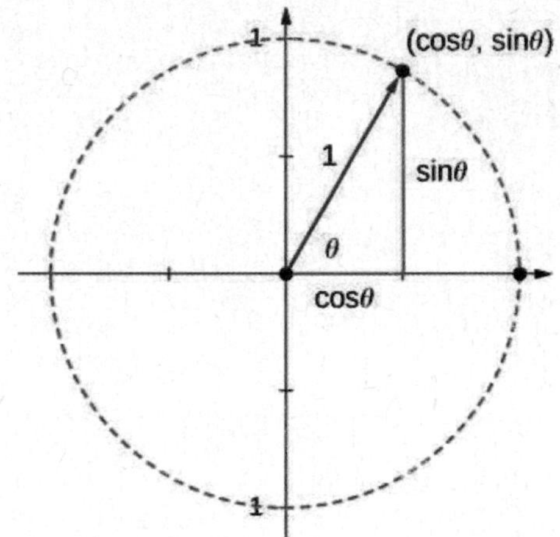

Figure 2.20 The terminal point of $\mathbf{u}$ lies on the unit circle $(\cos\theta, \sin\theta)$.

2.9 Let $\mathbf{a} = \langle 16, -11 \rangle$ and let $\mathbf{b}$ be a unit vector that forms an angle of $225°$ with the positive x-axis. Express $\mathbf{a}$ and $\mathbf{b}$ in terms of the standard unit vectors.

Applications of Vectors

Because vectors have both direction and magnitude, they are valuable tools for solving problems involving such applications as motion and force. Recall the boat example and the quarterback example we described earlier. Here we look at two other examples in detail.

Example 2.9

Finding Resultant Force

Jane's car is stuck in the mud. Lisa and Jed come along in a truck to help pull her out. They attach one end of a tow strap to the front of the car and the other end to the truck's trailer hitch, and the truck starts to pull. Meanwhile, Jane and Jed get behind the car and push. The truck generates a horizontal force of 300 lb on the car. Jane and Jed are pushing at a slight upward angle and generate a force of 150 lb on the car. These forces can be represented by vectors, as shown in **Figure 2.21**. The angle between these vectors is $15°$. Find the resultant force (the vector sum) and give its magnitude to the nearest tenth of a pound and its direction angle from the positive *x*-axis.

Figure 2.21 Two forces acting on a car in different directions.

Solution

To find the effect of combining the two forces, add their representative vectors. First, express each vector in component form or in terms of the standard unit vectors. For this purpose, it is easiest if we align one of the vectors with the positive *x*-axis. The horizontal vector, then, has initial point $(0, 0)$ and terminal point $(300, 0)$. It can be expressed as $\langle 300, 0 \rangle$ or $300\mathbf{i}$.

The second vector has magnitude 150 and makes an angle of $15°$ with the first, so we can express it as $\langle 150\cos(15°), 150\sin(15°) \rangle$, or $150\cos(15°)\mathbf{i} + 150\sin(15°)\mathbf{j}$. Then, the sum of the vectors, or resultant vector, is $\mathbf{r} = \langle 300, 0 \rangle + \langle 150\cos(15°), 150\sin(15°) \rangle$, and we have

$$\begin{aligned} \| \mathbf{r} \| &= \sqrt{(300 + 150\cos(15°))^2 + (150\sin(15°))^2} \\ &\approx 446.6. \end{aligned}$$

The angle θ made by $\mathbf{r}$ and the positive *x*-axis has $\tan\theta = \dfrac{150\sin 15°}{(300 + 150\cos 15°)} \approx 0.09$, so $\theta \approx tan^{-1}(0.09) \approx 5°$, which means the resultant force $\mathbf{r}$ has an angle of $5°$ above the horizontal axis.

Example 2.10

Finding Resultant Velocity

An airplane flies due west at an airspeed of 425 mph. The wind is blowing from the northeast at 40 mph. What is the ground speed of the airplane? What is the bearing of the airplane?

Solution

Let's start by sketching the situation described (**Figure 2.22**).

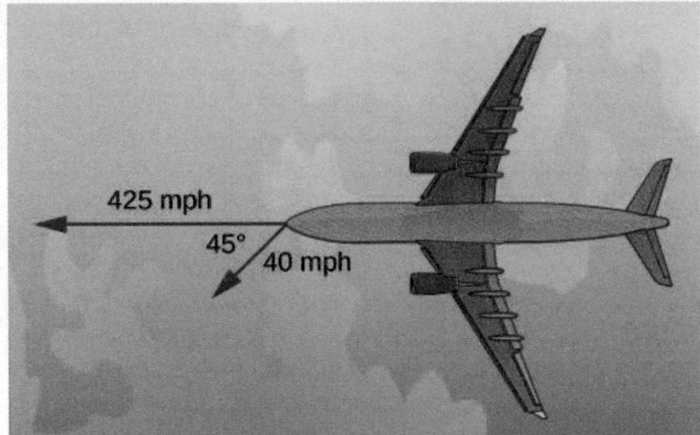

Figure 2.22 Initially, the plane travels due west. The wind is from the northeast, so it is blowing to the southwest. The angle between the plane's course and the wind is $45°$. (Figure not drawn to scale.)

Set up a sketch so that the initial points of the vectors lie at the origin. Then, the plane's velocity vector is $\mathbf{p} = -425\mathbf{i}$. The vector describing the wind makes an angle of $225°$ with the positive x-axis:

$$\mathbf{w} = \langle 40\cos(225°), 40\sin(225°) \rangle = \left\langle -\frac{40}{\sqrt{2}}, -\frac{40}{\sqrt{2}} \right\rangle = -\frac{40}{\sqrt{2}}\mathbf{i} - \frac{40}{\sqrt{2}}\mathbf{j}.$$

When the airspeed and the wind act together on the plane, we can add their vectors to find the resultant force:

$$\mathbf{p} + \mathbf{w} = -425\mathbf{i} + \left(-\frac{40}{\sqrt{2}}\mathbf{i} - \frac{40}{\sqrt{2}}\mathbf{j}\right) = \left(-425 - \frac{40}{\sqrt{2}}\right)\mathbf{i} - \frac{40}{\sqrt{2}}\mathbf{j}.$$

The magnitude of the resultant vector shows the effect of the wind on the ground speed of the airplane:

$$\|\mathbf{p} + \mathbf{w}\| = \sqrt{\left(-425 - \frac{40}{\sqrt{2}}\right)^2 + \left(-\frac{40}{\sqrt{2}}\right)^2} \approx 454.17 \text{ mph}$$

As a result of the wind, the plane is traveling at approximately 454 mph relative to the ground.

To determine the bearing of the airplane, we want to find the direction of the vector $\mathbf{p} + \mathbf{w}$:

$$\tan\theta = \frac{-\frac{40}{\sqrt{2}}}{\left(-425 - \frac{40}{\sqrt{2}}\right)} \approx 0.06$$
$$\theta \approx 3.57°.$$

The overall direction of the plane is $3.57°$ south of west.

2.10 An airplane flies due north at an airspeed of 550 mph. The wind is blowing from the northwest at 50 mph. What is the ground speed of the airplane?

2.1 EXERCISES

For the following exercises, consider points $P(-1, 3)$, $Q(1, 5)$, and $R(-3, 7)$. Determine the requested vectors and express each of them a. in component form and b. by using the standard unit vectors.

1. $\overrightarrow{PQ}$

2. $\overrightarrow{PR}$

3. $\overrightarrow{QP}$

4. $\overrightarrow{RP}$

5. $\overrightarrow{PQ} + \overrightarrow{PR}$

6. $\overrightarrow{PQ} - \overrightarrow{PR}$

7. $2\overrightarrow{PQ} - 2\overrightarrow{PR}$

8. $2\overrightarrow{PQ} + \frac{1}{2}\overrightarrow{PR}$

9. The unit vector in the direction of $\overrightarrow{PQ}$

10. The unit vector in the direction of $\overrightarrow{PR}$

11. A vector $\mathbf{v}$ has initial point $(-1, -3)$ and terminal point $(2, 1)$. Find the unit vector in the direction of $\mathbf{v}$. Express the answer in component form.

12. A vector $\mathbf{v}$ has initial point $(-2, 5)$ and terminal point $(3, -1)$. Find the unit vector in the direction of $\mathbf{v}$. Express the answer in component form.

13. The vector $\mathbf{v}$ has initial point $P(1, 0)$ and terminal point Q that is on the y-axis and above the initial point. Find the coordinates of terminal point Q such that the magnitude of the vector $\mathbf{v}$ is $\sqrt{5}$.

14. The vector $\mathbf{v}$ has initial point $P(1, 1)$ and terminal point Q that is on the x-axis and left of the initial point. Find the coordinates of terminal point Q such that the magnitude of the vector $\mathbf{v}$ is $\sqrt{10}$.

For the following exercises, use the given vectors $\mathbf{a}$ and $\mathbf{b}$.

a. Determine the vector sum $\mathbf{a} + \mathbf{b}$ and express it in both the component form and by using the standard unit vectors.

b. Find the vector difference $\mathbf{a} - \mathbf{b}$ and express it in both the component form and by using the standard unit vectors.

c. Verify that the vectors $\mathbf{a}$, $\mathbf{b}$, and $\mathbf{a} + \mathbf{b}$, and, respectively, $\mathbf{a}$, $\mathbf{b}$, and $\mathbf{a} - \mathbf{b}$ satisfy the triangle inequality.

d. Determine the vectors $2\mathbf{a}$, $-\mathbf{b}$, and $2\mathbf{a} - \mathbf{b}$. Express the vectors in both the component form and by using standard unit vectors.

15. $\mathbf{a} = 2\mathbf{i} + \mathbf{j}$, $\mathbf{b} = \mathbf{i} + 3\mathbf{j}$

16. $\mathbf{a} = 2\mathbf{i}$, $\mathbf{b} = -2\mathbf{i} + 2\mathbf{j}$

17. Let $\mathbf{a}$ be a standard-position vector with terminal point $(-2, -4)$. Let $\mathbf{b}$ be a vector with initial point $(1, 2)$ and terminal point $(-1, 4)$. Find the magnitude of vector $-3\mathbf{a} + \mathbf{b} - 4\mathbf{i} + \mathbf{j}$.

18. Let $\mathbf{a}$ be a standard-position vector with terminal point at $(2, 5)$. Let $\mathbf{b}$ be a vector with initial point $(-1, 3)$ and terminal point $(1, 0)$. Find the magnitude of vector $\mathbf{a} - 3\mathbf{b} + 14\mathbf{i} - 14\mathbf{j}$.

19. Let $\mathbf{u}$ and $\mathbf{v}$ be two nonzero vectors that are nonequivalent. Consider the vectors $\mathbf{a} = 4\mathbf{u} + 5\mathbf{v}$ and $\mathbf{b} = \mathbf{u} + 2\mathbf{v}$ defined in terms of $\mathbf{u}$ and $\mathbf{v}$. Find the scalar λ such that vectors $\mathbf{a} + \lambda\mathbf{b}$ and $\mathbf{u} - \mathbf{v}$ are equivalent.

20. Let $\mathbf{u}$ and $\mathbf{v}$ be two nonzero vectors that are nonequivalent. Consider the vectors $\mathbf{a} = 2\mathbf{u} - 4\mathbf{v}$ and $\mathbf{b} = 3\mathbf{u} - 7\mathbf{v}$ defined in terms of $\mathbf{u}$ and $\mathbf{v}$. Find the scalars α and β such that vectors $\alpha\mathbf{a} + \beta\mathbf{b}$ and $\mathbf{u} - \mathbf{v}$ are equivalent.

21. Consider the vector $\mathbf{a}(t) = \langle \cos t, \sin t \rangle$ with components that depend on a real number t. As the number t varies, the components of $\mathbf{a}(t)$ change as well, depending on the functions that define them.

a. Write the vectors $\mathbf{a}(0)$ and $\mathbf{a}(\pi)$ in component form.

b. Show that the magnitude $\| \mathbf{a}(t) \|$ of vector $\mathbf{a}(t)$ remains constant for any real number t.

c. As t varies, show that the terminal point of vector $\mathbf{a}(t)$ describes a circle centered at the origin of radius 1.

22. Consider vector $\mathbf{a}(x) = \langle x, \sqrt{1 - x^2} \rangle$ with components that depend on a real number $x \in [-1, 1]$. As the number x varies, the components of $\mathbf{a}(x)$ change as well, depending on the functions that define them.

a. Write the vectors $\mathbf{a}(0)$ and $\mathbf{a}(1)$ in component form.

b. Show that the magnitude $\| \mathbf{a}(x) \|$ of vector $\mathbf{a}(x)$ remains constant for any real number x

c. As x varies, show that the terminal point of vector $\mathbf{a}(x)$ describes a circle centered at the origin of radius 1.

23. Show that vectors $\mathbf{a}(t) = \langle \cos t, \sin t \rangle$ and $\mathbf{a}(x) = \langle x, \sqrt{1 - x^2} \rangle$ are equivalent for $x = r$ and $t = 2k\pi$, where k is an integer.

24. Show that vectors $\mathbf{a}(t) = \langle \cos t, \sin t \rangle$ and $\mathbf{a}(x) = \langle x, \sqrt{1 - x^2} \rangle$ are opposite for $x = r$ and $t = \pi + 2k\pi$, where k is an integer.

For the following exercises, find vector $\mathbf{v}$ with the given magnitude and in the same direction as vector $\mathbf{u}$.

25. $\| \mathbf{v} \| = 7, \mathbf{u} = \langle 3, 4 \rangle$

26. $\| \mathbf{v} \| = 3, \mathbf{u} = \langle -2, 5 \rangle$

27. $\| \mathbf{v} \| = 7, \mathbf{u} = \langle 3, -5 \rangle$

28. $\| \mathbf{v} \| = 10, \mathbf{u} = \langle 2, -1 \rangle$

For the following exercises, find the component form of vector $\mathbf{u}$, given its magnitude and the angle the vector makes with the positive *x*-axis. Give exact answers when possible.

29. $\| \mathbf{u} \| = 2, \quad \theta = 30°$

30. $\| \mathbf{u} \| = 6, \quad \theta = 60°$

31. $\| \mathbf{u} \| = 5, \quad \theta = \frac{\pi}{2}$

32. $\| \mathbf{u} \| = 8, \quad \theta = \pi$

33. $\| \mathbf{u} \| = 10, \quad \theta = \frac{5\pi}{6}$

34. $\| \mathbf{u} \| = 50, \quad \theta = \frac{3\pi}{4}$

For the following exercises, vector $\mathbf{u}$ is given. Find the angle $\theta \in [0, 2\pi)$ that vector $\mathbf{u}$ makes with the positive direction of the *x*-axis, in a counter-clockwise direction.

35. $\mathbf{u} = 5\sqrt{2}\mathbf{i} - 5\sqrt{2}\mathbf{j}$

36. $\mathbf{u} = -\sqrt{3}\mathbf{i} - \mathbf{j}$

37. Let $\mathbf{a} = \langle a_1, a_2 \rangle$, $\mathbf{b} = \langle b_1, b_2 \rangle$, and $\mathbf{c} = \langle c_1, c_2 \rangle$ be three nonzero vectors. If $a_1 b_2 - a_2 b_1 \neq 0$, then show there are two scalars, α and β, such that $\mathbf{c} = \alpha\mathbf{a} + \beta\mathbf{b}$.

38. Consider vectors $\mathbf{a} = \langle 2, -4 \rangle$, $\mathbf{b} = \langle -1, 2 \rangle$, and $\mathbf{c} = \mathbf{0}$ Determine the scalars α and β such that $\mathbf{c} = \alpha\mathbf{a} + \beta\mathbf{b}$.

39. Let $P(x_0, f(x_0))$ be a fixed point on the graph of the differential function f with a domain that is the set of real numbers.

a. Determine the real number z_0 such that point $Q(x_0 + 1, z_0)$ is situated on the line tangent to the graph of f at point P.

b. Determine the unit vector $\mathbf{u}$ with initial point P and terminal point Q.

40. Consider the function $f(x) = x^4$, where $x \in \mathbb{R}$.

a. Determine the real number z_0 such that point $Q(2, z_0)$ s situated on the line tangent to the graph of f at point $P(1, 1)$.

b. Determine the unit vector $\mathbf{u}$ with initial point P and terminal point Q.

41. Consider f and g two functions defined on the same set of real numbers D. Let $\mathbf{a} = \langle x, f(x) \rangle$ and $\mathbf{b} = \langle x, g(x) \rangle$ be two vectors that describe the graphs of the functions, where $x \in D$. Show that if the graphs of the functions f and g do not intersect, then the vectors $\mathbf{a}$ and $\mathbf{b}$ are not equivalent.

42. Find $x \in \mathbb{R}$ such that vectors $\mathbf{a} = \langle x, \sin x \rangle$ and $\mathbf{b} = \langle x, \cos x \rangle$ are equivalent.

43. Calculate the coordinates of point D such that $ABCD$ is a parallelogram, with $A(1, 1)$, $B(2, 4)$, and $C(7, 4)$.

44. Consider the points $A(2, 1)$, $B(10, 6)$, $C(13, 4)$, and $D(16, -2)$. Determine the component form of vector $\overrightarrow{AD}$.

45. The speed of an object is the magnitude of its related velocity vector. A football thrown by a quarterback has an initial speed of 70 mph and an angle of elevation of $30°$. Determine the velocity vector in mph and express it in component form. (Round to two decimal places.)

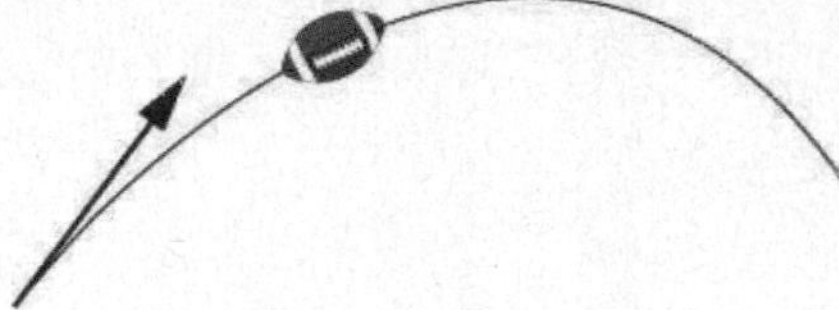

46. A baseball player throws a baseball at an angle of $30°$ with the horizontal. If the initial speed of the ball is 100 mph, find the horizontal and vertical components of the initial velocity vector of the baseball. (Round to two decimal places.)

47. A bullet is fired with an initial velocity of 1500 ft/sec at an angle of $60°$ with the horizontal. Find the horizontal and vertical components of the velocity vector of the bullet. (Round to two decimal places.)

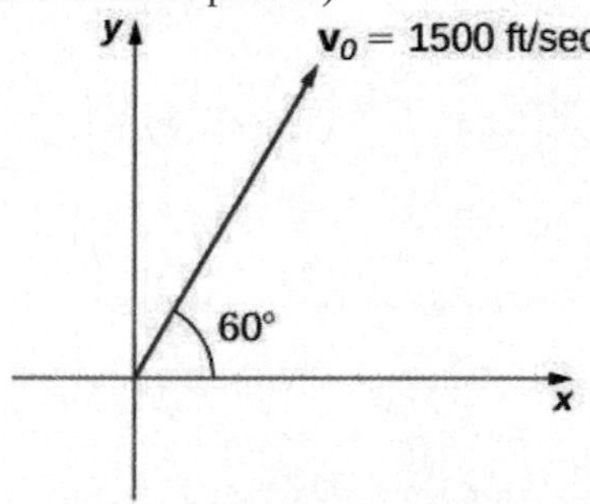

48. **[T]** A 65-kg sprinter exerts a force of 798 N at a $19°$ angle with respect to the ground on the starting block at the instant a race begins. Find the horizontal component of the force. (Round to two decimal places.)

49. **[T]** Two forces, a horizontal force of 45 lb and another of 52 lb, act on the same object. The angle between these forces is $25°$. Find the magnitude and direction angle from the positive *x*-axis of the resultant force that acts on the object. (Round to two decimal places.)

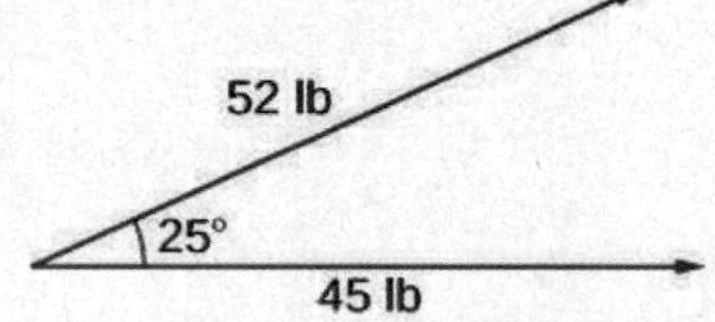

50. **[T]** Two forces, a vertical force of 26 lb and another of 45 lb, act on the same object. The angle between these forces is $55°$. Find the magnitude and direction angle from the positive *x*-axis of the resultant force that acts on the object. (Round to two decimal places.)

51. **[T]** Three forces act on object. Two of the forces have the magnitudes 58 N and 27 N, and make angles $53°$ and $152°$, respectively, with the positive *x*-axis. Find the magnitude and the direction angle from the positive *x*-axis of the third force such that the resultant force acting on the object is zero. (Round to two decimal places.)

52. Three forces with magnitudes 80 lb, 120 lb, and 60 lb act on an object at angles of $45°$, $60°$ and $30°$, respectively, with the positive *x*-axis. Find the magnitude and direction angle from the positive *x*-axis of the resultant force. (Round to two decimal places.)

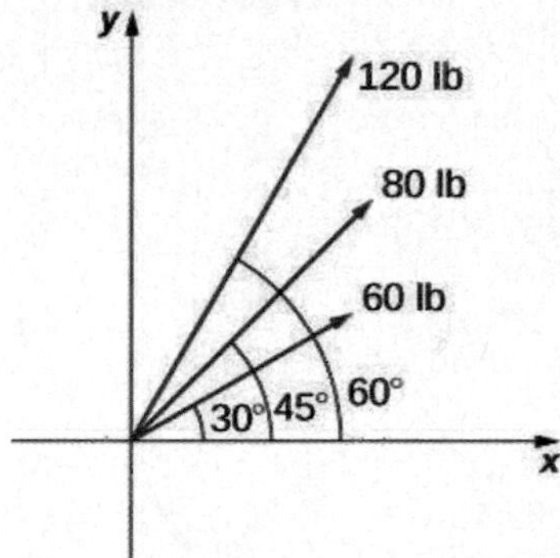

53. **[T]** An airplane is flying in the direction of $43°$ east of north (also abbreviated as N43E) at a speed of 550 mph. A wind with speed 25 mph comes from the southwest at a bearing of N15E. What are the ground speed and new direction of the airplane?

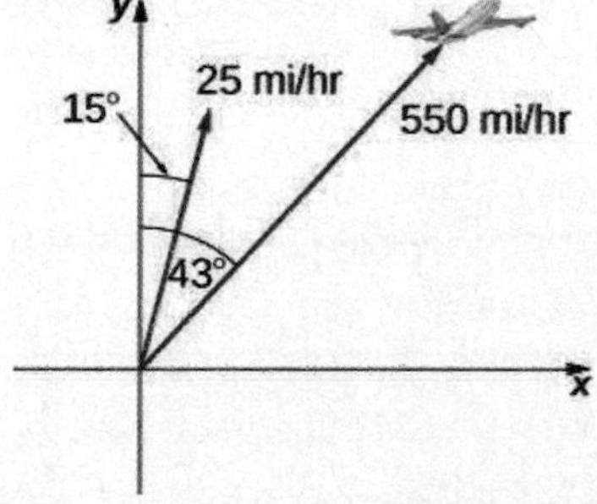

54. **[T]** A boat is traveling in the water at 30 mph in a direction of N20E (that is, 20° east of north). A strong current is moving at 15 mph in a direction of N45E. What are the new speed and direction of the boat?

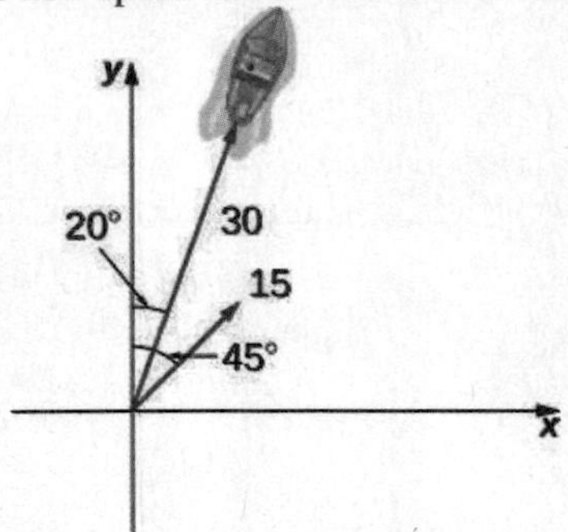

55. **[T]** A 50-lb weight is hung by a cable so that the two portions of the cable make angles of 40° and 53°, respectively, with the horizontal. Find the magnitudes of the forces of tension $\mathbf{T}_1$ and $\mathbf{T}_2$ in the cables if the resultant force acting on the object is zero. (Round to two decimal places.)

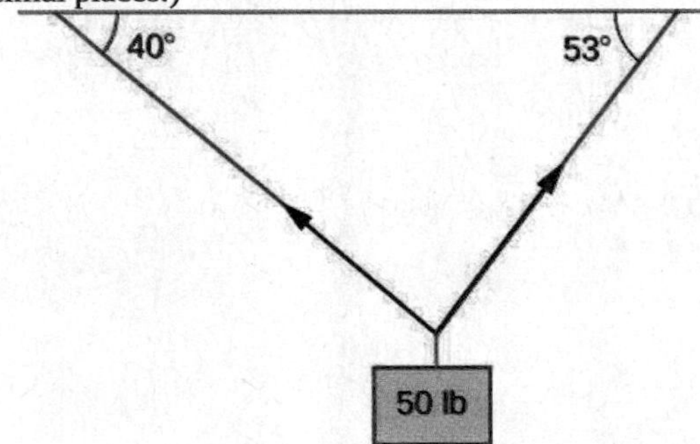

56. **[T]** A 62-lb weight hangs from a rope that makes the angles of 29° and 61°, respectively, with the horizontal. Find the magnitudes of the forces of tension $\mathbf{T}_1$ and $\mathbf{T}_2$ in the cables if the resultant force acting on the object is zero. (Round to two decimal places.)

57. **[T]** A 1500-lb boat is parked on a ramp that makes an angle of 30° with the horizontal. The boat's weight vector points downward and is a sum of two vectors: a horizontal vector $\mathbf{v}_1$ that is parallel to the ramp and a vertical vector $\mathbf{v}_2$ that is perpendicular to the inclined surface. The magnitudes of vectors $\mathbf{v}_1$ and $\mathbf{v}_2$ are the horizontal and vertical component, respectively, of the boat's weight vector. Find the magnitudes of $\mathbf{v}_1$ and $\mathbf{v}_2$. (Round to the nearest integer.)

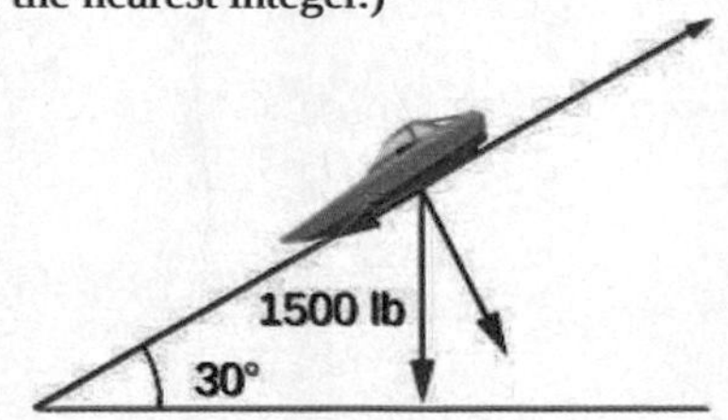

58. **[T]** An 85-lb box is at rest on a 26° incline. Determine the magnitude of the force parallel to the incline necessary to keep the box from sliding. (Round to the nearest integer.)

59. A guy-wire supports a pole that is 75 ft high. One end of the wire is attached to the top of the pole and the other end is anchored to the ground 50 ft from the base of the pole. Determine the horizontal and vertical components of the force of tension in the wire if its magnitude is 50 lb. (Round to the nearest integer.)

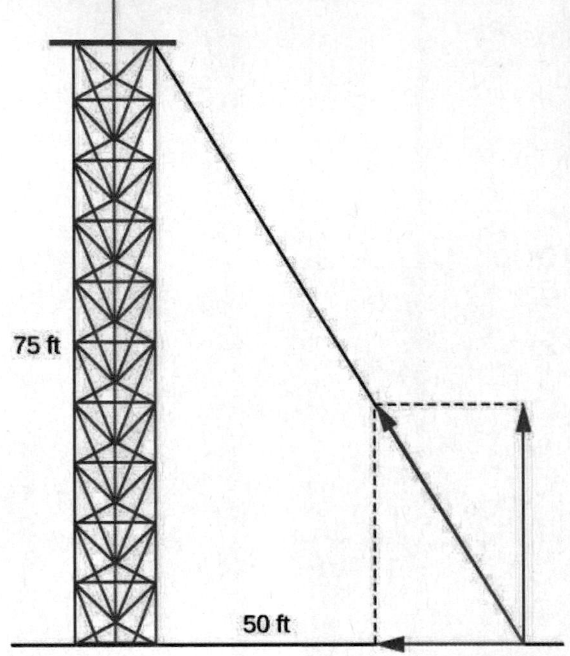

60. A telephone pole guy-wire has an angle of elevation of 35° with respect to the ground. The force of tension in the guy-wire is 120 lb. Find the horizontal and vertical components of the force of tension. (Round to the nearest integer.)

2.2 | Vectors in Three Dimensions

Learning Objectives

2.2.1 Describe three-dimensional space mathematically.
2.2.2 Locate points in space using coordinates.
2.2.3 Write the distance formula in three dimensions.
2.2.4 Write the equations for simple planes and spheres.
2.2.5 Perform vector operations in $\mathbb{R}^3$.

Vectors are useful tools for solving two-dimensional problems. Life, however, happens in three dimensions. To expand the use of vectors to more realistic applications, it is necessary to create a framework for describing three-dimensional space. For example, although a two-dimensional map is a useful tool for navigating from one place to another, in some cases the topography of the land is important. Does your planned route go through the mountains? Do you have to cross a river? To appreciate fully the impact of these geographic features, you must use three dimensions. This section presents a natural extension of the two-dimensional Cartesian coordinate plane into three dimensions.

Three-Dimensional Coordinate Systems

As we have learned, the two-dimensional rectangular coordinate system contains two perpendicular axes: the horizontal *x*-axis and the vertical *y*-axis. We can add a third dimension, the *z*-axis, which is perpendicular to both the *x*-axis and the *y*-axis. We call this system the three-dimensional rectangular coordinate system. It represents the three dimensions we encounter in real life.

Definition

The **three-dimensional rectangular coordinate system** consists of three perpendicular axes: the *x*-axis, the *y*-axis, and the *z*-axis. Because each axis is a number line representing all real numbers in $\mathbb{R}$, the three-dimensional system is often denoted by $\mathbb{R}^3$.

In **Figure 2.23**(a), the positive *z*-axis is shown above the plane containing the *x*- and *y*-axes. The positive *x*-axis appears to the left and the positive *y*-axis is to the right. A natural question to ask is: How was arrangement determined? The system displayed follows the **right-hand rule**. If we take our right hand and align the fingers with the positive *x*-axis, then curl the fingers so they point in the direction of the positive *y*-axis, our thumb points in the direction of the positive *z*-axis. In this text, we always work with coordinate systems set up in accordance with the right-hand rule. Some systems do follow a left-hand rule, but the right-hand rule is considered the standard representation.

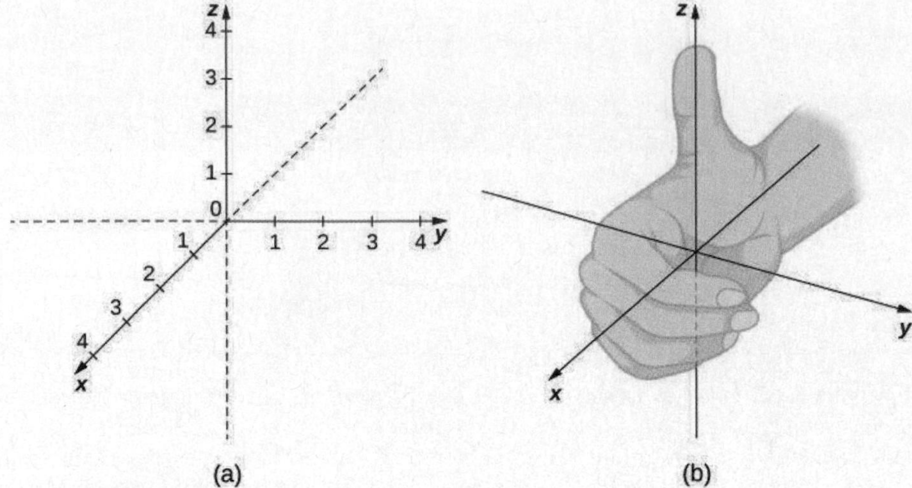

Figure 2.23 (a) We can extend the two-dimensional rectangular coordinate system by adding a third axis, the z-axis, that is perpendicular to both the x-axis and the y-axis. (b) The right-hand rule is used to determine the placement of the coordinate axes in the standard Cartesian plane.

In two dimensions, we describe a point in the plane with the coordinates (x, y). Each coordinate describes how the point aligns with the corresponding axis. In three dimensions, a new coordinate, z, is appended to indicate alignment with the z-axis: (x, y, z). A point in space is identified by all three coordinates (**Figure 2.24**). To plot the point (x, y, z), go x units along the x-axis, then y units in the direction of the y-axis, then z units in the direction of the z-axis.

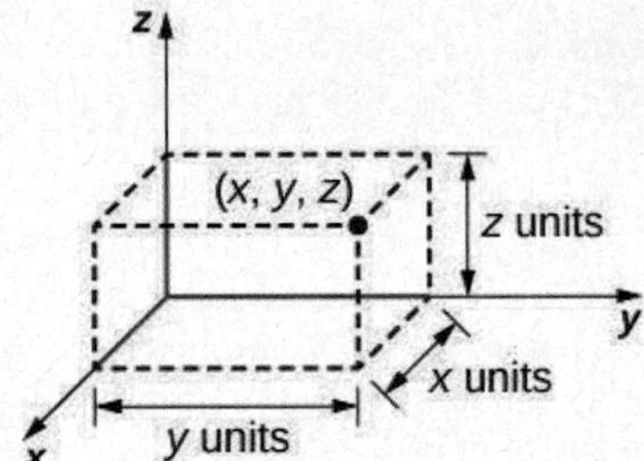

Figure 2.24 To plot the point (x, y, z) go x units along the x-axis, then y units in the direction of the y-axis, then z units in the direction of the z-axis.

Example 2.11

Locating Points in Space

Sketch the point $(1, -2, 3)$ in three-dimensional space.

Solution

To sketch a point, start by sketching three sides of a rectangular prism along the coordinate axes: one unit in the positive x direction, 2 units in the negative y direction, and 3 units in the positive z direction. Complete the prism to plot the point (**Figure 2.25**).

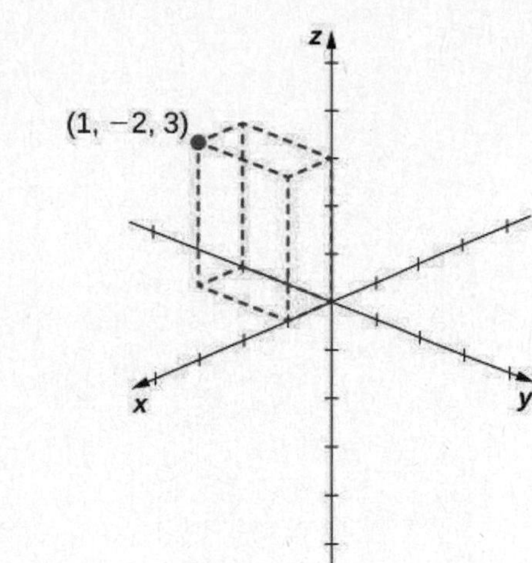

Figure 2.25 Sketching the point $(1, -2, 3)$.

2.11 Sketch the point $(-2, 3, -1)$ in three-dimensional space.

In two-dimensional space, the coordinate plane is defined by a pair of perpendicular axes. These axes allow us to name any location within the plane. In three dimensions, we define **coordinate planes** by the coordinate axes, just as in two dimensions. There are three axes now, so there are three intersecting pairs of axes. Each pair of axes forms a coordinate plane: the *xy*-plane, the *xz*-plane, and the *yz*-plane (**Figure 2.26**). We define the *xy*-plane formally as the following set: $\{(x, y, 0) : x, y \in \mathbb{R}\}$. Similarly, the *xz*-plane and the *yz*-plane are defined as $\{(x, 0, z) : x, z \in \mathbb{R}\}$ and $\{(0, y, z) : y, z \in \mathbb{R}\}$, respectively.

To visualize this, imagine you're building a house and are standing in a room with only two of the four walls finished. (Assume the two finished walls are adjacent to each other.) If you stand with your back to the corner where the two finished walls meet, facing out into the room, the floor is the *xy*-plane, the wall to your right is the *xz*-plane, and the wall to your left is the *yz*-plane.

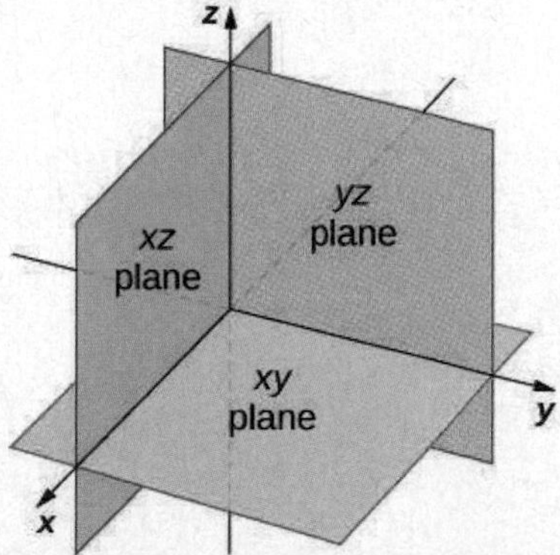

Figure 2.26 The plane containing the *x*- and *y*-axes is called the *xy*-plane. The plane containing the *x*- and *z*-axes is called the *xz*-plane, and the *y*- and *z*-axes define the *yz*-plane.

In two dimensions, the coordinate axes partition the plane into four quadrants. Similarly, the coordinate planes divide space between them into eight regions about the origin, called **octants**. The octants fill $\mathbb{R}^3$ in the same way that quadrants fill

$\mathbb{R}^2$, as shown in **Figure 2.27**.

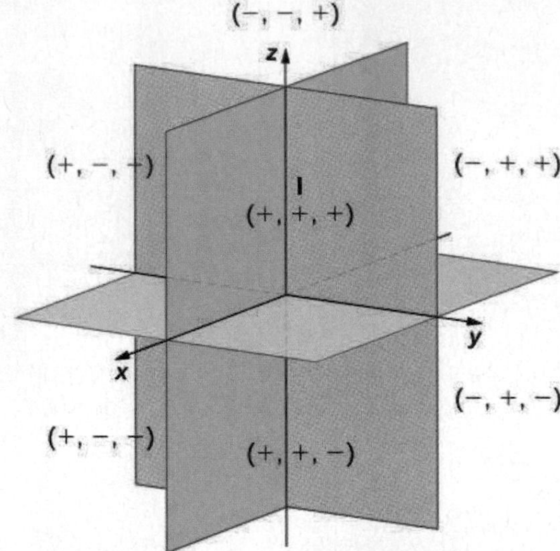

Figure 2.27 Points that lie in octants have three nonzero coordinates.

Most work in three-dimensional space is a comfortable extension of the corresponding concepts in two dimensions. In this section, we use our knowledge of circles to describe spheres, then we expand our understanding of vectors to three dimensions. To accomplish these goals, we begin by adapting the distance formula to three-dimensional space.

If two points lie in the same coordinate plane, then it is straightforward to calculate the distance between them. We that the distance d between two points (x_1, y_1) and (x_2, y_2) in the *xy*-coordinate plane is given by the formula

$$d = \sqrt{(x_2 - x_1)^2 + (y_2 - y_1)^2}.$$

The formula for the distance between two points in space is a natural extension of this formula.

Theorem 2.2: The Distance between Two Points in Space

The distance d between points (x_1, y_1, z_1) and (x_2, y_2, z_2) is given by the formula

$$d = \sqrt{(x_2 - x_1)^2 + (y_2 - y_1)^2 + (z_2 - z_1)^2}. \tag{2.1}$$

The proof of this theorem is left as an exercise. (*Hint:* First find the distance d_1 between the points (x_1, y_1, z_1) and (x_2, y_2, z_1) as shown in **Figure 2.28**.)

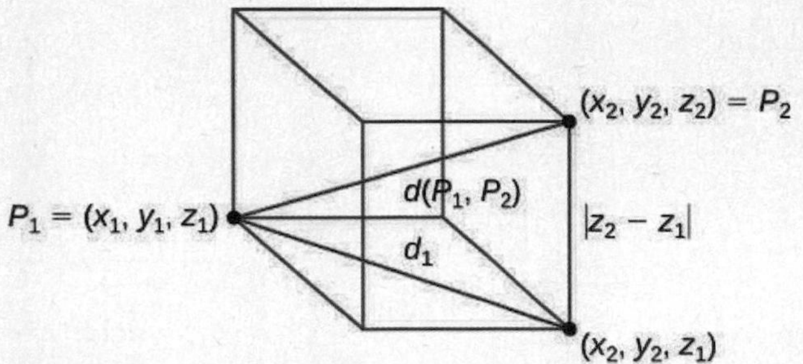

Figure 2.28 The distance between P_1 and P_2 is the length of the diagonal of the rectangular prism having P_1 and P_2 as opposite corners.

Example 2.12

Distance in Space

Find the distance between points $P_1 = (3, -1, 5)$ and $P_2 = (2, 1, -1)$.

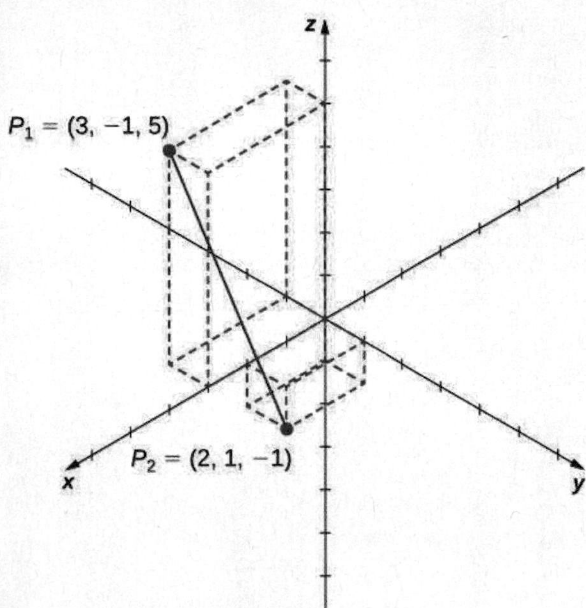

Figure 2.29 Find the distance between the two points.

Solution

Substitute values directly into the distance formula:

$$\begin{aligned} d(P_1, P_2) &= \sqrt{(x_2 - x_1)^2 + (y_2 - y_1)^2 + (z_2 - z_1)^2} \\ &= \sqrt{(2 - 3)^2 + (1 - (-1))^2 + (-1 - 5)^2} \\ &= \sqrt{1^2 + 2^2 + (-6)^2} \\ &= \sqrt{41}. \end{aligned}$$

2.12 Find the distance between points $P_1 = (1, -5, 4)$ and $P_2 = (4, -1, -1)$.

Before moving on to the next section, let's get a feel for how $\mathbb{R}^3$ differs from $\mathbb{R}^2$. For example, in $\mathbb{R}^2$, lines that are not parallel must always intersect. This is not the case in $\mathbb{R}^3$. For example, consider the line shown in **Figure 2.30**. These two lines are not parallel, nor do they intersect.

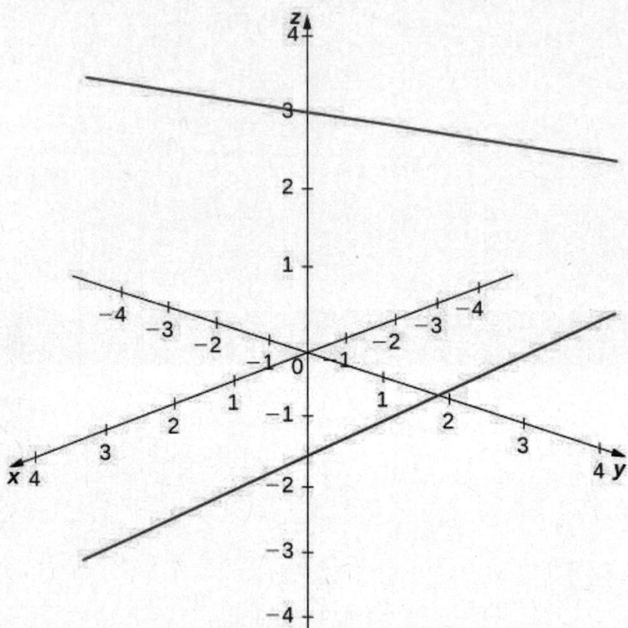

Figure 2.30 These two lines are not parallel, but still do not intersect.

You can also have circles that are interconnected but have no points in common, as in **Figure 2.31**.

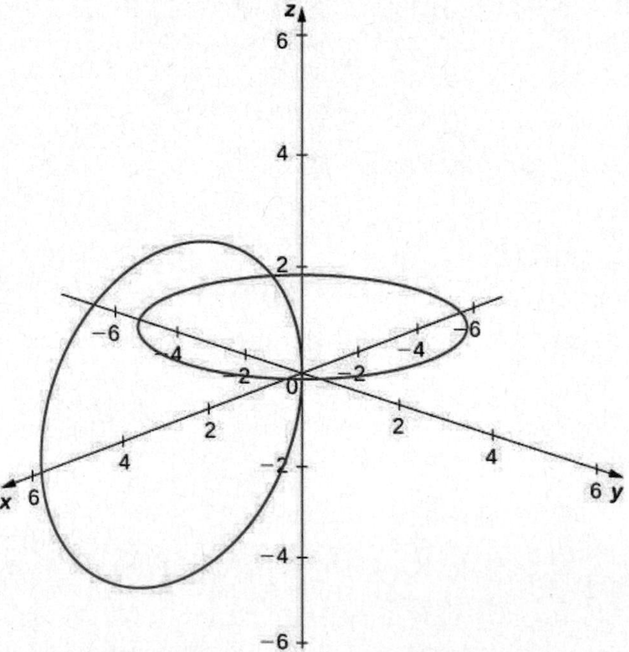

Figure 2.31 These circles are interconnected, but have no points in common.

We have a lot more flexibility working in three dimensions than we do if we stuck with only two dimensions.

Writing Equations in $\mathbb{R}^3$

Now that we can represent points in space and find the distance between them, we can learn how to write equations of geometric objects such as lines, planes, and curved surfaces in $\mathbb{R}^3$. First, we start with a simple equation. Compare the graphs of the equation $x = 0$ in $\mathbb{R}$, $\mathbb{R}^2$, and $\mathbb{R}^3$ (**Figure 2.32**). From these graphs, we can see the same equation can describe a point, a line, or a plane.

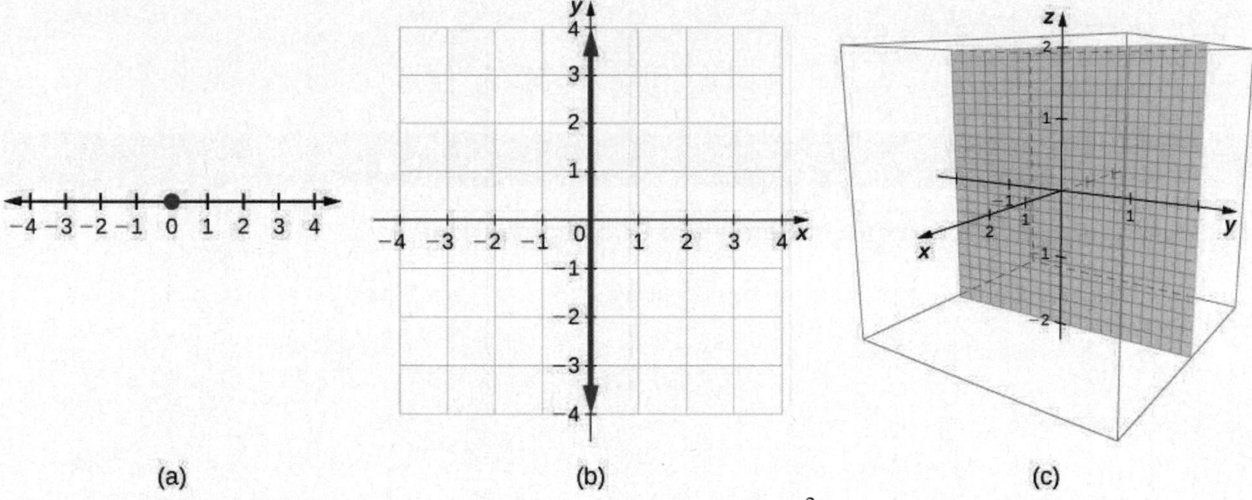

Figure 2.32 (a) In $\mathbb{R}$, the equation $x = 0$ describes a single point. (b) In $\mathbb{R}^2$, the equation $x = 0$ describes a line, the *y*-axis. (c) In $\mathbb{R}^3$, the equation $x = 0$ describes a plane, the *yz*-plane.

In space, the equation $x = 0$ describes all points $(0, y, z)$. This equation defines the *yz*-plane. Similarly, the *xy*-plane contains all points of the form $(x, y, 0)$. The equation $z = 0$ defines the *xy*-plane and the equation $y = 0$ describes the *xz*-plane (**Figure 2.33**).

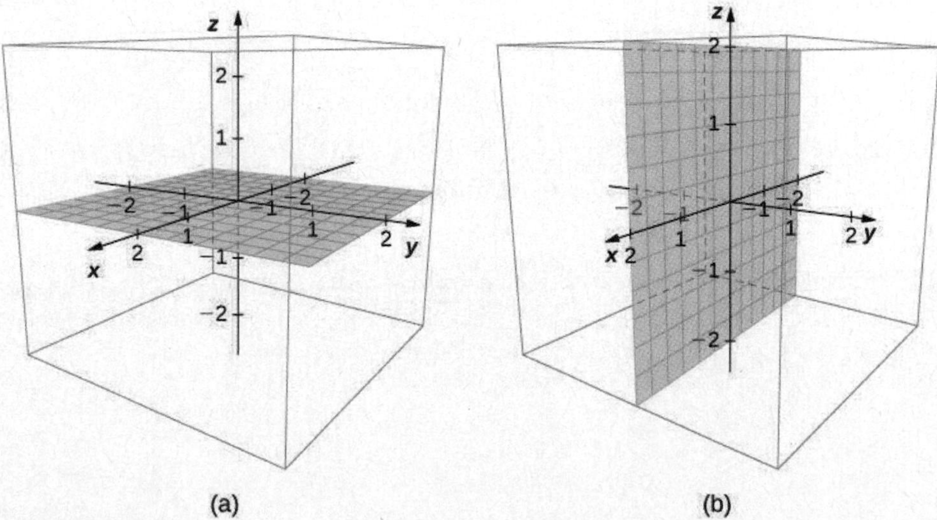

Figure 2.33 (a) In space, the equation $z = 0$ describes the *xy*-plane. (b) All points in the *xz*-plane satisfy the equation $y = 0$.

Understanding the equations of the coordinate planes allows us to write an equation for any plane that is parallel to one of the coordinate planes. When a plane is parallel to the *xy*-plane, for example, the *z*-coordinate of each point in the plane has the same constant value. Only the *x*- and *y*-coordinates of points in that plane vary from point to point.

Rule: Equations of Planes Parallel to Coordinate Planes

1. The plane in space that is parallel to the *xy*-plane and contains point (a, b, c) can be represented by the equation $z = c$.
2. The plane in space that is parallel to the *xz*-plane and contains point (a, b, c) can be represented by the equation $y = b$.
3. The plane in space that is parallel to the *yz*-plane and contains point (a, b, c) can be represented by the equation $x = a$.

Example 2.13

Writing Equations of Planes Parallel to Coordinate Planes

a. Write an equation of the plane passing through point $(3, 11, 7)$ that is parallel to the *yz*-plane.

b. Find an equation of the plane passing through points $(6, -2, 9)$, $(0, -2, 4)$, and $(1, -2, -3)$.

Solution

a. When a plane is parallel to the *yz*-plane, only the *y*- and *z*-coordinates may vary. The *x*-coordinate has the same constant value for all points in this plane, so this plane can be represented by the equation $x = 3$.

b. Each of the points $(6, -2, 9)$, $(0, -2, 4)$, and $(1, -2, -3)$ has the same *y*-coordinate. This plane can be represented by the equation $y = -2$.

2.13 Write an equation of the plane passing through point $(1, -6, -4)$ that is parallel to the *xy*-plane.

As we have seen, in $\mathbb{R}^2$ the equation $x = 5$ describes the vertical line passing through point $(5, 0)$. This line is parallel to the *y*-axis. In a natural extension, the equation $x = 5$ in $\mathbb{R}^3$ describes the plane passing through point $(5, 0, 0)$, which is parallel to the *yz*-plane. Another natural extension of a familiar equation is found in the equation of a sphere.

Definition

A **sphere** is the set of all points in space equidistant from a fixed point, the center of the sphere (**Figure 2.34**), just as the set of all points in a plane that are equidistant from the center represents a circle. In a sphere, as in a circle, the distance from the center to a point on the sphere is called the *radius*.

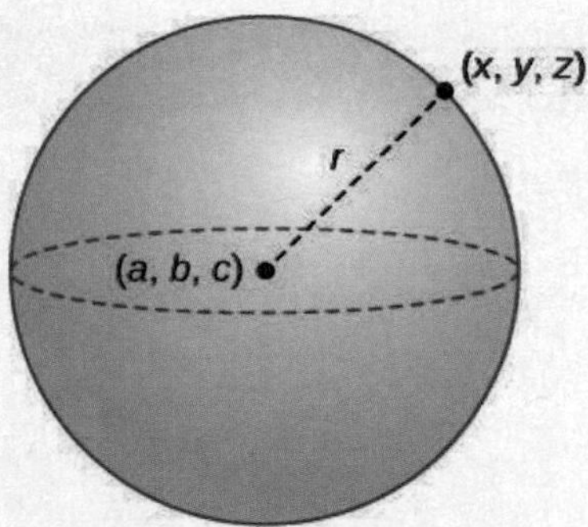

Figure 2.34 Each point (x, y, z) on the surface of a sphere is r units away from the center (a, b, c).

The equation of a circle is derived using the distance formula in two dimensions. In the same way, the equation of a sphere is based on the three-dimensional formula for distance.

Rule: Equation of a Sphere

The sphere with center (a, b, c) and radius r can be represented by the equation

$$(x-a)^2 + (y-b)^2 + (z-c)^2 = r^2. \tag{2.2}$$

This equation is known as the **standard equation of a sphere**.

Example 2.14

Finding an Equation of a Sphere

Find the standard equation of the sphere with center $(10, 7, 4)$ and point $(-1, 3, -2)$, as shown in **Figure 2.35**.

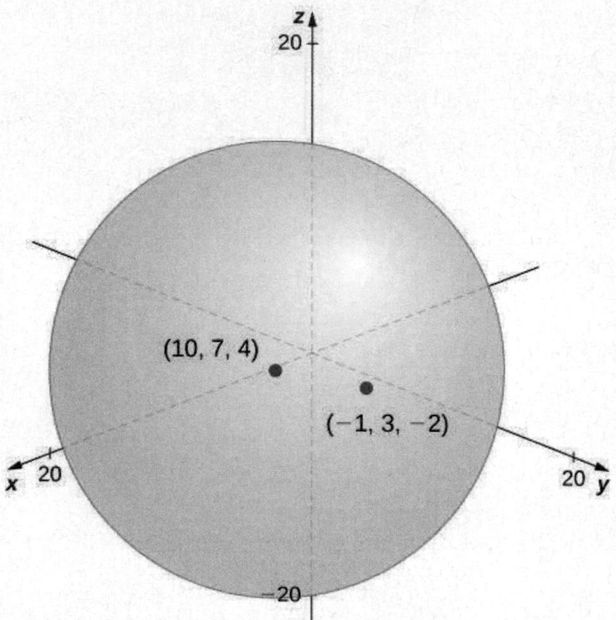

Figure 2.35 The sphere centered at $(10, 7, 4)$ containing point $(-1, 3, -2)$.

Solution

Use the distance formula to find the radius r of the sphere:

$$\begin{aligned} r &= \sqrt{(-1-10)^2 + (3-7)^2 + (-2-4)^2} \\ &= \sqrt{(-11)^2 + (-4)^2 + (-6)^2} \\ &= \sqrt{173}. \end{aligned}$$

The standard equation of the sphere is

$$(x-10)^2 + (y-7)^2 + (z-4)^2 = 173.$$

2.14 Find the standard equation of the sphere with center $(-2, 4, -5)$ containing point $(4, 4, -1)$.

Example 2.15

Finding the Equation of a Sphere

Let $P = (-5, 2, 3)$ and $Q = (3, 4, -1)$, and suppose line segment PQ forms the diameter of a sphere

(**Figure 2.36**). Find the equation of the sphere.

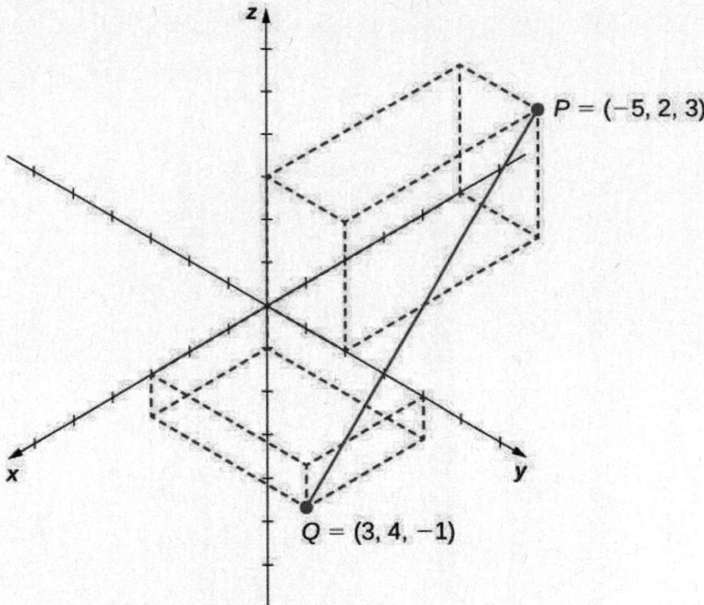

Figure 2.36 Line segment PQ.

Solution

Since PQ is a diameter of the sphere, we know the center of the sphere is the midpoint of PQ. Then,

$$\begin{aligned} C &= \left(\frac{-5+3}{2}, \frac{2+4}{2}, \frac{3+(-1)}{2}\right) \\ &= (-1, 3, 1). \end{aligned}$$

Furthermore, we know the radius of the sphere is half the length of the diameter. This gives

$$\begin{aligned} r &= \frac{1}{2}\sqrt{(-5-3)^2+(2-4)^2+(3-(-1))^2} \\ &= \frac{1}{2}\sqrt{64+4+16} \\ &= \sqrt{21}. \end{aligned}$$

Then, the equation of the sphere is $(x+1)^2+(y-3)^2+(z-1)^2=21.$

2.15 Find the equation of the sphere with diameter $PQ,$ where $P=(2, -1, -3)$ and $Q=(-2, 5, -1).$

Example 2.16

Graphing Other Equations in Three Dimensions

Describe the set of points that satisfies $(x-4)(z-2)=0,$ and graph the set.

Solution

We must have either $x - 4 = 0$ or $z - 2 = 0,$ so the set of points forms the two planes $x = 4$ and $z = 2$ (**Figure 2.37**).

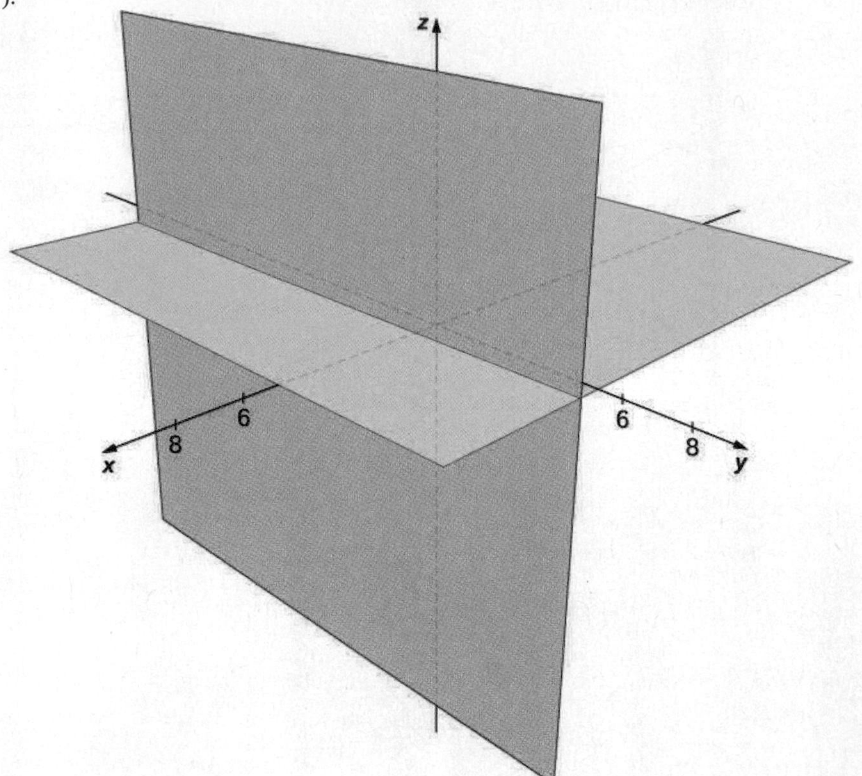

Figure 2.37 The set of points satisfying $(x - 4)(z - 2) = 0$ forms the two planes $x = 4$ and $z = 2.$

2.16 Describe the set of points that satisfies $(y + 2)(z - 3) = 0,$ and graph the set.

Example 2.17

Graphing Other Equations in Three Dimensions

Describe the set of points in three-dimensional space that satisfies $(x - 2)^2 + (y - 1)^2 = 4,$ and graph the set.

Solution

The x- and y-coordinates form a circle in the xy-plane of radius $2,$ centered at $(2, 1).$ Since there is no restriction on the z-coordinate, the three-dimensional result is a circular cylinder of radius 2 centered on the line with $x = 2$ and $y = 1.$ The cylinder extends indefinitely in the z-direction (**Figure 2.38**).

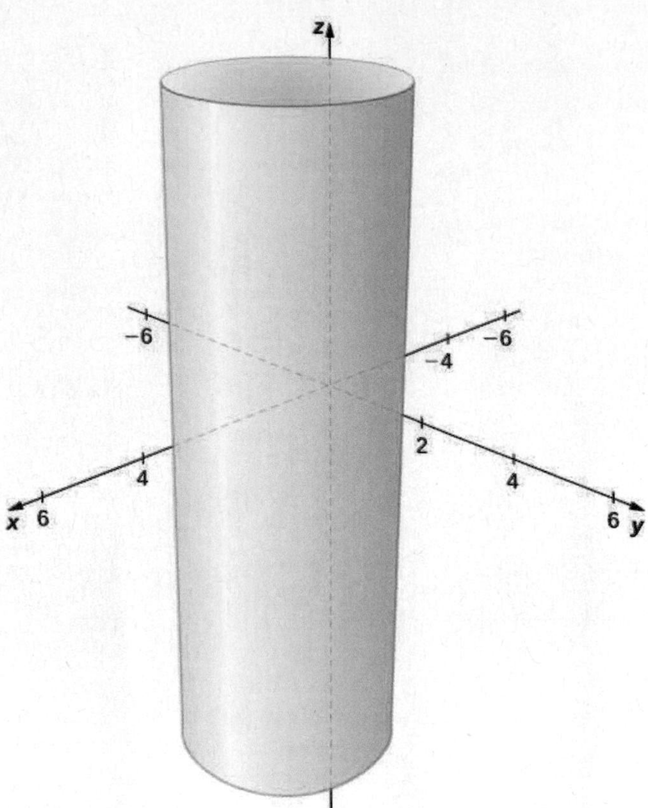

Figure 2.38 The set of points satisfying $(x-2)^2+(y-1)^2=4$. This is a cylinder of radius 2 centered on the line with $x=2$ and $y=1$.

2.17 Describe the set of points in three dimensional space that satisfies $x^2+(z-2)^2=16$, and graph the surface.

Working with Vectors in $\mathbb{R}^3$

Just like two-dimensional vectors, three-dimensional vectors are quantities with both magnitude and direction, and they are represented by directed line segments (arrows). With a three-dimensional vector, we use a three-dimensional arrow.

Three-dimensional vectors can also be represented in component form. The notation $\mathbf{v} = \langle x, y, z \rangle$ is a natural extension of the two-dimensional case, representing a vector with the initial point at the origin, $(0, 0, 0)$, and terminal point (x, y, z). The zero vector is $\mathbf{0} = \langle 0, 0, 0 \rangle$. So, for example, the three dimensional vector $\mathbf{v} = \langle 2, 4, 1 \rangle$ is represented by a directed line segment from point $(0, 0, 0)$ to point $(2, 4, 1)$ (**Figure 2.39**).

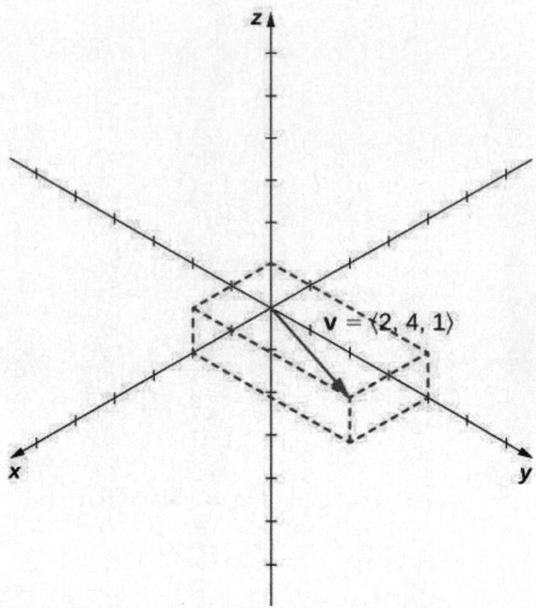

Figure 2.39 Vector $\mathbf{v} = \langle 2, 4, 1 \rangle$ is represented by a directed line segment from point $(0, 0, 0)$ to point $(2, 4, 1)$.

Vector addition and scalar multiplication are defined analogously to the two-dimensional case. If $\mathbf{v} = \langle x_1, y_1, z_1 \rangle$ and $\mathbf{w} = \langle x_2, y_2, z_2 \rangle$ are vectors, and k is a scalar, then

$$\mathbf{v} + \mathbf{w} = \langle x_1 + x_2, y_1 + y_2, z_1 + z_2 \rangle \text{ and } k\mathbf{v} = \langle kx_1, ky_1, kz_1 \rangle.$$

If $k = -1$, then $k\mathbf{v} = (-1)\mathbf{v}$ is written as $-\mathbf{v}$, and vector subtraction is defined by $\mathbf{v} - \mathbf{w} = \mathbf{v} + (-\mathbf{w}) = \mathbf{v} + (-1)\mathbf{w}$.

The standard unit vectors extend easily into three dimensions as well—$\mathbf{i} = \langle 1, 0, 0 \rangle$, $\mathbf{j} = \langle 0, 1, 0 \rangle$, and $\mathbf{k} = \langle 0, 0, 1 \rangle$—and we use them in the same way we used the standard unit vectors in two dimensions. Thus, we can represent a vector in $\mathbb{R}^3$ in the following ways:

$$\mathbf{v} = \langle x, y, z \rangle = x\mathbf{i} + y\mathbf{j} + z\mathbf{k}.$$

Example 2.18

Vector Representations

Let $\overrightarrow{PQ}$ be the vector with initial point $P = (3, 12, 6)$ and terminal point $Q = (-4, -3, 2)$ as shown in **Figure 2.40**. Express $\overrightarrow{PQ}$ in both component form and using standard unit vectors.

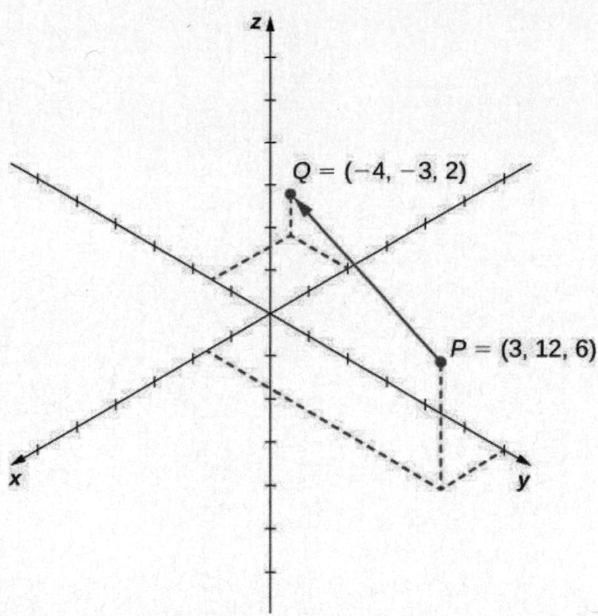

Figure 2.40 The vector with initial point $P = (3,\ 12,\ 6)$ and terminal point $Q = (-4,\ -3,\ 2)$.

Solution

In component form,

$$\begin{aligned}\overrightarrow{PQ} &= \langle x_2 - x_1, y_2 - y_1, z_2 - z_1 \rangle \\ &= \langle -4 - 3, -3 - 12, 2 - 6 \rangle = \langle -7, -15, -4 \rangle .\end{aligned}$$

In standard unit form,

$$\overrightarrow{PQ} = -7\mathbf{i} - 15\mathbf{j} - 4\mathbf{k}.$$

2.18 Let $S = (3,\ 8,\ 2)$ and $T = (2,\ -1,\ 3)$. Express $\overrightarrow{ST}$ in component form and in standard unit form.

As described earlier, vectors in three dimensions behave in the same way as vectors in a plane. The geometric interpretation of vector addition, for example, is the same in both two- and three-dimensional space (**Figure 2.41**).

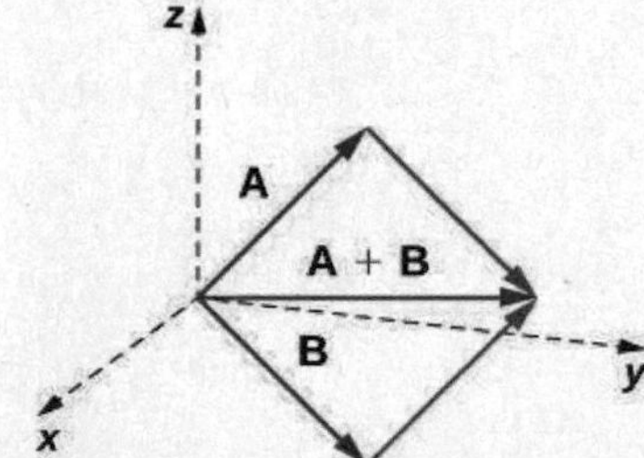

Figure 2.41 To add vectors in three dimensions, we follow the same procedures we learned for two dimensions.

We have already seen how some of the algebraic properties of vectors, such as vector addition and scalar multiplication, can be extended to three dimensions. Other properties can be extended in similar fashion. They are summarized here for our reference.

Rule: Properties of Vectors in Space

Let $\mathbf{v} = \langle x_1, y_1, z_1 \rangle$ and $\mathbf{w} = \langle x_2, y_2, z_2 \rangle$ be vectors, and let k be a scalar.

Scalar multiplication: $k\mathbf{v} = \langle kx_1, ky_1, kz_1 \rangle$

Vector addition: $\mathbf{v} + \mathbf{w} = \langle x_1, y_1, z_1 \rangle + \langle x_2, y_2, z_2 \rangle = \langle x_1 + x_2, y_1 + y_2, z_1 + z_2 \rangle$

Vector subtraction: $\mathbf{v} - \mathbf{w} = \langle x_1, y_1, z_1 \rangle - \langle x_2, y_2, z_2 \rangle = \langle x_1 - x_2, y_1 - y_2, z_1 - z_2 \rangle$

Vector magnitude: $\|\mathbf{v}\| = \sqrt{x_1^2 + y_1^2 + z_1^2}$

Unit vector in the direction of v: $\frac{1}{\|\mathbf{v}\|}\mathbf{v} = \frac{1}{\|\mathbf{v}\|}\langle x_1, y_1, z_1 \rangle = \langle \frac{x_1}{\|\mathbf{v}\|}, \frac{y_1}{\|\mathbf{v}\|}, \frac{z_1}{\|\mathbf{v}\|} \rangle, \text{ if } \mathbf{v} \neq \mathbf{0}$

We have seen that vector addition in two dimensions satisfies the commutative, associative, and additive inverse properties. These properties of vector operations are valid for three-dimensional vectors as well. Scalar multiplication of vectors satisfies the distributive property, and the zero vector acts as an additive identity. The proofs to verify these properties in three dimensions are straightforward extensions of the proofs in two dimensions.

Example 2.19

Vector Operations in Three Dimensions

Let $\mathbf{v} = \langle -2, 9, 5 \rangle$ and $\mathbf{w} = \langle 1, -1, 0 \rangle$ (**Figure 2.42**). Find the following vectors.

a. $3\mathbf{v} - 2\mathbf{w}$

b. $5\|\mathbf{w}\|$

c. $\|5\mathbf{w}\|$

d. A unit vector in the direction of $\mathbf{v}$

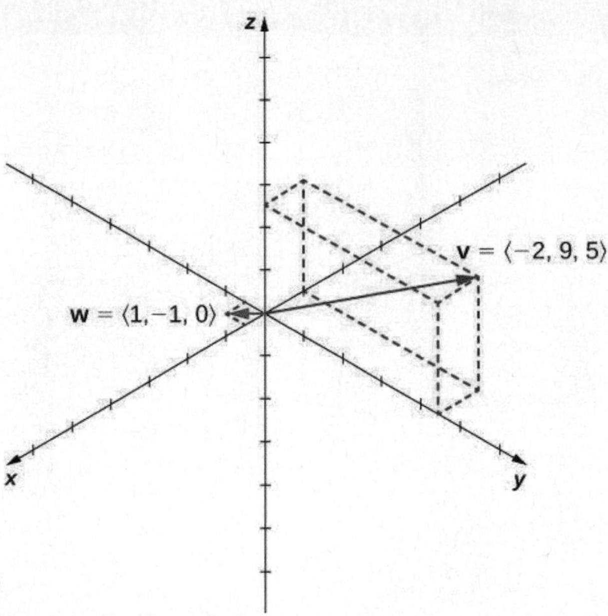

Figure 2.42 The vectors $\mathbf{v} = \langle -2, 9, 5 \rangle$ and $\mathbf{w} = \langle 1, -1, 0 \rangle$.

Solution

a. First, use scalar multiplication of each vector, then subtract:

$$\begin{aligned} 3\mathbf{v} - 2\mathbf{w} &= 3 \langle -2, 9, 5 \rangle - 2 \langle 1, -1, 0 \rangle \\ &= \langle -6, 27, 15 \rangle - \langle 2, -2, 0 \rangle \\ &= \langle -6 - 2, 27 - (-2), 15 - 0 \rangle \\ &= \langle -8, 29, 15 \rangle . \end{aligned}$$

b. Write the equation for the magnitude of the vector, then use scalar multiplication:

$$5 \| \mathbf{w} \| = 5\sqrt{1^2 + (-1)^2 + 0^2} = 5\sqrt{2}.$$

c. First, use scalar multiplication, then find the magnitude of the new vector. Note that the result is the same as for part b.:

$$\| 5\mathbf{w} \| = \| \langle 5, -5, 0 \rangle \| = \sqrt{5^2 + (-5)^2 + 0^2} = \sqrt{50} = 5\sqrt{2}.$$

d. Recall that to find a unit vector in two dimensions, we divide a vector by its magnitude. The procedure is the same in three dimensions:

$$\begin{aligned} \frac{\mathbf{v}}{\| \mathbf{v} \|} &= \frac{1}{\| \mathbf{v} \|} \langle -2, 9, 5 \rangle \\ &= \frac{1}{\sqrt{(-2)^2 + 9^2 + 5^2}} \langle -2, 9, 5 \rangle \\ &= \frac{1}{\sqrt{110}} \langle -2, 9, 5 \rangle \\ &= \langle \frac{-2}{\sqrt{110}}, \frac{9}{\sqrt{110}}, \frac{5}{\sqrt{110}} \rangle . \end{aligned}$$

2.19 Let $\mathbf{v} = \langle -1, -1, 1 \rangle$ and $\mathbf{w} = \langle 2, 0, 1 \rangle$. Find a unit vector in the direction of $5\mathbf{v} + 3\mathbf{w}$.

Example 2.20

Throwing a Forward Pass

A quarterback is standing on the football field preparing to throw a pass. His receiver is standing 20 yd down the field and 15 yd to the quarterback's left. The quarterback throws the ball at a velocity of 60 mph toward the receiver at an upward angle of $30°$ (see the following figure). Write the initial velocity vector of the ball, $\mathbf{v}$, in component form.

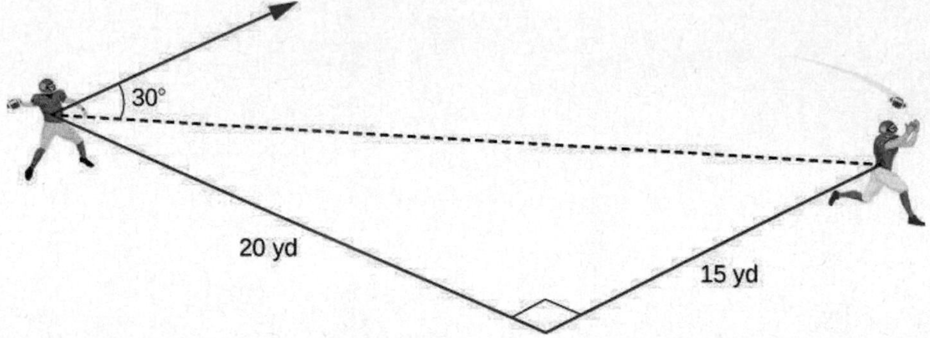

Solution

The first thing we want to do is find a vector in the same direction as the velocity vector of the ball. We then scale the vector appropriately so that it has the right magnitude. Consider the vector $\mathbf{w}$ extending from the quarterback's arm to a point directly above the receiver's head at an angle of $30°$ (see the following figure). This vector would have the same direction as $\mathbf{v}$, but it may not have the right magnitude.

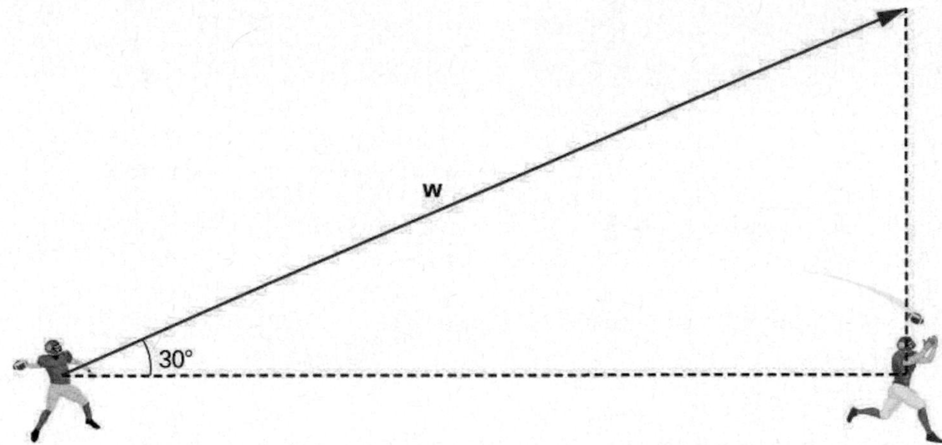

The receiver is 20 yd down the field and 15 yd to the quarterback's left. Therefore, the straight-line distance from the quarterback to the receiver is

$$\text{Dist from QB to receiver} = \sqrt{15^2 + 20^2} = \sqrt{225 + 400} = \sqrt{625} = 25 \text{ yd}.$$

We have $\dfrac{25}{\|\mathbf{w}\|} = \cos 30°$. Then the magnitude of $\mathbf{w}$ is given by

$$\|\mathbf{w}\| = \frac{25}{\cos 30°} = \frac{25 \cdot 2}{\sqrt{3}} = \frac{50}{\sqrt{3}} \text{ yd}$$

and the vertical distance from the receiver to the terminal point of $\mathbf{w}$ is

$$\text{Vert dist from receiver to terminal point of } \mathbf{w} = \|\mathbf{w}\| \sin 30° = \frac{50}{\sqrt{3}} \cdot \frac{1}{2} = \frac{25}{\sqrt{3}} \text{ yd.}$$

Then $\mathbf{w} = \langle 20, 15, \frac{25}{\sqrt{3}} \rangle$, and has the same direction as $\mathbf{v}$.

Recall, though, that we calculated the magnitude of $\mathbf{w}$ to be $\| \mathbf{w} \| = \frac{50}{\sqrt{3}}$, and $\mathbf{v}$ has magnitude 60 mph. So, we need to multiply vector $\mathbf{w}$ by an appropriate constant, k. We want to find a value of k so that $\| k\mathbf{w} \| = 60$ mph. We have

$$\| k\mathbf{w} \| = k \| \mathbf{w} \| = k\frac{50}{\sqrt{3}} \text{ mph},$$

so we want

$$\begin{aligned} k\frac{50}{\sqrt{3}} &= 60 \\ k &= \frac{60\sqrt{3}}{50} \\ k &= \frac{6\sqrt{3}}{5}. \end{aligned}$$

Then

$$\mathbf{v} = k\mathbf{w} = k \langle 20, 15, \frac{25}{\sqrt{3}} \rangle = \frac{6\sqrt{3}}{5} \langle 20, 15, \frac{25}{\sqrt{3}} \rangle = \langle 24\sqrt{3}, 18\sqrt{3}, 30 \rangle.$$

Let's double-check that $\| \mathbf{v} \| = 60$. We have

$$\| \mathbf{v} \| = \sqrt{(24\sqrt{3})^2 + (18\sqrt{3})^2 + (30)^2} = \sqrt{1728 + 972 + 900} = \sqrt{3600} = 60 \text{ mph}.$$

So, we have found the correct components for $\mathbf{v}$.

2.20 Assume the quarterback and the receiver are in the same place as in the previous example. This time, however, the quarterback throws the ball at velocity of 40 mph and an angle of $45°$. Write the initial velocity vector of the ball, $\mathbf{v}$, in component form.

2.2 EXERCISES

61. Consider a rectangular box with one of the vertices at the origin, as shown in the following figure. If point $A(2, 3, 5)$ is the opposite vertex to the origin, then find

a. the coordinates of the other six vertices of the box and
b. the length of the diagonal of the box determined by the vertices O and A.

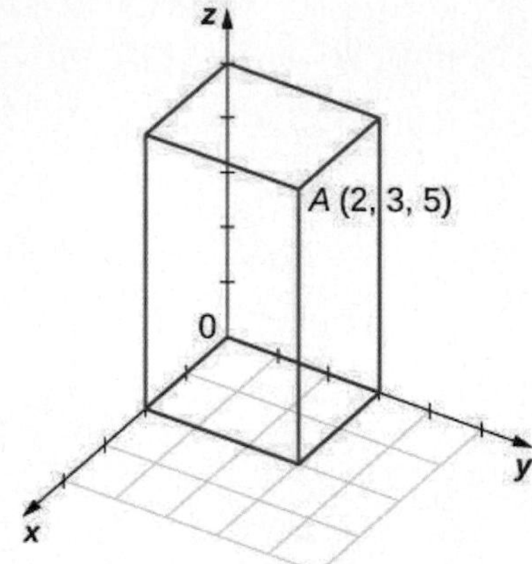

62. Find the coordinates of point P and determine its distance to the origin.

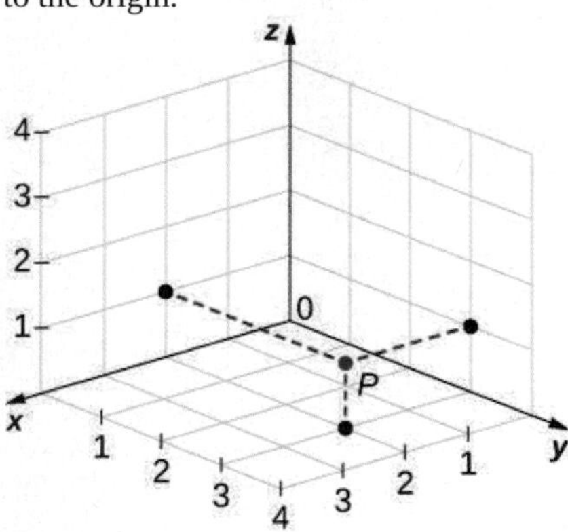

For the following exercises, describe and graph the set of points that satisfies the given equation.

63. $(y-5)(z-6)=0$

64. $(z-2)(z-5)=0$

65. $(y-1)^2+(z-1)^2=1$

66. $(x-2)^2+(z-5)^2=4$

67. Write the equation of the plane passing through point $(1, 1, 1)$ that is parallel to the xy-plane.

68. Write the equation of the plane passing through point $(1, -3, 2)$ that is parallel to the xz-plane.

69. Find an equation of the plane passing through points $(1, -3, -2)$, $(0, 3, -2)$, and $(1, 0, -2)$.

70. Find an equation of the plane passing through points $(1, 9, 2)$, $(1, 3, 6)$, and $(1, -7, 8)$.

For the following exercises, find the equation of the sphere in standard form that satisfies the given conditions.

71. Center $C(-1, 7, 4)$ and radius 4

72. Center $C(-4, 7, 2)$ and radius 6

73. Diameter PQ, where $P(-1, 5, 7)$ and $Q(-5, 2, 9)$

74. Diameter PQ, where $P(-16, -3, 9)$ and $Q(-2, 3, 5)$

For the following exercises, find the center and radius of the sphere with an equation in general form that is given.

75. $P(1, 2, 3)$ $x^2+y^2+z^2-4z+3=0$

76. $x^2+y^2+z^2-6x+8y-10z+25=0$

For the following exercises, express vector $\overrightarrow{PQ}$ with the initial point at P and the terminal point at Q

a. in component form and
b. by using standard unit vectors.

77. $P(3, 0, 2)$ and $Q(-1, -1, 4)$

78. $P(0, 10, 5)$ and $Q(1, 1, -3)$

79. $P(-2, 5, -8)$ and $M(1, -7, 4)$, where M is the midpoint of the line segment PQ

80. $Q(0, 7, -6)$ and $M(-1, 3, 2)$, where M is the midpoint of the line segment PQ

81. Find terminal point Q of vector $\overrightarrow{PQ} = \langle 7, -1, 3 \rangle$ with the initial point at $P(-2, 3, 5)$.

82. Find initial point P of vector $\overrightarrow{PQ} = \langle -9, 1, 2 \rangle$ with the terminal point at $Q(10, 0, -1)$.

For the following exercises, use the given vectors **a** and

b to find and express the vectors $\mathbf{a}+\mathbf{b}$, $4\mathbf{a}$, and $-5\mathbf{a}+3\mathbf{b}$ in component form.

83. $\mathbf{a} = \langle -1, -2, 4 \rangle$, $\mathbf{b} = \langle -5, 6, -7 \rangle$

84. $\mathbf{a} = \langle 3, -2, 4 \rangle$, $\mathbf{b} = \langle -5, 6, -9 \rangle$

85. $\mathbf{a} = -\mathbf{k}$, $\mathbf{b} = -\mathbf{i}$

86. $\mathbf{a} = \mathbf{i}+\mathbf{j}+\mathbf{k}$, $\mathbf{b} = 2\mathbf{i}-3\mathbf{j}+2\mathbf{k}$

For the following exercises, vectors **u** and **v** are given. Find the magnitudes of vectors $\mathbf{u}-\mathbf{v}$ and $-2\mathbf{u}$.

87. $\mathbf{u} = 2\mathbf{i}+3\mathbf{j}+4\mathbf{k}$, $\mathbf{v} = -\mathbf{i}+5\mathbf{j}-\mathbf{k}$

88. $\mathbf{u} = \mathbf{i}+\mathbf{j}$, $\mathbf{v} = \mathbf{j}-\mathbf{k}$

89. $\mathbf{u} = \langle 2\cos t, -2\sin t, 3 \rangle$, $\mathbf{v} = \langle 0, 0, 3 \rangle$, where t is a real number.

90. $\mathbf{u} = \langle 0, 1, \sinh t \rangle$, $\mathbf{v} = \langle 1, 1, 0 \rangle$, where t is a real number.

For the following exercises, find the unit vector in the direction of the given vector **a** and express it using standard unit vectors.

91. $\mathbf{a} = 3\mathbf{i}-4\mathbf{j}$

92. $\mathbf{a} = \langle 4, -3, 6 \rangle$

93. $\mathbf{a} = \overrightarrow{PQ}$, where $P(-2, 3, 1)$ and $Q(0, -4, 4)$

94. $\mathbf{a} = \overrightarrow{OP}$, where $P(-1, -1, 1)$

95. $\mathbf{a} = \mathbf{u}-\mathbf{v}+\mathbf{w}$, where $\mathbf{u} = \mathbf{i}-\mathbf{j}-\mathbf{k}$, $\mathbf{v} = 2\mathbf{i}-\mathbf{j}+\mathbf{k}$, and $\mathbf{w} = -\mathbf{i}+\mathbf{j}+3\mathbf{k}$

96. $\mathbf{a} = 2\mathbf{u}+\mathbf{v}-\mathbf{w}$, where $\mathbf{u} = \mathbf{i}-\mathbf{k}$, $\mathbf{v} = 2\mathbf{j}$, and $\mathbf{w} = \mathbf{i}-\mathbf{j}$

97. Determine whether $\overrightarrow{AB}$ and $\overrightarrow{PQ}$ are equivalent vectors, where $A(1, 1, 1)$, $B(3, 3, 3)$, $P(1, 4, 5)$, and $Q(3, 6, 7)$.

98. Determine whether the vectors $\overrightarrow{AB}$ and $\overrightarrow{PQ}$ are equivalent, where $A(1, 4, 1)$, $B(-2, 2, 0)$, $P(2, 5, 7)$, and $Q(-3, 2, 1)$.

For the following exercises, find vector **u** with a magnitude that is given and satisfies the given conditions.

99. $\mathbf{v} = \langle 7, -1, 3 \rangle$, $\|\mathbf{u}\| = 10$, **u** and **v** have the same direction

100. $\mathbf{v} = \langle 2, 4, 1 \rangle$, $\|\mathbf{u}\| = 15$, **u** and **v** have the same direction

101. $\mathbf{v} = \langle 2\sin t, 2\cos t, 1 \rangle$, $\|\mathbf{u}\| = 2$, **u** and **v** have opposite directions for any t, where t is a real number

102. $\mathbf{v} = \langle 3\sinh t, 0, 3 \rangle$, $\|\mathbf{u}\| = 5$, **u** and **v** have opposite directions for any t, where t is a real number

103. Determine a vector of magnitude 5 in the direction of vector $\overrightarrow{AB}$, where $A(2, 1, 5)$ and $B(3, 4, -7)$.

104. Find a vector of magnitude 2 that points in the opposite direction than vector $\overrightarrow{AB}$, where $A(-1, -1, 1)$ and $B(0, 1, 1)$. Express the answer in component form.

105. Consider the points $A(2, \alpha, 0)$, $B(0, 1, \beta)$, and $C(1, 1, \beta)$, where α and β are negative real numbers. Find α and β such that $\|\overrightarrow{OA}-\overrightarrow{OB}+\overrightarrow{OC}\| = \|\overrightarrow{OB}\| = 4$.

106. Consider points $A(\alpha, 0, 0)$, $B(0, \beta, 0)$, and $C(\alpha, \beta, \beta)$, where α and β are positive real numbers. Find α and β such that $\|\overline{OA}+\overline{OB}\| = \sqrt{2}$ and $\|\overline{OC}\| = \sqrt{3}$.

107. Let $P(x, y, z)$ be a point situated at an equal distance from points $A(1, -1, 0)$ and $B(-1, 2, 1)$. Show that point P lies on the plane of equation $-2x+3y+z=2$.

108. Let $P(x, y, z)$ be a point situated at an equal distance from the origin and point $A(4, 1, 2)$. Show that the coordinates of point P satisfy the equation $8x+2y+4z=21$.

109. The points A, B, and C are collinear (in this order) if the relation $\|\overrightarrow{AB}\| + \|\overrightarrow{BC}\| = \|\overrightarrow{AC}\|$ is satisfied. Show that $A(5, 3, -1)$, $B(-5, -3, 1)$, and $C(-15, -9, 3)$ are collinear points.

110. Show that points $A(1, 0, 1)$, $B(0, 1, 1)$, and $C(1, 1, 1)$ are not collinear.

111. **[T]** A force $\mathbf{F}$ of 50 N acts on a particle in the direction of the vector $\overrightarrow{OP}$, where $P(3, 4, 0)$.

a. Express the force as a vector in component form.
b. Find the angle between force $\mathbf{F}$ and the positive direction of the x-axis. Express the answer in degrees rounded to the nearest integer.

112. **[T]** A force $\mathbf{F}$ of 40 N acts on a box in the direction of the vector $\overrightarrow{OP}$, where $P(1, 0, 2)$.

a. Express the force as a vector by using standard unit vectors.
b. Find the angle between force $\mathbf{F}$ and the positive direction of the x-axis.

113. If $\mathbf{F}$ is a force that moves an object from point $P_1(x_1, y_1, z_1)$ to another point $P_2(x_2, y_2, z_2)$, then the displacement vector is defined as $\mathbf{D} = (x_2 - x_1)\mathbf{i} + (y_2 - y_1)\mathbf{j} + (z_2 - z_1)\mathbf{k}$. A metal container is lifted 10 m vertically by a constant force $\mathbf{F}$. Express the displacement vector $\mathbf{D}$ by using standard unit vectors.

114. A box is pulled 4 yd horizontally in the x-direction by a constant force $\mathbf{F}$. Find the displacement vector in component form.

115. The sum of the forces acting on an object is called the *resultant* or *net force*. An object is said to be in static equilibrium if the resultant force of the forces that act on it is zero. Let $\mathbf{F}_1 = \langle 10, 6, 3 \rangle$, $\mathbf{F}_2 = \langle 0, 4, 9 \rangle$, and $\mathbf{F}_3 = \langle 10, -3, -9 \rangle$ be three forces acting on a box. Find the force $\mathbf{F}_4$ acting on the box such that the box is in static equilibrium. Express the answer in component form.

116. **[T]** Let $\mathbf{F}_k = \langle 1, k, k^2 \rangle$, $k = 1,..., n$ be n forces acting on a particle, with $n \geq 2$.

a. Find the net force $\mathbf{F} = \sum_{k=1}^{n} F_k$. Express the answer using standard unit vectors.
b. Use a computer algebra system (CAS) to find n such that $\| \mathbf{F} \| < 100$.

117. The force of gravity $\mathbf{F}$ acting on an object is given by $\mathbf{F} = m\mathbf{g}$, where m is the mass of the object (expressed in kilograms) and $\mathbf{g}$ is acceleration resulting from gravity, with $\| \mathbf{g} \| = 9.8$ N/kg. A 2-kg disco ball hangs by a chain from the ceiling of a room.

a. Find the force of gravity $\mathbf{F}$ acting on the disco ball and find its magnitude.
b. Find the force of tension $\mathbf{T}$ in the chain and its magnitude.

Express the answers using standard unit vectors.

Figure 2.43 (credit: modification of work by Kenneth Lu, Flickr)

118. A 5-kg pendant chandelier is designed such that the alabaster bowl is held by four chains of equal length, as shown in the following figure.

a. Find the magnitude of the force of gravity acting on the chandelier.
b. Find the magnitudes of the forces of tension for each of the four chains (assume chains are essentially vertical).

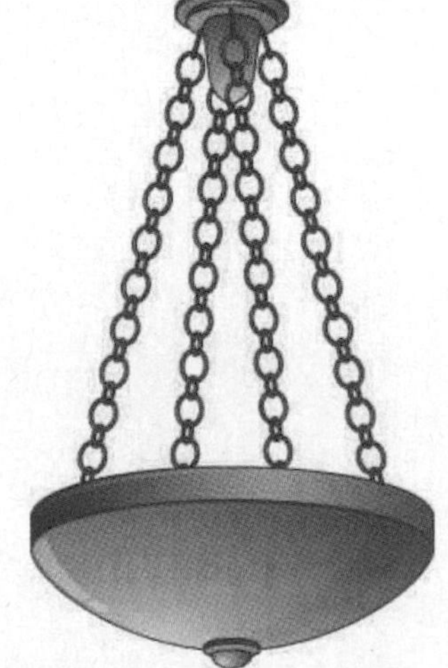

119. **[T]** A 30-kg block of cement is suspended by three cables of equal length that are anchored at points $P(-2, 0, 0)$, $Q(1, \sqrt{3}, 0)$, and $R(1, -\sqrt{3}, 0)$. The load is located at $S(0, 0, -2\sqrt{3})$, as shown in the following figure. Let $\mathbf{F}_1$, $\mathbf{F}_2$, and $\mathbf{F}_3$ be the forces of tension resulting from the load in cables RS, QS, and PS, respectively.

a. Find the gravitational force $\mathbf{F}$ acting on the block of cement that counterbalances the sum $\mathbf{F}_1 + \mathbf{F}_2 + \mathbf{F}_3$ of the forces of tension in the cables.

b. Find forces $\mathbf{F}_1$, $\mathbf{F}_2$, and $\mathbf{F}_3$. Express the answer in component form.

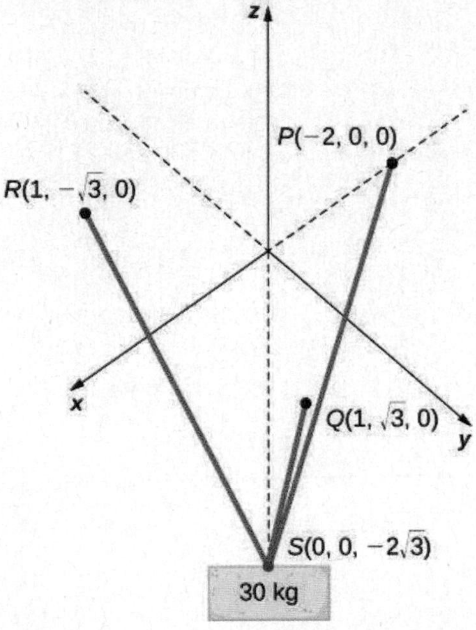

120. Two soccer players are practicing for an upcoming game. One of them runs 10 m from point *A* to point *B*. She then turns left at $90°$ and runs 10 m until she reaches point *C*. Then she kicks the ball with a speed of 10 m/sec at an upward angle of $45°$ to her teammate, who is located at point *A*. Write the velocity of the ball in component form.

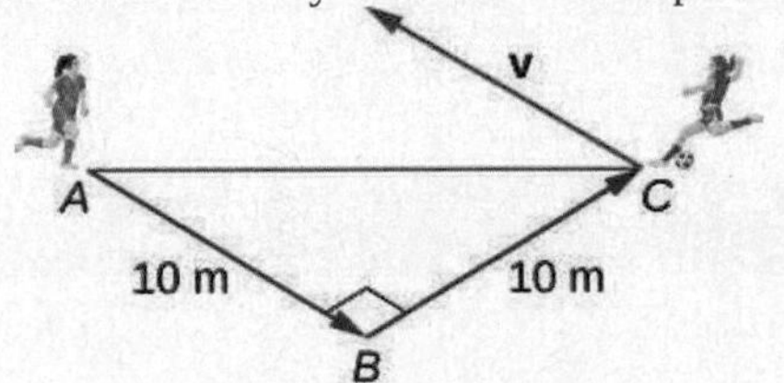

121. Let $\mathbf{r}(t) = \langle x(t), y(t), z(t) \rangle$ be the position vector of a particle at the time $t \in [0, T]$, where x, y, and z are smooth functions on $[0, T]$. The instantaneous velocity of the particle at time t is defined by vector $\mathbf{v}(t) = \langle x'(t), y'(t), z'(t) \rangle$, with components that are the derivatives with respect to t, of the functions x, y, and z, respectively. The magnitude $\| \mathbf{v}(t) \|$ of the instantaneous velocity vector is called the *speed of the particle at time* t. Vector $\mathbf{a}(t) = \langle x''(t), y''(t), z''(t) \rangle$, with components that are the second derivatives with respect to t, of the functions x, y, and z, respectively, gives the acceleration of the particle at time t. Consider $\mathbf{r}(t) = \langle \cos t, \sin t, 2t \rangle$ the position vector of a particle at time $t \in [0, 30]$, where the components of $\mathbf{r}$ are expressed in centimeters and time is expressed in seconds.

a. Find the instantaneous velocity, speed, and acceleration of the particle after the first second. Round your answer to two decimal places.

b. Use a CAS to visualize the path of the particle—that is, the set of all points of coordinates $(\cos t, \sin t, 2t)$, where $t \in [0, 30]$.

122. **[T]** Let $\mathbf{r}(t) = \langle t, 2t^2, 4t^2 \rangle$ be the position vector of a particle at time t (in seconds), where $t \in [0, 10]$ (here the components of $\mathbf{r}$ are expressed in centimeters).

a. Find the instantaneous velocity, speed, and acceleration of the particle after the first two seconds. Round your answer to two decimal places.

b. Use a CAS to visualize the path of the particle defined by the points $(t, 2t^2, 4t^2)$, where $t \in [0, 60]$.

2.3 | The Dot Product

Learning Objectives

2.3.1 Calculate the dot product of two given vectors.
2.3.2 Determine whether two given vectors are perpendicular.
2.3.3 Find the direction cosines of a given vector.
2.3.4 Explain what is meant by the vector projection of one vector onto another vector, and describe how to compute it.
2.3.5 Calculate the work done by a given force.

If we apply a force to an object so that the object moves, we say that *work* is done by the force. In **Introduction to Applications of Integration (http://cnx.org/content/m53638/latest/)** on integration applications, we looked at a constant force and we assumed the force was applied in the direction of motion of the object. Under those conditions, work can be expressed as the product of the force acting on an object and the distance the object moves. In this chapter, however, we have seen that both force and the motion of an object can be represented by vectors.

In this section, we develop an operation called the *dot product,* which allows us to calculate work in the case when the force vector and the motion vector have different directions. The dot product essentially tells us how much of the force vector is applied in the direction of the motion vector. The dot product can also help us measure the angle formed by a pair of vectors and the position of a vector relative to the coordinate axes. It even provides a simple test to determine whether two vectors meet at a right angle.

The Dot Product and Its Properties

We have already learned how to add and subtract vectors. In this chapter, we investigate two types of vector multiplication. The first type of vector multiplication is called the dot product, based on the notation we use for it, and it is defined as follows:

Definition

The **dot product** of vectors $\mathbf{u} = \langle u_1, u_2, u_3 \rangle$ and $\mathbf{v} = \langle v_1, v_2, v_3 \rangle$ is given by the sum of the products of the components

$$\mathbf{u} \cdot \mathbf{v} = u_1 v_1 + u_2 v_2 + u_3 v_3. \quad \textbf{(2.3)}$$

Note that if **u** and **v** are two-dimensional vectors, we calculate the dot product in a similar fashion. Thus, if $\mathbf{u} = \langle u_1, u_2 \rangle$ and $\mathbf{v} = \langle v_1, v_2 \rangle$, then

$$\mathbf{u} \cdot \mathbf{v} = u_1 v_1 + u_2 v_2.$$

When two vectors are combined under addition or subtraction, the result is a vector. When two vectors are combined using the dot product, the result is a scalar. For this reason, the dot product is often called the *scalar product*. It may also be called the *inner product*.

Example 2.21

Calculating Dot Products

a. Find the dot product of $\mathbf{u} = \langle 3, 5, 2 \rangle$ and $\mathbf{v} = \langle -1, 3, 0 \rangle$.

b. Find the scalar product of $\mathbf{p} = 10\mathbf{i} - 4\mathbf{j} + 7\mathbf{k}$ and $\mathbf{q} = -2\mathbf{i} + \mathbf{j} + 6\mathbf{k}$.

Solution

a. Substitute the vector components into the formula for the dot product:

$$\begin{aligned}\mathbf{u}\cdot\mathbf{v} &= u_1v_1 + u_2v_2 + u_3v_3 \\ &= 3(-1) + 5(3) + 2(0) = -3 + 15 + 0 = 12.\end{aligned}$$

b. The calculation is the same if the vectors are written using standard unit vectors. We still have three components for each vector to substitute into the formula for the dot product:

$$\begin{aligned}\mathbf{p}\cdot\mathbf{q} &= u_1v_1 + u_2v_2 + u_3v_3 \\ &= 10(-2) + (-4)(1) + (7)(6) = -20 - 4 + 42 = 18.\end{aligned}$$

2.21 Find $\mathbf{u}\cdot\mathbf{v}$, where $\mathbf{u} = \langle 2, 9, -1 \rangle$ and $\mathbf{v} = \langle -3, 1, -4 \rangle$.

Like vector addition and subtraction, the dot product has several algebraic properties. We prove three of these properties and leave the rest as exercises.

Theorem 2.3: Properties of the Dot Product

Let $\mathbf{u}$, $\mathbf{v}$, and $\mathbf{w}$ be vectors, and let c be a scalar.

i.	$\mathbf{u}\cdot\mathbf{v} = \mathbf{v}\cdot\mathbf{u}$	Commutative property
ii.	$\mathbf{u}\cdot(\mathbf{v}+\mathbf{w}) = \mathbf{u}\cdot\mathbf{v}+\mathbf{u}\cdot\mathbf{w}$	Distributive property
iii.	$c(\mathbf{u}\cdot\mathbf{v}) = (c\mathbf{u})\cdot\mathbf{v} = \mathbf{u}\cdot(c\mathbf{v})$	Associative property
iv.	$\mathbf{v}\cdot\mathbf{v} = \|\mathbf{v}\|^2$	Property of magnitude

Proof

Let $\mathbf{u} = \langle u_1, u_2, u_3 \rangle$ and $\mathbf{v} = \langle v_1, v_2, v_3 \rangle$. Then

$$\begin{aligned}\mathbf{u}\cdot\mathbf{v} &= \langle u_1, u_2, u_3 \rangle \cdot \langle v_1, v_2, v_3 \rangle \\ &= u_1v_1 + u_2v_2 + u_3v_3 \\ &= v_1u_1 + v_2u_2 + v_3u_3 \\ &= \langle v_1, v_2, v_3 \rangle \cdot \langle u_1, u_2, u_3 \rangle \\ &= \mathbf{v}\cdot\mathbf{u}.\end{aligned}$$

The associative property looks like the associative property for real-number multiplication, but pay close attention to the difference between scalar and vector objects:

$$\begin{aligned}c(\mathbf{u}\cdot\mathbf{v}) &= c(u_1v_1 + u_2v_2 + u_3v_3) \\ &= c(u_1v_1) + c(u_2v_2) + c(u_3v_3) \\ &= (cu_1)v_1 + (cu_2)v_2 + (cu_3)v_3 \\ &= \langle cu_1, cu_2, cu_3 \rangle \cdot \langle v_1, v_2, v_3 \rangle \\ &= c\langle u_1, u_2, u_3 \rangle \cdot \langle v_1, v_2, v_3 \rangle \\ &= (c\mathbf{u})\cdot\mathbf{v}.\end{aligned}$$

The proof that $c(\mathbf{u}\cdot\mathbf{v}) = \mathbf{u}\cdot(c\mathbf{v})$ is similar.

The fourth property shows the relationship between the magnitude of a vector and its dot product with itself:

$$\begin{aligned}\mathbf{v}\cdot\mathbf{v} &= \langle v_1, v_2, v_3 \rangle \cdot \langle v_1, v_2, v_3 \rangle \\ &= (v_1)^2 + (v_2)^2 + (v_3)^2 \\ &= \left[\sqrt{(v_1)^2 + (v_2)^2 + (v_3)^2}\right]^2 \\ &= \|\mathbf{v}\|^2.\end{aligned}$$

□

Note that the definition of the dot product yields $0 \cdot \mathbf{v} = \mathbf{0}$. By property iv., if $\mathbf{v} \cdot \mathbf{v} = 0$, then $\mathbf{v} = 0$.

Example 2.22

Using Properties of the Dot Product

Let $\mathbf{a} = \langle 1, 2, -3 \rangle$, $\mathbf{b} = \langle 0, 2, 4 \rangle$, and $\mathbf{c} = \langle 5, -1, 3 \rangle$. Find each of the following products.

a. $(\mathbf{a}\cdot\mathbf{b})\mathbf{c}$

b. $\mathbf{a}\cdot(2\mathbf{c})$

c. $\|\mathbf{b}\|^2$

Solution

a. Note that this expression asks for the scalar multiple of **c** by $\mathbf{a}\cdot\mathbf{b}$:

$$\begin{aligned}(\mathbf{a}\cdot\mathbf{b})\mathbf{c} &= (\langle 1, 2, -3 \rangle \cdot \langle 0, 2, 4 \rangle)\langle 5, -1, 3 \rangle \\ &= (1(0) + 2(2) + (-3)(4))\langle 5, -1, 3 \rangle \\ &= -8\langle 5, -1, 3 \rangle \\ &= \langle -40, 8, -24 \rangle.\end{aligned}$$

b. This expression is a dot product of vector **a** and scalar multiple 2**c**:

$$\begin{aligned}\mathbf{a}\cdot(2\mathbf{c}) &= 2(\mathbf{a}\cdot\mathbf{c}) \\ &= 2(\langle 1, 2, -3 \rangle \cdot \langle 5, -1, 3 \rangle) \\ &= 2(1(5) + 2(-1) + (-3)(3)) \\ &= 2(-6) = -12.\end{aligned}$$

c. Simplifying this expression is a straightforward application of the dot product:

$$\|\mathbf{b}\|^2 = \mathbf{b}\cdot\mathbf{b} = \langle 0, 2, 4 \rangle \cdot \langle 0, 2, 4 \rangle = 0^2 + 2^2 + 4^2 = 0 + 4 + 16 = 20.$$

2.22 Find the following products for $\mathbf{p} = \langle 7, 0, 2 \rangle$, $\mathbf{q} = \langle -2, 2, -2 \rangle$, and $\mathbf{r} = \langle 0, 2, -3 \rangle$.

a. $(\mathbf{r}\cdot\mathbf{p})\mathbf{q}$

b. $\|\mathbf{p}\|^2$

Using the Dot Product to Find the Angle between Two Vectors

When two nonzero vectors are placed in standard position, whether in two dimensions or three dimensions, they form an angle between them (**Figure 2.44**). The dot product provides a way to find the measure of this angle. This property is a result of the fact that we can express the dot product in terms of the cosine of the angle formed by two vectors.

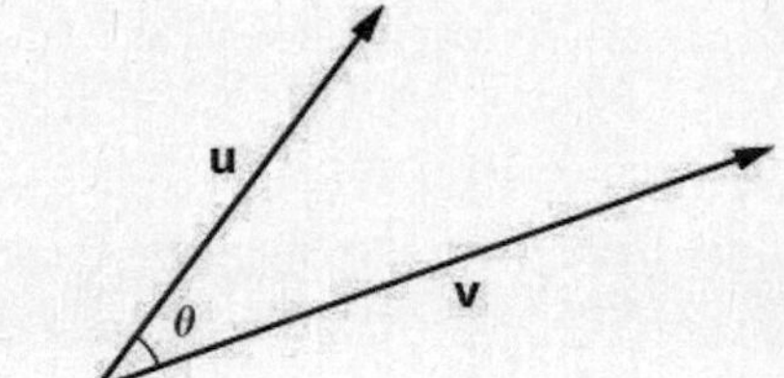

Figure 2.44 Let θ be the angle between two nonzero vectors **u** and **v** such that $0 \leq \theta \leq \pi$.

Theorem 2.4: Evaluating a Dot Product

The dot product of two vectors is the product of the magnitude of each vector and the cosine of the angle between them:

$$\mathbf{u} \cdot \mathbf{v} = \|\mathbf{u}\| \|\mathbf{v}\| \cos \theta. \tag{2.4}$$

Proof

Place vectors **u** and **v** in standard position and consider the vector $\mathbf{v} - \mathbf{u}$ (**Figure 2.45**). These three vectors form a triangle with side lengths $\|\mathbf{u}\|$, $\|\mathbf{v}\|$, and $\|\mathbf{v} - \mathbf{u}\|$.

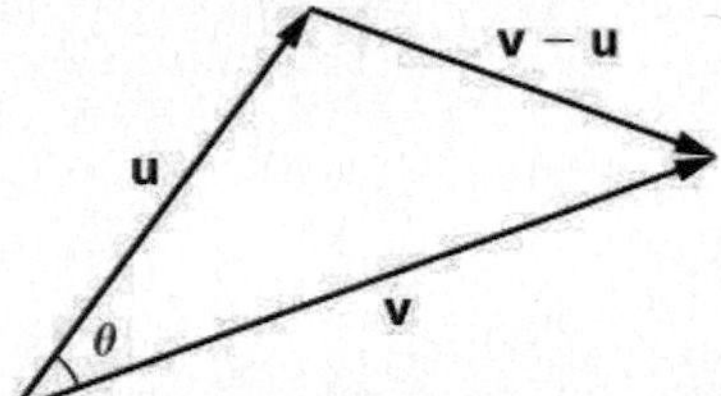

Figure 2.45 The lengths of the sides of the triangle are given by the magnitudes of the vectors that form the triangle.

Recall from trigonometry that the law of cosines describes the relationship among the side lengths of the triangle and the angle θ. Applying the law of cosines here gives

$$\|\mathbf{v} - \mathbf{u}\|^2 = \|\mathbf{u}\|^2 + \|\mathbf{v}\|^2 - 2\|\mathbf{u}\| \|\mathbf{v}\| \cos \theta.$$

The dot product provides a way to rewrite the left side of this equation:

$$\begin{aligned}
\|\mathbf{v} - \mathbf{u}\|^2 &= (\mathbf{v} - \mathbf{u}) \cdot (\mathbf{v} - \mathbf{u}) \\
&= (\mathbf{v} - \mathbf{u}) \cdot \mathbf{v} - (\mathbf{v} - \mathbf{u}) \cdot \mathbf{u} \\
&= \mathbf{v} \cdot \mathbf{v} - \mathbf{u} \cdot \mathbf{v} - \mathbf{v} \cdot \mathbf{u} + \mathbf{u} \cdot \mathbf{u} \\
&= \mathbf{v} \cdot \mathbf{v} - \mathbf{u} \cdot \mathbf{v} - \mathbf{u} \cdot \mathbf{v} + \mathbf{u} \cdot \mathbf{u} \\
&= \|\mathbf{v}\|^2 - 2\mathbf{u} \cdot \mathbf{v} + \|\mathbf{u}\|^2.
\end{aligned}$$

Substituting into the law of cosines yields

$$\begin{aligned}
\|\mathbf{v} - \mathbf{u}\|^2 &= \|\mathbf{u}\|^2 + \|\mathbf{v}\|^2 - 2\|\mathbf{u}\| \|\mathbf{v}\| \cos \theta \\
\|\mathbf{v}\|^2 - 2\mathbf{u} \cdot \mathbf{v} + \|\mathbf{u}\|^2 &= \|\mathbf{u}\|^2 + \|\mathbf{v}\|^2 - 2\|\mathbf{u}\| \|\mathbf{v}\| \cos \theta \\
-2\mathbf{u} \cdot \mathbf{v} &= -2\|\mathbf{u}\| \|\mathbf{v}\| \cos \theta \\
\mathbf{u} \cdot \mathbf{v} &= \|\mathbf{u}\| \|\mathbf{v}\| \cos \theta.
\end{aligned}$$

□

We can use this form of the dot product to find the measure of the angle between two nonzero vectors. The following equation rearranges **Equation 2.3** to solve for the cosine of the angle:

$$\cos \theta = \frac{\mathbf{u} \cdot \mathbf{v}}{\|\mathbf{u}\| \|\mathbf{v}\|}. \tag{2.5}$$

Using this equation, we can find the cosine of the angle between two nonzero vectors. Since we are considering the smallest angle between the vectors, we assume $0° \le \theta \le 180°$ (or $0 \le \theta \le \pi$ if we are working in radians). The inverse cosine is unique over this range, so we are then able to determine the measure of the angle θ.

Example 2.23

Finding the Angle between Two Vectors

Find the measure of the angle between each pair of vectors.

a. $\mathbf{i} + \mathbf{j} + \mathbf{k}$ and $2\mathbf{i} - \mathbf{j} - 3\mathbf{k}$

b. $\langle 2, 5, 6 \rangle$ and $\langle -2, -4, 4 \rangle$

Solution

a. To find the cosine of the angle formed by the two vectors, substitute the components of the vectors into **Equation 2.5**:

$$\begin{aligned} \cos\theta &= \frac{(\mathbf{i}+\mathbf{j}+\mathbf{k})\cdot(2\mathbf{i}-\mathbf{j}-3\mathbf{k})}{\| \mathbf{i}+\mathbf{j}+\mathbf{k} \| \cdot \| 2\mathbf{i}-\mathbf{j}-3\mathbf{k} \|} \\ &= \frac{1(2)+(1)(-1)+(1)(-3)}{\sqrt{1^2+1^2+1^2}\sqrt{2^2+(-1)^2+(-3)^2}} \\ &= \frac{-2}{\sqrt{3}\sqrt{14}} = \frac{-2}{\sqrt{42}}. \end{aligned}$$

Therefore, $\theta = \arccos \frac{-2}{\sqrt{42}}$ rad.

b. Start by finding the value of the cosine of the angle between the vectors:

$$\begin{aligned} \cos\theta &= \frac{\langle 2, 5, 6 \rangle \cdot \langle -2, -4, 4 \rangle}{\| \langle 2, 5, 6 \rangle \| \cdot \| \langle -2, -4, 4 \rangle \|} \\ &= \frac{2(-2)+(5)(-4)+(6)(4)}{\sqrt{2^2+5^2+6^2}\sqrt{(-2)^2+(-4)^2+4^2}} \\ &= \frac{0}{\sqrt{65}\sqrt{36}} = 0. \end{aligned}$$

Now, $\cos\theta = 0$ and $0 \le \theta \le \pi$, so $\theta = \pi/2$.

2.23 Find the measure of the angle, in radians, formed by vectors $\mathbf{a} = \langle 1, 2, 0 \rangle$ and $\mathbf{b} = \langle 2, 4, 1 \rangle$. Round to the nearest hundredth.

The angle between two vectors can be acute $(0 < \cos\theta < 1)$, obtuse $(-1 < \cos\theta < 0)$, or straight $(\cos\theta = -1)$. If $\cos\theta = 1$, then both vectors have the same direction. If $\cos\theta = 0$, then the vectors, when placed in standard position, form a right angle (**Figure 2.46**). We can formalize this result into a theorem regarding orthogonal (perpendicular) vectors.

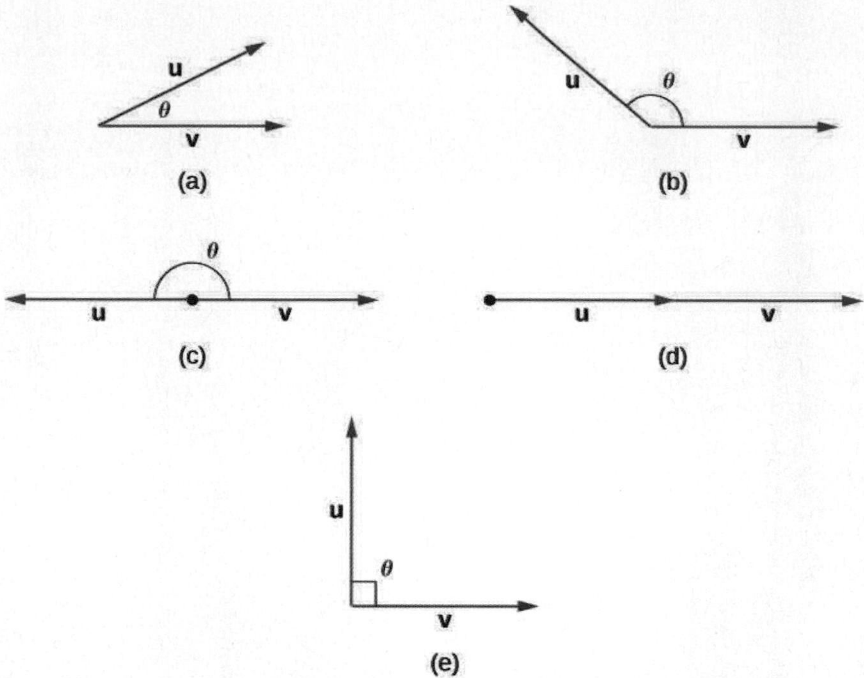

Figure 2.46 (a) An acute angle has $0 < \cos\theta < 1.$ (b) An obtuse angle has $-1 < \cos\theta < 0.$ (c) A straight line has $\cos\theta = -1.$ (d) If the vectors have the same direction, $\cos\theta = 1.$ (e) If the vectors are orthogonal (perpendicular), $\cos\theta = 0.$

Theorem 2.5: Orthogonal Vectors

The nonzero vectors **u** and **v** are **orthogonal vectors** if and only if $\mathbf{u} \cdot \mathbf{v} = 0.$

Proof

Let **u** and **v** be nonzero vectors, and let θ denote the angle between them. First, assume $\mathbf{u} \cdot \mathbf{v} = 0.$ Then

$$\| \mathbf{u} \| \ \| \mathbf{v} \| \cos\theta = 0.$$

However, $\| \mathbf{u} \| \neq 0$ and $\| \mathbf{v} \| \neq 0,$ so we must have $\cos\theta = 0.$ Hence, $\theta = 90°,$ and the vectors are orthogonal.

Now assume **u** and **v** are orthogonal. Then $\theta = 90°$ and we have

$$\mathbf{u} \cdot \mathbf{v} = \| \mathbf{u} \| \ \| \mathbf{v} \| \cos\theta = \| \mathbf{u} \| \ \| \mathbf{v} \| \cos 90° = \| \mathbf{u} \| \ \| \mathbf{v} \| (0) = 0.$$

□

The terms *orthogonal*, *perpendicular*, and *normal* each indicate that mathematical objects are intersecting at right angles. The use of each term is determined mainly by its context. We say that vectors are orthogonal and lines are perpendicular. The term *normal* is used most often when measuring the angle made with a plane or other surface.

Example 2.24

Identifying Orthogonal Vectors

Determine whether $\mathbf{p} = \langle 1, 0, 5 \rangle$ and $\mathbf{q} = \langle 10, 3, -2 \rangle$ are orthogonal vectors.

Solution

Using the definition, we need only check the dot product of the vectors:

$$\mathbf{p} \cdot \mathbf{q} = 1(10) + (0)(3) + (5)(-2) = 10 + 0 - 10 = 0.$$

Because $\mathbf{p} \cdot \mathbf{q} = 0,$ the vectors are orthogonal (**Figure 2.47**).

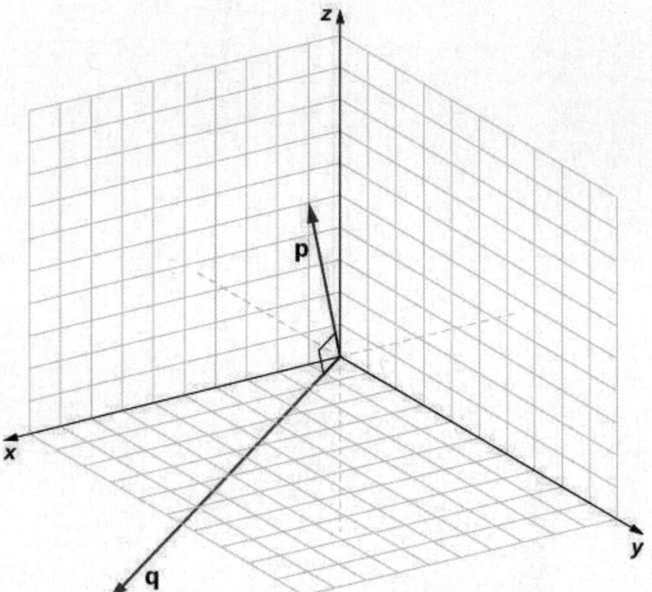

Figure 2.47 Vectors **p** and **q** form a right angle when their initial points are aligned.

2.24 For which value of x is $\mathbf{p} = \langle 2, 8, -1 \rangle$ orthogonal to $\mathbf{q} = \langle x, -1, 2 \rangle$?

Example 2.25

Measuring the Angle Formed by Two Vectors

Let $\mathbf{v} = \langle 2, 3, 3 \rangle$. Find the measures of the angles formed by the following vectors.

a. **v** and **i**

b. **v** and **j**

c. **v** and **k**

Solution

a. Let α be the angle formed by **v** and **i:**

$$\begin{aligned}\cos\alpha &= \frac{\mathbf{v}\cdot\mathbf{i}}{\|\mathbf{v}\|\cdot\|\mathbf{i}\|} \\ &= \frac{\langle 2, 3, 3\rangle\cdot\langle 1, 0, 0\rangle}{\sqrt{2^2+3^2+3^2}\sqrt{1}} \\ &= \frac{2}{\sqrt{22}}.\end{aligned}$$

$$\alpha = \arccos\frac{2}{\sqrt{22}} \approx 1.130 \text{ rad.}$$

b. Let β represent the angle formed by $\mathbf{v}$ and $\mathbf{j}$:

$$\begin{aligned}\cos\beta &= \frac{\mathbf{v}\cdot\mathbf{j}}{\|\mathbf{v}\|\cdot\|\mathbf{j}\|} \\ &= \frac{\langle 2, 3, 3\rangle\cdot\langle 0, 1, 0\rangle}{\sqrt{2^2+3^2+3^2}\sqrt{1}} \\ &= \frac{3}{\sqrt{22}}.\end{aligned}$$

$$\beta = \arccos\frac{3}{\sqrt{22}} \approx 0.877 \text{ rad.}$$

c. Let γ represent the angle formed by $\mathbf{v}$ and $\mathbf{k}$:

$$\begin{aligned}\cos\gamma &= \frac{\mathbf{v}\cdot\mathbf{k}}{\|\mathbf{v}\|\cdot\|\mathbf{k}\|} \\ &= \frac{\langle 2, 3, 3\rangle\cdot\langle 0, 0, 1\rangle}{\sqrt{2^2+3^2+3^2}\sqrt{1}} \\ &= \frac{3}{\sqrt{22}}.\end{aligned}$$

$$\gamma = \arccos\frac{3}{\sqrt{22}} \approx 0.877 \text{ rad.}$$

2.25 Let $\mathbf{v} = \langle 3, -5, 1\rangle$. Find the measure of the angles formed by each pair of vectors.

a. $\mathbf{v}$ and $\mathbf{i}$

b. $\mathbf{v}$ and $\mathbf{j}$

c. $\mathbf{v}$ and $\mathbf{k}$

The angle a vector makes with each of the coordinate axes, called a direction angle, is very important in practical computations, especially in a field such as engineering. For example, in astronautical engineering, the angle at which a rocket is launched must be determined very precisely. A very small error in the angle can lead to the rocket going hundreds of miles off course. Direction angles are often calculated by using the dot product and the cosines of the angles, called the direction cosines. Therefore, we define both these angles and their cosines.

Definition

The angles formed by a nonzero vector and the coordinate axes are called the **direction angles** for the vector (**Figure 2.48**). The cosines for these angles are called the **direction cosines**.

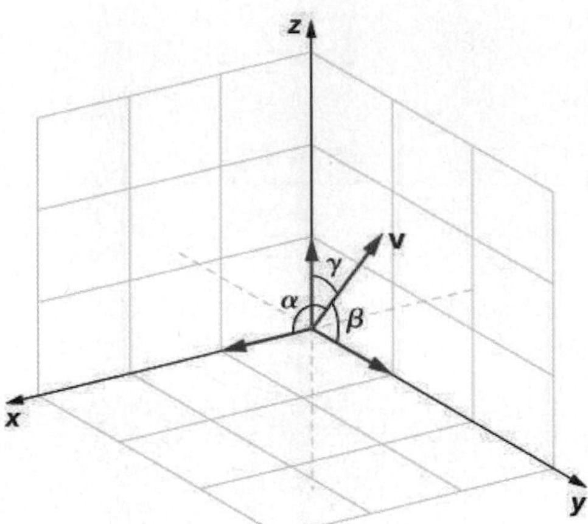

Figure 2.48 Angle α is formed by vector $\mathbf{v}$ and unit vector $\mathbf{i}$. Angle β is formed by vector $\mathbf{v}$ and unit vector $\mathbf{j}$. Angle γ is formed by vector $\mathbf{v}$ and unit vector $\mathbf{k}$.

In **Example 2.25**, the direction cosines of $\mathbf{v} = \langle 2, 3, 3 \rangle$ are $\cos\alpha = \frac{2}{\sqrt{22}}$, $\cos\beta = \frac{3}{\sqrt{22}}$, and $\cos\gamma = \frac{3}{\sqrt{22}}$. The direction angles of $\mathbf{v}$ are $\alpha = 1.130\text{ rad}$, $\beta = 0.877\text{ rad}$, and $\gamma = 0.877\text{ rad}$.

So far, we have focused mainly on vectors related to force, movement, and position in three-dimensional physical space. However, vectors are often used in more abstract ways. For example, suppose a fruit vendor sells apples, bananas, and oranges. On a given day, he sells 30 apples, 12 bananas, and 18 oranges. He might use a quantity vector, $\mathbf{q} = \langle 30, 12, 18 \rangle$, to represent the quantity of fruit he sold that day. Similarly, he might want to use a price vector, $\mathbf{p} = \langle 0.50, 0.25, 1 \rangle$, to indicate that he sells his apples for 50¢ each, bananas for 25¢ each, and oranges for $1 apiece. In this example, although we could still graph these vectors, we do not interpret them as literal representations of position in the physical world. We are simply using vectors to keep track of particular pieces of information about apples, bananas, and oranges.

This idea might seem a little strange, but if we simply regard vectors as a way to order and store data, we find they can be quite a powerful tool. Going back to the fruit vendor, let's think about the dot product, $\mathbf{q} \cdot \mathbf{p}$. We compute it by multiplying the number of apples sold (30) by the price per apple (50¢), the number of bananas sold by the price per banana, and the number of oranges sold by the price per orange. We then add all these values together. So, in this example, the dot product tells us how much money the fruit vendor had in sales on that particular day.

When we use vectors in this more general way, there is no reason to limit the number of components to three. What if the fruit vendor decides to start selling grapefruit? In that case, he would want to use four-dimensional quantity and price vectors to represent the number of apples, bananas, oranges, and grapefruit sold, and their unit prices. As you might expect, to calculate the dot product of four-dimensional vectors, we simply add the products of the components as before, but the sum has four terms instead of three.

Example 2.26

Using Vectors in an Economic Context

AAA Party Supply Store sells invitations, party favors, decorations, and food service items such as paper plates and napkins. When AAA buys its inventory, it pays 25¢ per package for invitations and party favors. Decorations cost AAA 50¢ each, and food service items cost 20¢ per package. AAA sells invitations for $2.50 per package and party favors for $1.50 per package. Decorations sell for $4.50 each and food service items for $1.25 per package.

During the month of May, AAA Party Supply Store sells 1258 invitations, 342 party favors, 2426 decorations, and 1354 food service items. Use vectors and dot products to calculate how much money AAA made in sales during the month of May. How much did the store make in profit?

Solution

The cost, price, and quantity vectors are

$$\begin{aligned}\mathbf{c} &= \langle 0.25, 0.25, 0.50, 0.20 \rangle \\ \mathbf{p} &= \langle 2.50, 1.50, 4.50, 1.25 \rangle \\ \mathbf{q} &= \langle 1258, 342, 2426, 1354 \rangle.\end{aligned}$$

AAA sales for the month of May can be calculated using the dot product $\mathbf{p} \cdot \mathbf{q}$. We have

$$\begin{aligned}\mathbf{p} \cdot \mathbf{q} &= \langle 2.50, 1.50, 4.50, 1.25 \rangle \cdot \langle 1258, 342, 2426, 1354 \rangle \\ &= 3145 + 513 + 10917 + 1692.5 \\ &= 16267.5.\end{aligned}$$

So, AAA took in \$16,267.50 during the month of May.

To calculate the profit, we must first calculate how much AAA paid for the items sold. We use the dot product $\mathbf{c} \cdot \mathbf{q}$ to get

$$\begin{aligned}\mathbf{c} \cdot \mathbf{q} &= \langle 0.25, 0.25, 0.50, 0.20 \rangle \cdot \langle 1258, 342, 2426, 1354 \rangle \\ &= 314.5 + 85.5 + 1213 + 270.8 \\ &= 1883.8.\end{aligned}$$

So, AAA paid \$1,883.30 for the items they sold. Their profit, then, is given by

$$\begin{aligned}\mathbf{p} \cdot \mathbf{q} - \mathbf{c} \cdot \mathbf{q} &= 16267.5 - 1883.8 \\ &= 14383.7.\end{aligned}$$

Therefore, AAA Party Supply Store made \$14,383.70 in May.

2.26 On June 1, AAA Party Supply Store decided to increase the price they charge for party favors to \$2 per package. They also changed suppliers for their invitations, and are now able to purchase invitations for only 10¢ per package. All their other costs and prices remain the same. If AAA sells 1408 invitations, 147 party favors, 2112 decorations, and 1894 food service items in the month of June, use vectors and dot products to calculate their total sales and profit for June.

Projections

As we have seen, addition combines two vectors to create a resultant vector. But what if we are given a vector and we need to find its component parts? We use vector projections to perform the opposite process; they can break down a vector into its components. The magnitude of a vector projection is a scalar projection. For example, if a child is pulling the handle of a wagon at a 55° angle, we can use projections to determine how much of the force on the handle is actually moving the wagon forward (**Figure 2.49**). We return to this example and learn how to solve it after we see how to calculate projections.

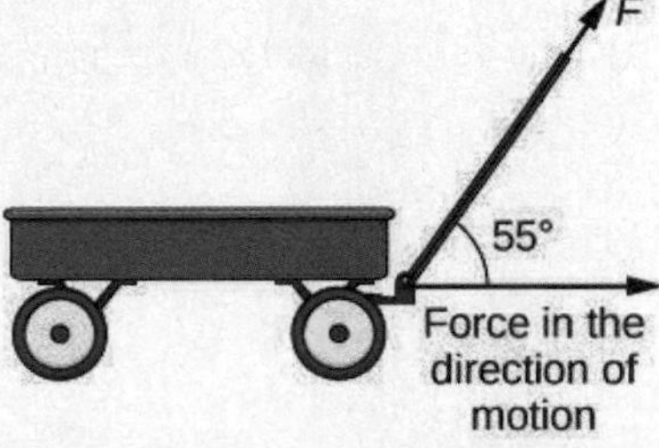

Figure 2.49 When a child pulls a wagon, only the horizontal component of the force propels the wagon forward.

Definition

The **vector projection** of $\mathbf{v}$ onto $\mathbf{u}$ is the vector labeled $\text{proj}_{\mathbf{u}}\mathbf{v}$ in **Figure 2.50**. It has the same initial point as $\mathbf{u}$ and $\mathbf{v}$ and the same direction as $\mathbf{u}$, and represents the component of $\mathbf{v}$ that acts in the direction of $\mathbf{u}$. If θ represents the angle between $\mathbf{u}$ and $\mathbf{v}$, then, by properties of triangles, we know the length of $\text{proj}_{\mathbf{u}}\mathbf{v}$ is $\|\text{proj}_{\mathbf{u}}\mathbf{v}\| = \|\mathbf{v}\|\cos\theta$. When expressing $\cos\theta$ in terms of the dot product, this becomes

$$\begin{aligned}\|\text{proj}_{\mathbf{u}}\mathbf{v}\| &= \|\mathbf{v}\|\cos\theta \\ &= \|\mathbf{v}\|\left(\frac{\mathbf{u}\cdot\mathbf{v}}{\|\mathbf{u}\|\,\|\mathbf{v}\|}\right) \\ &= \frac{\mathbf{u}\cdot\mathbf{v}}{\|\mathbf{u}\|}.\end{aligned}$$

We now multiply by a unit vector in the direction of $\mathbf{u}$ to get $\text{proj}_{\mathbf{u}}\mathbf{v}$:

$$\text{proj}_{\mathbf{u}}\mathbf{v} = \frac{\mathbf{u}\cdot\mathbf{v}}{\|\mathbf{u}\|}\left(\frac{1}{\|\mathbf{u}\|}\mathbf{u}\right) = \frac{\mathbf{u}\cdot\mathbf{v}}{\|\mathbf{u}\|^2}\mathbf{u}. \tag{2.6}$$

The length of this vector is also known as the **scalar projection** of $\mathbf{v}$ onto $\mathbf{u}$ and is denoted by

$$\|\text{proj}_{\mathbf{u}}\mathbf{v}\| = \text{comp}_{\mathbf{u}}\mathbf{v} = \frac{\mathbf{u}\cdot\mathbf{v}}{\|\mathbf{u}\|}. \tag{2.7}$$

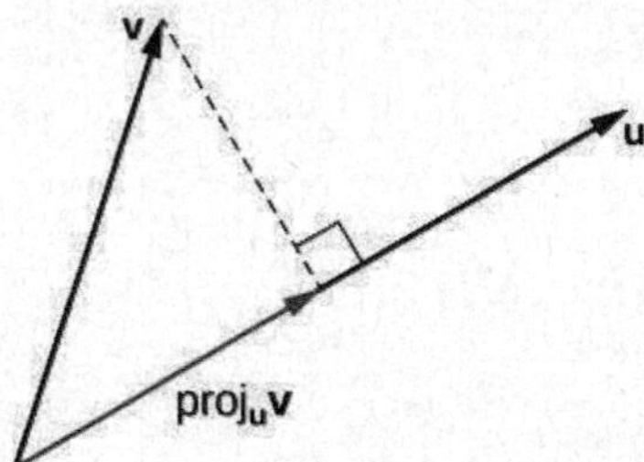

Figure 2.50 The projection of $\mathbf{v}$ onto $\mathbf{u}$ shows the component of vector $\mathbf{v}$ in the direction of $\mathbf{u}$.

Example 2.27

Finding Projections

Find the projection of $\mathbf{v}$ onto $\mathbf{u}$.

a. $\mathbf{v} = \langle 3, 5, 1\rangle$ and $\mathbf{u} = \langle -1, 4, 3\rangle$

b. $\mathbf{v} = 3\mathbf{i} - 2\mathbf{j}$ and $\mathbf{u} = \mathbf{i} + 6\mathbf{j}$

Solution

a. Substitute the components of $\mathbf{v}$ and $\mathbf{u}$ into the formula for the projection:

$$\begin{aligned}
\text{proj}_{\mathbf{u}}\mathbf{v} &= \frac{\mathbf{u}\cdot\mathbf{v}}{\|\mathbf{u}\|^2}\mathbf{u} \\
&= \frac{\langle -1, 4, 3\rangle \cdot \langle 3, 5, 1\rangle}{\|\langle -1, 4, 3\rangle\|^2}\langle -1, 4, 3\rangle \\
&= \frac{-3+20+3}{(-1)^2+4^2+3^2}\langle -1, 4, 3\rangle \\
&= \frac{20}{26}\langle -1, 4, 3\rangle \\
&= \left\langle -\frac{10}{13}, \frac{40}{13}, \frac{30}{13}\right\rangle.
\end{aligned}$$

b. To find the two-dimensional projection, simply adapt the formula to the two-dimensional case:

$$\begin{aligned}
\text{proj}_{\mathbf{u}}\mathbf{v} &= \frac{\mathbf{u}\cdot\mathbf{v}}{\|\mathbf{u}\|^2}\mathbf{u} \\
&= \frac{(\mathbf{i}+6\mathbf{j})\cdot(3\mathbf{i}-2\mathbf{j})}{\|\mathbf{i}+6\mathbf{j}\|^2}(\mathbf{i}+6\mathbf{j}) \\
&= \frac{1(3)+6(-2)}{1^2+6^2}(\mathbf{i}+6\mathbf{j}) \\
&= -\frac{9}{37}(\mathbf{i}+6\mathbf{j}) \\
&= -\frac{9}{37}\mathbf{i}-\frac{54}{37}\mathbf{j}.
\end{aligned}$$

Sometimes it is useful to decompose vectors—that is, to break a vector apart into a sum. This process is called the *resolution of a vector into components*. Projections allow us to identify two orthogonal vectors having a desired sum. For example, let $\mathbf{v} = \langle 6, -4\rangle$ and let $\mathbf{u} = \langle 3, 1\rangle$. We want to decompose the vector **v** into orthogonal components such that one of the component vectors has the same direction as **u**.

We first find the component that has the same direction as **u** by projecting **v** onto **u**. Let $\mathbf{p} = \text{proj}_{\mathbf{u}}\mathbf{v}$. Then, we have

$$\begin{aligned}
\mathbf{p} &= \frac{\mathbf{u}\cdot\mathbf{v}}{\|\mathbf{u}\|^2}\mathbf{u} \\
&= \frac{18-4}{9+1}\mathbf{u} \\
&= \frac{7}{5}\mathbf{u} = \frac{7}{5}\langle 3, 1\rangle = \left\langle \frac{21}{5}, \frac{7}{5}\right\rangle.
\end{aligned}$$

Now consider the vector $\mathbf{q} = \mathbf{v} - \mathbf{p}$. We have

$$\begin{aligned}
\mathbf{q} &= \mathbf{v}-\mathbf{p} \\
&= \langle 6, -4\rangle - \left\langle \frac{21}{5}, \frac{7}{5}\right\rangle \\
&= \left\langle \frac{9}{5}, -\frac{27}{5}\right\rangle.
\end{aligned}$$

Clearly, by the way we defined **q**, we have $\mathbf{v} = \mathbf{q} + \mathbf{p},$ and

$$\begin{aligned}
\mathbf{q}\cdot\mathbf{p} &= \left\langle \frac{9}{5}, -\frac{27}{5}\right\rangle \cdot \left\langle \frac{21}{5}, \frac{7}{5}\right\rangle \\
&= \frac{9(21)}{25} + \frac{-27(7)}{25} \\
&= \frac{189}{25} - \frac{189}{25} = 0.
\end{aligned}$$

Therefore, **q** and **p** are orthogonal.

Example 2.28

Resolving Vectors into Components

Express $\mathbf{v} = \langle 8, -3, -3 \rangle$ as a sum of orthogonal vectors such that one of the vectors has the same direction as $\mathbf{u} = \langle 2, 3, 2 \rangle$.

Solution

Let **p** represent the projection of **v** onto **u**:

$$\begin{aligned}\mathbf{p} &= \text{proj}_{\mathbf{u}}\mathbf{v} \\ &= \frac{\mathbf{u} \cdot \mathbf{v}}{\|\mathbf{u}\|^2}\mathbf{u} \\ &= \frac{\langle 2, 3, 2 \rangle \cdot \langle 8, -3, -3 \rangle}{\|\langle 2, 3, 2 \rangle\|^2}\langle 2, 3, 2 \rangle \\ &= \frac{16 - 9 - 6}{2^2 + 3^2 + 2^2}\langle 2, 3, 2 \rangle \\ &= \frac{1}{17}\langle 2, 3, 2 \rangle \\ &= \left\langle \frac{2}{17}, \frac{3}{17}, \frac{2}{17} \right\rangle.\end{aligned}$$

Then,

$$\mathbf{q} = \mathbf{v} - \mathbf{p} = \langle 8, -3, -3 \rangle - \left\langle \frac{2}{17}, \frac{3}{17}, \frac{2}{17} \right\rangle = \left\langle \frac{134}{17}, -\frac{54}{17}, -\frac{53}{17} \right\rangle.$$

To check our work, we can use the dot product to verify that **p** and **q** are orthogonal vectors:

$$\mathbf{p} \cdot \mathbf{q} = \left\langle \frac{2}{17}, \frac{3}{17}, \frac{2}{17} \right\rangle \cdot \left\langle \frac{134}{17}, -\frac{54}{17}, -\frac{53}{17} \right\rangle = \frac{268}{17} - \frac{162}{17} - \frac{106}{17} = 0.$$

Then,

$$\mathbf{v} = \mathbf{p} + \mathbf{q} = \left\langle \frac{2}{17}, \frac{3}{17}, \frac{2}{17} \right\rangle + \left\langle \frac{134}{17}, -\frac{54}{17}, -\frac{53}{17} \right\rangle.$$

2.27 Express $\mathbf{v} = 5\mathbf{i} - \mathbf{j}$ as a sum of orthogonal vectors such that one of the vectors has the same direction as $\mathbf{u} = 4\mathbf{i} + 2\mathbf{j}$.

Example 2.29

Scalar Projection of Velocity

A container ship leaves port traveling $15°$ north of east. Its engine generates a speed of 20 knots along that path (see the following figure). In addition, the ocean current moves the ship northeast at a speed of 2 knots. Considering both the engine and the current, how fast is the ship moving in the direction $15°$ north of east? Round the answer to two decimal places.

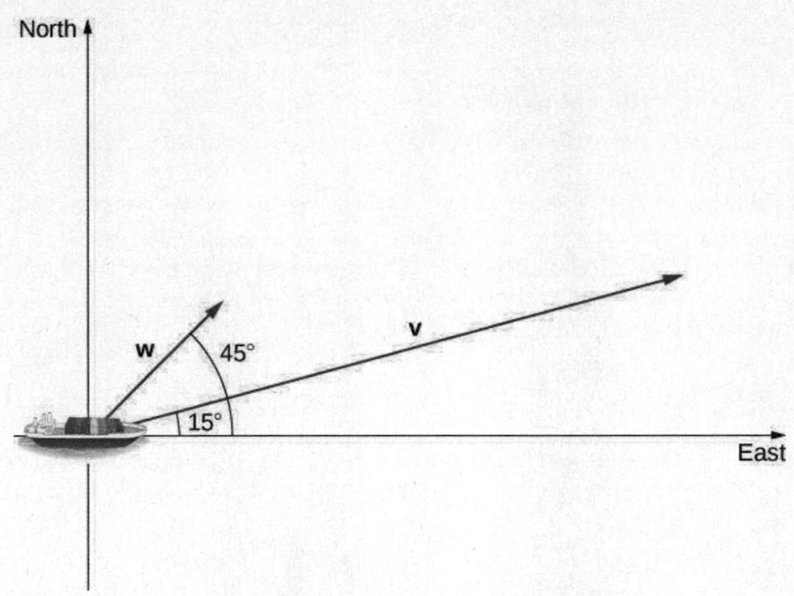

Solution

Let **v** be the velocity vector generated by the engine, and let **w** be the velocity vector of the current. We already know $\| \mathbf{v} \| = 20$ along the desired route. We just need to add in the scalar projection of **w** onto **v**. We get

$$\begin{aligned}\text{comp}_{\mathbf{v}} \mathbf{w} &= \frac{\mathbf{v} \cdot \mathbf{w}}{\| \mathbf{v} \|} \\ &= \frac{\| \mathbf{v} \| \ \| \mathbf{w} \| \cos(30°)}{\| \mathbf{v} \|} \\ &= \| \mathbf{w} \| \cos(30°) \\ &= 2\frac{\sqrt{3}}{2} = \sqrt{3} \approx 1.73 \text{ knots.}\end{aligned}$$

The ship is moving at 21.73 knots in the direction $15°$ north of east.

2.28 Repeat the previous example, but assume the ocean current is moving southeast instead of northeast, as shown in the following figure.

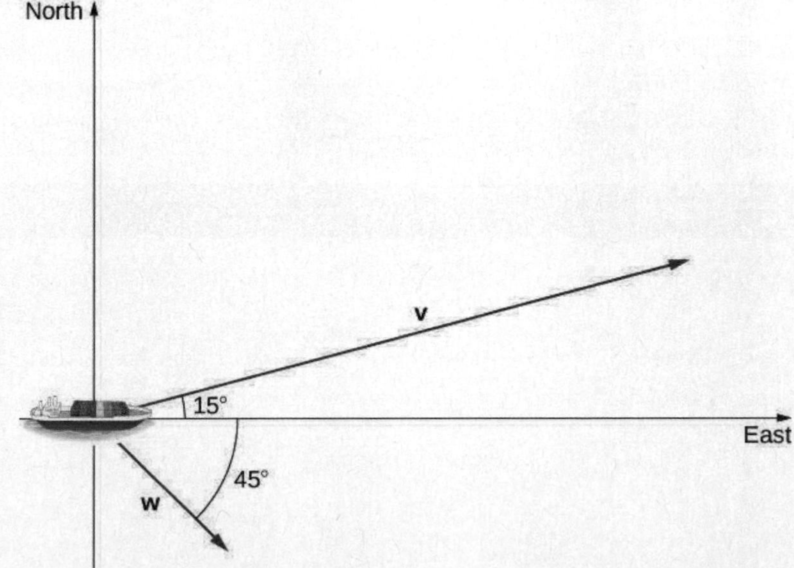

Work

Now that we understand dot products, we can see how to apply them to real-life situations. The most common application of the dot product of two vectors is in the calculation of work.

From physics, we know that work is done when an object is moved by a force. When the force is constant and applied in the same direction the object moves, then we define the work done as the product of the force and the distance the object travels: $W = Fd.$ We saw several examples of this type in earlier chapters. Now imagine the direction of the force is different from the direction of motion, as with the example of a child pulling a wagon. To find the work done, we need to multiply the component of the force that acts in the direction of the motion by the magnitude of the displacement. The dot product allows us to do just that. If we represent an applied force by a vector **F** and the displacement of an object by a vector **s**, then the **work done by the force** is the dot product of **F** and **s**.

Definition

When a constant force is applied to an object so the object moves in a straight line from point P to point Q, the work W done by the force **F**, acting at an angle θ from the line of motion, is given by

$$W = \mathbf{F} \cdot \overrightarrow{PQ} = \| \mathbf{F} \| \, \| \overrightarrow{PQ} \| \cos \theta. \tag{2.8}$$

Let's revisit the problem of the child's wagon introduced earlier. Suppose a child is pulling a wagon with a force having a magnitude of 8 lb on the handle at an angle of 55°. If the child pulls the wagon 50 ft, find the work done by the force (**Figure 2.51**).

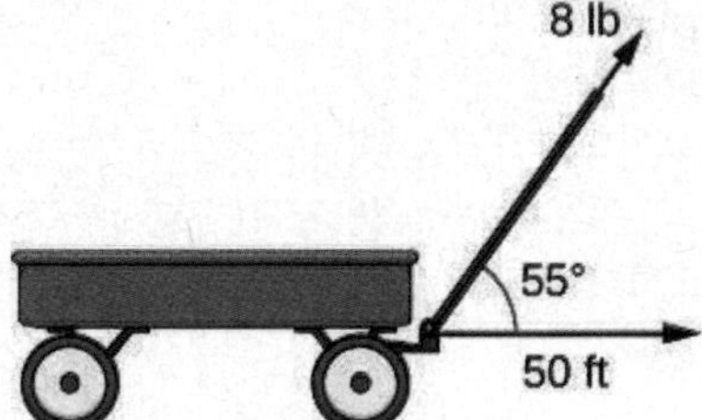

Figure 2.51 The horizontal component of the force is the projection of **F** onto the positive x-axis.

We have

$$W = \| \mathbf{F} \| \, \| \overrightarrow{PQ} \| \cos \theta = 8(50)(\cos(55°)) \approx 229 \text{ ft} \cdot \text{lb}.$$

In U.S. standard units, we measure the magnitude of force $\| \mathbf{F} \|$ in pounds. The magnitude of the displacement vector $\| \overrightarrow{PQ} \|$ tells us how far the object moved, and it is measured in feet. The customary unit of measure for work, then, is the foot-pound. One foot-pound is the amount of work required to move an object weighing 1 lb a distance of 1 ft straight up. In the metric system, the unit of measure for force is the newton (N), and the unit of measure of magnitude for work is a newton-meter (N·m), or a joule (J).

Example 2.30

Calculating Work

A conveyor belt generates a force $\mathbf{F} = 5\mathbf{i} - 3\mathbf{j} + \mathbf{k}$ that moves a suitcase from point $(1, 1, 1)$ to point $(9, 4, 7)$ along a straight line. Find the work done by the conveyor belt. The distance is measured in meters and the force is measured in newtons.

Solution

The displacement vector $\overrightarrow{PQ}$ has initial point $(1, 1, 1)$ and terminal point $(9, 4, 7)$:

$$\overrightarrow{PQ} = \langle 9-1, 4-1, 7-1 \rangle = \langle 8, 3, 6 \rangle = 8\mathbf{i} + 3\mathbf{j} + 6\mathbf{k}.$$

Work is the dot product of force and displacement:

$$\begin{aligned} W &= \mathbf{F} \cdot \overrightarrow{PQ} \\ &= (5\mathbf{i} - 3\mathbf{j} + \mathbf{k}) \cdot (8\mathbf{i} + 3\mathbf{j} + 6\mathbf{k}) \\ &= 5(8) + (-3)(3) + 1(6) \\ &= 37 \text{N} \cdot \text{m} \\ &= 37 \text{ J}. \end{aligned}$$

2.29 A constant force of 30 lb is applied at an angle of 60° to pull a handcart 10 ft across the ground (**Figure 2.52**). What is the work done by this force?

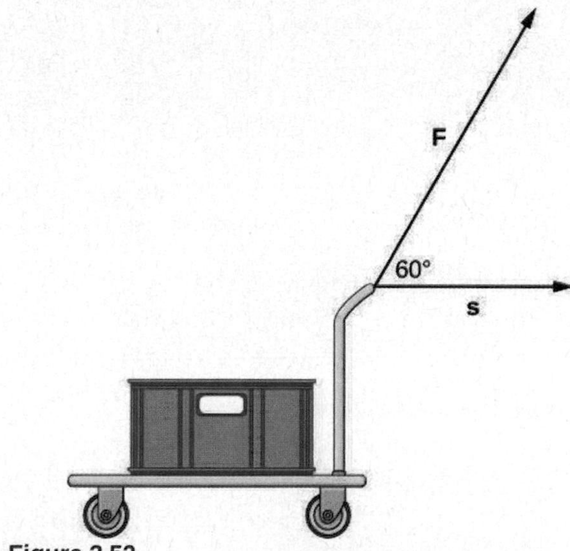

Figure 2.52

2.3 EXERCISES

For the following exercises, the vectors **u** and **v** are given. Calculate the dot product $\mathbf{u} \cdot \mathbf{v}$.

123. $\mathbf{u} = \langle 3, 0 \rangle, \quad \mathbf{v} = \langle 2, 2 \rangle$

124. $\mathbf{u} = \langle 3, -4 \rangle, \quad \mathbf{v} = \langle 4, 3 \rangle$

125. $\mathbf{u} = \langle 2, 2, -1 \rangle, \quad \mathbf{v} = \langle -1, 2, 2 \rangle$

126. $\mathbf{u} = \langle 4, 5, -6 \rangle, \quad \mathbf{v} = \langle 0, -2, -3 \rangle$

For the following exercises, the vectors **a**, **b**, and **c** are given. Determine the vectors $(\mathbf{a} \cdot \mathbf{b})\mathbf{c}$ and $(\mathbf{a} \cdot \mathbf{c})\mathbf{b}$. Express the vectors in component form.

127. $\mathbf{a} = \langle 2, 0, -3 \rangle, \quad \mathbf{b} = \langle -4, -7, 1 \rangle, \quad \mathbf{c} = \langle 1, 1, -1 \rangle$

128. $\mathbf{a} = \langle 0, 1, 2 \rangle, \quad \mathbf{b} = \langle -1, 0, 1 \rangle, \quad \mathbf{c} = \langle 1, 0, -1 \rangle$

129. $\mathbf{a} = \mathbf{i} + \mathbf{j}, \quad \mathbf{b} = \mathbf{i} - \mathbf{k}, \quad \mathbf{c} = \mathbf{i} - 2\mathbf{k}$

130. $\mathbf{a} = \mathbf{i} - \mathbf{j} + \mathbf{k}, \quad \mathbf{b} = \mathbf{j} + 3\mathbf{k}, \quad \mathbf{c} = -\mathbf{i} + 2\mathbf{j} - 4\mathbf{k}$

For the following exercises, the two-dimensional vectors **a** and **b** are given.

a. Find the measure of the angle θ between **a** and **b**. Express the answer in radians rounded to two decimal places, if it is not possible to express it exactly.
b. Is θ an acute angle?

131. **[T]** $\mathbf{a} = \langle 3, -1 \rangle, \quad \mathbf{b} = \langle -4, 0 \rangle$

132. **[T]** $\mathbf{a} = \langle 2, 1 \rangle, \quad \mathbf{b} = \langle -1, 3 \rangle$

133. $\mathbf{u} = 3\mathbf{i}, \quad \mathbf{v} = 4\mathbf{i} + 4\mathbf{j}$

134. $\mathbf{u} = 5\mathbf{i}, \quad \mathbf{v} = -6\mathbf{i} + 6\mathbf{j}$

For the following exercises, find the measure of the angle between the three-dimensional vectors **a** and **b**. Express the answer in radians rounded to two decimal places, if it is not possible to express it exactly.

135. $\mathbf{a} = \langle 3, -1, 2 \rangle, \quad \mathbf{b} = \langle 1, -1, -2 \rangle$

136. $\mathbf{a} = \langle 0, -1, -3 \rangle, \quad \mathbf{b} = \langle 2, 3, -1 \rangle$

137. $\mathbf{a} = \mathbf{i} + \mathbf{j}, \quad \mathbf{b} = \mathbf{j} - \mathbf{k}$

138. $\mathbf{a} = \mathbf{i} - 2\mathbf{j} + \mathbf{k}, \quad \mathbf{b} = \mathbf{i} + \mathbf{j} - 2\mathbf{k}$

139. **[T]** $\mathbf{a} = 3\mathbf{i} - \mathbf{j} - 2\mathbf{k}, \quad \mathbf{b} = \mathbf{v} + \mathbf{w},$ where $\mathbf{v} = -2\mathbf{i} - 3\mathbf{j} + 2\mathbf{k}$ and $\mathbf{w} = \mathbf{i} + 2\mathbf{k}$

140. **[T]** $\mathbf{a} = 3\mathbf{i} - \mathbf{j} + 2\mathbf{k}, \quad \mathbf{b} = \mathbf{v} - \mathbf{w},$ where $\mathbf{v} = 2\mathbf{i} + \mathbf{j} + 4\mathbf{k}$ and $\mathbf{w} = 6\mathbf{i} + \mathbf{j} + 2\mathbf{k}$

For the following exercises determine whether the given vectors are orthogonal.

141. $\mathbf{a} = \langle x, y \rangle, \quad \mathbf{b} = \langle -y, x \rangle,$ where x and y are nonzero real numbers

142. $\mathbf{a} = \langle x, x \rangle, \quad \mathbf{b} = \langle -y, y \rangle,$ where x and y are nonzero real numbers

143. $\mathbf{a} = 3\mathbf{i} - \mathbf{j} - 2\mathbf{k}, \quad \mathbf{b} = -2\mathbf{i} - 3\mathbf{j} + \mathbf{k}$

144. $\mathbf{a} = \mathbf{i} - \mathbf{j}, \quad \mathbf{b} = 7\mathbf{i} + 2\mathbf{j} - \mathbf{k}$

145. Find all two-dimensional vectors **a** orthogonal to vector $\mathbf{b} = \langle 3, 4 \rangle$. Express the answer in component form.

146. Find all two-dimensional vectors **a** orthogonal to vector $\mathbf{b} = \langle 5, -6 \rangle$. Express the answer by using standard unit vectors.

147. Determine all three-dimensional vectors **u** orthogonal to vector $\mathbf{v} = \langle 1, 1, 0 \rangle$. Express the answer by using standard unit vectors.

148. Determine all three-dimensional vectors **u** orthogonal to vector $\mathbf{v} = \mathbf{i} - \mathbf{j} - \mathbf{k}$. Express the answer in component form.

149. Determine the real number α such that vectors $\mathbf{a} = 2\mathbf{i} + 3\mathbf{j}$ and $\mathbf{b} = 9\mathbf{i} + \alpha\mathbf{j}$ are orthogonal.

150. Determine the real number α such that vectors $\mathbf{a} = -3\mathbf{i} + 2\mathbf{j}$ and $\mathbf{b} = 2\mathbf{i} + \alpha\mathbf{j}$ are orthogonal.

151. **[T]** Consider the points $P(4, 5)$ and $Q(5, -7)$.

a. Determine vectors $\overrightarrow{OP}$ and $\overrightarrow{OQ}$. Express the answer by using standard unit vectors.
b. Determine the measure of angle O in triangle OPQ. Express the answer in degrees rounded to two decimal places.

152. **[T]** Consider points $A(1, 1)$, $B(2, -7)$, and $C(6, 3)$.

a. Determine vectors $\overrightarrow{BA}$ and $\overrightarrow{BC}$. Express the answer in component form.
b. Determine the measure of angle B in triangle ABC. Express the answer in degrees rounded to two decimal places.

153. Determine the measure of angle A in triangle ABC, where $A(1, 1, 8)$, $B(4, -3, -4)$, and $C(-3, 1, 5)$. Express your answer in degrees rounded to two decimal places.

154. Consider points $P(3, 7, -2)$ and $Q(1, 1, -3)$. Determine the angle between vectors $\overrightarrow{OP}$ and $\overrightarrow{OQ}$. Express the answer in degrees rounded to two decimal places.

For the following exercises, determine which (if any) pairs of the following vectors are orthogonal.

155. $\mathbf{u} = \langle 3, 7, -2 \rangle$, $\mathbf{v} = \langle 5, -3, -3 \rangle$, $\mathbf{w} = \langle 0, 1, -1 \rangle$

156. $\mathbf{u} = \mathbf{i} - \mathbf{k}$, $\mathbf{v} = 5\mathbf{j} - 5\mathbf{k}$, $\mathbf{w} = 10\mathbf{j}$

157. Use vectors to show that a parallelogram with equal diagonals is a square.

158. Use vectors to show that the diagonals of a rhombus are perpendicular.

159. Show that $\mathbf{u} \cdot (\mathbf{v} + \mathbf{w}) = \mathbf{u} \cdot \mathbf{v} + \mathbf{u} \cdot \mathbf{w}$ is true for any vectors $\mathbf{u}$, $\mathbf{v}$, and $\mathbf{w}$.

160. Verify the identity $\mathbf{u} \cdot (\mathbf{v} + \mathbf{w}) = \mathbf{u} \cdot \mathbf{v} + \mathbf{u} \cdot \mathbf{w}$ for vectors $\mathbf{u} = \langle 1, 0, 4 \rangle$, $\mathbf{v} = \langle -2, 3, 5 \rangle$, and $\mathbf{w} = \langle 4, -2, 6 \rangle$.

For the following problems, the vector **u** is given.

a. Find the direction cosines for the vector u.
b. Find the direction angles for the vector u expressed in degrees. (Round the answer to the nearest integer.)

161. $\mathbf{u} = \langle 2, 2, 1 \rangle$

162. $\mathbf{u} = \mathbf{i} - 2\mathbf{j} + 2\mathbf{k}$

163. $\mathbf{u} = \langle -1, 5, 2 \rangle$

164. $\mathbf{u} = \langle 2, 3, 4 \rangle$

165. Consider $\mathbf{u} = \langle a, b, c \rangle$ a nonzero three-dimensional vector. Let $\cos\alpha$, $\cos\beta$, and $\cos\gamma$ be the directions of the cosines of **u**. Show that $\cos^2\alpha + \cos^2\beta + \cos^2\gamma = 1$.

166. Determine the direction cosines of vector $\mathbf{u} = \mathbf{i} + 2\mathbf{j} + 2\mathbf{k}$ and show they satisfy $\cos^2\alpha + \cos^2\beta + \cos^2\gamma = 1$.

For the following exercises, the vectors **u** and **v** are given.

a. Find the vector projection $\mathrm{w} = \text{proj}_{\mathbf{u}}\mathbf{v}$ of vector **v** onto vector **u**. Express your answer in component form.
b. Find the scalar projection $\text{comp}_{\mathrm{u}}\mathrm{v}$ of vector **v** onto vector **u**.

167. $\mathbf{u} = 5\mathbf{i} + 2\mathbf{j}$, $\mathbf{v} = 2\mathbf{i} + 3\mathbf{j}$

168. $\mathbf{u} = \langle -4, 7 \rangle$, $\mathbf{v} = \langle 3, 5 \rangle$

169. $\mathbf{u} = 3\mathbf{i} + 2\mathbf{k}$, $\mathbf{v} = 2\mathbf{j} + 4\mathbf{k}$

170. $\mathbf{u} = \langle 4, 4, 0 \rangle$, $\mathbf{v} = \langle 0, 4, 1 \rangle$

171. Consider the vectors $\mathbf{u} = 4\mathbf{i} - 3\mathbf{j}$ and $\mathbf{v} = 3\mathbf{i} + 2\mathbf{j}$.

a. Find the component form of vector $\mathbf{w} = \text{proj}_{\mathbf{u}}\mathbf{v}$ that represents the projection of **v** onto **u**.
b. Write the decomposition $\mathbf{v} = \mathbf{w} + \mathbf{q}$ of vector **v** into the orthogonal components **w** and **q**, where **w** is the projection of **v** onto **u** and **q** is a vector orthogonal to the direction of **u**.

172. Consider vectors $\mathbf{u} = 2\mathbf{i} + 4\mathbf{j}$ and $\mathbf{v} = 4\mathbf{j} + 2\mathbf{k}$.

a. Find the component form of vector $\mathbf{w} = \text{proj}_{\mathrm{u}}\mathbf{v}$ that represents the projection of **v** onto **u**.
b. Write the decomposition $\mathbf{v} = \mathbf{w} + \mathbf{q}$ of vector **v** into the orthogonal components **w** and **q**, where **w** is the projection of **v** onto **u** and **q** is a vector orthogonal to the direction of **u**.

173. A methane molecule has a carbon atom situated at the origin and four hydrogen atoms located at points $P(1, 1, -1)$, $Q(1, -1, 1)$, $R(-1, 1, 1)$, and $S(-1, -1, -1)$ (see figure).

a. Find the distance between the hydrogen atoms located at *P* and *R*.

b. Find the angle between vectors $\overrightarrow{OS}$ and $\overrightarrow{OR}$ that connect the carbon atom with the hydrogen atoms located at *S* and *R*, which is also called the *bond angle*. Express the answer in degrees rounded to two decimal places.

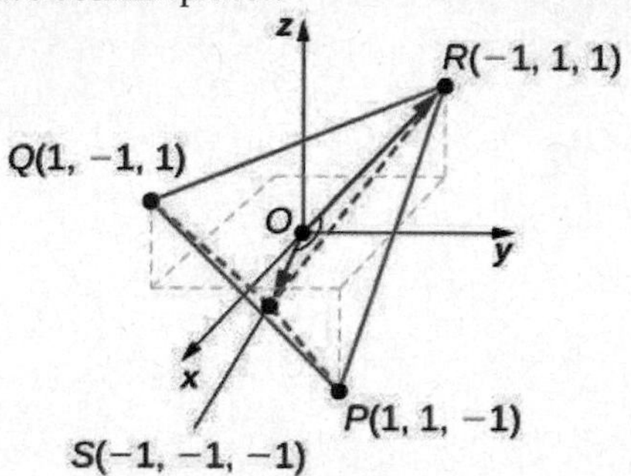

174. **[T]** Find the vectors that join the center of a clock to the hours 1:00, 2:00, and 3:00. Assume the clock is circular with a radius of 1 unit.

175. Find the work done by force $\mathbf{F} = \langle 5, 6, -2 \rangle$ (measured in Newtons) that moves a particle from point $P(3, -1, 0)$ to point $Q(2, 3, 1)$ along a straight line (the distance is measured in meters).

176. **[T]** A sled is pulled by exerting a force of 100 N on a rope that makes an angle of $25°$ with the horizontal. Find the work done in pulling the sled 40 m. (Round the answer to one decimal place.)

177. **[T]** A father is pulling his son on a sled at an angle of $20°$ with the horizontal with a force of 25 lb (see the following image). He pulls the sled in a straight path of 50 ft. How much work was done by the man pulling the sled? (Round the answer to the nearest integer.)

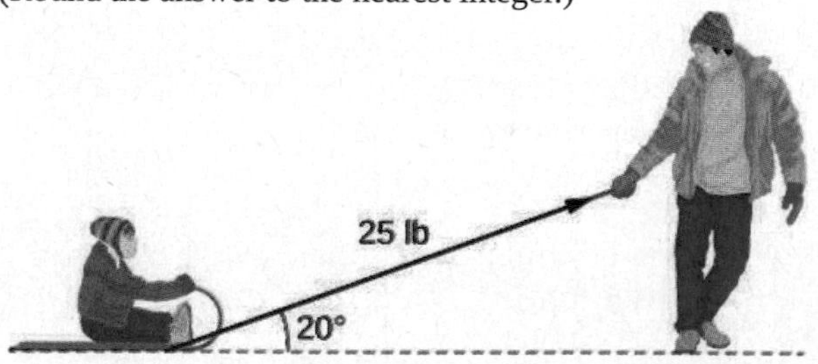

178. **[T]** A car is towed using a force of 1600 N. The rope used to pull the car makes an angle of 25° with the horizontal. Find the work done in towing the car 2 km. Express the answer in joules $(1\text{J} = 1\text{N} \cdot \text{m})$ rounded to the nearest integer.

179. **[T]** A boat sails north aided by a wind blowing in a direction of N30°E with a magnitude of 500 lb. How much work is performed by the wind as the boat moves 100 ft? (Round the answer to two decimal places.)

180. Vector $\mathbf{p} = \langle 150, 225, 375 \rangle$ represents the price of certain models of bicycles sold by a bicycle shop. Vector $\mathbf{n} = \langle 10, 7, 9 \rangle$ represents the number of bicycles sold of each model, respectively. Compute the dot product $\mathbf{p} \cdot \mathbf{n}$ and state its meaning.

181. **[T]** Two forces $\mathbf{F}_1$ and $\mathbf{F}_2$ are represented by vectors with initial points that are at the origin. The first force has a magnitude of 20 lb and the terminal point of the vector is point $P(1, 1, 0)$. The second force has a magnitude of 40 lb and the terminal point of its vector is point $Q(0, 1, 1)$. Let **F** be the resultant force of forces $\mathbf{F}_1$ and $\mathbf{F}_2$.

a. Find the magnitude of **F**. (Round the answer to one decimal place.)

b. Find the direction angles of **F**. (Express the answer in degrees rounded to one decimal place.)

182. **[T]** Consider $\mathbf{r}(t) = \langle \cos t, \sin t, 2t \rangle$ the position vector of a particle at time $t \in [0, 30]$, where the components of **r** are expressed in centimeters and time in seconds. Let $\overrightarrow{OP}$ be the position vector of the particle after 1 sec.

a. Show that all vectors $\overrightarrow{PQ}$, where $Q(x, y, z)$ is an arbitrary point, orthogonal to the instantaneous velocity vector $\mathbf{v}(1)$ of the particle after 1 sec, can be expressed as $\overrightarrow{PQ} = \langle x - \cos 1, y - \sin 1, z - 2 \rangle$, where $x \sin 1 - y \cos 1 - 2z + 4 = 0$. The set of point *Q* describes a plane called the *normal plane* to the path of the particle at point *P*.

b. Use a CAS to visualize the instantaneous velocity vector and the normal plane at point *P* along with the path of the particle.

2.4 | The Cross Product

Learning Objectives

2.4.1 Calculate the cross product of two given vectors.
2.4.2 Use determinants to calculate a cross product.
2.4.3 Find a vector orthogonal to two given vectors.
2.4.4 Determine areas and volumes by using the cross product.
2.4.5 Calculate the torque of a given force and position vector.

Imagine a mechanic turning a wrench to tighten a bolt. The mechanic applies a force at the end of the wrench. This creates rotation, or torque, which tightens the bolt. We can use vectors to represent the force applied by the mechanic, and the distance (radius) from the bolt to the end of the wrench. Then, we can represent torque by a vector oriented along the axis of rotation. Note that the torque vector is orthogonal to both the force vector and the radius vector.

In this section, we develop an operation called the *cross product,* which allows us to find a vector orthogonal to two given vectors. Calculating torque is an important application of cross products, and we examine torque in more detail later in the section.

The Cross Product and Its Properties

The dot product is a multiplication of two vectors that results in a scalar. In this section, we introduce a product of two vectors that generates a third vector orthogonal to the first two. Consider how we might find such a vector. Let $\mathbf{u} = \langle u_1, u_2, u_3 \rangle$ and $\mathbf{v} = \langle v_1, v_2, v_3 \rangle$ be nonzero vectors. We want to find a vector $\mathbf{w} = \langle w_1, w_2, w_3 \rangle$ orthogonal to both $\mathbf{u}$ and $\mathbf{v}$—that is, we want to find $\mathbf{w}$ such that $\mathbf{u} \cdot \mathbf{w} = 0$ and $\mathbf{v} \cdot \mathbf{w} = 0.$ Therefore, $w_1,$ $w_2,$ and w_3 must satisfy

$$\begin{aligned} u_1 w_1 + u_2 w_2 + u_3 w_3 &= 0 \\ v_1 w_1 + v_2 w_2 + v_3 w_3 &= 0. \end{aligned}$$

If we multiply the top equation by v_3 and the bottom equation by u_3 and subtract, we can eliminate the variable $w_3,$ which gives

$$(u_1 v_3 - v_1 u_3)w_1 + (u_2 v_3 - v_2 u_3)w_2 = 0.$$

If we select

$$\begin{aligned} w_1 &= u_2 v_3 - u_3 v_2 \\ w_2 &= -(u_1 v_3 - u_3 v_1), \end{aligned}$$

we get a possible solution vector. Substituting these values back into the original equations gives

$$w_3 = u_1 v_2 - u_2 v_1.$$

That is, vector

$$\mathbf{w} = \langle u_2 v_3 - u_3 v_2, -(u_1 v_3 - u_3 v_1), u_1 v_2 - u_2 v_1 \rangle$$

is orthogonal to both $\mathbf{u}$ and $\mathbf{v},$ which leads us to define the following operation, called the cross product.

Definition

Let $\mathbf{u} = \langle u_1, u_2, u_3 \rangle$ and $\mathbf{v} = \langle v_1, v_2, v_3 \rangle$. Then, the **cross product** $\mathbf{u} \times \mathbf{v}$ is vector

$$\begin{aligned} \mathbf{u} \times \mathbf{v} &= (u_2 v_3 - u_3 v_2)\mathbf{i} - (u_1 v_3 - u_3 v_1)\mathbf{j} + (u_1 v_2 - u_2 v_1)\mathbf{k} \\ &= \langle u_2 v_3 - u_3 v_2, -(u_1 v_3 - u_3 v_1), u_1 v_2 - u_2 v_1 \rangle. \end{aligned} \quad (2.9)$$

From the way we have developed $\mathbf{u} \times \mathbf{v},$ it should be clear that the cross product is orthogonal to both $\mathbf{u}$ and $\mathbf{v}.$ However, it never hurts to check. To show that $\mathbf{u} \times \mathbf{v}$ is orthogonal to $\mathbf{u}$, we calculate the dot product of $\mathbf{u}$ and $\mathbf{u} \times \mathbf{v}$.

$$\begin{aligned} \mathbf{u} \cdot (\mathbf{u} \times \mathbf{v}) &= \langle u_1, u_2, u_3 \rangle \cdot \langle u_2 v_3 - u_3 v_2, -u_1 v_3 + u_3 v_1, u_1 v_2 - u_2 v_1 \rangle \\ &= u_1 (u_2 v_3 - u_3 v_2) + u_2 (-u_1 v_3 + u_3 v_1) + u_3 (u_1 v_2 - u_2 v_1) \\ &= u_1 u_2 v_3 - u_1 u_3 v_2 - u_1 u_2 v_3 + u_2 u_3 v_1 + u_1 u_3 v_2 - u_2 u_3 v_1 \\ &= (u_1 u_2 v_3 - u_1 u_2 v_3) + (-u_1 u_3 v_2 + u_1 u_3 v_2) + (u_2 u_3 v_1 - u_2 u_3 v_1) \\ &= 0 \end{aligned}$$

In a similar manner, we can show that the cross product is also orthogonal to $\mathbf{v}$.

Example 2.31

Finding a Cross Product

Let $\mathbf{p} = \langle -1, 2, 5 \rangle$ and $\mathbf{q} = \langle 4, 0, -3 \rangle$ (**Figure 2.53**). Find $\mathbf{p} \times \mathbf{q}$.

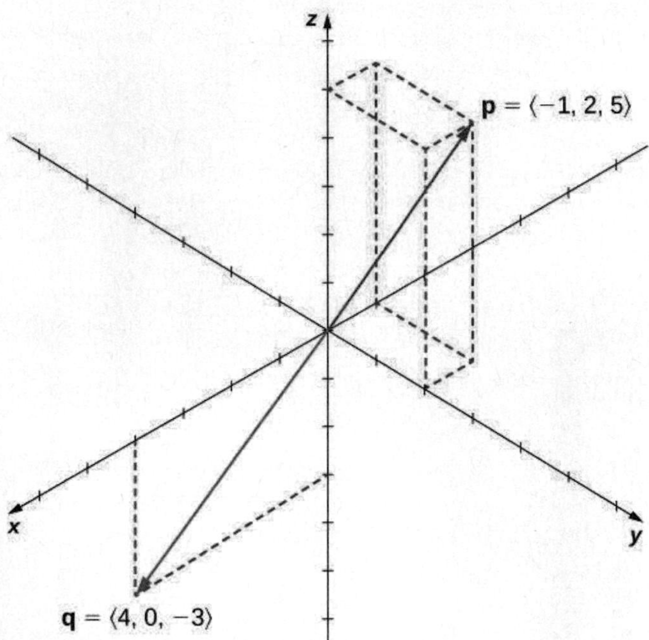

Figure 2.53 Finding a cross product to two given vectors.

Solution

Substitute the components of the vectors into **Equation 2.9**:

$$\begin{aligned} \mathbf{p} \times \mathbf{q} &= \langle -1, 2, 5 \rangle \times \langle 4, 0, -3 \rangle \\ &= \langle p_2 q_3 - p_3 q_2, p_1 q_3 - p_3 q_1, p_1 q_2 - p_2 q_1 \rangle \\ &= \langle 2(-3) - 5(0), -(-1)(-3) + 5(4), (-1)(0) - 2(4) \rangle \\ &= \langle -6, 17, -8 \rangle . \end{aligned}$$

2.30 Find $\mathbf{p} \times \mathbf{q}$ for $\mathbf{p} = \langle 5, 1, 2 \rangle$ and $\mathbf{q} = \langle -2, 0, 1 \rangle$. Express the answer using standard unit vectors.

Although it may not be obvious from **Equation 2.9**, the direction of $\mathbf{u} \times \mathbf{v}$ is given by the right-hand rule. If we hold the right hand out with the fingers pointing in the direction of $\mathbf{u}$, then curl the fingers toward vector $\mathbf{v}$, the thumb points in the direction of the cross product, as shown.

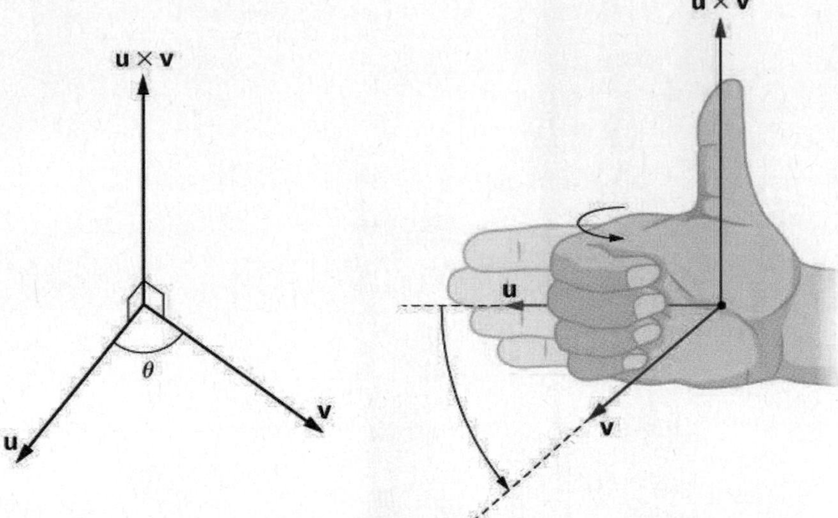

Figure 2.54 The direction of $\mathbf{u} \times \mathbf{v}$ is determined by the right-hand rule.

Notice what this means for the direction of $\mathbf{v} \times \mathbf{u}$. If we apply the right-hand rule to $\mathbf{v} \times \mathbf{u}$, we start with our fingers pointed in the direction of $\mathbf{v}$, then curl our fingers toward the vector $\mathbf{u}$. In this case, the thumb points in the opposite direction of $\mathbf{u} \times \mathbf{v}$. (Try it!)

Example 2.32

Anticommutativity of the Cross Product

Let $\mathbf{u} = \langle 0, 2, 1 \rangle$ and $\mathbf{v} = \langle 3, -1, 0 \rangle$. Calculate $\mathbf{u} \times \mathbf{v}$ and $\mathbf{v} \times \mathbf{u}$ and graph them.

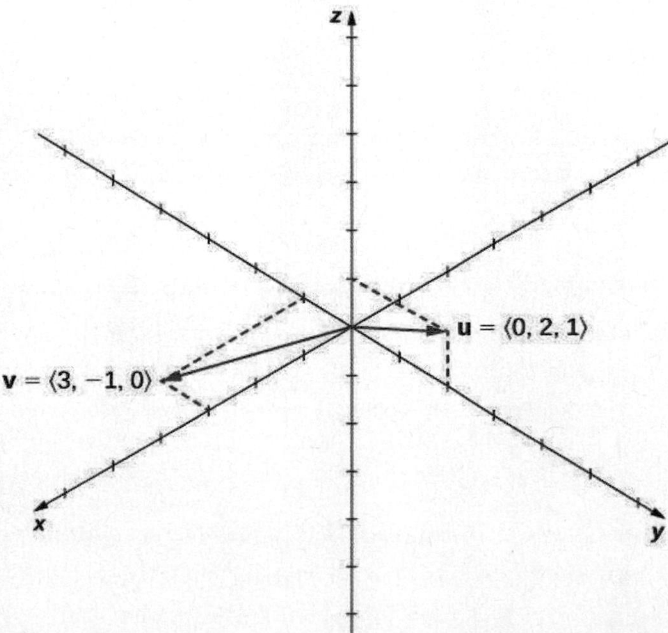

Figure 2.55 Are the cross products $\mathbf{u} \times \mathbf{v}$ and $\mathbf{v} \times \mathbf{u}$ in the same direction?

Solution

We have

$$\begin{aligned} \mathbf{u} \times \mathbf{v} &= \langle (0+1), -(0-3), (0-6) \rangle = \langle 1, 3, -6 \rangle \\ \mathbf{v} \times \mathbf{u} &= \langle (-1-0), -(3-0), (6-0) \rangle = \langle -1, -3, 6 \rangle. \end{aligned}$$

We see that, in this case, $\mathbf{u} \times \mathbf{v} = -(\mathbf{v} \times \mathbf{u})$ (**Figure 2.56**). We prove this in general later in this section.

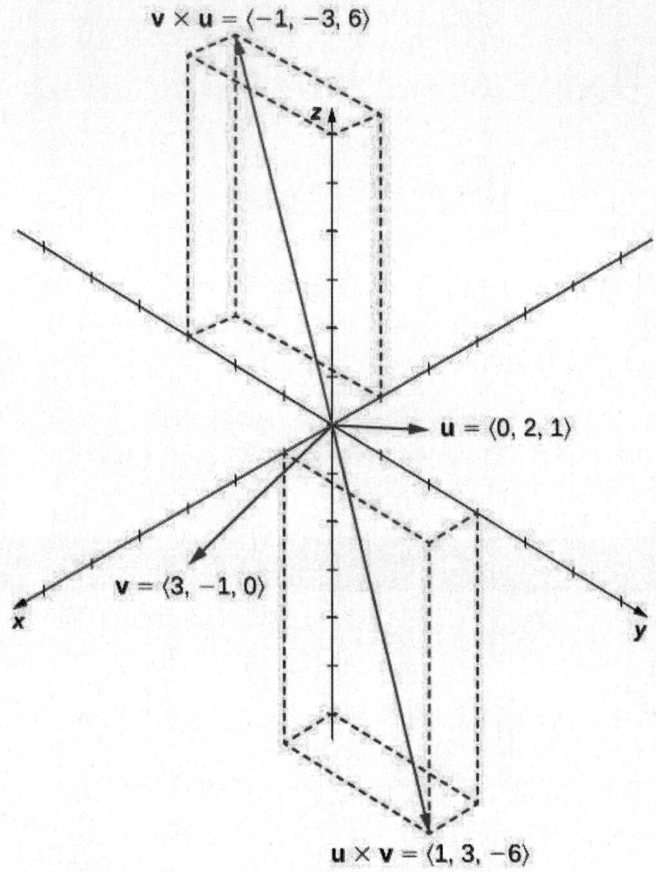

Figure 2.56 The cross products $\mathbf{u} \times \mathbf{v}$ and $\mathbf{v} \times \mathbf{u}$ are both orthogonal to $\mathbf{u}$ and $\mathbf{v},$ but in opposite directions.

2.31 Suppose vectors $\mathbf{u}$ and $\mathbf{v}$ lie in the *xy*-plane (the *z*-component of each vector is zero). Now suppose the *x*- and *y*-components of $\mathbf{u}$ and the *y*-component of $\mathbf{v}$ are all positive, whereas the *x*-component of $\mathbf{v}$ is negative. Assuming the coordinate axes are oriented in the usual positions, in which direction does $\mathbf{u} \times \mathbf{v}$ point?

The cross products of the standard unit vectors $\mathbf{i}, \mathbf{j},$ and $\mathbf{k}$ can be useful for simplifying some calculations, so let's consider these cross products. A straightforward application of the definition shows that

$$\mathbf{i} \times \mathbf{i} = \mathbf{j} \times \mathbf{j} = \mathbf{k} \times \mathbf{k} = \mathbf{0}.$$

(The cross product of two vectors is a vector, so each of these products results in the zero vector, not the scalar $0.$) It's up to you to verify the calculations on your own.

Furthermore, because the cross product of two vectors is orthogonal to each of these vectors, we know that the cross product of $\mathbf{i}$ and $\mathbf{j}$ is parallel to $\mathbf{k}$. Similarly, the vector product of $\mathbf{i}$ and $\mathbf{k}$ is parallel to $\mathbf{j}$, and the vector product of $\mathbf{j}$ and $\mathbf{k}$ is parallel to $\mathbf{i}$. We can use the right-hand rule to determine the direction of each product. Then we have

$$\begin{aligned} \mathbf{i}\times\mathbf{j} &= \mathbf{k} & \mathbf{j}\times\mathbf{i} &= -\mathbf{k} \\ \mathbf{j}\times\mathbf{k} &= \mathbf{i} & \mathbf{k}\times\mathbf{j} &= -\mathbf{i} \\ \mathbf{k}\times\mathbf{i} &= \mathbf{j} & \mathbf{i}\times\mathbf{k} &= -\mathbf{j}. \end{aligned}$$

These formulas come in handy later.

Example 2.33

Cross Product of Standard Unit Vectors

Find $\mathbf{i}\times(\mathbf{j}\times\mathbf{k})$.

Solution

We know that $\mathbf{j}\times\mathbf{k}=\mathbf{i}$. Therefore, $\mathbf{i}\times(\mathbf{j}\times\mathbf{k})=\mathbf{i}\times\mathbf{i}=\mathbf{0}$.

2.32 Find $(\mathbf{i}\times\mathbf{j})\times(\mathbf{k}\times\mathbf{i})$.

As we have seen, the dot product is often called the *scalar product* because it results in a scalar. The cross product results in a vector, so it is sometimes called the **vector product**. These operations are both versions of vector multiplication, but they have very different properties and applications. Let's explore some properties of the cross product. We prove only a few of them. Proofs of the other properties are left as exercises.

Theorem 2.6: Properties of the Cross Product

Let $\mathbf{u}$, $\mathbf{v}$, and $\mathbf{w}$ be vectors in space, and let c be a scalar.

i.	$\mathbf{u}\times\mathbf{v} = -(\mathbf{v}\times\mathbf{u})$	Anticommutative property
ii.	$\mathbf{u}\times(\mathbf{v}+\mathbf{w}) = \mathbf{u}\times\mathbf{v}+\mathbf{u}\times\mathbf{w}$	Distributive property
iii.	$c(\mathbf{u}\times\mathbf{v}) = (c\mathbf{u})\times\mathbf{v}=\mathbf{u}\times(c\mathbf{v})$	Multiplication by a constant
iv.	$\mathbf{u}\times\mathbf{0} = \mathbf{0}\times\mathbf{u}=\mathbf{0}$	Cross product of the zero vector
v.	$\mathbf{v}\times\mathbf{v} = \mathbf{0}$	Cross product of a vector with itself
vi.	$\mathbf{u}\cdot(\mathbf{v}\times\mathbf{w}) = (\mathbf{u}\times\mathbf{v})\cdot\mathbf{w}$	Scalar triple product

Proof

For property i., we want to show $\mathbf{u}\times\mathbf{v}=-(\mathbf{v}\times\mathbf{u})$. We have

$$\begin{aligned} \mathbf{u}\times\mathbf{v} &= \langle u_1, u_2, u_3\rangle\times\langle v_1, v_2, v_3\rangle \\ &= \langle u_2v_3-u_3v_2, -u_1v_3+u_3v_1, u_1v_2-u_2v_1\rangle \\ &= -\langle u_3v_2-u_2v_3, -u_3v_1+u_1v_3, u_2v_1-u_1v_2\rangle \\ &= -\langle v_1, v_2, v_3\rangle\times\langle u_1, u_2, u_3\rangle \\ &= -(\mathbf{v}\times\mathbf{u}). \end{aligned}$$

Unlike most operations we've seen, the cross product is not commutative. This makes sense if we think about the right-hand rule.

For property iv., this follows directly from the definition of the cross product. We have

$$\begin{aligned}\mathbf{u}\times\mathbf{0} &= \langle u_2(0)-u_3(0), -(u_2(0)-u_3(0)), u_1(0)-u_2(0)\rangle \\ &= \langle 0, 0, 0\rangle = \mathbf{0}.\end{aligned}$$

Then, by property i., $\mathbf{0}\times\mathbf{u}=\mathbf{0}$ as well. Remember that the dot product of a vector and the zero vector is the *scalar* 0, whereas the cross product of a vector with the zero vector is the *vector* $\mathbf{0}$.

Property vi. looks like the associative property, but note the change in operations:

$$\begin{aligned}\mathbf{u}\cdot(\mathbf{v}\times\mathbf{w}) &= \mathbf{u}\cdot\langle v_2w_3-v_3w_2, -v_1w_3+v_3w_1, v_1w_2-v_2w_1\rangle \\ &= u_1(v_2w_3-v_3w_2)+u_2(-v_1w_3+v_3w_1)+u_3(v_1w_2-v_2w_1) \\ &= u_1v_2w_3-u_1v_3w_2-u_2v_1w_3+u_2v_3w_1+u_3v_1w_2-u_3v_2w_1 \\ &= (u_2v_3-u_3v_2)w_1+(u_3v_1-u_1v_3)w_2+(u_1v_2-u_2v_1)w_3 \\ &= \langle u_2v_3-u_3v_2, u_3v_1-u_1v_3, u_1v_2-u_2v_1\rangle\cdot\langle w_1, w_2, w_3\rangle \\ &= (\mathbf{u}\times\mathbf{v})\cdot\mathbf{w}.\end{aligned}$$

□

Example 2.34

Using the Properties of the Cross Product

Use the cross product properties to calculate $(2\mathbf{i}\times 3\mathbf{j})\times\mathbf{j}$.

Solution

$$\begin{aligned}(2\mathbf{i}\times 3\mathbf{j})\times\mathbf{j} &= 2(\mathbf{i}\times 3\mathbf{j})\times\mathbf{j} \\ &= 2(3)(\mathbf{i}\times\mathbf{j})\times\mathbf{j} \\ &= (6\mathbf{k})\times\mathbf{j} \\ &= 6(\mathbf{k}\times\mathbf{j}) \\ &= 6(-\mathbf{i}) = -6\mathbf{i}.\end{aligned}$$

2.33 Use the properties of the cross product to calculate $(\mathbf{i}\times\mathbf{k})\times(\mathbf{k}\times\mathbf{j})$.

So far in this section, we have been concerned with the direction of the vector $\mathbf{u}\times\mathbf{v}$, but we have not discussed its magnitude. It turns out there is a simple expression for the magnitude of $\mathbf{u}\times\mathbf{v}$ involving the magnitudes of $\mathbf{u}$ and $\mathbf{v}$, and the sine of the angle between them.

Theorem 2.7: Magnitude of the Cross Product

Let $\mathbf{u}$ and $\mathbf{v}$ be vectors, and let θ be the angle between them. Then, $\|\mathbf{u}\times\mathbf{v}\| = \|\mathbf{u}\|\cdot\|\mathbf{v}\|\cdot\sin\theta$.

Proof

Let $\mathbf{u}=\langle u_1, u_2, u_3\rangle$ and $\mathbf{v}=\langle v_1, v_2, v_3\rangle$ be vectors, and let θ denote the angle between them. Then

$$\begin{aligned}
\|\mathbf{u}\times\mathbf{v}\|^2 &= (u_2v_3-u_3v_2)^2+(u_3v_1-u_1v_3)^2+(u_1v_2-u_2v_1)^2 \\
&= u_2^2v_3^2-2u_2u_3v_2v_3+u_3^2v_2^2+u_3^2v_1^2-2u_1u_3v_1v_3+u_1^2v_3^2+u_1^2v_2^2-2u_1u_2v_1v_2+u_2^2v_1^2 \\
&= u_1^2v_1^2+u_1^2v_2^2+u_1^2v_3^2+u_2^2v_1^2+u_2^2v_2^2+u_2^2v_3^2+u_3^2v_1^2+u_3^2v_2^2+u_3^2v_3^2 \\
&\quad -\left(u_1^2v_1^2+u_2^2v_2^2+u_3^2v_3^2+2u_1u_2v_1v_2+2u_1u_3v_1v_3+2u_2u_3v_2v_3\right) \\
&= \left(u_1^2+u_2^2+u_3^2\right)\left(v_1^2+v_2^2+v_3^2\right)-(u_1v_1+u_2v_2+u_3v_3)^2 \\
&= \|\mathbf{u}\|^2\|\mathbf{v}\|^2-(\mathbf{u}\cdot\mathbf{v})^2 \\
&= \|\mathbf{u}\|^2\|\mathbf{v}\|^2-\|\mathbf{u}\|^2\|\mathbf{v}\|^2\cos^2\theta \\
&= \|\mathbf{u}\|^2\|\mathbf{v}\|^2\left(1-\cos^2\theta\right) \\
&= \|\mathbf{u}\|^2\|\mathbf{v}\|^2\left(\sin^2\theta\right).
\end{aligned}$$

Taking square roots and noting that $\sqrt{\sin^2\theta}=\sin\theta$ for $0\le\theta\le 180°$, we have the desired result:

$$\|\mathbf{u}\times\mathbf{v}\| = \|\mathbf{u}\|\,\|\mathbf{v}\|\sin\theta.$$

□

This definition of the cross product allows us to visualize or interpret the product geometrically. It is clear, for example, that the cross product is defined only for vectors in three dimensions, not for vectors in two dimensions. In two dimensions, it is impossible to generate a vector simultaneously orthogonal to two nonparallel vectors.

Example 2.35

Calculating the Cross Product

Use **Properties of the Cross Product** to find the magnitude of the cross product of $\mathbf{u}=\langle 0, 4, 0\rangle$ and $\mathbf{v}=\langle 0, 0, -3\rangle$.

Solution

We have

$$\begin{aligned}
\|\mathbf{u}\times\mathbf{v}\| &= \|\mathbf{u}\|\cdot\|\mathbf{v}\|\cdot\sin\theta \\
&= \sqrt{0^2+4^2+0^2}\cdot\sqrt{0^2+0^2+(-3)^2}\cdot\sin\frac{\pi}{2} \\
&= 4(3)(1)=12.
\end{aligned}$$

2.34 Use **Properties of the Cross Product** to find the magnitude of $\mathbf{u}\times\mathbf{v}$, where $\mathbf{u}=\langle -8, 0, 0\rangle$ and $\mathbf{v}=\langle 0, 2, 0\rangle$.

Determinants and the Cross Product

Using **Equation 2.9** to find the cross product of two vectors is straightforward, and it presents the cross product in the useful component form. The formula, however, is complicated and difficult to remember. Fortunately, we have an alternative. We can calculate the cross product of two vectors using **determinant** notation.

A 2×2 determinant is defined by

$$\begin{vmatrix} a_1 & a_2 \\ b_1 & b_2 \end{vmatrix} = a_1b_2-b_1a_2.$$

For example,

$$\begin{vmatrix} 3 & -2 \\ 5 & 1 \end{vmatrix} = 3(1) - 5(-2) = 3 + 10 = 13.$$

A 3×3 determinant is defined in terms of 2×2 determinants as follows:

$$\begin{vmatrix} a_1 & a_2 & a_3 \\ b_1 & b_2 & b_3 \\ c_1 & c_2 & c_3 \end{vmatrix} = a_1 \begin{vmatrix} b_2 & b_3 \\ c_2 & c_3 \end{vmatrix} - a_2 \begin{vmatrix} b_1 & b_3 \\ c_1 & c_3 \end{vmatrix} + a_3 \begin{vmatrix} b_1 & b_2 \\ c_1 & c_2 \end{vmatrix}. \quad (2.10)$$

Equation 2.10 is referred to as the *expansion of the determinant along the first row*. Notice that the multipliers of each of the 2×2 determinants on the right side of this expression are the entries in the first row of the 3×3 determinant. Furthermore, each of the 2×2 determinants contains the entries from the 3×3 determinant that would remain if you crossed out the row and column containing the multiplier. Thus, for the first term on the right, a_1 is the multiplier, and the 2×2 determinant contains the entries that remain if you cross out the first row and first column of the 3×3 determinant. Similarly, for the second term, the multiplier is a_2, and the 2×2 determinant contains the entries that remain if you cross out the first row and second column of the 3×3 determinant. Notice, however, that the coefficient of the second term is negative. The third term can be calculated in similar fashion.

Example 2.36

Using Expansion Along the First Row to Compute a 3×3 Determinant

Evaluate the determinant $\begin{vmatrix} 2 & 5 & -1 \\ -1 & 1 & 3 \\ -2 & 3 & 4 \end{vmatrix}$.

Solution

We have

$$\begin{aligned} \begin{vmatrix} 2 & 5 & -1 \\ -1 & 1 & 3 \\ -2 & 3 & 4 \end{vmatrix} &= 2\begin{vmatrix} 1 & 3 \\ 3 & 4 \end{vmatrix} - 5\begin{vmatrix} -1 & 3 \\ -2 & 4 \end{vmatrix} - 1\begin{vmatrix} -1 & 1 \\ -2 & 3 \end{vmatrix} \\ &= 2(4-9) - 5(-4+6) - 1(-3+2) \\ &= 2(-5) - 5(2) - 1(-1) = -10 - 10 + 1 \\ &= -19. \end{aligned}$$

2.35 Evaluate the determinant $\begin{vmatrix} 1 & -2 & -1 \\ 3 & 2 & -3 \\ 1 & 5 & 4 \end{vmatrix}$.

Technically, determinants are defined only in terms of arrays of real numbers. However, the determinant notation provides a useful mnemonic device for the cross product formula.

Rule: Cross Product Calculated by a Determinant

Let $\mathbf{u} = \langle u_1, u_2, u_3 \rangle$ and $\mathbf{v} = \langle v_1, v_2, v_3 \rangle$ be vectors. Then the cross product $\mathbf{u} \times \mathbf{v}$ is given by

$$\mathbf{u} \times \mathbf{v} = \begin{vmatrix} \mathbf{i} & \mathbf{j} & \mathbf{k} \\ u_1 & u_2 & u_3 \\ v_1 & v_2 & v_3 \end{vmatrix} = \begin{vmatrix} u_2 & u_3 \\ v_2 & v_3 \end{vmatrix}\mathbf{i} - \begin{vmatrix} u_1 & u_3 \\ v_1 & v_3 \end{vmatrix}\mathbf{j} + \begin{vmatrix} u_1 & u_2 \\ v_1 & v_2 \end{vmatrix}\mathbf{k}.$$

Example 2.37

Using Determinant Notation to find $\mathbf{p} \times \mathbf{q}$

Let $\mathbf{p} = \langle -1, 2, 5 \rangle$ and $\mathbf{q} = \langle 4, 0, -3 \rangle$. Find $\mathbf{p} \times \mathbf{q}$.

Solution

We set up our determinant by putting the standard unit vectors across the first row, the components of $\mathbf{u}$ in the second row, and the components of $\mathbf{v}$ in the third row. Then, we have

$$\begin{aligned}\mathbf{p} \times \mathbf{q} &= \begin{vmatrix} \mathbf{i} & \mathbf{j} & \mathbf{k} \\ -1 & 2 & 5 \\ 4 & 0 & -3 \end{vmatrix} = \begin{vmatrix} 2 & 5 \\ 0 & -3 \end{vmatrix}\mathbf{i} - \begin{vmatrix} -1 & 5 \\ 4 & -3 \end{vmatrix}\mathbf{j} + \begin{vmatrix} -1 & 2 \\ 4 & 0 \end{vmatrix}\mathbf{k} \\ &= (-6 - 0)\mathbf{i} - (3 - 20)\mathbf{j} + (0 - 8)\mathbf{k} \\ &= -6\mathbf{i} + 17\mathbf{j} - 8\mathbf{k}.\end{aligned}$$

Notice that this answer confirms the calculation of the cross product in **Example 2.31**.

2.36 Use determinant notation to find $\mathbf{a} \times \mathbf{b}$, where $\mathbf{a} = \langle 8, 2, 3 \rangle$ and $\mathbf{b} = \langle -1, 0, 4 \rangle$.

Using the Cross Product

The cross product is very useful for several types of calculations, including finding a vector orthogonal to two given vectors, computing areas of triangles and parallelograms, and even determining the volume of the three-dimensional geometric shape made of parallelograms known as a *parallelepiped*. The following examples illustrate these calculations.

Example 2.38

Finding a Unit Vector Orthogonal to Two Given Vectors

Let $\mathbf{a} = \langle 5, 2, -1 \rangle$ and $\mathbf{b} = \langle 0, -1, 4 \rangle$. Find a unit vector orthogonal to both $\mathbf{a}$ and $\mathbf{b}$.

Solution

The cross product $\mathbf{a} \times \mathbf{b}$ is orthogonal to both vectors $\mathbf{a}$ and $\mathbf{b}$. We can calculate it with a determinant:

$$\begin{aligned}\mathbf{a} \times \mathbf{b} &= \begin{vmatrix} \mathbf{i} & \mathbf{j} & \mathbf{k} \\ 5 & 2 & -1 \\ 0 & -1 & 4 \end{vmatrix} = \begin{vmatrix} 2 & -1 \\ -1 & 4 \end{vmatrix}\mathbf{i} - \begin{vmatrix} 5 & -1 \\ 0 & 4 \end{vmatrix}\mathbf{j} + \begin{vmatrix} 5 & 2 \\ 0 & -1 \end{vmatrix}\mathbf{k} \\ &= (8 - 1)\mathbf{i} - (20 - 0)\mathbf{j} + (-5 - 0)\mathbf{k} \\ &= 7\mathbf{i} - 20\mathbf{j} - 5\mathbf{k}.\end{aligned}$$

Normalize this vector to find a unit vector in the same direction:

$$\| \mathbf{a} \times \mathbf{b} \| = \sqrt{(7)^2 + (-20)^2 + (-5)^2} = \sqrt{474}.$$

Thus, $\left\langle \frac{7}{\sqrt{474}}, \frac{-20}{\sqrt{474}}, \frac{-5}{\sqrt{474}} \right\rangle$ is a unit vector orthogonal to $\mathbf{a}$ and $\mathbf{b}$.

2.37 Find a unit vector orthogonal to both $\mathbf{a}$ and $\mathbf{b}$, where $\mathbf{a} = \langle 4, 0, 3 \rangle$ and $\mathbf{b} = \langle 1, 1, 4 \rangle$.

To use the cross product for calculating areas, we state and prove the following theorem.

Theorem 2.8: Area of a Parallelogram

If we locate vectors $\mathbf{u}$ and $\mathbf{v}$ such that they form adjacent sides of a parallelogram, then the area of the parallelogram is given by $\|\mathbf{u} \times \mathbf{v}\|$ (**Figure 2.57**).

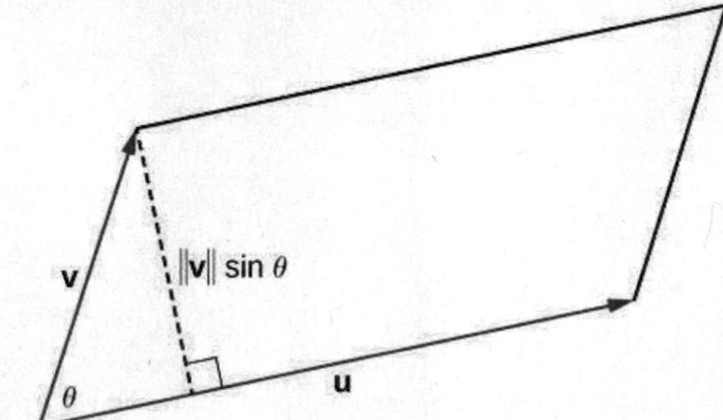

Figure 2.57 The parallelogram with adjacent sides $\mathbf{u}$ and $\mathbf{v}$ has base $\|\mathbf{u}\|$ and height $\|\mathbf{v}\| \sin \theta$.

Proof

We show that the magnitude of the cross product is equal to the base times height of the parallelogram.

$$\begin{aligned} \text{Area of a parallelogram} &= \text{base} \times \text{height} \\ &= \|\mathbf{u}\| (\|\mathbf{v}\| \sin \theta) \\ &= \|\mathbf{u} \times \mathbf{v}\| \end{aligned}$$

□

Example 2.39

Finding the Area of a Triangle

Let $P = (1, 0, 0)$, $Q = (0, 1, 0)$, and $R = (0, 0, 1)$ be the vertices of a triangle (**Figure 2.58**). Find its area.

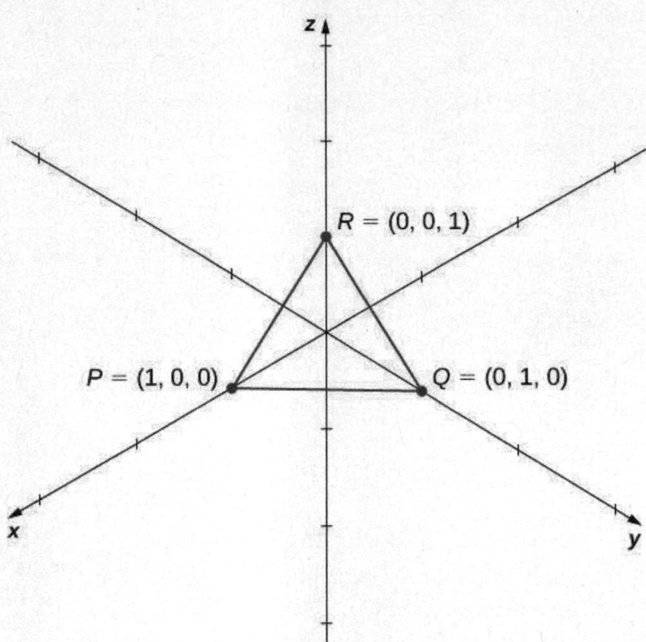

Figure 2.58 Finding the area of a triangle by using the cross product.

Solution

We have $\overrightarrow{PQ} = \langle 0-1, 1-0, 0-0 \rangle = \langle -1, 1, 0 \rangle$ and $\overrightarrow{PR} = \langle 0-1, 0-0, 1-0 \rangle = \langle -1, 0, 1 \rangle$. The area of the parallelogram with adjacent sides $\overrightarrow{PQ}$ and $\overrightarrow{PR}$ is given by $\| \overrightarrow{PQ} \times \overrightarrow{PR} \|$:

$$\begin{aligned} \overrightarrow{PQ} \times \overrightarrow{PR} &= \begin{vmatrix} \mathbf{i} & \mathbf{j} & \mathbf{k} \\ -1 & 1 & 0 \\ -1 & 0 & 1 \end{vmatrix} = (1-0)\mathbf{i} - (-1-0)\mathbf{j} + (0-(-1))\mathbf{k} = \mathbf{i} + \mathbf{j} + \mathbf{k} \\ \| \overrightarrow{PQ} \times \overrightarrow{PR} \| &= \| \langle 1, 1, 1 \rangle \| = \sqrt{1^2 + 1^2 + 1^2} = \sqrt{3}. \end{aligned}$$

The area of ΔPQR is half the area of the parallelogram, or $\sqrt{3}/2$.

2.38 Find the area of the parallelogram $PQRS$ with vertices $P(1, 1, 0)$, $Q(7, 1, 0)$, $R(9, 4, 2)$, and $S(3, 4, 2)$.

The Triple Scalar Product

Because the cross product of two vectors is a vector, it is possible to combine the dot product and the cross product. The dot product of a vector with the cross product of two other vectors is called the triple scalar product because the result is a scalar.

Definition

The **triple scalar product** of vectors $\mathbf{u}$, $\mathbf{v}$, and $\mathbf{w}$ is $\mathbf{u} \cdot (\mathbf{v} \times \mathbf{w})$.

Theorem 2.9: Calculating a Triple Scalar Product

The triple scalar product of vectors $\mathbf{u} = u_1\mathbf{i} + u_2\mathbf{j} + u_3\mathbf{k}$, $\mathbf{v} = v_1\mathbf{i} + v_2\mathbf{j} + v_3\mathbf{k}$, and $\mathbf{w} = w_1\mathbf{i} + w_2\mathbf{j} + w_3\mathbf{k}$ is the determinant of the 3×3 matrix formed by the components of the vectors:

$$\mathbf{u} \cdot (\mathbf{v} \times \mathbf{w}) = \begin{vmatrix} u_1 & u_2 & u_3 \\ v_1 & v_2 & v_3 \\ w_1 & w_2 & w_3 \end{vmatrix}.$$

Proof

The calculation is straightforward.

$$\begin{aligned} \mathbf{u} \cdot (\mathbf{v} \times \mathbf{w}) &= \langle u_1, u_2, u_3 \rangle \cdot \langle v_2w_3 - v_3w_2, -v_1w_3 + v_3w_1, v_1w_2 - v_2w_1 \rangle \\ &= u_1(v_2w_3 - v_3w_2) + u_2(-v_1w_3 + v_3w_1) + u_3(v_1w_2 - v_2w_1) \\ &= u_1(v_2w_3 - v_3w_2) - u_2(v_1w_3 - v_3w_1) + u_3(v_1w_2 - v_2w_1) \\ &= \begin{vmatrix} u_1 & u_2 & u_3 \\ v_1 & v_2 & v_3 \\ w_1 & w_2 & w_3 \end{vmatrix} \end{aligned}$$

□

Example 2.40

Calculating the Triple Scalar Product

Let $\mathbf{u} = \langle 1, 3, 5 \rangle$, $\mathbf{v} = \langle 2, -1, 0 \rangle$ and $\mathbf{w} = \langle -3, 0, -1 \rangle$. Calculate the triple scalar product $\mathbf{u} \cdot (\mathbf{v} \times \mathbf{w})$.

Solution

Apply **Calculating a Triple Scalar Product** directly:

$$\begin{aligned} \mathbf{u} \cdot (\mathbf{v} \times \mathbf{w}) &= \begin{vmatrix} 1 & 3 & 5 \\ 2 & -1 & 0 \\ -3 & 0 & -1 \end{vmatrix} \\ &= 1\begin{vmatrix} -1 & 0 \\ 0 & -1 \end{vmatrix} - 3\begin{vmatrix} 2 & 0 \\ -3 & -1 \end{vmatrix} + 5\begin{vmatrix} 2 & -1 \\ -3 & 0 \end{vmatrix} \\ &= (1 - 0) - 3(-2 - 0) + 5(0 - 3) \\ &= 1 + 6 - 15 = -8. \end{aligned}$$

2.39 Calculate the triple scalar product $\mathbf{a} \cdot (\mathbf{b} \times \mathbf{c})$, where $\mathbf{a} = \langle 2, -4, 1 \rangle$, $\mathbf{b} = \langle 0, 3, -1 \rangle$, and $\mathbf{c} = \langle 5, -3, 3 \rangle$.

When we create a matrix from three vectors, we must be careful about the order in which we list the vectors. If we list them in a matrix in one order and then rearrange the rows, the absolute value of the determinant remains unchanged. However, each time two rows switch places, the determinant changes sign:

$$\begin{vmatrix} a_1 & a_2 & a_3 \\ b_1 & b_2 & b_3 \\ c_1 & c_2 & c_3 \end{vmatrix} = d \quad \begin{vmatrix} b_1 & b_2 & b_3 \\ a_1 & a_2 & a_3 \\ c_1 & c_2 & c_3 \end{vmatrix} = -d \quad \begin{vmatrix} b_1 & b_2 & b_3 \\ c_1 & c_2 & c_3 \\ a_1 & a_2 & a_3 \end{vmatrix} = d \quad \begin{vmatrix} c_1 & c_2 & c_3 \\ b_1 & b_2 & b_3 \\ a_1 & a_2 & a_3 \end{vmatrix} = -d.$$

Verifying this fact is straightforward, but rather messy. Let's take a look at this with an example:

$$\begin{vmatrix} 1 & 2 & 1 \\ -2 & 0 & 3 \\ 4 & 1 & -1 \end{vmatrix} = \begin{vmatrix} 0 & 3 \\ 1 & -1 \end{vmatrix} - 2\begin{vmatrix} -2 & 3 \\ 4 & -1 \end{vmatrix} + \begin{vmatrix} -2 & 0 \\ 4 & 1 \end{vmatrix}$$
$$= (0-3) - 2(2-12) + (-2-0) = -3 + 20 - 2 = 15.$$

Switching the top two rows we have

$$\begin{vmatrix} -2 & 0 & 3 \\ 1 & 2 & 1 \\ 4 & 1 & -1 \end{vmatrix} = -2\begin{vmatrix} 2 & 1 \\ 1 & -1 \end{vmatrix} + 3\begin{vmatrix} 1 & 2 \\ 4 & 1 \end{vmatrix} = -2(-2-1) + 3(1-8) = 6 - 21 = -15.$$

Rearranging vectors in the triple products is equivalent to reordering the rows in the matrix of the determinant. Let $\mathbf{u} = u_1\mathbf{i} + u_2\mathbf{j} + u_3\mathbf{k}$, $\mathbf{v} = v_1\mathbf{i} + v_2\mathbf{j} + v_3\mathbf{k}$, and $\mathbf{w} = w_1\mathbf{i} + w_2\mathbf{j} + w_3\mathbf{k}$. Applying **Calculating a Triple Scalar Product**, we have

$$\mathbf{u} \cdot (\mathbf{v} \times \mathbf{w}) = \begin{vmatrix} u_1 & u_2 & u_3 \\ v_1 & v_2 & v_3 \\ w_1 & w_2 & w_3 \end{vmatrix} \quad \text{and} \quad \mathbf{u} \cdot (\mathbf{w} \times \mathbf{v}) = \begin{vmatrix} u_1 & u_2 & u_3 \\ w_1 & w_2 & w_3 \\ v_1 & v_2 & v_3 \end{vmatrix}.$$

We can obtain the determinant for calculating $\mathbf{u} \cdot (\mathbf{w} \times \mathbf{v})$ by switching the bottom two rows of $\mathbf{u} \cdot (\mathbf{v} \times \mathbf{w})$. Therefore, $\mathbf{u} \cdot (\mathbf{v} \times \mathbf{w}) = -\mathbf{u} \cdot (\mathbf{w} \times \mathbf{v})$.

Following this reasoning and exploring the different ways we can interchange variables in the triple scalar product lead to the following identities:

$$\begin{aligned} \mathbf{u} \cdot (\mathbf{v} \times \mathbf{w}) &= -\mathbf{u} \cdot (\mathbf{w} \times \mathbf{v}) \\ \mathbf{u} \cdot (\mathbf{v} \times \mathbf{w}) &= \mathbf{v} \cdot (\mathbf{w} \times \mathbf{u}) = \mathbf{w} \cdot (\mathbf{u} \times \mathbf{v}). \end{aligned}$$

Let $\mathbf{u}$ and $\mathbf{v}$ be two vectors in standard position. If $\mathbf{u}$ and $\mathbf{v}$ are not scalar multiples of each other, then these vectors form adjacent sides of a parallelogram. We saw in **Area of a Parallelogram** that the area of this parallelogram is $\| \mathbf{u} \times \mathbf{v} \|$. Now suppose we add a third vector $\mathbf{w}$ that does not lie in the same plane as $\mathbf{u}$ and $\mathbf{v}$ but still shares the same initial point. Then these vectors form three edges of a **parallelepiped**, a three-dimensional prism with six faces that are each parallelograms, as shown in **Figure 2.59**. The volume of this prism is the product of the figure's height and the area of its base. The triple scalar product of $\mathbf{u}$, $\mathbf{v}$, and $\mathbf{w}$ provides a simple method for calculating the volume of the parallelepiped defined by these vectors.

Theorem 2.10: Volume of a Parallelepiped

The volume of a parallelepiped with adjacent edges given by the vectors $\mathbf{u}$, $\mathbf{v}$, and $\mathbf{w}$ is the absolute value of the triple scalar product:

$$V = |\mathbf{u} \cdot (\mathbf{v} \times \mathbf{w})|.$$

See **Figure 2.59**.

Note that, as the name indicates, the triple scalar product produces a scalar. The volume formula just presented uses the absolute value of a scalar quantity.

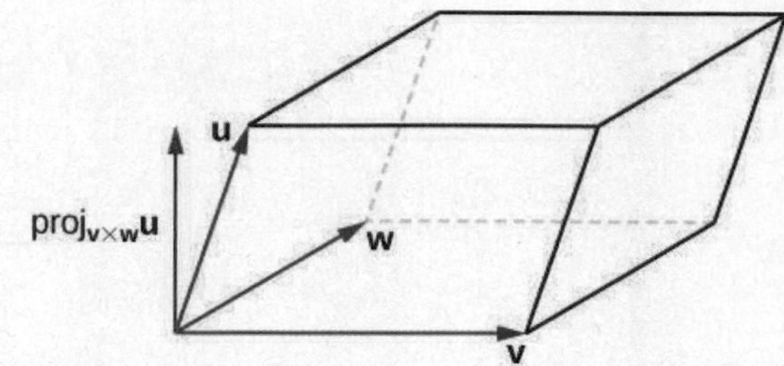

Figure 2.59 The height of the parallelepiped is given by $\|\text{proj}_{\mathbf{v}\times\mathbf{w}}\mathbf{u}\|$.

Proof

The area of the base of the parallelepiped is given by $\|\mathbf{v}\times\mathbf{w}\|$. The height of the figure is given by $\|\text{proj}_{\mathbf{v}\times\mathbf{w}}\mathbf{u}\|$. The volume of the parallelepiped is the product of the height and the area of the base, so we have

$$\begin{aligned} V &= \|\text{proj}_{\mathbf{v}\times\mathbf{w}}\mathbf{u}\|\ \|\mathbf{v}\times\mathbf{w}\| \\ &= \left|\frac{\mathbf{u}\cdot(\mathbf{v}\times\mathbf{w})}{\|\mathbf{v}\times\mathbf{w}\|}\right|\ \|\mathbf{v}\times\mathbf{w}\| \\ &= |\mathbf{u}\cdot(\mathbf{v}\times\mathbf{w})|. \end{aligned}$$

□

Example 2.41

Calculating the Volume of a Parallelepiped

Let $\mathbf{u} = \langle -1, -2, 1\rangle$, $\mathbf{v} = \langle 4, 3, 2\rangle$, and $\mathbf{w} = \langle 0, -5, -2\rangle$. Find the volume of the parallelepiped with adjacent edges $\mathbf{u}$, $\mathbf{v}$, and $\mathbf{w}$ (**Figure 2.60**).

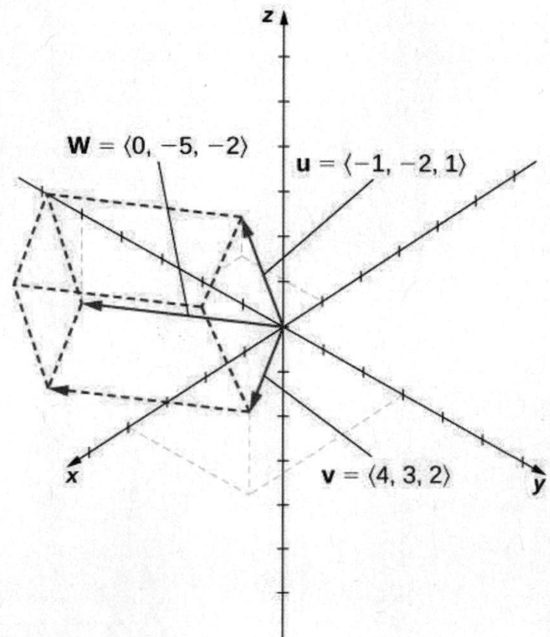

Figure 2.60

Solution

We have

$$\begin{aligned} \mathbf{u} \cdot (\mathbf{v} \times \mathbf{w}) &= \begin{vmatrix} -1 & -2 & 1 \\ 4 & 3 & 2 \\ 0 & -5 & -2 \end{vmatrix} = (-1)\begin{vmatrix} 3 & 2 \\ -5 & -2 \end{vmatrix} + 2\begin{vmatrix} 4 & 2 \\ 0 & -2 \end{vmatrix} + \begin{vmatrix} 4 & 3 \\ 0 & -5 \end{vmatrix} \\ &= (-1)(-6+10) + 2(-8-0) + (-20-0) \\ &= -4 - 16 - 20 \\ &= -40. \end{aligned}$$

Thus, the volume of the parallelepiped is $|-40| = 40$ units^3.

2.40 Find the volume of the parallelepiped formed by the vectors $\mathbf{a} = 3\mathbf{i} + 4\mathbf{j} - \mathbf{k}$, $\mathbf{b} = 2\mathbf{i} - \mathbf{j} - \mathbf{k}$, and $\mathbf{c} = 3\mathbf{j} + \mathbf{k}$.

Applications of the Cross Product

The cross product appears in many practical applications in mathematics, physics, and engineering. Let's examine some of these applications here, including the idea of torque, with which we began this section. Other applications show up in later chapters, particularly in our study of vector fields such as gravitational and electromagnetic fields (**Introduction to Vector Calculus**).

Example 2.42

Using the Triple Scalar Product

Use the triple scalar product to show that vectors $\mathbf{u} = \langle 2, 0, 5 \rangle$, $\mathbf{v} = \langle 2, 2, 4 \rangle$, and $\mathbf{w} = \langle 1, -1, 3 \rangle$ are coplanar—that is, show that these vectors lie in the same plane.

Solution

Start by calculating the triple scalar product to find the volume of the parallelepiped defined by $\mathbf{u}$, $\mathbf{v}$, and $\mathbf{w}$:

$$\begin{aligned} \mathbf{u} \cdot (\mathbf{v} \times \mathbf{w}) &= \begin{vmatrix} 2 & 0 & 5 \\ 2 & 2 & 4 \\ 1 & -1 & 3 \end{vmatrix} \\ &= [2(2)(3) + (0)(4)(1) + 5(2)(-1)] - [5(2)(1) + (2)(4)(-1) + (0)(2)(3)] \\ &= 2 - 2 \\ &= 0. \end{aligned}$$

The volume of the parallelepiped is 0 units^3, so one of the dimensions must be zero. Therefore, the three vectors all lie in the same plane.

2.41 Are the vectors $\mathbf{a} = \mathbf{i} + \mathbf{j} - \mathbf{k}$, $\mathbf{b} = \mathbf{i} - \mathbf{j} + \mathbf{k}$, and $\mathbf{c} = \mathbf{i} + \mathbf{j} + \mathbf{k}$ coplanar?

Example 2.43

Finding an Orthogonal Vector

Only a single plane can pass through any set of three noncolinear points. Find a vector orthogonal to the plane containing points $P = (9, -3, -2)$, $Q = (1, 3, 0)$, and $R = (-2, 5, 0)$.

Solution

The plane must contain vectors $\overrightarrow{PQ}$ and $\overrightarrow{QR}$:

$$\overrightarrow{PQ} = \langle 1 - 9, 3 - (-3), 0 - (-2) \rangle = \langle -8, 6, 2 \rangle$$
$$\overrightarrow{QR} = \langle -2 - 1, 5 - 3, 0 - 0 \rangle = \langle -3, 2, 0 \rangle.$$

The cross product $\overrightarrow{PQ} \times \overrightarrow{QR}$ produces a vector orthogonal to both $\overrightarrow{PQ}$ and $\overrightarrow{QR}$. Therefore, the cross product is orthogonal to the plane that contains these two vectors:

$$\begin{aligned}\overrightarrow{PQ} \times \overrightarrow{QR} &= \begin{vmatrix} \mathbf{i} & \mathbf{j} & \mathbf{k} \\ -8 & 6 & 2 \\ -3 & 2 & 0 \end{vmatrix} \\ &= 0\mathbf{i} - 6\mathbf{j} - 16\mathbf{k} - (-18\mathbf{k} + 4\mathbf{i} + 0\mathbf{j}) \\ &= -4\mathbf{i} - 6\mathbf{j} + 2\mathbf{k}.\end{aligned}$$

We have seen how to use the triple scalar product and how to find a vector orthogonal to a plane. Now we apply the cross product to real-world situations.

Sometimes a force causes an object to rotate. For example, turning a screwdriver or a wrench creates this kind of rotational effect, called torque.

Definition

Torque, τ (the Greek letter *tau*), measures the tendency of a force to produce rotation about an axis of rotation. Let $\mathbf{r}$ be a vector with an initial point located on the axis of rotation and with a terminal point located at the point where the force is applied, and let vector $\mathbf{F}$ represent the force. Then torque is equal to the cross product of $\mathbf{r}$ and $\mathbf{F}$:

$$\tau = \mathbf{r} \times \mathbf{F}.$$

See **Figure 2.61**.

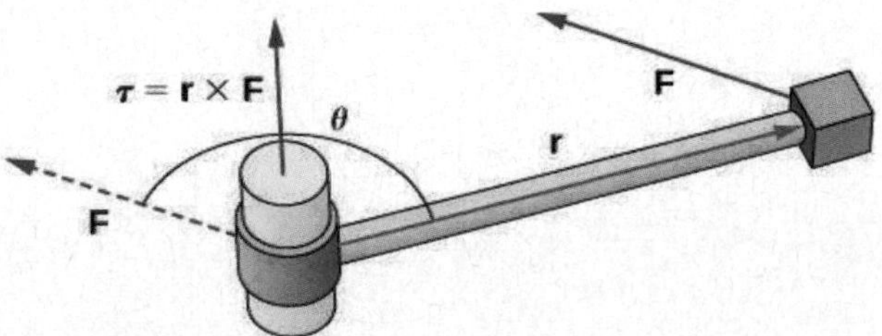

Figure 2.61 Torque measures how a force causes an object to rotate.

Think about using a wrench to tighten a bolt. The torque τ applied to the bolt depends on how hard we push the wrench (force) and how far up the handle we apply the force (distance). The torque increases with a greater force on the wrench at a greater distance from the bolt. Common units of torque are the newton-meter or foot-pound. Although torque is dimensionally equivalent to work (it has the same units), the two concepts are distinct. Torque is used specifically in the context of rotation, whereas work typically involves motion along a line.

Example 2.44

Evaluating Torque

A bolt is tightened by applying a force of 6 N to a 0.15-m wrench (**Figure 2.62**). The angle between the wrench and the force vector is $40°$. Find the magnitude of the torque about the center of the bolt. Round the answer to two decimal places.

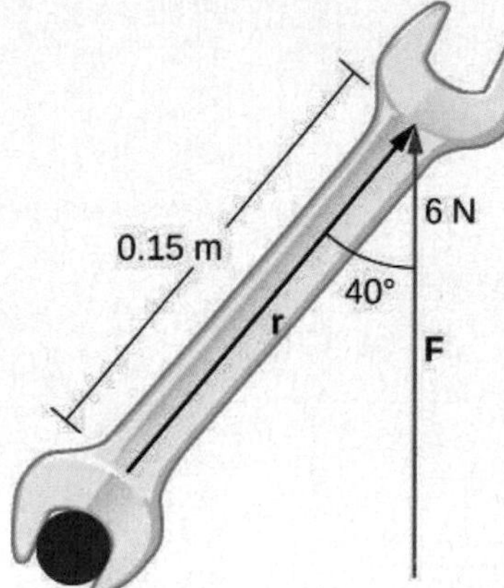

Figure 2.62 Torque describes the twisting action of the wrench.

Solution

Substitute the given information into the equation defining torque:

$$\| \tau \| = \| \mathbf{r} \times \mathbf{F} \| = \| \mathbf{r} \| \ \| \mathbf{F} \| \sin\theta = (0.15\text{ m})(6\text{ N})\sin 40° \approx 0.58\text{ N}\cdot\text{m}.$$

2.42 Calculate the force required to produce $15\text{ N}\cdot\text{m}$ torque at an angle of $30\,°$ from a 150-cm rod.

2.4 EXERCISES

For the following exercises, the vectors $\mathbf{u}$ and $\mathbf{v}$ are given.

a. Find the cross product $\mathbf{u} \times \mathbf{v}$ of the vectors $\mathbf{u}$ and $\mathbf{v}$. Express the answer in component form.

b. Sketch the vectors $\mathbf{u}$, $\mathbf{v}$, and $\mathbf{u} \times \mathbf{v}$.

183. $\mathbf{u} = \langle 2, 0, 0 \rangle$, $\mathbf{v} = \langle 2, 2, 0 \rangle$

184. $\mathbf{u} = \langle 3, 2, -1 \rangle$, $\mathbf{v} = \langle 1, 1, 0 \rangle$

185. $\mathbf{u} = 2\mathbf{i} + 3\mathbf{j}$, $\mathbf{v} = \mathbf{j} + 2\mathbf{k}$

186. $\mathbf{u} = 2\mathbf{j} + 3\mathbf{k}$, $\mathbf{v} = 3\mathbf{i} + \mathbf{k}$

187. Simplify $(\mathbf{i} \times \mathbf{i} - 2\mathbf{i} \times \mathbf{j} - 4\mathbf{i} \times \mathbf{k} + 3\mathbf{j} \times \mathbf{k}) \times \mathbf{i}$.

188. Simplify $\mathbf{j} \times (\mathbf{k} \times \mathbf{j} + 2\mathbf{j} \times \mathbf{i} - 3\mathbf{j} \times \mathbf{j} + 5\mathbf{i} \times \mathbf{k})$.

In the following exercises, vectors $\mathbf{u}$ and $\mathbf{v}$ are given. Find unit vector $\mathbf{w}$ in the direction of the cross product vector $\mathbf{u} \times \mathbf{v}$. Express your answer using standard unit vectors.

189. $\mathbf{u} = \langle 3, -1, 2 \rangle$, $\mathbf{v} = \langle -2, 0, 1 \rangle$

190. $\mathbf{u} = \langle 2, 6, 1 \rangle$, $\mathbf{v} = \langle 3, 0, 1 \rangle$

191. $\mathbf{u} = \overrightarrow{AB}$, $\mathbf{v} = \overrightarrow{AC}$, where $A(1, 0, 1)$, $B(1, -1, 3)$, and $C(0, 0, 5)$

192. $\mathbf{u} = \overrightarrow{OP}$, $\mathbf{v} = \overrightarrow{PQ}$, where $P(-1, 1, 0)$ and $Q(0, 2, 1)$

193. Determine the real number α such that $\mathbf{u} \times \mathbf{v}$ and $\mathbf{i}$ are orthogonal, where $\mathbf{u} = 3\mathbf{i} + \mathbf{j} - 5\mathbf{k}$ and $\mathbf{v} = 4\mathbf{i} - 2\mathbf{j} + \alpha\mathbf{k}$.

194. Show that $\mathbf{u} \times \mathbf{v}$ and $2\mathbf{i} - 14\mathbf{j} + 2\mathbf{k}$ cannot be orthogonal for any α real number, where $\mathbf{u} = \mathbf{i} + 7\mathbf{j} - \mathbf{k}$ and $\mathbf{v} = \alpha\mathbf{i} + 5\mathbf{j} + \mathbf{k}$.

195. Show that $\mathbf{u} \times \mathbf{v}$ is orthogonal to $\mathbf{u} + \mathbf{v}$ and $\mathbf{u} - \mathbf{v}$, where $\mathbf{u}$ and $\mathbf{v}$ are nonzero vectors.

196. Show that $\mathbf{v} \times \mathbf{u}$ is orthogonal to $(\mathbf{u} \cdot \mathbf{v})(\mathbf{u} + \mathbf{v}) + \mathbf{u}$, where $\mathbf{u}$ and $\mathbf{v}$ are nonzero vectors.

197. Calculate the determinant $\begin{vmatrix} \mathbf{i} & \mathbf{j} & \mathbf{k} \\ 1 & -1 & 7 \\ 2 & 0 & 3 \end{vmatrix}$.

198. Calculate the determinant $\begin{vmatrix} \mathbf{i} & \mathbf{j} & \mathbf{k} \\ 0 & 3 & -4 \\ 1 & 6 & -1 \end{vmatrix}$.

For the following exercises, the vectors $\mathbf{u}$ and $\mathbf{v}$ are given. Use determinant notation to find vector $\mathbf{w}$ orthogonal to vectors $\mathbf{u}$ and $\mathbf{v}$.

199. $\mathbf{u} = \langle -1, 0, e^t \rangle$, $\mathbf{v} = \langle 1, e^{-t}, 0 \rangle$, where t is a real number

200. $\mathbf{u} = \langle 1, 0, x \rangle$, $\mathbf{v} = \langle \frac{2}{x}, 1, 0 \rangle$, where x is a nonzero real number

201. Find vector $(\mathbf{a} - 2\mathbf{b}) \times \mathbf{c}$, where $\mathbf{a} = \begin{vmatrix} \mathbf{i} & \mathbf{j} & \mathbf{k} \\ 2 & -1 & 5 \\ 0 & 1 & 8 \end{vmatrix}$, $\mathbf{b} = \begin{vmatrix} \mathbf{i} & \mathbf{j} & \mathbf{k} \\ 0 & 1 & 1 \\ 2 & -1 & -2 \end{vmatrix}$, and $\mathbf{c} = \mathbf{i} + \mathbf{j} + \mathbf{k}$.

202. Find vector $\mathbf{c} \times (\mathbf{a} + 3\mathbf{b})$, where $\mathbf{a} = \begin{vmatrix} \mathbf{i} & \mathbf{j} & \mathbf{k} \\ 5 & 0 & 9 \\ 0 & 1 & 0 \end{vmatrix}$, $\mathbf{b} = \begin{vmatrix} \mathbf{i} & \mathbf{j} & \mathbf{k} \\ 0 & -1 & 1 \\ 7 & 1 & -1 \end{vmatrix}$, and $\mathbf{c} = \mathbf{i} - \mathbf{k}$.

203. **[T]** Use the cross product $\mathbf{u} \times \mathbf{v}$ to find the acute angle between vectors $\mathbf{u}$ and $\mathbf{v}$, where $\mathbf{u} = \mathbf{i} + 2\mathbf{j}$ and $\mathbf{v} = \mathbf{i} + \mathbf{k}$. Express the answer in degrees rounded to the nearest integer.

204. **[T]** Use the cross product $\mathbf{u} \times \mathbf{v}$ to find the obtuse angle between vectors $\mathbf{u}$ and $\mathbf{v}$, where $\mathbf{u} = -\mathbf{i} + 3\mathbf{j} + \mathbf{k}$ and $\mathbf{v} = \mathbf{i} - 2\mathbf{j}$. Express the answer in degrees rounded to the nearest integer.

205. Use the sine and cosine of the angle between two nonzero vectors $\mathbf{u}$ and $\mathbf{v}$ to prove Lagrange's identity: $\| \mathbf{u} \times \mathbf{v} \|^2 = \| \mathbf{u} \|^2 \| \mathbf{v} \|^2 - (\mathbf{u} \cdot \mathbf{v})^2$.

206. Verify Lagrange's identity $\| \mathbf{u} \times \mathbf{v} \|^2 = \| \mathbf{u} \|^2 \| \mathbf{v} \|^2 - (\mathbf{u} \cdot \mathbf{v})^2$ for vectors $\mathbf{u} = -\mathbf{i} + \mathbf{j} - 2\mathbf{k}$ and $\mathbf{v} = 2\mathbf{i} - \mathbf{j}$.

207. Nonzero vectors $\mathbf{u}$ and $\mathbf{v}$ are called *collinear* if there exists a nonzero scalar α such that $\mathbf{v} = \alpha\mathbf{u}$. Show that $\mathbf{u}$ and $\mathbf{v}$ are collinear if and only if $\mathbf{u} \times \mathbf{v} = \mathbf{0}$.

208. Nonzero vectors $\mathbf{u}$ and $\mathbf{v}$ are called *collinear* if there exists a nonzero scalar α such that $\mathbf{v} = \alpha\mathbf{u}$. Show that vectors $\overrightarrow{AB}$ and $\overrightarrow{AC}$ are collinear, where $A(4, 1, 0)$, $B(6, 5, -2)$, and $C(5, 3, -1)$.

209. Find the area of the parallelogram with adjacent sides $\mathbf{u} = \langle 3, 2, 0 \rangle$ and $\mathbf{v} = \langle 0, 2, 1 \rangle$.

210. Find the area of the parallelogram with adjacent sides $\mathbf{u} = \mathbf{i} + \mathbf{j}$ and $\mathbf{v} = \mathbf{i} + \mathbf{k}$.

211. Consider points $A(3, -1, 2)$, $B(2, 1, 5)$, and $C(1, -2, -2)$.

a. Find the area of parallelogram $ABCD$ with adjacent sides $\overrightarrow{AB}$ and $\overrightarrow{AC}$.
b. Find the area of triangle ABC.
c. Find the distance from point A to line BC.

212. Consider points $A(2, -3, 4)$, $B(0, 1, 2)$, and $C(-1, 2, 0)$.

a. Find the area of parallelogram $ABCD$ with adjacent sides $\overrightarrow{AB}$ and $\overrightarrow{AC}$.
b. Find the area of triangle ABC.
c. Find the distance from point B to line AC.

In the following exercises, vectors $\mathbf{u}$, $\mathbf{v}$, and $\mathbf{w}$ are given.

a. Find the triple scalar product $\mathbf{u} \cdot (\mathbf{v} \times \mathbf{w})$.
b. Find the volume of the parallelepiped with the adjacent edges $\mathbf{u}$, $\mathbf{v}$, and $\mathbf{w}$.

213. $\mathbf{u} = \mathbf{i} + \mathbf{j}$, $\mathbf{v} = \mathbf{j} + \mathbf{k}$, and $\mathbf{w} = \mathbf{i} + \mathbf{k}$

214. $\mathbf{u} = \langle -3, 5, -1 \rangle$, $\mathbf{v} = \langle 0, 2, -2 \rangle$, and $\mathbf{w} = \langle 3, 1, 1 \rangle$

215. Calculate the triple scalar products $\mathbf{v} \cdot (\mathbf{u} \times \mathbf{w})$ and $\mathbf{w} \cdot (\mathbf{u} \times \mathbf{v})$, where $\mathbf{u} = \langle 1, 1, 1 \rangle$, $\mathbf{v} = \langle 7, 6, 9 \rangle$, and $\mathbf{w} = \langle 4, 2, 7 \rangle$.

216. Calculate the triple scalar products $\mathbf{w} \cdot (\mathbf{v} \times \mathbf{u})$ and $\mathbf{u} \cdot (\mathbf{w} \times \mathbf{v})$, where $\mathbf{u} = \langle 4, 2, -1 \rangle$, $\mathbf{v} = \langle 2, 5, -3 \rangle$, and $\mathbf{w} = \langle 9, 5, -10 \rangle$.

217. Find vectors $\mathbf{a}$, $\mathbf{b}$, and $\mathbf{c}$ with a triple scalar product given by the determinant $\begin{vmatrix} 1 & 2 & 3 \\ 0 & 2 & 5 \\ 8 & 9 & 2 \end{vmatrix}$. Determine their triple scalar product.

218. The triple scalar product of vectors $\mathbf{a}$, $\mathbf{b}$, and $\mathbf{c}$ is given by the determinant $\begin{vmatrix} 0 & -2 & 1 \\ 0 & 1 & 4 \\ 1 & -3 & 7 \end{vmatrix}$. Find vector $\mathbf{a} - \mathbf{b} + \mathbf{c}$.

219. Consider the parallelepiped with edges OA, OB, and OC, where $A(2, 1, 0)$, $B(1, 2, 0)$, and $C(0, 1, \alpha)$.

a. Find the real number $\alpha > 0$ such that the volume of the parallelepiped is 3 units^3.
b. For $\alpha = 1$, find the height h from vertex C of the parallelepiped. Sketch the parallelepiped.

220. Consider points $A(\alpha, 0, 0)$, $B(0, \beta, 0)$, and $C(0, 0, \gamma)$, with α, β, and γ positive real numbers.

a. Determine the volume of the parallelepiped with adjacent sides $\overrightarrow{OA}$, $\overrightarrow{OB}$, and $\overrightarrow{OC}$.
b. Find the volume of the tetrahedron with vertices O, A, B, and C. (*Hint*: The volume of the tetrahedron is $1/6$ of the volume of the parallelepiped.)
c. Find the distance from the origin to the plane determined by A, B, and C. Sketch the parallelepiped and tetrahedron.

221. Let $\mathbf{u}$, $\mathbf{v}$, and $\mathbf{w}$ be three-dimensional vectors and c be a real number. Prove the following properties of the cross product.

a. $\mathbf{u} \times \mathbf{u} = 0$
b. $\mathbf{u} \times (\mathbf{v} + \mathbf{w}) = (\mathbf{u} \times \mathbf{v}) + (\mathbf{u} \times \mathbf{w})$
c. $c(\mathbf{u} \times \mathbf{v}) = (c\mathbf{u}) \times \mathbf{v} = \mathbf{u} \times (c\mathbf{v})$
d. $\mathbf{u} \cdot (\mathbf{u} \times \mathbf{v}) = \mathbf{0}$

222. Show that vectors $\mathbf{u} = \langle 1, 0, -8 \rangle$, $\mathbf{v} = \langle 0, 1, 6 \rangle$, and $\mathbf{w} = \langle -1, 9, 3 \rangle$ satisfy the following properties of the cross product.

a. $\mathbf{u} \times \mathbf{u} = 0$
b. $\mathbf{u} \times (\mathbf{v} + \mathbf{w}) = (\mathbf{u} \times \mathbf{v}) + (\mathbf{u} \times \mathbf{w})$
c. $c(\mathbf{u} \times \mathbf{v}) = (c\mathbf{u}) \times \mathbf{v} = \mathbf{u} \times (c\mathbf{v})$
d. $\mathbf{u} \cdot (\mathbf{u} \times \mathbf{v}) = \mathbf{0}$

223. Nonzero vectors $\mathbf{u}$, $\mathbf{v}$, and $\mathbf{w}$ are said to be *linearly dependent* if one of the vectors is a linear combination of the other two. For instance, there exist two nonzero real numbers α and β such that $\mathbf{w} = \alpha\mathbf{u} + \beta\mathbf{v}$. Otherwise, the vectors are called *linearly independent*. Show that $\mathbf{u}$, $\mathbf{v}$, and $\mathbf{w}$ are coplanar if and only if they are linear dependent.

224. Consider vectors $\mathbf{u} = \langle 1, 4, -7 \rangle$, $\mathbf{v} = \langle 2, -1, 4 \rangle$, $\mathbf{w} = \langle 0, -9, 18 \rangle$, and $\mathbf{p} = \langle 0, -9, 17 \rangle$.

a. Show that $\mathbf{u}$, $\mathbf{v}$, and $\mathbf{w}$ are coplanar by using their triple scalar product

b. Show that $\mathbf{u}$, $\mathbf{v}$, and $\mathbf{w}$ are coplanar, using the definition that there exist two nonzero real numbers α and β such that $\mathbf{w} = \alpha\mathbf{u} + \beta\mathbf{v}$.

c. Show that $\mathbf{u}$, $\mathbf{v}$, and $\mathbf{p}$ are linearly independent—that is, none of the vectors is a linear combination of the other two.

225. Consider points $A(0, 0, 2)$, $B(1, 0, 2)$, $C(1, 1, 2)$, and $D(0, 1, 2)$. Are vectors $\overrightarrow{AB}$, $\overrightarrow{AC}$, and $\overrightarrow{AD}$ linearly dependent (that is, one of the vectors is a linear combination of the other two)?

226. Show that vectors $\mathbf{i} + \mathbf{j}$, $\mathbf{i} - \mathbf{j}$, and $\mathbf{i} + \mathbf{j} + \mathbf{k}$ are linearly independent—that is, there exist two nonzero real numbers α and β such that $\mathbf{i} + \mathbf{j} + \mathbf{k} = \alpha(\mathbf{i} + \mathbf{j}) + \beta(\mathbf{i} - \mathbf{j})$.

227. Let $\mathbf{u} = \langle u_1, u_2 \rangle$ and $\mathbf{v} = \langle v_1, v_2 \rangle$ be two-dimensional vectors. The cross product of vectors $\mathbf{u}$ and $\mathbf{v}$ is not defined. However, if the vectors are regarded as the three-dimensional vectors $\tilde{\mathbf{u}} = \langle u_1, u_2, 0 \rangle$ and $\tilde{\mathbf{v}} = \langle v_1, v_2, 0 \rangle$, respectively, then, in this case, we can define the cross product of $\tilde{\mathbf{u}}$ and $\tilde{\mathbf{v}}$. In particular, in determinant notation, the cross product of $\tilde{\mathbf{u}}$ and $\tilde{\mathbf{v}}$ is given by

$$\tilde{\mathbf{u}} \times \tilde{\mathbf{v}} = \begin{vmatrix} \mathbf{i} & \mathbf{j} & \mathbf{k} \\ u_1 & u_2 & 0 \\ v_1 & v_2 & 0 \end{vmatrix}.$$

Use this result to compute $(\mathbf{i}\cos\theta + \mathbf{j}\sin\theta) \times (\mathbf{i}sin\theta - \mathbf{j}cos\theta)$, where θ is a real number.

228. Consider points $P(2, 1)$, $Q(4, 2)$, and $R(1, 2)$.

a. Find the area of triangle P, Q, and R.

b. Determine the distance from point R to the line passing through P and Q.

229. Determine a vector of magnitude 10 perpendicular to the plane passing through the x-axis and point $P(1, 2, 4)$.

230. Determine a unit vector perpendicular to the plane passing through the z-axis and point $A(3, 1, -2)$.

231. Consider $\mathbf{u}$ and $\mathbf{v}$ two three-dimensional vectors. If the magnitude of the cross product vector $\mathbf{u} \times \mathbf{v}$ is k times larger than the magnitude of vector $\mathbf{u}$, show that the magnitude of $\mathbf{v}$ is greater than or equal to k, where k is a natural number.

232. **[T]** Assume that the magnitudes of two nonzero vectors $\mathbf{u}$ and $\mathbf{v}$ are known. The function $f(\theta) = \|\mathbf{u}\| \, \|\mathbf{v}\| \sin\theta$ defines the magnitude of the cross product vector $\mathbf{u} \times \mathbf{v}$, where $\theta \in [0, \pi]$ is the angle between $\mathbf{u}$ and $\mathbf{v}$.

a. Graph the function f.

b. Find the absolute minimum and maximum of function f. Interpret the results.

c. If $\|\mathbf{u}\| = 5$ and $\|\mathbf{v}\| = 2$, find the angle between $\mathbf{u}$ and $\mathbf{v}$ if the magnitude of their cross product vector is equal to 9.

233. Find all vectors $\mathbf{w} = \langle w_1, w_2, w_3 \rangle$ that satisfy the equation $\langle 1, 1, 1 \rangle \times \mathbf{w} = \langle -1, -1, 2 \rangle$.

234. Solve the equation $\mathbf{w} \times \langle 1, 0, -1 \rangle = \langle 3, 0, 3 \rangle$, where $\mathbf{w} = \langle w_1, w_2, w_3 \rangle$ is a nonzero vector with a magnitude of 3.

235. **[T]** A mechanic uses a 12-in. wrench to turn a bolt. The wrench makes a $30°$ angle with the horizontal. If the mechanic applies a vertical force of 10 lb on the wrench handle, what is the magnitude of the torque at point P (see the following figure)? Express the answer in foot-pounds rounded to two decimal places.

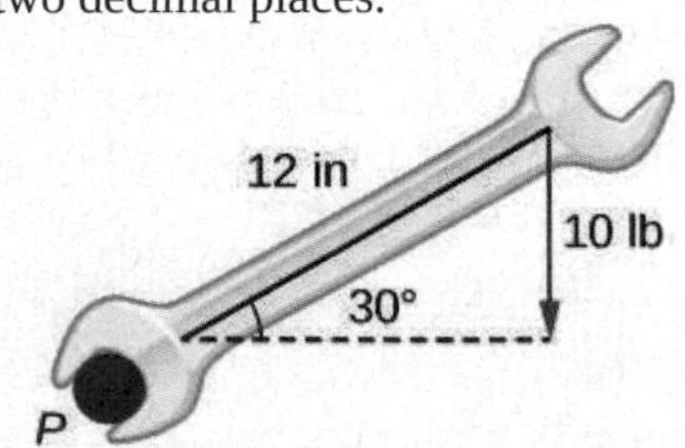

236. **[T]** A boy applies the brakes on a bicycle by applying a downward force of 20 lb on the pedal when the 6-in. crank makes a $40°$ angle with the horizontal (see the following figure). Find the torque at point P. Express your answer in foot-pounds rounded to two decimal places.

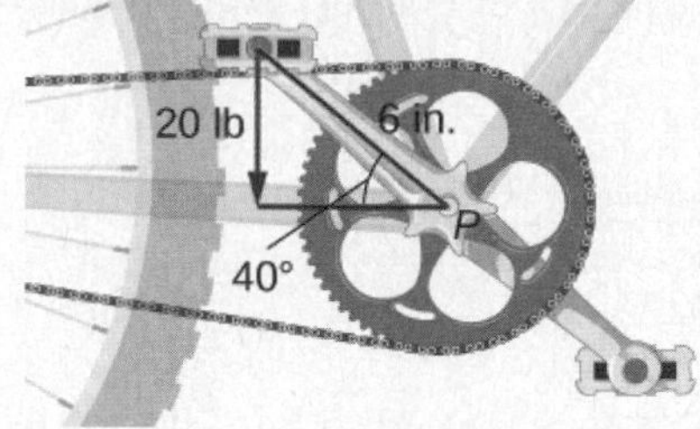

237. **[T]** Find the magnitude of the force that needs to be applied to the end of a 20-cm wrench located on the positive direction of the y-axis if the force is applied in the direction $\langle 0, 1, -2 \rangle$ and it produces a 100 N·m torque to the bolt located at the origin.

238. **[T]** What is the magnitude of the force required to be applied to the end of a 1-ft wrench at an angle of $35°$ to produce a torque of 20 N·m?

239. **[T]** The force vector $\mathbf{F}$ acting on a proton with an electric charge of $1.6 \times 10^{-19}\text{C}$ (in coulombs) moving in a magnetic field $\mathbf{B}$ where the velocity vector $\mathbf{v}$ is given by $\mathbf{F} = 1.6 \times 10^{-19}(\mathbf{v} \times \mathbf{B})$ (here, $\mathbf{v}$ is expressed in meters per second, $\mathbf{B}$ is in tesla [T], and $\mathbf{F}$ is in newtons [N]). Find the force that acts on a proton that moves in the xy-plane at velocity $\mathbf{v} = 10^5\mathbf{i} + 10^5\mathbf{j}$ (in meters per second) in a magnetic field given by $\mathbf{B} = 0.3\mathbf{j}$.

240. **[T]** The force vector $\mathbf{F}$ acting on a proton with an electric charge of $1.6 \times 10^{-19}\text{C}$ moving in a magnetic field $\mathbf{B}$ where the velocity vector $\mathbf{v}$ is given by $\mathbf{F} = 1.6 \times 10^{-19}(\mathbf{v} \times \mathbf{B})$ (here, $\mathbf{v}$ is expressed in meters per second, $\mathbf{B}$ in T, and $\mathbf{F}$ in N). If the magnitude of force $\mathbf{F}$ acting on a proton is 5.9×10^{-17} N and the proton is moving at the speed of 300 m/sec in magnetic field $\mathbf{B}$ of magnitude 2.4 T, find the angle between velocity vector $\mathbf{v}$ of the proton and magnetic field $\mathbf{B}$. Express the answer in degrees rounded to the nearest integer.

241. **[T]** Consider $\mathbf{r}(t) = \langle \cos t, \sin t, 2t \rangle$ the position vector of a particle at time $t \in [0, 30]$, where the components of $\mathbf{r}$ are expressed in centimeters and time in seconds. Let $\overrightarrow{OP}$ be the position vector of the particle after 1 sec.

a. Determine unit vector $\mathbf{B}(t)$ (called the *binormal unit vector*) that has the direction of cross product vector $\mathbf{v}(t) \times \mathbf{a}(t)$, where $\mathbf{v}(t)$ and $\mathbf{a}(t)$ are the instantaneous velocity vector and, respectively, the acceleration vector of the particle after t seconds.

b. Use a CAS to visualize vectors $\mathbf{v}(1)$, $\mathbf{a}(1)$, and $\mathbf{B}(1)$ as vectors starting at point P along with the path of the particle.

242. A solar panel is mounted on the roof of a house. The panel may be regarded as positioned at the points of coordinates (in meters) $A(8, 0, 0)$, $B(8, 18, 0)$, $C(0, 18, 8)$, and $D(0, 0, 8)$ (see the following figure).

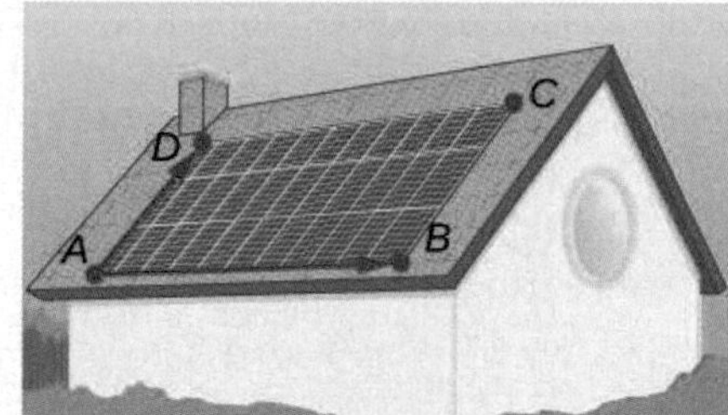

a. Find vector $\mathbf{n} = \overrightarrow{AB} \times \overrightarrow{AD}$ perpendicular to the surface of the solar panels. Express the answer using standard unit vectors.

b. Assume unit vector $\mathbf{s} = \frac{1}{\sqrt{3}}\mathbf{i} + \frac{1}{\sqrt{3}}\mathbf{j} + \frac{1}{\sqrt{3}}\mathbf{k}$ points toward the Sun at a particular time of the day and the flow of solar energy is $\mathbf{F} = 900\mathbf{s}$ (in watts per square meter [W/m^2]). Find the predicted amount of electrical power the panel can produce, which is given by the dot product of vectors $\mathbf{F}$ and $\mathbf{n}$ (expressed in watts).

c. Determine the angle of elevation of the Sun above the solar panel. Express the answer in degrees rounded to the nearest whole number. (*Hint*: The angle between vectors $\mathbf{n}$ and $\mathbf{s}$ and the angle of elevation are complementary.)

2.5 | Equations of Lines and Planes in Space

Learning Objectives

2.5.1 Write the vector, parametric, and symmetric of a line through a given point in a given direction, and a line through two given points.
2.5.2 Find the distance from a point to a given line.
2.5.3 Write the vector and scalar equations of a plane through a given point with a given normal.
2.5.4 Find the distance from a point to a given plane.
2.5.5 Find the angle between two planes.

By now, we are familiar with writing equations that describe a line in two dimensions. To write an equation for a line, we must know two points on the line, or we must know the direction of the line and at least one point through which the line passes. In two dimensions, we use the concept of slope to describe the orientation, or direction, of a line. In three dimensions, we describe the direction of a line using a vector parallel to the line. In this section, we examine how to use equations to describe lines and planes in space.

Equations for a Line in Space

Let's first explore what it means for two vectors to be parallel. Recall that parallel vectors must have the same or opposite directions. If two nonzero vectors, $\mathbf{u}$ and $\mathbf{v}$, are parallel, we claim there must be a scalar, k, such that $\mathbf{u} = k\mathbf{v}$. If $\mathbf{u}$ and $\mathbf{v}$ have the same direction, simply choose $k = \frac{\|\mathbf{u}\|}{\|\mathbf{v}\|}$. If $\mathbf{u}$ and $\mathbf{v}$ have opposite directions, choose $k = -\frac{\|\mathbf{u}\|}{\|\mathbf{v}\|}$. Note that the converse holds as well. If $\mathbf{u} = k\mathbf{v}$ for some scalar k, then either $\mathbf{u}$ and $\mathbf{v}$ have the same direction $(k > 0)$ or opposite directions $(k < 0)$, so $\mathbf{u}$ and $\mathbf{v}$ are parallel. Therefore, two nonzero vectors $\mathbf{u}$ and $\mathbf{v}$ are parallel if and only if $\mathbf{u} = k\mathbf{v}$ for some scalar k. By convention, the zero vector $\mathbf{0}$ is considered to be parallel to all vectors.

As in two dimensions, we can describe a line in space using a point on the line and the direction of the line, or a parallel vector, which we call the **direction vector** (**Figure 2.63**). Let L be a line in space passing through point $P(x_0, y_0, z_0)$. Let $\mathbf{v} = \langle a, b, c \rangle$ be a vector parallel to L. Then, for any point on line $Q(x, y, z)$, we know that $\overrightarrow{PQ}$ is parallel to $\mathbf{v}$. Thus, as we just discussed, there is a scalar, t, such that $\overrightarrow{PQ} = t\mathbf{v}$, which gives

$$\begin{aligned} \overrightarrow{PQ} &= t\mathbf{v} \\ \langle x - x_0, y - y_0, z - z_0 \rangle &= t\langle a, b, c \rangle \\ \langle x - x_0, y - y_0, z - z_0 \rangle &= \langle ta, tb, tc \rangle . \end{aligned} \tag{2.11}$$

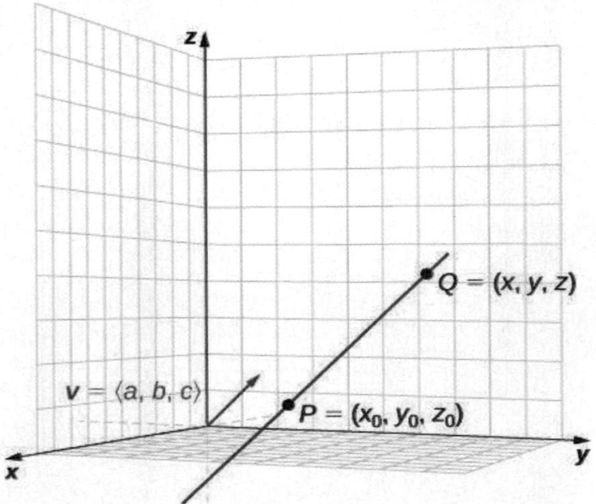

Figure 2.63 Vector $\mathbf{v}$ is the direction vector for $\overrightarrow{PQ}$.

Using vector operations, we can rewrite **Equation 2.11** as

$$\begin{aligned} \langle x - x_0, y - y_0, z - z_0 \rangle &= \langle ta, tb, tc \rangle \\ \langle x, y, z \rangle - \langle x_0, y_0, z_0 \rangle &= t \langle a, b, c \rangle \\ \langle x, y, z \rangle &= \langle x_0, y_0, z_0 \rangle + t \langle a, b, c \rangle . \end{aligned}$$

Setting $\mathbf{r} = \langle x, y, z \rangle$ and $\mathbf{r}_0 = \langle x_0, y_0, z_0 \rangle$, we now have the **vector equation of a line**:

$$\mathbf{r} = \mathbf{r}_0 + t\mathbf{v}. \tag{2.12}$$

Equating components, **Equation 2.11** shows that the following equations are simultaneously true: $x - x_0 = ta$, $y - y_0 = tb$, and $z - z_0 = tc$. If we solve each of these equations for the component variables x, y, and z, we get a set of equations in which each variable is defined in terms of the parameter t and that, together, describe the line. This set of three equations forms a set of **parametric equations of a line**:

$$x = x_0 + ta \quad y = y_0 + tb \quad z = z_0 + tc.$$

If we solve each of the equations for t assuming a, b, and c are nonzero, we get a different description of the same line:

$$\frac{x - x_0}{a} = t \quad \frac{y - y_0}{b} = t \quad \frac{z - z_0}{c} = t.$$

Because each expression equals t, they all have the same value. We can set them equal to each other to create **symmetric equations of a line**:

$$\frac{x - x_0}{a} = \frac{y - y_0}{b} = \frac{z - z_0}{c}.$$

We summarize the results in the following theorem.

Theorem 2.11: Parametric and Symmetric Equations of a Line

A line L parallel to vector $\mathbf{v} = \langle a, b, c \rangle$ and passing through point $P(x_0, y_0, z_0)$ can be described by the following parametric equations:

$$x = x_0 + ta, \ y = y_0 + tb, \ \text{and } z = z_0 + tc. \tag{2.13}$$

If the constants a, b, and c are all nonzero, then L can be described by the symmetric equation of the line:

$$\frac{x - x_0}{a} = \frac{y - y_0}{b} = \frac{z - z_0}{c}. \tag{2.14}$$

The parametric equations of a line are not unique. Using a different parallel vector or a different point on the line leads to a different, equivalent representation. Each set of parametric equations leads to a related set of symmetric equations, so it follows that a symmetric equation of a line is not unique either.

Example 2.45

Equations of a Line in Space

Find parametric and symmetric equations of the line passing through points $(1, 4, -2)$ and $(-3, 5, 0)$.

Solution

First, identify a vector parallel to the line:

$$\mathbf{v} = \langle -3-1, 5-4, 0-(-2) \rangle = \langle -4, 1, 2 \rangle.$$

Use either of the given points on the line to complete the parametric equations:

$$x = 1 - 4t, \; y = 4 + t, \; \text{and}\; z = -2 + 2t.$$

Solve each equation for t to create the symmetric equation of the line:

$$\frac{x-1}{-4} = y - 4 = \frac{z+2}{2}.$$

2.43 Find parametric and symmetric equations of the line passing through points $(1, -3, 2)$ and $(5, -2, 8)$.

Sometimes we don't want the equation of a whole line, just a line segment. In this case, we limit the values of our parameter t. For example, let $P(x_0, y_0, z_0)$ and $Q(x_1, y_1, z_1)$ be points on a line, and let $\mathbf{p} = \langle x_0, y_0, z_0 \rangle$ and $\mathbf{q} = \langle x_1, y_1, z_1 \rangle$ be the associated position vectors. In addition, let $\mathbf{r} = \langle x, y, z \rangle$. We want to find a vector equation for the line segment between P and Q. Using P as our known point on the line, and $\overrightarrow{PQ} = \langle x_1 - x_0, y_1 - y_0, z_1 - z_0 \rangle$ as the direction vector equation, **Equation 2.12** gives

$$\mathbf{r} = \mathbf{p} + t\left(\overrightarrow{PQ}\right).$$

Using properties of vectors, then

$$\begin{aligned}
\mathbf{r} &= \mathbf{p} + t\left(\overrightarrow{PQ}\right) \\
&= \langle x_0, y_0, z_0 \rangle + t \langle x_1 - x_0, y_1 - y_0, z_1 - z_0 \rangle \\
&= \langle x_0, y_0, z_0 \rangle + t(\langle x_1, y_1, z_1 \rangle - \langle x_0, y_0, z_0 \rangle) \\
&= \langle x_0, y_0, z_0 \rangle + t \langle x_1, y_1, z_1 \rangle - t \langle x_0, y_0, z_0 \rangle \\
&= (1-t) \langle x_0, y_0, z_0 \rangle + t \langle x_1, y_1, z_1 \rangle \\
&= (1-t)\mathbf{p} + t\mathbf{q}.
\end{aligned}$$

Thus, the vector equation of the line passing through P and Q is

$$\mathbf{r} = (1-t)\mathbf{p} + t\mathbf{q}.$$

Remember that we didn't want the equation of the whole line, just the line segment between P and Q. Notice that when $t = 0$, we have $\mathbf{r} = \mathbf{p}$, and when $t = 1$, we have $\mathbf{r} = \mathbf{q}$. Therefore, the vector equation of the line segment between P and Q is

$$\mathbf{r} = (1-t)\mathbf{p} + t\mathbf{q}, \; 0 \le t \le 1. \tag{2.15}$$

Going back to **Equation 2.12**, we can also find parametric equations for this line segment. We have

$$\begin{aligned}
\mathbf{r} &= \mathbf{p} + t\left(\overrightarrow{PQ}\right) \\
\langle x, y, z \rangle &= \langle x_0, y_0, z_0 \rangle + t \langle x_1 - x_0, y_1 - y_0, z_1 - z_0 \rangle \\
&= \langle x_0 + t(x_1 - x_0), y_0 + t(y_1 - y_0), z_0 + t(z_1 - z_0) \rangle.
\end{aligned}$$

Then, the parametric equations are

$$x = x_0 + t(x_1 - x_0), \; y = y_0 + t(y_1 - y_0), \; z = z_0 + t(z_1 - z_0), \; 0 \le t \le 1. \tag{2.16}$$

Example 2.46

Parametric Equations of a Line Segment

Find parametric equations of the line segment between the points $P(2, 1, 4)$ and $Q(3, -1, 3)$.

Solution

By **Equation 2.16**, we have

$$x = x_0 + t(x_1 - x_0),\ y = y_0 + t(y_1 - y_0),\ z = z_0 + t(z_1 - z_0),\ 0 \le t \le 1.$$

Working with each component separately, we get

$$\begin{aligned} x &= x_0 + t(x_1 - x_0) \\ &= 2 + t(3 - 2) \\ &= 2 + t, \\ y &= y_0 + t(y_1 - y_0) \\ &= 1 + t(-1 - 1) \\ &= 1 - 2t, \end{aligned}$$

and

$$\begin{aligned} z &= z_0 + t(z_1 - z_0) \\ &= 4 + t(3 - 4) \\ &= 4 - t. \end{aligned}$$

Therefore, the parametric equations for the line segment are

$$x = 2 + t,\ y = 1 - 2t,\ z = 4 - t,\ 0 \le t \le 1.$$

2.44 Find parametric equations of the line segment between points $P(-1, 3, 6)$ and $Q(-8, 2, 4)$.

Distance between a Point and a Line

We already know how to calculate the distance between two points in space. We now expand this definition to describe the distance between a point and a line in space. Several real-world contexts exist when it is important to be able to calculate these distances. When building a home, for example, builders must consider "setback" requirements, when structures or fixtures have to be a certain distance from the property line. Air travel offers another example. Airlines are concerned about the distances between populated areas and proposed flight paths.

Let L be a line in the plane and let M be any point not on the line. Then, we define distance d from M to L as the length of line segment $\overline{MP}$, where P is a point on L such that $\overline{MP}$ is perpendicular to L (**Figure 2.64**).

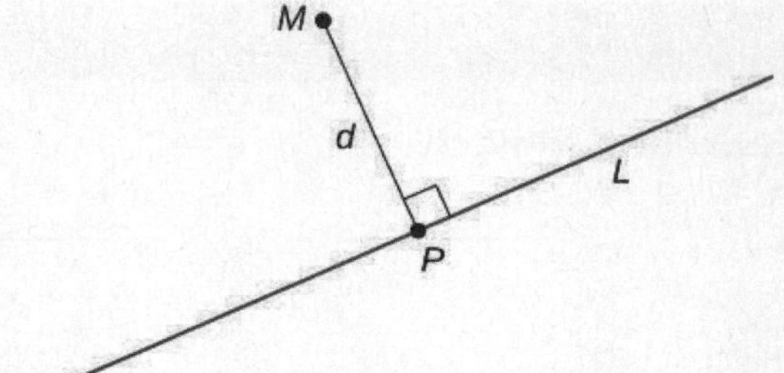

Figure 2.64 The distance from point M to line L is the length of $\overline{MP}$.

When we're looking for the distance between a line and a point in space, **Figure 2.64** still applies. We still define the distance as the length of the perpendicular line segment connecting the point to the line. In space, however, there is no clear way to know which point on the line creates such a perpendicular line segment, so we select an arbitrary point on the line and use properties of vectors to calculate the distance. Therefore, let P be an arbitrary point on line L and let $\mathbf{v}$ be a direction vector for L (**Figure 2.65**).

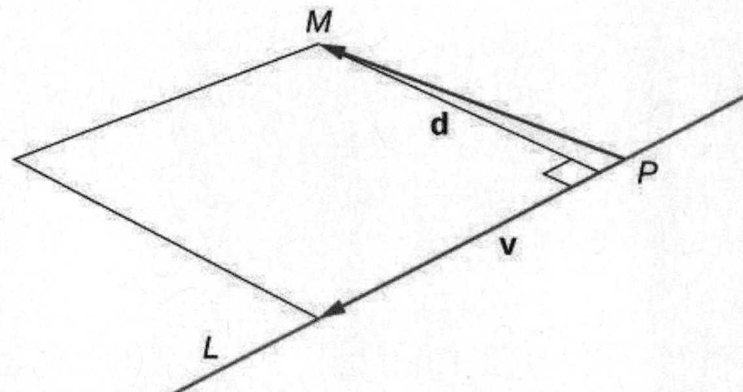

Figure 2.65 Vectors $\overrightarrow{PM}$ and $\mathbf{v}$ form two sides of a parallelogram with base $\|\mathbf{v}\|$ and height $d,$ which is the distance between a line and a point in space.

By **Area of a Parallelogram**, vectors $\overrightarrow{PM}$ and $\mathbf{v}$ form two sides of a parallelogram with area $\|\overrightarrow{PM} \times \mathbf{v}\|$. Using a formula from geometry, the area of this parallelogram can also be calculated as the product of its base and height:

$$\|\overrightarrow{PM} \times \mathbf{v}\| = \|\mathbf{v}\| d.$$

We can use this formula to find a general formula for the distance between a line in space and any point not on the line.

Theorem 2.12: Distance from a Point to a Line

Let L be a line in space passing through point P with direction vector $\mathbf{v}$. If M is any point not on $L,$ then the distance from M to L is

$$d = \frac{\|\overrightarrow{PM} \times \mathbf{v}\|}{\|\mathbf{v}\|}.$$

Example 2.47

Calculating the Distance from a Point to a Line

Find the distance between t point $M = (1, 1, 3)$ and line $\frac{x-3}{4} = \frac{y+1}{2} = z - 3.$

Solution

From the symmetric equations of the line, we know that vector $\mathbf{v} = \langle 4, 2, 1 \rangle$ is a direction vector for the line. Setting the symmetric equations of the line equal to zero, we see that point $P(3, -1, 3)$ lies on the line. Then,

$$\overrightarrow{PM} = \langle 1-3, 1-(-1), 3-3 \rangle = \langle -2, 2, 0 \rangle.$$

To calculate the distance, we need to find $\overrightarrow{PM} \times \mathbf{v}$:

$$\begin{aligned}\overrightarrow{PM} \times \mathbf{v} &= \begin{vmatrix} \mathbf{i} & \mathbf{j} & \mathbf{k} \\ -2 & 2 & 0 \\ 4 & 2 & 1 \end{vmatrix} \\ &= (2-0)\mathbf{i} - (-2-0)\mathbf{j} + (-4-8)\mathbf{k} \\ &= 2\mathbf{i} + 2\mathbf{j} - 12\mathbf{k}.\end{aligned}$$

Therefore, the distance between the point and the line is (**Figure 2.66**)

$$\begin{aligned} d &= \frac{\| \overrightarrow{PM} \times \mathbf{v} \|}{\| \mathbf{v} \|} \\ &= \frac{\sqrt{2^2 + 2^2 + 12^2}}{\sqrt{4^2 + 2^2 + 1^2}} \\ &= \frac{2\sqrt{38}}{\sqrt{21}}. \end{aligned}$$

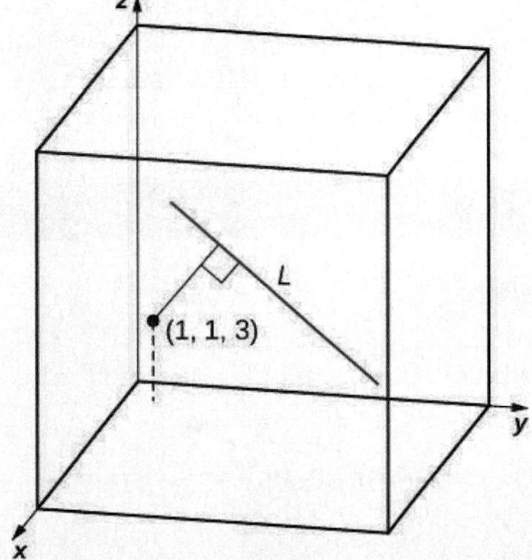

Figure 2.66 Point $(1, 1, 3)$ is approximately 2.7 units from the line with symmetric equations $\frac{x-3}{4} = \frac{y+1}{2} = z - 3.$

2.45 Find the distance between point $(0, 3, 6)$ and the line with parametric equations $x = 1 - t, y = 1 + 2t, z = 5 + 3t.$

Relationships between Lines

Given two lines in the two-dimensional plane, the lines are equal, they are parallel but not equal, or they intersect in a single point. In three dimensions, a fourth case is possible. If two lines in space are not parallel, but do not intersect, then the lines are said to be **skew lines** (**Figure 2.67**).

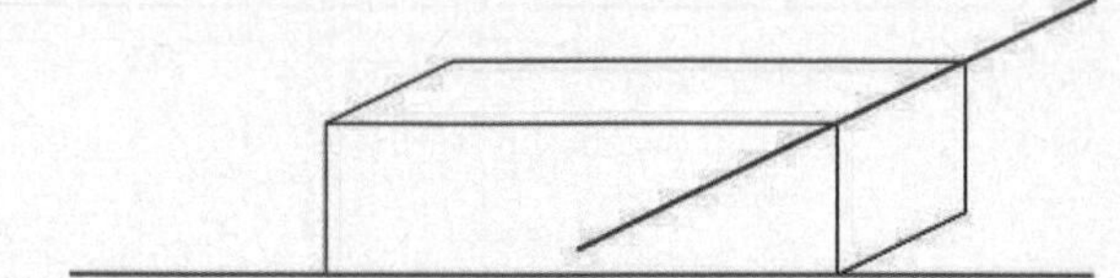

Figure 2.67 In three dimensions, it is possible that two lines do not cross, even when they have different directions.

To classify lines as parallel but not equal, equal, intersecting, or skew, we need to know two things: whether the direction vectors are parallel and whether the lines share a point (**Figure 2.68**).

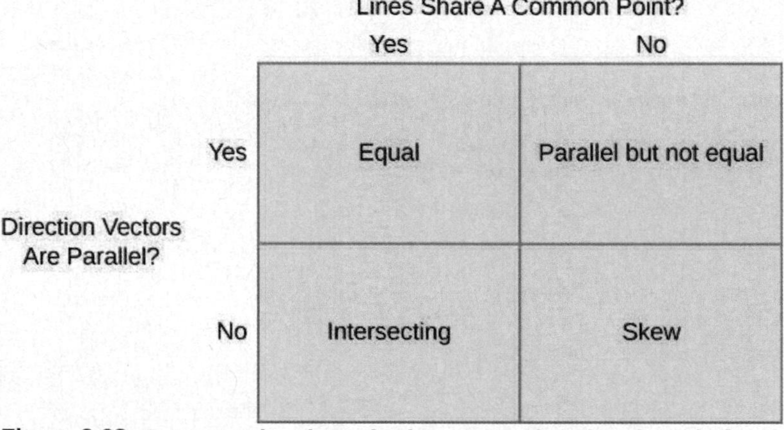

Lines Share A Common Point?
Yes
No
Direction Vectors Are Parallel?
Yes
No
Equal
Parallel but not equal
Intersecting
Skew

Figure 2.68 Determine the relationship between two lines based on whether their direction vectors are parallel and whether they share a point.

Example 2.48

Classifying Lines in Space

For each pair of lines, determine whether the lines are equal, parallel but not equal, skew, or intersecting.

a. $L_1 : x = 2s - 1,\ y = s - 1,\ z = s - 4$

$L_2 : x = t - 3,\ y = 3t + 8,\ z = 5 - 2t$

b. $L_1 :\ x = -y = z$

$L_2 : \dfrac{x-3}{2} = y = z - 2$

c. $L_1 : x = 6s - 1,\ y = -2s,\ z = 3s + 1$

$L_2 : \dfrac{x-4}{6} = \dfrac{y+3}{-2} = \dfrac{z-1}{3}$

Solution

a. Line L_1 has direction vector $\mathbf{v_1} = \langle 2, 1, 1 \rangle$; line L_2 has direction vector $\mathbf{v_2} = \langle 1, 3, -2 \rangle$. Because the direction vectors are not parallel vectors, the lines are either intersecting or skew. To determine whether the lines intersect, we see if there is a point, (x, y, z), that lies on both lines. To find this point, we use the parametric equations to create a system of equalities:

$$2s - 1 = t - 3; \quad s - 1 = 3t + 8; \quad s - 4 = 5 - 2t.$$

By the first equation, $t = 2s + 2$. Substituting into the second equation yields

$$\begin{aligned} s - 1 &= 3(2s + 2) + 8 \\ s - 1 &= 6s + 6 + 8 \\ 5s &= -15 \\ s &= -3. \end{aligned}$$

Substitution into the third equation, however, yields a contradiction:

$$\begin{aligned} s - 4 &= 5 - 2(2s + 2) \\ s - 4 &= 5 - 4s - 4 \\ 5s &= 5 \\ s &= 1. \end{aligned}$$

There is no single point that satisfies the parametric equations for L_1 and L_2 simultaneously. These lines do not intersect, so they are skew (see the following figure).

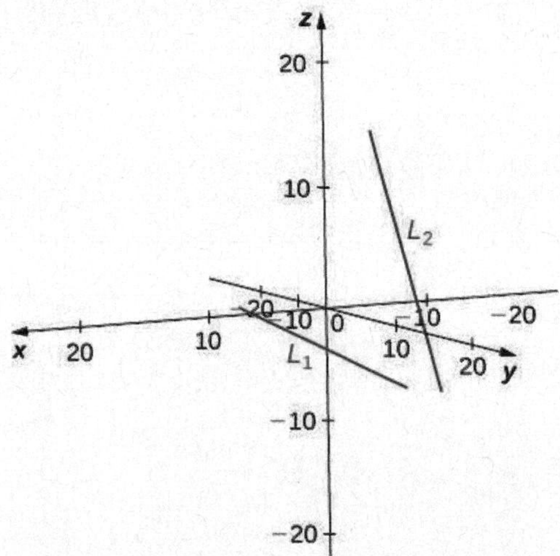

b. Line L_1 has direction vector $\mathbf{v_1} = \langle 1, -1, 1 \rangle$ and passes through the origin, $(0, 0, 0)$. Line L_2 has a different direction vector, $\mathbf{v_2} = \langle 2, 1, 1 \rangle$, so these lines are not parallel or equal. Let r represent the parameter for line L_1 and let s represent the parameter for L_2:

$$\begin{aligned} x &= r & x &= 2s + 3 \\ y &= -r & y &= s \\ z &= r & z &= s + 2. \end{aligned}$$

Solve the system of equations to find $r = 1$ and $s = -1$. If we need to find the point of intersection, we can substitute these parameters into the original equations to get $(1, -1, 1)$ (see the following figure).

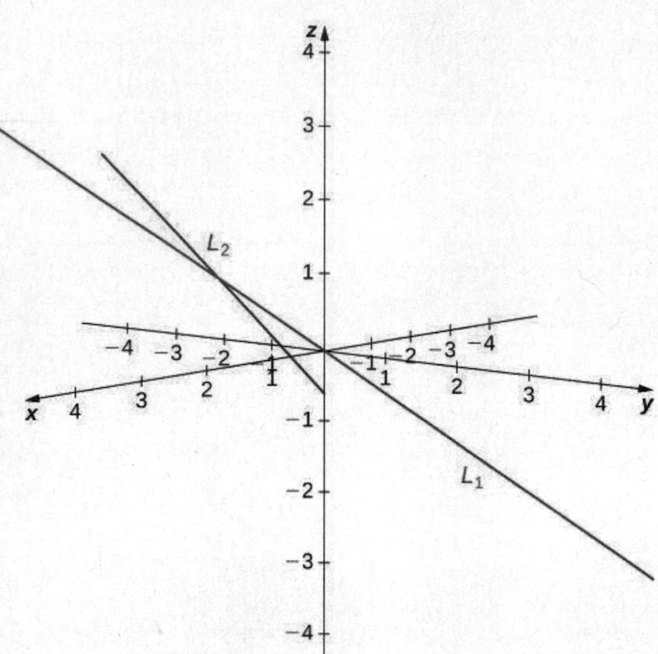

c. Lines L_1 and L_2 have equivalent direction vectors: $\mathbf{v} = \langle 6, -2, 3 \rangle$. These two lines are parallel (see the following figure).

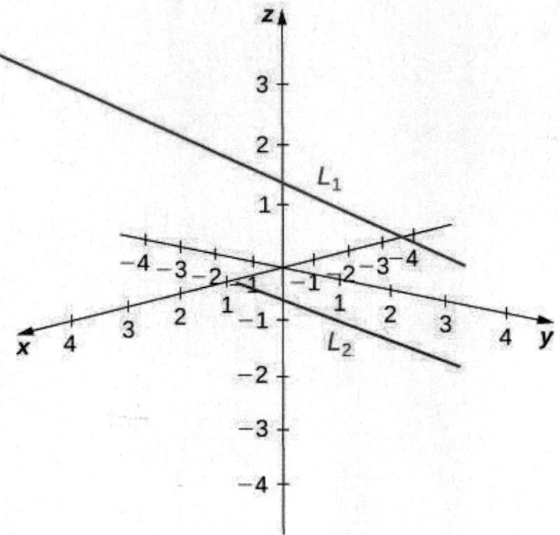

2.46 Describe the relationship between the lines with the following parametric equations:

$$x = 1 - 4t,\ y = 3 + t,\ z = 8 - 6t$$

$$x = 2 + 3s,\ y = 2s,\ z = -1 - 3s.$$

Equations for a Plane

We know that a line is determined by two points. In other words, for any two distinct points, there is exactly one line that passes through those points, whether in two dimensions or three. Similarly, given any three points that do not all lie on the same line, there is a unique plane that passes through these points. Just as a line is determined by two points, a plane is determined by three.

This may be the simplest way to characterize a plane, but we can use other descriptions as well. For example, given two distinct, intersecting lines, there is exactly one plane containing both lines. A plane is also determined by a line and any point that does not lie on the line. These characterizations arise naturally from the idea that a plane is determined by three points. Perhaps the most surprising characterization of a plane is actually the most useful.

Imagine a pair of orthogonal vectors that share an initial point. Visualize grabbing one of the vectors and twisting it. As you twist, the other vector spins around and sweeps out a plane. Here, we describe that concept mathematically. Let $\mathbf{n} = \langle a, b, c \rangle$ be a vector and $P = (x_0, y_0, z_0)$ be a point. Then the set of all points $Q = (x, y, z)$ such that $\overrightarrow{PQ}$ is orthogonal to $\mathbf{n}$ forms a plane (**Figure 2.69**). We say that $\mathbf{n}$ is a **normal vector**, or perpendicular to the plane. Remember, the dot product of orthogonal vectors is zero. This fact generates the **vector equation of a plane**: $\mathbf{n} \cdot \overrightarrow{PQ} = 0.$ Rewriting this equation provides additional ways to describe the plane:

$$\begin{aligned} \mathbf{n} \cdot \overrightarrow{PQ} &= 0 \\ \langle a, b, c \rangle \cdot \langle x - x_0, y - y_0, z - z_0 \rangle &= 0 \\ a(x - x_0) + b(y - y_0) + c(z - z_0) &= 0. \end{aligned}$$

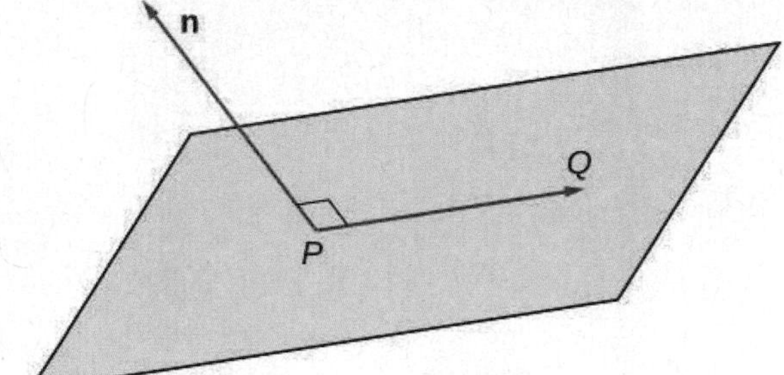

Figure 2.69 Given a point P and vector $\mathbf{n},$ the set of all points Q with $\overrightarrow{PQ}$ orthogonal to $\mathbf{n}$ forms a plane.

Definition

Given a point P and vector $\mathbf{n},$ the set of all points Q satisfying the equation $\mathbf{n} \cdot \overrightarrow{PQ} = 0$ forms a plane. The equation

$$\mathbf{n} \cdot \overrightarrow{PQ} = 0 \tag{2.17}$$

is known as the vector equation of a plane.

The **scalar equation of a plane** containing point $P = (x_0, y_0, z_0)$ with normal vector $\mathbf{n} = \langle a, b, c \rangle$ is

$$a(x - x_0) + b(y - y_0) + c(z - z_0) = 0. \tag{2.18}$$

This equation can be expressed as $ax + by + cz + d = 0,$ where $d = -ax_0 - by_0 - cz_0.$ This form of the equation is sometimes called the **general form of the equation of a plane**.

As described earlier in this section, any three points that do not all lie on the same line determine a plane. Given three such points, we can find an equation for the plane containing these points.

Example 2.49

Writing an Equation of a Plane Given Three Points in the Plane

Write an equation for the plane containing points $P = (1, 1, -2),$ $Q = (0, 2, 1),$ and $R = (-1, -1, 0)$ in both standard and general forms.

Solution

To write an equation for a plane, we must find a normal vector for the plane. We start by identifying two vectors in the plane:

$$\begin{aligned}\overrightarrow{PQ} &= \langle 0-1, 2-1, 1-(-2) \rangle = \langle -1, 1, 3 \rangle \\ \overrightarrow{QR} &= \langle -1-0, -1-2, 0-1 \rangle = \langle -1, -3, -1 \rangle .\end{aligned}$$

The cross product $\overrightarrow{PQ} \times \overrightarrow{QR}$ is orthogonal to both $\overrightarrow{PQ}$ and $\overrightarrow{QR}$, so it is normal to the plane that contains these two vectors:

$$\begin{aligned}\mathbf{n} &= \overrightarrow{PQ} \times \overrightarrow{QR} \\ &= \begin{vmatrix} \mathbf{i} & \mathbf{j} & \mathbf{k} \\ -1 & 1 & 3 \\ -1 & -3 & -1 \end{vmatrix} \\ &= (-1+9)\mathbf{i} - (1+3)\mathbf{j} + (3+1)\mathbf{k} \\ &= 8\mathbf{i} - 4\mathbf{j} + 4\mathbf{k}.\end{aligned}$$

Thus, $\mathbf{n} = \langle 8, -4, 4 \rangle$, and we can choose any of the three given points to write an equation of the plane:

$$\begin{aligned}8(x-1) - 4(y-1) + 4(z+2) &= 0 \\ 8x - 4y + 4z + 4 &= 0.\end{aligned}$$

The scalar equations of a plane vary depending on the normal vector and point chosen.

Example 2.50

Writing an Equation for a Plane Given a Point and a Line

Find an equation of the plane that passes through point $(1, 4, 3)$ and contains the line given by $x = \frac{y-1}{2} = z+1.$

Solution

Symmetric equations describe the line that passes through point $(0, 1, -1)$ parallel to vector $\mathbf{v}_1 = \langle 1, 2, 1 \rangle$ (see the following figure). Use this point and the given point, $(1, 4, 3),$ to identify a second vector parallel to the plane:

$$\mathbf{v}_2 = \langle 1-0, 4-1, 3-(-1) \rangle = \langle 1, 3, 4 \rangle .$$

Use the cross product of these vectors to identify a normal vector for the plane:

$$\begin{aligned}\mathbf{n} &= \mathbf{v}_1 \times \mathbf{v}_2 \\ &= \begin{vmatrix} \mathbf{i} & \mathbf{j} & \mathbf{k} \\ 1 & 2 & 1 \\ 1 & 3 & 4 \end{vmatrix} \\ &= (8-3)\mathbf{i} - (4-1)\mathbf{j} + (3-2)\mathbf{k} \\ &= 5\mathbf{i} - 3\mathbf{j} + \mathbf{k}.\end{aligned}$$

The scalar equations for the plane are $5x - 3(y - 1) + (z + 1) = 0$ and $5x - 3y + z + 4 = 0.$

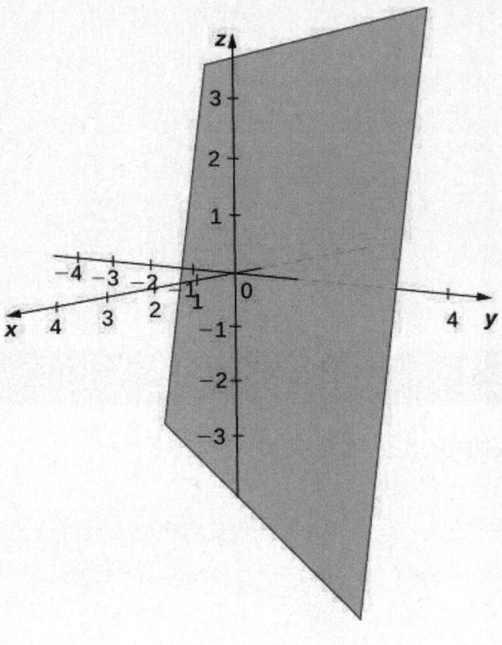

2.47 Find an equation of the plane containing the lines L_1 and L_2:

$$L_1 : x = -y = z$$
$$L_2 : \frac{x - 3}{2} = y = z - 2.$$

Now that we can write an equation for a plane, we can use the equation to find the distance d between a point P and the plane. It is defined as the shortest possible distance from P to a point on the plane.

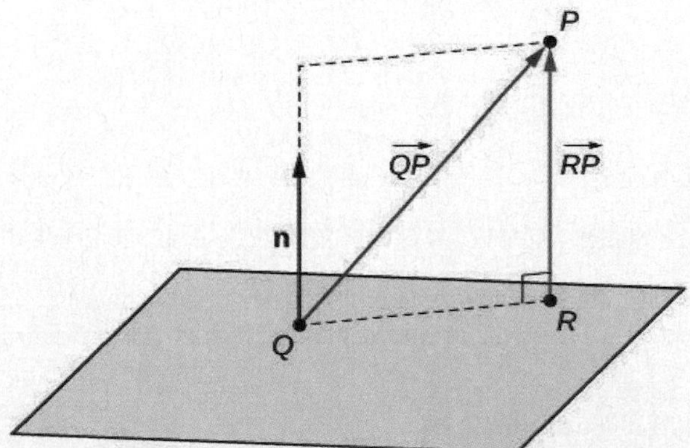

Figure 2.70 We want to find the shortest distance from point P to the plane. Let point R be the point in the plane such that, for any other point in the plane Q, $\| \overrightarrow{RP} \| < \| \overrightarrow{QP} \|$.

Just as we find the two-dimensional distance between a point and a line by calculating the length of a line segment perpendicular to the line, we find the three-dimensional distance between a point and a plane by calculating the length of a line segment perpendicular to the plane. Let R bet the point in the plane such that $\overrightarrow{RP}$ is orthogonal to the plane, and let

Q be an arbitrary point in the plane. Then the projection of vector $\vec{QP}$ onto the normal vector describes vector $\vec{RP}$, as shown in **Figure 2.70**.

Theorem 2.13: The Distance between a Plane and a Point

Suppose a plane with normal vector $\mathbf{n}$ passes through point Q. The distance d from the plane to a point P not in the plane is given by

$$d = \|\text{proj}_{\mathbf{n}} \vec{QP}\| = \left|\text{comp}_{\mathbf{n}} \vec{QP}\right| = \frac{\left|\vec{QP} \cdot \mathbf{n}\right|}{\|\mathbf{n}\|}. \tag{2.19}$$

Example 2.51

Distance between a Point and a Plane

Find the distance between point $P = (3,\ 1,\ 2)$ and the plane given by $x - 2y + z = 5$ (see the following figure).

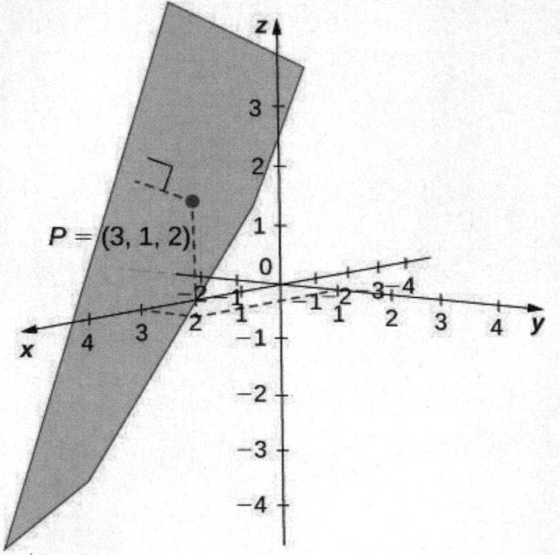

Solution

The coefficients of the plane's equation provide a normal vector for the plane: $\mathbf{n} = \langle 1, -2, 1 \rangle$. To find vector $\vec{QP}$, we need a point in the plane. Any point will work, so set $y = z = 0$ to see that point $Q = (5,\ 0,\ 0)$ lies in the plane. Find the component form of the vector from Q to P:

$$\vec{QP} = \langle 3 - 5, 1 - 0, 2 - 0 \rangle = \langle -2, 1, 2 \rangle.$$

Apply the distance formula from **Equation 2.19**:

$$\begin{aligned} d &= \frac{\left|\overrightarrow{QP} \cdot \mathbf{n}\right|}{\|\mathbf{n}\|} \\ &= \frac{|\langle -2, 1, 2 \rangle \cdot \langle 1, -2, 1 \rangle|}{\sqrt{1^2 + (-2)^2 + 1^2}} \\ &= \frac{|-2 - 2 + 2|}{\sqrt{6}} \\ &= \frac{2}{\sqrt{6}}. \end{aligned}$$

2.48 Find the distance between point $P = (5, -1, 0)$ and the plane given by $4x + 2y - z = 3.$

Parallel and Intersecting Planes

We have discussed the various possible relationships between two lines in two dimensions and three dimensions. When we describe the relationship between two planes in space, we have only two possibilities: the two distinct planes are parallel or they intersect. When two planes are parallel, their normal vectors are parallel. When two planes intersect, the intersection is a line (**Figure 2.71**).

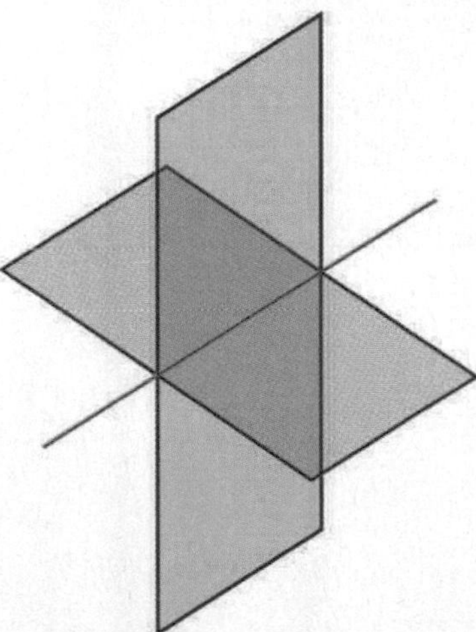

Figure 2.71 The intersection of two nonparallel planes is always a line.

We can use the equations of the two planes to find parametric equations for the line of intersection.

Example 2.52

Finding the Line of Intersection for Two Planes

Find parametric and symmetric equations for the line formed by the intersection of the planes given by $x + y + z = 0$ and $2x - y + z = 0$ (see the following figure).

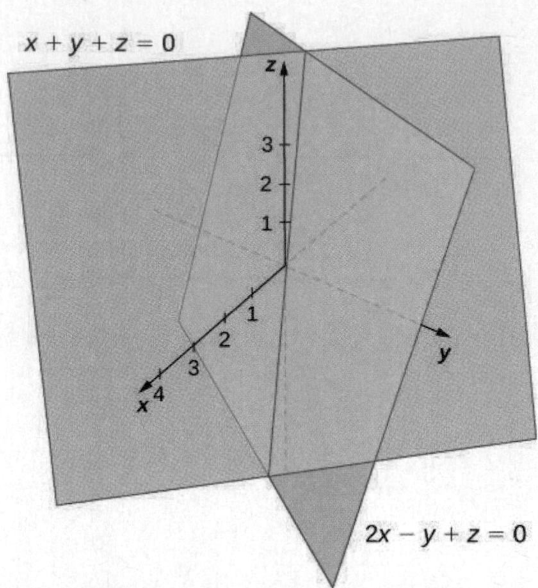

Solution

Note that the two planes have nonparallel normals, so the planes intersect. Further, the origin satisfies each equation, so we know the line of intersection passes through the origin. Add the plane equations so we can eliminate the one of the variables, in this case, y:

$$\begin{array}{rcrcrcl} x & + & y & + & z & = & 0 \\ 2x & - & y & + & z & = & 0 \\ \hline 3x & & & + & 2z & = & 0. \end{array}$$

This gives us $x = -\frac{2}{3}z.$ We substitute this value into the first equation to express y in terms of z:

$$\begin{aligned} x + y + z &= 0 \\ -\frac{2}{3}z + y + z &= 0 \\ y + \frac{1}{3}z &= 0 \\ y &= -\frac{1}{3}z. \end{aligned}$$

We now have the first two variables, x and $y,$ in terms of the third variable, $z.$ Now we define z in terms of $t.$ To eliminate the need for fractions, we choose to define the parameter t as $t = -\frac{1}{3}z.$ Then, $z = -3t.$ Substituting the parametric representation of z back into the other two equations, we see that the parametric equations for the line of intersection are $x = 2t,\ y = t,\ z = -3t.$ The symmetric equations for the line are $\frac{x}{2} = y = \frac{z}{-3}.$

2.49 Find parametric equations for the line formed by the intersection of planes $x + y - z = 3$ and $3x - y + 3z = 5.$

In addition to finding the equation of the line of intersection between two planes, we may need to find the angle formed by the intersection of two planes. For example, builders constructing a house need to know the angle where different sections of the roof meet to know whether the roof will look good and drain properly. We can use normal vectors to calculate the angle between the two planes. We can do this because the angle between the normal vectors is the same as the angle between the planes. **Figure 2.72** shows why this is true.

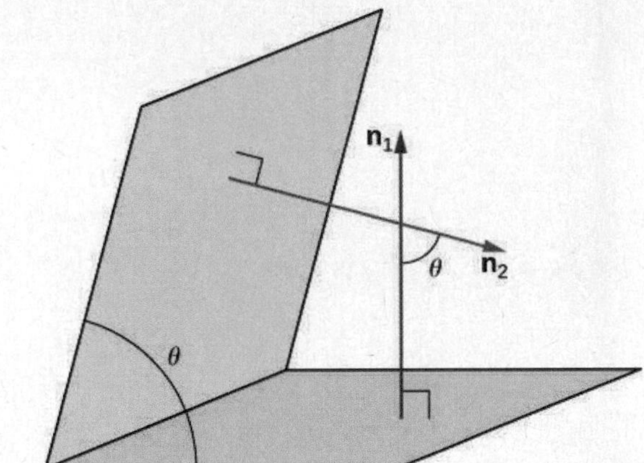

Figure 2.72 The angle between two planes has the same measure as the angle between the normal vectors for the planes.

We can find the measure of the angle θ between two intersecting planes by first finding the cosine of the angle, using the following equation:

$$\cos\theta = \frac{|\mathbf{n}_1 \cdot \mathbf{n}_2|}{\|\mathbf{n}_1\| \, \|\mathbf{n}_2\|}.$$

We can then use the angle to determine whether two planes are parallel or orthogonal or if they intersect at some other angle.

Example 2.53

Finding the Angle between Two Planes

Determine whether each pair of planes is parallel, orthogonal, or neither. If the planes are intersecting, but not orthogonal, find the measure of the angle between them. Give the answer in radians and round to two decimal places.

a. $x + 2y - z = 8$ and $2x + 4y - 2z = 10$

b. $2x - 3y + 2z = 3$ and $6x + 2y - 3z = 1$

c. $x + y + z = 4$ and $x - 3y + 5z = 1$

Solution

a. The normal vectors for these planes are $\mathbf{n}_1 = \langle 1, 2, -1 \rangle$ and $\mathbf{n}_2 = \langle 2, 4, -2 \rangle$. These two vectors are scalar multiples of each other. The normal vectors are parallel, so the planes are parallel.

b. The normal vectors for these planes are $\mathbf{n}_1 = \langle 2, -3, 2 \rangle$ and $\mathbf{n}_2 = \langle 6, 2, -3 \rangle$. Taking the dot product of these vectors, we have

$$\mathbf{n}_1 \cdot \mathbf{n}_2 = \langle 2, -3, 2 \rangle \cdot \langle 6, 2, -3 \rangle = 2(6) - 3(2) + 2(-3) = 0.$$

The normal vectors are orthogonal, so the corresponding planes are orthogonal as well.

c. The normal vectors for these planes are $\mathbf{n}_1 = \langle 1, 1, 1 \rangle$ and $\mathbf{n}_2 = \langle 1, -3, 5 \rangle$:

$$\begin{aligned}\cos\theta &= \frac{|\mathbf{n}_1 \cdot \mathbf{n}_2|}{\|\mathbf{n}_1\| \ \|\mathbf{n}_2\|} \\ &= \frac{|\langle 1, 1, 1 \rangle \cdot \langle 1, -3, 5 \rangle|}{\sqrt{1^2+1^2+1^2}\sqrt{1^2+(-3)^2+5^2}} \\ &= \frac{3}{\sqrt{105}}.\end{aligned}$$

The angle between the two planes is 1.27 rad, or approximately $73°$.

2.50 Find the measure of the angle between planes $x + y - z = 3$ and $3x - y + 3z = 5$. Give the answer in radians and round to two decimal places.

When we find that two planes are parallel, we may need to find the distance between them. To find this distance, we simply select a point in one of the planes. The distance from this point to the other plane is the distance between the planes.

Previously, we introduced the formula for calculating this distance in **Equation 2.19**:

$$d = \frac{\overrightarrow{QP} \cdot \mathbf{n}}{\|\mathbf{n}\|},$$

where Q is a point on the plane, P is a point not on the plane, and $\mathbf{n}$ is the normal vector that passes through point Q. Consider the distance from point (x_0, y_0, z_0) to plane $ax + by + cz + k = 0$. Let (x_1, y_1, z_1) be any point in the plane. Substituting into the formula yields

$$\begin{aligned}d &= \frac{|a(x_0 - x_1) + b(y_0 - y_1) + c(z_0 - z_1)|}{\sqrt{a^2+b^2+c^2}} \\ &= \frac{|ax_0 + by_0 + cz_0 + k|}{\sqrt{a^2+b^2+c^2}}.\end{aligned}$$

We state this result formally in the following theorem.

Theorem 2.14: Distance from a Point to a Plane

Let $P(x_0, y_0, z_0)$ be a point. The distance from P to plane $ax + by + cz + k = 0$ is given by

$$d = \frac{|ax_0 + by_0 + cz_0 + k|}{\sqrt{a^2+b^2+c^2}}.$$

Example 2.54

Finding the Distance between Parallel Planes

Find the distance between the two parallel planes given by $2x + y - z = 2$ and $2x + y - z = 8$.

Solution

Point $(1, 0, 0)$ lies in the first plane. The desired distance, then, is

$$\begin{aligned} d &= \frac{|ax_0 + by_0 + cz_0 + k|}{\sqrt{a^2 + b^2 + c^2}} \\ &= \frac{|2(1) + 1(0) + (-1)(0) + (-8)|}{\sqrt{2^2 + 1^2 + (-1)^2}} \\ &= \frac{6}{\sqrt{6}} = \sqrt{6}. \end{aligned}$$

2.51 Find the distance between parallel planes $5x - 2y + z = 6$ and $5x - 2y + z = -3$.

Student PROJECT

Distance between Two Skew Lines

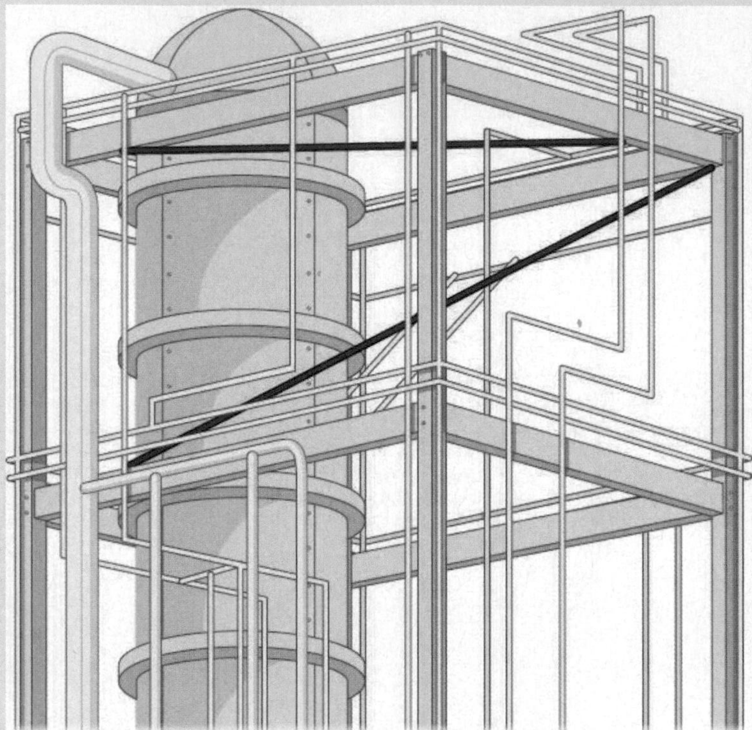

Figure 2.73 Industrial pipe installations often feature pipes running in different directions. How can we find the distance between two skew pipes?

Finding the distance from a point to a line or from a line to a plane seems like a pretty abstract procedure. But, if the lines represent pipes in a chemical plant or tubes in an oil refinery or roads at an intersection of highways, confirming that the distance between them meets specifications can be both important and awkward to measure. One way is to model the two pipes as lines, using the techniques in this chapter, and then calculate the distance between them. The calculation involves forming vectors along the directions of the lines and using both the cross product and the dot product.

The symmetric forms of two lines, L_1 and $L_2,$ are

$$L_1 : \frac{x - x_1}{a_1} = \frac{y - y_1}{b_1} = \frac{z - z_1}{c_1}$$
$$L_2 : \frac{x - x_2}{a_2} = \frac{y - y_2}{b_2} = \frac{z - z_2}{c_2}.$$

You are to develop a formula for the distance d between these two lines, in terms of the values $a_1, b_1, c_1; a_2, b_2, c_2; x_1, y_1, z_1;$ and $x_2, y_2, z_2.$ The distance between two lines is usually taken to mean the minimum distance, so this is the length of a line segment or the length of a vector that is perpendicular to both lines and intersects both lines.

1. First, write down two vectors, $\mathbf{v}_1$ and $\mathbf{v}_2,$ that lie along L_1 and $L_2,$ respectively.
2. Find the cross product of these two vectors and call it $\mathbf{N}$. This vector is perpendicular to $\mathbf{v}_1$ and $\mathbf{v}_2,$ and

hence is perpendicular to both lines.

3. From vector **N**, form a unit vector **n** in the same direction.
4. Use symmetric equations to find a convenient vector $\mathbf{v}_{12}$ that lies between any two points, one on each line. Again, this can be done directly from the symmetric equations.
5. The dot product of two vectors is the magnitude of the projection of one vector onto the other—that is, $\mathbf{A} \cdot \mathbf{B} = \|\mathbf{A}\| \|\mathbf{B}\| \cos\theta,$ where θ is the angle between the vectors. Using the dot product, find the projection of vector $\mathbf{v}_{12}$ found in step 4 onto unit vector **n** found in step 3. This projection is perpendicular to both lines, and hence its length must be the perpendicular distance d between them. Note that the value of d may be negative, depending on your choice of vector $\mathbf{v}_{12}$ or the order of the cross product, so use absolute value signs around the numerator.
6. Check that your formula gives the correct distance of $|-25|/\sqrt{198} \approx 1.78$ between the following two lines:

$$L_1 : \frac{x-5}{2} = \frac{y-3}{4} = \frac{z-1}{3}$$
$$L_2 : \frac{x-6}{3} = \frac{y-1}{5} = \frac{z}{7}.$$

7. Is your general expression valid when the lines are parallel? If not, why not? (*Hint:* What do you know about the value of the cross product of two parallel vectors? Where would that result show up in your expression for d?)
8. Demonstrate that your expression for the distance is zero when the lines intersect. Recall that two lines intersect if they are not parallel and they are in the same plane. Hence, consider the direction of **n** and $\mathbf{v}_{12}$. What is the result of their dot product?
9. Consider the following application. Engineers at a refinery have determined they need to install support struts between many of the gas pipes to reduce damaging vibrations. To minimize cost, they plan to install these struts at the closest points between adjacent skewed pipes. Because they have detailed schematics of the structure, they are able to determine the correct lengths of the struts needed, and hence manufacture and distribute them to the installation crews without spending valuable time making measurements.
The rectangular frame structure has the dimensions $4.0 \times 15.0 \times 10.0$ m (height, width, and depth). One sector has a pipe entering the lower corner of the standard frame unit and exiting at the diametrically opposed corner (the one farthest away at the top); call this L_1. A second pipe enters and exits at the two different opposite lower corners; call this L_2 (**Figure 2.74**).

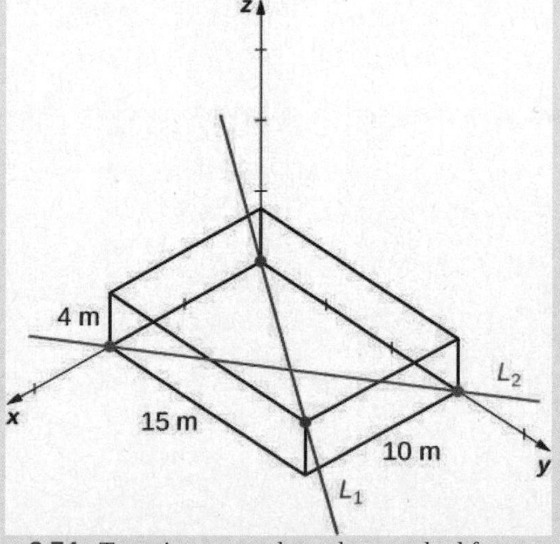

Figure 2.74 Two pipes cross through a standard frame unit.

Write down the vectors along the lines representing those pipes, find the cross product between them from which to create the unit vector **n**, define a vector that spans two points on each line, and finally determine the minimum distance between the lines. (Take the origin to be at the lower corner of the first pipe.) Similarly, you may also develop the symmetric equations for each line and substitute directly into your formula.

2.5 EXERCISES

In the following exercises, points P and Q are given. Let L be the line passing through points P and Q.

a. Find the vector equation of line L.

b. Find parametric equations of line L.

c. Find symmetric equations of line L.

d. Find parametric equations of the line segment determined by P and Q.

243. $P(-3, 5, 9)$, $Q(4, -7, 2)$

244. $P(4, 0, 5)$, $Q(2, 3, 1)$

245. $P(-1, 0, 5)$, $Q(4, 0, 3)$

246. $P(7, -2, 6)$, $Q(-3, 0, 6)$

For the following exercises, point P and vector $\mathbf{v}$ are given. Let L be the line passing through point P with direction $\mathbf{v}$.

a. Find parametric equations of line L.

b. Find symmetric equations of line L.

c. Find the intersection of the line with the xy-plane.

247. $P(1, -2, 3)$, $\mathbf{v} = \langle 1, 2, 3 \rangle$

248. $P(3, 1, 5)$, $\mathbf{v} = \langle 1, 1, 1 \rangle$

249. $P(3, 1, 5)$, $\mathbf{v} = \overrightarrow{QR}$, where $Q(2, 2, 3)$ and $R(3, 2, 3)$

250. $P(2, 3, 0)$, $\mathbf{v} = \overrightarrow{QR}$, where $Q(0, 4, 5)$ and $R(0, 4, 6)$

For the following exercises, line L is given.

a. Find point P that belongs to the line and direction vector $\mathbf{v}$ of the line. Express $\mathbf{v}$ in component form.

b. Find the distance from the origin to line L.

251. $x = 1 + t,\ y = 3 + t,\ z = 5 + 4t, \quad t \in \mathbb{R}$

252. $-x = y + 1,\ z = 2$

253. Find the distance between point $A(-3, 1, 1)$ and the line of symmetric equations $x = -y = -z$.

254. Find the distance between point $A(4, 2, 5)$ and the line of parametric equations $x = -1 - t,\ y = -t,\ z = 2,$ $t \in \mathbb{R}$.

For the following exercises, lines L_1 and L_2 are given.

a. Verify whether lines L_1 and L_2 are parallel.

b. If the lines L_1 and L_2 are parallel, then find the distance between them.

255. $L_1 : x = 1 + t,\ y = t,\ z = 2 + t, \quad t \in \mathbb{R}$, $L_2 : x - 3 = y - 1 = z - 3$

256. $L_1 : x = 2,\ y = 1,\ z = t,$ $L_2 : x = 1,\ y = 1,\ z = 2 - 3t, \quad t \in \mathbb{R}$

257. Show that the line passing through points $P(3, 1, 0)$ and $Q(1, 4, -3)$ is perpendicular to the line with equation $x = 3t,\ y = 3 + 8t,\ z = -7 + 6t, \quad t \in \mathbb{R}$.

258. Are the lines of equations $x = -2 + 2t,\ y = -6,\ z = 2 + 6t$ and $x = -1 + t,\ y = 1 + t,\ z = t, \quad t \in \mathbb{R}$, perpendicular to each other?

259. Find the point of intersection of the lines of equations $x = -2y = 3z$ and $x = -5 - t,\ y = -1 + t,\ z = t - 11,$ $t \in \mathbb{R}$.

260. Find the intersection point of the x-axis with the line of parametric equations $x = 10 + t,\ y = 2 - 2t,\ z = -3 + 3t, \quad t \in \mathbb{R}$.

For the following exercises, lines L_1 and L_2 are given. Determine whether the lines are equal, parallel but not equal, skew, or intersecting.

261. $L_1 : x = y - 1 = -z$ and $L_2 : x - 2 = -y = \frac{z}{2}$

262. $L_1 : x = 2t,\ y = 0,\ z = 3, \quad t \in \mathbb{R}$ and $L_2 : x = 0,\ y = 8 + s,\ z = 7 + s, \quad s \in \mathbb{R}$

263. $L_1 : x = -1 + 2t,\ y = 1 + 3t,\ z = 7t, \quad t \in \mathbb{R}$ and $L_2 : x - 1 = \frac{2}{3}(y - 4) = \frac{2}{7}z - 2$

264. $L_1 : 3x = y + 1 = 2z$ and $L_2 : x = 6 + 2t,\ y = 17 + 6t,\ z = 9 + 3t, \quad t \in \mathbb{R}$

265. Consider line L of symmetric equations $x-2=-y=\frac{z}{2}$ and point $A(1, 1, 1)$.

a. Find parametric equations for a line parallel to L that passes through point A.
b. Find symmetric equations of a line skew to L and that passes through point A.
c. Find symmetric equations of a line that intersects L and passes through point A.

266. Consider line L of parametric equations $x=t,\ y=2t,\ z=3,\quad t\in\mathbb{R}$.

a. Find parametric equations for a line parallel to L that passes through the origin.
b. Find parametric equations of a line skew to L that passes through the origin.
c. Find symmetric equations of a line that intersects L and passes through the origin.

For the following exercises, point P and vector $\mathbf{n}$ are given.

a. Find the scalar equation of the plane that passes through P and has normal vector $\mathbf{n}$.
b. Find the general form of the equation of the plane that passes through P and has normal vector $\mathbf{n}$.

267. $P(0, 0, 0),\quad \mathbf{n}=3\mathbf{i}-2\mathbf{j}+4\mathbf{k}$

268. $P(3, 2, 2),\quad \mathbf{n}=2\mathbf{i}+3\mathbf{j}-\mathbf{k}$

269. $P(1, 2, 3),\quad \mathbf{n}=\langle 1, 2, 3\rangle$

270. $P(0, 0, 0),\quad \mathbf{n}=\langle -3, 2, -1\rangle$

For the following exercises, the equation of a plane is given.

a. Find normal vector $\mathbf{n}$ to the plane. Express $\mathbf{n}$ using standard unit vectors.
b. Find the intersections of the plane with the axes of coordinates.
c. Sketch the plane.

271. **[T]** $4x+5y+10z-20=0$

272. $3x+4y-12=0$

273. $3x-2y+4z=0$

274. $x+z=0$

275. Given point $P(1, 2, 3)$ and vector $\mathbf{n}=\mathbf{i}+\mathbf{j}$, find point Q on the x-axis such that $\overrightarrow{PQ}$ and $\mathbf{n}$ are orthogonal.

276. Show there is no plane perpendicular to $\mathbf{n}=\mathbf{i}+\mathbf{j}$ that passes through points $P(1, 2, 3)$ and $Q(2, 3, 4)$.

277. Find parametric equations of the line passing through point $P(-2, 1, 3)$ that is perpendicular to the plane of equation $2x-3y+z=7$.

278. Find symmetric equations of the line passing through point $P(2, 5, 4)$ that is perpendicular to the plane of equation $2x+3y-5z=0$.

279. Show that line $\frac{x-1}{2}=\frac{y+1}{3}=\frac{z-2}{4}$ is parallel to plane $x-2y+z=6$.

280. Find the real number α such that the line of parametric equations $x=t,\ y=2-t,\ z=3+t,$ $t\in\mathbb{R}$ is parallel to the plane of equation $\alpha x+5y+z-10=0$.

For the following exercises, points $P, Q,$ and R are given.

a. Find the general equation of the plane passing through $P, Q,$ and R.
b. Write the vector equation $\mathbf{n}\cdot\overrightarrow{PS}=0$ of the plane at a., where $S(x, y, z)$ is an arbitrary point of the plane.
c. Find parametric equations of the line passing through the origin that is perpendicular to the plane passing through $P, Q,$ and R.

281. $P(1, 1, 1), Q(2, 4, 3),$ and $R(-1, -2, -1)$

282. $P(-2, 1, 4), Q(3, 1, 3),$ and $R(-2, 1, 0)$

283. Consider the planes of equations $x+y+z=1$ and $x+z=0$.

a. Show that the planes intersect.
b. Find symmetric equations of the line passing through point $P(1, 4, 6)$ that is parallel to the line of intersection of the planes.

284. Consider the planes of equations $-y+z-2=0$ and $x-y=0$.

a. Show that the planes intersect.
b. Find parametric equations of the line passing through point $P(-8, 0, 2)$ that is parallel to the line of intersection of the planes.

285. Find the scalar equation of the plane that passes through point $P(-1, 2, 1)$ and is perpendicular to the line of intersection of planes $x+y-z-2=0$ and $2x-y+3z-1=0$.

286. Find the general equation of the plane that passes through the origin and is perpendicular to the line of intersection of planes $-x+y+2=0$ and $z-3=0$.

287. Determine whether the line of parametric equations $x=1+2t, y=-2t, z=2+t, \quad t\in\mathbb{R}$ intersects the plane with equation $3x+4y+6z-7=0$. If it does intersect, find the point of intersection.

288. Determine whether the line of parametric equations $x=5, y=4-t, z=2t, \quad t\in\mathbb{R}$ intersects the plane with equation $2x-y+z=5$. If it does intersect, find the point of intersection.

289. Find the distance from point $P(1, 5, -4)$ to the plane of equation $3x-y+2z-6=0$.

290. Find the distance from point $P(1, -2, 3)$ to the plane of equation $(x-3)+2(y+1)-4z=0$.

For the following exercises, the equations of two planes are given.

a. Determine whether the planes are parallel, orthogonal, or neither.
b. If the planes are neither parallel nor orthogonal, then find the measure of the angle between the planes. Express the answer in degrees rounded to the nearest integer.

291. **[T]** $x+y+z=0, \quad 2x-y+z-7=0$

292. $5x-3y+z=4, \quad x+4y+7z=1$

293. $x-5y-z=1, \quad 5x-25y-5z=-3$

294. **[T]** $x-3y+6z=4, \quad 5x+y-z=4$

295. Show that the lines of equations $x=t, y=1+t, z=2+t, \quad t\in\mathbb{R}$, and $\frac{x}{2}=\frac{y-1}{3}=z-3$ are skew, and find the distance between them.

296. Show that the lines of equations $x=-1+t, y=-2+t, z=3t, \quad t\in\mathbb{R}$, and $x=5+s, y=-8+2s, z=7s, \quad s\in\mathbb{R}$ are skew, and find the distance between them.

297. Consider point $C(-3, 2, 4)$ and the plane of equation $2x+4y-3z=8$.

a. Find the radius of the sphere with center C tangent to the given plane.
b. Find point P of tangency.

298. Consider the plane of equation $x-y-z-8=0$.

a. Find the equation of the sphere with center C at the origin that is tangent to the given plane.
b. Find parametric equations of the line passing through the origin and the point of tangency.

299. Two children are playing with a ball. The girl throws the ball to the boy. The ball travels in the air, curves 3 ft to the right, and falls 5 ft away from the girl (see the following figure). If the plane that contains the trajectory of the ball is perpendicular to the ground, find its equation.

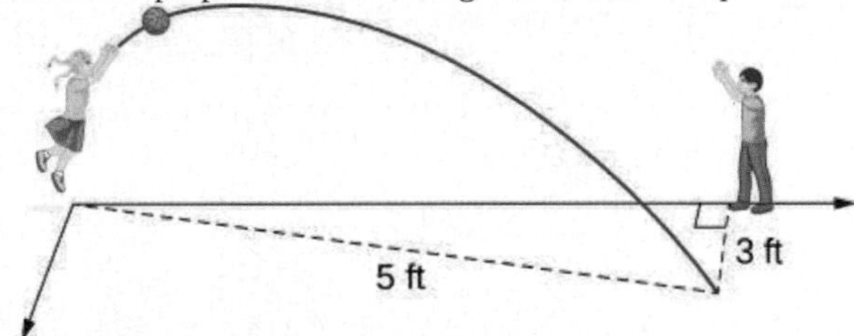

300. **[T]** John allocates d dollars to consume monthly three goods of prices $a, b,$ and c. In this context, the budget equation is defined as $ax+by+cz=d$, where $x\geq 0, y\geq 0,$ and $z\geq 0$ represent the number of items bought from each of the goods. The budget set is given by $\{(x, y, z)|ax+by+cz\leq d, x\geq 0, y\geq 0, z\geq 0\}$, and the budget plane is the part of the plane of equation $ax+by+cz=d$ for which $x\geq 0, y\geq 0,$ and $z\geq 0$. Consider $a=\$8, \quad b=\$5, \quad c=\$10,$ and $d=\$500$.

a. Use a CAS to graph the budget set and budget plane.
b. For $z=25$, find the new budget equation and graph the budget set in the same system of coordinates.

301. **[T]** Consider $\mathbf{r}(t) = \langle \sin t, \cos t, 2t \rangle$ the position vector of a particle at time $t \in [0, 3]$, where the components of $\mathbf{r}$ are expressed in centimeters and time is measured in seconds. Let $\overrightarrow{OP}$ be the position vector of the particle after 1 sec.

a. Determine the velocity vector $\mathbf{v}(1)$ of the particle after 1 sec.
b. Find the scalar equation of the plane that is perpendicular to $\mathbf{v}(1)$ and passes through point P. This plane is called the *normal plane* to the path of the particle at point P.
c. Use a CAS to visualize the path of the particle along with the velocity vector and normal plane at point P.

302. **[T]** A solar panel is mounted on the roof of a house. The panel may be regarded as positioned at the points of coordinates (in meters) $A(8, 0, 0)$, $B(8, 18, 0)$, $C(0, 18, 8)$, and $D(0, 0, 8)$ (see the following figure).

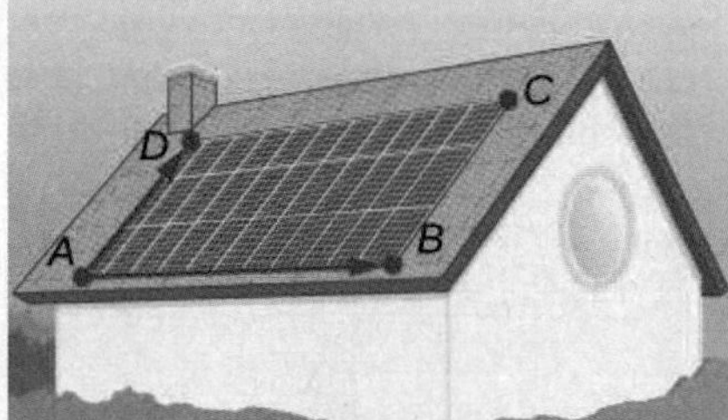

a. Find the general form of the equation of the plane that contains the solar panel by using points A, B, and C, and show that its normal vector is equivalent to $\overrightarrow{AB} \times \overrightarrow{AD}$.
b. Find parametric equations of line L_1 that passes through the center of the solar panel and has direction vector $\mathbf{s} = \frac{1}{\sqrt{3}}\mathbf{i} + \frac{1}{\sqrt{3}}\mathbf{j} + \frac{1}{\sqrt{3}}\mathbf{k}$, which points toward the position of the Sun at a particular time of day.
c. Find symmetric equations of line L_2 that passes through the center of the solar panel and is perpendicular to it.
d. Determine the angle of elevation of the Sun above the solar panel by using the angle between lines L_1 and L_2.

2.6 | Quadric Surfaces

Learning Objectives

2.6.1 Identify a cylinder as a type of three-dimensional surface.
2.6.2 Recognize the main features of ellipsoids, paraboloids, and hyperboloids.
2.6.3 Use traces to draw the intersections of quadric surfaces with the coordinate planes.

We have been exploring vectors and vector operations in three-dimensional space, and we have developed equations to describe lines, planes, and spheres. In this section, we use our knowledge of planes and spheres, which are examples of three-dimensional figures called *surfaces*, to explore a variety of other surfaces that can be graphed in a three-dimensional coordinate system.

Identifying Cylinders

The first surface we'll examine is the cylinder. Although most people immediately think of a hollow pipe or a soda straw when they hear the word *cylinder*, here we use the broad mathematical meaning of the term. As we have seen, cylindrical surfaces don't have to be circular. A rectangular heating duct is a cylinder, as is a rolled-up yoga mat, the cross-section of which is a spiral shape.

In the two-dimensional coordinate plane, the equation $x^2 + y^2 = 9$ describes a circle centered at the origin with radius 3. In three-dimensional space, this same equation represents a surface. Imagine copies of a circle stacked on top of each other centered on the *z*-axis (**Figure 2.75**), forming a hollow tube. We can then construct a cylinder from the set of lines parallel to the *z*-axis passing through circle $x^2 + y^2 = 9$ in the *xy*-plane, as shown in the figure. In this way, any curve in one of the coordinate planes can be extended to become a surface.

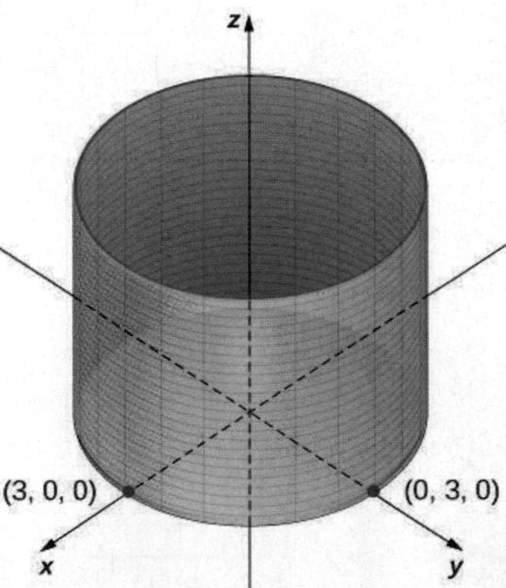

Figure 2.75 In three-dimensional space, the graph of equation $x^2 + y^2 = 9$ is a cylinder with radius 3 centered on the *z*-axis. It continues indefinitely in the positive and negative directions.

Definition

A set of lines parallel to a given line passing through a given curve is known as a cylindrical surface, or **cylinder**. The parallel lines are called **rulings**.

From this definition, we can see that we still have a cylinder in three-dimensional space, even if the curve is not a circle. Any curve can form a cylinder, and the rulings that compose the cylinder may be parallel to any given line (**Figure 2.76**).

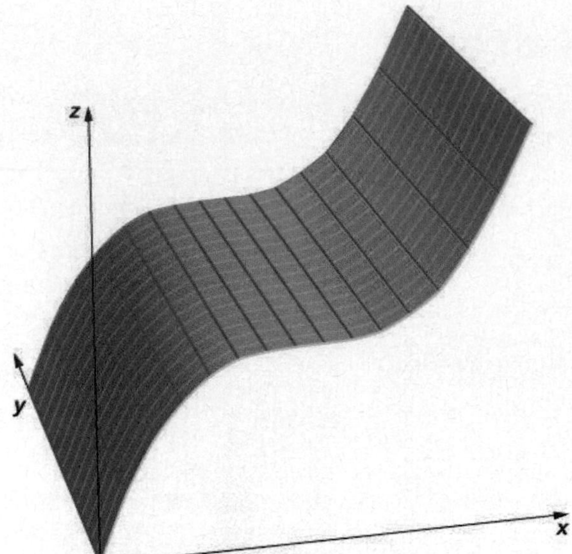

Figure 2.76 In three-dimensional space, the graph of equation $z = x^3$ is a cylinder, or a cylindrical surface with rulings parallel to the *y*-axis.

Example 2.55

Graphing Cylindrical Surfaces

Sketch the graphs of the following cylindrical surfaces.

a. $x^2 + z^2 = 25$

b. $z = 2x^2 - y$

c. $y = \sin x$

Solution

a. The variable y can take on any value without limit. Therefore, the lines ruling this surface are parallel to the *y*-axis. The intersection of this surface with the *xz*-plane forms a circle centered at the origin with radius 5 (see the following figure).

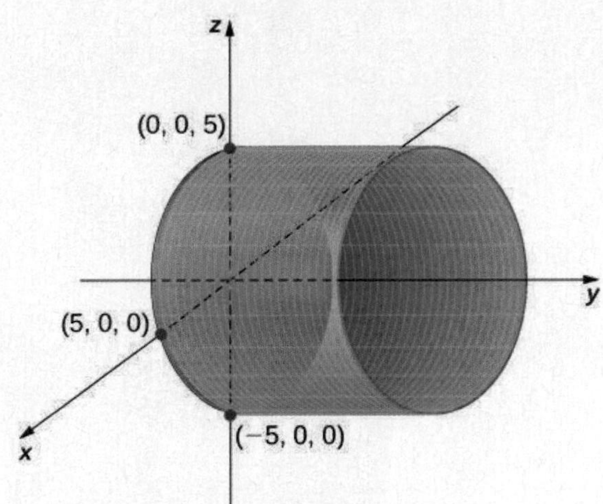

Figure 2.77 The graph of equation $x^2 + z^2 = 25$ is a cylinder with radius 5 centered on the y-axis.

b. In this case, the equation contains all three variables —x, y, and z— so none of the variables can vary arbitrarily. The easiest way to visualize this surface is to use a computer graphing utility (see the following figure).

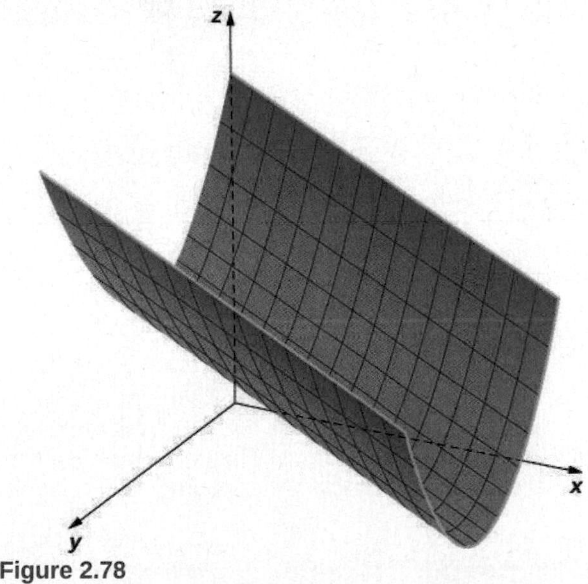

Figure 2.78

c. In this equation, the variable z can take on any value without limit. Therefore, the lines composing this surface are parallel to the z-axis. The intersection of this surface with the yz-plane outlines curve $y = \sin x$ (see the following figure).

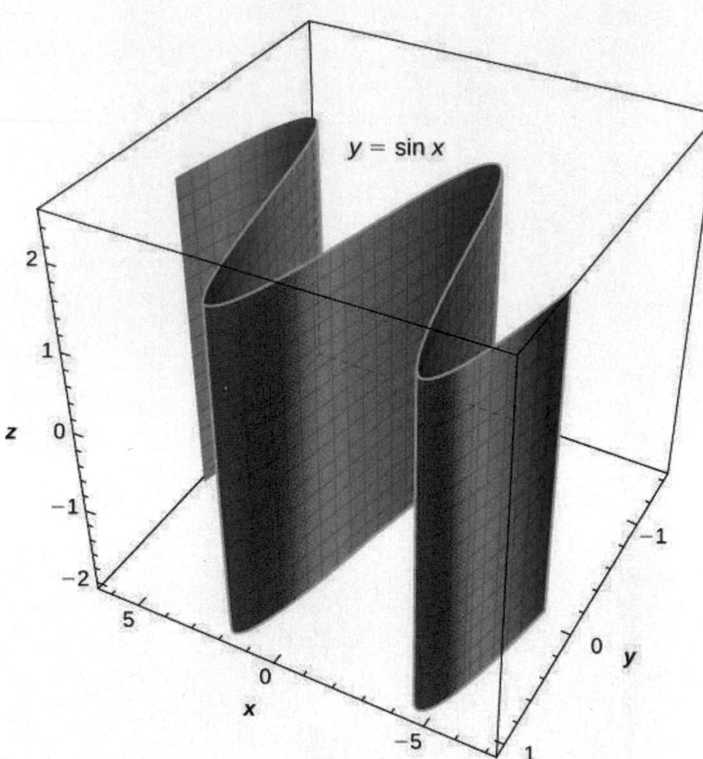

Figure 2.79 The graph of equation $y = \sin x$ is formed by a set of lines parallel to the z-axis passing through curve $y = \sin x$ in the xy-plane.

2.52 Sketch or use a graphing tool to view the graph of the cylindrical surface defined by equation $z = y^2$.

When sketching surfaces, we have seen that it is useful to sketch the intersection of the surface with a plane parallel to one of the coordinate planes. These curves are called traces. We can see them in the plot of the cylinder in **Figure 2.80**.

Definition

The **traces** of a surface are the cross-sections created when the surface intersects a plane parallel to one of the coordinate planes.

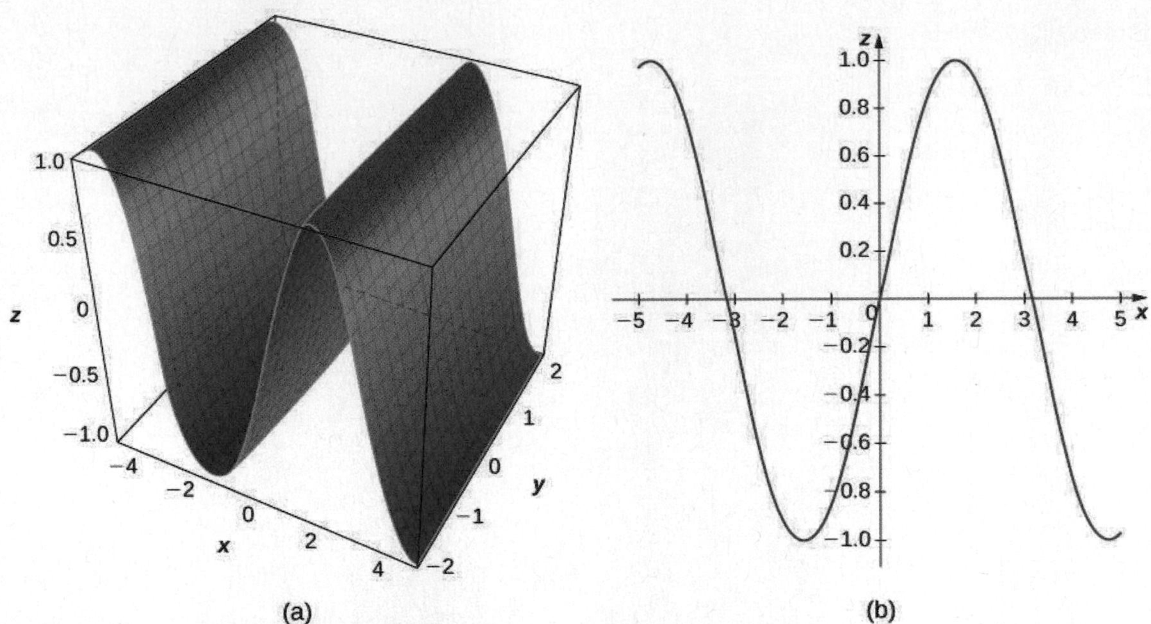

Figure 2.80 (a) This is one view of the graph of equation $z = \sin x$. (b) To find the trace of the graph in the *xz*-plane, set $y = 0$. The trace is simply a two-dimensional sine wave.

Traces are useful in sketching cylindrical surfaces. For a cylinder in three dimensions, though, only one set of traces is useful. Notice, in **Figure 2.80**, that the trace of the graph of $z = \sin x$ in the *xz*-plane is useful in constructing the graph. The trace in the *xy*-plane, though, is just a series of parallel lines, and the trace in the *yz*-plane is simply one line.

Cylindrical surfaces are formed by a set of parallel lines. Not all surfaces in three dimensions are constructed so simply, however. We now explore more complex surfaces, and traces are an important tool in this investigation.

Quadric Surfaces

We have learned about surfaces in three dimensions described by first-order equations; these are planes. Some other common types of surfaces can be described by second-order equations. We can view these surfaces as three-dimensional extensions of the conic sections we discussed earlier: the ellipse, the parabola, and the hyperbola. We call these graphs quadric surfaces.

Definition

Quadric surfaces are the graphs of equations that can be expressed in the form

$$Ax^2 + By^2 + Cz^2 + Dxy + Exz + Fyz + Gx + Hy + Jz + K = 0.$$

When a quadric surface intersects a coordinate plane, the trace is a conic section.

An **ellipsoid** is a surface described by an equation of the form $\frac{x^2}{a^2} + \frac{y^2}{b^2} + \frac{z^2}{c^2} = 1.$ Set $x = 0$ to see the trace of the ellipsoid in the *yz*-plane. To see the traces in the *y*- and *xz*-planes, set $z = 0$ and $y = 0,$ respectively. Notice that, if $a = b,$ the trace in the *xy*-plane is a circle. Similarly, if $a = c,$ the trace in the *xz*-plane is a circle and, if $b = c,$ then the trace in the *yz*-plane is a circle. A sphere, then, is an ellipsoid with $a = b = c.$

Example 2.56

Sketching an Ellipsoid

Sketch the ellipsoid $\frac{x^2}{2^2} + \frac{y^2}{3^2} + \frac{z^2}{5^2} = 1.$

Solution

Start by sketching the traces. To find the trace in the xy-plane, set $z = 0$: $\frac{x^2}{2^2} + \frac{y^2}{3^2} = 1$ (see **Figure 2.81**). To find the other traces, first set $y = 0$ and then set $x = 0.$

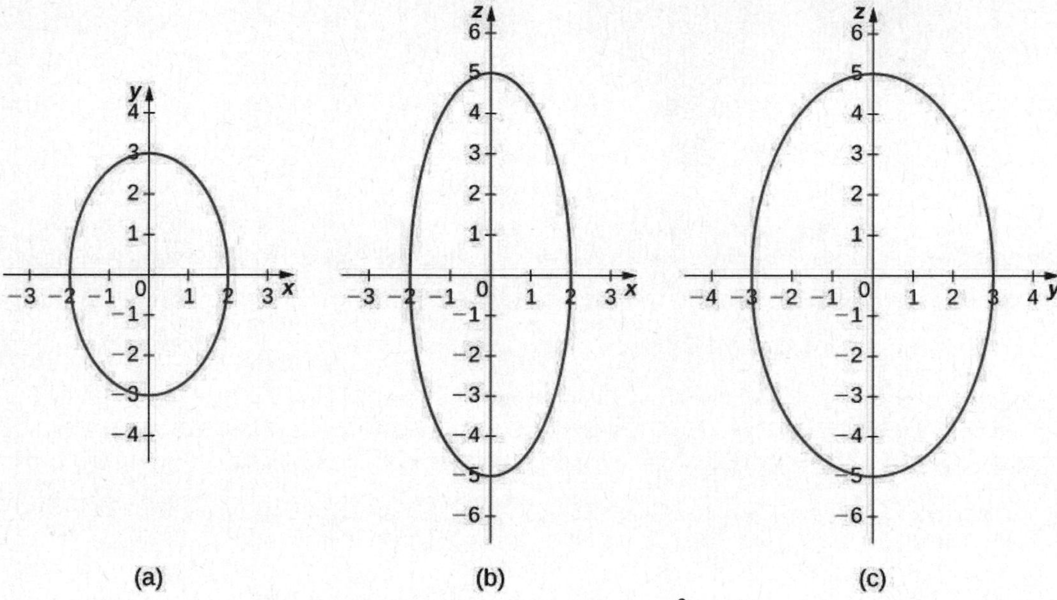

Figure 2.81 (a) This graph represents the trace of equation $\frac{x^2}{2^2} + \frac{y^2}{3^2} + \frac{z^2}{5^2} = 1$ in the xy-plane, when we set $z = 0.$ (b) When we set $y = 0,$ we get the trace of the ellipsoid in the xz-plane, which is an ellipse. (c) When we set $x = 0,$ we get the trace of the ellipsoid in the yz-plane, which is also an ellipse.

Now that we know what traces of this solid look like, we can sketch the surface in three dimensions (**Figure 2.82**).

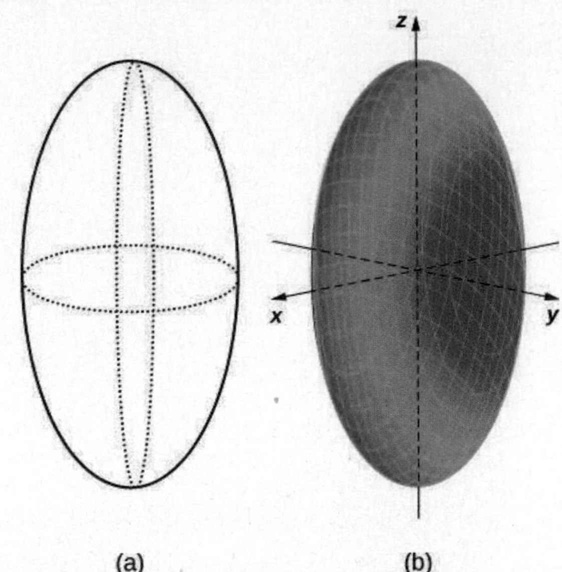

Figure 2.82 (a) The traces provide a framework for the surface. (b) The center of this ellipsoid is the origin.

The trace of an ellipsoid is an ellipse in each of the coordinate planes. However, this does not have to be the case for all quadric surfaces. Many quadric surfaces have traces that are different kinds of conic sections, and this is usually indicated by the name of the surface. For example, if a surface can be described by an equation of the form $\frac{x^2}{a^2} + \frac{y^2}{b^2} = \frac{z}{c}$, then we call that surface an **elliptic paraboloid**. The trace in the *xy*-plane is an ellipse, but the traces in the *xz*-plane and *yz*-plane are parabolas (**Figure 2.83**). Other elliptic paraboloids can have other orientations simply by interchanging the variables to give us a different variable in the linear term of the equation $\frac{x^2}{a^2} + \frac{z^2}{c^2} = \frac{y}{b}$ or $\frac{y^2}{b^2} + \frac{z^2}{c^2} = \frac{x}{a}$.

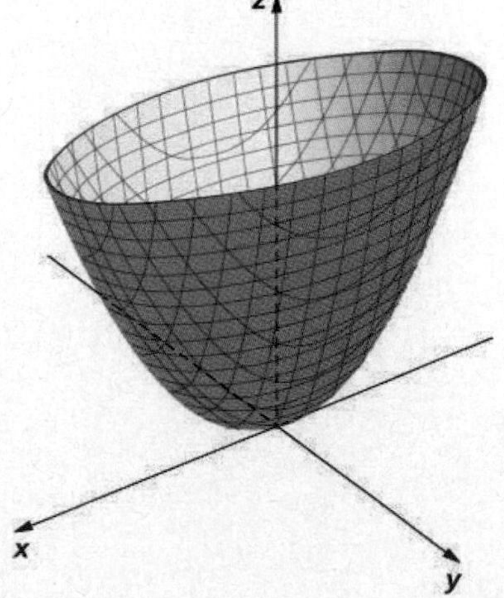

Figure 2.83 This quadric surface is called an *elliptic paraboloid.*

Example 2.57

Identifying Traces of Quadric Surfaces

Describe the traces of the elliptic paraboloid $x^2 + \frac{y^2}{2^2} = \frac{z}{5}$.

Solution

To find the trace in the *xy*-plane, set $z = 0$: $x^2 + \frac{y^2}{2^2} = 0$. The trace in the plane $z = 0$ is simply one point, the origin. Since a single point does not tell us what the shape is, we can move up the *z*-axis to an arbitrary plane to find the shape of other traces of the figure.

The trace in plane $z = 5$ is the graph of equation $x^2 + \frac{y^2}{2^2} = 1$, which is an ellipse. In the *xz*-plane, the equation becomes $z = 5x^2$. The trace is a parabola in this plane and in any plane with the equation $y = b$.

In planes parallel to the *yz*-plane, the traces are also parabolas, as we can see in the following figure.

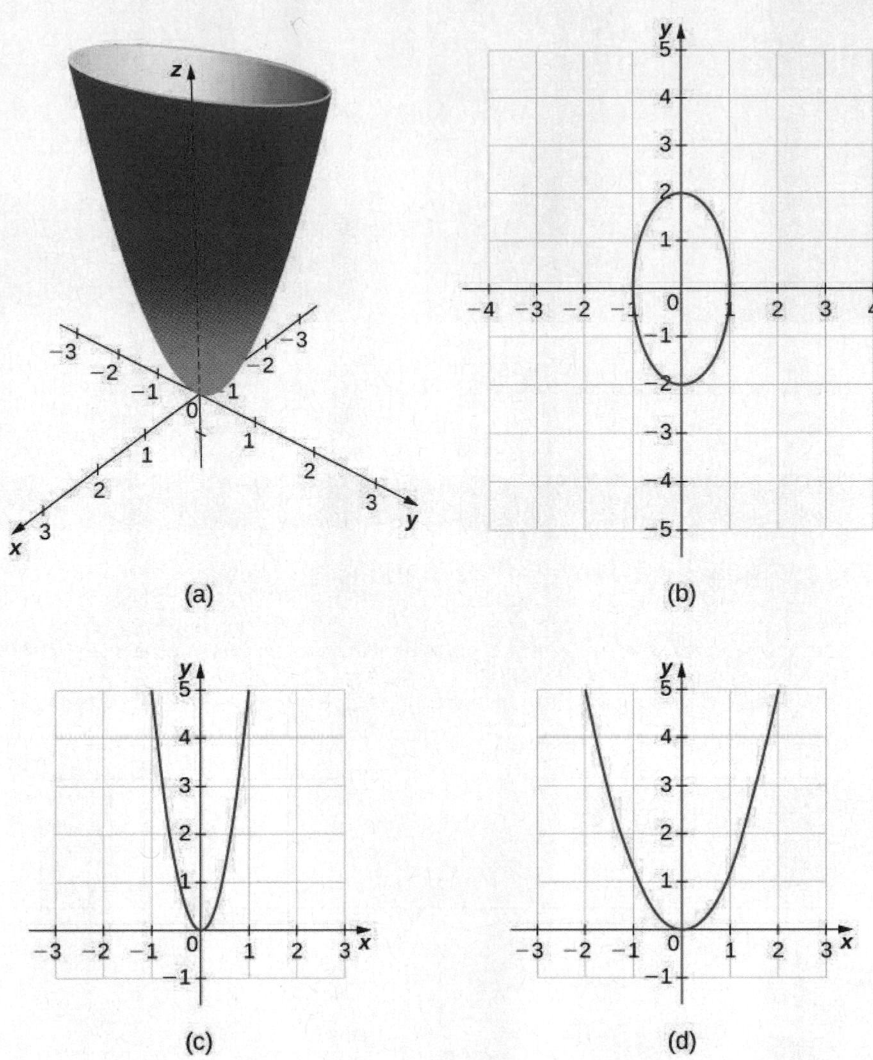

Figure 2.84 (a) The paraboloid $x^2 + \frac{y^2}{2^2} = \frac{z}{5}$. (b) The trace in plane $z = 5$. (c) The trace in the *xz*-plane. (d) The trace in the *yz*-plane.

2.53 A hyperboloid of one sheet is any surface that can be described with an equation of the form $\frac{x^2}{a^2} + \frac{y^2}{b^2} - \frac{z^2}{c^2} = 1$. Describe the traces of the hyperboloid of one sheet given by equation $\frac{x^2}{3^2} + \frac{y^2}{2^2} - \frac{z^2}{5^2} = 1$.

Hyperboloids of one sheet have some fascinating properties. For example, they can be constructed using straight lines, such as in the sculpture in **Figure 2.85**(a). In fact, cooling towers for nuclear power plants are often constructed in the shape of a hyperboloid. The builders are able to use straight steel beams in the construction, which makes the towers very strong while using relatively little material (**Figure 2.85**(b)).

Figure 2.85 (a) A sculpture in the shape of a hyperboloid can be constructed of straight lines. (b) Cooling towers for nuclear power plants are often built in the shape of a hyperboloid.

Example 2.58

Chapter Opener: Finding the Focus of a Parabolic Reflector

Energy hitting the surface of a parabolic reflector is concentrated at the focal point of the reflector (**Figure 2.86**). If the surface of a parabolic reflector is described by equation $\frac{x^2}{100} + \frac{y^2}{100} = \frac{z}{4}$, where is the focal point of the reflector?

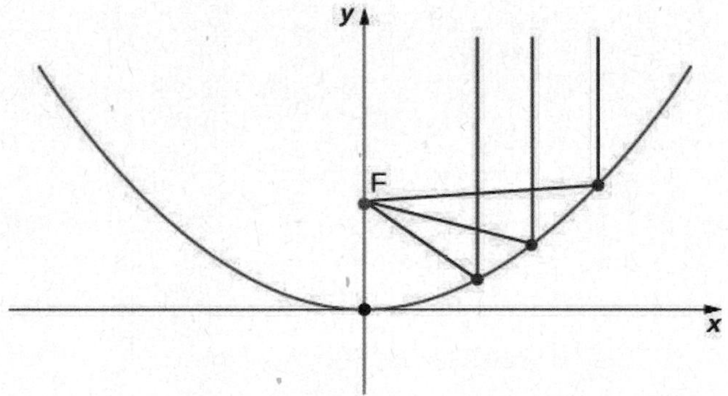

Figure 2.86 Energy reflects off of the parabolic reflector and is collected at the focal point. (credit: modification of CGP Grey, Wikimedia Commons)

Solution

Since z is the first-power variable, the axis of the reflector corresponds to the z-axis. The coefficients of x^2 and y^2 are equal, so the cross-section of the paraboloid perpendicular to the z-axis is a circle. We can consider a trace in the xz-plane or the yz-plane; the result is the same. Setting $y = 0$, the trace is a parabola opening up along the z-axis, with standard equation $x^2 = 4pz$, where p is the focal length of the parabola. In this case, this equation becomes $x^2 = 100 \cdot \frac{z}{4} = 4pz$ or $25 = 4p$. So p is 6.25 m, which tells us that the focus of the paraboloid is 6.25 m up the axis from the vertex. Because the vertex of this surface is the origin, the focal point is $(0, 0, 6.25)$.

Seventeen standard quadric surfaces can be derived from the general equation

$$Ax^2 + By^2 + Cz^2 + Dxy + Exz + Fyz + Gx + Hy + Jz + K = 0.$$

The following figures summarizes the most important ones.

Characteristics of Common Quadric Surfaces

Ellipsoid

$$\frac{x^2}{a^2} + \frac{y^2}{b^2} + \frac{z^2}{c^2} = 1$$

Traces
In plane $z = p$: an ellipse
In plane $y = q$: an ellipse
In plane $x = r$: an ellipse

If $a = b = c$, then this surface is a sphere.

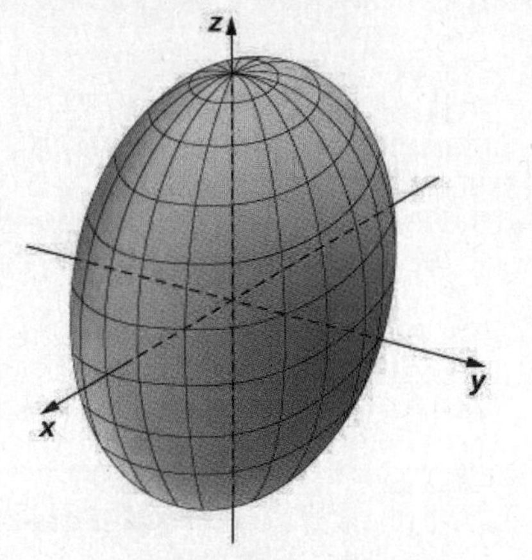

Hyperboloid of One Sheet

$$\frac{x^2}{a^2} + \frac{y^2}{b^2} - \frac{z^2}{c^2} = 1$$

Traces
In plane $z = p$: an ellipse
In plane $y = q$: a hyperbola
In plane $x = r$: a hyperbola

In the equation for this surface, two of the variables have positive coefficients and one has a negative coefficient. The axis of the surface corresponds to the variable with the negative coefficient.

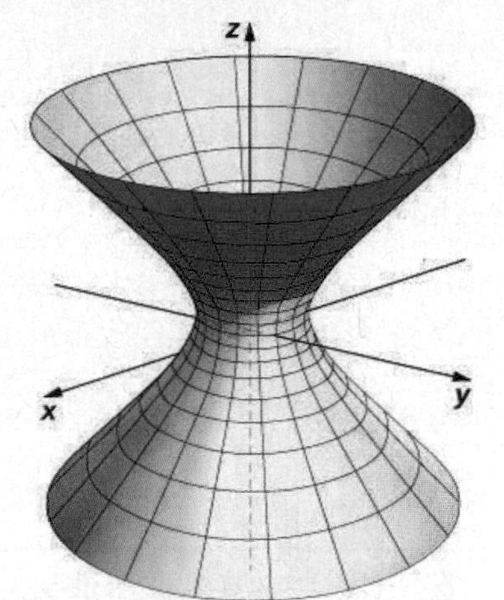

Hyperboloid of Two Sheets

$$\frac{z^2}{c^2} - \frac{x^2}{a^2} - \frac{y^2}{b^2} = 1$$

Traces
In plane $z = p$: an ellipse or the empty set (no trace)
In plane $y = q$: a hyperbola
In plane $x = r$: a hyperbola

In the equation for this surface, two of the variables have negative coefficients and one has a positive coefficient. The axis of the surface corresponds to the variable with a positive coefficient. The surface does not intersect the coordinate plane perpendicular to the axis.

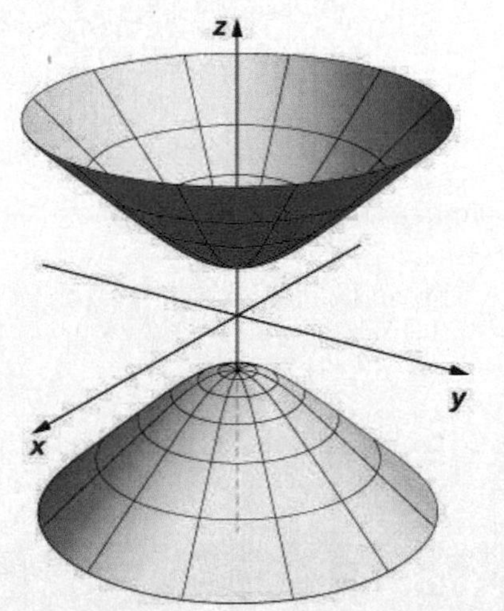

Figure 2.87 Characteristics of Common Quadratic Surfaces: Ellipsoid, **Hyperboloid of One Sheet**, **Hyperboloid of Two Sheets**.

Characteristics of Common Quadric Surfaces

Elliptic Cone $$\frac{x^2}{a^2} + \frac{y^2}{b^2} - \frac{z^2}{c^2} = 0$$ *Traces* In plane $z = p$: an ellipse In plane $y = q$: a hyperbola In plane $x = r$: a hyperbola In the xz – plane: a pair of lines that intersect at the origin In the yz – plane: a pair of lines that intersect at the origin The axis of the surface corresponds to the variable with a negative coefficient. The traces in the coordinate planes parallel to the axis are intersecting lines.	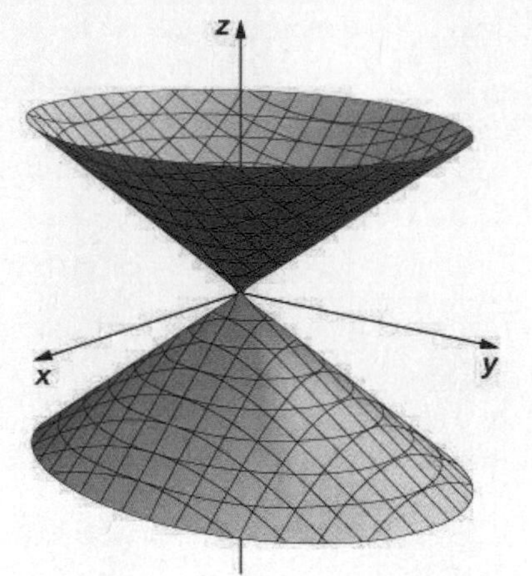
Elliptic Paraboloid $$z = \frac{x^2}{a^2} + \frac{y^2}{b^2}$$ *Traces* In plane $z = p$: an ellipse In plane $y = q$: a parabola In plane $x = r$: a parabola The axis of the surface corresponds to the linear variable.	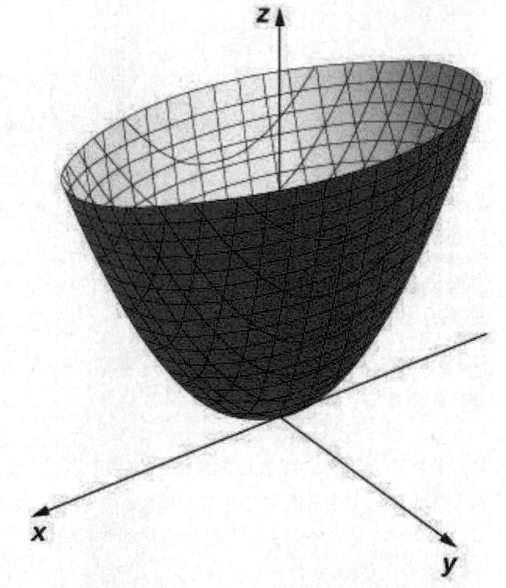
Hyperbolic Paraboloid $$z = \frac{x^2}{a^2} - \frac{y^2}{b^2}$$ *Traces* In plane $z = p$: a hyperbola In plane $y = q$: a parabola In plane $x = r$: a parabola The axis of the surface corresponds to the linear variable.	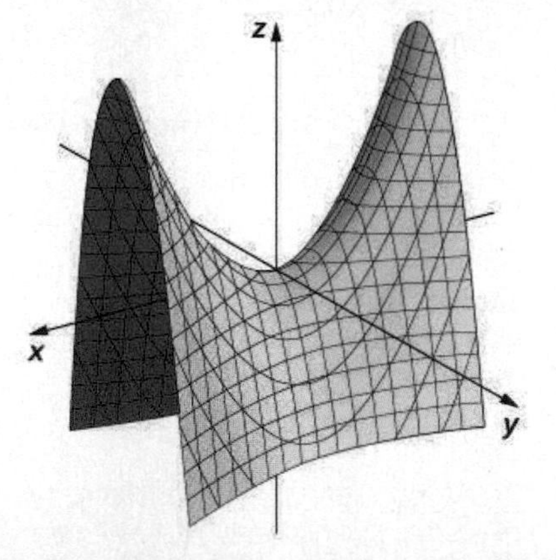

Figure 2.88 Characteristics of Common Quadratic Surfaces: **Elliptic Cone**, **Elliptic Paraboloid**, Hyperbolic Paraboloid.

Example 2.59

Identifying Equations of Quadric Surfaces

Identify the surfaces represented by the given equations.

a. $16x^2 + 9y^2 + 16z^2 = 144$

b. $9x^2 - 18x + 4y^2 + 16y - 36z + 25 = 0$

Solution

a. The $x, y,$ and z terms are all squared, and are all positive, so this is probably an ellipsoid. However, let's put the equation into the standard form for an ellipsoid just to be sure. We have

$$16x^2 + 9y^2 + 16z^2 = 144.$$

Dividing through by 144 gives

$$\frac{x^2}{9} + \frac{y^2}{16} + \frac{z^2}{9} = 1.$$

So, this is, in fact, an ellipsoid, centered at the origin.

b. We first notice that the z term is raised only to the first power, so this is either an elliptic paraboloid or a hyperbolic paraboloid. We also note there are x terms and y terms that are not squared, so this quadric surface is not centered at the origin. We need to complete the square to put this equation in one of the standard forms. We have

$$\begin{aligned} 9x^2 - 18x + 4y^2 + 16y - 36z + 25 &= 0 \\ 9x^2 - 18x + 4y^2 + 16y + 25 &= 36z \\ 9\left(x^2 - 2x\right) + 4\left(y^2 + 4y\right) + 25 &= 36z \\ 9\left(x^2 - 2x + 1 - 1\right) + 4\left(y^2 + 4y + 4 - 4\right) + 25 &= 36z \\ 9(x-1)^2 - 9 + 4(y+2)^2 - 16 + 25 &= 36z \\ 9(x-1)^2 + 4(y+2)^2 &= 36z \\ \frac{(x-1)^2}{4} + \frac{(y-2)^2}{9} &= z. \end{aligned}$$

This is an elliptic paraboloid centered at $(1, 2, 0)$.

2.54 Identify the surface represented by equation $9x^2 + y^2 - z^2 + 2z - 10 = 0$.

2.6 EXERCISES

For the following exercises, sketch and describe the cylindrical surface of the given equation.

303. **[T]** $x^2 + z^2 = 1$

304. **[T]** $x^2 + y^2 = 9$

305. **[T]** $z = \cos\left(\frac{\pi}{2} + x\right)$

306. **[T]** $z = e^x$

307. **[T]** $z = 9 - y^2$

308. **[T]** $z = \ln(x)$

For the following exercises, the graph of a quadric surface is given.

a. Specify the name of the quadric surface.

b. Determine the axis of symmetry of the quadric surface.

309.

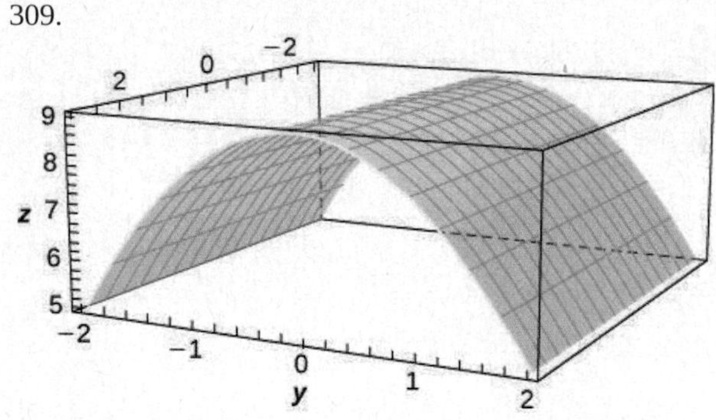

310.

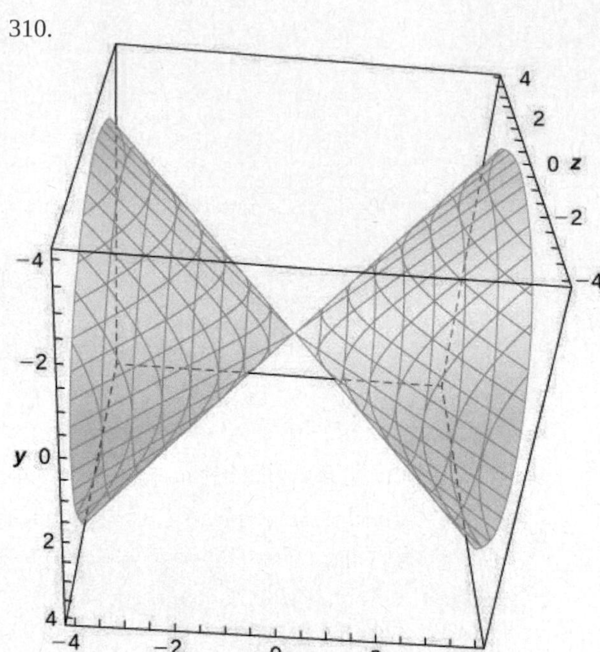

311.

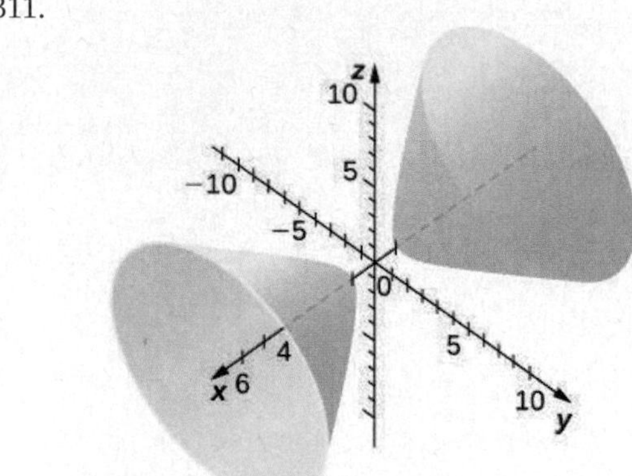

312.

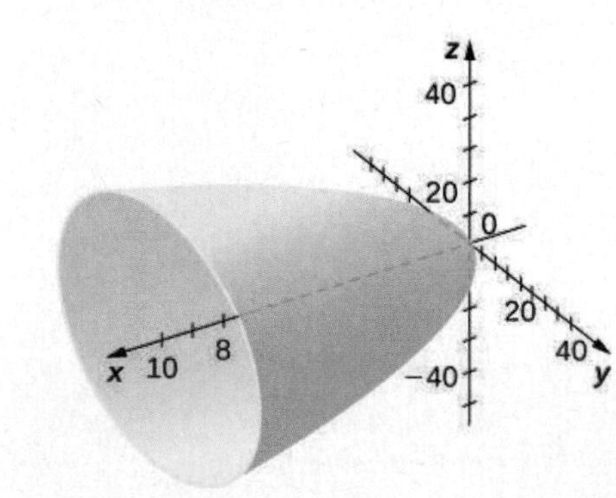

For the following exercises, match the given quadric surface with its corresponding equation in standard form.

a. $\frac{x^2}{4} + \frac{y^2}{9} - \frac{z^2}{12} = 1$

b. $\frac{x^2}{4} - \frac{y^2}{9} - \frac{z^2}{12} = 1$

c. $\frac{x^2}{4} + \frac{y^2}{9} + \frac{z^2}{12} = 1$

d. $z^2 = 4x^2 + 3y^2$

e. $z = 4x^2 - y^2$

f. $4x^2 + y^2 - z^2 = 0$

313. Hyperboloid of two sheets

314. Ellipsoid

315. Elliptic paraboloid

316. Hyperbolic paraboloid

317. Hyperboloid of one sheet

318. Elliptic cone

For the following exercises, rewrite the given equation of the quadric surface in standard form. Identify the surface.

319. $-x^2 + 36y^2 + 36z^2 = 9$

320. $-4x^2 + 25y^2 + z^2 = 100$

321. $-3x^2 + 5y^2 - z^2 = 10$

322. $3x^2 - y^2 - 6z^2 = 18$

323. $5y = x^2 - z^2$

324. $8x^2 - 5y^2 - 10z = 0$

325. $x^2 + 5y^2 + 3z^2 - 15 = 0$

326. $63x^2 + 7y^2 + 9z^2 - 63 = 0$

327. $x^2 + 5y^2 - 8z^2 = 0$

328. $5x^2 - 4y^2 + 20z^2 = 0$

329. $6x = 3y^2 + 2z^2$

330. $49y = x^2 + 7z^2$

For the following exercises, find the trace of the given quadric surface in the specified plane of coordinates and sketch it.

331. **[T]** $x^2 + z^2 + 4y = 0,\ z = 0$

332. **[T]** $x^2 + z^2 + 4y = 0,\ x = 0$

333. **[T]** $-4x^2 + 25y^2 + z^2 = 100,\ x = 0$

334. **[T]** $-4x^2 + 25y^2 + z^2 = 100,\ y = 0$

335. **[T]** $x^2 + \frac{y^2}{4} + \frac{z^2}{100} = 1,\ x = 0$

336. **[T]** $x^2 - y - z^2 = 1,\ y = 0$

337. Use the graph of the given quadric surface to answer the questions.

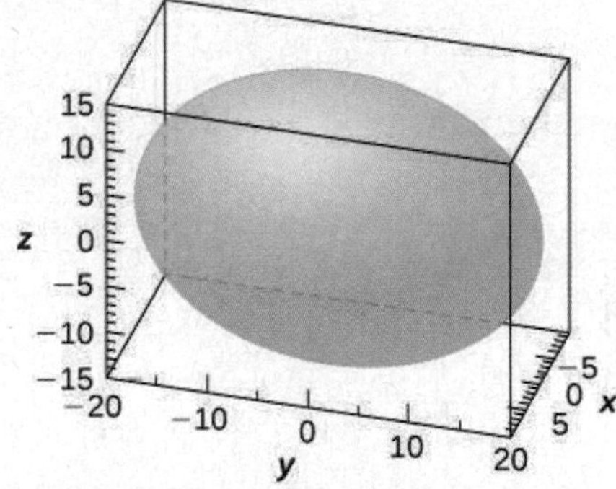

a. Specify the name of the quadric surface.
b. Which of the equations—$16x^2 + 9y^2 + 36z^2 = 3600$, $9x^2 + 36y^2 + 16z^2 = 3600$, or $36x^2 + 9y^2 + 16z^2 = 3600$—corresponds to the graph?
c. Use b. to write the equation of the quadric surface in standard form.

338. Use the graph of the given quadric surface to answer the questions.

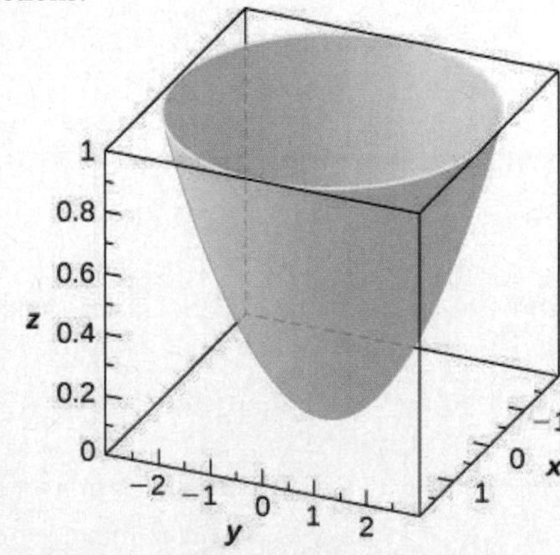

a. Specify the name of the quadric surface.
b. Which of the equations—$36z = 9x^2 + y^2$, $9x^2 + 4y^2 = 36z$, or $-36z = -81x^2 + 4y^2$—corresponds to the graph above?
c. Use b. to write the equation of the quadric surface in standard form.

For the following exercises, the equation of a quadric surface is given.

a. Use the method of completing the square to write the equation in standard form.

b. Identify the surface.

339. $x^2 + 2z^2 + 6x - 8z + 1 = 0$

340. $4x^2 - y^2 + z^2 - 8x + 2y + 2z + 3 = 0$

341. $x^2 + 4y^2 - 4z^2 - 6x - 16y - 16z + 5 = 0$

342. $x^2 + z^2 - 4y + 4 = 0$

343. $x^2 + \frac{y^2}{4} - \frac{z^2}{3} + 6x + 9 = 0$

344. $x^2 - y^2 + z^2 - 12z + 2x + 37 = 0$

345. Write the standard form of the equation of the ellipsoid centered at the origin that passes through points $A(2, 0, 0)$, $B(0, 0, 1)$, and $C\left(\frac{1}{2}, \sqrt{11}, \frac{1}{2}\right)$.

346. Write the standard form of the equation of the ellipsoid centered at point $P(1, 1, 0)$ that passes through points $A(6, 1, 0)$, $B(4, 2, 0)$ and $C(1, 2, 1)$.

347. Determine the intersection points of elliptic cone $x^2 - y^2 - z^2 = 0$ with the line of symmetric equations $\frac{x-1}{2} = \frac{y+1}{3} = z$.

348. Determine the intersection points of parabolic hyperboloid $z = 3x^2 - 2y^2$ with the line of parametric equations $x = 3t$, $y = 2t$, $z = 19t$, where $t \in \mathbb{R}$.

349. Find the equation of the quadric surface with points $P(x, y, z)$ that are equidistant from point $Q(0, -1, 0)$ and plane of equation $y = 1$. Identify the surface.

350. Find the equation of the quadric surface with points $P(x, y, z)$ that are equidistant from point $Q(0, 2, 0)$ and plane of equation $y = -2$. Identify the surface.

351. If the surface of a parabolic reflector is described by equation $400z = x^2 + y^2$, find the focal point of the reflector.

352. Consider the parabolic reflector described by equation $z = 20x^2 + 20y^2$. Find its focal point.

353. Show that quadric surface $x^2 + y^2 + z^2 + 2xy + 2xz + 2yz + x + y + z = 0$ reduces to two parallel planes.

354. Show that quadric surface $x^2 + y^2 + z^2 - 2xy - 2xz + 2yz - 1 = 0$ reduces to two parallel planes passing.

355. **[T]** The intersection between cylinder $(x-1)^2 + y^2 = 1$ and sphere $x^2 + y^2 + z^2 = 4$ is called a *Viviani curve*.

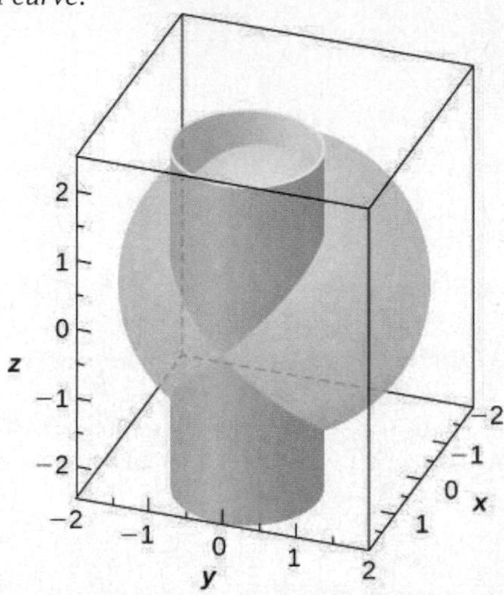

a. Solve the system consisting of the equations of the surfaces to find the equation of the intersection curve. (*Hint:* Find x and y in terms of z.)

b. Use a computer algebra system (CAS) to visualize the intersection curve on sphere $x^2 + y^2 + z^2 = 4$.

356. Hyperboloid of one sheet $25x^2 + 25y^2 - z^2 = 25$ and elliptic cone $-25x^2 + 75y^2 + z^2 = 0$ are represented in the following figure along with their intersection curves. Identify the intersection curves and find their equations (*Hint:* Find y from the system consisting of the equations of the surfaces.)

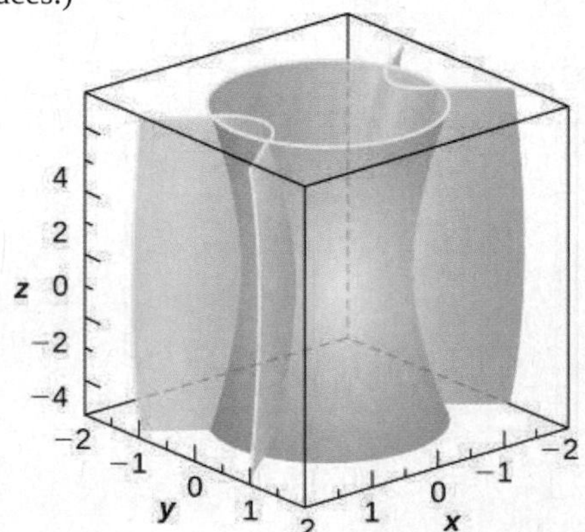

357. **[T]** Use a CAS to create the intersection between cylinder $9x^2 + 4y^2 = 18$ and ellipsoid $36x^2 + 16y^2 + 9z^2 = 144$, and find the equations of the intersection curves.

358. **[T]** A spheroid is an ellipsoid with two equal semiaxes. For instance, the equation of a spheroid with the z-axis as its axis of symmetry is given by $\frac{x^2}{a^2} + \frac{y^2}{a^2} + \frac{z^2}{c^2} = 1$, where a and c are positive real numbers. The spheroid is called *oblate* if $c < a$, and *prolate* for $c > a$.

a. The eye cornea is approximated as a prolate spheroid with an axis that is the eye, where $a = 8.7$ mm and $c = 9.6$ mm. Write the equation of the spheroid that models the cornea and sketch the surface.
b. Give two examples of objects with prolate spheroid shapes.

359. **[T]** In cartography, Earth is approximated by an oblate spheroid rather than a sphere. The radii at the equator and poles are approximately 3963 mi and 3950 mi, respectively.

a. Write the equation in standard form of the ellipsoid that represents the shape of Earth. Assume the center of Earth is at the origin and that the trace formed by plane $z = 0$ corresponds to the equator.
b. Sketch the graph.
c. Find the equation of the intersection curve of the surface with plane $z = 1000$ that is parallel to the xy-plane. The intersection curve is called a *parallel*.
d. Find the equation of the intersection curve of the surface with plane $x + y = 0$ that passes through the z-axis. The intersection curve is called a *meridian*.

360. **[T]** A set of buzzing stunt magnets (or "rattlesnake eggs") includes two sparkling, polished, superstrong spheroid-shaped magnets well-known for children's entertainment. Each magnet is 1.625 in. long and 0.5 in. wide at the middle. While tossing them into the air, they create a buzzing sound as they attract each other.

a. Write the equation of the prolate spheroid centered at the origin that describes the shape of one of the magnets.
b. Write the equations of the prolate spheroids that model the shape of the buzzing stunt magnets. Use a CAS to create the graphs.

361. **[T]** A heart-shaped surface is given by equation $\left(x^2 + \frac{9}{4}y^2 + z^2 - 1\right)^3 - x^2z^3 - \frac{9}{80}y^2z^3 = 0.$

a. Use a CAS to graph the surface that models this shape.
b. Determine and sketch the trace of the heart-shaped surface on the xz-plane.

362. **[T]** The ring torus symmetric about the z-axis is a special type of surface in topology and its equation is given by $\left(x^2 + y^2 + z^2 + R^2 - r^2\right)^2 = 4R^2\left(x^2 + y^2\right)$, where $R > r > 0$. The numbers R and r are called are the major and minor radii, respectively, of the surface. The following figure shows a ring torus for which $R = 2$ and $r = 1$.

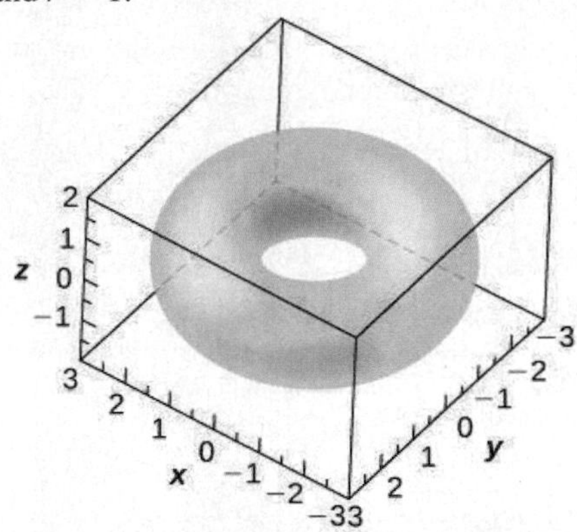

a. Write the equation of the ring torus with $R = 2$ and $r = 1$, and use a CAS to graph the surface. Compare the graph with the figure given.
b. Determine the equation and sketch the trace of the ring torus from a. on the xy-plane.
c. Give two examples of objects with ring torus shapes.

2.7 | Cylindrical and Spherical Coordinates

Learning Objectives

2.7.1 Convert from cylindrical to rectangular coordinates.
2.7.2 Convert from rectangular to cylindrical coordinates.
2.7.3 Convert from spherical to rectangular coordinates.
2.7.4 Convert from rectangular to spherical coordinates.

The Cartesian coordinate system provides a straightforward way to describe the location of points in space. Some surfaces, however, can be difficult to model with equations based on the Cartesian system. This is a familiar problem; recall that in two dimensions, polar coordinates often provide a useful alternative system for describing the location of a point in the plane, particularly in cases involving circles. In this section, we look at two different ways of describing the location of points in space, both of them based on extensions of polar coordinates. As the name suggests, cylindrical coordinates are useful for dealing with problems involving cylinders, such as calculating the volume of a round water tank or the amount of oil flowing through a pipe. Similarly, spherical coordinates are useful for dealing with problems involving spheres, such as finding the volume of domed structures.

Cylindrical Coordinates

When we expanded the traditional Cartesian coordinate system from two dimensions to three, we simply added a new axis to model the third dimension. Starting with polar coordinates, we can follow this same process to create a new three-dimensional coordinate system, called the cylindrical coordinate system. In this way, cylindrical coordinates provide a natural extension of polar coordinates to three dimensions.

Definition

In the **cylindrical coordinate system**, a point in space (**Figure 2.89**) is represented by the ordered triple (r, θ, z), where

- (r, θ) are the polar coordinates of the point's projection in the xy-plane
- z is the usual z-coordinate in the Cartesian coordinate system

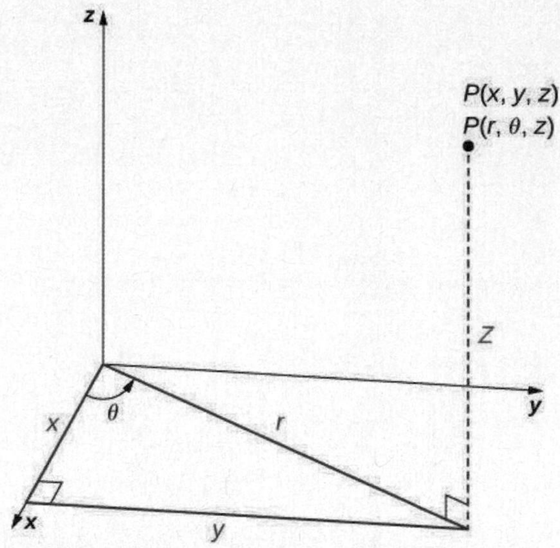

Figure 2.89 The right triangle lies in the *xy*-plane. The length of the hypotenuse is r and θ is the measure of the angle formed by the positive *x*-axis and the hypotenuse. The *z*-coordinate describes the location of the point above or below the *xy*-plane.

In the *xy*-plane, the right triangle shown in **Figure 2.89** provides the key to transformation between cylindrical and Cartesian, or rectangular, coordinates.

Theorem 2.15: Conversion between Cylindrical and Cartesian Coordinates

The rectangular coordinates (x, y, z) and the cylindrical coordinates (r, θ, z) of a point are related as follows:

$$\begin{aligned} x &= r\cos\theta \\ y &= r\sin\theta \\ z &= z \end{aligned}$$

These equations are used to convert from cylindrical coordinates to rectangular coordinates.

and

$$\begin{aligned} r^2 &= x^2 + y^2 \\ \tan\theta &= \frac{y}{x} \\ z &= z \end{aligned}$$

These equations are used to convert from rectangular coordinates to cylindrical coordinates.

As when we discussed conversion from rectangular coordinates to polar coordinates in two dimensions, it should be noted that the equation $\tan\theta = \frac{y}{x}$ has an infinite number of solutions. However, if we restrict θ to values between 0 and 2π, then we can find a unique solution based on the quadrant of the *xy*-plane in which original point (x, y, z) is located. Note that if $x = 0,$ then the value of θ is either $\frac{\pi}{2}, \frac{3\pi}{2},$ or $0,$ depending on the value of y.

Notice that these equations are derived from properties of right triangles. To make this easy to see, consider point P in the *xy*-plane with rectangular coordinates $(x, y, 0)$ and with cylindrical coordinates $(r, \theta, 0),$ as shown in the following figure.

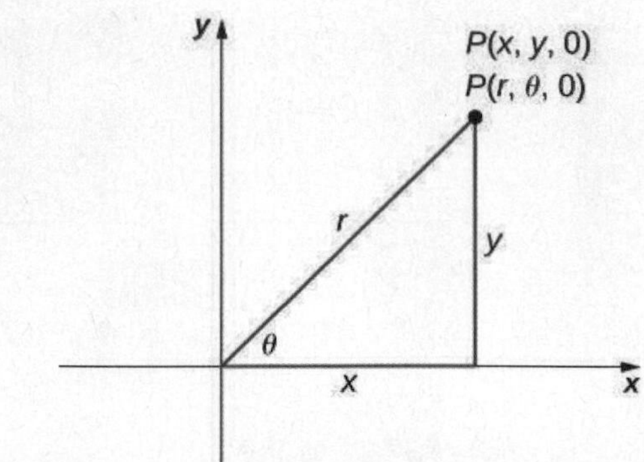

Figure 2.90 The Pythagorean theorem provides equation $r^2 = x^2 + y^2$. Right-triangle relationships tell us that $x = r\cos\theta,\ \ y = r\sin\theta,$ and $\tan\theta = y/x.$

Let's consider the differences between rectangular and cylindrical coordinates by looking at the surfaces generated when each of the coordinates is held constant. If c is a constant, then in rectangular coordinates, surfaces of the form $x = c,$ $y = c,$ or $z = c$ are all planes. Planes of these forms are parallel to the *yz*-plane, the *xz*-plane, and the *xy*-plane, respectively. When we convert to cylindrical coordinates, the *z*-coordinate does not change. Therefore, in cylindrical coordinates, surfaces of the form $z = c$ are planes parallel to the *xy*-plane. Now, let's think about surfaces of the form $r = c.$ The points on these surfaces are at a fixed distance from the *z*-axis. In other words, these surfaces are vertical circular cylinders. Last, what about $\theta = c$? The points on a surface of the form $\theta = c$ are at a fixed angle from the *x*-axis, which gives us a half-plane that starts at the *z*-axis (**Figure 2.91** and **Figure 2.92**).

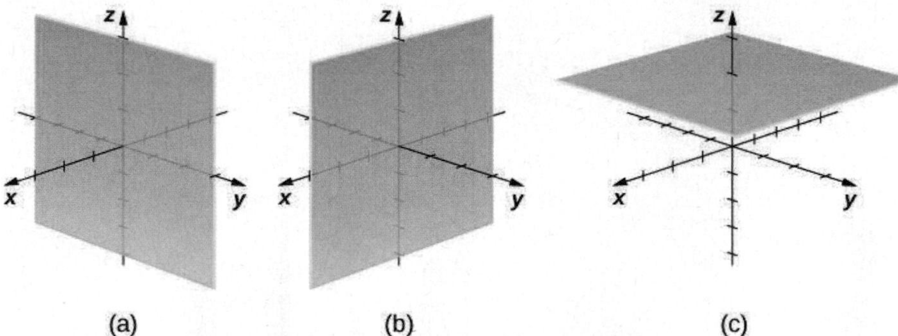

Figure 2.91 In rectangular coordinates, (a) surfaces of the form $x = c$ are planes parallel to the *yz*-plane, (b) surfaces of the form $y = c$ are planes parallel to the *xz*-plane, and (c) surfaces of the form $z = c$ are planes parallel to the *xy*-plane.

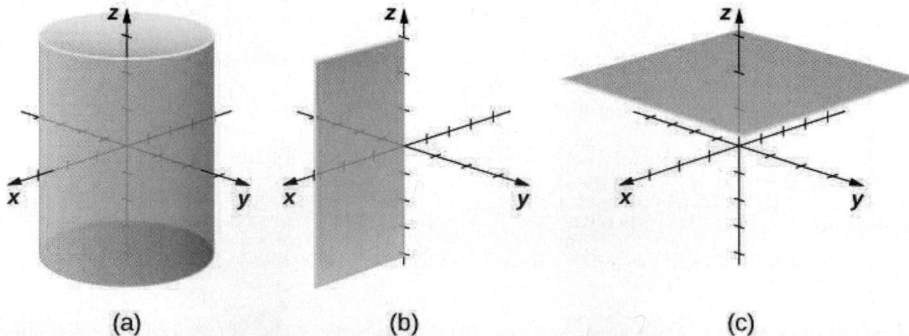

Figure 2.92 In cylindrical coordinates, (a) surfaces of the form $r = c$ are vertical cylinders of radius $r,$ (b) surfaces of the form $\theta = c$ are half-planes at angle θ from the *x*-axis, and (c) surfaces of the form $z = c$ are planes parallel to the *xy*-plane.

Example 2.60

Converting from Cylindrical to Rectangular Coordinates

Plot the point with cylindrical coordinates $\left(4, \frac{2\pi}{3}, -2\right)$ and express its location in rectangular coordinates.

Solution

Conversion from cylindrical to rectangular coordinates requires a simple application of the equations listed in **Conversion between Cylindrical and Cartesian Coordinates**:

$$\begin{aligned} x &= r\cos\theta = 4\cos\frac{2\pi}{3} = -2 \\ y &= r\sin\theta = 4\sin\frac{2\pi}{3} = 2\sqrt{3} \\ z &= -2. \end{aligned}$$

The point with cylindrical coordinates $\left(4, \frac{2\pi}{3}, -2\right)$ has rectangular coordinates $\left(-2, 2\sqrt{3}, -2\right)$ (see the following figure).

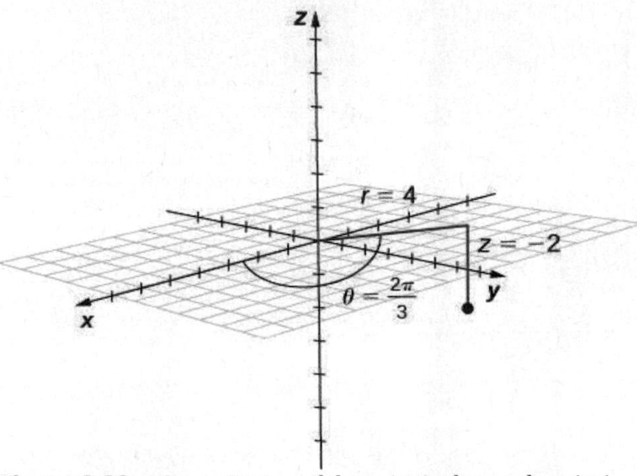

Figure 2.93 The projection of the point in the xy-plane is 4 units from the origin. The line from the origin to the point's projection forms an angle of $\frac{2\pi}{3}$ with the positive x-axis. The point lies 2 units below the xy-plane.

2.55 Point R has cylindrical coordinates $\left(5, \frac{\pi}{6}, 4\right)$. Plot R and describe its location in space using rectangular, or Cartesian, coordinates.

If this process seems familiar, it is with good reason. This is exactly the same process that we followed in **Introduction to Parametric Equations and Polar Coordinates** to convert from polar coordinates to two-dimensional rectangular coordinates.

Example 2.61

Converting from Rectangular to Cylindrical Coordinates

Convert the rectangular coordinates $(1, -3, 5)$ to cylindrical coordinates.

Solution

Use the second set of equations from **Conversion between Cylindrical and Cartesian Coordinates** to translate from rectangular to cylindrical coordinates:

$$\begin{aligned} r^2 &= x^2 + y^2 \\ r &= \pm\sqrt{1^2 + (-3)^2} = \pm\sqrt{10}. \end{aligned}$$

We choose the positive square root, so $r = \sqrt{10}$. Now, we apply the formula to find θ. In this case, y is negative and x is positive, which means we must select the value of θ between $\frac{3\pi}{2}$ and 2π:

$$\begin{aligned} \tan\theta &= \frac{y}{x} = \frac{-3}{1} \\ \theta &= \arctan(-3) \approx 5.03 \text{ rad}. \end{aligned}$$

In this case, the *z*-coordinates are the same in both rectangular and cylindrical coordinates:

$$z = 5.$$

The point with rectangular coordinates $(1, -3, 5)$ has cylindrical coordinates approximately equal to $(\sqrt{10}, 5.03, 5)$.

2.56 Convert point $(-8, 8, -7)$ from Cartesian coordinates to cylindrical coordinates.

The use of cylindrical coordinates is common in fields such as physics. Physicists studying electrical charges and the capacitors used to store these charges have discovered that these systems sometimes have a cylindrical symmetry. These systems have complicated modeling equations in the Cartesian coordinate system, which make them difficult to describe and analyze. The equations can often be expressed in more simple terms using cylindrical coordinates. For example, the cylinder described by equation $x^2 + y^2 = 25$ in the Cartesian system can be represented by cylindrical equation $r = 5$.

Example 2.62

Identifying Surfaces in the Cylindrical Coordinate System

Describe the surfaces with the given cylindrical equations.

a. $\theta = \frac{\pi}{4}$

b. $r^2 + z^2 = 9$

c. $z = r$

Solution

a. When the angle θ is held constant while r and z are allowed to vary, the result is a half-plane (see the following figure).

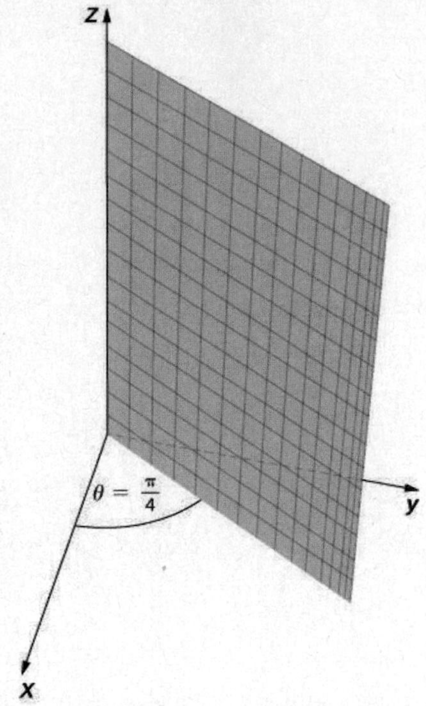

Figure 2.94 In polar coordinates, the equation $\theta = \pi/4$ describes the ray extending diagonally through the first quadrant. In three dimensions, this same equation describes a half-plane.

b. Substitute $r^2 = x^2 + y^2$ into equation $r^2 + z^2 = 9$ to express the rectangular form of the equation: $x^2 + y^2 + z^2 = 9$. This equation describes a sphere centered at the origin with radius 3 (see the following figure).

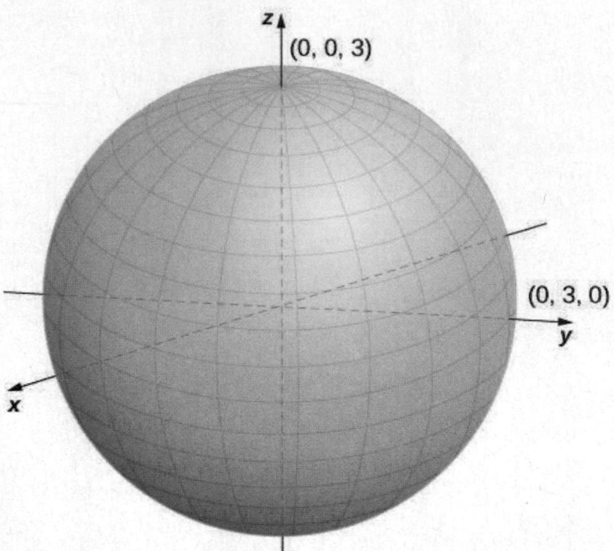

Figure 2.95 The sphere centered at the origin with radius 3 can be described by the cylindrical equation $r^2 + z^2 = 9.$

c. To describe the surface defined by equation $z = r,$ is it useful to examine traces parallel to the *xy*-plane. For example, the trace in plane $z = 1$ is circle $r = 1,$ the trace in plane $z = 3$ is circle $r = 3,$ and so on. Each trace is a circle. As the value of z increases, the radius of the circle also increases. The resulting surface is a cone (see the following figure).

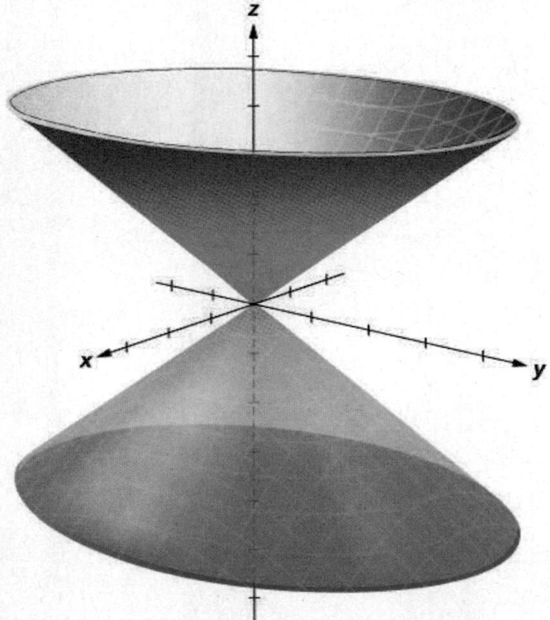

Figure 2.96 The traces in planes parallel to the *xy*-plane are circles. The radius of the circles increases as z increases.

2.57 Describe the surface with cylindrical equation $r = 6.$

Spherical Coordinates

In the Cartesian coordinate system, the location of a point in space is described using an ordered triple in which each coordinate represents a distance. In the cylindrical coordinate system, location of a point in space is described using two distances (r and z) and an angle measure (θ). In the spherical coordinate system, we again use an ordered triple to describe the location of a point in space. In this case, the triple describes one distance and two angles. Spherical coordinates make it simple to describe a sphere, just as cylindrical coordinates make it easy to describe a cylinder. Grid lines for spherical coordinates are based on angle measures, like those for polar coordinates.

Definition

In the **spherical coordinate system**, a point P in space (**Figure 2.97**) is represented by the ordered triple (ρ, θ, φ) where

- ρ (the Greek letter rho) is the distance between P and the origin $(\rho \neq 0)$;
- θ is the same angle used to describe the location in cylindrical coordinates;
- φ (the Greek letter phi) is the angle formed by the positive z-axis and line segment $\overline{OP}$, where O is the origin and $0 \leq \varphi \leq \pi$.

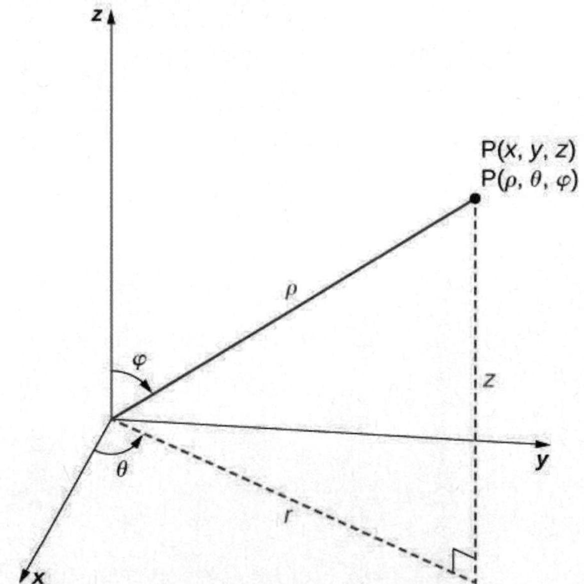

Figure 2.97 The relationship among spherical, rectangular, and cylindrical coordinates.

By convention, the origin is represented as $(0, 0, 0)$ in spherical coordinates.

Theorem 2.16: Converting among Spherical, Cylindrical, and Rectangular Coordinates

Rectangular coordinates (x, y, z) and spherical coordinates (ρ, θ, φ) of a point are related as follows:

$$\begin{aligned} x &= \rho \sin \varphi \cos \theta \\ y &= \rho \sin \varphi \sin \theta \\ z &= \rho \cos \varphi \end{aligned}$$

These equations are used to convert from spherical coordinates to rectangular coordinates.

and

$$\begin{aligned} \rho^2 &= x^2 + y^2 + z^2 \\ \tan \theta &= \frac{y}{x} \\ \varphi &= \arccos\left(\frac{z}{\sqrt{x^2 + y^2 + z^2}}\right). \end{aligned}$$

These equations are used to convert from rectangular coordinates to spherical coordinates.

If a point has cylindrical coordinates (r, θ, z), then these equations define the relationship between cylindrical and spherical coordinates.

$$\begin{aligned} r &= \rho \sin \varphi \\ \theta &= \theta \\ z &= \rho \cos \varphi \end{aligned}$$

These equations are used to convert from spherical coordinates to cylindrical coordinates.

and

$$\begin{aligned} \rho &= \sqrt{r^2 + z^2} \\ \theta &= \theta \\ \varphi &= \arccos\left(\frac{z}{\sqrt{r^2 + z^2}}\right) \end{aligned}$$

These equations are used to convert from cylindrical coordinates to spherical coordinates.

The formulas to convert from spherical coordinates to rectangular coordinates may seem complex, but they are straightforward applications of trigonometry. Looking at **Figure 2.98**, it is easy to see that $r = \rho \sin \varphi$. Then, looking at the triangle in the *xy*-plane with r as its hypotenuse, we have $x = r \cos \theta = \rho \sin \varphi \cos \theta$. The derivation of the formula for y is similar. **Figure 2.96** also shows that $\rho^2 = r^2 + z^2 = x^2 + y^2 + z^2$ and $z = \rho \cos \varphi$. Solving this last equation for φ and then substituting $\rho = \sqrt{r^2 + z^2}$ (from the first equation) yields $\varphi = \arccos\left(\frac{z}{\sqrt{r^2 + z^2}}\right)$. Also, note that, as before, we must be careful when using the formula $\tan \theta = \frac{y}{x}$ to choose the correct value of θ.

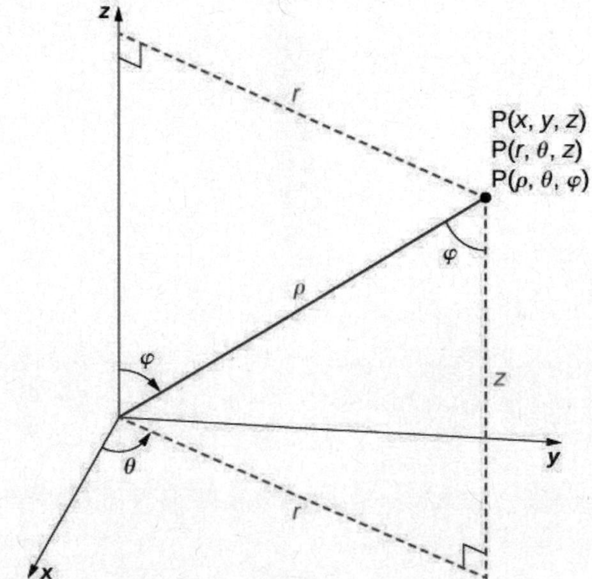

Figure 2.98 The equations that convert from one system to another are derived from right-triangle relationships.

As we did with cylindrical coordinates, let's consider the surfaces that are generated when each of the coordinates is held constant. Let c be a constant, and consider surfaces of the form $\rho = c.$ Points on these surfaces are at a fixed distance from the origin and form a sphere. The coordinate θ in the spherical coordinate system is the same as in the cylindrical coordinate system, so surfaces of the form $\theta = c$ are half-planes, as before. Last, consider surfaces of the form $\varphi = 0.$ The points on these surfaces are at a fixed angle from the z-axis and form a half-cone (**Figure 2.99**).

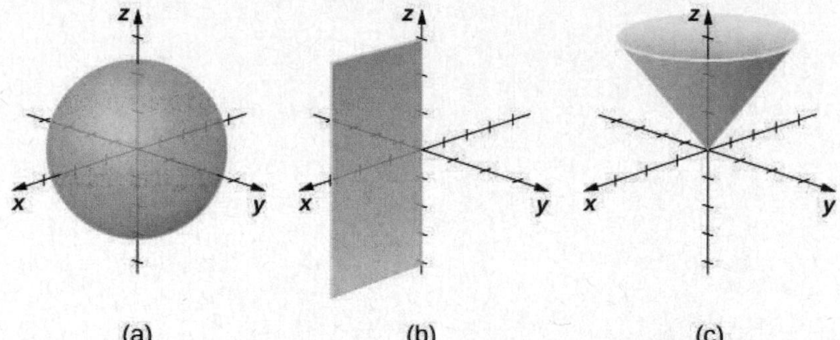

Figure 2.99 In spherical coordinates, surfaces of the form $\rho = c$ are spheres of radius ρ (a), surfaces of the form $\theta = c$ are half-planes at an angle θ from the x-axis (b), and surfaces of the form $\phi = c$ are half-cones at an angle ϕ from the z-axis (c).

Example 2.63

Converting from Spherical Coordinates

Plot the point with spherical coordinates $\left(8, \frac{\pi}{3}, \frac{\pi}{6}\right)$ and express its location in both rectangular and cylindrical coordinates.

Solution

Use the equations in **Converting among Spherical, Cylindrical, and Rectangular Coordinates** to translate between spherical and cylindrical coordinates (**Figure 2.100**):

$$\begin{aligned} x &= \rho \sin \varphi \cos \theta = 8 \sin\left(\frac{\pi}{6}\right)\cos\left(\frac{\pi}{3}\right) = 8\left(\frac{1}{2}\right)\frac{1}{2} = 2 \\ y &= \rho \sin \varphi \sin \theta = 8 \sin\left(\frac{\pi}{6}\right)\sin\left(\frac{\pi}{3}\right) = 8\left(\frac{1}{2}\right)\frac{\sqrt{3}}{2} = 2\sqrt{3} \\ z &= \rho \cos \varphi = 8 \cos\left(\frac{\pi}{6}\right) = 8\left(\frac{\sqrt{3}}{2}\right) = 4\sqrt{3}. \end{aligned}$$

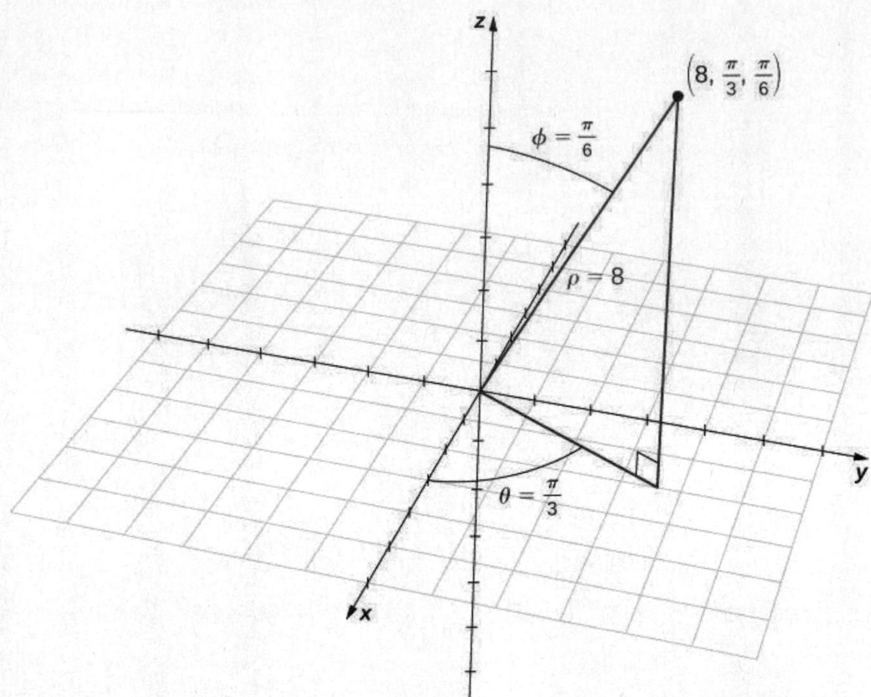

Figure 2.100 The projection of the point in the xy-plane is 4 units from the origin. The line from the origin to the point's projection forms an angle of $\pi/3$ with the positive x-axis. The point lies $4\sqrt{3}$ units above the xy-plane.

The point with spherical coordinates $\left(8, \frac{\pi}{3}, \frac{\pi}{6}\right)$ has rectangular coordinates $\left(2, 2\sqrt{3}, 4\sqrt{3}\right)$.

Finding the values in cylindrical coordinates is equally straightforward:

$$\begin{aligned} r &= \rho \sin \varphi = 8 \sin \frac{\pi}{6} = 4 \\ \theta &= \theta \\ z &= \rho \cos \varphi = 8 \cos \frac{\pi}{6} = 4\sqrt{3}. \end{aligned}$$

Thus, cylindrical coordinates for the point are $\left(4, \frac{\pi}{3}, 4\sqrt{3}\right)$.

2.58 Plot the point with spherical coordinates $\left(2, -\frac{5\pi}{6}, \frac{\pi}{6}\right)$ and describe its location in both rectangular and cylindrical coordinates.

Example 2.64

Converting from Rectangular Coordinates

Convert the rectangular coordinates $\left(-1, 1, \sqrt{6}\right)$ to both spherical and cylindrical coordinates.

Solution

Start by converting from rectangular to spherical coordinates:

$$\begin{aligned} \rho^2 &= x^2 + y^2 + z^2 = (-1)^2 + 1^2 + (\sqrt{6})^2 = 8 \qquad & \tan\theta &= \frac{1}{-1} \\ \rho &= 2\sqrt{2} & \theta &= \arctan(-1) = \frac{3\pi}{4}. \end{aligned}$$

Because $(x, y) = (-1, 1),$ then the correct choice for θ is $\frac{3\pi}{4}.$

There are actually two ways to identify φ. We can use the equation $\varphi = \arccos\left(\frac{z}{\sqrt{x^2 + y^2 + z^2}}\right)$. A more simple approach, however, is to use equation $z = \rho\cos\varphi$. We know that $z = \sqrt{6}$ and $\rho = 2\sqrt{2},$ so

$$\sqrt{6} = 2\sqrt{2}\cos\varphi, \text{ so } \cos\varphi = \frac{\sqrt{6}}{2\sqrt{2}} = \frac{\sqrt{3}}{2}$$

and therefore $\varphi = \frac{\pi}{6}$. The spherical coordinates of the point are $\left(2\sqrt{2}, \frac{3\pi}{4}, \frac{\pi}{6}\right)$.

To find the cylindrical coordinates for the point, we need only find r:

$$r = \rho\sin\varphi = 2\sqrt{2}\sin\left(\frac{\pi}{6}\right) = \sqrt{2}.$$

The cylindrical coordinates for the point are $\left(\sqrt{2}, \frac{3\pi}{4}, \sqrt{6}\right)$.

Example 2.65

Identifying Surfaces in the Spherical Coordinate System

Describe the surfaces with the given spherical equations.

a. $\theta = \frac{\pi}{3}$

b. $\varphi = \frac{5\pi}{6}$

c. $\rho = 6$

d. $\rho = \sin\theta\sin\varphi$

Solution

a. The variable θ represents the measure of the same angle in both the cylindrical and spherical coordinate systems. Points with coordinates $\left(\rho, \frac{\pi}{3}, \varphi\right)$ lie on the plane that forms angle $\theta = \frac{\pi}{3}$ with the positive x-axis. Because $\rho > 0,$ the surface described by equation $\theta = \frac{\pi}{3}$ is the half-plane shown in **Figure 2.101**.

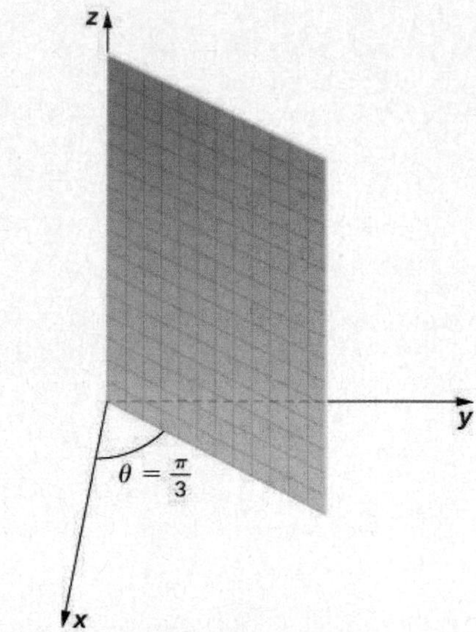

Figure 2.101 The surface described by equation $\theta = \frac{\pi}{3}$ is a half-plane.

b. Equation $\varphi = \frac{5\pi}{6}$ describes all points in the spherical coordinate system that lie on a line from the origin forming an angle measuring $\frac{5\pi}{6}$ rad with the positive z-axis. These points form a half-cone (**Figure 2.102**). Because there is only one value for φ that is measured from the positive z-axis, we do not get the full cone (with two pieces).

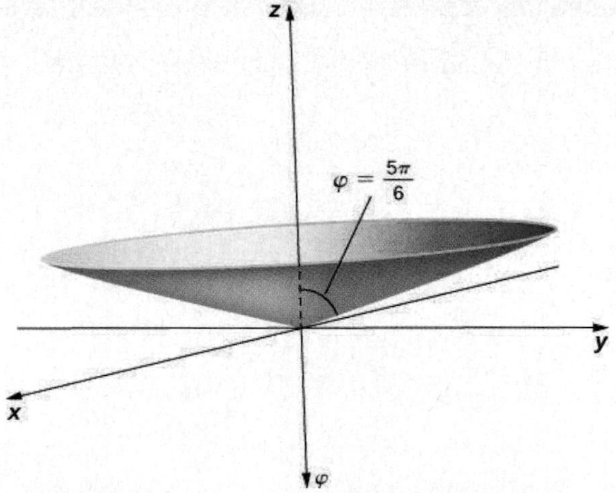

Figure 2.102 The equation $\varphi = \frac{5\pi}{6}$ describes a cone.

To find the equation in rectangular coordinates, use equation $\varphi = \arccos\left(\frac{z}{\sqrt{x^2 + y^2 + z^2}}\right)$.

$$\begin{aligned}
\frac{5\pi}{6} &= \arccos\left(\frac{z}{\sqrt{x^2+y^2+z^2}}\right)\\
\cos\frac{5\pi}{6} &= \frac{z}{\sqrt{x^2+y^2+z^2}}\\
-\frac{\sqrt{3}}{2} &= \frac{z}{\sqrt{x^2+y^2+z^2}}\\
\frac{3}{4} &= \frac{z^2}{x^2+y^2+z^2}\\
\frac{3x^2}{4}+\frac{3y^2}{4}+\frac{3z^2}{4} &= z^2\\
\frac{3x^2}{4}+\frac{3y^2}{4}-\frac{z^2}{4} &= 0.
\end{aligned}$$

This is the equation of a cone centered on the z-axis.

c. Equation $\rho = 6$ describes the set of all points 6 units away from the origin—a sphere with radius 6 (**Figure 2.103**).

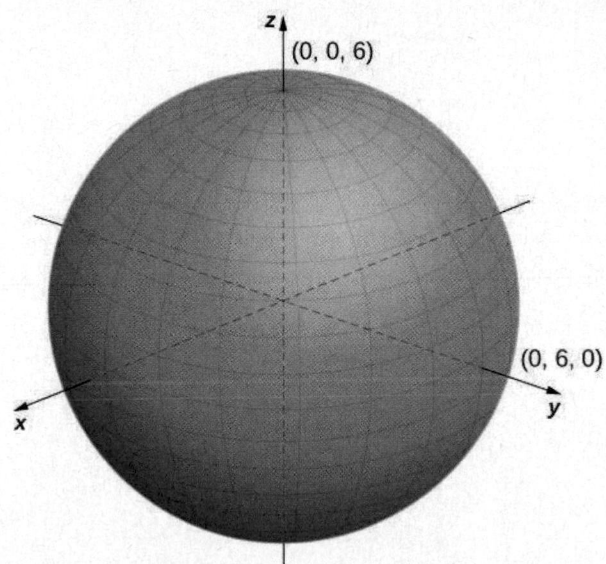

Figure 2.103 Equation $\rho = 6$ describes a sphere with radius 6.

d. To identify this surface, convert the equation from spherical to rectangular coordinates, using equations $y = \rho \sin\varphi \sin\theta$ and $\rho^2 = x^2 + y^2 + z^2$:

$$\begin{aligned}
\rho &= \sin\theta\sin\varphi \\
\rho^2 &= \rho\sin\theta\sin\varphi && \text{Multiply both sides of the equation by } \rho. \\
x^2+y^2+z^2 &= y && \text{Substitute rectangular variables using the equations above.} \\
x^2+y^2-y+z^2 &= 0 && \text{Subtract } y \text{ from both sides of the equation.} \\
x^2+y^2-y+\frac{1}{4}+z^2 &= \frac{1}{4} && \text{Complete the square.} \\
x^2+\left(y-\frac{1}{2}\right)^2+z^2 &= \frac{1}{4}. && \text{Rewrite the middle terms as a perfect square.}
\end{aligned}$$

The equation describes a sphere centered at point $\left(0, \frac{1}{2}, 0\right)$ with radius $\frac{1}{2}$.

2.59 Describe the surfaces defined by the following equations.

a. $\rho = 13$

b. $\theta = \frac{2\pi}{3}$

c. $\varphi = \frac{\pi}{4}$

Spherical coordinates are useful in analyzing systems that have some degree of symmetry about a point, such as the volume of the space inside a domed stadium or wind speeds in a planet's atmosphere. A sphere that has Cartesian equation $x^2 + y^2 + z^2 = c^2$ has the simple equation $\rho = c$ in spherical coordinates.

In geography, latitude and longitude are used to describe locations on Earth's surface, as shown in **Figure 2.104**. Although the shape of Earth is not a perfect sphere, we use spherical coordinates to communicate the locations of points on Earth. Let's assume Earth has the shape of a sphere with radius 4000 mi. We express angle measures in degrees rather than radians because latitude and longitude are measured in degrees.

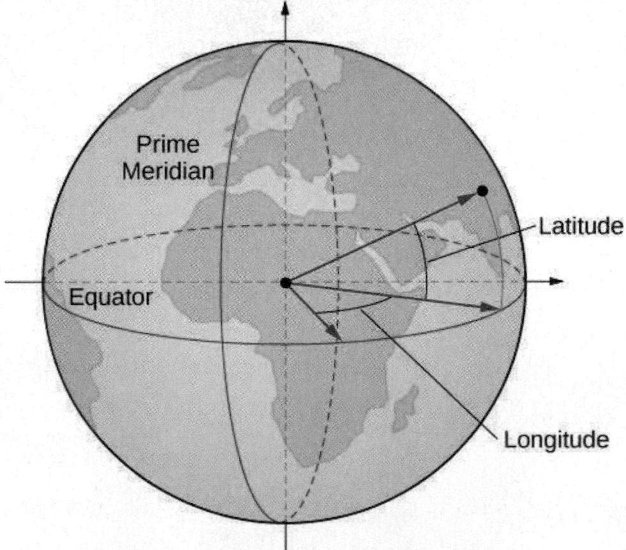

Figure 2.104 In the latitude–longitude system, angles describe the location of a point on Earth relative to the equator and the prime meridian.

Let the center of Earth be the center of the sphere, with the ray from the center through the North Pole representing the positive *z*-axis. The prime meridian represents the trace of the surface as it intersects the *xz*-plane. The equator is the trace of the sphere intersecting the *xy*-plane.

Example 2.66

Converting Latitude and Longitude to Spherical Coordinates

The latitude of Columbus, Ohio, is $40°$ N and the longitude is $83°$ W, which means that Columbus is $40°$ north of the equator. Imagine a ray from the center of Earth through Columbus and a ray from the center of Earth through the equator directly south of Columbus. The measure of the angle formed by the rays is $40°$. In the same way, measuring from the prime meridian, Columbus lies $83°$ to the west. Express the location of Columbus in spherical coordinates.

Solution

The radius of Earth is 4000 mi, so $\rho = 4000$. The intersection of the prime meridian and the equator lies on the positive *x*-axis. Movement to the west is then described with negative angle measures, which shows that $\theta = -83°$, Because Columbus lies $40°$ north of the equator, it lies $50°$ south of the North Pole, so $\varphi = 50°$. In spherical coordinates, Columbus lies at point $(4000, -83°, 50°)$.

2.60 Sydney, Australia is at $34°\text{S}$ and $151°\text{E}$. Express Sydney's location in spherical coordinates.

Cylindrical and spherical coordinates give us the flexibility to select a coordinate system appropriate to the problem at hand. A thoughtful choice of coordinate system can make a problem much easier to solve, whereas a poor choice can lead to unnecessarily complex calculations. In the following example, we examine several different problems and discuss how to select the best coordinate system for each one.

Example 2.67

Choosing the Best Coordinate System

In each of the following situations, we determine which coordinate system is most appropriate and describe how we would orient the coordinate axes. There could be more than one right answer for how the axes should be oriented, but we select an orientation that makes sense in the context of the problem. *Note*: There is not enough information to set up or solve these problems; we simply select the coordinate system (**Figure 2.105**).

a. Find the center of gravity of a bowling ball.

b. Determine the velocity of a submarine subjected to an ocean current.

c. Calculate the pressure in a conical water tank.

d. Find the volume of oil flowing through a pipeline.

e. Determine the amount of leather required to make a football.

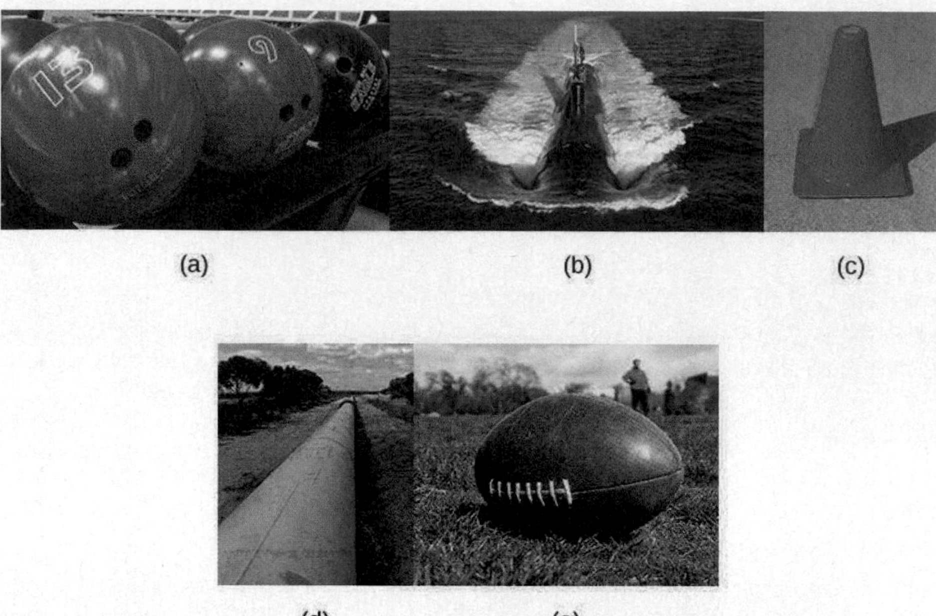

Figure 2.105 (credit: (a) modification of work by scl hua, Wikimedia, (b) modification of work by DVIDSHUB, Flickr, (c) modification of work by Michael Malak, Wikimedia, (d) modification of work by Sean Mack, Wikimedia, (e) modification of work by Elvert Barnes, Flickr)

Solution

a. Clearly, a bowling ball is a sphere, so spherical coordinates would probably work best here. The origin should be located at the physical center of the ball. There is no obvious choice for how the *x*-, *y*- and *z*-axes should be oriented. Bowling balls normally have a weight block in the center. One possible choice is to align the *z*-axis with the axis of symmetry of the weight block.

b. A submarine generally moves in a straight line. There is no rotational or spherical symmetry that applies in this situation, so rectangular coordinates are a good choice. The *z*-axis should probably point upward. The *x*- and *y*-axes could be aligned to point east and north, respectively. The origin should be some convenient physical location, such as the starting position of the submarine or the location of a particular port.

c. A cone has several kinds of symmetry. In cylindrical coordinates, a cone can be represented by equation $z = kr,$ where k is a constant. In spherical coordinates, we have seen that surfaces of the form $\varphi = c$ are half-cones. Last, in rectangular coordinates, elliptic cones are quadric surfaces and can be represented by equations of the form $z^2 = \frac{x^2}{a^2} + \frac{y^2}{b^2}.$ In this case, we could choose any of the three. However, the equation for the surface is more complicated in rectangular coordinates than in the other two systems, so we might want to avoid that choice. In addition, we are talking about a water tank, and the depth of the water might come into play at some point in our calculations, so it might be nice to have a component that represents height and depth directly. Based on this reasoning, cylindrical coordinates might be the best choice. Choose the *z*-axis to align with the axis of the cone. The orientation of the other two axes is arbitrary. The origin should be the bottom point of the cone.

d. A pipeline is a cylinder, so cylindrical coordinates would be best the best choice. In this case, however, we would likely choose to orient our *z*-axis with the center axis of the pipeline. The *x*-axis could be chosen to point straight downward or to some other logical direction. The origin should be chosen based on the problem statement. Note that this puts the *z*-axis in a horizontal orientation, which is a little different from what we usually do. It may make sense to choose an unusual orientation for the axes if it makes sense for the problem.

e. A football has rotational symmetry about a central axis, so cylindrical coordinates would work best. The z-axis should align with the axis of the ball. The origin could be the center of the ball or perhaps one of the ends. The position of the x-axis is arbitrary.

2.61 Which coordinate system is most appropriate for creating a star map, as viewed from Earth (see the following figure)?

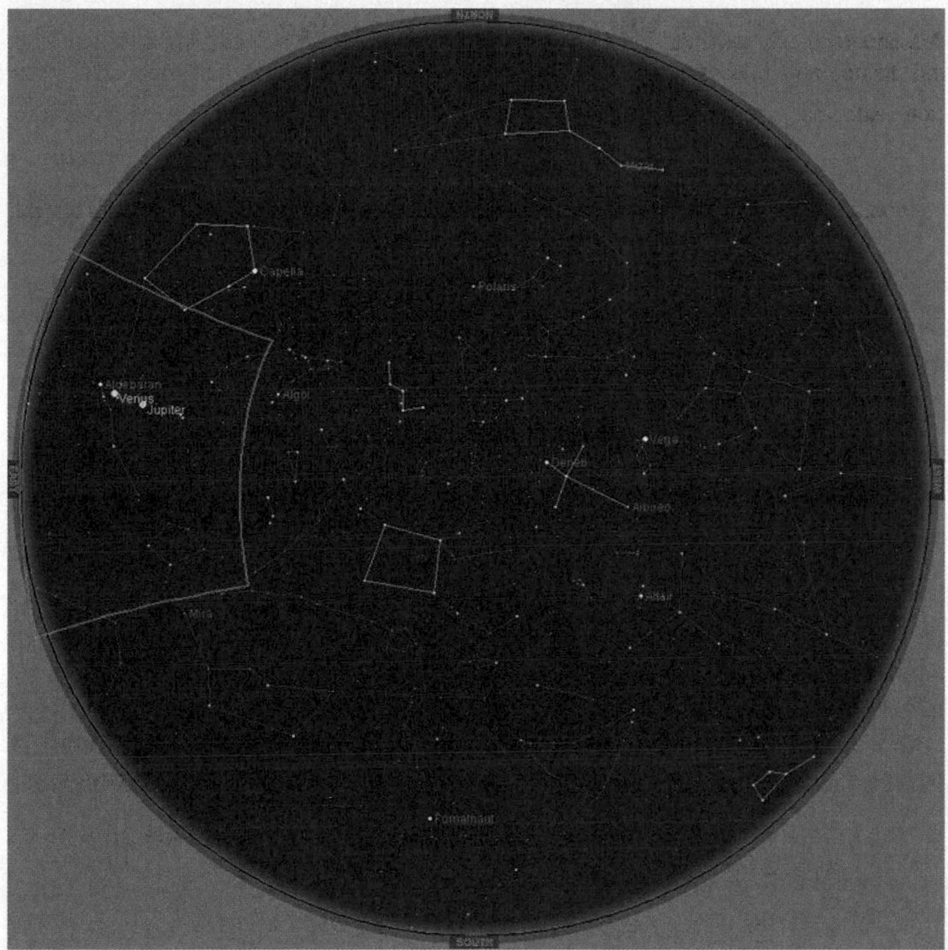

How should we orient the coordinate axes?

2.7 EXERCISES

Use the following figure as an aid in identifying the relationship between the rectangular, cylindrical, and spherical coordinate systems.

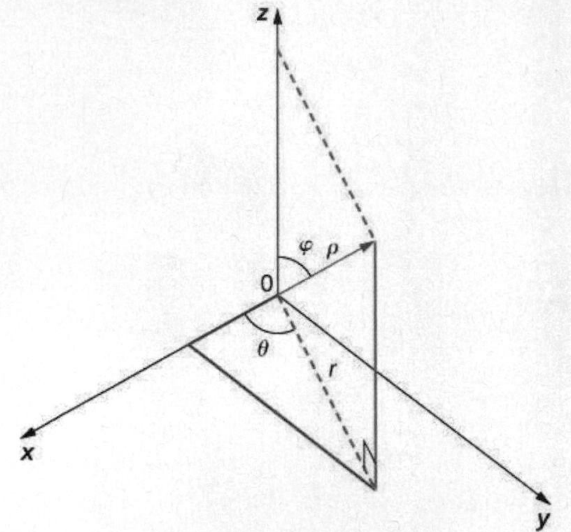

For the following exercises, the cylindrical coordinates (r, θ, z) of a point are given. Find the rectangular coordinates (x, y, z) of the point.

363. $\left(4, \frac{\pi}{6}, 3\right)$

364. $\left(3, \frac{\pi}{3}, 5\right)$

365. $\left(4, \frac{7\pi}{6}, 3\right)$

366. $(2, \pi, -4)$

For the following exercises, the rectangular coordinates (x, y, z) of a point are given. Find the cylindrical coordinates (r, θ, z) of the point.

367. $(1, \sqrt{3}, 2)$

368. $(1, 1, 5)$

369. $(3, -3, 7)$

370. $\left(-2\sqrt{2}, 2\sqrt{2}, 4\right)$

For the following exercises, the equation of a surface in cylindrical coordinates is given.

Find the equation of the surface in rectangular coordinates. Identify and graph the surface.

371. **[T]** $r = 4$

372. **[T]** $z = r^2 \cos^2 \theta$

373. **[T]** $r^2 \cos(2\theta) + z^2 + 1 = 0$

374. **[T]** $r = 3 \sin \theta$

375. **[T]** $r = 2 \cos \theta$

376. **[T]** $r^2 + z^2 = 5$

377. **[T]** $r = 2 \sec \theta$

378. **[T]** $r = 3 \csc \theta$

For the following exercises, the equation of a surface in rectangular coordinates is given. Find the equation of the surface in cylindrical coordinates.

379. $z = 3$

380. $x = 6$

381. $x^2 + y^2 + z^2 = 9$

382. $y = 2x^2$

383. $x^2 + y^2 - 16x = 0$

384. $x^2 + y^2 - 3\sqrt{x^2 + y^2} + 2 = 0$

For the following exercises, the spherical coordinates (ρ, θ, φ) of a point are given. Find the rectangular coordinates (x, y, z) of the point.

385. $(3, 0, \pi)$

386. $\left(1, \frac{\pi}{6}, \frac{\pi}{6}\right)$

387. $\left(12, -\frac{\pi}{4}, \frac{\pi}{4}\right)$

388. $\left(3, \frac{\pi}{4}, \frac{\pi}{6}\right)$

For the following exercises, the rectangular coordinates (x, y, z) of a point are given. Find the spherical coordinates (ρ, θ, φ) of the point. Express the measure of the angles in degrees rounded to the nearest integer.

389. $(4, 0, 0)$

390. $(-1, 2, 1)$

391. $(0, 3, 0)$

392. $\left(-2, 2\sqrt{3}, 4\right)$

For the following exercises, the equation of a surface in spherical coordinates is given. Find the equation of the surface in rectangular coordinates. Identify and graph the surface.

393. **[T]** $\rho = 3$

394. **[T]** $\varphi = \frac{\pi}{3}$

395. **[T]** $\rho = 2\cos\varphi$

396. **[T]** $\rho = 4\csc\varphi$

397. **[T]** $\varphi = \frac{\pi}{2}$

398. **[T]** $\rho = 6\csc\varphi\sec\theta$

For the following exercises, the equation of a surface in rectangular coordinates is given. Find the equation of the surface in spherical coordinates. Identify the surface.

399. $x^2 + y^2 - 3z^2 = 0, \quad z \neq 0$

400. $x^2 + y^2 + z^2 - 4z = 0$

401. $z = 6$

402. $x^2 + y^2 = 9$

For the following exercises, the cylindrical coordinates of a point are given. Find its associated spherical coordinates, with the measure of the angle φ in radians rounded to four decimal places.

403. **[T]** $\left(1, \frac{\pi}{4}, 3\right)$

404. **[T]** $(5, \pi, 12)$

405. $\left(3, \frac{\pi}{2}, 3\right)$

406. $\left(3, -\frac{\pi}{6}, 3\right)$

For the following exercises, the spherical coordinates of a point are given. Find its associated cylindrical coordinates.

407. $\left(2, -\frac{\pi}{4}, \frac{\pi}{2}\right)$

408. $\left(4, \frac{\pi}{4}, \frac{\pi}{6}\right)$

409. $\left(8, \frac{\pi}{3}, \frac{\pi}{2}\right)$

410. $\left(9, -\frac{\pi}{6}, \frac{\pi}{3}\right)$

For the following exercises, find the most suitable system of coordinates to describe the solids.

411. The solid situated in the first octant with a vertex at the origin and enclosed by a cube of edge length a, where $a > 0$

412. A spherical shell determined by the region between two concentric spheres centered at the origin, of radii of a and b, respectively, where $b > a > 0$

413. A solid inside sphere $x^2 + y^2 + z^2 = 9$ and outside cylinder $\left(x - \frac{3}{2}\right)^2 + y^2 = \frac{9}{4}$

414. A cylindrical shell of height 10 determined by the region between two cylinders with the same center, parallel rulings, and radii of 2 and 5, respectively

415. **[T]** Use a CAS to graph in cylindrical coordinates the region between elliptic paraboloid $z = x^2 + y^2$ and cone $x^2 + y^2 - z^2 = 0$.

416. **[T]** Use a CAS to graph in spherical coordinates the “ice cream-cone region” situated above the *xy*-plane between sphere $x^2 + y^2 + z^2 = 4$ and elliptical cone $x^2 + y^2 - z^2 = 0$.

417. Washington, DC, is located at $39°$ N and $77°$ W (see the following figure). Assume the radius of Earth is 4000 mi. Express the location of Washington, DC, in spherical coordinates.

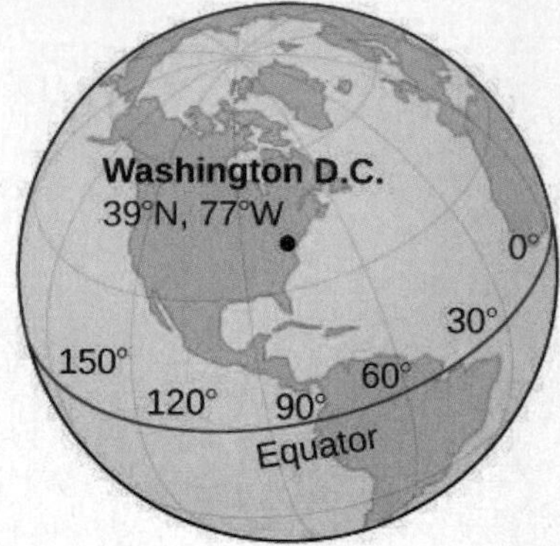

418. San Francisco is located at $37.78°\text{N}$ and $122.42°\text{W}$. Assume the radius of Earth is 4000 mi. Express the location of San Francisco in spherical coordinates.

419. Find the latitude and longitude of Rio de Janeiro if its spherical coordinates are $(4000, -43.17°, 102.91°)$.

420. Find the latitude and longitude of Berlin if its spherical coordinates are $(4000, 13.38°, 37.48°)$.

421. **[T]** Consider the torus of equation $\left(x^2+y^2+z^2+R^2-r^2\right)^2=4R^2\left(x^2+y^2\right),$ where $R \geq r > 0.$

a. Write the equation of the torus in spherical coordinates.
b. If $R=r,$ the surface is called a *horn torus*. Show that the equation of a horn torus in spherical coordinates is $\rho = 2R\sin\varphi$.
c. Use a CAS to graph the horn torus with $R=r=2$ in spherical coordinates.

422. **[T]** The “bumpy sphere” with an equation in spherical coordinates is $\rho = a + b\cos(m\theta)\sin(n\varphi),$ with $\theta \in [0, 2\pi]$ and $\varphi \in [0, \pi],$ where a and b are positive numbers and m and n are positive integers, may be used in applied mathematics to model tumor growth.

a. Show that the “bumpy sphere” is contained inside a sphere of equation $\rho = a + b$. Find the values of θ and φ at which the two surfaces intersect.
b. Use a CAS to graph the surface for $a=14,$ $b=2,$ $m=4,$ and $n=6$ along with sphere $\rho = a + b.$
c. Find the equation of the intersection curve of the surface at b. with the cone $\varphi = \frac{\pi}{12}$. Graph the intersection curve in the plane of intersection.

CHAPTER 2 REVIEW

KEY TERMS

component a scalar that describes either the vertical or horizontal direction of a vector

coordinate plane a plane containing two of the three coordinate axes in the three-dimensional coordinate system, named by the axes it contains: the *xy*-plane, *xz*-plane, or the *yz*-plane

cross product $\mathbf{u} \times \mathbf{v} = (u_2 v_3 - u_3 v_2)\mathbf{i} - (u_1 v_3 - u_3 v_1)\mathbf{j} + (u_1 v_2 - u_2 v_1)\mathbf{k},$ where $\mathbf{u} = \langle u_1, u_2, u_3 \rangle$ and $\mathbf{v} = \langle v_1, v_2, v_3 \rangle$

cylinder a set of lines parallel to a given line passing through a given curve

cylindrical coordinate system a way to describe a location in space with an ordered triple $(r, \theta, z),$ where (r, θ) represents the polar coordinates of the point's projection in the *xy*-plane, and z represents the point's projection onto the *z*-axis

determinant a real number associated with a square matrix

direction angles the angles formed by a nonzero vector and the coordinate axes

direction cosines the cosines of the angles formed by a nonzero vector and the coordinate axes

direction vector a vector parallel to a line that is used to describe the direction, or orientation, of the line in space

dot product or scalar product $\mathbf{u} \cdot \mathbf{v} = u_1 v_1 + u_2 v_2 + u_3 v_3$ where $\mathbf{u} = \langle u_1, u_2, u_3 \rangle$ and $\mathbf{v} = \langle v_1, v_2, v_3 \rangle$

ellipsoid a three-dimensional surface described by an equation of the form $\frac{x^2}{a^2} + \frac{y^2}{b^2} + \frac{z^2}{c^2} = 1;$ all traces of this surface are ellipses

elliptic cone a three-dimensional surface described by an equation of the form $\frac{x^2}{a^2} + \frac{y^2}{b^2} - \frac{z^2}{c^2} = 0;$ traces of this surface include ellipses and intersecting lines

elliptic paraboloid a three-dimensional surface described by an equation of the form $z = \frac{x^2}{a^2} + \frac{y^2}{b^2};$ traces of this surface include ellipses and parabolas

equivalent vectors vectors that have the same magnitude and the same direction

general form of the equation of a plane an equation in the form $ax + by + cz + d = 0,$ where $\mathbf{n} = \langle a, b, c \rangle$ is a normal vector of the plane, $P = (x_0, y_0, z_0)$ is a point on the plane, and $d = -ax_0 - by_0 - cz_0$

hyperboloid of one sheet a three-dimensional surface described by an equation of the form $\frac{x^2}{a^2} + \frac{y^2}{b^2} - \frac{z^2}{c^2} = 1;$ traces of this surface include ellipses and hyperbolas

hyperboloid of two sheets a three-dimensional surface described by an equation of the form $\frac{z^2}{c^2} - \frac{x^2}{a^2} - \frac{y^2}{b^2} = 1;$ traces of this surface include ellipses and hyperbolas

initial point the starting point of a vector

magnitude the length of a vector

normal vector a vector perpendicular to a plane

normalization using scalar multiplication to find a unit vector with a given direction

octants the eight regions of space created by the coordinate planes

orthogonal vectors vectors that form a right angle when placed in standard position

parallelepiped a three-dimensional prism with six faces that are parallelograms

parallelogram method a method for finding the sum of two vectors; position the vectors so they share the same initial point; the vectors then form two adjacent sides of a parallelogram; the sum of the vectors is the diagonal of that parallelogram

parametric equations of a line the set of equations $x = x_0 + ta,\quad y = y_0 + tb,$ and $z = z_0 + tc$ describing the line with direction vector $\mathbf{v} = \langle a, b, c \rangle$ passing through point (x_0, y_0, z_0)

quadric surfaces surfaces in three dimensions having the property that the traces of the surface are conic sections (ellipses, hyperbolas, and parabolas)

right-hand rule a common way to define the orientation of the three-dimensional coordinate system; when the right hand is curved around the *z*-axis in such a way that the fingers curl from the positive *x*-axis to the positive *y*-axis, the thumb points in the direction of the positive *z*-axis

rulings parallel lines that make up a cylindrical surface

scalar a real number

scalar equation of a plane the equation $a(x - x_0) + b(y - y_0) + c(z - z_0) = 0$ used to describe a plane containing point $P = (x_0, y_0, z_0)$ with normal vector $\mathbf{n} = \langle a, b, c \rangle$ or its alternate form $ax + by + cz + d = 0,$ where $d = -ax_0 - by_0 - cz_0$

scalar multiplication a vector operation that defines the product of a scalar and a vector

scalar projection the magnitude of the vector projection of a vector

skew lines two lines that are not parallel but do not intersect

sphere the set of all points equidistant from a given point known as the *center*

spherical coordinate system a way to describe a location in space with an ordered triple $(\rho, \theta, \varphi),$ where ρ is the distance between P and the origin $(\rho \neq 0),$ θ is the same angle used to describe the location in cylindrical coordinates, and φ is the angle formed by the positive *z*-axis and line segment $\overline{OP},$ where O is the origin and $0 \leq \varphi \leq \pi$

standard equation of a sphere $(x - a)^2 + (y - b)^2 + (z - c)^2 = r^2$ describes a sphere with center (a, b, c) and radius r

standard unit vectors unit vectors along the coordinate axes: $\mathbf{i} = \langle 1, 0 \rangle, \mathbf{j} = \langle 0, 1 \rangle$

standard-position vector a vector with initial point $(0, 0)$

symmetric equations of a line the equations $\frac{x - x_0}{a} = \frac{y - y_0}{b} = \frac{z - z_0}{c}$ describing the line with direction vector $\mathbf{v} = \langle a, b, c \rangle$ passing through point (x_0, y_0, z_0)

terminal point the endpoint of a vector

three-dimensional rectangular coordinate system a coordinate system defined by three lines that intersect at right angles; every point in space is described by an ordered triple (x, y, z) that plots its location relative to the defining axes

torque the effect of a force that causes an object to rotate

trace the intersection of a three-dimensional surface with a coordinate plane

triangle inequality the length of any side of a triangle is less than the sum of the lengths of the other two sides

triangle method a method for finding the sum of two vectors; position the vectors so the terminal point of one vector is the initial point of the other; these vectors then form two sides of a triangle; the sum of the vectors is the vector that forms the third side; the initial point of the sum is the initial point of the first vector; the terminal point of the sum is the terminal point of the second vector

triple scalar product the dot product of a vector with the cross product of two other vectors: $\mathbf{u} \cdot (\mathbf{v} \times \mathbf{w})$

unit vector a vector with margnitude 1

vector a mathematical object that has both magnitude and direction

vector addition a vector operation that defines the sum of two vectors

vector difference the vector difference $\mathbf{v} - \mathbf{w}$ is defined as $\mathbf{v} + (-\mathbf{w}) = \mathbf{v} + (-1)\mathbf{w}$

vector equation of a line the equation $\mathbf{r} = \mathbf{r}_0 + t\mathbf{v}$ used to describe a line with direction vector $\mathbf{v} = \langle a, b, c \rangle$ passing through point $P = (x_0, y_0, z_0)$, where $\mathbf{r}_0 = \langle x_0, y_0, z_0 \rangle$, is the position vector of point P

vector equation of a plane the equation $\mathbf{n} \cdot \overrightarrow{PQ} = 0$, where P is a given point in the plane, Q is any point in the plane, and $\mathbf{n}$ is a normal vector of the plane

vector product the cross product of two vectors

vector projection the component of a vector that follows a given direction

vector sum the sum of two vectors, $\mathbf{v}$ and $\mathbf{w}$, can be constructed graphically by placing the initial point of $\mathbf{w}$ at the terminal point of $\mathbf{v}$; then the vector sum $\mathbf{v} + \mathbf{w}$ is the vector with an initial point that coincides with the initial point of $\mathbf{v}$, and with a terminal point that coincides with the terminal point of $\mathbf{w}$

work done by a force work is generally thought of as the amount of energy it takes to move an object; if we represent an applied force by a vector **F** and the displacement of an object by a vector **s**, then the work done by the force is the dot product of **F** and **s**.

zero vector the vector with both initial point and terminal point $(0, 0)$

KEY EQUATIONS

- **Distance between two points in space:**
  $d = \sqrt{(x_2 - x_1)^2 + (y_2 - y_1)^2 + (z_2 - z_1)^2}$
- **Sphere with center (a, b, c) and radius r:**
  $(x - a)^2 + (y - b)^2 + (z - c)^2 = r^2$
- **Dot product of u and v**
  $$\begin{aligned}\mathbf{u} \cdot \mathbf{v} &= u_1 v_1 + u_2 v_2 + u_3 v_3 \\ &= \|\mathbf{u}\| \, \|\mathbf{v}\| \cos\theta\end{aligned}$$
- **Cosine of the angle formed by u and v**
  $\cos\theta = \dfrac{\mathbf{u} \cdot \mathbf{v}}{\|\mathbf{u}\| \, \|\mathbf{v}\|}$
- **Vector projection of v onto u**
  $\text{proj}_{\mathbf{u}} \mathbf{v} = \dfrac{\mathbf{u} \cdot \mathbf{v}}{\|\mathbf{u}\|^2} \mathbf{u}$
- **Scalar projection of v onto u**
  $\text{comp}_{\mathbf{u}} \mathbf{v} = \dfrac{\mathbf{u} \cdot \mathbf{v}}{\|\mathbf{u}\|}$
- **Work done by a force F to move an object through displacement vector $\overrightarrow{PQ}$**
  $W = \mathbf{F} \cdot \overrightarrow{PQ} = \|\mathbf{F}\| \, \|\overrightarrow{PQ}\| \cos\theta$
- **The cross product of two vectors in terms of the unit vectors**

$$\mathbf{u} \times \mathbf{v} = (u_2 v_3 - u_3 v_2)\mathbf{i} - (u_1 v_3 - u_3 v_1)\mathbf{j} + (u_1 v_2 - u_2 v_1)\mathbf{k}$$

- **Vector Equation of a Line**
  $\mathbf{r} = \mathbf{r}_0 + t\mathbf{v}$
- **Parametric Equations of a Line**
  $x = x_0 + ta, \quad y = y_0 + tb, \quad \text{and } z = z_0 + tc$
- **Symmetric Equations of a Line**
  $\dfrac{x - x_0}{a} = \dfrac{y - y_0}{b} = \dfrac{z - z_0}{c}$
- **Vector Equation of a Plane**
  $\mathbf{n} \cdot \overrightarrow{PQ} = 0$
- **Scalar Equation of a Plane**
  $a(x - x_0) + b(y - y_0) + c(z - z_0) = 0$
- **Distance between a Plane and a Point**
  $d = \left\| \text{proj}_{\mathbf{n}} \overrightarrow{QP} \right\| = \left|\text{comp}_{\mathbf{n}} \overrightarrow{QP}\right| = \dfrac{\left|\overrightarrow{QP} \cdot \mathbf{n}\right|}{\|\mathbf{n}\|}$

KEY CONCEPTS

2.1 Vectors in the Plane

- Vectors are used to represent quantities that have both magnitude and direction.
- We can add vectors by using the parallelogram method or the triangle method to find the sum. We can multiply a vector by a scalar to change its length or give it the opposite direction.
- Subtraction of vectors is defined in terms of adding the negative of the vector.
- A vector is written in component form as $\mathbf{v} = \langle x, y \rangle$.
- The magnitude of a vector is a scalar: $\|\mathbf{v}\| = \sqrt{x^2 + y^2}$.
- A unit vector $\mathbf{u}$ has magnitude 1 and can be found by dividing a vector by its magnitude: $\mathbf{u} = \dfrac{1}{\|\mathbf{v}\|}\mathbf{v}$. The standard unit vectors are $\mathbf{i} = \langle 1, 0 \rangle$ and $\mathbf{j} = \langle 0, 1 \rangle$. A vector $\mathbf{v} = \langle x, y \rangle$ can be expressed in terms of the standard unit vectors as $\mathbf{v} = x\mathbf{i} + y\mathbf{j}$.
- Vectors are often used in physics and engineering to represent forces and velocities, among other quantities.

2.2 Vectors in Three Dimensions

- The three-dimensional coordinate system is built around a set of three axes that intersect at right angles at a single point, the origin. Ordered triples (x, y, z) are used to describe the location of a point in space.
- The distance d between points (x_1, y_1, z_1) and (x_2, y_2, z_2) is given by the formula
  $$d = \sqrt{(x_2 - x_1)^2 + (y_2 - y_1)^2 + (z_2 - z_1)^2}.$$
- In three dimensions, the equations $x = a$, $y = b$, and $z = c$ describe planes that are parallel to the coordinate planes.
- The standard equation of a sphere with center (a, b, c) and radius r is
  $$(x - a)^2 + (y - b)^2 + (z - c)^2 = r^2.$$
- In three dimensions, as in two, vectors are commonly expressed in component form, $\mathbf{v} = \langle x, y, z \rangle$, or in terms

of the standard unit vectors, $x\mathbf{i} + y\mathbf{j} + z\mathbf{k}$.

- Properties of vectors in space are a natural extension of the properties for vectors in a plane. Let $\mathbf{v} = \langle x_1, y_1, z_1 \rangle$ and $\mathbf{w} = \langle x_2, y_2, z_2 \rangle$ be vectors, and let k be a scalar.
  - **Scalar multiplication:** $k\mathbf{v} = \langle kx_1, ky_1, kz_1 \rangle$
  - **Vector addition:** $\mathbf{v} + \mathbf{w} = \langle x_1, y_1, z_1 \rangle + \langle x_2, y_2, z_2 \rangle = \langle x_1 + x_2, y_1 + y_2, z_1 + z_2 \rangle$
  - **Vector subtraction:** $\mathbf{v} - \mathbf{w} = \langle x_1, y_1, z_1 \rangle - \langle x_2, y_2, z_2 \rangle = \langle x_1 - x_2, y_1 - y_2, z_1 - z_2 \rangle$
  - **Vector magnitude:** $\| \mathbf{v} \| = \sqrt{x_1^2 + y_1^2 + z_1^2}$
  - **Unit vector in the direction of v:** $\dfrac{\mathbf{v}}{\| \mathbf{v} \|} = \dfrac{1}{\| \mathbf{v} \|} \langle x_1, y_1, z_1 \rangle = \langle \dfrac{x_1}{\| \mathbf{v} \|}, \dfrac{y_1}{\| \mathbf{v} \|}, \dfrac{z_1}{\| \mathbf{v} \|} \rangle$, $\mathbf{v} \neq \mathbf{0}$

2.3 The Dot Product

- The dot product, or scalar product, of two vectors $\mathbf{u} = \langle u_1, u_2, u_3 \rangle$ and $\mathbf{v} = \langle v_1, v_2, v_3 \rangle$ is $\mathbf{u} \cdot \mathbf{v} = u_1 v_1 + u_2 v_2 + u_3 v_3$.
- The dot product satisfies the following properties:
  - $\mathbf{u} \cdot \mathbf{v} = \mathbf{v} \cdot \mathbf{u}$
  - $\mathbf{u} \cdot (\mathbf{v} + \mathbf{w}) = \mathbf{u} \cdot \mathbf{v} + \mathbf{u} \cdot \mathbf{w}$
  - $c(\mathbf{u} \cdot \mathbf{v}) = (c\mathbf{u}) \cdot \mathbf{v} = \mathbf{u} \cdot (c\mathbf{v})$
  - $\mathbf{v} \cdot \mathbf{v} = \| \mathbf{v} \|^2$
- The dot product of two vectors can be expressed, alternatively, as $\mathbf{u} \cdot \mathbf{v} = \| \mathbf{u} \| \, \| \mathbf{v} \| \cos \theta$. This form of the dot product is useful for finding the measure of the angle formed by two vectors.
- Vectors **u** and **v** are orthogonal if $\mathbf{u} \cdot \mathbf{v} = 0$.
- The angles formed by a nonzero vector and the coordinate axes are called the *direction angles* for the vector. The cosines of these angles are known as the *direction cosines*.
- The vector projection of **v** onto **u** is the vector $\text{proj}_{\mathbf{u}} \mathbf{v} = \dfrac{\mathbf{u} \cdot \mathbf{v}}{\| \mathbf{u} \|^2} \mathbf{u}$. The magnitude of this vector is known as the *scalar projection* of **v** onto **u**, given by $\text{comp}_{\mathbf{u}} \mathbf{v} = \dfrac{\mathbf{u} \cdot \mathbf{v}}{\| \mathbf{u} \|}$.
- Work is done when a force is applied to an object, causing displacement. When the force is represented by the vector **F** and the displacement is represented by the vector **s**, then the work done W is given by the formula $W = \mathbf{F} \cdot s = \| \mathbf{F} \| \, \| \mathbf{s} \| \cos \theta$.

2.4 The Cross Product

- The cross product $\mathbf{u} \times \mathbf{v}$ of two vectors $\mathbf{u} = \langle u_1, u_2, u_3 \rangle$ and $\mathbf{v} = \langle v_1, v_2, v_3 \rangle$ is a vector orthogonal to both **u** and **v**. Its length is given by $\| \mathbf{u} \times \mathbf{v} \| = \| \mathbf{u} \| \cdot \| \mathbf{v} \| \cdot \sin \theta$, where θ is the angle between **u** and **v**. Its direction is given by the right-hand rule.
- The algebraic formula for calculating the cross product of two vectors, $\mathbf{u} = \langle u_1, u_2, u_3 \rangle$ and $\mathbf{v} = \langle v_1, v_2, v_3 \rangle$, is $\mathbf{u} \times \mathbf{v} = (u_2 v_3 - u_3 v_2)\mathbf{i} - (u_1 v_3 - u_3 v_1)\mathbf{j} + (u_1 v_2 - u_2 v_1)\mathbf{k}$.

- The cross product satisfies the following properties for vectors $\mathbf{u}$, $\mathbf{v}$, and $\mathbf{w}$, and scalar c:
    - $\mathbf{u} \times \mathbf{v} = -(\mathbf{v} \times \mathbf{u})$
    - $\mathbf{u} \times (\mathbf{v} + \mathbf{w}) = \mathbf{u} \times \mathbf{v} + \mathbf{u} \times \mathbf{w}$
    - $c(\mathbf{u} \times \mathbf{v}) = (c\mathbf{u}) \times \mathbf{v} = \mathbf{u} \times (c\mathbf{v})$
    - $\mathbf{u} \times \mathbf{0} = \mathbf{0} \times \mathbf{u} = \mathbf{0}$
    - $\mathbf{v} \times \mathbf{v} = 0$
    - $\mathbf{u} \cdot (\mathbf{v} \times \mathbf{w}) = (\mathbf{u} \times \mathbf{v}) \cdot \mathbf{w}$
- The cross product of vectors $\mathbf{u} = \langle u_1, u_2, u_3 \rangle$ and $\mathbf{v} = \langle v_1, v_2, v_3 \rangle$ is the determinant $\begin{vmatrix} \mathbf{i} & \mathbf{j} & \mathbf{k} \\ u_1 & u_2 & u_3 \\ v_1 & v_2 & v_3 \end{vmatrix}$.
- If vectors $\mathbf{u}$ and $\mathbf{v}$ form adjacent sides of a parallelogram, then the area of the parallelogram is given by $\| \mathbf{u} \times \mathbf{v} \|$.
- The triple scalar product of vectors $\mathbf{u}$, $\mathbf{v}$, and $\mathbf{w}$ is $\mathbf{u} \cdot (\mathbf{v} \times \mathbf{w})$.
- The volume of a parallelepiped with adjacent edges given by vectors $\mathbf{u}$, $\mathbf{v}$, and $\mathbf{w}$ is $V = |\mathbf{u} \cdot (\mathbf{v} \times \mathbf{w})|$.
- If the triple scalar product of vectors $\mathbf{u}$, $\mathbf{v}$, and $\mathbf{w}$ is zero, then the vectors are coplanar. The converse is also true: If the vectors are coplanar, then their triple scalar product is zero.
- The cross product can be used to identify a vector orthogonal to two given vectors or to a plane.
- Torque τ measures the tendency of a force to produce rotation about an axis of rotation. If force $\mathbf{F}$ is acting at a distance $\mathbf{r}$ from the axis, then torque is equal to the cross product of $\mathbf{r}$ and $\mathbf{F}$: $\tau = \mathbf{r} \times \mathbf{F}$.

2.5 Equations of Lines and Planes in Space

- In three dimensions, the direction of a line is described by a direction vector. The vector equation of a line with direction vector $\mathbf{v} = \langle a, b, c \rangle$ passing through point $P = (x_0, y_0, z_0)$ is $\mathbf{r} = \mathbf{r}_0 + t\mathbf{v}$, where $\mathbf{r}_0 = \langle x_0, y_0, z_0 \rangle$ is the position vector of point P. This equation can be rewritten to form the parametric equations of the line: $x = x_0 + ta$, $y = y_0 + tb$, and $z = z_0 + tc$. The line can also be described with the symmetric equations $\frac{x - x_0}{a} = \frac{y - y_0}{b} = \frac{z - z_0}{c}$.
- Let L be a line in space passing through point P with direction vector $\mathbf{v}$. If Q is any point not on L, then the distance from Q to L is $d = \frac{\| \overrightarrow{PQ} \times \mathbf{v} \|}{\| \mathbf{v} \|}$.
- In three dimensions, two lines may be parallel but not equal, equal, intersecting, or skew.
- Given a point P and vector $\mathbf{n}$, the set of all points Q satisfying equation $\mathbf{n} \cdot \overrightarrow{PQ} = 0$ forms a plane. Equation $\mathbf{n} \cdot \overrightarrow{PQ} = 0$ is known as the *vector equation of a plane.*
- The scalar equation of a plane containing point $P = (x_0, y_0, z_0)$ with normal vector $\mathbf{n} = \langle a, b, c \rangle$ is $a(x - x_0) + b(y - y_0) + c(z - z_0) = 0$. This equation can be expressed as $ax + by + cz + d = 0$, where $d = -ax_0 - by_0 - cz_0$. This form of the equation is sometimes called the *general form of the equation of a plane*.
- Suppose a plane with normal vector $\mathbf{n}$ passes through point Q. The distance D from the plane to point P not in the plane is given by

$$D = \| \text{proj}_{\mathbf{n}} \overrightarrow{QP} \| = \left| \text{comp}_{\mathbf{n}} \overrightarrow{QP} \right| = \frac{\left| \overrightarrow{QP} \cdot \mathbf{n} \right|}{\| \mathbf{n} \|}.$$

- The normal vectors of parallel planes are parallel. When two planes intersect, they form a line.
- The measure of the angle θ between two intersecting planes can be found using the equation: $\cos \theta = \frac{|\mathbf{n}_1 \cdot \mathbf{n}_2|}{\| \mathbf{n}_1 \| \, \| \mathbf{n}_2 \|}$, where $\mathbf{n}_1$ and $\mathbf{n}_2$ are normal vectors to the planes.
- The distance D from point (x_0, y_0, z_0) to plane $ax + by + cz + d = 0$ is given by

$$D = \frac{|a(x_0 - x_1) + b(y_0 - y_1) + c(z_0 - z_1)|}{\sqrt{a^2 + b^2 + c^2}} = \frac{|ax_0 + by_0 + cz_0 + d|}{\sqrt{a^2 + b^2 + c^2}}.$$

2.6 Quadric Surfaces

- A set of lines parallel to a given line passing through a given curve is called a *cylinder*, or a *cylindrical surface*. The parallel lines are called *rulings*.
- The intersection of a three-dimensional surface and a plane is called a *trace*. To find the trace in the *xy*-, *yz*-, or *xz*-planes, set $z = 0, \; x = 0,$ or $y = 0,$ respectively.
- Quadric surfaces are three-dimensional surfaces with traces composed of conic sections. Every quadric surface can be expressed with an equation of the form $Ax^2 + By^2 + Cz^2 + Dxy + Exz + Fyz + Gx + Hy + Jz + K = 0.$
- To sketch the graph of a quadric surface, start by sketching the traces to understand the framework of the surface.
- Important quadric surfaces are summarized in **Figure 2.87** and **Figure 2.88**.

2.7 Cylindrical and Spherical Coordinates

- In the cylindrical coordinate system, a point in space is represented by the ordered triple $(r, \theta, z),$ where (r, θ) represents the polar coordinates of the point's projection in the *xy*-plane and z represents the point's projection onto the *z*-axis.
- To convert a point from cylindrical coordinates to Cartesian coordinates, use equations $x = r \cos \theta,$ $y = r \sin \theta,$ and $z = z.$
- To convert a point from Cartesian coordinates to cylindrical coordinates, use equations $r^2 = x^2 + y^2,$ $\tan \theta = \frac{y}{x},$ and $z = z.$
- In the spherical coordinate system, a point P in space is represented by the ordered triple $(\rho, \theta, \varphi),$ where ρ is the distance between P and the origin $(\rho \neq 0),$ θ is the same angle used to describe the location in cylindrical coordinates, and φ is the angle formed by the positive *z*-axis and line segment $\overline{OP},$ where O is the origin and $0 \le \varphi \le \pi.$
- To convert a point from spherical coordinates to Cartesian coordinates, use equations $x = \rho \sin \varphi \cos \theta,$ $y = \rho \sin \varphi \sin \theta,$ and $z = \rho \cos \varphi.$
- To convert a point from Cartesian coordinates to spherical coordinates, use equations $\rho^2 = x^2 + y^2 + z^2,$ $\tan \theta = \frac{y}{x},$ and $\varphi = \arccos\left(\frac{z}{\sqrt{x^2 + y^2 + z^2}}\right).$
- To convert a point from spherical coordinates to cylindrical coordinates, use equations $r = \rho \sin \varphi,$ $\theta = \theta,$ and $z = \rho \cos \varphi.$

- To convert a point from cylindrical coordinates to spherical coordinates, use equations $\rho = \sqrt{r^2 + z^2}, \quad \theta = \theta,$ and $\varphi = \arccos\left(\frac{z}{\sqrt{r^2 + z^2}}\right).$

CHAPTER 2 REVIEW EXERCISES

For the following exercises, determine whether the statement is *true or false*. Justify the answer with a proof or a counterexample.

423. For vectors $\mathbf{a}$ and $\mathbf{b}$ and any given scalar c, $c(\mathbf{a} \cdot \mathbf{b}) = (c\mathbf{a}) \cdot \mathbf{b}.$

424. For vectors $\mathbf{a}$ and $\mathbf{b}$ and any given scalar c, $c(\mathbf{a} \times \mathbf{b}) = (c\mathbf{a}) \times \mathbf{b}.$

425. The symmetric equation for the line of intersection between two planes $x + y + z = 2$ and $x + 2y - 4z = 5$ is given by $-\frac{x-1}{6} = \frac{y-1}{5} = z.$

426. If $\mathbf{a} \cdot \mathbf{b} = 0,$ then $\mathbf{a}$ is perpendicular to $\mathbf{b}.$

For the following exercises, use the given vectors to find the quantities.

427. $\mathbf{a} = 9\mathbf{i} - 2\mathbf{j},\ \mathbf{b} = -3\mathbf{i} + \mathbf{j}$

a. $3\mathbf{a} + \mathbf{b}$
b. $|\mathbf{a}|$
c. $\mathbf{a} \times |\mathbf{b} \times |\mathbf{a}$
d. $\mathbf{b} \times |\mathbf{a}$

428. $\mathbf{a} = 2\mathbf{i} + \mathbf{j} - 9\mathbf{k},\ \mathbf{b} = -\mathbf{i} + 2\mathbf{k},\ \mathbf{c} = 4\mathbf{i} - 2\mathbf{j} + \mathbf{k}$

a. $2\mathbf{a} - \mathbf{b}$
b. $|\mathbf{b} \times \mathbf{c}|$
c. $\mathbf{b} \times |\mathbf{b} \times \mathbf{c}|$
d. $\mathbf{c} \times |\mathbf{b} \times \mathbf{a}|$
e. $\text{proj}_{\mathbf{a}}\mathbf{b}$

429. Find the values of a such that vectors $\langle 2, 4, a \rangle$ and $\langle 0, -1, a \rangle$ are orthogonal.

For the following exercises, find the unit vectors.

430. Find the unit vector that has the same direction as vector $\mathbf{v}$ that begins at $(0, -3)$ and ends at $(4, 10).$

431. Find the unit vector that has the same direction as vector $\mathbf{v}$ that begins at $(1, 4, 10)$ and ends at $(3, 0, 4).$

For the following exercises, find the area or volume of the given shapes.

432. The parallelogram spanned by vectors $\mathbf{a} = \langle 1, 13 \rangle$ and $\mathbf{b} = \langle 3, 21 \rangle$

433. The parallelepiped formed by $\mathbf{a} = \langle 1, 4, 1 \rangle$ and $\mathbf{b} = \langle 3, 6, 2 \rangle,$ and $\mathbf{c} = \langle -2, 1, -5 \rangle$

For the following exercises, find the vector and parametric equations of the line with the given properties.

434. The line that passes through point $(2, -3, 7)$ that is parallel to vector $\langle 1, 3, -2 \rangle$

435. The line that passes through points $(1, 3, 5)$ and $(-2, 6, -3)$

For the following exercises, find the equation of the plane with the given properties.

436. The plane that passes through point $(4, 7, -1)$ and has normal vector $\mathbf{n} = \langle 3, 4, 2 \rangle$

437. The plane that passes through points $(0, 1, 5), (2, -1, 6),$ and $(3, 2, 5).$

For the following exercises, find the traces for the surfaces in planes $x = k,\ y = k,$ and $z = k.$ Then, describe and draw the surfaces.

438. $9x^2 + 4y^2 - 16y + 36z^2 = 20$

439. $x^2 = y^2 + z^2$

For the following exercises, write the given equation in cylindrical coordinates and spherical coordinates.

440. $x^2 + y^2 + z^2 = 144$

441. $z = x^2 + y^2 - 1$

For the following exercises, convert the given equations from cylindrical or spherical coordinates to rectangular coordinates. Identify the given surface.

442. $\rho^2\left(\sin^2(\varphi) - \cos^2(\varphi)\right) = 1$

443. $r^2 - 2r\cos(\theta) + z^2 = 1$

For the following exercises, consider a small boat crossing a river.

444. If the boat velocity is 5 km/h due north in still water and the water has a current of 2 km/h due west (see the following figure), what is the velocity of the boat relative to shore? What is the angle θ that the boat is actually traveling?

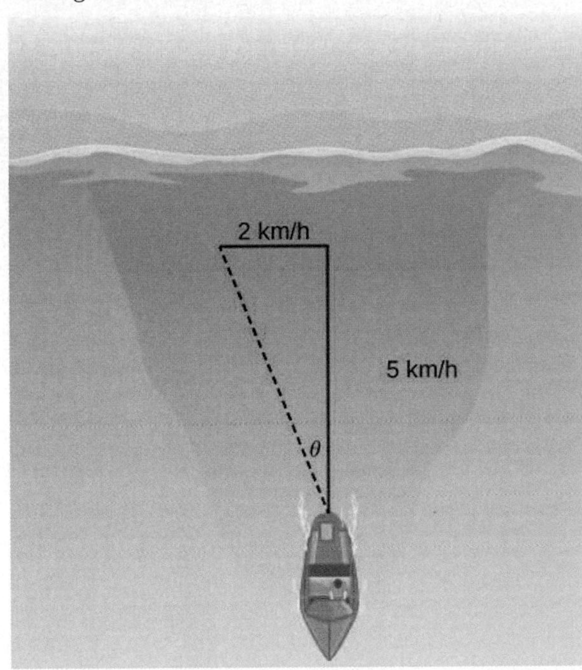

445. When the boat reaches the shore, two ropes are thrown to people to help pull the boat ashore. One rope is at an angle of $25°$ and the other is at $35°$. If the boat must be pulled straight and at a force of $500\text{N},$ find the magnitude of force for each rope (see the following figure).

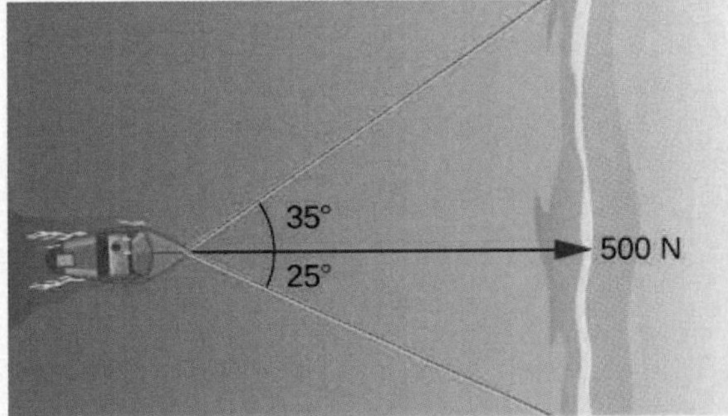

446. An airplane is flying in the direction of 52° east of north with a speed of 450 mph. A strong wind has a bearing 33° east of north with a speed of 50 mph. What is the resultant ground speed and bearing of the airplane?

447. Calculate the work done by moving a particle from position $(1, 2, 0)$ to $(8, 4, 5)$ along a straight line with a force $\mathbf{F} = 2\mathbf{i} + 3\mathbf{j} - \mathbf{k}$.

The following problems consider your unsuccessful attempt to take the tire off your car using a wrench to loosen the bolts. Assume the wrench is 0.3 m long and you are able to apply a 200-N force.

448. Because your tire is flat, you are only able to apply your force at a $60°$ angle. What is the torque at the center of the bolt? Assume this force is not enough to loosen the bolt.

449. Someone lends you a tire jack and you are now able to apply a 200-N force at an $80°$ angle. Is your resulting torque going to be more or less? What is the new resulting torque at the center of the bolt? Assume this force is not enough to loosen the bolt.

3 | VECTOR-VALUED FUNCTIONS

Figure 3.1 Halley's Comet appeared in view of Earth in 1986 and will appear again in 2061.

Chapter Outline

Introduction

In 1705, using Sir Isaac Newton's new laws of motion, the astronomer Edmond Halley made a prediction. He stated that comets that had appeared in 1531, 1607, and 1682 were actually the same comet and that it would reappear in 1758. Halley was proved to be correct, although he did not live to see it. However, the comet was later named in his honor.

Halley's Comet follows an elliptical path through the solar system, with the Sun appearing at one focus of the ellipse. This motion is predicted by Johannes Kepler's first law of planetary motion, which we mentioned briefly in the **Introduction to Parametric Equations and Polar Coordinates**. In **Example 3.15**, we show how to use Kepler's third law of planetary motion along with the calculus of vector-valued functions to find the average distance of Halley's Comet from the Sun.

Vector-valued functions provide a useful method for studying various curves both in the plane and in three-dimensional space. We can apply this concept to calculate the velocity, acceleration, arc length, and curvature of an object's trajectory. In this chapter, we examine these methods and show how they are used.

3.1 | Vector-Valued Functions and Space Curves

Learning Objectives

3.1.1 Write the general equation of a vector-valued function in component form and unit-vector form.
3.1.2 Recognize parametric equations for a space curve.
3.1.3 Describe the shape of a helix and write its equation.
3.1.4 Define the limit of a vector-valued function.

Our study of vector-valued functions combines ideas from our earlier examination of single-variable calculus with our description of vectors in three dimensions from the preceding chapter. In this section we extend concepts from earlier chapters and also examine new ideas concerning curves in three-dimensional space. These definitions and theorems support the presentation of material in the rest of this chapter and also in the remaining chapters of the text.

Definition of a Vector-Valued Function

Our first step in studying the calculus of vector-valued functions is to define what exactly a vector-valued function is. We can then look at graphs of vector-valued functions and see how they define curves in both two and three dimensions.

Definition

A **vector-valued function** is a function of the form

$$\mathbf{r}(t) = f(t)\mathbf{i} + g(t)\mathbf{j} \quad \text{or} \quad \mathbf{r}(t) = f(t)\mathbf{i} + g(t)\mathbf{j} + h(t)\mathbf{k}, \tag{3.1}$$

where the **component functions** *f*, *g*, and *h*, are real-valued functions of the parameter *t*. Vector-valued functions are also written in the form

$$\mathbf{r}(t) = \langle f(t), g(t) \rangle \quad \text{or} \quad \mathbf{r}(t) = \langle f(t), g(t), h(t) \rangle. \tag{3.2}$$

In both cases, the first form of the function defines a two-dimensional vector-valued function; the second form describes a three-dimensional vector-valued function.

The parameter t can lie between two real numbers: $a \le t \le b$. Another possibility is that the value of t might take on all real numbers. Last, the component functions themselves may have domain restrictions that enforce restrictions on the value of t. We often use t as a parameter because t can represent time.

Example 3.1

Evaluating Vector-Valued Functions and Determining Domains

For each of the following vector-valued functions, evaluate $\mathbf{r}(0)$, $\mathbf{r}\left(\frac{\pi}{2}\right)$, and $\mathbf{r}\left(\frac{2\pi}{3}\right)$. Do any of these functions have domain restrictions?

a. $\mathbf{r}(t) = 4\cos t\,\mathbf{i} + 3\sin t\,\mathbf{j}$

b. $\mathbf{r}(t) = 3\tan t\,\mathbf{i} + 4\sec t\,\mathbf{j} + 5t\,\mathbf{k}$

Solution

a. To calculate each of the function values, substitute the appropriate value of t into the function:

$$\begin{aligned}
\mathbf{r}(0) &= 4\cos(0)\mathbf{i} + 3\sin(0)\mathbf{j} \\
&= 4\mathbf{i} + 0\mathbf{j} = 4\mathbf{i} \\
\mathbf{r}\left(\frac{\pi}{2}\right) &= 4\cos\left(\frac{\pi}{2}\right)\mathbf{i} + 3\sin\left(\frac{\pi}{2}\right)\mathbf{j} \\
&= 0\mathbf{i} + 3\mathbf{j} = 3\mathbf{j} \\
\mathbf{r}\left(\frac{2\pi}{3}\right) &= 4\cos\left(\frac{2\pi}{3}\right)\mathbf{i} + 3\sin\left(\frac{2\pi}{3}\right)\mathbf{j} \\
&= 4\left(-\frac{1}{2}\right)\mathbf{i} + 3\left(\frac{\sqrt{3}}{2}\right)\mathbf{j} = -2\mathbf{i} + \frac{3\sqrt{3}}{2}\mathbf{j}.
\end{aligned}$$

To determine whether this function has any domain restrictions, consider the component functions separately. The first component function is $f(t) = 4\cos t$ and the second component function is $g(t) = 3\sin t$. Neither of these functions has a domain restriction, so the domain of $\mathbf{r}(t) = 4\cos t\mathbf{i} + 3\sin t\mathbf{j}$ is all real numbers.

b. To calculate each of the function values, substitute the appropriate value of t into the function:

$$\begin{aligned}
\mathbf{r}(0) &= 3\tan(0)\mathbf{i} + 4\sec(0)\mathbf{j} + 5(0)\mathbf{k} \\
&= 0\mathbf{i} + 4\mathbf{j} + 0\mathbf{k} = 4\mathbf{j} \\
\mathbf{r}\left(\frac{\pi}{2}\right) &= 3\tan\left(\frac{\pi}{2}\right)\mathbf{i} + 4\sec\left(\frac{\pi}{2}\right)\mathbf{j} + 5\left(\frac{\pi}{2}\right)\mathbf{k}, \text{ which does not exist} \\
\mathbf{r}\left(\frac{2\pi}{3}\right) &= 3\tan\left(\frac{2\pi}{3}\right)\mathbf{i} + 4\sec\left(\frac{2\pi}{3}\right)\mathbf{j} + 5\left(\frac{2\pi}{3}\right)\mathbf{k} \\
&= 3(-\sqrt{3})\mathbf{i} + 4(-2)\mathbf{j} + \frac{10\pi}{3}\mathbf{k} \\
&= -3\sqrt{3}\mathbf{i} - 8\mathbf{j} + \frac{10\pi}{3}\mathbf{k}.
\end{aligned}$$

To determine whether this function has any domain restrictions, consider the component functions separately. The first component function is $f(t) = 3\tan t$, the second component function is $g(t) = 4\sec t$, and the third component function is $h(t) = 5t$. The first two functions are not defined for odd multiples of $\pi/2$, so the function is not defined for odd multiples of $\pi/2$. Therefore, $\text{dom}(\mathbf{r}(t)) = \left\{t \middle| t \neq \frac{(2n+1)\pi}{2}\right\}$, where n is any integer.

3.1 For the vector-valued function $\mathbf{r}(t) = \left(t^2 - 3t\right)\mathbf{i} + (4t + 1)\mathbf{j}$, evaluate $\mathbf{r}(0)$, $\mathbf{r}(1)$, and $\mathbf{r}(-4)$. Does this function have any domain restrictions?

Example 3.1 illustrates an important concept. The domain of a vector-valued function consists of real numbers. The domain can be all real numbers or a subset of the real numbers. The range of a vector-valued function consists of vectors. Each real number in the domain of a vector-valued function is mapped to either a two- or a three-dimensional vector.

Graphing Vector-Valued Functions

Recall that a plane vector consists of two quantities: direction and magnitude. Given any point in the plane (the *initial point*), if we move in a specific direction for a specific distance, we arrive at a second point. This represents the *terminal point* of the vector. We calculate the components of the vector by subtracting the coordinates of the initial point from the coordinates of the terminal point.

A vector is considered to be in *standard position* if the initial point is located at the origin. When graphing a vector-valued function, we typically graph the vectors in the domain of the function in standard position, because doing so guarantees the uniqueness of the graph. This convention applies to the graphs of three-dimensional vector-valued functions as well. The graph of a vector-valued function of the form $\mathbf{r}(t) = f(t)\mathbf{i} + g(t)\mathbf{j}$ consists of the set of all $(t, \mathbf{r}(t))$, and the path it traces is called a **plane curve**. The graph of a vector-valued function of the form $\mathbf{r}(t) = f(t)\mathbf{i} + g(t)\mathbf{j} + h(t)\mathbf{k}$ consists of the set of all $(t, \mathbf{r}(t))$, and the path it traces is called a **space curve**. Any representation of a plane curve or space curve using a vector-valued function is called a **vector parameterization** of the curve.

Example 3.2

Graphing a Vector-Valued Function

Create a graph of each of the following vector-valued functions:

a. The plane curve represented by $\mathbf{r}(t) = 4\cos t\,\mathbf{i} + 3\sin t\,\mathbf{j}, \quad 0 \le t \le 2\pi$

b. The plane curve represented by $\mathbf{r}(t) = 4\cos t^3\,\mathbf{i} + 3\sin t^3\,\mathbf{j}, \quad 0 \le t \le 2\pi$

c. The space curve represented by $\mathbf{r}(t) = \cos t\,\mathbf{i} + \sin t\,\mathbf{j} + t\mathbf{k}, \quad 0 \le t \le 4\pi$

Solution

a. As with any graph, we start with a table of values. We then graph each of the vectors in the second column of the table in standard position and connect the terminal points of each vector to form a curve (**Figure 3.2**). This curve turns out to be an ellipse centered at the origin.

t	$\mathbf{r}(t)$	t	$\mathbf{r}(t)$
0	$4\mathbf{i}$	π	$-4\mathbf{i}$
$\frac{\pi}{4}$	$2\sqrt{2}\mathbf{i} + \frac{3\sqrt{2}}{2}\mathbf{j}$	$\frac{5\pi}{4}$	$-2\sqrt{2}\mathbf{i} - \frac{3\sqrt{2}}{2}\mathbf{j}$
$\frac{\pi}{2}$	$3\mathbf{j}$	$\frac{3\pi}{2}$	$-3\mathbf{j}$
$\frac{3\pi}{4}$	$-2\sqrt{2}\mathbf{i} + \frac{3\sqrt{2}}{2}\mathbf{j}$	$\frac{7\pi}{4}$	$2\sqrt{2}\mathbf{i} - \frac{3\sqrt{2}}{2}\mathbf{j}$
2π	$4\mathbf{i}$		

Table 3.1
Table of Values for $\mathbf{r}(t) = 4\cos t\,\mathbf{i} + 3\sin t\,\mathbf{j}, \quad 0 \le t \le 2\pi$

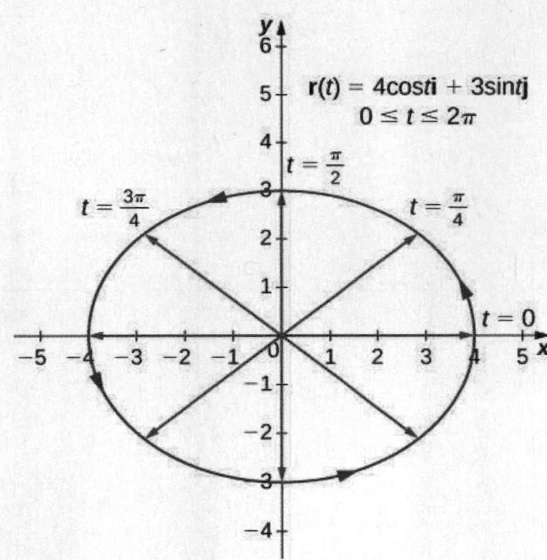

Figure 3.2 The graph of the first vector-valued function is an ellipse.

b. The table of values for $\mathbf{r}(t) = 4\cos t\,\mathbf{i} + 3\sin t\,\mathbf{j}, \quad 0 \le t \le 2\pi$ is as follows:

t	$\mathbf{r}(t)$	t	$\mathbf{r}(t)$
0	$4\mathbf{i}$	π	$-4\mathbf{i}$
$\frac{\pi}{4}$	$2\sqrt{2}\mathbf{i} + \frac{3\sqrt{2}}{2}\mathbf{j}$	$\frac{5\pi}{4}$	$-2\sqrt{2}\mathbf{i} - \frac{3\sqrt{2}}{2}\mathbf{j}$
$\frac{\pi}{2}$	$3\mathbf{j}$	$\frac{3\pi}{2}$	$-3\mathbf{j}$
$\frac{3\pi}{4}$	$-2\sqrt{2}\mathbf{i} + \frac{3\sqrt{2}}{2}\mathbf{j}$	$\frac{7\pi}{4}$	$2\sqrt{2}\mathbf{i} - \frac{3\sqrt{2}}{2}\mathbf{j}$
2π	$4\mathbf{i}$		

Table 3.2
Table of Values for $\mathbf{r}(t) = 4\cos t\,\mathbf{i} + 3\sin t\,\mathbf{j}, \quad 0 \le t \le 2\pi$

The graph of this curve is also an ellipse centered at the origin.

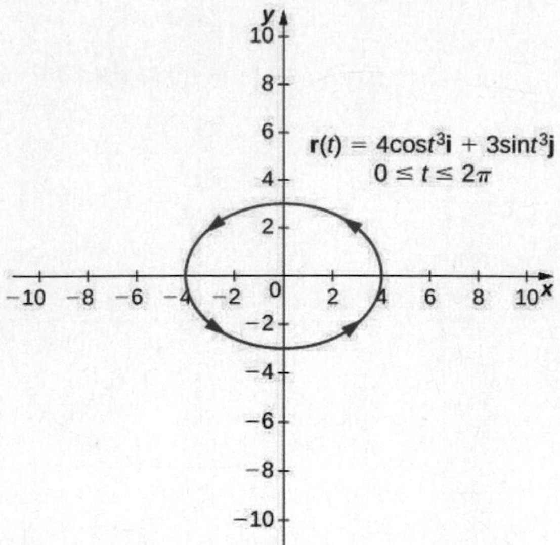

Figure 3.3 The graph of the second vector-valued function is also an ellipse.

c. We go through the same procedure for a three-dimensional vector function.

t	$\mathbf{r}(t)$	t	$\mathbf{r}(t)$
0	$4\mathbf{i}$	π	$-4\mathbf{j}+\pi\mathbf{k}$
$\frac{\pi}{4}$	$2\sqrt{2}\mathbf{i}+2\sqrt{2}\mathbf{j}+\frac{\pi}{4}\mathbf{k}$	$\frac{5\pi}{4}$	$-2\sqrt{2}\mathbf{i}-2\sqrt{2}\mathbf{j}+\frac{5\pi}{4}\mathbf{k}$
$\frac{\pi}{2}$	$4\mathbf{j}+\frac{\pi}{2}\mathbf{k}$	$\frac{3\pi}{2}$	$-4\mathbf{j}+\frac{3\pi}{2}\mathbf{k}$
$\frac{3\pi}{4}$	$-2\sqrt{2}\mathbf{i}+2\sqrt{2}\mathbf{j}+\frac{3\pi}{4}\mathbf{k}$	$\frac{7\pi}{4}$	$2\sqrt{2}\mathbf{i}-2\sqrt{2}\mathbf{j}+\frac{7\pi}{4}\mathbf{k}$
2π	$4\mathbf{i}+2\pi\mathbf{k}$		

Table 3.3
Table of Values for $\mathbf{r}(t)=\cos t\,\mathbf{i}+\sin t\,\mathbf{j}+t\mathbf{k},\quad 0\le t\le 4\pi$

The values then repeat themselves, except for the fact that the coefficient of k is always increasing (**Figure 3.4**). This curve is called a **helix**. Notice that if the **k** component is eliminated, then the function becomes $\mathbf{r}(t)=\cos t\,\mathbf{i}+\sin t\,\mathbf{j},$ which is a unit circle centered at the origin.

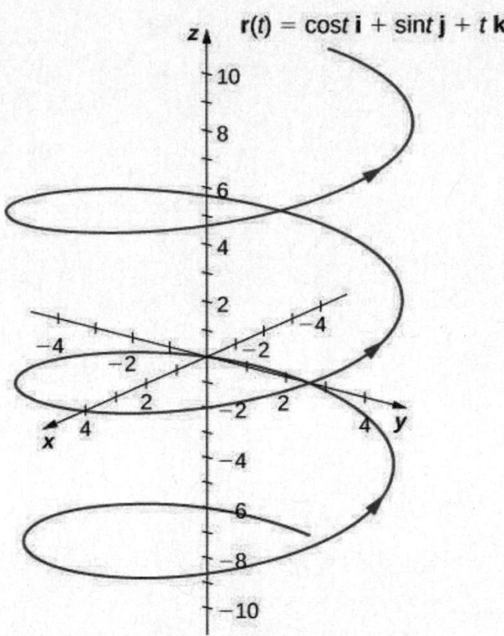

Figure 3.4 The graph of the third vector-valued function is a helix.

You may notice that the graphs in parts a. and b. are identical. This happens because the function describing curve b is a so-called **reparameterization** of the function describing curve a. In fact, any curve has an infinite number of reparameterizations; for example, we can replace *t* with $2t$ in any of the three previous curves without changing the shape of the curve. The interval over which *t* is defined may change, but that is all. We return to this idea later in this chapter when we study arc-length parameterization.

As mentioned, the name of the shape of the curve of the graph in **Example 3.2**c. is a **helix** (**Figure 3.4**). The curve resembles a spring, with a circular cross-section looking down along the *z*-axis. It is possible for a helix to be elliptical in cross-section as well. For example, the vector-valued function $\mathbf{r}(t) = 4\cos t\,\mathbf{i} + 3\sin t\,\mathbf{j} + t\,\mathbf{k}$ describes an elliptical helix. The projection of this helix into the x, y-plane is an ellipse. Last, the arrows in the graph of this helix indicate the orientation of the curve as *t* progresses from 0 to 4π.

3.2 Create a graph of the vector-valued function $\mathbf{r}(t) = \left(t^2 - 1\right)\mathbf{i} + (2t - 3)\,\mathbf{j}, \quad 0 \le t \le 3.$

At this point, you may notice a similarity between vector-valued functions and parameterized curves. Indeed, given a vector-valued function $\mathbf{r}(t) = f(t)\,\mathbf{i} + g(t)\,\mathbf{j},$ we can define $x = f(t)$ and $y = g(t)$. If a restriction exists on the values of *t* (for example, *t* is restricted to the interval $[a, b]$ for some constants $a < b$), then this restriction is enforced on the parameter. The graph of the parameterized function would then agree with the graph of the vector-valued function, except that the vector-valued graph would represent vectors rather than points. Since we can parameterize a curve defined by a function $y = f(x)$, it is also possible to represent an arbitrary plane curve by a vector-valued function.

Limits and Continuity of a Vector-Valued Function

We now take a look at the **limit of a vector-valued function**. This is important to understand to study the calculus of vector-valued functions.

Definition

A vector-valued function **r** approaches the limit **L** as t approaches a, written

$$\lim_{t \to a} \mathbf{r}(t) = \mathbf{L},$$

provided

$$\lim_{t \to a} \|\mathbf{r}(t) - \mathbf{L}\| = 0.$$

This is a rigorous definition of the limit of a vector-valued function. In practice, we use the following theorem:

Theorem 3.1: Limit of a Vector-Valued Function

Let f, g, and h be functions of t. Then the limit of the vector-valued function $\mathbf{r}(t) = f(t)\mathbf{i} + g(t)\mathbf{j}$ as t approaches a is given by

$$\lim_{t \to a} \mathbf{r}(t) = \left[\lim_{t \to a} f(t)\right]\mathbf{i} + \left[\lim_{t \to a} g(t)\right]\mathbf{j}, \tag{3.3}$$

provided the limits $\lim_{t \to a} f(t)$ and $\lim_{t \to a} g(t)$ exist. Similarly, the limit of the vector-valued function $\mathbf{r}(t) = f(t)\mathbf{i} + g(t)\mathbf{j} + h(t)\mathbf{k}$ as t approaches a is given by

$$\lim_{t \to a} \mathbf{r}(t) = \left[\lim_{t \to a} f(t)\right]\mathbf{i} + \left[\lim_{t \to a} g(t)\right]\mathbf{j} + \left[\lim_{t \to a} h(t)\right]\mathbf{k}, \tag{3.4}$$

provided the limits $\lim_{t \to a} f(t)$, $\lim_{t \to a} g(t)$and $\lim_{t \to a} h(t)$ exist.

In the following example, we show how to calculate the limit of a vector-valued function.

Example 3.3

Evaluating the Limit of a Vector-Valued Function

For each of the following vector-valued functions, calculate $\lim_{t \to 3} \mathbf{r}(t)$ for

a. $\mathbf{r}(t) = \left(t^2 - 3t + 4\right)\mathbf{i} + (4t + 3)\mathbf{j}$

b. $\mathbf{r}(t) = \dfrac{2t - 4}{t + 1}\mathbf{i} + \dfrac{t}{t^2 + 1}\mathbf{j} + (4t - 3)\mathbf{k}$

Solution

a. Use **Equation 3.3** and substitute the value $t = 3$ into the two component expressions:

$$\begin{aligned} \lim_{t \to 3} \mathbf{r}(t) &= \lim_{t \to 3}\left[\left(t^2 - 3t + 4\right)\mathbf{i} + (4t + 3)\mathbf{j}\right] \\ &= \left[\lim_{t \to 3}\left(t^2 - 3t + 4\right)\right]\mathbf{i} + \left[\lim_{t \to 3}(4t + 3)\right]\mathbf{j} \\ &= 4\mathbf{i} + 15\mathbf{j}. \end{aligned}$$

b. Use **Equation 3.4** and substitute the value $t = 3$ into the three component expressions:

$$\begin{aligned}\lim_{t\to 3}\mathbf{r}(t) &= \lim_{t\to 3}\left(\frac{2t-4}{t+1}\mathbf{i}+\frac{t}{t^2+1}\mathbf{j}+(4t-3)\mathbf{k}\right)\\ &= \left[\lim_{t\to 3}\left(\frac{2t-4}{t+1}\right)\right]\mathbf{i}+\left[\lim_{t\to 3}\left(\frac{t}{t^2+1}\right)\right]\mathbf{j}+\left[\lim_{t\to 3}(4t-3)\right]\mathbf{k}\\ &= \frac{1}{2}\mathbf{i}+\frac{3}{10}\mathbf{j}+9\mathbf{k}.\end{aligned}$$

3.3 Calculate $\lim_{t\to -2}\mathbf{r}(t)$ for the function $\mathbf{r}(t)=\sqrt{t^2-3t-1}\,\mathbf{i}+(4t+3)\mathbf{j}+\sin\frac{(t+1)\pi}{2}\mathbf{k}.$

Now that we know how to calculate the limit of a vector-valued function, we can define continuity at a point for such a function.

Definition

Let *f*, *g*, and *h* be functions of *t*. Then, the vector-valued function $\mathbf{r}(t)=f(t)\mathbf{i}+g(t)\mathbf{j}$ is continuous at point $t=a$ if the following three conditions hold:

1. $\mathbf{r}(a)$ exists
2. $\lim_{t\to a}\mathbf{r}(t)$ exists
3. $\lim_{t\to a}\mathbf{r}(t)=\mathbf{r}(a)$

Similarly, the vector-valued function $\mathbf{r}(t)=f(t)\mathbf{i}+g(t)\mathbf{j}+h(t)\mathbf{k}$ is continuous at point $t=a$ if the following three conditions hold:

1. $\mathbf{r}(a)$ exists
2. $\lim_{t\to a}\mathbf{r}(t)$ exists
3. $\lim_{t\to a}\mathbf{r}(t)=\mathbf{r}(a)$

3.1 EXERCISES

1. Give the component functions $x = f(t)$ and $y = g(t)$ for the vector-valued function $\mathbf{r}(t) = 3\sec t\,\mathbf{i} + 2\tan t\,\mathbf{j}$.

2. Given $\mathbf{r}(t) = 3\sec t\,\mathbf{i} + 2\tan t\,\mathbf{j}$, find the following values (if possible).
   a. $\mathbf{r}\left(\frac{\pi}{4}\right)$
   b. $\mathbf{r}(\pi)$
   c. $\mathbf{r}\left(\frac{\pi}{2}\right)$

3. Sketch the curve of the vector-valued function $\mathbf{r}(t) = 3\sec t\,\mathbf{i} + 2\tan t\,\mathbf{j}$ and give the orientation of the curve. Sketch asymptotes as a guide to the graph.

4. Evaluate $\lim\limits_{t \to 0} \left\langle e^t\,\mathbf{i} + \frac{\sin t}{t}\mathbf{j} + e^{-t}\,\mathbf{k} \right\rangle$.

5. Given the vector-valued function $\mathbf{r}(t) = \langle \cos t, \sin t \rangle$, find the following values:
   a. $\lim\limits_{t \to \frac{\pi}{4}} \mathbf{r}(t)$
   b. $\mathbf{r}\left(\frac{\pi}{3}\right)$
   c. Is $\mathbf{r}(t)$ continuous at $t = \frac{\pi}{3}$?
   d. Graph $\mathbf{r}(t)$.

6. Given the vector-valued function $\mathbf{r}(t) = \langle t, t^2 + 1 \rangle$, find the following values:
   a. $\lim\limits_{t \to -3} \mathbf{r}(t)$
   b. $\mathbf{r}(-3)$
   c. Is $\mathbf{r}(t)$ continuous at $x = -3$?
   d. $\mathbf{r}(t + 2) - \mathbf{r}(t)$

7. Let $\mathbf{r}(t) = e^t\,\mathbf{i} + \sin t\,\mathbf{j} + \ln t\,\mathbf{k}$. Find the following values:
   a. $\mathbf{r}\left(\frac{\pi}{4}\right)$
   b. $\lim\limits_{t \to \pi/4} \mathbf{r}(t)$
   c. Is $\mathbf{r}(t)$ continuous at $t = t = \frac{\pi}{4}$?

Find the limit of the following vector-valued functions at the indicated value of t.

8. $\lim\limits_{t \to 4} \left\langle \sqrt{t-3}, \frac{\sqrt{t}-2}{t-4}, \tan\left(\frac{\pi}{t}\right) \right\rangle$

9. $\lim\limits_{t \to \pi/2} \mathbf{r}(t)$ for $\mathbf{r}(t) = e^t\,\mathbf{i} + \sin t\,\mathbf{j} + \ln t\,\mathbf{k}$

10. $\lim\limits_{t \to \infty} \left\langle e^{-2t}, \frac{2t+3}{3t-1}, \arctan(2t) \right\rangle$

11. $\lim\limits_{t \to e^2} \left\langle t\ln(t), \frac{\ln t}{t^2}, \sqrt{\ln\left(t^2\right)} \right\rangle$

12. $\lim\limits_{t \to \pi/6} \langle \cos^2 t, \sin^2 t, 1 \rangle$

13. $\lim\limits_{t \to \infty} \mathbf{r}(t)$ for $\mathbf{r}(t) = 2e^{-t}\,\mathbf{i} + e^{-t}\,\mathbf{j} + \ln(t-1)\mathbf{k}$

14. Describe the curve defined by the vector-valued function $\mathbf{r}(t) = (1+t)\mathbf{i} + (2+5t)\mathbf{j} + (-1+6t)\mathbf{k}$.

Find the domain of the vector-valued functions.

15. Domain: $\mathbf{r}(t) = \langle t^2, \tan t, \ln t \rangle$

16. Domain: $\mathbf{r}(t) = \left\langle t^2, \sqrt{t-3}, \frac{3}{2t+1} \right\rangle$

17. Domain: $\mathbf{r}(t) = \left\langle \csc(t), \frac{1}{\sqrt{t-3}}, \ln(t-2) \right\rangle$

Let $\mathbf{r}(t) = \langle \cos t, t, \sin t \rangle$ and use it to answer the following questions.

18. For what values of t is $\mathbf{r}(t)$ continuous?

19. Sketch the graph of $\mathbf{r}(t)$.

20. Find the domain of $\mathbf{r}(t) = 2e^{-t}\,\mathbf{i} + e^{-t}\,\mathbf{j} + \ln(t-1)\mathbf{k}$.

21. For what values of t is $\mathbf{r}(t) = 2e^{-t}\,\mathbf{i} + e^{-t}\,\mathbf{j} + \ln(t-1)\mathbf{k}$ continuous?

Eliminate the parameter t, write the equation in Cartesian coordinates, then sketch the graphs of the vector-valued functions.

22. $\mathbf{r}(t) = 2t\,\mathbf{i} + t^2\,\mathbf{j}$ (*Hint:* Let $x = 2t$ and $y = t^2$. Solve the first equation for x in terms of t and substitute this result into the second equation.)

23. $\mathbf{r}(t) = t^3\,\mathbf{i} + 2t\,\mathbf{j}$

24. $\mathbf{r}(t) = 2(\sinh t)\mathbf{i} + 2(\cosh t)\mathbf{j}$, $t > 0$

25. $\mathbf{r}(t) = 3(\cos t)\mathbf{i} + 3(\sin t)\mathbf{j}$

26. $\mathbf{r}(t) = \langle 3\sin t, 3\cos t \rangle$

Use a graphing utility to sketch each of the following vector-valued functions:

27. **[T]** $\mathbf{r}(t) = 2\cos t^2\,\mathbf{i} + (2 - \sqrt{t})\,\mathbf{j}$

28. **[T]** $\mathbf{r}(t) = \langle e^{\cos(3t)}, e^{-\sin(t)} \rangle$

29. **[T]** $\mathbf{r}(t) = \langle 2 - \sin(2t), 3 + 2\cos t \rangle$

30. $4x^2 + 9y^2 = 36$; clockwise and counterclockwise

31. $\mathbf{r}(t) = \langle t, t^2 \rangle$; from left to right

32. The line through P and Q where P is $(1, 4, -2)$ and Q is $(3, 9, 6)$

Consider the curve described by the vector-valued function $\mathbf{r}(t) = (50e^{-t}\cos t)\mathbf{i} + (50e^{-t}\sin t)\mathbf{j} + (5 - 5e^{-t})\mathbf{k}$.

33. What is the initial point of the path corresponding to $\mathbf{r}(0)$?

34. What is $\lim\limits_{t \to \infty} \mathbf{r}(t)$?

35. **[T]** Use technology to sketch the curve.

36. Eliminate the parameter t to show that $z = 5 - \frac{r}{10}$ where $r^2 = x^2 + y^2$.

37. **[T]** Let $r(t) = \cos t\mathbf{i} + \sin t\mathbf{j} + 0.3\sin(2t)\mathbf{k}$. Use technology to graph the curve (called the *roller-coaster curve*) over the interval $[0, 2\pi)$. Choose at least two views to determine the peaks and valleys.

38. **[T]** Use the result of the preceding problem to construct an equation of a roller coaster with a steep drop from the peak and steep incline from the "valley." Then, use technology to graph the equation.

39. Use the results of the preceding two problems to construct an equation of a path of a roller coaster with more than two turning points (peaks and valleys).

40.
   a. Graph the curve $\mathbf{r}(t) = (4 + \cos(18t))\cos(t)\mathbf{i} + (4 + \cos(18t)\sin(t))\mathbf{j} + 0.3\sin(18t)\mathbf{k}$ using two viewing angles of your choice to see the overall shape of the curve.
   b. Does the curve resemble a "slinky"?
   c. What changes to the equation should be made to increase the number of coils of the slinky?

3.2 | Calculus of Vector-Valued Functions

Learning Objectives

3.2.1 Write an expression for the derivative of a vector-valued function.
3.2.2 Find the tangent vector at a point for a given position vector.
3.2.3 Find the unit tangent vector at a point for a given position vector and explain its significance.
3.2.4 Calculate the definite integral of a vector-valued function.

To study the calculus of vector-valued functions, we follow a similar path to the one we took in studying real-valued functions. First, we define the derivative, then we examine applications of the derivative, then we move on to defining integrals. However, we will find some interesting new ideas along the way as a result of the vector nature of these functions and the properties of space curves.

Derivatives of Vector-Valued Functions

Now that we have seen what a vector-valued function is and how to take its limit, the next step is to learn how to differentiate a vector-valued function. The definition of the derivative of a vector-valued function is nearly identical to the definition of a real-valued function of one variable. However, because the range of a vector-valued function consists of vectors, the same is true for the range of the derivative of a vector-valued function.

Definition

The **derivative of a vector-valued function** $\mathbf{r}(t)$ is

$$\mathbf{r}'(t) = \lim_{\Delta t \to 0} \frac{\mathbf{r}(t + \Delta t) - \mathbf{r}(t)}{\Delta t}, \tag{3.5}$$

provided the limit exists. If $\mathbf{r}'(t)$ exists, then $\mathbf{r}$ is differentiable at t. If $\mathbf{r}'(t)$ exists for all t in an open interval (a, b), then $\mathbf{r}$ is differentiable over the interval (a, b). For the function to be differentiable over the closed interval $[a, b]$, the following two limits must exist as well:

$$\mathbf{r}'(a) = \lim_{\Delta t \to 0^+} \frac{\mathbf{r}(a + \Delta t) - \mathbf{r}(a)}{\Delta t} \text{ and } \mathbf{r}'(b) = \lim_{\Delta t \to 0^-} \frac{\mathbf{r}(b + \Delta t) - \mathbf{r}(b)}{\Delta t}.$$

Many of the rules for calculating derivatives of real-valued functions can be applied to calculating the derivatives of vector-valued functions as well. Recall that the derivative of a real-valued function can be interpreted as the slope of a tangent line or the instantaneous rate of change of the function. The derivative of a vector-valued function can be understood to be an instantaneous rate of change as well; for example, when the function represents the position of an object at a given point in time, the derivative represents its velocity at that same point in time.

We now demonstrate taking the derivative of a vector-valued function.

Example 3.4

Finding the Derivative of a Vector-Valued Function

Use the definition to calculate the derivative of the function

$$\mathbf{r}(t) = (3t + 4)\mathbf{i} + \left(t^2 - 4t + 3\right)\mathbf{j}.$$

Solution

Let's use **Equation 3.5**:

$$\begin{aligned}
\mathbf{r}'(t) &= \lim_{\Delta t \to 0} \frac{\mathbf{r}(t+\Delta t) - \mathbf{r}(t)}{\Delta t} \\
&= \lim_{\Delta t \to 0} \frac{\left[(3(t+\Delta t)+4)\mathbf{i} + \left((t+\Delta t)^2 - 4(t+\Delta t)+3\right)\mathbf{j}\right] - \left[(3t+4)\mathbf{i} + \left(t^2-4t+3\right)\mathbf{j}\right]}{\Delta t} \\
&= \lim_{\Delta t \to 0} \frac{(3t+3\Delta t+4)\mathbf{i} - (3t+4)\mathbf{i} + \left(t^2+2t\Delta t+(\Delta t)^2-4t-4\Delta t+3\right)\mathbf{j} - \left(t^2-4t+3\right)\mathbf{j}}{\Delta t} \\
&= \lim_{\Delta t \to 0} \frac{(3\Delta t)\mathbf{i} + \left(2t\Delta t + (\Delta t)^2 - 4\Delta t\right)\mathbf{j}}{\Delta t} \\
&= \lim_{\Delta t \to 0} \left(3\mathbf{i} + (2t+\Delta t-4)\mathbf{j}\right) \\
&= 3\mathbf{i} + (2t-4)\mathbf{j}.
\end{aligned}$$

3.4 Use the definition to calculate the derivative of the function $\mathbf{r}(t) = \left(2t^2+3\right)\mathbf{i} + (5t-6)\mathbf{j}$.

Notice that in the calculations in **Example 3.4**, we could also obtain the answer by first calculating the derivative of each component function, then putting these derivatives back into the vector-valued function. This is always true for calculating the derivative of a vector-valued function, whether it is in two or three dimensions. We state this in the following theorem. The proof of this theorem follows directly from the definitions of the limit of a vector-valued function and the derivative of a vector-valued function.

Theorem 3.2: Differentiation of Vector-Valued Functions

Let f, g, and h be differentiable functions of t.

i. If $\mathbf{r}(t) = f(t)\mathbf{i} + g(t)\mathbf{j}$, then $\mathbf{r}'(t) = f'(t)\mathbf{i} + g'(t)\mathbf{j}$.

ii. If $\mathbf{r}(t) = f(t)\mathbf{i} + g(t)\mathbf{j} + h(t)\mathbf{k}$, then $\mathbf{r}'(t) = f'(t)\mathbf{i} + g'(t)\mathbf{j} + h'(t)\mathbf{k}$.

Example 3.5

Calculating the Derivative of Vector-Valued Functions

Use **Differentiation of Vector-Valued Functions** to calculate the derivative of each of the following functions.

a. $\mathbf{r}(t) = (6t+8)\mathbf{i} + \left(4t^2+2t-3\right)\mathbf{j}$

b. $\mathbf{r}(t) = 3\cos t\,\mathbf{i} + 4\sin t\,\mathbf{j}$

c. $\mathbf{r}(t) = e^t \sin t\,\mathbf{i} + e^t \cos t\,\mathbf{j} - e^{2t}\,\mathbf{k}$

Solution

We use **Differentiation of Vector-Valued Functions** and what we know about differentiating functions of one variable.

a. The first component of $\mathbf{r}(t) = (6t+8)\mathbf{i} + \left(4t^2+2t-3\right)\mathbf{j}$ is $f(t) = 6t+8$. The second component is $g(t) = 4t^2+2t-3$. We have $f'(t) = 6$ and $g'(t) = 8t+2$, so the theorem gives $\mathbf{r}'(t) = 6\mathbf{i} + (8t+2)\mathbf{j}$.

b. The first component is $f(t) = 3\cos t$ and the second component is $g(t) = 4\sin t$. We have $f'(t) = -3\sin t$ and $g'(t) = 4\cos t$, so we obtain $\mathbf{r}'(t) = -3\sin t\,\mathbf{i} + 4\cos t\,\mathbf{j}$.

c. The first component of $\mathbf{r}(t) = e^t\sin t\,\mathbf{i} + e^t\cos t\,\mathbf{j} - e^{2t}\,\mathbf{k}$ is $f(t) = e^t\sin t$, the second component is $g(t) = e^t\cos t$, and the third component is $h(t) = -e^{2t}$. We have $f'(t) = e^t(\sin t + \cos t)$, $g'(t) = e^t(\cos t - \sin t)$, and $h'(t) = -2e^{2t}$, so the theorem gives $\mathbf{r}'(t) = e^t(\sin t + \cos t)\mathbf{i} + e^t(\cos t - \sin t)\mathbf{j} - 2e^{2t}\,\mathbf{k}$.

3.5 Calculate the derivative of the function

$$\mathbf{r}(t) = (t\ln t)\mathbf{i} + \left(5e^t\right)\mathbf{j} + (\cos t - \sin t)\mathbf{k}.$$

We can extend to vector-valued functions the properties of the derivative that we presented in the **Introduction to Derivatives (http://cnx.org/content/m53494/latest/)**. In particular, the constant multiple rule, the sum and difference rules, the product rule, and the chain rule all extend to vector-valued functions. However, in the case of the product rule, there are actually three extensions: (1) for a real-valued function multiplied by a vector-valued function, (2) for the dot product of two vector-valued functions, and (3) for the cross product of two vector-valued functions.

Theorem 3.3: Properties of the Derivative of Vector-Valued Functions

Let **r** and **u** be differentiable vector-valued functions of t, let f be a differentiable real-valued function of t, and let c be a scalar.

i.	$\frac{d}{dt}[c\mathbf{r}(t)]$	$=$	$c\mathbf{r}'(t)$	Scalar multiple
ii.	$\frac{d}{dt}[\mathbf{r}(t) \pm \mathbf{u}(t)]$	$=$	$\mathbf{r}'(t) \pm \mathbf{u}'(t)$	Sum and difference
iii.	$\frac{d}{dt}[f(t)\mathbf{u}(t)]$	$=$	$f'(t)\mathbf{u}(t) + f(t)\mathbf{u}'(t)$	Scalar product
iv.	$\frac{d}{dt}[\mathbf{r}(t)\cdot\mathbf{u}(t)]$	$=$	$\mathbf{r}'(t)\cdot\mathbf{u}(t) + \mathbf{r}(t)\cdot\mathbf{u}'(t)$	Dot product
v.	$\frac{d}{dt}[\mathbf{r}(t)\times\mathbf{u}(t)]$	$=$	$\mathbf{r}'(t)\times\mathbf{u}(t) + \mathbf{r}(t)\times\mathbf{u}'(t)$	Cross product
vi.	$\frac{d}{dt}[\mathbf{r}(f(t))]$	$=$	$\mathbf{r}'(f(t))\cdot f'(t)$	Chain rule
vii.	If $\mathbf{r}(t)\cdot\mathbf{r}(t)$	$=$	c, then $\mathbf{r}(t)\cdot\mathbf{r}'(t) = 0$.	

Proof

The proofs of the first two properties follow directly from the definition of the derivative of a vector-valued function. The third property can be derived from the first two properties, along with the product rule from the **Introduction to Derivatives (http://cnx.org/content/m53494/latest/)**. Let $\mathbf{u}(t) = g(t)\mathbf{i} + h(t)\mathbf{j}$. Then

$$\begin{aligned}
\frac{d}{dt}[f(t)\mathbf{u}(t)] &= \frac{d}{dt}[f(t)(g(t)\mathbf{i} + h(t)\mathbf{j})] \\
&= \frac{d}{dt}[f(t)g(t)\mathbf{i} + f(t)h(t)\mathbf{j}] \\
&= \frac{d}{dt}[f(t)g(t)]\mathbf{i} + \frac{d}{dt}[f(t)h(t)]\mathbf{j} \\
&= (f'(t)g(t) + f(t)g'(t))\mathbf{i} + (f'(t)h(t) + f(t)h'(t))\mathbf{j} \\
&= f'(t)\mathbf{u}(t) + f(t)\mathbf{u}'(t).
\end{aligned}$$

To prove property iv. let $\mathbf{r}(t) = f_1(t)\mathbf{i} + g_1(t)\mathbf{j}$ and $\mathbf{u}(t) = f_2(t)\mathbf{i} + g_2(t)\mathbf{j}$. Then

$$\begin{aligned}
\frac{d}{dt}[\mathbf{r}(t) \cdot \mathbf{u}(t)] &= \frac{d}{dt}[f_1(t)f_2(t) + g_1(t)g_2(t)] \\
&= f_1{}'(t)f_2(t) + f_1(t)f_2{}'(t) + g_1{}'(t)g_2(t) + g_1(t)g_2{}'(t) \\
&= f_1{}'(t)f_2(t) + g_1{}'(t)g_2(t) + f_1(t)f_2{}'(t) + g_1(t)g_2{}'(t) \\
&= (f_1{}'\,\mathbf{i} + g_1{}'\,\mathbf{j})\cdot(f_2\,\mathbf{i} + g_2\,\mathbf{j}) + (f_1\,\mathbf{i} + g_1\,\mathbf{j})\cdot(f_2{}'\,\mathbf{i} + g_2{}'\,\mathbf{j}) \\
&= \mathbf{r}'(t) \cdot \mathbf{u}(t) + \mathbf{r}(t) \cdot \mathbf{u}'(t).
\end{aligned}$$

The proof of property v. is similar to that of property iv. Property vi. can be proved using the chain rule. Last, property vii. follows from property iv:

$$\begin{aligned}
\frac{d}{dt}[\mathbf{r}(t) \cdot \mathbf{r}(t)] &= \frac{d}{dt}[c] \\
\mathbf{r}'(t) \cdot \mathbf{r}(t) + \mathbf{r}(t) \cdot \mathbf{r}'(t) &= 0 \\
2\mathbf{r}(t) \cdot \mathbf{r}'(t) &= 0 \\
\mathbf{r}(t) \cdot \mathbf{r}'(t) &= 0.
\end{aligned}$$

□

Now for some examples using these properties.

Example 3.6

Using the Properties of Derivatives of Vector-Valued Functions

Given the vector-valued functions

$$\mathbf{r}(t) = (6t + 8)\mathbf{i} + \left(4t^2 + 2t - 3\right)\mathbf{j} + 5t\mathbf{k}$$

and

$$\mathbf{u}(t) = \left(t^2 - 3\right)\mathbf{i} + (2t + 4)\mathbf{j} + \left(t^3 - 3t\right)\mathbf{k},$$

calculate each of the following derivatives using the properties of the derivative of vector-valued functions.

a. $\frac{d}{dt}[\mathbf{r}(t) \cdot \mathbf{u}(t)]$

b. $\frac{d}{dt}[\mathbf{u}(t) \times \mathbf{u}'(t)]$

Solution

a. We have $\mathbf{r}'(t) = 6\mathbf{i} + (8t + 2)\mathbf{j} + 5\mathbf{k}$ and $\mathbf{u}'(t) = 2t\mathbf{i} + 2\mathbf{j} + \left(3t^2 - 3\right)\mathbf{k}$. Therefore, according to property iv.:

$$\begin{aligned}\frac{d}{dt}[\mathbf{r}(t)\cdot\mathbf{u}(t)] &= \mathbf{r}'(t)\cdot\mathbf{u}(t)+\mathbf{r}(t)\cdot\mathbf{u}'(t)\\ &= (6\mathbf{i}+(8t+2)\mathbf{j}+5\mathbf{k})\cdot\left((t^2-3)\mathbf{i}+(2t+4)\mathbf{j}+\left(t^3-3t\right)\mathbf{k}\right)\\ &\quad+\left((6t+8)\mathbf{i}+\left(4t^2+2t-3\right)\mathbf{j}+5t\mathbf{k}\right)\cdot\left(2t\mathbf{i}+2\mathbf{j}+\left(3t^2-3\right)\mathbf{k}\right)\\ &= 6\left(t^2-3\right)+(8t+2)(2t+4)+5\left(t^3-3t\right)\\ &\quad+2t(6t+8)+2\left(4t^2+2t-3\right)+5t\left(3t^2-3\right)\\ &= 20t^3+42t^2+26t-16.\end{aligned}$$

b. First, we need to adapt property v. for this problem:

$$\frac{d}{dt}[\mathbf{u}(t)\times\mathbf{u}'(t)]=\mathbf{u}'(t)\times\mathbf{u}'(t)+\mathbf{u}(t)\times\mathbf{u}''(t).$$

Recall that the cross product of any vector with itself is zero. Furthermore, $\mathbf{u}''(t)$ represents the second derivative of $\mathbf{u}(t)$:

$$\mathbf{u}''(t)=\frac{d}{dt}[\mathbf{u}'(t)]=\frac{d}{dt}\left[2t\mathbf{i}+2\mathbf{j}+\left(3t^2-3\right)\mathbf{k}\right]=2\mathbf{i}+6t\mathbf{k}.$$

Therefore,

$$\begin{aligned}\frac{d}{dt}[\mathbf{u}(t)\times\mathbf{u}'(t)] &= \mathbf{0}+\left((t^2-3)\mathbf{i}+(2t+4)\mathbf{j}+\left(t^3-3t\right)\mathbf{k}\right)\times(2\mathbf{i}+6t\mathbf{k})\\ &= \begin{vmatrix}\mathbf{i} & \mathbf{j} & \mathbf{k}\\ t^2-3 & 2t+4 & t^3-3t\\ 2 & 0 & 6t\end{vmatrix}\\ &= 6t(2t+4)\mathbf{i}-\left(6t\left(t^2-3\right)-2\left(t^3-3t\right)\right)\mathbf{j}-2(2t+4)\mathbf{k}\\ &= \left(12t^2+24t\right)\mathbf{i}+\left(12t-4t^3\right)\mathbf{j}-(4t+8)\mathbf{k}.\end{aligned}$$

3.6 Given the vector-valued functions $\mathbf{r}(t)=\cos t\,\mathbf{i}+\sin t\,\mathbf{j}-e^{2t}\,\mathbf{k}$ and $\mathbf{u}(t)=t\,\mathbf{i}+\sin t\,\mathbf{j}+\cos t\,\mathbf{k}$, calculate $\frac{d}{dt}[\mathbf{r}(t)\cdot\mathbf{r}'(t)]$ and $\frac{d}{dt}[\mathbf{u}(t)\times\mathbf{r}(t)]$.

Tangent Vectors and Unit Tangent Vectors

Recall from the **Introduction to Derivatives (http://cnx.org/content/m53494/latest/)** that the derivative at a point can be interpreted as the slope of the tangent line to the graph at that point. In the case of a vector-valued function, the derivative provides a tangent vector to the curve represented by the function. Consider the vector-valued function $\mathbf{r}(t)=\cos t\,\mathbf{i}+\sin t\,\mathbf{j}$. The derivative of this function is $\mathbf{r}'(t)=-\sin t\,\mathbf{i}+\cos t\,\mathbf{j}$. If we substitute the value $t=\pi/6$ into both functions we get

$$\mathbf{r}\left(\frac{\pi}{6}\right)=\frac{\sqrt{3}}{2}\mathbf{i}+\frac{1}{2}\mathbf{j}\quad\text{and}\quad\mathbf{r}'\left(\frac{\pi}{6}\right)=-\frac{1}{2}\mathbf{i}+\frac{\sqrt{3}}{2}\mathbf{j}.$$

The graph of this function appears in **Figure 3.5**, along with the vectors $\mathbf{r}\left(\frac{\pi}{6}\right)$ and $\mathbf{r}'\left(\frac{\pi}{6}\right)$.

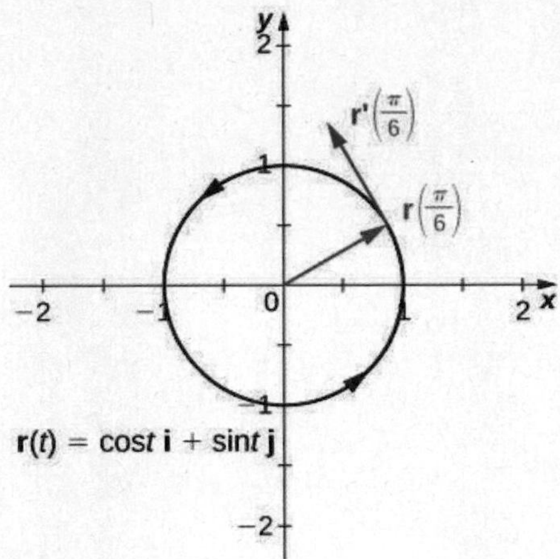

Figure 3.5 The tangent line at a point is calculated from the derivative of the vector-valued function $\mathbf{r}(t)$.

Notice that the vector $\mathbf{r}'\left(\frac{\pi}{6}\right)$ is tangent to the circle at the point corresponding to $t = \pi/6$. This is an example of a **tangent vector** to the plane curve defined by $\mathbf{r}(t) = \cos t\,\mathbf{i} + \sin t\,\mathbf{j}$.

Definition

Let C be a curve defined by a vector-valued function **r**, and assume that $\mathbf{r}'(t)$ exists when $t = t_0$. A tangent vector **v** at $t = t_0$ is any vector such that, when the tail of the vector is placed at point $\mathbf{r}(t_0)$ on the graph, vector **v** is tangent to curve *C*. Vector $\mathbf{r}'(t_0)$ is an example of a tangent vector at point $t = t_0$. Furthermore, assume that $\mathbf{r}'(t) \neq \mathbf{0}$. The **principal unit tangent vector** at *t* is defined to be

$$\mathbf{T}(t) = \frac{\mathbf{r}'(t)}{\|\mathbf{r}'(t)\|}, \tag{3.6}$$

provided $\|\mathbf{r}'(t)\| \neq 0$.

The unit tangent vector is exactly what it sounds like: a unit vector that is tangent to the curve. To calculate a unit tangent vector, first find the derivative $\mathbf{r}'(t)$. Second, calculate the magnitude of the derivative. The third step is to divide the derivative by its magnitude.

Example 3.7

Finding a Unit Tangent Vector

Find the unit tangent vector for each of the following vector-valued functions:

a. $\mathbf{r}(t) = \cos t\,\mathbf{i} + \sin t\,\mathbf{j}$

b. $\mathbf{u}(t) = \left(3t^2 + 2t\right)\mathbf{i} + \left(2 - 4t^3\right)\mathbf{j} + (6t + 5)\mathbf{k}$

Solution

a.

$$\begin{aligned}\text{First step:} \quad \mathbf{r}'(t) &= -\sin t\,\mathbf{i} + \cos t\,\mathbf{j} \\ \text{Second step:} \quad \|\mathbf{r}'(t)\| &= \sqrt{(-\sin t)^2 + (\cos t)^2} = 1 \\ \text{Third step:} \quad \mathbf{T}(t) &= \frac{\mathbf{r}'(t)}{\|\mathbf{r}'(t)\|} = \frac{-\sin t\,\mathbf{i} + \cos t\,\mathbf{j}}{1} = -\sin t\,\mathbf{i} + \cos t\,\mathbf{j}\end{aligned}$$

b.

$$\begin{aligned}\text{First step:} \quad \mathbf{u}'(t) &= (6t+2)\mathbf{i} - 12t^2\,\mathbf{j} + 6\mathbf{k} \\ \text{Second step:} \quad \|\mathbf{u}'(t)\| &= \sqrt{(6t+2)^2 + \left(-12t^2\right)^2 + 6^2} \\ &= \sqrt{144t^4 + 36t^2 + 24t + 40} \\ &= 2\sqrt{36t^4 + 9t^2 + 6t + 10} \\ \text{Third step:} \quad \mathbf{T}(t) &= \frac{\mathbf{u}'(t)}{\|\mathbf{u}'(t)\|} = \frac{(6t+2)\mathbf{i} - 12t^2\,\mathbf{j} + 6\mathbf{k}}{2\sqrt{36t^4 + 9t^2 + 6t + 10}} \\ &= \frac{3t+1}{\sqrt{36t^4 + 9t^2 + 6t + 10}}\mathbf{i} - \frac{6t^2}{\sqrt{36t^4 + 9t^2 + 6t + 10}}\mathbf{j} + \frac{3}{\sqrt{36t^4 + 9t^2 + 6t + 10}}\mathbf{k}\end{aligned}$$

3.7 Find the unit tangent vector for the vector-valued function

$$\mathbf{r}(t) = \left(t^2 - 3\right)\mathbf{i} + (2t+1)\,\mathbf{j} + (t-2)\mathbf{k}.$$

Integrals of Vector-Valued Functions

We introduced antiderivatives of real-valued functions in **Antiderivatives (http://cnx.org/content/m53621/latest/)** and definite integrals of real-valued functions in **The Definite Integral (http://cnx.org/content/m53631/latest/)** . Each of these concepts can be extended to vector-valued functions. Also, just as we can calculate the derivative of a vector-valued function by differentiating the component functions separately, we can calculate the antiderivative in the same manner. Furthermore, the Fundamental Theorem of Calculus applies to vector-valued functions as well.

The antiderivative of a vector-valued function appears in applications. For example, if a vector-valued function represents the velocity of an object at time *t*, then its antiderivative represents position. Or, if the function represents the acceleration of the object at a given time, then the antiderivative represents its velocity.

Definition

Let *f*, *g*, and *h* be integrable real-valued functions over the closed interval $[a, b]$.

1. The **indefinite integral of a vector-valued function** $\mathbf{r}(t) = f(t)\mathbf{i} + g(t)\mathbf{j}$ is

$$\int [f(t)\mathbf{i} + g(t)\mathbf{j}]dt = \left[\int f(t)dt\right]\mathbf{i} + \left[\int g(t)dt\right]\mathbf{j}. \quad (3.7)$$

The **definite integral of a vector-valued function** is

$$\int_a^b [f(t)\mathbf{i} + g(t)\mathbf{j}]dt = \left[\int_a^b f(t)dt\right]\mathbf{i} + \left[\int_a^b g(t)dt\right]\mathbf{j}. \quad (3.8)$$

2. The indefinite integral of a vector-valued function $\mathbf{r}(t) = f(t)\mathbf{i} + g(t)\mathbf{j} + h(t)\mathbf{k}$ is

$$\int [f(t)\mathbf{i} + g(t)\mathbf{j} + h(t)\mathbf{k}]dt = \left[\int f(t)dt\right]\mathbf{i} + \left[\int g(t)dt\right]\mathbf{j} + \left[\int h(t)dt\right]\mathbf{k}. \quad (3.9)$$

The definite integral of the vector-valued function is

$$\int_a^b [f(t)\mathbf{i} + g(t)\mathbf{j} + h(t)\mathbf{k}]dt = \left[\int_a^b f(t)dt\right]\mathbf{i} + \left[\int_a^b g(t)dt\right]\mathbf{j} + \left[\int_a^b h(t)dt\right]\mathbf{k}. \tag{3.10}$$

Since the indefinite integral of a vector-valued function involves indefinite integrals of the component functions, each of these component integrals contains an integration constant. They can all be different. For example, in the two-dimensional case, we can have

$$\int f(t)dt = F(t) + C_1 \text{ and } \int g(t)dt = G(t) + C_2,$$

where F and G are antiderivatives of f and g, respectively. Then

$$\begin{aligned}\int [f(t)\mathbf{i} + g(t)\mathbf{j}]dt &= \left[\int f(t)dt\right]\mathbf{i} + \left[\int g(t)dt\right]\mathbf{j} \\ &= (F(t) + C_1)\mathbf{i} + (G(t) + C_2)\mathbf{j} \\ &= F(t)\mathbf{i} + G(t)\mathbf{j} + C_1\mathbf{i} + C_2\mathbf{j} \\ &= F(t)\mathbf{i} + G(t)\mathbf{j} + \mathbf{C},\end{aligned}$$

where $\mathbf{C} = C_1\mathbf{i} + C_2\mathbf{j}$. Therefore, the integration constant becomes a constant vector.

Example 3.8

Integrating Vector-Valued Functions

Calculate each of the following integrals:

a. $\int \left[(3t^2 + 2t)\mathbf{i} + (3t - 6)\mathbf{j} + (6t^3 + 5t^2 - 4)\mathbf{k}\right]dt$

b. $\int \left[\langle t, t^2, t^3 \rangle \times \langle t^3, t^2, t \rangle\right]dt$

c. $\int_0^{\pi/3} \left[\sin 2t\,\mathbf{i} + \tan t\,\mathbf{j} + e^{-2t}\,\mathbf{k}\right]dt$

Solution

a. We use the first part of the definition of the integral of a space curve:

$$\begin{aligned}&\int \left[(3t^2 + 2t)\mathbf{i} + (3t - 6)\mathbf{j} + (6t^3 + 5t^2 - 4)\mathbf{k}\right]dt \\ &= \left[\int 3t^2 + 2t\,dt\right]\mathbf{i} + \left[\int 3t - 6dt\right]\mathbf{j} + \left[\int 6t^3 + 5t^2 - 4dt\right]\mathbf{k} \\ &= (t^3 + t^2)\mathbf{i} + \left(\tfrac{3}{2}t^2 - 6t\right)\mathbf{j} + \left(\tfrac{3}{2}t^4 + \tfrac{5}{3}t^3 - 4t\right)\mathbf{k} + \mathbf{C}.\end{aligned}$$

b. First calculate $\langle t, t^2, t^3 \rangle \times \langle t^3, t^2, t \rangle$:

$$\begin{aligned}\langle t, t^2, t^3 \rangle \times \langle t^3, t^2, t \rangle &= \begin{vmatrix} \mathbf{i} & \mathbf{j} & \mathbf{k} \\ t & t^2 & t^3 \\ t^3 & t^2 & t \end{vmatrix} \\ &= \left(t^2(t) - t^3(t^2)\right)\mathbf{i} - \left(t^2 - t^3(t^3)\right)\mathbf{j} + \left(t(t^2) - t^2(t^3)\right)\mathbf{k} \\ &= (t^3 - t^5)\mathbf{i} + (t^6 - t^2)\mathbf{j} + (t^3 - t^5)\mathbf{k}.\end{aligned}$$

Next, substitute this back into the integral and integrate:

$$\begin{aligned}\int\left[\langle t, t^2, t^3\rangle \times \langle t^3, t^2, t\rangle\right]dt &= \int\left(t^3 - t^5\right)\mathbf{i} + \left(t^6 - t^2\right)\mathbf{j} + \left(t^3 - t^5\right)\mathbf{k}\,dt \\ &= \left(\frac{t^4}{4} - \frac{t^6}{6}\right)\mathbf{i} + \left(\frac{t^7}{7} - \frac{t^3}{3}\right)\mathbf{j} + \left(\frac{t^4}{4} - \frac{t^6}{6}\right)\mathbf{k} + \mathbf{C}.\end{aligned}$$

c. Use the second part of the definition of the integral of a space curve:

$$\begin{aligned}&\int_0^{\pi/3}\left[\sin 2t\,\mathbf{i} + \tan t\,\mathbf{j} + e^{-2t}\,\mathbf{k}\right]dt \\ &= \left[\int_0^{\pi/3}\sin 2t\,dt\right]\mathbf{i} + \left[\int_0^{\pi/3}\tan t\,dt\right]\mathbf{j} + \left[\int_0^{\pi/3}e^{-2t}dt\right]\mathbf{k} \\ &= \left(-\frac{1}{2}\cos 2t\right)\Big|_0^{\pi/3}\,\mathbf{i} - \left(\ln(\cos t)\right)\Big|_0^{\pi/3}\,\mathbf{j} - \left(\frac{1}{2}e^{-2t}\right)\Big|_0^{\pi/3}\,\mathbf{k} \\ &= \left(-\frac{1}{2}\cos\frac{2\pi}{3} + \frac{1}{2}\cos 0\right)\mathbf{i} - \left(\ln\left(\cos\frac{\pi}{3}\right) - \ln(\cos 0)\right)\mathbf{j} - \left(\frac{1}{2}e^{-2\pi/3} - \frac{1}{2}e^{-2(0)}\right)\mathbf{k} \\ &= \left(\frac{1}{4} + \frac{1}{2}\right)\mathbf{i} - (-\ln 2)\,\mathbf{j} - \left(\frac{1}{2}e^{-2\pi/3} - \frac{1}{2}\right)\mathbf{k} \\ &= \frac{3}{4}\mathbf{i} + (\ln 2)\,\mathbf{j} + \left(\frac{1}{2} - \frac{1}{2}e^{-2\pi/3}\right)\mathbf{k}.\end{aligned}$$

3.8 Calculate the following integral:

$$\int_1^3\left[(2t + 4)\mathbf{i} + \left(3t^2 - 4t\right)\mathbf{j}\right]dt.$$

3.2 EXERCISES

Compute the derivatives of the vector-valued functions.

41. $\mathbf{r}(t) = t^3\,\mathbf{i} + 3t^2\,\mathbf{j} + \frac{t^3}{6}\mathbf{k}$

42. $\mathbf{r}(t) = \sin(t)\mathbf{i} + \cos(t)\mathbf{j} + e^t\,\mathbf{k}$

43. $\mathbf{r}(t) = e^{-t}\,\mathbf{i} + \sin(3t)\mathbf{j} + 10\sqrt{t}\mathbf{k}$. A sketch of the graph is shown here. Notice the varying periodic nature of the graph.

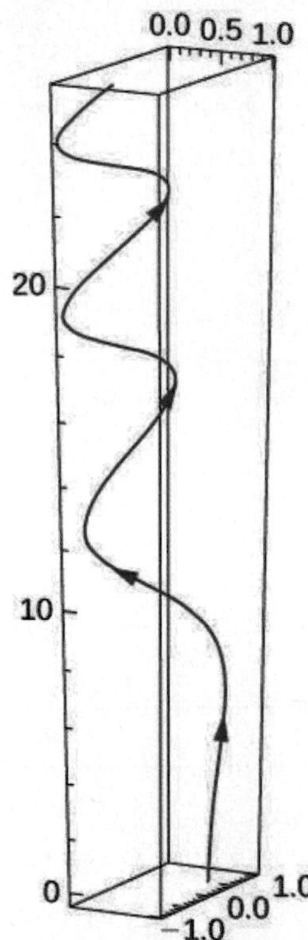

44. $\mathbf{r}(t) = e^t\,\mathbf{i} + 2e^t\,\mathbf{j} + \mathbf{k}$

45. $\mathbf{r}(t) = \mathbf{i} + \mathbf{j} + \mathbf{k}$

46. $\mathbf{r}(t) = te^t\,\mathbf{i} + t\ln(t)\mathbf{j} + \sin(3t)\mathbf{k}$

47. $\mathbf{r}(t) = \frac{1}{t+1}\mathbf{i} + \arctan(t)\mathbf{j} + \ln t^3\,\mathbf{k}$

48. $\mathbf{r}(t) = \tan(2t)\mathbf{i} + \sec(2t)\mathbf{j} + \sin^2(t)\mathbf{k}$

49. $\mathbf{r}(t) = 3\mathbf{i} + 4\sin(3t)\mathbf{j} + t\cos(t)\mathbf{k}$

50. $\mathbf{r}(t) = t^2\,\mathbf{i} + te^{-2t}\,\mathbf{j} - 5e^{-4t}\,\mathbf{k}$

For the following problems, find a tangent vector at the indicated value of *t*.

51. $\mathbf{r}(t) = t\mathbf{i} + \sin(2t)\mathbf{j} + \cos(3t)\mathbf{k};\ t = \frac{\pi}{3}$

52. $\mathbf{r}(t) = 3t^3\,\mathbf{i} + 2t^2\,\mathbf{j} + \frac{1}{t}\mathbf{k};\ t = 1$

53. $\mathbf{r}(t) = 3e^t\,\mathbf{i} + 2e^{-3t}\,\mathbf{j} + 4e^{2t}\,\mathbf{k};\ \ t = \ln(2)$

54. $\mathbf{r}(t) = \cos(2t)\mathbf{i} + 2\sin t\mathbf{j} + t^2\,\mathbf{k};\ t = \frac{\pi}{2}$

Find the unit tangent vector for the following parameterized curves.

55. $\mathbf{r}(t) = 6\mathbf{i} + \cos(3t)\mathbf{j} + 3\sin(4t)\mathbf{k},\quad 0 \le t < 2\pi$

56. $\mathbf{r}(t) = \cos t\mathbf{i} + \sin t\mathbf{j} + \sin t\mathbf{k},\quad 0 \le t < 2\pi$. Two views of this curve are presented here:

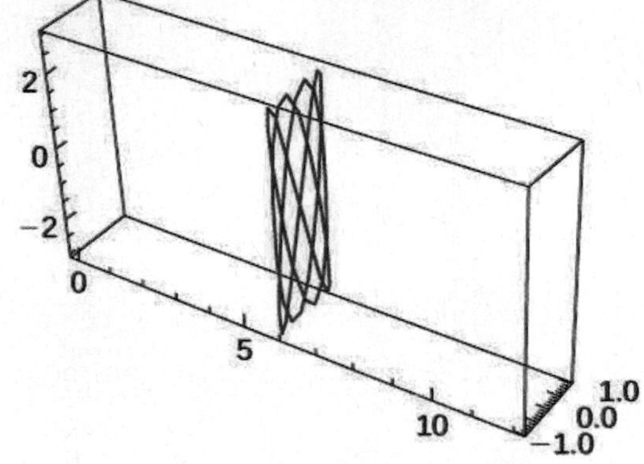

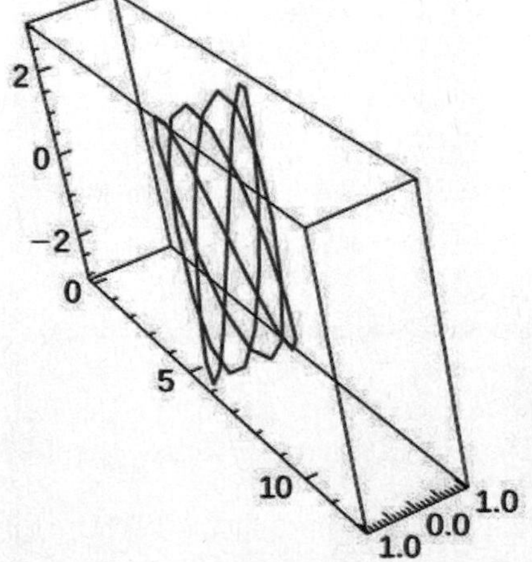

57. $\mathbf{r}(t) = 3\cos(4t)\mathbf{i} + 3\sin(4t)\mathbf{j} + 5t\mathbf{k},\ 1 \le t \le 2$

58. $\mathbf{r}(t) = t\mathbf{i} + 3t\mathbf{j} + t^2\,\mathbf{k}$

Let $\mathbf{r}(t) = t\mathbf{i} + t^2\,\mathbf{j} - t^4\,\mathbf{k}$ and $s(t) = \sin(t)\mathbf{i} + e^t\,\mathbf{j} + \cos(t)\mathbf{k}$. Here is the graph of the function:

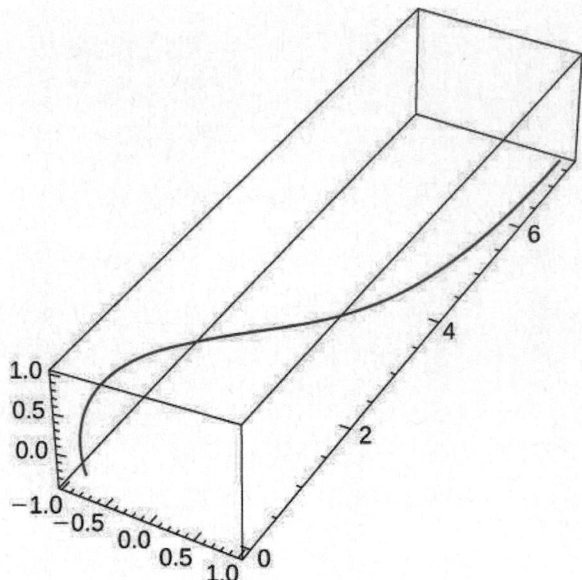

Find the following.

59. $\frac{d}{dt}\left[r\left(t^2\right)\right]$

60. $\frac{d}{dt}\left[t^2 \cdot s(t)\right]$

61. $\frac{d}{dt}[r(t) \cdot s(t)]$

62. Compute the first, second, and third derivatives of $\mathbf{r}(t) = 3t\,\mathbf{i} + 6\ln(t)\,\mathbf{j} + 5e^{-3t}\,\mathbf{k}$.

63. Find $\mathbf{r}'(t) \cdot \mathbf{r}''(t)$ for $\mathbf{r}(t) = -3t^5\,\mathbf{i} + 5t\,\mathbf{j} + 2t^2\,\mathbf{k}$.

64. The acceleration function, initial velocity, and initial position of a particle are $\mathbf{a}(t) = -5\cos t\,\mathbf{i} - 5\sin t\,\mathbf{j}$, $\mathbf{v}(0) = 9\,\mathbf{i} + 2\,\mathbf{j}$, and $\mathbf{r}(0) = 5\,\mathbf{i}$. Find $\mathbf{v}(t)$ and $\mathbf{r}(t)$.

65. The position vector of a particle is $\mathbf{r}(t) = 5\sec(2t)\,\mathbf{i} - 4\tan(t)\,\mathbf{j} + 7t^2\,\mathbf{k}$.

a. Graph the position function and display a view of the graph that illustrates the asymptotic behavior of the function.

b. Find the velocity as t approaches but is not equal to $\pi/4$ (if it exists).

66. Find the velocity and the speed of a particle with the position function $\mathbf{r}(t) = \left(\frac{2t-1}{2t+1}\right)\mathbf{i} + \ln(1-4t^2)\,\mathbf{j}$. The speed of a particle is the magnitude of the velocity and is represented by $\|r'(t)\|$.

A particle moves on a circular path of radius b according to the function $\mathbf{r}(t) = b\cos(\omega t)\,\mathbf{i} + b\sin(\omega t)\,\mathbf{j}$, where ω is the angular velocity, $d\theta/dt$.

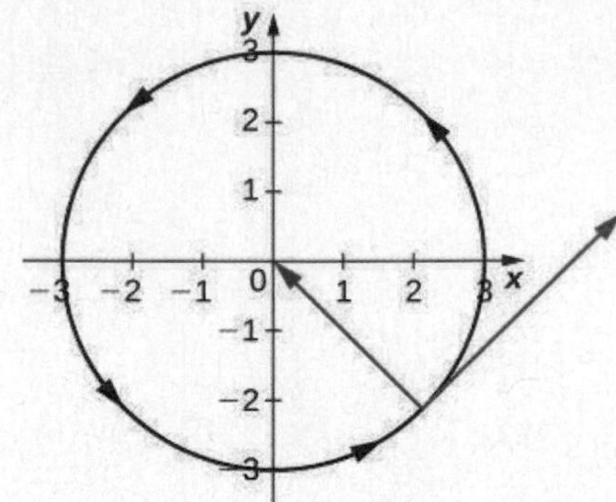

67. Find the velocity function and show that $\mathbf{v}(t)$ is always orthogonal to $\mathbf{r}(t)$.

68. Show that the speed of the particle is proportional to the angular velocity.

69. Evaluate $\frac{d}{dt}[\mathbf{u}(t) \times \mathbf{u}'(t)]$ given $\mathbf{u}(t) = t^2\,\mathbf{i} - 2t\,\mathbf{j} + \mathbf{k}$.

70. Find the antiderivative of $\mathbf{r}'(t) = \cos(2t)\,\mathbf{i} - 2\sin t\,\mathbf{j} + \frac{1}{1+t^2}\mathbf{k}$ that satisfies the initial condition $\mathbf{r}(0) = 3\,\mathbf{i} - 2\,\mathbf{j} + \mathbf{k}$.

71. Evaluate $\int_0^3 \|t\,\mathbf{i} + t^2\,\mathbf{j}\|dt$.

72. An object starts from rest at point $P(1, 2, 0)$ and moves with an acceleration of $\mathbf{a}(t) = \mathbf{j} + 2\mathbf{k}$, where $\|\mathbf{a}(t)\|$ is measured in feet per second per second. Find the location of the object after $t = 2$ sec.

73. Show that if the speed of a particle traveling along a curve represented by a vector-valued function is constant, then the velocity function is always perpendicular to the acceleration function.

74. Given $\mathbf{r}(t) = t\,\mathbf{i} + 3t\,\mathbf{j} + t^2\,\mathbf{k}$ and $\mathbf{u}(t) = 4t\,\mathbf{i} + t^2\,\mathbf{j} + t^3\,\mathbf{k}$, find $\frac{d}{dt}(\mathbf{r}(t) \times \mathbf{u}(t))$.

75. Given $\mathbf{r}(t) = \langle t + \cos t, t - \sin t \rangle$, find the velocity and the speed at any time.

76. Find the velocity vector for the function $\mathbf{r}(t) = \langle e^t, e^{-t}, 0 \rangle$.

77. Find the equation of the tangent line to the curve $\mathbf{r}(t) = \langle e^t, e^{-t}, 0 \rangle$ at $t = 0$.

78. Describe and sketch the curve represented by the vector-valued function $\mathbf{r}(t) = \langle 6t, 6t - t^2 \rangle$.

79. Locate the highest point on the curve $\mathbf{r}(t) = \langle 6t, 6t - t^2 \rangle$ and give the value of the function at this point.

The position vector for a particle is $\mathbf{r}(t) = t\mathbf{i} + t^2\mathbf{j} + t^3\mathbf{k}$. The graph is shown here:

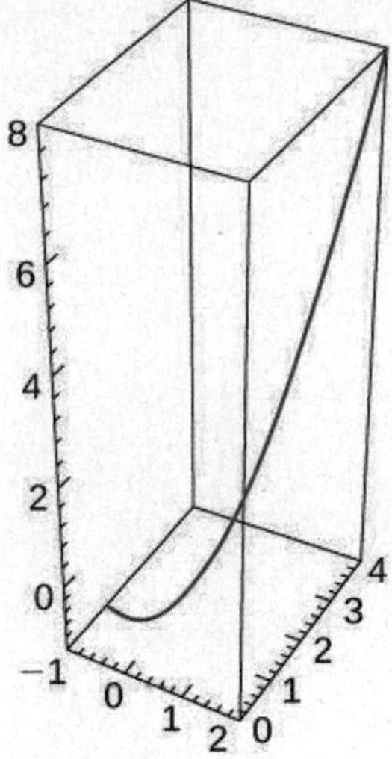

80. Find the velocity vector at any time.

81. Find the speed of the particle at time $t = 2$ sec.

82. Find the acceleration at time $t = 2$ sec.

A particle travels along the path of a helix with the equation $\mathbf{r}(t) = \cos(t)\mathbf{i} + \sin(t)\mathbf{j} + t\mathbf{k}$. See the graph presented here:

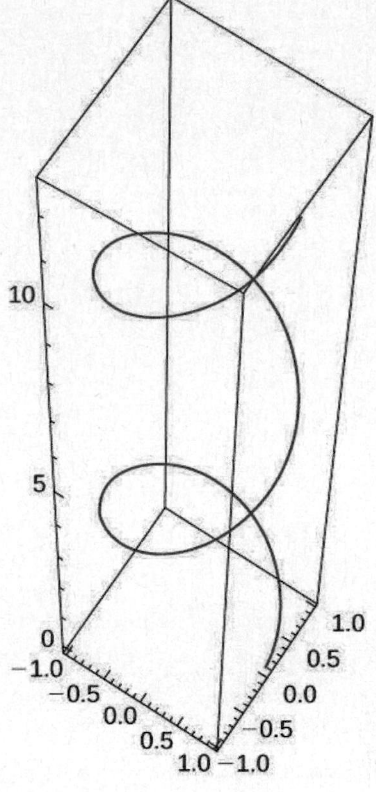

Find the following:

83. Velocity of the particle at any time

84. Speed of the particle at any time

85. Acceleration of the particle at any time

86. Find the unit tangent vector for the helix.

A particle travels along the path of an ellipse with the equation $\mathbf{r}(t) = \cos t\mathbf{i} + 2\sin t\mathbf{j} + 0\mathbf{k}$. Find the following:

87. Velocity of the particle

88. Speed of the particle at $t = \frac{\pi}{4}$

89. Acceleration of the particle at $t = \frac{\pi}{4}$

Given the vector-valued function $\mathbf{r}(t) = \langle \tan t, \sec t, 0 \rangle$ (graph is shown here), find the following:

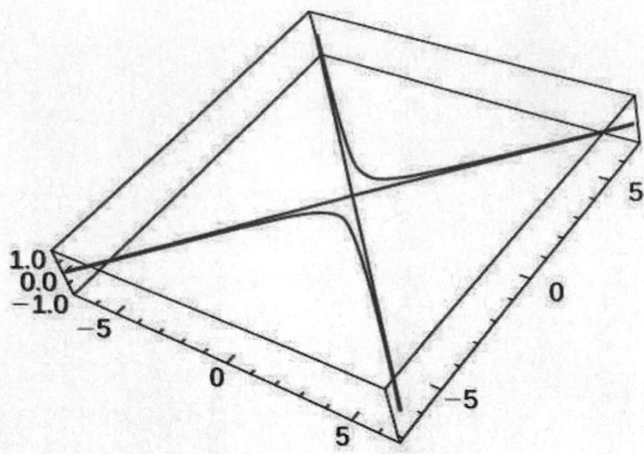

90. Velocity

91. Speed

92. Acceleration

93. Find the minimum speed of a particle traveling along the curve $\mathbf{r}(t) = \langle t + \cos t, t - \sin t \rangle \quad t \in [0, 2\pi)$.

Given $\mathbf{r}(t) = t\mathbf{i} + 2\sin t\mathbf{j} + 2\cos t\mathbf{k}$ and $\mathbf{u}(t) = \frac{1}{t}\mathbf{i} + 2\sin t\mathbf{j} + 2\cos t\mathbf{k}$, find the following:

94. $\mathbf{r}(t) \times \mathbf{u}(t)$

95. $\frac{d}{dt}(\mathbf{r}(t) \times \mathbf{u}(t))$

96. Now, use the product rule for the derivative of the cross product of two vectors and show this result is the same as the answer for the preceding problem.

Find the unit tangent vector $\mathbf{T}$(t) for the following vector-valued functions.

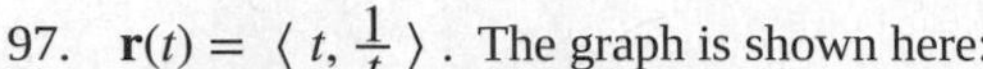
97. $\mathbf{r}(t) = \langle t, \frac{1}{t} \rangle$. The graph is shown here:

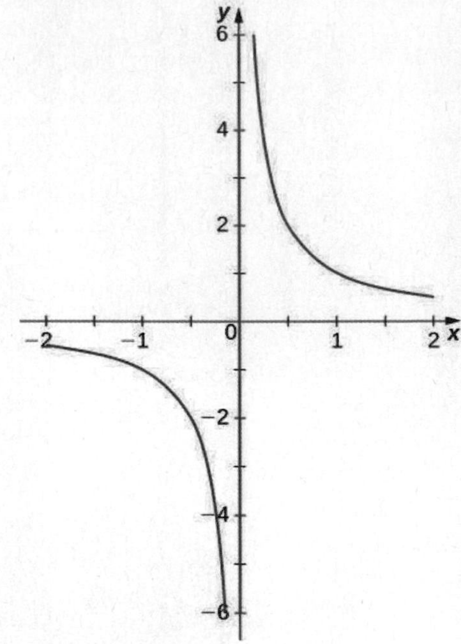

98. $\mathbf{r}(t) = \langle t\cos t, t\sin t \rangle$

99. $\mathbf{r}(t) = \langle t + 1, 2t + 1, 2t + 2 \rangle$

Evaluate the following integrals:

100. $\int \left(e^t\,\mathbf{i} + \sin t\,\mathbf{j} + \frac{1}{2t - 1}\mathbf{k}\right)dt$

101. $\int_0^1 \mathbf{r}(t)dt$, where $\mathbf{r}(t) = \langle \sqrt[3]{t}, \frac{1}{t + 1}, e^{-t} \rangle$

3.3 | Arc Length and Curvature

Learning Objectives

3.3.1 Determine the length of a particle's path in space by using the arc-length function.
3.3.2 Explain the meaning of the curvature of a curve in space and state its formula.
3.3.3 Describe the meaning of the normal and binormal vectors of a curve in space.

In this section, we study formulas related to curves in both two and three dimensions, and see how they are related to various properties of the same curve. For example, suppose a vector-valued function describes the motion of a particle in space. We would like to determine how far the particle has traveled over a given time interval, which can be described by the arc length of the path it follows. Or, suppose that the vector-valued function describes a road we are building and we want to determine how sharply the road curves at a given point. This is described by the curvature of the function at that point. We explore each of these concepts in this section.

Arc Length for Vector Functions

We have seen how a vector-valued function describes a curve in either two or three dimensions. Recall **Alternative Formulas for Curvature**, which states that the formula for the arc length of a curve defined by the parametric functions $x = x(t),\ y = y(t),\ t_1 \leq t \leq t_2$ is given by

$$s = \int_{t_1}^{t_2} \sqrt{(x'(t))^2 + (y'(t))^2}\,dt.$$

In a similar fashion, if we define a smooth curve using a vector-valued function $\mathbf{r}(t) = f(t)\,\mathbf{i} + g(t)\,\mathbf{j},$ where $a \leq t \leq b,$ the arc length is given by the formula

$$s = \int_a^b \sqrt{(f'(t))^2 + (g'(t))^2}\,dt.$$

In three dimensions, if the vector-valued function is described by $\mathbf{r}(t) = f(t)\,\mathbf{i} + g(t)\,\mathbf{j} + h(t)\,\mathbf{k}$ over the same interval $a \leq t \leq b,$ the arc length is given by

$$s = \int_a^b \sqrt{(f'(t))^2 + (g'(t))^2 + (h'(t))^2}\,dt.$$

Theorem 3.4: Arc-Length Formulas

i. *Plane curve*: Given a smooth curve C defined by the function $\mathbf{r}(t) = f(t)\,\mathbf{i} + g(t)\,\mathbf{j},$ where t lies within the interval $[a, b],$ the arc length of C over the interval is

$$s = \int_a^b \sqrt{[f'(t)]^2 + [g'(t)]^2}\,dt = \int_a^b \|\mathbf{r}'(t)\|\,dt. \quad \textbf{(3.11)}$$

ii. *Space curve*: Given a smooth curve C defined by the function $\mathbf{r}(t) = f(t)\,\mathbf{i} + g(t)\,\mathbf{j} + h(t)\,\mathbf{k},$ where t lies within the interval $[a, b],$ the arc length of C over the interval is

$$s = \int_a^b \sqrt{[f'(t)]^2 + [g'(t)]^2 + [h'(t)]^2}\,dt = \int_a^b \|\mathbf{r}'(t)\|\,dt. \quad \textbf{(3.12)}$$

The two formulas are very similar; they differ only in the fact that a space curve has three component functions instead of two. Note that the formulas are defined for smooth curves: curves where the vector-valued function $\mathbf{r}(t)$ is differentiable with a non-zero derivative. The smoothness condition guarantees that the curve has no cusps (or corners) that could make the formula problematic.

Example 3.9

Finding the Arc Length

Calculate the arc length for each of the following vector-valued functions:

a. $\mathbf{r}(t) = (3t - 2)\mathbf{i} + (4t + 5)\mathbf{j},\ 1 \le t \le 5$

b. $\mathbf{r}(t) = \langle t\cos t, t\sin t, 2t \rangle,\ 0 \le t \le 2\pi$

Solution

a. Using **Equation 3.11**, $\mathbf{r}'(t) = 3\mathbf{i} + 4\mathbf{j}$, so

$$\begin{aligned} s &= \int_a^b \| \mathbf{r}'(t) \| \, dt \\ &= \int_a^5 \sqrt{3^2 + 4^2} dt \\ &= \int_1^5 5\, dt = 5t|_1^5 = 20. \end{aligned}$$

b. Using **Equation 3.12**, $\mathbf{r}'(t) = \langle \cos t - t\sin t, \sin t + t\cos t, 2 \rangle$, so

$$\begin{aligned} s &= \int_a^b \| \mathbf{r}'(t) \| \, dt \\ &= \int_0^{2\pi} \sqrt{(\cos t - t\sin t)^2 + (\sin t + t\cos t)^2 + 2^2} dt \\ &= \int_0^{2\pi} \sqrt{\left(\cos^2 t - 2t\sin t\cos t + t^2\sin^2 t\right) + \left(\sin^2 t + 2t\sin t\cos t + t^2\cos^2 t\right) + 4}\, dt \\ &= \int_0^{2\pi} \sqrt{\cos^2 t + \sin^2 t + t^2\left(\cos^2 t + \sin^2 t\right) + 4}\, dt \\ &= \int_0^{2\pi} \sqrt{t^2 + 5}\, dt. \end{aligned}$$

Here we can use a table integration formula

$$\int \sqrt{u^2 + a^2}\, du = \frac{u}{2}\sqrt{u^2 + a^2} + \frac{a^2}{2}\ln\left|u + \sqrt{u^2 + a^2}\right| + C,$$

so we obtain

$$\begin{aligned} \int_0^{2\pi} \sqrt{t^2 + 5}\, dt &= \frac{1}{2}\left(t\sqrt{t^2 + 5} + 5\ln\left|t + \sqrt{t^2 + 5}\right|\right)_0^{2\pi} \\ &= \frac{1}{2}\left(2\pi\sqrt{4\pi^2 + 5} + 5\ln\left(2\pi + \sqrt{4\pi^2 + 5}\right)\right) - \frac{5}{2}\ln\sqrt{5} \\ &\approx 25.343. \end{aligned}$$

3.9 Calculate the arc length of the parameterized curve

$$\mathbf{r}(t) = \langle 2t^2 + 1, 2t^2 - 1, t^3 \rangle,\ 0 \le t \le 3.$$

We now return to the helix introduced earlier in this chapter. A vector-valued function that describes a helix can be written in the form

$$\mathbf{r}(t) = R\cos\left(\frac{2\pi Nt}{h}\right)\mathbf{i} + R\sin\left(\frac{2\pi Nt}{h}\right)\mathbf{j} + t\,\mathbf{k},\ 0 \le t \le h,$$

where R represents the radius of the helix, h represents the height (distance between two consecutive turns), and the helix completes N turns. Let's derive a formula for the arc length of this helix using **Equation 3.12**. First of all,

$$\mathbf{r}'(t) = -\frac{2\pi NR}{h}\sin\left(\frac{2\pi Nt}{h}\right)\mathbf{i} + \frac{2\pi NR}{h}\cos\left(\frac{2\pi Nt}{h}\right)\mathbf{j} + \mathbf{k}.$$

Therefore,

$$\begin{aligned}
s &= \int_a^b \|\mathbf{r}'(t)\|\,dt \\
&= \int_0^h \sqrt{\left(-\frac{2\pi NR}{h}\sin\left(\frac{2\pi Nt}{h}\right)\right)^2 + \left(\frac{2\pi NR}{h}\cos\left(\frac{2\pi Nt}{h}\right)\right)^2 + 1^2}\,dt \\
&= \int_0^h \sqrt{\frac{4\pi^2N^2R^2}{h^2}\left(\sin^2\left(\frac{2\pi Nt}{h}\right) + \cos^2\left(\frac{2\pi Nt}{h}\right)\right) + 1}\,dt \\
&= \int_0^h \sqrt{\frac{4\pi^2N^2R^2}{h^2} + 1}\,dt \\
&= \left[t\sqrt{\frac{4\pi^2N^2R^2}{h^2} + 1}\right]_0^h \\
&= h\sqrt{\frac{4\pi^2N^2R^2 + h^2}{h^2}} \\
&= \sqrt{4\pi^2N^2R^2 + h^2}.
\end{aligned}$$

This gives a formula for the length of a wire needed to form a helix with N turns that has radius R and height h.

Arc-Length Parameterization

We now have a formula for the arc length of a curve defined by a vector-valued function. Let's take this one step further and examine what an **arc-length function** is.

If a vector-valued function represents the position of a particle in space as a function of time, then the arc-length function measures how far that particle travels as a function of time. The formula for the arc-length function follows directly from the formula for arc length:

$$s(t) = \int_a^t \sqrt{(f'(u))^2 + (g'(u))^2 + (h'(u))^2}\,du. \tag{3.13}$$

If the curve is in two dimensions, then only two terms appear under the square root inside the integral. The reason for using the independent variable u is to distinguish between time and the variable of integration. Since $s(t)$ measures distance traveled as a function of time, $s'(t)$ measures the speed of the particle at any given time. Since we have a formula for $s(t)$ in **Equation 3.13**, we can differentiate both sides of the equation:

$$\begin{aligned}
s'(t) &= \frac{d}{dt}\left[\int_a^t \sqrt{(f'(u))^2 + (g'(u))^2 + (h'(u))^2}\,du\right] \\
&= \frac{d}{dt}\left[\int_a^t \|\mathbf{r}'(u)\|\,du\right] \\
&= \|\mathbf{r}'(t)\|.
\end{aligned}$$

If we assume that $\mathbf{r}(t)$ defines a smooth curve, then the arc length is always increasing, so $s'(t) > 0$ for $t > a$. Last, if $\mathbf{r}(t)$ is a curve on which $\|\mathbf{r}'(t)\| = 1$ for all t, then

$$s(t) = \int_a^t \|\mathbf{r}'(u)\|\,du = \int_a^t 1\,du = t - a,$$

which means that t represents the arc length as long as $a = 0$.

Theorem 3.5: Arc-Length Function

Let $\mathbf{r}(t)$ describe a smooth curve for $t \geq a$. Then the arc-length function is given by

$$s(t) = \int_a^t \| \mathbf{r}'(u) \| \, du. \tag{3.14}$$

Furthermore, $\frac{ds}{dt} = \| \mathbf{r}'(t) \| > 0$. If $\| \mathbf{r}'(t) \| = 1$ for all $t \geq a$, then the parameter t represents the arc length from the starting point at $t = a$.

A useful application of this theorem is to find an alternative parameterization of a given curve, called an **arc-length parameterization**. Recall that any vector-valued function can be reparameterized via a change of variables. For example, if we have a function $\mathbf{r}(t) = \langle 3\cos t, 3\sin t \rangle, 0 \leq t \leq 2\pi$ that parameterizes a circle of radius 3, we can change the parameter from t to $4t$, obtaining a new parameterization $\mathbf{r}(t) = \langle 3\cos 4t, 3\sin 4t \rangle$. The new parameterization still defines a circle of radius 3, but now we need only use the values $0 \leq t \leq \pi/2$ to traverse the circle once.

Suppose that we find the arc-length function $s(t)$ and are able to solve this function for t as a function of s. We can then reparameterize the original function $\mathbf{r}(t)$ by substituting the expression for t back into $\mathbf{r}(t)$. The vector-valued function is now written in terms of the parameter s. Since the variable s represents the arc length, we call this an *arc-length parameterization* of the original function $\mathbf{r}(t)$. One advantage of finding the arc-length parameterization is that the distance traveled along the curve starting from $s = 0$ is now equal to the parameter s. The arc-length parameterization also appears in the context of curvature (which we examine later in this section) and line integrals, which we study in the **Introduction to Vector Calculus**.

Example 3.10

Finding an Arc-Length Parameterization

Find the arc-length parameterization for each of the following curves:

a. $\mathbf{r}(t) = 4\cos t\,\mathbf{i} + 4\sin t\,\mathbf{j},\ t \geq 0$

b. $\mathbf{r}(t) = \langle t+3,\ 2t-4,\ 2t \rangle,\ t \geq 3$

Solution

a. First we find the arc-length function using **Equation 3.14**:

$$\begin{aligned} s(t) &= \int_a^t \| \mathbf{r}'(u) \| \, du \\ &= \int_0^t \| \langle -4\sin u, 4\cos u \rangle \| \, du \\ &= \int_0^t \sqrt{(-4\sin u)^2 + (4\cos u)^2} \, du \\ &= \int_0^t \sqrt{16\sin^2 u + 16\cos^2 u} \, du \\ &= \int_0^t 4 \, du = 4t, \end{aligned}$$

which gives the relationship between the arc length s and the parameter t as $s = 4t$; so, $t = s/4$. Next we replace the variable t in the original function $\mathbf{r}(t) = 4\cos t\,\mathbf{i} + 4\sin t\,\mathbf{j}$ with the expression $s/4$ to obtain

$$\mathbf{r}(s) = 4\cos\left(\frac{s}{4}\right)\mathbf{i} + 4\sin\left(\frac{s}{4}\right)\mathbf{j}.$$

This is the arc-length parameterization of $\mathbf{r}(t)$. Since the original restriction on t was given by $t \geq 0,$ the restriction on s becomes $s/4 \geq 0,$ or $s \geq 0.$

b. The arc-length function is given by **Equation 3.14**:

$$\begin{aligned} s(t) &= \int_a^t \| \mathbf{r}'(u) \| \, du \\ &= \int_3^t \| \langle 1, 2, 2 \rangle \| \, du \\ &= \int_3^t \sqrt{1^2 + 2^2 + 2^2}\, du \\ &= \int_3^t 3\, du \\ &= 3t - 9. \end{aligned}$$

Therefore, the relationship between the arc length s and the parameter t is $s = 3t - 9,$ so $t = \frac{s}{3} + 3.$ Substituting this into the original function $\mathbf{r}(t) = \langle t + 3, 2t - 4, 2t \rangle$ yields

$$\mathbf{r}(s) = \left\langle \left(\frac{s}{3} + 3\right) + 3,\ 2\left(\frac{s}{3} + 3\right) - 4,\ 2\left(\frac{s}{3} + 3\right) \right\rangle = \left\langle \frac{s}{3} + 6,\ \frac{2s}{3} + 2,\ \frac{2s}{3} + 6 \right\rangle.$$

This is an arc-length parameterization of $\mathbf{r}(t)$. The original restriction on the parameter t was $t \geq 3,$ so the restriction on s is $(s/3) + 3 \geq 3,$ or $s \geq 0.$

3.10 Find the arc-length function for the helix

$$\mathbf{r}(t) = \langle 3\cos t, 3\sin t, 4t \rangle, \ t \geq 0.$$

Then, use the relationship between the arc length and the parameter t to find an arc-length parameterization of $\mathbf{r}(t)$.

Curvature

An important topic related to arc length is curvature. The concept of curvature provides a way to measure how sharply a smooth curve turns. A circle has constant curvature. The smaller the radius of the circle, the greater the curvature.

Think of driving down a road. Suppose the road lies on an arc of a large circle. In this case you would barely have to turn the wheel to stay on the road. Now suppose the radius is smaller. In this case you would need to turn more sharply to stay on the road. In the case of a curve other than a circle, it is often useful first to inscribe a circle to the curve at a given point so that it is tangent to the curve at that point and "hugs" the curve as closely as possible in a neighborhood of the point (**Figure 3.6**). The curvature of the graph at that point is then defined to be the same as the curvature of the inscribed circle.

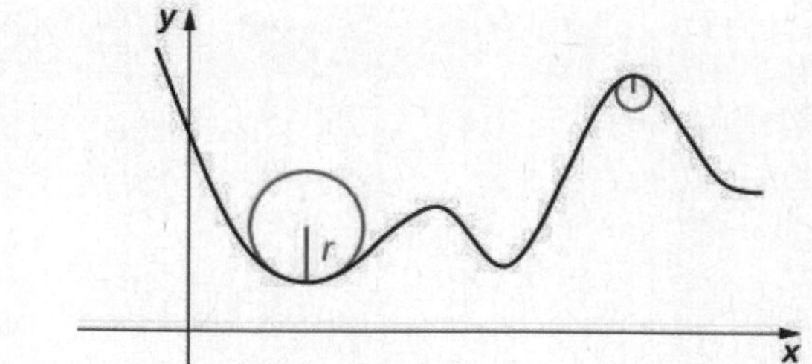

Figure 3.6 The graph represents the curvature of a function $y = f(x)$. The sharper the turn in the graph, the greater the curvature, and the smaller the radius of the inscribed circle.

Definition

Let C be a smooth curve in the plane or in space given by $\mathbf{r}(s)$, where s is the arc-length parameter. The **curvature** κ at s is

$$\kappa = \left\| \frac{d\mathbf{T}}{ds} \right\| = \| \mathbf{T}'(s) \|.$$

Visit this **website (http://www.openstaxcollege.org/l/20_spacecurve)** for more information about the curvature of a space curve.

The formula in the definition of curvature is not very useful in terms of calculation. In particular, recall that $\mathbf{T}(t)$ represents the unit tangent vector to a given vector-valued function $\mathbf{r}(t)$, and the formula for $\mathbf{T}(t)$ is $\mathbf{T}(t) = \frac{\mathbf{r}'(t)}{\| \mathbf{r}'(t) \|}$. To use the formula for curvature, it is first necessary to express $\mathbf{r}(t)$ in terms of the arc-length parameter s, then find the unit tangent vector $\mathbf{T}(s)$ for the function $\mathbf{r}(s)$, then take the derivative of $\mathbf{T}(s)$ with respect to s. This is a tedious process. Fortunately, there are equivalent formulas for curvature.

Theorem 3.6: Alternative Formulas for Curvature

If C is a smooth curve given by $\mathbf{r}(t)$, then the curvature κ of C at t is given by

$$\kappa = \frac{\| \mathbf{T}'(t) \|}{\| \mathbf{r}'(t) \|}. \quad \textbf{(3.15)}$$

If C is a three-dimensional curve, then the curvature can be given by the formula

$$\kappa = \frac{\| \mathbf{r}'(t) \times \mathbf{r}''(t) \|}{\| \mathbf{r}'(t) \|^3}. \quad \textbf{(3.16)}$$

If C is the graph of a function $y = f(x)$ and both y' and y'' exist, then the curvature κ at point (x, y) is given by

$$\kappa = \frac{|y''|}{\left[1 + (y')^2\right]^{3/2}}. \quad \textbf{(3.17)}$$

Proof

The first formula follows directly from the chain rule:

$$\frac{d\mathbf{T}}{dt} = \frac{d\mathbf{T}}{ds}\frac{ds}{dt},$$

where s is the arc length along the curve C. Dividing both sides by ds/dt, and taking the magnitude of both sides gives

$$\left\| \frac{d\mathbf{T}}{ds} \right\| = \left\| \frac{\mathbf{T}'(t)}{\frac{ds}{dt}} \right\|.$$

Since $ds/dt = \| \mathbf{r}'(t) \|$, this gives the formula for the curvature κ of a curve C in terms of any parameterization of C:

$$\kappa = \frac{\| \mathbf{T}'(t) \|}{\| \mathbf{r}'(t) \|}.$$

In the case of a three-dimensional curve, we start with the formulas $\mathbf{T}(t) = (\mathbf{r}'(t))/\| \mathbf{r}'(t) \|$ and $ds/dt = \| \mathbf{r}'(t) \|$. Therefore, $\mathbf{r}'(t) = (ds/dt)\mathbf{T}(t)$. We can take the derivative of this function using the scalar product formula:

$$\mathbf{r}''(t) = \frac{d^2 s}{dt^2}\mathbf{T}(t) + \frac{ds}{dt}\mathbf{T}'(t).$$

Using these last two equations we get

$$\begin{aligned} \mathbf{r}'(t) \times \mathbf{r}''(t) &= \frac{ds}{dt}\mathbf{T}(t) \times \left(\frac{d^2 s}{dt^2}\mathbf{T}(t) + \frac{ds}{dt}\mathbf{T}'(t)\right) \\ &= \frac{ds}{dt}\frac{d^2 s}{dt^2}\mathbf{T}(t) \times \mathbf{T}(t) + \left(\frac{ds}{dt}\right)^2 \mathbf{T}(t) \times \mathbf{T}'(t). \end{aligned}$$

Since $\mathbf{T}(t) \times \mathbf{T}(t) = \mathbf{0}$, this reduces to

$$\mathbf{r}'(t) \times \mathbf{r}''(t) = \left(\frac{ds}{dt}\right)^2 \mathbf{T}(t) \times \mathbf{T}'(t).$$

Since $\mathbf{T}'$ is parallel to $\mathbf{N}$, and $\mathbf{T}$ is orthogonal to $\mathbf{N}$, it follows that $\mathbf{T}$ and $\mathbf{T}'$ are orthogonal. This means that $\| \mathbf{T} \times \mathbf{T}' \| = \| \mathbf{T} \| \, \| \mathbf{T}' \| \sin(\pi/2) = \| \mathbf{T}' \|$, so

$$\mathbf{r}'(t) \times \mathbf{r}''(t) = \left(\frac{ds}{dt}\right)^2 \| \mathbf{T}'(t) \|.$$

Now we solve this equation for $\| \mathbf{T}'(t) \|$ and use the fact that $ds/dt = \| \mathbf{r}'(t) \|$:

$$\| \mathbf{T}'(t) \| = \frac{\| \mathbf{r}'(t) \times \mathbf{r}''(t) \|}{\| \mathbf{r}'(t) \|^2}.$$

Then, we divide both sides by $\| \mathbf{r}'(t) \|$. This gives

$$\kappa = \frac{\| \mathbf{T}'(t) \|}{\| \mathbf{r}'(t) \|} = \frac{\| \mathbf{r}'(t) \times \mathbf{r}''(t) \|}{\| \mathbf{r}'(t) \|^3}.$$

This proves **Equation 3.16**. To prove **Equation 3.17**, we start with the assumption that curve C is defined by the function $y = f(x)$. Then, we can define $\mathbf{r}(t) = x\,\mathbf{i} + f(x)\,\mathbf{j} + 0\,\mathbf{k}$. Using the previous formula for curvature:

$$\begin{aligned} \mathbf{r}'(t) &= \mathbf{i} + f'(x)\,\mathbf{j} \\ \mathbf{r}''(t) &= f''(x)\,\mathbf{j} \\ \mathbf{r}'(t) \times \mathbf{r}''(t) &= \begin{vmatrix} \mathbf{i} & \mathbf{j} & \mathbf{k} \\ 1 & f'(x) & 0 \\ 0 & f''(x) & 0 \end{vmatrix} = f''(x)\,\mathbf{k}. \end{aligned}$$

Therefore,

$$\kappa = \frac{\| \mathbf{r}'(t) \times \mathbf{r}''(t) \|}{\| \mathbf{r}'(t) \|^3} = \frac{|f''(x)|}{\left(1 + \left[(f'(x))^2\right]\right)^{3/2}}.$$

□

Example 3.11

Finding Curvature

Find the curvature for each of the following curves at the given point:

a. $\mathbf{r}(t) = 4\cos t\,\mathbf{i} + 4\sin t\,\mathbf{j} + 3t\,\mathbf{k},\ t = \frac{4\pi}{3}$

b. $f(x) = \sqrt{4x - x^2},\ x = 2$

Solution

a. This function describes a helix.

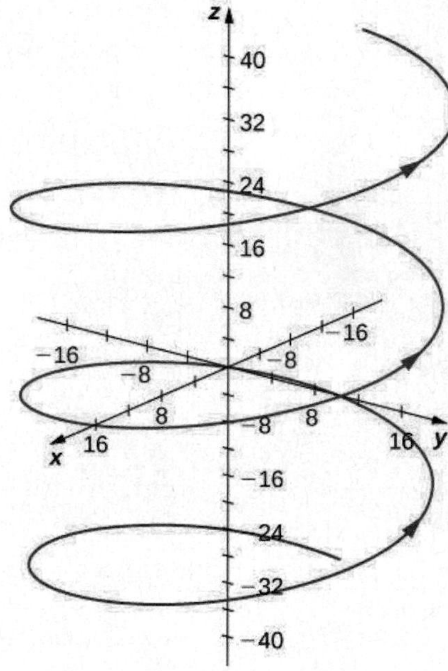

The curvature of the helix at $t = (4\pi)/3$ can be found by using **Equation 3.15**. First, calculate $\mathbf{T}(t)$:

$$\begin{aligned}\mathbf{T}(t) &= \frac{\mathbf{r}'(t)}{\|\mathbf{r}'(t)\|} \\ &= \frac{\langle -4\sin t,\ 4\cos t,\ 3\rangle}{\sqrt{(-4\sin t)^2 + (4\cos t)^2 + 3^2}} \\ &= \langle -\tfrac{4}{5}\sin t,\ \tfrac{4}{5}\cos t,\ \tfrac{3}{5}\rangle.\end{aligned}$$

Next, calculate $\mathbf{T}'(t)$:

$$\mathbf{T}'(t) = \langle -\tfrac{4}{5}\cos t,\ -\tfrac{4}{5}\sin t,\ 0\rangle.$$

Last, apply **Equation 3.15**:

$$\begin{aligned}\kappa &= \frac{\|\mathbf{T}'(t)\|}{\|\mathbf{r}'(t)\|} = \frac{\|\langle -\frac{4}{5}\cos t, -\frac{4}{5}\sin t, 0\rangle\|}{\|\langle -4\sin t, 4\cos t, 3\rangle\|} \\ &= \frac{\sqrt{\left(-\frac{4}{5}\cos t\right)^2 + \left(-\frac{4}{5}\sin t\right)^2 + 0^2}}{\sqrt{(-4\sin t)^2 + (4\cos t)^2 + 3^2}} \\ &= \frac{4/5}{5} = \frac{4}{25}.\end{aligned}$$

The curvature of this helix is constant at all points on the helix.

b. This function describes a semicircle.

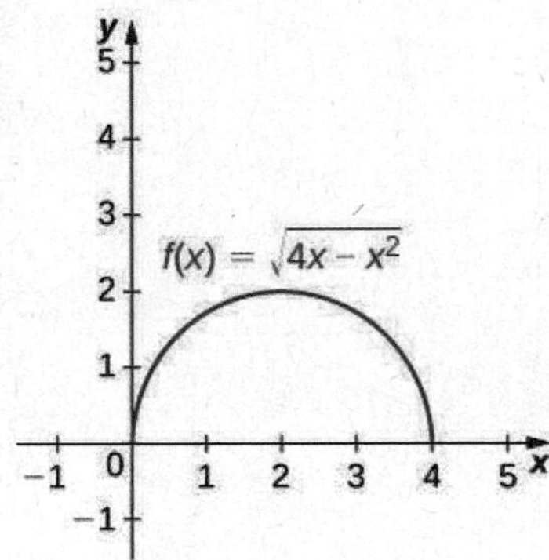

To find the curvature of this graph, we must use **Equation 3.16**. First, we calculate y' and y'':

$$\begin{aligned}y &= \sqrt{4x - x^2} = \left(4x - x^2\right)^{1/2} \\ y' &= \frac{1}{2}\left(4x - x^2\right)^{-1/2}(4 - 2x) = (2 - x)\left(4x - x^2\right)^{-1/2} \\ y'' &= -\left(4x - x^2\right)^{-1/2} + (2 - x)\left(-\frac{1}{2}\right)\left(4x - x^2\right)^{-3/2}(4 - 2x) \\ &= -\frac{4x - x^2}{\left(4x - x^2\right)^{3/2}} - \frac{(2 - x)^2}{\left(4x - x^2\right)^{3/2}} \\ &= \frac{x^2 - 4x - \left(4 - 4x + x^2\right)}{\left(4x - x^2\right)^{3/2}} \\ &= -\frac{4}{\left(4x - x^2\right)^{3/2}}.\end{aligned}$$

Then, we apply **Equation 3.17**:

$$\begin{aligned}\kappa &= \frac{|y''|}{\left[1+(y')^2\right]^{3/2}} \\ &= \frac{\left|-\frac{4}{(4x-x^2)^{3/2}}\right|}{\left[1+\left((2-x)(4x-x^2)^{-1/2}\right)^2\right]^{3/2}} = \frac{\left|\frac{4}{(4x-x^2)^{3/2}}\right|}{\left[1+\frac{(2-x)^2}{4x-x^2}\right]^{3/2}} \\ &= \frac{\left|\frac{4}{(4x-x^2)^{3/2}}\right|}{\left[\frac{4x-x^2+x^2-4x+4}{4x-x^2}\right]^{3/2}} = \left|\frac{4}{(4x-x^2)^{3/2}}\right| \cdot \frac{(4x-x^2)^{3/2}}{8} \\ &= \frac{1}{2}.\end{aligned}$$

The curvature of this circle is equal to the reciprocal of its radius. There is a minor issue with the absolute value in **Equation 3.16**; however, a closer look at the calculation reveals that the denominator is positive for any value of x.

3.11 Find the curvature of the curve defined by the function

$$y = 3x^2 - 2x + 4$$

at the point $x = 2$.

The Normal and Binormal Vectors

We have seen that the derivative $\mathbf{r}'(t)$ of a vector-valued function is a tangent vector to the curve defined by $\mathbf{r}(t)$, and the unit tangent vector $\mathbf{T}(t)$ can be calculated by dividing $\mathbf{r}'(t)$ by its magnitude. When studying motion in three dimensions, two other vectors are useful in describing the motion of a particle along a path in space: the **principal unit normal vector** and the **binormal vector**.

Definition

Let C be a three-dimensional **smooth** curve represented by **r** over an open interval I. If $\mathbf{T}'(t) \neq \mathbf{0}$, then the principal unit normal vector at t is defined to be

$$\mathbf{N}(t) = \frac{\mathbf{T}'(t)}{\|\mathbf{T}'(t)\|}. \tag{3.18}$$

The binormal vector at t is defined as

$$\mathbf{B}(t) = \mathbf{T}(t) \times \mathbf{N}(t), \tag{3.19}$$

where $\mathbf{T}(t)$ is the unit tangent vector.

Note that, by definition, the binormal vector is orthogonal to both the unit tangent vector and the normal vector. Furthermore, $\mathbf{B}(t)$ is always a unit vector. This can be shown using the formula for the magnitude of a cross product

$$\| \mathbf{B}(t) \| = \| \mathbf{T}(t) \times \mathbf{N}(t) \| = \| \mathbf{T}(t) \| \, \| \mathbf{N}(t) \| \sin\theta,$$

where θ is the angle between $\mathbf{T}(t)$ and $\mathbf{N}(t)$. Since $\mathbf{N}(t)$ is the derivative of a unit vector, property (vii) of the derivative of a vector-valued function tells us that $\mathbf{T}(t)$ and $\mathbf{N}(t)$ are orthogonal to each other, so $\theta = \pi/2$. Furthermore, they are both unit vectors, so their magnitude is 1. Therefore, $\| \mathbf{T}(t) \| \, \| \mathbf{N}(t) \| \sin\theta = (1)(1)\sin(\pi/2) = 1$ and $\mathbf{B}(t)$ is a unit vector.

The principal unit normal vector can be challenging to calculate because the unit tangent vector involves a quotient, and this quotient often has a square root in the denominator. In the three-dimensional case, finding the cross product of the unit tangent vector and the unit normal vector can be even more cumbersome. Fortunately, we have alternative formulas for finding these two vectors, and they are presented in **Motion in Space**.

Example 3.12

Finding the Principal Unit Normal Vector and Binormal Vector

For each of the following vector-valued functions, find the principal unit normal vector. Then, if possible, find the binormal vector.

a. $\mathbf{r}(t) = 4\cos t\,\mathbf{i} - 4\sin t\,\mathbf{j}$

b. $\mathbf{r}(t) = (6t + 2)\,\mathbf{i} + 5t^2\,\mathbf{j} - 8t\,\mathbf{k}$

Solution

a. This function describes a circle.

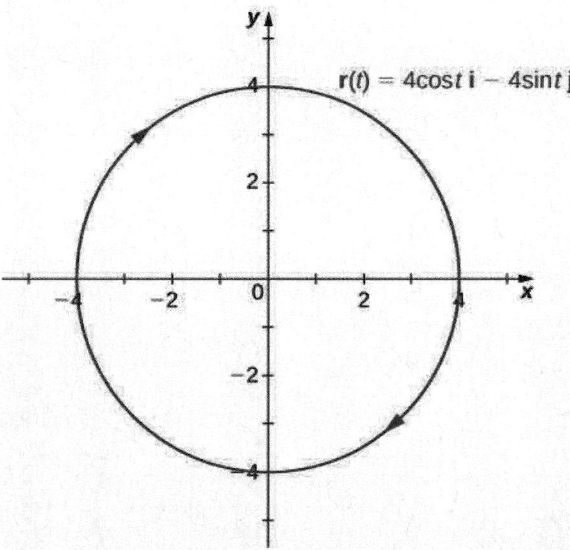

To find the principal unit normal vector, we first must find the unit tangent vector $\mathbf{T}(t)$:

$$\begin{aligned}\mathbf{T}(t) &= \frac{\mathbf{r}'(t)}{\|\mathbf{r}'(t)\|} \\ &= \frac{-4\sin t\,\mathbf{i} - 4\cos t\,\mathbf{j}}{\sqrt{(-4\sin t)^2 + (-4\cos t)^2}} \\ &= \frac{-4\sin t\,\mathbf{i} - 4\cos t\,\mathbf{j}}{\sqrt{16\sin^2 t + 16\cos^2 t}} \\ &= \frac{-4\sin t\,\mathbf{i} - 4\cos t\,\mathbf{j}}{\sqrt{16\left(\sin^2 t + \cos^2 t\right)}} \\ &= \frac{-4\sin t\,\mathbf{i} - 4\cos t\,\mathbf{j}}{4} \\ &= -\sin t\,\mathbf{i} - \cos t\,\mathbf{j}.\end{aligned}$$

Next, we use **Equation 3.18**:

$$\begin{aligned}\mathbf{N}(t) &= \frac{\mathbf{T}'(t)}{\|\mathbf{T}'(t)\|} \\ &= \frac{-\cos t\,\mathbf{i} + \sin t\,\mathbf{j}}{\sqrt{(-\cos t)^2 + (\sin t)^2}} \\ &= \frac{-\cos t\,\mathbf{i} + \sin t\,\mathbf{j}}{\sqrt{\cos^2 t + \sin^2 t}} \\ &= -\cos t\,\mathbf{i} + \sin t\,\mathbf{j}.\end{aligned}$$

Notice that the unit tangent vector and the principal unit normal vector are orthogonal to each other for all values of t:

$$\begin{aligned}\mathbf{T}(t)\cdot\mathbf{N}(t) &= \langle -\sin t,\ -\cos t \rangle \cdot \langle -\cos t,\ \sin t \rangle \\ &= \sin t\cos t - \cos t\sin t \\ &= 0.\end{aligned}$$

Furthermore, the principal unit normal vector points toward the center of the circle from every point on the circle. Since $\mathbf{r}(t)$ defines a curve in two dimensions, we cannot calculate the binormal vector.

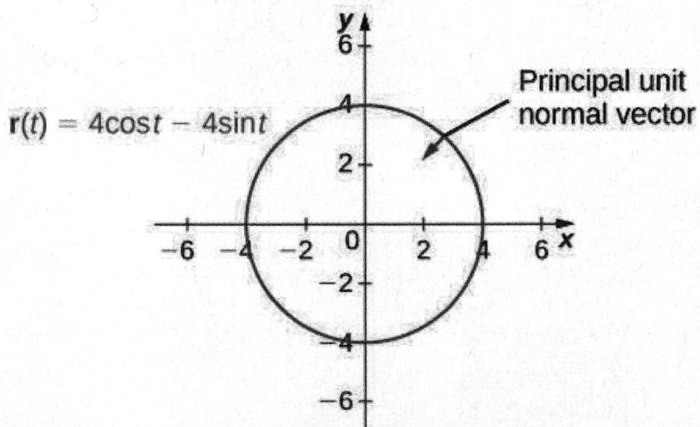

b. This function looks like this:

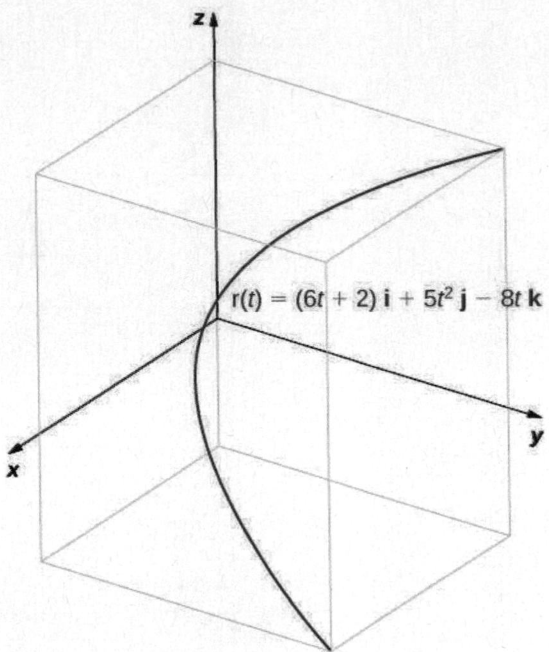

To find the principal unit normal vector, we first find the unit tangent vector $\mathbf{T}(t)$:

$$\begin{aligned}
\mathbf{T}(t) &= \frac{\mathbf{r}'(t)}{\|\mathbf{r}'(t)\|} \\
&= \frac{6\,\mathbf{i} + 10t\,\mathbf{j} - 8\,\mathbf{k}}{\sqrt{6^2 + (10t)^2 + (-8)^2}} \\
&= \frac{6\,\mathbf{i} + 10t\,\mathbf{j} - 8\,\mathbf{k}}{\sqrt{36 + 100t^2 + 64}} \\
&= \frac{6\,\mathbf{i} + 10t\,\mathbf{j} - 8\mathbf{k}}{\sqrt{100\left(t^2 + 1\right)}} \\
&= \frac{3\,\mathbf{i} - 5t\,\mathbf{j} - 4\mathbf{k}}{5\sqrt{t^2 + 1}} \\
&= \frac{3}{5}\left(t^2 + 1\right)^{-1/2}\mathbf{i} - t\left(t^2 + 1\right)^{-1/2}\mathbf{j} - \frac{4}{5}\left(t^2 + 1\right)^{-1/2}\mathbf{k}.
\end{aligned}$$

Next, we calculate $\mathbf{T}'(t)$ and $\|\mathbf{T}'(t)\|$:

$$\begin{aligned}
\mathbf{T}'(t) &= \tfrac{3}{5}\left(-\tfrac{1}{2}\right)\left(t^2+1\right)^{-3/2}(2t)\,\mathbf{i} - \left(\left(t^2+1\right)^{-1/2} - t\left(\tfrac{1}{2}\right)\left(t^2+1\right)^{-3/2}(2t)\right)\mathbf{j} \\
&\quad -\tfrac{4}{5}\left(-\tfrac{1}{2}\right)\left(t^2+1\right)^{-3/2}(2t)\,\mathbf{k} \\
&= -\frac{3t}{5\left(t^2+1\right)^{3/2}}\mathbf{i} - \frac{1}{\left(t^2+1\right)^{3/2}}\mathbf{j} + \frac{4t}{5\left(t^2+1\right)^{3/2}}\mathbf{k} \\
\|\,\mathbf{T}'(t)\,\| &= \sqrt{\left(-\frac{3t}{5\left(t^2+1\right)^{3/2}}\right)^2 + \left(-\frac{1}{\left(t^2+1\right)^{3/2}}\right)^2 + \left(\frac{4t}{5\left(t^2+1\right)^{3/2}}\right)^2} \\
&= \sqrt{\frac{9t^2}{25\left(t^2+1\right)^3} + \frac{1}{\left(t^2+1\right)^3} + \frac{16t^2}{25\left(t^2+1\right)^3}} \\
&= \sqrt{\frac{25t^2+25}{25\left(t^2+1\right)^3}} \\
&= \sqrt{\frac{1}{\left(t^2+1\right)^2}} \\
&= \frac{1}{t^2+1}.
\end{aligned}$$

Therefore, according to **Equation 3.18**:

$$\begin{aligned}
\mathbf{N}(t) &= \frac{\mathbf{T}'(t)}{\|\,\mathbf{T}'(t)\,\|} \\
&= \left(-\frac{3t}{5\left(t^2+1\right)^{3/2}}\mathbf{i} - \frac{1}{\left(t^2+1\right)^{3/2}}\mathbf{j} + \frac{4t}{5\left(t^2+1\right)^{3/2}}\mathbf{k}\right)\left(t^2+1\right) \\
&= -\frac{3t}{5\left(t^2+1\right)^{1/2}}\mathbf{i} - \frac{5}{5\left(t^2+1\right)^{1/2}}\mathbf{j} + \frac{4t}{5\left(t^2+1\right)^{1/2}}\mathbf{k} \\
&= -\frac{3t\,\mathbf{i} + 5\mathbf{j} - 4t\,\mathbf{k}}{5\sqrt{t^2+1}}.
\end{aligned}$$

Once again, the unit tangent vector and the principal unit normal vector are orthogonal to each other for all values of t:

$$\begin{aligned}
\mathbf{T}(t)\cdot\mathbf{N}(t) &= \left(\frac{3\,\mathbf{i} - 5t\,\mathbf{j} - 4\mathbf{k}}{5\sqrt{t^2+1}}\right)\cdot\left(-\frac{3t\,\mathbf{i} + 5\mathbf{j} - 4t\,\mathbf{k}}{5\sqrt{t^2+1}}\right) \\
&= \frac{3(-3t) - 5t(-5) - 4(4t)}{5\sqrt{t^2+1}} \\
&= \frac{-9t + 25t - 16t}{5\sqrt{t^2+1}} \\
&= 0.
\end{aligned}$$

Last, since $\mathbf{r}(t)$ represents a three-dimensional curve, we can calculate the binormal vector using **Equation 3.17**:

$$\begin{aligned}
\mathbf{B}(t) &= \mathbf{T}(t) \times \mathbf{N}(t) \\
&= \begin{vmatrix} \mathbf{i} & \mathbf{j} & \mathbf{k} \\ \dfrac{3}{5\sqrt{t^2+1}} & -\dfrac{5t}{5\sqrt{t^2+1}} & -\dfrac{4}{5\sqrt{t^2+1}} \\ -\dfrac{3t}{5\sqrt{t^2+1}} & -\dfrac{5}{5\sqrt{t^2+1}} & \dfrac{4t}{5\sqrt{t^2+1}} \end{vmatrix} \\
&= \left(\left(-\frac{5t}{5\sqrt{t^2+1}}\right)\left(\frac{4t}{5\sqrt{t^2+1}}\right) - \left(-\frac{4}{5\sqrt{t^2+1}}\right)\left(-\frac{5}{5\sqrt{t^2+1}}\right)\right)\mathbf{i} \\
&\quad -\left(\left(\frac{3}{5\sqrt{t^2+1}}\right)\left(\frac{4t}{5\sqrt{t^2+1}}\right) - \left(-\frac{4}{5\sqrt{t^2+1}}\right)\left(-\frac{3t}{5\sqrt{t^2+1}}\right)\right)\mathbf{j} \\
&\quad +\left(\left(\frac{3}{5\sqrt{t^2+1}}\right)\left(-\frac{5}{5\sqrt{t^2+1}}\right) - \left(-\frac{5t}{5\sqrt{t^2+1}}\right)\left(-\frac{3t}{5\sqrt{t^2+1}}\right)\right)\mathbf{k} \\
&= \left(\frac{-20t^2-20}{25\left(t^2+1\right)}\right)\mathbf{i} + \left(\frac{-15-15t^2}{25\left(t^2+1\right)}\right)\mathbf{k} \\
&= -20\left(\frac{t^2+1}{25\left(t^2+1\right)}\right)\mathbf{i} - 15\left(\frac{t^2+1}{25\left(t^2+1\right)}\right)\mathbf{k} \\
&= -\tfrac{4}{5}\mathbf{i} - \tfrac{3}{5}\mathbf{k}.
\end{aligned}$$

3.12 Find the unit normal vector for the vector-valued function $\mathbf{r}(t) = \left(t^2 - 3t\right)\mathbf{i} + (4t + 1)\,\mathbf{j}$ and evaluate it at $t = 2$.

For any smooth curve in three dimensions that is defined by a vector-valued function, we now have formulas for the unit tangent vector **T**, the unit normal vector **N**, and the binormal vector **B**. The unit normal vector and the binormal vector form a plane that is perpendicular to the curve at any point on the curve, called the **normal plane**. In addition, these three vectors form a frame of reference in three-dimensional space called the **Frenet frame of reference** (also called the **TNB** frame) (**Figure 3.7**). Lat, the plane determined by the vectors **T** and **N** forms the osculating plane of C at any point P on the curve.

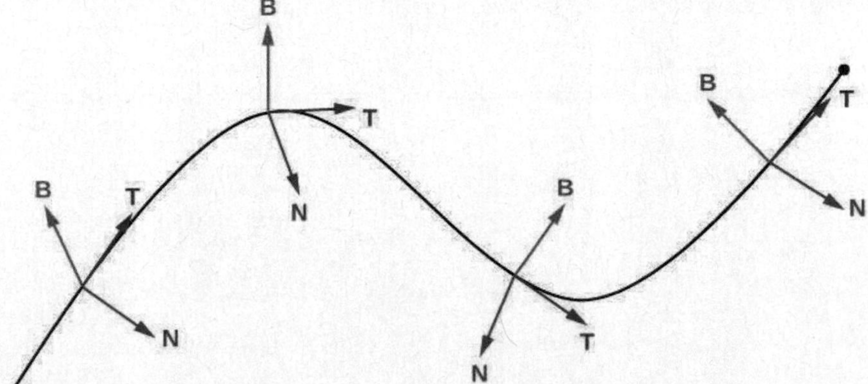

Figure 3.7 This figure depicts a Frenet frame of reference. At every point P on a three-dimensional curve, the unit tangent, unit normal, and binormal vectors form a three-dimensional frame of reference.

Suppose we form a circle in the osculating plane of C at point P on the curve. Assume that the circle has the same curvature as the curve does at point P and let the circle have radius r. Then, the curvature of the circle is given by $1/r$. We call r the **radius of curvature** of the curve, and it is equal to the reciprocal of the curvature. If this circle lies on the concave side of the curve and is tangent to the curve at point P, then this circle is called the **osculating circle** of C at P, as shown in the following figure.

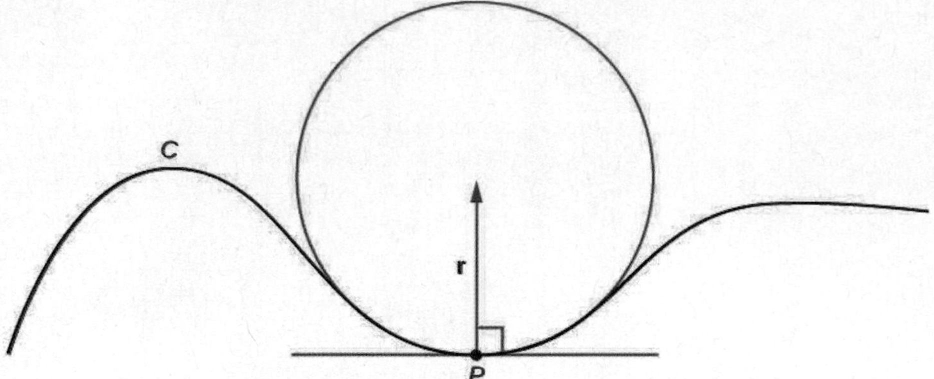

Figure 3.8 In this osculating circle, the circle is tangent to curve C at point P and shares the same curvature.

For more information on osculating circles, see this **demonstration (http://www.openstaxcollege.org/l/20_OsculCircle1)** on curvature and torsion, this **article (http://www.openstaxcollege.org/l/20_OsculCircle3)** on osculating circles, and this **discussion (http://www.openstaxcollege.org/l/20_OsculCircle2)** of Serret formulas.

To find the equation of an osculating circle in two dimensions, we need find only the center and radius of the circle.

Example 3.13

Finding the Equation of an Osculating Circle

Find the equation of the osculating circle of the helix defined by the function $y = x^3 - 3x + 1$ at $x = 1$.

Solution

Figure 3.9 shows the graph of $y = x^3 - 3x + 1$.

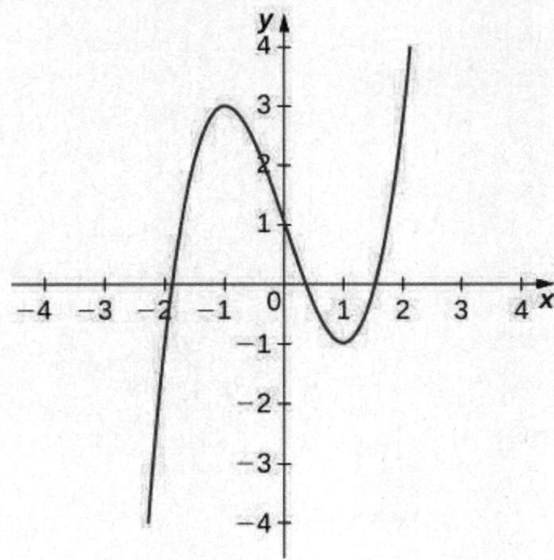

Figure 3.9 We want to find the osculating circle of this graph at the point where $t = 1$.

First, let's calculate the curvature at $x = 1$:

$$\kappa = \frac{|f''(x)|}{\left(1 + [f'(x)]^2\right)^{3/2}} = \frac{|6x|}{\left(1 + \left[3x^2 - 3\right]^2\right)^{3/2}}.$$

This gives $\kappa = 6$. Therefore, the radius of the osculating circle is given by $R = \frac{1}{\kappa} = \frac{1}{6}$. Next, we then calculate the coordinates of the center of the circle. When $x = 1$, the slope of the tangent line is zero. Therefore, the center of the osculating circle is directly above the point on the graph with coordinates $(1, -1)$. The center is located at $\left(1, -\frac{5}{6}\right)$. The formula for a circle with radius r and center (h, k) is given by $(x - h)^2 + (y - k)^2 = r^2$. Therefore, the equation of the osculating circle is $(x - 1)^2 + \left(y + \frac{5}{6}\right)^2 = \frac{1}{36}$. The graph and its osculating circle appears in the following graph.

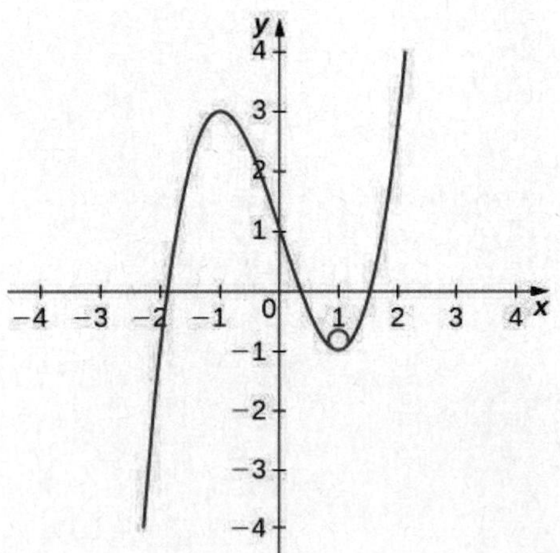

Figure 3.10 The osculating circle has radius $R = 1/6$.

3.13 Find the equation of the osculating circle of the curve defined by the vector-valued function $y = 2x^2 - 4x + 5$ at $x = 1$.

3.3 EXERCISES

Find the arc length of the curve on the given interval.

102. $\mathbf{r}(t) = t^2\mathbf{i} + 14t\mathbf{j},\ 0 \le t \le 7$. This portion of the graph is shown here:

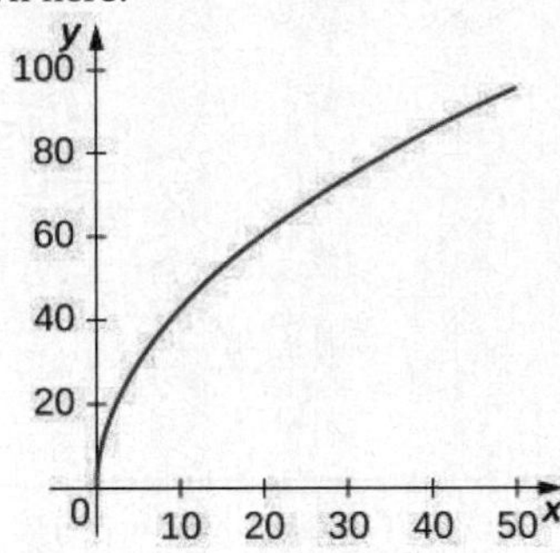

103. $\mathbf{r}(t) = t^2\mathbf{i} + (2t^2 + 1)\mathbf{j},\ 1 \le t \le 3$

104. $\mathbf{r}(t) = \langle 2\sin t, 5t, 2\cos t \rangle,\ 0 \le t \le \pi$. This portion of the graph is shown here:

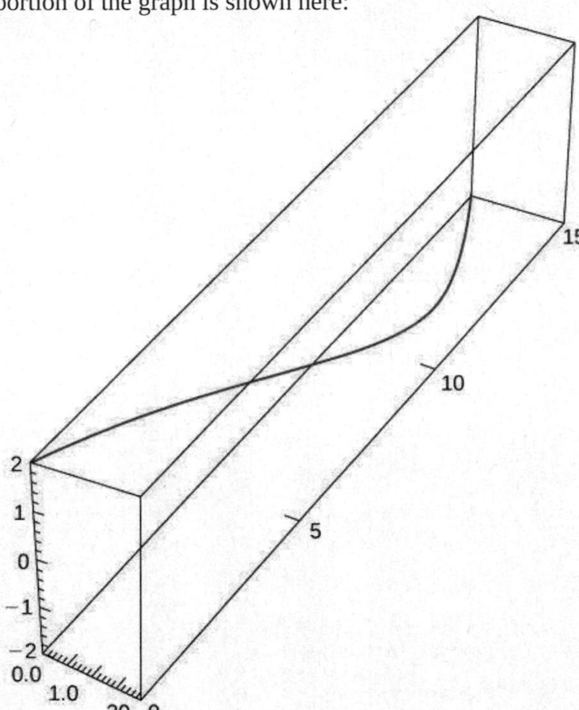

105. $\mathbf{r}(t) = \langle t^2 + 1, 4t^3 + 3 \rangle,\ -1 \le t \le 0$

106. $\mathbf{r}(t) = \langle e^{-t}\cos t, e^{-t}\sin t \rangle$ over the interval $\left[0, \frac{\pi}{2}\right]$. Here is the portion of the graph on the indicated interval:

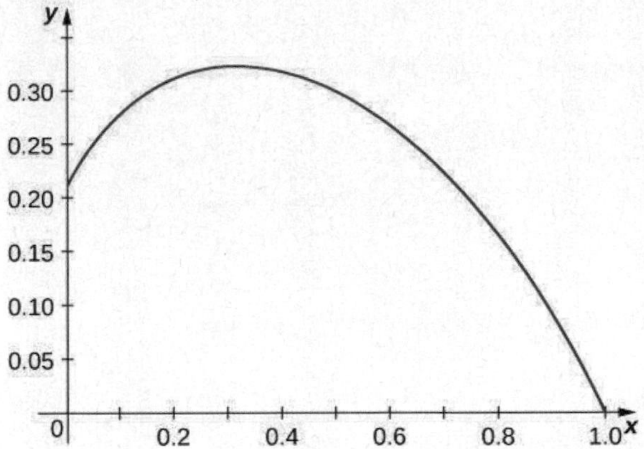

107. Find the length of one turn of the helix given by $\mathbf{r}(t) = \frac{1}{2}\cos t\mathbf{i} + \frac{1}{2}\sin t\mathbf{j} + \sqrt{\frac{3}{4}}\,t\,\mathbf{k}$.

108. Find the arc length of the vector-valued function $\mathbf{r}(t) = -t\mathbf{i} + 4t\mathbf{j} + 3t\mathbf{k}$ over $[0, 1]$.

109. A particle travels in a circle with the equation of motion $\mathbf{r}(t) = 3\cos t\mathbf{i} + 3\sin t\mathbf{j} + 0\mathbf{k}$. Find the distance traveled around the circle by the particle.

110. Set up an integral to find the circumference of the ellipse with the equation $\mathbf{r}(t) = \cos t\mathbf{i} + 2\sin t\mathbf{j} + 0\mathbf{k}$.

111. Find the length of the curve $\mathbf{r}(t) = \langle \sqrt{2}t, e^t, e^{-t} \rangle$ over the interval $0 \le t \le 1$. The graph is shown here:

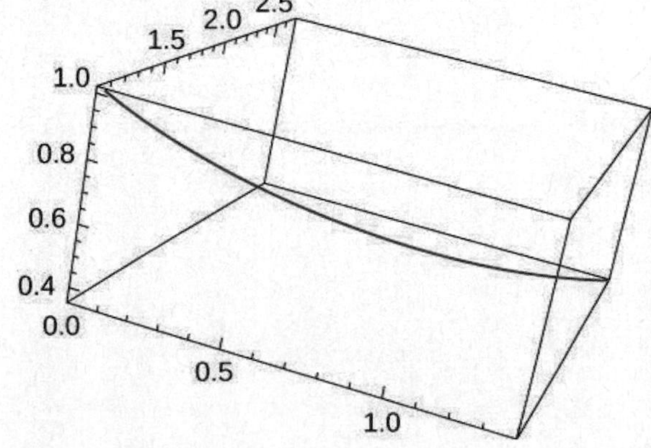

112. Find the length of the curve $\mathbf{r}(t) = \langle 2\sin t, 5t, 2\cos t \rangle$ for $t \in [-10, 10]$.

113. The position function for a particle is $\mathbf{r}(t) = a\cos(\omega t)\mathbf{i} + b\sin(\omega t)\mathbf{j}$. Find the unit tangent vector and the unit normal vector at $t = 0$.

114. Given $\mathbf{r}(t) = a\cos(\omega t)\mathbf{i} + b\sin(\omega t)\mathbf{j}$, find the binormal vector $\mathbf{B}(0)$.

115. Given $\mathbf{r}(t) = \langle 2e^t, e^t\cos t, e^t\sin t \rangle$, determine the tangent vector $\mathbf{T}(t)$.

116. Given $\mathbf{r}(t) = \langle 2e^t, e^t\cos t, e^t\sin t \rangle$, determine the unit tangent vector $\mathbf{T}(t)$ evaluated at $t = 0$.

117. Given $\mathbf{r}(t) = \langle 2e^t, e^t\cos t, e^t\sin t \rangle$, find the unit normal vector $\mathbf{N}(t)$ evaluated at $t = 0$, $\mathbf{N}(0)$.

118. Given $\mathbf{r}(t) = \langle 2e^t, e^t\cos t, e^t\sin t \rangle$, find the unit normal vector evaluated at $t = 0$.

119. Given $\mathbf{r}(t) = t\mathbf{i} + t^2\mathbf{j} + t\mathbf{k}$, find the unit tangent vector $\mathbf{T}(t)$. The graph is shown here:

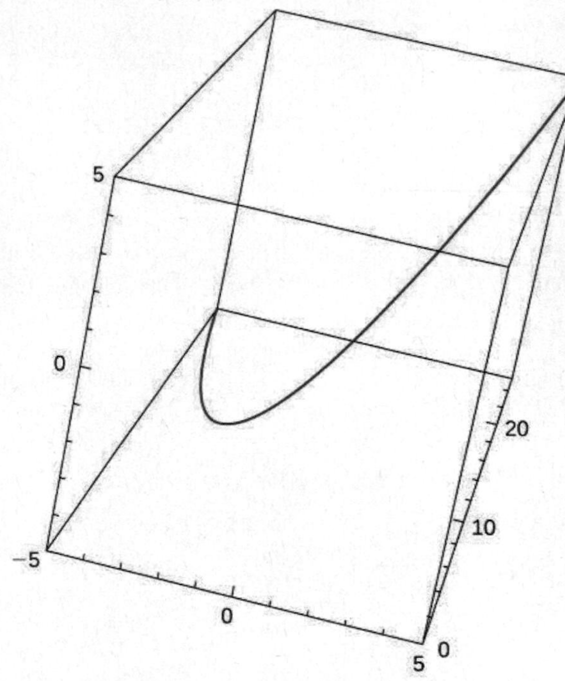

120. Find the unit tangent vector $\mathbf{T}(t)$ and unit normal vector $\mathbf{N}(t)$ at $t = 0$ for the plane curve $\mathbf{r}(t) = \langle t^3 - 4t, 5t^2 - 2 \rangle$. The graph is shown here:

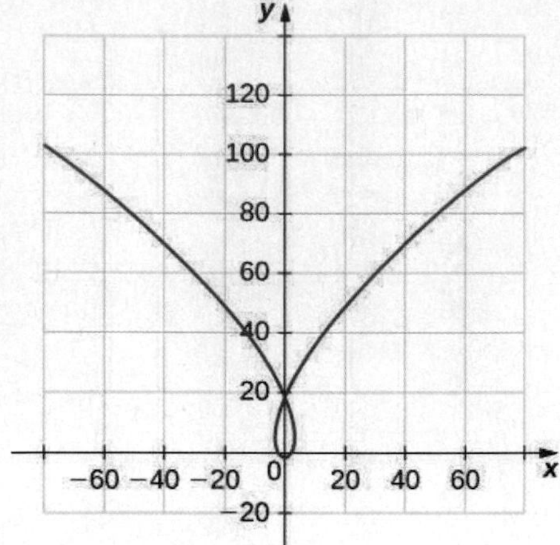

121. Find the unit tangent vector $\mathbf{T}(t)$ for $\mathbf{r}(t) = 3t\mathbf{i} + 5t^2\mathbf{j} + 2t\mathbf{k}$

122. Find the principal normal vector to the curve $\mathbf{r}(t) = \langle 6\cos t, 6\sin t \rangle$ at the point determined by $t = \pi/3$.

123. Find $\mathbf{T}(t)$ for the curve $\mathbf{r}(t) = (t^3 - 4t)\mathbf{i} + (5t^2 - 2)\mathbf{j}$.

124. Find $\mathbf{N}(t)$ for the curve $\mathbf{r}(t) = (t^3 - 4t)\mathbf{i} + (5t^2 - 2)\mathbf{j}$.

125. Find the unit normal vector $\mathbf{N}(t)$ for $\mathbf{r}(t) = \langle 2\sin t, 5t, 2\cos t \rangle$.

126. Find the unit tangent vector $\mathbf{T}(t)$ for $\mathbf{r}(t) = \langle 2\sin t, 5t, 2\cos t \rangle$.

127. Find the arc-length function $s(t)$ for the line segment given by $\mathbf{r}(t) = \langle 3 - 3t, 4t \rangle$. Write *r* as a parameter of *s*.

128. Parameterize the helix $\mathbf{r}(t) = \cos t\mathbf{i} + \sin t\mathbf{j} + t\mathbf{k}$ using the arc-length parameter *s*, from $t = 0$.

129. Parameterize the curve using the arc-length parameter *s*, at the point at which $t = 0$ for $\mathbf{r}(t) = e^t\sin t\mathbf{i} + e^t\cos t\mathbf{j}$.

130. Find the curvature of the curve $\mathbf{r}(t) = 5\cos t\mathbf{i} + 4\sin t\mathbf{j}$ at $t = \pi/3$. (*Note:* The graph is an ellipse.)

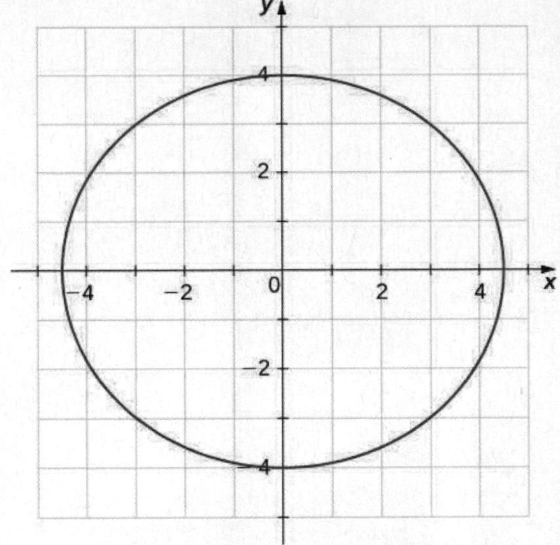

131. Find the x-coordinate at which the curvature of the curve $y = 1/x$ is a maximum value.

132. Find the curvature of the curve $\mathbf{r}(t) = 5\cos t\mathbf{i} + 5\sin t\mathbf{j}$. Does the curvature depend upon the parameter t?

133. Find the curvature κ for the curve $y = x - \frac{1}{4}x^2$ at the point $x = 2$.

134. Find the curvature κ for the curve $y = \frac{1}{3}x^3$ at the point $x = 1$.

135. Find the curvature κ of the curve $\mathbf{r}(t) = t\mathbf{i} + 6t^2\mathbf{j} + 4t\mathbf{k}$. The graph is shown here:

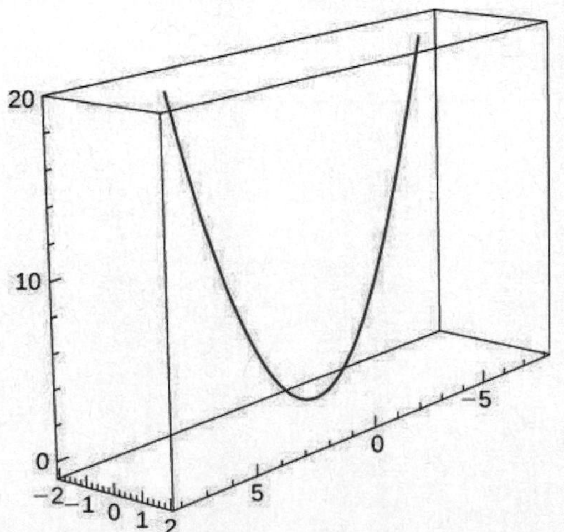

136. Find the curvature of $\mathbf{r}(t) = \langle 2\sin t, 5t, 2\cos t \rangle$.

137. Find the curvature of $\mathbf{r}(t) = \sqrt{2}t\mathbf{i} + e^t\mathbf{j} + e^{-t}\mathbf{k}$ at point $P(0, 1, 1)$.

138. At what point does the curve $y = e^x$ have maximum curvature?

139. What happens to the curvature as $x \to \infty$ for the curve $y = e^x$?

140. Find the point of maximum curvature on the curve $y = \ln x$.

141. Find the equations of the normal plane and the osculating plane of the curve $\mathbf{r}(t) = \langle 2\sin(3t), t, 2\cos(3t) \rangle$ at point $(0, \pi, -2)$.

142. Find equations of the osculating circles of the ellipse $4y^2 + 9x^2 = 36$ at the points $(2, 0)$ and $(0, 3)$.

143. Find the equation for the osculating plane at point $t = \pi/4$ on the curve $\mathbf{r}(t) = \cos(2t)\mathbf{i} + \sin(2t)\mathbf{j} + t$.

144. Find the radius of curvature of $6y = x^3$ at the point $\left(2, \frac{4}{3}\right)$.

145. Find the curvature at each point (x, y) on the hyperbola $\mathbf{r}(t) = \langle a\cosh(t), b\sinh(t) \rangle$.

146. Calculate the curvature of the circular helix $\mathbf{r}(t) = r\sin(t)\mathbf{i} + r\cos(t)\mathbf{j} + t\mathbf{k}$.

147. Find the radius of curvature of $y = \ln(x + 1)$ at point $(2, \ln 3)$.

148. Find the radius of curvature of the hyperbola $xy = 1$ at point $(1, 1)$.

A particle moves along the plane curve C described by $\mathbf{r}(t) = t\mathbf{i} + t^2\mathbf{j}$. Solve the following problems.

149. Find the length of the curve over the interval $[0, 2]$.

150. Find the curvature of the plane curve at $t = 0, 1, 2$.

151. Describe the curvature as t increases from $t = 0$ to $t = 2$.

The surface of a large cup is formed by revolving the graph of the function $y = 0.25x^{1.6}$ from $x = 0$ to $x = 5$ about the y-axis (measured in centimeters).

152. **[T]** Use technology to graph the surface.

153. Find the curvature κ of the generating curve as a function of x.

154. **[T]** Use technology to graph the curvature function.

3.4 | Motion in Space

Learning Objectives

- **3.4.1** Describe the velocity and acceleration vectors of a particle moving in space.
- **3.4.2** Explain the tangential and normal components of acceleration.
- **3.4.3** State Kepler's laws of planetary motion.

We have now seen how to describe curves in the plane and in space, and how to determine their properties, such as arc length and curvature. All of this leads to the main goal of this chapter, which is the description of motion along plane curves and space curves. We now have all the tools we need; in this section, we put these ideas together and look at how to use them.

Motion Vectors in the Plane and in Space

Our starting point is using vector-valued functions to represent the position of an object as a function of time. All of the following material can be applied either to curves in the plane or to space curves. For example, when we look at the orbit of the planets, the curves defining these orbits all lie in a plane because they are elliptical. However, a particle traveling along a helix moves on a curve in three dimensions.

Definition

Let $\mathbf{r}(t)$ be a twice-differentiable vector-valued function of the parameter t that represents the position of an object as a function of time. The **velocity vector** $\mathbf{v}(t)$ of the object is given by

$$\text{Velocity} = \mathbf{v}(t) = \mathbf{r}'(t). \tag{3.20}$$

The **acceleration vector** $\mathbf{a}(t)$ is defined to be

$$\text{Acceleration} = \mathbf{a}(t) = \mathbf{v}'(t) = \mathbf{r}''(t). \tag{3.21}$$

The *speed* is defined to be

$$\text{Speed} = v(t) = \|\mathbf{v}(t)\| = \|\mathbf{r}'(t)\| = \frac{ds}{dt}. \tag{3.22}$$

Since $\mathbf{r}(t)$ can be in either two or three dimensions, these vector-valued functions can have either two or three components. In two dimensions, we define $\mathbf{r}(t) = x(t)\mathbf{i} + y(t)\mathbf{j}$ and in three dimensions $\mathbf{r}(t) = x(t)\mathbf{i} + y(t)\mathbf{j} + z(t)\mathbf{k}$. Then the velocity, acceleration, and speed can be written as shown in the following table.

Quantity	Two Dimensions	Three Dimensions
Position	$\mathbf{r}(t) = x(t)\mathbf{i} + y(t)\mathbf{j}$	$\mathbf{r}(t) = x(t)\mathbf{i} + y(t)\mathbf{j} + z(t)\mathbf{k}$
Velocity	$\mathbf{v}(t) = x'(t)\mathbf{i} + y'(t)\mathbf{j}$	$\mathbf{v}(t) = x'(t)\mathbf{i} + y'(t)\mathbf{j} + z'(t)\mathbf{k}$
Acceleration	$\mathbf{a}(t) = x''(t)\mathbf{i} + y''(t)\mathbf{j}$	$\mathbf{a}(t) = x''(t)\mathbf{i} + y''(t)\mathbf{j} + z''(t)\mathbf{k}$
Speed	$v(t) = \sqrt{(x'(t))^2 + (y'(t))^2}$	$v(t) = \sqrt{(x'(t))^2 + (y'(t))^2 + (z'(t))^2}$

Table 3.4 Formulas for Position, Velocity, Acceleration, and Speed

Example 3.14

Studying Motion Along a Parabola

A particle moves in a parabolic path defined by the vector-valued function $\mathbf{r}(t) = t^2\mathbf{i} + \sqrt{5 - t^2}\mathbf{j},$ where t measures time in seconds.

a. Find the velocity, acceleration, and speed as functions of time.
b. Sketch the curve along with the velocity vector at time $t = 1.$

Solution

a. We use **Equation 3.20**, **Equation 3.21**, and **Equation 3.22**:

$$\begin{aligned} \mathbf{v}(t) &= \mathbf{r}'(t) = 2t\mathbf{i} - \frac{t}{\sqrt{5 - t^2}}\mathbf{j} \\ \mathbf{a}(t) &= \mathbf{v}'(t) = 2\mathbf{i} - 5\left(5 - t^2\right)^{-\frac{3}{2}}\mathbf{j} \\ v(t) &= \|\mathbf{r}'(t)\| \\ &= \sqrt{(2t)^2 + \left(-\frac{t}{\sqrt{5 - t^2}}\right)^2} \\ &= \sqrt{4t^2 + \frac{t^2}{5 - t^2}} \\ &= \sqrt{\frac{21t^2 - 4t^4}{5 - t^2}}. \end{aligned}$$

b. The graph of $\mathbf{r}(t) = t^2\mathbf{i} + \sqrt{5 - t^2}\mathbf{j}$ is a portion of a parabola (**Figure 3.11**). The velocity vector at $t = 1$ is

$$\mathbf{v}(1) = \mathbf{r}'(1) = 2(1)\mathbf{i} - \frac{1}{\sqrt{5 - (1)^2}}\mathbf{j} = 2\mathbf{i} - \frac{1}{2}\mathbf{j}$$

and the acceleration vector at $t = 1$ is

$$\mathbf{a}(1) = \mathbf{v}'(1) = 2\mathbf{i} - 5\left(5 - (1)^2\right)^{-3/2}\mathbf{j} = 2\mathbf{i} - \frac{5}{8}\mathbf{j}.$$

Notice that the velocity vector is tangent to the path, as is always the case.

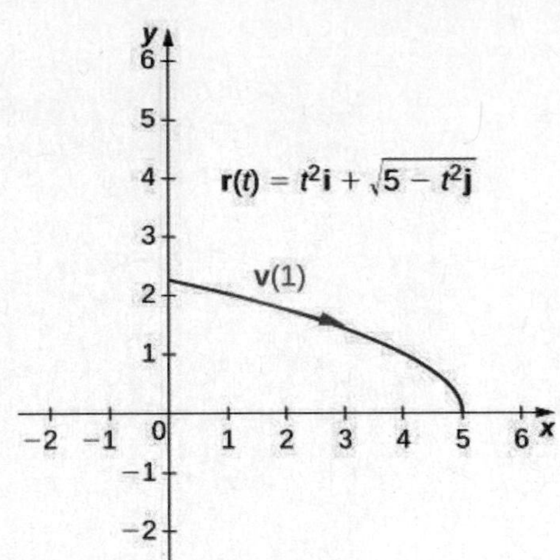

Figure 3.11 This graph depicts the velocity vector at time $t = 1$ for a particle moving in a parabolic path.

3.14 A particle moves in a path defined by the vector-valued function $\mathbf{r}(t) = \left(t^2 - 3t\right)\mathbf{i} + (2t - 4)\,\mathbf{j} + (t + 2)\mathbf{k}$, where t measures time in seconds and where distance is measured in feet. Find the velocity, acceleration, and speed as functions of time.

To gain a better understanding of the velocity and acceleration vectors, imagine you are driving along a curvy road. If you do not turn the steering wheel, you would continue in a straight line and run off the road. The speed at which you are traveling when you run off the road, coupled with the direction, gives a vector representing your velocity, as illustrated in the following figure.

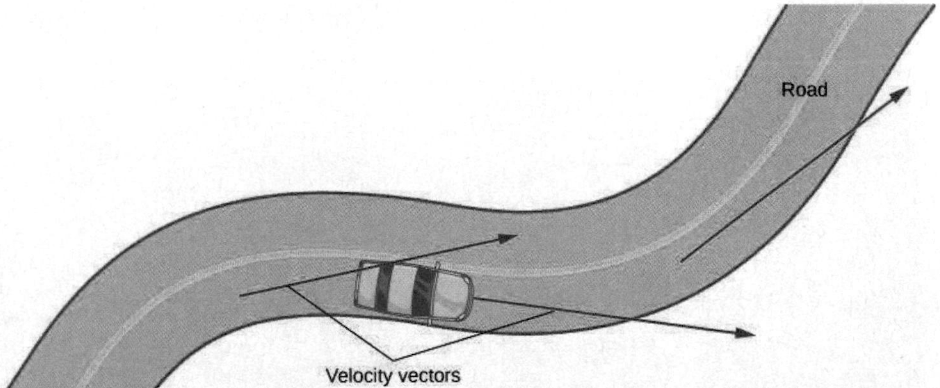

Figure 3.12 At each point along a road traveled by a car, the velocity vector of the car is tangent to the path traveled by the car.

However, the fact that you must turn the steering wheel to stay on the road indicates that your velocity is always changing (even if your speed is not) because your *direction* is constantly changing to keep you on the road. As you turn to the right, your acceleration vector also points to the right. As you turn to the left, your acceleration vector points to the left. This indicates that your velocity and acceleration vectors are constantly changing, regardless of whether your actual speed varies (**Figure 3.13**).

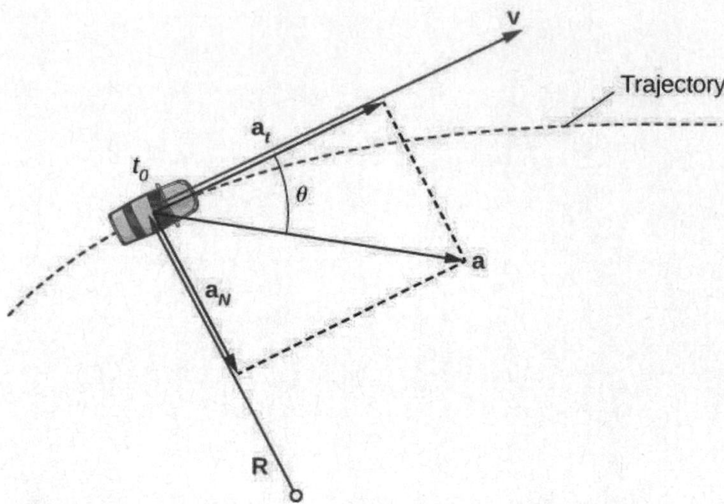

Figure 3.13 The dashed line represents the trajectory of an object (a car, for example). The acceleration vector points toward the inside of the turn at all times.

Components of the Acceleration Vector

We can combine some of the concepts discussed in **Arc Length and Curvature** with the acceleration vector to gain a deeper understanding of how this vector relates to motion in the plane and in space. Recall that the unit tangent vector **T** and the unit normal vector **N** form an osculating plane at any point *P* on the curve defined by a vector-valued function $\mathbf{r}(t)$. The following theorem shows that the acceleration vector $\mathbf{a}(t)$ lies in the osculating plane and can be written as a linear combination of the unit tangent and the unit normal vectors.

Theorem 3.7: The Plane of the Acceleration Vector

The acceleration vector $\mathbf{a}(t)$ of an object moving along a curve traced out by a twice-differentiable function $\mathbf{r}(t)$ lies in the plane formed by the unit tangent vector $\mathbf{T}(t)$ and the principal unit normal vector $\mathbf{N}(t)$ to *C*. Furthermore,

$$\mathbf{a}(t) = v'(t)\mathbf{T}(t) + [v(t)]^2 \kappa \mathbf{N}(t).$$

Here, $v(t)$ is the speed of the object and κ is the curvature of *C* traced out by $\mathbf{r}(t)$.

Proof

Because $\mathbf{v}(t) = \mathbf{r}'(t)$ and $\mathbf{T}(t) = \dfrac{\mathbf{r}'(t)}{\|\mathbf{r}'(t)\|}$, we have $\mathbf{v}(t) = \|\mathbf{r}'(t)\|\mathbf{T}(t) = v(t)\mathbf{T}(t)$. Now we differentiate this equation:

$$\mathbf{a}(t) = \mathbf{v}'(t) = \frac{d}{dt}(v(t)\mathbf{T}(t)) = v'(t)\mathbf{T}(t) + v(t)\mathbf{T}'(t).$$

Since $\mathbf{N}(t) = \dfrac{\mathbf{T}'(t)}{\|\mathbf{T}'(t)\|}$, we know $\mathbf{T}'(t) = \|\mathbf{T}'(t)\|\mathbf{N}(t)$, so

$$\mathbf{a}(t) = v'(t)\mathbf{T}(t) + v(t)\|\mathbf{T}'(t)\|\mathbf{N}(t).$$

A formula for curvature is $\kappa = \dfrac{\|\mathbf{T}'(t)\|}{\|\mathbf{r}'(t)\|}$, so $\|\mathbf{T}'(t)\| = \kappa\|\mathbf{r}'(t)\| = \kappa v(t)$. This gives $\mathbf{a}(t) = v'(t)\mathbf{T}(t) + \kappa(v(t))^2\mathbf{N}(t)$.

□

The coefficients of $\mathbf{T}(t)$ and $\mathbf{N}(t)$ are referred to as the **tangential component of acceleration** and the **normal component**

of acceleration, respectively. We write $a_{\mathbf{T}}$ to denote the tangential component and $a_{\mathbf{N}}$ to denote the normal component.

Theorem 3.8: Tangential and Normal Components of Acceleration

Let $\mathbf{r}(t)$ be a vector-valued function that denotes the position of an object as a function of time. Then $\mathbf{a}(t) = \mathbf{r}''(t)$ is the acceleration vector. The tangential and normal components of acceleration $a_{\mathbf{T}}$ and $a_{\mathbf{N}}$ are given by the formulas

$$a_{\mathbf{T}} = \mathbf{a} \cdot \mathbf{T} = \frac{\mathbf{v} \cdot \mathbf{a}}{\| \mathbf{v} \|} \quad (3.23)$$

and

$$a_{\mathbf{N}} = \mathbf{a} \cdot \mathbf{N} = \frac{\| \mathbf{v} \times \mathbf{a} \|}{\| \mathbf{v} \|} = \sqrt{\| \mathbf{a} \|^2 - a_{\mathbf{T}}^2}. \quad (3.24)$$

These components are related by the formula

$$\mathbf{a}(t) = a_{\mathbf{T}} \mathbf{T}(t) + a_{\mathbf{N}} \mathbf{N}(t). \quad (3.25)$$

Here $\mathbf{T}(t)$ is the unit tangent vector to the curve defined by $\mathbf{r}(t)$, and $\mathbf{N}(t)$ is the unit normal vector to the curve defined by $\mathbf{r}(t)$.

The normal component of acceleration is also called the *centripetal component of acceleration* or sometimes the *radial component of acceleration*. To understand centripetal acceleration, suppose you are traveling in a car on a circular track at a constant speed. Then, as we saw earlier, the acceleration vector points toward the center of the track at all times. As a rider in the car, you feel a pull toward the *outside* of the track because you are constantly turning. This sensation acts in the opposite direction of centripetal acceleration. The same holds true for noncircular paths. The reason is that your body tends to travel in a straight line and resists the force resulting from acceleration that push it toward the side. Note that at point B in **Figure 3.14** the acceleration vector is pointing backward. This is because the car is decelerating as it goes into the curve.

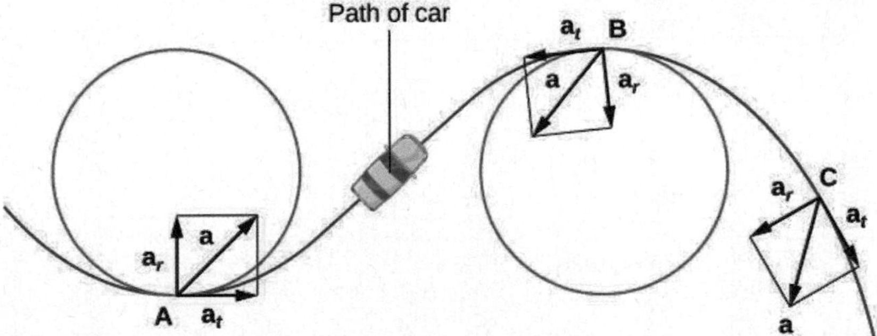

Figure 3.14 The tangential and normal components of acceleration can be used to describe the acceleration vector.

The tangential and normal unit vectors at any given point on the curve provide a frame of reference at that point. The tangential and normal components of acceleration are the projections of the acceleration vector onto **T** and **N**, respectively.

Example 3.15

Finding Components of Acceleration

A particle moves in a path defined by the vector-valued function $\mathbf{r}(t) = t^2\mathbf{i} + (2t - 3)\mathbf{j} + \left(3t^2 - 3t\right)\mathbf{k}$, where t measures time in seconds and distance is measured in feet.

a. Find $a_{\mathbf{T}}$ and $a_{\mathbf{N}}$ as functions of t.

b. Find $a_{\mathbf{T}}$ and $a_{\mathbf{N}}$ at time $t = 2$.

Solution

a. Let's start with **Equation 3.23**:

$$\begin{aligned}
\mathbf{v}(t) &= \mathbf{r}'(t) = 2t\mathbf{i} + 2\mathbf{j} + (6t - 3)\mathbf{k} \\
\mathbf{a}(t) &= \mathbf{v}'(t) = 2\mathbf{i} + 6\mathbf{k} \\
a_{\mathbf{T}} &= \frac{\mathbf{v} \cdot \mathbf{a}}{\| \mathbf{v} \|} \\
&= \frac{(2t\mathbf{i} + 2\mathbf{j} + (6t - 3)\mathbf{k}) \cdot (2\mathbf{i} + 6\mathbf{k})}{\| 2t\mathbf{i} + 2\mathbf{j} + (6t - 3)\mathbf{k} \|} \\
&= \frac{4t + 6(6t - 3)}{\sqrt{(2t)^2 + 2^2 + (6t - 3)^2}} \\
&= \frac{40t - 18}{\sqrt{40t^2 - 36t + 13}}.
\end{aligned}$$

Then we apply **Equation 3.24**:

$$\begin{aligned}
a_{\mathbf{N}} &= \sqrt{\| \mathbf{a} \|^2 - a} \\
&= \sqrt{\| 2\mathbf{i} + 6\mathbf{k} \|^2 - \left(\frac{40t - 18}{\sqrt{40t^2 - 36t + 13}} \right)^2} \\
&= \sqrt{4 + 36 - \frac{(40t - 18)^2}{40t^2 - 36t + 13}} \\
&= \sqrt{\frac{40\left(40t^2 - 36t + 13\right) - \left(1600t^2 - 1440t + 324\right)}{40t^2 - 36t + 13}} \\
&= \sqrt{\frac{196}{40t^2 - 36t + 13}} \\
&= \frac{14}{\sqrt{40t^2 - 36t + 13}}.
\end{aligned}$$

b. We must evaluate each of the answers from part a. at $t = 2$:

$$\begin{aligned}
a_{\mathbf{T}}(2) &= \frac{40(2) - 18}{\sqrt{40(2)^2 - 36(2) + 13}} \\
&= \frac{80 - 18}{\sqrt{160 - 72 + 13}} = \frac{62}{\sqrt{101}} \\
a_{\mathbf{N}}(2) &= \frac{14}{\sqrt{40(2)^2 - 36(2) + 13}} \\
&= \frac{14}{\sqrt{160 - 72 + 13}} = \frac{14}{\sqrt{101}}.
\end{aligned}$$

The units of acceleration are feet per second squared, as are the units of the normal and tangential components of acceleration.

3.15 An object moves in a path defined by the vector-valued function $\mathbf{r}(t) = 4t\mathbf{i} + t^2\mathbf{j},$ where t measures time in seconds.

a. Find a_{T} and a_{N} as functions of t.

b. Find a_{T} and a_{N} at time $t = -3$.

Projectile Motion

Now let's look at an application of vector functions. In particular, let's consider the effect of gravity on the motion of an object as it travels through the air, and how it determines the resulting trajectory of that object. In the following, we ignore the effect of air resistance. This situation, with an object moving with an initial velocity but with no forces acting on it other than gravity, is known as **projectile motion**. It describes the motion of objects from golf balls to baseballs, and from arrows to cannonballs.

First we need to choose a coordinate system. If we are standing at the origin of this coordinate system, then we choose the positive y-axis to be up, the negative y-axis to be down, and the positive x-axis to be forward (i.e., away from the thrower of the object). The effect of gravity is in a downward direction, so Newton's second law tells us that the force on the object resulting from gravity is equal to the mass of the object times the acceleration resulting from to gravity, or $F_g = mg,$ where F_g represents the force from gravity and g represents the acceleration resulting from gravity at Earth's surface. The value of g in the English system of measurement is approximately 32 ft/sec^2 and it is approximately 9.8 m/sec^2 in the metric system. This is the only force acting on the object. Since gravity acts in a downward direction, we can write the force resulting from gravity in the form $F_g = -mg\,\mathbf{j},$ as shown in the following figure.

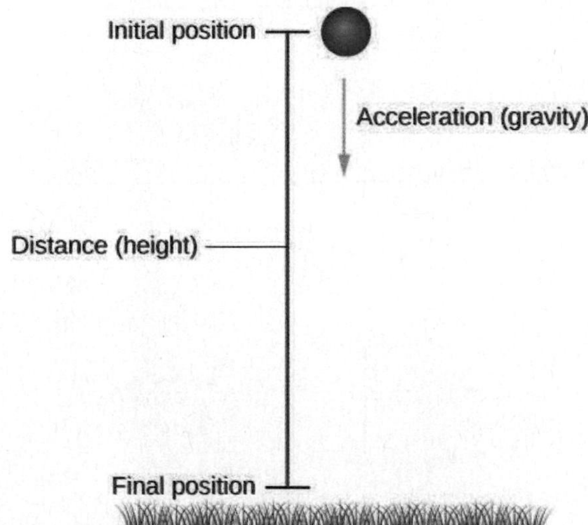

Figure 3.15 An object is falling under the influence of gravity.

Visit this **website (http://www.openstaxcollege.org/l/20_projectile)** for a video showing projectile motion.

Newton's second law also tells us that $F = m\mathbf{a},$ where **a** represents the acceleration vector of the object. This force must be equal to the force of gravity at all times, so we therefore know that

$$\begin{aligned} F &= F_g \\ m\mathbf{a} &= -mg\,\mathbf{j} \\ \mathbf{a} &= -g\,\mathbf{j}. \end{aligned}$$

Now we use the fact that the acceleration vector is the first derivative of the velocity vector. Therefore, we can rewrite the last equation in the form

$$\mathbf{v}'(t) = -g\,\mathbf{j}.$$

By taking the antiderivative of each side of this equation we obtain

$$\begin{aligned}\mathbf{v}(t) &= \int -g\,\mathbf{j}dt \\ &= -gt\,\mathbf{j} + \mathbf{C}_1\end{aligned}$$

for some constant vector $\mathbf{C}_1$. To determine the value of this vector, we can use the velocity of the object at a fixed time, say at time $t = 0$. We call this velocity the *initial velocity*: $\mathbf{v}(0) = \mathbf{v}_0$. Therefore, $\mathbf{v}(0) = -g(0)\,\mathbf{j} + \mathbf{C}_1 = \mathbf{v}_0$ and $\mathbf{C}_1 = \mathbf{v}_0$. This gives the velocity vector as $\mathbf{v}(t) = -gt\,\mathbf{j} + \mathbf{v}_0$.

Next we use the fact that velocity $\mathbf{v}(t)$ is the derivative of position $\mathbf{s}(t)$. This gives the equation

$$\mathbf{s}'(t) = -gt\,\mathbf{j} + \mathbf{v}_0.$$

Taking the antiderivative of both sides of this equation leads to

$$\begin{aligned}\mathbf{s}(t) &= \int -gt\,\mathbf{j} + \mathbf{v}_0\,dt \\ &= -\frac{1}{2}gt^2\,\mathbf{j} + \mathbf{v}_0 t + \mathbf{C}_2,\end{aligned}$$

with another unknown constant vector $\mathbf{C}_2$. To determine the value of $\mathbf{C}_2$, we can use the position of the object at a given time, say at time $t = 0$. We call this position the *initial position*: $\mathbf{s}(0) = \mathbf{s}_0$. Therefore, $\mathbf{s}(0) = -(1/2)g(0)^2\,\mathbf{j} + \mathbf{v}_0(0) + \mathbf{C}_2 = \mathbf{s}_0$ and $\mathbf{C}_2 = \mathbf{s}_0$. This gives the position of the object at any time as

$$\mathbf{s}(t) = -\frac{1}{2}gt^2\,\mathbf{j} + \mathbf{v}_0 t + \mathbf{s}_0.$$

Let's take a closer look at the initial velocity and initial position. In particular, suppose the object is thrown upward from the origin at an angle θ to the horizontal, with initial speed v_0. How can we modify the previous result to reflect this scenario? First, we can assume it is thrown from the origin. If not, then we can move the origin to the point from where it is thrown. Therefore, $\mathbf{s}_0 = \mathbf{0}$, as shown in the following figure.

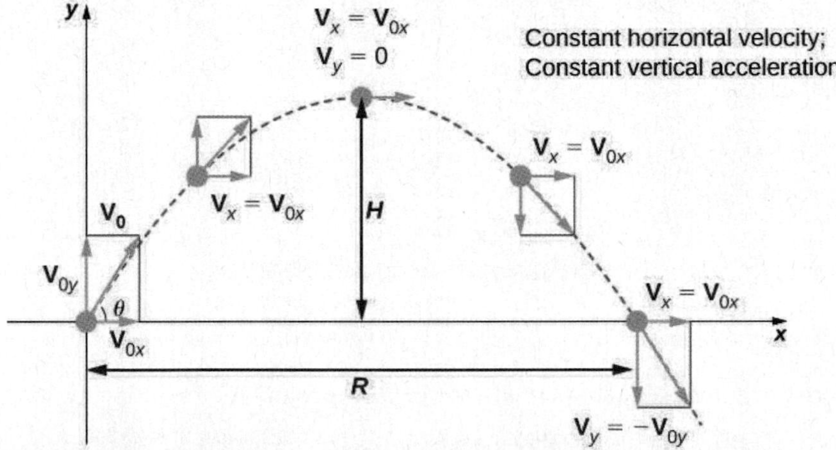

Figure 3.16 Projectile motion when the object is thrown upward at an angle θ. The horizontal motion is at constant velocity and the vertical motion is at constant acceleration.

We can rewrite the initial velocity vector in the form $\mathbf{v}_0 = v_0\cos\theta\,\mathbf{i} + v_0\sin\theta\,\mathbf{j}$. Then the equation for the position function $\mathbf{s}(t)$ becomes

$$\begin{aligned}\mathbf{s}(t) &= -\frac{1}{2}gt^2\,\mathbf{j} + v_0 t\cos\theta\,\mathbf{i} + v_0 t\sin\theta\,\mathbf{j} \\ &= v_0 t\cos\theta\,\mathbf{i} + v_0 t\sin\theta\,\mathbf{j} - \frac{1}{2}gt^2\,\mathbf{j} \\ &= v_0 t\cos\theta\,\mathbf{i} + \left(v_0 t\sin\theta - \frac{1}{2}gt^2\right)\mathbf{j}.\end{aligned}$$

The coefficient of **i** represents the horizontal component of $\mathbf{s}(t)$ and is the horizontal distance of the object from the origin at time *t*. The maximum value of the horizontal distance (measured at the same initial and final altitude) is called the range *R*. The coefficient of **j** represents the vertical component of $\mathbf{s}(t)$ and is the altitude of the object at time *t*. The maximum value of the vertical distance is the height *H*.

Example 3.16

Motion of a Cannonball

During an Independence Day celebration, a cannonball is fired from a cannon on a cliff toward the water. The cannon is aimed at an angle of 30° above horizontal and the initial speed of the cannonball is 600 ft/sec. The cliff is 100 ft above the water (**Figure 3.17**).

a. Find the maximum height of the cannonball.

b. How long will it take for the cannonball to splash into the sea?

c. How far out to sea will the cannonball hit the water?

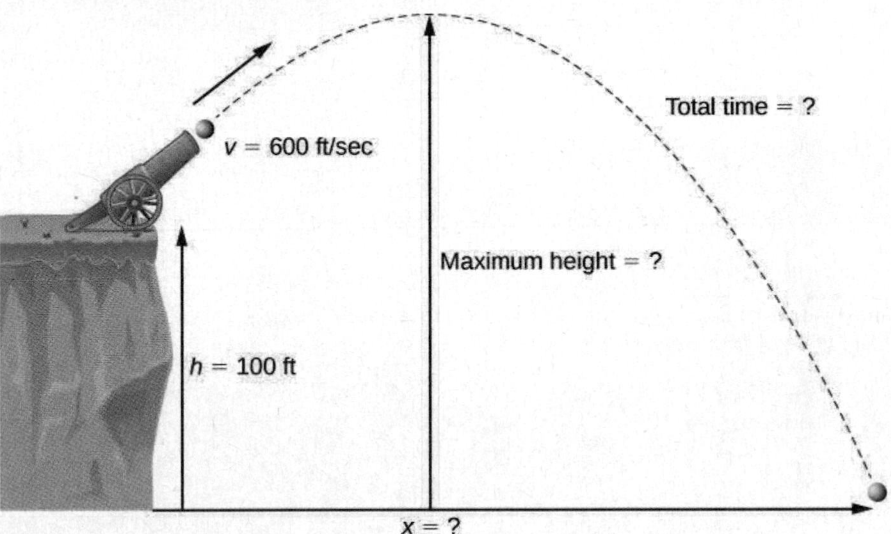

Figure 3.17 The flight of a cannonball (ignoring air resistance) is projectile motion.

Solution

We use the equation

$$\mathbf{s}(t) = v_0 t\cos\theta\,\mathbf{i} + \left(v_0 t\sin\theta - \frac{1}{2}gt^2\right)\mathbf{j}$$

with $\theta = 30°$, $g = 32$ ft/sec^2, and $v_0 = 600$ ft/sec. Then the position equation becomes

$$\begin{aligned}\mathbf{s}(t) &= 600t(\cos 30)\mathbf{i} + \left(600t\sin 30 - \frac{1}{2}(32)t^2\right)\mathbf{j} \\ &= 300t\sqrt{3}\mathbf{i} + \left(300t - 16t^2\right)\mathbf{j}.\end{aligned}$$

a. The cannonball reaches its maximum height when the vertical component of its velocity is zero, because the cannonball is neither rising nor falling at that point. The velocity vector is

$$\begin{aligned} \mathbf{v}(t) &= \mathbf{s}'(t) \\ &= 300\sqrt{3}\mathbf{i} + (300 - 32t)\mathbf{j}. \end{aligned}$$

Therefore, the vertical component of velocity is given by the expression $300 - 32t$. Setting this expression equal to zero and solving for t gives $t = 9.375$ sec. The height of the cannonball at this time is given by the vertical component of the position vector, evaluated at $t = 9.375$.

$$\begin{aligned} \mathbf{s}(9.375) &= 300(9.375)\sqrt{3}\mathbf{i} + \left(300(9.375) - 16(9.375)^2\right)\mathbf{j} \\ &= 4871.39\mathbf{i} + 1406.25\mathbf{j} \end{aligned}$$

Therefore, the maximum height of the cannonball is 1406.39 ft above the cannon, or 1506.39 ft above sea level.

b. When the cannonball lands in the water, it is 100 ft below the cannon. Therefore, the vertical component of the position vector is equal to -100. Setting the vertical component of $\mathbf{s}(t)$ equal to -100 and solving, we obtain

$$\begin{aligned} 300t - 16t^2 &= -100 \\ 16t^2 - 300t - 100 &= 0 \\ 4t^2 - 75t - 25 &= 0 \\ t &= \frac{75 \pm \sqrt{(-75)^2 - 4(4)(-25)}}{2(4)} \\ &= \frac{75 \pm \sqrt{6025}}{8} \\ &= \frac{75 \pm 5\sqrt{241}}{8}. \end{aligned}$$

The positive value of t that solves this equation is approximately 19.08. Therefore, the cannonball hits the water after approximately 19.08 sec.

c. To find the distance out to sea, we simply substitute the answer from part (b) into $\mathbf{s}(t)$:

$$\begin{aligned} \mathbf{s}(19.08) &= 300(19.08)\sqrt{3}\mathbf{i} + \left(300(19.08) - 16(19.08)^2\right)\mathbf{j} \\ &= 9914.26\mathbf{i} - 100.7424\mathbf{j}. \end{aligned}$$

Therefore, the ball hits the water about 9914.26 ft away from the base of the cliff. Notice that the vertical component of the position vector is very close to -100, which tells us that the ball just hit the water. Note that 9914.26 feet is not the true range of the cannon since the cannonball lands in the ocean at a location below the cannon. The range of the cannon would be determined by finding how far out the cannonball is when its height is 100 ft above the water (the same as the altitude of the cannon).

3.16 An archer fires an arrow at an angle of 40° above the horizontal with an initial speed of 98 m/sec. The height of the archer is 171.5 cm. Find the horizontal distance the arrow travels before it hits the ground.

One final question remains: In general, what is the maximum distance a projectile can travel, given its initial speed? To determine this distance, we assume the projectile is fired from ground level and we wish it to return to ground level. In other words, we want to determine an equation for the range. In this case, the equation of projectile motion is

$$\mathbf{s}(t) = v_0 t \cos\theta \mathbf{i} + \left(v_0 t \sin\theta - \frac{1}{2}gt^2\right)\mathbf{j}.$$

Setting the second component equal to zero and solving for t yields

$$\begin{aligned} v_0 t \sin\theta - \frac{1}{2}gt^2 &= 0 \\ t\left(v_0 \sin\theta - \frac{1}{2}gt\right) &= 0. \end{aligned}$$

Therefore, either $t = 0$ or $t = \frac{2v_0 \sin\theta}{g}$. We are interested in the second value of t, so we substitute this into $\mathbf{s}(t)$, which gives

$$\begin{aligned} \mathbf{s}\left(\frac{2v_0 \sin\theta}{g}\right) &= v_0\left(\frac{2v_0 \sin\theta}{g}\right)\cos\theta \mathbf{i} + \left(v_0\left(\frac{2v_0 \sin\theta}{g}\right)\sin\theta - \frac{1}{2}g\left(\frac{2v_0 \sin\theta}{g}\right)^2\right)\mathbf{j} \\ &= \left(\frac{2v_0^2 \sin\theta \cos\theta}{g}\right)\mathbf{i} \\ &= \frac{v_0^2 \sin 2\theta}{g}\mathbf{i}. \end{aligned}$$

Thus, the expression for the range of a projectile fired at an angle θ is

$$R = \frac{v_0^2 \sin 2\theta}{g}\mathbf{i}.$$

The only variable in this expression is θ. To maximize the distance traveled, take the derivative of the coefficient of **i** with respect to θ and set it equal to zero:

$$\begin{aligned} \frac{d}{d\theta}\left(\frac{v_0^2 \sin 2\theta}{g}\right) &= 0 \\ \frac{2v_0^2 \cos 2\theta}{g} &= 0 \\ \theta &= 45°. \end{aligned}$$

This value of θ is the smallest positive value that makes the derivative equal to zero. Therefore, in the absence of air resistance, the best angle to fire a projectile (to maximize the range) is at a $45°$ angle. The distance it travels is given by

$$\mathbf{s}\left(\frac{2v_0 \sin 45}{g}\right) = \frac{v_0^2 \sin 90}{g}\mathbf{i} = \frac{v_0^2}{g}\mathbf{j}.$$

Therefore, the range for an angle of $45°$ is v_0^2/g.

Kepler's Laws

During the early 1600s, Johannes Kepler was able to use the amazingly accurate data from his mentor Tycho Brahe to formulate his three laws of planetary motion, now known as **Kepler's laws of planetary motion**. These laws also apply to other objects in the solar system in orbit around the Sun, such as comets (e.g., Halley's comet) and asteroids. Variations of these laws apply to satellites in orbit around Earth.

Theorem 3.9: Kepler's Laws of Planetary Motion

i. The path of any planet about the Sun is elliptical in shape, with the center of the Sun located at one focus of the ellipse (the law of ellipses).

ii. A line drawn from the center of the Sun to the center of a planet sweeps out equal areas in equal time intervals (the law of equal areas) (**Figure 3.18**).

iii. The ratio of the squares of the periods of any two planets is equal to the ratio of the cubes of the lengths of their semimajor orbital axes (the law of harmonies).

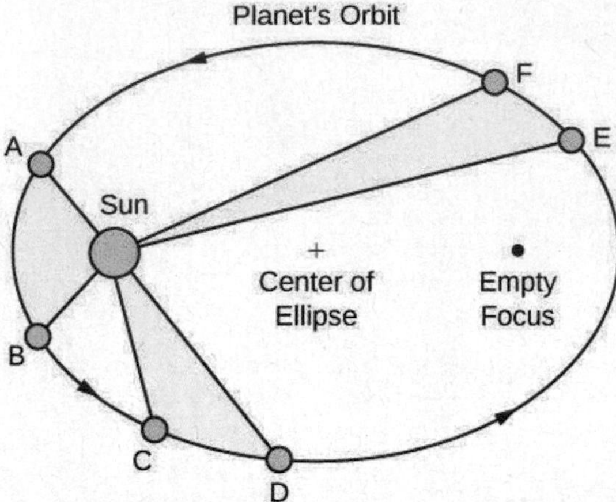

Figure 3.18 Kepler's first and second laws are pictured here. The Sun is located at a focus of the elliptical orbit of any planet. Furthermore, the shaded areas are all equal, assuming that the amount of time measured as the planet moves is the same for each region.

Kepler's third law is especially useful when using appropriate units. In particular, *1 astronomical unit* is defined to be the average distance from Earth to the Sun, and is now recognized to be 149,597,870,700 m or, approximately 93,000,000 mi. We therefore write 1 A.U. = 93,000,000 mi. Since the time it takes for Earth to orbit the Sun is 1 year, we use Earth years for units of time. Then, substituting 1 year for the period of Earth and 1 A.U. for the average distance to the Sun, Kepler's third law can be written as

$$T_P^2 = D_P^3$$

for any planet in the solar system, where T_P is the period of that planet measured in Earth years and D_P is the average distance from that planet to the Sun measured in astronomical units. Therefore, if we know the average distance from a planet to the Sun (in astronomical units), we can then calculate the length of its year (in Earth years), and vice versa.

Kepler's laws were formulated based on observations from Brahe; however, they were not proved formally until Sir Isaac Newton was able to apply calculus. Furthermore, Newton was able to generalize Kepler's third law to other orbital systems, such as a moon orbiting around a planet. Kepler's original third law only applies to objects orbiting the Sun.

Proof

Let's now prove Kepler's first law using the calculus of vector-valued functions. First we need a coordinate system. Let's place the Sun at the origin of the coordinate system and let the vector-valued function $\mathbf{r}(t)$ represent the location of a planet as a function of time. Newton proved Kepler's law using his second law of motion and his law of universal gravitation. Newton's second law of motion can be written as $\mathbf{F} = m\mathbf{a},$ where $\mathbf{F}$ represents the net force acting on the planet. His law of universal gravitation can be written in the form $\mathbf{F} = -\frac{GmM}{\|\mathbf{r}\|^2} \cdot \frac{\mathbf{r}}{\|\mathbf{r}\|},$ which indicates that the force resulting from the gravitational attraction of the Sun points back toward the Sun, and has magnitude $\frac{GmM}{\|\mathbf{r}\|^2}$ (**Figure 3.19**).

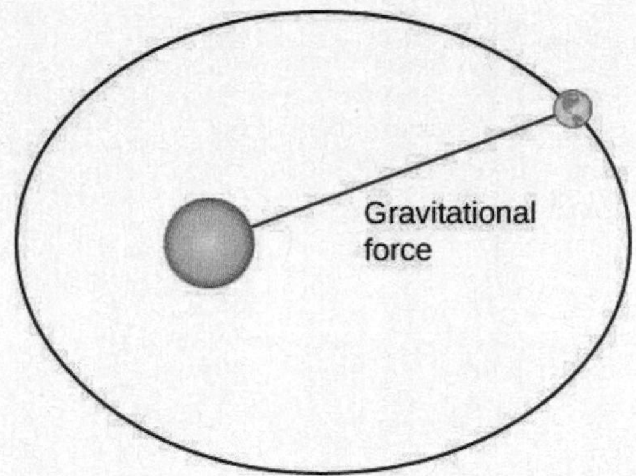

Figure 3.19 The gravitational force between Earth and the Sun is equal to the mass of the earth times its acceleration.

Setting these two forces equal to each other, and using the fact that $\mathbf{a}(t) = \mathbf{v}'(t),$ we obtain

$$m\mathbf{v}'(t) = -\frac{GmM}{\|\mathbf{r}\|^2} \cdot \frac{\mathbf{r}}{\|\mathbf{r}\|},$$

which can be rewritten as

$$\frac{d\mathbf{v}}{dt} = -\frac{GM}{\|\mathbf{r}\|^3}\mathbf{r}.$$

This equation shows that the vectors $d\mathbf{v}/dt$ and $\mathbf{r}$ are parallel to each other, so $d\mathbf{v}/dt \times \mathbf{r} = \mathbf{0}$. Next, let's differentiate $\mathbf{r} \times \mathbf{v}$ with respect to time:

$$\frac{d}{dt}(\mathbf{r} \times \mathbf{v}) = \frac{d\mathbf{r}}{dt} \times \mathbf{v} + \mathbf{r} \times \frac{d\mathbf{v}}{dt} = \mathbf{v} \times \mathbf{v} + \mathbf{0} = \mathbf{0}.$$

This proves that $\mathbf{r} \times \mathbf{v}$ is a constant vector, which we call $\mathbf{C}$. Since $\mathbf{r}$ and $\mathbf{v}$ are both perpendicular to $\mathbf{C}$ for all values of t, they must lie in a plane perpendicular to $\mathbf{C}$. Therefore, the motion of the planet lies in a plane.

Next we calculate the expression $d\mathbf{v}/dt \times \mathbf{C}$:

$$\frac{d\mathbf{v}}{dt} \times \mathbf{C} = -\frac{GM}{\|\mathbf{r}\|^3}\mathbf{r} \times (\mathbf{r} \times \mathbf{v}) = -\frac{GM}{\|\mathbf{r}\|^3}[(\mathbf{r} \cdot \mathbf{v})\mathbf{r} - (\mathbf{r} \cdot \mathbf{r})\mathbf{v}]. \quad \textbf{(3.26)}$$

The last equality in **Equation 3.26** is from the triple cross product formula (**Introduction to Vectors in Space**). We need an expression for $\mathbf{r} \cdot \mathbf{v}$. To calculate this, we differentiate $\mathbf{r} \cdot \mathbf{r}$ with respect to time:

$$\frac{d}{dt}(\mathbf{r} \cdot \mathbf{r}) = \frac{d\mathbf{r}}{dt} \cdot \mathbf{r} + \mathbf{r} \cdot \frac{d\mathbf{r}}{dt} = 2\mathbf{r} \cdot \frac{d\mathbf{r}}{dt} = 2\mathbf{r} \cdot \mathbf{v}. \quad \textbf{(3.27)}$$

Since $\mathbf{r} \cdot \mathbf{r} = \|\mathbf{r}\|^2,$ we also have

$$\frac{d}{dt}(\mathbf{r} \cdot \mathbf{r}) = \frac{d}{dt}\|\mathbf{r}\|^2 = 2\|\mathbf{r}\|\frac{d}{dt}\|\mathbf{r}\|. \quad \textbf{(3.28)}$$

Combining **Equation 3.27** and **Equation 3.28**, we get

$$\begin{aligned} 2\mathbf{r} \cdot \mathbf{v} &= 2\|\mathbf{r}\|\frac{d}{dt}\|\mathbf{r}\| \\ \mathbf{r} \cdot \mathbf{v} &= \|\mathbf{r}\|\frac{d}{dt}\|\mathbf{r}\|. \end{aligned}$$

Substituting this into **Equation 3.26** gives us

$$\begin{aligned}\frac{d\mathbf{v}}{dt}\times\mathbf{C} &= -\frac{GM}{\|\mathbf{r}\|^3}[(\mathbf{r}\cdot\mathbf{v})\mathbf{r}-(\mathbf{r}\cdot\mathbf{r})\mathbf{v}] \\ &= -\frac{GM}{\|\mathbf{r}\|^3}\left[\|\mathbf{r}\|\left(\frac{d}{dt}\|\mathbf{r}\|\right)\mathbf{r}-\|\mathbf{r}\|^2\mathbf{v}\right] \\ &= -GM\left[\frac{1}{\|\mathbf{r}\|^2}\left(\frac{d}{dt}\|\mathbf{r}\|\right)\mathbf{r}-\frac{1}{\|\mathbf{r}\|}\mathbf{v}\right] \\ &= GM\left[\frac{\mathbf{v}}{\|\mathbf{r}\|}-\frac{\mathbf{r}}{\|\mathbf{r}\|^2}\left(\frac{d}{dt}\|\mathbf{r}\|\right)\right].\end{aligned} \tag{3.29}$$

However,

$$\begin{aligned}\frac{d}{dt}\frac{\mathbf{r}}{\|\mathbf{r}\|} &= \frac{\frac{d}{dt}(\mathbf{r})\|\mathbf{r}\|-\mathbf{r}\frac{d}{dt}\|\mathbf{r}\|}{\|\mathbf{r}\|^2} \\ &= \frac{\frac{d\mathbf{r}}{dt}}{\|\mathbf{r}\|}-\frac{\mathbf{r}}{\|\mathbf{r}\|^2}\frac{d}{dt}\|\mathbf{r}\| \\ &= \frac{\mathbf{v}}{\|\mathbf{r}\|}-\frac{\mathbf{r}}{\|\mathbf{r}\|^2}\frac{d}{dt}\|\mathbf{r}\|.\end{aligned}$$

Therefore, **Equation 3.29** becomes

$$\frac{d\mathbf{v}}{dt}\times\mathbf{C}=GM\left(\frac{d}{dt}\frac{\mathbf{r}}{\|\mathbf{r}\|}\right).$$

Since **C** is a constant vector, we can integrate both sides and obtain

$$\mathbf{v}\times\mathbf{C}=GM\frac{\mathbf{r}}{\|\mathbf{r}\|}+\mathbf{D},$$

where **D** is a constant vector. Our goal is to solve for $\|\mathbf{r}\|$. Let's start by calculating $\mathbf{r}\cdot(\mathbf{v}\times\mathbf{C})$:

$$\mathbf{r}\cdot(\mathbf{v}\times\mathbf{C})=\mathbf{r}\cdot\left(GM\frac{\mathbf{r}}{\|\mathbf{r}\|}+\mathbf{D}\right)=GM\frac{\|\mathbf{r}\|^2}{\|\mathbf{r}\|}+\mathbf{r}\cdot\mathbf{D}=GM\|\mathbf{r}\|+\mathbf{r}\cdot\mathbf{D}.$$

However, $\mathbf{r}\cdot(\mathbf{v}\times\mathbf{C})=(\mathbf{r}\times\mathbf{v})\cdot\mathbf{C},$ so

$$(\mathbf{r}\times\mathbf{v})\cdot\mathbf{C}=GM\|\mathbf{r}\|+\mathbf{r}\cdot\mathbf{D}.$$

Since $\mathbf{r}\times\mathbf{v}=\mathbf{C},$ we have

$$\|\mathbf{C}\|^2=GM\|\mathbf{r}\|+\mathbf{r}\cdot\mathbf{D}.$$

Note that $\mathbf{r}\cdot\mathbf{D}=\|\mathbf{r}\|\,\|\mathbf{D}\|\cos\theta,$ where θ is the angle between **r** and **D.** Therefore,

$$\|\mathbf{C}\|^2=GM\|\mathbf{r}\|+\|\mathbf{r}\|\,\|\mathbf{D}\|\cos\theta.$$

Solving for $\|\mathbf{r}\|$,

$$\|\mathbf{r}\|=\frac{\|\mathbf{C}\|^2}{GM+\|\mathbf{D}\|\cos\theta}=\frac{\|\mathbf{C}\|^2}{GM}\left(\frac{1}{1+e\cos\theta}\right),$$

where $e=\|\mathbf{D}\|/GM.$ This is the polar equation of a conic with a focus at the origin, which we set up to be the Sun. It is a hyperbola if $e>1,$ a parabola if $e=1,$ or an ellipse if $e<1.$ Since planets have closed orbits, the only possibility is an ellipse. However, at this point it should be mentioned that hyperbolic comets do exist. These are objects that are merely passing through the solar system at speeds too great to be trapped into orbit around the Sun. As they pass close enough to the Sun, the gravitational field of the Sun deflects the trajectory enough so the path becomes hyperbolic.

□

Example 3.17

Using Kepler's Third Law for Nonheliocentric Orbits

Kepler's third law of planetary motion can be modified to the case of one object in orbit around an object other than the Sun, such as the Moon around the Earth. In this case, Kepler's third law becomes

$$P^2 = \frac{4\pi^2 a^3}{G(m+M)}, \qquad \textbf{(3.30)}$$

where m is the mass of the Moon and M is the mass of Earth, a represents the length of the major axis of the elliptical orbit, and P represents the period.

Given that the mass of the Moon is 7.35×10^{22} kg, the mass of Earth is 5.97×10^{24} kg, $G = 6.67 \times 10^{-11}\,\text{m}/\text{kg} \cdot \text{sec}^2,$ and the period of the moon is 27.3 days, let's find the length of the major axis of the orbit of the Moon around Earth.

Solution

It is important to be consistent with units. Since the universal gravitational constant contains seconds in the units, we need to use seconds for the period of the Moon as well:

$$27.3 \text{ days} \times \frac{24 \text{ hr}}{1 \text{ day}} \times \frac{3600 \text{ sec}}{1 \text{ hour}} = 2{,}358{,}720 \text{ sec}.$$

Substitute all the data into **Equation 3.30** and solve for a:

$$\begin{aligned}
(2{,}358{,}720 \text{ sec})^2 &= \frac{4\pi^2 a^3}{\left(6.67 \times 10^{-11} \frac{\text{m}}{\text{kg} \cdot \text{sec}^2}\right)\left(7.35\, x\, 10^{22}\,\text{kg} + 5.97\, x\, 10^{24}\,\text{kg}\right)} \\
5.563 \times 10^{12} &= \frac{4\pi^2 a^3}{\left(6.67 \times 10^{-11}\,\text{m}^3\right)\left(6.04\, x\, 10^{24}\right)} \\
\left(5.563 \times 10^{12}\right)\left(6.67 \times 10^{-11}\,\text{m}^3\right)\left(6.04 \times 10^{24}\right) &= 4\pi^2 a^3 \\
a^3 &= \frac{2.241 \times 10^{27}}{4\pi^2}\text{m}^3 \\
a &= 3.84 \times 10^8\,\text{m} \\
&\approx 384{,}000 \text{ km}.
\end{aligned}$$

Analysis

According to solarsystem.nasa.gov, the actual average distance from the Moon to Earth is 384,400 km. This is calculated using reflectors left on the Moon by Apollo astronauts back in the 1960s.

3.17 Titan is the largest moon of Saturn. The mass of Titan is approximately 1.35×10^{23} kg. The mass of Saturn is approximately 5.68×10^{26} kg. Titan takes approximately 16 days to orbit Saturn. Use this information, along with the universal gravitation constant $G = 6.67 \times 10^{-11}\,\text{m}/\text{kg} \cdot \text{sec}^2$ to estimate the distance from Titan to Saturn.

Example 3.18

Chapter Opener: Halley's Comet

We now return to the chapter opener, which discusses the motion of Halley's comet around the Sun. Kepler's first law states that Halley's comet follows an elliptical path around the Sun, with the Sun as one focus of the ellipse. The period of Halley's comet is approximately 76.1 years, depending on how closely it passes by Jupiter and Saturn as it passes through the outer solar system. Let's use $T = 76.1$ years. What is the average distance of Halley's comet from the Sun?

Solution

Using the equation $T^2 = D^3$ with $T = 76.1,$ we obtain $D^3 = 5791.21,$ so $D \approx 17.96$ A.U. This comes out to approximately 1.67×10^9 mi.

A natural question to ask is: What are the maximum (aphelion) and minimum (perihelion) distances from Halley's Comet to the Sun? The eccentricity of the orbit of Halley's Comet is 0.967 (Source: http://nssdc.gsfc.nasa.gov/planetary/factsheet/cometfact.html). Recall that the formula for the eccentricity of an ellipse is $e = c/a,$ where a is the length of the semimajor axis and c is the distance from the center to either focus. Therefore, $0.967 = c/17.96$ and $c \approx 17.37$ A.U. Subtracting this from a gives the perihelion distance $p = a - c = 17.96 - 17.37 = 0.59$ A.U. According to the National Space Science Data Center (Source: http://nssdc.gsfc.nasa.gov/planetary/factsheet/cometfact.html), the perihelion distance for Halley's comet is 0.587 A.U. To calculate the aphelion distance, we add

$$P = a + c = 17.96 + 17.37 = 35.33 \text{ A.U.}$$

This is approximately 3.3×10^9 mi. The average distance from Pluto to the Sun is 39.5 A.U. (Source: http://www.oarval.org/furthest.htm), so it would appear that Halley's Comet stays just within the orbit of Pluto.

Student PROJECT

Navigating a Banked Turn

How fast can a racecar travel through a circular turn without skidding and hitting the wall? The answer could depend on several factors:

- The weight of the car;
- The friction between the tires and the road;
- The radius of the circle;
- The “steepness” of the turn.

In this project we investigate this question for NASCAR racecars at the Bristol Motor Speedway in Tennessee. Before considering this track in particular, we use vector functions to develop the mathematics and physics necessary for answering questions such as this.

A car of mass m moves with constant angular speed ω around a circular curve of radius R (**Figure 3.20**). The curve is banked at an angle θ. If the height of the car off the ground is h, then the position of the car at time t is given by the function $r(t) = \langle R\cos(\omega t), R\sin(\omega t), h \rangle$.

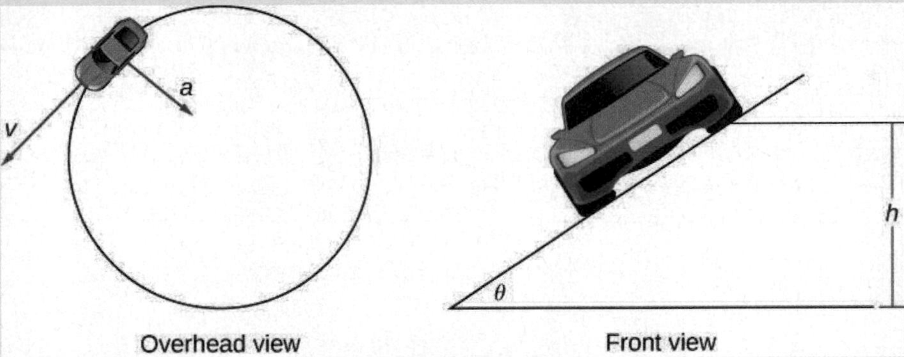

Figure 3.20 Views of a race car moving around a track.

1. Find the velocity function $\mathbf{v}(t)$ of the car. Show that $\mathbf{v}$ is tangent to the circular curve. This means that, without a force to keep the car on the curve, the car will shoot off of it.
2. Show that the speed of the car is ωR. Use this to show that $(2\pi 4)/|\mathbf{v}| = (2\pi)/\omega$.
3. Find the acceleration $\mathbf{a}$. Show that this vector points toward the center of the circle and that $|\mathbf{a}| = R\omega^2$.
4. The force required to produce this circular motion is called the *centripetal force*, and it is denoted $\mathbf{F}_{\text{cent}}$. This force points toward the center of the circle (not toward the ground). Show that $|\mathbf{F}_{\text{cent}}| = \left(m|\mathbf{v}|^2\right)/R$.

   As the car moves around the curve, three forces act on it: gravity, the force exerted by the road (this force is perpendicular to the ground), and the friction force (**Figure 3.21**). Because describing the frictional force generated by the tires and the road is complex, we use a standard approximation for the frictional force. Assume that $\mathbf{f} = \mu\mathbf{N}$ for some positive constant μ. The constant μ is called the *coefficient of friction*.

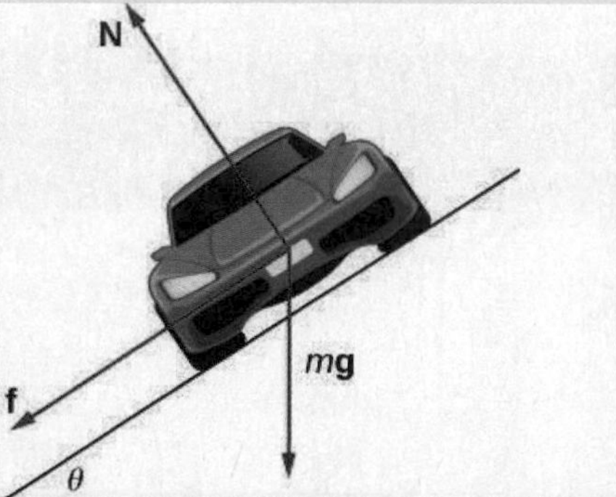

Figure 3.21 The car has three forces acting on it: gravity (denoted by $m\mathbf{g}$), the friction force $\mathbf{f}$, and the force exerted by the road $\mathbf{N}$.

Let v_{max} denote the maximum speed the car can attain through the curve without skidding. In other words, v_{max} is the fastest speed at which the car can navigate the turn. When the car is traveling at this speed, the magnitude of the centripetal force is

$$|\mathbf{F}_{cent}| = \frac{mv_{max}^2}{R}.$$

The next three questions deal with developing a formula that relates the speed v_{max} to the banking angle θ.

5. Show that $\mathbf{N}\cos\theta = mg + \mathbf{f}\sin\theta$. Conclude that $\mathbf{N} = (mg)/(\cos\theta - \mu\sin\theta)$.

6. The centripetal force is the sum of the forces in the horizontal direction, since the centripetal force points toward the center of the circular curve. Show that

$$\mathbf{F}_{cent} = \mathbf{N}\sin\theta + \mathbf{f}\cos\theta.$$

Conclude that

$$\mathbf{F}_{cent} = \frac{\sin\theta + \mu\cos\theta}{\cos\theta - \mu\sin\theta}mg.$$

7. Show that $v_{max}^2 = ((\sin\theta + \mu\cos\theta)/(\cos\theta - \mu\sin\theta))gR$. Conclude that the maximum speed does not actually depend on the mass of the car.

Now that we have a formula relating the maximum speed of the car and the banking angle, we are in a position to answer the questions like the one posed at the beginning of the project.

The Bristol Motor Speedway is a NASCAR short track in Bristol, Tennessee. The track has the approximate shape shown in **Figure 3.22**. Each end of the track is approximately semicircular, so when cars make turns they are traveling along an approximately circular curve. If a car takes the inside track and speeds along the bottom of turn 1, the car travels along a semicircle of radius approximately 211 ft with a banking angle of 24°. If the car decides to take the outside track and speeds along the top of turn 1, then the car travels along a semicircle with a banking angle of 28°. (The track has variable angle banking.)

Figure 3.22 At the Bristol Motor Speedway, Bristol, Tennessee (a), the turns have an inner radius of about 211 ft and a width of 40 ft (b). (credit: part (a) photo by Raniel Diaz, Flickr)

The coefficient of friction for a normal tire in dry conditions is approximately 0.7. Therefore, we assume the coefficient for a NASCAR tire in dry conditions is approximately 0.98.

Before answering the following questions, note that it is easier to do computations in terms of feet and seconds, and then convert the answers to miles per hour as a final step.

8. In dry conditions, how fast can the car travel through the bottom of the turn without skidding?
9. In dry conditions, how fast can the car travel through the top of the turn without skidding?
10. In wet conditions, the coefficient of friction can become as low as 0.1. If this is the case, how fast can the car travel through the bottom of the turn without skidding?
11. Suppose the measured speed of a car going along the outside edge of the turn is 105 mph. Estimate the coefficient of friction for the car's tires.

3.4 EXERCISES

155. Given $\mathbf{r}(t) = (3t^2 - 2)\mathbf{i} + (2t - \sin(t))\mathbf{j}$, find the velocity of a particle moving along this curve.

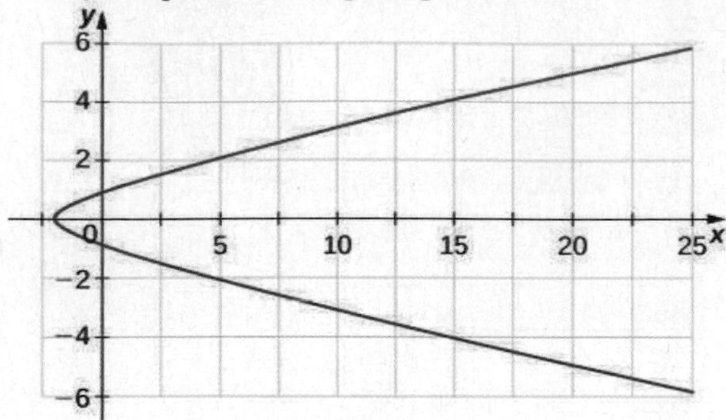

156. Given $\mathbf{r}(t) = (3t^2 - 2)\mathbf{i} + (2t - \sin(t))\mathbf{j}$, find the acceleration vector of a particle moving along the curve in the preceding exercise.

Given the following position functions, find the velocity, acceleration, and speed in terms of the parameter t.

157. $\mathbf{r}(t) = \langle 3\cos t, 3\sin t, t^2 \rangle$

158. $\mathbf{r}(t) = e^{-t}\mathbf{i} + t^2\mathbf{j} + \tan t\mathbf{k}$

159. $\mathbf{r}(t) = 2\cos t\,\mathbf{j} + 3\sin t\,\mathbf{k}$. The graph is shown here:

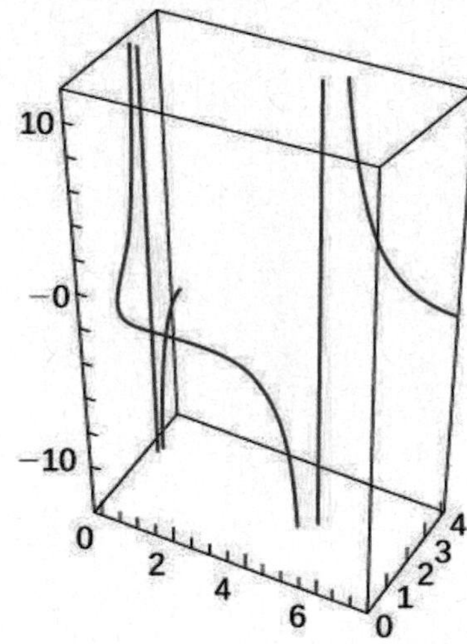

Find the velocity, acceleration, and speed of a particle with the given position function.

160. $\mathbf{r}(t) = \langle t^2 - 1, t \rangle$

161. $\mathbf{r}(t) = \langle e^t, e^{-t} \rangle$

162. $\mathbf{r}(t) = \langle \sin t, t, \cos t \rangle$. The graph is shown here:

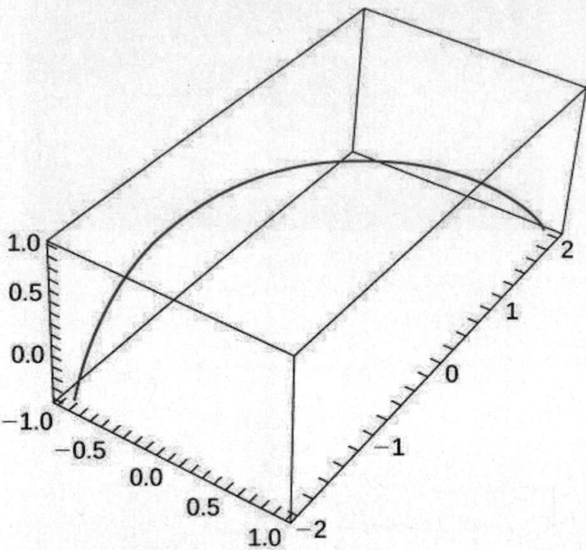

163. The position function of an object is given by $\mathbf{r}(t) = \langle t^2, 5t, t^2 - 16t \rangle$. At what time is the speed a minimum?

164. Let $\mathbf{r}(t) = r\cosh(\omega t)\mathbf{i} + r\sinh(\omega t)\mathbf{j}$. Find the velocity and acceleration vectors and show that the acceleration is proportional to $\mathbf{r}(t)$.

Consider the motion of a point on the circumference of a rolling circle. As the circle rolls, it generates the cycloid $\mathbf{r}(t) = (\omega t - \sin(\omega t))\mathbf{i} + (1 - \cos(\omega t))\mathbf{j}$, where ω is the angular velocity of the circle and b is the radius of the circle:

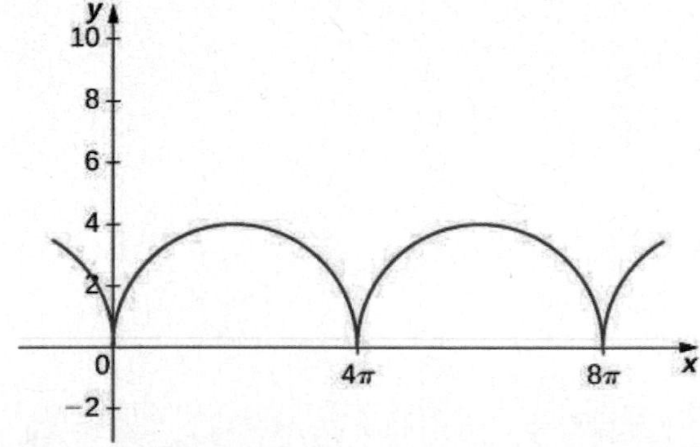

165. Find the equations for the velocity, acceleration, and speed of the particle at any time.

A person on a hang glider is spiraling upward as a result of the rapidly rising air on a path having position vector $\mathbf{r}(t) = (3\cos t)\mathbf{i} + (3\sin t)\mathbf{j} + t^2\mathbf{k}$. The path is similar to that of a helix, although it is not a helix. The graph is shown here:

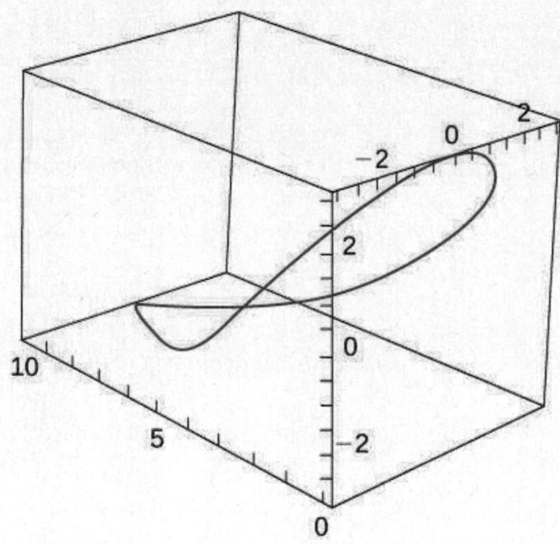

Find the following quantities:

166. The velocity and acceleration vectors

167. The glider's speed at any time

168. The times, if any, at which the glider's acceleration is orthogonal to its velocity

Given that $\mathbf{r}(t) = \langle e^{-5t}\sin t, e^{-5t}\cos t, 4e^{-5t}\rangle$ is the position vector of a moving particle, find the following quantities:

169. The velocity of the particle

170. The speed of the particle

171. The acceleration of the particle

172. Find the maximum speed of a point on the circumference of an automobile tire of radius 1 ft when the automobile is traveling at 55 mph.

A projectile is shot in the air from ground level with an initial velocity of 500 m/sec at an angle of 60° with the horizontal. The graph is shown here:

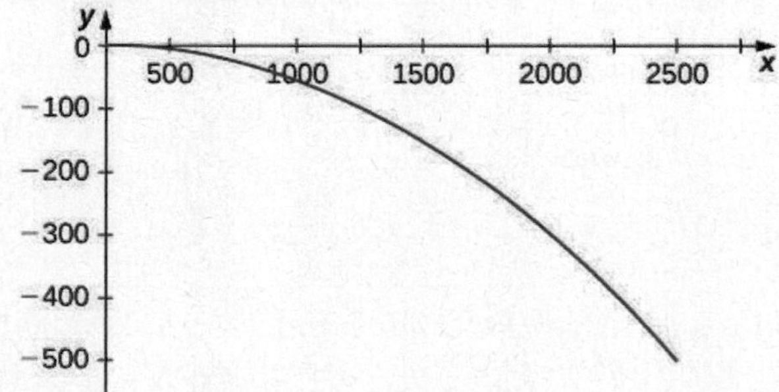

173. At what time does the projectile reach maximum height?

174. What is the approximate maximum height of the projectile?

175. At what time is the maximum range of the projectile attained?

176. What is the maximum range?

177. What is the total flight time of the projectile?

A projectile is fired at a height of 1.5 m above the ground with an initial velocity of 100 m/sec and at an angle of 30° above the horizontal. Use this information to answer the following questions:

178. Determine the maximum height of the projectile.

179. Determine the range of the projectile.

180. A golf ball is hit in a horizontal direction off the top edge of a building that is 100 ft tall. How fast must the ball be launched to land 450 ft away?

181. A projectile is fired from ground level at an angle of 8° with the horizontal. The projectile is to have a range of 50 m. Find the minimum velocity necessary to achieve this range.

182. Prove that an object moving in a straight line at a constant speed has an acceleration of zero.

183. The acceleration of an object is given by $\mathbf{a}(t) = t\mathbf{j} + t\mathbf{k}$. The velocity at $t = 1$ sec is $\mathbf{v}(1) = 5\mathbf{j}$ and the position of the object at $t = 1$ sec is $\mathbf{r}(1) = 0\mathbf{i} + 0\mathbf{j} + 0\mathbf{k}$. Find the object's position at any time.

184. Find $\mathbf{r}(t)$ given that $\mathbf{a}(t) = -32\mathbf{j}$, $\mathbf{v}(0) = 600\sqrt{3}\mathbf{i} + 600\mathbf{j}$, and $\mathbf{r}(0) = \mathbf{0}$.

185. Find the tangential and normal components of acceleration for $\mathbf{r}(t) = a\cos(\omega t)\mathbf{i} + b\sin(\omega t)\mathbf{j}$ at $t = 0$.

186. Given $\mathbf{r}(t) = t^2\mathbf{i} + 2t\mathbf{j}$ and $t = 1$, find the tangential and normal components of acceleration.

For each of the following problems, find the tangential and normal components of acceleration.

187. $\mathbf{r}(t) = \langle e^t \cos t, e^t \sin t, e^t \rangle$. The graph is shown here:

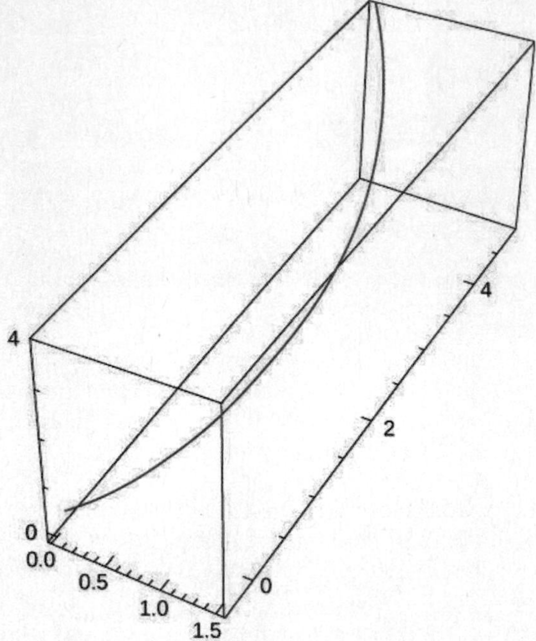

188. $\mathbf{r}(t) = \langle \cos(2t), \sin(2t), 1 \rangle$

189. $\mathbf{r}(t) = \langle 2t, t^2, \frac{t^3}{3} \rangle$

190. $\mathbf{r}(t) = \langle \frac{2}{3}(1+t)^{3/2}, \frac{2}{3}(1-t)^{3/2}, \sqrt{2}t \rangle$

191. $\mathbf{r}(t) = \langle 6t, 3t^2, 2t^3 \rangle$

192. $\mathbf{r}(t) = t^2\mathbf{i} + t^2\mathbf{j} + t^3\mathbf{k}$

193. $\mathbf{r}(t) = 3\cos(2\pi t)\mathbf{i} + 3\sin(2\pi t)\mathbf{j}$

194. Find the position vector-valued function $\mathbf{r}(t)$, given that $\mathbf{a}(t) = \mathbf{i} + e^t\mathbf{j}$, $\mathbf{v}(0) = 2\mathbf{j}$, and $\mathbf{r}(0) = 2\mathbf{i}$.

195. The force on a particle is given by $\mathbf{f}(t) = (\cos t)\mathbf{i} + (\sin t)\mathbf{j}$. The particle is located at point $(c, 0)$ at $t = 0$. The initial velocity of the particle is given by $\mathbf{v}(0) = v_0\mathbf{j}$. Find the path of the particle of mass $\mathbf{m}$. (Recall, $\mathbf{F} = m \cdot \mathbf{a}$.)

196. An automobile that weighs 2700 lb makes a turn on a flat road while traveling at 56 ft/sec. If the radius of the turn is 70 ft, what is the required frictional force to keep the car from skidding?

197. Using Kepler's laws, it can be shown that $v_0 = \sqrt{\frac{2GM}{r_0}}$ is the minimum speed needed when $\theta = 0$ so that an object will escape from the pull of a central force resulting from mass M. Use this result to find the minimum speed when $\theta = 0$ for a space capsule to escape from the gravitational pull of Earth if the probe is at an altitude of 300 km above Earth's surface.

198. Find the time in years it takes the dwarf planet Pluto to make one orbit about the Sun given that $a = 39.5$ A.U.

Suppose that the position function for an object in three dimensions is given by the equation $\mathbf{r}(t) = t\cos(t)\mathbf{i} + t\sin(t)\mathbf{j} + 3t\mathbf{k}$.

199. Show that the particle moves on a circular cone.

200. Find the angle between the velocity and acceleration vectors when $t = 1.5$.

201. Find the tangential and normal components of acceleration when $t = 1.5$.

CHAPTER 3 REVIEW

KEY TERMS

acceleration vector the second derivative of the position vector

arc-length function a function $s(t)$ that describes the arc length of curve C as a function of t

arc-length parameterization a reparameterization of a vector-valued function in which the parameter is equal to the arc length

binormal vector a unit vector orthogonal to the unit tangent vector and the unit normal vector

component functions the component functions of the vector-valued function $\mathbf{r}(t) = f(t)\mathbf{i} + g(t)\mathbf{j}$ are $f(t)$ and $g(t)$, and the component functions of the vector-valued function $\mathbf{r}(t) = f(t)\mathbf{i} + g(t)\mathbf{j} + h(t)\mathbf{k}$ are $f(t)$, $g(t)$ and $h(t)$

curvature the derivative of the unit tangent vector with respect to the arc-length parameter

definite integral of a vector-valued function the vector obtained by calculating the definite integral of each of the component functions of a given vector-valued function, then using the results as the components of the resulting function

derivative of a vector-valued function the derivative of a vector-valued function $\mathbf{r}(t)$ is $\mathbf{r}'(t) = \lim_{\Delta t \to 0} \frac{\mathbf{r}(t + \Delta t) - \mathbf{r}(t)}{\Delta t}$, provided the limit exists

Frenet frame of reference (TNB frame) a frame of reference in three-dimensional space formed by the unit tangent vector, the unit normal vector, and the binormal vector

helix a three-dimensional curve in the shape of a spiral

indefinite integral of a vector-valued function a vector-valued function with a derivative that is equal to a given vector-valued function

Kepler's laws of planetary motion three laws governing the motion of planets, asteroids, and comets in orbit around the Sun

limit of a vector-valued function a vector-valued function $\mathbf{r}(t)$ has a limit $\mathbf{L}$ as t approaches a if $\lim_{t \to a} |\mathbf{r}(t) - \mathbf{L}| = 0$

normal component of acceleration the coefficient of the unit normal vector $\mathbf{N}$ when the acceleration vector is written as a linear combination of $\mathbf{T}$ and $\mathbf{N}$

normal plane a plane that is perpendicular to a curve at any point on the curve

osculating circle a circle that is tangent to a curve C at a point P and that shares the same curvature

osculating plane the plane determined by the unit tangent and the unit normal vector

plane curve the set of ordered pairs $(f(t), g(t))$ together with their defining parametric equations $x = f(t)$ and $y = g(t)$

principal unit normal vector a vector orthogonal to the unit tangent vector, given by the formula $\frac{\mathbf{T}'(t)}{\| \mathbf{T}'(t) \|}$

principal unit tangent vector a unit vector tangent to a curve C

projectile motion motion of an object with an initial velocity but no force acting on it other than gravity

radius of curvature the reciprocal of the curvature

reparameterization an alternative parameterization of a given vector-valued function

smooth curves where the vector-valued function $\mathbf{r}(t)$ is differentiable with a non-zero derivative

space curve the set of ordered triples $(f(t), g(t), h(t))$ together with their defining parametric equations $x = f(t)$, $y = g(t)$ and $z = h(t)$

tangent vector to $\mathbf{r}(t)$ at $t = t_0$ any vector **v** such that, when the tail of the vector is placed at point $\mathbf{r}(t_0)$ on the graph, vector **v** is tangent to curve C

tangential component of acceleration the coefficient of the unit tangent vector $\mathbf{T}$ when the acceleration vector is written as a linear combination of $\mathbf{T}$ and $\mathbf{N}$

vector parameterization any representation of a plane or space curve using a vector-valued function

vector-valued function a function of the form $\mathbf{r}(t) = f(t)\mathbf{i} + g(t)\mathbf{j}$ or $\mathbf{r}(t) = f(t)\mathbf{i} + g(t)\mathbf{j} + h(t)\mathbf{k}$, where the component functions f, g, and h are real-valued functions of the parameter t

velocity vector the derivative of the position vector

KEY EQUATIONS

- **Vector-valued function**
  $\mathbf{r}(t) = f(t)\mathbf{i} + g(t)\mathbf{j}$ or $\mathbf{r}(t) = f(t)\mathbf{i} + g(t)\mathbf{j} + h(t)\mathbf{k}$, or $\mathbf{r}(t) = \langle f(t), g(t) \rangle$ or $\mathbf{r}(t) = \langle f(t), g(t), h(t) \rangle$
- **Limit of a vector-valued function**
  $\lim_{t \to a} \mathbf{r}(t) = \left[\lim_{t \to a} f(t)\right]\mathbf{i} + \left[\lim_{t \to a} g(t)\right]\mathbf{j}$ or $\lim_{t \to a} \mathbf{r}(t) = \left[\lim_{t \to a} f(t)\right]\mathbf{i} + \left[\lim_{t \to a} g(t)\right]\mathbf{j} + \left[\lim_{t \to a} h(t)\right]\mathbf{k}$
- **Derivative of a vector-valued function**
  $$\mathbf{r}'(t) = \lim_{\Delta t \to 0} \frac{\mathbf{r}(t + \Delta t) - \mathbf{r}(t)}{\Delta t}$$
- **Principal unit tangent vector**
  $$\mathbf{T}(t) = \frac{\mathbf{r}'(t)}{\|\mathbf{r}'(t)\|}$$
- **Indefinite integral of a vector-valued function**
  $$\int [f(t)\mathbf{i} + g(t)\mathbf{j} + h(t)\mathbf{k}]dt = \left[\int f(t)dt\right]\mathbf{i} + \left[\int g(t)dt\right]\mathbf{j} + \left[\int h(t)dt\right]\mathbf{k}$$
- **Definite integral of a vector-valued function**
  $$\int_a^b [f(t)\mathbf{i} + g(t)\mathbf{j} + h(t)\mathbf{k}]dt = \left[\int_a^b f(t)dt\right]\mathbf{i} + \left[\int_a^b g(t)dt\right]\mathbf{j} + \left[\int_a^b h(t)dt\right]\mathbf{k}$$
- **Arc length of space curve**
  $$s = \int_a^b \sqrt{[f'(t)]^2 + [g'(t)]^2 + [h'(t)]^2}\, dt = \int_a^b \|\mathbf{r}'(t)\|\, dt$$
- **Arc-length function**
  $$s(t) = \int_a^t \sqrt{(f'(u))^2 + (g'(u))^2 + (h'(u))^2} du \text{ or } s(t) = \int_a^t \|\mathbf{r}'(u)\|\, du$$
- **Curvature**
  $$\kappa = \frac{\|\mathbf{T}'(t)\|}{\|\mathbf{r}'(t)\|} \text{ or } \kappa = \frac{\|\mathbf{r}'(t) \times \mathbf{r}''(t)\|}{\|\mathbf{r}'(t)\|^3} \text{ or } \kappa = \frac{|y''|}{\left[1 + (y')^2\right]^{3/2}}$$
- **Principal unit normal vector**
  $$\mathbf{N}(t) = \frac{\mathbf{T}'(t)}{\|\mathbf{T}'(t)\|}$$
- **Binormal vector**
  $\mathbf{B}(t) = \mathbf{T}(t) \times \mathbf{N}(t)$
- **Velocity**

$\mathbf{v}(t) = \mathbf{r}'(t)$

- **Acceleration**
$\mathbf{a}(t) = \mathbf{v}'(t) = \mathbf{r}''(t)$
- **Speed**
$v(t) = \|\mathbf{v}(t)\| = \|\mathbf{r}'(t)\| = \frac{ds}{dt}$
- **Tangential component of acceleration**
$a_{\mathbf{T}} = \mathbf{a} \cdot \mathbf{T} = \frac{\mathbf{v} \cdot \mathbf{a}}{\|\mathbf{v}\|}$
- **Normal component of acceleration**
$a_{\mathbf{N}} = \mathbf{a} \cdot \mathbf{N} = \frac{\|\mathbf{v} \times \mathbf{a}\|}{\|\mathbf{v}\|} = \sqrt{\|\mathbf{a}\|^2 - a^{\mathbf{T}}}$

KEY CONCEPTS

3.1 Vector-Valued Functions and Space Curves

- A vector-valued function is a function of the form $\mathbf{r}(t) = f(t)\mathbf{i} + g(t)\mathbf{j}$ or $\mathbf{r}(t) = f(t)\mathbf{i} + g(t)\mathbf{j} + h(t)\mathbf{k}$, where the component functions *f*, *g*, and *h* are real-valued functions of the parameter *t*.
- The graph of a vector-valued function of the form $\mathbf{r}(t) = f(t)\mathbf{i} + g(t)\mathbf{j}$ is called a *plane curve*. The graph of a vector-valued function of the form $\mathbf{r}(t) = f(t)\mathbf{i} + g(t)\mathbf{j} + h(t)\mathbf{k}$ is called a *space curve*.
- It is possible to represent an arbitrary plane curve by a vector-valued function.
- To calculate the limit of a vector-valued function, calculate the limits of the component functions separately.

3.2 Calculus of Vector-Valued Functions

- To calculate the derivative of a vector-valued function, calculate the derivatives of the component functions, then put them back into a new vector-valued function.
- Many of the properties of differentiation from the **Introduction to Derivatives (http://cnx.org/content/m53494/latest/)** also apply to vector-valued functions.
- The derivative of a vector-valued function $\mathbf{r}(t)$ is also a tangent vector to the curve. The unit tangent vector $\mathbf{T}(t)$ is calculated by dividing the derivative of a vector-valued function by its magnitude.
- The antiderivative of a vector-valued function is found by finding the antiderivatives of the component functions, then putting them back together in a vector-valued function.
- The definite integral of a vector-valued function is found by finding the definite integrals of the component functions, then putting them back together in a vector-valued function.

3.3 Arc Length and Curvature

- The arc-length function for a vector-valued function is calculated using the integral formula $s(t) = \int_a^t \|\mathbf{r}'(u)\|\, du$. This formula is valid in both two and three dimensions.
- The curvature of a curve at a point in either two or three dimensions is defined to be the curvature of the inscribed circle at that point. The arc-length parameterization is used in the definition of curvature.
- There are several different formulas for curvature. The curvature of a circle is equal to the reciprocal of its radius.
- The principal unit normal vector at *t* is defined to be

$$\mathbf{N}(t) = \frac{\mathbf{T}'(t)}{\|\mathbf{T}'(t)\|}.$$

- The binormal vector at t is defined as $\mathbf{B}(t) = \mathbf{T}(t) \times \mathbf{N}(t)$, where $\mathbf{T}(t)$ is the unit tangent vector.
- The Frenet frame of reference is formed by the unit tangent vector, the principal unit normal vector, and the binormal vector.
- The osculating circle is tangent to a curve at a point and has the same curvature as the tangent curve at that point.

3.4 Motion in Space

- If $\mathbf{r}(t)$ represents the position of an object at time t, then $\mathbf{r}'(t)$ represents the velocity and $\mathbf{r}''(t)$ represents the acceleration of the object at time t. The magnitude of the velocity vector is speed.
- The acceleration vector always points toward the concave side of the curve defined by $\mathbf{r}(t)$. The tangential and normal components of acceleration $a_{\mathbf{T}}$ and $a_{\mathbf{N}}$ are the projections of the acceleration vector onto the unit tangent and unit normal vectors to the curve.
- Kepler's three laws of planetary motion describe the motion of objects in orbit around the Sun. His third law can be modified to describe motion of objects in orbit around other celestial objects as well.
- Newton was able to use his law of universal gravitation in conjunction with his second law of motion and calculus to prove Kepler's three laws.

CHAPTER 3 REVIEW EXERCISES

True or False? Justify your answer with a proof or a counterexample.

202. A parametric equation that passes through points P and Q can be given by $\mathbf{r}(t) = \langle t^2, 3t+1, t-2 \rangle$, where $P(1, 4, -1)$ and $Q(16, 11, 2)$.

203. $\frac{d}{dt}[\mathbf{u}(t) \times \mathbf{u}(t)] = 2\mathbf{u}'(t) \times \mathbf{u}(t)$

204. The curvature of a circle of radius r is constant everywhere. Furthermore, the curvature is equal to $1/r$.

205. The speed of a particle with a position function $\mathbf{r}(t)$ is $(\mathbf{r}'(t))/(|\mathbf{r}'(t)|)$.

Find the domains of the vector-valued functions.

206. $\mathbf{r}(t) = \langle \sin(t), \ln(t), \sqrt{t} \rangle$

207. $\mathbf{r}(t) = \langle e^t, \frac{1}{\sqrt{4-t}}, \sec(t) \rangle$

Sketch the curves for the following vector equations. Use a calculator if needed.

208. **[T]** $\mathbf{r}(t) = \langle t^2, t^3 \rangle$

209. **[T]** $\mathbf{r}(t) = \langle \sin(20t)e^{-t}, \cos(20t)e^{-t}, e^{-t} \rangle$

Find a vector function that describes the following curves.

210. Intersection of the cylinder $x^2 + y^2 = 4$ with the plane $x + z = 6$

211. Intersection of the cone $z = \sqrt{x^2 + y^2}$ and plane $z = y - 4$

Find the derivatives of $\mathbf{u}(t)$, $\mathbf{u}'(t)$, $\mathbf{u}'(t) \times \mathbf{u}(t)$, $\mathbf{u}(t) \times \mathbf{u}'(t)$, and $\mathbf{u}(t) \cdot \mathbf{u}'(t)$. Find the unit tangent vector.

212. $\mathbf{u}(t) = \langle e^t, e^{-t} \rangle$

213. $\mathbf{u}(t) = \langle t^2, 2t+6, 4t^5 - 12 \rangle$

Evaluate the following integrals.

214. $\int \left(\tan(t)\sec(t)\mathbf{i} - te^{3t}\mathbf{j}\right)dt$

215. $\int_1^4 \mathbf{u}(t)dt$, with $\mathbf{u}(t) = \langle \frac{\ln(t)}{t}, \frac{1}{\sqrt{t}}, \sin\left(\frac{t\pi}{4}\right) \rangle$

Find the length for the following curves.

216. $\mathbf{r}(t) = \langle 3(t), 4\cos(t), 4\sin(t) \rangle$ for $1 \le t \le 4$

217. $\mathbf{r}(t) = 2\mathbf{i} + t\,\mathbf{j} + 3t^2\mathbf{k}$ for $0 \le t \le 1$

Reparameterize the following functions with respect to their arc length measured from $t = 0$ in direction of increasing t.

218. $\mathbf{r}(t) = 2t\mathbf{i} + (4t - 5)\mathbf{j} + (1 - 3t)\mathbf{k}$

219. $\mathbf{r}(t) = \cos(2t)\mathbf{i} + 8t\,\mathbf{j} - \sin(2t)\mathbf{k}$

Find the curvature for the following vector functions.

220. $\mathbf{r}(t) = (2\sin t)\mathbf{i} - 4t\,\mathbf{j} + (2\cos t)\mathbf{k}$

221. $\mathbf{r}(t) = \sqrt{2}e^{t}\mathbf{i} + \sqrt{2}e^{-t}\mathbf{j} + 2t\mathbf{k}$

222. Find the unit tangent vector, the unit normal vector, and the binormal vector for $\mathbf{r}(t) = 2\cos t\,\mathbf{i} + 3t\,\mathbf{j} + 2\sin t\,\mathbf{k}$.

223. Find the tangential and normal acceleration components with the position vector $\mathbf{r}(t) = \langle \cos t, \sin t, e^{t} \rangle$.

224. A Ferris wheel car is moving at a constant speed v and has a constant radius r. Find the tangential and normal acceleration of the Ferris wheel car.

225. The position of a particle is given by $\mathbf{r}(t) = \langle t^2, \ln(t), \sin(\pi t) \rangle$, where t is measured in seconds and $\mathbf{r}$ is measured in meters. Find the velocity, acceleration, and speed functions. What are the position, velocity, speed, and acceleration of the particle at 1 sec?

The following problems consider launching a cannonball out of a cannon. The cannonball is shot out of the cannon with an angle θ and initial velocity $\mathbf{v}_0$. The only force acting on the cannonball is gravity, so we begin with a constant acceleration $\mathbf{a}(t) = -g\,\mathbf{j}$.

226. Find the velocity vector function $\mathbf{v}(t)$.

227. Find the position vector $\mathbf{r}(t)$ and the parametric representation for the position.

228. At what angle do you need to fire the cannonball for the horizontal distance to be greatest? What is the total distance it would travel?

4 | DIFFERENTIATION OF FUNCTIONS OF SEVERAL VARIABLES

Figure 4.1 Americans use (and lose) millions of golf balls a year, which keeps golf ball manufacturers in business. In this chapter, we study a profit model and learn methods for calculating optimal production levels for a typical golf ball manufacturing company. (credit: modification of work by oatsy40, Flickr)

Chapter Outline

Introduction

In **Introduction to Applications of Derivatives (http://cnx.org/content/m53602/latest/)** , we studied how to determine the maximum and minimum of a function of one variable over a closed interval. This function might represent the temperature over a given time interval, the position of a car as a function of time, or the altitude of a jet plane as it travels from New York to San Francisco. In each of these examples, the function has one independent variable.

Suppose, however, that we have a quantity that depends on more than one variable. For example, temperature can depend on location and the time of day, or a company's profit model might depend on the number of units sold and the amount of money spent on advertising. In this chapter, we look at a company that produces golf balls. We develop a profit model and, under various restrictions, we find that the optimal level of production and advertising dollars spent determines the maximum possible profit. Depending on the nature of the restrictions, both the method of solution and the solution itself changes (see **Example 4.41**).

When dealing with a function of more than one independent variable, several questions naturally arise. For example, how do we calculate limits of functions of more than one variable? The definition of *derivative* we used before involved a limit. Does the new definition of derivative involve limits as well? Do the rules of differentiation apply in this context? Can we find relative extrema of functions using derivatives? All these questions are answered in this chapter.

4.1 | Functions of Several Variables

Learning Objectives

4.1.1 Recognize a function of two variables and identify its domain and range.
4.1.2 Sketch a graph of a function of two variables.
4.1.3 Sketch several traces or level curves of a function of two variables.
4.1.4 Recognize a function of three or more variables and identify its level surfaces.

Our first step is to explain what a function of more than one variable is, starting with functions of two independent variables. This step includes identifying the domain and range of such functions and learning how to graph them. We also examine ways to relate the graphs of functions in three dimensions to graphs of more familiar planar functions.

Functions of Two Variables

The definition of a function of two variables is very similar to the definition for a function of one variable. The main difference is that, instead of mapping values of one variable to values of another variable, we map ordered pairs of variables to another variable.

Definition

A **function of two variables** $z = f(x, y)$ maps each ordered pair (x, y) in a subset D of the real plane $\mathbb{R}^2$ to a unique real number z. The set D is called the *domain* of the function. The *range* of f is the set of all real numbers

z that has at least one ordered pair $(x, y) \in D$ such that $f(x, y) = z$ as shown in the following figure.

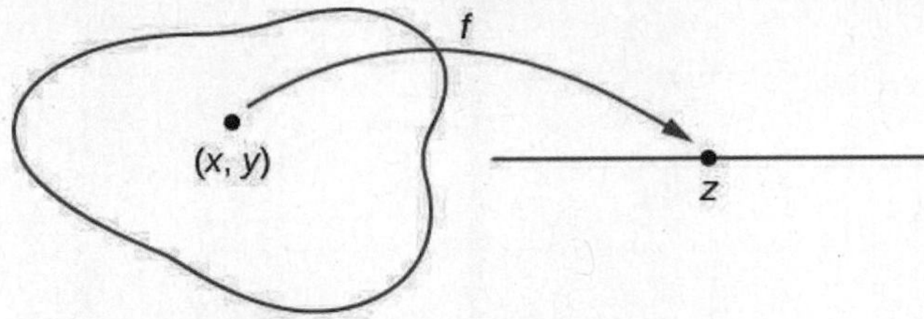

Figure 4.2 The domain of a function of two variables consists of ordered pairs (x, y).

Determining the domain of a function of two variables involves taking into account any domain restrictions that may exist. Let's take a look.

Example 4.1

Domains and Ranges for Functions of Two Variables

Find the domain and range of each of the following functions:

a. $f(x, y) = 3x + 5y + 2$

b. $g(x, y) = \sqrt{9 - x^2 - y^2}$

Solution

a. This is an example of a linear function in two variables. There are no values or combinations of x and y that cause $f(x, y)$ to be undefined, so the domain of f is $\mathbb{R}^2$. To determine the range, first pick a value for z. We need to find a solution to the equation $f(x, y) = z$, or $3x - 5y + 2 = z$. One such solution can be obtained by first setting $y = 0$, which yields the equation $3x + 2 = z$. The solution to this equation is $x = \frac{z - 2}{3}$, which gives the ordered pair $\left(\frac{z - 2}{3}, 0\right)$ as a solution to the equation $f(x, y) = z$ for any value of z. Therefore, the range of the function is all real numbers, or $\mathbb{R}$.

b. For the function $g(x, y)$ to have a real value, the quantity under the square root must be nonnegative:

$$9 - x^2 - y^2 \geq 0.$$

This inequality can be written in the form

$$x^2 + y^2 \leq 9.$$

Therefore, the domain of $g(x, y)$ is $\{(x, y) \in \mathbb{R}^2 | x^2 + y^2 \leq 9\}$. The graph of this set of points can be described as a disk of radius 3 centered at the origin. The domain includes the boundary circle as shown in the following graph.

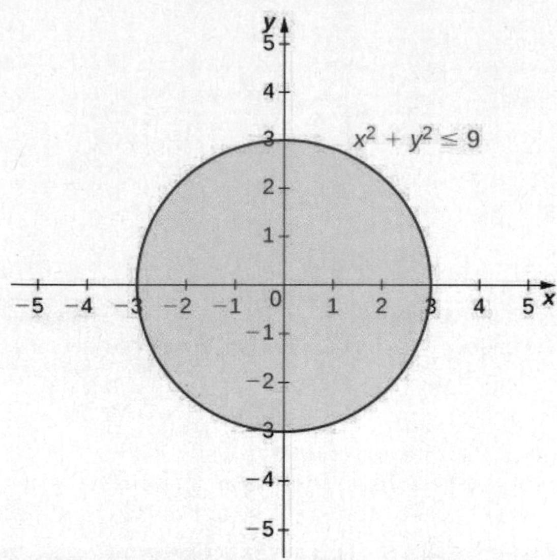

Figure 4.3 The domain of the function $g(x, y) = \sqrt{9 - x^2 - y^2}$ is a closed disk of radius 3.

To determine the range of $g(x, y) = \sqrt{9 - x^2 - y^2}$ we start with a point (x_0, y_0) on the boundary of the domain, which is defined by the relation $x^2 + y^2 = 9.$ It follows that $x_0^2 + y_0^2 = 9$ and

$$g(x_0, y_0) = \sqrt{9 - x_0^2 - y_0^2} = \sqrt{9 - \left(x_0^2 + y_0^2\right)} = \sqrt{9 - 9} = 0.$$

If $x_0^2 + y_0^2 = 0$ (in other words, $x_0 = y_0 = 0$), then

$$g(x_0, y_0) = \sqrt{9 - x_0^2 - y_0^2} = \sqrt{9 - \left(x_0^2 + y_0^2\right)} = \sqrt{9 - 0} = 3.$$

This is the maximum value of the function. Given any value c between 0 and 3, we can find an entire set of points inside the domain of g such that $g(x, y) = c$:

$$\begin{aligned} \sqrt{9 - x^2 - y^2} &= c \\ 9 - x^2 - y^2 &= c^2 \\ x^2 + y^2 &= 9 - c^2. \end{aligned}$$

Since $9 - c^2 > 0,$ this describes a circle of radius $\sqrt{9 - c^2}$ centered at the origin. Any point on this circle satisfies the equation $g(x, y) = c.$ Therefore, the range of this function can be written in interval notation as $[0, 3].$

4.1 Find the domain and range of the function $f(x, y) = \sqrt{36 - 9x^2 - 9y^2}.$

Graphing Functions of Two Variables

Suppose we wish to graph the function $z = (x, y)$. This function has two independent variables (x and y) and one dependent variable (z). When graphing a function $y = f(x)$ of one variable, we use the Cartesian plane. We are able to graph any ordered pair (x, y) in the plane, and every point in the plane has an ordered pair (x, y) associated with it. With a function of two variables, each ordered pair (x, y) in the domain of the function is mapped to a real number z. Therefore, the graph of the function f consists of ordered triples (x, y, z). The graph of a function $z = (x, y)$ of two variables is called a **surface**.

To understand more completely the concept of plotting a set of ordered triples to obtain a surface in three-dimensional space, imagine the (x, y) coordinate system laying flat. Then, every point in the domain of the function f has a unique z-value associated with it. If z is positive, then the graphed point is located above the xy-plane, if z is negative, then the graphed point is located below the xy-plane. The set of all the graphed points becomes the two-dimensional surface that is the graph of the function f.

Example 4.2

Graphing Functions of Two Variables

Create a graph of each of the following functions:

a. $g(x, y) = \sqrt{9 - x^2 - y^2}$

b. $f(x, y) = x^2 + y^2$

Solution

a. In **Example 4.1**, we determined that the domain of $g(x, y) = \sqrt{9 - x^2 - y^2}$ is $\{(x, y) \in \mathbb{R}^2 | x^2 + y^2 \le 9\}$ and the range is $\{z \in \mathbb{R}^2 | 0 \le z \le 3\}$. When $x^2 + y^2 = 9$ we have $g(x, y) = 0$. Therefore any point on the circle of radius 3 centered at the origin in the x, y-plane maps to $z = 0$ in $\mathbb{R}^3$. If $x^2 + y^2 = 8$, then $g(x, y) = 1$, so any point on the circle of radius $2\sqrt{2}$ centered at the origin in the x, y-plane maps to $z = 1$ in $\mathbb{R}^3$. As $x^2 + y^2$ gets closer to zero, the value of z approaches 3. When $x^2 + y^2 = 0$, then $g(x, y) = 3$. This is the origin in the x, y-plane. If $x^2 + y^2$ is equal to any other value between 0 and 9, then $g(x, y)$ equals some other constant between 0 and 3. The surface described by this function is a hemisphere centered at the origin with radius 3 as shown in the following graph.

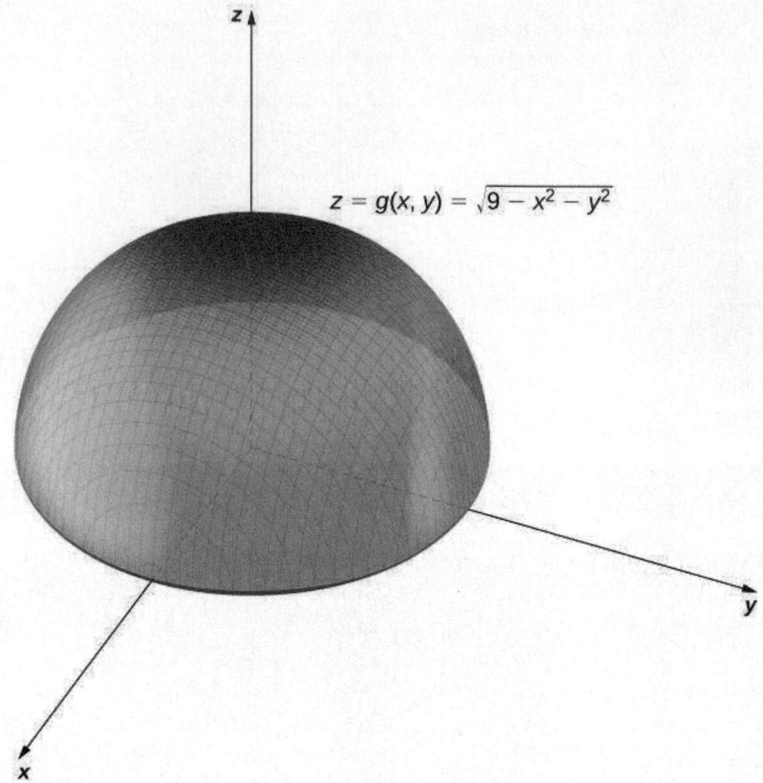

Figure 4.4 Graph of the hemisphere represented by the given function of two variables.

b. This function also contains the expression $x^2 + y^2$. Setting this expression equal to various values starting at zero, we obtain circles of increasing radius. The minimum value of $f(x, y) = x^2 + y^2$ is zero (attained when $x = y = 0.$). When $x = 0,$ the function becomes $z = y^2,$ and when $y = 0,$ then the function becomes $z = x^2$. These are cross-sections of the graph, and are parabolas. Recall from **Introduction to Vectors in Space** that the name of the graph of $f(x, y) = x^2 + y^2$ is a *paraboloid*. The graph of f appears in the following graph.

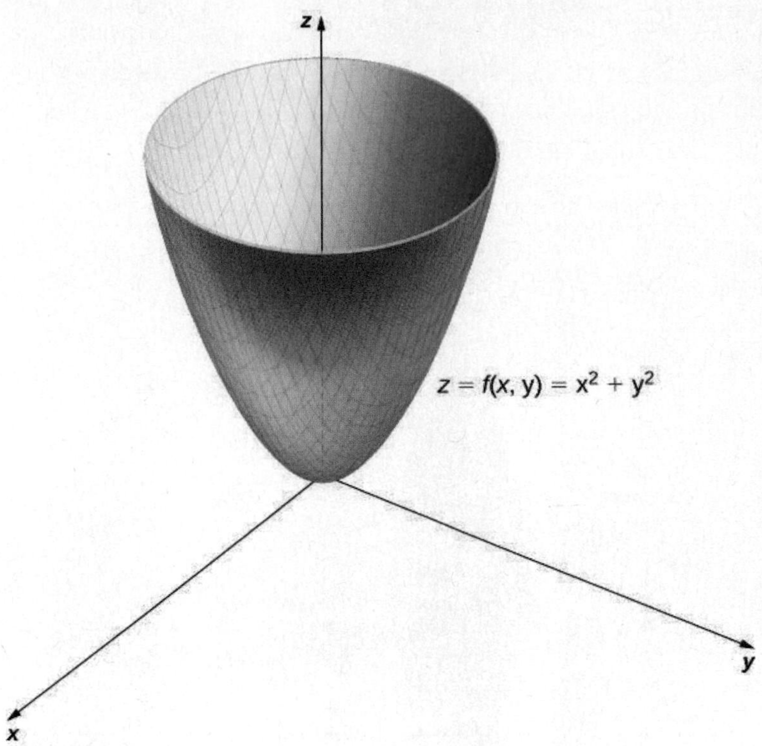

Figure 4.5 A paraboloid is the graph of the given function of two variables.

Example 4.3

Nuts and Bolts

A profit function for a hardware manufacturer is given by

$$f(x, y) = 16 - (x-3)^2 - (y-2)^2,$$

where x is the number of nuts sold per month (measured in thousands) and y represents the number of bolts sold per month (measured in thousands). Profit is measured in thousands of dollars. Sketch a graph of this function.

Solution

This function is a polynomial function in two variables. The domain of f consists of (x, y) coordinate pairs that yield a nonnegative profit:

$$16 - (x-3)^2 - (y-2)^2 \geq 0$$
$$(x-3)^2 + (y-2)^2 \leq 16.$$

This is a disk of radius 4 centered at $(3, 2)$. A further restriction is that both x and y must be nonnegative. When $x = 3$ and $y = 2$, $f(x, y) = 16$. Note that it is possible for either value to be a noninteger; for example, it is possible to sell 2.5 thousand nuts in a month. The domain, therefore, contains thousands of points, so we can consider all points within the disk. For any $z < 16,$ we can solve the equation $f(x, y) = 16:$

$$\begin{aligned} 16 - (x-3)^2 - (y-2)^2 &= z \\ (x-3)^2 + (y-2)^2 &= 16 - z. \end{aligned}$$

Since $z < 16,$ we know that $16 - z > 0,$ so the previous equation describes a circle with radius $\sqrt{16 - z}$ centered at the point $(3, 2)$. Therefore. the range of $f(x, y)$ is $\{z \in \mathbb{R} | z \le 16\}$. The graph of $f(x, y)$ is also a paraboloid, and this paraboloid points downward as shown.

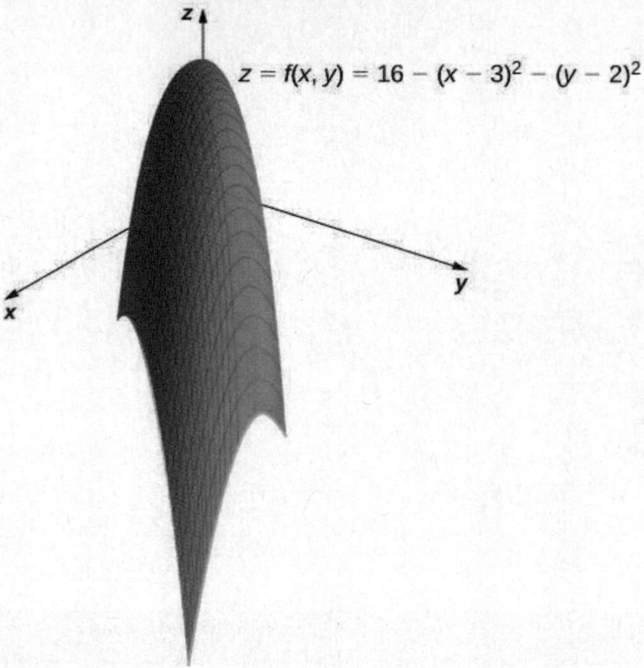

Figure 4.6 The graph of the given function of two variables is also a paraboloid.

Level Curves

If hikers walk along rugged trails, they might use a topographical map that shows how steeply the trails change. A topographical map contains curved lines called *contour lines*. Each contour line corresponds to the points on the map that have equal elevation (**Figure 4.7**). A level curve of a function of two variables $f(x, y)$ is completely analogous to a contour line on a topographical map.

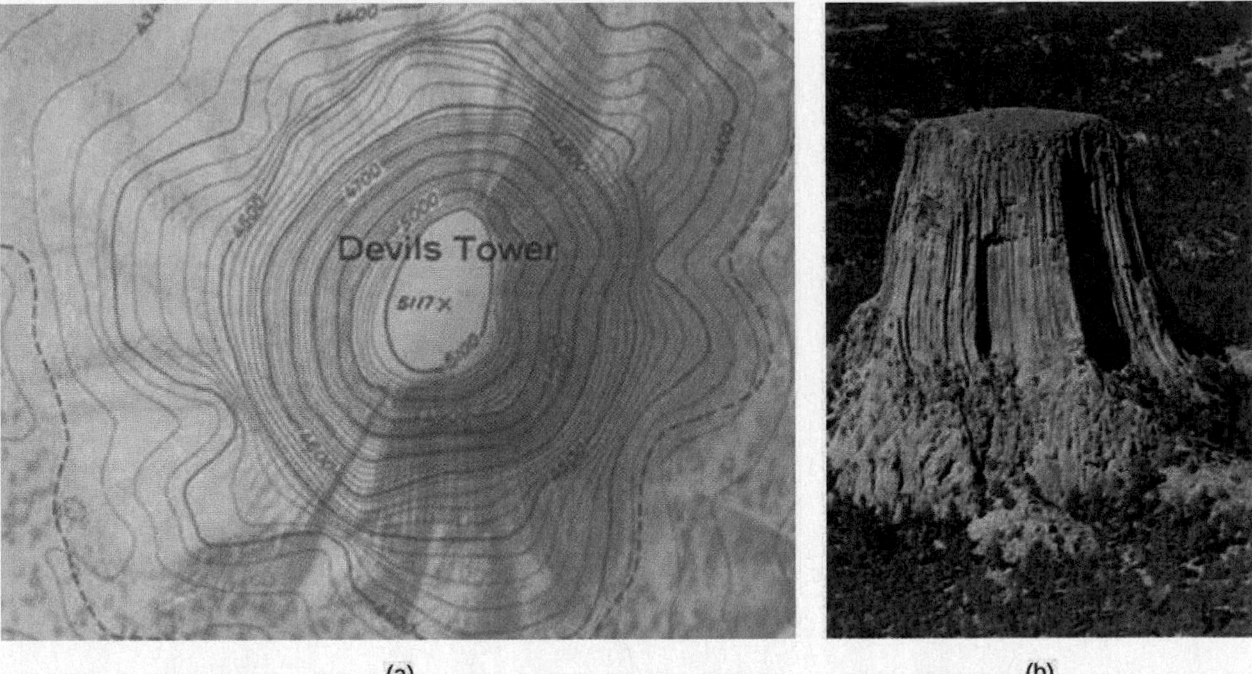

(a) (b)

Figure 4.7 (a) A topographical map of Devil's Tower, Wyoming. Lines that are close together indicate very steep terrain. (b) A perspective photo of Devil's Tower shows just how steep its sides are. Notice the top of the tower has the same shape as the center of the topographical map.

Definition

Given a function $f(x, y)$ and a number c in the range of f, a **level curve of a function of two variables** for the value c is defined to be the set of points satisfying the equation $f(x, y) = c$.

Returning to the function $g(x, y) = \sqrt{9 - x^2 - y^2}$, we can determine the level curves of this function. The range of g is the closed interval $[0, 3]$. First, we choose any number in this closed interval—say, $c = 2$. The level curve corresponding to $c = 2$ is described by the equation

$$\sqrt{9 - x^2 - y^2} = 2.$$

To simplify, square both sides of this equation:

$$9 - x^2 - y^2 = 4.$$

Now, multiply both sides of the equation by -1 and add 9 to each side:

$$x^2 + y^2 = 5.$$

This equation describes a circle centered at the origin with radius $\sqrt{5}$. Using values of c between 0 and 3 yields other circles also centered at the origin. If $c = 3$, then the circle has radius 0, so it consists solely of the origin. **Figure 4.8** is a graph of the level curves of this function corresponding to $c = 0, 1, 2,$ and 3. Note that in the previous derivation it may be possible that we introduced extra solutions by squaring both sides. This is not the case here because the range of the square root function is nonnegative.

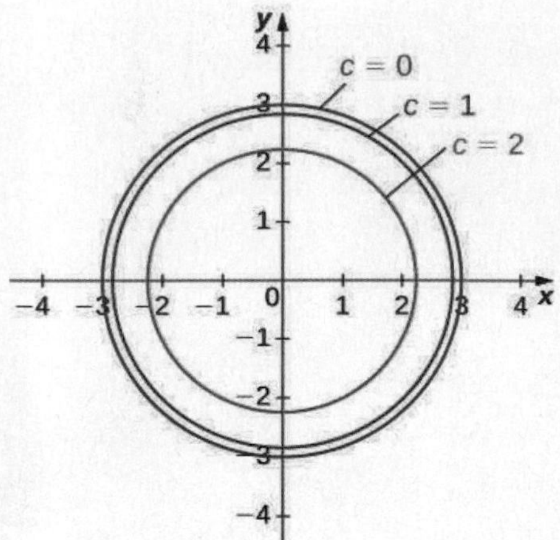

Figure 4.8 Level curves of the function $g(x, y) = \sqrt{9 - x^2 - y^2}$, using $c = 0, 1, 2,$ and 3 ($c = 3$ corresponds to the origin).

A graph of the various level curves of a function is called a **contour map**.

Example 4.4

Making a Contour Map

Given the function $f(x, y) = \sqrt{8 + 8x - 4y - 4x^2 - y^2}$, find the level curve corresponding to $c = 0$. Then create a contour map for this function. What are the domain and range of f?

Solution

To find the level curve for $c = 0$, we set $f(x, y) = 0$ and solve. This gives

$$0 = \sqrt{8 + 8x - 4y - 4x^2 - y^2}.$$

We then square both sides and multiply both sides of the equation by -1:

$$4x^2 + y^2 - 8x + 4y - 8 = 0.$$

Now, we rearrange the terms, putting the x terms together and the y terms together, and add 8 to each side:

$$4x^2 - 8x + y^2 + 4y = 8.$$

Next, we group the pairs of terms containing the same variable in parentheses, and factor 4 from the first pair:

$$4\left(x^2 - 2x\right) + \left(y^2 + 4y\right) = 8.$$

Then we complete the square in each pair of parentheses and add the correct value to the right-hand side:

$$4\left(x^2 - 2x + 1\right) + \left(y^2 + 4y + 4\right) = 8 + 4(1) + 4.$$

Next, we factor the left-hand side and simplify the right-hand side:

$$4(x - 1)^2 + (y + 2)^2 = 16.$$

Last, we divide both sides by 16:

$$\frac{(x-1)^2}{4} + \frac{(y+2)^2}{16} = 1. \tag{4.1}$$

This equation describes an ellipse centered at $(1, -2)$. The graph of this ellipse appears in the following graph.

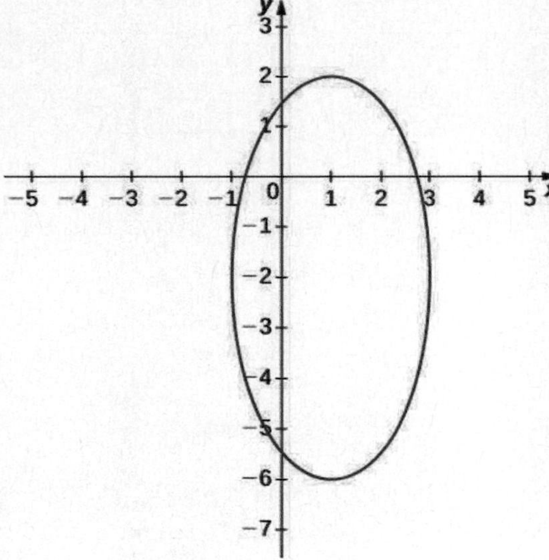

Figure 4.9 Level curve of the function $f(x, y) = \sqrt{8 + 8x - 4y - 4x^2 - y^2}$ corresponding to $c = 0$.

We can repeat the same derivation for values of c less than 4. Then, **Equation 4.1** becomes

$$\frac{4(x-1)^2}{16 - c^2} + \frac{(y+2)^2}{16 - c^2} = 1$$

for an arbitrary value of c. **Figure 4.10** shows a contour map for $f(x, y)$ using the values $c = 0, 1, 2,$ and 3. When $c = 4,$ the level curve is the point $(-1, 2)$.

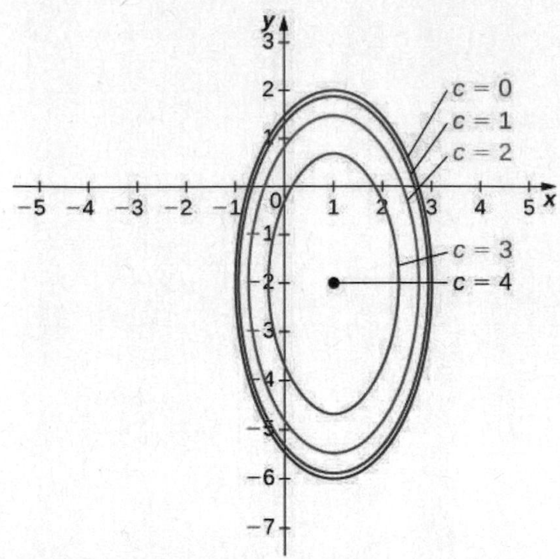

Figure 4.10 Contour map for the function $f(x, y) = \sqrt{8 + 8x - 4y - 4x^2 - y^2}$ using the values $c = 0,\ 1,\ 2,\ 3,$ and $4.$

4.2 Find and graph the level curve of the function $g(x, y) = x^2 + y^2 - 6x + 2y$ corresponding to $c = 15.$

Another useful tool for understanding the **graph of a function of two variables** is called a vertical trace. Level curves are always graphed in the xy-plane, but as their name implies, vertical traces are graphed in the xz- or yz-planes.

Definition

Consider a function $z = f(x, y)$ with domain $D \subseteq \mathbb{R}^2$. A **vertical trace** of the function can be either the set of points that solves the equation $f(a, y) = z$ for a given constant $x = a$ or $f(x, b) = z$ for a given constant $y = b$.

Example 4.5

Finding Vertical Traces

Find vertical traces for the function $f(x, y) = \sin x \cos y$ corresponding to $x = -\frac{\pi}{4},\ 0,$ and $\frac{\pi}{4},$ and $y = -\frac{\pi}{4},\ 0,$ and $\frac{\pi}{4}.$

Solution

First set $x = -\frac{\pi}{4}$ in the equation $z = \sin x \cos y$:

$$z = \sin\left(-\frac{\pi}{4}\right)\cos y = -\frac{\sqrt{2}\cos y}{2} \approx -0.7071 \cos y.$$

This describes a cosine graph in the plane $x = -\frac{\pi}{4}$. The other values of z appear in the following table.

c	***Vertical Trace for*** $x = c$
$-\frac{\pi}{4}$	$z = -\frac{\sqrt{2}\cos y}{2}$
0	$z = 0$
$\frac{\pi}{4}$	$z = \frac{\sqrt{2}\cos y}{2}$

Table 4.1
Vertical Traces Parallel to the xz-Plane for the Function $f(x, y) = \sin x \cos y$

In a similar fashion, we can substitute the y-values in the equation $f(x, y)$ to obtain the traces in the yz-plane, as listed in the following table.

d	***Vertical Trace for*** $y = d$
$-\frac{\pi}{4}$	$z = -\frac{\sqrt{2}\sin x}{2}$
0	$z = \sin x$
$\frac{\pi}{4}$	$z = \frac{\sqrt{2}\sin x}{2}$

Table 4.2
Vertical Traces Parallel to the yz-Plane for the Function $f(x, y) = \sin x \cos y$

The three traces in the xz-plane are cosine functions; the three traces in the yz-plane are sine functions. These curves appear in the intersections of the surface with the planes $x = -\frac{\pi}{4}, x = 0, x = \frac{\pi}{4}$ and $y = -\frac{\pi}{4}, y = 0, y = \frac{\pi}{4}$ as shown in the following figure.

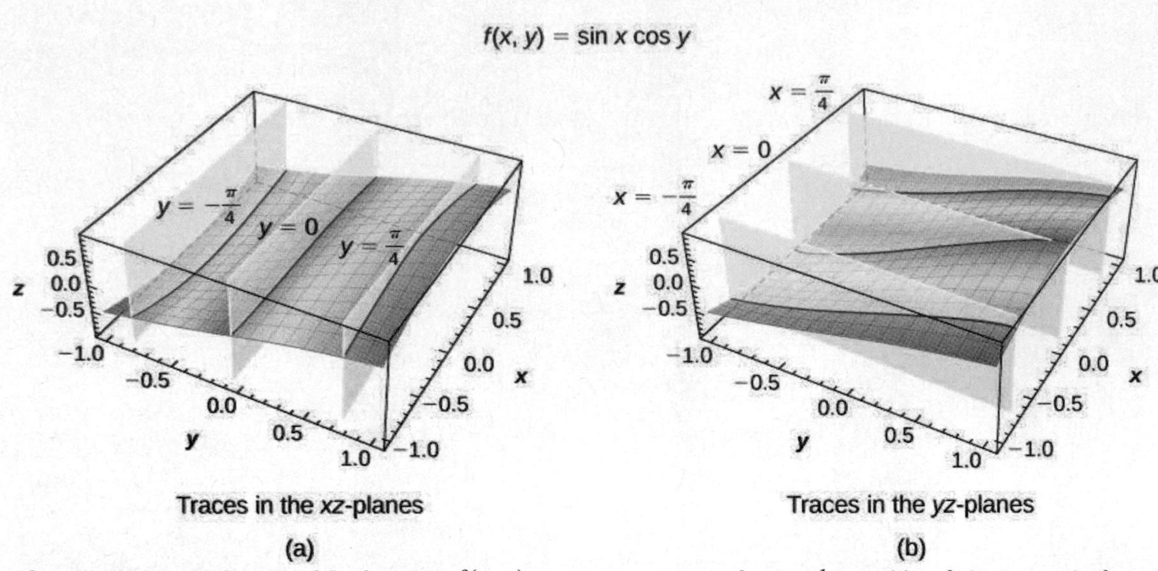

Figure 4.11 Vertical traces of the function $f(x, y)$ are cosine curves in the xz-planes (a) and sine curves in the yz-planes (b).

4.3 Determine the equation of the vertical trace of the function $g(x, y) = -x^2 - y^2 + 2x + 4y - 1$ corresponding to $y = 3,$ and describe its graph.

Functions of two variables can produce some striking-looking surfaces. The following figure shows two examples.

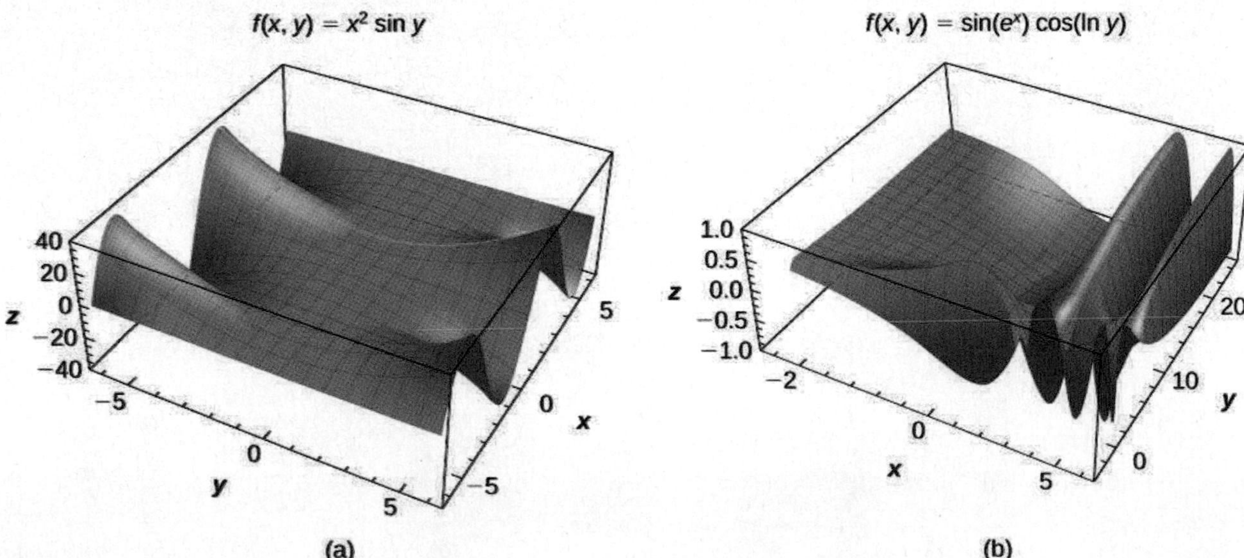

Figure 4.12 Examples of surfaces representing functions of two variables: (a) a combination of a power function and a sine function and (b) a combination of trigonometric, exponential, and logarithmic functions.

Functions of More Than Two Variables

So far, we have examined only functions of two variables. However, it is useful to take a brief look at functions of more than two variables. Two such examples are

$$f(x, y, z) = x^2 - 2xy + y^2 + 3yz - z^2 + 4x - 2y + 3x - 6 \text{ (a polynomial in three variables)}$$

and

$$g(x, y, t) = (x^2 - 4xy + y^2)\sin t - (3x + 5y)\cos t.$$

In the first function, (x, y, z) represents a point in space, and the function f maps each point in space to a fourth quantity, such as temperature or wind speed. In the second function, (x, y) can represent a point in the plane, and t can represent time. The function might map a point in the plane to a third quantity (for example, pressure) at a given time t. The method for finding the domain of a function of more than two variables is analogous to the method for functions of one or two variables.

Example 4.6

Domains for Functions of Three Variables

Find the domain of each of the following functions:

a. $f(x, y, z) = \dfrac{3x - 4y + 2z}{\sqrt{9 - x^2 - y^2 - z^2}}$

b. $g(x, y, t) = \dfrac{\sqrt{2t - 4}}{x^2 - y^2}$

Solution

a. For the function $f(x, y, z) = \dfrac{3x - 4y + 2z}{\sqrt{9 - x^2 - y^2 - z^2}}$ to be defined (and be a real value), two conditions must hold:

1. The denominator cannot be zero.
2. The radicand cannot be negative.

Combining these conditions leads to the inequality

$$9 - x^2 - y^2 - z^2 > 0.$$

Moving the variables to the other side and reversing the inequality gives the domain as

$$\text{domain}(f) = \{(x, y, z) \in \mathbb{R}^3 \mid x^2 + y^2 + z^2 < 9\},$$

which describes a ball of radius 3 centered at the origin. (*Note*: The surface of the ball is not included in this domain.)

b. For the function $g(x, y, t) = \dfrac{\sqrt{2t - 4}}{x^2 - y^2}$ to be defined (and be a real value), two conditions must hold:

1. The radicand cannot be negative.
2. The denominator cannot be zero.

Since the radicand cannot be negative, this implies $2t - 4 \geq 0$, and therefore that $t \geq 2$. Since the denominator cannot be zero, $x^2 - y^2 \neq 0$, or $x^2 \neq y^2$, Which can be rewritten as $y = \pm x$, which are the equations of two lines passing through the origin. Therefore, the domain of g is

$$\text{domain}(g) = \{(x, y, t) \mid y \neq \pm x, t \geq 2\}.$$

4.4 Find the domain of the function $h(x, y, t) = (3t - 6)\sqrt{y - 4x^2 + 4}.$

Functions of two variables have level curves, which are shown as curves in the xy-plane. However, when the function has three variables, the curves become surfaces, so we can define level surfaces for functions of three variables.

Definition

Given a function $f(x, y, z)$ and a number c in the range of f, a **level surface of a function of three variables** is defined to be the set of points satisfying the equation $f(x, y, z) = c.$

Example 4.7

Finding a Level Surface

Find the level surface for the function $f(x, y, z) = 4x^2 + 9y^2 - z^2$ corresponding to $c = 1.$

Solution

The level surface is defined by the equation $4x^2 + 9y^2 - z^2 = 1.$ This equation describes a hyperboloid of one sheet as shown in the following figure.

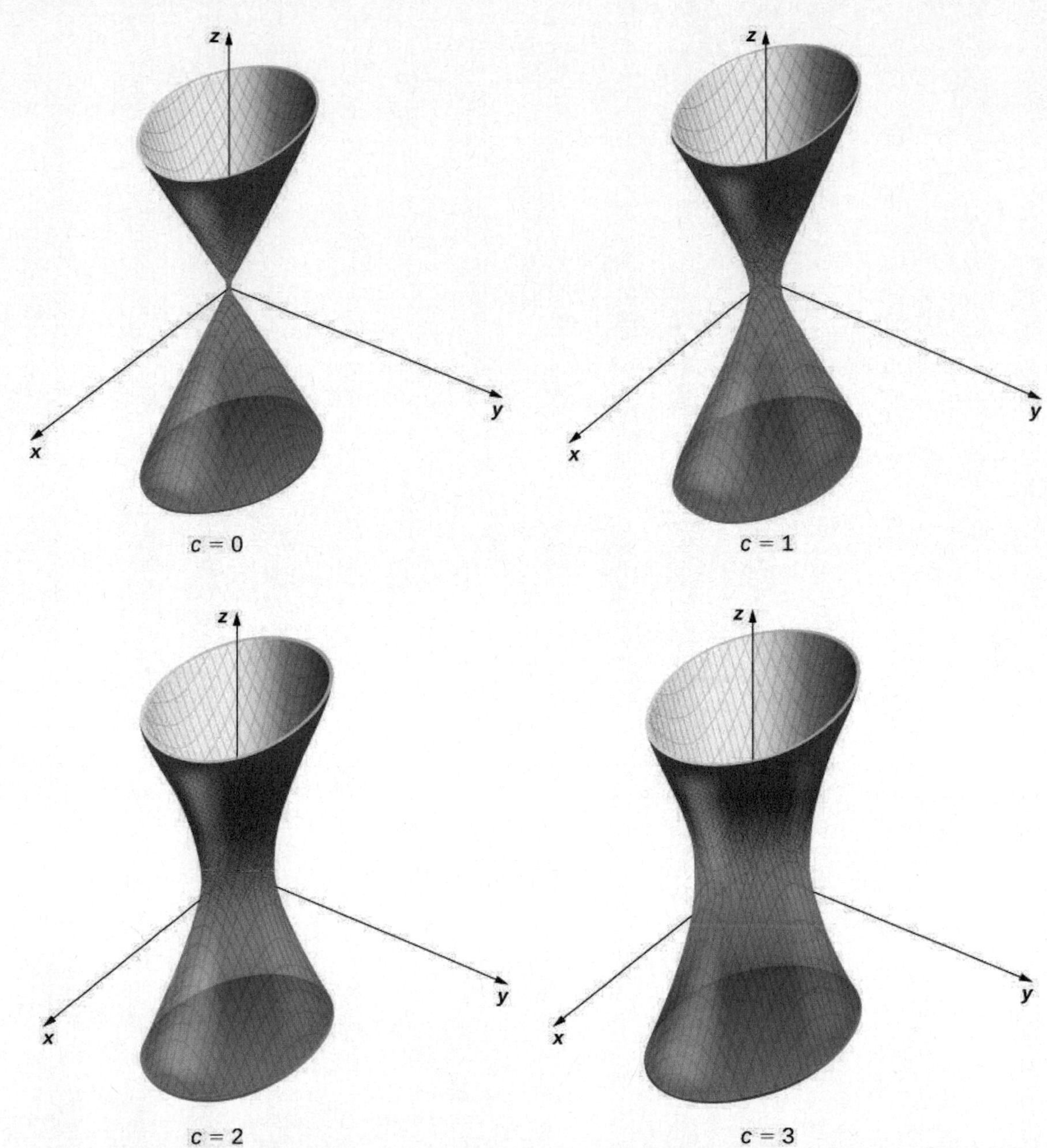

Figure 4.13 A hyperboloid of one sheet with some of its level surfaces.

4.5 Find the equation of the level surface of the function

$$g(x,\ y,\ z) = x^2 + y^2 + z^2 - 2x + 4y - 6z$$

corresponding to $c = 2,$ and describe the surface, if possible.

4.1 EXERCISES

For the following exercises, evaluate each function at the indicated values.

1. $W(x, y) = 4x^2 + y^2$. Find $W(2, -1)$, $W(-3, 6)$.

2. $W(x, y) = 4x^2 + y^2$. Find $W(2 + h, 3 + h)$.

3. The volume of a right circular cylinder is calculated by a function of two variables, $V(x, y) = \pi x^2 y$, where x is the radius of the right circular cylinder and y represents the height of the cylinder. Evaluate $V(2, 5)$ and explain what this means.

4. An oxygen tank is constructed of a right cylinder of height y and radius x with two hemispheres of radius x mounted on the top and bottom of the cylinder. Express the volume of the cylinder as a function of two variables, x and y, find $V(10, 2)$, and explain what this means.

For the following exercises, find the domain of the function.

5. $V(x, y) = 4x^2 + y^2$

6. $f(x, y) = \sqrt{x^2 + y^2 - 4}$

7. $f(x, y) = 4\ln(y^2 - x)$

8. $g(x, y) = \sqrt{16 - 4x^2 - y^2}$

9. $z(x, y) = y^2 - x^2$

10. $f(x, y) = \dfrac{y + 2}{x^2}$

Find the range of the functions.

11. $g(x, y) = \sqrt{16 - 4x^2 - y^2}$

12. $V(x, y) = 4x^2 + y^2$

13. $z = y^2 - x^2$

For the following exercises, find the level curves of each function at the indicated value of c to visualize the given function.

14. $z(x, y) = y^2 - x^2, \quad c = 1$

15. $z(x, y) = y^2 - x^2, \quad c = 4$

16. $g(x, y) = x^2 + y^2;\ c = 4,\ c = 9$

17. $g(x, y) = 4 - x - y;\ c = 0, 4$

18. $f(x, y) = xy;\ c = 1;\ c = -1$

19. $h(x, y) = 2x - y;\ c = 0, -2, 2$

20. $f(x, y) = x^2 - y;\ c = 1, 2$

21. $g(x, y) = \dfrac{x}{x + y};\ c = -1, 0, 2$

22. $g(x, y) = x^3 - y;\ c = -1, 0, 2$

23. $g(x, y) = e^{xy};\ c = \dfrac{1}{2}, 3$

24. $f(x, y) = x^2;\ c = 4, 9$

25. $f(x, y) = xy - x;\ c = -2, 0, 2$

26. $h(x, y) = \ln(x^2 + y^2);\ c = -1, 0, 1$

27. $g(x, y) = \ln\left(\dfrac{y}{x^2}\right);\ c = -2, 0, 2$

28. $z = f(x, y) = \sqrt{x^2 + y^2}, \quad c = 3$

29. $f(x, y) = \dfrac{y + 2}{x^2}, \quad c =$ any constant

For the following exercises, find the vertical traces of the functions at the indicated values of x and y, and plot the traces.

30. $z = 4 - x - y;\ x = 2$

31. $f(x, y) = 3x + y^3,\ x = 1$

32. $z = \cos\sqrt{x^2 + y^2} \quad x = 1$

Find the domain of the following functions.

33. $z = \sqrt{100 - 4x^2 - 25y^2}$

34. $z = \ln\left(x - y^2\right)$

35. $f(x, y, z) = \frac{1}{\sqrt{36 - 4x^2 - 9y^2 - z^2}}$

36. $f(x, y, z) = \sqrt{49 - x^2 - y^2 - z^2}$

37. $f(x, y, z) = \sqrt[3]{16 - x^2 - y^2 - z^2}$

38. $f(x, y) = \cos\sqrt{x^2 + y^2}$

For the following exercises, plot a graph of the function.

39. $z = f(x, y) = \sqrt{x^2 + y^2}$

40. $z = x^2 + y^2$

41. Use technology to graph $z = x^2 y$.

Sketch the following by finding the level curves. Verify the graph using technology.

42. $f(x, y) = \sqrt{4 - x^2 - y^2}$

43. $f(x, y) = 2 - \sqrt{x^2 + y^2}$

44. $z = 1 + e^{-x^2 - y^2}$

45. $z = \cos\sqrt{x^2 + y^2}$

46. $z = y^2 - x^2$

47. Describe the contour lines for several values of c for $z = x^2 + y^2 - 2x - 2y$.

Find the level surface for the functions of three variables and describe it.

48. $w(x, y, z) = x - 2y + z,\ c = 4$

49. $w(x, y, z) = x^2 + y^2 + z^2,\ c = 9$

50. $w(x, y, z) = x^2 + y^2 - z^2,\ c = -4$

51. $w(x, y, z) = x^2 + y^2 - z^2,\ c = 4$

52. $w(x, y, z) = 9x^2 - 4y^2 + 36z^2,\ c = 0$

For the following exercises, find an equation of the level curve of f that contains the point P.

53. $f(x, y) = 1 - 4x^2 - y^2,\ P(0, 1)$

54. $g(x, y) = y^2 \arctan x,\ P(1, 2)$

55. $g(x, y) = e^{xy}(x^2 + y^2),\ P(1, 0)$

56. The strength E of an electric field at point (x, y, z) resulting from an infinitely long charged wire lying along the y-axis is given by $E(x, y, z) = k/\sqrt{x^2 + y^2}$, where k is a positive constant. For simplicity, let $k = 1$ and find the equations of the level surfaces for $E = 10$ and $E = 100$.

57. A thin plate made of iron is located in the xy-plane. The temperature T in degrees Celsius at a point $P(x, y)$ is inversely proportional to the square of its distance from the origin. Express T as a function of x and y.

58. Refer to the preceding problem. Using the temperature function found there, determine the proportionality constant if the temperature at point $P(1, 2)$ *is* 50°C. Use this constant to determine the temperature at point $Q(3, 4)$.

59. Refer to the preceding problem. Find the level curves for $T = 40°\text{C}$ and $T = 100°\text{C}$, and describe what the level curves represent.

4.2 | Limits and Continuity

Learning Objectives

4.2.1 Calculate the limit of a function of two variables.

4.2.2 Learn how a function of two variables can approach different values at a boundary point, depending on the path of approach.

4.2.3 State the conditions for continuity of a function of two variables.

4.2.4 Verify the continuity of a function of two variables at a point.

4.2.5 Calculate the limit of a function of three or more variables and verify the continuity of the function at a point.

We have now examined functions of more than one variable and seen how to graph them. In this section, we see how to take the limit of a function of more than one variable, and what it means for a function of more than one variable to be continuous at a point in its domain. It turns out these concepts have aspects that just don't occur with functions of one variable.

Limit of a Function of Two Variables

Recall from Section 2.2 the definition of a limit of a function of one variable:

Let $f(x)$ be defined for all $x \neq a$ in an open interval containing a. Let L be a real number. Then

$$\lim_{x \to a} f(x) = L$$

if for every $\varepsilon > 0,$ there exists a $\delta > 0,$ such that if $0 < |x - a| < \delta$ for all x in the domain of $f,$ then

$$|f(x) - L| > \varepsilon.$$

Before we can adapt this definition to define a limit of a function of two variables, we first need to see how to extend the idea of an open interval in one variable to an open interval in two variables.

Definition

Consider a point $(a, b) \in \mathbb{R}^2$. A **δ disk** centered at point (a, b) is defined to be an open disk of radius δ centered at point (a, b)—that is,

$$\left\{(x, y) \in \mathbb{R}^2 \middle| (x - a)^2 + (y - b)^2 < \delta^2\right\}$$

as shown in the following graph.

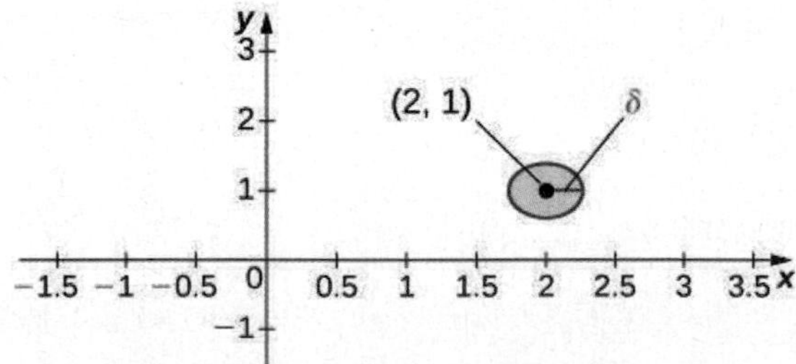

Figure 4.14 A δ disk centered around the point $(2, 1)$.

The idea of a δ disk appears in the definition of the limit of a function of two variables. If δ is small, then all the points (x, y) in the δ disk are close to (a, b). This is completely analogous to x being close to a in the definition of a limit of a function of one variable. In one dimension, we express this restriction as

$$a - \delta < x < a + \delta.$$

In more than one dimension, we use a δ disk.

Definition

Let f be a function of two variables, x and y. The limit of $f(x, y)$ as (x, y) approaches (a, b) is L, written

$$\lim_{(x, y) \to (a, b)} f(x, y) = L$$

if for each $\varepsilon > 0$ there exists a small enough $\delta > 0$ such that for all points (x, y) in a δ disk around (a, b), except possibly for (a, b) itself, the value of $f(x, y)$ is no more than ε away from L (**Figure 4.15**). Using symbols, we write the following: For any $\varepsilon > 0$, there exists a number $\delta > 0$ such that

$$|f(x, y) - L| < \varepsilon \text{ whenever } 0 < \sqrt{(x-a)^2 + (y-b)^2} < \delta.$$

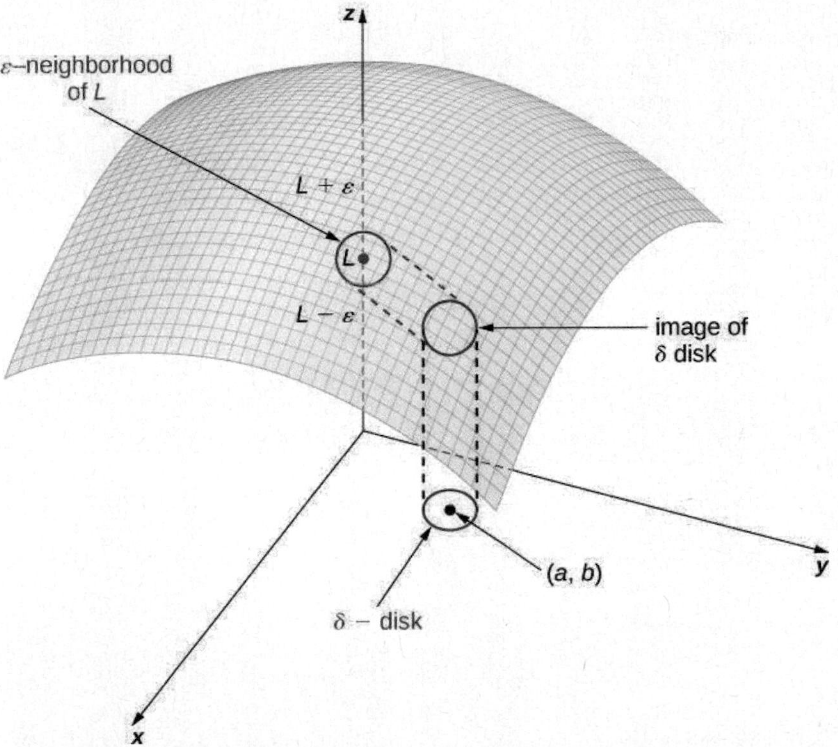

Figure 4.15 The limit of a function involving two variables requires that $f(x, y)$ be within ε of L whenever (x, y) is within δ of (a, b). The smaller the value of ε, the smaller the value of δ.

Proving that a limit exists using the definition of a limit of a function of two variables can be challenging. Instead, we use the following theorem, which gives us shortcuts to finding limits. The formulas in this theorem are an extension of the formulas in the limit laws theorem in **The Limit Laws (http://cnx.org/content/m53492/latest/)** .

Theorem 4.1: Limit laws for functions of two variables

Let $f(x, y)$ and $g(x, y)$ be defined for all $(x, y) \neq (a, b)$ in a neighborhood around (a, b), and assume the neighborhood is contained completely inside the domain of f. Assume that L and M are real numbers such that $\lim_{(x, y) \to (a, b)} f(x, y) = L$ and $\lim_{(x, y) \to (a, b)} g(x, y) = M$, and let c be a constant. Then each of the following statements holds:

Constant Law:

$$\lim_{(x, y) \to (a, b)} c = c \tag{4.2}$$

Identity Laws:

$$\lim_{(x, y) \to (a, b)} x = a \tag{4.3}$$

$$\lim_{(x, y) \to (a, b)} y = b \tag{4.4}$$

Sum Law:

$$\lim_{(x, y) \to (a, b)} (f(x, y) + g(x, y)) = L + M \tag{4.5}$$

Difference Law:

$$\lim_{(x, y) \to (a, b)} (f(x, y) - g(x, y)) = L - M \tag{4.6}$$

Constant Multiple Law:

$$\lim_{(x, y) \to (a, b)} (cf(x, y)) = cL \tag{4.7}$$

Product Law:

$$\lim_{(x, y) \to (a, b)} (f(x, y)g(x, y)) = LM \tag{4.8}$$

Quotient Law:

$$\lim_{(x, y) \to (a, b)} \frac{f(x, y)}{g(x, y)} = \frac{L}{M} \text{ for } M \neq 0 \tag{4.9}$$

Power Law:

$$\lim_{(x, y) \to (a, b)} (f(x, y))^n = L^n \tag{4.10}$$

for any positive integer n.

Root Law:

$$\lim_{(x, y) \to (a, b)} \sqrt[n]{f(x, y)} = \sqrt[n]{L} \tag{4.11}$$

for all L if n is odd and positive, and for $L \geq 0$ if n is even and positive.

The proofs of these properties are similar to those for the limits of functions of one variable. We can apply these laws to finding limits of various functions.

Example 4.8

Finding the Limit of a Function of Two Variables

Find each of the following limits:

a. $\lim_{(x, y) \to (2, -1)} \left(x^2 - 2xy + 3y^2 - 4x + 3y - 6\right)$

b. $\lim_{(x, y) \to (2, -1)} \frac{2x + 3y}{4x - 3y}$

Solution

a. First use the sum and difference laws to separate the terms:

$$\begin{aligned}&\lim_{(x, y) \to (2, -1)} \left(x^2 - 2xy + 3y^2 - 4x + 3y - 6\right) \\ &= \left(\lim_{(x, y) \to (2, -1)} x^2\right) - \left(\lim_{(x, y) \to (2, -1)} 2xy\right) + \left(\lim_{(x, y) \to (2, -1)} 3y^2\right) - \left(\lim_{(x, y) \to (2, -1)} 4x\right) \\ &\quad + \left(\lim_{(x, y) \to (2, -1)} 3y\right) - \left(\lim_{(x, y) \to (2, -1)} 6\right).\end{aligned}$$

Next, use the constant multiple law on the second, third, fourth, and fifth limits:

$$\begin{aligned}&= \left(\lim_{(x, y) \to (2, -1)} x^2\right) - 2\left(\lim_{(x, y) \to (2, -1)} xy\right) + 3\left(\lim_{(x, y) \to (2, -1)} y^2\right) - 4\left(\lim_{(x, y) \to (2, -1)} x\right) \\ &\quad + 3\left(\lim_{(x, y) \to (2, -1)} y\right) - \lim_{(x, y) \to (2, -1)} 6.\end{aligned}$$

Now, use the power law on the first and third limits, and the product law on the second limit:

$$\begin{aligned}&= \left(\lim_{(x, y) \to (2, -1)} x\right)^2 - 2\left(\lim_{(x, y) \to (2, -1)} x\right)\left(\lim_{(x, y) \to (2, -1)} y\right) + 3\left(\lim_{(x, y) \to (2, -1)} y\right)^2 \\ &\quad - 4\left(\lim_{(x, y) \to (2, -1)} x\right) + 3\left(\lim_{(x, y) \to (2, -1)} y\right) - \lim_{(x, y) \to (2, -1)} 6.\end{aligned}$$

Last, use the identity laws on the first six limits and the constant law on the last limit:

$$\begin{aligned}\lim_{(x, y) \to (2, -1)} \left(x^2 - 2xy + 3y^2 - 4x + 3y - 6\right) &= (2)^2 - 2(2)(-1) + 3(-1)^2 - 4(2) + 3(-1) - 6 \\ &= -6.\end{aligned}$$

b. Before applying the quotient law, we need to verify that the limit of the denominator is nonzero. Using the difference law, constant multiple law, and identity law,

$$\begin{aligned}\lim_{(x, y) \to (2, -1)} (4x - 3y) &= \lim_{(x, y) \to (2, -1)} 4x - \lim_{(x, y) \to (2, -1)} 3y \\ &= 4\left(\lim_{(x, y) \to (2, -1)} x\right) - 3\left(\lim_{(x, y) \to (2, -1)} y\right) \\ &= 4(2) - 3(-1) = 11.\end{aligned}$$

Since the limit of the denominator is nonzero, the quotient law applies. We now calculate the limit of the numerator using the difference law, constant multiple law, and identity law:

$$\begin{aligned}\lim_{(x, y) \to (2, -1)} (2x + 3y) &= \lim_{(x, y) \to (2, -1)} 2x + \lim_{(x, y) \to (2, -1)} 3y \\ &= 2\left(\lim_{(x, y) \to (2, -1)} x\right) + 3\left(\lim_{(x, y) \to (2, -1)} y\right) \\ &= 2(2) + 3(-1) \\ &= 1.\end{aligned}$$

Therefore, according to the quotient law we have

$$\lim_{(x,\,y)\to(2,\,-1)} \frac{2x+3y}{4x-3y} = \frac{\lim_{(x,\,y)\to(2,\,-1)}(2x+3y)}{\lim_{(x,\,y)\to(2,\,-1)}(4x-3y)} = \frac{1}{11}.$$

4.6 Evaluate the following limit:

$$\lim_{(x,\,y)\to(5,\,-2)} \sqrt[3]{\frac{x^2-y}{y^2+x-1}}.$$

Since we are taking the limit of a function of two variables, the point $(a,\,b)$ is in $\mathbb{R}^2$, and it is possible to approach this point from an infinite number of directions. Sometimes when calculating a limit, the answer varies depending on the path taken toward $(a,\,b)$. If this is the case, then the limit fails to exist. In other words, the limit must be unique, regardless of path taken.

Example 4.9

Limits That Fail to Exist

Show that neither of the following limits exist:

a. $\lim_{(x,\,y)\to(0,\,0)} \frac{2xy}{3x^2+y^2}$

b. $\lim_{(x,\,y)\to(0,\,0)} \frac{4xy^2}{x^2+3y^4}$

Solution

a. The domain of the function $f(x,\,y) = \frac{2xy}{3x^2+y^2}$ consists of all points in the xy-plane except for the point $(0,\,0)$ (**Figure 4.16**). To show that the limit does not exist as $(x,\,y)$ approaches $(0,\,0)$, we note that it is impossible to satisfy the definition of a limit of a function of two variables because of the fact that the function takes different values along different lines passing through point $(0,\,0)$. First, consider the line $y=0$ in the xy-plane. Substituting $y=0$ into $f(x,\,y)$ gives

$$f(x,\,0) = \frac{2x(0)}{3x^2+0^2} = 0$$

for any value of x. Therefore the value of f remains constant for any point on the x-axis, and as y approaches zero, the function remains fixed at zero.
Next, consider the line $y=x$. Substituting $y=x$ into $f(x,\,y)$ gives

$$f(x,\,x) = \frac{2x(x)}{3x^2+x^2} = \frac{2x^2}{4x^2} = \frac{1}{2}.$$

This is true for any point on the line $y=x$. If we let x approach zero while staying on this line, the value of the function remains fixed at $\frac{1}{2}$, regardless of how small x is.

Choose a value for ε that is less than $1/2$—say, $1/4$. Then, no matter how small a δ disk we draw around $(0, 0)$, the values of $f(x, y)$ for points inside that δ disk will include both 0 and $\frac{1}{2}$. Therefore, the definition of limit at a point is never satisfied and the limit fails to exist.

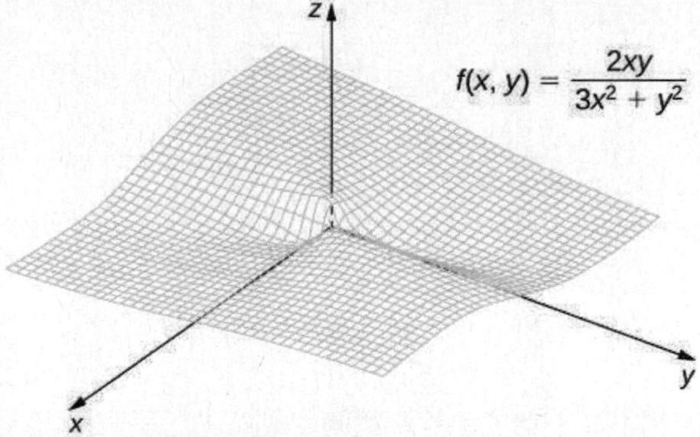

Figure 4.16 Graph of the function $f(x, y) = (2xy)/(3x^2 + y^2)$. Along the line $y = 0$, the function is equal to zero; along the line $y = x$, the function is equal to $\frac{1}{2}$.

In a similar fashion to a., we can approach the origin along any straight line passing through the origin. If we try the x-axis (i.e., $y = 0$), then the function remains fixed at zero. The same is true for the y-axis. Suppose we approach the origin along a straight line of slope k. The equation of this line is $y = kx$. Then the limit becomes

$$\begin{aligned}
\lim_{(x, y) \to (0, 0)} \frac{4xy^2}{x^2 + 3y^4} &= \lim_{(x, y) \to (0, 0)} \frac{4x(kx)^2}{x^2 + 3(kx)^4} \\
&= \lim_{(x, y) \to (0, 0)} \frac{4k^2x^3}{x^2 + 3k^4x^4} \\
&= \lim_{(x, y) \to (0, 0)} \frac{4k^2x}{1 + 3k^4x^2} \\
&= \frac{\lim_{(x, y) \to (0, 0)} (4k^2x)}{\lim_{(x, y) \to (0, 0)} (1 + 3k^4x^2)} \\
&= 0
\end{aligned}$$

regardless of the value of k. It would seem that the limit is equal to zero. What if we chose a curve passing through the origin instead? For example, we can consider the parabola given by the equation $x = y^2$. Substituting y^2 in place of x in $f(x, y)$ gives

$$\begin{aligned}\lim_{(x,\,y)\to(0,\,0)}\frac{4xy^2}{x^2+3y^4} &= \lim_{(x,\,y)\to(0,\,0)}\frac{4(y^2)y^2}{(y^2)^2+3y^4}\\ &= \lim_{(x,\,y)\to(0,\,0)}\frac{4y^4}{y^4+3y^4}\\ &= \lim_{(x,\,y)\to(0,\,0)} 1\\ &= 1.\end{aligned}$$

By the same logic in a., it is impossible to find a δ disk around the origin that satisfies the definition of the limit for any value of $\varepsilon < 1$. Therefore, $\lim_{(x,\,y)\to(0,\,0)}\frac{4xy^2}{x^2+3y^4}$ does not exist.

4.7 Show that

$$\lim_{(x,\,y)\to(2,\,1)}\frac{(x-2)(y-1)}{(x-2)^2+(y-1)^2}$$

does not exist.

Interior Points and Boundary Points

To study continuity and differentiability of a function of two or more variables, we first need to learn some new terminology.

Definition

Let S be a subset of $\mathbb{R}^2$ (**Figure 4.17**).

1. A point P_0 is called an **interior point** of S if there is a δ disk centered around P_0 contained completely in S.
2. A point P_0 is called a **boundary point** of S if every δ disk centered around P_0 contains points both inside and outside S.

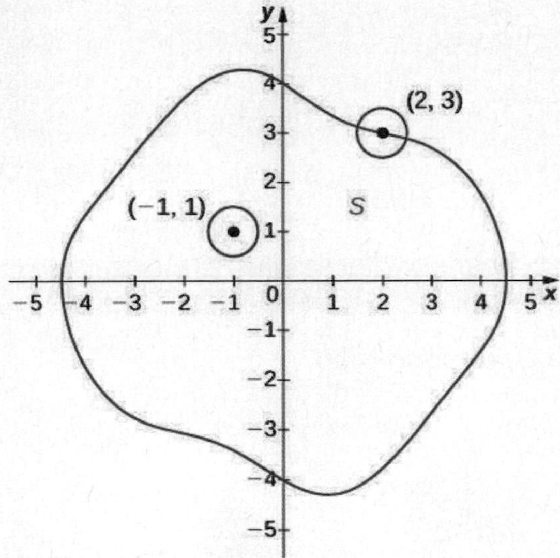

Figure 4.17 In the set S shown, $(-1,\ 1)$ is an interior point and $(2,\ 3)$ is a boundary point.

Definition

Let S be a subset of $\mathbb{R}^2$ (**Figure 4.17**).

1. S is called an **open set** if every point of S is an interior point.
2. S is called a **closed set** if it contains all its boundary points.

An example of an open set is a δ disk. If we include the boundary of the disk, then it becomes a closed set. A set that contains some, but not all, of its boundary points is neither open nor closed. For example if we include half the boundary of a δ disk but not the other half, then the set is neither open nor closed.

Definition

Let S be a subset of $\mathbb{R}^2$ (**Figure 4.17**).

1. An open set S is a **connected set** if it cannot be represented as the union of two or more disjoint, nonempty open subsets.
2. A set S is a **region** if it is open, connected, and nonempty.

The definition of a limit of a function of two variables requires the δ disk to be contained inside the domain of the function. However, if we wish to find the limit of a function at a boundary point of the domain, the δ disk is not contained inside the domain. By definition, some of the points of the δ disk are inside the domain and some are outside. Therefore, we need only consider points that are inside both the δ disk and the domain of the function. This leads to the definition of the limit of a function at a boundary point.

Definition

Let f be a function of two variables, x and y, and suppose $(a,\ b)$ is on the boundary of the domain of f. Then, the limit of $f(x,\ y)$ as $(x,\ y)$ approaches $(a,\ b)$ is L, written

$$\lim_{(x,\ y) \to (a,\ b)} f(x,\ y) = L,$$

if for any $\varepsilon > 0,$ there exists a number $\delta > 0$ such that for any point (x, y) inside the domain of f and within a suitably small distance positive δ of $(a, b),$ the value of $f(x, y)$ is no more than ε away from L (**Figure 4.15**). Using symbols, we can write: For any $\varepsilon > 0,$ there exists a number $\delta > 0$ such that

$$|f(x, y) - L| < \varepsilon \text{ whenever } 0 < \sqrt{(x-a)^2 + (y-b)^2} < \delta.$$

Example 4.10

Limit of a Function at a Boundary Point

Prove $\lim_{(x, y) \to (4, 3)} \sqrt{25 - x^2 - y^2} = 0.$

Solution

The domain of the function $f(x, y) = \sqrt{25 - x^2 - y^2}$ is $\left\{(x, y) \in \mathbb{R}^2 \middle| x^2 + y^2 \le 25\right\},$ which is a circle of radius 5 centered at the origin, along with its interior as shown in the following graph.

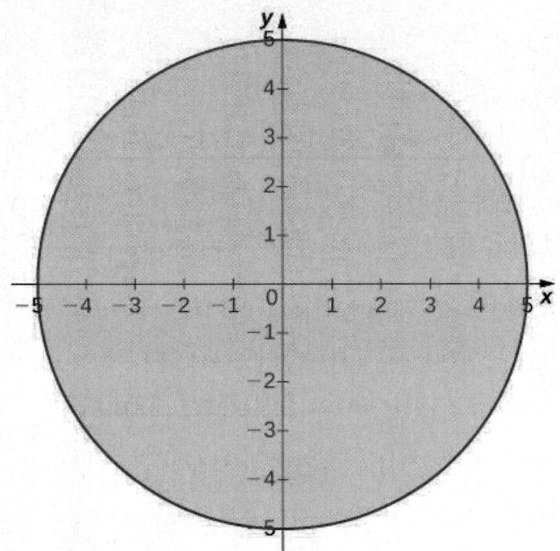

Figure 4.18 Domain of the function $f(x, y) = \sqrt{25 - x^2 - y^2}.$

We can use the limit laws, which apply to limits at the boundary of domains as well as interior points:

$$\begin{aligned}\lim_{(x, y) \to (4, 3)} \sqrt{25 - x^2 - y^2} &= \sqrt{\lim_{(x, y) \to (4, 3)} \left(25 - x^2 - y^2\right)} \\ &= \sqrt{\lim_{(x, y) \to (4, 3)} 25 - \lim_{(x, y) \to (4, 3)} x^2 - \lim_{(x, y) \to (4, 3)} y^2} \\ &= \sqrt{25 - 4^2 - 3^2} \\ &= 0.\end{aligned}$$

See the following graph.

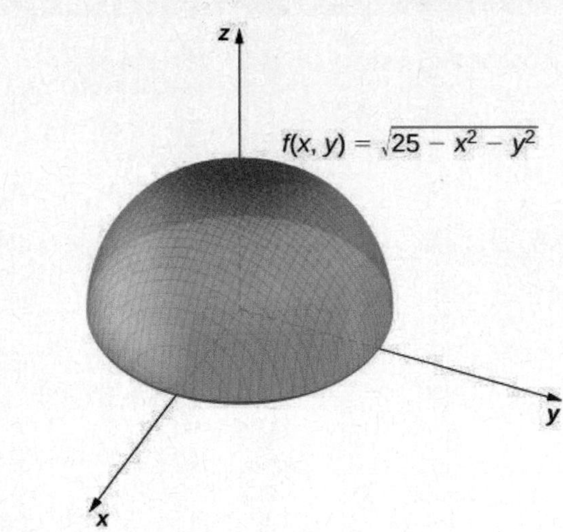

Figure 4.19 Graph of the function $f(x, y) = \sqrt{25 - x^2 - y^2}$.

4.8 Evaluate the following limit:

$$\lim_{(x, y) \to (5, -2)} \sqrt{29 - x^2 - y^2}.$$

Continuity of Functions of Two Variables

In **Continuity (http://cnx.org/content/m53489/latest/)** , we defined the continuity of a function of one variable and saw how it relied on the limit of a function of one variable. In particular, three conditions are necessary for $f(x)$ to be continuous at point $x = a$:

1. $f(a)$ exists.
2. $\lim_{x \to a} f(x)$ exists.
3. $\lim_{x \to a} f(x) = f(a)$.

These three conditions are necessary for continuity of a function of two variables as well.

Definition

A function $f(x, y)$ is continuous at a point (a, b) in its domain if the following conditions are satisfied:

1. $f(a, b)$ exists.
2. $\lim_{(x, y) \to (a, b)} f(x, y)$ exists.
3. $\lim_{(x, y) \to (a, b)} f(x, y) = f(a, b)$.

Example 4.11

Demonstrating Continuity for a Function of Two Variables

Show that the function $f(x, y) = \dfrac{3x + 2y}{x + y + 1}$ is continuous at point $(5, -3)$.

Solution

There are three conditions to be satisfied, per the definition of continuity. In this example, $a = 5$ and $b = -3$.

1. $f(a, b)$ exists. This is true because the domain of the function f consists of those ordered pairs for which the denominator is nonzero (i.e., $x + y + 1 \neq 0$). Point $(5, -3)$ satisfies this condition. Furthermore,

$$f(a, b) = f(5, -3) = \frac{3(5) + 2(-3)}{5 + (-3) + 1} = \frac{15 - 6}{2 + 1} = 3.$$

2. $\lim_{(x, y) \to (a, b)} f(x, y)$ exists. This is also true:

$$\begin{aligned} \lim_{(x, y) \to (a, b)} f(x, y) &= \lim_{(x, y) \to (5, -3)} \frac{3x + 2y}{x + y + 1} \\ &= \frac{\lim_{(x, y) \to (5, -3)} (3x + 2y)}{\lim_{(x, y) \to (5, -3)} (x + y + 1)} \\ &= \frac{15 - 6}{5 - 3 + 1} \\ &= 3. \end{aligned}$$

3. $\lim_{(x, y) \to (a, b)} f(x, y) = f(a, b)$. This is true because we have just shown that both sides of this equation equal three.

4.9 Show that the function $f(x, y) = \sqrt{26 - 2x^2 - y^2}$ is continuous at point $(2, -3)$.

Continuity of a function of any number of variables can also be defined in terms of delta and epsilon. A function of two variables is continuous at a point (x_0, y_0) in its domain if for every $\varepsilon > 0$ there exists a $\delta > 0$ such that, whenever $\sqrt{(x - x_0)^2 + (y - y_0)^2} < \delta$ it is true, $|f(x, y) - f(a, b)| < \varepsilon$. This definition can be combined with the formal definition (that is, the *epsilon–delta definition*) of continuity of a function of one variable to prove the following theorems:

Theorem 4.2: The Sum of Continuous Functions Is Continuous

If $f(x, y)$ is continuous at (x_0, y_0), and $g(x, y)$ is continuous at (x_0, y_0), then $f(x, y) + g(x, y)$ is continuous at (x_0, y_0).

Theorem 4.3: The Product of Continuous Functions Is Continuous

If $g(x)$ is continuous at x_0 and $h(y)$ is continuous at y_0, then $f(x, y) = g(x)h(y)$ is continuous at (x_0, y_0).

Theorem 4.4: The Composition of Continuous Functions Is Continuous

Let g be a function of two variables from a domain $D \subseteq \mathbb{R}^2$ to a range $R \subseteq \mathbb{R}$. Suppose g is continuous at some point $(x_0, y_0) \in D$ and define $z_0 = g(x_0, y_0)$. Let f be a function that maps $\mathbb{R}$ to $\mathbb{R}$ such that z_0 is in the domain of f. Last, assume f is continuous at z_0. Then $f \circ g$ is continuous at (x_0, y_0) as shown in the following figure.

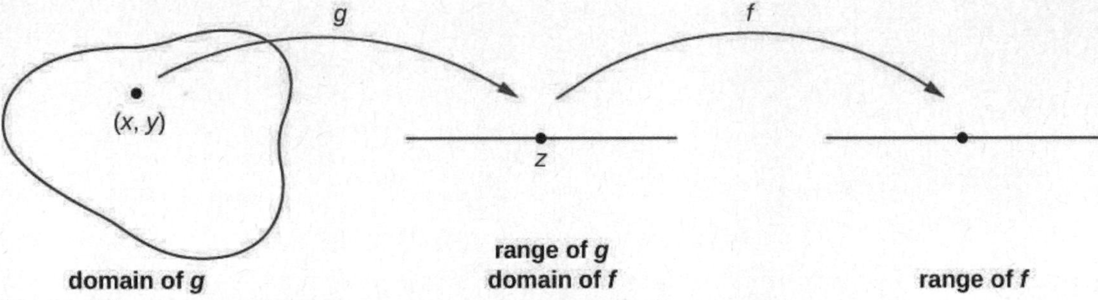

Figure 4.20 The composition of two continuous functions is continuous.

Let's now use the previous theorems to show continuity of functions in the following examples.

Example 4.12

More Examples of Continuity of a Function of Two Variables

Show that the functions $f(x, y) = 4x^3y^2$ and $g(x, y) = \cos\left(4x^3y^2\right)$ are continuous everywhere.

Solution

The polynomials $g(x) = 4x^3$ and $h(y) = y^2$ are continuous at every real number, and therefore by the product of continuous functions theorem, $f(x, y) = 4x^3y^2$ is continuous at every point (x, y) in the xy-plane. Since $f(x, y) = 4x^3y^2$ is continuous at every point (x, y) in the xy-plane and $g(x) = \cos x$ is continuous at every real number x, the continuity of the composition of functions tells us that $g(x, y) = \cos\left(4x^3y^2\right)$ is continuous at every point (x, y) in the xy-plane.

4.10 Show that the functions $f(x, y) = 2x^2y^3 + 3$ and $g(x, y) = \left(2x^2y^3 + 3\right)^4$ are continuous everywhere.

Functions of Three or More Variables

The limit of a function of three or more variables occurs readily in applications. For example, suppose we have a function $f(x, y, z)$ that gives the temperature at a physical location (x, y, z) in three dimensions. Or perhaps a function $g(x, y, z, t)$ can indicate air pressure at a location (x, y, z) at time t. How can we take a limit at a point in $\mathbb{R}^3$? What does it mean to be continuous at a point in four dimensions?

The answers to these questions rely on extending the concept of a δ disk into more than two dimensions. Then, the ideas of the limit of a function of three or more variables and the continuity of a function of three or more variables are very similar to the definitions given earlier for a function of two variables.

Definition

Let (x_0, y_0, z_0) be a point in $\mathbb{R}^3$. Then, a **δ ball** in three dimensions consists of all points in $\mathbb{R}^3$ lying at a distance of less than δ from (x_0, y_0, z_0)—that is,

$$\left\{(x, y, z) \in \mathbb{R}^3 \middle| \sqrt{(x - x_0)^2 + (y - y_0)^2 + (z - z_0)^2} < \delta\right\}.$$

To define a δ ball in higher dimensions, add additional terms under the radical to correspond to each additional dimension. For example, given a point $P = (w_0, x_0, y_0, z_0)$ in $\mathbb{R}^4$, a δ ball around P can be described by

$$\left\{(w, x, y, z) \in \mathbb{R}^4 \middle| \sqrt{(w - w_0)^2 + (x - x_0)^2 + (y - y_0)^2 + (z - z_0)^2} < \delta\right\}.$$

To show that a limit of a function of three variables exists at a point (x_0, y_0, z_0), it suffices to show that for any point in a δ ball centered at (x_0, y_0, z_0), the value of the function at that point is arbitrarily close to a fixed value (the limit value). All the limit laws for functions of two variables hold for functions of more than two variables as well.

Example 4.13

Finding the Limit of a Function of Three Variables

Find $\lim_{(x, y, z) \to (4, 1, -3)} \dfrac{x^2 y - 3z}{2x + 5y - z}$.

Solution

Before we can apply the quotient law, we need to verify that the limit of the denominator is nonzero. Using the difference law, the identity law, and the constant law,

$$\begin{aligned} \lim_{(x, y, z) \to (4, 1, -3)} (2x + 5y - z) &= 2\left(\lim_{(x, y, z) \to (4, 1, -3)} x\right) + 5\left(\lim_{(x, y, z) \to (4, 1, -3)} y\right) - \left(\lim_{(x, y, z) \to (4, 1, -3)} z\right) \\ &= 2(4) + 5(1) - (-3) \\ &= 16. \end{aligned}$$

Since this is nonzero, we next find the limit of the numerator. Using the product law, difference law, constant multiple law, and identity law,

$$\begin{aligned} \lim_{(x, y, z) \to (4, 1, -3)} \left(x^2 y - 3z\right) &= \left(\lim_{(x, y, z) \to (4, 1, -3)} x\right)^2 \left(\lim_{(x, y, z) \to (4, 1, -3)} y\right) - 3 \lim_{(x, y, z) \to (4, 1, -3)} z \\ &= \left(4^2\right)(1) - 3(-3) \\ &= 16 + 9 \\ &= 25. \end{aligned}$$

Last, applying the quotient law:

$$\begin{aligned} \lim_{(x, y, z) \to (4, 1, -3)} \frac{x^2 y - 3z}{2x + 5y - z} &= \frac{\lim_{(x, y, z) \to (4, 1, -3)} \left(x^2 y - 3z\right)}{\lim_{(x, y, z) \to (4, 1, -3)} (2x + 5y - z)} \\ &= \frac{25}{16}. \end{aligned}$$

4.11 Find $\lim_{(x, y, z) \to (4, -1, 3)} \sqrt{13 - x^2 - 2y^2 + z^2}$.

4.2 EXERCISES

For the following exercises, find the limit of the function.

60. $\lim_{(x, y) \to (1, 2)} x$

61. $\lim_{(x, y) \to (1, 2)} \frac{5x^2 y}{x^2 + y^2}$

62. Show that the limit $\lim_{(x, y) \to (0, 0)} \frac{5x^2 y}{x^2 + y^2}$ exists and is the same along the paths: y-axis and x-axis, and along $y = x$.

For the following exercises, evaluate the limits at the indicated values of x and y. If the limit does not exist, state this and explain why the limit does not exist.

63. $\lim_{(x, y) \to (0, 0)} \frac{4x^2 + 10y^2 + 4}{4x^2 - 10y^2 + 6}$

64. $\lim_{(x, y) \to (11, 13)} \sqrt{\frac{1}{xy}}$

65. $\lim_{(x, y) \to (0, 1)} \frac{y^2 \sin x}{x}$

66. $\lim_{(x, y) \to (0, 0)} \sin\left(\frac{x^8 + y^7}{x - y + 10}\right)$

67. $\lim_{(x, y) \to (\pi/4, 1)} \frac{y \tan x}{y + 1}$

68. $\lim_{(x, y) \to (0, \pi/4)} \frac{\sec x + 2}{3x - \tan y}$

69. $\lim_{(x, y) \to (2, 5)} \left(\frac{1}{x} - \frac{5}{y}\right)$

70. $\lim_{(x, y) \to (4, 4)} x \ln y$

71. $\lim_{(x, y) \to (4, 4)} e^{-x^2 - y^2}$

72. $\lim_{(x, y) \to (0, 0)} \sqrt{9 - x^2 - y^2}$

73. $\lim_{(x, y) \to (1, 2)} \left(x^2 y^3 - x^3 y^2 + 3x + 2y\right)$

74. $\lim_{(x, y) \to (\pi, \pi)} x \sin\left(\frac{x + y}{4}\right)$

75. $\lim_{(x, y) \to (0, 0)} \frac{xy + 1}{x^2 + y^2 + 1}$

76. $\lim_{(x, y) \to (0, 0)} \frac{x^2 + y^2}{\sqrt{x^2 + y^2 + 1} - 1}$

77. $\lim_{(x, y) \to (0, 0)} \ln\left(x^2 + y^2\right)$

For the following exercises, complete the statement.

78. A point (x_0, y_0) in a plane region R is an interior point of R if _________________.

79. A point (x_0, y_0) in a plane region R is called a boundary point of R if ___________.

For the following exercises, use algebraic techniques to evaluate the limit.

80. $\lim_{(x, y) \to (2, 1)} \frac{x - y - 1}{\sqrt{x - y} - 1}$

81. $\lim_{(x, y) \to (0, 0)} \frac{x^4 - 4y^4}{x^2 + 2y^2}$

82. $\lim_{(x, y) \to (0, 0)} \frac{x^3 - y^3}{x - y}$

83. $\lim_{(x, y) \to (0, 0)} \frac{x^2 - xy}{\sqrt{x} - \sqrt{y}}$

For the following exercises, evaluate the limits of the functions of three variables.

84. $\lim_{(x, y, z) \to (1, 2, 3)} \frac{xz^2 - y^2 z}{xyz - 1}$

85. $\lim_{(x, y, z) \to (0, 0, 0)} \frac{x^2 - y^2 - z^2}{x^2 + y^2 - z^2}$

For the following exercises, evaluate the limit of the function by determining the value the function approaches along the indicated paths. If the limit does not exist, explain why not.

86. $\lim_{(x, y) \to (0, 0)} \frac{xy + y^3}{x^2 + y^2}$

a. Along the x-axis $(y = 0)$

b. Along the y-axis $(x = 0)$

c. Along the path $y = 2x$

87. Evaluate $\lim_{(x, y) \to (0, 0)} \frac{xy + y^3}{x^2 + y^2}$ using the results of previous problem.

88. $\lim_{(x, y) \to (0, 0)} \frac{x^2 y}{x^4 + y^2}$

a. Along the x-axis $(y = 0)$

b. Along the y-axis $(x = 0)$

c. Along the path $y = x^2$

89. Evaluate $\lim_{(x, y) \to (0, 0)} \frac{x^2 y}{x^4 + y^2}$ using the results of previous problem.

Discuss the continuity of the following functions. Find the largest region in the xy-plane in which the following functions are continuous.

90. $f(x, y) = \sin(xy)$

91. $f(x, y) = \ln(x + y)$

92. $f(x, y) = e^{3xy}$

93. $f(x, y) = \frac{1}{xy}$

For the following exercises, determine the region in which the function is continuous. Explain your answer.

94. $f(x, y) = \frac{x^2 y}{x^2 + y^2}$

95. $f(x, y) = \begin{cases} \frac{x^2 y}{x^2 + y^2} & \text{if } (x, y) \neq (0, 0) \\ 0 & \text{if } (x, y) = (0, 0) \end{cases}$ (*Hint*: Show that the function approaches different values along two different paths.)

96. $f(x, y) = \frac{\sin(x^2 + y^2)}{x^2 + y^2}$

97. Determine whether $g(x, y) = \frac{x^2 - y^2}{x^2 + y^2}$ is continuous at $(0, 0)$.

98. Create a plot using graphing software to determine where the limit does not exist. Determine the region of the coordinate plane in which $f(x, y) = \frac{1}{x^2 - y}$ is continuous.

99. Determine the region of the xy-plane in which the composite function $g(x, y) = \arctan\left(\frac{xy^2}{x + y}\right)$ is continuous. Use technology to support your conclusion.

100. Determine the region of the xy-plane in which $f(x, y) = \ln(x^2 + y^2 - 1)$ is continuous. Use technology to support your conclusion. (*Hint*: Choose the range of values for x and y carefully!)

101. At what points in space is $g(x, y, z) = x^2 + y^2 - 2z^2$ continuous?

102. At what points in space is $g(x, y, z) = \frac{1}{x^2 + z^2 - 1}$ continuous?

103. Show that $\lim_{(x, y) \to (0, 0)} \frac{1}{x^2 + y^2}$ does not exist at $(0, 0)$ by plotting the graph of the function.

104. **[T]** Evaluate $\lim_{(x, y) \to (0, 0)} \frac{-xy^2}{x^2 + y^4}$ by plotting the function using a CAS. Determine analytically the limit along the path $x = y^2$.

105. **[T]**

a. Use a CAS to draw a contour map of $z = \sqrt{9 - x^2 - y^2}$.

b. What is the name of the geometric shape of the level curves?

c. Give the general equation of the level curves.

d. What is the maximum value of z?

e. What is the domain of the function?

f. What is the range of the function?

106. *True or False*: If we evaluate $\lim_{(x, y) \to (0, 0)} f(x)$ along several paths and each time the limit is 1, we can conclude that $\lim_{(x, y) \to (0, 0)} f(x) = 1$.

107. Use polar coordinates to find $\lim_{(x,\, y) \to (0,\, 0)} \frac{\sin\sqrt{x^2 + y^2}}{\sqrt{x^2 + y^2}}$. You can also find the limit using L'Hôpital's rule.

108. Use polar coordinates to find $\lim_{(x,\, y) \to (0,\, 0)} \cos\left(x^2 + y^2\right)$.

109. Discuss the continuity of $f(g(x, y))$ where $f(t) = 1/t$ and $g(x, y) = 2x - 5y$.

110. Given $f(x, y) = x^2 - 4y$, find $\lim_{h \to 0} \frac{f(x + h, y) - f(x, y)}{h}$.

111. Given $f(x, y) = x^2 - 4y$, find $\lim_{h \to 0} \frac{f(1 + h, y) - f(1, y)}{h}$.

4.3 | Partial Derivatives

Learning Objectives

4.3.1 Calculate the partial derivatives of a function of two variables.
4.3.2 Calculate the partial derivatives of a function of more than two variables.
4.3.3 Determine the higher-order derivatives of a function of two variables.
4.3.4 Explain the meaning of a partial differential equation and give an example.

Now that we have examined limits and continuity of functions of two variables, we can proceed to study derivatives. Finding derivatives of functions of two variables is the key concept in this chapter, with as many applications in mathematics, science, and engineering as differentiation of single-variable functions. However, we have already seen that limits and continuity of multivariable functions have new issues and require new terminology and ideas to deal with them. This carries over into differentiation as well.

Derivatives of a Function of Two Variables

When studying derivatives of functions of one variable, we found that one interpretation of the derivative is an instantaneous rate of change of y as a function of x. Leibniz notation for the derivative is dy/dx, which implies that y is the dependent variable and x is the independent variable. For a function $z = f(x, y)$ of two variables, x and y are the independent variables and z is the dependent variable. This raises two questions right away: How do we adapt Leibniz notation for functions of two variables? Also, what is an interpretation of the derivative? The answer lies in partial derivatives.

Definition

Let $f(x, y)$ be a function of two variables. Then the **partial derivative** of f with respect to x, written as $\partial f/\partial x$, or f_x, is defined as

$$\frac{\partial f}{\partial x} = \lim_{h \to 0} \frac{f(x + h, y) - f(x, y)}{h}. \quad \textbf{(4.12)}$$

The partial derivative of f with respect to y, written as $\partial f/\partial y$, or f_y, is defined as

$$\frac{\partial f}{\partial y} = \lim_{k \to 0} \frac{f(x, y + k) - f(x, y)}{k}. \quad \textbf{(4.13)}$$

This definition shows two differences already. First, the notation changes, in the sense that we still use a version of Leibniz notation, but the d in the original notation is replaced with the symbol ∂. (This rounded "d" is usually called "partial," so $\partial f/\partial x$ is spoken as the "partial of f with respect to x.") This is the first hint that we are dealing with partial derivatives. Second, we now have two different derivatives we can take, since there are two different independent variables. Depending on which variable we choose, we can come up with different partial derivatives altogether, and often do.

Example 4.14

Calculating Partial Derivatives from the Definition

Use the definition of the partial derivative as a limit to calculate $\partial f/\partial x$ and $\partial f/\partial y$ for the function

$$f(x, y) = x^2 - 3xy + 2y^2 - 4x + 5y - 12.$$

Solution

First, calculate $f(x+h,\ y)$.

$$\begin{aligned} f(x+h,\ y) &= (x+h)^2 - 3(x+h)y + 2y^2 - 4(x+h) + 5y - 12 \\ &= x^2 + 2xh + h^2 - 3xy - 3hy + 2y^2 - 4x - 4h + 5y - 12. \end{aligned}$$

Next, substitute this into **Equation 4.12** and simplify:

$$\begin{aligned} \frac{\partial f}{\partial x} &= \lim_{h \to 0} \frac{f(x+h,\ y) - f(x,\ y)}{h} \\ &= \lim_{h \to 0} \frac{\left(x^2 + 2xh + h^2 - 3xy - 3hy + 2y^2 - 4x - 4h + 5y - 12\right) - \left(x^2 - 3xy + 2y^2 - 4x + 5y - 12\right)}{h} \\ &= \lim_{h \to 0} \frac{x^2 + 2xh + h^2 - 3xy - 3hy + 2y^2 - 4x - 4h + 5y - 12 - x^2 + 3xy - 2y^2 + 4x - 5y + 12}{h} \\ &= \lim_{h \to 0} \frac{2xh + h^2 - 3hy - 4h}{h} \\ &= \lim_{h \to 0} \frac{h(2x + h - 3y - 4)}{h} \\ &= \lim_{h \to 0} (2x + h - 3y - 4) \\ &= 2x - 3y - 4. \end{aligned}$$

To calculate $\frac{\partial f}{\partial y}$, first calculate $f(x,\ y+h)$:

$$\begin{aligned} f(x+h,\ y) &= x^2 - 3x(y+h) + 2(y+h)^2 - 4x + 5(y+h) - 12 \\ &= x^2 - 3xy - 3xh + 2y^2 + 4yh + 2h^2 - 4x + 5y + 5h - 12. \end{aligned}$$

Next, substitute this into **Equation 4.13** and simplify:

$$\begin{aligned} \frac{\partial f}{\partial y} &= \lim_{h \to 0} \frac{f(x,\ y+h) - f(x,\ y)}{h} \\ &= \lim_{h \to 0} \frac{\left(x^2 - 3xy - 3xh + 2y^2 + 4yh + 2h^2 - 4x + 5y + 5h - 12\right) - \left(x^2 - 3xy + 2y^2 - 4x + 5y - 12\right)}{h} \\ &= \lim_{h \to 0} \frac{x^2 - 3xy - 3xh + 2y^2 + 4yh + 2h^2 - 4x + 5y + 5h - 12 - x^2 + 3xy - 2y^2 + 4x - 5y + 12}{h} \\ &= \lim_{h \to 0} \frac{-3xh + 4yh + 2h^2 + 5h}{h} \\ &= \lim_{h \to 0} \frac{h(-3x + 4y + 2h + 5)}{h} \\ &= \lim_{h \to 0} (-3x + 4y + 2h + 5) \\ &= -3x + 4y + 5. \end{aligned}$$

4.12 Use the definition of the partial derivative as a limit to calculate $\partial f/\partial x$ and $\partial f/\partial y$ for the function

$$f(x,\ y) = 4x^2 + 2xy - y^2 + 3x - 2y + 5.$$

The idea to keep in mind when calculating partial derivatives is to treat all independent variables, other than the variable with respect to which we are differentiating, as constants. Then proceed to differentiate as with a function of a single variable. To see why this is true, first fix y and define $g(x) = f(x,\ y)$ as a function of x. Then

$$g'(x) = \lim_{h \to 0} \frac{g(x+h) - g(x)}{h} = \lim_{h \to 0} \frac{f(x+h,\, y) - f(x,\, y)}{h} = \frac{\partial f}{\partial x}.$$

The same is true for calculating the partial derivative of f with respect to y. This time, fix x and define $h(y) = f(x, y)$ as a function of y. Then

$$h'(x) = \lim_{k \to 0} \frac{h(x+k) - h(x)}{k} = \lim_{k \to 0} \frac{f(x,\, y+k) - f(x,\, y)}{k} = \frac{\partial f}{\partial y}.$$

All differentiation rules from **Introduction to Derivatives (http://cnx.org/content/m53494/latest/)** apply.

Example 4.15

Calculating Partial Derivatives

Calculate $\partial f/\partial x$ and $\partial f/\partial y$ for the following functions by holding the opposite variable constant then differentiating:

a. $f(x, y) = x^2 - 3xy + 2y^2 - 4x + 5y - 12$

b. $g(x, y) = \sin\left(x^2 y - 2x + 4\right)$

Solution

a. To calculate $\partial f/\partial x$, treat the variable y as a constant. Then differentiate $f(x, y)$ with respect to x using the sum, difference, and power rules:

$$\begin{aligned}\frac{\partial f}{\partial x} &= \frac{\partial}{\partial x}\left[x^2 - 3xy + 2y^2 - 4x + 5y - 12\right] \\ &= \frac{\partial}{\partial x}\left[x^2\right] - \frac{\partial}{\partial x}[3xy] + \frac{\partial}{\partial x}\left[2y^2\right] - \frac{\partial}{\partial x}[4x] + \frac{\partial}{\partial x}[5y] - \frac{\partial}{\partial x}[12] \\ &= 2x - 3y + 0 - 4 + 0 - 0 \\ &= 2x - 3y - 4.\end{aligned}$$

The derivatives of the third, fifth, and sixth terms are all zero because they do not contain the variable x, so they are treated as constant terms. The derivative of the second term is equal to the coefficient of x, which is $-3y$. Calculating $\partial f/\partial y$:

$$\begin{aligned}\frac{\partial f}{\partial y} &= \frac{\partial}{\partial y}\left[x^2 - 3xy + 2y^2 - 4x + 5y - 12\right] \\ &= \frac{\partial}{\partial y}\left[x^2\right] - \frac{\partial}{\partial y}[3xy] + \frac{\partial}{\partial y}\left[2y^2\right] - \frac{\partial}{\partial y}[4x] + \frac{\partial}{\partial y}[5y] - \frac{\partial}{\partial y}[12] \\ &= -3x + 4y - 0 + 5 - 0 \\ &= -3x + 4y + 5.\end{aligned}$$

These are the same answers obtained in **Example 4.14**.

b. To calculate $\partial g/\partial x$, treat the variable y as a constant. Then differentiate $g(x, y)$ with respect to x using the chain rule and power rule:

$$\begin{aligned}\frac{\partial g}{\partial x} &= \frac{\partial}{\partial x}\left[\sin\left(x^2 y - 2x + 4\right)\right] \\ &= \cos\left(x^2 y - 2x + 4\right)\frac{\partial}{\partial x}\left[x^2 y - 2x + 4\right] \\ &= (2xy - 2)\cos\left(x^2 y - 2x + 4\right).\end{aligned}$$

To calculate $\partial g/\partial y$, treat the variable x as a constant. Then differentiate $g(x, y)$ with respect to y using the chain rule and power rule:

$$\begin{aligned}\frac{\partial g}{\partial y} &= \frac{\partial}{\partial y}\left[\sin\left(x^2 y - 2x + 4\right)\right] \\ &= \cos\left(x^2 y - 2x + 4\right)\frac{\partial}{\partial y}\left[x^2 y - 2x + 4\right] \\ &= x^2 \cos\left(x^2 y - 2x + 4\right).\end{aligned}$$

4.13 Calculate $\partial f/\partial x$ and $\partial f/\partial y$ for the function $f(x, y) = \tan\left(x^3 - 3x^2 y^2 + 2y^4\right)$ by holding the opposite variable constant, then differentiating.

How can we interpret these partial derivatives? Recall that the graph of a function of two variables is a surface in $\mathbb{R}^3$. If we remove the limit from the definition of the partial derivative with respect to x, the difference quotient remains:

$$\frac{f(x+h, y) - f(x, y)}{h}.$$

This resembles the difference quotient for the derivative of a function of one variable, except for the presence of the y variable. **Figure 4.21** illustrates a surface described by an arbitrary function $z = f(x, y)$.

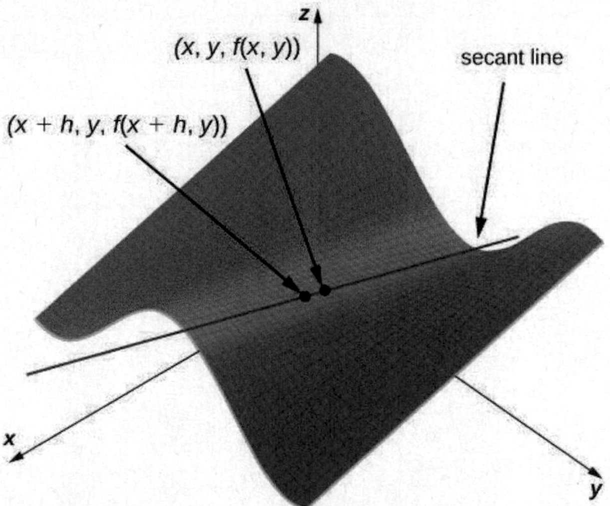

Figure 4.21 Secant line passing through the points $(x, y, f(x, y))$ and $(x+h, y, f(x+h, y))$.

In **Figure 4.21**, the value of h is positive. If we graph $f(x, y)$ and $f(x+h, y)$ for an arbitrary point (x, y), then the slope of the secant line passing through these two points is given by

$$\frac{f(x+h, y) - f(x, y)}{h}.$$

This line is parallel to the x-axis. Therefore, the slope of the secant line represents an average rate of change of the function f as we travel parallel to the x-axis. As h approaches zero, the slope of the secant line approaches the slope of the tangent line.

If we choose to change y instead of x by the same incremental value $h,$ then the secant line is parallel to the y-axis and so is the tangent line. Therefore, $\partial f / \partial x$ represents the slope of the tangent line passing through the point $(x, y, f(x, y))$ parallel to the x-axis and $\partial f / \partial y$ represents the slope of the tangent line passing through the point $(x, y, f(x, y))$ parallel to the y-axis. If we wish to find the slope of a tangent line passing through the same point in any other direction, then we need what are called *directional derivatives*, which we discuss in **Directional Derivatives and the Gradient**.

We now return to the idea of contour maps, which we introduced in **Functions of Several Variables**. We can use a contour map to estimate partial derivatives of a function $g(x, y).$

Example 4.16

Partial Derivatives from a Contour Map

Use a contour map to estimate $\partial g / \partial x$ at the point $(\sqrt{5}, 0)$ for the function $g(x, y) = \sqrt{9 - x^2 - y^2}.$

Solution

The following graph represents a contour map for the function $g(x, y) = \sqrt{9 - x^2 - y^2}.$

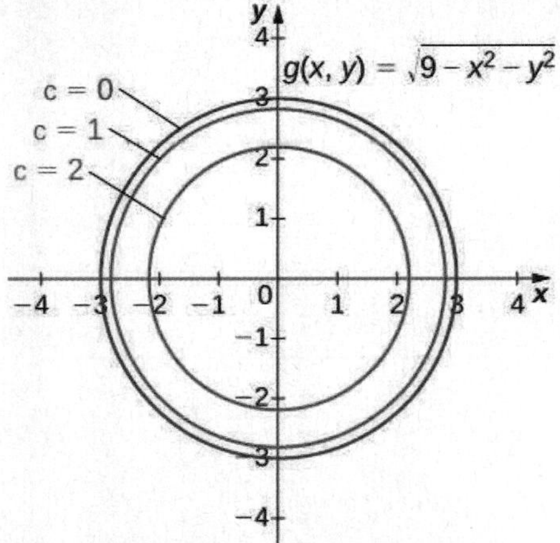

Figure 4.22 Contour map for the function $g(x, y) = \sqrt{9 - x^2 - y^2},$ using $c = 0, 1, 2,$ and 3 ($c = 3$ corresponds to the origin).

The inner circle on the contour map corresponds to $c = 2$ and the next circle out corresponds to $c = 1.$ The first circle is given by the equation $2 = \sqrt{9 - x^2 - y^2};$ the second circle is given by the equation $1 = \sqrt{9 - x^2 - y^2}.$ The first equation simplifies to $x^2 + y^2 = 5$ and the second equation simplifies to $x^2 + y^2 = 8.$ The x-intercept of the first circle is $(\sqrt{5}, 0)$ and the x-intercept of the second circle is $(2\sqrt{2}, 0).$ We can estimate the value of $\partial g / \partial x$ evaluated at the point $(\sqrt{5}, 0)$ using the slope formula:

$$\left.\frac{\partial g}{\partial x}\right|_{(x, y) = (\sqrt{5}, 0)} \approx \frac{g(\sqrt{5}, 0) - g(2\sqrt{2}, 0)}{\sqrt{5} - 2\sqrt{2}} = \frac{2 - 1}{\sqrt{5} - 2\sqrt{2}} = \frac{1}{\sqrt{5} - 2\sqrt{2}} \approx -1.688.$$

To calculate the exact value of $\partial g / \partial x$ evaluated at the point $(\sqrt{5}, 0),$ we start by finding $\partial g / \partial x$ using the chain rule. First, we rewrite the function as $g(x, y) = \sqrt{9 - x^2 - y^2} = \left(9 - x^2 - y^2\right)^{1/2}$ and then differentiate with respect to x while holding y constant:

$$\frac{\partial g}{\partial x} = \frac{1}{2}\left(9 - x^2 - y^2\right)^{-1/2}(-2x) = -\frac{x}{\sqrt{9 - x^2 - y^2}}.$$

Next, we evaluate this expression using $x = \sqrt{5}$ and $y = 0$:

$$\left.\frac{\partial g}{\partial x}\right|_{(x, y) = (\sqrt{5}, 0)} = -\frac{\sqrt{5}}{\sqrt{9 - (\sqrt{5})^2 - (0)^2}} = -\frac{\sqrt{5}}{\sqrt{4}} = -\frac{\sqrt{5}}{2} \approx -1.118.$$

The estimate for the partial derivative corresponds to the slope of the secant line passing through the points $\left(\sqrt{5}, 0, g(\sqrt{5}, 0)\right)$ and $\left(2\sqrt{2}, 0, g(2\sqrt{2}, 0)\right)$. It represents an approximation to the slope of the tangent line to the surface through the point $\left(\sqrt{5}, 0, g(\sqrt{5}, 0)\right)$, which is parallel to the x-axis.

4.14 Use a contour map to estimate $\partial f / \partial y$ at point $\left(0, \sqrt{2}\right)$ for the function

$$f(x, y) = x^2 - y^2.$$

Compare this with the exact answer.

Functions of More Than Two Variables

Suppose we have a function of three variables, such as $w = f(x, y, z)$. We can calculate partial derivatives of w with respect to any of the independent variables, simply as extensions of the definitions for partial derivatives of functions of two variables.

Definition

Let $f(x, y, z)$ be a function of three variables. Then, the *partial derivative of* f *with respect to x*, written as $\partial f / \partial x$, or f_x, is defined to be

$$\frac{\partial f}{\partial x} = \lim_{h \to 0} \frac{f(x + h, y, z) - f(x, y, z)}{h}. \tag{4.14}$$

The *partial derivative of* f *with respect to* y, written as $\partial f / \partial y$, or f_y, is defined to be

$$\frac{\partial f}{\partial y} = \lim_{k \to 0} \frac{f(x, y + k, z) - f(x, y, z)}{k}. \tag{4.15}$$

The *partial derivative of* f *with respect to* z, written as $\partial f / \partial z$, or f_z, is defined to be

$$\frac{\partial f}{\partial z} = \lim_{m \to 0} \frac{f(x, y, z + m) - f(x, y, z)}{m}. \tag{4.16}$$

We can calculate a partial derivative of a function of three variables using the same idea we used for a function of two variables. For example, if we have a function f of x, y, and z, and we wish to calculate $\partial f / \partial x$, then we treat the other two independent variables as if they are constants, then differentiate with respect to x.

Example 4.17

Calculating Partial Derivatives for a Function of Three Variables

Use the limit definition of partial derivatives to calculate $\partial f/\partial x$ for the function

$$f(x,\ y,\ z) = x^2 - 3xy + 2y^2 - 4xz + 5yz^2 - 12x + 4y - 3z.$$

Then, find $\partial f/\partial y$ and $\partial f/\partial z$ by setting the other two variables constant and differentiating accordingly.

Solution

We first calculate $\partial f/\partial x$ using **Equation 4.14**, then we calculate the other two partial derivatives by holding the remaining variables constant. To use the equation to find $\partial f/\partial x$, we first need to calculate $f(x+h,\ y,\ z)$:

$$\begin{aligned} f(x+h,\ y,\ z) &= (x+h)^2 - 3(x+h)y + 2y^2 - 4(x+h)z + 5yz^2 - 12(x+h) + 4y - 3z \\ &= x^2 + 2xh + h^2 - 3xy - 3xh + 2y^2 - 4xz - 4hz + 5yz^2 - 12x - 12h + 4y - 3z \end{aligned}$$

and recall that $f(x,\ y,\ z) = x^2 - 3xy + 2y^2 - 4zx + 5yz^2 - 12x + 4y - 3z.$ Next, we substitute these two expressions into the equation:

$$\begin{aligned} \frac{\partial f}{\partial x} &= \lim_{h \to 0}\Bigg[\frac{x^2 + 2xh + h^2 - 3xy - 3hy + 2y^2 - 4xz - 4hz + 5yz^2 - 12x - 12h + 4y - 3z}{h} \\ &\quad - \frac{x^2 - 3xy + 2y^2 - 4xz + 5yz^2 - 12x + 4y - 3z}{h}\Bigg] \\ &= \lim_{h \to 0}\left[\frac{2xh + h^2 - 3hy - 4hz - 12h}{h}\right] \\ &= \lim_{h \to 0}\left[\frac{h(2x + h - 3y - 4z - 12)}{h}\right] \\ &= \lim_{h \to 0}(2x + h - 3y - 4z - 12) \\ &= 2x - 3y - 4z - 12. \end{aligned}$$

Then we find $\partial f/\partial y$ by holding x and z constant. Therefore, any term that does not include the variable y is constant, and its derivative is zero. We can apply the sum, difference, and power rules for functions of one variable:

$$\begin{aligned} &\frac{\partial}{\partial y}\left[x^2 - 3xy + 2y^2 - 4xz + 5yz^2 - 12x + 4y - 3z\right] \\ &= \frac{\partial}{\partial y}\left[x^2\right] - \frac{\partial}{\partial y}[3xy] + \frac{\partial}{\partial y}\left[2y^2\right] - \frac{\partial}{\partial y}[4xz] + \frac{\partial}{\partial y}\left[5yz^2\right] - \frac{\partial}{\partial y}[12x] + \frac{\partial}{\partial y}[4y] - \frac{\partial}{\partial y}[3z] \\ &= 0 - 3x + 4y - 0 + 5z^2 - 0 + 4 - 0 \\ &= -3x + 4y + 5z^2 + 4. \end{aligned}$$

To calculate $\partial f/\partial z$, we hold x and y constant and apply the sum, difference, and power rules for functions of one variable:

$$\begin{aligned} &\frac{\partial}{\partial z}\left[x^2 - 3xy + 2y^2 - 4xz + 5yz^2 - 12x + 4y - 3z\right] \\ &= \frac{\partial}{\partial z}\left[x^2\right] - \frac{\partial}{\partial z}[3xy] + \frac{\partial}{\partial z}\left[2y^2\right] - \frac{\partial}{\partial z}[4xz] + \frac{\partial}{\partial z}\left[5yz^2\right] - \frac{\partial}{\partial z}[12x] + \frac{\partial}{\partial z}[4y] - \frac{\partial}{\partial z}[3z] \\ &= 0 - 0 + 0 - 4x + 10yz - 0 + 0 - 3 \\ &= -4x + 10yz - 3. \end{aligned}$$

4.15 Use the limit definition of partial derivatives to calculate $\partial f / \partial x$ for the function

$$f(x, y, z) = 2x^2 - 4x^2 y + 2y^2 + 5xz^2 - 6x + 3z - 8.$$

Then find $\partial f / \partial y$ and $\partial f / \partial z$ by setting the other two variables constant and differentiating accordingly.

Example 4.18

Calculating Partial Derivatives for a Function of Three Variables

Calculate the three partial derivatives of the following functions.

a. $f(x, y, z) = \dfrac{x^2 y - 4xz + y^2}{x - 3yz}$

b. $g(x, y, z) = \sin\left(x^2 y - z\right) + \cos\left(x^2 - yz\right)$

Solution

In each case, treat all variables as constants except the one whose partial derivative you are calculating.

a.

$$\begin{aligned}
\frac{\partial f}{\partial x} &= \frac{\partial}{\partial x}\left[\frac{x^2 y - 4xz + y^2}{x - 3yz}\right] \\
&= \frac{\frac{\partial}{\partial x}\left(x^2 y - 4xz + y^2\right)(x - 3yz) - \left(x^2 y - 4xz + y^2\right)\frac{\partial}{\partial x}(x - 3yz)}{(x - 3yz)^2} \\
&= \frac{(2xy - 4z)(x - 3yz) - \left(x^2 y - 4xz + y^2\right)(1)}{(x - 3yz)^2} \\
&= \frac{2x^2 y - 6xy^2 z - 4xz + 12yz^2 - x^2 y + 4xz - y^2}{(x - 3yz)^2} \\
&= \frac{x^2 y - 6xy^2 z - 4xz + 12yz^2 + 4xz - y^2}{(x - 3yz)^2}
\end{aligned}$$

$$\begin{aligned}
\frac{\partial f}{\partial y} &= \frac{\partial}{\partial y}\left[\frac{x^2 y - 4xz + y^2}{x - 3yz}\right] \\
&= \frac{\frac{\partial}{\partial y}\left(x^2 y - 4xz + y^2\right)(x - 3yz) - \left(x^2 y - 4xz + y^2\right)\frac{\partial}{\partial y}(x - 3yz)}{(x - 3yz)^2} \\
&= \frac{\left(x^2 + 2y\right)(x - 3yz) - \left(x^2 y - 4xz + y^2\right)(-3z)}{(x - 3yz)^2} \\
&= \frac{x^3 - 3x^2 yz + 2xy - 6y^2 z + 3x^2 yz - 12xz^2 + 3y^2 z}{(x - 3yz)^2} \\
&= \frac{x^3 + 2xy - 3y^2 z - 12xz^2}{(x - 3yz)^2}
\end{aligned}$$

$$\begin{aligned}
\frac{\partial f}{\partial z} &= \frac{\partial}{\partial z}\left[\frac{x^2y-4xz+y^2}{x-3yz}\right] \\
&= \frac{\frac{\partial}{\partial z}\left(x^2y-4xz+y^2\right)(x-3yz)-\left(x^2y-4xz+y^2\right)\frac{\partial}{\partial z}(x-3yz)}{(x-3yz)^2} \\
&= \frac{(-4x)(x-3yz)-\left(x^2y-4xz+y^2\right)(-3y)}{(x-3yz)^2} \\
&= \frac{-4x^2+12xyz+3x^2y^2-12xyz+3y^3}{(x-3yz)^2} \\
&= \frac{-4x^2+3x^2y^2+3y^3}{(x-3yz)^2}
\end{aligned}$$

b.

$$\begin{aligned}
\frac{\partial f}{\partial x} &= \frac{\partial}{\partial x}\left[\sin\left(x^2y-z\right)+\cos\left(x^2-yz\right)\right] \\
&= \left(\cos\left(x^2y-z\right)\right)\frac{\partial}{\partial x}\left(x^2y-z\right)-\left(\sin\left(x^2-yz\right)\right)\frac{\partial}{\partial x}\left(x^2-yz\right) \\
&= 2xy\cos\left(x^2y-z\right)-2x\sin\left(x^2-yz\right) \\
\frac{\partial f}{\partial y} &= \frac{\partial}{\partial y}\left[\sin\left(x^2y-z\right)+\cos\left(x^2-yz\right)\right] \\
&= \left(\cos\left(x^2y-z\right)\right)\frac{\partial}{\partial y}\left(x^2y-z\right)-\left(\sin\left(x^2-yz\right)\right)\frac{\partial}{\partial y}\left(x^2-yz\right) \\
&= x^2\cos\left(x^2y-z\right)+z\sin\left(x^2-yz\right) \\
\frac{\partial f}{\partial z} &= \frac{\partial}{\partial z}\left[\sin\left(x^2y-z\right)+\cos\left(x^2-yz\right)\right] \\
&= \left(\cos\left(x^2y-z\right)\right)\frac{\partial}{\partial z}\left(x^2y-z\right)-\left(\sin\left(x^2-yz\right)\right)\frac{\partial}{\partial z}\left(x^2-yz\right) \\
&= -\cos\left(x^2y-z\right)+y\sin\left(x^2-yz\right)
\end{aligned}$$

4.16 Calculate $\partial f/\partial x,\ \ \partial f/\partial y,$ and $\partial f/\partial z$ for the function $f(x,\ y,\ z)=\sec\left(x^2y\right)-\tan\left(x^3yz^2\right).$

Higher-Order Partial Derivatives

Consider the function

$$f(x,\ y)=2x^3-4xy^2+5y^3-6xy+5x-4y+12.$$

Its partial derivatives are

$$\frac{\partial f}{\partial x}=6x^2-4y^2-6y+5 \text{ and } \frac{\partial f}{\partial y}=-8xy+15y^2-6x-4.$$

Each of these partial derivatives is a function of two variables, so we can calculate partial derivatives of these functions. Just as with derivatives of single-variable functions, we can call these *second-order derivatives*, *third-order derivatives*, and so on. In general, they are referred to as **higher-order partial derivatives**. There are four second-order partial derivatives for any function (provided they all exist):

$$\frac{\partial^2 f}{\partial x^2}=\frac{\partial}{\partial x}\left[\frac{\partial f}{\partial x}\right],\quad \frac{\partial^2 f}{\partial x\partial y}=\frac{\partial}{\partial x}\left[\frac{\partial f}{\partial y}\right],\quad \frac{\partial^2 f}{\partial y\partial x}=\frac{\partial}{\partial y}\left[\frac{\partial f}{\partial x}\right],\quad \frac{\partial^2 f}{\partial y^2}=\frac{\partial}{\partial y}\left[\frac{\partial f}{\partial y}\right].$$

An alternative notation for each is $f_{xx}, f_{yx}, f_{xy},$ and $f_{yy},$ respectively. Higher-order partial derivatives calculated with respect to different variables, such as f_{xy} and $f_{yx},$ are commonly called **mixed partial derivatives**.

Example 4.19

Calculating Second Partial Derivatives

Calculate all four second partial derivatives for the function

$$f(x, y) = xe^{-3y} + \sin(2x - 5y).$$

Solution

To calculate $\partial^2 f/dx^2$ and $\partial^2 f/\partial y \partial x,$ we first calculate $\partial f/\partial x$:

$$\frac{\partial f}{\partial x} = e^{-3y} + 2\cos(2x - 5y).$$

To calculate $\partial^2 f/dx^2,$ differentiate $\partial f/\partial x$ with respect to x:

$$\begin{aligned} \frac{\partial^2 f}{\partial x^2} &= \frac{\partial}{\partial x}\left[\frac{\partial f}{\partial x}\right] \\ &= \frac{\partial}{\partial x}\left[e^{-3y} + 2\cos(2x - 5y)\right] \\ &= -4\sin(2x - 5y). \end{aligned}$$

To calculate $\partial^2 f/\partial y \partial x,$ differentiate $\partial f/\partial x$ with respect to y:

$$\begin{aligned} \frac{\partial^2 f}{\partial y \partial x} &= \frac{\partial}{\partial y}\left[\frac{\partial f}{\partial x}\right] \\ &= \frac{\partial}{\partial y}\left[e^{-3y} + 2\cos(2x - 5y)\right] \\ &= -3e^{-3y} + 10\sin(2x - 5y). \end{aligned}$$

To calculate $\partial^2 f/\partial x \partial y$ and $\partial^2 f/dy^2,$ first calculate $\partial f/\partial y$:

$$\frac{\partial f}{\partial y} = -3xe^{-3y} - 5\cos(2x - 5y).$$

To calculate $\partial^2 f/\partial x \partial y,$ differentiate $\partial f/\partial y$ with respect to x:

$$\begin{aligned} \frac{\partial^2 f}{\partial x \partial y} &= \frac{\partial}{\partial x}\left[\frac{\partial f}{\partial y}\right] \\ &= \frac{\partial}{\partial x}\left[-3xe^{-3y} - 5\cos(2x - 5y)\right] \\ &= -3e^{-3y} + 10\sin(2x - 5y). \end{aligned}$$

To calculate $\partial^2 f/\partial y^2,$ differentiate $\partial f/\partial y$ with respect to y:

$$\begin{aligned}\frac{\partial^2 f}{\partial y^2} &= \frac{\partial}{\partial y}\left[\frac{\partial f}{\partial y}\right] \\ &= \frac{\partial}{\partial y}\left[-3xe^{-3y} - 5\cos(2x - 5y)\right] \\ &= 9xe^{-3y} - 25\sin(2x - 5y).\end{aligned}$$

4.17 Calculate all four second partial derivatives for the function

$$f(x, y) = \sin(3x - 2y) + \cos(x + 4y).$$

At this point we should notice that, in both **Example 4.19** and the checkpoint, it was true that $\partial^2 f/\partial x\partial y = \partial^2 f/\partial y\partial x$. Under certain conditions, this is always true. In fact, it is a direct consequence of the following theorem.

Theorem 4.5: Equality of Mixed Partial Derivatives (Clairaut's Theorem)

Suppose that $f(x, y)$ is defined on an open disk D that contains the point (a, b). If the functions f_{xy} and f_{yx} are continuous on D, then $f_{xy} = f_{yx}$.

Clairaut's theorem guarantees that as long as mixed second-order derivatives are continuous, the order in which we choose to differentiate the functions (i.e., which variable goes first, then second, and so on) does not matter. It can be extended to higher-order derivatives as well. The proof of Clairaut's theorem can be found in most advanced calculus books.

Two other second-order partial derivatives can be calculated for any function $f(x, y)$. The partial derivative f_{xx} is equal to the partial derivative of f_x with respect to x, and f_{yy} is equal to the partial derivative of f_y with respect to y.

Partial Differential Equations

In **Introduction to Differential Equations (http://cnx.org/content/m53696/latest/)** , we studied differential equations in which the unknown function had one independent variable. A **partial differential equation** is an equation that involves an unknown function of more than one independent variable and one or more of its partial derivatives. Examples of partial differential equations are

$$u_t = c^2(u_{xx} + u_{yy}) \tag{4.17}$$

(heat equation in two dimensions)

$$u_{tt} = c^2(u_{xx} + u_{yy}) \tag{4.18}$$

(wave equation in two dimensions)

$$u_{xx} + u_{yy} = 0 \tag{4.19}$$

(Laplace's equation in two dimensions)

In the first two equations, the unknown function u has three independent variables— t, x, and y—and c is an arbitrary constant. The independent variables x and y are considered to be spatial variables, and the variable t represents time. In Laplace's equation, the unknown function u has two independent variables x and y.

Example 4.20

A Solution to the Wave Equation

Verify that

$$u(x, y, t) = 5\sin(3\pi x)\sin(4\pi y)\cos(10\pi t)$$

is a solution to the wave equation

$$u_{tt} = 4(u_{xx} + u_{yy}). \tag{4.20}$$

Solution

First, we calculate $u_{tt}, u_{xx},$ and u_{yy}:

$$\begin{aligned} u_{tt} &= \frac{\partial}{\partial t}\left[\frac{\partial u}{\partial t}\right] \\ &= \frac{\partial}{\partial t}[5\sin(3\pi x)\sin(4\pi y)(-10\pi\sin(10\pi t))] \\ &= \frac{\partial}{\partial t}[-50\pi\sin(3\pi x)\sin(4\pi y)\sin(10\pi t)] \\ &= -500\pi^2\sin(3\pi x)\sin(4\pi y)\cos(10\pi t) \\ u_{xx} &= \frac{\partial}{\partial x}\left[\frac{\partial u}{\partial x}\right] \\ &= \frac{\partial}{\partial x}[15\pi\cos(3\pi x)\sin(4\pi y)\cos(10\pi t)] \\ &= -45\pi^2\sin(3\pi x)\sin(4\pi y)\cos(10\pi t) \\ u_{yy} &= \frac{\partial}{\partial y}\left[\frac{\partial u}{\partial y}\right] \\ &= \frac{\partial}{\partial y}[5\sin(3\pi x)(4\pi\cos(4\pi y))\cos(10\pi t)] \\ &= \frac{\partial}{\partial y}[20\pi\sin(3\pi x)\cos(4\pi y)\cos(10\pi t)] \\ &= -80\pi^2\sin(3\pi x)\sin(4\pi y)\cos(10\pi t). \end{aligned}$$

Next, we substitute each of these into the right-hand side of **Equation 4.20** and simplify:

$$\begin{aligned} 4(u_{xx} + u_{yy}) &= 4(-45\pi^2\sin(3\pi x)\sin(4\pi y)\cos(10\pi t) + -80\pi^2\sin(3\pi x)\sin(4\pi y)\cos(10\pi t)) \\ &= 4(-125\pi^2\sin(3\pi x)\sin(4\pi y)\cos(10\pi t)) \\ &= -500\pi^2\sin(3\pi x)\sin(4\pi y)\cos(10\pi t) \\ &= u_{tt}. \end{aligned}$$

This verifies the solution.

4.18 Verify that $u(x, y, t) = 2\sin\left(\frac{x}{3}\right)\sin\left(\frac{y}{4}\right)e^{-25t/16}$ is a solution to the heat equation

$$u_t = 9(u_{xx} + u_{yy}). \tag{4.21}$$

Since the solution to the two-dimensional heat equation is a function of three variables, it is not easy to create a visual representation of the solution. We can graph the solution for fixed values of t, which amounts to snapshots of the heat distributions at fixed times. These snapshots show how the heat is distributed over a two-dimensional surface as time progresses. The graph of the preceding solution at time $t = 0$ appears in the following figure. As time progresses, the extremes level out, approaching zero as t approaches infinity.

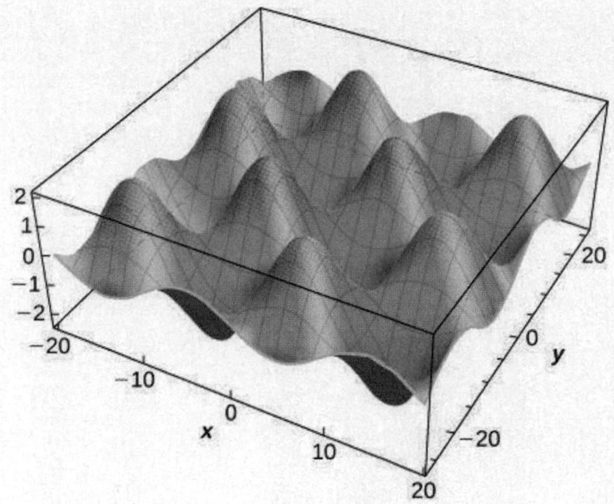

Figure 4.23

If we consider the heat equation in one dimension, then it is possible to graph the solution over time. The heat equation in one dimension becomes

$$u_t = c^2 u_{xx},$$

where c^2 represents the thermal diffusivity of the material in question. A solution of this differential equation can be written in the form

$$u_m(x, t) = e^{-\pi^2 m^2 c^2 t} \sin(m\pi x) \tag{4.22}$$

where m is any positive integer. A graph of this solution using $m = 1$ appears in **Figure 4.24**, where the initial temperature distribution over a wire of length 1 is given by $u(x, 0) = \sin \pi x$. Notice that as time progresses, the wire cools off. This is seen because, from left to right, the highest temperature (which occurs in the middle of the wire) decreases and changes color from red to blue.

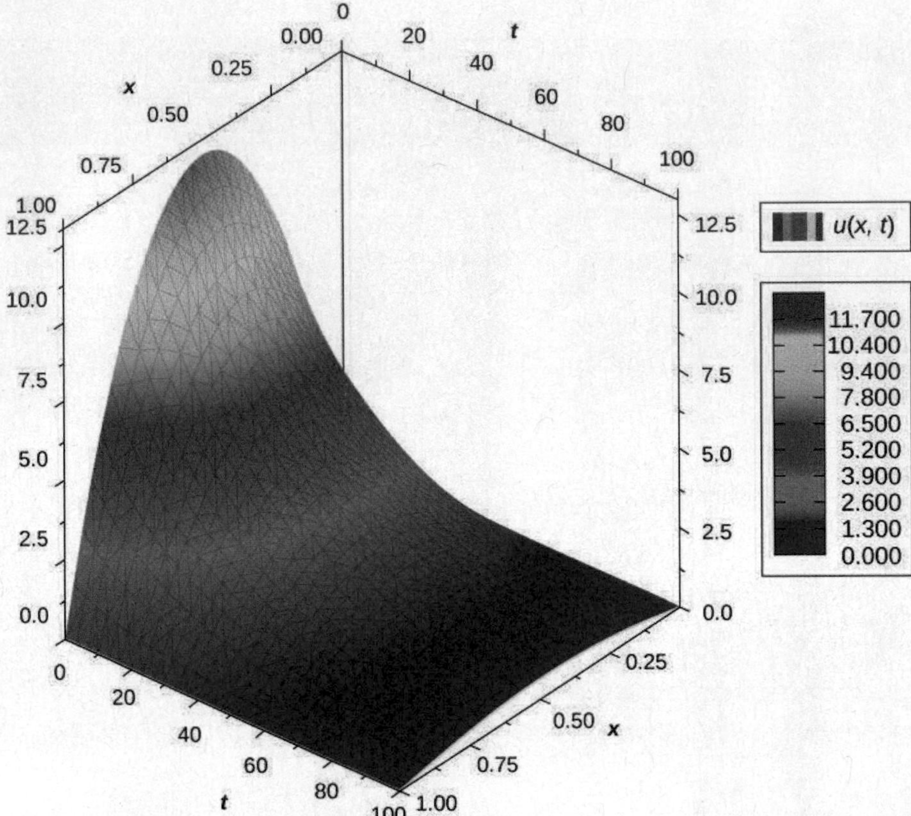

Figure 4.24 Graph of a solution of the heat equation in one dimension over time.

Student PROJECT

Lord Kelvin and the Age of Earth

(a) (b)

Figure 4.25 (a) William Thomson (Lord Kelvin), 1824-1907, was a British physicist and electrical engineer; (b) Kelvin used the heat diffusion equation to estimate the age of Earth (credit: modification of work by NASA).

During the late 1800s, the scientists of the new field of geology were coming to the conclusion that Earth must be "millions and millions" of years old. At about the same time, Charles Darwin had published his treatise on evolution. Darwin's view was that evolution needed many millions of years to take place, and he made a bold claim that the Weald chalk fields, where important fossils were found, were the result of 300 million years of erosion.

At that time, eminent physicist William Thomson (Lord Kelvin) used an important partial differential equation, known as the *heat diffusion equation,* to estimate the age of Earth by determining how long it would take Earth to cool from molten rock to what we had at that time. His conclusion was a range of $20 \text{ to } 400$ million years, but most likely about 50 million years. For many decades, the proclamations of this irrefutable icon of science did not sit well with geologists or with Darwin.

 Read Kelvin's **paper (http://www.openstaxcollege.org/l/20_KelEarthAge)** on estimating the age of the Earth.

Kelvin made reasonable assumptions based on what was known in his time, but he also made several assumptions that turned out to be wrong. One incorrect assumption was that Earth is solid and that the cooling was therefore via conduction only, hence justifying the use of the diffusion equation. But the most serious error was a forgivable one—omission of the fact that Earth contains radioactive elements that continually supply heat beneath Earth's mantle. The discovery of radioactivity came near the end of Kelvin's life and he acknowledged that his calculation would have to be modified.

Kelvin used the simple one-dimensional model applied only to Earth's outer shell, and derived the age from graphs and the roughly known temperature gradient near Earth's surface. Let's take a look at a more appropriate version of the diffusion equation in radial coordinates, which has the form

$$\frac{\partial T}{\partial t} = K\left[\frac{\partial^2 T}{\partial^2 r} + \frac{2}{r}\frac{\partial T}{\partial r}\right]. \quad (4.23)$$

Here, $T(r, t)$ is temperature as a function of r (measured from the center of Earth) and time t. K is the heat conductivity—for molten rock, in this case. The standard method of solving such a partial differential equation is by separation of variables, where we express the solution as the product of functions containing each variable separately. In this case, we would write the temperature as

$$T(r, t) = R(r)f(t).$$

1. Substitute this form into **Equation 4.13** and, noting that $f(t)$ is constant with respect to distance (r) and $R(r)$ is constant with respect to time (t), show that
$$\frac{1}{f}\frac{\partial f}{\partial t} = \frac{K}{R}\left[\frac{\partial^2 R}{\partial r^2} + \frac{2}{r}\frac{\partial R}{\partial r}\right].$$
2. This equation represents the separation of variables we want. The left-hand side is only a function of t and the right-hand side is only a function of r, and they must be equal for all values of r and t. Therefore, they both must be equal to a constant. Let's call that constant $-\lambda^2$. (The convenience of this choice is seen on substitution.) So, we have
$$\frac{1}{f}\frac{\partial f}{\partial t} = -\lambda^2 \quad \text{and} \quad \frac{K}{R}\left[\frac{\partial^2 R}{\partial r^2} + \frac{2}{r}\frac{\partial R}{\partial r}\right] = -\lambda^2.$$
Now, we can verify through direct substitution for each equation that the solutions are $f(t) = Ae^{-\lambda^2 t}$ and $R(r) = B\left(\frac{\sin \alpha r}{r}\right) + C\left(\frac{\cos \alpha r}{r}\right)$, where $\alpha = \lambda/\sqrt{K}$. Note that $f(t) = Ae^{+\lambda n^2 t}$ is also a valid solution, so we could have chosen $+\lambda^2$ for our constant. Can you see why it would not be valid for this case as time increases?
3. Let's now apply boundary conditions.
    a. The temperature must be finite at the center of Earth, $r = 0$. Which of the two constants, B or C, must therefore be zero to keep R finite at $r = 0$? (Recall that $\sin(\alpha r)/r \to \alpha =$ as $r \to 0$, but $\cos(\alpha r)/r$ behaves very differently.)
    b. Kelvin argued that when magma reaches Earth's surface, it cools very rapidly. A person can often touch the surface within weeks of the flow. Therefore, the surface reached a moderate temperature very early and remained nearly constant at a surface temperature T_s. For simplicity, let's set $T = 0$ at $r = R_E$ and find α such that this is the temperature there for all time t. (Kelvin took the value to be $300\text{ K} \approx 80°\text{F}$. We can add this 300 K constant to our solution later.) For this to be true, the sine argument must be zero at $r = R_E$. Note that α has an infinite series of values that satisfies this condition. Each value of α represents a valid solution (each with its own value for A). The total or general solution is the sum of all these solutions.
    c. At $t = 0$, we assume that all of Earth was at an initial hot temperature T_0 (Kelvin took this to be about 7000 K.) The application of this boundary condition involves the more advanced application of Fourier coefficients. As noted in part b. each value of α_n represents a valid solution, and the general solution is a sum of all these solutions. This results in a series solution:
    $$T(r, t) = \left(\frac{T_0 R_{\text{E}}}{\pi}\right)\sum_n \frac{(-1)^{n-1}}{n} e^{-\lambda n^2 t}\frac{\sin(\alpha_n r)}{r}, \text{ where } \alpha_n = n\pi/R_{\text{E}}.$$

Note how the values of α_n come from the boundary condition applied in part b. The term $\frac{-1^{n-1}}{n}$ is the constant A_n for each term in the series, determined from applying the Fourier method. Letting $\beta = \frac{\pi}{R_{\text{E}}}$, examine the first few terms of this solution shown here and note how λ^2 in the exponential causes the higher terms to decrease quickly as time progresses:

$$T(r,t) = \frac{T_0 R_E}{\pi r}\begin{pmatrix} e^{-K\beta^2 t}(\sin \beta r) - \frac{1}{2}e^{-4K\beta^2 t}(\sin 2\beta r) + \frac{1}{3}e^{-9K\beta^2 t}(\sin 3\beta r) \\ -\frac{1}{4}e^{-16K\beta^2 t}(\sin 4\beta r) + \frac{1}{5}e^{-25K\beta^2 t}(\sin 5\beta r)... \end{pmatrix}.$$

Near time $t = 0,$ many terms of the solution are needed for accuracy. Inserting values for the conductivity K and $\beta = \pi / R_E$ for time approaching merely thousands of years, only the first few terms make a significant contribution. Kelvin only needed to look at the solution near Earth's surface (**Figure 4.26**) and, after a long time, determine what time best yielded the estimated temperature gradient known during his era $(1°F$ increase per $50 \text{ ft})$. He simply chose a range of times with a gradient close to this value. In **Figure 4.26**, the solutions are plotted and scaled, with the $300 - \text{K}$ surface temperature added. Note that the center of Earth would be relatively cool. At the time, it was thought Earth must be solid.

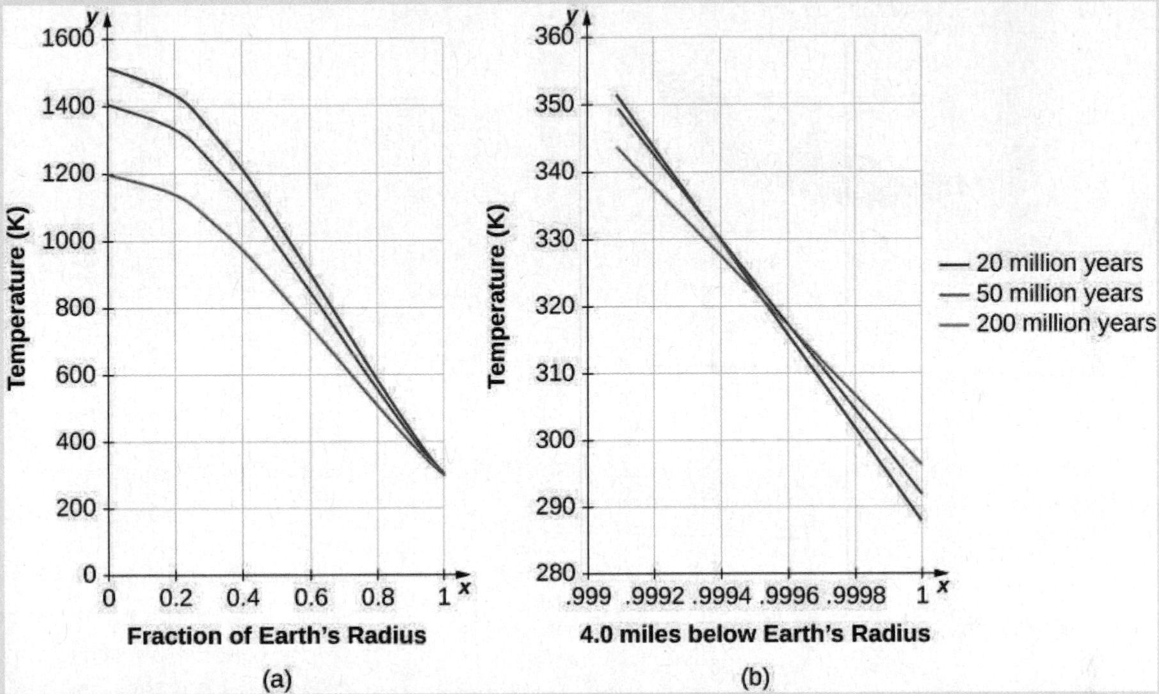

Figure 4.26 Temperature versus radial distance from the center of Earth. (a) Kelvin's results, plotted to scale. (b) A close-up of the results at a depth of 4.0 mi below Earth's surface.

Epilog

On May $20, 1904,$ physicist Ernest Rutherford spoke at the Royal Institution to announce a revised calculation that included the contribution of radioactivity as a source of Earth's heat. In Rutherford's own words:

"I came into the room, which was half-dark, and presently spotted Lord Kelvin in the audience, and realised that I was in for trouble at the last part of my speech dealing with the age of the Earth, where my views conflicted with his. To my relief, Kelvin fell fast asleep, but as I came to the important point, I saw the old bird sit up, open an eye and cock a baleful glance at me.

Then a sudden inspiration came, and I said Lord Kelvin had limited the age of the Earth, *provided no new source* [*of heat*] *was discovered*. That prophetic utterance referred to what we are now considering tonight, radium! Behold! The old boy beamed upon me."

Rutherford calculated an age for Earth of about 500 million years. Today's accepted value of Earth's age is about 4.6 billion years.

4.3 EXERCISES

For the following exercises, calculate the partial derivative using the limit definitions only.

112. $\frac{\partial z}{\partial x}$ for $z = x^2 - 3xy + y^2$

113. $\frac{\partial z}{\partial y}$ for $z = x^2 - 3xy + y^2$

For the following exercises, calculate the sign of the partial derivative using the graph of the surface.

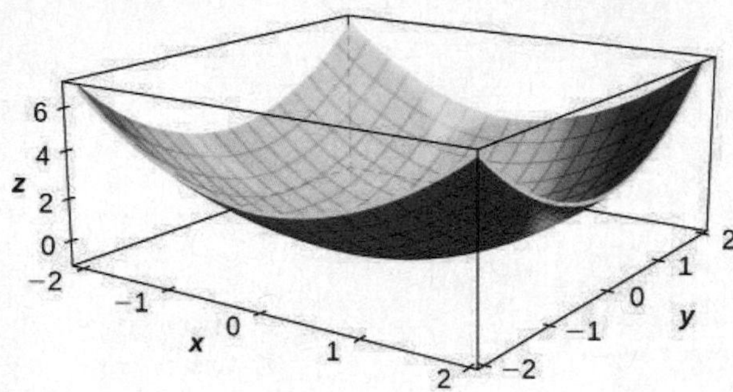

114. $f_x(1, 1)$

115. $f_x(-1, 1)$

116. $f_y(1, 1)$

117. $f_x(0, 0)$

For the following exercises, calculate the partial derivatives.

118. $\frac{\partial z}{\partial x}$ for $z = \sin(3x)\cos(3y)$

119. $\frac{\partial z}{\partial y}$ for $z = \sin(3x)\cos(3y)$

120. $\frac{\partial z}{\partial x}$ and $\frac{\partial z}{\partial y}$ for $z = x^8 e^{3y}$

121. $\frac{\partial z}{\partial x}$ and $\frac{\partial z}{\partial y}$ for $z = \ln\left(x^6 + y^4\right)$

122. Find $f_y(x, y)$ for $f(x, y) = e^{xy}\cos(x)\sin(y)$.

123. Let $z = e^{xy}$. Find $\frac{\partial z}{\partial x}$ and $\frac{\partial z}{\partial y}$.

124. Let $z = \ln\left(\frac{x}{y}\right)$. Find $\frac{\partial z}{\partial x}$ and $\frac{\partial z}{\partial y}$.

125. Let $z = \tan(2x - y)$. Find $\frac{\partial z}{\partial x}$ and $\frac{\partial z}{\partial y}$.

126. Let $z = \sinh(2x + 3y)$. Find $\frac{\partial z}{\partial x}$ and $\frac{\partial z}{\partial y}$.

127. Let $f(x, y) = \arctan\left(\frac{y}{x}\right)$. Evaluate $f_x(2, -2)$ and $f_y(2, -2)$.

128. Let $f(x, y) = \frac{xy}{x - y}$. Find $f_x(2, -2)$ and $f_y(2, -2)$.

Evaluate the partial derivatives at point $P(0, 1)$.

129. Find $\frac{\partial z}{\partial x}$ at $(0, 1)$ for $z = e^{-x}\cos(y)$.

130. Given $f(x, y, z) = x^3 yz^2$, find $\frac{\partial^2 f}{\partial x \partial y}$ and $f_z(1, 1, 1)$.

131. Given $f(x, y, z) = 2\sin(x + y)$, find $f_x\left(0, \frac{\pi}{2}, -4\right)$, $f_y\left(0, \frac{\pi}{2}, -4\right)$, and $f_z\left(0, \frac{\pi}{2}, -4\right)$.

132. The area of a parallelogram with adjacent side lengths that are a and b, and in which the angle between these two sides is θ, is given by the function $A(a, b, \theta) = ba\sin(\theta)$. Find the rate of change of the area of the parallelogram with respect to the following:

a. Side a
b. Side b
c. Angle θ

133. Express the volume of a right circular cylinder as a function of two variables:

a. its radius r and its height h.
b. Show that the rate of change of the volume of the cylinder with respect to its radius is the product of its circumference multiplied by its height.
c. Show that the rate of change of the volume of the cylinder with respect to its height is equal to the area of the circular base.

134. Calculate $\frac{\partial w}{\partial z}$ for $w = z\sin(xy^2 + 2z)$.

Find the indicated higher-order partial derivatives.

135. f_{xy} for $z = \ln(x - y)$

136. f_{yx} for $z = \ln(x - y)$

137. Let $z = x^2 + 3xy + 2y^2$. Find $\frac{\partial^2 z}{\partial x^2}$ and $\frac{\partial^2 z}{\partial y^2}$.

138. Given $z = e^x \tan y$, find $\frac{\partial^2 z}{\partial x \partial y}$ and $\frac{\partial^2 z}{\partial y \partial x}$.

139. Given $f(x, y, z) = xyz$, find f_{xyy}, f_{yxy}, and f_{yyx}.

140. Given $f(x, y, z) = e^{-2x}\sin\left(z^2 y\right)$, show that $f_{xyy} = f_{yxy}$.

141. Show that $z = \frac{1}{2}\left(e^y - e^{-y}\right)\sin x$ is a solution of the differential equation $\frac{\partial^2 z}{\partial x^2} + \frac{\partial^2 z}{\partial y^2} = 0$.

142. Find $f_{xx}(x, y)$ for $f(x, y) = \frac{4x^2}{y} + \frac{y^2}{2x}$.

143. Let $f(x, y, z) = x^2 y^3 z - 3xy^2 z^3 + 5x^2 z - y^3 z$. Find f_{xyz}.

144. Let $F(x, y, z) = x^3 yz^2 - 2x^2 yz + 3xz - 2y^3 z$. Find F_{xyz}.

145. Given $f(x, y) = x^2 + x - 3xy + y^3 - 5$, find all points at which $f_x = f_y = 0$ simultaneously.

146. Given $f(x, y) = 2x^2 + 2xy + y^2 + 2x - 3$, find all points at which $\frac{\partial f}{\partial x} = 0$ and $\frac{\partial f}{\partial y} = 0$ simultaneously.

147. Given $f(x, y) = y^3 - 3yx^2 - 3y^2 - 3x^2 + 1$, find all points on f at which $f_x = f_y = 0$ simultaneously.

148. Given $f(x, y) = 15x^3 - 3xy + 15y^3$, find all points at which $f_x(x, y) = f_y(x, y) = 0$ simultaneously.

149. Show that $z = e^x \sin y$ satisfies the equation $\frac{\partial^2 z}{\partial x^2} + \frac{\partial^2 z}{\partial y^2} = 0$.

150. Show that $f(x, y) = \ln\left(x^2 + y^2\right)$ solves Laplace's equation $\frac{\partial^2 z}{\partial x^2} + \frac{\partial^2 z}{\partial y^2} = 0$.

151. Show that $z = e^{-t}\cos\left(\frac{x}{c}\right)$ satisfies the heat equation $\frac{\partial z}{\partial t} = -e^{-t}\cos\left(\frac{x}{c}\right)$.

152. Find $\lim\limits_{\Delta x \to 0} \frac{f(x + \Delta x) - f(x, y)}{\Delta x}$ for $f(x, y) = -7x - 2xy + 7y$.

153. Find $\lim\limits_{\Delta y \to 0} \frac{f(x, y + \Delta y) - f(x, y)}{\Delta y}$ for $f(x, y) = -7x - 2xy + 7y$.

154. Find $\lim\limits_{\Delta x \to 0} \frac{\Delta f}{\Delta x} = \lim\limits_{\Delta x \to 0} \frac{f(x + \Delta x, y) - f(x, y)}{\Delta x}$ for $f(x, y) = x^2 y^2 + xy + y$.

155. Find $\lim\limits_{\Delta x \to 0} \frac{\Delta f}{\Delta x} = \lim\limits_{\Delta x \to 0} \frac{f(x + \Delta x, y) - f(x, y)}{\Delta x}$ for $f(x, y) = \sin(xy)$.

156. The function $P(T, V) = \frac{nRT}{V}$ gives the pressure at a point in a gas as a function of temperature T and volume V. The letters n and R are constants. Find $\frac{\partial P}{\partial V}$ and $\frac{\partial P}{\partial T}$, and explain what these quantities represent.

157. The equation for heat flow in the xy-plane is $\frac{\partial f}{\partial t} = \frac{\partial^2 f}{\partial x^2} + \frac{\partial^2 f}{\partial y^2}$. Show that $f(x, y, t) = e^{-2t}\sin x \sin y$ is a solution.

158. The basic wave equation is $f_{tt} = f_{xx}$. Verify that $f(x, t) = \sin(x + t)$ and $f(x, t) = \sin(x - t)$ are solutions.

159. The law of cosines can be thought of as a function of three variables. Let x, y, and θ be two sides of any triangle where the angle θ is the included angle between the two sides. Then, $F(x, y, \theta) = x^2 + y^2 - 2xy\cos\theta$ gives the square of the third side of the triangle. Find $\frac{\partial F}{\partial \theta}$ and $\frac{\partial F}{\partial x}$ when $x = 2$, $y = 3$, and $\theta = \frac{\pi}{6}$.

160. Suppose the sides of a rectangle are changing with respect to time. The first side is changing at a rate of 2 in./sec whereas the second side is changing at the rate of 4 in/sec. How fast is the diagonal of the rectangle changing when the first side measures 16 in. and the second side measures 20 in.? (Round answer to three decimal places.)

161. A Cobb-Douglas production function is $f(x, y) = 200x^{0.7}y^{0.3}$, where x and y represent the amount of labor and capital available. Let $x = 500$ and $y = 1000$. Find $\frac{\delta f}{\delta x}$ and $\frac{\delta f}{\delta y}$ at these values, which represent the marginal productivity of labor and capital, respectively.

162. The apparent temperature index is a measure of how the temperature feels, and it is based on two variables: h, which is relative humidity, and t, which is the air temperature. $A = 0.885t - 22.4h + 1.20th - 0.544$. Find $\frac{\partial A}{\partial t}$ and $\frac{\partial A}{\partial h}$ when $t = 20°\text{F}$ and $h = 0.90$.

4.4 | Tangent Planes and Linear Approximations

Learning Objectives

- **4.4.1** Determine the equation of a plane tangent to a given surface at a point.
- **4.4.2** Use the tangent plane to approximate a function of two variables at a point.
- **4.4.3** Explain when a function of two variables is differentiable.
- **4.4.4** Use the total differential to approximate the change in a function of two variables.

In this section, we consider the problem of finding the tangent plane to a surface, which is analogous to finding the equation of a tangent line to a curve when the curve is defined by the graph of a function of one variable, $y = f(x)$. The slope of the tangent line at the point $x = a$ is given by $m = f'(a)$; what is the slope of a tangent plane? We learned about the equation of a plane in **Equations of Lines and Planes in Space**; in this section, we see how it can be applied to the problem at hand.

Tangent Planes

Intuitively, it seems clear that, in a plane, only one line can be tangent to a curve at a point. However, in three-dimensional space, many lines can be tangent to a given point. If these lines lie in the same plane, they determine the tangent plane at that point. A tangent plane at a regular point contains all of the lines tangent to that point. A more intuitive way to think of a tangent plane is to assume the surface is smooth at that point (no corners). Then, a tangent line to the surface at that point in any direction does not have any abrupt changes in slope because the direction changes smoothly.

Definition

Let $P_0 = (x_0, y_0, z_0)$ be a point on a surface S, and let C be any curve passing through P_0 and lying entirely in S. If the tangent lines to all such curves C at P_0 lie in the same plane, then this plane is called the **tangent plane** to S at P_0 (**Figure 4.27**).

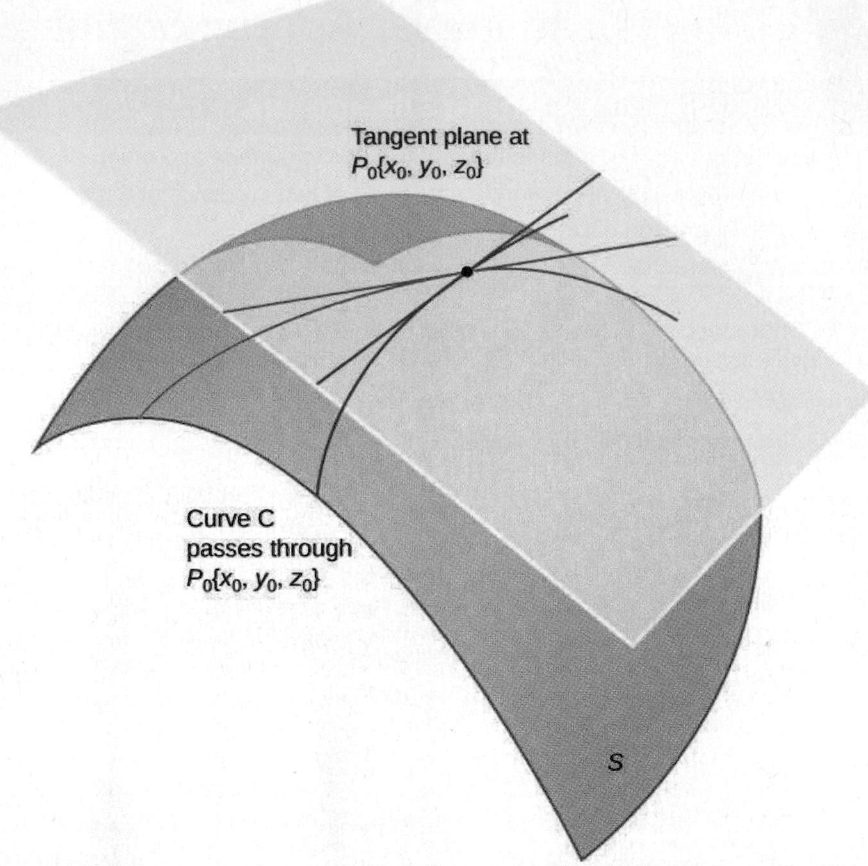

Figure 4.27 The tangent plane to a surface S at a point P_0 contains all the tangent lines to curves in S that pass through P_0.

For a tangent plane to a surface to exist at a point on that surface, it is sufficient for the function that defines the surface to be differentiable at that point. We define the term tangent plane here and then explore the idea intuitively.

Definition

Let S be a surface defined by a differentiable function $z = f(x, y)$, and let $P_0 = (x_0, y_0)$ be a point in the domain of f. Then, the equation of the tangent plane to S at P_0 is given by

$$z = f(x_0, y_0) + f_x(x_0, y_0)(x - x_0) + f_y(x_0, y_0)(y - y_0). \quad \textbf{(4.24)}$$

To see why this formula is correct, let's first find two tangent lines to the surface S. The equation of the tangent line to the curve that is represented by the intersection of S with the vertical trace given by $x = x_0$ is $z = f(x_0, y_0) + f_y(x_0, y_0)(y - y_0)$. Similarly, the equation of the tangent line to the curve that is represented by the intersection of S with the vertical trace given by $y = y_0$ is $z = f(x_0, y_0) + f_x(x_0, y_0)(x - x_0)$. A parallel vector to the first tangent line is $\mathbf{a} = \mathbf{j} + f_y(x_0, y_0)\mathbf{k}$; a parallel vector to the second tangent line is $\mathbf{b} = \mathbf{i} + f_x(x_0, y_0)\mathbf{k}$. We can take the cross product of these two vectors:

$$\begin{aligned}
\mathbf{a} \times \mathbf{b} &= \left(\mathbf{j} + f_y(x_0, y_0)\mathbf{k}\right) \times \left(\mathbf{i} + f_x(x_0, y_0)\mathbf{k}\right) \\
&= \begin{vmatrix} \mathbf{i} & \mathbf{j} & \mathbf{k} \\ 0 & 1 & f_y(x_0, y_0) \\ 1 & 0 & f_x(x_0, y_0) \end{vmatrix} \\
&= f_x(x_0, y_0)\mathbf{i} + f_y(x_0, y_0)\mathbf{j} - \mathbf{k}.
\end{aligned}$$

This vector is perpendicular to both lines and is therefore perpendicular to the tangent plane. We can use this vector as a normal vector to the tangent plane, along with the point $P_0 = \left(x_0, y_0, f(x_0, y_0)\right)$ in the equation for a plane:

$$\begin{aligned}
\mathbf{n} \cdot \left((x - x_0)\mathbf{i} + (y - y_0)\mathbf{j} + \left(z - f(x_0, y_0)\right)\mathbf{k}\right) &= 0 \\
\left(f_x(x_0, y_0)\mathbf{i} + f_y(x_0, y_0)\mathbf{j}\text{-}\mathbf{k}\right) \cdot \left((x - x_0)\mathbf{i} + (y - y_0)\mathbf{j} + \left(z - f(x_0, y_0)\right)\mathbf{k}\right) &= 0 \\
f_x(x_0, y_0)(x - x_0) + f_y(x_0, y_0)(y - y_0) - \left(z - f(x_0, y_0)\right) &= 0.
\end{aligned}$$

Solving this equation for z gives **Equation 4.24**.

Example 4.21

Finding a Tangent Plane

Find the equation of the tangent plane to the surface defined by the function $f(x, y) = 2x^2 - 3xy + 8y^2 + 2x - 4y + 4$ at point $(2, -1)$.

Solution

First, we must calculate $f_x(x, y)$ and $f_y(x, y)$, then use **Equation 4.24** with $x_0 = 2$ and $y_0 = -1$:

$$\begin{aligned}
f_x(x, y) &= 4x - 3y + 2 \\
f_y(x, y) &= -3x + 16y - 4 \\
f(2, -1) &= 2(2)^2 - 3(2)(-1) + 8(-1)^2 + 2(2) - 4(-1) + 4 = 34. \\
f_x(2, -1) &= 4(2) - 3(-1) + 2 = 13 \\
f_y(2, -1) &= -3(2) + 16(-1) - 4 = -26.
\end{aligned}$$

Then **Equation 4.24** becomes

$$\begin{aligned}
z &= f(x_0, y_0) + f_x(x_0, y_0)(x - x_0) + f_y(x_0, y_0)(y - y_0) \\
z &= 34 + 13(x - 2) - 26(y - (-1)) \\
z &= 34 + 13x - 26 - 26y - 26 \\
z &= 13x - 26y - 18.
\end{aligned}$$

(See the following figure).

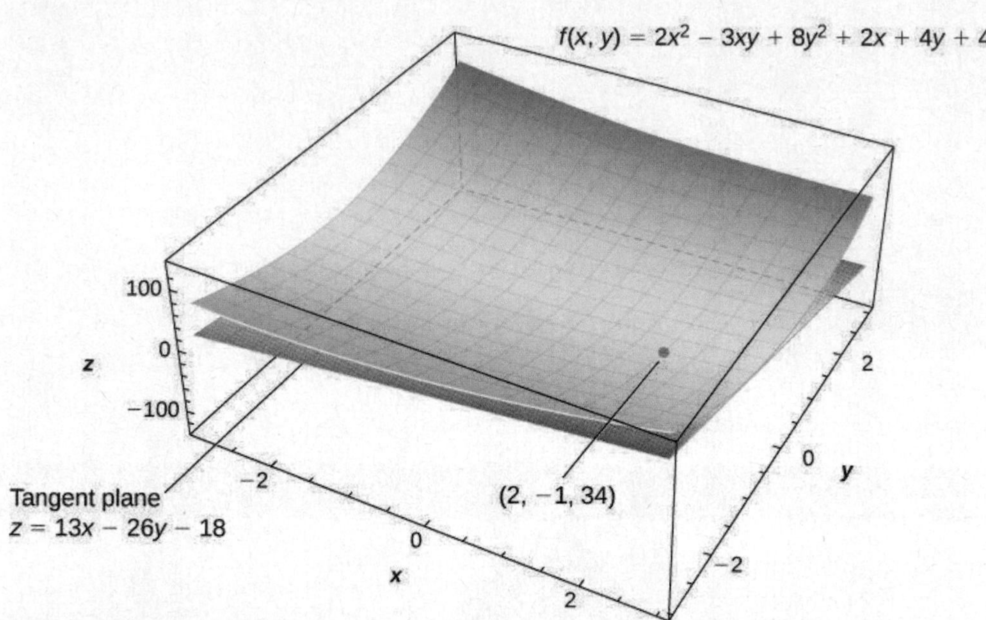

Figure 4.28 Calculating the equation of a tangent plane to a given surface at a given point.

4.19 Find the equation of the tangent plane to the surface defined by the function $f(x, y) = x^3 - x^2 y + y^2 - 2x + 3y - 2$ at point $(-1, 3)$.

Example 4.22

Finding Another Tangent Plane

Find the equation of the tangent plane to the surface defined by the function $f(x, y) = \sin(2x)\cos(3y)$ at the point $(\pi/3, \pi/4)$.

Solution

First, calculate $f_x(x, y)$ and $f_y(x, y)$, then use **Equation 4.24** with $x_0 = \pi/3$ and $y_0 = \pi/4$:

$$\begin{aligned}
f_x(x, y) &= 2\cos(2x)\cos(3y) \\
f_y(x, y) &= -3\sin(2x)\sin(3y) \\
f\left(\frac{\pi}{3}, \frac{\pi}{4}\right) &= \sin\left(2\left(\frac{\pi}{3}\right)\right)\cos\left(3\left(\frac{\pi}{4}\right)\right) = \left(\frac{\sqrt{3}}{2}\right)\left(-\frac{\sqrt{2}}{2}\right) = -\frac{\sqrt{6}}{4} \\
f_x\left(\frac{\pi}{3}, \frac{\pi}{4}\right) &= 2\cos\left(2\left(\frac{\pi}{3}\right)\right)\cos\left(3\left(\frac{\pi}{4}\right)\right) = 2\left(-\frac{1}{2}\right)\left(-\frac{\sqrt{2}}{2}\right) = \frac{\sqrt{2}}{2} \\
f_y\left(\frac{\pi}{3}, \frac{\pi}{4}\right) &= -3\sin\left(2\left(\frac{\pi}{3}\right)\right)\sin\left(3\left(\frac{\pi}{4}\right)\right) = -3\left(\frac{\sqrt{3}}{2}\right)\left(\frac{\sqrt{2}}{2}\right) = -\frac{3\sqrt{6}}{4}.
\end{aligned}$$

Then **Equation 4.24** becomes

$$z = f(x_0, y_0) + f_x(x_0, y_0)(x - x_0) + f_y(x_0, y_0)(y - y_0)$$
$$z = -\frac{\sqrt{6}}{4} + \frac{\sqrt{2}}{2}\left(x - \frac{\pi}{3}\right) - \frac{3\sqrt{6}}{4}\left(y - \frac{\pi}{4}\right)$$
$$z = \frac{\sqrt{2}}{2}x - \frac{3\sqrt{6}}{4}y - \frac{\sqrt{6}}{4} - \frac{\pi\sqrt{2}}{6} + \frac{3\pi\sqrt{6}}{16}.$$

A tangent plane to a surface does not always exist at every point on the surface. Consider the function

$$f(x, y) = \begin{cases} \frac{xy}{\sqrt{x^2 + y^2}} & (x, y) \neq (0, 0) \\ 0 & (x, y) = (0, 0). \end{cases}$$

The graph of this function follows.

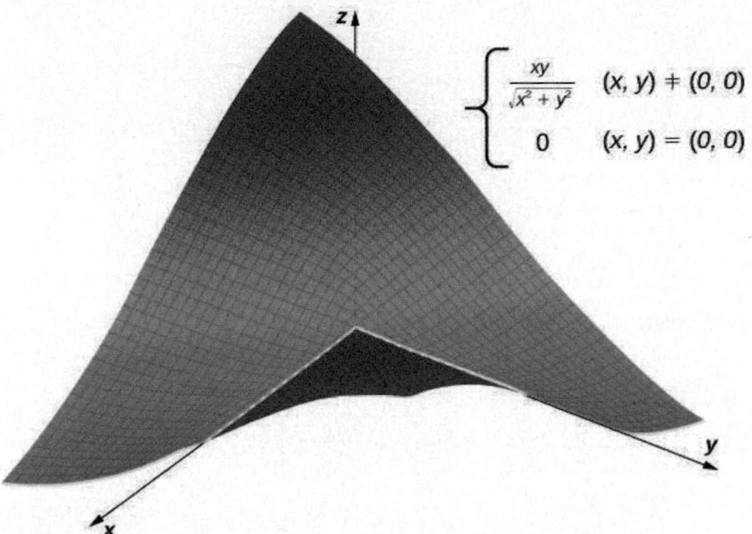

Figure 4.29 Graph of a function that does not have a tangent plane at the origin.

If either $x = 0$ or $y = 0,$ then $f(x, y) = 0,$ so the value of the function does not change on either the x- or y-axis. Therefore, $f_x(x, 0) = f_y(0, y) = 0,$ so as either $x\, or\, y$ approach zero, these partial derivatives stay equal to zero. Substituting them into **Equation 4.24** gives $z = 0$ as the equation of the tangent line. However, if we approach the origin from a different direction, we get a different story. For example, suppose we approach the origin along the line $y = x.$ If we put $y = x$ into the original function, it becomes

$$f(x, x) = \frac{x(x)}{\sqrt{x^2 + (x)^2}} = \frac{x^2}{\sqrt{2x^2}} = \frac{|x|}{\sqrt{2}}.$$

When $x > 0,$ the slope of this curve is equal to $\sqrt{2}/2;$ when $x < 0,$ the slope of this curve is equal to $-\left(\sqrt{2}/2\right).$ This presents a problem. In the definition of *tangent plane*, we presumed that all tangent lines through point P (in this case, the origin) lay in the same plane. This is clearly not the case here. When we study differentiable functions, we will see that this function is not differentiable at the origin.

Linear Approximations

Recall from **Linear Approximations and Differentials (http://cnx.org/content/m53605/latest/)** that the formula for the linear approximation of a function $f(x)$ at the point $x = a$ is given by

$$y \approx f(a) + f'(a)(x - a).$$

The diagram for the linear approximation of a function of one variable appears in the following graph.

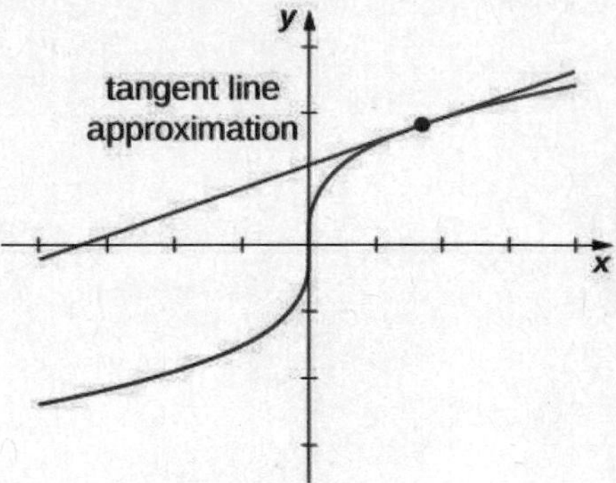

Figure 4.30 Linear approximation of a function in one variable.

The tangent line can be used as an approximation to the function $f(x)$ for values of x reasonably close to $x = a.$ When working with a function of two variables, the tangent line is replaced by a tangent plane, but the approximation idea is much the same.

Definition

Given a function $z = f(x, y)$ with continuous partial derivatives that exist at the point $(x_0, y_0),$ the **linear approximation** of f at the point (x_0, y_0) is given by the equation

$$L(x, y) = f(x_0, y_0) + f_x(x_0, y_0)(x - x_0) + f_y(x_0, y_0)(y - y_0). \tag{4.25}$$

Notice that this equation also represents the tangent plane to the surface defined by $z = f(x, y)$ at the point $(x_0, y_0).$ The idea behind using a linear approximation is that, if there is a point (x_0, y_0) at which the precise value of $f(x, y)$ is known, then for values of (x, y) reasonably close to $(x_0, y_0),$ the linear approximation (i.e., tangent plane) yields a value that is also reasonably close to the exact value of $f(x, y)$ (**Figure 4.31**). Furthermore the plane that is used to find the linear approximation is also the tangent plane to the surface at the point $(x_0, y_0).$

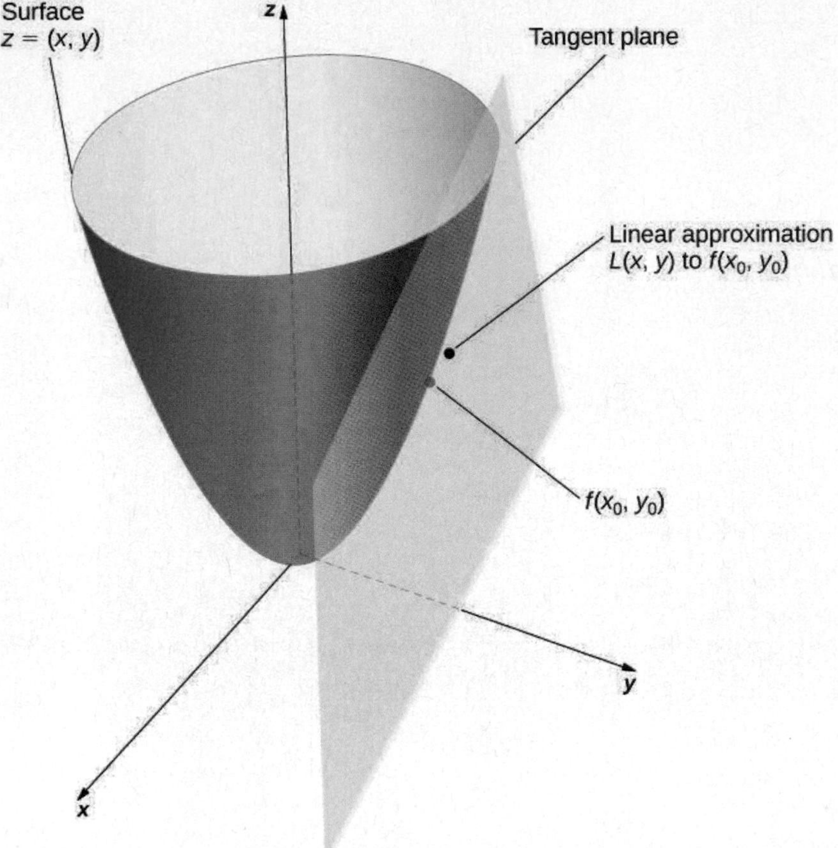

Figure 4.31 Using a tangent plane for linear approximation at a point.

Example 4.23

Using a Tangent Plane Approximation

Given the function $f(x, y) = \sqrt{41 - 4x^2 - y^2}$, approximate $f(2.1, 2.9)$ using point $(2, 3)$ for (x_0, y_0). What is the approximate value of $f(2.1, 2.9)$ to four decimal places?

Solution

To apply **Equation 4.25**, we first must calculate $f(x_0, y_0)$, $f_x(x_0, y_0)$, and $f_y(x_0, y_0)$ using $x_0 = 2$ and $y_0 = 3$:

$$\begin{aligned} f(x_0, y_0) &= f(2, 3) = \sqrt{41 - 4(2)^2 - (3)^2} = \sqrt{41 - 16 - 9} = \sqrt{16} = 4 \\ f_x(x, y) &= -\frac{4x}{\sqrt{41 - 4x^2 - y^2}} \text{ so } f_x(x_0, y_0) = -\frac{4(2)}{\sqrt{41 - 4(2)^2 - (3)^2}} = -2 \\ f_y(x, y) &= -\frac{y}{\sqrt{41 - 4x^2 - y^2}} \text{ so } f_y(x_0, y_0) = -\frac{3}{\sqrt{41 - 4(2)^2 - (3)^2}} = -\frac{3}{4}. \end{aligned}$$

Now we substitute these values into **Equation 4.25**:

$$\begin{aligned} L(x, y) &= f(x_0, y_0) + f_x(x_0, y_0)(x - x_0) + f_y(x_0, y_0)(y - y_0) \\ &= 4 - 2(x - 2) - \frac{3}{4}(y - 3) \\ &= \frac{41}{4} - 2x - \frac{3}{4}y. \end{aligned}$$

Last, we substitute $x = 2.1$ and $y = 2.9$ into $L(x, y)$:

$$L(2.1, 2.9) = \frac{41}{4} - 2(2.1) - \frac{3}{4}(2.9) = 10.25 - 4.2 - 2.175 = 3.875.$$

The approximate value of $f(2.1, 2.9)$ to four decimal places is

$$f(2.1, 2.9) = \sqrt{41 - 4(2.1)^2 - (2.9)^2} = \sqrt{14.95} \approx 3.8665,$$

which corresponds to a 0.2% error in approximation.

4.20 Given the function $f(x, y) = e^{5 - 2x + 3y}$, approximate $f(4.1, 0.9)$ using point $(4, 1)$ for (x_0, y_0). What is the approximate value of $f(4.1, 0.9)$ to four decimal places?

Differentiability

When working with a function $y = f(x)$ of one variable, the function is said to be differentiable at a point $x = a$ if $f'(a)$ exists. Furthermore, if a function of one variable is differentiable at a point, the graph is "smooth" at that point (i.e., no corners exist) and a tangent line is well-defined at that point.

The idea behind differentiability of a function of two variables is connected to the idea of smoothness at that point. In this case, a surface is considered to be smooth at point P if a tangent plane to the surface exists at that point. If a function is differentiable at a point, then a tangent plane to the surface exists at that point. Recall the formula for a tangent plane at a point (x_0, y_0) is given by

$$z = f(x_0, y_0) + f_x(x_0, y_0)(x - x_0) + f_y(x_0, y_0)(y - y_0),$$

For a tangent plane to exist at the point (x_0, y_0), the partial derivatives must therefore exist at that point. However, this is not a sufficient condition for smoothness, as was illustrated in **Figure 4.29**. In that case, the partial derivatives existed at the origin, but the function also had a corner on the graph at the origin.

Definition

A function $f(x, y)$ is **differentiable** at a point $P(x_0, y_0)$ if, for all points (x, y) in a δ disk around P, we can write

$$f(x, y) = f(x_0, y_0) + f_x(x_0, y_0)(x - x_0) + f_y(x_0, y_0)(y - y_0) + E(x, y), \tag{4.26}$$

where the error term E satisfies

$$\lim_{(x, y) \to (x_0, y_0)} \frac{E(x, y)}{\sqrt{(x - x_0)^2 + (y - y_0)^2}} = 0.$$

The last term in **Equation 4.26** is referred to as the *error term* and it represents how closely the tangent plane comes to the surface in a small neighborhood (δ disk) of point P. For the function f to be differentiable at P, the function must be smooth—that is, the graph of f must be close to the tangent plane for points near P.

Example 4.24

Demonstrating Differentiability

Show that the function $f(x, y) = 2x^2 - 4y$ is differentiable at point $(2, -3)$.

Solution

First, we calculate $f(x_0, y_0)$, $f_x(x_0, y_0)$, and $f_y(x_0, y_0)$ using $x_0 = 2$ and $y_0 = -3$, then we use **Equation 4.26**:

$$\begin{aligned} f(2, -3) &= 2(2)^2 - 4(-3) = 8 + 12 = 20 \\ f_x(2, -3) &= 4(2) = 8 \\ f_y(2, -3) &= -4. \end{aligned}$$

Therefore $m_1 = 8$ and $m_2 = -4$, and **Equation 4.26** becomes

$$\begin{aligned} f(x, y) &= f(2, -3) + f_x(2, -3)(x - 2) + f_y(2, -3)(y + 3) + E(x, y) \\ 2x^2 - 4y &= 20 + 8(x - 2) - 4(y + 3) + E(x, y) \\ 2x^2 - 4y &= 20 + 8x - 16 - 4y - 12 + E(x, y) \\ 2x^2 - 4y &= 8x - 4y - 8 + E(x, y) \\ E(x, y) &= 2x^2 - 8x + 8. \end{aligned}$$

Next, we calculate $\lim\limits_{(x, y) \to (x_0, y_0)} \dfrac{E(x, y)}{\sqrt{(x - x_0)^2 + (y - y_0)^2}}$:

$$\begin{aligned} \lim_{(x, y) \to (x_0, y_0)} \frac{E(x, y)}{\sqrt{(x - x_0)^2 + (y - y_0)^2}} &= \lim_{(x, y) \to (2, -3)} \frac{2x^2 - 8x + 8}{\sqrt{(x - 2)^2 + (y + 3)^2}} \\ &= \lim_{(x, y) \to (2, -3)} \frac{2\left(x^2 - 4x + 4\right)}{\sqrt{(x - 2)^2 + (y + 3)^2}} \\ &= \lim_{(x, y) \to (2, -3)} \frac{2(x - 2)^2}{\sqrt{(x - 2)^2 + (y + 3)^2}} \\ &\le \lim_{(x, y) \to (2, -3)} \frac{2\left((x - 2)^2 + (y + 3)^2\right)}{\sqrt{(x - 2)^2 + (y + 3)^2}} \\ &= \lim_{(x, y) \to (2, -3)} 2\sqrt{(x - 2)^2 + (y + 3)^2} \\ &= 0. \end{aligned}$$

Since $E(x, y) \ge 0$ for any value of x or y, the original limit must be equal to zero. Therefore, $f(x, y) = 2x^2 - 4y$ is differentiable at point $(2, -3)$.

4.21 Show that the function $f(x, y) = 3x - 4y^2$ is differentiable at point $(-1, 2)$.

The function $f(x, y) = \begin{cases} \dfrac{xy}{\sqrt{x^2 + y^2}} & (x, y) \neq (0, 0) \\ 0 & (x, y) = (0, 0) \end{cases}$ is not differentiable at the origin. We can see this by calculating the partial derivatives. This function appeared earlier in the section, where we showed that $f_x(0, 0) = f_y(0, 0) = 0.$ Substituting this information into **Equation 4.26** using $x_0 = 0$ and $y_0 = 0,$ we get

$$\begin{aligned} f(x, y) &= f(0, 0) + f_x(0, 0)(x - 0) + f_y(0, 0)(y - 0) + E(x, y) \\ E(x, y) &= \frac{xy}{\sqrt{x^2 + y^2}}. \end{aligned}$$

Calculating $\lim_{(x, y) \to (x_0, y_0)} \frac{E(x, y)}{\sqrt{(x - x_0)^2 + (y - y_0)^2}}$ gives

$$\begin{aligned} \lim_{(x, y) \to (x_0, y_0)} \frac{E(x, y)}{\sqrt{(x - x_0)^2 + (y - y_0)^2}} &= \lim_{(x, y) \to (0, 0)} \frac{\frac{xy}{\sqrt{x^2 + y^2}}}{\sqrt{x^2 + y^2}} \\ &= \lim_{(x, y) \to (0, 0)} \frac{xy}{x^2 + y^2}. \end{aligned}$$

Depending on the path taken toward the origin, this limit takes different values. Therefore, the limit does not exist and the function f is not differentiable at the origin as shown in the following figure.

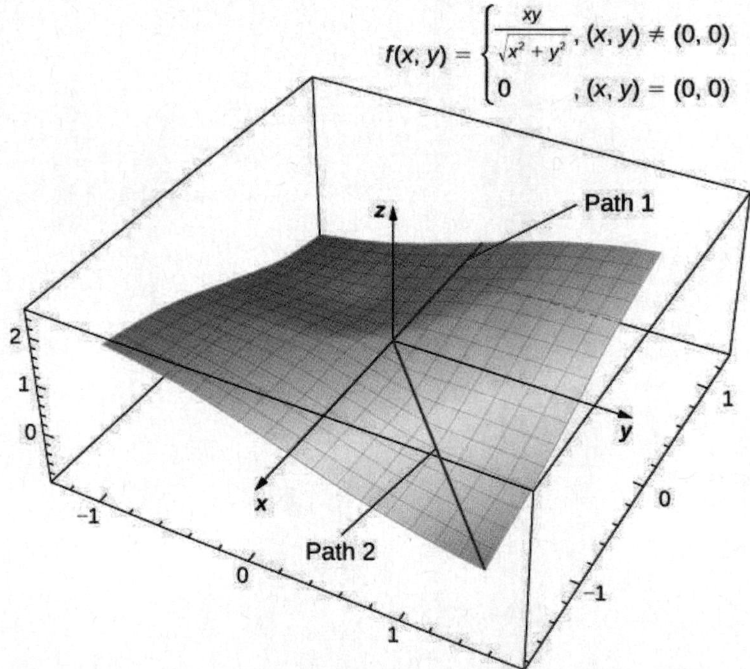

Figure 4.32 This function $f(x, y)$ is not differentiable at the origin.

Differentiability and continuity for functions of two or more variables are connected, the same as for functions of one variable. In fact, with some adjustments of notation, the basic theorem is the same.

Theorem 4.6: Differentiability Implies Continuity

Let $z = f(x, y)$ be a function of two variables with (x_0, y_0) in the domain of f. If $f(x, y)$ is differentiable at $(x_0, y_0),$ then $f(x, y)$ is continuous at (x_0, y_0).

Differentiability Implies Continuity shows that if a function is differentiable at a point, then it is continuous there. However, if a function is continuous at a point, then it is not necessarily differentiable at that point. For example,

$$f(x, y) = \begin{cases} \dfrac{xy}{\sqrt{x^2 + y^2}} & (x, y) \neq (0, 0) \\ 0 & (x, y) = (0, 0) \end{cases}$$

is continuous at the origin, but it is not differentiable at the origin. This observation is also similar to the situation in single-variable calculus.

Continuity of First Partials Implies Differentiability further explores the connection between continuity and differentiability at a point. This theorem says that if the function and its partial derivatives are continuous at a point, the function is differentiable.

Theorem 4.7: Continuity of First Partials Implies Differentiability

Let $z = f(x, y)$ be a function of two variables with (x_0, y_0) in the domain of f. If $f(x, y)$, $f_x(x, y)$, and $f_y(x, y)$ all exist in a neighborhood of (x_0, y_0) and are continuous at (x_0, y_0), then $f(x, y)$ is differentiable there.

Recall that earlier we showed that the function

$$f(x, y) = \begin{cases} \dfrac{xy}{\sqrt{x^2 + y^2}} & (x, y) \neq (0, 0) \\ 0 & (x, y) = (0, 0) \end{cases}$$

was not differentiable at the origin. Let's calculate the partial derivatives f_x and f_y:

$$\frac{\partial f}{\partial x} = \frac{y^3}{\left(x^2 + y^2\right)^{3/2}} \quad \text{and} \quad \frac{\partial f}{\partial y} = \frac{x^3}{\left(x^2 + y^2\right)^{3/2}}.$$

The contrapositive of the preceding theorem states that if a function is not differentiable, then at least one of the hypotheses must be false. Let's explore the condition that $f_x(0, 0)$ must be continuous. For this to be true, it must be true that $\lim_{(x, y) \to (0, 0)} f_x(0, 0) = f_x(0, 0)$:

$$\lim_{(x, y) \to (0, 0)} f_x(x, y) = \lim_{(x, y) \to (0, 0)} \frac{y^3}{\left(x^2 + y^2\right)^{3/2}}.$$

Let $x = ky$. Then

$$\begin{aligned} \lim_{(x, y) \to (0, 0)} \frac{y^3}{\left(x^2 + y^2\right)^{3/2}} &= \lim_{y \to 0} \frac{y^3}{\left((ky)^2 + y^2\right)^{3/2}} \\ &= \lim_{y \to 0} \frac{y^3}{\left(k^2 y^2 + y^2\right)^{3/2}} \\ &= \lim_{y \to 0} \frac{y^3}{|y|^3 \left(k^2 + 1\right)^{3/2}} \\ &= \frac{1}{\left(k^2 + 1\right)^{3/2}} \lim_{y \to 0} \frac{|y|}{y}. \end{aligned}$$

If $y > 0$, then this expression equals $1/\left(k^2 + 1\right)^{3/2}$; if $y < 0$, then it equals $-\left(1/\left(k^2 + 1\right)^{3/2}\right)$. In either case, the value depends on $k,$ so the limit fails to exist.

Differentials

In **Linear Approximations and Differentials (http://cnx.org/content/m53605/latest/)** we first studied the concept of differentials. The differential of $y,$ written $dy,$ is defined as $f'(x)dx.$ The differential is used to approximate $\Delta y = f(x + \Delta x) - f(x),$ where $\Delta x = dx.$ Extending this idea to the linear approximation of a function of two variables at the point (x_0, y_0) yields the formula for the total differential for a function of two variables.

Definition

Let $z = f(x, y)$ be a function of two variables with (x_0, y_0) in the domain of $f,$ and let Δx and Δy be chosen so that $(x_0 + \Delta x, y_0 + \Delta y)$ is also in the domain of $f.$ If f is differentiable at the point $(x_0, y_0),$ then the differentials dx and dy are defined as

$$dx = \Delta x \text{ and } dy = \Delta y.$$

The differential $dz,$ also called the **total differential** of $z = f(x, y)$ at $(x_0, y_0),$ is defined as

$$dz = f_x(x_0, y_0)dx + f_y(x_0, y_0)dy. \tag{4.27}$$

Notice that the symbol ∂ is not used to denote the total differential; rather, d appears in front of $z.$ Now, let's define $\Delta z = f(x + \Delta x, y + \Delta y) - f(x, y).$ We use dz to approximate $\Delta z,$ so

$$\Delta z \approx dz = f_x(x_0, y_0)dx + f_y(x_0, y_0)dy.$$

Therefore, the differential is used to approximate the change in the function $z = f(x_0, y_0)$ at the point (x_0, y_0) for given values of Δx and $\Delta y.$ Since $\Delta z = f(x + \Delta x, y + \Delta y) - f(x, y),$ this can be used further to approximate $f(x + \Delta x, y + \Delta y)$:

$$\begin{aligned} f(x + \Delta x, y + \Delta y) &= f(x, y) + \Delta z \\ &\approx f(x, y) + f_x(x_0, y_0)\Delta x + f_y(x_0, y_0)\Delta y. \end{aligned}$$

See the following figure.

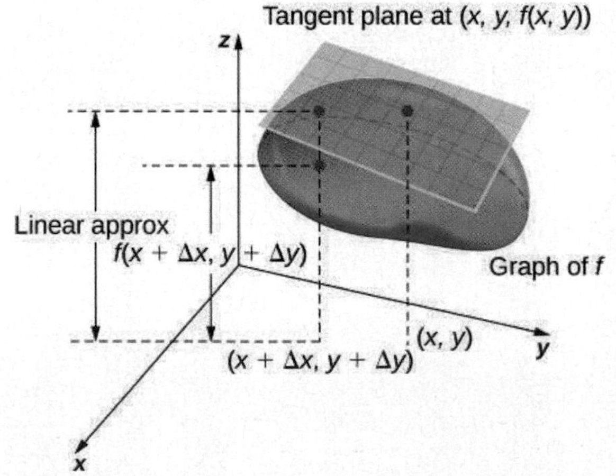

Figure 4.33 The linear approximation is calculated via the formula
$f(x + \Delta x, y + \Delta y) \approx f(x, y) + f_x(x_0, y_0)\Delta x + f_y(x_0, y_0)\Delta y.$

One such application of this idea is to determine error propagation. For example, if we are manufacturing a gadget and are off by a certain amount in measuring a given quantity, the differential can be used to estimate the error in the total volume of the gadget.

Example 4.25

Approximation by Differentials

Find the differential dz of the function $f(x, y) = 3x^2 - 2xy + y^2$ and use it to approximate Δz at point $(2, -3)$. Use $\Delta x = 0.1$ and $\Delta y = -0.05$. What is the exact value of Δz?

Solution

First, we must calculate $f(x_0, y_0)$, $f_x(x_0, y_0)$, and $f_y(x_0, y_0)$ using $x_0 = 2$ and $y_0 = -3$:

$$\begin{aligned}
f(x_0, y_0) &= f(2, -3) = 3(2)^2 - 2(2)(-3) + (-3)^2 = 12 + 12 + 9 = 33 \\
f_x(x, y) &= 6x - 2y \\
f_y(x, y) &= -2x + 2y \\
f_x(x_0, y_0) &= f_x(2, -3) = 6(2) - 2(-3) = 12 + 6 = 18 \\
f_y(x_0, y_0) &= f_y(2, -3) = -2(2) + 2(-3) = -4 - 6 = -10.
\end{aligned}$$

Then, we substitute these quantities into **Equation 4.27**:

$$\begin{aligned}
dz &= f_x(x_0, y_0)dx + f_y(x_0, y_0)dy \\
dz &= 18(0.1) - 10(-0.05) = 1.8 + 0.5 = 2.3.
\end{aligned}$$

This is the approximation to $\Delta z = f(x_0 + \Delta x, y_0 + \Delta y) - f(x_0, y_0)$. The exact value of Δz is given by

$$\begin{aligned}
\Delta z &= f(x_0 + \Delta x, y_0 + \Delta y) - f(x_0, y_0) \\
&= f(2 + 0.1, -3 - 0.05) - f(2, -3) \\
&= f(2.1, -3.05) - f(2, -3) \\
&= 2.3425.
\end{aligned}$$

4.22 Find the differential dz of the function $f(x, y) = 4y^2 + x^2 y - 2xy$ and use it to approximate Δz at point $(1, -1)$. Use $\Delta x = 0.03$ and $\Delta y = -0.02$. What is the exact value of Δz?

Differentiability of a Function of Three Variables

All of the preceding results for differentiability of functions of two variables can be generalized to functions of three variables. First, the definition:

Definition

A function $f(x, y, z)$ is differentiable at a point $P(x_0, y_0, z_0)$ if for all points (x, y, z) in a δ disk around P we can write

$$\begin{aligned}
f(x, y) &= f(x_0, y_0, z_0) + f_x(x_0, y_0, z_0)(x - x_0) + f_y(x_0, y_0, z_0)(y - y_0) \\
&\quad + f_z(x_0, y_0, z_0)(z - z_0) + E(x, y, z),
\end{aligned} \tag{4.28}$$

where the error term E satisfies

$$\lim_{(x,\ y,\ z) \to (x_0,\ y_0,\ z_0)} \frac{E(x,\ y,\ z)}{\sqrt{(x - x_0)^2 + (y - y_0)^2 + (z - z_0)^2}} = 0.$$

If a function of three variables is differentiable at a point $(x_0,\ y_0,\ z_0)$, then it is continuous there. Furthermore, continuity of first partial derivatives at that point guarantees differentiability.

4.4 EXERCISES

For the following exercises, find a unit normal vector to the surface at the indicated point.

163. $f(x, y) = x^3$, $(2, -1, 8)$

164. $\ln\left(\frac{x}{y-z}\right) = 0$ when $x = y = 1$

For the following exercises, as a useful review for techniques used in this section, find a normal vector and a tangent vector at point P.

165. $x^2 + xy + y^2 = 3$, $P(-1, -1)$

166. $\left(x^2 + y^2\right)^2 = 9\left(x^2 - y^2\right)$, $P(\sqrt{2}, 1)$

167. $xy^2 - 2x^2 + y + 5x = 6$, $P(4, 2)$

168. $2x^3 - x^2y^2 = 3x - y - 7$, $P(1, -2)$

169. $ze^{x^2 - y^2} - 3 = 0$, $P(2, 2, 3)$

For the following exercises, find the equation for the tangent plane to the surface at the indicated point. (*Hint:* Solve for z in terms of x and y.)

170. $-8x - 3y - 7z = -19$, $P(1, -1, 2)$

171. $z = -9x^2 - 3y^2$, $P(2, 1, -39)$

172. $x^2 + 10xyz + y^2 + 8z^2 = 0$, $P(-1, -1, -1)$

173. $z = \ln(10x^2 + 2y^2 + 1)$, $P(0, 0, 0)$

174. $z = e^{7x^2 + 4y^2}$, $P(0, 0, 1)$

175. $xy + yz + zx = 11$, $P(1, 2, 3)$

176. $x^2 + 4y^2 = z^2$, $P(3, 2, 5)$

177. $x^3 + y^3 = 3xyz$, $P\left(1, 2, \frac{3}{2}\right)$

178. $z = axy$, $P\left(1, \frac{1}{a}, 1\right)$

179. $z = \sin x + \sin y + \sin(x + y)$, $P(0, 0, 0)$

180. $h(x, y) = \ln\sqrt{x^2 + y^2}$, $P(3, 4)$

181. $z = x^2 - 2xy + y^2$, $P(1, 2, 1)$

For the following exercises, find parametric equations for the normal line to the surface at the indicated point. (Recall that to find the equation of a line in space, you need a point on the line, $P_0(x_0, y_0, z_0)$, and a vector $\mathbf{n} = \langle a, b, c \rangle$ that is parallel to the line. Then the equation of the line is $x - x_0 = at$, $y - y_0 = bt$, $z - z_0 = ct$.)

182. $-3x + 9y + 4z = -4$, $P(1, -1, 2)$

183. $z = 5x^2 - 2y^2$, $P(2, 1, 18)$

184. $x^2 - 8xyz + y^2 + 6z^2 = 0$, $P(1, 1, 1)$

185. $z = \ln\left(3x^2 + 7y^2 + 1\right)$, $P(0, 0, 0)$

186. $z = e^{4x^2 + 6y^2}$, $P(0, 0, 1)$

187. $z = x^2 - 2xy + y^2$ at point $P(1, 2, 1)$

For the following exercises, use the figure shown here.

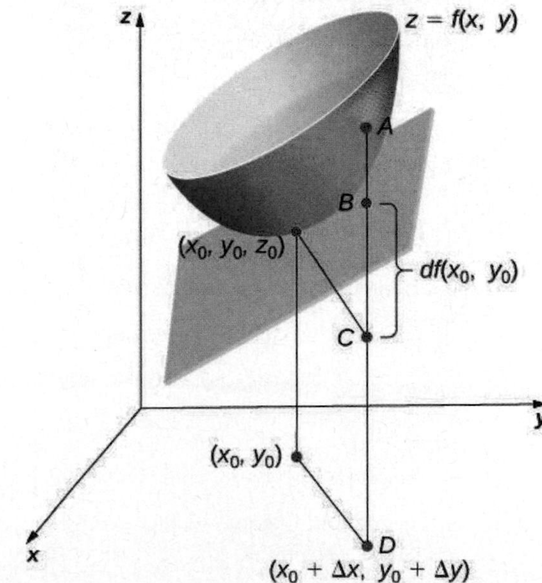

188. The length of line segment AC is equal to what mathematical expression?

189. The length of line segment BC is equal to what mathematical expression?

190. Using the figure, explain what the length of line segment AB represents.

For the following exercises, complete each task.

191. Show that $f(x, y) = e^{xy} x$ is differentiable at point $(1, 0)$.

192. Find the total differential of the function $w = e^y \cos(x) + z^2$.

193. Show that $f(x, y) = x^2 + 3y$ is differentiable at every point. In other words, show that $\Delta z = f(x + \Delta x, y + \Delta y) - f(x, y) = f_x \Delta x + f_y \Delta y + \varepsilon_1 \Delta x + \varepsilon_2 \Delta y$, where both ε_1 and ε_2 approach zero as $(\Delta x, \Delta y)$ approaches $(0, 0)$.

194. Find the total differential of the function $z = \frac{xy}{y + x}$ where x changes from 10 to 10.5 and y changes from 15 to 13.

195. Let $z = f(x, y) = xe^y$. Compute Δz from $P(1, 2)$ to $Q(1.05, 2.1)$ and then find the approximate change in z from point P to point Q. Recall $\Delta z = f(x + \Delta x, y + \Delta y) - f(x, y)$, and dz and Δz are approximately equal.

196. The volume of a right circular cylinder is given by $V(r, h) = \pi r^2 h$. Find the differential dV. Interpret the formula geometrically.

197. See the preceding problem. Use differentials to estimate the amount of aluminum in an enclosed aluminum can with diameter $8.0\,\text{cm}$ and height $12\,\text{cm}$ if the aluminum is 0.04 cm thick.

198. Use the differential dz to approximate the change in $z = \sqrt{4 - x^2 - y^2}$ as (x, y) moves from point $(1, 1)$ to point $(1.01, 0.97)$. Compare this approximation with the actual change in the function.

199. Let $z = f(x, y) = x^2 + 3xy - y^2$. Find the exact change in the function and the approximate change in the function as x changes from 2.00 to 2.05 and y changes from 3.00 to 2.96.

200. The centripetal acceleration of a particle moving in a circle is given by $a(r, v) = \frac{v^2}{r}$, where v is the velocity and r is the radius of the circle. Approximate the maximum percent error in measuring the acceleration resulting from errors of 3% in v and 2% in r. (Recall that the percentage error is the ratio of the amount of error over the original amount. So, in this case, the percentage error in a is given by $\frac{da}{a}$.)

201. The radius r and height h of a right circular cylinder are measured with possible errors of 4% and 5%, respectively. Approximate the maximum possible percentage error in measuring the volume (Recall that the percentage error is the ratio of the amount of error over the original amount. So, in this case, the percentage error in V is given by $\frac{dV}{V}$.)

202. The base radius and height of a right circular cone are measured as 10 in. and 25 in., respectively, with a possible error in measurement of as much as 0.1 in. each. Use differentials to estimate the maximum error in the calculated volume of the cone.

203. The electrical resistance R produced by wiring resistors R_1 and R_2 in parallel can be calculated from the formula $\frac{1}{R} = \frac{1}{R_1} + \frac{1}{R_2}$. If R_1 and R_2 are measured to be 7Ω and 6Ω, respectively, and if these measurements are accurate to within 0.05Ω, estimate the maximum possible error in computing R. (The symbol Ω represents an ohm, the unit of electrical resistance.)

204. The area of an ellipse with axes of length $2a$ and $2b$ is given by the formula $A = \pi ab$. Approximate the percent change in the area when a increases by 2% and b increases by 1.5%.

205. The period T of a simple pendulum with small oscillations is calculated from the formula $T = 2\pi\sqrt{\frac{L}{g}}$, where L is the length of the pendulum and g is the acceleration resulting from gravity. Suppose that L and g have errors of, at most, 0.5% and 0.1%, respectively. Use differentials to approximate the maximum percentage error in the calculated value of T.

206. Electrical power P is given by $P = \frac{V^2}{R}$, where V is the voltage and R is the resistance. Approximate the maximum percentage error in calculating power if 120 V is applied to a $2000 - \Omega$ resistor and the possible percent errors in measuring V and R are 3% and 4%, respectively.

For the following exercises, find the linear approximation of each function at the indicated point.

207. $f(x, y) = x\sqrt{y}$, $P(1, 4)$

208. $f(x, y) = e^x \cos y$; $P(0, 0)$

209. $f(x, y) = \arctan(x + 2y)$, $P(1, 0)$

210. $f(x, y) = \sqrt{20 - x^2 - 7y^2}$, $P(2, 1)$

211. $f(x, y, z) = \sqrt{x^2 + y^2 + z^2}$, $P(3, 2, 6)$

212. **[T]** Find the equation of the tangent plane to the surface $f(x, y) = x^2 + y^2$ at point $(1, 2, 5)$, and graph the surface and the tangent plane at the point.

213. **[T]** Find the equation for the tangent plane to the surface at the indicated point, and graph the surface and the tangent plane: $z = \ln(10x^2 + 2y^2 + 1)$, $P(0, 0, 0)$.

214. **[T]** Find the equation of the tangent plane to the surface $z = f(x, y) = \sin(x + y^2)$ at point $\left(\frac{\pi}{4}, 0, \frac{\sqrt{2}}{2}\right)$, and graph the surface and the tangent plane.

4.5 | The Chain Rule

Learning Objectives

4.5.1 State the chain rules for one or two independent variables.
4.5.2 Use tree diagrams as an aid to understanding the chain rule for several independent and intermediate variables.
4.5.3 Perform implicit differentiation of a function of two or more variables.

In single-variable calculus, we found that one of the most useful differentiation rules is the chain rule, which allows us to find the derivative of the composition of two functions. The same thing is true for multivariable calculus, but this time we have to deal with more than one form of the chain rule. In this section, we study extensions of the chain rule and learn how to take derivatives of compositions of functions of more than one variable.

Chain Rules for One or Two Independent Variables

Recall that the chain rule for the derivative of a composite of two functions can be written in the form

$$\frac{d}{dx}(f(g(x))) = f'(g(x))g'(x).$$

In this equation, both $f(x)$ and $g(x)$ are functions of one variable. Now suppose that f is a function of two variables and g is a function of one variable. Or perhaps they are both functions of two variables, or even more. How would we calculate the derivative in these cases? The following theorem gives us the answer for the case of one independent variable.

Theorem 4.8: Chain Rule for One Independent Variable

Suppose that $x = g(t)$ and $y = h(t)$ are differentiable functions of t and $z = f(x, y)$ is a differentiable function of x and y. Then $z = f(x(t), y(t))$ is a differentiable function of t and

$$\frac{dz}{dt} = \frac{\partial z}{\partial x} \cdot \frac{dx}{dt} + \frac{\partial z}{\partial y} \cdot \frac{dy}{dt}, \qquad \textbf{(4.29)}$$

where the ordinary derivatives are evaluated at t and the partial derivatives are evaluated at (x, y).

Proof

The proof of this theorem uses the definition of differentiability of a function of two variables. Suppose that f is differentiable at the point $P(x_0, y_0)$, where $x_0 = g(t_0)$ and $y_0 = h(t_0)$ for a fixed value of t_0. We wish to prove that $z = f(x(t), y(t))$ is differentiable at $t = t_0$ and that **Equation 4.29** holds at that point as well.

Since f is differentiable at P, we know that

$$z(t) = f(x, y) = f(x_0, y_0) + f_x(x_0, y_0)(x - x_0) + f_y(x_0, y_0)(y - y_0) + E(x, y), \qquad \textbf{(4.30)}$$

where $\lim_{(x, y) \to (x_0, y_0)} \frac{E(x, y)}{\sqrt{(x - x_0)^2 + (y - y_0)^2}} = 0.$ We then subtract $z_0 = f(x_0, y_0)$ from both sides of this equation:

$$\begin{aligned} z(t) - z(t_0) &= f(x(t), y(t)) - f(x(t_0), y(t_0)) \\ &= f_x(x_0, y_0)(x(t) - x(t_0)) + f_y(x_0, y_0)(y(t) - y(t_0)) + E(x(t), y(t)). \end{aligned}$$

Next, we divide both sides by $t - t_0$:

$$\frac{z(t) - z(t_0)}{t - t_0} = f_x(x_0, y_0)\left(\frac{x(t) - x(t_0)}{t - t_0}\right) + f_y(x_0, y_0)\left(\frac{y(t) - y(t_0)}{t - t_0}\right) + \frac{E(x(t), y(t))}{t - t_0}.$$

Then we take the limit as t approaches t_0:

$$\lim_{t \to t_0} \frac{z(t) - z(t_0)}{t - t_0} = f_x(x_0, y_0) \lim_{t \to t_0}\left(\frac{x(t) - x(t_0)}{t - t_0}\right) + f_y(x_0, y_0) \lim_{t \to t_0}\left(\frac{y(t) - y(t_0)}{t - t_0}\right) + \lim_{t \to t_0} \frac{E(x(t), y(t))}{t - t_0}.$$

The left-hand side of this equation is equal to dz/dt, which leads to

$$\frac{dz}{dt} = f_x(x_0, y_0)\frac{dx}{dt} + f_y(x_0, y_0)\frac{dy}{dt} + \lim_{t \to t_0} \frac{E(x(t), y(t))}{t - t_0}.$$

The last term can be rewritten as

$$\begin{aligned} \lim_{t \to t_0} \frac{E(x(t), y(t))}{t - t_0} &= \lim_{t \to t_0}\left(\frac{E(x, y)}{\sqrt{(x - x_0)^2 + (y - y_0)^2}} \frac{\sqrt{(x - x_0)^2 + (y - y_0)^2}}{t - t_0}\right) \\ &= \lim_{t \to t_0}\left(\frac{E(x, y)}{\sqrt{(x - x_0)^2 + (y - y_0)^2}}\right) \lim_{t \to t_0}\left(\frac{\sqrt{(x - x_0)^2 + (y - y_0)^2}}{t - t_0}\right). \end{aligned}$$

As t approaches t_0, $(x(t), y(t))$ approaches $(x(t_0), y(t_0))$, so we can rewrite the last product as

$$\lim_{(x, y) \to (x_0, y_0)}\left(\frac{E(x, y)}{\sqrt{(x - x_0)^2 + (y - y_0)^2}}\right) \lim_{(x, y) \to (x_0, y_0)}\left(\frac{\sqrt{(x - x_0)^2 + (y - y_0)^2}}{t - t_0}\right).$$

Since the first limit is equal to zero, we need only show that the second limit is finite:

$$\begin{aligned} \lim_{(x, y) \to (x_0, y_0)}\left(\frac{\sqrt{(x - x_0)^2 + (y - y_0)^2}}{t - t_0}\right) &= \lim_{(x, y) \to (x_0, y_0)}\left(\sqrt{\frac{(x - x_0)^2 + (y - y_0)^2}{(t - t_0)^2}}\right) \\ &= \lim_{(x, y) \to (x_0, y_0)}\left(\sqrt{\left(\frac{x - x_0}{t - t_0}\right)^2 + \left(\frac{y - y_0}{t - t_0}\right)^2}\right) \\ &= \sqrt{\left(\lim_{(x, y) \to (x_0, y_0)}\left(\frac{x - x_0}{t - t_0}\right)\right)^2 + \left(\lim_{(x, y) \to (x_0, y_0)}\left(\frac{y - y_0}{t - t_0}\right)\right)^2}. \end{aligned}$$

Since $x(t)$ and $y(t)$ are both differentiable functions of t, both limits inside the last radical exist. Therefore, this value is finite. This proves the chain rule at $t = t_0$; the rest of the theorem follows from the assumption that all functions are differentiable over their entire domains.

□

Closer examination of **Equation 4.29** reveals an interesting pattern. The first term in the equation is $\frac{\partial f}{\partial x} \cdot \frac{dx}{dt}$ and the second term is $\frac{\partial f}{\partial y} \cdot \frac{dy}{dt}$. Recall that when multiplying fractions, cancelation can be used. If we treat these derivatives as fractions, then each product "simplifies" to something resembling $\partial f/dt$. The variables x and y that disappear in this simplification are often called **intermediate variables**: they are independent variables for the function f, but are dependent variables for the variable t. Two terms appear on the right-hand side of the formula, and f is a function of two variables. This pattern works with functions of more than two variables as well, as we see later in this section.

Example 4.26

Using the Chain Rule

Calculate dz/dt for each of the following functions:

a. $z = f(x, y) = 4x^2 + 3y^2, \; x = x(t) = \sin t, \; y = y(t) = \cos t$

b. $z = f(x, y) = \sqrt{x^2 - y^2}, \; x = x(t) = e^{2t}, \; y = y(t) = e^{-t}$

Solution

a. To use the chain rule, we need four quantities— $\partial z/\partial x, \; \partial z/\partial y, \; dx/dt,$ and dy/dt:

$$\frac{\partial z}{\partial x} = 8x \qquad \frac{\partial z}{\partial y} = 6y$$
$$\frac{dx}{dt} = \cos t \qquad \frac{dy}{dt} = -\sin t$$

Now, we substitute each of these into **Equation 4.29**:

$$\begin{aligned}\frac{dz}{dt} &= \frac{\partial z}{\partial x} \cdot \frac{dx}{dt} + \frac{\partial z}{\partial y} \cdot \frac{dy}{dt} \\ &= (8x)(\cos t) + (6y)(-\sin t) \\ &= 8x \cos t - 6y \sin t.\end{aligned}$$

This answer has three variables in it. To reduce it to one variable, use the fact that $x(t) = \sin t$ and $y(t) = \cos t$. We obtain

$$\begin{aligned}\frac{dz}{dt} &= 8x \cos t - 6y \sin t \\ &= 8(\sin t)\cos t - 6(\cos t)\sin t \\ &= 2 \sin t \cos t.\end{aligned}$$

This derivative can also be calculated by first substituting $x(t)$ and $y(t)$ into $f(x, y),$ then differentiating with respect to t:

$$\begin{aligned}z &= f(x, y) \\ &= f(x(t), y(t)) \\ &= 4(x(t))^2 + 3(y(t))^2 \\ &= 4\sin^2 t + 3\cos^2 t.\end{aligned}$$

Then

$$\begin{aligned}\frac{dz}{dt} &= 2(4 \sin t)(\cos t) + 2(3 \cos t)(-\sin t) \\ &= 8 \sin t \cos t - 6 \sin t \cos t \\ &= 2 \sin t \cos t,\end{aligned}$$

which is the same solution. However, it may not always be this easy to differentiate in this form.

b. To use the chain rule, we again need four quantities— $\partial z/\partial x, \; \partial z/dy, \; dx/dt,$ and dy/dt:

$$\frac{\partial z}{\partial x} = \frac{x}{\sqrt{x^2 - y^2}} \qquad \frac{\partial z}{\partial y} = \frac{-y}{\sqrt{x^2 - y^2}}$$
$$\frac{dx}{dt} = 2e^{2t} \qquad \frac{dx}{dt} = -e^{-t}.$$

We substitute each of these into **Equation 4.29**:

$$\begin{aligned}\frac{dz}{dt} &= \frac{\partial z}{\partial x} \cdot \frac{dx}{dt} + \frac{\partial z}{\partial y} \cdot \frac{dy}{dt} \\ &= \left(\frac{x}{\sqrt{x^2 - y^2}}\right)(2e^{2t}) + \left(\frac{-y}{\sqrt{x^2 - y^2}}\right)(-e^{-t}) \\ &= \frac{2xe^{2t} - ye^{-t}}{\sqrt{x^2 - y^2}}.\end{aligned}$$

To reduce this to one variable, we use the fact that $x(t) = e^{2t}$ and $y(t) = e^{-t}$. Therefore,

$$\begin{aligned}\frac{dz}{dt} &= \frac{2xe^{2t} + ye^{-t}}{\sqrt{x^2 - y^2}} \\ &= \frac{2(e^{2t})e^{2t} + (e^{-t})e^{-t}}{\sqrt{e^{4t} - e^{-2t}}} \\ &= \frac{2e^{4t} + e^{-2t}}{\sqrt{e^{4t} - e^{-2t}}}.\end{aligned}$$

To eliminate negative exponents, we multiply the top by e^{2t} and the bottom by $\sqrt{e^{4t}}$:

$$\begin{aligned}\frac{dz}{dt} &= \frac{2e^{4t} + e^{-2t}}{\sqrt{e^{4t} - e^{-2t}}} \cdot \frac{e^{2t}}{\sqrt{e^{4t}}} \\ &= \frac{2e^{6t} + 1}{\sqrt{e^{8t} - e^{2t}}} \\ &= \frac{2e^{6t} + 1}{\sqrt{e^{2t}(e^{6t} - 1)}} \\ &= \frac{2e^{6t} + 1}{e^t\sqrt{e^{6t} - 1}}.\end{aligned}$$

Again, this derivative can also be calculated by first substituting $x(t)$ and $y(t)$ into $f(x, y)$, then differentiating with respect to t:

$$\begin{aligned}z &= f(x, y) \\ &= f(x(t), y(t)) \\ &= \sqrt{(x(t))^2 - (y(t))^2} \\ &= \sqrt{e^{4t} - e^{-2t}} \\ &= \left(e^{4t} - e^{-2t}\right)^{1/2}.\end{aligned}$$

Then

$$\begin{aligned}\frac{dz}{dt} &= \frac{1}{2}\left(e^{4t} - e^{-2t}\right)^{-1/2}\left(4e^{4t} + 2e^{-2t}\right) \\ &= \frac{2e^{4t} + e^{-2t}}{\sqrt{e^{4t} - e^{-2t}}}.\end{aligned}$$

This is the same solution.

4.23 Calculate dz/dt given the following functions. Express the final answer in terms of t.

$$z = f(x, y) = x^2 - 3xy + 2y^2, \; x = x(t) = 3 \sin 2t, \; y = y(t) = 4 \cos 2t$$

It is often useful to create a visual representation of **Equation 4.29** for the chain rule. This is called a **tree diagram** for the chain rule for functions of one variable and it provides a way to remember the formula (**Figure 4.34**). This diagram can be expanded for functions of more than one variable, as we shall see very shortly.

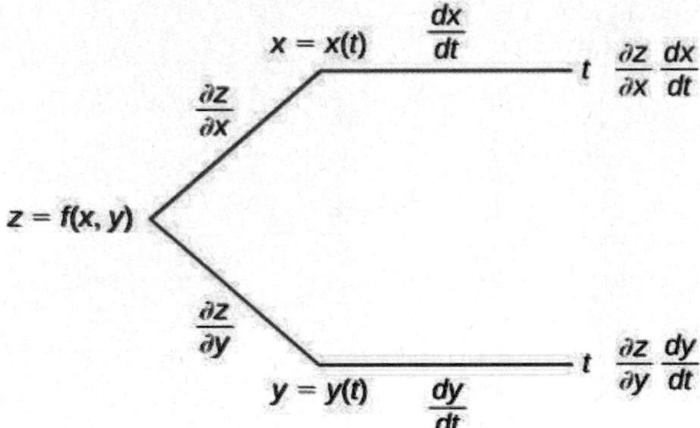

Figure 4.34 Tree diagram for the case $\frac{dz}{dt} = \frac{\partial z}{\partial x} \cdot \frac{dx}{dt} + \frac{\partial z}{\partial y} \cdot \frac{dy}{dt}$.

In this diagram, the leftmost corner corresponds to $z = f(x, y)$. Since f has two independent variables, there are two lines coming from this corner. The upper branch corresponds to the variable x and the lower branch corresponds to the variable y. Since each of these variables is then dependent on one variable t, one branch then comes from x and one branch comes from y. Last, each of the branches on the far right has a label that represents the path traveled to reach that branch. The top branch is reached by following the x branch, then the t branch; therefore, it is labeled $(\partial z/\partial x) \times (dx/dt)$. The bottom branch is similar: first the y branch, then the t branch. This branch is labeled $(\partial z/\partial y) \times (dy/dt)$. To get the formula for dz/dt, add all the terms that appear on the rightmost side of the diagram. This gives us **Equation 4.29**.

In **Chain Rule for Two Independent Variables**, $z = f(x, y)$ is a function of x and y, and both $x = g(u, v)$ and $y = h(u, v)$ are functions of the independent variables u and v.

Theorem 4.9: Chain Rule for Two Independent Variables

Suppose $x = g(u, v)$ and $y = h(u, v)$ are differentiable functions of u and v, and $z = f(x, y)$ is a differentiable function of x and y. Then, $z = f(g(u, v), h(u, v))$ is a differentiable function of u and v, and

$$\frac{\partial z}{\partial u} = \frac{\partial z}{\partial x}\frac{\partial x}{\partial u} + \frac{\partial z}{\partial y}\frac{\partial x}{\partial u} \qquad \textbf{(4.31)}$$

and

$$\frac{\partial z}{\partial v} = \frac{\partial z}{\partial x}\frac{\partial x}{\partial v} + \frac{\partial z}{\partial y}\frac{\partial y}{\partial v}. \qquad \textbf{(4.32)}$$

We can draw a tree diagram for each of these formulas as well as follows.

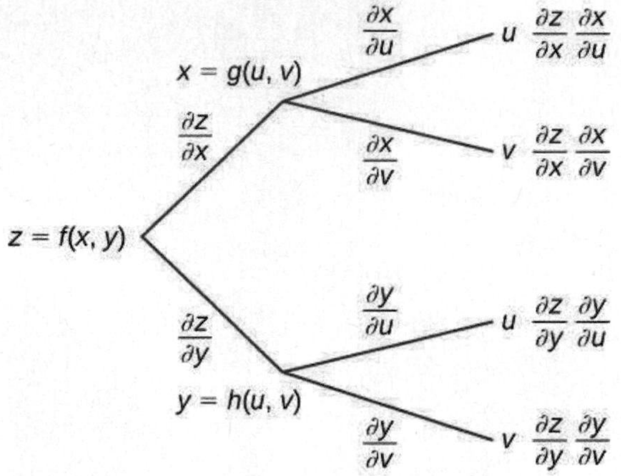

Figure 4.35 Tree diagram for $\frac{\partial z}{\partial u} = \frac{\partial z}{\partial x} \cdot \frac{\partial x}{\partial u} + \frac{\partial z}{\partial y} \cdot \frac{\partial y}{\partial u}$ and $\frac{\partial z}{\partial v} = \frac{\partial z}{\partial x} \cdot \frac{\partial x}{\partial v} + \frac{\partial z}{\partial y} \cdot \frac{\partial y}{\partial v}.$

To derive the formula for $\partial z/\partial u,$ start from the left side of the diagram, then follow only the branches that end with u and add the terms that appear at the end of those branches. For the formula for $\partial z/\partial v,$ follow only the branches that end with v and add the terms that appear at the end of those branches.

There is an important difference between these two chain rule theorems. In **Chain Rule for One Independent Variable**, the left-hand side of the formula for the derivative is not a partial derivative, but in **Chain Rule for Two Independent Variables** it is. The reason is that, in **Chain Rule for One Independent Variable**, z is ultimately a function of t alone, whereas in **Chain Rule for Two Independent Variables**, z is a function of both u and v.

Example 4.27

Using the Chain Rule for Two Variables

Calculate $\partial z/\partial u$ and $\partial z/\partial v$ using the following functions:

$$z = f(x, y) = 3x^2 - 2xy + y^2, \; x = x(u, v) = 3u + 2v, \; y = y(u, v) = 4u - v.$$

Solution

To implement the chain rule for two variables, we need six partial derivatives—$\partial z/\partial x, \partial z/\partial y, \partial x/\partial u, \partial x/\partial v, \partial y/\partial u,$ and $\partial y/\partial v$:

$$\frac{\partial z}{\partial x} = 6x - 2y \qquad \frac{\partial z}{\partial y} = -2x + 2y$$
$$\frac{\partial x}{\partial u} = 3 \qquad \frac{\partial x}{\partial v} = 2$$
$$\frac{\partial y}{\partial u} = 4 \qquad \frac{\partial y}{\partial v} = -1.$$

To find $\partial z/\partial u,$ we use **Equation 4.31**:

$$\begin{aligned}\frac{\partial z}{\partial u} &= \frac{\partial z}{\partial x}\cdot\frac{\partial x}{\partial u} + \frac{\partial z}{\partial y}\cdot\frac{\partial y}{\partial u}\\ &= 3(6x - 2y) + 4(-2x + 2y)\\ &= 10x + 2y.\end{aligned}$$

Next, we substitute $x(u, v) = 3u + 2v$ and $y(u, v) = 4u - v$:

$$\begin{aligned}\frac{\partial z}{\partial u} &= 10x + 2y\\ &= 10(3u + 2v) + 2(4u - v)\\ &= 38u + 18v.\end{aligned}$$

To find $\partial z/\partial v,$ we use **Equation 4.32**:

$$\begin{aligned}\frac{\partial z}{\partial v} &= \frac{\partial z}{\partial x}\frac{\partial x}{\partial v} + \frac{\partial z}{\partial y}\frac{\partial y}{\partial v}\\ &= 2(6x - 2y) + (-1)(-2x + 2y)\\ &= 14x - 6y.\end{aligned}$$

Then we substitute $x(u, v) = 3u + 2v$ and $y(u, v) = 4u - v$:

$$\begin{aligned}\frac{\partial z}{\partial v} &= 14x - 6y\\ &= 14(3u + 2v) - 6(4u - v)\\ &= 18u + 34v.\end{aligned}$$

4.24 Calculate $\partial z/\partial u$ and $\partial z/\partial v$ given the following functions:

$$z = f(x, y) = \frac{2x - y}{x + 3y},\ x(u, v) = e^{2u}\cos 3v,\ y(u, v) = e^{2u}\sin 3v.$$

The Generalized Chain Rule

Now that we've see how to extend the original chain rule to functions of two variables, it is natural to ask: Can we extend the rule to more than two variables? The answer is yes, as the **generalized chain rule** states.

Theorem 4.10: Generalized Chain Rule

Let $w = f(x_1, x_2,\ldots, x_m)$ be a differentiable function of m independent variables, and for each $i \in \{1,\ldots, m\},$ let $x_i = x_i(t_1, t_2,\ldots, t_n)$ be a differentiable function of n independent variables. Then

$$\frac{\partial w}{\partial t_j} = \frac{\partial w}{\partial x_1}\frac{\partial x_1}{\partial t_j} + \frac{\partial w}{\partial x_2}\frac{\partial x_2}{\partial t_j} + \cdots + \frac{\partial w}{\partial x_m}\frac{\partial x_m}{\partial t_j} \qquad (4.33)$$

for any $j \in \{1, 2, \ldots, n\}$.

In the next example we calculate the derivative of a function of three independent variables in which each of the three variables is dependent on two other variables.

Example 4.28

Using the Generalized Chain Rule

Calculate $\partial w/\partial u$ and $\partial w/\partial v$ using the following functions:

$$\begin{aligned} w &= f(x, y, z) = 3x^2 - 2xy + 4z^2 \\ x &= x(u, v) = e^u \sin v \\ y &= y(u, v) = e^u \cos v \\ z &= z(u, v) = e^u. \end{aligned}$$

Solution

The formulas for $\partial w/\partial u$ and $\partial w/\partial v$ are

$$\frac{\partial w}{\partial u} = \frac{\partial w}{\partial x} \cdot \frac{\partial x}{\partial u} + \frac{\partial w}{\partial y} \cdot \frac{\partial y}{\partial u} + \frac{\partial w}{\partial z} \cdot \frac{\partial z}{\partial u}$$
$$\frac{\partial w}{\partial v} = \frac{\partial w}{\partial x} \cdot \frac{\partial x}{\partial v} + \frac{\partial w}{\partial y} \cdot \frac{\partial y}{\partial v} + \frac{\partial w}{\partial z} \cdot \frac{\partial z}{\partial v}.$$

Therefore, there are nine different partial derivatives that need to be calculated and substituted. We need to calculate each of them:

$$\begin{aligned} \frac{\partial w}{\partial x} &= 6x - 2y & \frac{\partial w}{\partial y} &= -2x & \frac{\partial w}{\partial z} &= 8z \\ \frac{\partial x}{\partial u} &= e^u \sin v & \frac{\partial y}{\partial u} &= e^u \cos v & \frac{\partial z}{\partial u} &= e^u \\ \frac{\partial x}{\partial v} &= e^u \cos v & \frac{\partial y}{\partial v} &= -e^u \sin v & \frac{\partial z}{\partial v} &= 0. \end{aligned}$$

Now, we substitute each of them into the first formula to calculate $\partial w/\partial u$:

$$\begin{aligned} \frac{\partial w}{\partial u} &= \frac{\partial w}{\partial x} \cdot \frac{\partial x}{\partial u} + \frac{\partial w}{\partial y} \cdot \frac{\partial y}{\partial u} + \frac{\partial w}{\partial z} \cdot \frac{\partial z}{\partial u} \\ &= (6x - 2y)e^u \sin v - 2xe^u \cos v + 8ze^u, \end{aligned}$$

then substitute $x(u, v) = e^u \sin v$, $y(u, v) = e^u \cos v$, and $z(u, v) = e^u$ into this equation:

$$\begin{aligned} \frac{\partial w}{\partial u} &= (6x - 2y)e^u \sin v - 2xe^u \cos v + 8ze^u \\ &= (6e^u \sin v - 2e^u \cos v)e^u \sin v - 2(e^u \sin v)e^u \cos v + 8e^{2u} \\ &= 6e^{2u} \sin^2 v - 4e^{2u} \sin v \cos v + 8e^{2u} \\ &= 2e^{2u}\left(3 \sin^2 v - 2 \sin v \cos v + 4\right). \end{aligned}$$

Next, we calculate $\partial w/\partial v$:

$$\begin{aligned}\frac{\partial w}{\partial v} &= \frac{\partial w}{\partial x}\cdot\frac{\partial x}{\partial v}+\frac{\partial w}{\partial y}\cdot\frac{\partial y}{\partial v}+\frac{\partial w}{\partial z}\cdot\frac{\partial z}{\partial v}\\ &= (6x-2y)e^u\cos v-2x(-e^u\sin v)+8z(0),\end{aligned}$$

then we substitute $x(u, v) = e^u \sin v$, $y(u, v) = e^u \cos v$, and $z(u, v) = e^u$ into this equation:

$$\begin{aligned}\frac{\partial w}{\partial v} &= (6x-2y)e^u\cos v-2x(-e^u\sin v)\\ &= (6e^u\sin v-2e^u\cos v)e^u\cos v+2(e^u\sin v)(e^u\sin v)\\ &= 2e^{2u}\sin^2 v+6e^{2u}\sin v\cos v-2e^{2u}\cos^2 v\\ &= 2e^{2u}\left(\sin^2 v+\sin v\cos v-\cos^2 v\right).\end{aligned}$$

4.25 Calculate $\partial w/\partial u$ and $\partial w/\partial v$ given the following functions:

$$\begin{aligned} w &= f(x, y, z) = \frac{x+2y-4z}{2x-y+3z}\\ x &= x(u, v) = e^{2u}\cos 3v\\ y &= y(u, v) = e^{2u}\sin 3v\\ z &= z(u, v) = e^{2u}.\end{aligned}$$

Example 4.29

Drawing a Tree Diagram

Create a tree diagram for the case when

$$w = f(x, y, z),\ x = x(t, u, v),\ y = y(t, u, v),\ z = z(t, u, v)$$

and write out the formulas for the three partial derivatives of w.

Solution

Starting from the left, the function f has three independent variables: x, y, and z. Therefore, three branches must be emanating from the first node. Each of these three branches also has three branches, for each of the variables t, u, and v.

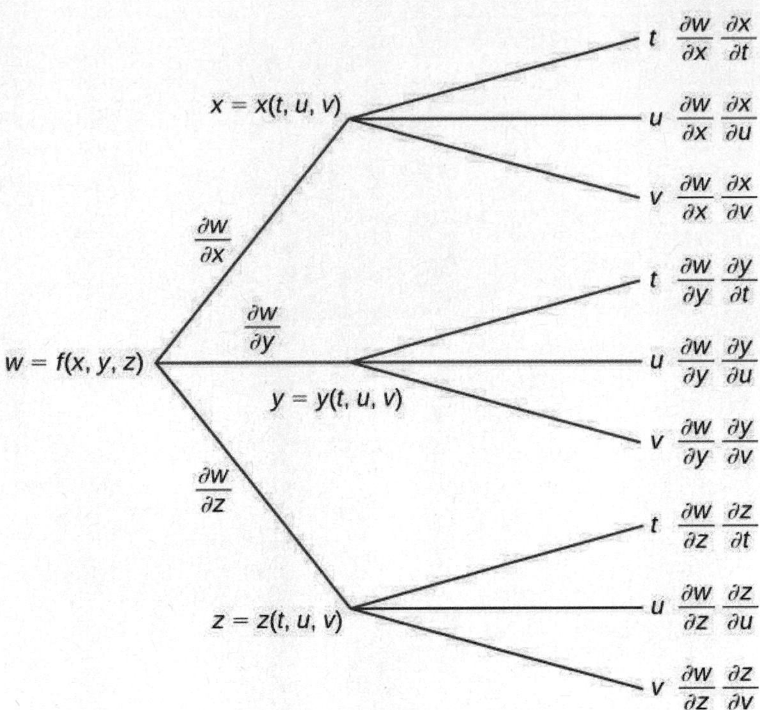

Figure 4.36 Tree diagram for a function of three variables, each of which is a function of three independent variables.

The three formulas are

$$\frac{\partial w}{\partial t} = \frac{\partial w}{\partial x}\frac{\partial x}{\partial t} + \frac{\partial w}{\partial y}\frac{\partial y}{\partial t} + \frac{\partial w}{\partial z}\frac{\partial z}{\partial t}$$
$$\frac{\partial w}{\partial u} = \frac{\partial w}{\partial x}\frac{\partial x}{\partial u} + \frac{\partial w}{\partial y}\frac{\partial y}{\partial u} + \frac{\partial w}{\partial z}\frac{\partial z}{\partial u}$$
$$\frac{\partial w}{\partial v} = \frac{\partial w}{\partial x}\frac{\partial x}{\partial v} + \frac{\partial w}{\partial y}\frac{\partial y}{\partial v} + \frac{\partial w}{\partial z}\frac{\partial z}{\partial v}.$$

4.26 Create a tree diagram for the case when

$$w = f(x, y),\ x = x(t, u, v),\ y = y(t, u, v)$$

and write out the formulas for the three partial derivatives of w.

Implicit Differentiation

Recall from **Implicit Differentiation (http://cnx.org/content/m53585/latest/)** that implicit differentiation provides a method for finding dy/dx when y is defined implicitly as a function of x. The method involves differentiating both sides of the equation defining the function with respect to x, then solving for dy/dx. Partial derivatives provide an alternative to this method.

Consider the ellipse defined by the equation $x^2 + 3y^2 + 4y - 4 = 0$ as follows.

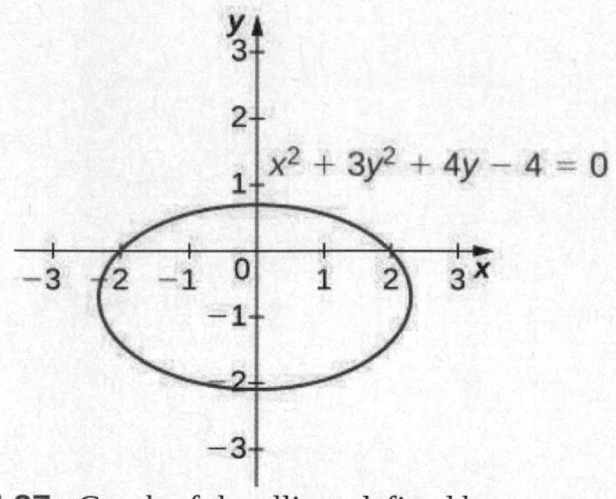

Figure 4.37 Graph of the ellipse defined by $x^2 + 3y^2 + 4y - 4 = 0$.

This equation implicitly defines y as a function of x. As such, we can find the derivative dy/dx using the method of implicit differentiation:

$$\begin{aligned}
\frac{d}{dx}\left(x^2 + 3y^2 + 4y - 4\right) &= \frac{d}{dx}(0) \\
2x + 6y\frac{dy}{dx} + 4\frac{dy}{dx} &= 0 \\
(6y + 4)\frac{dy}{dx} &= -2x \\
\frac{dy}{dx} &= -\frac{x}{3y + 2}.
\end{aligned}$$

We can also define a function $z = f(x, y)$ by using the left-hand side of the equation defining the ellipse. Then $f(x, y) = x^2 + 3y^2 + 4y - 4$. The ellipse $x^2 + 3y^2 + 4y - 4 = 0$ can then be described by the equation $f(x, y) = 0$. Using this function and the following theorem gives us an alternative approach to calculating dy/dx.

Theorem 4.11: Implicit Differentiation of a Function of Two or More Variables

Suppose the function $z = f(x, y)$ defines y implicitly as a function $y = g(x)$ of x via the equation $f(x, y) = 0$. Then

$$\frac{dy}{dx} = -\frac{\partial f/\partial x}{\partial f/\partial y} \tag{4.34}$$

provided $f_y(x, y) \neq 0$.

If the equation $f(x, y, z) = 0$ defines z implicitly as a differentiable function of x and y, then

$$\frac{\partial z}{\partial x} = -\frac{\partial f/\partial x}{\partial f/\partial z} \quad \text{and} \quad \frac{\partial z}{\partial y} = -\frac{\partial f/\partial y}{\partial f/\partial z} \tag{4.35}$$

as long as $f_z(x, y, z) \neq 0$.

Equation 4.34 is a direct consequence of **Equation 4.31**. In particular, if we assume that y is defined implicitly as a function of x via the equation $f(x, y) = 0$, we can apply the chain rule to find dy/dx:

$$\begin{aligned} \frac{d}{dx} f(x, y) &= \frac{d}{dx}(0) \\ \frac{\partial f}{\partial x} \cdot \frac{dx}{dx} + \frac{\partial f}{\partial y} \cdot \frac{dy}{dx} &= 0 \\ \frac{\partial f}{\partial x} + \frac{\partial f}{\partial y} \cdot \frac{dy}{dx} &= 0. \end{aligned}$$

Solving this equation for dy/dx gives **Equation 4.34**. **Equation 4.35** can be derived in a similar fashion.

Let's now return to the problem that we started before the previous theorem. Using **Implicit Differentiation of a Function of Two or More Variables** and the function $f(x, y) = x^2 + 3y^2 + 4y - 4,$ we obtain

$$\begin{aligned} \frac{\partial f}{\partial x} &= 2x \\ \frac{\partial f}{\partial y} &= 6y + 4. \end{aligned}$$

Then **Equation 4.34** gives

$$\frac{dy}{dx} = -\frac{\partial f / \partial x}{\partial f / \partial y} = -\frac{2x}{6y + 4} = -\frac{x}{3y + 2},$$

which is the same result obtained by the earlier use of implicit differentiation.

Example 4.30

Implicit Differentiation by Partial Derivatives

a. Calculate dy/dx if y is defined implicitly as a function of x via the equation $3x^2 - 2xy + y^2 + 4x - 6y - 11 = 0.$ What is the equation of the tangent line to the graph of this curve at point $(2, 1)$?

b. Calculate $\partial z/\partial x$ and $\partial z/\partial y,$ given $x^2 e^y - yze^x = 0.$

Solution

a. Set $f(x, y) = 3x^2 - 2xy + y^2 + 4x - 6y - 11 = 0,$ then calculate f_x and f_y: $\begin{aligned} f_x &= 6x - 2y + 4 \\ f_y &= -2x + 2y - 6. \end{aligned}$

The derivative is given by

$$\frac{dy}{dx} = -\frac{\partial f / \partial x}{\partial f / \partial y} = -\frac{6x - 2y + 4}{-2x + 2y - 6} = \frac{3x - y + 2}{x - y + 3}.$$

The slope of the tangent line at point $(2, 1)$ is given by

$$\left.\frac{dy}{dx}\right|_{(x, y) = (2, 1)} = \frac{3(2) - 1 + 2}{2 - 1 + 3} = \frac{7}{4}.$$

To find the equation of the tangent line, we use the point-slope form (**Figure 4.38**):

$$\begin{aligned} y - y_0 &= m(x - x_0) \\ y - 1 &= \frac{7}{4}(x - 2) \\ y &= \frac{7}{4}x - \frac{7}{2} + 1 \\ y &= \frac{7}{4}x - \frac{5}{2}. \end{aligned}$$

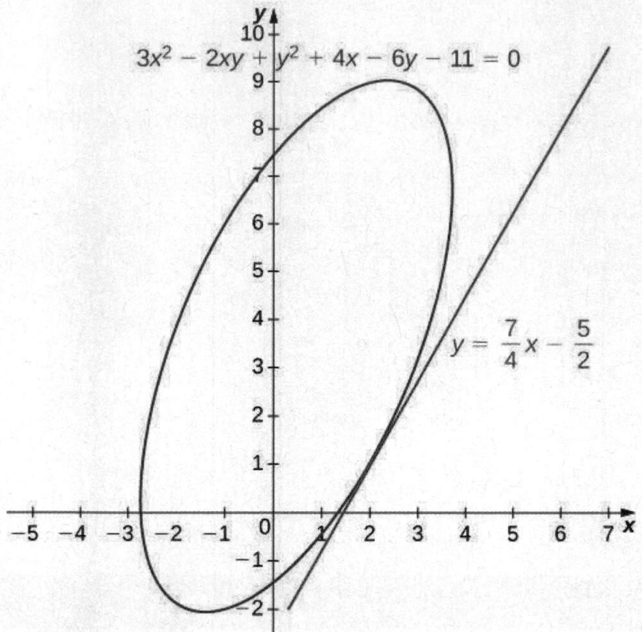

Figure 4.38 Graph of the rotated ellipse defined by $3x^2 - 2xy + y^2 + 4x - 6y - 11 = 0.$

b. We have $f(x, y, z) = x^2 e^y - yze^x$. Therefore,

$$\frac{\partial f}{\partial x} = 2xe^y - yze^x$$
$$\frac{\partial f}{\partial y} = x^2 e^y - ze^x$$
$$\frac{\partial f}{\partial z} = -ye^x.$$

Using **Equation 4.35**,

$$\begin{aligned} \frac{\partial z}{\partial x} &= -\frac{\partial f/\partial x}{\partial f/\partial y} \\ &= -\frac{2xe^y - yze^x}{-ye^x} \\ &= \frac{2xe^y - yze^x}{ye^x} \end{aligned} \quad \text{and} \quad \begin{aligned} \frac{\partial z}{\partial y} &= -\frac{\partial f/\partial y}{\partial f/\partial z} \\ &= -\frac{x^2 e^y - ze^x}{-ye^x} \\ &= \frac{x^2 e^y - ze^x}{ye^x}. \end{aligned}$$

4.27 Find dy/dx if y is defined implicitly as a function of x by the equation $x^2 + xy - y^2 + 7x - 3y - 26 = 0$. What is the equation of the tangent line to the graph of this curve at point $(3, -2)$?

4.5 EXERCISES

For the following exercises, use the information provided to solve the problem.

215. Let $w(x, y, z) = xy\cos z$, where $x = t$, $y = t^2$, and $z = \arcsin t$. Find $\frac{dw}{dt}$.

216. Let $w(t, v) = e^{tv}$ where $t = r + s$ and $v = rs$. Find $\frac{\partial w}{\partial r}$ and $\frac{\partial w}{\partial s}$.

217. If $w = 5x^2 + 2y^2$, $x = -3s + t$, and $y = s - 4t$, find $\frac{\partial w}{\partial s}$ and $\frac{\partial w}{\partial t}$.

218. If $w = xy^2$, $x = 5\cos(2t)$, and $y = 5\sin(2t)$, find $\frac{\partial w}{\partial t}$.

219. If $f(x, y) = xy$, $x = r\cos\theta$, and $y = r\sin\theta$, find $\frac{\partial f}{\partial r}$ and express the answer in terms of r and θ.

220. Suppose $f(x, y) = x + y$, $u = e^x \sin y$, $x = t^2$, and $y = \pi t$, where $x = r\cos\theta$ and $y = r\sin\theta$. Find $\frac{\partial f}{\partial \theta}$.

For the following exercises, find $\frac{df}{dt}$ using the chain rule and direct substitution.

221. $f(x, y) = x^2 + y^2$, $x = t$, $y = t^2$

222. $f(x, y) = \sqrt{x^2 + y^2}$, $y = t^2$, $x = t$

223. $f(x, y) = xy$, $x = 1 - \sqrt{t}$, $y = 1 + \sqrt{t}$

224. $f(x, y) = \frac{x}{y}$, $x = e^t$, $y = 2e^t$

225. $f(x, y) = \ln(x + y)$, $x = e^t$, $y = e^t$

226. $f(x, y) = x^4$, $x = t$, $y = t$

227. Let $w(x, y, z) = x^2 + y^2 + z^2$, $x = \cos t$, $y = \sin t$, and $z = e^t$. Express w as a function of t and find $\frac{dw}{dt}$ directly. Then, find $\frac{dw}{dt}$ using the chain rule.

228. Let $z = x^2 y$, where $x = t^2$ and $y = t^3$. Find $\frac{dz}{dt}$.

229. Let $u = e^x \sin y$, where $x = t^2$ and $y = \pi t$. Find $\frac{du}{dt}$ when $x = \ln 2$ and $y = \frac{\pi}{4}$.

For the following exercises, find $\frac{dy}{dx}$ using partial derivatives.

230. $\sin(6x) + \tan(8y) + 5 = 0$

231. $x^3 + y^2 x - 3 = 0$

232. $\sin(x + y) + \cos(x - y) = 4$

233. $x^2 - 2xy + y^4 = 4$

234. $xe^y + ye^x - 2x^2 y = 0$

235. $x^{2/3} + y^{2/3} = a^{2/3}$

236. $x\cos(xy) + y\cos x = 2$

237. $e^{xy} + ye^y = 1$

238. $x^2 y^3 + \cos y = 0$

239. Find $\frac{dz}{dt}$ using the chain rule where $z = 3x^2 y^3$, $x = t^4$, and $y = t^2$.

240. Let $z = 3\cos x - \sin(xy)$, $x = \frac{1}{t}$, and $y = 3t$. Find $\frac{dz}{dt}$.

241. Let $z = e^{1 - xy}$, $x = t^{1/3}$, and $y = t^3$. Find $\frac{dz}{dt}$.

242. Find $\frac{dz}{dt}$ by the chain rule where $z = \cosh^2(xy)$, $x = \frac{1}{2}t$, and $y = e^t$.

243. Let $z = \frac{x}{y}$, $x = 2\cos u$, and $y = 3\sin v$. Find $\frac{\partial z}{\partial u}$ and $\frac{\partial z}{\partial v}$.

244. Let $z = e^{x^2 y}$, where $x = \sqrt{uv}$ and $y = \frac{1}{v}$. Find $\frac{\partial z}{\partial u}$ and $\frac{\partial z}{\partial v}$.

245. If $z = xye^{x/y}$, $x = r\cos\theta$, and $y = r\sin\theta$, find $\frac{\partial z}{\partial r}$ and $\frac{\partial z}{\partial \theta}$ when $r = 2$ and $\theta = \frac{\pi}{6}$.

246. Find $\frac{\partial w}{\partial s}$ if $w = 4x + y^2 + z^3$, $x = e^{rs^2}$, $y = \ln\left(\frac{r+s}{t}\right)$, and $z = rst^2$.

247. If $w = \sin(xyz)$, $x = 1 - 3t$, $y = e^{1-t}$, and $z = 4t$, find $\frac{\partial w}{\partial t}$.

For the following exercises, use this information: A function $f(x, y)$ is said to be homogeneous of degree n if $f(tx, ty) = t^n f(x, y)$. For all homogeneous functions of degree n, the following equation is true: $x\frac{\partial f}{\partial x} + y\frac{\partial f}{\partial y} = nf(x, y)$. Show that the given function is homogeneous and verify that $x\frac{\partial f}{\partial x} + y\frac{\partial f}{\partial y} = nf(x, y)$.

248. $f(x, y) = 3x^2 + y^2$

249. $f(x, y) = \sqrt{x^2 + y^2}$

250. $f(x, y) = x^2 y - 2y^3$

251. The volume of a right circular cylinder is given by $V(x, y) = \pi x^2 y$, where x is the radius of the cylinder and y is the cylinder height. Suppose x and y are functions of t given by $x = \frac{1}{2}t$ and $y = \frac{1}{3}t$ so that x and y are both increasing with time. How fast is the volume increasing when $x = 2$ and $y = 5$?

252. The pressure P of a gas is related to the volume and temperature by the formula $PV = kT$, where temperature is expressed in kelvins. Express the pressure of the gas as a function of both V and T. Find $\frac{dP}{dt}$ when $k = 1$, $\frac{dV}{dt} = 2$ cm^3/min, $\frac{dT}{dt} = \frac{1}{2}$ K/min, $V = 20$ cm^3, and $T = 20°$F.

253. The radius of a right circular cone is increasing at 3 cm/min whereas the height of the cone is decreasing at 2 cm/min. Find the rate of change of the volume of the cone when the radius is 13 cm and the height is 18 cm.

254. The volume of a frustum of a cone is given by the formula $V = \frac{1}{3}\pi z(x^2 + y^2 + xy)$, where x is the radius of the smaller circle, y is the radius of the larger circle, and z is the height of the frustum (see figure). Find the rate of change of the volume of this frustum when $x = 10$ in., $y = 12$ in., and $z = 18$ in.

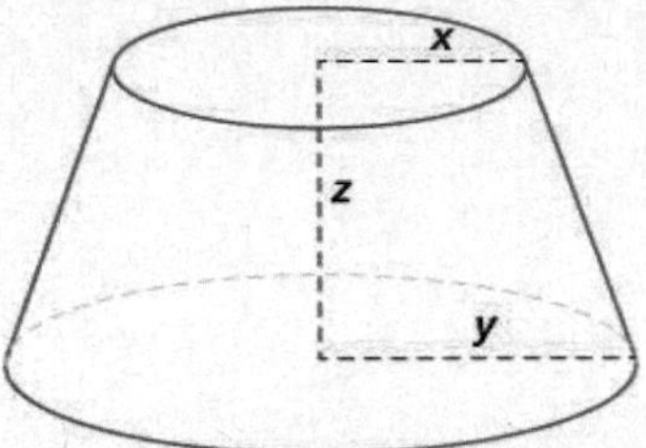

255. A closed box is in the shape of a rectangular solid with dimensions x, y, and z. (Dimensions are in inches.) Suppose each dimension is changing at the rate of 0.5 in./min. Find the rate of change of the total surface area of the box when $x = 2$ in., $y = 3$ in., and $z = 1$ in.

256. The total resistance in a circuit that has three individual resistances represented by x, y, and z is given by the formula $R(x, y, z) = \frac{xyz}{yz + xz + xy}$. Suppose at a given time the x resistance is 100Ω, the y resistance is 200Ω, and the z resistance is 300Ω. Also, suppose the x resistance is changing at a rate of 2Ω/min, the y resistance is changing at the rate of 1Ω/min, and the z resistance has no change. Find the rate of change of the total resistance in this circuit at this time.

257. The temperature T at a point (x, y) is $T(x, y)$ and is measured using the Celsius scale. A fly crawls so that its position after t seconds is given by $x = \sqrt{1+t}$ and $y = 2 + \frac{1}{3}t$, where x and y are measured in centimeters. The temperature function satisfies $T_x(2, 3) = 4$ and $T_y(2, 3) = 3$. How fast is the temperature increasing on the fly's path after 3 sec?

258. The x and y components of a fluid moving in two dimensions are given by the following functions: $u(x, y) = 2y$ and $v(x, y) = -2x;$ $x \geq 0; y \geq 0.$ The speed of the fluid at the point (x, y) is $s(x, y) = \sqrt{u(x, y)^2 + v(x, y)^2}.$ Find $\frac{\partial s}{\partial x}$ and $\frac{\partial s}{\partial y}$ using the chain rule.

259. Let $u = u(x, y, z),$ where $x = x(w, t),\ y = y(w, t),\ z = z(w, t),\ w = w(r, s),$ and $t = t(r, s).$ Use a tree diagram and the chain rule to find an expression for $\frac{\partial u}{\partial r}.$

4.6 | Directional Derivatives and the Gradient

Learning Objectives

4.6.1 Determine the directional derivative in a given direction for a function of two variables.
4.6.2 Determine the gradient vector of a given real-valued function.
4.6.3 Explain the significance of the gradient vector with regard to direction of change along a surface.
4.6.4 Use the gradient to find the tangent to a level curve of a given function.
4.6.5 Calculate directional derivatives and gradients in three dimensions.

In **Partial Derivatives** we introduced the partial derivative. A function $z = f(x, y)$ has two partial derivatives: $\partial z/\partial x$ and $\partial z/\partial y$. These derivatives correspond to each of the independent variables and can be interpreted as instantaneous rates of change (that is, as slopes of a tangent line). For example, $\partial z/\partial x$ represents the slope of a tangent line passing through a given point on the surface defined by $z = f(x, y)$, assuming the tangent line is parallel to the x-axis. Similarly, $\partial z/\partial y$ represents the slope of the tangent line parallel to the y-axis. Now we consider the possibility of a tangent line parallel to neither axis.

Directional Derivatives

We start with the graph of a surface defined by the equation $z = f(x, y)$. Given a point (a, b) in the domain of f, we choose a direction to travel from that point. We measure the direction using an angle θ, which is measured counterclockwise in the x, y-plane, starting at zero from the positive x-axis (**Figure 4.39**). The distance we travel is h and the direction we travel is given by the unit vector $\mathbf{u} = (\cos\theta)\mathbf{i} + (\sin\theta)\mathbf{j}$. Therefore, the z-coordinate of the second point on the graph is given by $z = f(a + h\cos\theta, b + h\sin\theta)$.

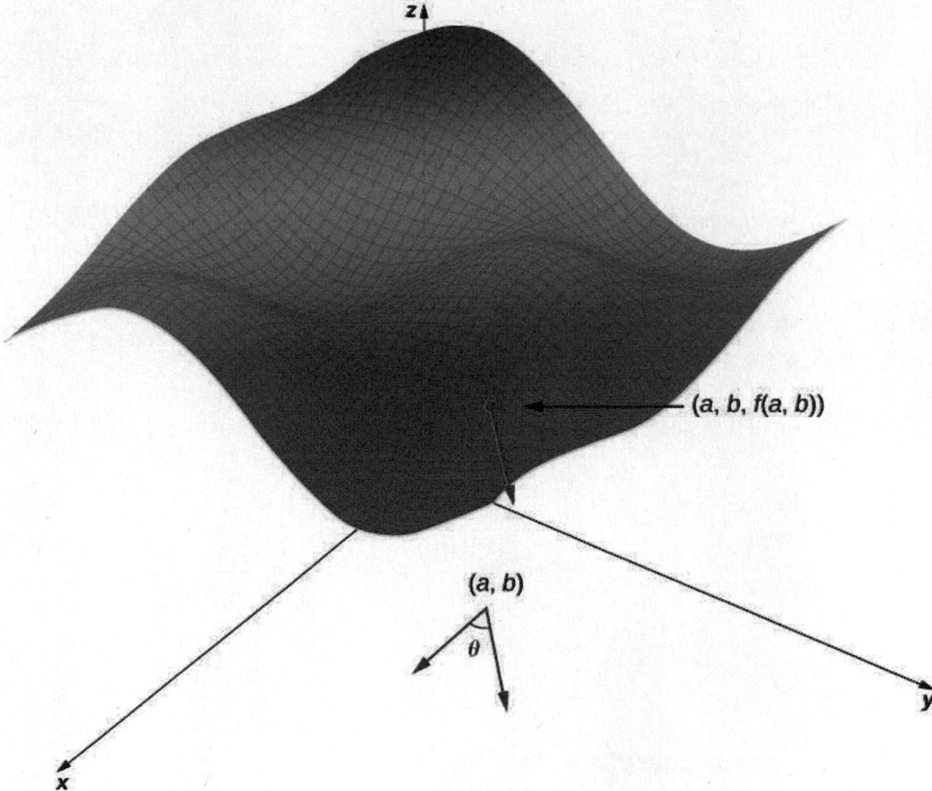

Figure 4.39 Finding the directional derivative at a point on the graph of $z = f(x, y)$. The slope of the black arrow on the graph indicates the value of the directional derivative at that point.

We can calculate the slope of the secant line by dividing the difference in z-values by the length of the line segment connecting the two points in the domain. The length of the line segment is h. Therefore, the slope of the secant line is

$$m_{\text{sec}} = \frac{f(a + h\cos\theta, b + h\sin\theta) - f(a, b)}{h}.$$

To find the slope of the tangent line in the same direction, we take the limit as h approaches zero.

Definition

Suppose $z = f(x, y)$ is a function of two variables with a domain of D. Let $(a, b) \in D$ and define $\mathbf{u} = \cos\theta\mathbf{i} + \sin\theta\mathbf{j}$. Then the **directional derivative** of f in the direction of u is given by

$$D_{\mathbf{u}} f(a, b) = \lim_{h \to 0} \frac{f(a + h\cos\theta, b + h\sin\theta) - f(a, b)}{h}, \tag{4.36}$$

provided the limit exists.

Equation 4.36 provides a formal definition of the directional derivative that can be used in many cases to calculate a directional derivative.

Example 4.31

Finding a Directional Derivative from the Definition

Let $\theta = \arccos(3/5)$. Find the directional derivative $D_{\mathbf{u}} f(x, y)$ of $f(x, y) = x^2 - xy + 3y^2$ in the direction of $\mathbf{u} = (\cos\theta)\mathbf{i} + (\sin\theta)\mathbf{j}$. What is $D_{\mathbf{u}} f(-1, 2)$?

Solution

First of all, since $\cos\theta = 3/5$ and θ is acute, this implies

$$\sin\theta = \sqrt{1 - \left(\frac{3}{5}\right)^2} = \sqrt{\frac{16}{25}} = \frac{4}{5}.$$

Using $f(x, y) = x^2 - xy + 3y^2$, we first calculate $f(x + h\cos\theta, y + h\sin\theta)$:

$$\begin{aligned}
f(x + h\cos\theta, y + h\sin\theta) &= (x + h\cos\theta)^2 - (x + h\cos\theta)(y + h\sin\theta) + 3(y + h\sin\theta)^2 \\
&= x^2 + 2xh\cos\theta + h^2\cos^2\theta - xy - xh\sin\theta - yh\cos\theta \\
&\quad -h^2\sin\theta\cos\theta + 3y^2 + 6yh\sin\theta + 3h^2\sin^2\theta \\
&= x^2 + 2xh\left(\frac{3}{5}\right) + \frac{9h^2}{25} - xy - \frac{4xh}{5} - \frac{3yh}{5} - \frac{12h^2}{25} + 3y^2 \\
&\quad +6yh\left(\frac{4}{5}\right) + 3h^2\left(\frac{16}{25}\right) \\
&= x^2 - xy + 3y^2 + \frac{2xh}{5} + \frac{9h^2}{5} + \frac{21yh}{5}.
\end{aligned}$$

We substitute this expression into **Equation 4.36**:

$$\begin{aligned}
D_{\mathbf{u}} f(a, b) &= \lim_{h \to 0} \frac{f(a + h\cos\theta, b + h\sin\theta) - f(a, b)}{h} \\
&= \lim_{h \to 0} \frac{\left(x^2 - xy + 3y^2 + \frac{2xh}{5} + \frac{9h^2}{5} + \frac{21yh}{5}\right) - \left(x^2 - xy + 3y^2\right)}{h} \\
&= \lim_{h \to 0} \frac{\frac{2xh}{5} + \frac{9h^2}{5} + \frac{21yh}{5}}{h} \\
&= \lim_{h \to 0} \frac{2x}{5} + \frac{9h}{5} + \frac{21y}{5} \\
&= \frac{2x + 21y}{5}.
\end{aligned}$$

To calculate $D_{\mathbf{u}} f(-1, 2)$, we substitute $x = -1$ and $y = 2$ into this answer:

$$\begin{aligned}
D_{\mathbf{u}} f(-1, 2) &= \frac{2(-1) + 21(2)}{5} \\
&= \frac{-2 + 42}{5} \\
&= 8.
\end{aligned}$$

(See the following figure.)

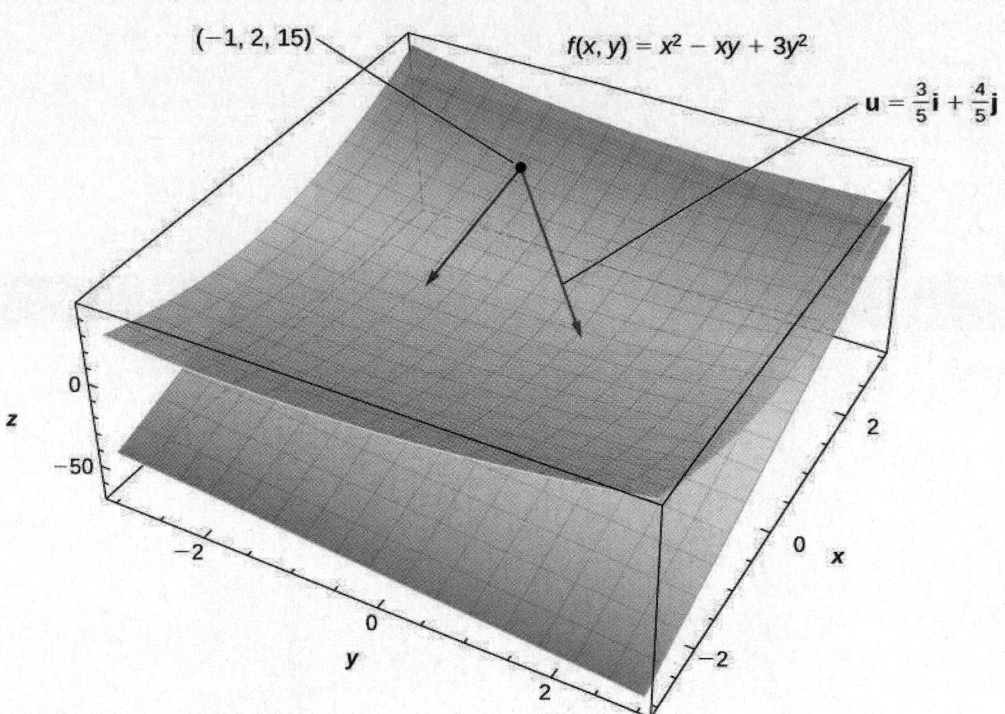

Figure 4.40 Finding the directional derivative in a given direction $\mathbf{u}$ at a given point on a surface. The plane is tangent to the surface at the given point $(-1, 2, 15)$.

Another approach to calculating a directional derivative involves partial derivatives, as outlined in the following theorem.

Theorem 4.12: Directional Derivative of a Function of Two Variables

Let $z = f(x, y)$ be a function of two variables x and y, and assume that f_x and f_y exist. Then the directional derivative of f in the direction of $\mathrm{u} = \cos\theta\mathrm{i} + \sin\theta\mathrm{j}$ is given by

$$D_{\mathbf{u}}f(x, y) = f_x(x, y)\cos\theta + f_y(x, y)\sin\theta. \tag{4.37}$$

Proof

Equation 4.36 states that the directional derivative of f in the direction of $\mathbf{u} = \cos\theta\mathbf{i} + \sin\theta\mathbf{j}$ is given by

$$D_{\mathbf{u}}f(a, b) = \lim_{t \to 0}\frac{f(a + t\cos\theta, b + t\sin\theta) - f(a, b)}{t}.$$

Let $x = a + t\cos\theta$ and $y = b + t\sin\theta$, and define $g(t) = f(x, y)$. Since f_x and f_y both exist, we can use the chain rule for functions of two variables to calculate $g'(t)$:

$$\begin{aligned} g'(t) &= \frac{\partial f}{\partial x}\frac{dx}{dt} + \frac{\partial f}{\partial y}\frac{dy}{dt} \\ &= f_x(x, y)\cos\theta + f_y(x, y)\sin\theta. \end{aligned}$$

If $t = 0$, then $x = x_0$ and $y = y_0$, so

$$g'(0) = f_x(x_0, y_0)\cos\theta + f_y(x_0, y_0)\sin\theta.$$

By the definition of $g'(t)$, it is also true that

$$\begin{aligned} g'(0) &= \lim_{t \to 0} \frac{g(t) - g(0)}{t} \\ &= \lim_{t \to 0} \frac{f(x_0 + t\cos\theta,\ y_0 + t\sin\theta) - f(x_0,\ y_0)}{t}. \end{aligned}$$

Therefore, $D_{\mathbf{u}} f(x_0, y_0) = f_x(x, y)\cos\theta + f_y(x, y)\sin\theta$.

□

Example 4.32

Finding a Directional Derivative: Alternative Method

Let $\theta = \arccos(3/5)$. Find the directional derivative $D_{\mathbf{u}} f(x, y)$ of $f(x, y) = x^2 - xy + 3y^2$ in the direction of $\mathbf{u} = (\cos\theta)\mathbf{i} + (\sin\theta)\mathbf{j}$. What is $D_{\mathbf{u}} f(-1, 2)$?

Solution

First, we must calculate the partial derivatives of f:

$$\begin{aligned} f_x &= 2x - y \\ f_y &= -x + 6y, \end{aligned}$$

Then we use **Equation 4.37** with $\theta = \arccos(3/5)$:

$$\begin{aligned} D_{\mathbf{u}} f(x, y) &= f_x(x, y)\cos\theta + f_y(x, y)\sin\theta \\ &= (2x - y)\frac{3}{5} + (-x + 6y)\frac{4}{5} \\ &= \frac{6x}{5} - \frac{3y}{5} - \frac{4x}{5} + \frac{24y}{5} \\ &= \frac{2x + 21y}{5}. \end{aligned}$$

To calculate $D_{\mathbf{u}} f(-1, 2)$, let $x = -1$ and $y = 2$:

$$D_{\mathbf{u}} f(-1, 2) = \frac{2(-1) + 21(2)}{5} = \frac{-2 + 42}{5} = 8.$$

This is the same answer obtained in **Example 4.31**.

4.28 Find the directional derivative $D_{\mathbf{u}} f(x, y)$ of $f(x, y) = 3x^2 y - 4xy^3 + 3y^2 - 4x$ in the direction of $\mathbf{u} = \left(\cos\frac{\pi}{3}\right)\mathbf{i} + \left(\sin\frac{\pi}{3}\right)\mathbf{j}$ using **Equation 4.37**. What is $D_{\mathbf{u}} f(3, 4)$?

If the vector that is given for the direction of the derivative is not a unit vector, then it is only necessary to divide by the norm of the vector. For example, if we wished to find the directional derivative of the function in **Example 4.32** in the direction of the vector $\langle -5, 12 \rangle$, we would first divide by its magnitude to get $\mathbf{u}$. This gives us $\mathbf{u} = \langle -(5/13), 12/13 \rangle$. Then

$$\begin{aligned} D_{\mathbf{u}} f(x, y) &= \nabla f(x, y) \cdot \mathbf{u} \\ &= -\frac{5}{13}(2x - y) + \frac{12}{13}(-x + 6y) \\ &= -\frac{22}{13}x + \frac{17}{13}y. \end{aligned}$$

Gradient

The right-hand side of **Equation 4.37** is equal to $f_x(x, y)\cos\theta + f_y(x, y)\sin\theta$, which can be written as the dot product of two vectors. Define the first vector as $\nabla f(x, y) = f_x(x, y)\mathrm{i} + f_y(x, y)\mathrm{j}$ and the second vector as $\mathbf{u} = (\cos\theta)\mathbf{i} + (\sin\theta)\mathbf{j}$. Then the right-hand side of the equation can be written as the dot product of these two vectors:

$$D_{\mathbf{u}} f(x, y) = \nabla f(x, y) \cdot \mathbf{u}. \tag{4.38}$$

The first vector in **Equation 4.38** has a special name: the gradient of the function f. The symbol ∇ is called *nabla* and the vector ∇f is read "del f."

Definition

Let $z = f(x, y)$ be a function of x and y such that f_x and f_y exist. The vector $\nabla f(x, y)$ is called the **gradient** of f and is defined as

$$\nabla f(x, y) = f_x(x, y)\mathbf{i} + f_y(x, y)\mathbf{j}. \tag{4.39}$$

The vector $\nabla f(x, y)$ is also written as "grad f."

Example 4.33

Finding Gradients

Find the gradient $\nabla f(x, y)$ of each of the following functions:

a. $f(x, y) = x^2 - xy + 3y^2$

b. $f(x, y) = \sin 3x \cos 3y$

Solution

For both parts a. and b., we first calculate the partial derivatives f_x and f_y, then use **Equation 4.39**.

a.

$$\begin{aligned} f_x(x, y) &= 2x - y \text{ and } f_y(x, y) = -x + 6y, \text{ so} \\ \nabla f(x, y) &= f_x(x, y)\mathbf{i} + f_y(x, y)\mathbf{j} \\ &= (2x - y)\mathbf{i} + (-x + 6y)\mathbf{j}. \end{aligned}$$

b.

$$\begin{aligned} f_x(x, y) &= 3\cos 3x \cos 3y \text{ and } f_y(x, y) = -3\sin 3x \sin 3y, \text{ so} \\ \nabla f(x, y) &= f_x(x, y)\mathbf{i} + f_y(x, y)\mathbf{j} \\ &= (3\cos 3x \cos 3y)\mathbf{i} - (3\sin 3x \sin 3y)\mathbf{j}. \end{aligned}$$

4.29 Find the gradient $\nabla f(x, y)$ of $f(x, y) = \left(x^2 - 3y^2\right)/(2x + y)$.

The gradient has some important properties. We have already seen one formula that uses the gradient: the formula for the directional derivative. Recall from **The Dot Product** that if the angle between two vectors $\mathbf{a}$ and $\mathbf{b}$ is φ, then $\mathbf{a} \cdot \mathrm{b} = \| \mathbf{a} \| \, \| \mathrm{b} \| \cos \varphi$. Therefore, if the angle between $\nabla f(x_0, y_0)$ and $\mathbf{u} = (\cos \theta)\mathbf{i} + (\sin \theta)\mathbf{j}$ is φ, we have

$$D_{\mathbf{u}} f(x_0, y_0) = \nabla f(x_0, y_0) \cdot \mathbf{u} = \| \nabla f(x_0, y_0) \| \, \| \mathbf{u} \| \cos \varphi = \| \nabla f(x_0, y_0) \| \cos \varphi.$$

The $\| \mathbf{u} \|$ disappears because $\mathbf{u}$ is a unit vector. Therefore, the directional derivative is equal to the magnitude of the gradient evaluated at (x_0, y_0) multiplied by $\cos \varphi$. Recall that $\cos \varphi$ ranges from -1 to 1. If $\varphi = 0$, then $\cos \varphi = 1$ and $\nabla f(x_0, y_0)$ and $\mathbf{u}$ both point in the same direction. If $\varphi = \pi$, then $\cos \varphi = -1$ and $\nabla f(x_0, y_0)$ and $\mathbf{u}$ point in opposite directions. In the first case, the value of $D_{\mathrm{u}} f(x_0, y_0)$ is maximized; in the second case, the value of $D_{\mathrm{u}} f(x_0, y_0)$ is minimized. If $\nabla f(x_0, y_0) = 0$, then $D_{\mathbf{u}} f(x_0, y_0) = \nabla f(x_0, y_0) \cdot \mathbf{u} = 0$ for any vector $\mathbf{u}$. These three cases are outlined in the following theorem.

Theorem 4.13: Properties of the Gradient

Suppose the function $z = f(x, y)$ is differentiable at (x_0, y_0) (**Figure 4.41**).

i. If $\nabla f(x_0, y_0) = \mathbf{0}$, then $D_{\mathbf{u}} f(x_0, y_0) = 0$ for any unit vector $\mathbf{u}$.

ii. If $\nabla f(x_0, y_0) \neq \mathbf{0}$, then $D_{\mathbf{u}} f(x_0, y_0)$ is maximized when $\mathbf{u}$ points in the same direction as $\nabla f(x_0, y_0)$. The maximum value of $D_{\mathbf{u}} f(x_0, y_0)$ is $\| \nabla f(x_0, y_0) \|$.

iii. If $\nabla f(x_0, y_0) \neq \mathbf{0}$, then $D_{\mathbf{u}} f(x_0, y_0)$ is minimized when $\mathbf{u}$ points in the opposite direction from $\nabla f(x_0, y_0)$. The minimum value of $D_{\mathbf{u}} f(x_0, y_0)$ is $-\| \nabla f(x_0, y_0) \|$.

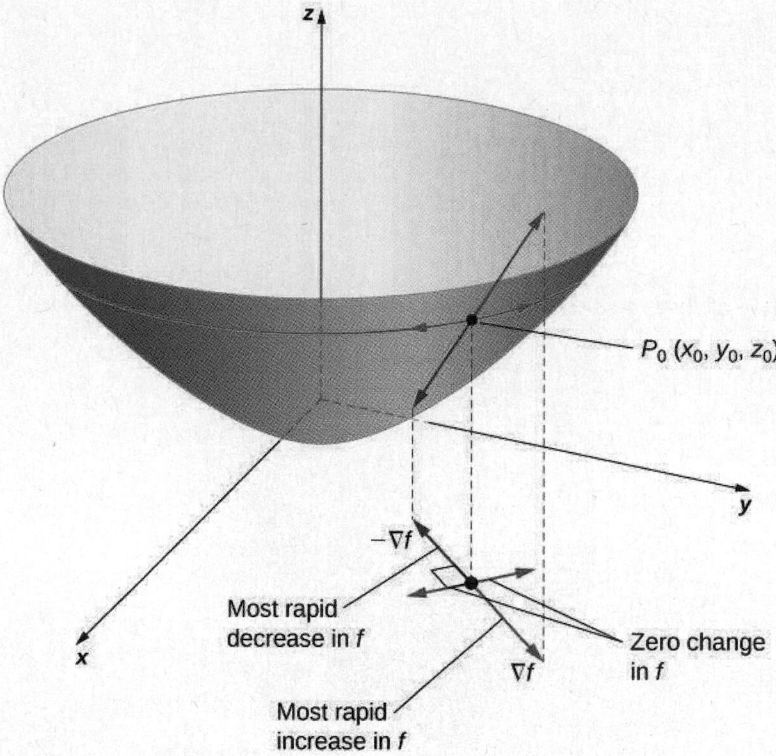

Figure 4.41 The gradient indicates the maximum and minimum values of the directional derivative at a point.

Example 4.34

Finding a Maximum Directional Derivative

Find the direction for which the directional derivative of $f(x, y) = 3x^2 - 4xy + 2y^2$ at $(-2, 3)$ is a maximum. What is the maximum value?

Solution

The maximum value of the directional derivative occurs when ∇f and the unit vector point in the same direction. Therefore, we start by calculating $\nabla f(x, y)$:

$$\begin{aligned} f_x(x, y) &= 6x - 4y \text{ and } f_y(x, y) = -4x + 4y, \text{ so} \\ \nabla f(x, y) &= f_x(x, y)\mathbf{i} + f_y(x, y)\mathbf{j} = (6x - 4y)\mathbf{i} + (-4x + 4y)\mathbf{j}. \end{aligned}$$

Next, we evaluate the gradient at $(-2, 3)$:

$$\nabla f(-2, 3) = (6(-2) - 4(3))\mathbf{i} + (-4(-2) + 4(3))\mathbf{j} = -24\mathbf{i} + 20\mathbf{j}.$$

We need to find a unit vector that points in the same direction as $\nabla f(-2, 3)$, so the next step is to divide $\nabla f(-2, 3)$ by its magnitude, which is $\sqrt{(-24)^2 + (20)^2} = \sqrt{976} = 4\sqrt{61}$. Therefore,

$$\frac{\nabla f(-2, 3)}{\| \nabla f(-2, 3) \|} = \frac{-24}{4\sqrt{61}}\mathbf{i} + \frac{20}{4\sqrt{61}}\mathbf{j} = \frac{-6\sqrt{61}}{61}\mathbf{i} + \frac{5\sqrt{61}}{61}\mathbf{j}.$$

This is the unit vector that points in the same direction as $\nabla f(-2, 3)$. To find the angle corresponding to this unit vector, we solve the equations

$$\cos\theta = \frac{-6\sqrt{61}}{61} \text{ and } \sin\theta = \frac{5\sqrt{61}}{61}$$

for θ. Since cosine is negative and sine is positive, the angle must be in the second quadrant. Therefore, $\theta = \pi - \arcsin\left((5\sqrt{61})/61\right) \approx 2.45$ rad.

The maximum value of the directional derivative at $(-2, 3)$ is $\|\nabla f(-2, 3)\| = 4\sqrt{61}$ (see the following figure).

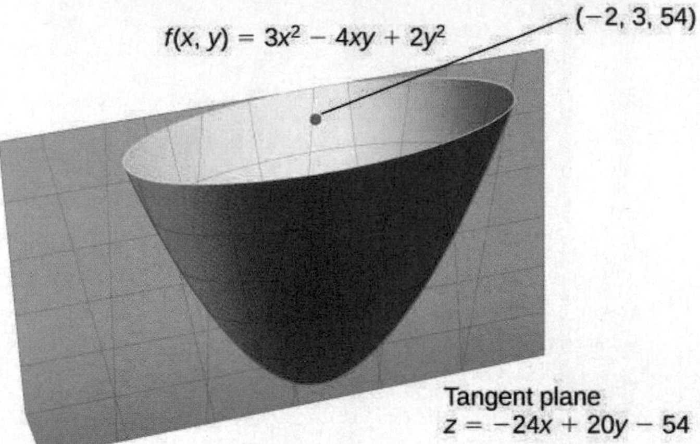

Figure 4.42 The maximum value of the directional derivative at $(-2, 3)$ is in the direction of the gradient.

4.30 Find the direction for which the directional derivative of $g(x, y) = 4x - xy + 2y^2$ at $(-2, 3)$ is a maximum. What is the maximum value?

Figure 4.43 shows a portion of the graph of the function $f(x, y) = 3 + \sin x \sin y$. Given a point (a, b) in the domain of f, the maximum value of the gradient at that point is given by $\|\nabla f(a, b)\|$. This would equal the rate of greatest ascent if the surface represented a topographical map. If we went in the opposite direction, it would be the rate of greatest descent.

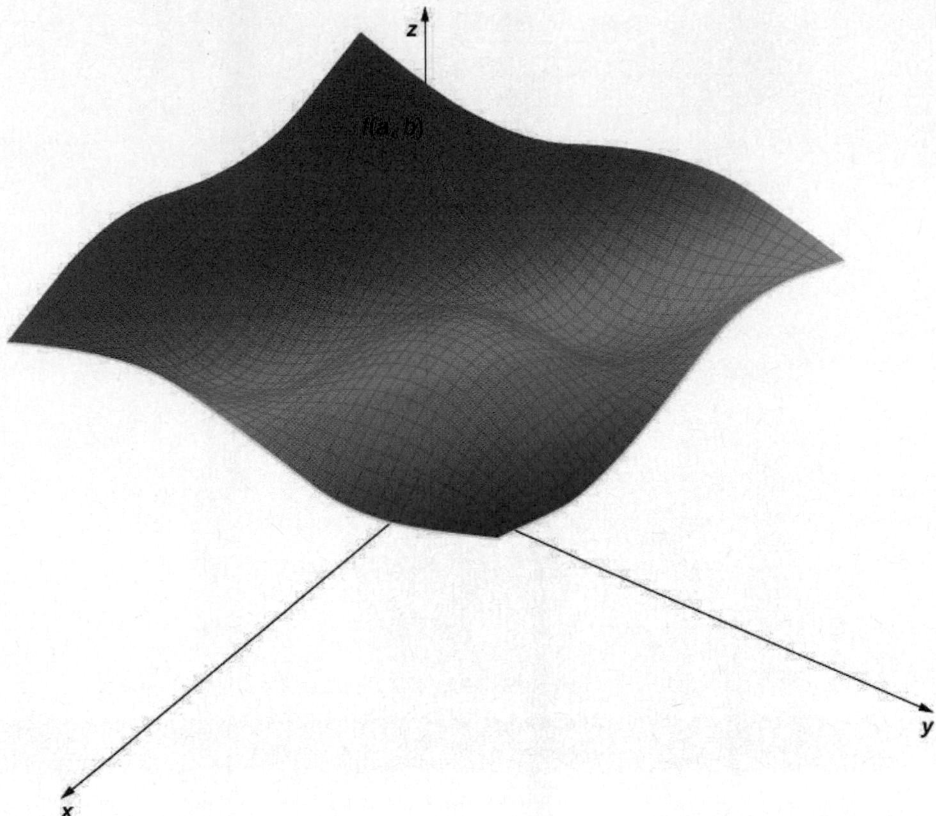

Figure 4.43 A typical surface in $\mathbb{R}^3$. Given a point on the surface, the directional derivative can be calculated using the gradient.

When using a topographical map, the steepest slope is always in the direction where the contour lines are closest together (see **Figure 4.44**). This is analogous to the contour map of a function, assuming the level curves are obtained for equally spaced values throughout the range of that function.

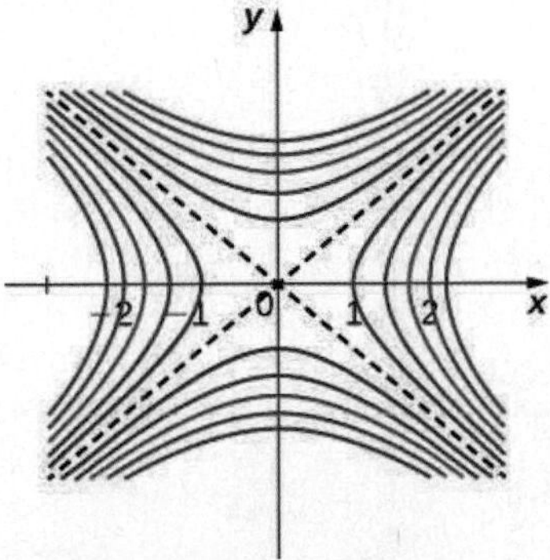

Figure 4.44 Contour map for the function $f(x, y) = x^2 - y^2$ using level values between -5 and 5.

Gradients and Level Curves

Recall that if a curve is defined parametrically by the function pair $(x(t), y(t)),$ then the vector $x'(t)\mathbf{i} + y'(t)\mathbf{j}$ is tangent to the curve for every value of t in the domain. Now let's assume $z = f(x, y)$ is a differentiable function of x and $y,$ and (x_0, y_0) is in its domain. Let's suppose further that $x_0 = x(t_0)$ and $y_0 = y(t_0)$ for some value of $t,$ and consider the level curve $f(x, y) = k.$ Define $g(t) = f(x(t), y(t))$ and calculate $g'(t)$ on the level curve. By the chain Rule,

$$g'(t) = f_x(x(t), y(t))x'(t) + f_y(x(t), y(t))y'(t).$$

But $g'(t) = 0$ because $g(t) = k$ for all t. Therefore, on the one hand,

$$f_x(x(t), y(t))x'(t) + f_y(x(t), y(t))y'(t) = 0;$$

on the other hand,

$$f_x(x(t), y(t))x'(t) + f_y(x(t), y(t))y'(t) = \nabla f(x, y) \cdot \langle x'(t), y'(t) \rangle .$$

Therefore,

$$\nabla f(x, y) \cdot \langle x'(t), y'(t) \rangle = 0.$$

Thus, the dot product of these vectors is equal to zero, which implies they are orthogonal. However, the second vector is tangent to the level curve, which implies the gradient must be normal to the level curve, which gives rise to the following theorem.

Theorem 4.14: Gradient Is Normal to the Level Curve

Suppose the function $z = f(x, y)$ has continuous first-order partial derivatives in an open disk centered at a point (x_0, y_0). If $\nabla f(x_0, y_0) \neq \mathbf{0}$, then $\nabla f(x_0, y_0)$ is normal to the level curve of f at (x_0, y_0).

We can use this theorem to find tangent and normal vectors to level curves of a function.

Example 4.35

Finding Tangents to Level Curves

For the function $f(x, y) = 2x^2 - 3xy + 8y^2 + 2x - 4y + 4$, find a tangent vector to the level curve at point $(-2, 1)$. Graph the level curve corresponding to $f(x, y) = 18$ and draw in $\nabla f(-2, 1)$ and a tangent vector.

Solution

First, we must calculate $\nabla f(x, y)$:

$$f_x(x, y) = 4x - 3y + 2 \text{ and } f_y = -3x + 16y - 4 \text{ so } \nabla f(x, y) = (4x - 3y + 2)\mathbf{i} + (-3x + 16y - 4)\mathbf{j}.$$

Next, we evaluate $\nabla f(x, y)$ at $(-2, 1)$:

$$\nabla f(-2, 1) = (4(-2) - 3(1) + 2)\mathbf{i} + (-3(-2) + 16(1) - 4)\mathbf{j} = -9\mathbf{i} + 18\mathbf{j}.$$

This vector is orthogonal to the curve at point $(-2, 1)$. We can obtain a tangent vector by reversing the components and multiplying either one by -1. Thus, for example, $-18\mathbf{i} - 9\mathbf{j}$ is a tangent vector (see the following graph).

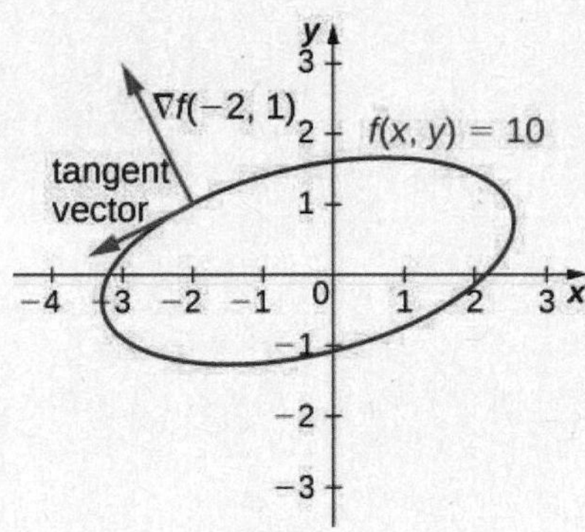

Figure 4.45 Tangent and normal vectors to $2x^2 - 3xy + 8y^2 + 2x - 4y + 4 = 18$ at point $(-2, 1)$.

4.31 For the function $f(x, y) = x^2 - 2xy + 5y^2 + 3x - 2y + 4,$ find the tangent to the level curve at point $(1, 1)$. Draw the graph of the level curve corresponding to $f(x, y) = 8$ and draw $\nabla f(1, 1)$ and a tangent vector.

Three-Dimensional Gradients and Directional Derivatives

The definition of a gradient can be extended to functions of more than two variables.

Definition

Let $w = f(x, y, z)$ be a function of three variables such that $f_x, f_y,$ and f_z exist. The vector $\nabla f(x, y, z)$ is called the gradient of f and is defined as

$$\nabla f(x, y, z) = f_x(x, y, z)\mathbf{i} + f_y(x, y, z)\mathbf{j} + f_z(x, y, z)\mathbf{k}. \tag{4.40}$$

$\nabla f(x, y, z)$ can also be written as $\text{grad } f(x, y, z)$.

Calculating the gradient of a function in three variables is very similar to calculating the gradient of a function in two variables. First, we calculate the partial derivatives $f_x, f_y,$ and $f_z,$ and then we use **Equation 4.40**.

Example 4.36

Finding Gradients in Three Dimensions

Find the gradient $\nabla f(x, y, z)$ of each of the following functions:

a. $f(x, y) = 5x^2 - 2xy + y^2 - 4yz + z^2 + 3xz$

b. $f(x, y, z) = e^{-2z} \sin 2x \cos 2y$

Solution

For both parts a. and b., we first calculate the partial derivatives $f_x,\ f_y,$ and $f_z,$ then use **Equation 4.40**.

a.

$$\begin{aligned} f_z(x, y, z) &= 10x - 2y + 3z,\ f_y(x, y, z) = -2x + 2y - 4z \text{ and } f_z(x, y, z) = 3x - 4y + 2z, \text{ so} \\ \nabla f(x, y, z) &= f_x(x, y, z)\mathbf{i} + f_y(x, y, z)\mathbf{j} + f_z(x, y, z)\mathbf{k} \\ &= (10x - 2y + 3z)\mathbf{i} + (-2x + 2y - 4z)\mathbf{j} + (-4x + 3y + 2z)\mathbf{k}. \end{aligned}$$

b.

$$\begin{aligned} f_x(x, y, z) &= -2e^{-2z}\cos 2x \cos 2y,\ f_y(x, y, z) = -2e^{-2z}\sin 2x \sin 2y \text{ and} \\ f_z(x, y, z) &= -2e^{-2z}\sin 2x \cos 2y, \text{ so} \\ \nabla f(x, y, z) &= f_x(x, y, z)\mathbf{i} + f_y(x, y, z)\mathbf{j} + f_z(x, y, z)\mathbf{k} \\ &= \left(2e^{-2z}\cos 2x \cos 2y\right)\mathbf{i} + \left(-2e^{-2z}\right)\mathbf{j} + \left(-2e^{-2z}\right) \\ &= 2e^{-2z}(\cos 2x \cos 2y\, \mathrm{i} - \sin 2x \sin 2y\, \mathrm{j} - \sin 2x \cos 2y\, \mathrm{k}). \end{aligned}$$

4.32 Find the gradient $\nabla f(x, y, z)$ of $f(x, y, z) = \dfrac{x^2 - 3y^2 + z^2}{2x + y - 4z}.$

The directional derivative can also be generalized to functions of three variables. To determine a direction in three dimensions, a vector with three components is needed. This vector is a unit vector, and the components of the unit vector are called *directional cosines*. Given a three-dimensional unit vector $\mathbf{u}$ in standard form (i.e., the initial point is at the origin), this vector forms three different angles with the positive $x-,\ y-,$ and z-axes. Let's call these angles $\alpha,\ \beta,$ and $\gamma.$ Then the directional cosines are given by $\cos \alpha,\ \cos \beta,$ and $\cos \gamma.$ These are the components of the unit vector $\mathbf{u}$; since $\mathbf{u}$ is a unit vector, it is true that $\cos^2 \alpha + \cos^2 \beta + \cos^2 \gamma = 1.$

Definition

Suppose $w = f(x, y, z)$ is a function of three variables with a domain of $D.$ Let $(x_0, y_0, z_0) \in D$ and let $\mathrm{u} = \cos \alpha \mathbf{i} + \cos \beta \mathbf{j} + \cos \gamma \mathbf{k}$ be a unit vector. Then, the directional derivative of f in the direction of u is given by

$$D_{\mathbf{u}} f(x_0, y_0, z_0) = \lim_{t \to 0} \frac{f(x_0 + t\cos \alpha,\ y_0 + t\cos \beta,\ z_0 + t\cos \gamma) - f(x_0, y_0, z_0)}{t}, \tag{4.41}$$

provided the limit exists.

We can calculate the directional derivative of a function of three variables by using the gradient, leading to a formula that is analogous to **Equation 4.38**.

Theorem 4.15: Directional Derivative of a Function of Three Variables

Let $f(x, y, z)$ be a differentiable function of three variables and let $\mathbf{u} = \cos \alpha \mathbf{i} + \cos \beta \mathbf{j} + \cos \gamma \mathbf{k}$ be a unit vector. Then, the directional derivative of f in the direction of $\mathbf{u}$ is given by

$$\begin{aligned} D_{\mathbf{u}} f(x, y, z) &= \nabla f(x, y, z) \cdot \mathbf{u} \\ &= f_x(x, y, z)\cos \alpha + f_y(x, y, z)\cos \beta + f_z(x, y, z)\cos \gamma. \end{aligned} \tag{4.42}$$

The three angles α, β, and γ determine the unit vector **u**. In practice, we can use an arbitrary (nonunit) vector, then divide by its magnitude to obtain a unit vector in the desired direction.

Example 4.37

Finding a Directional Derivative in Three Dimensions

Calculate $D_{\mathbf{u}} f(1, -2, 3)$ in the direction of $\mathbf{v} = -\mathbf{i} + 2\mathbf{j} + 2\mathbf{k}$ for the function

$$f(x, y, z) = 5x^2 - 2xy + y^2 - 4yz + z^2 + 3xz.$$

Solution

First, we find the magnitude of $\mathbf{v}$:

$$\| \mathbf{v} \| = \sqrt{(-1)^2 + (2)^2} = 3.$$

Therefore, $\frac{\mathbf{v}}{\| \mathbf{v} \|} = \frac{-\mathbf{i} + 2\mathbf{j} + 2\mathbf{k}}{3} = -\frac{1}{3}\mathbf{i} + \frac{2}{3}\mathbf{j} + \frac{2}{3}\mathbf{k}$ is a unit vector in the direction of $\mathbf{v}$, so $\cos\alpha = -\frac{1}{3}$, $\cos\beta = \frac{2}{3}$, and $\cos\gamma = \frac{2}{3}$. Next, we calculate the partial derivatives of f:

$$\begin{aligned} f_x(x, y, z) &= 10x - 2y + 3z \\ f_y(x, y, z) &= -2x + 2y - 4z \\ f_z(x, y, z) &= -4y + 2z + 3x, \end{aligned}$$

then substitute them into **Equation 4.42**:

$$\begin{aligned} D_{\mathbf{u}} f(x, y, z) &= f_x(x, y, z)\cos\alpha + f_y(x, y, z)\cos\beta + f_z(x, y, z)\cos\gamma \\ &= (10x - 2y + 3z)\left(-\frac{1}{3}\right) + (-2x + 2y - 4z)\left(\frac{2}{3}\right) + (-4y + 2z + 3x)\left(\frac{2}{3}\right) \\ &= -\frac{10x}{3} + \frac{2y}{3} - \frac{3z}{3} - \frac{4x}{3} + \frac{4y}{3} - \frac{8z}{3} - \frac{8y}{3} + \frac{4z}{3} + \frac{6x}{3} \\ &= -\frac{8x}{3} - \frac{2y}{3} - \frac{7z}{3}. \end{aligned}$$

Last, to find $D_{\mathbf{u}} f(1, -2, 3)$, we substitute $x = 1$, $y = -2$, and $z = 3$:

$$\begin{aligned} D_{\mathbf{u}} f(1, -2, 3) &= -\frac{8(1)}{3} - \frac{2(-2)}{3} - \frac{7(3)}{3} \\ &= -\frac{8}{3} + \frac{4}{3} - \frac{21}{3} \\ &= -\frac{25}{3}. \end{aligned}$$

4.33 Calculate $D_{\mathbf{u}} f(x, y, z)$ and $D_{\mathbf{u}} f(0, -2, 5)$ in the direction of $\mathbf{v} = -3\mathbf{i} + 12\mathbf{j} - 4\mathbf{k}$ for the function $f(x, y, z) = 3x^2 + xy - 2y^2 + 4yz - z^2 + 2xz.$

4.6 EXERCISES

For the following exercises, find the directional derivative using the limit definition only.

260. $f(x, y) = 5 - 2x^2 - \frac{1}{2}y^2$ at point $P(3, 4)$ in the direction of $\mathrm{u} = \left(\cos\frac{\pi}{4}\right)\mathbf{i} + \left(\sin\frac{\pi}{4}\right)\mathbf{j}$

261. $f(x, y) = y^2\cos(2x)$ at point $P\left(\frac{\pi}{3}, 2\right)$ in the direction of $\mathrm{u} = \left(\cos\frac{\pi}{4}\right)\mathbf{i} + \left(\sin\frac{\pi}{4}\right)\mathbf{j}$

262. Find the directional derivative of $f(x, y) = y^2\sin(2x)$ at point $P\left(\frac{\pi}{4}, 2\right)$ in the direction of $\mathbf{u} = 5\mathbf{i} + 12\mathbf{j}$.

For the following exercises, find the directional derivative of the function at point P in the direction of $\mathbf{v}$.

263. $f(x, y) = xy, \quad P(0, -2), \quad \mathrm{v} = \frac{1}{2}\mathbf{i} + \frac{\sqrt{3}}{2}\mathbf{j}$

264. $h(x, y) = e^x\sin y,\ P\left(1, \frac{\pi}{2}\right),\ \mathbf{v} = -\mathbf{i}$

265. $h(x, y, z) = xyz,\ P(2, 1, 1),\ \mathrm{v} = 2\mathbf{i} + \mathbf{j} - \mathbf{k}$

266. $f(x, y) = xy,\ P(1, 1),\ \mathbf{u} = \left\langle \frac{\sqrt{2}}{2}, \frac{\sqrt{2}}{2} \right\rangle$

267. $f(x, y) = x^2 - y^2,\ \mathbf{u} = \left\langle \frac{\sqrt{3}}{2}, \frac{1}{2} \right\rangle,\ P(1, 0)$

268. $f(x, y) = 3x + 4y + 7,\ \mathbf{u} = \left\langle \frac{3}{5}, \frac{4}{5} \right\rangle,\ P\left(0, \frac{\pi}{2}\right)$

269. $f(x, y) = e^x\cos y, \quad \mathbf{u} = \langle 0, 1 \rangle, \quad P = \left(0, \frac{\pi}{2}\right)$

270. $f(x, y) = y^{10}, \quad \mathbf{u} = \langle 0, -1 \rangle, \quad P = (1, -1)$

271. $f(x, y) = \ln(x^2 + y^2),\ \mathbf{u} = \left\langle \frac{3}{5}, \frac{4}{5} \right\rangle,\ P(1, 2)$

272. $f(x, y) = x^2y,\ P(-5, 5), \quad \mathbf{v} = 3\mathbf{i} - 4\mathbf{j}$

273. $f(x, y) = y^2 + xz,\ P(1, 2, 2), \quad \mathbf{v} = \langle 2, -1, 2 \rangle$

For the following exercises, find the directional derivative of the function in the direction of the unit vector $\mathbf{u} = \cos\theta\mathbf{i} + \sin\theta\mathbf{j}$.

274. $f(x, y) = x^2 + 2y^2,\ \theta = \frac{\pi}{6}$

275. $f(x, y) = \frac{y}{x + 2y},\ \theta = -\frac{\pi}{4}$

276. $f(x, y) = \cos(3x + y),\ \theta = \frac{\pi}{4}$

277. $w(x, y) = ye^x,\ \theta = \frac{\pi}{3}$

278. $f(x, y) = x\arctan(y), \quad \theta = \frac{\pi}{2}$

279. $f(x, y) = \ln(x + 2y), \quad \theta = \frac{\pi}{3}$

For the following exercises, find the gradient.

280. Find the gradient of $f(x, y) = \frac{14 - x^2 - y^2}{3}$. Then, find the gradient at point $P(1, 2)$.

281. Find the gradient of $f(x, y, z) = xy + yz + xz$ at point $P(1, 2, 3)$.

282. Find the gradient of $f(x, y, z)$ at P and in the direction of $\mathbf{u}$: $f(x, y, z) = \ln(x^2 + 2y^2 + 3z^2),\ P(2, 1, 4), \quad \mathbf{u} = \frac{-3}{13}\mathbf{i} - \frac{4}{13}\mathbf{j} - \frac{12}{13}\mathbf{k}$.

283. $f(x, y, z) = 4x^5y^2z^3,\ P(2, -1, 1), \quad \mathbf{u} = \frac{1}{3}\mathbf{i} + \frac{2}{3}\mathbf{j} - \frac{2}{3}\mathbf{k}$

For the following exercises, find the directional derivative of the function at point P in the direction of Q.

284. $f(x, y) = x^2 + 3y^2,\ P(1, 1), \quad Q(4, 5)$

285. $f(x, y, z) = \frac{y}{x + z},\ P(2, 1, -1), \quad Q(-1, 2, 0)$

For the following exercises, find the derivative of the function at P in the direction of $\mathbf{u}$.

286. $f(x, y) = -7x + 2y,\ P(2, -4), \quad \mathbf{u} = 4\mathbf{i} - 3\mathbf{j}$

287. $f(x, y) = \ln(5x + 4y),\ P(3, 9), \quad \mathbf{u} = 6\mathbf{i} + 8\mathbf{j}$

288. **[T]** Use technology to sketch the level curve of $f(x, y) = 4x - 2y + 3$ that passes through $P(1, 2)$ and draw the gradient vector at P.

289. **[T]** Use technology to sketch the level curve of $f(x, y) = x^2 + 4y^2$ that passes through $P(-2, 0)$ and draw the gradient vector at P.

For the following exercises, find the gradient vector at the indicated point.

290. $f(x, y) = xy^2 - yx^2, P(-1, 1)$

291. $f(x, y) = xe^y - \ln(x), P(-3, 0)$

292. $f(x, y, z) = xy - \ln(z), P(2, -2, 2)$

293. $f(x, y, z) = x\sqrt{y^2 + z^2}, P(-2, -1, -1)$

For the following exercises, find the derivative of the function.

294. $f(x, y) = x^2 + xy + y^2$ at point $(-5, -4)$ in the direction the function increases most rapidly

295. $f(x, y) = e^{xy}$ at point $(6, 7)$ in the direction the function increases most rapidly

296. $f(x, y) = \arctan\left(\frac{y}{x}\right)$ at point $(-9, 9)$ in the direction the function increases most rapidly

297. $f(x, y, z) = \ln(xy + yz + zx)$ at point $(-9, -18, -27)$ in the direction the function increases most rapidly

298. $f(x, y, z) = \frac{x}{y} + \frac{y}{z} + \frac{z}{x}$ at point $(5, -5, 5)$ in the direction the function increases most rapidly

For the following exercises, find the maximum rate of change of f at the given point and the direction in which it occurs.

299. $f(x, y) = xe^{-y}, \quad (1, 0)$

300. $f(x, y) = \sqrt{x^2 + 2y}, \quad (4, 10)$

301. $f(x, y) = \cos(3x + 2y), \left(\frac{\pi}{6}, -\frac{\pi}{8}\right)$

For the following exercises, find equations of

a. the tangent plane and
b. the normal line to the given surface at the given point.

302. The level curve $f(x, y, z) = 12$ for $f(x, y, z) = 4x^2 - 2y^2 + z^2$ at point $(2, 2, 2)$.

303. $f(x, y, z) = xy + yz + xz = 3$ at point $(1, 1, 1)$

304. $f(x, y, z) = xyz = 6$ at point $(1, 2, 3)$

305. $f(x, y, z) = xe^y \cos z - z = 1$ at point $(1, 0, 0)$

For the following exercises, solve the problem.

306. The temperature T in a metal sphere is inversely proportional to the distance from the center of the sphere (the origin: $(0, 0, 0)$). The temperature at point $(1, 2, 2)$ is 120°C.

a. Find the rate of change of the temperature at point $(1, 2, 2)$ in the direction toward point $(2, 1, 3)$.
b. Show that, at any point in the sphere, the direction of greatest increase in temperature is given by a vector that points toward the origin.

307. The electrical potential (voltage) in a certain region of space is given by the function $V(x, y, z) = 5x^2 - 3xy + xyz$.

a. Find the rate of change of the voltage at point $(3, 4, 5)$ in the direction of the vector $\langle 1, 1, -1 \rangle$.
b. In which direction does the voltage change most rapidly at point $(3, 4, 5)$?
c. What is the maximum rate of change of the voltage at point $(3, 4, 5)$?

308. If the electric potential at a point (x, y) in the xy-plane is $V(x, y) = e^{-2x}\cos(2y)$, then the electric intensity vector at (x, y) is $\mathbf{E} = -\nabla V(x, y)$.

a. Find the electric intensity vector at $\left(\frac{\pi}{4}, 0\right)$.
b. Show that, at each point in the plane, the electric potential decreases most rapidly in the direction of the vector $\mathbf{E}$.

309. In two dimensions, the motion of an ideal fluid is governed by a velocity potential φ. The velocity components of the fluid u in the x-direction and v in the y-direction, are given by $\langle u, v \rangle = \nabla\varphi$. Find the velocity components associated with the velocity potential $\varphi(x, y) = \sin \pi x \sin 2\pi y$.

4.7 | Maxima/Minima Problems

Learning Objectives

4.7.1 Use partial derivatives to locate critical points for a function of two variables.

4.7.2 Apply a second derivative test to identify a critical point as a local maximum, local minimum, or saddle point for a function of two variables.

4.7.3 Examine critical points and boundary points to find absolute maximum and minimum values for a function of two variables.

One of the most useful applications for derivatives of a function of one variable is the determination of maximum and/or minimum values. This application is also important for functions of two or more variables, but as we have seen in earlier sections of this chapter, the introduction of more independent variables leads to more possible outcomes for the calculations. The main ideas of finding critical points and using derivative tests are still valid, but new wrinkles appear when assessing the results.

Critical Points

For functions of a single variable, we defined critical points as the values of the function when the derivative equals zero or does not exist. For functions of two or more variables, the concept is essentially the same, except for the fact that we are now working with partial derivatives.

Definition

Let $z = f(x, y)$ be a function of two variables that is defined on an open set containing the point (x_0, y_0). The point (x_0, y_0) is called a **critical point of a function of two variables** f if one of the two following conditions holds:

1. $f_x(x_0, y_0) = f_y(x_0, y_0) = 0$
2. Either $f_x(x_0, y_0)$ or $f_y(x_0, y_0)$ does not exist.

Example 4.38

Finding Critical Points

Find the critical points of each of the following functions:

a. $f(x, y) = \sqrt{4y^2 - 9x^2 + 24y + 36x + 36}$

b. $g(x, y) = x^2 + 2xy - 4y^2 + 4x - 6y + 4$

Solution

a. First, we calculate $f_x(x, y)$ and $f_y(x, y)$:

$$\begin{aligned} f_x(x, y) &= \tfrac{1}{2}(-18x + 36)\left(4y^2 - 9x^2 + 24y + 36x + 36\right)^{-1/2} \\ &= \frac{-9x + 18}{\sqrt{4y^2 - 9x^2 + 24y + 36x + 36}} \\ f_y(x, y) &= \tfrac{1}{2}(8y + 24)\left(4y^2 - 9x^2 + 24y + 36x + 36\right)^{-1/2} \\ &= \frac{4y + 12}{\sqrt{4y^2 - 9x^2 + 24y + 36x + 36}}. \end{aligned}$$

Next, we set each of these expressions equal to zero:

$$\begin{aligned} \frac{-9x + 18}{\sqrt{4y^2 - 9x^2 + 24y + 36x + 36}} &= 0 \\ \frac{4y + 12}{\sqrt{4y^2 - 9x^2 + 24y + 36x + 36}} &= 0. \end{aligned}$$

Then, multiply each equation by its common denominator:

$$\begin{aligned} -9x + 18 &= 0 \\ 4y + 12 &= 0. \end{aligned}$$

Therefore, $x = 2$ and $y = -3,$ so $(2, -3)$ is a critical point of f.

We must also check for the possibility that the denominator of each partial derivative can equal zero, thus causing the partial derivative not to exist. Since the denominator is the same in each partial derivative, we need only do this once:

$$4y^2 - 9x^2 + 24y + 36x + 36 = 0.$$

This equation represents a hyperbola. We should also note that the domain of f consists of points satisfying the inequality

$$4y^2 - 9x^2 + 24y + 36x + 36 \geq 0.$$

Therefore, any points on the hyperbola are not only critical points, they are also on the boundary of the domain. To put the hyperbola in standard form, we use the method of completing the square:

$$\begin{aligned} 4y^2 - 9x^2 + 24y + 36x + 36 &= 0 \\ 4y^2 - 9x^2 + 24y + 36x &= -36 \\ 4y^2 + 24y - 9x^2 + 36x &= -36 \\ 4\left(y^2 + 6y\right) - 9\left(x^2 - 4x\right) &= -36 \\ 4\left(y^2 + 6y + 9\right) - 9\left(x^2 - 4x + 4\right) &= -36 + 36 - 36 \\ 4(y + 3)^2 - 9(x - 2)^2 &= -36. \end{aligned}$$

Dividing both sides by -36 puts the equation in standard form:

$$\begin{aligned}\frac{4(y+3)^2}{-36} - \frac{9(x-2)^2}{-36} &= 1 \\ \frac{(x-2)^2}{4} - \frac{(y+3)^2}{9} &= 1.\end{aligned}$$

Notice that point $(2, -3)$ is the center of the hyperbola.

b. First, we calculate $g_x(x, y)$ and $g_y(x, y)$:

$$\begin{aligned}g_x(x, y) &= 2x + 2y + 4 \\ g_y(x, y) &= 2x - 8y - 6.\end{aligned}$$

Next, we set each of these expressions equal to zero, which gives a system of equations in x and y:

$$\begin{aligned}2x + 2y + 4 &= 0 \\ 2x - 8y - 6 &= 0.\end{aligned}$$

Subtracting the second equation from the first gives $10y + 10 = 0$, so $y = -1$. Substituting this into the first equation gives $2x + 2(-1) + 4 = 0$, so $x = -1$. Therefore $(-1, -1)$ is a critical point of g (**Figure 4.46**). There are no points in $\mathbb{R}^2$ that make either partial derivative not exist.

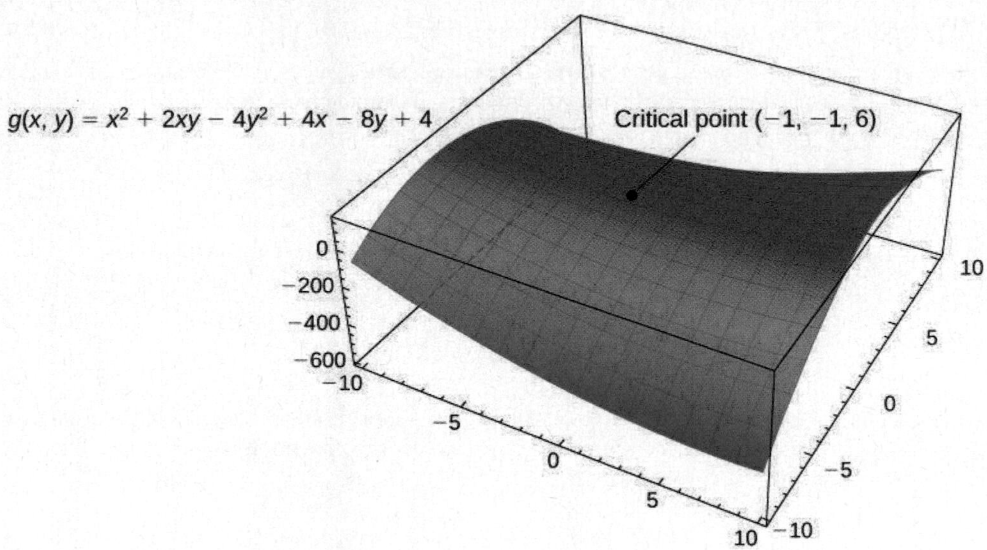

Figure 4.46 The function $g(x, y)$ has a critical point at $(-1, -1, 6)$.

 **4.34** Find the critical point of the function $f(x, y) = x^3 + 2xy - 2x - 4y$.

The main purpose for determining critical points is to locate relative maxima and minima, as in single-variable calculus. When working with a function of one variable, the definition of a local extremum involves finding an interval around the critical point such that the function value is either greater than or less than all the other function values in that interval. When working with a function of two or more variables, we work with an open disk around the point.

Definition

Let $z = f(x, y)$ be a function of two variables that is defined and continuous on an open set containing the point (x_0, y_0). Then f has a *local maximum* at (x_0, y_0) if

$$f(x_0, y_0) \geq f(x, y)$$

for all points (x, y) within some disk centered at (x_0, y_0). The number $f(x_0, y_0)$ is called a *local maximum value*. If the preceding inequality holds for every point (x, y) in the domain of f, then f has a *global maximum* (also called an *absolute maximum*) at (x_0, y_0).

The function f has a *local minimum* at (x_0, y_0) if

$$f(x_0, y_0) \leq f(x, y)$$

for all points (x, y) within some disk centered at (x_0, y_0). The number $f(x_0, y_0)$ is called a *local minimum value*. If the preceding inequality holds for every point (x, y) in the domain of f, then f has a *global minimum* (also called an *absolute minimum*) at (x_0, y_0).

If $f(x_0, y_0)$ is either a local maximum or local minimum value, then it is called a *local extremum* (see the following figure).

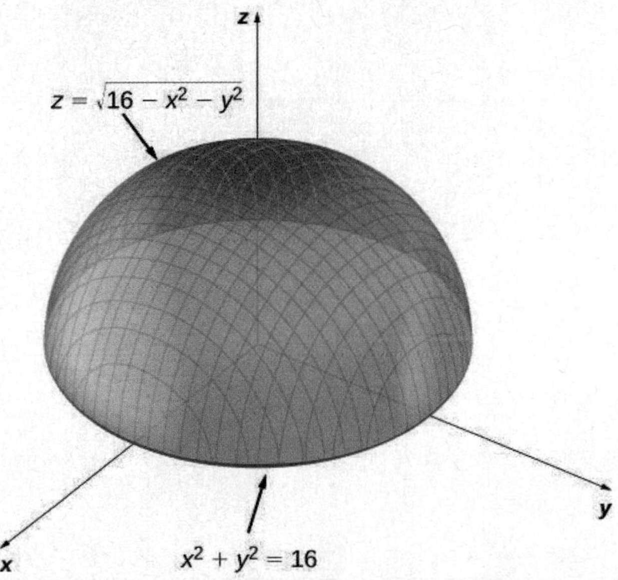

Figure 4.47 The graph of $z = \sqrt{16 - x^2 - y^2}$ has a maximum value when $(x, y) = (0, 0)$. It attains its minimum value at the boundary of its domain, which is the circle $x^2 + y^2 = 16$.

In **Maxima and Minima (http://cnx.org/content/m53611/latest/)** , we showed that extrema of functions of one variable occur at critical points. The same is true for functions of more than one variable, as stated in the following theorem.

Theorem 4.16: Fermat's Theorem for Functions of Two Variables

Let $z = f(x, y)$ be a function of two variables that is defined and continuous on an open set containing the point

(x_0, y_0). Suppose f_x and f_y each exists at (x_0, y_0). If f has a local extremum at (x_0, y_0), then (x_0, y_0) is a critical point of f.

Second Derivative Test

Consider the function $f(x) = x^3$. This function has a critical point at $x = 0$, since $f'(0) = 3(0)^2 = 0$. However, f does not have an extreme value at $x = 0$. Therefore, the existence of a critical value at $x = x_0$ does not guarantee a local extremum at $x = x_0$. The same is true for a function of two or more variables. One way this can happen is at a **saddle point**. An example of a saddle point appears in the following figure.

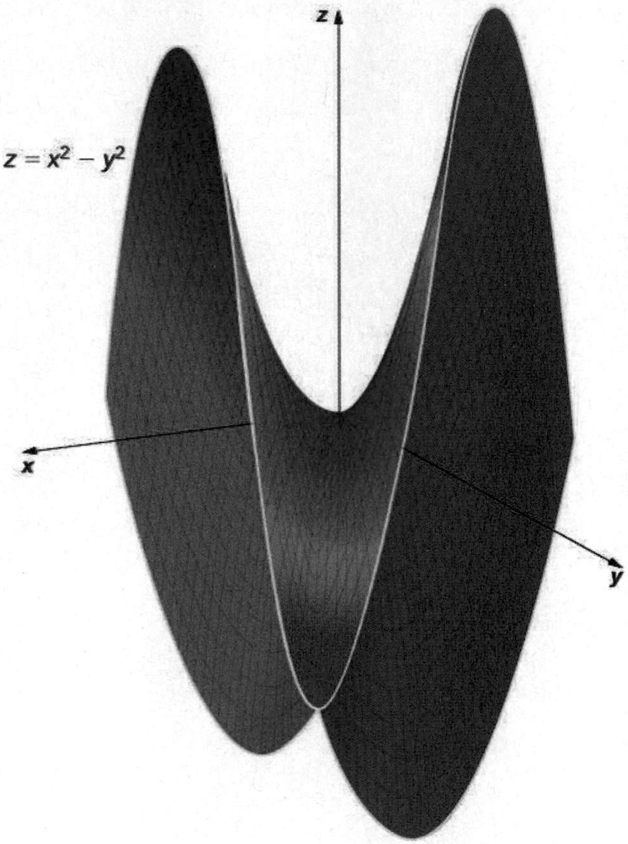

Figure 4.48 Graph of the function $z = x^2 - y^2$. This graph has a saddle point at the origin.

In this graph, the origin is a saddle point. This is because the first partial derivatives of $f(x, y) = x^2 - y^2$ are both equal to zero at this point, but it is neither a maximum nor a minimum for the function. Furthermore the vertical trace corresponding to $y = 0$ is $z = x^2$ (a parabola opening upward), but the vertical trace corresponding to $x = 0$ is $z = -y^2$ (a parabola opening downward). Therefore, it is both a global maximum for one trace and a global minimum for another.

Definition

Given the function $z = f(x, y)$, the point $\left(x_0, y_0, f(x_0, y_0)\right)$ is a saddle point if both $f_0(x_0, y_0) = 0$ and $f_y(x_0, y_0) = 0$, but f does not have a local extremum at (x_0, y_0).

The second derivative test for a function of one variable provides a method for determining whether an extremum occurs at a critical point of a function. When extending this result to a function of two variables, an issue arises related to the fact that there are, in fact, four different second-order partial derivatives, although equality of mixed partials reduces this to three. The second derivative test for a function of two variables, stated in the following theorem, uses a **discriminant** D that replaces $f''(x_0)$ in the second derivative test for a function of one variable.

Theorem 4.17: Second Derivative Test

Let $z = f(x, y)$ be a function of two variables for which the first- and second-order partial derivatives are continuous on some disk containing the point (x_0, y_0). Suppose $f_x(x_0, y_0) = 0$ and $f_y(x_0, y_0) = 0$. Define the quantity

$$D = f_{xx}(x_0, y_0)f_{yy}(x_0, y_0) - \left(f_{xy}(x_0, y_0)\right)^2. \quad \textbf{(4.43)}$$

i. If $D > 0$ and $f_{xx}(x_0, y_0) > 0,$ then f has a local minimum at (x_0, y_0).

ii. If $D > 0$ and $f_{xx}(x_0, y_0) < 0,$ then f has a local maximum at (x_0, y_0).

iii. If $D < 0,$, then f has a saddle point at (x_0, y_0).

iv. If $D = 0,$ then the test is inconclusive.

See **Figure 4.49**.

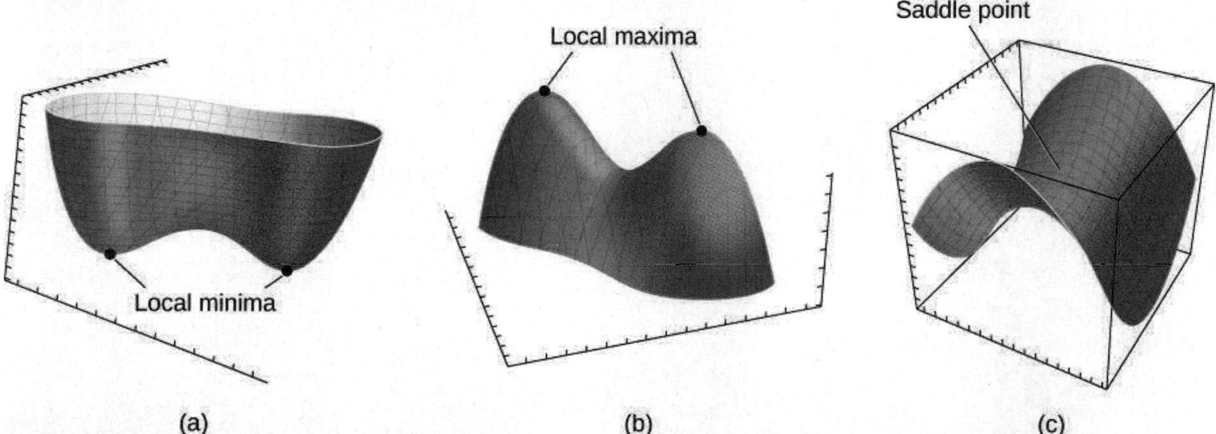

Figure 4.49 The second derivative test can often determine whether a function of two variables has a local minima (a), a local maxima (b), or a saddle point (c).

To apply the second derivative test, it is necessary that we first find the critical points of the function. There are several steps involved in the entire procedure, which are outlined in a problem-solving strategy.

Problem-Solving Strategy: Using the Second Derivative Test for Functions of Two Variables

Let $z = f(x, y)$ be a function of two variables for which the first- and second-order partial derivatives are continuous on some disk containing the point (x_0, y_0). To apply the second derivative test to find local extrema, use the following steps:

1. Determine the critical points (x_0, y_0) of the function f where $f_x(x_0, y_0) = f_y(x_0, y_0) = 0$. Discard any points where at least one of the partial derivatives does not exist.
2. Calculate the discriminant $D = f_{xx}(x_0, y_0)f_{yy}(x_0, y_0) - \left(f_{xy}(x_0, y_0)\right)^2$ for each critical point of f.

3. Apply **Second Derivative Test** to determine whether each critical point is a local maximum, local minimum, or saddle point, or whether the theorem is inconclusive.

Example 4.39

Using the Second Derivative Test

Find the critical points for each of the following functions, and use the second derivative test to find the local extrema:

a. $f(x, y) = 4x^2 + 9y^2 + 8x - 36y + 24$

b. $g(x, y) = \frac{1}{3}x^3 + y^2 + 2xy - 6x - 3y + 4$

Solution

a. Step 1 of the problem-solving strategy involves finding the critical points of f. To do this, we first calculate $f_x(x, y)$ and $f_y(x, y)$, then set each of them equal to zero:

$$\begin{aligned} f_x(x, y) &= 8x + 8 \\ f_y(x, y) &= 18y - 36. \end{aligned}$$

Setting them equal to zero yields the system of equations

$$\begin{aligned} 8x + 8 &= 0 \\ 18y - 36 &= 0. \end{aligned}$$

The solution to this system is $x = -1$ and $y = 2$. Therefore $(-1, 2)$ is a critical point of f.

Step 2 of the problem-solving strategy involves calculating D. To do this, we first calculate the second partial derivatives of f:

$$\begin{aligned} f_{xx}(x, y) &= 8 \\ f_{xy}(x, y) &= 0 \\ f_{yy}(x, y) &= 18. \end{aligned}$$

Therefore, $D = f_{xx}(-1, 2)f_{yy}(-1, 2) - \left(f_{xy}(-1, 2)\right)^2 = (8)(18) - (0)^2 = 144.$

Step 3 states to check **Fermat's Theorem for Functions of Two Variables.** Since $D > 0$ and $f_{xx}(-1, 2) > 0,$ this corresponds to case 1. Therefore, f has a local minimum at $(-1, 2)$ as shown in the following figure.

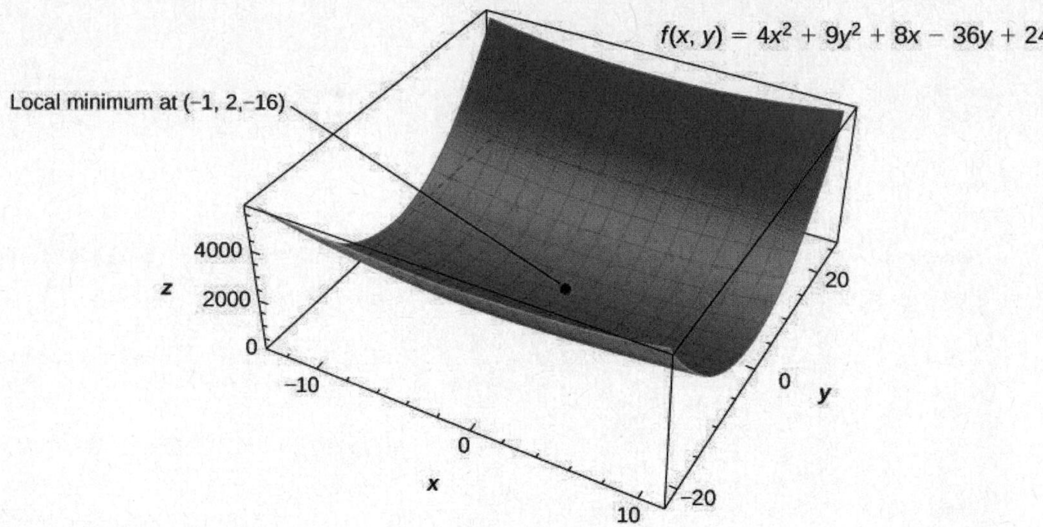

Figure 4.50 The function $f(x, y)$ has a local minimum at $(-1, 2, -16)$.

b. For step 1, we first calculate $g_x(x, y)$ and $g_y(x, y)$, then set each of them equal to zero:

$$\begin{aligned} g_x(x, y) &= x^2 + 2y - 6 \\ g_y(x, y) &= 2y + 2x - 3. \end{aligned}$$

Setting them equal to zero yields the system of equations

$$\begin{aligned} x^2 + 2y - 6 &= 0 \\ 2y + 2x - 3 &= 0. \end{aligned}$$

To solve this system, first solve the second equation for *y*. This gives $y = \frac{3 - 2x}{2}$. Substituting this into the first equation gives

$$\begin{aligned} x^2 + 3 - 2x - 6 &= 0 \\ x^2 - 2x - 3 &= 0 \\ (x - 3)(x + 1) &= 0. \end{aligned}$$

Therefore, $x = -1$ or $x = 3$. Substituting these values into the equation $y = \frac{3 - 2x}{2}$ yields the critical points $\left(-1, \frac{5}{2}\right)$ and $\left(3, -\frac{3}{2}\right)$.

Step 2 involves calculating the second partial derivatives of g:

$$\begin{aligned} g_{xx}(x, y) &= 2x \\ g_{xy}(x, y) &= 2 \\ g_{yy}(x, y) &= 2. \end{aligned}$$

Then, we find a general formula for D:

$$\begin{aligned} D &= g_{xx}(x_0, y_0)g_{yy}(x_0, y_0) - \left(g_{xy}(x_0, y_0)\right)^2 \\ &= (2x_0)(2) - 2^2 \\ &= 4x_0 - 4. \end{aligned}$$

Next, we substitute each critical point into this formula:

$$D\left(-1, \frac{5}{2}\right) = (2(-1))(2) - (2)^2 = -4 - 4 = -8$$

$$D\left(3, -\frac{3}{2}\right) = (2(3))(2) - (2)^2 = 12 - 4 = 8.$$

In step 3, we note that, applying **Fermat's Theorem for Functions of Two Variables** to point $\left(-1, \frac{5}{2}\right)$ leads to case 3, which means that $\left(-1, \frac{5}{2}\right)$ is a saddle point. Applying the theorem to point $\left(3, -\frac{3}{2}\right)$ leads to case 1, which means that $\left(3, -\frac{3}{2}\right)$ corresponds to a local minimum as shown in the following figure.

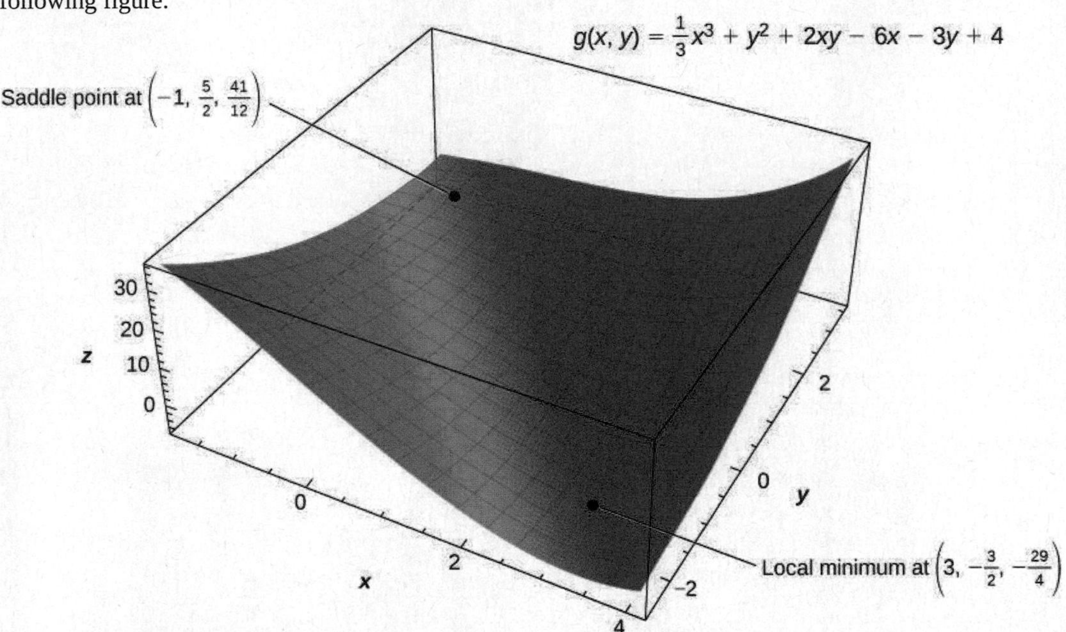

Figure 4.51 The function $g(x, y)$ has a local minimum and a saddle point.

4.35 Use the second derivative to find the local extrema of the function

$$f(x, y) = x^3 + 2xy - 6x - 4y^2.$$

Absolute Maxima and Minima

When finding global extrema of functions of one variable on a closed interval, we start by checking the critical values over that interval and then evaluate the function at the endpoints of the interval. When working with a function of two variables, the closed interval is replaced by a closed, bounded set. A set is *bounded* if all the points in that set can be contained within a ball (or disk) of finite radius. First, we need to find the critical points inside the set and calculate the corresponding critical values. Then, it is necessary to find the maximum and minimum value of the function on the boundary of the set. When we have all these values, the largest function value corresponds to the global maximum and the smallest function value corresponds to the absolute minimum. First, however, we need to be assured that such values exist. The following theorem does this.

Theorem 4.18: Extreme Value Theorem

A continuous function $f(x, y)$ on a closed and bounded set D in the plane attains an absolute maximum value at some point of D and an absolute minimum value at some point of D.

Now that we know any continuous function f defined on a closed, bounded set attains its extreme values, we need to know how to find them.

Theorem 4.19: Finding Extreme Values of a Function of Two Variables

Assume $z = f(x, y)$ is a differentiable function of two variables defined on a closed, bounded set D. Then f will attain the absolute maximum value and the absolute minimum value, which are, respectively, the largest and smallest values found among the following:

i. The values of f at the critical points of f in D.

ii. The values of f on the boundary of D.

The proof of this theorem is a direct consequence of the extreme value theorem and Fermat's theorem. In particular, if either extremum is not located on the boundary of D, then it is located at an interior point of D. But an interior point (x_0, y_0) of D that's an absolute extremum is also a local extremum; hence, (x_0, y_0) is a critical point of f by Fermat's theorem. Therefore the only possible values for the global extrema of f on D are the extreme values of f on the interior or boundary of D.

Problem-Solving Strategy: Finding Absolute Maximum and Minimum Values

Let $z = f(x, y)$ be a continuous function of two variables defined on a closed, bounded set D, and assume f is differentiable on D. To find the absolute maximum and minimum values of f on D, do the following:

1. Determine the critical points of f in D.
2. Calculate f at each of these critical points.
3. Determine the maximum and minimum values of f on the boundary of its domain.
4. The maximum and minimum values of f will occur at one of the values obtained in steps 2 and 3.

Finding the maximum and minimum values of f on the boundary of D can be challenging. If the boundary is a rectangle or set of straight lines, then it is possible to parameterize the line segments and determine the maxima on each of these segments, as seen in **Example 4.40**. The same approach can be used for other shapes such as circles and ellipses.

If the boundary of the set D is a more complicated curve defined by a function $g(x, y) = c$ for some constant c, and the first-order partial derivatives of g exist, then the method of Lagrange multipliers can prove useful for determining the extrema of f on the boundary. The method of Lagrange multipliers is introduced in **Lagrange Multipliers**.

Example 4.40

Finding Absolute Extrema

Use the problem-solving strategy for finding absolute extrema of a function to determine the absolute extrema of each of the following functions:

a. $f(x, y) = x^2 - 2xy + 4y^2 - 4x - 2y + 24$ on the domain defined by $0 \le x \le 4$ and $0 \le y \le 2$

b. $g(x, y) = x^2 + y^2 + 4x - 6y$ on the domain defined by $x^2 + y^2 \le 16$

Solution

a. Using the problem-solving strategy, step 1 involves finding the critical points of f on its domain. Therefore, we first calculate $f_x(x, y)$ and $f_y(x, y)$, then set them each equal to zero:

$$\begin{aligned} f_x(x, y) &= 2x - 2y - 4 \\ f_y(x, y) &= -2x + 8y - 2. \end{aligned}$$

Setting them equal to zero yields the system of equations

$$\begin{aligned} 2x - 2y - 4 &= 0 \\ -2x + 8y - 2 &= 0. \end{aligned}$$

The solution to this system is $x = 3$ and $y = 1$. Therefore $(3, 1)$ is a critical point of f. Calculating $f(3, 1)$ gives $f(3, 1) = 17$.

The next step involves finding the extrema of f on the boundary of its domain. The boundary of its domain consists of four line segments as shown in the following graph:

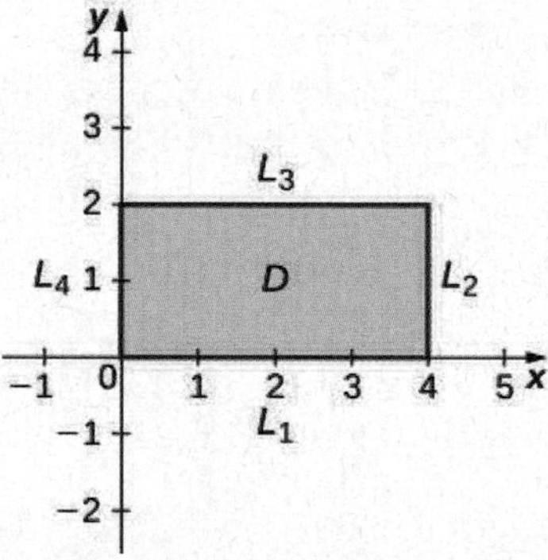

Figure 4.52 Graph of the domain of the function $f(x, y) = x^2 - 2xy + 4y^2 - 4x - 2y + 24$.

L_1 is the line segment connecting $(0, 0)$ and $(4, 0)$, and it can be parameterized by the equations $x(t) = t, y(t) = 0$ for $0 \le t \le 4$. Define $g(t) = f(x(t), y(t))$. This gives $g(t) = t^2 - 4t + 24$. Differentiating g leads to $g'(t) = 2t - 4$. Therefore, g has a critical value at $t = 2$, which corresponds to the point $(2, 0)$. Calculating $f(2, 0)$ gives the z-value 20.

L_2 is the line segment connecting $(4, 0)$ and $(4, 2)$, and it can be parameterized by the equations $x(t) = 4, y(t) = t$ for $0 \le t \le 2$. Again, define $g(t) = f(x(t), y(t))$. This gives $g(t) = 4t^2 - 10t + 24$. Then, $g'(t) = 8t - 10$. g has a critical value at $t = \frac{5}{4}$, which corresponds to the point $\left(0, \frac{5}{4}\right)$.

Calculating $f\left(0, \frac{5}{4}\right)$ gives the z-value 27.75.

L_3 is the line segment connecting $(0, 2)$ and $(4, 2)$, and it can be parameterized by the equations $x(t) = t,\ y(t) = 2$ for $0 \le t \le 4$. Again, define $g(t) = f(x(t), y(t))$. This gives $g(t) = t^2 - 8t + 36$. The critical value corresponds to the point $(4, 2)$. So, calculating $f(4, 2)$ gives the z-value 20.

L_4 is the line segment connecting $(0, 0)$ and $(0, 2)$, and it can be parameterized by the equations $x(t) = 0,\ y(t) = t$ for $0 \le t \le 2$. This time, $g(t) = 4t^2 - 2t + 24$ and the critical value $t = \frac{1}{4}$ correspond to the point $\left(0, \frac{1}{4}\right)$. Calculating $f\left(0, \frac{1}{4}\right)$ gives the z-value 23.75.

We also need to find the values of $f(x, y)$ at the corners of its domain. These corners are located at $(0, 0), (4, 0), (4, 2)$ and $(0, 2)$:

$$\begin{aligned} f(0, 0) &= (0)^2 - 2(0)(0) + 4(0)^2 - 4(0) - 2(0) + 24 &= 24 \\ f(4, 0) &= (4)^2 - 2(4)(0) + 4(0)^2 - 4(4) - 2(0) + 24 &= 24 \\ f(4, 2) &= (4)^2 - 2(4)(2) + 4(2)^2 - 4(4) - 2(2) + 24 &= 20 \\ f(0, 2) &= (0)^2 - 2(0)(2) + 4(2)^2 - 4(0) - 2(2) + 24 &= 36. \end{aligned}$$

The absolute maximum value is 36, which occurs at $(0, 2)$, and the global minimum value is 20, which occurs at both $(4, 2)$ and $(2, 0)$ as shown in the following figure.

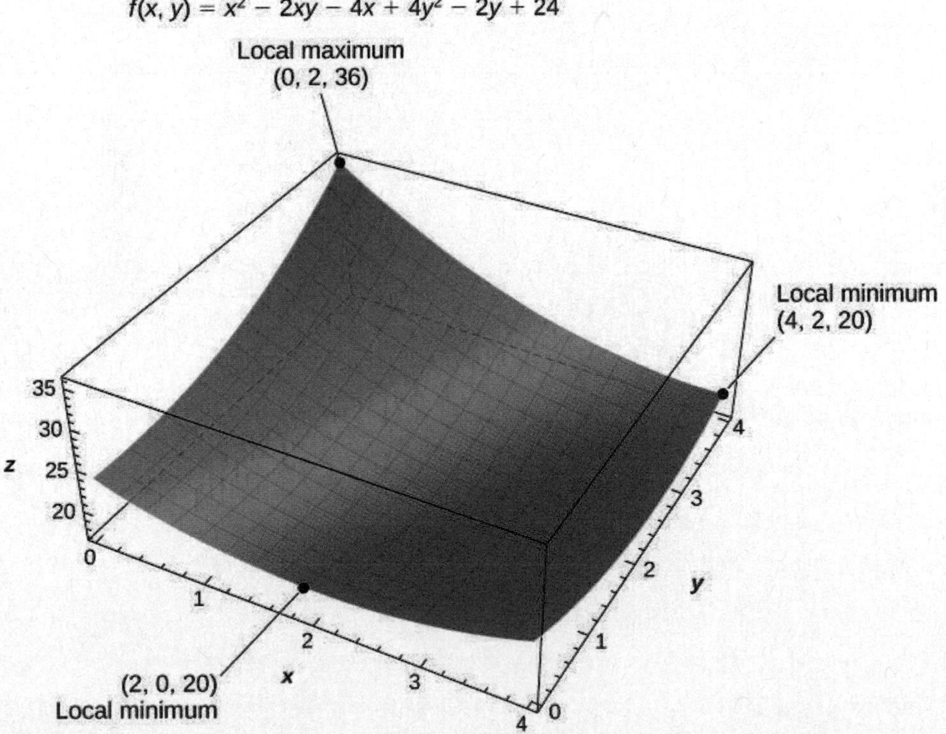

Figure 4.53 The function $f(x, y)$ has two global minima and one global maximum over its domain.

b. Using the problem-solving strategy, step 1 involves finding the critical points of g on its domain. Therefore, we first calculate $g_x(x, y)$ and $g_y(x, y)$, then set them each equal to zero:

$$\begin{aligned} g_x(x, y) &= 2x + 4 \\ g_y(x, y) &= 2y - 6. \end{aligned}$$

Setting them equal to zero yields the system of equations

$$\begin{aligned} 2x + 4 &= 0 \\ 2y - 6 &= 0. \end{aligned}$$

The solution to this system is $x = -2$ and $y = 3$. Therefore, $(-2, 3)$ is a critical point of g. Calculating $g(-2, 3)$, we get

$$g(-2, 3) = (-2)^2 + 3^2 + 4(-2) - 6(3) = 4 + 9 - 8 - 18 = -13.$$

The next step involves finding the extrema of g on the boundary of its domain. The boundary of its domain consists of a circle of radius 4 centered at the origin as shown in the following graph.

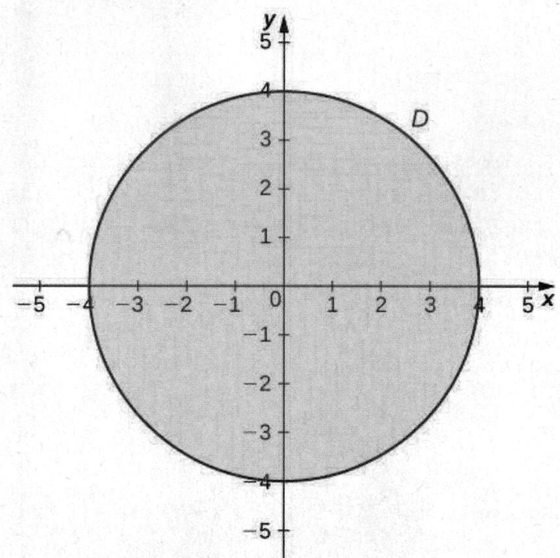

Figure 4.54 Graph of the domain of the function $g(x, y) = x^2 + y^2 + 4x - 6y$.

The boundary of the domain of g can be parameterized using the functions $x(t) = 4\cos t,\ y(t) = 4\sin t$ for $0 \le t \le 2\pi$. Define $h(t) = g(x(t), y(t))$:

$$\begin{aligned} h(t) &= g(x(t), y(t)) \\ &= (4\cos t)^2 + (4\sin t)^2 + 4(4\cos t) - 6(4\sin t) \\ &= 16\cos^2 t + 16\sin^2 t + 16\cos t - 24\sin t \\ &= 16 + 16\cos t - 24\sin t. \end{aligned}$$

Setting $h'(t) = 0$ leads to

$$\begin{aligned} -16 \sin t - 24 \cos t &= 0 \\ -16 \sin t &= 24 \cos t \\ \frac{-16 \sin t}{-16 \cos t} &= \frac{24 \cos t}{-16 \cos t} \\ \tan t &= -\frac{3}{2}. \end{aligned}$$

This equation has two solutions over the interval $0 \le t \le 2\pi$. One is $t = \pi - \arctan\left(\frac{3}{2}\right)$ and the other is $t = 2\pi - \arctan\left(\frac{3}{2}\right)$. For the first angle,

$$\begin{aligned} \sin t &= \sin\left(\pi - \arctan\left(\frac{3}{2}\right)\right) = \sin\left(\arctan\left(\frac{3}{2}\right)\right) = \frac{3\sqrt{13}}{13} \\ \cos t &= \cos\left(\pi - \arctan\left(\frac{3}{2}\right)\right) = -\cos\left(\arctan\left(\frac{3}{2}\right)\right) = -\frac{2\sqrt{13}}{13}. \end{aligned}$$

Therefore, $x(t) = 4 \cos t = -\frac{8\sqrt{13}}{13}$ and $y(t) = 4 \sin t = \frac{12\sqrt{13}}{13}$, so $\left(-\frac{8\sqrt{13}}{13}, \frac{12\sqrt{13}}{13}\right)$ is a critical point on the boundary and

$$\begin{aligned} g\left(-\frac{8\sqrt{13}}{13}, \frac{12\sqrt{13}}{13}\right) &= \left(-\frac{8\sqrt{13}}{13}\right)^2 + \left(\frac{12\sqrt{13}}{13}\right)^2 + 4\left(-\frac{8\sqrt{13}}{13}\right) - 6\left(\frac{12\sqrt{13}}{13}\right) \\ &= \frac{144}{13} + \frac{64}{13} - \frac{32\sqrt{13}}{13} - \frac{72\sqrt{13}}{13} \\ &= \frac{208 - 104\sqrt{13}}{13} \approx -12.844. \end{aligned}$$

For the second angle,

$$\begin{aligned} \sin t &= \sin\left(2\pi - \arctan\left(\frac{3}{2}\right)\right) = -\sin\left(\arctan\left(\frac{3}{2}\right)\right) = -\frac{3\sqrt{13}}{13} \\ \cos t &= \cos\left(2\pi - \arctan\left(\frac{3}{2}\right)\right) = \cos\left(\arctan\left(\frac{3}{2}\right)\right) = \frac{2\sqrt{13}}{13}. \end{aligned}$$

Therefore, $x(t) = 4 \cos t = \frac{8\sqrt{13}}{13}$ and $y(t) = 4 \sin t = -\frac{12\sqrt{13}}{13}$, so $\left(\frac{8\sqrt{13}}{13}, -\frac{12\sqrt{13}}{13}\right)$ is a critical point on the boundary and

$$\begin{aligned} g\left(\frac{8\sqrt{13}}{13}, -\frac{12\sqrt{13}}{13}\right) &= \left(\frac{8\sqrt{13}}{13}\right)^2 + \left(-\frac{12\sqrt{13}}{13}\right)^2 + 4\left(\frac{8\sqrt{13}}{13}\right) - 6\left(-\frac{12\sqrt{13}}{13}\right) \\ &= \frac{144}{13} + \frac{64}{13} + \frac{32\sqrt{13}}{13} + \frac{72\sqrt{13}}{13} \\ &= \frac{208 + 104\sqrt{13}}{13} \approx 44.844. \end{aligned}$$

The absolute minimum of g is -13, which is attained at the point $(-2, 3)$, which is an interior point of D. The absolute maximum of g is approximately equal to 44.844, which is attained at the boundary point $\left(\frac{8\sqrt{13}}{13}, -\frac{12\sqrt{13}}{13}\right)$. These are the absolute extrema of g on D as shown in the following figure.

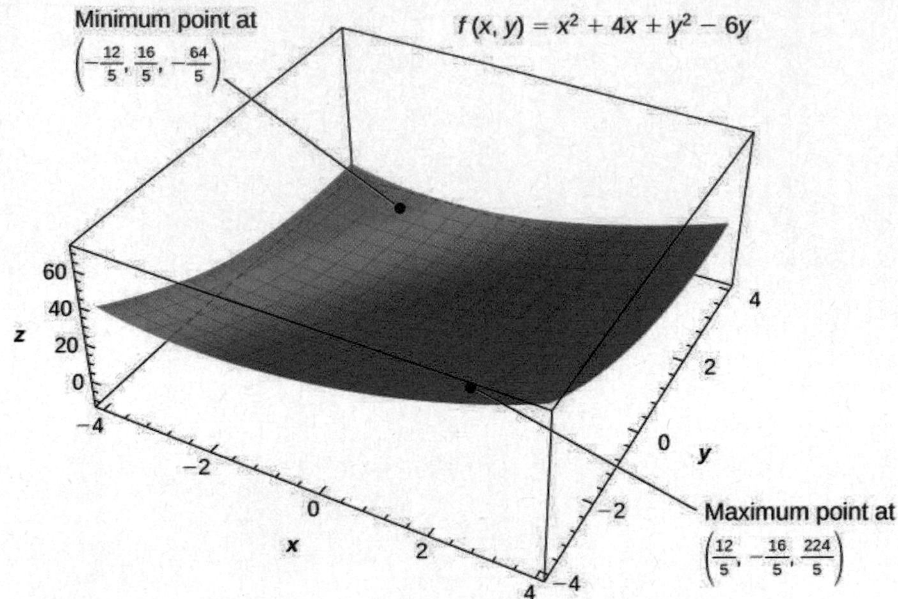

Figure 4.55 The function $f(x, y)$ has a local minimum and a local maximum.

4.36 Use the problem-solving strategy for finding absolute extrema of a function to find the absolute extrema of the function

$$f(x, y) = 4x^2 - 2xy + 6y^2 - 8x + 2y + 3$$

on the domain defined by $0 \le x \le 2$ and $-1 \le y \le 3$.

Example 4.41

Chapter Opener: Profitable Golf Balls

Figure 4.56 (credit: modification of work by oatsy40, Flickr)

Pro- T company has developed a profit model that depends on the number x of golf balls sold per month (measured in thousands), and the number of hours per month of advertising y, according to the function

$$z = f(x, y) = 48x + 96y - x^2 - 2xy - 9y^2,$$

where z is measured in thousands of dollars. The maximum number of golf balls that can be produced and sold is $50{,}000,$ and the maximum number of hours of advertising that can be purchased is $25.$ Find the values of x and y that maximize profit, and find the maximum profit.

Solution

Using the problem-solving strategy, step 1 involves finding the critical points of f on its domain. Therefore, we first calculate $f_x(x, y)$ and $f_y(x, y),$ then set them each equal to zero:

$$\begin{aligned} f_x(x, y) &= 48 - 2x - 2y \\ f_y(x, y) &= 96 - 2x - 18y. \end{aligned}$$

Setting them equal to zero yields the system of equations

$$\begin{aligned} 48 - 2x - 2y &= 0 \\ 96 - 2x - 18y &= 0. \end{aligned}$$

The solution to this system is $x = 21$ and $y = 3.$ Therefore $(21, 3)$ is a critical point of $f.$ Calculating $f(21, 3)$ gives $f(21, 3) = 48(21) + 96(3) - 21^2 - 2(21)(3) - 9(3)^2 = 648.$

The domain of this function is $0 \le x \le 50$ and $0 \le y \le 25$ as shown in the following graph.

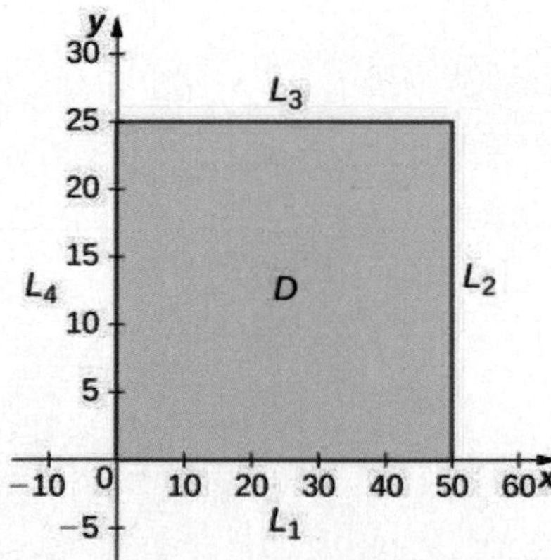

Figure 4.57 Graph of the domain of the function $f(x, y) = 48x + 96y - x^2 - 2xy - 9y^2.$

L_1 is the line segment connecting $(0, 0)$ and $(50, 0),$ and it can be parameterized by the equations $x(t) = t,\ y(t) = 0$ for $0 \le t \le 50.$ We then define $g(t) = f(x(t), y(t))$:

$$\begin{aligned} g(t) &= f(x(t), y(t)) \\ &= f(t, 0) \\ &= 48t + 96(0) - y^2 - 2(t)(0) - 9(0)^2 \\ &= 48t - t^2. \end{aligned}$$

Setting $g'(t) = 0$ yields the critical point $t = 24,$ which corresponds to the point $(24, 0)$ in the domain of $f.$

Calculating $f(24, 0)$ gives 576.

L_2 is the line segment connecting and $(50, 25)$, and it can be parameterized by the equations $x(t) = 50, \ y(t) = t$ for $0 \le t \le 25$. Once again, we define $g(t) = f(x(t), y(t))$:

$$\begin{aligned} g(t) &= f(x(t), y(t)) \\ &= f(50, t) \\ &= 48(50) + 96t - 50^2 - 2(50)t - 9t^2 \\ &= -9t^2 - 4t - 100. \end{aligned}$$

This function has a critical point at $t = -\frac{2}{9}$, which corresponds to the point $\left(50, \ -\frac{2}{9}\right)$. This point is not in the domain of f.

L_3 is the line segment connecting $(0, 25)$ and $(50, 25)$, and it can be parameterized by the equations $x(t) = t, \ y(t) = 25$ for $0 \le t \le 50$. We define $g(t) = f(x(t), y(t))$:

$$\begin{aligned} g(t) &= f(x(t), y(t)) \\ &= f(t, 25) \\ &= 48t + 96(25) - t^2 - 2t(25) - 9\left(25^2\right) \\ &= -t^2 - 2t - 3225. \end{aligned}$$

This function has a critical point at $t = -1$, which corresponds to the point $(-1, 25)$, which is not in the domain.

L_4 is the line segment connecting $(0, 0)$ to $(0, 25)$, and it can be parameterized by the equations $x(t) = 0, \ y(t) = t$ for $0 \le t \le 25$. We define $g(t) = f(x(t), y(t))$:

$$\begin{aligned} g(t) &= f(x(t), y(t)) \\ &= f(0, t) \\ &= 48(0) + 96t - (0)^2 - 2(0)t - 9t^2 \\ &= 96t - t^2. \end{aligned}$$

This function has a critical point at $t = \frac{16}{3}$, which corresponds to the point $\left(0, \ \frac{16}{3}\right)$, which is on the boundary of the domain. Calculating $f\left(0, \ \frac{16}{3}\right)$ gives 256.

We also need to find the values of $f(x, y)$ at the corners of its domain. These corners are located at $(0, 0), (50, 0), (50, 25)$ and $(0, 25)$:

$$\begin{aligned} f(0, 0) &= 48(0) + 96(0) - (0)^2 - 2(0)(0) - 9(0)^2 = 0 \\ f(50, 0) &= 48(50) + 96(0) - (50)^2 - 2(50)(0) - 9(0)^2 = -100 \\ f(50, 25) &= 48(50) + 96(25) - (50)^2 - 2(50)(25) - 9(25)^2 = -5825 \\ f(0, 25) &= 48(0) + 96(25) - (0)^2 - 2(0)(25) - 9(25)^2 = -3225. \end{aligned}$$

The maximum critical value is 648, which occurs at $(21, 3)$. Therefore, a maximum profit of $\$648{,}000$ is realized when $21{,}000$ golf balls are sold and 3 hours of advertising are purchased per month as shown in the following figure.

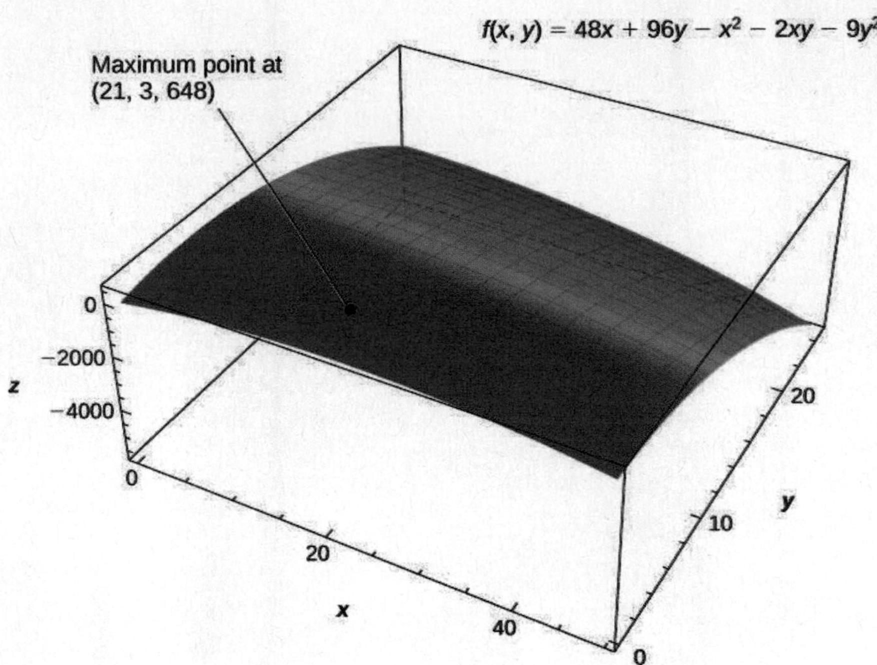

Figure 4.58 The profit function $f(x, y)$ has a maximum at $(21, 3, 648)$.

4.7 EXERCISES

For the following exercises, find all critical points.

310. $f(x, y) = 1 + x^2 + y^2$

311. $f(x, y) = (3x - 2)^2 + (y - 4)^2$

312. $f(x, y) = x^4 + y^4 - 16xy$

313. $f(x, y) = 15x^3 - 3xy + 15y^3$

For the following exercises, find the critical points of the function by using algebraic techniques (completing the square) or by examining the form of the equation. Verify your results using the partial derivatives test.

314. $f(x, y) = \sqrt{x^2 + y^2 + 1}$

315. $f(x, y) = -x^2 - 5y^2 + 8x - 10y - 13$

316. $f(x, y) = x^2 + y^2 + 2x - 6y + 6$

317. $f(x, y) = \sqrt{x^2 + y^2} + 1$

For the following exercises, use the second derivative test to identify any critical points and determine whether each critical point is a maximum, minimum, saddle point, or none of these.

318. $f(x, y) = -x^3 + 4xy - 2y^2 + 1$

319. $f(x, y) = x^2 y^2$

320. $f(x, y) = x^2 - 6x + y^2 + 4y - 8$

321. $f(x, y) = 2xy + 3x + 4y$

322. $f(x, y) = 8xy(x + y) + 7$

323. $f(x, y) = x^2 + 4xy + y^2$

324. $f(x, y) = x^3 + y^3 - 300x - 75y - 3$

325. $f(x, y) = 9 - x^4 y^4$

326. $f(x, y) = 7x^2 y + 9xy^2$

327. $f(x, y) = 3x^2 - 2xy + y^2 - 8y$

328. $f(x, y) = 3x^2 + 2xy + y^2$

329. $f(x, y) = y^2 + xy + 3y + 2x + 3$

330. $f(x, y) = x^2 + xy + y^2 - 3x$

331. $f(x, y) = x^2 + 2y^2 - x^2 y$

332. $f(x, y) = x^2 + y - e^y$

333. $f(x, y) = e^{-(x^2 + y^2 + 2x)}$

334. $f(x, y) = x^2 + xy + y^2 - x - y + 1$

335. $f(x, y) = x^2 + 10xy + y^2$

336. $f(x, y) = -x^2 - 5y^2 + 10x - 30y - 62$

337. $f(x, y) = 120x + 120y - xy - x^2 - y^2$

338. $f(x, y) = 2x^2 + 2xy + y^2 + 2x - 3$

339. $f(x, y) = x^2 + x - 3xy + y^3 - 5$

340. $f(x, y) = 2xye^{-x^2 - y^2}$

For the following exercises, determine the extreme values and the saddle points. Use a CAS to graph the function.

341. **[T]** $f(x, y) = ye^x - e^y$

342. **[T]** $f(x, y) = x \sin(y)$

343. **[T]** $f(x, y) = \sin(x)\sin(y),\ x \in (0, 2\pi),\ y \in (0, 2\pi)$

Find the absolute extrema of the given function on the indicated closed and bounded set R.

344. $f(x, y) = xy - x - 3y$; R is the triangular region with vertices $(0, 0)$, $(0, 4)$, and $(5, 0)$.

345. Find the absolute maximum and minimum values of $f(x, y) = x^2 + y^2 - 2y + 1$ on the region $R = \{(x, y) | x^2 + y^2 \le 4\}$.

346. $f(x, y) = x^3 - 3xy - y^3$ on $R = \{(x, y): -2 \le x \le 2,\ -2 \le y \le 2\}$

347. $f(x, y) = \dfrac{-2y}{x^2 + y^2 + 1}$ on $R = \{(x, y): x^2 + y^2 \leq 4\}$

348. Find three positive numbers the sum of which is $27,$ such that the sum of their squares is as small as possible.

349. Find the points on the surface $x^2 - yz = 5$ that are closest to the origin.

350. Find the maximum volume of a rectangular box with three faces in the coordinate planes and a vertex in the first octant on the plane $x + y + z = 1.$

351. The sum of the length and the girth (perimeter of a cross-section) of a package carried by a delivery service cannot exceed 108 in. Find the dimensions of the rectangular package of largest volume that can be sent.

352. A cardboard box without a lid is to be made with a volume of 4 ft^3. Find the dimensions of the box that requires the least amount of cardboard.

353. Find the point on the surface $f(x, y) = x^2 + y^2 + 10$ nearest the plane $x + 2y - z = 0.$ Identify the point on the plane.

354. Find the point in the plane $2x - y + 2z = 16$ that is closest to the origin.

355. A company manufactures two types of athletic shoes: jogging shoes and cross-trainers. The total revenue from x units of jogging shoes and y units of cross-trainers is given by $R(x, y) = -5x^2 - 8y^2 - 2xy + 42x + 102y,$ where x and y are in thousands of units. Find the values of *x* and *y* to maximize the total revenue.

356. A shipping company handles rectangular boxes provided the sum of the length, width, and height of the box does not exceed 96 in. Find the dimensions of the box that meets this condition and has the largest volume.

357. Find the maximum volume of a cylindrical soda can such that the sum of its height and circumference is 120 cm.

4.8 | Lagrange Multipliers

Learning Objectives

4.8.1 Use the method of Lagrange multipliers to solve optimization problems with one constraint.

4.8.2 Use the method of Lagrange multipliers to solve optimization problems with two constraints.

Solving optimization problems for functions of two or more variables can be similar to solving such problems in single-variable calculus. However, techniques for dealing with multiple variables allow us to solve more varied optimization problems for which we need to deal with additional conditions or constraints. In this section, we examine one of the more common and useful methods for solving optimization problems with constraints.

Lagrange Multipliers

Example 4.41 was an applied situation involving maximizing a profit function, subject to certain **constraints**. In that example, the constraints involved a maximum number of golf balls that could be produced and sold in 1 month (x), and a maximum number of advertising hours that could be purchased per month (y). Suppose these were combined into a budgetary constraint, such as $20x + 4y \leq 216$, that took into account the cost of producing the golf balls and the number of advertising hours purchased per month. The goal is, still, be to maximize profit, but now there is a different type of constraint on the values of x and y. This constraint, when combined with the profit function $f(x, y) = 48x + 96y - x^2 - 2xy - 9y^2$, is an example of an **optimization problem**, and the function $f(x, y)$ is called the **objective function**. A graph of various level curves of the function $f(x, y)$ follows.

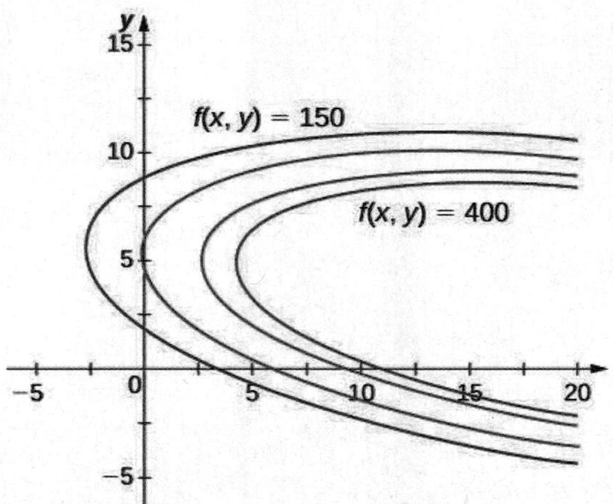

Figure 4.59 Graph of level curves of the function $f(x, y) = 48x + 96y - x^2 - 2xy - 9y^2$ corresponding to $c = 150, 250, 350,$ and $400.$

In **Figure 4.59**, the value c represents different profit levels (i.e., values of the function f). As the value of c increases, the curve shifts to the right. Since our goal is to maximize profit, we want to choose a curve as far to the right as possible. If there was no restriction on the number of golf balls the company could produce, or the number of units of advertising available, then we could produce as many golf balls as we want, and advertise as much as we want, and there would be not be a maximum profit for the company. Unfortunately, we have a budgetary constraint that is modeled by the inequality $20x + 4y \leq 216.$ To see how this constraint interacts with the profit function, **Figure 4.60** shows the graph of the line $20x + 4y = 216$ superimposed on the previous graph.

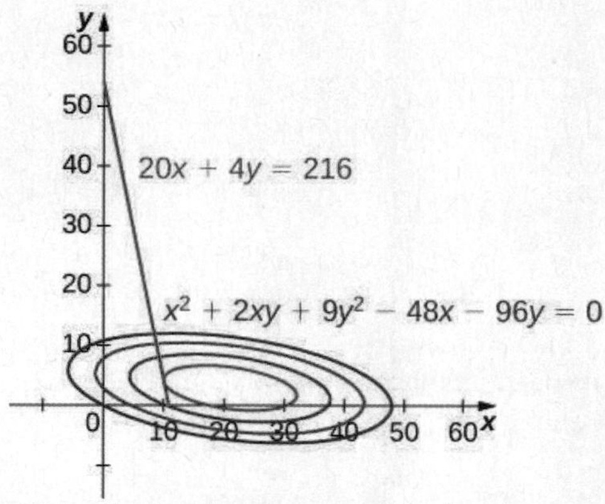

Figure 4.60 Graph of level curves of the function $f(x, y) = 48x + 96y - x^2 - 2xy - 9y^2$ corresponding to $c = 150, 250, 350,$ and 395. The red graph is the constraint function.

As mentioned previously, the maximum profit occurs when the level curve is as far to the right as possible. However, the level of production corresponding to this maximum profit must also satisfy the budgetary constraint, so the point at which this profit occurs must also lie on (or to the left of) the red line in **Figure 4.60**. Inspection of this graph reveals that this point exists where the line is tangent to the level curve of f. Trial and error reveals that this profit level seems to be around 395, when x and y are both just less than 5. We return to the solution of this problem later in this section. From a theoretical standpoint, at the point where the profit curve is tangent to the constraint line, the gradient of both of the functions evaluated at that point must point in the same (or opposite) direction. Recall that the gradient of a function of more than one variable is a vector. If two vectors point in the same (or opposite) directions, then one must be a constant multiple of the other. This idea is the basis of the **method of Lagrange multipliers**.

Theorem 4.20: Method of Lagrange Multipliers: One Constraint

Let f and g be functions of two variables with continuous partial derivatives at every point of some open set containing the smooth curve $g(x, y) = 0$. Suppose that f, when restricted to points on the curve $g(x, y) = 0$, has a local extremum at the point (x_0, y_0) and that $\nabla g(x_0, y_0) \neq 0$. Then there is a number λ called a **Lagrange multiplier**, for which

$$\nabla f(x_0, y_0) = \lambda \nabla g(x_0, y_0).$$

Proof

Assume that a constrained extremum occurs at the point (x_0, y_0). Furthermore, we assume that the equation $g(x, y) = 0$ can be smoothly parameterized as

$$x = x(s) \text{ and } y = y(s)$$

where s is an arc length parameter with reference point (x_0, y_0) at $s = 0$. Therefore, the quantity $z = f(x(s), y(s))$ has a relative maximum or relative minimum at $s = 0$, and this implies that $\frac{dz}{ds} = 0$ at that point. From the chain rule,

$$\frac{dz}{ds} = \frac{\partial f}{\partial x} \cdot \frac{\partial x}{\partial s} + \frac{\partial f}{\partial y} \cdot \frac{\partial y}{\partial s} = \left(\frac{\partial f}{\partial x}\mathbf{i} + \mathbf{j}\frac{\partial x}{\partial s}\right) + \left(\frac{\partial f}{\partial y} \cdot \frac{\partial y}{\partial s}\right) = 0,$$

where the derivatives are all evaluated at $s = 0$. However, the first factor in the dot product is the gradient of f, and the second factor is the unit tangent vector $\mathrm{T}(0)$ to the constraint curve. Since the point (x_0, y_0) corresponds to $s = 0$, it follows from this equation that

$$\nabla f(x_0, y_0) \cdot \mathrm{T}(0) = 0,$$

which implies that the gradient is either $\mathbf{0}$ or is normal to the constraint curve at a constrained relative extremum. However, the constraint curve $g(x, y) = 0$ is a level curve for the function $g(x, y)$ so that if $\nabla g(x_0, y_0) \neq 0$ then $\nabla g(x_0, y_0)$ is normal to this curve at (x_0, y_0) It follows, then, that there is some scalar λ such that

$$\nabla f(x_0, y_0) = \lambda \nabla g(x_0, y_0)$$

□

To apply **Method of Lagrange Multipliers: One Constraint** to an optimization problem similar to that for the golf ball manufacturer, we need a problem-solving strategy.

Problem-Solving Strategy: Steps for Using Lagrange Multipliers

1. Determine the objective function $f(x, y)$ and the constraint function $g(x, y)$. Does the optimization problem involve maximizing or minimizing the objective function?
2. Set up a system of equations using the following template:
$$\begin{aligned}\nabla f(x_0, y_0) &= \lambda \nabla g(x_0, y_0) \\ g(x_0, y_0) &= 0.\end{aligned}$$
3. Solve for x_0 and y_0.
4. The largest of the values of f at the solutions found in step 3 maximizes f; the smallest of those values minimizes f.

Example 4.42

Using Lagrange Multipliers

Use the method of Lagrange multipliers to find the minimum value of $f(x, y) = x^2 + 4y^2 - 2x + 8y$ subject to the constraint $x + 2y = 7$.

Solution

Let’s follow the problem-solving strategy:

1. The optimization function is $f(x, y) = x^2 + 4y^2 - 2x + 8y$. To determine the constraint function, we must first subtract 7 from both sides of the constraint. This gives $x + 2y - 7 = 0$. The constraint function is equal to the left-hand side, so $g(x, y) = x + 2y - 7$. The problem asks us to solve for the minimum value of f, subject to the constraint (see the following graph).

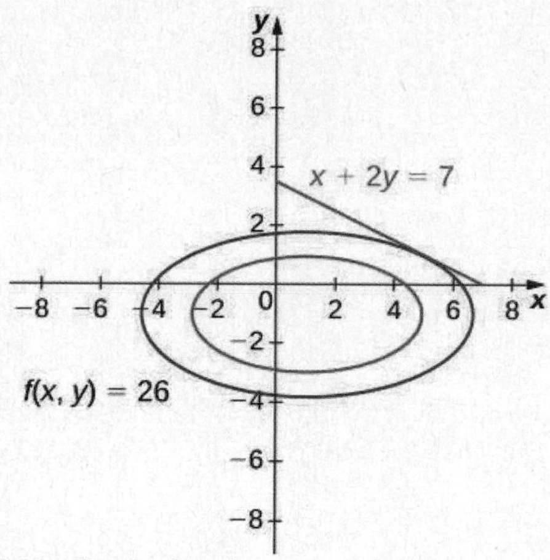

Figure 4.61 Graph of level curves of the function $f(x, y) = x^2 + 4y^2 - 2x + 8y$ corresponding to $c = 10$ and 26. The red graph is the constraint function.

2. We then must calculate the gradients of both f and g:

$$\nabla f(x, y) = (2x - 2)\mathbf{i} + (8y + 8)\mathbf{j}$$
$$\nabla g(x, y) = \mathbf{i} + 2\mathbf{j}.$$

The equation $\nabla f(x_0, y_0) = \lambda \nabla g(x_0, y_0)$ becomes

$$(2x_0 - 2)\mathbf{i} + (8y_0 + 8)\mathbf{j} = \lambda(\mathbf{i} + 2\mathbf{j}),$$

which can be rewritten as

$$(2x_0 - 2)\mathbf{i} + (8y_0 + 8)\mathbf{j} = \lambda\mathbf{i} + 2\lambda\mathbf{j}.$$

Next, we set the coefficients of $\mathbf{i}$ and $\mathbf{j}$ equal to each other:

$$2x_0 - 2 = \lambda$$
$$8y_0 + 8 = 2\lambda.$$

The equation $g(x_0, y_0) = 0$ becomes $x_0 + 2y_0 - 7 = 0$. Therefore, the system of equations that needs to be solved is

$$\begin{aligned} 2x_0 - 2 &= \lambda \\ 8y_0 + 8 &= 2\lambda \\ x_0 + 2y_0 - 7 &= 0. \end{aligned}$$

3. This is a linear system of three equations in three variables. We start by solving the second equation for λ and substituting it into the first equation. This gives $\lambda = 4y_0 + 4,$ so substituting this into the first equation gives

$$2x_0 - 2 = 4y_0 + 4.$$

Solving this equation for x_0 gives $x_0 = 2y_0 + 3.$ We then substitute this into the third equation:

$$\begin{aligned} (2y_0 + 3) + 2y_0 - 7 &= 0 \\ 4y_0 - 4 &= 0 \\ y_0 &= 1. \end{aligned}$$

Since $x_0 = 2y_0 + 3,$ this gives $x_0 = 5.$

4. Next, we substitute $(5, 1)$ into $f(x, y) = x^2 + 4y^2 - 2x + 8y,$ gives $f(5, 1) = 5^2 + 4(1)^2 - 2(5) + 8(1) = 27.$ To ensure this corresponds to a minimum value on the constraint function, let's try some other values, such as the intercepts of $g(x, y) = 0,$ Which are $(7, 0)$ and $(0, 3.5)$. We get $f(7, 0) = 35$ and $f(0, 3.5) = 77,$ so it appears f has a minimum at $(5, 1)$.

4.37 Use the method of Lagrange multipliers to find the maximum value of $f(x, y) = 9x^2 + 36xy - 4y^2 - 18x - 8y$ subject to the constraint $3x + 4y = 32.$

Let's now return to the problem posed at the beginning of the section.

Example 4.43

Golf Balls and Lagrange Multipliers

The golf ball manufacturer, Pro-T, has developed a profit model that depends on the number x of golf balls sold per month (measured in thousands), and the number of hours per month of advertising y, according to the function

$$z = f(x, y) = 48x + 96y - x^2 - 2xy - 9y^2,$$

where z is measured in thousands of dollars. The budgetary constraint function relating the cost of the production of thousands golf balls and advertising units is given by $20x + 4y = 216.$ Find the values of x and y that maximize profit, and find the maximum profit.

Solution

Again, we follow the problem-solving strategy:

1. The optimization function is $f(x, y) = 48x + 96y - x^2 - 2xy - 9y^2.$ To determine the constraint function, we first subtract 216 from both sides of the constraint, then divide both sides by $4,$ which gives $5x + y - 54 = 0.$ The constraint function is equal to the left-hand side, so $g(x, y) = 5x + y - 54.$ The problem asks us to solve for the maximum value of $f,$ subject to this constraint.

2. So, we calculate the gradients of both f and g:

$$\begin{aligned} \nabla f(x, y) &= (48 - 2x - 2y)\mathbf{i} + (96 - 2x - 18y)\mathbf{j} \\ \nabla g(x, y) &= 5\mathbf{i} + \mathbf{j}. \end{aligned}$$

The equation $\nabla f(x_0, y_0) = \lambda \nabla g(x_0, y_0)$ becomes

$$(48 - 2x_0 - 2y_0)\mathbf{i} + (96 - 2x_0 - 18y_0)\mathbf{j} = \lambda(5\mathbf{i} + \mathbf{j}),$$

which can be rewritten as

$$(48 - 2x_0 - 2y_0)\mathbf{i} + (96 - 2x_0 - 18y_0)\mathbf{j} = \lambda 5\mathbf{i} + \lambda\mathbf{j}.$$

We then set the coefficients of **i** and **j** equal to each other:

$$\begin{aligned} 48 - 2x_0 - 2y_0 &= 5\lambda \\ 96 - 2x_0 - 18y_0 &= \lambda. \end{aligned}$$

The equation $g(x_0, y_0) = 0$ becomes $5x_0 + y_0 - 54 = 0$. Therefore, the system of equations that needs to be solved is

$$\begin{aligned} 48 - 2x_0 - 2y_0 &= 5\lambda \\ 96 - 2x_0 - 18y_0 &= \lambda \\ 5x_0 + y_0 - 54 &= 0. \end{aligned}$$

3. We use the left-hand side of the second equation to replace λ in the first equation:

$$\begin{aligned} 48 - 2x_0 - 2y_0 &= 5(96 - 2x_0 - 18y_0) \\ 48 - 2x_0 - 2y_0 &= 480 - 10x_0 - 90y_0 \\ 8x_0 &= 432 - 88y_0 \\ x_0 &= 54 - 11y_0. \end{aligned}$$

Then we substitute this into the third equation:

$$\begin{aligned} 5(54 - 11y_0) + y_0 - 54 &= 0 \\ 270 - 55y_0 + y_0 &= 0 \\ 216 - 54y_0 &= 0 \\ y_0 &= 4. \end{aligned}$$

Since $x_0 = 54 - 11y_0$, this gives $x_0 = 10$.

4. We then substitute $(10, 4)$ into $f(x, y) = 48x + 96y - x^2 - 2xy - 9y^2$, which gives

$$\begin{aligned} f(10, 4) &= 48(10) + 96(4) - (10)^2 - 2(10)(4) - 9(4)^2 \\ &= 480 + 384 - 100 - 80 - 144 = 540. \end{aligned}$$

Therefore the maximum profit that can be attained, subject to budgetary constraints, is $\$540{,}000$ with a production level of $10{,}000$ golf balls and 4 hours of advertising bought per month. Let's check to make sure this truly is a maximum. The endpoints of the line that defines the constraint are $(10.8, 0)$ and $(0, 54)$ Let's evaluate f at both of these points:

$$\begin{aligned} f(10.8, 0) &= 48(10.8) + 96(0) - 10.8^2 - 2(10.8)(0) - 9\left(0^2\right) = 401.76 \\ f(0, 54) &= 48(0) + 96(54) - 0^2 - 2(0)(54) - 9\left(54^2\right) = -21, 060. \end{aligned}$$

The second value represents a loss, since no golf balls are produced. Neither of these values exceed 540, so it seems that our extremum is a maximum value of f.

4.38 A company has determined that its production level is given by the Cobb-Douglas function $f(x, y) = 2.5x^{0.45}y^{0.55}$ where x represents the total number of labor hours in 1 year and y represents the total capital input for the company. Suppose 1 unit of labor costs \$40 and 1 unit of capital costs \$50. Use the method of Lagrange multipliers to find the maximum value of $f(x, y) = 2.5x^{0.45}y^{0.55}$ subject to a budgetary constraint of \$500,000 per year.

In the case of an optimization function with three variables and a single constraint function, it is possible to use the method of Lagrange multipliers to solve an optimization problem as well. An example of an optimization function with three variables could be the Cobb-Douglas function in the previous example: $f(x, y, z) = x^{0.2}y^{0.4}z^{0.4}$, where x represents the cost of labor, y represents capital input, and z represents the cost of advertising. The method is the same as for the method with a function of two variables; the equations to be solved are

$$\begin{aligned} \nabla f(x, y, z) &= \lambda \nabla g(x, y, z) \\ g(x, y, z) &= 0. \end{aligned}$$

Example 4.44

Lagrange Multipliers with a Three-Variable Optimization Function

Maximize the function $f(x, y, z) = x^2 + y^2 + z^2$ subject to the constraint $x + y + z = 1$.

Solution

1. The optimization function is $f(x, y, z) = x^2 + y^2 + z^2$. To determine the constraint function, we subtract 1 from each side of the constraint: $x + y + z - 1 = 0$ which gives the constraint function as $g(x, y, z) = x + y + z - 1$.

2. Next, we calculate $\nabla f(x, y, z)$ and $\nabla g(x, y, z)$:

$$\begin{aligned} \nabla f(x, y, z) &= \langle 2x, 2y, 2z \rangle \\ \nabla g(x, y, z) &= \langle 1, 1, 1 \rangle. \end{aligned}$$

This leads to the equations

$$\begin{aligned} \langle 2x_0, 2y_0, 2z_0 \rangle &= \lambda \langle 1, 1, 1 \rangle \\ x_0 + y_0 + z_0 - 1 &= 0 \end{aligned}$$

which can be rewritten in the following form:

$$\begin{aligned} 2x_0 &= \lambda \\ 2y_0 &= \lambda \\ 2z_0 &= \lambda \\ x_0 + y_0 + z_0 - 1 &= 0. \end{aligned}$$

3. Since each of the first three equations has λ on the right-hand side, we know that $2x_0 = 2y_0 = 2z_0$ and all three variables are equal to each other. Substituting $y_0 = x_0$ and $z_0 = x_0$ into the last equation yields $3x_0 - 1 = 0$, so $x_0 = \frac{1}{3}$ and $y_0 = \frac{1}{3}$ and $z_0 = \frac{1}{3}$ which corresponds to a critical point on the constraint curve.

4. Then, we evaluate f at the point $\left(\frac{1}{3}, \frac{1}{3}, \frac{1}{3}\right)$:

$$f\left(\frac{1}{3}, \frac{1}{3}, \frac{1}{3}\right) = \left(\frac{1}{3}\right)^2 + \left(\frac{1}{3}\right)^2 + \left(\frac{1}{3}\right)^2 = \frac{3}{9} = \frac{1}{3}.$$

Therefore, an extremum of the function is $\frac{1}{3}$. To verify it is a minimum, choose other points that satisfy the constraint and calculate f at that point. For example,

$$\begin{aligned} f(1, 0, 0) &= 1^2 + 0^2 + 0^2 = 1 \\ f(0, -2, 3) &= 0^2 + +(-2)^2 + 3^2 = 13. \end{aligned}$$

Both of these values are greater than $\frac{1}{3}$, leading us to believe the extremum is a minimum.

4.39 Use the method of Lagrange multipliers to find the minimum value of the function

$$f(x, y, z) = x + y + z$$

subject to the constraint $x^2 + y^2 + z^2 = 1$.

Problems with Two Constraints

The method of Lagrange multipliers can be applied to problems with more than one constraint. In this case the optimization function, w is a function of three variables:

$$w = f(x, y, z)$$

and it is subject to two constraints:

$$g(x, y, z) = 0 \text{ and } h(x, y, z) = 0.$$

There are two Lagrange multipliers, λ_1 and λ_2, and the system of equations becomes

$$\begin{aligned} \nabla f(x_0, y_0, z_0) &= \lambda_1 \nabla g(x_0, y_0, z_0) + \lambda_2 \nabla h(x_0, y_0, z_0) \\ g(x_0, y_0, z_0) &= 0 \\ h(x_0, y_0, z_0) &= 0. \end{aligned}$$

Example 4.45

Lagrange Multipliers with Two Constraints

Find the maximum and minimum values of the function

$$f(x, y, z) = x^2 + y^2 + z^2$$

subject to the constraints $z^2 = x^2 + y^2$ and $x + y - z + 1 = 0$.

Solution

Let's follow the problem-solving strategy:

1. The optimization function is $f(x, y, z) = x^2 + y^2 + z^2$. To determine the constraint functions, we first subtract z^2 from both sides of the first constraint, which gives $x^2 + y^2 - z^2 = 0$, so $g(x, y, z) = x^2 + y^2 - z^2$. The second constraint function is $h(x, y, z) = x + y - z + 1$.
2. We then calculate the gradients of $f, g,$ and h:
$$\begin{aligned}\nabla f(x, y, z) &= 2x\mathbf{i} + 2y\mathbf{j} + 2z\mathbf{k}\\ \nabla g(x, y, z) &= 2x\mathbf{i} + 2y\mathbf{j} - 2z\mathbf{k}\\ \nabla h(x, y, z) &= \mathbf{i} + \mathbf{j} - \mathbf{k}.\end{aligned}$$
The equation $\nabla f(x_0, y_0, z_0) = \lambda_1 \nabla g(x_0, y_0, z_0) + \lambda_2 \nabla h(x_0, y_0, z_0)$ becomes
$$2x_0\mathbf{i} + 2y_0\mathbf{j} + 2z_0\mathbf{k} = \lambda_1(2x_0\mathbf{i} + 2y_0\mathbf{j} - 2z_0\mathbf{k}) + \lambda_2(\mathbf{i} + \mathbf{j} - \mathbf{k}),$$
which can be rewritten as
$$2x_0\mathbf{i} + 2y_0\mathbf{j} + 2z_0\mathbf{k} = (2\lambda_1 x_0 + \lambda_2)\mathbf{i} + (2\lambda_1 y_0 + \lambda_2)\mathbf{j} - (2\lambda_1 z_0 + \lambda_2)\mathbf{k}.$$
Next, we set the coefficients of $\mathbf{i}$ and $\mathbf{j}$ equal to each other:
$$\begin{aligned}2x_0 &= 2\lambda_1 x_0 + \lambda_2\\ 2y_0 &= 2\lambda_1 y_0 + \lambda_2\\ 2z_0 &= -2\lambda_1 z_0 - \lambda_2.\end{aligned}$$
The two equations that arise from the constraints are $z_0^2 = x_0^2 + y_0^2$ and $x_0 + y_0 - z_0 + 1 = 0$. Combining these equations with the previous three equations gives
$$\begin{aligned}2x_0 &= 2\lambda_1 x_0 + \lambda_2\\ 2y_0 &= 2\lambda_1 y_0 + \lambda_2\\ 2z_0 &= -2\lambda_1 z_0 - \lambda_2\\ z_0^2 &= x_0^2 + y_0^2\\ x_0 + y_0 - z_0 + 1 &= 0.\end{aligned}$$
3. The first three equations contain the variable λ_2. Solving the third equation for λ_2 and replacing into the first and second equations reduces the number of equations to four:
$$\begin{aligned}2x_0 &= 2\lambda_1 x_0 - 2\lambda_1 z_0 - 2z_0\\ 2y_0 &= 2\lambda_1 y_0 - 2\lambda_1 z_0 - 2z_0\\ z_0^2 &= x_0^2 + y_0^2\\ x_0 + y_0 - z_0 + 1 &= 0.\end{aligned}$$
Next, we solve the first and second equation for λ_1. The first equation gives $\lambda_1 = \dfrac{x_0 + z_0}{x_0 - z_0}$, the second equation gives $\lambda_1 = \dfrac{y_0 + z_0}{y_0 - z_0}$. We set the right-hand side of each equation equal to each other and cross-multiply:

$$\begin{aligned}
\frac{x_0+z_0}{x_0-z_0} &= \frac{y_0+z_0}{y_0-z_0} \\
(x_0+z_0)(y_0-z_0) &= (x_0-z_0)(y_0+z_0) \\
x_0y_0-x_0z_0+y_0z_0-z_0^2 &= x_0y_0+x_0z_0-y_0z_0-z_0 2. \\
2y_0z_0-2x_0z_0 &= 0 \\
2z_0(y_0-x_0) &= 0.
\end{aligned}$$

Therefore, either $z_0=0$ or $y_0=x_0$. If $z_0=0$, then the first constraint becomes $0=x_0{}^2+y_0{}^2$. The only real solution to this equation is $x_0=0$ and $y_0=0$, which gives the ordered triple $(0, 0, 0)$. This point does not satisfy the second constraint, so it is not a solution.

Next, we consider $y_0=x_0$, which reduces the number of equations to three:

$$\begin{aligned}
y_0 &= x_0 \\
z_0{}^2 &= x_0{}^2+y_0{}^2 \\
x_0+y_0-z_0+1 &= 0.
\end{aligned}$$

We substitute the first equation into the second and third equations:

$$\begin{aligned}
z_0{}^2 &= x_0{}^2+x_0{}^2 \\
x_0+x_0-z_0+1 &= 0.
\end{aligned}$$

Then, we solve the second equation for z_0, which gives $z_0=2x_0+1$. We then substitute this into the first equation,

$$\begin{aligned}
z_0{}^2 &= 2x_0{}^2 \\
(2x_0+1)^2 &= 2x_0{}^2 \\
4x_0{}^2+4x_0+1 &= 2x_0{}^2 \\
2x_0{}^2+4x_0+1 &= 0,
\end{aligned}$$

and use the quadratic formula to solve for x_0:

$$x_0=\frac{-4\pm\sqrt{4^2-4(2)(1)}}{2(2)}=\frac{-4\pm\sqrt{8}}{4}=\frac{-4\pm2\sqrt{2}}{4}=-1\pm\frac{\sqrt{2}}{2}.$$

Recall $y_0=x_0$, so this solves for y_0 as well. Then, $z_0=2x_0+1$, so

$$z_0=2x_0+1=2\left(-1\pm\frac{\sqrt{2}}{2}\right)+1=-2+1\pm\sqrt{2}=-1\pm\sqrt{2}.$$

Therefore, there are two ordered triplet solutions:

$$\left(-1+\frac{\sqrt{2}}{2}, -1+\frac{\sqrt{2}}{2}, -1+\sqrt{2}\right) \text{ and } \left(-1-\frac{\sqrt{2}}{2}, -1-\frac{\sqrt{2}}{2}, -1-\sqrt{2}\right).$$

4. We substitute $\left(-1+\frac{\sqrt{2}}{2}, -1+\frac{\sqrt{2}}{2}, -1+\sqrt{2}\right)$ into $f(x, y, z)=x^2+y^2+z^2$, which gives

$$\begin{aligned} f\left(-1+\frac{\sqrt{2}}{2}, -1+\frac{\sqrt{2}}{2}, -1+\sqrt{2}\right) &= \left(-1+\frac{\sqrt{2}}{2}\right)^2 + \left(-1+\frac{\sqrt{2}}{2}\right)^2 + (-1+\sqrt{2})^2 \\ &= \left(1-\sqrt{2}+\frac{1}{2}\right) + \left(1-\sqrt{2}+\frac{1}{2}\right) + (1-2\sqrt{2}+2) \\ &= 6-4\sqrt{2}. \end{aligned}$$

Then, we substitute $\left(-1-\frac{\sqrt{2}}{2}, -1-\frac{\sqrt{2}}{2}, -1-\sqrt{2}\right)$ into $f(x, y, z) = x^2 + y^2 + z^2$, which gives

$$\begin{aligned} f\left(-1-\frac{\sqrt{2}}{2}, -1-\frac{\sqrt{2}}{2}, -1-\sqrt{2}\right) &= \left(-1-\frac{\sqrt{2}}{2}\right)^2 + \left(-1-\frac{\sqrt{2}}{2}\right)^2 + (-1-\sqrt{2})^2 \\ &= \left(1+\sqrt{2}+\frac{1}{2}\right) + \left(1+\sqrt{2}+\frac{1}{2}\right) + (1+2\sqrt{2}+2) \\ &= 6+4\sqrt{2}. \end{aligned}$$

$6+4\sqrt{2}$ is the maximum value and $6-4\sqrt{2}$ is the minimum value of $f(x, y, z)$, subject to the given constraints.

4.40 Use the method of Lagrange multipliers to find the minimum value of the function

$$f(x, y, z) = x^2 + y^2 + z^2$$

subject to the constraints $2x + y + 2z = 9$ and $5x + 5y + 7z = 29$.

4.8 EXERCISES

For the following exercises, use the method of Lagrange multipliers to find the maximum and minimum values of the function subject to the given constraints.

358. $f(x, y) = x^2 y;\ x^2 + 2y^2 = 6$

359. $f(x, y, z) = xyz,\ x^2 + 2y^2 + 3z^2 = 6$

360. $f(x, y) = xy;\ 4x^2 + 8y^2 = 16$

361. $f(x, y) = 4x^3 + y^2;\ 2x^2 + y^2 = 1$

362. $f(x, y, z) = x^2 + y^2 + z^2,\ x^4 + y^4 + z^4 = 1$

363. $f(x, y, z) = yz + xy,\ xy = 1,\ y^2 + z^2 = 1$

364. $f(x, y) = x^2 + y^2,\ (x - 1)^2 + 4y^2 = 4$

365. $f(x, y) = 4xy,\ \frac{x^2}{9} + \frac{y^2}{16} = 1$

366. $f(x, y, z) = x + y + z,\ \frac{1}{x} + \frac{1}{y} + \frac{1}{z} = 1$

367. $f(x, y, z) = x + 3y - z,\ x^2 + y^2 + z^2 = 4$

368. $f(x, y, z) = x^2 + y^2 + z^2,\ xyz = 4$

369. Minimize $f(x, y) = x^2 + y^2$ on the hyperbola $xy = 1$.

370. Minimize $f(x, y) = xy$ on the ellipse $b^2x^2 + a^2y^2 = a^2b^2$.

371. Maximize $f(x, y, z) = 2x + 3y + 5z$ on the sphere $x^2 + y^2 + z^2 = 19$.

372. Maximize $\begin{array}{l} f(x, y) = x^2 - y^2;\ x > 0,\ y > 0; \\ g(x, y) = y - x^2 = 0 \end{array}$

373. The curve $x^3 - y^3 = 1$ is asymptotic to the line $y = x$. Find the point(s) on the curve $x^3 - y^3 = 1$ farthest from the line $y = x$.

374. Maximize $U(x, y) = 8x^{4/5}y^{1/5};\ 4x + 2y = 12$

375. Minimize $f(x, y) = x^2 + y^2,\ x + 2y - 5 = 0$.

376. Maximize $f(x, y) = \sqrt{6 - x^2 - y^2},\ x + y - 2 = 0$.

377. Minimize $f(x, y, z) = x^2 + y^2 + z^2,\ x + y + z = 1$.

378. Minimize $f(x, y) = x^2 - y^2$ subject to the constraint $x - 2y + 6 = 0$.

379. Minimize $f(x, y, z) = x^2 + y^2 + z^2$ when $x + y + z = 9$ and $x + 2y + 3z = 20$.

For the next group of exercises, use the method of Lagrange multipliers to solve the following applied problems.

380. A pentagon is formed by placing an isosceles triangle on a rectangle, as shown in the diagram. If the perimeter of the pentagon is 10 in., find the lengths of the sides of the pentagon that will maximize the area of the pentagon.

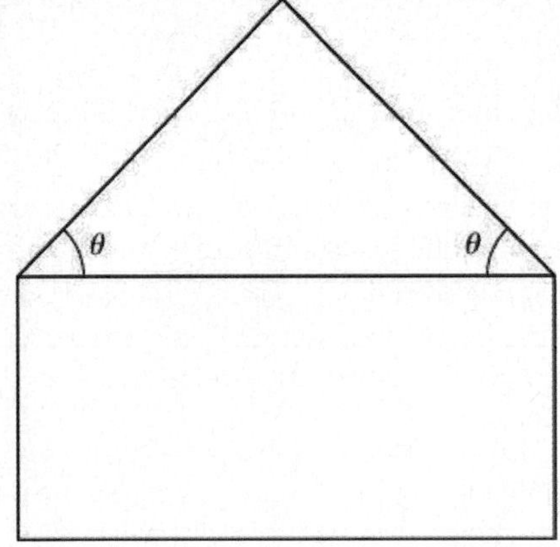

381. A rectangular box without a top (a topless box) is to be made from 12 ft^2 of cardboard. Find the maximum volume of such a box.

382. Find the minimum and maximum distances between the ellipse $x^2 + xy + 2y^2 = 1$ and the origin.

383. Find the point on the surface $x^2 - 2xy + y^2 - x + y = 0$ closest to the point $(1, 2, -3)$.

384. Show that, of all the triangles inscribed in a circle of radius R (see diagram), the equilateral triangle has the largest perimeter.

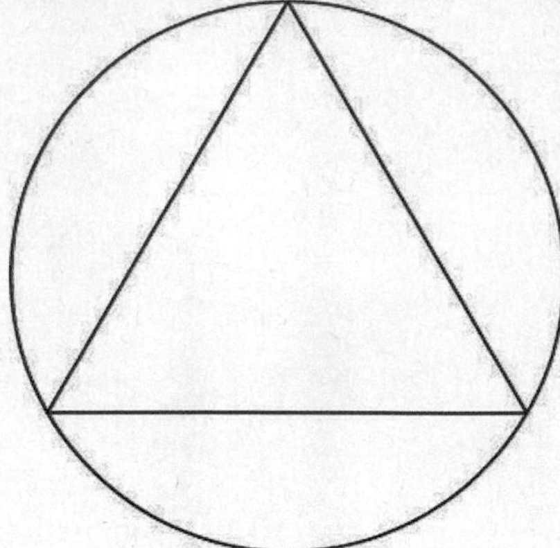

385. Find the minimum distance from point $(0, 1)$ to the parabola $x^2 = 4y$.

386. Find the minimum distance from the parabola $y = x^2$ to point $(0, 3)$.

387. Find the minimum distance from the plane $x + y + z = 1$ to point $(2, 1, 1)$.

388. A large container in the shape of a rectangular solid must have a volume of 480 m^3. The bottom of the container costs \$5/m^2 to construct whereas the top and sides cost \$3/m^2 to construct. Use Lagrange multipliers to find the dimensions of the container of this size that has the minimum cost.

389. Find the point on the line $y = 2x + 3$ that is closest to point $(4, 2)$.

390. Find the point on the plane $4x + 3y + z = 2$ that is closest to the point $(1, -1, 1)$.

391. Find the maximum value of $f(x, y) = \sin x \sin y$, where x and y denote the acute angles of a right triangle. Draw the contours of the function using a CAS.

392. A rectangular solid is contained within a tetrahedron with vertices at $(1, 0, 0), (0, 1, 0), (0, 0, 1),$ and the origin. The base of the box has dimensions $x, y,$ and the height of the box is z. If the sum of $x, y,$ and z is 1.0, find the dimensions that maximizes the volume of the rectangular solid.

393. **[T]** By investing x units of labor and y units of capital, a watch manufacturer can produce $P(x, y) = 50x^{0.4}y^{0.6}$ watches. Find the maximum number of watches that can be produced on a budget of \$20,000 if labor costs \$100/unit and capital costs \$200/unit. Use a CAS to sketch a contour plot of the function.

CHAPTER 4 REVIEW

KEY TERMS

boundary point a point P_0 of R is a boundary point if every δ disk centered around P_0 contains points both inside and outside R

closed set a set S that contains all its boundary points

connected set an open set S that cannot be represented as the union of two or more disjoint, nonempty open subsets

constraint an inequality or equation involving one or more variables that is used in an optimization problem; the constraint enforces a limit on the possible solutions for the problem

contour map a plot of the various level curves of a given function $f(x, y)$

critical point of a function of two variables the point (x_0, y_0) is called a critical point of $f(x, y)$ if one of the two following conditions holds:

1. $f_x(x_0, y_0) = f_y(x_0, y_0) = 0$
2. At least one of $f_x(x_0, y_0)$ and $f_y(x_0, y_0)$ do not exist

differentiable a function $f(x, y)$ is differentiable at (x_0, y_0) if $f(x, y)$ can be expressed in the form $f(x, y) = f(x_0, y_0) + f_x(x_0, y_0)(x - x_0) + f_y(x_0, y_0)(y - y_0) + E(x, y),$

where the error term $E(x, y)$ satisfies $\lim_{(x, y) \to (x_0, y_0)} \frac{E(x, y)}{\sqrt{(x - x_0)^2 + (y - y_0)^2}} = 0$

directional derivative the derivative of a function in the direction of a given unit vector

discriminant the discriminant of the function $f(x, y)$ is given by the formula $D = f_{xx}(x_0, y_0)f_{yy}(x_0, y_0) - \left(f_{xy}(x_0, y_0)\right)^2$

function of two variables a function $z = f(x, y)$ that maps each ordered pair (x, y) in a subset D of $\mathbb{R}^2$ to a unique real number z

generalized chain rule the chain rule extended to functions of more than one independent variable, in which each independent variable may depend on one or more other variables

gradient the gradient of the function $f(x, y)$ is defined to be $\nabla f(x, y) = (\partial f/\partial x)\mathbf{i} + (\partial f/\partial y)\mathbf{j},$ which can be generalized to a function of any number of independent variables

graph of a function of two variables a set of ordered triples (x, y, z) that satisfies the equation $z = f(x, y)$ plotted in three-dimensional Cartesian space

higher-order partial derivatives second-order or higher partial derivatives, regardless of whether they are mixed partial derivatives

interior point a point P_0 of R is a boundary point if there is a δ disk centered around P_0 contained completely in R

intermediate variable given a composition of functions (e.g., $f(x(t), y(t))$), the intermediate variables are the variables that are independent in the outer function but dependent on other variables as well; in the function $f(x(t), y(t)),$ the variables x and y are examples of intermediate variables

Lagrange multiplier the constant (or constants) used in the method of Lagrange multipliers; in the case of one constant, it is represented by the variable λ

level curve of a function of two variables the set of points satisfying the equation $f(x, y) = c$ for some real number c in the range of f

level surface of a function of three variables the set of points satisfying the equation $f(x, y, z) = c$ for some real number c in the range of f

linear approximation given a function $f(x, y)$ and a tangent plane to the function at a point (x_0, y_0), we can approximate $f(x, y)$ for points near (x_0, y_0) using the tangent plane formula

method of Lagrange multipliers a method of solving an optimization problem subject to one or more constraints

mixed partial derivatives second-order or higher partial derivatives, in which at least two of the differentiations are with respect to different variables

objective function the function that is to be maximized or minimized in an optimization problem

open set a set S that contains none of its boundary points

optimization problem calculation of a maximum or minimum value of a function of several variables, often using Lagrange multipliers

partial derivative a derivative of a function of more than one independent variable in which all the variables but one are held constant

partial differential equation an equation that involves an unknown function of more than one independent variable and one or more of its partial derivatives

region an open, connected, nonempty subset of $\mathbb{R}^2$

saddle point given the function $z = f(x, y)$, the point $(x_0, y_0, f(x_0, y_0))$ is a saddle point if both $f_x(x_0, y_0) = 0$ and $f_y(x_0, y_0) = 0$, but f does not have a local extremum at (x_0, y_0)

surface the graph of a function of two variables, $z = f(x, y)$

tangent plane given a function $f(x, y)$ that is differentiable at a point (x_0, y_0), the equation of the tangent plane to the surface $z = f(x, y)$ is given by $z = f(x_0, y_0) + f_x(x_0, y_0)(x - x_0) + f_y(x_0, y_0)(y - y_0)$

total differential the total differential of the function $f(x, y)$ at (x_0, y_0) is given by the formula $dz = f_x(x_0, y_0)dx + f_y(x_0, y_0)dy$

tree diagram illustrates and derives formulas for the generalized chain rule, in which each independent variable is accounted for

vertical trace the set of ordered triples (c, y, z) that solves the equation $f(c, y) = z$ for a given constant $x = c$ or the set of ordered triples (x, d, z) that solves the equation $f(x, d) = z$ for a given constant $y = d$

δ ball all points in $\mathbb{R}^3$ lying at a distance of less than δ from (x_0, y_0, z_0)

δ disk an open disk of radius δ centered at point (a, b)

KEY EQUATIONS

- **Vertical trace**
  $f(a, y) = z$ for $x = a$ or $f(x, b) = z$ for $y = b$
- **Level surface of a function of three variables**
  $f(x, y, z) = c$
- **Partial derivative of f with respect to x**
  $$\frac{\partial f}{\partial x} = \lim_{h \to 0} \frac{f(x + h, y) - f(x, y)}{h}$$

- **Partial derivative of f with respect to y**
$$\frac{\partial f}{\partial y} = \lim_{k \to 0} \frac{f(x, y+k) - f(x, y)}{k}$$

- **Tangent plane**
$z = f(x_0, y_0) + f_x(x_0, y_0)(x - x_0) + f_y(x_0, y_0)(y - y_0)$

- **Linear approximation**
$L(x, y) = f(x_0, y_0) + f_x(x_0, y_0)(x - x_0) + f_y(x_0, y_0)(y - y_0)$

- **Total differential**
$dz = f_x(x_0, y_0)dx + f_y(x_0, y_0)dy.$

- **Differentiability (two variables)**
$f(x, y) = f(x_0, y_0) + f_x(x_0, y_0)(x - x_0) + f_y(x_0, y_0)(y - y_0) + E(x, y),$
where the error term E satisfies
$$\lim_{(x, y) \to (x_0, y_0)} \frac{E(x, y)}{\sqrt{(x - x_0)^2 + (y - y_0)^2}} = 0.$$

- **Differentiability (three variables)**
$$\begin{aligned} f(x, y) &= f(x_0, y_0, z_0) + f_x(x_0, y_0, z_0)(x - x_0) + f_y(x_0, y_0, z_0)(y - y_0) \\ &\quad + f_z(x_0, y_0, z_0)(z - z_0) + E(x, y, z), \end{aligned}$$
where the error term E satisfies
$$\lim_{(x, y, z) \to (x_0, y_0, z_0)} \frac{E(x, y, z)}{\sqrt{(x - x_0)^2 + (y - y_0)^2 + (z - z_0)^2}} = 0.$$

- **Chain rule, one independent variable**
$$\frac{dz}{dt} = \frac{\partial z}{\partial x} \cdot \frac{dx}{dt} + \frac{\partial z}{\partial y} \cdot \frac{dy}{dt}$$

- **Chain rule, two independent variables**
$$\frac{dz}{du} = \frac{\partial z}{\partial x} \cdot \frac{\partial x}{\partial u} + \frac{\partial z}{\partial y} \cdot \frac{\partial y}{\partial u}$$
$$\frac{dz}{dv} = \frac{\partial z}{\partial x} \cdot \frac{\partial x}{\partial v} + \frac{\partial z}{\partial y} \cdot \frac{\partial y}{\partial v}$$

- **Generalized chain rule**
$$\frac{\partial w}{\partial t_j} = \frac{\partial w}{\partial x_1} \frac{\partial x_1}{\partial t_j} + \frac{\partial w}{\partial x_2} \frac{\partial x_1}{\partial t_j} + \cdots + \frac{\partial w}{\partial x_m} \frac{\partial x_m}{\partial t_j}$$

- **directional derivative (two dimensions)**
$$D_{\mathbf{u}} f(a, b) = \lim_{h \to 0} \frac{f(a + h\cos\theta, b + h\sin\theta) - f(a, b)}{h}$$
or
$D_{\mathbf{u}} f(x, y) = f_x(x, y)\cos\theta + f_y(x, y)\sin\theta$

- **gradient (two dimensions)**
$\nabla f(x, y) = f_x(x, y)\mathbf{i} + f_y(x, y)\mathbf{j}$

- **gradient (three dimensions)**
$\nabla f(x, y, z) = f_x(x, y, z)\mathbf{i} + f_y(x, y, z)\mathbf{j} + f_z(x, y, z)\mathbf{k}$

- **directional derivative (three dimensions)**
$$\begin{aligned} D_{\mathbf{u}} f(x, y, z) &= \nabla f(x, y, z) \cdot \mathbf{u} \\ &= f_x(x, y, z)\cos\alpha + f_y(x, y, z)\cos\beta + f_x(x, y, z)\cos\gamma \end{aligned}$$

- **Discriminant**

$$D = f_{xx}(x_0, y_0) f_{yy}(x_0, y_0) - \left(f_{xy}(x_0, y_0)\right)^2$$

- **Method of Lagrange multipliers, one constraint**
$$\begin{aligned} \nabla f(x_0, y_0) &= \lambda \nabla g(x_0, y_0) \\ g(x_0, y_0) &= 0 \end{aligned}$$

- **Method of Lagrange multipliers, two constraints**
$$\begin{aligned} \nabla f(x_0, y_0, z_0) &= \lambda_1 \nabla g(x_0, y_0, z_0) + \lambda_2 \nabla h(x_0, y_0, z_0) \\ g(x_0, y_0, z_0) &= 0 \\ h(x_0, y_0, z_0) &= 0 \end{aligned}$$

KEY CONCEPTS

4.1 Functions of Several Variables

- The graph of a function of two variables is a surface in $\mathbb{R}^3$ and can be studied using level curves and vertical traces.
- A set of level curves is called a contour map.

4.2 Limits and Continuity

- To study limits and continuity for functions of two variables, we use a δ disk centered around a given point.
- A function of several variables has a limit if for any point in a δ ball centered at a point $P,$ the value of the function at that point is arbitrarily close to a fixed value (the limit value).
- The limit laws established for a function of one variable have natural extensions to functions of more than one variable.
- A function of two variables is continuous at a point if the limit exists at that point, the function exists at that point, and the limit and function are equal at that point.

4.3 Partial Derivatives

- A partial derivative is a derivative involving a function of more than one independent variable.
- To calculate a partial derivative with respect to a given variable, treat all the other variables as constants and use the usual differentiation rules.
- Higher-order partial derivatives can be calculated in the same way as higher-order derivatives.

4.4 Tangent Planes and Linear Approximations

- The analog of a tangent line to a curve is a tangent plane to a surface for functions of two variables.
- Tangent planes can be used to approximate values of functions near known values.
- A function is differentiable at a point if it is ”smooth” at that point (i.e., no corners or discontinuities exist at that point).
- The total differential can be used to approximate the change in a function $z = f(x_0, y_0)$ at the point (x_0, y_0) for given values of Δx and $\Delta y.$

4.5 The Chain Rule

- The chain rule for functions of more than one variable involves the partial derivatives with respect to all the independent variables.
- Tree diagrams are useful for deriving formulas for the chain rule for functions of more than one variable, where each independent variable also depends on other variables.

4.6 Directional Derivatives and the Gradient

- A directional derivative represents a rate of change of a function in any given direction.
- The gradient can be used in a formula to calculate the directional derivative.
- The gradient indicates the direction of greatest change of a function of more than one variable.

4.7 Maxima/Minima Problems

- A critical point of the function $f(x, y)$ is any point (x_0, y_0) where either $f_x(x_0, y_0) = f_y(x_0, y_0) = 0,$ or at least one of $f_x(x_0, y_0)$ and $f_y(x_0, y_0)$ do not exist.
- A saddle point is a point (x_0, y_0) where $f_x(x_0, y_0) = f_y(x_0, y_0) = 0,$ but (x_0, y_0) is neither a maximum nor a minimum at that point.
- To find extrema of functions of two variables, first find the critical points, then calculate the discriminant and apply the second derivative test.

4.8 Lagrange Multipliers

- An objective function combined with one or more constraints is an example of an optimization problem.
- To solve optimization problems, we apply the method of Lagrange multipliers using a four-step problem-solving strategy.

CHAPTER 4 REVIEW EXERCISES

For the following exercises, determine whether the statement is *true or false*. Justify your answer with a proof or a counterexample.

394. The domain of $f(x, y) = x^3 \sin^{-1}(y)$ is $x =$ all real numbers, and $-\pi \leq y \leq \pi.$

395. If the function $f(x, y)$ is continuous everywhere, then $f_{xy} = f_{yx}.$

396. The linear approximation to the function of $f(x, y) = 5x^2 + x\tan(y)$ at $(2, \pi)$ is given by $L(x, y) = 22 + 21(x - 2) + (y - \pi).$

397. $\left(\frac{3}{4}, \frac{9}{16}\right)$ is a critical point of $g(x, y) = 4x^3 - 2x^2 y + y^2 - 2.$

For the following exercises, sketch the function in one graph and, in a second, sketch several level curves.

398. $f(x, y) = e^{-\left(x^2 + 2y^2\right)}.$

399. $f(x, y) = x + 4y^2.$

For the following exercises, evaluate the following limits, if they exist. If they do not exist, prove it.

400. $\lim\limits_{(x, y) \to (1, 1)} \frac{4xy}{x - 2y^2}$

401. $\lim\limits_{(x, y) \to (0, 0)} \frac{4xy}{x - 2y^2}$

For the following exercises, find the largest interval of continuity for the function.

402. $f(x, y) = x^3 \sin^{-1}(y)$

403. $g(x, y) = \ln\left(4 - x^2 - y^2\right)$

For the following exercises, find all first partial derivatives.

404. $f(x, y) = \sqrt{x^2 - y^2}$

405. $u(x, y) = x^4 - 3xy + 1, \; x = 2t, \; y = t^3$

For the following exercises, find all second partial derivatives.

406. $g(t, x) = 3t^2 - \sin(x + t)$

407. $h(x, y, z) = \frac{x^3 e^{2y}}{z}$

For the following exercises, find the equation of the tangent plane to the specified surface at the given point.

408. $z = x^3 - 2y^2 + y - 1$ at point $(1, 1, -1)$

409. $3z^3 = e^x + \frac{2}{y}$ at point $(0, 1, 3)$

410. Approximate $f(x, y) = e^{x^2} + \sqrt{y}$ at $(0.1, 9.1)$. Write down your linear approximation function $L(x, y)$. How accurate is the approximation to the exact answer, rounded to four digits?

411. Find the differential dz of $h(x, y) = 4x^2 + 2xy - 3y$ and approximate Δz at the point $(1, -2)$. Let $\Delta x = 0.1$ and $\Delta y = 0.01$.

412. Find the directional derivative of $f(x, y) = x^2 + 6xy - y^2$ in the direction $v = \mathbf{i} + 4\mathbf{j}$.

413. Find the maximal directional derivative magnitude and direction for the function $f(x, y) = x^3 + 2xy - \cos(\pi y)$ at point $(3, 0)$.

For the following exercises, find the gradient.

414. $c(x, t) = e(t - x)^2 + 3\cos(t)$

415. $f(x, y) = \frac{\sqrt{x} + y^2}{xy}$

For the following exercises, find and classify the critical points.

416. $z = x^3 - xy + y^2 - 1$

For the following exercises, use Lagrange multipliers to find the maximum and minimum values for the functions with the given constraints.

417. $f(x, y) = x^2 y,\ x^2 + y^2 = 4$

418. $f(x, y) = x^2 - y^2,\ x + 6y = 4$

419. A machinist is constructing a right circular cone out of a block of aluminum. The machine gives an error of 5% in height and 2% in radius. Find the maximum error in the volume of the cone if the machinist creates a cone of height 6 cm and radius 2 cm.

420. A trash compactor is in the shape of a cuboid. Assume the trash compactor is filled with incompressible liquid. The length and width are decreasing at rates of 2 ft/sec and 3 ft/sec, respectively. Find the rate at which the liquid level is rising when the length is 14 ft, the width is 10 ft, and the height is 4 ft.

5 | MULTIPLE INTEGRATION

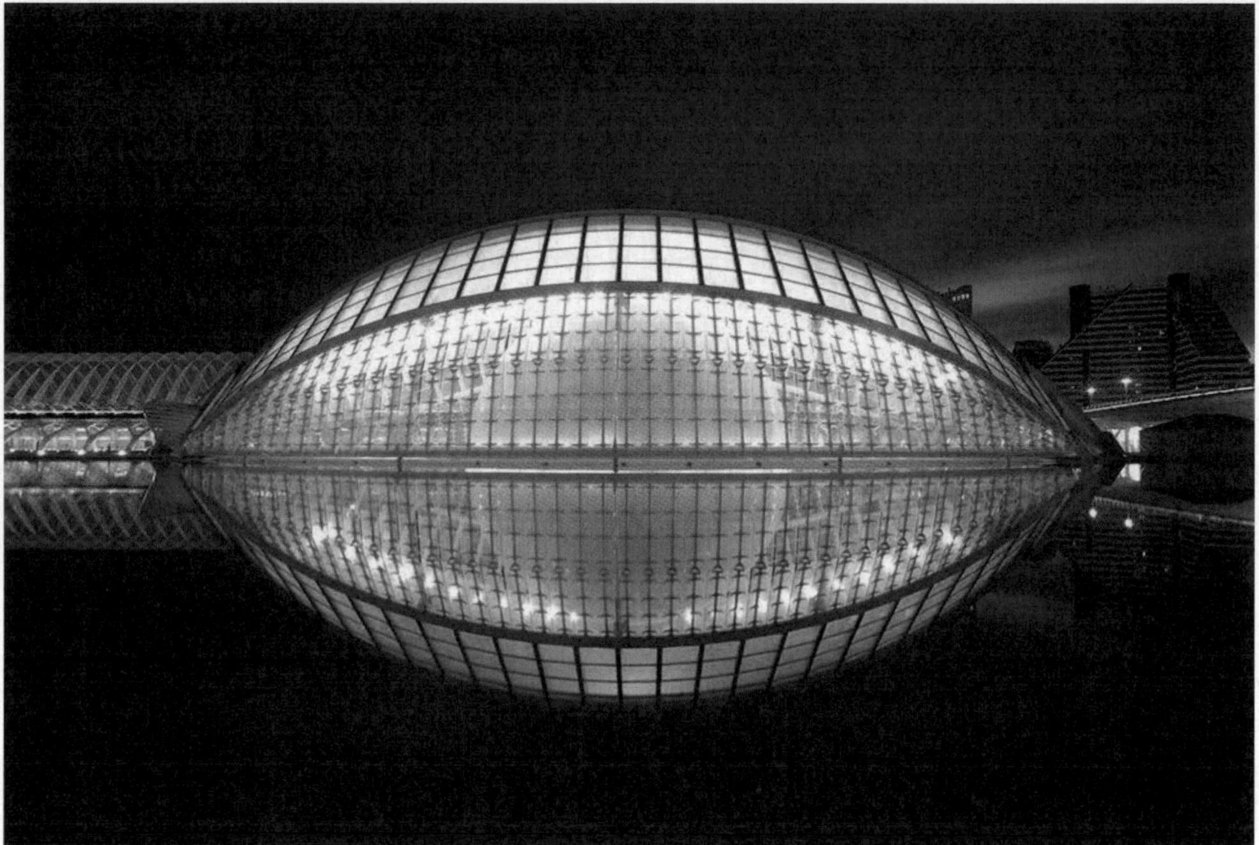

Figure 5.1 The City of Arts and Sciences in Valencia, Spain, has a unique structure along an axis of just two kilometers that was formerly the bed of the River Turia. The l'Hemisfèric has an IMAX cinema with three systems of modern digital projections onto a concave screen of 900 square meters. An oval roof over 100 meters long has been made to look like a huge human eye that comes alive and opens up to the world as the "Eye of Wisdom." (credit: modification of work by Javier Yaya Tur, Wikimedia Commons)

Chapter Outline

Introduction

In this chapter we extend the concept of a definite integral of a single variable to double and triple integrals of functions of two and three variables, respectively. We examine applications involving integration to compute volumes, masses, and centroids of more general regions. We will also see how the use of other coordinate systems (such as polar, cylindrical, and spherical coordinates) makes it simpler to compute multiple integrals over some types of regions and functions. As an example, we will use polar coordinates to find the volume of structures such as l'Hemisfèric. (See **Example 5.51**.)

In the preceding chapter, we discussed differential calculus with multiple independent variables. Now we examine integral calculus in multiple dimensions. Just as a partial derivative allows us to differentiate a function with respect to one variable while holding the other variables constant, we will see that an iterated integral allows us to integrate a function with respect to one variable while holding the other variables constant.

5.1 | Double Integrals over Rectangular Regions

Learning Objectives

5.1.1 Recognize when a function of two variables is integrable over a rectangular region.
5.1.2 Recognize and use some of the properties of double integrals.
5.1.3 Evaluate a double integral over a rectangular region by writing it as an iterated integral.
5.1.4 Use a double integral to calculate the area of a region, volume under a surface, or average value of a function over a plane region.

In this section we investigate double integrals and show how we can use them to find the volume of a solid over a rectangular region in the xy-plane. Many of the properties of double integrals are similar to those we have already discussed for single integrals.

Volumes and Double Integrals

We begin by considering the space above a rectangular region *R*. Consider a continuous function $f(x, y) \geq 0$ of two variables defined on the closed rectangle *R*:

$$R = [a, b] \times [c, d] = \{(x, y) \in \mathbb{R}^2 \,|\, a \leq x \leq b,\ c \leq y \leq d\}$$

Here $[a, b] \times [c, d]$ denotes the Cartesian product of the two closed intervals $[a, b]$ and $[c, d]$. It consists of rectangular pairs (x, y) such that $a \leq x \leq b$ and $c \leq y \leq d$. The graph of f represents a surface above the xy-plane with equation $z = f(x, y)$ where z is the height of the surface at the point (x, y). Let S be the solid that lies above R and under the graph of f (**Figure 5.2**). The base of the solid is the rectangle R in the xy-plane. We want to find the volume V of the solid S.

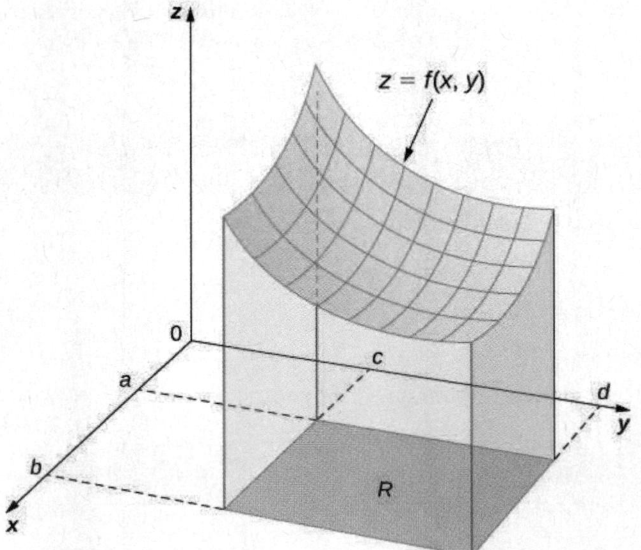

Figure 5.2 The graph of $f(x, y)$ over the rectangle R in the xy-plane is a curved surface.

We divide the region R into small rectangles R_{ij}, each with area ΔA and with sides Δx and Δy (**Figure 5.3**). We do this by dividing the interval $[a, b]$ into m subintervals and dividing the interval $[c, d]$ into n subintervals. Hence $\Delta x = \frac{b-a}{m}$, $\Delta y = \frac{d-c}{n}$, and $\Delta A = \Delta x \Delta y$.

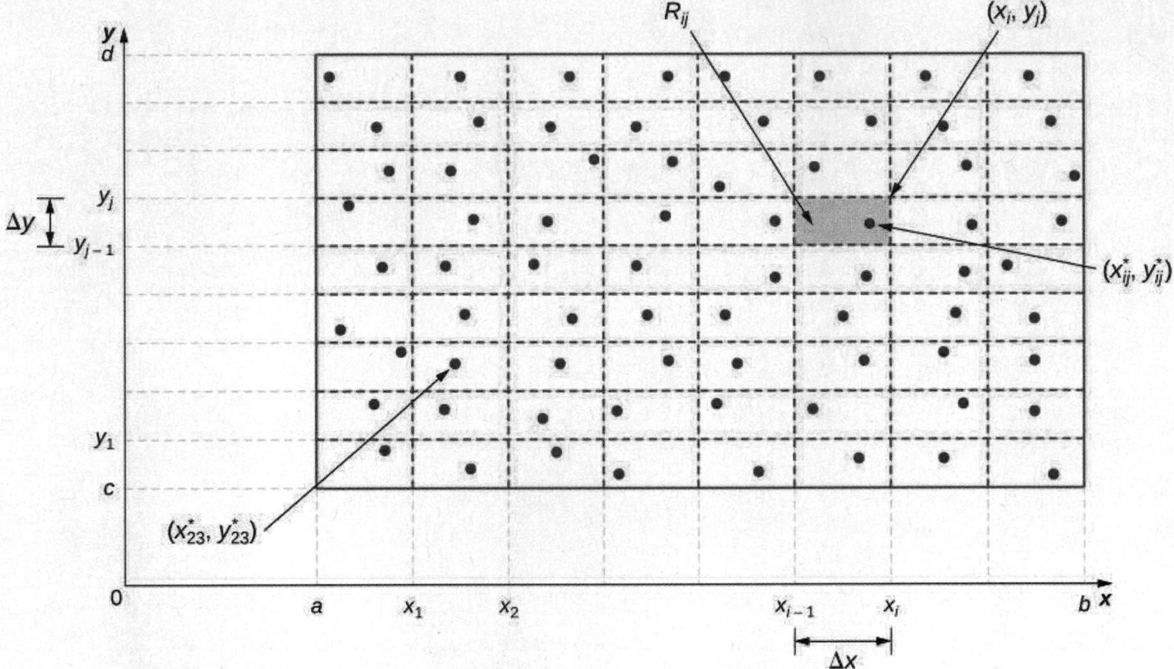

Figure 5.3 Rectangle R is divided into small rectangles R_{ij}, each with area ΔA.

The volume of a thin rectangular box above R_{ij} is $f(x^*_{ij}, y^*_{ij})\Delta A$, where (x^*_{ij}, y^*_{ij}) is an arbitrary sample point in each R_{ij} as shown in the following figure.

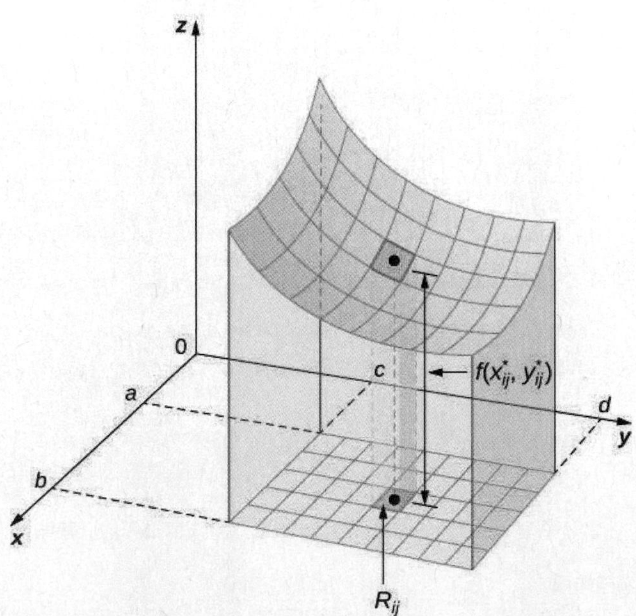

Figure 5.4 A thin rectangular box above R_{ij} with height $f\left(x^*_{ij}, y^*_{ij}\right)$.

Using the same idea for all the subrectangles, we obtain an approximate volume of the solid S as $V \approx \sum_{i=1}^{m} \sum_{j=1}^{n} f(x_{ij}^*, y_{ij}^*)\Delta A$. This sum is known as a **double Riemann sum** and can be used to approximate the value of the volume of the solid. Here the double sum means that for each subrectangle we evaluate the function at the chosen point, multiply by the area of each rectangle, and then add all the results.

As we have seen in the single-variable case, we obtain a better approximation to the actual volume if m and n become larger.

$$V = \lim_{m, n \to \infty} \sum_{i=1}^{m} \sum_{j=1}^{n} f(x_{ij}^*, y_{ij}^*)\Delta A \text{ or } V = \lim_{\Delta x, \Delta y \to 0} \sum_{i=1}^{m} \sum_{j=1}^{n} f(x_{ij}^*, y_{ij}^*)\Delta A.$$

Note that the sum approaches a limit in either case and the limit is the volume of the solid with the base R. Now we are ready to define the double integral.

Definition

The **double integral** of the function $f(x, y)$ over the rectangular region R in the xy-plane is defined as

$$\iint_R f(x, y)dA = \lim_{m, n \to \infty} \sum_{i=1}^{m} \sum_{j=1}^{n} f(x_{ij}^*, y_{ij}^*)\Delta A. \tag{5.1}$$

If $f(x, y) \geq 0$, then the volume V of the solid S, which lies above R in the xy-plane and under the graph of f, is the double integral of the function $f(x, y)$ over the rectangle R. If the function is ever negative, then the double integral can be considered a “signed” volume in a manner similar to the way we defined net signed area in **The Definite Integral (http://cnx.org/content/m53631/latest/)** .

Example 5.1

Setting up a Double Integral and Approximating It by Double Sums

Consider the function $z = f(x, y) = 3x^2 - y$ over the rectangular region $R = [0, 2] \times [0, 2]$ (**Figure 5.5**).

a. Set up a double integral for finding the value of the signed volume of the solid S that lies above R and “under” the graph of f.

b. Divide R into four squares with $m = n = 2$, and choose the sample point as the upper right corner point of each square $(1, 1), (2, 1), (1, 2)$, and $(2, 2)$ (**Figure 5.6**) to approximate the signed volume of the solid S that lies above R and “under” the graph of f.

c. Divide R into four squares with $m = n = 2$, and choose the sample point as the midpoint of each square: $(1/2, 1/2), (3/2, 1/2), (1/2, 3/2)$, and $(3/2, 3/2)$ to approximate the signed volume.

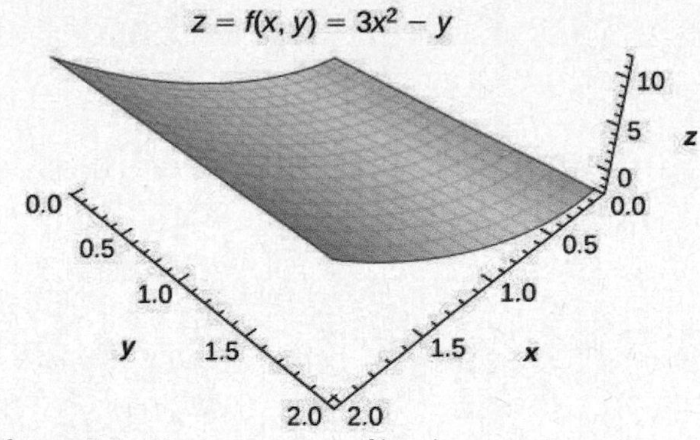

Figure 5.5 The function $z = f(x, y)$ graphed over the rectangular region $R = [0, 2] \times [0, 2]$.

Solution

a. As we can see, the function $z = f(x, y) = 3x^2 - y$ is above the plane. To find the signed volume of S, we need to divide the region R into small rectangles R_{ij}, each with area ΔA and with sides Δx and Δy, and choose (x_{ij}^*, y_{ij}^*) as sample points in each R_{ij}. Hence, a double integral is set up as

$$V = \iint_R (3x^2 - y)dA = \lim_{m, n \to \infty} \sum_{i=1}^{m} \sum_{j=1}^{n} \left[3\left(x_{ij}^*\right)^2 - y_{ij}^*\right]\Delta A.$$

b. Approximating the signed volume using a Riemann sum with $m = n = 2$ we have $\Delta A = \Delta x \Delta y = 1 \times 1 = 1$. Also, the sample points are (1, 1), (2, 1), (1, 2), and (2, 2) as shown in the following figure.

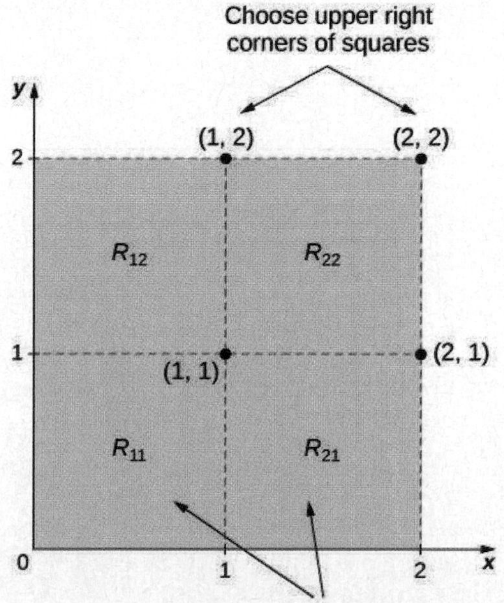

Figure 5.6 Subrectangles for the rectangular region $R = [0, 2] \times [0, 2]$.

Hence,

$$\begin{aligned} V &= \sum_{i=1}^{2} \sum_{j=1}^{2} f(x_{ij}^*, y_{ij}^*)\Delta A \\ &= \sum_{i=1}^{2} (f(x_{i1}^*, y_{i1}^*) + f(x_{i2}^*, y_{i2}^*))\Delta A \\ &= f(x_{11}^*, y_{11}^*)\Delta A + f(x_{21}^*, y_{21}^*)\Delta A + f(x_{12}^*, y_{12}^*)\Delta A + f(x_{22}^*, y_{22}^*)\Delta A \\ &= f(1, 1)(1) + f(2, 1)(1) + f(1, 2)(1) + f(2, 2)(1) \\ &= (3 - 1)(1) + (12 - 1)(1) + (3 - 2)(1) + (12 - 2)(1) \\ &= 2 + 11 + 1 + 10 = 24. \end{aligned}$$

c. Approximating the signed volume using a Riemann sum with $m = n = 2,$ we have $\Delta A = \Delta x \Delta y = 1 \times 1 = 1.$ In this case the sample points are (1/2, 1/2), (3/2, 1/2), (1/2, 3/2), and (3/2, 3/2).
Hence

$$\begin{aligned} V &= \sum_{i=1}^{2} \sum_{j=1}^{2} f(x_{ij}^*, y_{ij}^*)\Delta A \\ &= f(x_{11}^*, y_{11}^*)\Delta A + f(x_{21}^*, y_{21}^*)\Delta A + f(x_{12}^*, y_{12}^*)\Delta A + f(x_{22}^*, y_{22}^*)\Delta A \\ &= f(1/2, 1/2)(1) + f(3/2, 1/2)(1) + f(1/2, 3/2)(1) + f(3/2, 3/2)(1) \\ &= \left(\tfrac{3}{4} - \tfrac{1}{4}\right)(1) + \left(\tfrac{27}{4} - \tfrac{1}{2}\right)(1) + \left(\tfrac{3}{4} - \tfrac{3}{2}\right)(1) + \left(\tfrac{27}{4} - \tfrac{3}{2}\right)(1) \\ &= \tfrac{2}{4} + \tfrac{25}{4} + \left(-\tfrac{3}{4}\right) + \tfrac{21}{4} = \tfrac{45}{4} = 11. \end{aligned}$$

Analysis

Notice that the approximate answers differ due to the choices of the sample points. In either case, we are introducing some error because we are using only a few sample points. Thus, we need to investigate how we can achieve an accurate answer.

5.1 Use the same function $z = f(x, y) = 3x^2 - y$ over the rectangular region $R = [0, 2] \times [0, 2].$

Divide R into the same four squares with $m = n = 2,$ and choose the sample points as the upper left corner point of each square $(0, 1), (1, 1), (0, 2),$ and $(1, 2)$ (**Figure 5.6**) to approximate the signed volume of the solid S that lies above R and "under" the graph of f.

Note that we developed the concept of double integral using a rectangular region R. This concept can be extended to any general region. However, when a region is not rectangular, the subrectangles may not all fit perfectly into R, particularly if the base area is curved. We examine this situation in more detail in the next section, where we study regions that are not always rectangular and subrectangles may not fit perfectly in the region R. Also, the heights may not be exact if the surface $z = f(x, y)$ is curved. However, the errors on the sides and the height where the pieces may not fit perfectly within the solid S approach 0 as m and n approach infinity. Also, the double integral of the function $z = f(x, y)$ exists provided that the function f is not too discontinuous. If the function is bounded and continuous over R except on a finite number of smooth curves, then the double integral exists and we say that f is integrable over R.

Since $\Delta A = \Delta x \Delta y = \Delta y \Delta x,$ we can express dA as $dx\,dy$ or $dy\,dx.$ This means that, when we are using rectangular coordinates, the double integral over a region R denoted by $\iint_R f(x, y)dA$ can be written as $\iint_R f(x, y)dx\,dy$ or

$$\iint_R f(x, y)dy\,dx.$$

Now let's list some of the properties that can be helpful to compute double integrals.

Properties of Double Integrals

The properties of double integrals are very helpful when computing them or otherwise working with them. We list here six properties of double integrals. Properties 1 and 2 are referred to as the linearity of the integral, property 3 is the additivity of the integral, property 4 is the monotonicity of the integral, and property 5 is used to find the bounds of the integral. Property 6 is used if $f(x, y)$ is a product of two functions $g(x)$ and $h(y)$.

Theorem 5.1: Properties of Double Integrals

Assume that the functions $f(x, y)$ and $g(x, y)$ are integrable over the rectangular region *R*; *S* and *T* are subregions of *R*; and assume that *m* and *M* are real numbers.

i. The sum $f(x, y) + g(x, y)$ is integrable and

$$\iint_R [f(x, y) + g(x, y)]dA = \iint_R f(x, y)dA + \iint_R g(x, y)dA.$$

ii. If *c* is a constant, then $cf(x, y)$ is integrable and

$$\iint_R cf(x, y)dA = c\iint_R f(x, y)dA.$$

iii. If $R = S \cup T$ and $S \cap T = \varnothing$ except an overlap on the boundaries, then

$$\iint_R f(x, y)dA = \iint_S f(x, y)dA + \iint_T f(x, y)dA.$$

iv. If $f(x, y) \ge g(x, y)$ for (x, y) in $R,$ then

$$\iint_R f(x, y)dA \ge \iint_R g(x, y)dA.$$

v. If $m \le f(x, y) \le M,$ then

$$m \times A(R) \le \iint_R f(x, y)dA \le M \times A(R).$$

vi. In the case where $f(x, y)$ can be factored as a product of a function $g(x)$ of x only and a function $h(y)$ of y only, then over the region $R = \{(x, y)|a \le x \le b, c \le y \le d\},$ the double integral can be written as

$$\iint_R f(x, y)dA = \left(\int_a^b g(x)dx\right)\left(\int_c^d h(y)dy\right).$$

These properties are used in the evaluation of double integrals, as we will see later. We will become skilled in using these properties once we become familiar with the computational tools of double integrals. So let's get to that now.

Iterated Integrals

So far, we have seen how to set up a double integral and how to obtain an approximate value for it. We can also imagine that evaluating double integrals by using the definition can be a very lengthy process if we choose larger values for m and n. Therefore, we need a practical and convenient technique for computing double integrals. In other words, we need to learn how to compute double integrals without employing the definition that uses limits and double sums.

The basic idea is that the evaluation becomes easier if we can break a double integral into single integrals by integrating first with respect to one variable and then with respect to the other. The key tool we need is called an iterated integral.

Definition

Assume $a, b, c,$ and d are real numbers. We define an **iterated integral** for a function $f(x, y)$ over the rectangular region $R = [a, b] \times [c, d]$ as

a.

$$\int_a^b \int_c^d f(x, y)\,dy\,dx = \int_a^b \left[\int_c^d f(x, y)\,dy\right] dx \tag{5.2}$$

b.

$$\int_c^d \int_a^b f(x, y)\,dx\,dy = \int_c^d \left[\int_a^b f(x, y)\,dx\right] dy. \tag{5.3}$$

The notation $\int_a^b \left[\int_c^d f(x, y)\,dy\right] dx$ means that we integrate $f(x, y)$ with respect to y while holding x constant. Similarly, the notation $\int_c^d \left[\int_a^b f(x, y)\,dx\right] dy$ means that we integrate $f(x, y)$ with respect to x while holding y constant. The fact that double integrals can be split into iterated integrals is expressed in Fubini's theorem. Think of this theorem as an essential tool for evaluating double integrals.

Theorem 5.2: Fubini's Theorem

Suppose that $f(x, y)$ is a function of two variables that is continuous over a rectangular region $R = \{(x, y) \in \mathbb{R}^2 \,|\, a \le x \le b, \mathrm{c} \le \mathrm{y} \le \mathrm{d}\}$. Then we see from **Figure 5.7** that the double integral of f over the region equals an iterated integral,

$$\iint_R f(x, y)\,dA = \iint_R f(x, y)\,dx\,dy = \int_a^b \int_c^d f(x, y)\,dy\,dx = \int_c^d \int_a^b f(x, y)\,dx\,dy.$$

More generally, **Fubini's theorem** is true if f is bounded on R and f is discontinuous only on a finite number of continuous curves. In other words, f has to be integrable over R.

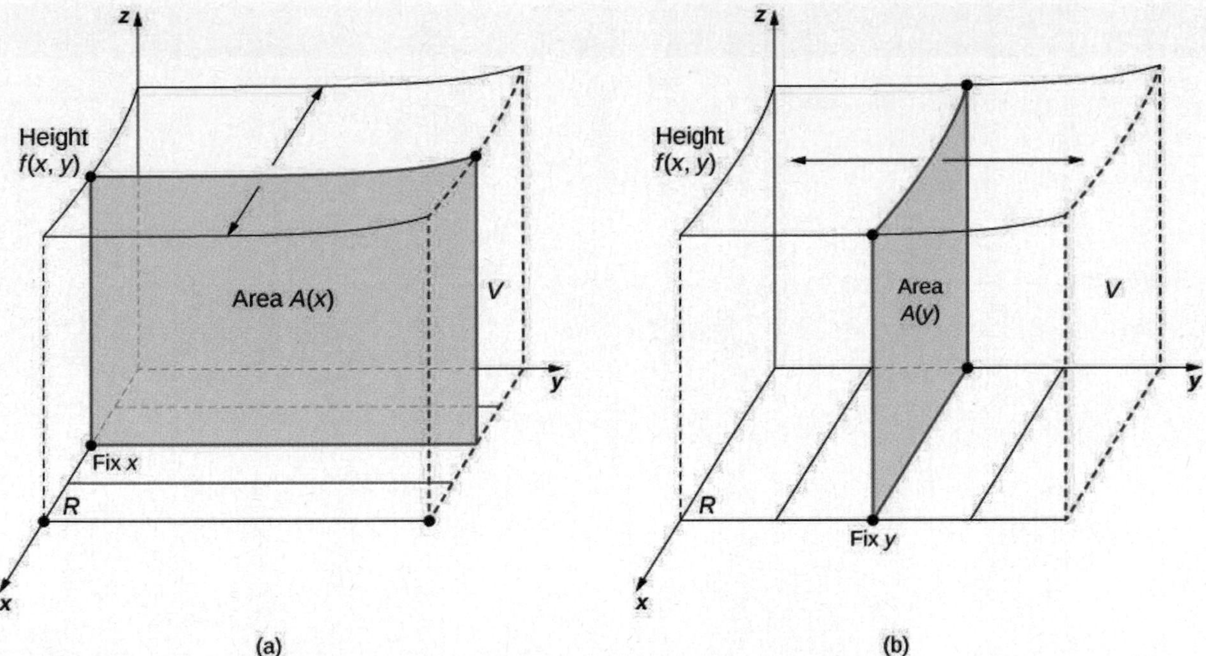

Figure 5.7 (a) Integrating first with respect to y and then with respect to x to find the area $A(x)$ and then the volume V; (b) integrating first with respect to x and then with respect to y to find the area $A(y)$ and then the volume V.

Example 5.2

Using Fubini's Theorem

Use Fubini's theorem to compute the double integral $\iint_R f(x, y)dA$ where $f(x, y) = x$ and $R = [0, 2] \times [0, 1]$.

Solution

Fubini's theorem offers an easier way to evaluate the double integral by the use of an iterated integral. Note how the boundary values of the region R become the upper and lower limits of integration.

$$\begin{aligned} \iint_R f(x, y)dA &= \iint_R f(x, y)dx\,dy \\ &= \int_{y=0}^{y=1} \int_{x=0}^{x=2} x\,dx\,dy \\ &= \int_{y=0}^{y=1} \left[\frac{x^2}{2} \Big|_{x=0}^{x=2} \right] dy \\ &= \int_{y=0}^{y=1} 2dy = 2y\Big|_{y=0}^{y=1} = 2. \end{aligned}$$

The double integration in this example is simple enough to use Fubini's theorem directly, allowing us to convert a double integral into an iterated integral. Consequently, we are now ready to convert all double integrals to iterated integrals and demonstrate how the properties listed earlier can help us evaluate double integrals when the function $f(x, y)$ is more complex. Note that the order of integration can be changed (see **Example 5.7**).

Example 5.3

Illustrating Properties i and ii

Evaluate the double integral $\iint_R (xy - 3xy^2)\,dA$ where $R = \{(x, y) | 0 \le x \le 2, 1 \le y \le 2\}$.

Solution

This function has two pieces: one piece is xy and the other is $3xy^2$. Also, the second piece has a constant 3. Notice how we use properties i and ii to help evaluate the double integral.

$$\iint_R (xy - 3xy^2)\,dA$$

$$= \iint_R xy\,dA + \iint_R (-3xy^2)\,dA$$ Property i: Integral of a sum is the sum of the integrals.

$$= \int_{y=1}^{y=2} \int_{x=0}^{x=2} xy\,dx\,dy - \int_{y=1}^{y=2} \int_{x=0}^{x=2} 3xy^2\,dx\,dy$$ Convert double integrals to iterated integrals.

$$= \int_{y=1}^{y=2} \left(\frac{x^2}{2}y\right)\Big|_{x=0}^{x=2} dy - 3\int_{y=1}^{y=2} \left(\frac{x^2}{2}y^2\right)\Big|_{x=0}^{x=2} dy$$ Integrate with respect to x, holding y constant.

$$= \int_{y=1}^{y=2} 2y\,dy - \int_{y=1}^{y=2} 6y^2\,dy$$ Property ii: Placing the constant before the integral.

$$= \int_1^2 y\,dy - 6\int_1^2 y^2\,dy$$ Integrate with respect to y.

$$= 2\frac{y^2}{2}\Big|_1^2 - 6\frac{y^3}{3}\Big|_1^2$$

$$= y^2\Big|_1^2 - 2y^3\Big|_1^2$$

$$= (4 - 1) - 2(8 - 1)$$
$$= 3 - 2(7) = 3 - 14 = -11.$$

Example 5.4

Illustrating Property v.

Over the region $R = \{(x, y) | 1 \le x \le 3, 1 \le y \le 2\}$, we have $2 \le x^2 + y^2 \le 13$. Find a lower and an upper bound for the integral $\iint_R (x^2 + y^2)\,dA$.

Solution

For a lower bound, integrate the constant function 2 over the region R. For an upper bound, integrate the constant function 13 over the region R.

$$\int_1^2 \int_1^3 2dx\,dy = \int_1^2 \left[2x|_1^3\right]dy = \int_1^2 2(2)dy = 4y|_1^2 = 4(2-1) = 4$$
$$\int_1^2 \int_1^3 13dx\,dy = \int_1^2 \left[13x|_1^3\right]dy = \int_1^2 13(2)dy = 26y|_1^2 = 26(2-1) = 26.$$

Hence, we obtain $4 \le \iint_R \left(x^2 + y^2\right)dA \le 26.$

Example 5.5

Illustrating Property vi

Evaluate the integral $\iint_R e^y \cos x\,dA$ over the region $R = \left\{(x, y)\middle|0 \le x \le \frac{\pi}{2}, 0 \le y \le 1\right\}.$

Solution

This is a great example for property vi because the function $f(x, y)$ is clearly the product of two single-variable functions e^y and $\cos x$. Thus we can split the integral into two parts and then integrate each one as a single-variable integration problem.

$$\begin{aligned}\iint_R e^y \cos x\,dA &= \int_0^1 \int_0^{\pi/2} e^y \cos x\,dx\,dy \\ &= \left(\int_0^1 e^y\,dy\right)\left(\int_0^{\pi/2} \cos x\,dx\right) \\ &= \left(e^y|_0^1\right)\left(\sin x|_0^{\pi/2}\right) \\ &= e - 1.\end{aligned}$$

5.2 a. Use the properties of the double integral and Fubini's theorem to evaluate the integral

$$\int_0^1 \int_{-1}^3 (3 - x + 4y)dy\,dx.$$

b. Show that $0 \le \iint_R \sin \pi x \cos \pi y\,dA \le \frac{1}{32}$ where $R = \left(0, \frac{1}{4}\right)\left(\frac{1}{4}, \frac{1}{2}\right).$

As we mentioned before, when we are using rectangular coordinates, the double integral over a region R denoted by $\iint_R f(x, y)dA$ can be written as $\iint_R f(x, y)dx\,dy$ or $\iint_R f(x, y)dy\,dx.$ The next example shows that the results are the same regardless of which order of integration we choose.

Example 5.6

Evaluating an Iterated Integral in Two Ways

Let's return to the function $f(x, y) = 3x^2 - y$ from **Example 5.1**, this time over the rectangular region $R = [0, 2] \times [0, 3]$. Use Fubini's theorem to evaluate $\iint_R f(x, y)dA$ in two different ways:

a. First integrate with respect to y and then with respect to x;
b. First integrate with respect to x and then with respect to y.

Solution

Figure 5.7 shows how the calculation works in two different ways.

a. First integrate with respect to y and then integrate with respect to x:

$$\begin{aligned}\iint_R f(x, y)dA &= \int_{x=0}^{x=2}\int_{y=0}^{y=3}(3x^2 - y)dy\,dx \\ &= \int_{x=0}^{x=2}\left(\int_{y=0}^{y=3}(3x^2 - y)dy\right)dx = \int_{x=0}^{x=2}\left[3x^2y - \frac{y^2}{2}\Big|_{y=0}^{y=3}\right]dx \\ &= \int_{x=0}^{x=2}\left(9x^2 - \frac{9}{2}\right)dx = 3x^3 - \frac{9}{2}x\Big|_{x=0}^{x=2} = 15.\end{aligned}$$

b. First integrate with respect to x and then integrate with respect to y:

$$\begin{aligned}\iint_R f(x, y)dA &= \int_{y=0}^{y=3}\int_{x=0}^{x=2}(3x^2 - y)dx\,dy \\ &= \int_{y=0}^{y=3}\left(\int_{x=0}^{x=2}(3x^2 - y)dx\right)dy = \int_{y=0}^{y=3}\left[x^3 - xy\Big|_{x=0}^{x=2}\right]dy \\ &= \int_{y=0}^{y=3}(8 - 2y)dy = 8y - y^2\Big|_{y=0}^{y=3} = 15.\end{aligned}$$

Analysis

With either order of integration, the double integral gives us an answer of 15. We might wish to interpret this answer as a volume in cubic units of the solid S below the function $f(x, y) = 3x^2 - y$ over the region $R = [0, 2] \times [0, 3]$. However, remember that the interpretation of a double integral as a (non-signed) volume works only when the integrand f is a nonnegative function over the base region R.

5.3 Evaluate $\int_{y=-3}^{y=2}\int_{x=3}^{x=5}\left(2 - 3x^2 + y^2\right)dx\,dy.$

In the next example we see that it can actually be beneficial to switch the order of integration to make the computation easier. We will come back to this idea several times in this chapter.

Example 5.7

Switching the Order of Integration

Consider the double integral $\iint_R x\sin(xy)dA$ over the region $R = \{(x, y)|0 \le x \le 3, 0 \le y \le 2\}$ (**Figure 5.8**).

a. Express the double integral in two different ways.

b. Analyze whether evaluating the double integral in one way is easier than the other and why.

c. Evaluate the integral.

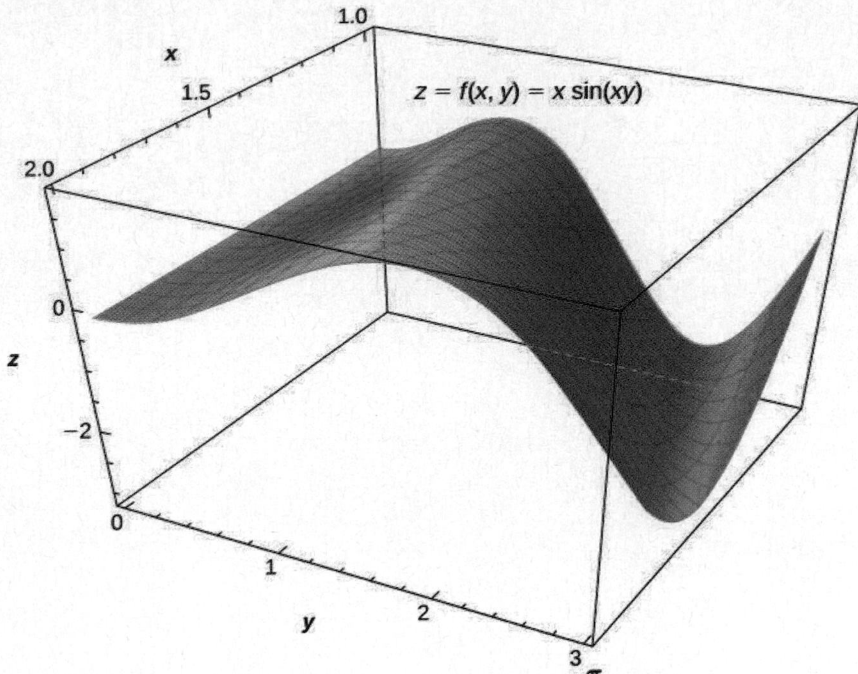

Figure 5.8 The function $z = f(x, y) = x\sin(xy)$ over the rectangular region $R = [0, \pi] \times [1, 2]$.

Solution

a. We can express $\iint_R x\sin(xy)dA$ in the following two ways: first by integrating with respect to y and then with respect to x; second by integrating with respect to x and then with respect to y.

$$\begin{aligned} &\iint_R x\sin(xy)dA \\ &= \int_{x=0}^{x=\pi}\int_{y=1}^{y=2} x\sin(xy)dy\,dx && \text{Integrate first with respect to } y. \\ &= \int_{y=1}^{y=2}\int_{x=0}^{x=\pi} x\sin(xy)dx\,dy && \text{Integrate first with respect to } x. \end{aligned}$$

b. If we want to integrate with respect to y first and then integrate with respect to x, we see that we can use the substitution $u = xy$, which gives $du = x\,dy$. Hence the inner integral is simply $\int \sin u\,du$ and we can change the limits to be functions of x,

$$\iint_R x\sin(xy)dA = \int_{x=0}^{x=\pi}\int_{y=1}^{y=2} x\sin(xy)dy\,dx = \int_{x=0}^{x=\pi}\left[\int_{u=x}^{u=2x}\sin(u)du\right]dx.$$

However, integrating with respect to x first and then integrating with respect to y requires integration by parts for the inner integral, with $u = x$ and $dv = \sin(xy)dx$.

Then $du = dx$ and $v = -\dfrac{\cos(xy)}{y}$, so

$$\iint_R x\sin(xy)dA = \int_{y=1}^{y=2}\int_{x=0}^{x=\pi} x\sin(xy)dx\,dy = \int_{y=1}^{y=2}\left[-\frac{x\cos(xy)}{y}\Big|_{x=0}^{x=\pi} + \frac{1}{y}\int_{x=0}^{x=\pi}\cos(xy)dx\right]dy.$$

Since the evaluation is getting complicated, we will only do the computation that is easier to do, which is clearly the first method.

c. Evaluate the double integral using the easier way.

$$\begin{aligned}\iint_R x\sin(xy)dA &= \int_{x=0}^{x=\pi}\int_{y=1}^{y=2} x\sin(xy)dy\,dx \\ &= \int_{x=0}^{x=\pi}\left[\int_{u=x}^{u=2x}\sin(u)du\right]dx = \int_{x=0}^{x=\pi}\left[-\cos u\big|_{u=x}^{u=2x}\right]dx = \int_{x=0}^{x=\pi}(-\cos 2x + \cos x)dx \\ &= -\tfrac{1}{2}\sin 2x + \sin x\Big|_{x=0}^{x=\pi} = 0.\end{aligned}$$

5.4 Evaluate the integral $\iint_R xe^{xy}\,dA$ where $R = [0, 1] \times [0, \ln 5]$.

Applications of Double Integrals

Double integrals are very useful for finding the area of a region bounded by curves of functions. We describe this situation in more detail in the next section. However, if the region is a rectangular shape, we can find its area by integrating the constant function $f(x, y) = 1$ over the region R.

Definition

The area of the region R is given by $A(R) = \iint_R 1dA$.

This definition makes sense because using $f(x, y) = 1$ and evaluating the integral make it a product of length and width. Let's check this formula with an example and see how this works.

Example 5.8

Finding Area Using a Double Integral

Find the area of the region $R = \{(x, y)|0 \le x \le 3, 0 \le y \le 2\}$ by using a double integral, that is, by integrating 1 over the region R.

Solution

The region is rectangular with length 3 and width 2, so we know that the area is 6. We get the same answer when we use a double integral:

$$A(R) = \int_0^2 \int_0^3 1dx\,dy = \int_0^2 \left[x|_0^3\right] dy = \int_0^2 3dy = 3\int_0^2 dy = 3y|_0^2 = 3(2) = 6.$$

We have already seen how double integrals can be used to find the volume of a solid bounded above by a function $f(x, y)$ over a region R provided $f(x, y) \geq 0$ for all (x, y) in R. Here is another example to illustrate this concept.

Example 5.9

Volume of an Elliptic Paraboloid

Find the volume V of the solid S that is bounded by the elliptic paraboloid $2x^2 + y^2 + z = 27,$ the planes $x = 3$ and $y = 3,$ and the three coordinate planes.

Solution

First notice the graph of the surface $z = 27 - 2x^2 - y^2$ in **Figure 5.9**(a) and above the square region $R_1 = [-3, 3] \times [-3, 3].$ However, we need the volume of the solid bounded by the elliptic paraboloid $2x^2 + y^2 + z = 27,$ the planes $x = 3$ and $y = 3,$ and the three coordinate planes.

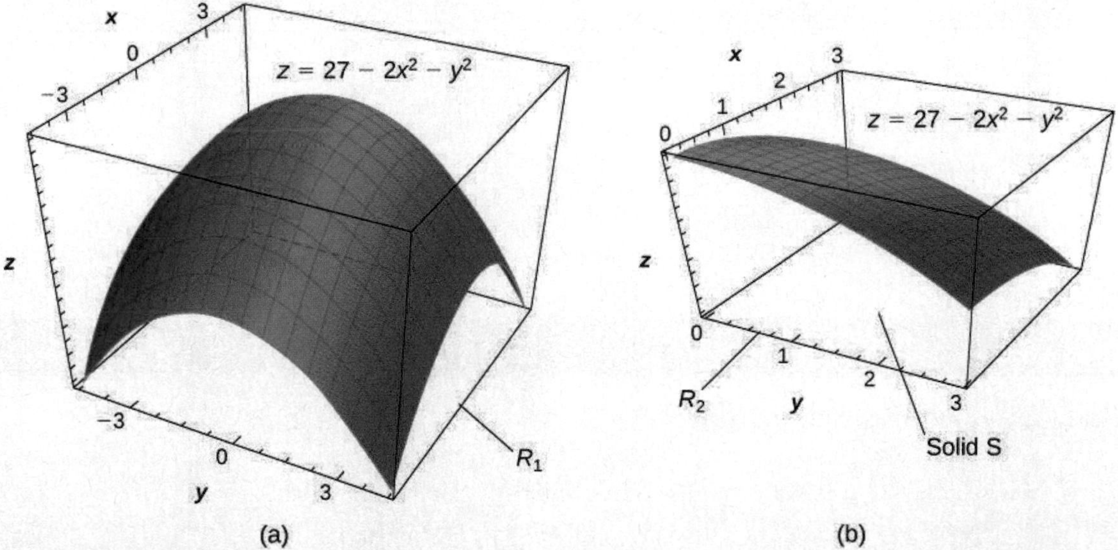

Figure 5.9 (a) The surface $z = 27 - 2x^2 - y^2$ above the square region $R_1 = [-3, 3] \times [-3, 3].$ (b) The solid S lies under the surface $z = 27 - 2x^2 - y^2$ above the square region $R_2 = [0, 3] \times [0, 3].$

Now let's look at the graph of the surface in **Figure 5.9**(b). We determine the volume V by evaluating the double integral over R_2:

$$\begin{aligned} V &= \iint_R z\,dA = \iint_R \left(27 - 2x^2 - y^2\right)dA \\ &= \int_{y=0}^{y=3}\int_{x=0}^{x=3} \left(27 - 2x^2 - y^2\right)dx\,dy && \text{Convert to iterated integral.} \\ &= \int_{y=0}^{y=3} \left[27x - \tfrac{2}{3}x^3 - y^2 x\right]\Big|_{x=0}^{x=3} dy && \text{Integrate with respect to } x. \\ &= \int_{y=0}^{y=3} \left(64 - 3y^2\right)dy = 63y - y^3\Big|_{y=0}^{y=3} = 162. \end{aligned}$$

5.5 Find the volume of the solid bounded above by the graph of $f(x, y) = xy\sin(x^2 y)$ and below by the xy-plane on the rectangular region $R = [0, 1] \times [0, \pi]$.

Recall that we defined the average value of a function of one variable on an interval $[a, b]$ as

$$f_{\text{ave}} = \frac{1}{b-a}\int_a^b f(x)dx.$$

Similarly, we can define the average value of a function of two variables over a region R. The main difference is that we divide by an area instead of the width of an interval.

Definition

The average value of a function of two variables over a region R is

$$f_{\text{ave}} = \frac{1}{\text{Area } R}\iint_R f(x, y)dA. \quad (5.4)$$

In the next example we find the average value of a function over a rectangular region. This is a good example of obtaining useful information for an integration by making individual measurements over a grid, instead of trying to find an algebraic expression for a function.

Example 5.10

Calculating Average Storm Rainfall

The weather map in **Figure 5.10** shows an unusually moist storm system associated with the remnants of Hurricane Karl, which dumped 4–8 inches (100–200 mm) of rain in some parts of the Midwest on September 22–23, 2010. The area of rainfall measured 300 miles east to west and 250 miles north to south. Estimate the average rainfall over the entire area in those two days.

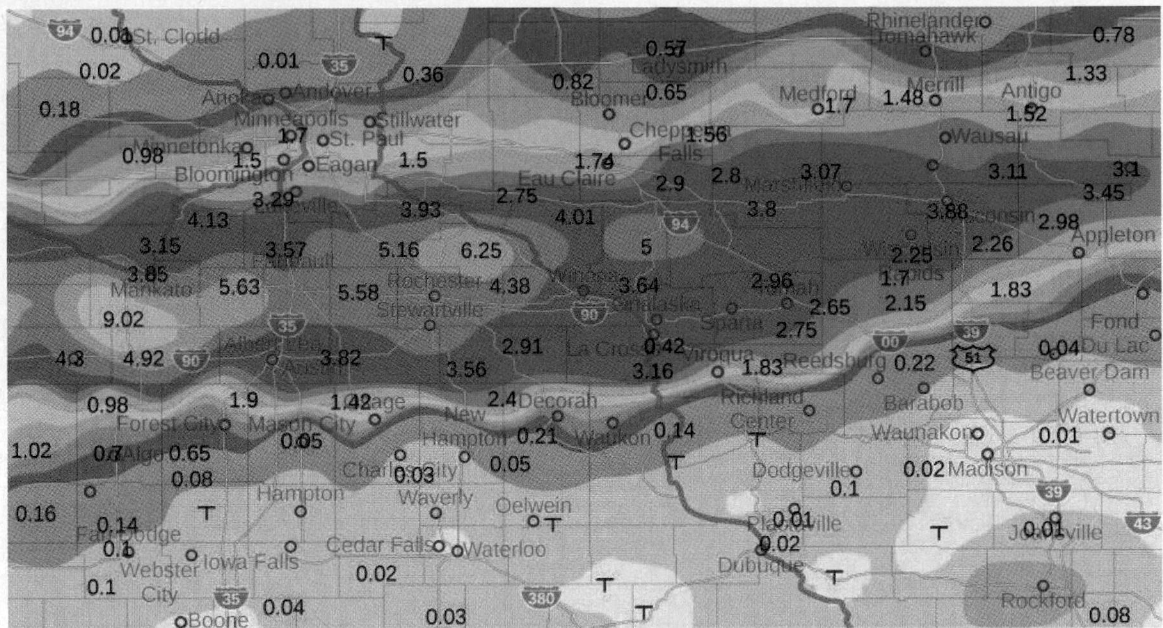

Figure 5.10 Effects of Hurricane Karl, which dumped 4–8 inches (100–200 mm) of rain in some parts of southwest Wisconsin, southern Minnesota, and southeast South Dakota over a span of 300 miles east to west and 250 miles north to south.

Solution

Place the origin at the southwest corner of the map so that all the values can be considered as being in the first quadrant and hence all are positive. Now divide the entire map into six rectangles $(m = 2 \text{ and } n = 3),$ as shown in **Figure 5.11**. Assume $f(x, y)$ denotes the storm rainfall in inches at a point approximately x miles to the east of the origin and y miles to the north of the origin. Let R represent the entire area of $250 \times 300 = 75000$ square miles. Then the area of each subrectangle is

$$\Delta A = \frac{1}{6}(75000) = 12500.$$

Assume (x_{ij}^*, y_{ij}^*) are approximately the midpoints of each subrectangle R_{ij}. Note the color-coded region at each of these points, and estimate the rainfall. The rainfall at each of these points can be estimated as:

At (x_{11}, y_{11}) the rainfall is 0.08.

At (x_{12}, y_{12}) the rainfall is 0.08.

At (x_{13}, y_{13}) the rainfall is 0.01.

At (x_{21}, y_{21}) the rainfall is 1.70.

At (x_{22}, y_{22}) the rainfall is 1.74.

At (x_{23}, y_{23}) the rainfall is 3.00.

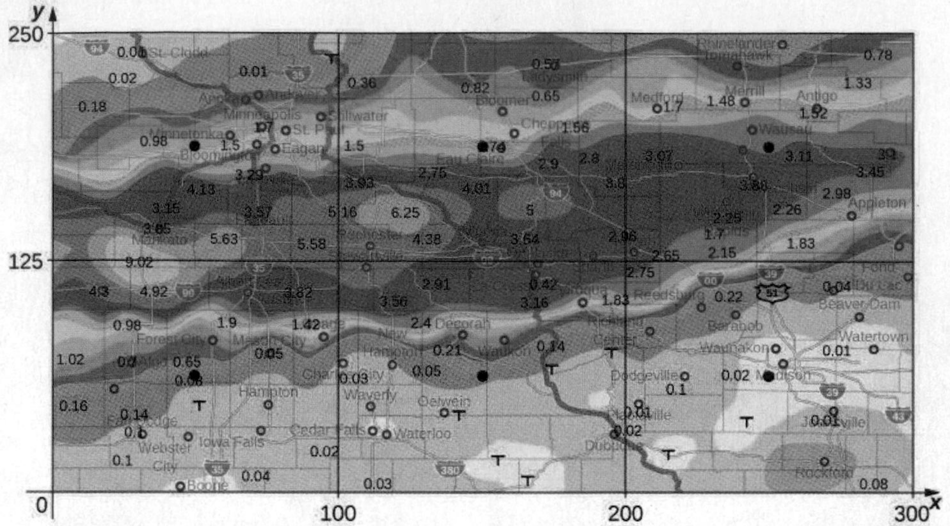

Figure 5.11 Storm rainfall with rectangular axes and showing the midpoints of each subrectangle.

According to our definition, the average storm rainfall in the entire area during those two days was

$$\begin{aligned}
f_{\text{ave}} &= \frac{1}{\text{Area } R}\iint_R f(x, y)dx\,dy = \frac{1}{75000}\iint_R f(x, y)dx\,dy \\
&\cong \frac{1}{75{,}000}\sum_{i=1}^{3}\sum_{j=1}^{2} f(x_{ij}^*, y_{ij}^*)\Delta A \\
&\cong \frac{1}{75{,}000}\big[f(x_{11}^*, y_{11}^*)\Delta A + f(x_{12}^*, y_{12}^*)\Delta A \\
&\quad + f(x_{13}^*, y_{13}^*)\Delta A + f(x_{21}^*, y_{21}^*)\Delta A + f(x_{22}^*, y_{22}^*)\Delta A + f(x_{23}^*, y_{23}^*)\Delta A\big] \\
&\cong \frac{1}{75{,}000}[0.08 + 0.08 + 0.01 + 1.70 + 1.74 + 3.00]\Delta A \\
&\cong \frac{1}{75{,}000}[0.08 + 0.08 + 0.01 + 1.70 + 1.74 + 3.00]12500 \\
&\cong \frac{5}{30}[0.08 + 0.08 + 0.01 + 1.70 + 1.74 + 3.00] \\
&\cong 1.10.
\end{aligned}$$

During September 22–23, 2010 this area had an average storm rainfall of approximately 1.10 inches.

5.6 A contour map is shown for a function $f(x, y)$ on the rectangle $R = [-3, 6] \times [-1, 4]$.

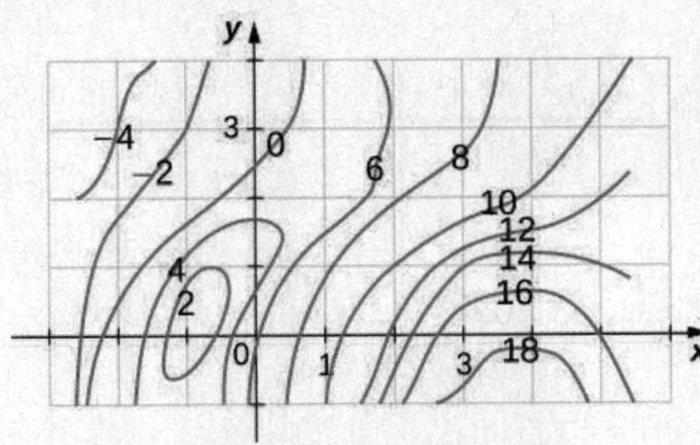

a. Use the midpoint rule with $m = 3$ and $n = 2$ to estimate the value of $\iint\limits_R f(x, y)dA$.

b. Estimate the average value of the function $f(x, y)$.

5.1 EXERCISES

In the following exercises, use the midpoint rule with $m=4$ and $n=2$ to estimate the volume of the solid bounded by the surface $z=f(x, y)$, the vertical planes $x=1$, $x=2$, $y=1$, and $y=2$, and the horizontal plane $z=0$.

1. $f(x, y)=4x+2y+8xy$

2. $f(x, y)=16x^2+\frac{y}{2}$

In the following exercises, estimate the volume of the solid under the surface $z=f(x, y)$ and above the rectangular region R by using a Riemann sum with $m=n=2$ and the sample points to be the lower left corners of the subrectangles of the partition.

3. $f(x, y)=\sin x-\cos y$, $R=[0, \pi]\times[0, \pi]$

4. $f(x, y)=\cos x+\cos y$, $R=[0, \pi]\times\left[0, \frac{\pi}{2}\right]$

5. Use the midpoint rule with $m=n=2$ to estimate $\iint_R f(x, y)dA$, where the values of the function f on $R=[8, 10]\times[9, 11]$ are given in the following table.

	y				
x	9	9.5	10	10.5	11
8	9.8	5	6.7	5	5.6
8.5	9.4	4.5	8	5.4	3.4
9	8.7	4.6	6	5.5	3.4
9.5	6.7	6	4.5	5.4	6.7
10	6.8	6.4	5.5	5.7	6.8

6. The values of the function f on the rectangle $R=[0, 2]\times[7, 9]$ are given in the following table. Estimate the double integral $\iint_R f(x, y)dA$ by using a Riemann sum with $m=n=2$. Select the sample points to be the upper right corners of the subsquares of R.

	$y_0=7$	$y_1=8$	$y_2=9$
$x_0=0$	10.22	10.21	9.85
$x_1=1$	6.73	9.75	9.63
$x_2=2$	5.62	7.83	8.21

7. The depth of a children's 4-ft by 4-ft swimming pool, measured at 1-ft intervals, is given in the following table.

a. Estimate the volume of water in the swimming pool by using a Riemann sum with $m=n=2$. Select the sample points using the midpoint rule on $R=[0, 4]\times[0, 4]$.

b. Find the average depth of the swimming pool.

	y				
x	0	1	2	3	4
0	1	1.5	2	2.5	3
1	1	1.5	2	2.5	3
2	1	1.5	1.5	2.5	3
3	1	1	1.5	2	2.5
4	1	1	1	1.5	2

8. The depth of a 3-ft by 3-ft hole in the ground, measured at 1-ft intervals, is given in the following table.
   a. Estimate the volume of the hole by using a Riemann sum with $m = n = 3$ and the sample points to be the upper left corners of the subsquares of R.
   b. Find the average depth of the hole.

	y			
x	0	1	2	3
0	6	6.5	6.4	6
1	6.5	7	7.5	6.5
2	6.5	6.7	6.5	6
3	6	6.5	5	5.6

9. The level curves $f(x, y) = k$ of the function f are given in the following graph, where k is a constant.
   a. Apply the midpoint rule with $m = n = 2$ to estimate the double integral $\iint_R f(x, y)dA$, where $R = [0.2, 1] \times [0, 0.8]$.
   b. Estimate the average value of the function f on R.

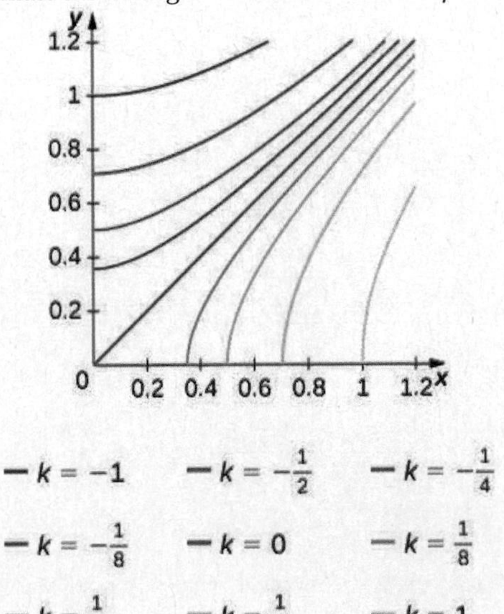

10. The level curves $f(x, y) = k$ of the function f are given in the following graph, where k is a constant.
   a. Apply the midpoint rule with $m = n = 2$ to estimate the double integral $\iint_R f(x, y)dA$, where $R = [0.1, 0.5] \times [0.1, 0.5]$.
   b. Estimate the average value of the function f on R.

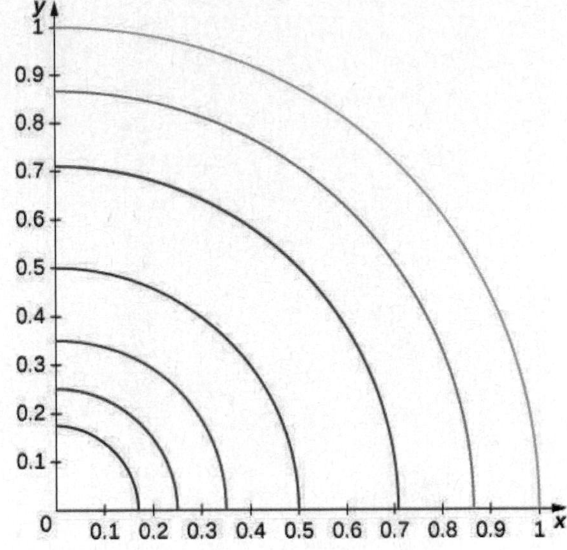

11. The solid lying under the surface $z = \sqrt{4 - y^2}$ and above the rectangular region $R = [0, 2] \times [0, 2]$ is illustrated in the following graph. Evaluate the double integral $\iint_R f(x, y)dA$, where $f(x, y) = \sqrt{4 - y^2}$, by finding the volume of the corresponding solid.

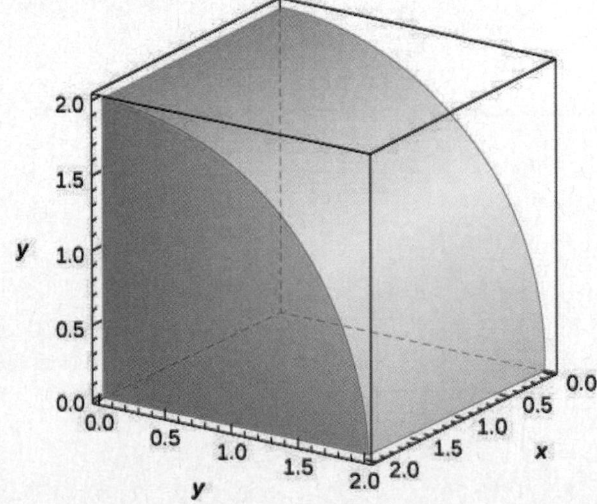

12. The solid lying under the plane $z = y + 4$ and above the rectangular region $R = [0, 2] \times [0, 4]$ is illustrated in the following graph. Evaluate the double integral $\iint_R f(x, y)dA$, where $f(x, y) = y + 4$, by finding the volume of the corresponding solid.

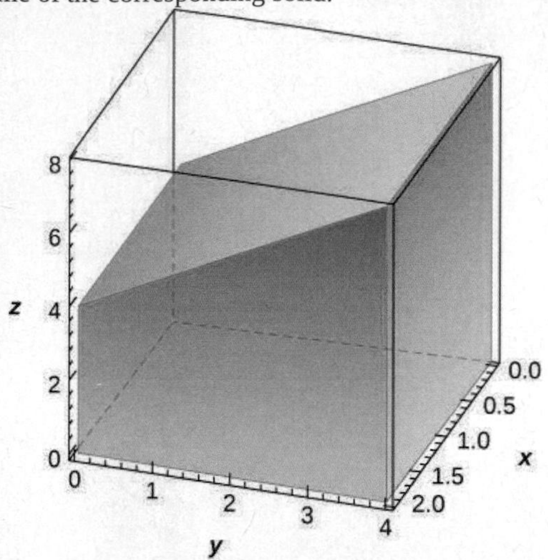

In the following exercises, calculate the integrals by interchanging the order of integration.

13. $\int_{-1}^{1}\left(\int_{-2}^{2}(2x + 3y + 5)dx\right)dy$

14. $\int_{0}^{2}\left(\int_{0}^{1}(x + 2e^y - 3)dx\right)dy$

15. $\int_{1}^{27}\left(\int_{1}^{2}(\sqrt[3]{x} + \sqrt[3]{y})dy\right)dx$

16. $\int_{1}^{16}\left(\int_{1}^{8}(\sqrt[4]{x} + 2\sqrt[3]{y})dy\right)dx$

17. $\int_{\ln 2}^{\ln 3}\left(\int_{0}^{1}e^{x+y}\,dy\right)dx$

18. $\int_{0}^{2}\left(\int_{0}^{1}3^{x+y}\,dy\right)dx$

19. $\int_{1}^{6}\left(\int_{2}^{9}\frac{\sqrt{y}}{x^2}dy\right)dx$

20. $\int_{1}^{9}\left(\int_{4}^{2}\frac{\sqrt{x}}{y^2}dy\right)dx$

In the following exercises, evaluate the iterated integrals by choosing the order of integration.

21. $\int_{0}^{\pi}\int_{0}^{\pi/2}\sin(2x)\cos(3y)dx\,dy$

22. $\int_{\pi/12}^{\pi/8}\int_{\pi/4}^{\pi/3}[\cot x + \tan(2y)]dx\,dy$

23. $\int_{1}^{e}\int_{1}^{e}\left[\frac{1}{x}\sin(\ln x) + \frac{1}{y}\cos(\ln y)\right]dx\,dy$

24. $\int_{1}^{e}\int_{1}^{e}\frac{\sin(\ln x)\cos(\ln y)}{xy}dx\,dy$

25. $\int_{1}^{2}\int_{1}^{2}\left(\frac{\ln y}{x} + \frac{x}{2y+1}\right)dy\,dx$

26. $\int_{1}^{e}\int_{1}^{2}x^2\ln(x)dy\,dx$

27. $\int_{1}^{\sqrt{3}}\int_{1}^{2}y\arctan\left(\frac{1}{x}\right)dy\,dx$

28. $\int_{0}^{1}\int_{0}^{1/2}(\arcsin x + \arcsin y)dy\,dx$

29. $\int_{0}^{1}\int_{1}^{2}xe^{x+4y}dy\,dx$

30. $\int_{1}^{2}\int_{0}^{1}xe^{x-y}dy\,dx$

31. $\int_{1}^{e}\int_{1}^{e}\left(\frac{\ln y}{\sqrt{y}} + \frac{\ln x}{\sqrt{x}}\right)dy\,dx$

32. $\int_{1}^{e}\int_{1}^{e}\left(\frac{x\ln y}{\sqrt{y}} + \frac{y\ln x}{\sqrt{x}}\right)dy\,dx$

33. $\int_{0}^{1}\int_{1}^{2}\left(\frac{x}{x^2 + y^2}\right)dy\,dx$

34. $\int_{0}^{1}\int_{1}^{2}\frac{y}{x + y^2}dy\,dx$

In the following exercises, find the average value of the

function over the given rectangles.

35. $f(x, y) = -x + 2y, \quad R = [0, 1] \times [0, 1]$

36. $f(x, y) = x^4 + 2y^3, \quad R = [1, 2] \times [2, 3]$

37. $f(x, y) = \sinh x + \sinh y, \quad R = [0, 1] \times [0, 2]$

38. $f(x, y) = \arctan(xy), \quad R = [0, 1] \times [0, 1]$

39. Let f and g be two continuous functions such that $0 \le m_1 \le f(x) \le M_1$ for any $x \in [a, b]$ and $0 \le m_2 \le g(y) \le M_2$ for any $y \in [c, d]$. Show that the following inequality is true: $m_1 m_2(b-a)(c-d) \le \int_a^b \int_c^d f(x)g(y)\,dy\,dx \le M_1 M_2(b-a)(c-d)$.

In the following exercises, use property v. of double integrals and the answer from the preceding exercise to show that the following inequalities are true.

40. $\frac{1}{e^2} \le \iint_R e^{-x^2-y^2}\,dA \le 1,$ where $R = [0, 1] \times [0, 1]$

41. $\frac{\pi^2}{144} \le \iint_R \sin x \cos y\,dA \le \frac{\pi^2}{48},$ where $R = \left[\frac{\pi}{6}, \frac{\pi}{3}\right] \times \left[\frac{\pi}{6}, \frac{\pi}{3}\right]$

42. $0 \le \iint_R e^{-y} \cos x\,dA \le \frac{\pi}{2},$ where $R = \left[0, \frac{\pi}{2}\right] \times \left[0, \frac{\pi}{2}\right]$

43. $0 \le \iint_R (\ln x)(\ln y)\,dA \le (e-1)^2,$ where $R = [1, e] \times [1, e]$

44. Let f and g be two continuous functions such that $0 \le m_1 \le f(x) \le M_1$ for any $x \in [a, b]$ and $0 \le m_2 \le g(y) \le M_2$ for any $y \in [c, d]$. Show that the following inequality is true: $(m_1 + m_2)(b-a)(c-d) \le \int_a^b \int_c^d [f(x) + g(y)]\,dy\,dx \le (M_1 + M_2)(b-a)(c-d)$.

In the following exercises, use property v. of double integrals and the answer from the preceding exercise to show that the following inequalities are true.

45. $\frac{2}{e} \le \iint_R \left(e^{-x^2} + e^{-y^2}\right)dA \le 2,$ where $R = [0, 1] \times [0, 1]$

46. $\frac{\pi^2}{36} \le \iint_R (\sin x + \cos y)\,dA \le \frac{\pi^2\sqrt{3}}{36},$ where $R = \left[\frac{\pi}{6}, \frac{\pi}{3}\right] \times \left[\frac{\pi}{6}, \frac{\pi}{3}\right]$

47. $\frac{\pi}{2}e^{-\pi/2} \le \iint_R \left(\cos x + e^{-y}\right)dA \le \pi,$ where $R = \left[0, \frac{\pi}{2}\right] \times \left[0, \frac{\pi}{2}\right]$

48. $\frac{1}{e} \le \iint_R \left(e^{-y} - \ln x\right)dA \le 2,$ where $R = [0, 1] \times [0, 1]$

In the following exercises, the function f is given in terms of double integrals.

a. Determine the explicit form of the function f.

b. Find the volume of the solid under the surface $z = f(x, y)$ and above the region R.

c. Find the average value of the function f on R.

d. Use a computer algebra system (CAS) to plot $z = f(x, y)$ and $z = f_{\text{ave}}$ in the same system of coordinates.

49. **[T]** $f(x, y) = \int_0^y \int_0^x (xs + yt)\,ds\,dt,$ where $(x, y) \in R = [0, 1] \times [0, 1]$

50. **[T]** $f(x, y) = \int_0^x \int_0^y [\cos(s) + \cos(t)]\,dt\,ds,$ where $(x, y) \in R = [0, 3] \times [0, 3]$

51. Show that if f and g are continuous on $[a, b]$ and $[c, d]$, respectively, then

$$\int_a^b \int_c^d [f(x) + g(y)]\,dy\,dx = (d-c)\int_a^b f(x)\,dx + \int_a^b \int_c^d g(y)\,dy\,dx = (b-a)\int_c^d g(y)\,dy + \int_c^d \int_a^b f(x)\,dx\,dy.$$

52. Show that $\int_a^b \int_c^d yf(x) + xg(y)\,dy\,dx = \frac{1}{2}(d^2 - c^2)\left(\int_a^b f(x)\,dx\right) + \frac{1}{2}(b^2 - a^2)\left(\int_c^d g(y)\,dy\right).$

53. **[T]** Consider the function $f(x, y) = e^{-x^2 - y^2}$, where $(x, y) \in R = [-1, 1] \times [-1, 1]$.

a. Use the midpoint rule with $m = n = 2, 4,\ldots, 10$ to estimate the double integral $I = \iint_R e^{-x^2 - y^2}\, dA$. Round your answers to the nearest hundredths.
b. For $m = n = 2$, find the average value of f over the region R. Round your answer to the nearest hundredths.
c. Use a CAS to graph in the same coordinate system the solid whose volume is given by $\iint_R e^{-x^2 - y^2}\, dA$ and the plane $z = f_{\text{ave}}$.

54. **[T]** Consider the function $f(x, y) = \sin(x^2)\cos(y^2)$, where $(x, y) \in R = [-1, 1] \times [-1, 1]$.

a. Use the midpoint rule with $m = n = 2, 4,\ldots, 10$ to estimate the double integral $I = \iint_R \sin(x^2)\cos(y^2)\, dA$. Round your answers to the nearest hundredths.
b. For $m = n = 2$, find the average value of f over the region R. Round your answer to the nearest hundredths.
c. Use a CAS to graph in the same coordinate system the solid whose volume is given by $\iint_R \sin(x^2)\cos(y^2)\, dA$ and the plane $z = f_{\text{ave}}$.

In the following exercises, the functions f_n are given, where $n \geq 1$ is a natural number.

a. Find the volume of the solids S_n under the surfaces $z = f_n(x, y)$ and above the region R.
b. Determine the limit of the volumes of the solids S_n as n increases without bound.

55. $f(x, y) = x^n + y^n + xy, \ (x, y) \in R = [0, 1] \times [0, 1]$

56. $f(x, y) = \frac{1}{x^n} + \frac{1}{y^n}, \ (x, y) \in R = [1, 2] \times [1, 2]$

57. Show that the average value of a function f on a rectangular region $R = [a, b] \times [c, d]$ is $f_{\text{ave}} \approx \frac{1}{mn} \sum_{i=1}^{m} \sum_{j=1}^{n} f(x_{ij}^*, y_{ij}^*)$, where (x_{ij}^*, y_{ij}^*) are the sample points of the partition of R, where $1 \leq i \leq m$ and $1 \leq j \leq n$.

58. Use the midpoint rule with $m = n$ to show that the average value of a function f on a rectangular region $R = [a, b] \times [c, d]$ is approximated by

$$f_{\text{ave}} \approx \frac{1}{n^2} \sum_{i,\, j=1}^{n} f\left(\frac{1}{2}(x_{i-1} + x_i), \frac{1}{2}(y_{j-1} + y_j)\right).$$

59. An isotherm map is a chart connecting points having the same temperature at a given time for a given period of time. Use the preceding exercise and apply the midpoint rule with $m = n = 2$ to find the average temperature over the region given in the following figure.

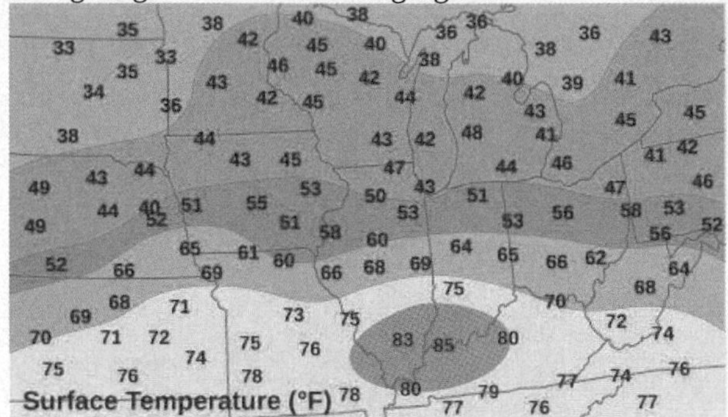

5.2 | Double Integrals over General Regions

Learning Objectives

5.2.1 Recognize when a function of two variables is integrable over a general region.

5.2.2 Evaluate a double integral by computing an iterated integral over a region bounded by two vertical lines and two functions of x, or two horizontal lines and two functions of y.

5.2.3 Simplify the calculation of an iterated integral by changing the order of integration.

5.2.4 Use double integrals to calculate the volume of a region between two surfaces or the area of a plane region.

5.2.5 Solve problems involving double improper integrals.

In **Double Integrals over Rectangular Regions**, we studied the concept of double integrals and examined the tools needed to compute them. We learned techniques and properties to integrate functions of two variables over rectangular regions. We also discussed several applications, such as finding the volume bounded above by a function over a rectangular region, finding area by integration, and calculating the average value of a function of two variables.

In this section we consider double integrals of functions defined over a general bounded region D on the plane. Most of the previous results hold in this situation as well, but some techniques need to be extended to cover this more general case.

General Regions of Integration

An example of a general bounded region D on a plane is shown in **Figure 5.12**. Since D is bounded on the plane, there must exist a rectangular region R on the same plane that encloses the region D, that is, a rectangular region R exists such that D is a subset of $R (D \subseteq R)$.

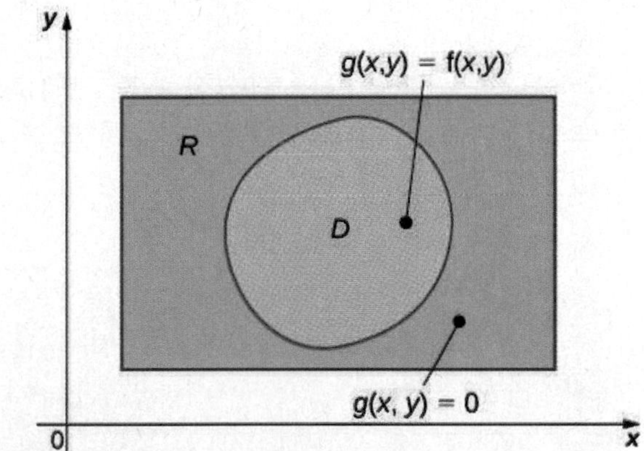

Figure 5.12 For a region D that is a subset of R, we can define a function $g(x, y)$ to equal $f(x, y)$ at every point in D and 0 at every point of R not in D.

Suppose $z = f(x, y)$ is defined on a general planar bounded region D as in **Figure 5.12**. In order to develop double integrals of f over D, we extend the definition of the function to include all points on the rectangular region R and then use the concepts and tools from the preceding section. But how do we extend the definition of f to include all the points on R? We do this by defining a new function $g(x, y)$ on R as follows:

$$g(x, y) = \begin{cases} f(x, y) & \text{if } (x, y) \text{ is in } D \\ 0 & \text{if } (x, y) \text{ is in } R \text{ but not in } D \end{cases}$$

Note that we might have some technical difficulties if the boundary of D is complicated. So we assume the boundary to be a piecewise smooth and continuous simple closed curve. Also, since all the results developed in **Double Integrals over Rectangular Regions** used an integrable function $f(x, y)$, we must be careful about $g(x, y)$ and verify that

$g(x, y)$ is an integrable function over the rectangular region R. This happens as long as the region D is bounded by simple closed curves. For now we will concentrate on the descriptions of the regions rather than the function and extend our theory appropriately for integration.

We consider two types of planar bounded regions.

Definition

A region D in the (x, y)-plane is of **Type I** if it lies between two vertical lines and the graphs of two continuous functions $g_1(x)$ and $g_2(x)$. That is (**Figure 5.13**),

$$D = \{(x, y) | a \leq x \leq b, g_1(x) \leq y \leq g_2(x)\}.$$

A region D in the xy plane is of **Type II** if it lies between two horizontal lines and the graphs of two continuous functions $h_1(y)$ and $h_2(y)$. That is (**Figure 5.14**),

$$D = \{(x, y) | c \leq y \leq d, h_1(y) \leq x \leq h_2(y)\}.$$

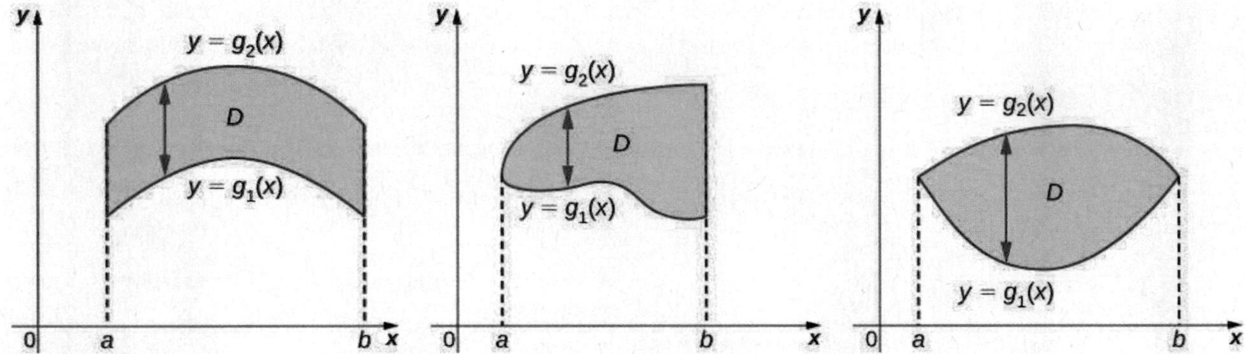

Figure 5.13 A Type I region lies between two vertical lines and the graphs of two functions of x.

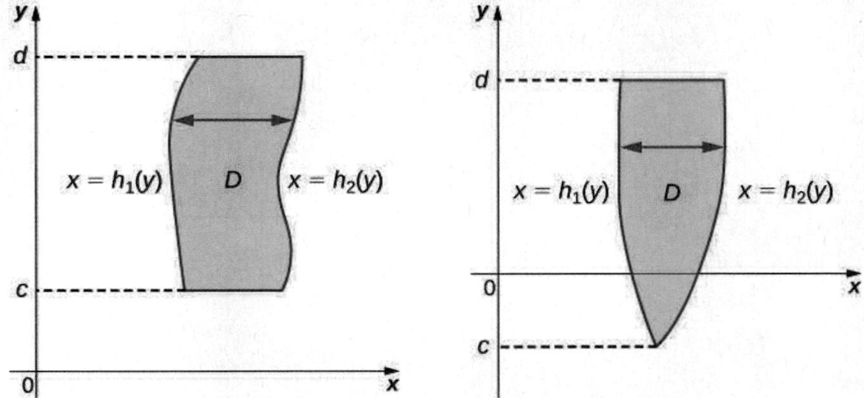

Figure 5.14 A Type II region lies between two horizontal lines and the graphs of two functions of y.

Example 5.11

Describing a Region as Type I and Also as Type II

Consider the region in the first quadrant between the functions $y = \sqrt{x}$ and $y = x^3$ (**Figure 5.15**). Describe the region first as Type I and then as Type II.

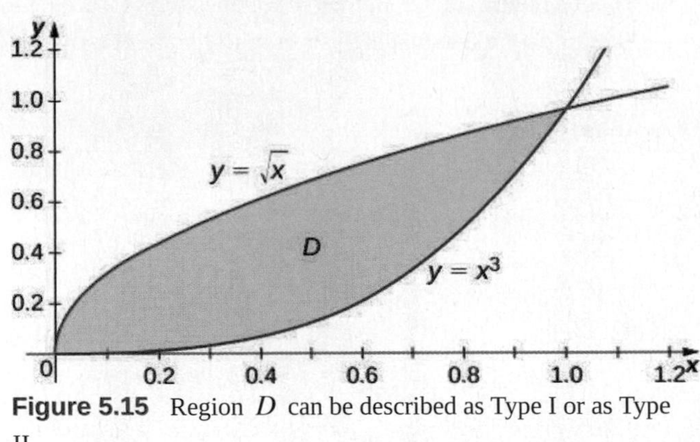

Figure 5.15 Region D can be described as Type I or as Type II.

Solution

When describing a region as Type I, we need to identify the function that lies above the region and the function that lies below the region. Here, region D is bounded above by $y = \sqrt{x}$ and below by $y = x^3$ in the interval for x in $[0, 1]$. Hence, as Type I, D is described as the set $\{(x, y)|0 \le x \le 1, x^3 \le y \le \sqrt{x}\}$.

However, when describing a region as Type II, we need to identify the function that lies on the left of the region and the function that lies on the right of the region. Here, the region D is bounded on the left by $x = y^2$ and on the right by $x = \sqrt[3]{y}$ in the interval for y in $[0, 1]$. Hence, as Type II, D is described as the set $\{(x, y)|0 \le y \le 1, y^2 \le x \le \sqrt[3]{y}\}$.

5.7 Consider the region in the first quadrant between the functions $y = 2x$ and $y = x^2$. Describe the region first as Type I and then as Type II.

Double Integrals over Nonrectangular Regions

To develop the concept and tools for evaluation of a double integral over a general, nonrectangular region, we need to first understand the region and be able to express it as Type I or Type II or a combination of both. Without understanding the regions, we will not be able to decide the limits of integrations in double integrals. As a first step, let us look at the following theorem.

Theorem 5.3: Double Integrals over Nonrectangular Regions

Suppose $g(x, y)$ is the extension to the rectangle R of the function $f(x, y)$ defined on the regions D and R as shown in **Figure 5.12** inside R. Then $g(x, y)$ is integrable and we define the double integral of $f(x, y)$ over D by

$$\iint_D f(x, y)dA = \iint_R g(x, y)dA.$$

The right-hand side of this equation is what we have seen before, so this theorem is reasonable because R is a rectangle and $\iint_R g(x, y)dA$ has been discussed in the preceding section. Also, the equality works because the values of $g(x, y)$ are 0 for any point (x, y) that lies outside $D,$ and hence these points do not add anything to the integral. However, it is important that the rectangle R contains the region $D.$

As a matter of fact, if the region D is bounded by smooth curves on a plane and we are able to describe it as Type I or Type II or a mix of both, then we can use the following theorem and not have to find a rectangle R containing the region.

Theorem 5.4: Fubini's Theorem (Strong Form)

For a function $f(x, y)$ that is continuous on a region D of Type I, we have

$$\iint_D f(x, y)dA = \iint_D f(x, y)dy\,dx = \int_a^b \left[\int_{g_1(x)}^{g_2(x)} f(x, y)dy \right] dx. \tag{5.5}$$

Similarly, for a function $f(x, y)$ that is continuous on a region D of Type II, we have

$$\iint_D f(x, y)dA = \iint_D f(x, y)dx\,dy = \int_c^d \left[\int_{h_1(y)}^{h_2(y)} f(x, y)dx \right] dy. \tag{5.6}$$

The integral in each of these expressions is an iterated integral, similar to those we have seen before. Notice that, in the inner integral in the first expression, we integrate $f(x, y)$ with x being held constant and the limits of integration being $g_1(x)$ and $g_2(x)$. In the inner integral in the second expression, we integrate $f(x, y)$ with y being held constant and the limits of integration are $h_1(x)$ and $h_2(x)$.

Example 5.12

Evaluating an Iterated Integral over a Type I Region

Evaluate the integral $\iint_D x^2 e^{xy}\,dA$ where D is shown in **Figure 5.16**.

Solution

First construct the region D as a Type I region (**Figure 5.16**). Here $D = \left\{(x, y)|0 \le x \le 2, \frac{1}{2}x \le y \le 1\right\}$. Then we have

$$\iint_D x^2 e^{xy}\,dA = \int_{x=0}^{x=2} \int_{y=1/2x}^{y=1} x^2 e^{xy}\,dy\,dx.$$

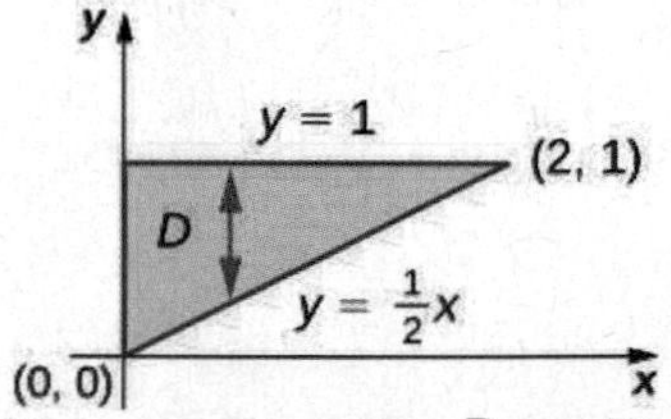

Figure 5.16 We can express region D as a Type I region and integrate from $y = \frac{1}{2}x$ to $y = 1,$ between the lines $x = 0$ and $x = 2.$

Therefore, we have

$$\int_{x=0}^{x=2}\int_{y=\frac{1}{2}x}^{y=1} x^2 e^{xy}\,dy\,dx = \int_{x=0}^{x=2}\left[\int_{y=1/2x}^{y=1} x^2 e^{xy}\,dy\right]dx$$ Iterated integral for a Type I region.

$$= \int_{x=0}^{x=2}\left[x^2\frac{e^{xy}}{x}\right]\Bigg|_{y=1/2x}^{y=1} dx$$ Integrate with respect to y using u-substitution with $u = xy$ where x is held constant.

$$= \int_{x=0}^{x=2}\left[xe^x - xe^{x^2/2}\right]dx$$ Integrate with respect to x using u-substitution with $u = \frac{1}{2}x^2$.

$$= \left[xe^x - e^x - e^{\frac{1}{2}x^2}\right]\Bigg|_{x=0}^{x=2} = 2$$

In **Example 5.12**, we could have looked at the region in another way, such as $D = \{(x, y)|0 \le y \le 1,\ 0 \le x \le 2y\}$ (**Figure 5.17**).

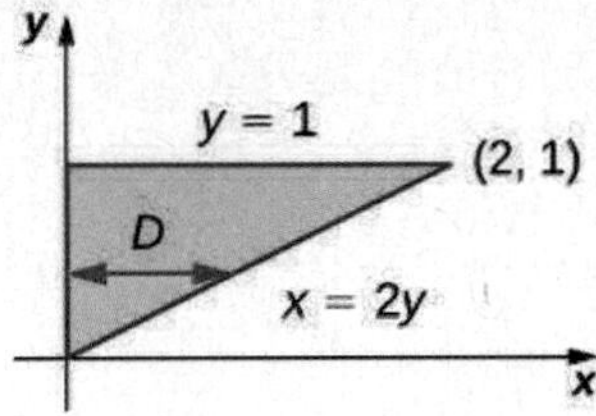

Figure 5.17

This is a Type II region and the integral would then look like

$$\iint_D x^2 e^{xy}\,dA = \int_{y=0}^{y=1}\int_{x=0}^{x=2y} x^2 e^{xy}\,dx\,dy.$$

However, if we integrate first with respect to x, this integral is lengthy to compute because we have to use integration by parts twice.

Example 5.13

Evaluating an Iterated Integral over a Type II Region

Evaluate the integral $\iint_D \left(3x^2 + y^2\right)dA$ where $= \left\{(x, y)| - 2 \le y \le 3,\ y^2 - 3 \le x \le y + 3\right\}$.

Solution

Notice that D can be seen as either a Type I or a Type II region, as shown in **Figure 5.18**. However, in this case describing D as Type I is more complicated than describing it as Type II. Therefore, we use D as a Type II region for the integration.

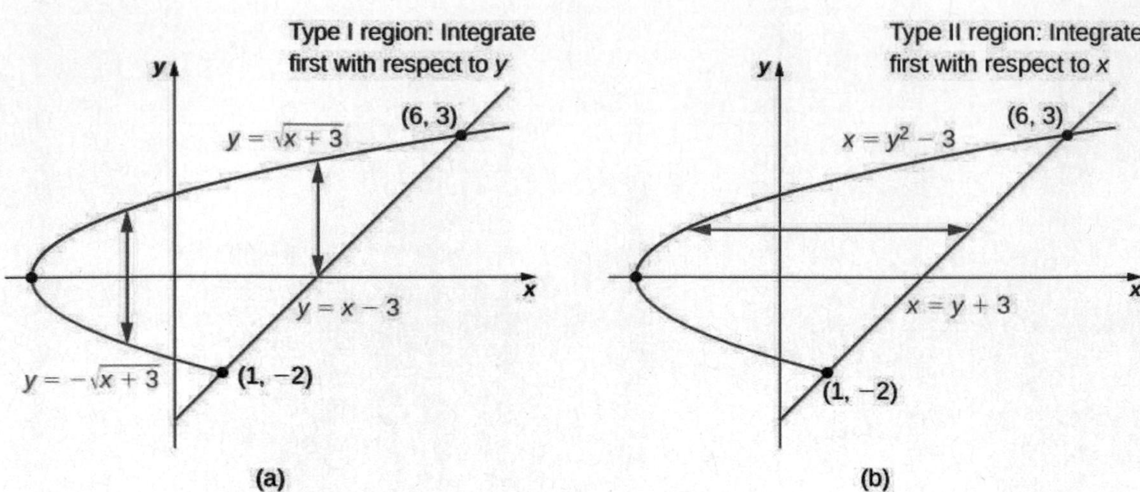

Figure 5.18 The region D in this example can be either (a) Type I or (b) Type II.

Choosing this order of integration, we have

$$\begin{aligned}
\iint_D \left(3x^2 + y^2\right)dA &= \int_{y=-2}^{y=3} \int_{x=y^2-3}^{x=y+3} \left(3x^2 + y^2\right)dx\,dy && \text{Iterated integral, Type II region.} \\
&= \int_{y=-2}^{y=3} \left(x^3 + xy^2\right)\Big|_{y^2-3}^{y+3} dy && \text{Integrate with respect to } x. \\
&= \int_{y=-2}^{y=3} \left((y+3)^3 + (y+3)y^2 - \left(y^2-3\right)^3 - \left(y^2-3\right)y^2\right)dy \\
&= \int_{-2}^{3} \left(54 + 27y - 12y^2 + 2y^3 + 8y^4 - y^6\right)dy && \text{Integrate with respect to } y. \\
&= \left[54y + \frac{27y^2}{2} - 4y^3 + \frac{y^4}{2} + \frac{8y^5}{5} - \frac{y^7}{7}\right]_{-2}^{3} \\
&= \frac{2375}{7}.
\end{aligned}$$

5.8 Sketch the region D and evaluate the iterated integral $\iint_D xy\,dy\,dx$ where D is the region bounded by the curves $y = \cos x$ and $y = \sin x$ in the interval $[-3\pi/4, \pi/4]$.

Recall from **Double Integrals over Rectangular Regions** the properties of double integrals. As we have seen from the examples here, all these properties are also valid for a function defined on a nonrectangular bounded region on a plane. In particular, property 3 states:

If $R = S \cup T$ and $S \cap T = \varnothing$ except at their boundaries, then

$$\iint_R f(x, y)dA = \iint_S f(x, y)dA + \iint_T f(x, y)dA.$$

Similarly, we have the following property of double integrals over a nonrectangular bounded region on a plane.

Theorem 5.5: Decomposing Regions into Smaller Regions

Suppose the region D can be expressed as $D = D_1 \cup D_2$ where D_1 and D_2 do not overlap except at their boundaries. Then

$$\iint_D f(x, y)dA = \iint_{D_1} f(x, y)dA + \iint_{D_2} f(x, y)dA. \quad (5.7)$$

This theorem is particularly useful for nonrectangular regions because it allows us to split a region into a union of regions of Type I and Type II. Then we can compute the double integral on each piece in a convenient way, as in the next example.

Example 5.14

Decomposing Regions

Express the region D shown in **Figure 5.19** as a union of regions of Type I or Type II, and evaluate the integral

$$\iint_D (2x + 5y)dA.$$

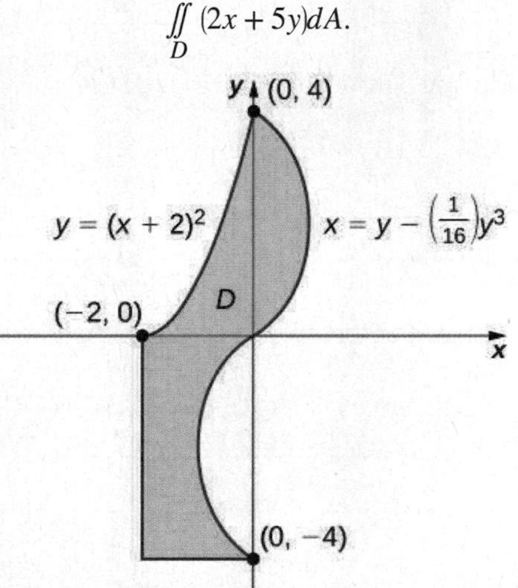

Figure 5.19 This region can be decomposed into a union of three regions of Type I or Type II.

Solution

The region D is not easy to decompose into any one type; it is actually a combination of different types. So we can write it as a union of three regions D_1, D_2, and D_3 where, $D_1 = \left\{(x, y)| - 2 \le x \le 0, 0 \le y \le (x+2)^2\right\}$, $D_2 = \left\{(x, y)|0 \le y \le 4, 0 \le x \le \left(y - \frac{1}{16}y^3\right)\right\}$. These regions are illustrated more clearly in **Figure 5.20**.

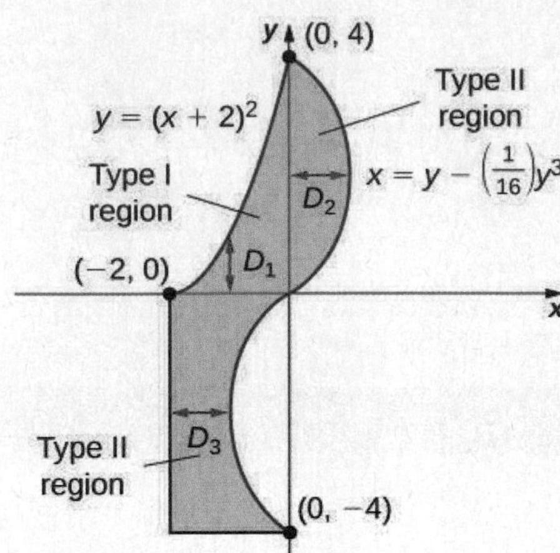

Figure 5.20 Breaking the region into three subregions makes it easier to set up the integration.

Here D_1 is Type I and D_2 and D_3 are both of Type II. Hence,

$$\begin{aligned}
\iint_D (2x+5y)dA &= \iint_{D_1}(2x+5y)dA + \iint_{D_2}(2x+5y)dA + \iint_{D_3}(2x+5y)dA \\
&= \int_{x=-2}^{x=0}\int_{y=0}^{y=(x+2)^2}(2x+5y)dy\,dx + \int_{y=0}^{y=4}\int_{x=0}^{x=y-(1/16)y^3}(2+5y)dx\,dy + \int_{y=-4}^{y=0}\int_{x=-2}^{x=y-(1/16)y^3}(2x+5y)dx\,dy \\
&= \int_{x=-2}^{x=0}\left[\frac{1}{2}(2+x)^2(20+24x+5x^2)\right] + \int_{y=0}^{y=4}\left[\frac{1}{256}y^6 - \frac{7}{16}y^4 + 6y^2\right] \\
&\quad + \int_{y=-4}^{y=0}\left[\frac{1}{256}y^6 - \frac{7}{16}y^4 + 6y^2 + 10y - 4\right] \\
&= \frac{40}{3} + \frac{1664}{35} - \frac{1696}{35} = \frac{1304}{105}.
\end{aligned}$$

Now we could redo this example using a union of two Type II regions (see the Checkpoint).

5.9 Consider the region bounded by the curves $y = \ln x$ and $y = e^x$ in the interval $[1, 2]$. Decompose the region into smaller regions of Type II.

5.10 Redo **Example 5.14** using a union of two Type II regions.

Changing the Order of Integration

As we have already seen when we evaluate an iterated integral, sometimes one order of integration leads to a computation that is significantly simpler than the other order of integration. Sometimes the order of integration does not matter, but it is important to learn to recognize when a change in order will simplify our work.

Example 5.15

Changing the Order of Integration

Reverse the order of integration in the iterated integral $\int_{x=0}^{x=\sqrt{2}} \int_{y=0}^{y=2-x^2} xe^{x^2}\, dy\, dx$. Then evaluate the new iterated integral.

Solution

The region as presented is of Type I. To reverse the order of integration, we must first express the region as Type II. Refer to **Figure 5.21**.

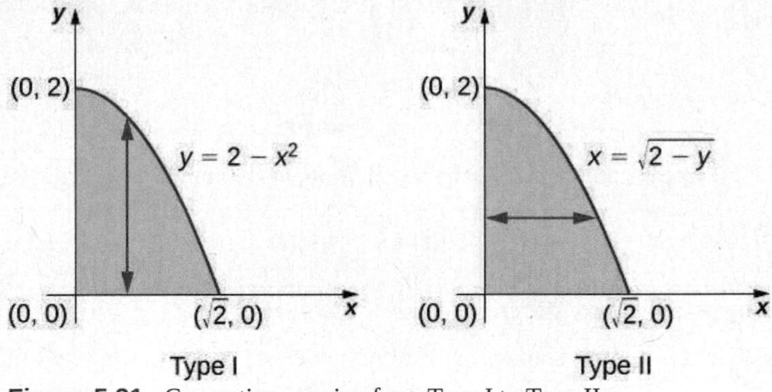

Figure 5.21 Converting a region from Type I to Type II.

We can see from the limits of integration that the region is bounded above by $y = 2 - x^2$ and below by $y = 0$, where x is in the interval $\left[0, \sqrt{2}\right]$. By reversing the order, we have the region bounded on the left by $x = 0$ and on the right by $x = \sqrt{2 - y}$ where y is in the interval $[0, 2]$. We solved $y = 2 - x^2$ in terms of x to obtain $x = \sqrt{2 - y}$.

Hence

$$\int_0^{\sqrt{2}} \int_0^{2-x^2} xe^{x^2}\, dy\, dx = \int_0^2 \int_0^{\sqrt{2-y}} xe^{x^2}\, dx\, dy$$

Reverse the order of integration then use substitution.

$$= \int_0^2 \left[\frac{1}{2} e^{x^2} \Big|_0^{\sqrt{2-y}} \right] dy = \int_0^2 \frac{1}{2}\left(e^{2-y} - 1\right) dy = -\frac{1}{2}\left(e^{2-y} + y\right)\Big|_0^2$$

$$= \frac{1}{2}\left(e^2 - 3\right).$$

Example 5.16

Evaluating an Iterated Integral by Reversing the Order of Integration

Consider the iterated integral $\iint_R f(x, y)dx\, dy$ where $z = f(x, y) = x - 2y$ over a triangular region R that has sides on $x = 0,\ y = 0,$ and the line $x + y = 1$. Sketch the region, and then evaluate the iterated integral by

a. integrating first with respect to y and then

b. integrating first with respect to x.

Solution

A sketch of the region appears in **Figure 5.22**.

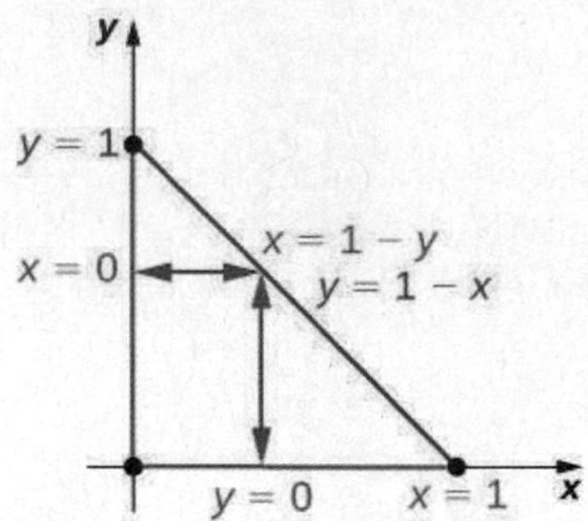

Figure 5.22 A triangular region R for integrating in two ways.

We can complete this integration in two different ways.

a. One way to look at it is by first integrating y from $y = 0$ to $y = 1 - x$ vertically and then integrating x from $x = 0$ to $x = 1$:

$$\begin{aligned}\iint_R f(x, y)dx\,dy &= \int_{x=0}^{x=1}\int_{y=0}^{y=1-x}(x - 2y)dy\,dx = \int_{x=0}^{x=1}\left[xy - 2y^2\right]_{y=0}^{y=1-x}dx \\ &= \int_{x=0}^{x=1}\left[x(1-x) - (1-x)^2\right]dx = \int_{x=0}^{x=1}\left[-1 + 3x - 2x^2\right]dx = \left[-x + \tfrac{3}{2}x^2 - \tfrac{2}{3}x^3\right]_{x=0}^{x=1} = -\tfrac{1}{6}.\end{aligned}$$

b. The other way to do this problem is by first integrating x from $x = 0$ to $x = 1 - y$ horizontally and then integrating y from $y = 0$ to $y = 1$:

$$\begin{aligned}\iint_R f(x, y)dx\,dy &= \int_{y=0}^{y=1}\int_{x=0}^{x=1-y}(x - 2y)dx\,dy = \int_{y=0}^{y=1}\left[\tfrac{1}{2}x^2 - 2xy\right]_{x=0}^{x=1-y}dy \\ &= \int_{y=0}^{y=1}\left[\tfrac{1}{2}(1-y)^2 - 2y(1-y)\right]dy = \int_{y=0}^{y=1}\left[\tfrac{1}{2} - 3y + \tfrac{5}{2}y^2\right]dy \\ &= \left[\tfrac{1}{2}y - \tfrac{3}{2}y^2 + \tfrac{5}{6}y^3\right]_{y=0}^{y=1} = -\tfrac{1}{6}.\end{aligned}$$

5.11 Evaluate the iterated integral $\iint_D \left(x^2 + y^2\right)dA$ over the region D in the first quadrant between the functions $y = 2x$ and $y = x^2$. Evaluate the iterated integral by integrating first with respect to y and then integrating first with resect to x.

Calculating Volumes, Areas, and Average Values

We can use double integrals over general regions to compute volumes, areas, and average values. The methods are the same as those in **Double Integrals over Rectangular Regions**, but without the restriction to a rectangular region, we can now solve a wider variety of problems.

Example 5.17

Finding the Volume of a Tetrahedron

Find the volume of the solid bounded by the planes $x = 0,\ y = 0,\ z = 0,$ and $2x + 3y + z = 6.$

Solution

The solid is a tetrahedron with the base on the xy-plane and a height $z = 6 - 2x - 3y.$ The base is the region D bounded by the lines, $x = 0,\ y = 0$ and $2x + 3y = 6$ where $z = 0$ (**Figure 5.23**). Note that we can consider the region D as Type I or as Type II, and we can integrate in both ways.

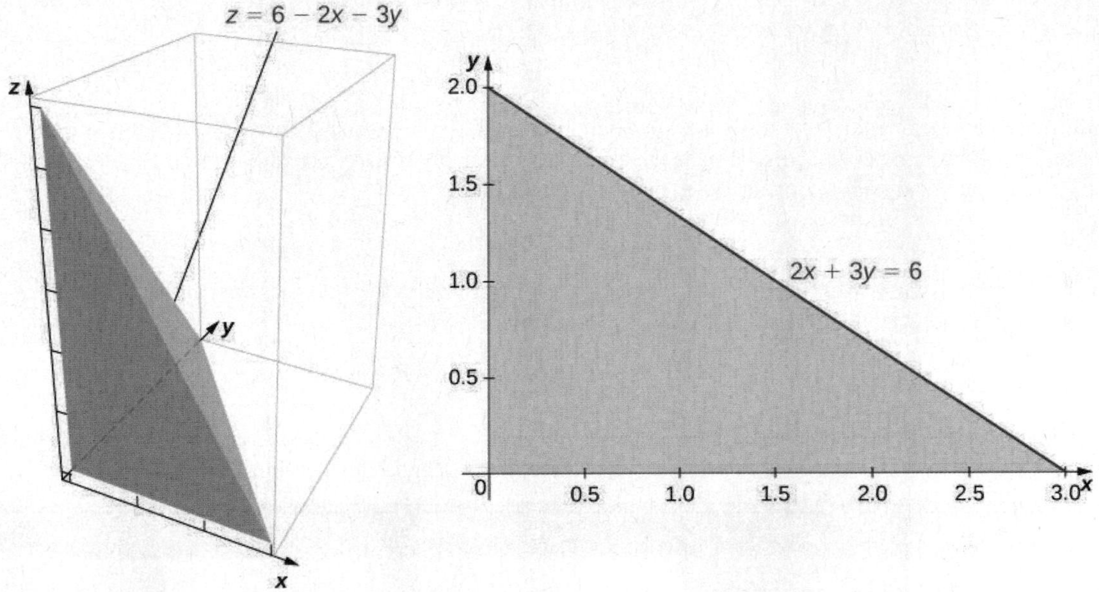

Figure 5.23 A tetrahedron consisting of the three coordinate planes and the plane $z = 6 - 2x - 3y,$ with the base bound by $x = 0,\ y = 0,$ and $2x + 3y = 6.$

First, consider D as a Type I region, and hence $D = \left\{(x,\ y)|0 \le x \le 3,\ 0 \le y \le 2 - \frac{2}{3}x\right\}.$

Therefore, the volume is

$$\begin{aligned} V &= \int_{x=0}^{x=3}\int_{y=0}^{y=2-(2x/3)} (6 - 2x - 3y)\,dy\,dx = \int_{x=0}^{x=3}\left[\left(6y - 2xy - \frac{3}{2}y^2\right)\Big|_{y=0}^{y=2-(2x/3)}\right]dx \\ &= \int_{x=0}^{x=3}\left[\frac{2}{3}(x-3)^2\right]dx = 6. \end{aligned}$$

Now consider D as a Type II region, so $D = \left\{(x,\ y)\middle|0 \le y \le 2,\ 0 \le x \le 3 - \frac{3}{2}y\right\}.$ In this calculation, the volume is

$$V = \int_{y=0}^{y=2} \int_{x=0}^{x=3-(3y/2)} (6 - 2x - 3y)\,dx\,dy = \int_{y=0}^{y=2} \left[\left(6x - x^2 - 3xy\right)\Big|_{x=0}^{x=3-(3y/2)} \right] dy$$
$$= \int_{y=0}^{y=2} \left[\frac{9}{4}(y-2)^2 \right] dy = 6.$$

Therefore, the volume is 6 cubic units.

5.12 Find the volume of the solid bounded above by $f(x, y) = 10 - 2x + y$ over the region enclosed by the curves $y = 0$ and $y = e^x$, where x is in the interval $[0, 1]$.

Finding the area of a rectangular region is easy, but finding the area of a nonrectangular region is not so easy. As we have seen, we can use double integrals to find a rectangular area. As a matter of fact, this comes in very handy for finding the area of a general nonrectangular region, as stated in the next definition.

Definition

The area of a plane-bounded region D is defined as the double integral $\iint_D 1 dA$.

We have already seen how to find areas in terms of single integration. Here we are seeing another way of finding areas by using double integrals, which can be very useful, as we will see in the later sections of this chapter.

Example 5.18

Finding the Area of a Region

Find the area of the region bounded below by the curve $y = x^2$ and above by the line $y = 2x$ in the first quadrant (**Figure 5.24**).

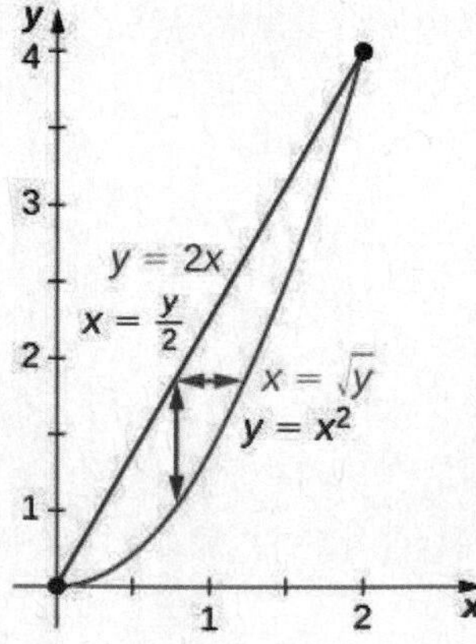

Figure 5.24 The region bounded by $y = x^2$ and $y = 2x$.

Solution

We just have to integrate the constant function $f(x, y) = 1$ over the region. Thus, the area A of the bounded region is $\int_{x=0}^{x=2} \int_{y=x^2}^{y=2x} dy\,dx$ or $\int_{y=0}^{x=4} \int_{x=y/2}^{x=\sqrt{y}} dx\,dy$:

$$A = \iint_D 1dx\,dy = \int_{x=0}^{x=2} \int_{y=x^2}^{y=2x} 1dy\,dx = \int_{x=0}^{x=2} \left[y|_{y=x^2}^{y=2x} \right] dx = \int_{x=0}^{x=2} \left(2x - x^2\right) dx = x^2 - \frac{x^3}{3}\Big|_0^2 = \frac{4}{3}.$$

5.13 Find the area of a region bounded above by the curve $y = x^3$ and below by $y = 0$ over the interval $[0, 3]$.

We can also use a double integral to find the average value of a function over a general region. The definition is a direct extension of the earlier formula.

Definition

If $f(x, y)$ is integrable over a plane-bounded region D with positive area $A(D)$, then the average value of the function is

$$f_{ave} = \frac{1}{A(D)} \iint_D f(x, y)dA.$$

Note that the area is $A(D) = \iint_D 1dA$.

Example 5.19

Finding an Average Value

Find the average value of the function $f(x, y) = 7xy^2$ on the region bounded by the line $x = y$ and the curve $x = \sqrt{y}$ (**Figure 5.25**).

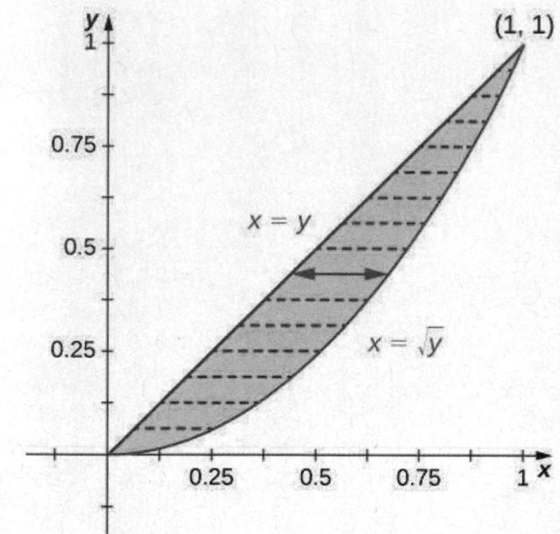

Figure 5.25 The region bounded by $x = y$ and $x = \sqrt{y}$.

Solution

First find the area $A(D)$ where the region D is given by the figure. We have

$$A(D) = \iint_D 1dA = \int_{y=0}^{y=1} \int_{x=y}^{x=\sqrt{y}} 1dx\,dy = \int_{y=0}^{y=1} \left[x\Big|_{x=y}^{x=\sqrt{y}}\right]dy = \int_{y=0}^{y=1} (\sqrt{y} - y)dy = \frac{2}{3}y^{3/2} - \frac{y^2}{2}\Big|_0^1 = \frac{1}{6}.$$

Then the average value of the given function over this region is

$$\begin{aligned} f_{ave} &= \frac{1}{A(D)} \iint_D f(x, y)dA = \frac{1}{A(D)} \int_{y=0}^{y=1} \int_{x=y}^{x=\sqrt{y}} 7xy^2\,dx\,dy = \frac{1}{1/6} \int_{y=0}^{y=1} \left[\frac{7}{2}x^2 y^2\Big|_{x=y}^{x=\sqrt{y}}\right]dy \\ &= 6 \int_{y=0}^{y=1} \left[\frac{7}{2}y^2\left(y - y^2\right)\right]dy = 6 \int_{y=0}^{y=1} \left[\frac{7}{2}\left(y^3 - y^4\right)\right]dy = \frac{42}{2}\left(\frac{y^4}{4} - \frac{y^5}{5}\right)\Big|_0^1 = \frac{42}{40} = \frac{21}{20}. \end{aligned}$$

5.14 Find the average value of the function $f(x, y) = xy$ over the triangle with vertices $(0, 0)$, $(1, 0)$ and $(1, 3)$.

Improper Double Integrals

An **improper double integral** is an integral $\iint_D f\,dA$ where either D is an unbounded region or f is an unbounded function. For example, $D = \{(x, y) \mid |x - y| \geq 2\}$ is an unbounded region, and the function $f(x, y) = 1/\left(1 - x^2 - 2y^2\right)$ over the ellipse $x^2 + 3y^2 \leq 1$ is an unbounded function. Hence, both of the following integrals are improper integrals:

i. $\iint_D xy\,dA$ where $D = \{(x, y) \mid |x - y| \geq 2\}$;

ii. $\iint_D \frac{1}{1 - x^2 - 2y^2}dA$ where $D = \left\{(x, y) \mid x^2 + 3y^2 \leq 1\right\}$.

In this section we would like to deal with improper integrals of functions over rectangles or simple regions such that f has only finitely many discontinuities. Not all such improper integrals can be evaluated; however, a form of Fubini's theorem does apply for some types of improper integrals.

Theorem 5.6: Fubini's Theorem for Improper Integrals

If D is a bounded rectangle or simple region in the plane defined by $\{(x, y): a \le x \le b, g(x) \le y \le h(x)\}$ and also by $\{(x, y): c \le y \le d, j(y) \le x \le k(y)\}$ and f is a nonnegative function on D with finitely many discontinuities in the interior of D, then

$$\iint_D f\,dA = \int_{x=a}^{x=b} \int_{y=g(x)}^{y=h(x)} f(x, y)dy\,dx = \int_{y=c}^{y=d} \int_{x=j(y)}^{x=k(y)} f(x, y)dx\,dy.$$

It is very important to note that we required that the function be nonnegative on D for the theorem to work. We consider only the case where the function has finitely many discontinuities inside D.

Example 5.20

Evaluating a Double Improper Integral

Consider the function $f(x, y) = \frac{e^y}{y}$ over the region $D = \{(x, y): 0 \le x \le 1, x \le y \le \sqrt{x}\}$.

Notice that the function is nonnegative and continuous at all points on D except $(0, 0)$. Use Fubini's theorem to evaluate the improper integral.

Solution

First we plot the region D (**Figure 5.26**); then we express it in another way.

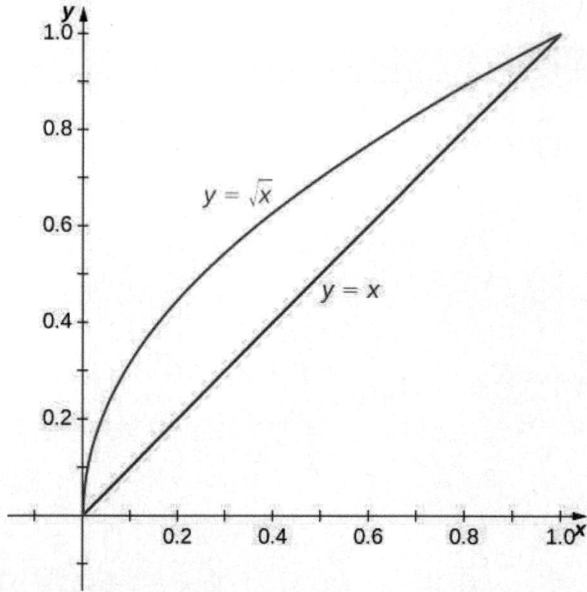

Figure 5.26 The function f is continuous at all points of the region D except $(0, 0)$.

The other way to express the same region D is

$$D = \{(x, y): 0 \le y \le 1, y^2 \le x \le y\}.$$

Thus we can use Fubini's theorem for improper integrals and evaluate the integral as

$$\int_{y=0}^{y=1} \int_{x=y^2}^{x=y} \frac{e^y}{y} dx\, dy.$$

Therefore, we have

$$\int_{y=0}^{y=1} \int_{x=y^2}^{x=y} \frac{e^y}{y} dx\, dy = \int_{y=0}^{y=1} \frac{e^y}{y} x \Big|_{x=y^2}^{x=y} dy = \int_{y=0}^{y=1} \frac{ey}{y}\left(y - y^2\right) dy = \int_0^1 \left(ey - ye^y\right) dy = e - 2.$$

As mentioned before, we also have an improper integral if the region of integration is unbounded. Suppose now that the function f is continuous in an unbounded rectangle R.

Theorem 5.7: Improper Integrals on an Unbounded Region

If R is an unbounded rectangle such as $R = \{(x, y): a \le x \le \infty, c \le y \le \infty\}$, then when the limit exists, we have

$$\iint_R f(x, y)dA = \lim_{(b, d) \to (\infty, \infty)} \int_a^b \left(\int_c^d f(x, y) dy \right) dx = \lim_{(b, d) \to (\infty, \infty)} \int_c^d \left(\int_a^b f(x, y) dy \right) dy.$$

The following example shows how this theorem can be used in certain cases of improper integrals.

Example 5.21

Evaluating a Double Improper Integral

Evaluate the integral $\iint_R xye^{-x^2 - y^2} dA$ where R is the first quadrant of the plane.

Solution

The region R is the first quadrant of the plane, which is unbounded. So

$$\begin{aligned}\iint_R xye^{-x^2 - y^2} dA &= \lim_{(b, d) \to (\infty, \infty)} \int_{x=0}^{x=b} \left(\int_{y=0}^{y=d} xye^{-x^2 - y^2} dy \right) dx = \lim_{(b, d) \to (\infty, \infty)} \int_{y=0}^{y=d} \left(\int_{x=0}^{x=b} xye^{-x^2 - y^2} dy \right) dy \\ &= \lim_{(b, d) \to (\infty, \infty)} \frac{1}{4}\left(1 - e^{-b^2}\right)\left(1 - e^{-d^2}\right) = \frac{1}{4}\end{aligned}$$

Thus, $\iint_R xye^{-x^2 - y^2} dA$ is convergent and the value is $\frac{1}{4}$.

5.15 Evaluate the improper integral $\iint_D \frac{y}{\sqrt{1 - x^2 - y^2}} dA$ where $D = \left\{(x, y)x \ge 0, y \ge 0, x^2 + y^2 \le 1\right\}$.

In some situations in probability theory, we can gain insight into a problem when we are able to use double integrals over general regions. Before we go over an example with a double integral, we need to set a few definitions and become familiar with some important properties.

Definition

Consider a pair of continuous random variables X and Y, such as the birthdays of two people or the number of sunny and rainy days in a month. The joint density function f of X and Y satisfies the probability that (X, Y) lies in a certain region D:

$$P((X, Y) \in D) = \iint_D f(x, y)dA.$$

Since the probabilities can never be negative and must lie between 0 and 1, the joint density function satisfies the following inequality and equation:

$$f(x, y) \geq 0 \text{ and } \iint_{R^2} f(x, y)dA = 1.$$

Definition

The variables X and Y are said to be independent random variables if their joint density function is the product of their individual density functions:

$$f(x, y) = f_1(x)f_2(y).$$

Example 5.22

Application to Probability

At Sydney's Restaurant, customers must wait an average of 15 minutes for a table. From the time they are seated until they have finished their meal requires an additional 40 minutes, on average. What is the probability that a customer spends less than an hour and a half at the diner, assuming that waiting for a table and completing the meal are independent events?

Solution

Waiting times are mathematically modeled by exponential density functions, with m being the average waiting time, as

$$f(t) = \begin{cases} 0 & \text{if } t < 0, \\ \frac{1}{m}e^{-t/m} & \text{if } t \geq 0. \end{cases}$$

If X and Y are random variables for 'waiting for a table' and 'completing the meal,' then the probability density functions are, respectively,

$$f_1(x) = \begin{cases} 0 & \text{if } x < 0, \\ \frac{1}{15}e^{-x/15} & \text{if } x \geq 0. \end{cases} \text{ and } f_2(y) = \begin{cases} 0 & \text{if } y < 0, \\ \frac{1}{40}e^{-y/40} & \text{if } y \geq 0. \end{cases}$$

Clearly, the events are independent and hence the joint density function is the product of the individual functions

$$f(x, y) = f_1(x)f_2(y) = \begin{cases} 0 & \text{if } x < 0 \text{ or } y < 0, \\ \frac{1}{600}e^{-x/15}e^{-y/60} & \text{if } x, y \geq 0. \end{cases}$$

We want to find the probability that the combined time $X+Y$ is less than 90 minutes. In terms of geometry, it means that the region D is in the first quadrant bounded by the line $x+y=90$ (**Figure 5.27**).

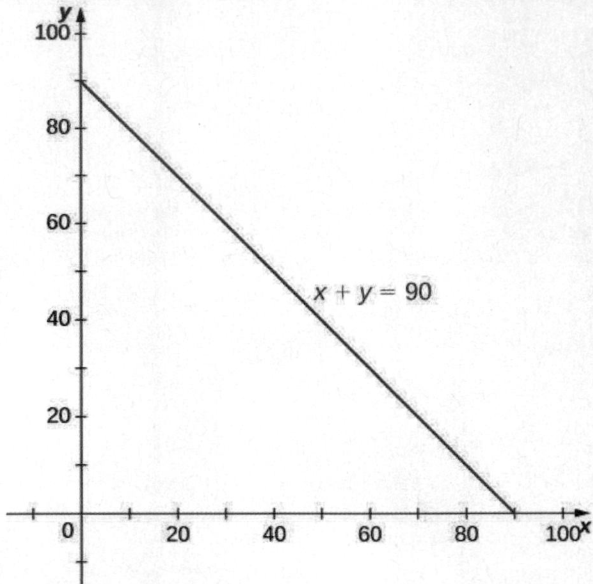

Figure 5.27 The region of integration for a joint probability density function.

Hence, the probability that (X, Y) is in the region D is

$$P(X+Y \le 90) = P((X, Y) \in D) = \iint_D f(x, y)dA = \iint_D \frac{1}{600}e^{-x/15}e^{-y/40}dA.$$

Since $x+y=90$ is the same as $y=90-x$, we have a region of Type I, so

$$\begin{aligned} D &= \{(x, y)|0 \le x \le 90, 0 \le y \le 90-x\}, \\ P(X+Y \le 90) &= \frac{1}{600}\int_{x=0}^{x=90}\int_{y=0}^{y=90-x} e^{-x/15}e^{-y/40}dx\,dy = \frac{1}{600}\int_{x=0}^{x=90}\int_{y=0}^{y=90-x} e^{-x/15}e^{-y/40}dx\,dy \\ &= \frac{1}{600}\int_{x=0}^{x=90}\int_{y=0}^{y=90-x} e^{-(x/15+y/40)}dx\,dy = 0.8328. \end{aligned}$$

Thus, there is an 83.2% chance that a customer spends less than an hour and a half at the restaurant.

Another important application in probability that can involve improper double integrals is the calculation of expected values. First we define this concept and then show an example of a calculation.

Definition

In probability theory, we denote the expected values $E(X)$ and $E(Y)$, respectively, as the most likely outcomes of the events. The expected values $E(X)$ and $E(Y)$ are given by

$$E(X) = \iint_S xf(x, y)dA \text{ and } E(Y) = \iint_S yf(x, y)dA,$$

where S is the sample space of the random variables X and Y.

Example 5.23

Finding Expected Value

Find the expected time for the events 'waiting for a table' and 'completing the meal' in **Example 5.22**.

Solution

Using the first quadrant of the rectangular coordinate plane as the sample space, we have improper integrals for $E(X)$ and $E(Y)$. The expected time for a table is

$$\begin{aligned}
E(X) &= \iint_S x\frac{1}{600}e^{-x/15}e^{-y/40}\,dA = \frac{1}{600}\int_{x=0}^{x=\infty}\int_{y=0}^{y=\infty} xe^{-x/15}e^{-y/40}\,dA \\
&= \frac{1}{600}\lim_{(a,\,b)\to(\infty,\,\infty)}\int_{x=0}^{x=a}\int_{y=0}^{y=b} xe^{-x/15}e^{-y/40}\,dx\,dy \\
&= \frac{1}{600}\left(\lim_{a\to\infty}\int_{x=0}^{x=a} xe^{-x/15}\,dx\right)\left(\lim_{b\to\infty}\int_{y=0}^{y=b} e^{-y/40}\,dy\right) \\
&= \frac{1}{600}\left(\left(\lim_{a\to\infty}\left(-15e^{-x/15}(x+15)\right)\right)\Big|_{x=0}^{x=a}\right)\left(\left(\lim_{b\to\infty}\left(-40e^{-y/40}\right)\right)\Big|_{y=0}^{y=b}\right) \\
&= \frac{1}{600}\left(\lim_{a\to\infty}\left(-15e^{-a/15}(x+15)+225\right)\right)\left(\lim_{b\to\infty}\left(-40e^{-b/40}+40\right)\right) \\
&= \frac{1}{600}(225)(40) \\
&= 15.
\end{aligned}$$

A similar calculation shows that $E(Y) = 40$. This means that the expected values of the two random events are the average waiting time and the average dining time, respectively.

5.16 The joint density function for two random variables X and Y is given by

$$f(x,\,y) = \begin{cases} \frac{1}{600}\left(x^2+y^2\right) & \text{if } 0 \le x \le 15,\ 0 \le y \le 10 \\ 0 & \text{otherwise} \end{cases}$$

Find the probability that X is at most 10 and Y is at least 5.

5.2 EXERCISES

In the following exercises, specify whether the region is of Type I or Type II.

60. The region D bounded by $y = x^3$, $y = x^3 + 1$, $x = 0$, and $x = 1$ as given in the following figure.

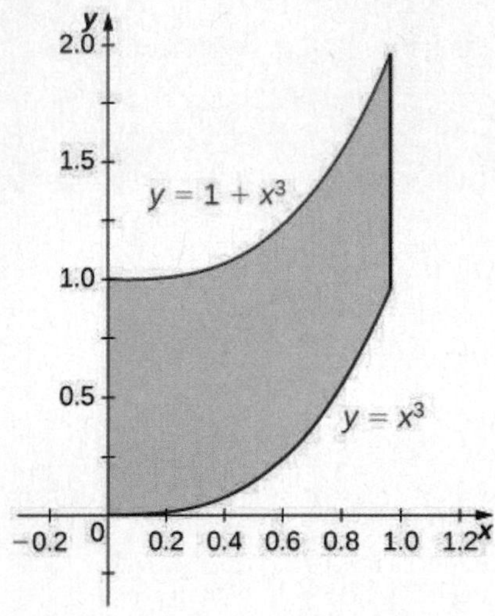

61. Find the average value of the function $f(x, y) = 3xy$ on the region graphed in the previous exercise.

62. Find the area of the region D given in the previous exercise.

63. The region D bounded by $y = \sin x$, $y = 1 + \sin x$, $x = 0$, and $x = \frac{\pi}{2}$ as given in the following figure.

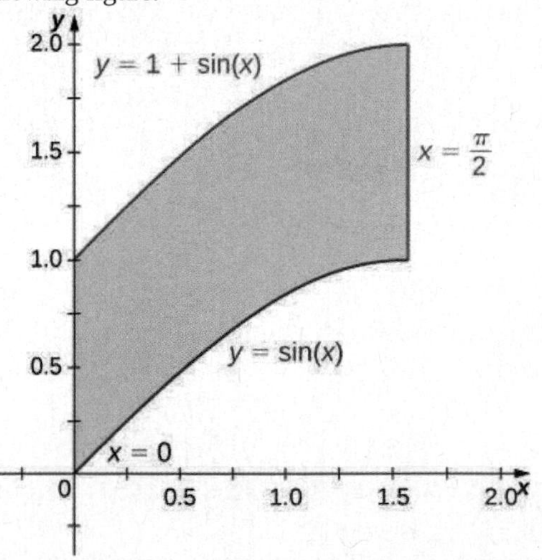

64. Find the average value of the function $f(x, y) = \cos x$ on the region graphed in the previous exercise.

65. Find the area of the region D given in the previous exercise.

66. The region D bounded by $x = y^2 - 1$ and $x = \sqrt{1 - y^2}$ as given in the following figure.

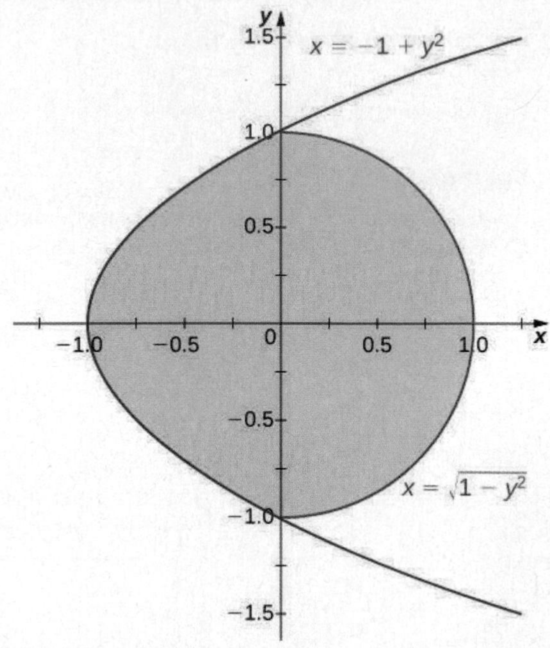

67. Find the volume of the solid under the graph of the function $f(x, y) = xy + 1$ and above the region in the figure in the previous exercise.

68. The region D bounded by $y = 0$, $x = -10 + y$, and $x = 10 - y$ as given in the following figure.

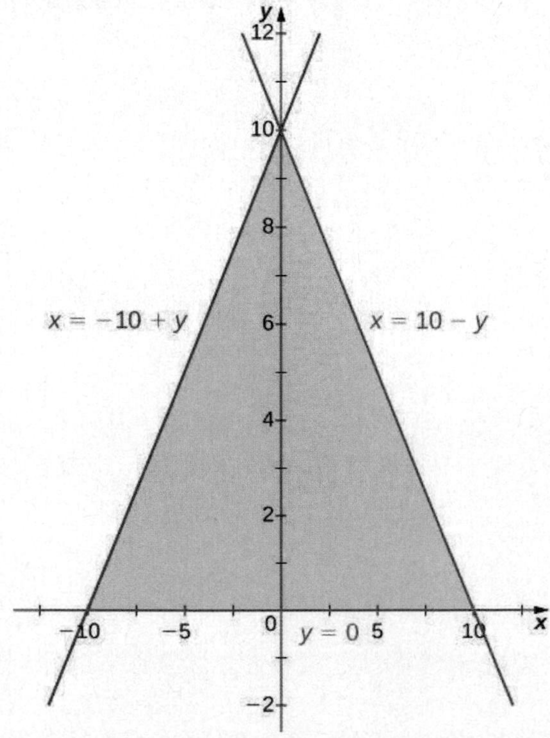

69. Find the volume of the solid under the graph of the function $f(x, y) = x + y$ and above the region in the figure from the previous exercise.

70. The region D bounded by $y = 0,\ x = y - 1,\ x = \frac{\pi}{2}$ as given in the following figure.

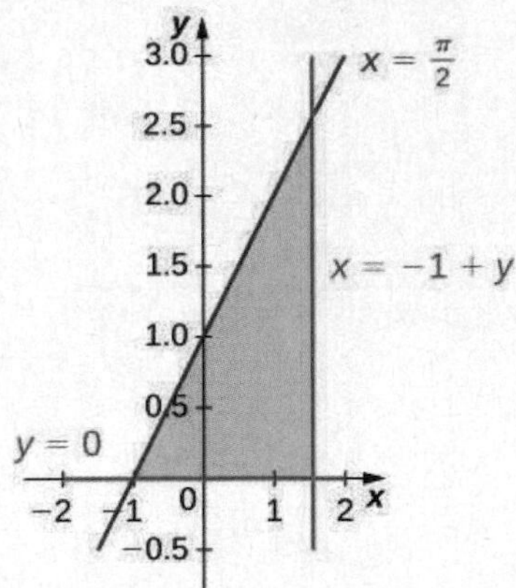

71. The region D bounded by $y = 0$ and $y = x^2 - 1$ as given in the following figure.

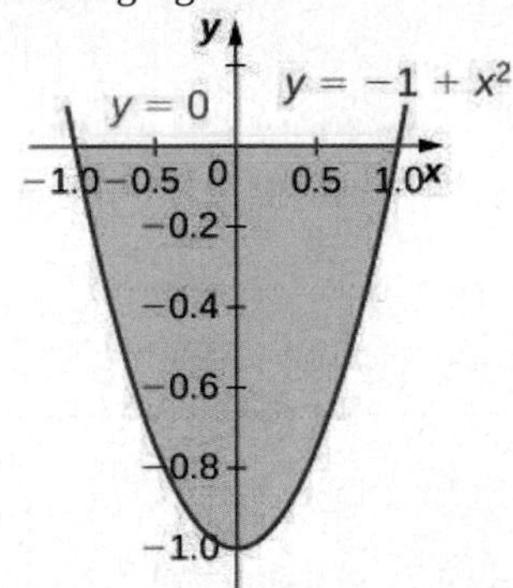

72. Let D be the region bounded by the curves of equations $y = x,\ y = -x,$ and $y = 2 - x^2$. Explain why D is neither of Type I nor II.

73. Let D be the region bounded by the curves of equations $y = \cos x$ and $y = 4 - x^2$ and the x-axis. Explain why D is neither of Type I nor II.

In the following exercises, evaluate the double integral $\iint_D f(x, y)dA$ over the region D.

74. $f(x, y) = 2x + 5y$ and $D = \left\{(x, y)|0 \le x \le 1,\ x^3 \le y \le x^3 + 1\right\}$

75. $f(x, y) = 1$ and $D = \left\{(x, y)|0 \le x \le \frac{\pi}{2},\ \sin x \le y \le 1 + \sin x\right\}$

76. $f(x, y) = 2$ and $D = \{(x, y)|0 \le y \le 1,\ y - 1 \le x \le \arccos y\}$

77. $f(x, y) = xy$ and $D = \left\{(x, y)| -1 \le y \le 1,\ y^2 - 1 \le x \le \sqrt{1 - y^2}\right\}$

78. $f(x, y) = \sin y$ and D is the triangular region with vertices $(0, 0),\ (0, 3),$ and $(3, 0)$

79. $f(x, y) = -x + 1$ and D is the triangular region with vertices $(0, 0),\ (0, 2),$ and $(2, 2)$

Evaluate the iterated integrals.

80. $\displaystyle\int_0^1 \int_{2x}^{3x} \left(x + y^2\right)dy\, dx$

81. $\displaystyle\int_0^1 \int_{2\sqrt{x}}^{2\sqrt{x}+1} (xy + 1)dy\, dx$

82. $\displaystyle\int_e^{e^2} \int_{\ln u}^{2} (v + \ln u)dv\, du$

83. $\displaystyle\int_1^2 \int_{-u^2-1}^{-u} (8uv)dv\, du$

84. $\displaystyle\int_0^1 \int_{-\sqrt{1-y^2}}^{\sqrt{1-y^2}} \left(2x + 4x^3\right)dx\, dy$

85. $\displaystyle\int_0^{1/2} \int_{-\sqrt{1-4y^2}}^{\sqrt{1-4y^2}} 4dx\, dy$

86. Let D be the region bounded by $y = 1 - x^2,\ y = 4 - x^2,$ and the x- and y-axes.

a. Show that $\displaystyle\iint_D x\, dA = \int_0^1 \int_{1-x^2}^{4-x^2} x\, dy\, dx + \int_1^2 \int_0^{4-x^2} x\, dy\, dx$ by dividing the region D into two regions of Type I.

b. Evaluate the integral $\iint_D x\, dA$.

87. Let D be the region bounded by $y = 1,\ y = x,\ y = \ln x,$ and the x-axis.

a. Show that $\iint\limits_D y\,dA = \int_0^1 \int_0^x y\,dy\,dx + \int_1^e \int_{\ln x}^1 y\,dy\,dx$ by dividing D into two regions of Type I.

b. Evaluate the integral $\iint\limits_D y\,dA.$

88.

a. Show that $\iint\limits_D y^2\,dA = \int_{-1}^0 \int_{-x}^{2-x^2} y^2\,dy\,dx + \int_0^1 \int_x^{2-x^2} y^2\,dy\,dx$ by dividing the region D into two regions of Type I, where $D = \{(x, y)|y \geq x, y \geq -x, y \leq 2 - x^2\}.$

b. Evaluate the integral $\iint\limits_D y^2 dA.$

89. Let D be the region bounded by $y = x^2,\ y = x + 2,$ and $y = -x.$

a. Show that $\iint\limits_D x\,dA = \int_0^1 \int_{-y}^{\sqrt{y}} x\,dx\,dy + \int_1^2 \int_{y-2}^{\sqrt{y}} x\,dx\,dy$ by dividing the region D into two regions of Type II, where $D = \{(x, y)|y \geq x^2, y \geq -x, y \leq x + 2\}.$

b. Evaluate the integral $\iint\limits_D x\,dA.$

90. The region D bounded by $x = 0,\ y = x^5 + 1,$ and $y = 3 - x^2$ is shown in the following figure. Find the area $A(D)$ of the region $D.$

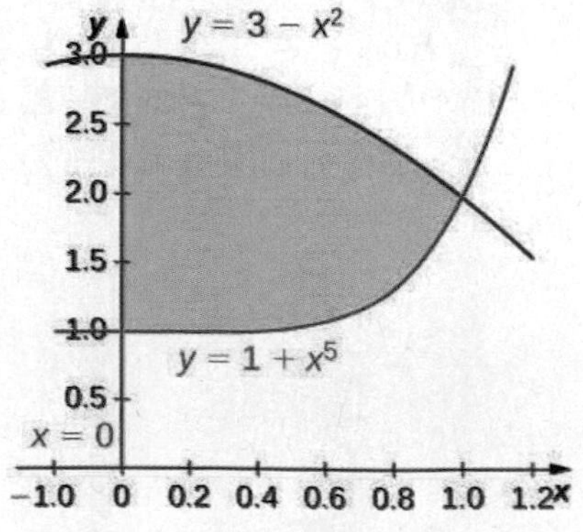

91. The region D bounded by $y = \cos x,\ y = 4\cos x,$ and $x = \pm\frac{\pi}{3}$ is shown in the following figure. Find the area $A(D)$ of the region $D.$

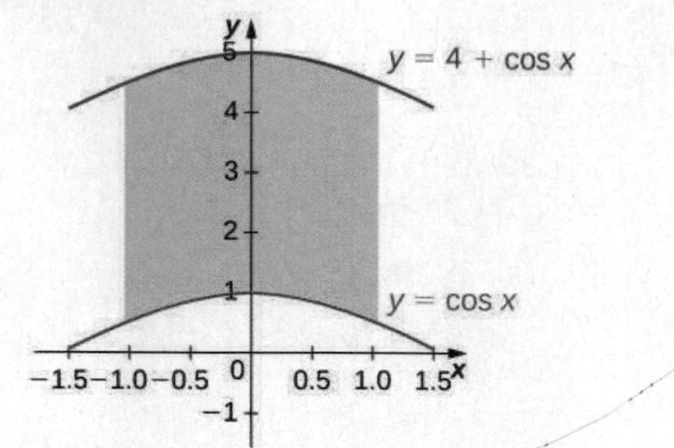

92. Find the area $A(D)$ of the region $D = \{(x, y)|y \geq 1 - x^2, y \leq 4 - x^2, y \geq 0, x \geq 0\}.$

93. Let D be the region bounded by $y = 1,\ y = x,\ y = \ln x,$ and the x-axis. Find the area $A(D)$ of the region $D.$

94. Find the average value of the function $f(x, y) = \sin y$ on the triangular region with vertices $(0, 0),\ (0, 3),$ and $(3, 0).$

95. Find the average value of the function $f(x, y) = -x + 1$ on the triangular region with vertices $(0, 0),\ (0, 2),$ and $(2, 2).$

In the following exercises, change the order of integration and evaluate the integral.

96. $\int_{-1}^{\pi/2} \int_0^{x+1} \sin x\,dy\,dx$

97. $\int_0^1 \int_{x-1}^{1-x} x\,dy\,dx$

98. $\int_{-1}^0 \int_{-\sqrt{y+1}}^{\sqrt{y+1}} y^2\,dx\,dy$

99. $\int_{-1/2}^{1/2} \int_{-\sqrt{y^2+1}}^{\sqrt{y^2+1}} y\,dx\,dy$

100. The region D is shown in the following figure. Evaluate the double integral $\iint\limits_D (x^2 + y)dA$ by using the easier order of integration.

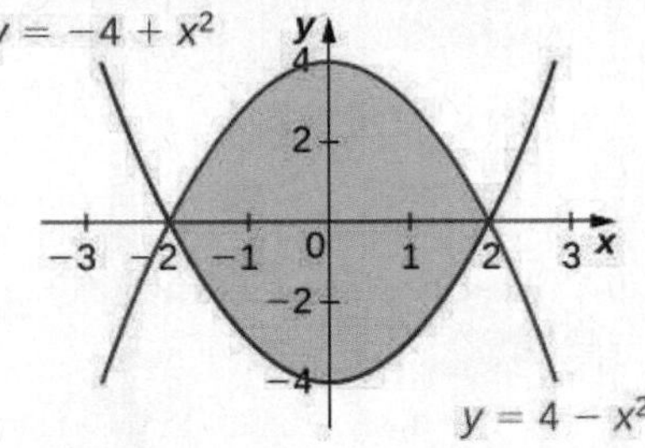

101. The region D is given in the following figure. Evaluate the double integral $\iint\limits_D (x^2 - y^2)dA$ by using the easier order of integration.

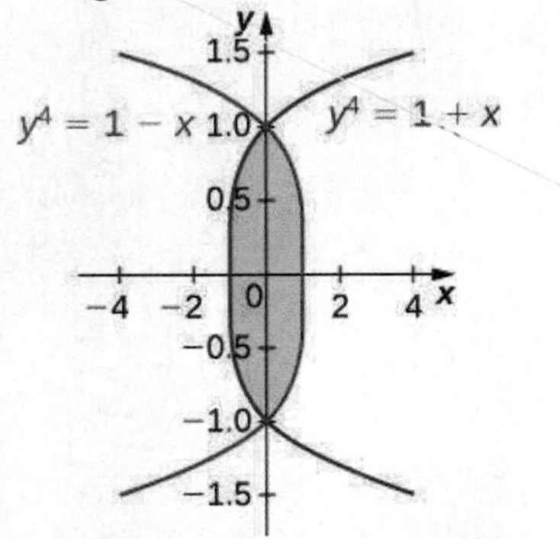

102. Find the volume of the solid under the surface $z = 2x + y^2$ and above the region bounded by $y = x^5$ and $y = x$.

103. Find the volume of the solid under the plane $z = 3x + y$ and above the region determined by $y = x^7$ and $y = x$.

104. Find the volume of the solid under the plane $z = x - y$ and above the region bounded by $x = \tan y$, $x = -\tan y$, and $x = 1$.

105. Find the volume of the solid under the surface $z = x^3$ and above the plane region bounded by $x = \sin y$, $x = -\sin y$, and $x = 1$.

106. Let g be a positive, increasing, and differentiable function on the interval $[a, b]$. Show that the volume of the solid under the surface $z = g'(x)$ and above the region bounded by $y = 0$, $y = g(x)$, $x = a$, and $x = b$ is given by $\frac{1}{2}\left(g^2(b) - g^2(a)\right)$.

107. Let g be a positive, increasing, and differentiable function on the interval $[a, b]$, and let k be a positive real number. Show that the volume of the solid under the surface $z = g'(x)$ and above the region bounded by $y = g(x)$, $y = g(x) + k$, $x = a$, and $x = b$ is given by $k(g(b) - g(a))$.

108. Find the volume of the solid situated in the first octant and determined by the planes $z = 2$, $z = 0$, $x + y = 1$, $x = 0$, and $y = 0$.

109. Find the volume of the solid situated in the first octant and bounded by the planes $x + 2y = 1$, $x = 0$, $y = 0$, $z = 4$, and $z = 0$.

110. Find the volume of the solid bounded by the planes $x + y = 1$, $x - y = 1$, $x = 0$, $z = 0$, and $z = 10$.

111. Find the volume of the solid bounded by the planes $x + y = 1$, $x - y = 1$, $x + y = -1$, $x - y = -1$, $z = 1$ and $z = 0$.

112. Let S_1 and S_2 be the solids situated in the first octant under the planes $x + y + z = 1$ and $x + y + 2z = 1$, respectively, and let S be the solid situated between S_1, S_2, $x = 0$, and $y = 0$.

a. Find the volume of the solid S_1.
b. Find the volume of the solid S_2.
c. Find the volume of the solid S by subtracting the volumes of the solids S_1 and S_2.

113. Let S_1 and S_2 be the solids situated in the first octant under the planes $2x + 2y + z = 2$ and $x + y + z = 1$, respectively, and let S be the solid situated between S_1, S_2, $x = 0$, and $y = 0$.

a. Find the volume of the solid S_1.
b. Find the volume of the solid S_2.
c. Find the volume of the solid S by subtracting the volumes of the solids S_1 and S_2.

114. Let S_1 and S_2 be the solids situated in the first octant under the plane $x + y + z = 2$ and under the sphere $x^2 + y^2 + z^2 = 4$, respectively. If the volume of the solid S_2 is $\frac{4\pi}{3}$, determine the volume of the solid S situated between S_1 and S_2 by subtracting the volumes of these solids.

115. Let S_1 and S_2 be the solids situated in the first octant under the plane $x + y + z = 2$ and bounded by the cylinder $x^2 + y^2 = 4,$ respectively.

a. Find the volume of the solid S_1.
b. Find the volume of the solid S_2.
c. Find the volume of the solid S situated between S_1 and S_2 by subtracting the volumes of the solids S_1 and S_2.

116. **[T]** The following figure shows the region D bounded by the curves $y = \sin x,$ $x = 0,$ and $y = x^4$. Use a graphing calculator or CAS to find the x-coordinates of the intersection points of the curves and to determine the area of the region D. Round your answers to six decimal places.

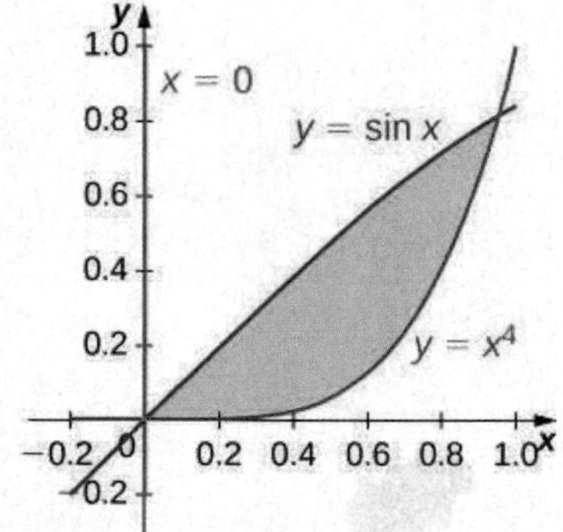

117. **[T]** The region D bounded by the curves $y = \cos x,$ $x = 0,$ and $y = x^3$ is shown in the following figure. Use a graphing calculator or CAS to find the x-coordinates of the intersection points of the curves and to determine the area of the region D. Round your answers to six decimal places.

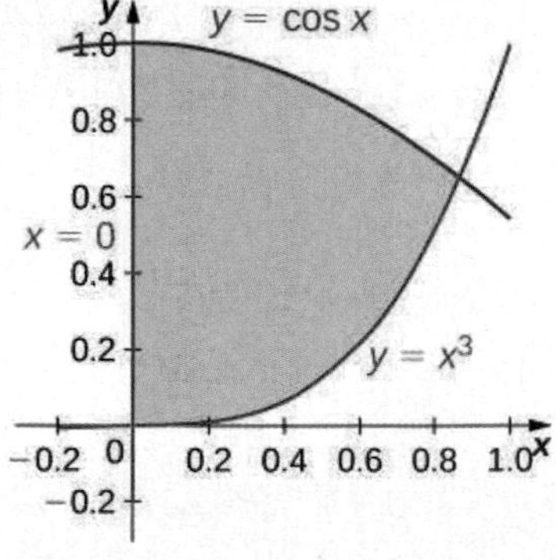

118. Suppose that (X, Y) is the outcome of an experiment that must occur in a particular region S in the xy-plane. In this context, the region S is called the sample space of the experiment and X and Y are random variables. If D is a region included in $S,$ then the probability of (X, Y) being in D is defined as $P[(X, Y) \in D] = \iint_D p(x, y)dx\,dy,$ where $p(x, y)$ is the joint probability density of the experiment. Here, $p(x, y)$ is a nonnegative function for which $\iint_S p(x, y)dx\,dy = 1$. Assume that a point (X, Y) is chosen arbitrarily in the square $[0, 3] \times [0, 3]$ with the probability density $p(x, y) = \begin{cases} \frac{1}{9} & (x, y) \in [0, 3] \times [0, 3], \\ 0 & \text{otherwise.} \end{cases}$ Find the probability that the point (X, Y) is inside the unit square and interpret the result.

119. Consider X and Y two random variables of probability densities $p_1(x)$ and $p_2(x),$ respectively. The random variables X and Y are said to be independent if their joint density function is given by $p(x, y) = p_1(x)p_2(y)$. At a drive-thru restaurant, customers spend, on average, 3 minutes placing their orders and an additional 5 minutes paying for and picking up their meals. Assume that placing the order and paying for/picking up the meal are two independent events X and Y. If the waiting times are modeled by the exponential probability densities

$$p_1(x) = \begin{cases} \frac{1}{3}e^{-x/3} & x \geq 0, \\ 0 & \text{otherwise,} \end{cases} \quad \text{and} \quad p_2(y) = \begin{cases} \frac{1}{5}e^{-y/5} & y \geq 0, \\ 0 & \text{otherwise,} \end{cases}$$

respectively, the probability that a customer will spend less than 6 minutes in the drive-thru line is given by $P[X + Y \leq 6] = \iint_D p(x, y)dx\,dy,$ where $D = \{(x, y)|x \geq 0, y \geq 0, x + y \leq 6\}$. Find $P[X + Y \leq 6]$ and interpret the result.

120. **[T]** The Reuleaux triangle consists of an equilateral triangle and three regions, each of them bounded by a side of the triangle and an arc of a circle of radius s centered at the opposite vertex of the triangle. Show that the area of the Reuleaux triangle in the following figure of side length s is $\frac{s^2}{2}(\pi - \sqrt{3})$.

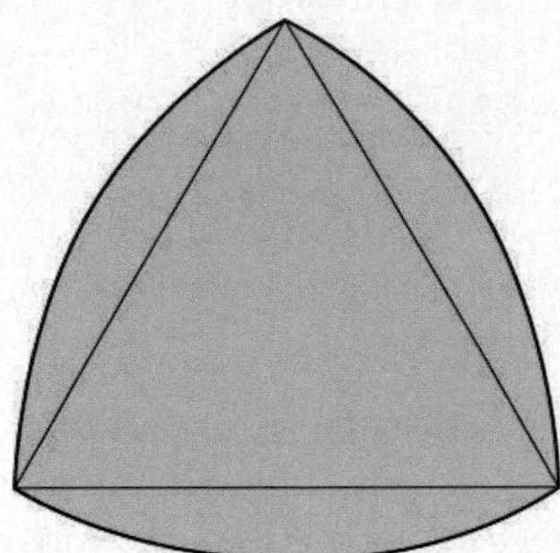

121. **[T]** Show that the area of the lunes of Alhazen, the two blue lunes in the following figure, is the same as the area of the right triangle ABC. The outer boundaries of the lunes are semicircles of diameters AB and AC, respectively, and the inner boundaries are formed by the circumcircle of the triangle ABC.

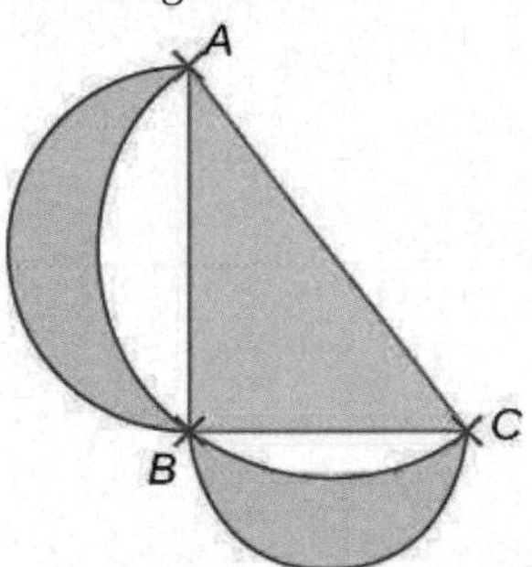

5.3 | Double Integrals in Polar Coordinates

Learning Objectives

- **5.3.1** Recognize the format of a double integral over a polar rectangular region.
- **5.3.2** Evaluate a double integral in polar coordinates by using an iterated integral.
- **5.3.3** Recognize the format of a double integral over a general polar region.
- **5.3.4** Use double integrals in polar coordinates to calculate areas and volumes.

Double integrals are sometimes much easier to evaluate if we change rectangular coordinates to polar coordinates. However, before we describe how to make this change, we need to establish the concept of a double integral in a polar rectangular region.

Polar Rectangular Regions of Integration

When we defined the double integral for a continuous function in rectangular coordinates—say, g over a region R in the xy-plane—we divided R into subrectangles with sides parallel to the coordinate axes. These sides have either constant x-values and/or constant y-values. In polar coordinates, the shape we work with is a **polar rectangle**, whose sides have constant r-values and/or constant θ-values. This means we can describe a polar rectangle as in **Figure 5.28**(a), with $R = \{(r, \theta) | a \le r \le b, \alpha \le \theta \le \beta\}$.

In this section, we are looking to integrate over polar rectangles. Consider a function $f(r, \theta)$ over a polar rectangle R. We divide the interval $[a, b]$ into m subintervals $[r_{i-1}, r_i]$ of length $\Delta r = (b - a)/m$ and divide the interval $[\alpha, \beta]$ into n subintervals $[\theta_{i-1}, \theta_i]$ of width $\Delta\theta = (\beta - \alpha)/n$. This means that the circles $r = r_i$ and rays $\theta = \theta_i$ for $1 \le i \le m$ and $1 \le j \le n$ divide the polar rectangle R into smaller polar subrectangles R_{ij} (**Figure 5.28**(b)).

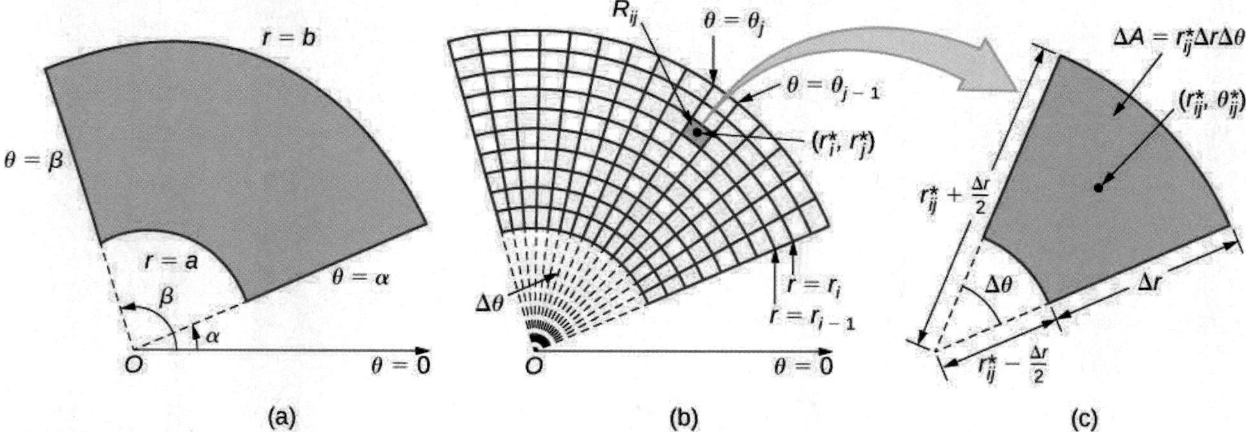

Figure 5.28 (a) A polar rectangle R (b) divided into subrectangles R_{ij}. (c) Close-up of a subrectangle.

As before, we need to find the area ΔA of the polar subrectangle R_{ij} and the "polar" volume of the thin box above R_{ij}. Recall that, in a circle of radius r, the length s of an arc subtended by a central angle of θ radians is $s = r\theta$. Notice that the polar rectangle R_{ij} looks a lot like a trapezoid with parallel sides $r_{i-1}\Delta\theta$ and $r_i\Delta\theta$ and with a width Δr. Hence the area of the polar subrectangle R_{ij} is

$$\Delta A = \frac{1}{2}\Delta r(r_{i-1}\Delta\theta + r_1\Delta\theta).$$

Simplifying and letting $r_{ij}^* = \frac{1}{2}(r_{i-1} + r_i)$, we have $\Delta A = r_{ij}^*\,\Delta r\Delta\theta$. Therefore, the polar volume of the thin box above R_{ij} (**Figure 5.29**) is

$$f(r_{ij}^*, \theta_{ij}^*)\Delta A = f(r_{ij}^*, \theta_{ij}^*)r_{ij}^* \Delta r \Delta \theta.$$

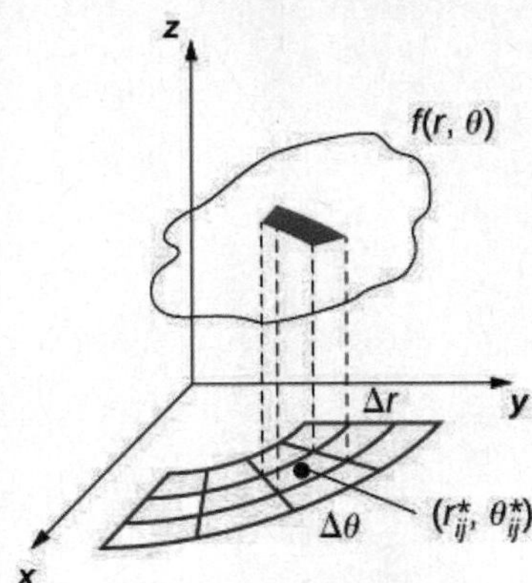

Figure 5.29 Finding the volume of the thin box above polar rectangle R_{ij}.

Using the same idea for all the subrectangles and summing the volumes of the rectangular boxes, we obtain a double Riemann sum as

$$\sum_{i=1}^{m} \sum_{j=1}^{n} f(r_{ij}^*, \theta_{ij}^*)r_{ij}^* \Delta r \Delta \theta.$$

As we have seen before, we obtain a better approximation to the polar volume of the solid above the region R when we let m and n become larger. Hence, we define the polar volume as the limit of the double Riemann sum,

$$V = \lim_{m, n \to \infty} \sum_{i=1}^{m} \sum_{j=1}^{n} f(r_{ij}^*, \theta_{ij}^*)r_{ij}^* \Delta r \Delta \theta.$$

This becomes the expression for the double integral.

Definition

The double integral of the function $f(r, \theta)$ over the polar rectangular region R in the $r\theta$-plane is defined as

$$\iint_R f(r, \theta)dA = \lim_{m, n \to \infty} \sum_{i=1}^{m} \sum_{j=1}^{n} f(r_{ij}^*, \theta_{ij}^*)\Delta A = \lim_{m, n \to \infty} \sum_{i=1}^{m} \sum_{j=1}^{n} f(r_{ij}^*, \theta_{ij}^*)r_{ij}^* \Delta r \Delta \theta. \quad (5.8)$$

Again, just as in **Double Integrals over Rectangular Regions**, the double integral over a polar rectangular region can be expressed as an iterated integral in polar coordinates. Hence,

$$\iint_R f(r, \theta)dA = \iint_R f(r, \theta)r\,dr\,d\theta = \int_{\theta=\alpha}^{\theta=\beta} \int_{r=a}^{r=b} f(r, \theta)r\,dr\,d\theta.$$

Notice that the expression for dA is replaced by $r\,dr\,d\theta$ when working in polar coordinates. Another way to look at the polar double integral is to change the double integral in rectangular coordinates by substitution. When the function f is given in terms of x and y, using $x = r\cos\theta$, $y = r\sin\theta$, and $dA = r\,dr\,d\theta$ changes it to

$$\iint_R f(x, y)dA = \iint_R f(r\cos\theta, r\sin\theta)r\,dr\,d\theta.$$

Note that all the properties listed in **Double Integrals over Rectangular Regions** for the double integral in rectangular coordinates hold true for the double integral in polar coordinates as well, so we can use them without hesitation.

Example 5.24

Sketching a Polar Rectangular Region

Sketch the polar rectangular region $R = \{(r, \theta) | 1 \le r \le 3, 0 \le \theta \le \pi\}$.

Solution

As we can see from **Figure 5.30**, $r = 1$ and $r = 3$ are circles of radius 1 and 3 and $0 \le \theta \le \pi$ covers the entire top half of the plane. Hence the region R looks like a semicircular band.

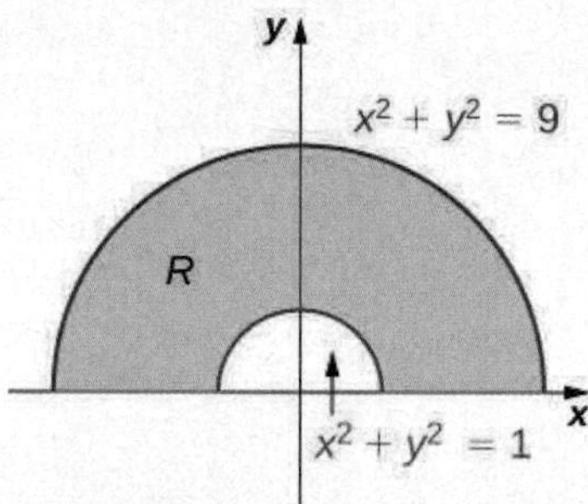

Figure 5.30 The polar region R lies between two semicircles.

Now that we have sketched a polar rectangular region, let us demonstrate how to evaluate a double integral over this region by using polar coordinates.

Example 5.25

Evaluating a Double Integral over a Polar Rectangular Region

Evaluate the integral $\iint\limits_R 3x\, dA$ over the region $R = \{(r, \theta) | 1 \le r \le 2, 0 \le \theta \le \pi\}$.

Solution

First we sketch a figure similar to **Figure 5.30** but with outer radius 2. From the figure we can see that we have

$$\iint\limits_R 3x\, dA = \int_{\theta=0}^{\theta=\pi} \int_{r=1}^{r=2} 3r \cos \theta r\, dr\, d\theta$$

Use an iterated integral with correct limits of integration.

$$= \int_{\theta=0}^{\theta=\pi} \cos \theta \left[r^3 \Big|_{r=1}^{r=2} \right] d\theta$$

Integrate first with respect to r.

$$= \int_{\theta=0}^{\theta=\pi} 7 \cos \theta\, d\theta = 7 \sin \theta \Big|_{\theta=0}^{\theta=\pi} = 0.$$

5.17 Sketch the region $R = \left\{(r, \theta) | 1 \le r \le 2, -\frac{\pi}{2} \le \theta \le \frac{\pi}{2}\right\}$, and evaluate $\iint\limits_R x\, dA$.

Example 5.26

Evaluating a Double Integral by Converting from Rectangular Coordinates

Evaluate the integral $\iint_R (1 - x^2 - y^2)dA$ where R is the unit circle on the xy -plane.

Solution

The region R is a unit circle, so we can describe it as $R = \{(r, \theta)|0 \le r \le 1, 0 \le \theta \le 2\pi\}$.

Using the conversion $x = r\cos\theta$, $y = r\sin\theta$, and $dA = r\,dr\,d\theta$, we have

$$\begin{aligned}\iint_R (1 - x^2 - y^2)dA &= \int_0^{2\pi}\int_0^1 (1 - r^2)r\,dr\,d\theta = \int_0^{2\pi}\int_0^1 (r - r^3)dr\,d\theta \\ &= \int_0^{2\pi}\left[\frac{r^2}{2} - \frac{r^4}{4}\right]_0^1 d\theta = \int_0^{2\pi}\frac{1}{4}d\theta = \frac{\pi}{2}.\end{aligned}$$

Example 5.27

Evaluating a Double Integral by Converting from Rectangular Coordinates

Evaluate the integral $\iint_R (x + y)dA$ where $R = \left\{(x, y)|1 \le x^2 + y^2 \le 4, x \le 0\right\}$.

Solution

We can see that R is an annular region that can be converted to polar coordinates and described as $R = \left\{(r, \theta)|1 \le r \le 2, \frac{\pi}{2} \le \theta \le \frac{3\pi}{2}\right\}$ (see the following graph).

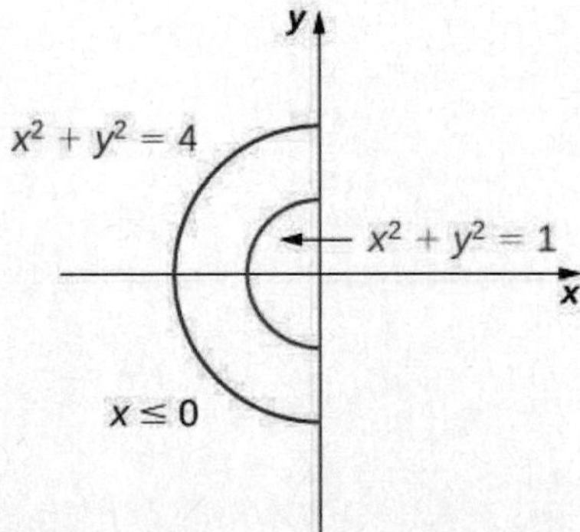

Figure 5.31 The annular region of integration R.

Hence, using the conversion $x = r\cos\theta$, $y = r\sin\theta$, and $dA = r\,dr\,d\theta$, we have

$$\begin{aligned}\iint_R (x+y)dA &= \int_{\theta=\pi/2}^{\theta=3\pi/2}\int_{r=1}^{r=2}(r\cos\theta + r\sin\theta)r\,dr\,d\theta \\ &= \left(\int_{r=1}^{r=2} r^2 dr\right)\left(\int_{\pi/2}^{3\pi/2}(\cos\theta+\sin\theta)d\theta\right) \\ &= \left[\frac{r^3}{3}\right]_1^2 [\sin\theta - \cos\theta]\Big|_{\pi/2}^{3\pi/2} \\ &= -\frac{14}{3}.\end{aligned}$$

5.18 Evaluate the integral $\iint_R (4 - x^2 - y^2)dA$ where R is the circle of radius 2 on the xy-plane.

General Polar Regions of Integration

To evaluate the double integral of a continuous function by iterated integrals over general polar regions, we consider two types of regions, analogous to Type I and Type II as discussed for rectangular coordinates in **Double Integrals over General Regions**. It is more common to write polar equations as $r = f(\theta)$ than $\theta = f(r)$, so we describe a general polar region as $R = \{(r, \theta) | \alpha \le \theta \le \beta, h_1(\theta) \le r \le h_2(\theta)\}$ (see the following figure).

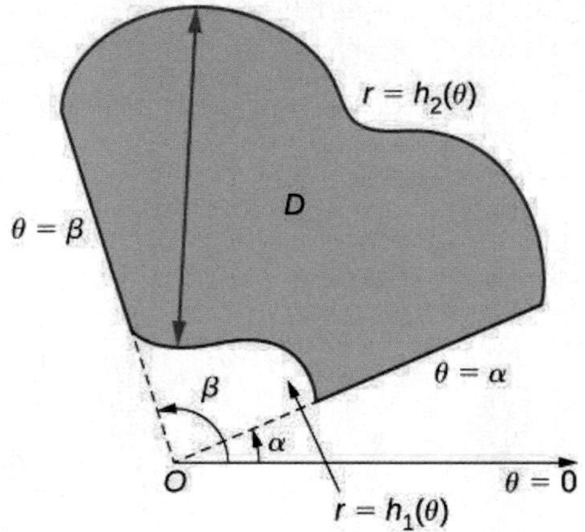

Figure 5.32 A general polar region between $\alpha < \theta < \beta$ and $h_1(\theta) < r < h_2(\theta)$.

Theorem 5.8: Double Integrals over General Polar Regions

If $f(r, \theta)$ is continuous on a general polar region D as described above, then

$$\iint_D f(r, \theta)r\,dr\,d\theta = \int_{\theta=\alpha}^{\theta=\beta}\int_{r=h_1(\theta)}^{r=h_2(\theta)} f(r, \theta)r\,dr\,d\theta \tag{5.9}$$

Example 5.28

Evaluating a Double Integral over a General Polar Region

Evaluate the integral $\iint_D r^2 \sin\theta r\,dr\,d\theta$ where D is the region bounded by the polar axis and the upper half of the cardioid $r = 1 + \cos\theta$.

Solution

We can describe the region D as $\{(r, \theta)|0 \le \theta \le \pi, 0 \le r \le 1 + \cos\theta\}$ as shown in the following figure.

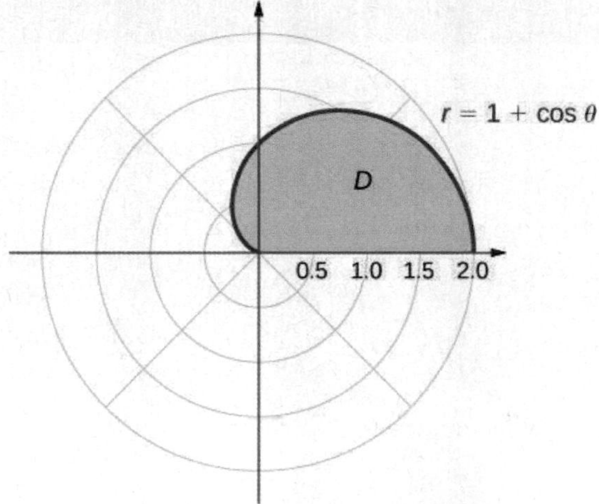

Figure 5.33 The region D is the top half of a cardioid.

Hence, we have

$$\begin{aligned}\iint_D r^2 \sin\theta r\,dr\,d\theta &= \int_{\theta=0}^{\theta=\pi}\int_{r=0}^{r=1+\cos\theta}\left(r^2\sin\theta\right)r\,dr\,d\theta \\ &= \frac{1}{4}\int_{\theta=0}^{\theta=\pi}\left[r^4\right]_{r=0}^{r=1+\cos\theta}\sin\theta\,d\theta \\ &= \frac{1}{4}\int_{\theta=0}^{\theta=\pi}(1+\cos\theta)^4\sin\theta\,d\theta \\ &= -\frac{1}{4}\left[\frac{(1+\cos\theta)^5}{5}\right]_0^{\pi} = \frac{8}{5}.\end{aligned}$$

5.19 Evaluate the integral

$$\iint_D r^2 \sin^2 2\theta r\,dr\,d\theta \text{ where } D = \left\{(r, \theta)|0 \le \theta \le \pi, 0 \le r \le 2\sqrt{\cos 2\theta}\right\}.$$

Polar Areas and Volumes

As in rectangular coordinates, if a solid S is bounded by the surface $z = f(r, \theta)$, as well as by the surfaces $r = a, r = b, \theta = \alpha,$ and $\theta = \beta,$ we can find the volume V of S by double integration, as

$$V = \iint_R f(r, \theta) r \, dr \, d\theta = \int_{\theta=\alpha}^{\theta=\beta} \int_{r=a}^{r=b} f(r, \theta) r \, dr \, d\theta.$$

If the base of the solid can be described as $D = \{(r, \theta) | \alpha \le \theta \le \beta, h_1(\theta) \le r \le h_2(\theta)\}$, then the double integral for the volume becomes

$$V = \iint_D f(r, \theta) r \, dr \, d\theta = \int_{\theta=\alpha}^{\theta=\beta} \int_{r=h_1(\theta)}^{r=h_2(\theta)} f(r, \theta) r \, dr \, d\theta.$$

We illustrate this idea with some examples.

Example 5.29

Finding a Volume Using a Double Integral

Find the volume of the solid that lies under the paraboloid $z = 1 - x^2 - y^2$ and above the unit circle on the xy -plane (see the following figure).

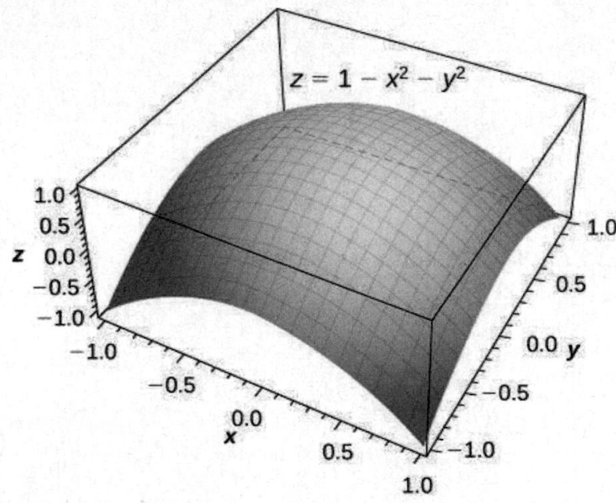

Figure 5.34 The paraboloid $z = 1 - x^2 - y^2$.

Solution

By the method of double integration, we can see that the volume is the iterated integral of the form $\iint_R \left(1 - x^2 - y^2\right) dA$ where $R = \{(r, \theta) | 0 \le r \le 1, 0 \le \theta \le 2\pi\}$.

This integration was shown before in **Example 5.26**, so the volume is $\frac{\pi}{2}$ cubic units.

Example 5.30

Finding a Volume Using Double Integration

Find the volume of the solid that lies under the paraboloid $z = 4 - x^2 - y^2$ and above the disk

$(x-1)^2+y^2=1$ on the xy-plane. See the paraboloid in **Figure 5.35** intersecting the cylinder $(x-1)^2+y^2=1$ above the xy-plane.

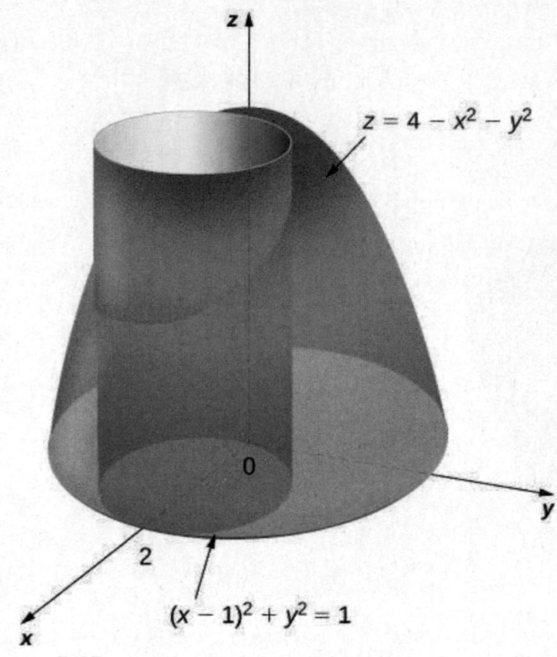

Figure 5.35 Finding the volume of a solid with a paraboloid cap and a circular base.

Solution

First change the disk $(x-1)^2+y^2=1$ to polar coordinates. Expanding the square term, we have $x^2-2x+1+y^2=1$. Then simplify to get $x^2+y^2=2x$, which in polar coordinates becomes $r^2=2r\cos\theta$ and then either $r=0$ or $r=2\cos\theta$. Similarly, the equation of the paraboloid changes to $z=4-r^2$. Therefore we can describe the disk $(x-1)^2+y^2=1$ on the xy-plane as the region

$$D=\{(r,\theta)|0\le\theta\le\pi,\ 0\le r\le 2\cos\theta\}.$$

Hence the volume of the solid bounded above by the paraboloid $z=4-x^2-y^2$ and below by $r=2\cos\theta$ is

$$\begin{aligned}V &= \iint\limits_D f(r,\theta)r\,dr\,d\theta=\int\limits_{\theta=0}^{\theta=\pi}\int\limits_{r=0}^{r=2\cos\theta}\left(4-r^2\right)r\,dr\,d\theta \\ &= \int\limits_{\theta=0}^{\theta=\pi}\left[4\frac{r^2}{2}-\frac{r^4}{4}\Big|_0^{2\cos\theta}\right]d\theta \\ &= \int\limits_0^{\pi}\left[8\cos^2\theta-4\cos^2\theta\right]d\theta=\left[\frac{5}{2}\theta+\frac{5}{2}\sin\theta\cos\theta-\sin\theta\cos^3\theta\right]_0^{\pi}=\frac{5}{2}\pi.\end{aligned}$$

Notice in the next example that integration is not always easy with polar coordinates. Complexity of integration depends on the function and also on the region over which we need to perform the integration. If the region has a more natural expression in polar coordinates or if f has a simpler antiderivative in polar coordinates, then the change in polar coordinates is appropriate; otherwise, use rectangular coordinates.

Example 5.31

Finding a Volume Using a Double Integral

Find the volume of the region that lies under the paraboloid $z = x^2 + y^2$ and above the triangle enclosed by the lines $y = x, x = 0,$ and $x + y = 2$ in the xy-plane (**Figure 5.36**).

Solution

First examine the region over which we need to set up the double integral and the accompanying paraboloid.

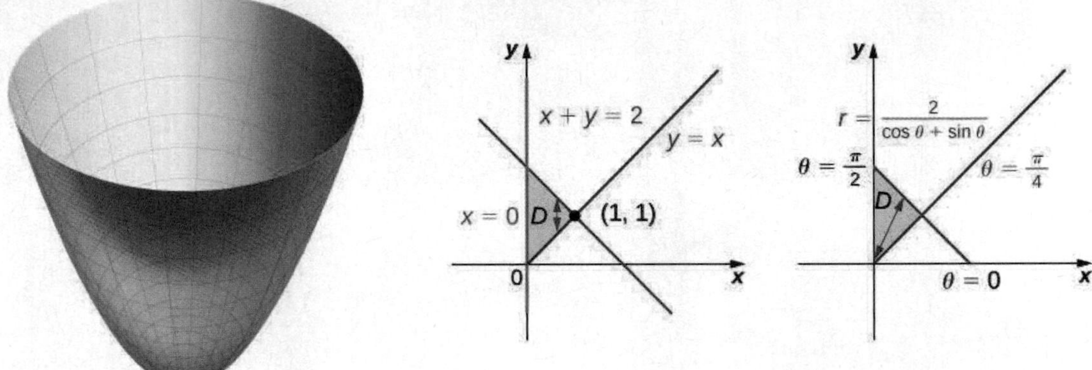

Figure 5.36 Finding the volume of a solid under a paraboloid and above a given triangle.

The region D is $\{(x, y)|0 \le x \le 1, x \le y \le 2 - x\}$. Converting the lines $y = x, x = 0,$ and $x + y = 2$ in the xy-plane to functions of r and $\theta,$ we have $\theta = \pi/4, \quad \theta = \pi/2,$ and $r = 2/(\cos\theta + \sin\theta),$ respectively. Graphing the region on the xy-plane, we see that it looks like $D = \{(r, \theta)|\pi/4 \le \theta \le \pi/2, 0 \le r \le 2/(\cos\theta + \sin\theta)\}$. Now converting the equation of the surface gives $z = x^2 + y^2 = r^2$. Therefore, the volume of the solid is given by the double integral

$$\begin{aligned} V &= \iint_D f(r, \theta) r\,dr\,d\theta = \int_{\theta=\pi/4}^{\theta=\pi/2} \int_{r=0}^{r=2/(\cos\theta+\sin\theta)} r^2 r\,dr\,d\theta = \int_{\pi/4}^{\pi/2} \left[\frac{r^4}{4}\right]_0^{2/(\cos\theta+\sin\theta)} d\theta \\ &= \frac{1}{4}\int_{\pi/4}^{\pi/2} \left(\frac{2}{\cos\theta + \sin\theta}\right)^4 d\theta = \frac{16}{4}\int_{\pi/4}^{\pi/2} \left(\frac{1}{\cos\theta + \sin\theta}\right)^4 d\theta = 4\int_{\pi/4}^{\pi/2} \left(\frac{1}{\cos\theta + \sin\theta}\right)^4 d\theta. \end{aligned}$$

As you can see, this integral is very complicated. So, we can instead evaluate this double integral in rectangular coordinates as

$$V = \int_0^1 \int_x^{2-x} (x^2 + y^2) dy\,dx.$$

Evaluating gives

$$\begin{aligned} V &= \int_0^1 \int_x^{2-x} (x^2 + y^2)\,dy\,dx = \int_0^1 \left[x^2 y + \frac{y^3}{3}\right]_x^{2-x} dx \\ &= \int_0^1 \frac{8}{3} - 4x + 4x^2 - \frac{8x^3}{3}\,dx \\ &= \left[\frac{8x}{3} - 2x^2 + \frac{4x^3}{3} - \frac{2x^4}{3}\right]_0^1 = \frac{4}{3}. \end{aligned}$$

To answer the question of how the formulas for the volumes of different standard solids such as a sphere, a cone, or a cylinder are found, we want to demonstrate an example and find the volume of an arbitrary cone.

Example 5.32

Finding a Volume Using a Double Integral

Use polar coordinates to find the volume inside the cone $z = 2 - \sqrt{x^2 + y^2}$ and above the xy-plane.

Solution

The region D for the integration is the base of the cone, which appears to be a circle on the xy-plane (see the following figure).

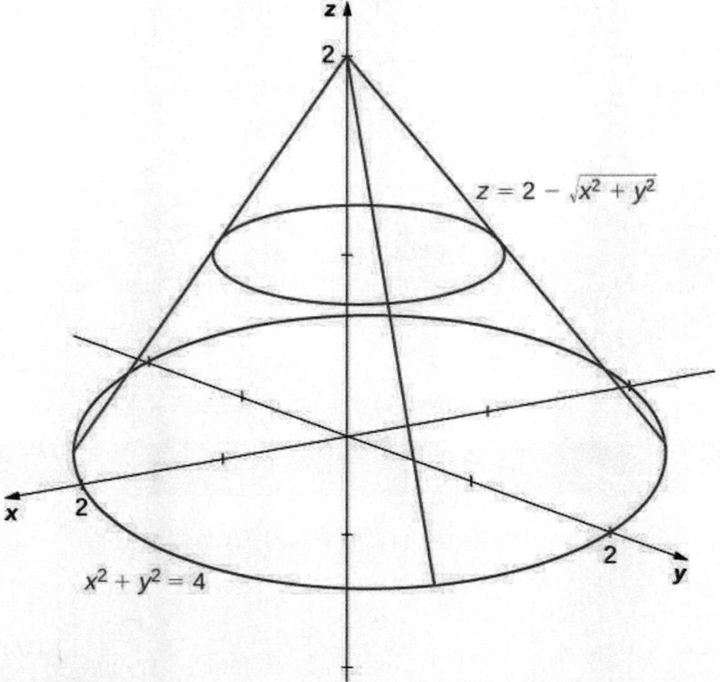

Figure 5.37 Finding the volume of a solid inside the cone and above the xy-plane.

We find the equation of the circle by setting $z = 0$:

$$\begin{aligned} 0 &= 2 - \sqrt{x^2 + y^2} \\ 2 &= \sqrt{x^2 + y^2} \\ x^2 + y^2 &= 4. \end{aligned}$$

This means the radius of the circle is 2, so for the integration we have $0 \le \theta \le 2\pi$ and $0 \le r \le 2$. Substituting $x = r\cos\theta$ and $y = r\sin\theta$ in the equation $z = 2 - \sqrt{x^2 + y^2}$ we have $z = 2 - r$. Therefore, the volume of the cone is

$$\int_{\theta=0}^{\theta=2\pi}\int_{r=0}^{r=2} (2 - r)r\,dr\,d\theta = 2\pi\frac{4}{3} = \frac{8\pi}{3} \text{ cubic units.}$$

Analysis

Note that if we were to find the volume of an arbitrary cone with radius a units and height h units, then the equation of the cone would be $z = h - \frac{h}{a}\sqrt{x^2 + y^2}$.

We can still use **Figure 5.37** and set up the integral as $\int_{\theta=0}^{\theta=2\pi}\int_{r=0}^{r=a}\left(h - \frac{h}{a}r\right)r\,dr\,d\theta$.

Evaluating the integral, we get $\frac{1}{3}\pi a^2 h$.

5.20 Use polar coordinates to find an iterated integral for finding the volume of the solid enclosed by the paraboloids $z = x^2 + y^2$ and $z = 16 - x^2 - y^2$.

As with rectangular coordinates, we can also use polar coordinates to find areas of certain regions using a double integral. As before, we need to understand the region whose area we want to compute. Sketching a graph and identifying the region can be helpful to realize the limits of integration. Generally, the area formula in double integration will look like

$$\text{Area } A = \int_{\alpha}^{\beta}\int_{h_1(\theta)}^{h_2(\theta)} 1r\,dr\,d\theta.$$

Example 5.33

Finding an Area Using a Double Integral in Polar Coordinates

Evaluate the area bounded by the curve $r = \cos 4\theta$.

Solution

Sketching the graph of the function $r = \cos 4\theta$ reveals that it is a polar rose with eight petals (see the following figure).

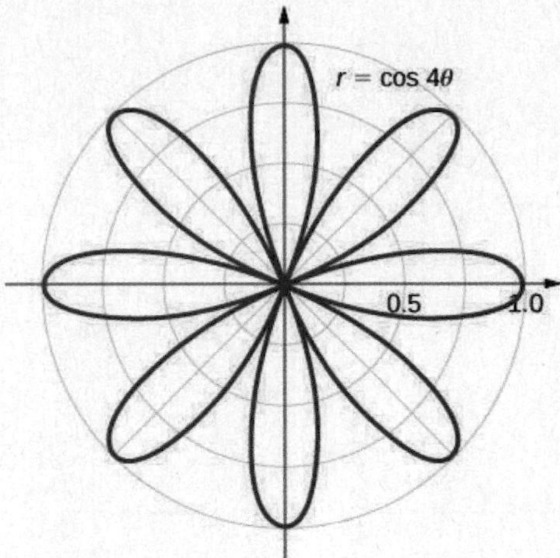

Figure 5.38 Finding the area of a polar rose with eight petals.

Using symmetry, we can see that we need to find the area of one petal and then multiply it by 8. Notice that the values of θ for which the graph passes through the origin are the zeros of the function $\cos 4\theta$, and these are odd multiples of $\pi/8$. Thus, one of the petals corresponds to the values of θ in the interval $[-\pi/8, \pi/8]$. Therefore, the area bounded by the curve $r = \cos 4\theta$ is

$$\begin{aligned} A &= 8 \int_{\theta=-\pi/8}^{\theta=\pi/8} \int_{r=0}^{r=\cos 4\theta} 1r\,dr\,d\theta \\ &= 8 \int_{-\pi/8}^{\pi/8} \left[\frac{1}{2}r^2\Big|_0^{\cos 4\theta}\right] d\theta = 8 \int_{-\pi/8}^{\pi/8} \frac{1}{2}\cos^2 4\theta\,d\theta = 8\left[\frac{1}{4}\theta + \frac{1}{16}\sin 4\theta \cos 4\theta\Big|_{-\pi/8}^{\pi/8}\right] = 8\left[\frac{\pi}{16}\right] = \frac{\pi}{2}. \end{aligned}$$

Example 5.34

Finding Area Between Two Polar Curves

Find the area enclosed by the circle $r = 3\cos\theta$ and the cardioid $r = 1 + \cos\theta$.

Solution

First and foremost, sketch the graphs of the region (**Figure 5.39**).

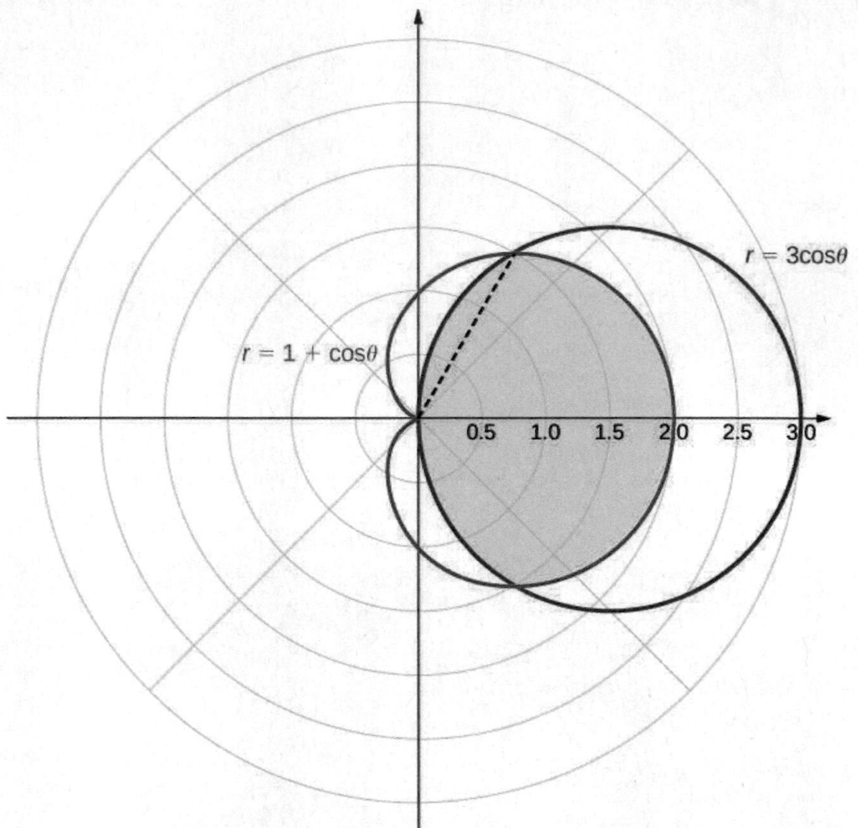

Figure 5.39 Finding the area enclosed by both a circle and a cardioid.

We can from see the symmetry of the graph that we need to find the points of intersection. Setting the two equations equal to each other gives

$$3\cos\theta = 1 + \cos\theta.$$

One of the points of intersection is $\theta = \pi/3$. The area above the polar axis consists of two parts, with one part defined by the cardioid from $\theta = 0$ to $\theta = \pi/3$ and the other part defined by the circle from $\theta = \pi/3$ to $\theta = \pi/2$. By symmetry, the total area is twice the area above the polar axis. Thus, we have

$$A = 2\left[\int_{\theta=0}^{\theta=\pi/3} \int_{r=0}^{r=1+\cos\theta} 1r\,dr\,d\theta + \int_{\theta=\pi/3}^{\theta=\pi/2} \int_{r=0}^{r=3\cos\theta} 1r\,dr\,d\theta\right].$$

Evaluating each piece separately, we find that the area is

$$A = 2\left(\frac{1}{4}\pi + \frac{9}{16}\sqrt{3} + \frac{3}{8}\pi - \frac{9}{16}\sqrt{3}\right) = 2\left(\frac{5}{8}\pi\right) = \frac{5}{4}\pi \text{ square units.}$$

5.21 Find the area enclosed inside the cardioid $r = 3 - 3\sin\theta$ and outside the cardioid $r = 1 + \sin\theta$.

Example 5.35

Evaluating an Improper Double Integral in Polar Coordinates

Evaluate the integral $\iint_{R^2} e^{-10(x^2+y^2)}\,dx\,dy.$

Solution

This is an improper integral because we are integrating over an unbounded region R^2. In polar coordinates, the entire plane R^2 can be seen as $0 \le \theta \le 2\pi, \quad 0 \le r \le \infty$.

Using the changes of variables from rectangular coordinates to polar coordinates, we have

$$\begin{aligned}
\iint_{R^2} e^{-10(x^2+y^2)}\,dx\,dy &= \int_{\theta=0}^{\theta=2\pi}\int_{r=0}^{r=\infty} e^{-10r^2}\,r\,dr\,d\theta = \int_{\theta=0}^{\theta=2\pi}\left(\lim_{a\to\infty}\int_{r=0}^{r=a} e^{-10r^2}\,r\,dr\right)d\theta \\
&= \left(\int_{\theta=0}^{\theta=2\pi} d\theta\right)\left(\lim_{a\to\infty}\int_{r=0}^{r=a} e^{-10r^2}\,r\,dr\right) \\
&= 2\pi\left(\lim_{a\to\infty}\int_{r=0}^{r=a} e^{-10r^2}\,r\,dr\right) \\
&= 2\pi\lim_{a\to\infty}\left(-\frac{1}{20}\right)\left(e^{-10r^2}\Big|_0^a\right) \\
&= 2\pi\left(-\frac{1}{20}\right)\lim_{a\to\infty}\left(e^{-10a^2}-1\right) \\
&= \frac{\pi}{10}.
\end{aligned}$$

5.22 Evaluate the integral $\iint_{R^2} e^{-4(x^2+y^2)}\,dx\,dy.$

5.3 EXERCISES

In the following exercises, express the region D in polar coordinates.

122. D is the region of the disk of radius 2 centered at the origin that lies in the first quadrant.

123. D is the region between the circles of radius 4 and radius 5 centered at the origin that lies in the second quadrant.

124. D is the region bounded by the y-axis and $x = \sqrt{1 - y^2}$.

125. D is the region bounded by the x-axis and $y = \sqrt{2 - x^2}$.

126. $D = \{(x, y)|x^2 + y^2 \leq 4x\}$

127. $D = \{(x, y)|x^2 + y^2 \leq 4y\}$

In the following exercises, the graph of the polar rectangular region D is given. Express D in polar coordinates.

128.

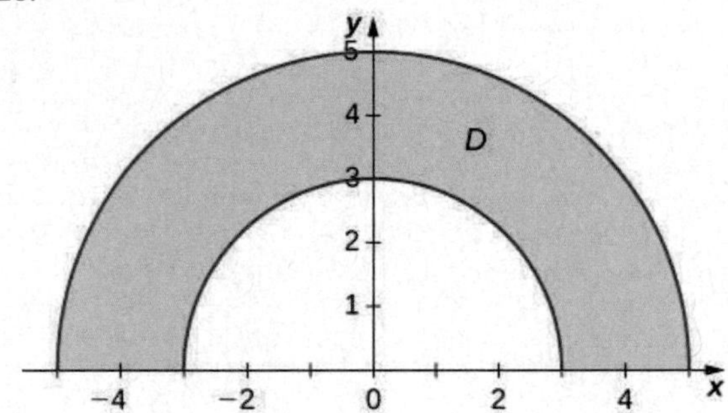

129.

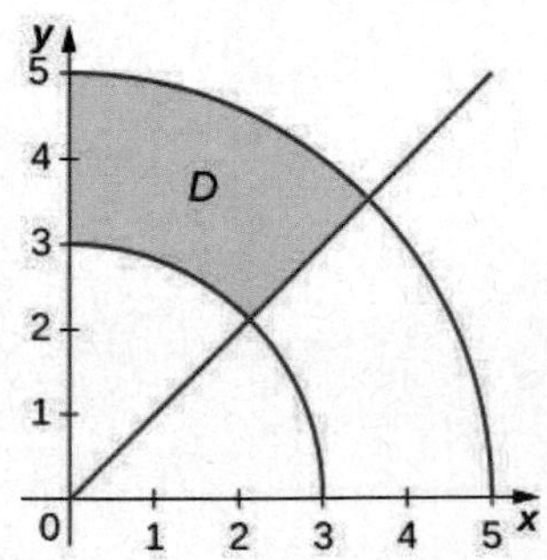

130.

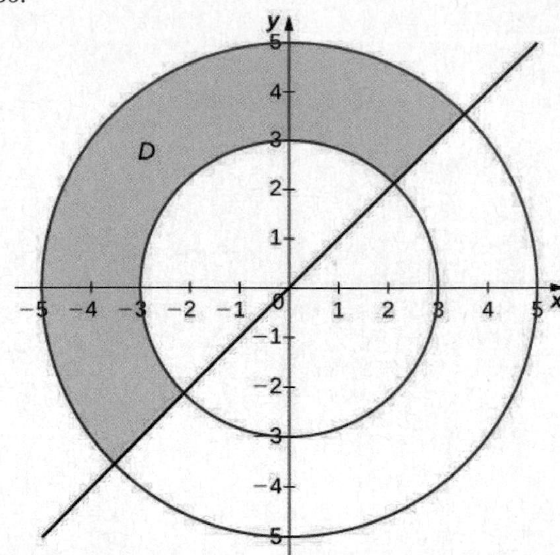

131.

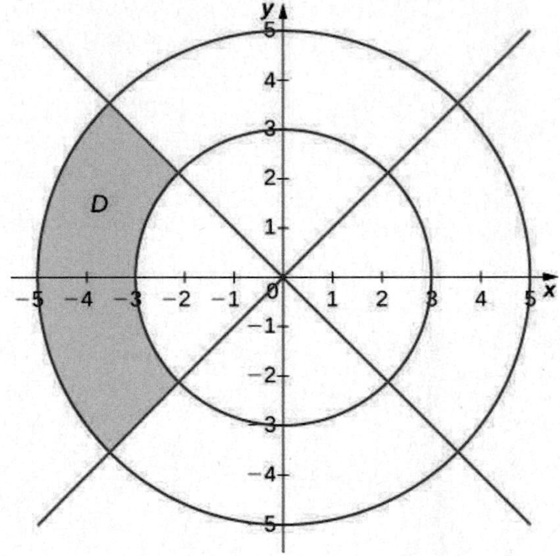

132. In the following graph, the region D is situated below $y = x$ and is bounded by $x = 1, x = 5,$ and $y = 0.$

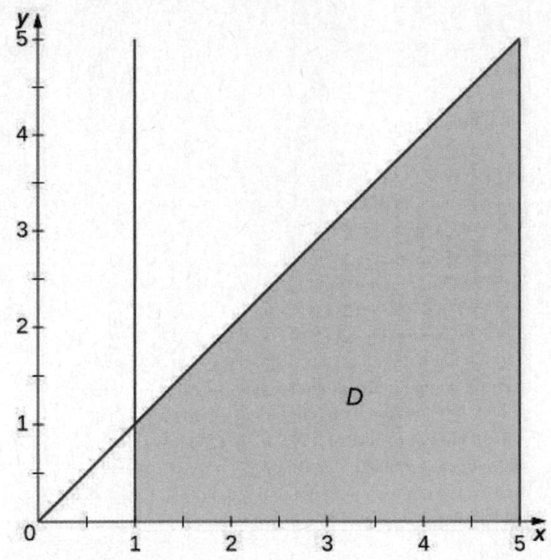

133. In the following graph, the region D is bounded by $y = x$ and $y = x^2.$

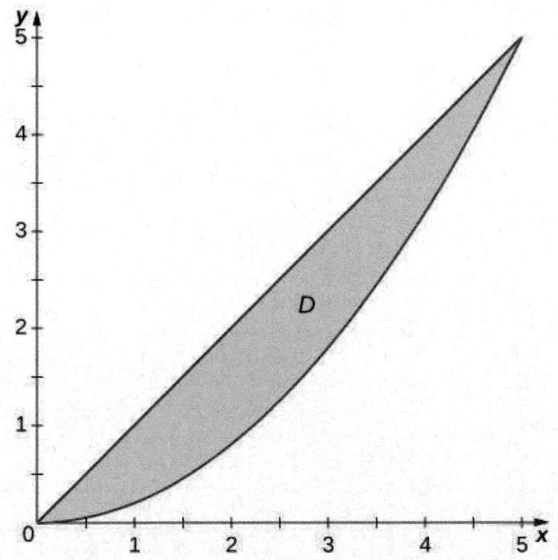

In the following exercises, evaluate the double integral $\iint_R f(x, y)dA$ over the polar rectangular region D.

134. $f(x, y) = x^2 + y^2, D = \{(r, \theta)|3 \le r \le 5, 0 \le \theta \le 2\pi\}$

135. $f(x, y) = x + y, \ D = \{(r, \theta)|3 \le r \le 5, 0 \le \theta \le 2\pi\}$

136. $f(x, y) = x^2 + xy, D = \{(r, \theta)|1 \le r \le 2, \pi \le \theta \le 2\pi\}$

137. $f(x, y) = x^4 + y^4, D = \left\{(r, \theta)|1 \le r \le 2, \frac{3\pi}{2} \le \theta \le 2\pi\right\}$

138. $f(x, y) = \sqrt[3]{x^2 + y^2},$ where $D = \left\{(r, \theta)|0 \le r \le 1, \frac{\pi}{2} \le \theta \le \pi\right\}.$

139. $f(x, y) = x^4 + 2x^2y^2 + y^4,$ where $D = \left\{(r, \theta)|3 \le r \le 4, \frac{\pi}{3} \le \theta \le \frac{2\pi}{3}\right\}.$

140. $f(x, y) = \sin\left(\arctan \frac{y}{x}\right),$ where $D = \left\{(r, \theta)\middle|1 \le r \le 2, \frac{\pi}{6} \le \theta \le \frac{\pi}{3}\right\}$

141. $f(x, y) = \arctan\left(\frac{y}{x}\right),$ where $D = \left\{(r, \theta)\middle|2 \le r \le 3, \frac{\pi}{4} \le \theta \le \frac{\pi}{3}\right\}$

142. $\iint_D e^{x^2 + y^2}\left[1 + 2\arctan\left(\frac{y}{x}\right)\right]dA, D = \left\{(r, \theta)|1 \le r \le 2, \frac{\pi}{6} \le \theta \le \frac{\pi}{3}\right\}$

143. $\iint_D \left(e^{x^2 + y^2} + x^4 + 2x^2y^2 + y^4\right)\arctan\left(\frac{y}{x}\right)dA, D = \left\{(r, \theta)|1 \le r \le 2, \frac{\pi}{4} \le \theta \le \frac{\pi}{3}\right\}$

In the following exercises, the integrals have been converted to polar coordinates. Verify that the identities are true and choose the easiest way to evaluate the integrals, in rectangular or polar coordinates.

144. $\int_1^2 \int_0^x (x^2 + y^2)dy\,dx = \int_0^{\frac{\pi}{4}} \int_{\sec\theta}^{2\sec\theta} r^3\,dr\,d\theta$

145. $\int_2^3 \int_0^x \frac{x}{\sqrt{x^2 + y^2}}dy\,dx = \int_0^{\pi/4} \int_0^{\tan\theta\sec\theta} r\cos\theta\,dr\,d\theta$

146. $\int_0^1 \int_{x^2}^x \frac{1}{\sqrt{x^2 + y^2}}dy\,dx = \int_0^{\pi/4} \int_0^{\tan\theta\sec\theta} dr\,d\theta$

147. $\int_0^1 \int_{x^2}^x \frac{y}{\sqrt{x^2 + y^2}}dy\,dx = \int_0^{\pi/4} \int_0^{\tan\theta\sec\theta} r\sin\theta\,dr\,d\theta$

In the following exercises, convert the integrals to polar coordinates and evaluate them.

148. $\int_0^3 \int_0^{\sqrt{9-y^2}} (x^2+y^2)dx\,dy$

149. $\int_0^2 \int_{-\sqrt{4-y^2}}^{\sqrt{4-y^2}} (x^2+y^2)^2\,dx\,dy$

150. $\int_0^1 \int_0^{\sqrt{1-x^2}} (x+y)dy\,dx$

151. $\int_0^4 \int_{-\sqrt{16-x^2}}^{\sqrt{16-x^2}} \sin(x^2+y^2)dy\,dx$

152. Evaluate the integral $\iint_D r\,dA$ where D is the region bounded by the polar axis and the upper half of the cardioid $r = 1 + \cos\theta$.

153. Find the area of the region D bounded by the polar axis and the upper half of the cardioid $r = 1 + \cos\theta$.

154. Evaluate the integral $\iint_D r\,dA$, where D is the region bounded by the part of the four-leaved rose $r = \sin 2\theta$ situated in the first quadrant (see the following figure).

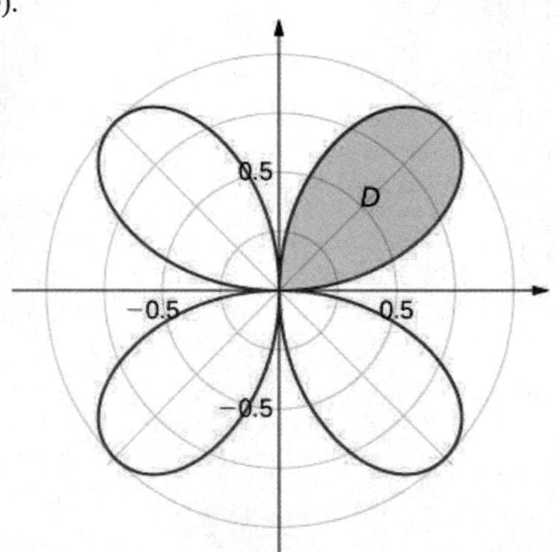

155. Find the total area of the region enclosed by the four-leaved rose $r = \sin 2\theta$ (see the figure in the previous exercise).

156. Find the area of the region D, which is the region bounded by $y = \sqrt{4-x^2}$, $x = \sqrt{3}$, $x = 2$, and $y = 0$.

157. Find the area of the region D, which is the region inside the disk $x^2 + y^2 \leq 4$ and to the right of the line $x = 1$.

158. Determine the average value of the function $f(x, y) = x^2 + y^2$ over the region D bounded by the polar curve $r = \cos 2\theta$, where $-\frac{\pi}{4} \leq \theta \leq \frac{\pi}{4}$ (see the following graph).

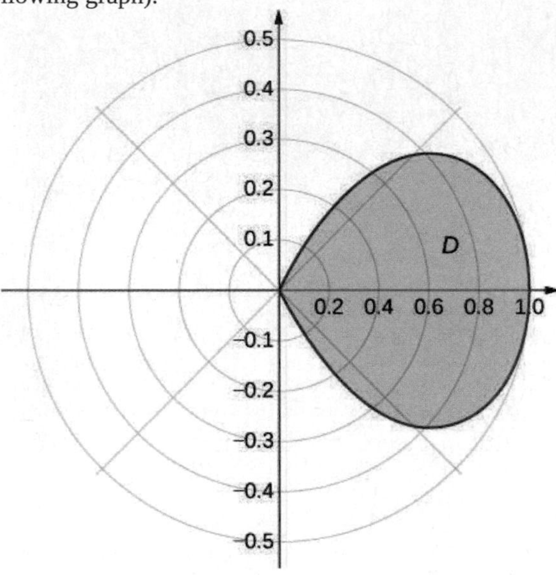

159. Determine the average value of the function $f(x, y) = \sqrt{x^2 + y^2}$ over the region D bounded by the polar curve $r = 3\sin 2\theta$, where $0 \leq \theta \leq \frac{\pi}{2}$ (see the following graph).

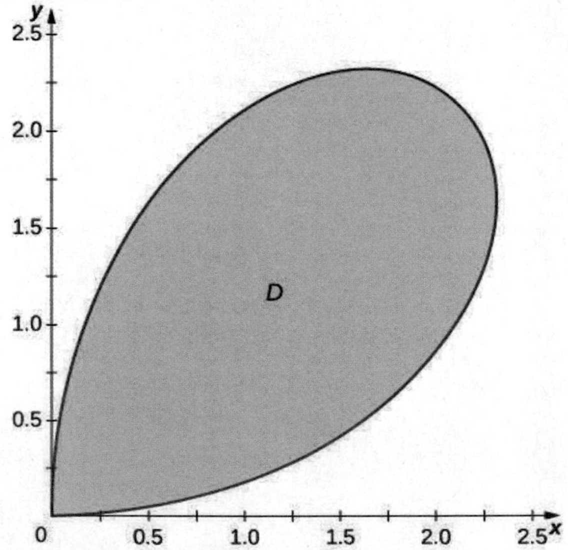

160. Find the volume of the solid situated in the first octant and bounded by the paraboloid $z = 1 - 4x^2 - 4y^2$ and the planes $x = 0$, $y = 0$, and $z = 0$.

161. Find the volume of the solid bounded by the paraboloid $z = 2 - 9x^2 - 9y^2$ and the plane $z = 1$.

162.

a. Find the volume of the solid S_1 bounded by the cylinder $x^2 + y^2 = 1$ and the planes $z = 0$ and $z = 1$.

b. Find the volume of the solid S_2 outside the double cone $z^2 = x^2 + y^2$, inside the cylinder $x^2 + y^2 = 1$, and above the plane $z = 0$.

c. Find the volume of the solid inside the cone $z^2 = x^2 + y^2$ and below the plane $z = 1$ by subtracting the volumes of the solids S_1 and S_2.

163.

a. Find the volume of the solid S_1 inside the unit sphere $x^2 + y^2 + z^2 = 1$ and above the plane $z = 0$.

b. Find the volume of the solid S_2 inside the double cone $(z - 1)^2 = x^2 + y^2$ and above the plane $z = 0$.

c. Find the volume of the solid outside the double cone $(z - 1)^2 = x^2 + y^2$ and inside the sphere $x^2 + y^2 + z^2 = 1$.

For the following two exercises, consider a spherical ring, which is a sphere with a cylindrical hole cut so that the axis of the cylinder passes through the center of the sphere (see the following figure).

164. If the sphere has radius 4 and the cylinder has radius 2, find the volume of the spherical ring.

165. A cylindrical hole of diameter 6 cm is bored through a sphere of radius 5 cm such that the axis of the cylinder passes through the center of the sphere. Find the volume of the resulting spherical ring.

166. Find the volume of the solid that lies under the double cone $z^2 = 4x^2 + 4y^2$, inside the cylinder $x^2 + y^2 = x$, and above the plane $z = 0$.

167. Find the volume of the solid that lies under the paraboloid $z = x^2 + y^2$, inside the cylinder $x^2 + y^2 = x$, and above the plane $z = 0$.

168. Find the volume of the solid that lies under the plane $x + y + z = 10$ and above the disk $x^2 + y^2 = 4x$.

169. Find the volume of the solid that lies under the plane $2x + y + 2z = 8$ and above the unit disk $x^2 + y^2 = 1$.

170. A radial function f is a function whose value at each point depends only on the distance between that point and the origin of the system of coordinates; that is, $f(x, y) = g(r)$, where $r = \sqrt{x^2 + y^2}$. Show that if f is a continuous radial function, then $\iint_D f(x, y)dA = (\theta_2 - \theta_1)[G(R_2) - G(R_1)]$, where $G'(r) = rg(r)$ and $(x, y) \in D = \{(r, \theta) | R_1 \le r \le R_2, 0 \le \theta \le 2\pi\}$, with $0 \le R_1 < R_2$ and $0 \le \theta_1 < \theta_2 \le 2\pi$.

171. Use the information from the preceding exercise to calculate the integral $\iint_D \left(x^2 + y^2\right)^3 dA$, where D is the unit disk.

172. Let $f(x, y) = \dfrac{F'(r)}{r}$ be a continuous radial function defined on the annular region $D = \{(r, \theta) | R_1 \le r \le R_2, 0 \le \theta \le 2\pi\}$, where $r = \sqrt{x^2 + y^2}$, $0 < R_1 < R_2$, and F is a differentiable function. Show that $\iint_D f(x, y)dA = 2\pi[F(R_2) - F(R_1)]$.

173. Apply the preceding exercise to calculate the integral $\iint_D \dfrac{e^{\sqrt{x^2 + y^2}}}{\sqrt{x^2 + y^2}} dx\, dy$, where D is the annular region between the circles of radii 1 and 2 situated in the third quadrant.

174. Let f be a continuous function that can be expressed in polar coordinates as a function of θ only; that is, $f(x, y) = h(\theta)$, where $(x, y) \in D = \{(r, \theta) | R_1 \le r \le R_2, \theta_1 \le \theta \le \theta_2\}$, with $0 \le R_1 < R_2$ and $0 \le \theta_1 < \theta_2 \le 2\pi$. Show that $\iint_D f(x, y)dA = \frac{1}{2}(R_2^2 - R_1^2)[H(\theta_2) - H(\theta_1)]$, where H is an antiderivative of h.

175. Apply the preceding exercise to calculate the integral $\iint_D \frac{y^2}{x^2} dA$, where $D = \left\{(r, \theta) \middle| 1 \le r \le 2, \frac{\pi}{6} \le \theta \le \frac{\pi}{3}\right\}$.

176. Let f be a continuous function that can be expressed in polar coordinates as a function of θ only; that is, $f(x, y) = g(r)h(\theta)$, where $(x, y) \in D = \{(r, \theta) | R_1 \le r \le R_2, \theta_1 \le \theta \le \theta_2\}$ with $0 \le R_1 < R_2$ and $0 \le \theta_1 < \theta_2 \le 2\pi$. Show that $\iint_D f(x, y)dA = [G(R_2) - G(R_1)][H(\theta_2) - H(\theta_1)]$, where G and H are antiderivatives of g and h, respectively.

177. Evaluate $\iint_D \arctan\left(\frac{y}{x}\right)\sqrt{x^2 + y^2} dA$, where $D = \left\{(r, \theta) \middle| 2 \le r \le 3, \frac{\pi}{4} \le \theta \le \frac{\pi}{3}\right\}$.

178. A spherical cap is the region of a sphere that lies above or below a given plane.

a. Show that the volume of the spherical cap in the figure below is $\frac{1}{6}\pi h\left(3a^2 + h^2\right)$.

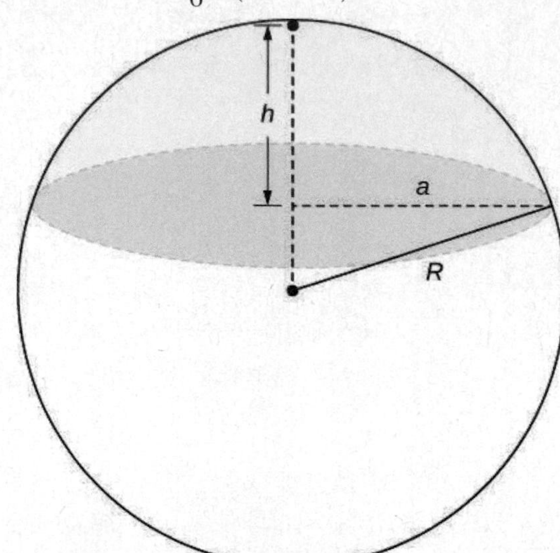

b. A spherical segment is the solid defined by intersecting a sphere with two parallel planes. If the distance between the planes is h, show that the volume of the spherical segment in the figure below is $\frac{1}{6}\pi h\left(3a^2 + 3b^2 + h^2\right)$.

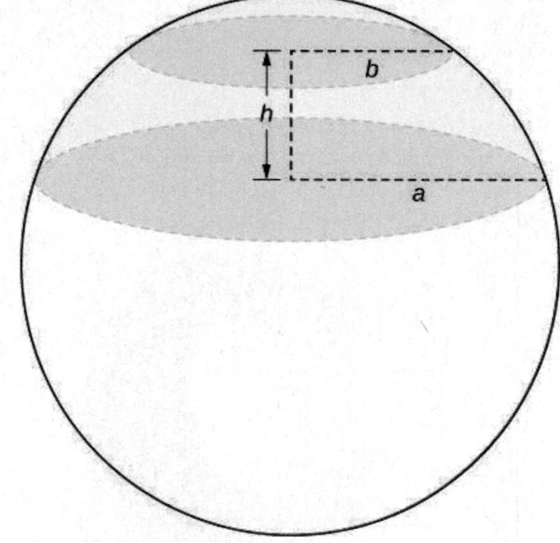

179. In statistics, the joint density for two independent, normally distributed events with a mean $\mu = 0$ and a standard distribution σ is defined by $p(x, y) = \frac{1}{2\pi\sigma^2} e^{-\frac{x^2 + y^2}{2\sigma^2}}$. Consider (X, Y), the Cartesian coordinates of a ball in the resting position after it was released from a position on the z-axis toward the xy-plane. Assume that the coordinates of the ball are independently normally distributed with a mean $\mu = 0$ and a standard deviation of σ (in feet). The probability that the ball will stop no more than a feet from the origin is given by $P[X^2 + Y^2 \le a^2] = \iint_D p(x, y)dy\,dx,$ where D is the disk of radius a centered at the origin. Show that $P[X^2 + Y^2 \le a^2] = 1 - e^{-a^2/2\sigma^2}$.

180. The double improper integral $\int_{-\infty}^{\infty}\int_{-\infty}^{\infty} e^{(-x^2 + y^2/2)} dy\,dx$ may be defined as the limit value of the double integrals $\iint_{D_a} e^{(-x^2 + y^2/2)} dA$ over disks D_a of radii a centered at the origin, as a increases without bound; that is, $\int_{-\infty}^{\infty}\int_{-\infty}^{\infty} e^{(-x^2 + y^2/2)} dy\,dx = \lim_{a \to \infty} \iint_{D_a} e^{(-x^2 + y^2/2)} dA.$

a. Use polar coordinates to show that $\int_{-\infty}^{\infty}\int_{-\infty}^{\infty} e^{(-x^2 + y^2/2)} dy\,dx = 2\pi.$

b. Show that $\int_{-\infty}^{\infty} e^{-x^2/2} dx = \sqrt{2\pi}$, by using the relation $\int_{-\infty}^{\infty}\int_{-\infty}^{\infty} e^{(-x^2 + y^2/2)} dy\,dx = \left(\int_{-\infty}^{\infty} e^{-x^2/2} dx\right)\left(\int_{-\infty}^{\infty} e^{-y^2/2} dy\right).$

5.4 | Triple Integrals

Learning Objectives

5.4.1 Recognize when a function of three variables is integrable over a rectangular box.
5.4.2 Evaluate a triple integral by expressing it as an iterated integral.
5.4.3 Recognize when a function of three variables is integrable over a closed and bounded region.
5.4.4 Simplify a calculation by changing the order of integration of a triple integral.
5.4.5 Calculate the average value of a function of three variables.

In **Double Integrals over Rectangular Regions**, we discussed the double integral of a function $f(x, y)$ of two variables over a rectangular region in the plane. In this section we define the triple integral of a function $f(x, y, z)$ of three variables over a rectangular solid box in space, $\mathbb{R}^3$. Later in this section we extend the definition to more general regions in $\mathbb{R}^3$.

Integrable Functions of Three Variables

We can define a rectangular box B in $\mathbb{R}^3$ as $B = \{(x, y, z) | a \le x \le b, c \le y \le d, e \le z \le f\}$. We follow a similar procedure to what we did in **Double Integrals over Rectangular Regions**. We divide the interval $[a, b]$ into l subintervals $[x_{i-1}, x_i]$ of equal length $\Delta x = \frac{x_i - x_{i-1}}{l}$, divide the interval $[c, d]$ into m subintervals $[y_{i-1}, y_i]$ of equal length $\Delta y = \frac{y_j - y_{j-1}}{m}$, and divide the interval $[e, f]$ into n subintervals $[z_{i-1}, z_i]$ of equal length $\Delta z = \frac{z_k - z_{k-1}}{n}$. Then the rectangular box B is subdivided into lmn subboxes $B_{ijk} = [x_{i-1}, x_i] \times [y_{i-1}, y_i] \times [z_{i-1}, z_i]$, as shown in **Figure 5.40**.

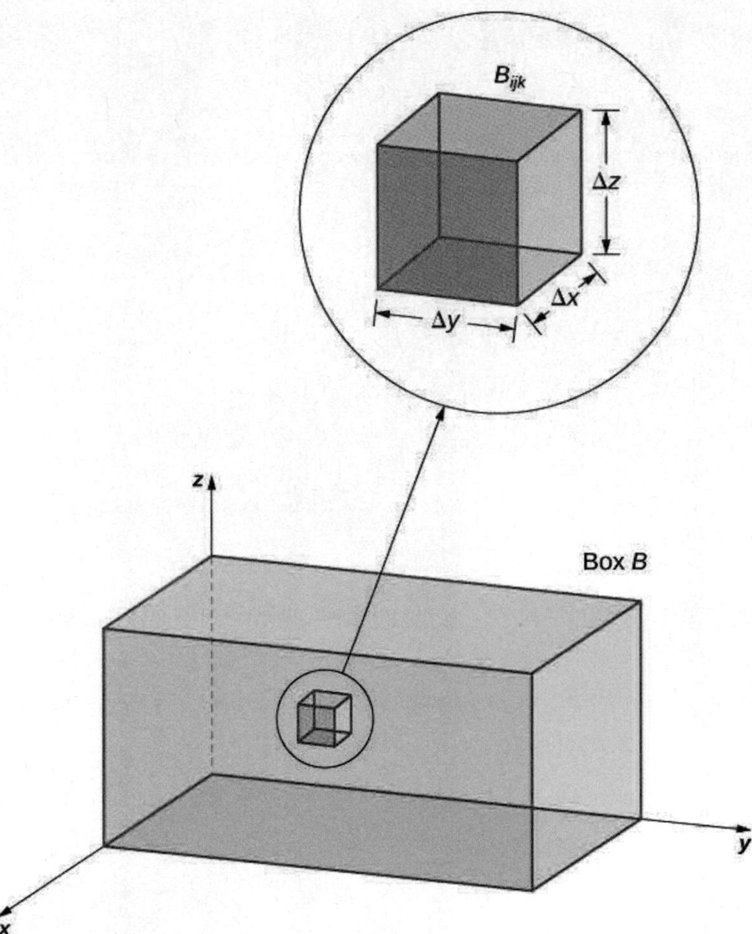

Figure 5.40 A rectangular box in $\mathbb{R}^3$ divided into subboxes by planes parallel to the coordinate planes.

For each $i, j,$ and $k,$ consider a sample point $(x^*_{ijk}, y^*_{ijk}, z^*_{ijk})$ in each sub-box B_{ijk}. We see that its volume is $\Delta V = \Delta x \Delta y \Delta z$. Form the triple Riemann sum

$$\sum_{i=1}^{l} \sum_{j=1}^{m} \sum_{k=1}^{n} f(x^*_{ijk}, y^*_{ijk}, z^*_{ijk}) \Delta x \Delta y \Delta z.$$

We define the triple integral in terms of the limit of a triple Riemann sum, as we did for the double integral in terms of a double Riemann sum.

Definition

The **triple integral** of a function $f(x, y, z)$ over a rectangular box B is defined as

$$\lim_{l, m, n \to \infty} \sum_{i=1}^{l} \sum_{j=1}^{m} \sum_{k=1}^{n} f(x^*_{ijk}, y^*_{ijk}, z^*_{ijk}) \Delta x \Delta y \Delta z = \iiint_B f(x, y, z) dV \quad (5.10)$$

if this limit exists.

When the triple integral exists on $B,$ the function $f(x, y, z)$ is said to be integrable on B. Also, the triple integral exists if $f(x, y, z)$ is continuous on B. Therefore, we will use continuous functions for our examples. However, continuity is sufficient but not necessary; in other words, f is bounded on B and continuous except possibly on the boundary of B.

The sample point $(x^*_{ijk}, y^*_{ijk}, z^*_{ijk})$ can be any point in the rectangular sub-box B_{ijk} and all the properties of a double integral apply to a triple integral. Just as the double integral has many practical applications, the triple integral also has many applications, which we discuss in later sections.

Now that we have developed the concept of the triple integral, we need to know how to compute it. Just as in the case of the double integral, we can have an iterated triple integral, and consequently, a version of Fubini's thereom for triple integrals exists.

Theorem 5.9: Fubini's Theorem for Triple Integrals

If $f(x, y, z)$ is continuous on a rectangular box $B = [a, b] \times [c, d] \times [e, f]$, then

$$\iiint_B f(x, y, z)dV = \int_e^f \int_c^d \int_a^b f(x, y, z)dx\,dy\,dz.$$

This integral is also equal to any of the other five possible orderings for the iterated triple integral.

For $a, b, c, d, e,$ and f real numbers, the iterated triple integral can be expressed in six different orderings:

$$\begin{aligned}\int_e^f \int_c^d \int_a^b f(x, y, z)dx\,dy\,dz &= \int_e^f \left(\int_c^d \left(\int_a^b f(x, y, z)dx\right)dy\right)dz = \int_c^d \left(\int_e^f \left(\int_a^b f(x, y, z)dx\right)dz\right)dy \\ &= \int_a^b \left(\int_e^f \left(\int_c^d f(x, y, z)dy\right)dz\right)dx = \int_e^f \left(\int_a^b \left(\int_c^d f(x, y, z)dy\right)dx\right)dz \\ &= \int_c^e \left(\int_a^b \left(\int_e^f f(x, y, z)dz\right)dx\right)dy = \int_a^b \left(\int_c^e \left(\int_e^f f(x, y, z)dz\right)dy\right)dx.\end{aligned}$$

For a rectangular box, the order of integration does not make any significant difference in the level of difficulty in computation. We compute triple integrals using Fubini's Theorem rather than using the Riemann sum definition. We follow the order of integration in the same way as we did for double integrals (that is, from inside to outside).

Example 5.36

Evaluating a Triple Integral

Evaluate the triple integral $\int_{z=0}^{z=1} \int_{y=2}^{y=4} \int_{x=-1}^{x=5} (x + yz^2)dx\,dy\,dz.$

Solution

The order of integration is specified in the problem, so integrate with respect to x first, then y, and then z.

$$\int_{z=0}^{z=1}\int_{y=2}^{y=4}\int_{x=-1}^{x=5}(x+yz^2)dx\,dy\,dz$$

$$=\int_{z=0}^{z=1}\int_{y=2}^{y=4}\left[\frac{x^2}{2}+xyz^2\Big|_{x=-1}^{x=5}\right]dy\,dz \qquad \text{Integrate with respect to } x.$$

$$=\int_{z=0}^{z=1}\int_{y=2}^{y=4}\left[12+6yz^2\right]dy\,dz \qquad \text{Evaluate.}$$

$$=\int_{z=0}^{z=1}\left[12y+6\frac{y^2}{2}z^2\Big|_{y=2}^{y=4}\right]dz \qquad \text{Integrate with respect to } y.$$

$$=\int_{z=0}^{z=1}\left[24+36z^2\right]dz \qquad \text{Evaluate.}$$

$$=\left[24z+36\frac{z^3}{3}\right]_{z=0}^{z=1}=36. \qquad \text{Integrate with respect to } z.$$

Example 5.37

Evaluating a Triple Integral

Evaluate the triple integral $\iiint\limits_B x^2yz\,dV$ where $B=\{(x,y,z)\,|-2\le x\le 1,\ 0\le y\le 3,\ 1\le z\le 5\}$ as shown in the following figure.

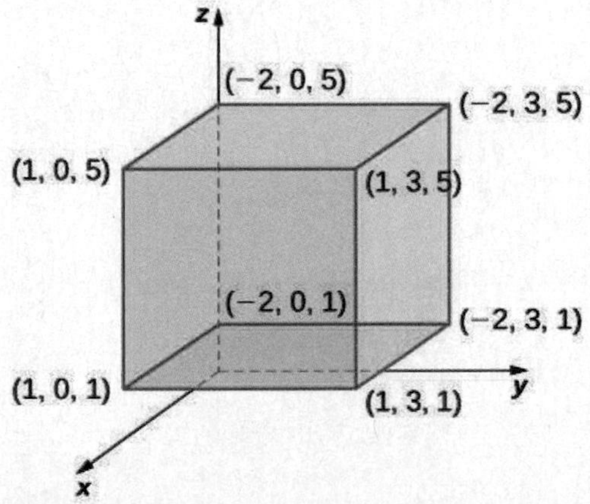

Figure 5.41 Evaluating a triple integral over a given rectangular box.

Solution

The order is not specified, but we can use the iterated integral in any order without changing the level of difficulty. Choose, say, to integrate y first, then x, and then z.

$$\begin{aligned}\iiint_B x^2 yz\,dV &= \int_1^5 \int_{-2}^1 \int_0^3 \left[x^2 yz\right] dy\,dx\,dz = \int_1^5 \int_{-2}^1 \left[x^2 \frac{y^2}{2} z \Big|_0^3\right] dx\,dz \\ &= \int_1^5 \int_{-2}^1 \frac{9}{2} x^2 z\,dx\,dz = \int_1^5 \left[\frac{9}{2}\frac{x^3}{3} z\Big|_{-2}^1\right] dz = \int_1^5 \frac{27}{2} z\,dz = \frac{27}{2}\frac{z^2}{2}\Big|_1^5 = 162.\end{aligned}$$

Now try to integrate in a different order just to see that we get the same answer. Choose to integrate with respect to x first, then z, and then y.

$$\begin{aligned}\iiint_B x^2 yz\,dV &= \int_0^3 \int_1^5 \int_{-2}^1 \left[x^2 yz\right] dx\,dz\,dy = \int_0^3 \int_1^5 \left[\frac{x^3}{3} yz\Big|_{-2}^1\right] dz\,dy \\ &= \int_0^3 \int_1^5 3yz\,dz\,dy = \int_0^3 \left[3y\frac{z^2}{2}\Big|_1^5\right] dy = \int_0^3 36y\,dy = 36\frac{y^2}{2}\Big|_0^3 = 18(9-0) = 162.\end{aligned}$$

5.23 Evaluate the triple integral $\iiint_B z \sin x \cos y\,dV$ where $B = \left\{(x, y, z) \middle| 0 \le x \le \pi, \frac{3\pi}{2} \le y \le 2\pi, 1 \le z \le 3\right\}$.

Triple Integrals over a General Bounded Region

We now expand the definition of the triple integral to compute a triple integral over a more general bounded region E in $\mathbb{R}^3$. The general bounded regions we will consider are of three types. First, let D be the bounded region that is a projection of E onto the xy-plane. Suppose the region E in $\mathbb{R}^3$ has the form

$$E = \{(x, y, z) | (x, y) \in D, u_1(x, y) \le z \le u_2(x, y)\}.$$

For two functions $z = u_1(x, y)$ and $z = u_2(x, y)$, such that $u_1(x, y) \le u_2(x, y)$ for all (x, y) in D as shown in the following figure.

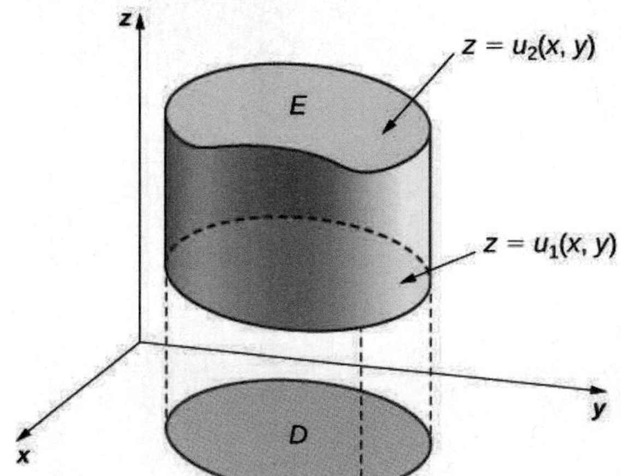

Figure 5.42 We can describe region E as the space between $u_1(x, y)$ and $u_2(x, y)$ above the projection D of E onto the xy-plane.

Theorem 5.10: Triple Integral over a General Region

The triple integral of a continuous function $f(x, y, z)$ over a general three-dimensional region

$$E = \{(x, y, z) | (x, y) \in D, u_1(x, y) \le z \le u_2(x, y)\}$$

in $\mathbb{R}^3$, where D is the projection of E onto the xy-plane, is

$$\iiint_E f(x, y, z) dV = \iint_D \left[\int_{u_1(x, y)}^{u_2(x, y)} f(x, y, z) dz \right] dA.$$

Similarly, we can consider a general bounded region D in the xy-plane and two functions $y = u_1(x, z)$ and $y = u_2(x, z)$ such that $u_1(x, z) \le u_2(x, z)$ for all (x, z) in D. Then we can describe the solid region E in $\mathbb{R}^3$ as

$$E = \{(x, y, z) | (x, z) \in D, u_1(x, z) \le y \le u_2(x, z)\}$$

where D is the projection of E onto the xy-plane and the triple integral is

$$\iiint_E f(x, y, z) dV = \iint_D \left[\int_{u_1(x, z)}^{u_2(x, z)} f(x, y, z) dy \right] dA.$$

Finally, if D is a general bounded region in the yz-plane and we have two functions $x = u_1(y, z)$ and $x = u_2(y, z)$ such that $u_1(y, z) \le u_2(y, z)$ for all (y, z) in D, then the solid region E in $\mathbb{R}^3$ can be described as

$$E = \{(x, y, z) | (y, z) \in D, u_1(y, z) \le x \le u_2(y, z)\}$$

where D is the projection of E onto the yz-plane and the triple integral is

$$\iiint_E f(x, y, z) dV = \iint_D \left[\int_{u_1(y, z)}^{u_2(y, z)} f(x, y, z) dx \right] dA.$$

Note that the region D in any of the planes may be of Type I or Type II as described in **Double Integrals over General Regions**. If D in the xy-plane is of Type I (**Figure 5.43**), then

$$E = \{(x, y, z) | a \le x \le b, g_1(x) \le y \le g_2(x), u_1(x, y) \le z \le u_2(x, y)\}.$$

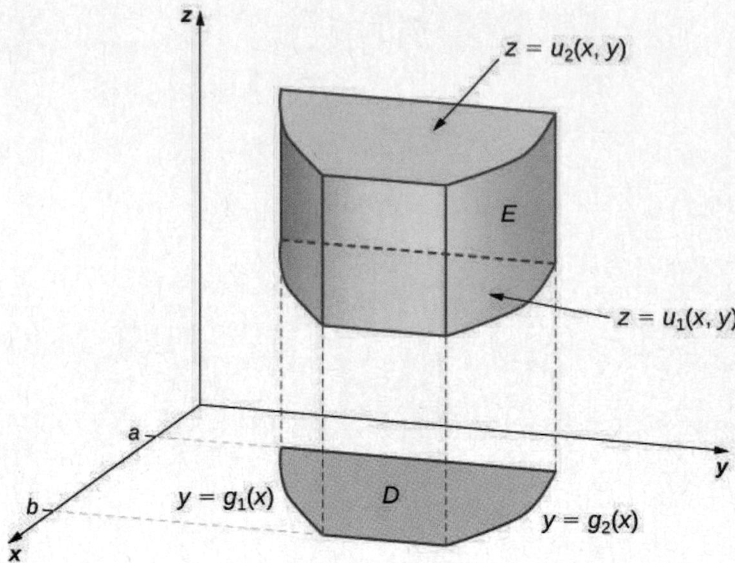

Figure 5.43 A box E where the projection D in the xy -plane is of Type I.

Then the triple integral becomes

$$\iiint_E f(x, y, z)dV = \int_a^b \int_{g_1(x)}^{g_2(x)} \int_{u_1(x, y)}^{u_2(x, y)} f(x, y, z)dz\,dy\,dx.$$

If D in the xy -plane is of Type II (**Figure 5.44**), then

$$E = \{(x, y, z)|c \le x \le d, h_1(x) \le y \le h_2(x), u_1(x, y) \le z \le u_2(x, y)\}.$$

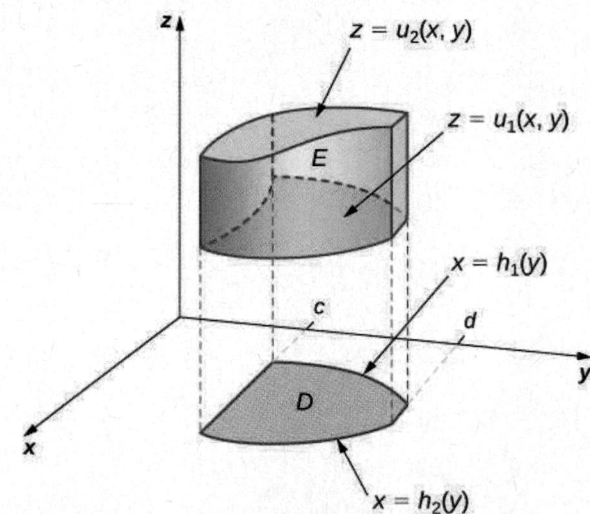

Figure 5.44 A box E where the projection D in the xy -plane is of Type II.

Then the triple integral becomes

$$\iiint_E f(x, y, z)dV = \int_{y=c}^{y=d} \int_{x=h_1(y)}^{x=h_2(y)} \int_{z=u_1(x, y)}^{z=u_2(x, y)} f(x, y, z)dz\,dx\,dy.$$

Example 5.38

Evaluating a Triple Integral over a General Bounded Region

Evaluate the triple integral of the function $f(x, y, z) = 5x - 3y$ over the solid tetrahedron bounded by the planes $x = 0, y = 0, z = 0,$ and $x + y + z = 1.$

Solution

Figure 5.45 shows the solid tetrahedron E and its projection D on the xy -plane.

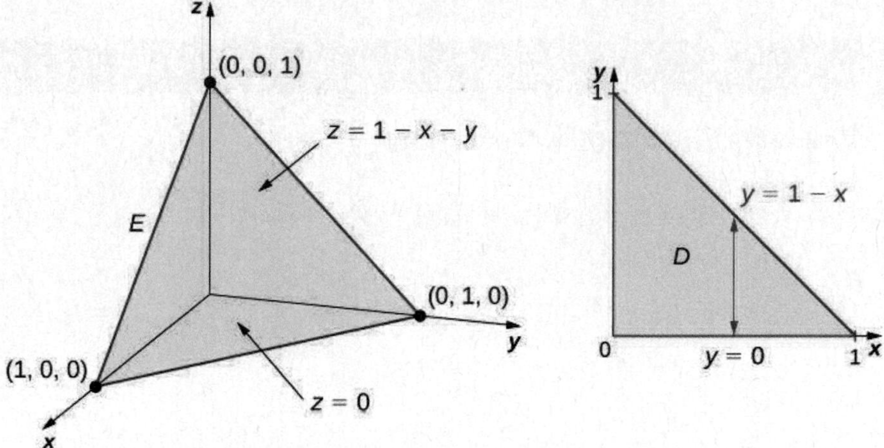

Figure 5.45 The solid E has a projection D on the xy -plane of Type I.

We can describe the solid region tetrahedron as

$$E = \{(x, y, z)|0 \le x \le 1, 0 \le y \le 1 - x, 0 \le z \le 1 - x - y\}.$$

Hence, the triple integral is

$$\iiint_E f(x, y, z)dV = \int_{x=0}^{x=1} \int_{y=0}^{y=1-x} \int_{z=0}^{z=1-x-y} (5x - 3y)dz\, dy\, dx.$$

To simplify the calculation, first evaluate the integral $\int_{z=0}^{z=1-x-y} (5x - 3y)dz.$ We have

$$\int_{z=0}^{z=1-x-y} (5x - 3y)dz = (5x - 3y)(1 - x - y).$$

Now evaluate the integral $\int_{y=0}^{y=1-x} (5x - 3y)(1 - x - y)dy,$ obtaining

$$\int_{y=0}^{y=1-x} (5x - 3y)(1 - x - y)dy = \frac{1}{2}(x - 1)^2(6x - 1).$$

Finally, evaluate

$$\int_{x=0}^{x=1} \frac{1}{2}(x - 1)^2(6x - 1)dx = \frac{1}{12}.$$

Putting it all together, we have

$$\iiint_E f(x, y, z)dV = \int_{x=0}^{x=1} \int_{y=0}^{y=1-x} \int_{z=0}^{z=1-x-y} (5x - 3y)dz\, dy\, dx = \frac{1}{12}.$$

Just as we used the double integral $\iint_D 1dA$ to find the area of a general bounded region $D,$ we can use $\iiint_E 1dV$ to find the volume of a general solid bounded region $E.$ The next example illustrates the method.

Example 5.39

Finding a Volume by Evaluating a Triple Integral

Find the volume of a right pyramid that has the square base in the xy-plane $[-1, 1] \times [-1, 1]$ and vertex at the point $(0, 0, 1)$ as shown in the following figure.

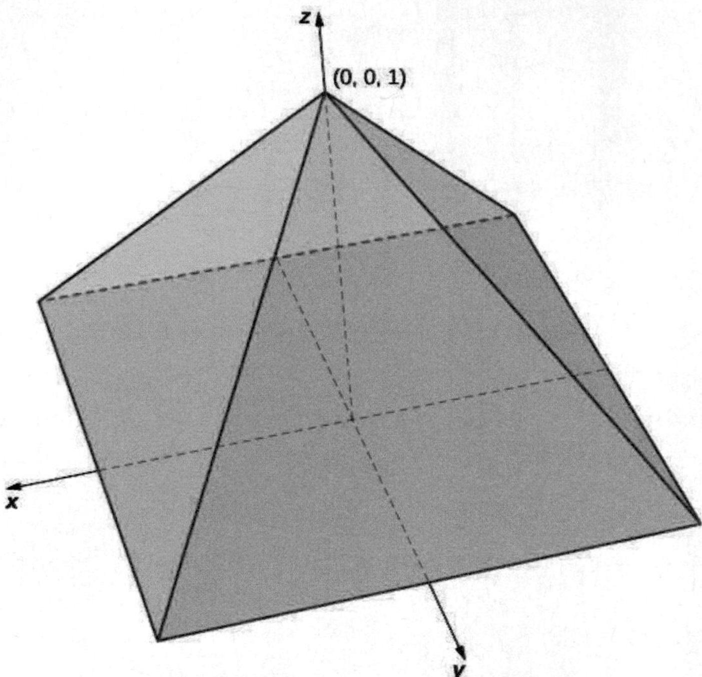

Figure 5.46 Finding the volume of a pyramid with a square base.

Solution

In this pyramid the value of z changes from 0 to 1, and at each height $z,$ the cross section of the pyramid for any value of z is the square $[-1 + z, 1 - z] \times [-1 + z, 1 - z].$ Hence, the volume of the pyramid is $\iiint_E 1dV$ where

$$E = \{(x, y, z)|0 \le z \le 1, -1 + z \le y \le 1 - z, -1 + z \le x \le 1 - z\}.$$

Thus, we have

$$\iiint_E 1dV = \int_{z=0}^{z=1} \int_{y=1+z}^{y=1-z} \int_{x=1+z}^{x=1-z} 1dx\,dy\,dz = \int_{z=0}^{z=1} \int_{y=1+z}^{y=1-z} (2-2z)dy\,dz = \int_{z=0}^{z=1} (2-2z)^2 dz = \frac{4}{3}.$$

Hence, the volume of the pyramid is $\frac{4}{3}$ cubic units.

5.24 Consider the solid sphere $E = \{(x, y, z)|x^2 + y^2 + z^2 = 9\}$. Write the triple integral $\iiint_E f(x, y, z)dV$ for an arbitrary function f as an iterated integral. Then evaluate this triple integral with $f(x, y, z) = 1$. Notice that this gives the volume of a sphere using a triple integral.

Changing the Order of Integration

As we have already seen in double integrals over general bounded regions, changing the order of the integration is done quite often to simplify the computation. With a triple integral over a rectangular box, the order of integration does not change the level of difficulty of the calculation. However, with a triple integral over a general bounded region, choosing an appropriate order of integration can simplify the computation quite a bit. Sometimes making the change to polar coordinates can also be very helpful. We demonstrate two examples here.

Example 5.40

Changing the Order of Integration

Consider the iterated integral

$$\int_{x=0}^{x=1} \int_{y=0}^{y=x^2} \int_{z=0}^{z=y} f(x, y, z)dz\,dy\,dx.$$

The order of integration here is first with respect to z, then y, and then x. Express this integral by changing the order of integration to be first with respect to x, then z, and then y. Verify that the value of the integral is the same if we let $f(x, y, z) = xyz$.

Solution

The best way to do this is to sketch the region E and its projections onto each of the three coordinate planes. Thus, let

$$E = \{(x, y, z)|0 \le x \le 1, 0 \le y \le x^2, 0 \le z \le y\}.$$

and

$$\int_{x=0}^{x=1} \int_{y=0}^{y=x^2} \int_{z=0}^{z=y^2} f(x, y, z)dz\,dy\,dx = \iiint_E f(x, y, z)dV.$$

We need to express this triple integral as

$$\int_{y=c}^{y=d} \int_{z=v_1(y)}^{z=v_2(y)} \int_{x=u_1(y,z)}^{x=u_2(y,z)} f(x, y, z)dx\, dz\, dy.$$

Knowing the region E we can draw the following projections (**Figure 5.47**):

on the xy -plane is $D_1 = \left\{(x, y) \middle| 0 \le x \le 1, 0 \le y \le x^2\right\} = \{(x, y)| 0 \le y \le 1, \sqrt{y} \le x \le 1\}$,

on the yz -plane is $D_2 = \left\{(y, z) \middle| 0 \le y \le 1, 0 \le z \le y^2\right\}$, and

on the xz -plane is $D_3 = \left\{(x, z) \middle| 0 \le x \le 1, 0 \le z \le x^2\right\}$.

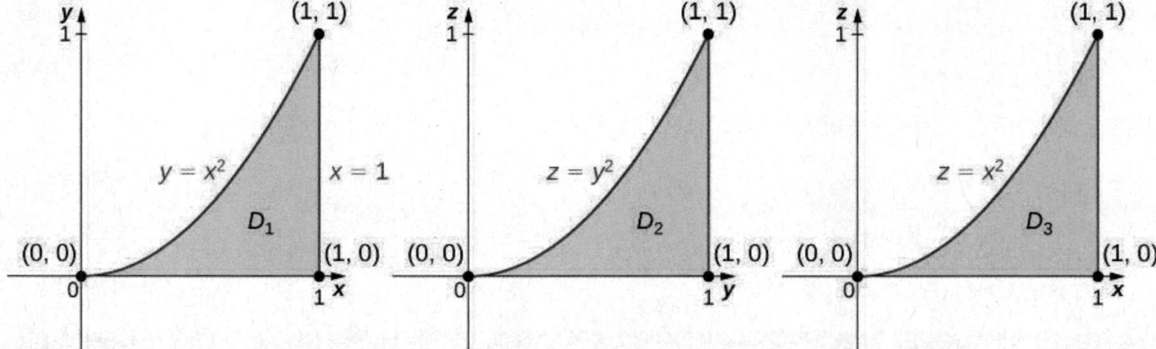

Figure 5.47 The three cross sections of E on the three coordinate planes.

Now we can describe the same region E as $\left\{(x, y, z) \middle| 0 \le y \le 1, 0 \le z \le y^2, \sqrt{y} \le x \le 1\right\}$, and consequently, the triple integral becomes

$$\int_{y=c}^{y=d} \int_{z=v_1(y)}^{z=v_2(y)} \int_{x=u_1(y,z)}^{x=u_2(y,z)} f(x, y, z)dx\, dz\, dy = \int_{y=0}^{y=1} \int_{z=0}^{z=x^2} \int_{x=\sqrt{y}}^{x=1} f(x, y, z)dx\, dz\, dy.$$

Now assume that $f(x, y, z) = xyz$ in each of the integrals. Then we have

$$\int_{x=0}^{x=1} \int_{y=0}^{y=x^2} \int_{z=0}^{z=y^2} xyz \, dz \, dy \, dx$$

$$= \int_{x=0}^{x=1} \int_{y=0}^{y=x^2} \left[xy\frac{z^2}{2} \Big|_{z=0}^{z=y^2} \right] dy \, dx = \int_{x=0}^{x=1} \int_{y=0}^{y=x^2} \left(x\frac{y^5}{2} \right) dy \, dx = \int_{x=0}^{x=1} \left[x\frac{y^6}{12} \Big|_{y=0}^{y=x^2} \right] dx = \int_{x=0}^{x=1} \frac{x^{13}}{12} dx = \frac{1}{168},$$

$$\int_{y=0}^{y=1} \int_{z=0}^{z=y^2} \int_{x=\sqrt{y}}^{x=1} xyz \, dx \, dz \, dy$$

$$= \int_{y=0}^{y=1} \int_{z=0}^{z=y^2} \left[yz\frac{x^2}{2} \Big|_{\sqrt{y}}^{1} \right] dz \, dy$$

$$= \int_{y=0}^{y=1} \int_{z=0}^{z=y^2} \left(\frac{yz}{2} - \frac{y^2 z}{2} \right) dz \, dy = \int_{y=0}^{y=1} \left[\frac{yz^2}{4} - \frac{y^2 z^2}{4} \Big|_{z=0}^{z=y^2} \right] dy = \int_{y=0}^{y=1} \left(\frac{y^5}{4} - \frac{y^6}{4} \right) dy = \frac{1}{168}.$$

The answers match.

5.25 Write five different iterated integrals equal to the given integral

$$\int_{z=0}^{z=4} \int_{y=0}^{y=4-z} \int_{x=0}^{x=\sqrt{y}} f(x, y, z) dx \, dy \, dz.$$

Example 5.41

Changing Integration Order and Coordinate Systems

Evaluate the triple integral $\iiint\limits_E \sqrt{x^2 + z^2} dV,$ where E is the region bounded by the paraboloid $y = x^2 + z^2$ (**Figure 5.48**) and the plane $y = 4.$

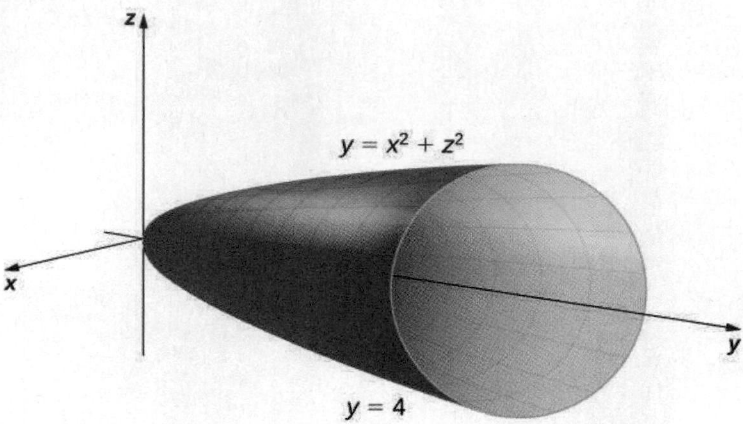

Figure 5.48 Integrating a triple integral over a paraboloid.

Solution

The projection of the solid region E onto the xy-plane is the region bounded above by $y = 4$ and below by the parabola $y = x^2$ as shown.

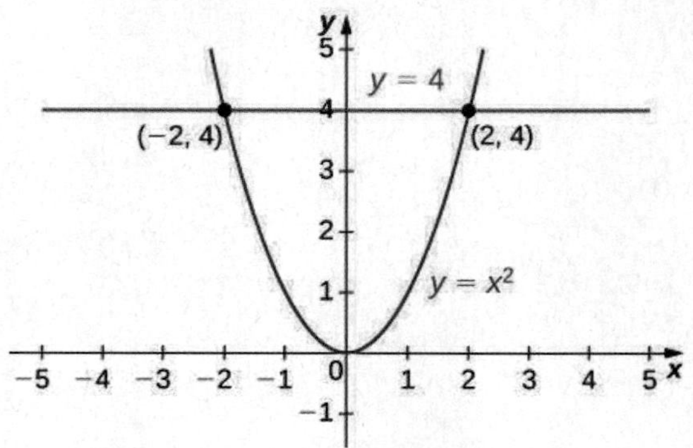

Figure 5.49 Cross section in the xy-plane of the paraboloid in **Figure 5.48**.

Thus, we have

$$E = \left\{(x, y, z) | -2 \le x \le 2, x^2 \le y \le 4, -\sqrt{y - x^2} \le z \le \sqrt{y - x^2}\right\}.$$

The triple integral becomes

$$\iiint_E \sqrt{x^2 + z^2} dV = \int_{x=-2}^{x=2} \int_{y=x^2}^{y=4} \int_{z=-\sqrt{y-x^2}}^{z=\sqrt{y-x^2}} \sqrt{x^2 + z^2} dz\, dy\, dx.$$

This expression is difficult to compute, so consider the projection of E onto the xz-plane. This is a circular disc $x^2 + z^2 \le 4.$ So we obtain

$$\iiint_E \sqrt{x^2 + z^2} dV = \int_{x=-2}^{x=2} \int_{y=x^2}^{y=4} \int_{z=-\sqrt{y-x^2}}^{z=\sqrt{y-x^2}} \sqrt{x^2 + z^2} dz\, dy\, dx = \int_{x=-2}^{x=2} \int_{z=-\sqrt{4-x^2}}^{z=\sqrt{4-x^2}} \int_{y=x^2+z^2}^{y=4} \sqrt{x^2 + z^2} dy\, dz\, dx.$$

Here the order of integration changes from being first with respect to $z,$ then $y,$ and then x to being first with respect to $y,$ then to $z,$ and then to $x.$ It will soon be clear how this change can be beneficial for computation. We have

$$\int_{x=-2}^{x=2}\int_{z=-\sqrt{4-x^2}}^{z=\sqrt{4-x^2}}\int_{y=x^2+z^2}^{y=4}\sqrt{x^2+z^2}\,dy\,dz\,dx=\int_{x=-2}^{x=2}\int_{z=-\sqrt{4-x^2}}^{z=\sqrt{4-x^2}}(4-x^2-z^2)\sqrt{x^2+z^2}\,dz\,dx.$$

Now use the polar substitution $x=r\cos\theta,\ z=r\sin\theta,$ and $dz\,dx=r\,dr\,d\theta$ in the xz-plane. This is essentially the same thing as when we used polar coordinates in the xy-plane, except we are replacing y by $z.$ Consequently the limits of integration change and we have, by using $r^2=x^2+z^2,$

$$\begin{aligned}\int_{x=-2}^{x=2}\int_{z=-\sqrt{4-x^2}}^{z=\sqrt{4-x^2}}(4-x^2-z^2)\sqrt{x^2+z^2}\,dz\,dx &= \int_{\theta=0}^{\theta=2\pi}\int_{r=0}^{r=2}(4-r^2)rr\,dr\,d\theta \\ &= \int_0^{2\pi}\left[\frac{4r^3}{3}-\frac{r^5}{5}\Big|_0^2\right]d\theta=\int_0^{2\pi}\frac{64}{15}d\theta=\frac{128\pi}{15}.\end{aligned}$$

Average Value of a Function of Three Variables

Recall that we found the average value of a function of two variables by evaluating the double integral over a region on the plane and then dividing by the area of the region. Similarly, we can find the average value of a function in three variables by evaluating the triple integral over a solid region and then dividing by the volume of the solid.

Theorem 5.11: Average Value of a Function of Three Variables

If $f(x,\,y,\,z)$ is integrable over a solid bounded region E with positive volume $V(E),$ then the average value of the function is

$$f_{\text{ave}}=\frac{1}{V(E)}\iiint_E f(x,\,y,\,z)dV.$$

Note that the volume is $V(E)=\iiint_E 1dV.$

Example 5.42

Finding an Average Temperature

The temperature at a point $(x,\,y,\,z)$ of a solid E bounded by the coordinate planes and the plane $x+y+z=1$ is $T(x,\,y,\,z)=(xy+8z+20)°\text{C}.$ Find the average temperature over the solid.

Solution

Use the theorem given above and the triple integral to find the numerator and the denominator. Then do the division. Notice that the plane $x + y + z = 1$ has intercepts $(1, 0, 0)$, $(0, 1, 0)$, and $(0, 0, 1)$. The region E looks like

$$E = \{(x, y, z) | 0 \le x \le 1, 0 \le y \le 1 - x, 0 \le z \le 1 - x - y\}.$$

Hence the triple integral of the temperature is

$$\iiint_E f(x, y, z) dV = \int_{x=0}^{x=1} \int_{y=0}^{y=1-x} \int_{z=0}^{z=1-x-y} (xy + 8z + 20) dz\, dy\, dx = \frac{147}{40}.$$

The volume evaluation is $V(E) = \iiint_E 1 dV = \int_{x=0}^{x=1} \int_{y=0}^{y=1-x} \int_{z=0}^{z=1-x-y} 1 dz\, dy\, dx = \frac{1}{6}.$

Hence the average value is $T_{\text{ave}} = \frac{147/40}{1/6} = \frac{6(147)}{40} = \frac{441}{20}$ degrees Celsius.

5.26 Find the average value of the function $f(x, y, z) = xyz$ over the cube with sides of length 4 units in the first octant with one vertex at the origin and edges parallel to the coordinate axes.

5.4 EXERCISES

In the following exercises, evaluate the triple integrals over the rectangular solid box B.

181. $\iiint_B \left(2x + 3y^2 + 4z^3\right)dV,$ where $B = \{(x, y, z)|0 \le x \le 1, 0 \le y \le 2, 0 \le z \le 3\}$

182. $\iiint_B (xy + yz + xz)dV,$ where $B = \{(x, y, z)|1 \le x \le 2, 0 \le y \le 2, 1 \le z \le 3\}$

183. $\iiint_B (x \cos y + z)dV,$ where $B = \{(x, y, z)|0 \le x \le 1, 0 \le y \le \pi, -1 \le z \le 1\}$

184. $\iiint_B \left(z \sin x + y^2\right)dV,$ where $B = \{(x, y, z)|0 \le x \le \pi, 0 \le y \le 1, -1 \le z \le 2\}$

In the following exercises, change the order of integration by integrating first with respect to $z,$ then $x,$ then $y.$

185. $\int_0^1 \int_1^2 \int_2^3 \left(x^2 + \ln y + z\right)dx\, dy\, dz$

186. $\int_0^1 \int_{-1}^1 \int_0^3 \left(ze^x + 2y\right)dx\, dy\, dz$

187. $\int_{-1}^2 \int_1^3 \int_0^4 \left(x^2 z + \frac{1}{y}\right)dx\, dy\, dz$

188. $\int_1^2 \int_{-2}^{-1} \int_0^1 \frac{x + y}{z}dx\, dy\, dz$

189. Let $F, G,$ and H be continuous functions on $[a, b], [c, d],$ and $[e, f],$ respectively, where $a, b, c, d, e,$ and f are real numbers such that $a < b, c < d,$ and $e < f.$ Show that

$$\int_a^b \int_c^d \int_e^f F(x)G(y)H(z)dz\, dy\, dx = \left(\int_a^b F(x)dx\right)\left(\int_c^d G(y)dy\right)\left(\int_e^f H(z)dz\right).$$

190. Let $F, G,$ and H be differential functions on $[a, b], [c, d],$ and $[e, f],$ respectively, where $a, b, c, d, e,$ and f are real numbers such that $a < b, c < d,$ and $e < f.$ Show that

$$\int_a^b \int_c^d \int_e^f F'(x)G'(y)H'(z)dz\, dy\, dx = [F(b) - F(a)][G(d) - G(c)][H(f) - H(e)].$$

In the following exercises, evaluate the triple integrals over the bounded region $E = \{(x, y, z)|a \le x \le b, h_1(x) \le y \le h_2(x), e \le z \le f\}.$

191. $\iiint_E (2x + 5y + 7z)dV,$ where $E = \{(x, y, z)|0 \le x \le 1, 0 \le y \le -x + 1, 1 \le z \le 2\}$

192. $\iiint_E (y \ln x + z)dV,$ where $E = \{(x, y, z)|1 \le x \le e, 0 \le y \le \ln x, 0 \le z \le 1\}$

193. $\iiint_E (\sin x + \sin y)dV,$ where $E = \left\{(x, y, z)|0 \le x \le \frac{\pi}{2}, -\cos x \le y \le \cos x, -1 \le z \le 1\right\}$

194. $\iiint_E (xy + yz + xz)dV,$ where $E = \left\{(x, y, z)|0 \le x \le 1, -x^2 \le y \le x^2, 0 \le z \le 1\right\}$

In the following exercises, evaluate the triple integrals over the indicated bounded region $E.$

195. $\iiint_E (x + 2yz)dV,$ where $E = \{(x, y, z)|0 \le x \le 1, 0 \le y \le x, 0 \le z \le 5 - x - y\}$

196. $\iiint_E \left(x^3 + y^3 + z^3\right)dV,$ where $E = \{(x, y, z)|0 \le x \le 2, 0 \le y \le 2x, 0 \le z \le 4 - x - y\}$

197. $\iiint_E y\, dV,$ where $E = \left\{(x, y, z)\middle| -1 \le x \le 1, -\sqrt{1 - x^2} \le y \le \sqrt{1 - x^2}, 0 \le z \le 1 - x^2 - y^2\right\}$

198. $\iiint_E x\, dV,$ where $E = \left\{(x, y, z)\middle| -2 \le x \le 2, -4\sqrt{1 - x^2} \le y \le \sqrt{4 - x^2}, 0 \le z \le 4 - x^2 - y^2\right\}$

In the following exercises, evaluate the triple integrals over the bounded region E of the form $E = \{(x, y, z)|g_1(y) \le x \le g_2(y), c \le y \le d, e \le z \le f\}.$

199. $\iiint\limits_E x^2\,dV,$ where $E = \{(x, y, z)|1 - y^2 \le x \le y^2 - 1, -1 \le y \le 1, 1 \le z \le 2\}$

200. $\iiint\limits_E (\sin x + y)dV,$ where $E = \{(x, y, z)| - y^4 \le x \le y^4, 0 \le y \le 2, 0 \le z \le 4\}$

201. $\iiint\limits_E (x - yz)dV,$ where $E = \{(x, y, z)| - y^6 \le x \le \sqrt{y}, 0 \le y \le 1x, -1 \le z \le 1\}$

202. $\iiint\limits_E z dV,$ where $E = \{(x, y, z)|2 - 2y \le x \le 2 + \sqrt{y}, 0 \le y \le 1x, 2 \le z \le 3\}$

In the following exercises, evaluate the triple integrals over the bounded region

$E = \{(x, y, z)|g_1(y) \le x \le g_2(y), c \le y \le d, u_1(x, y) \le z \le u_2(x, y)\}.$

203. $\iiint\limits_E z dV,$ where $E = \{(x, y, z)| - y \le x \le y, 0 \le y \le 1, 0 \le z \le 1 - x^4 - y^4\}$

204. $\iiint\limits_E (xz + 1)dV,$ where $E = \{(x, y, z)|0 \le x \le \sqrt{y}, 0 \le y \le 2, 0 \le z \le 1 - x^2 - y^2\}$

205. $\iiint\limits_E (x - z)dV,$ where $E = \{(x, y, z)| - \sqrt{1 - y^2} \le x \le y, 0 \le y \le \frac{1}{2}x, 0 \le z \le 1 - x^2 - y^2\}$

206. $\iiint\limits_E (x + y)dV,$ where $E = \{(x, y, z)|0 \le x \le \sqrt{1 - y^2}, 0 \le y \le 1x, 0 \le z \le 1 - x\}$

In the following exercises, evaluate the triple integrals over the bounded region $E = \{(x, y, z)|(x, y) \in D, u_1(x, y)x \le z \le u_2(x, y)\},$ where D is the projection of E onto the xy-plane.

207. $\iint\limits_D \left(\int_1^2 (x + z)dz\right)dA,$ where $D = \{(x, y)|x^2 + y^2 \le 1\}$

208. $\iint\limits_D \left(\int_1^3 x(z + 1)dz\right)dA,$ where $D = \{(x, y)|x^2 - y^2 \ge 1, x \le \sqrt{5}\}$

209. $\iint\limits_D \left(\int_0^{10 - x - y} (x + 2z)dz\right)dA,$ where $D = \{(x, y)|y \ge 0, x \ge 0, x + y \le 10\}$

210. $\iint\limits_D \left(\int_0^{4x^2 + 4y^2} y\,dz\right)dA,$ where $D = \{(x, y)|x^2 + y^2 \le 4, y \ge 1, x \ge 0\}$

211. The solid E bounded by $y^2 + z^2 = 9, z = 0,$ and $x = 5$ is shown in the following figure. Evaluate the integral $\iiint\limits_E z\,dV$ by integrating first with respect to $z,$ then $y,$ and then $x.$

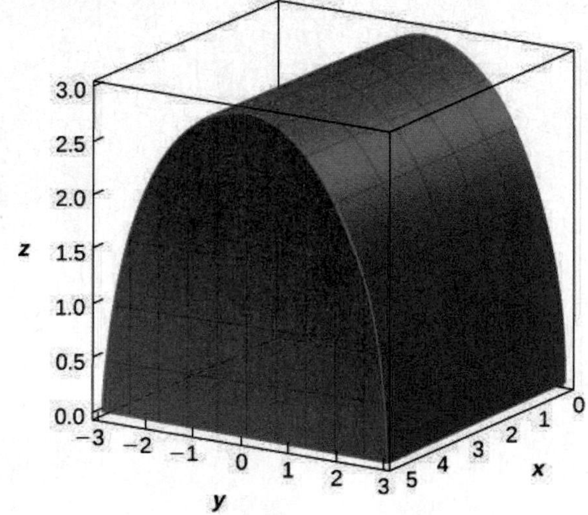

212. The solid E bounded by $y = \sqrt{x}$, $x = 4$, $y = 0$, and $z = 1$ is given in the following figure. Evaluate the integral $\iiint_E xyz\,dV$ by integrating first with respect to x, then y, and then z.

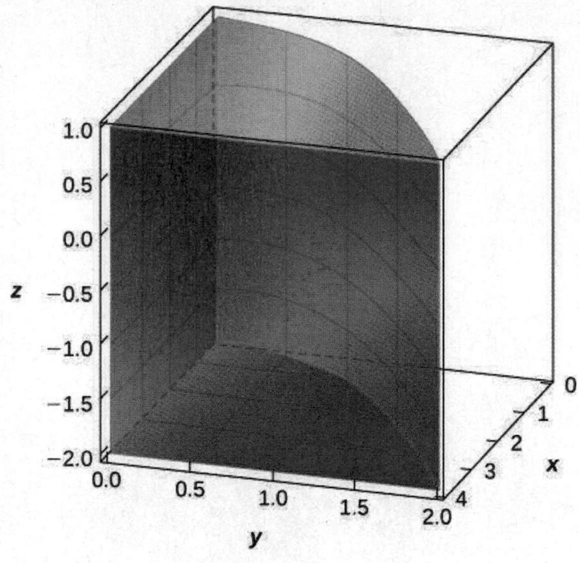

213. **[T]** The volume of a solid E is given by the integral $\int_{-2}^{0}\int_{x}^{0}\int_{0}^{x^2+y^2} dz\,dy\,dx$. Use a computer algebra system (CAS) to graph E and find its volume. Round your answer to two decimal places.

214. **[T]** The volume of a solid E is given by the integral $\int_{-1}^{0}\int_{-x^2}^{0}\int_{0}^{1+\sqrt{x^2+y^2}} dz\,dy\,dx$. Use a CAS to graph E and find its volume V. Round your answer to two decimal places.

In the following exercises, use two circular permutations of the variables x, y, and z to write new integrals whose values equal the value of the original integral. A circular permutation of x, y, and z is the arrangement of the numbers in one of the following orders: y, z, and x or z, x, and y.

215. $\int_{0}^{1}\int_{1}^{3}\int_{2}^{4}\left(x^2z^2+1\right)dx\,dy\,dz$

216. $\int_{1}^{3}\int_{0}^{1}\int_{0}^{-x+1}(2x+5y+7z)dy\,dx\,dz$

217. $\int_{0}^{1}\int_{-y}^{y}\int_{0}^{1-x^4-y^4} \ln x\,dz\,dx\,dy$

218. $\int_{-1}^{1}\int_{0}^{1}\int_{-y^6}^{\sqrt{y}}(x+yz)dx\,dy\,dz$

219. Set up the integral that gives the volume of the solid E bounded by $y^2 = x^2 + z^2$ and $y = a^2$, where $a > 0$.

220. Set up the integral that gives the volume of the solid E bounded by $x = y^2 + z^2$ and $x = a^2$, where $a > 0$.

221. Find the average value of the function $f(x, y, z) = x + y + z$ over the parallelepiped determined by $x = 0$, $x = 1$, $y = 0$, $y = 3$, $z = 0$, and $z = 5$.

222. Find the average value of the function $f(x, y, z) = xyz$ over the solid $E = [0, 1] \times [0, 1] \times [0, 1]$ situated in the first octant.

223. Find the volume of the solid E that lies under the plane $x + y + z = 9$ and whose projection onto the xy-plane is bounded by $x = \sqrt{y-1}$, $x = 0$, and $x + y = 7$.

224. Find the volume of the solid E that lies under the plane $2x + y + z = 8$ and whose projection onto the xy-plane is bounded by $x = \sin^{-1} y$, $y = 0$, and $x = \frac{\pi}{2}$.

225. Consider the pyramid with the base in the xy-plane of $[-2, 2] \times [-2, 2]$ and the vertex at the point $(0, 0, 8)$.

a. Show that the equations of the planes of the lateral faces of the pyramid are $4y + z = 8$, $4y - z = -8$, $4x + z = 8$, and $-4x + z = 8$.

b. Find the volume of the pyramid.

226. Consider the pyramid with the base in the xy-plane of $[-3, 3] \times [-3, 3]$ and the vertex at the point $(0, 0, 9)$.

a. Show that the equations of the planes of the side faces of the pyramid are $3y + z = 9$, $3y + z = 9$, $y = 0$ and $x = 0$.

b. Find the volume of the pyramid.

227. The solid E bounded by the sphere of equation $x^2 + y^2 + z^2 = r^2$ with $r > 0$ and located in the first octant is represented in the following figure.

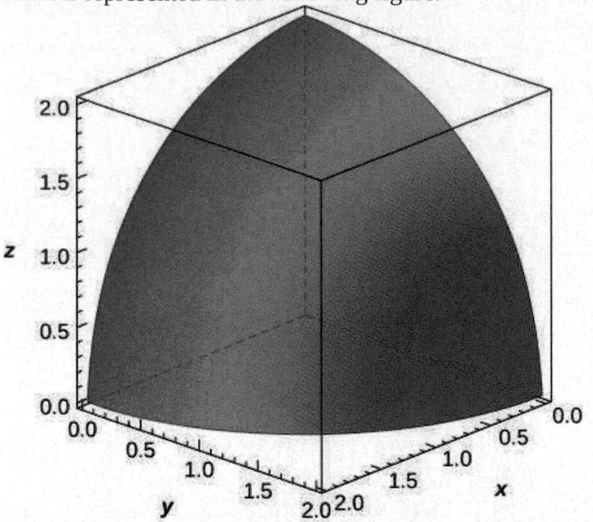

a. Write the triple integral that gives the volume of E by integrating first with respect to $z,$ then with $y,$ and then with $x.$
b. Rewrite the integral in part a. as an equivalent integral in five other orders.

228. The solid E bounded by the equation $9x^2 + 4y^2 + z^2 = 1$ and located in the first octant is represented in the following figure.

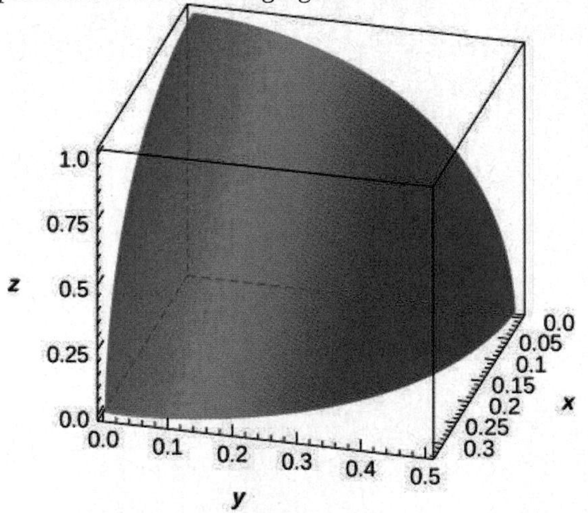

a. Write the triple integral that gives the volume of E by integrating first with respect to $z,$ then with $y,$ and then with $x.$
b. Rewrite the integral in part a. as an equivalent integral in five other orders.

229. Find the volume of the prism with vertices $(0, 0, 0), (2, 0, 0), (2, 3, 0),$ $(0, 3, 0), (0, 0, 1),$ and $(2, 0, 1).$

230. Find the volume of the prism with vertices $(0, 0, 0), (4, 0, 0), (4, 6, 0),$ $(0, 6, 0), (0, 0, 1),$ and $(4, 0, 1).$

231. The solid E bounded by $z = 10 - 2x - y$ and situated in the first octant is given in the following figure. Find the volume of the solid.

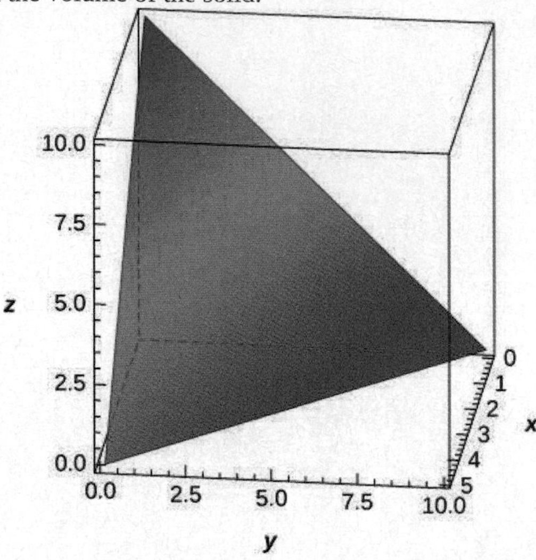

232. The solid E bounded by $z = 1 - x^2$ and situated in the first octant is given in the following figure. Find the volume of the solid.

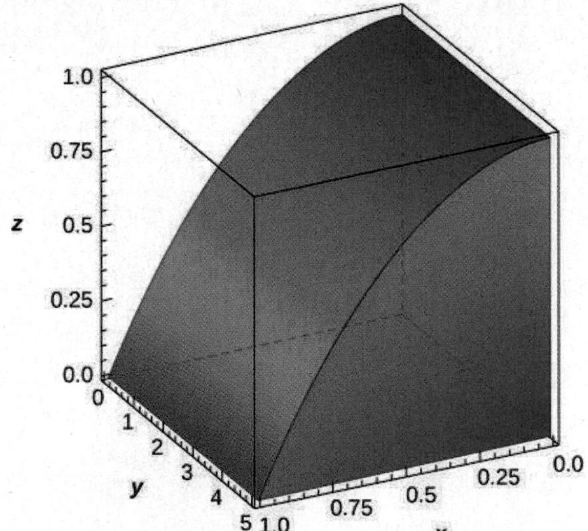

233. The midpoint rule for the triple integral $\iiint_B f(x, y, z)dV$ over the rectangular solid box B is a generalization of the midpoint rule for double integrals. The region B is divided into subboxes of equal sizes and the integral is approximated by the triple Riemann sum $\sum_{i=1}^{l} \sum_{j=1}^{m} \sum_{k=1}^{n} f(\bar{x}_i, \bar{y}_j, \bar{z}_k)\Delta V$, where $(\bar{x}_i, \bar{y}_j, \bar{z}_k)$ is the center of the box B_{ijk} and ΔV is the volume of each subbox. Apply the midpoint rule to approximate $\iiint_B x^2 dV$ over the solid $B = \{(x, y, z)|0 \le x \le 1, 0 \le y \le 1, 0 \le z \le 1\}$ by using a partition of eight cubes of equal size. Round your answer to three decimal places.

234. **[T]**

a. Apply the midpoint rule to approximate $\iiint_B e^{-x^2} dV$ over the solid $B = \{(x, y, z)|0 \le x \le 1, 0 \le y \le 1, 0 \le z \le 1\}$ by using a partition of eight cubes of equal size. Round your answer to three decimal places.

b. Use a CAS to improve the above integral approximation in the case of a partition of n^3 cubes of equal size, where $n = 3, 4,\ldots, 10$.

235. Suppose that the temperature in degrees Celsius at a point (x, y, z) of a solid E bounded by the coordinate planes and $x + y + z = 5$ is $T(x, y, z) = xz + 5z + 10$. Find the average temperature over the solid.

236. Suppose that the temperature in degrees Fahrenheit at a point (x, y, z) of a solid E bounded by the coordinate planes and $x + y + z = 5$ is $T(x, y, z) = x + y + xy$. Find the average temperature over the solid.

237. Show that the volume of a right square pyramid of height h and side length a is $v = \frac{ha^2}{3}$ by using triple integrals.

238. Show that the volume of a regular right hexagonal prism of edge length a is $\frac{3a^3\sqrt{3}}{2}$ by using triple integrals.

239. Show that the volume of a regular right hexagonal pyramid of edge length a is $\frac{a^3\sqrt{3}}{2}$ by using triple integrals.

240. If the charge density at an arbitrary point (x, y, z) of a solid E is given by the function $\rho(x, y, z)$, then the total charge inside the solid is defined as the triple integral $\iiint_E \rho(x, y, z)dV$. Assume that the charge density of the solid E enclosed by the paraboloids $x = 5 - y^2 - z^2$ and $x = y^2 + z^2 - 5$ is equal to the distance from an arbitrary point of E to the origin. Set up the integral that gives the total charge inside the solid E.

5.5 | Triple Integrals in Cylindrical and Spherical Coordinates

Learning Objectives

5.5.1 Evaluate a triple integral by changing to cylindrical coordinates.
5.5.2 Evaluate a triple integral by changing to spherical coordinates.

Earlier in this chapter we showed how to convert a double integral in rectangular coordinates into a double integral in polar coordinates in order to deal more conveniently with problems involving circular symmetry. A similar situation occurs with triple integrals, but here we need to distinguish between cylindrical symmetry and spherical symmetry. In this section we convert triple integrals in rectangular coordinates into a triple integral in either cylindrical or spherical coordinates.

Also recall the chapter opener, which showed the opera house l'Hemisphèric in Valencia, Spain. It has four sections with one of the sections being a theater in a five-story-high sphere (ball) under an oval roof as long as a football field. Inside is an IMAX screen that changes the sphere into a planetarium with a sky full of 9000 twinkling stars. Using triple integrals in spherical coordinates, we can find the volumes of different geometric shapes like these.

Review of Cylindrical Coordinates

As we have seen earlier, in two-dimensional space $\mathbb{R}^2$, a point with rectangular coordinates (x, y) can be identified with (r, θ) in polar coordinates and vice versa, where $x = r\cos\theta$, $y = r\sin\theta$, $r^2 = x^2 + y^2$ and $\tan\theta = \left(\frac{y}{x}\right)$ are the relationships between the variables.

In three-dimensional space $\mathbb{R}^3$, a point with rectangular coordinates (x, y, z) can be identified with cylindrical coordinates (r, θ, z) and vice versa. We can use these same conversion relationships, adding z as the vertical distance to the point from the xy-plane as shown in the following figure.

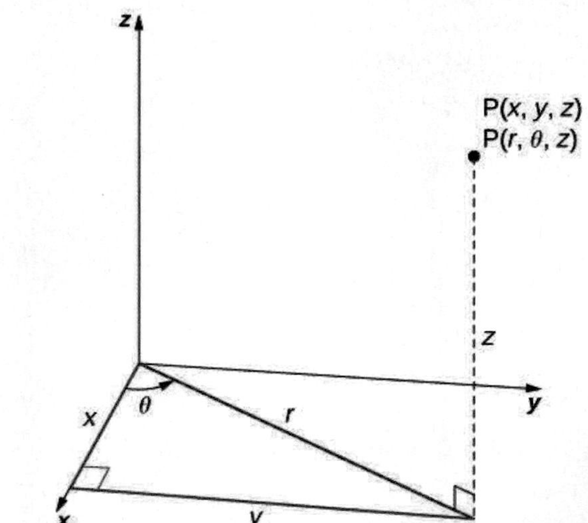

Figure 5.50 Cylindrical coordinates are similar to polar coordinates with a vertical z coordinate added.

To convert from rectangular to cylindrical coordinates, we use the conversion $x = r\cos\theta$ and $y = r\sin\theta$. To convert from cylindrical to rectangular coordinates, we use $r^2 = x^2 + y^2$ and $\theta = \tan^{-1}\left(\frac{y}{x}\right)$. The z-coordinate remains the same in both cases.

In the two-dimensional plane with a rectangular coordinate system, when we say $x = k$ (constant) we mean an unbounded vertical line parallel to the y-axis and when $y = l$ (constant) we mean an unbounded horizontal line parallel to the x-axis.

With the polar coordinate system, when we say $r = c$ (constant), we mean a circle of radius c units and when $\theta = \alpha$ (constant) we mean an infinite ray making an angle α with the positive x-axis.

Similarly, in three-dimensional space with rectangular coordinates (x, y, z), the equations $x = k, y = l,$ and $z = m,$ where $k, l,$ and m are constants, represent unbounded planes parallel to the yz-plane, xz-plane and xy-plane, respectively. With cylindrical coordinates (r, θ, z), by $r = c, \theta = \alpha,$ and $z = m,$ where $c, \alpha,$ and m are constants, we mean an unbounded vertical cylinder with the z-axis as its radial axis; a plane making a constant angle α with the xy-plane; and an unbounded horizontal plane parallel to the xy-plane, respectively. This means that the circular cylinder $x^2 + y^2 = c^2$ in rectangular coordinates can be represented simply as $r = c$ in cylindrical coordinates. (Refer to **Cylindrical and Spherical Coordinates** for more review.)

Integration in Cylindrical Coordinates

Triple integrals can often be more readily evaluated by using cylindrical coordinates instead of rectangular coordinates. Some common equations of surfaces in rectangular coordinates along with corresponding equations in cylindrical coordinates are listed in **Table 5.1**. These equations will become handy as we proceed with solving problems using triple integrals.

	Circular cylinder	Circular cone	Sphere	Paraboloid
Rectangular	$x^2 + y^2 = c^2$	$z^2 = c^2(x^2 + y^2)$	$x^2 + y^2 + z^2 = c^2$	$z = c(x^2 + y^2)$
Cylindrical	$r = c$	$z = cr$	$r^2 + z^2 = c^2$	$z = cr^2$

Table 5.1 Equations of Some Common Shapes

As before, we start with the simplest bounded region B in $\mathbb{R}^3$, to describe in cylindrical coordinates, in the form of a cylindrical box, $B = \{(r, \theta, z)|a \le r \le b, \alpha \le \theta \le \beta, c \le z \le d\}$ (**Figure 5.51**). Suppose we divide each interval into l, m and n subdivisions such that $\Delta r = \frac{b-a}{l}, \Delta\theta = \frac{\beta - \alpha}{m},$ and $\Delta z = \frac{d-c}{n}$. Then we can state the following definition for a triple integral in cylindrical coordinates.

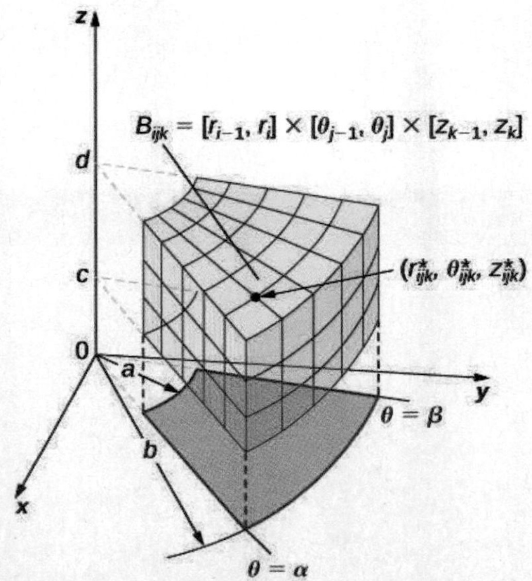

Figure 5.51 A cylindrical box B described by cylindrical coordinates.

Definition

Consider the cylindrical box (expressed in cylindrical coordinates)

$$B = \{(r, \theta, z) | a \le r \le b, \alpha \le \theta \le \beta, c \le z \le d\}.$$

If the function $f(r, \theta, z)$ is continuous on B and if $(r^*_{ijk}, \theta^*_{ijk}, z^*_{ijk})$ is any sample point in the cylindrical subbox $B_{ijk} = [r_{i-1}, r_i] \times [\theta_{j-1}, \theta_j] \times [z_{k-1}, z_k]$ (**Figure 5.51**), then we can define the **triple integral in cylindrical coordinates** as the limit of a triple Riemann sum, provided the following limit exists:

$$\lim_{l, m, n \to \infty} \sum_{i=1}^{l} \sum_{j=1}^{m} \sum_{k=1}^{n} f(r^*_{ijk}, \theta^*_{ijk}, z^*_{ijk}) r^*_{ijk} \Delta r \Delta\theta \Delta z.$$

Note that if $g(x, y, z)$ is the function in rectangular coordinates and the box B is expressed in rectangular coordinates, then the triple integral $\iiint\limits_B g(x, y, z)dV$ is equal to the triple integral $\iiint\limits_B g(r\cos\theta, r\sin\theta, z)r\,dr\,d\theta\,dz$ and we have

$$\iiint\limits_B g(x, y, z)dV = \iiint\limits_B g(r\cos\theta, r\sin\theta, z)r\,dr\,d\theta\,dz = \iiint\limits_B f(r, \theta, z)r\,dr\,d\theta\,dz. \quad \textbf{(5.11)}$$

As mentioned in the preceding section, all the properties of a double integral work well in triple integrals, whether in rectangular coordinates or cylindrical coordinates. They also hold for iterated integrals. To reiterate, in cylindrical coordinates, Fubini's theorem takes the following form:

Theorem 5.12: Fubini's Theorem in Cylindrical Coordinates

Suppose that $g(x, y, z)$ is continuous on a rectangular box B, which when described in cylindrical coordinates looks like $B = \{(r, \theta, z) | a \le r \le b, \alpha \le \theta \le \beta, c \le z \le d\}$.

Then $g(x, y, z) = g(r\cos\theta, r\sin\theta, z) = f(r, \theta, z)$ and

$$\iiint\limits_B g(x, y, z)dV = \int_c^d \int_\alpha^\beta \int_a^b f(r, \theta, z)r\,dr\,d\theta\,dz.$$

The iterated integral may be replaced equivalently by any one of the other five iterated integrals obtained by integrating with respect to the three variables in other orders.

Cylindrical coordinate systems work well for solids that are symmetric around an axis, such as cylinders and cones. Let us look at some examples before we define the triple integral in cylindrical coordinates on general cylindrical regions.

Example 5.43

Evaluating a Triple Integral over a Cylindrical Box

Evaluate the triple integral $\iiint\limits_B (zr\sin\theta)r\,dr\,d\theta\,dz$ where the cylindrical box B is $B = \{(r, \theta, z) | 0 \le r \le 2, 0 \le \theta \le \pi/2, 0 \le z \le 4\}$.

Solution

As stated in Fubini's theorem, we can write the triple integral as the iterated integral

$$\iiint_B (zr \sin \theta) r \, dr \, d\theta \, dz = \int_{\theta=0}^{\theta=\pi/2} \int_{r=0}^{r=2} \int_{z=0}^{z=4} (zr \sin \theta) r \, dz \, dr \, d\theta.$$

The evaluation of the iterated integral is straightforward. Each variable in the integral is independent of the others, so we can integrate each variable separately and multiply the results together. This makes the computation much easier:

$$\int_{\theta=0}^{\theta=\pi/2} \int_{r=0}^{r=2} \int_{z=0}^{z=4} (zr \sin \theta) r \, dz \, dr \, d\theta$$
$$= \left(\int_0^{\pi/2} \sin \theta \, d\theta\right)\left(\int_0^2 r^2 \, dr\right)\left(\int_0^4 z \, dz\right) = \left(-\cos \theta\big|_0^{\pi/2}\right)\left(\frac{r^3}{3}\bigg|_0^2\right)\left(\frac{z^2}{2}\bigg|_0^4\right) = \frac{64}{3}.$$

5.27 Evaluate the triple integral $\int_{\theta=0}^{\theta=\pi} \int_{r=0}^{r=1} \int_{z=0}^{z=4} rz \sin \theta r \, dz \, dr \, d\theta.$

If the cylindrical region over which we have to integrate is a general solid, we look at the projections onto the coordinate planes. Hence the triple integral of a continuous function $f(r, \theta, z)$ over a general solid region $E = \{(r, \theta, z) | (r, \theta) \in D, u_1(r, \theta) \le z \le u_2(r, \theta)\}$ in $\mathbb{R}^3$, where D is the projection of E onto the $r\theta$-plane, is

$$\iiint_E f(r, \theta, z) r \, dr \, d\theta \, dz = \iint_D \left[\int_{u_1(r, \theta)}^{u_2(r, \theta)} f(r, \theta, z) dz\right] r \, dr \, d\theta.$$

In particular, if $D = \{(r, \theta) | g_1(\theta) \le r \le g_2(\theta), \alpha \le \theta \le \beta\}$, then we have

$$\iiint_E f(r, \theta, z) r \, dr \, d\theta = \int_{\theta=\alpha}^{\theta=\beta} \int_{r=g_1(\theta)}^{r=g_2(\theta)} \int_{z=u_1(r, \theta)}^{z=u_2(r, \theta)} f(r, \theta, z) r \, dz \, dr \, d\theta.$$

Similar formulas exist for projections onto the other coordinate planes. We can use polar coordinates in those planes if necessary.

Example 5.44

Setting up a Triple Integral in Cylindrical Coordinates over a General Region

Consider the region E inside the right circular cylinder with equation $r = 2 \sin \theta$, bounded below by the $r\theta$-plane and bounded above by the sphere with radius 4 centered at the origin (**Figure 5.52**). Set up a triple integral over this region with a function $f(r, \theta, z)$ in cylindrical coordinates.

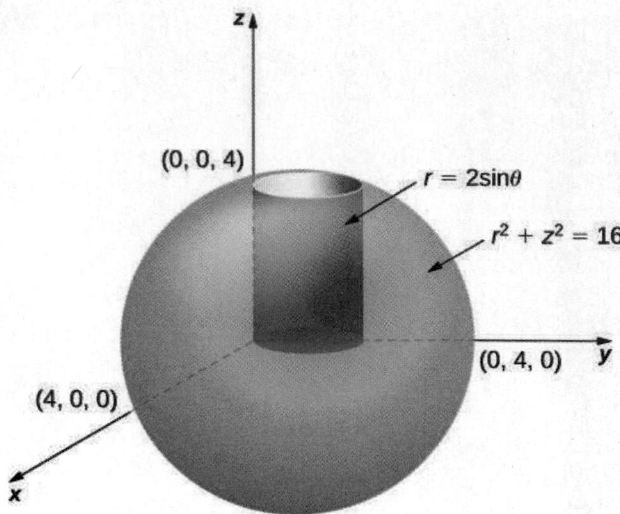

Figure 5.52 Setting up a triple integral in cylindrical coordinates over a cylindrical region.

Solution

First, identify that the equation for the sphere is $r^2 + z^2 = 16$. We can see that the limits for z are from 0 to $z = \sqrt{16 - r^2}$. Then the limits for r are from 0 to $r = 2\sin\theta$. Finally, the limits for θ are from 0 to π. Hence the region is

$$E = \left\{(r, \theta, z) | 0 \le \theta \le \pi, \ 0 \le r \le 2\sin\theta, \ 0 \le z \le \sqrt{16 - r^2}\right\}.$$

Therefore, the triple integral is

$$\iiint_E f(r, \theta, z) r \, dz \, dr \, d\theta = \int_{\theta=0}^{\theta=\pi} \int_{r=0}^{r=2\sin\theta} \int_{z=0}^{z=\sqrt{16-r^2}} f(r, \theta, z) r \, dz \, dr \, d\theta.$$

5.28 Consider the region E inside the right circular cylinder with equation $r = 2\sin\theta$, bounded below by the $r\theta$-plane and bounded above by $z = 4 - y$. Set up a triple integral with a function $f(r, \theta, z)$ in cylindrical coordinates.

Example 5.45

Setting up a Triple Integral in Two Ways

Let E be the region bounded below by the cone $z = \sqrt{x^2 + y^2}$ and above by the paraboloid $z = 2 - x^2 - y^2$. (**Figure 5.53**). Set up a triple integral in cylindrical coordinates to find the volume of the region, using the following orders of integration:

a. $dz \, dr \, d\theta$

b. $dr \, dz \, d\theta$.

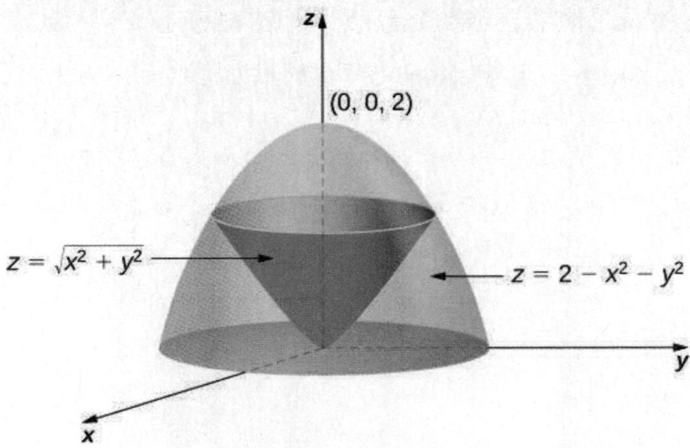

Figure 5.53 Setting up a triple integral in cylindrical coordinates over a conical region.

Solution

a. The cone is of radius 1 where it meets the paraboloid. Since $z = 2 - x^2 - y^2 = 2 - r^2$ and $z = \sqrt{x^2 + y^2} = r$ (assuming r is nonnegative), we have $2 - r^2 = r.$ Solving, we have $r^2 + r - 2 = (r + 2)(r - 1) = 0.$ Since $r \geq 0,$ we have $r = 1.$ Therefore $z = 1.$ So the intersection of these two surfaces is a circle of radius 1 in the plane $z = 1.$ The cone is the lower bound for z and the paraboloid is the upper bound. The projection of the region onto the xy-plane is the circle of radius 1 centered at the origin.
Thus, we can describe the region as

$$E = \{(r, \theta, z)|0 \leq \theta \leq 2\pi, 0 \leq r \leq 1, r \leq z \leq 2 - r^2\}.$$

Hence the integral for the volume is

$$V = \int_{\theta=0}^{\theta=2\pi} \int_{r=0}^{r=1} \int_{z=r}^{z=2-r^2} r\, dz\, dr\, d\theta.$$

b. We can also write the cone surface as $r = z$ and the paraboloid as $r^2 = 2 - z.$ The lower bound for r is zero, but the upper bound is sometimes the cone and the other times it is the paraboloid. The plane $z = 1$ divides the region into two regions. Then the region can be described as

$$\begin{aligned} E &= \{(r, \theta, z)|0 \leq \theta \leq 2\pi, 0 \leq z \leq 1, 0 \leq r \leq z\} \\ &\cup \{(r, \theta, z)|0 \leq \theta \leq 2\pi, 1 \leq z \leq 2, 0 \leq r \leq \sqrt{2 - z}\}. \end{aligned}$$

Now the integral for the volume becomes

$$V = \int_{\theta=0}^{\theta=2\pi} \int_{z=0}^{z=1} \int_{r=0}^{r=z} r\, dr\, dz\, d\theta + \int_{\theta=0}^{\theta=2\pi} \int_{z=1}^{z=2} \int_{r=0}^{r=\sqrt{2-z}} r\, dr\, dz\, d\theta.$$

5.29 Redo the previous example with the order of integration $d\theta\, dz\, dr.$

Example 5.46

Finding a Volume with Triple Integrals in Two Ways

Let E be the region bounded below by the $r\theta$-plane, above by the sphere $x^2 + y^2 + z^2 = 4,$ and on the sides by the cylinder $x^2 + y^2 = 1$ (**Figure 5.54**). Set up a triple integral in cylindrical coordinates to find the volume of the region using the following orders of integration, and in each case find the volume and check that the answers are the same:

a. $dz\, dr\, d\theta$

b. $dr\, dz\, d\theta.$

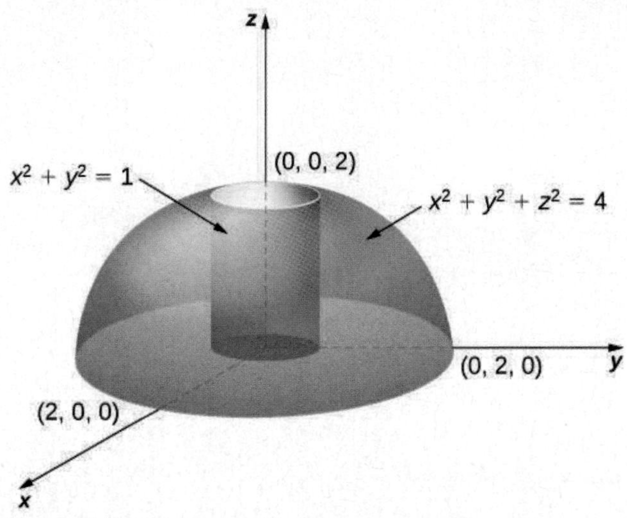

Figure 5.54 Finding a cylindrical volume with a triple integral in cylindrical coordinates.

Solution

a. Note that the equation for the sphere is

$$x^2 + y^2 + z^2 = 4 \text{ or } r^2 + z^2 = 4$$

and the equation for the cylinder is

$$x^2 + y^2 = 1 \text{ or } r^2 = 1.$$

Thus, we have for the region E

$$E = \left\{(r, \theta, z) | 0 \leq z \leq \sqrt{4 - r^2}, 0 \leq r \leq 1, 0 \leq \theta \leq 2\pi\right\}$$

Hence the integral for the volume is

$$\begin{aligned} V(E) &= \int_{\theta=0}^{\theta=2\pi} \int_{r=0}^{r=1} \int_{z=0}^{z=\sqrt{4-r^2}} r\,dz\,dr\,d\theta \\ &= \int_{\theta=0}^{\theta=2\pi} \int_{r=0}^{r=1} \left[rz|_{z=0}^{z=\sqrt{4-r^2}} \right] dr\,d\theta = \int_{\theta=0}^{\theta=2\pi} \int_{r=0}^{r=1} \left(r\sqrt{4-r^2} \right) dr\,d\theta \\ &= \int_0^{2\pi} \left(\frac{8}{3} - \sqrt{3} \right) d\theta = 2\pi \left(\frac{8}{3} - \sqrt{3} \right) \text{cubic units.} \end{aligned}$$

b. Since the sphere is $x^2 + y^2 + z^2 = 4$, which is $r^2 + z^2 = 4$, and the cylinder is $x^2 + y^2 = 1$, which is $r^2 = 1$, we have $1 + z^2 = 4$, that is, $z^2 = 3$. Thus we have two regions, since the sphere and the cylinder intersect at $(1, \sqrt{3})$ in the rz-plane

$$E_1 = \left\{ (r, \theta, z) | 0 \le r \le \sqrt{4-r^2}, \sqrt{3} \le z \le 2, 0 \le \theta \le 2\pi \right\}$$

and

$$E_2 = \{(r, \theta, z) | 0 \le r \le 1, 0 \le z \le \sqrt{3}, 0 \le \theta \le 2\pi\}.$$

Hence the integral for the volume is

$$\begin{aligned} V(E) &= \int_{\theta=0}^{\theta=2\pi} \int_{z=\sqrt{3}}^{z=2} \int_{r=0}^{r=\sqrt{4-r^2}} r\,dr\,dz\,d\theta + \int_{\theta=0}^{\theta=2\pi} \int_{z=0}^{z=\sqrt{3}} \int_{r=0}^{r=1} r\,dr\,dz\,d\theta \\ &= \sqrt{3}\pi + \left(\frac{16}{3} - 3\sqrt{3} \right) \pi = 2\pi \left(\frac{8}{3} - \sqrt{3} \right) \text{cubic units.} \end{aligned}$$

5.30 Redo the previous example with the order of integration $d\theta\,dz\,dr$.

Review of Spherical Coordinates

In three-dimensional space $\mathbb{R}^3$ in the spherical coordinate system, we specify a point P by its distance ρ from the origin, the polar angle θ from the positive x-axis (same as in the cylindrical coordinate system), and the angle φ from the positive z-axis and the line OP (**Figure 5.55**). Note that $\rho \ge 0$ and $0 \le \varphi \le \pi$. (Refer to **Cylindrical and Spherical Coordinates** for a review.) Spherical coordinates are useful for triple integrals over regions that are symmetric with respect to the origin.

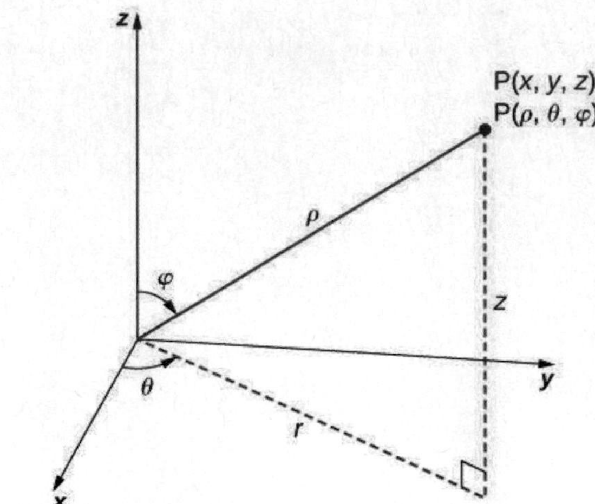

Figure 5.55 The spherical coordinate system locates points with two angles and a distance from the origin.

Recall the relationships that connect rectangular coordinates with spherical coordinates.

From spherical coordinates to rectangular coordinates:

$$x = \rho \sin \varphi \cos \theta, \; y = \rho \sin \varphi \sin \theta, \; \text{and } z = \rho \cos \varphi.$$

From rectangular coordinates to spherical coordinates:

$$\rho^2 = x^2 + y^2 + z^2, \; \tan \theta = \frac{y}{x}, \; \varphi = \arccos\left(\frac{z}{\sqrt{x^2 + y^2 + z^2}}\right).$$

Other relationships that are important to know for conversions are

- $r = \rho \sin \varphi$
- $\theta = \theta$
- $z = \rho \cos \varphi$

These equations are used to convert from spherical coordinates to cylindrical coordinates

and

- $\rho = \sqrt{r^2 + z^2}$
- $\theta = \theta$
- $\varphi = \arccos\left(\frac{z}{\sqrt{r^2 + z^2}}\right)$

These equations are used to convert from cylindrical coordinates to spherical coordinates.

The following figure shows a few solid regions that are convenient to express in spherical coordinates.

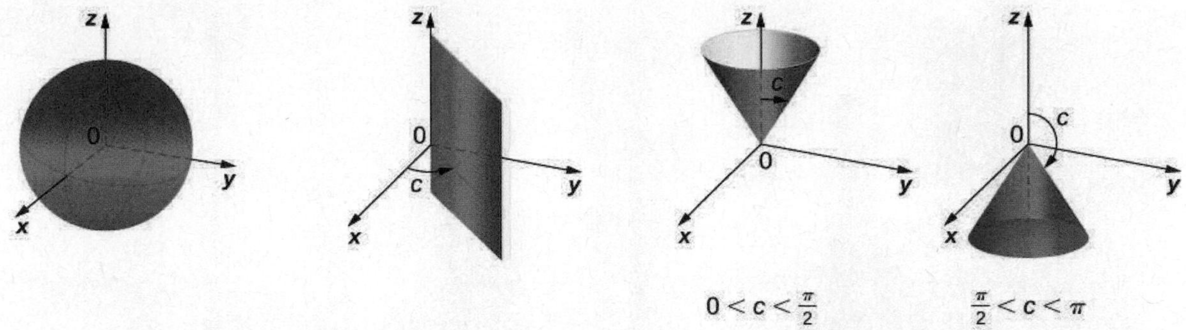

Figure 5.56 Spherical coordinates are especially convenient for working with solids bounded by these types of surfaces. (The letter c indicates a constant.)

Integration in Spherical Coordinates

We now establish a triple integral in the spherical coordinate system, as we did before in the cylindrical coordinate system. Let the function $f(\rho, \theta, \varphi)$ be continuous in a bounded spherical box, $B = \{(\rho, \theta, \varphi)|a \le \rho \le b, \alpha \le \theta \le \beta, \gamma \le \varphi \le \psi\}$. We then divide each interval into l, m and n subdivisions such that $\Delta\rho = \frac{b-a}{l}$, $\Delta\theta = \frac{\beta - \alpha}{m}$, $\Delta\varphi = \frac{\psi - \gamma}{n}$.

Now we can illustrate the following theorem for triple integrals in spherical coordinates with $(\rho^*_{ijk}, \theta^*_{ijk}, \varphi^*_{ijk})$ being any sample point in the spherical subbox B_{ijk}. For the volume element of the subbox ΔV in spherical coordinates, we have $\Delta V = (\Delta\rho)(\rho\Delta\varphi)(\rho \sin \varphi\Delta\theta)$, , as shown in the following figure.

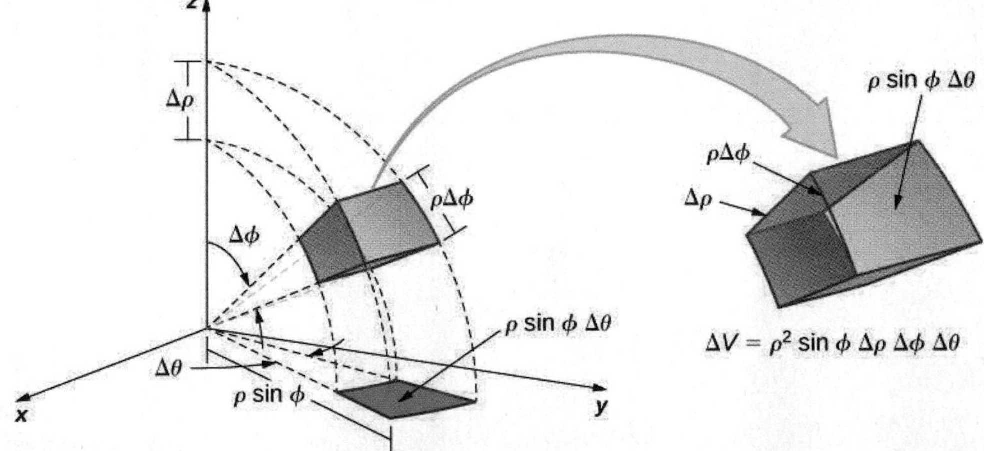

Figure 5.57 The volume element of a box in spherical coordinates.

Definition

The **triple integral in spherical coordinates** is the limit of a triple Riemann sum,

$$\lim_{l, m, n \to \infty} \sum_{i=1}^{l} \sum_{j=1}^{m} \sum_{k=1}^{n} f(\rho^*_{ijk}, \theta^*_{ijk}, \varphi^*_{ijk})(\rho^*_{ijk})^2 \sin \varphi\Delta\rho\Delta\theta\Delta\varphi$$

provided the limit exists.

As with the other multiple integrals we have examined, all the properties work similarly for a triple integral in the spherical coordinate system, and so do the iterated integrals. Fubini's theorem takes the following form.

Theorem 5.13: Fubini's Theorem for Spherical Coordinates

If $f(\rho, \theta, \varphi)$ is continuous on a spherical solid box $B = [a, b] \times [\alpha, \beta] \times [\gamma, \psi]$, then

$$\iiint_B f(\rho, \theta, \varphi)\rho^2 \sin \varphi \, d\rho \, d\varphi \, d\theta = \int_{\varphi=\gamma}^{\varphi=\psi} \int_{\theta=\alpha}^{\theta=\beta} \int_{\rho=a}^{\rho=b} f(\rho, \theta, \varphi)\rho^2 \sin \varphi \, d\rho \, d\varphi \, d\theta. \quad \textbf{(5.12)}$$

This iterated integral may be replaced by other iterated integrals by integrating with respect to the three variables in other orders.

As stated before, spherical coordinate systems work well for solids that are symmetric around a point, such as spheres and cones. Let us look at some examples before we consider triple integrals in spherical coordinates on general spherical regions.

Example 5.47

Evaluating a Triple Integral in Spherical Coordinates

Evaluate the iterated triple integral $\int_{\theta=0}^{\theta=2\pi} \int_{\varphi=0}^{\varphi=\pi/2} \int_{\rho=0}^{\rho=1} \rho^2 \sin \varphi \, d\rho \, d\varphi \, d\theta.$

Solution

As before, in this case the variables in the iterated integral are actually independent of each other and hence we can integrate each piece and multiply:

$$\int_0^{2\pi} \int_0^{\pi/2} \int_0^1 \rho^2 \sin \varphi \, d\rho \, d\varphi \, d\theta = \int_0^{2\pi} d\theta \int_0^{\pi/2} \sin \varphi \, d\varphi \int_0^1 \rho^2 \, d\rho = (2\pi)(1)\left(\frac{1}{3}\right) = \frac{2\pi}{3}.$$

The concept of triple integration in spherical coordinates can be extended to integration over a general solid, using the projections onto the coordinate planes. Note that dV and dA mean the increments in volume and area, respectively. The variables V and A are used as the variables for integration to express the integrals.

The triple integral of a continuous function $f(\rho, \theta, \varphi)$ over a general solid region

$$E = \{(\rho, \theta, \varphi) | (\rho, \theta) \in D, u_1(\rho, \theta) \le \varphi \le u_2(\rho, \theta)\}$$

in $\mathbb{R}^3$, where D is the projection of E onto the $\rho\theta$-plane, is

$$\iiint_E f(\rho, \theta, \varphi) dV = \iint_D \left[\int_{u_1(\rho, \theta)}^{u_2(\rho, \theta)} f(\rho, \theta, \varphi) d\varphi \right] dA.$$

In particular, if $D = \{(\rho, \theta) | g_1(\theta) \le \rho \le g_2(\theta), \alpha \le \theta \le \beta\}$, then we have

$$\iiint_E f(\rho, \theta, \varphi) dV = \int_\alpha^\beta \int_{g_1(\theta)}^{g_2(\theta)} \int_{u_1(\rho, \theta)}^{u_2(\rho, \theta)} f(\rho, \theta, \varphi)\rho^2 \sin \varphi \, d\varphi \, d\rho \, d\theta.$$

Similar formulas occur for projections onto the other coordinate planes.

Example 5.48

Setting up a Triple Integral in Spherical Coordinates

Set up an integral for the volume of the region bounded by the cone $z = \sqrt{3(x^2 + y^2)}$ and the hemisphere $z = \sqrt{4 - x^2 - y^2}$ (see the figure below).

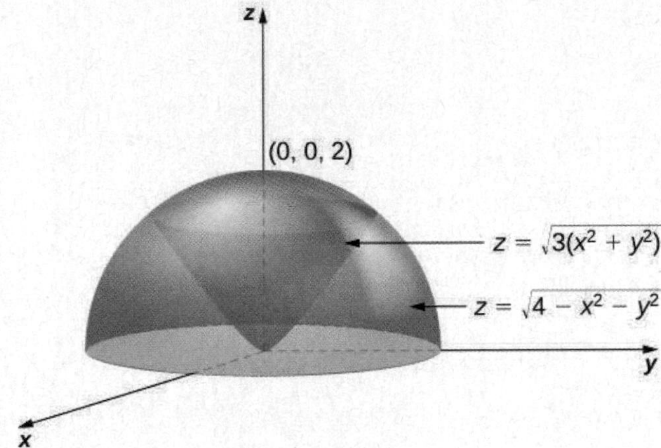

Figure 5.58 A region bounded below by a cone and above by a hemisphere.

Solution

Using the conversion formulas from rectangular coordinates to spherical coordinates, we have:

For the cone: $z = \sqrt{3(x^2 + y^2)}$ or $\rho \cos \varphi = \sqrt{3}\rho \sin \varphi$ or $\tan \varphi = \frac{1}{\sqrt{3}}$ or $\varphi = \frac{\pi}{6}$.

For the sphere: $z = \sqrt{4 - x^2 - y^2}$ or $z^2 + x^2 + y^2 = 4$ or $\rho^2 = 4$ or $\rho = 2$.

Thus, the triple integral for the volume is $V(E) = \int_{\theta=0}^{\theta=2\pi} \int_{\phi=0}^{\varphi=\pi/6} \int_{\rho=0}^{\rho=2} \rho^2 \sin \varphi \, d\rho \, d\varphi \, d\theta.$

5.31 Set up a triple integral for the volume of the solid region bounded above by the sphere $\rho = 2$ and bounded below by the cone $\varphi = \pi/3$.

Example 5.49

Interchanging Order of Integration in Spherical Coordinates

Let E be the region bounded below by the cone $z = \sqrt{x^2 + y^2}$ and above by the sphere $z = x^2 + y^2 + z^2$ (**Figure 5.59**). Set up a triple integral in spherical coordinates and find the volume of the region using the following orders of integration:

a. $d\rho \, d\phi \, d\theta$,

b. $d\varphi\, d\rho\, d\theta.$

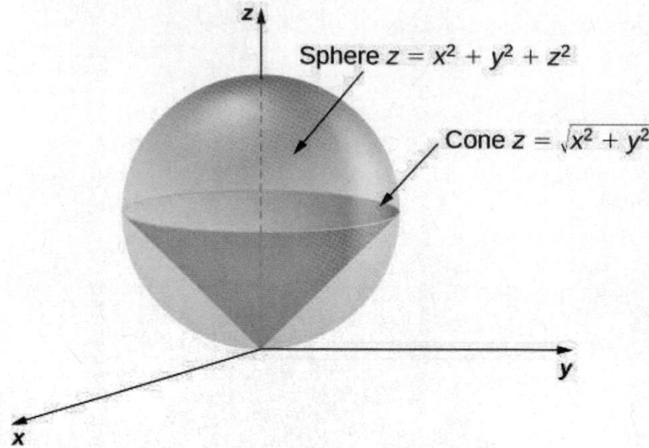

Figure 5.59 A region bounded below by a cone and above by a sphere.

Solution

a. Use the conversion formulas to write the equations of the sphere and cone in spherical coordinates. For the sphere:

$$\begin{aligned} x^2 + y^2 + z^2 &= z \\ \rho^2 &= \rho \cos \varphi \\ \rho &= \cos \varphi. \end{aligned}$$

For the cone:

$$\begin{aligned} z &= \sqrt{x^2 + y^2} \\ \rho \cos \varphi &= \sqrt{\rho^2 \sin^2 \varphi \cos^2 \phi + \rho^2 \sin^2 \varphi \sin^2 \phi} \\ \rho \cos \varphi &= \sqrt{\rho^2 \sin^2 \varphi (\cos^2 \phi + \sin^2 \phi)} \\ \rho \cos \varphi &= \rho \sin \varphi \\ \cos \varphi &= \sin \varphi \\ \varphi &= \pi/4. \end{aligned}$$

Hence the integral for the volume of the solid region E becomes

$$V(E) = \int_{\theta = 0}^{\theta = 2\pi} \int_{\varphi = 0}^{\varphi = \pi/4} \int_{\rho = 0}^{\rho = \cos \varphi} \rho^2 \sin \varphi \, d\rho \, d\varphi \, d\theta.$$

b. Consider the $\varphi\rho$ -plane. Note that the ranges for φ and ρ (from part a.) are

$$\begin{aligned} 0 \le \varphi \le \pi/4 \\ 0 \le \rho \le \cos \varphi. \end{aligned}$$

The curve $\rho = \cos \varphi$ meets the line $\varphi = \pi/4$ at the point $(\pi/4, \sqrt{2}/2)$. Thus, to change the order of integration, we need to use two pieces:

$$\begin{aligned} 0 \le \rho \le \sqrt{2}/2 \\ 0 \le \varphi \le \pi/4 \end{aligned} \quad \text{and} \quad \begin{aligned} \sqrt{2}/2 \ \le \ \rho \le 1 \\ 0 \ \le \ \varphi \le \cos^{-1} \rho. \end{aligned}$$

Hence the integral for the volume of the solid region E becomes

$$V(E) = \int_{\theta=0}^{\theta=2\pi} \int_{\rho=0}^{\rho=\sqrt{2}/2} \int_{\varphi=0}^{\varphi=\pi/4} \rho^2 \sin\varphi \, d\varphi \, d\rho \, d\theta + \int_{\theta=0}^{\theta=2\pi} \int_{\rho=\sqrt{2}/2}^{\rho=1} \int_{\varphi=0}^{\varphi=\cos^{-1}\rho} \rho^2 \sin\varphi \, d\varphi \, d\rho \, d\theta.$$

In each case, the integration results in $V(E) = \frac{\pi}{8}$.

Before we end this section, we present a couple of examples that can illustrate the conversion from rectangular coordinates to cylindrical coordinates and from rectangular coordinates to spherical coordinates.

Example 5.50

Converting from Rectangular Coordinates to Cylindrical Coordinates

Convert the following integral into cylindrical coordinates:

$$\int_{y=-1}^{y=1} \int_{x=0}^{x=\sqrt{1-y^2}} \int_{z=x^2+y^2}^{z=\sqrt{x^2+y^2}} xyz \, dz \, dx \, dy.$$

Solution

The ranges of the variables are

$$\begin{aligned} -1 &\le y \le 1 \\ 0 &\le x \le \sqrt{1-y^2} \\ x^2+y^2 &\le z \le \sqrt{x^2+y^2}. \end{aligned}$$

The first two inequalities describe the right half of a circle of radius 1. Therefore, the ranges for θ and r are

$$-\frac{\pi}{2} \le \theta \le \frac{\pi}{2} \text{ and } 0 \le r \le 1.$$

The limits of z are $r^2 \le z \le r$, hence

$$\int_{y=-1}^{y=1} \int_{x=0}^{x=\sqrt{1-y^2}} \int_{z=x^2+y^2}^{z=\sqrt{x^2+y^2}} xyz \, dz \, dx \, dy = \int_{\theta=-\pi/2}^{\theta=\pi/2} \int_{r=0}^{r=1} \int_{z=r^2}^{z=r} r(r\cos\theta)(r\sin\theta)z \, dz \, dr \, d\theta.$$

Example 5.51

Converting from Rectangular Coordinates to Spherical Coordinates

Convert the following integral into spherical coordinates:

$$\int_{y=0}^{y=3} \int_{x=0}^{x=\sqrt{9-y^2}} \int_{z=\sqrt{x^2+y^2}}^{z=\sqrt{18-x^2-y^2}} \left(x^2+y^2+z^2\right) dz\, dx\, dy.$$

Solution

The ranges of the variables are

$$\begin{aligned} 0 &\le y \le 3 \\ 0 &\le x \le \sqrt{9-y^2} \\ \sqrt{x^2+y^2} &\le z \le \sqrt{18-x^2-y^2}. \end{aligned}$$

The first two ranges of variables describe a quarter disk in the first quadrant of the xy -plane. Hence the range for θ is $0 \le \theta \le \frac{\pi}{2}.$

The lower bound $z=\sqrt{x^2+y^2}$ is the upper half of a cone and the upper bound $z=\sqrt{18-x^2-y^2}$ is the upper half of a sphere. Therefore, we have $0 \le \rho \le \sqrt{18},$ which is $0 \le \rho \le 3\sqrt{2}.$

For the ranges of $\varphi,$ we need to find where the cone and the sphere intersect, so solve the equation

$$\begin{aligned} r^2+z^2 &= 18 \\ \left(\sqrt{x^2+y^2}\right)^2+z^2 &= 18 \\ z^2+z^2 &= 18 \\ 2z^2 &= 18 \\ z^2 &= 9 \\ z &= 3. \end{aligned}$$

This gives

$$\begin{aligned} 3\sqrt{2}\cos\varphi &= 3 \\ \cos\varphi &= \frac{1}{\sqrt{2}} \\ \varphi &= \frac{\pi}{4}. \end{aligned}$$

Putting this together, we obtain

$$\int_{y=0}^{y=3} \int_{x=0}^{x=\sqrt{9-y^2}} \int_{z=\sqrt{x^2+y^2}}^{z=\sqrt{18-x^2-y^2}} \left(x^2+y^2+z^2\right) dz\, dx\, dy = \int_{\varphi=0}^{\varphi=\pi/4} \int_{\theta=0}^{\theta=\pi/2} \int_{\rho=0}^{\rho=3\sqrt{2}} \rho^4 \sin\varphi\, d\rho\, d\theta\, d\varphi.$$

5.32 Use rectangular, cylindrical, and spherical coordinates to set up triple integrals for finding the volume of the region inside the sphere $x^2 + y^2 + z^2 = 4$ but outside the cylinder $x^2 + y^2 = 1$.

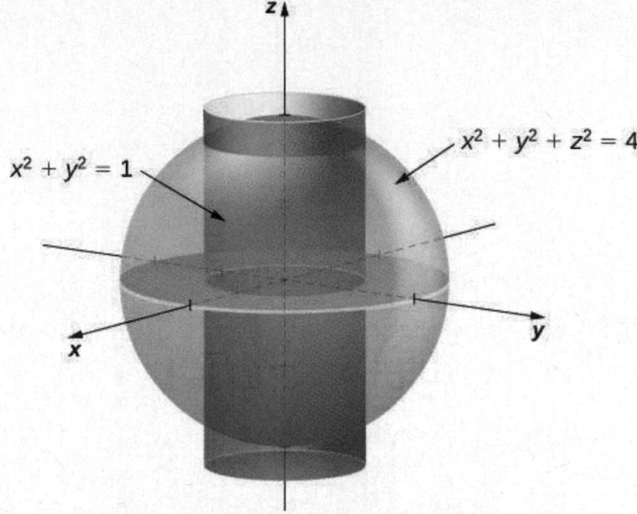

Now that we are familiar with the spherical coordinate system, let's find the volume of some known geometric figures, such as spheres and ellipsoids.

Example 5.52

Chapter Opener: Finding the Volume of l'Hemisphèric

Find the volume of the spherical planetarium in l'Hemisphèric in Valencia, Spain, which is five stories tall and has a radius of approximately 50 ft, using the equation $x^2 + y^2 + z^2 = r^2$.

Figure 5.60 (credit: modification of work by Javier Yaya Tur, Wikimedia Commons)

Solution

We calculate the volume of the ball in the first octant, where $x \geq 0, y \geq 0,$ and $z \geq 0,$ using spherical coordinates, and then multiply the result by 8 for symmetry. Since we consider the region D as the first octant in the integral, the ranges of the variables are

$$0 \leq \varphi \leq \frac{\pi}{2}, 0 \leq \rho \leq r, 0 \leq \theta \leq \frac{\pi}{2}.$$

Therefore,

$$\begin{aligned} V &= \iiint_D dx\,dy\,dz = 8 \int_{\theta=0}^{\theta=\pi/2} \int_{\rho=0}^{\rho=\pi} \int_{\varphi=0}^{\varphi=\pi/2} \rho^2 \sin\theta\, d\varphi\, d\rho\, d\theta \\ &= 8 \int_{\varphi=0}^{\varphi=\pi/2} d\varphi \int_{\rho=0}^{\rho=r} \rho^2\, d\rho \int_{\theta=0}^{\theta=\pi/2} \sin\theta\, d\theta \\ &= 8\left(\frac{\pi}{2}\right)\left(\frac{r^3}{3}\right)(1) \\ &= \frac{4}{3}\pi r^3. \end{aligned}$$

This exactly matches with what we knew. So for a sphere with a radius of approximately 50 ft, the volume is $\frac{4}{3}\pi(50)^3 \approx 523{,}600\ \text{ft}^3$.

For the next example we find the volume of an ellipsoid.

Example 5.53

Finding the Volume of an Ellipsoid

Find the volume of the ellipsoid $\frac{x^2}{a^2} + \frac{y^2}{b^2} + \frac{z^2}{c^2} = 1.$

Solution

We again use symmetry and evaluate the volume of the ellipsoid using spherical coordinates. As before, we use the first octant $x \geq 0,\ y \geq 0,$ and $z \geq 0$ and then multiply the result by $8.$

In this case the ranges of the variables are

$$0 \leq \varphi \leq \frac{\pi}{2},\ 0 \leq \rho \leq \frac{\pi}{2},\ 0 \leq \rho \leq 1, \text{ and } 0 \leq \theta \leq \frac{\pi}{2}.$$

Also, we need to change the rectangular to spherical coordinates in this way:

$$x = a\rho \cos\varphi \sin\theta,\ y = b\rho \sin\varphi \sin\theta, \text{ and } z = c\rho \cos\theta.$$

Then the volume of the ellipsoid becomes

$$\begin{aligned} V &= \iiint_D dx\,dy\,dz \\ &= 8 \int_{\theta=0}^{\theta=\pi/2} \int_{\rho=0}^{\rho=1} \int_{\varphi=0}^{\varphi=\pi/2} abc\rho^2 \sin\theta\, d\varphi\, d\rho\, d\theta \\ &= 8abc \int_{\varphi=0}^{\varphi=\pi/2} d\varphi \int_{\rho=0}^{\rho=1} \rho^2\, d\rho \int_{\theta=0}^{\theta=\pi/2} \sin\theta\, d\theta \\ &= 8abc\left(\frac{\pi}{2}\right)\left(\frac{1}{3}\right)(1) \\ &= \frac{4}{3}\pi abc. \end{aligned}$$

Example 5.54

Finding the Volume of the Space Inside an Ellipsoid and Outside a Sphere

Find the volume of the space inside the ellipsoid $\frac{x^2}{75^2} + \frac{y^2}{80^2} + \frac{z^2}{90^2} = 1$ and outside the sphere $x^2 + y^2 + z^2 = 50^2$.

Solution

This problem is directly related to the l'Hemisphèric structure. The volume of space inside the ellipsoid and outside the sphere might be useful to find the expense of heating or cooling that space. We can use the preceding two examples for the volume of the sphere and ellipsoid and then substract.

First we find the volume of the ellipsoid using $a = 75$ ft, $b = 80$ ft, and $c = 90$ ft in the result from **Example 5.53**. Hence the volume of the ellipsoid is

$$V_{\text{ellipsoid}} = \frac{4}{3}\pi(75)(80)(90) \approx 2{,}262{,}000 \text{ ft}^3.$$

From **Example 5.52**, the volume of the sphere is

$$V_{\text{sphere}} \approx 523{,}600 \text{ ft}^3.$$

Therefore, the volume of the space inside the ellipsoid $\frac{x^2}{75^2} + \frac{y^2}{80^2} + \frac{z^2}{90^2} = 1$ and outside the sphere $x^2 + y^2 + z^2 = 50^2$ is approximately

$$V_{\text{Hemisferic}} = V_{\text{ellipsoid}} - V_{\text{sphere}} = 1{,}738{,}400 \text{ ft}^3.$$

Student PROJECT

Hot air balloons

Hot air ballooning is a relaxing, peaceful pastime that many people enjoy. Many balloonist gatherings take place around the world, such as the Albuquerque International Balloon Fiesta. The Albuquerque event is the largest hot air balloon festival in the world, with over 500 balloons participating each year.

Figure 5.61 Balloons lift off at the 2001 Albuquerque International Balloon Fiesta. (credit: David Herrera, Flickr)

As the name implies, hot air balloons use hot air to generate lift. (Hot air is less dense than cooler air, so the balloon floats as long as the hot air stays hot.) The heat is generated by a propane burner suspended below the opening of the basket. Once the balloon takes off, the pilot controls the altitude of the balloon, either by using the burner to heat the air and ascend or by using a vent near the top of the balloon to release heated air and descend. The pilot has very little control over where the balloon goes, however—balloons are at the mercy of the winds. The uncertainty over where we will end up is one of the reasons balloonists are attracted to the sport.

In this project we use triple integrals to learn more about hot air balloons. We model the balloon in two pieces. The top of the balloon is modeled by a half sphere of radius 28 feet. The bottom of the balloon is modeled by a frustum of a cone (think of an ice cream cone with the pointy end cut off). The radius of the large end of the frustum is 28 feet and the radius of the small end of the frustum is 6 feet. A graph of our balloon model and a cross-sectional diagram showing the dimensions are shown in the following figure.

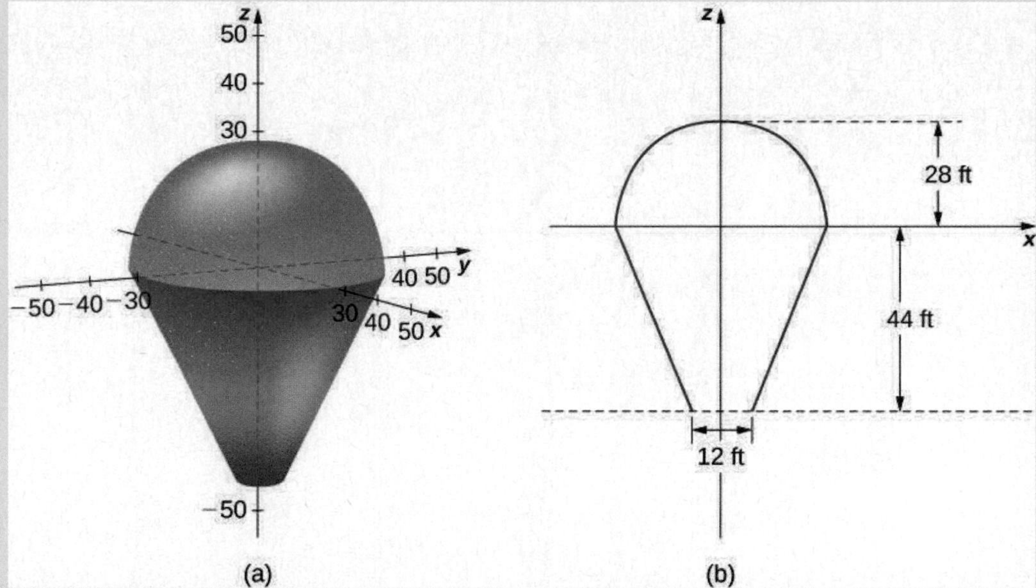

Figure 5.62 (a) Use a half sphere to model the top part of the balloon and a frustum of a cone to model the bottom part of the balloon. (b) A cross section of the balloon showing its dimensions.

We first want to find the volume of the balloon. If we look at the top part and the bottom part of the balloon separately, we see that they are geometric solids with known volume formulas. However, it is still worthwhile to set up and evaluate the integrals we would need to find the volume. If we calculate the volume using integration, we can use the known volume formulas to check our answers. This will help ensure that we have the integrals set up correctly for the later, more complicated stages of the project.

1. Find the volume of the balloon in two ways.
    a. Use triple integrals to calculate the volume. Consider each part of the balloon separately. (Consider using spherical coordinates for the top part and cylindrical coordinates for the bottom part.)
    b. Verify the answer using the formulas for the volume of a sphere, $V = \frac{4}{3}\pi r^3$, and for the volume of a cone, $V = \frac{1}{3}\pi r^2 h$.

In reality, calculating the temperature at a point inside the balloon is a tremendously complicated endeavor. In fact, an entire branch of physics (thermodynamics) is devoted to studying heat and temperature. For the purposes of this project, however, we are going to make some simplifying assumptions about how temperature varies from point to point within the balloon. Assume that just prior to liftoff, the temperature (in degrees Fahrenheit) of the air inside the balloon varies according to the function

$$T_0(r, \theta, z) = \frac{z - r}{10} + 210.$$

2. What is the average temperature of the air in the balloon just prior to liftoff? (Again, look at each part of the balloon separately, and do not forget to convert the function into spherical coordinates when looking at the top part of the balloon.)
Now the pilot activates the burner for 10 seconds. This action affects the temperature in a 12-foot-wide column 20 feet high, directly above the burner. A cross section of the balloon depicting this column in shown in the following figure.

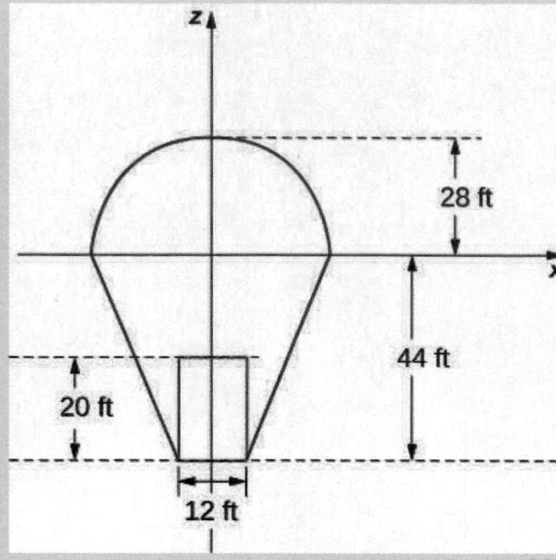

Figure 5.63 Activating the burner heats the air in a 20-foot-high, 12-foot-wide column directly above the burner.

Assume that after the pilot activates the burner for 10 seconds, the temperature of the air in the column described above *increases* according to the formula

$$H(r, \theta, z) = -2z - 48.$$

Then the temperature of the air in the column is given by

$$T_1(r, \theta, z) = \frac{z - r}{10} + 210 + (-2z - 48),$$

while the temperature in the remainder of the balloon is still given by

$$T_0(r, \theta, z) = \frac{z - r}{10} + 210.$$

3. Find the average temperature of the air in the balloon after the pilot has activated the burner for 10 seconds.

5.5 EXERCISES

In the following exercises, evaluate the triple integrals $\iiint_E f(x, y, z)dV$ over the solid E.

241. $f(x, y, z) = z,$ $B = \{(x, y, z)|x^2 + y^2 \le 9, x \ge 0, y \ge 0, 0 \le z \le 1\}$

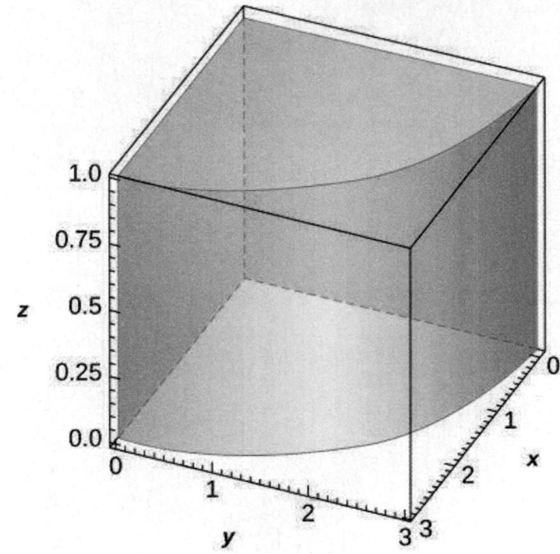

242. $f(x, y, z) = xz^2,$ $B = \{(x, y, z)|x^2 + y^2 \le 16, x \ge 0, y \le 0, -1 \le z \le 1\}$

243. $f(x, y, z) = xy,$ $B = \{(x, y, z)|x^2 + y^2 \le 1, x \ge 0, x \ge y, -1 \le z \le 1\}$

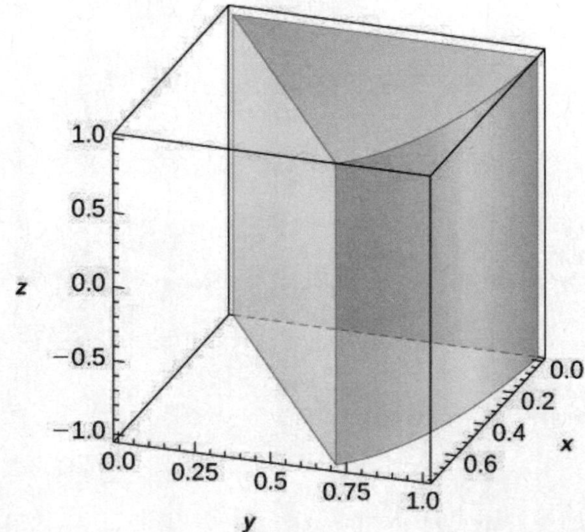

244. $f(x, y, z) = x^2 + y^2,$ $B = \{(x, y, z)|x^2 + y^2 \le 4, x \ge 0, x \le y, 0 \le z \le 3\}$

245. $f(x, y, z) = e^{\sqrt{x^2 + y^2}},$ $B = \{(x, y, z)|1 \le x^2 + y^2 \le 4, y \le 0, x \le y\sqrt{3}, 2 \le z \le 3\}$

246. $f(x, y, z) = \sqrt{x^2 + y^2},$ $B = \{(x, y, z)|1 \le x^2 + y^2 \le 9, y \le 0, 0 \le z \le 1\}$

247.

a. Let B be a cylindrical shell with inner radius $a,$ outer radius $b,$ and height $c,$ where $0 < a < b$ and $c > 0.$ Assume that a function F defined on B can be expressed in cylindrical coordinates as $F(x, y, z) = f(r) + h(z),$ where f and h are differentiable functions. If $\int_a^b \tilde{f}(r)dr = 0$ and $\tilde{h}(0) = 0,$ where $\tilde{f}$ and $\tilde{h}$ are antiderivatives of f and $h,$ respectively, show that $\iiint_B F(x, y, z)dV = 2\pi c\left(b\tilde{f}(b) - a\tilde{f}(a)\right) + \pi\left(b^2 - a^2\right)\tilde{h}(c).$

b. Use the previous result to show that $\iiint_B \left(z + \sin\sqrt{x^2 + y^2}\right)dx\,dy\,dz = 6\pi^2(\pi - 2),$ where B is a cylindrical shell with inner radius $\pi,$ outer radius $2\pi,$ and height $2.$

248.

a. Let B be a cylindrical shell with inner radius $a,$ outer radius $b,$ and height $c,$ where $0 < a < b$ and $c > 0.$ Assume that a function F defined on B can be expressed in cylindrical coordinates as $F(x, y, z) = f(r)g(\theta)h(z),$ where $f, g,$ and h are differentiable functions. If $\int_a^b \tilde{f}(r)dr = 0,$ where $\tilde{f}$ is an antiderivative of $f,$ show that $\iiint_B F(x, y, z)dV = \left[b\tilde{f}(b) - a\tilde{f}(a)\right]\left[\tilde{g}(2\pi) - \tilde{g}(0)\right]\left[\tilde{h}(c) - \tilde{h}(0)\right],$ where $\tilde{g}$ and $\tilde{h}$ are antiderivatives of g and $h,$ respectively.

b. Use the previous result to show that $\iiint_B z\sin\sqrt{x^2 + y^2}dx\,dy\,dz = -12\pi^2,$ where B is a cylindrical shell with inner radius $\pi,$ outer radius $2\pi,$ and height $2.$

In the following exercises, the boundaries of the solid E are given in cylindrical coordinates.

a. Express the region E in cylindrical coordinates.

b. Convert the integral $\iiint_E f(x, y, z)dV$ to cylindrical coordinates.

249. E is bounded by the right circular cylinder $r = 4\sin\theta$, the $r\theta$-plane, and the sphere $r^2 + z^2 = 16$.

250. E is bounded by the right circular cylinder $r = \cos\theta$, the $r\theta$-plane, and the sphere $r^2 + z^2 = 9$.

251. E is located in the first octant and is bounded by the circular paraboloid $z = 9 - 3r^2$, the cylinder $r = \sqrt{3}$, and the plane $r(\cos\theta + \sin\theta) = 20 - z$.

252. E is located in the first octant outside the circular paraboloid $z = 10 - 2r^2$ and inside the cylinder $r = \sqrt{5}$ and is bounded also by the planes $z = 20$ and $\theta = \frac{\pi}{4}$.

In the following exercises, the function f and region E are given.

a. Express the region E and the function f in cylindrical coordinates.

b. Convert the integral $\iiint_B f(x, y, z)dV$ into cylindrical coordinates and evaluate it.

253. $f(x, y, z) = \frac{1}{x+3}$, $E = \{(x, y, z)|0 \le x^2 + y^2 \le 9, x \ge 0, y \ge 0, 0 \le z \le x + 3\}$

254. $f(x, y, z) = x^2 + y^2$, $E = \{(x, y, z)|0 \le x^2 + y^2 \le 4, y \ge 0, 0 \le z \le 3 - x\}$

255. $f(x, y, z) = x$, $E = \{(x, y, z)|1 \le y^2 + z^2 \le 9, 0 \le x \le 1 - y^2 - z^2\}$

256. $f(x, y, z) = y$, $E = \{(x, y, z)|1 \le x^2 + z^2 \le 9, 0 \le y \le 1 - x^2 - z^2\}$

In the following exercises, find the volume of the solid E whose boundaries are given in rectangular coordinates.

257. E is above the xy-plane, inside the cylinder $x^2 + y^2 = 1$, and below the plane $z = 1$.

258. E is below the plane $z = 1$ and inside the paraboloid $z = x^2 + y^2$.

259. E is bounded by the circular cone $z = \sqrt{x^2 + y^2}$ and $z = 1$.

260. E is located above the xy-plane, below $z = 1$, outside the one-sheeted hyperboloid $x^2 + y^2 - z^2 = 1$, and inside the cylinder $x^2 + y^2 = 2$.

261. E is located inside the cylinder $x^2 + y^2 = 1$ and between the circular paraboloids $z = 1 - x^2 - y^2$ and $z = x^2 + y^2$.

262. E is located inside the sphere $x^2 + y^2 + z^2 = 1$, above the xy-plane, and inside the circular cone $z = \sqrt{x^2 + y^2}$.

263. E is located outside the circular cone $x^2 + y^2 = (z - 1)^2$ and between the planes $z = 0$ and $z = 2$.

264. E is located outside the circular cone $z = 1 - \sqrt{x^2 + y^2}$, above the xy-plane, below the circular paraboloid, and between the planes $z = 0$ and $z = 2$.

265. **[T]** Use a computer algebra system (CAS) to graph the solid whose volume is given by the iterated integral in cylindrical coordinates $\int_{-\pi/2}^{\pi/2} \int_0^1 \int_{r^2}^{r} r\,dz\,dr\,d\theta$. Find the volume V of the solid. Round your answer to four decimal places.

266. **[T]** Use a CAS to graph the solid whose volume is given by the iterated integral in cylindrical coordinates $\int_0^{\pi/2} \int_0^1 \int_{r^4}^{r} r\,dz\,dr\,d\theta$. Find the volume V of the solid. Round your answer to four decimal places.

267. Convert the integral $\int_0^1 \int_{-\sqrt{1-y^2}}^{\sqrt{1-y^2}} \int_{x^2+y^2}^{\sqrt{x^2+y^2}} xz\,dz\,dx\,dy$ into an integral in cylindrical coordinates.

268. Convert the integral $\int_0^2 \int_0^x \int_0^1 (xy + z)dz\,dx\,dy$ into an integral in cylindrical coordinates.

In the following exercises, evaluate the triple integral $\iiint_B f(x, y, z)dV$ over the solid B.

269. $f(x, y, z) = 1$, $B = \{(x, y, z)|x^2 + y^2 + z^2 \le 90,\ z \ge 0\}$

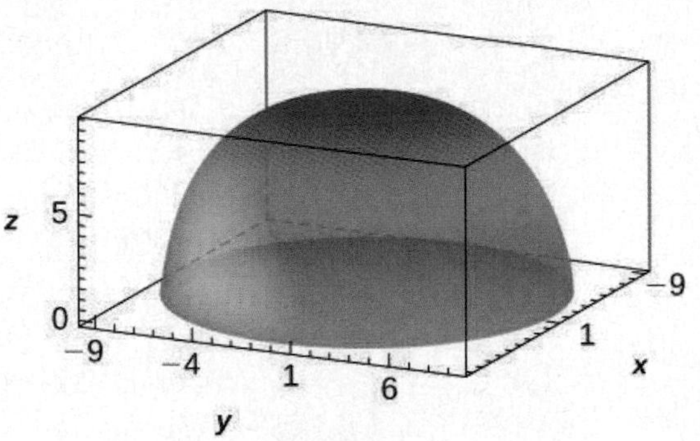

270. $f(x, y, z) = 1 - \sqrt{x^2 + y^2 + z^2}$, $B = \{(x, y, z)|x^2 + y^2 + z^2 \le 9,\ y \ge 0,\ z \ge 0\}$

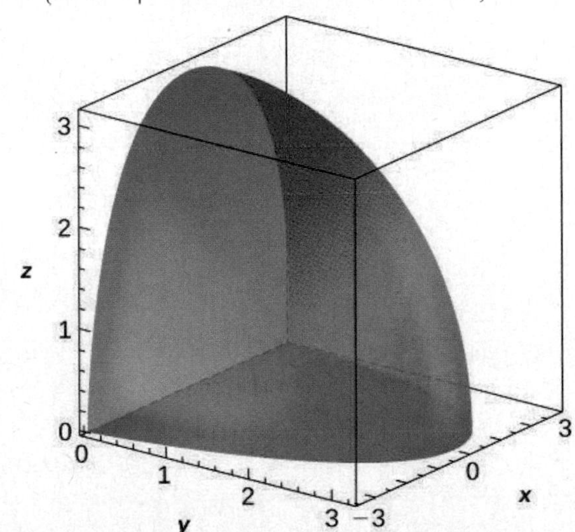

271. $f(x, y, z) = \sqrt{x^2 + y^2}$, B is bounded above by the half-sphere $x^2 + y^2 + z^2 = 9$ with $z \ge 0$ and below by the cone $2z^2 = x^2 + y^2$.

272. $f(x, y, z) = z$, B is bounded above by the half-sphere $x^2 + y^2 + z^2 = 16$ with $z \ge 0$ and below by the cone $2z^2 = x^2 + y^2$.

273. Show that if $F(\rho, \theta, \varphi) = f(\rho)g(\theta)h(\varphi)$ is a continuous function on the spherical box $B = \{(\rho, \theta, \varphi)|a \le \rho \le b,\ \alpha \le \theta \le \beta,\ \gamma \le \varphi \le \psi\}$, then

$$\iiint_B F\,dV = \left(\int_a^b \rho^2 f(\rho)dr\right)\left(\int_\alpha^\beta g(\theta)d\theta\right)\left(\int_\gamma^\psi h(\varphi)\sin\varphi\,d\varphi\right).$$

274.

a. A function F is said to have spherical symmetry if it depends on the distance to the origin only, that is, it can be expressed in spherical coordinates as $F(x, y, z) = f(\rho)$, where $\rho = \sqrt{x^2 + y^2 + z^2}$. Show that

$$\iiint_B F(x, y, z)dV = 2\pi \int_a^b \rho^2 f(\rho)d\rho,$$

where B is the region between the upper concentric hemispheres of radii a and b centered at the origin, with $0 < a < b$ and F a spherical function defined on B.

b. Use the previous result to show that $\iiint_B \left(x^2 + y^2 + z^2\right)\sqrt{x^2 + y^2 + z^2}\,dV = 21\pi$, where $B = \{(x, y, z)|1 \le x^2 + y^2 + z^2 \le 2,\ z \ge 0\}$.

275.

a. Let B be the region between the upper concentric hemispheres of radii a and b centered at the origin and situated in the first octant, where $0 < a < b$. Consider F a function defined on B whose form in spherical coordinates (ρ, θ, φ) is $F(x, y, z) = f(\rho)\cos\varphi$. Show that if $g(a) = g(b) = 0$ and $\int_a^b h(\rho)d\rho = 0$, then

$$\iiint_B F(x, y, z)dV = \frac{\pi^2}{4}[ah(a) - bh(b)],$$

where g is an antiderivative of f and h is an antiderivative of g.

b. Use the previous result to show that $\iiint_B \frac{z\cos\sqrt{x^2 + y^2 + z^2}}{\sqrt{x^2 + y^2 + z^2}}dV = \frac{3\pi^2}{2}$, where B is the region between the upper concentric hemispheres of radii π and 2π centered at the origin and situated in the first octant.

In the following exercises, the function f and region E are given.

a. Express the region E and function f in cylindrical coordinates.

b. Convert the integral $\iiint_B f(x, y, z)dV$ into cylindrical coordinates and evaluate it.

276. $f(x, y, z) = z$; $E = \{(x, y, z) | 0 \le x^2 + y^2 + z^2 \le 1, z \ge 0\}$

277. $f(x, y, z) = x + y$; $E = \{(x, y, z) | 1 \le x^2 + y^2 + z^2 \le 2, z \ge 0, y \ge 0\}$

278. $f(x, y, z) = 2xy$; $E = \left\{(x, y, z) \middle| \sqrt{x^2 + y^2} \le z \le \sqrt{1 - x^2 - y^2}, x \ge 0, y \ge 0\right\}$

279. $f(x, y, z) = z$; $E = \left\{(x, y, z) \middle| x^2 + y^2 + z^2 - 2z \le 0, \sqrt{x^2 + y^2} \le z\right\}$

In the following exercises, find the volume of the solid E whose boundaries are given in rectangular coordinates.

280. $E = \left\{(x, y, z) \middle| \sqrt{x^2 + y^2} \le z \le \sqrt{16 - x^2 - y^2}, x \ge 0, y \ge 0\right\}$

281. $E = \left\{(x, y, z) \middle| x^2 + y^2 + z^2 - 2z \le 0, \sqrt{x^2 + y^2} \le z\right\}$

282. Use spherical coordinates to find the volume of the solid situated outside the sphere $\rho = 1$ and inside the sphere $\rho = \cos \varphi$, with $\varphi \in \left[0, \frac{\pi}{2}\right]$.

283. Use spherical coordinates to find the volume of the ball $\rho \le 3$ that is situated between the cones $\varphi = \frac{\pi}{4}$ and $\varphi = \frac{\pi}{3}$.

284. Convert the integral $\int_{-4}^{4} \int_{-\sqrt{16 - y^2}}^{\sqrt{16 - y^2}} \int_{-\sqrt{16 - x^2 - y^2}}^{\sqrt{16 - x^2 - y^2}} \left(x^2 + y^2 + z^2\right) dz\, dx\, dy$ into an integral in spherical coordinates.

285. Convert the integral $\int_{0}^{4} \int_{0}^{\sqrt{16 - x^2}} \int_{-\sqrt{16 - x^2 - y^2}}^{\sqrt{16 - x^2 - y^2}} \left(x^2 + y^2 + z^2\right)^2 dz\, dy\, dx$ into an integral in spherical coordinates.

286. Convert the integral $\int_{-2}^{2} \int_{-\sqrt{4 - x^2}}^{\sqrt{4 - x^2}} \int_{\sqrt{x^2 + y^2}}^{\sqrt{16 - x^2 - y^2}} dz\, dy\, dx$ into an integral in spherical coordinates and evaluate it.

287. **[T]** Use a CAS to graph the solid whose volume is given by the iterated integral in spherical coordinates $\int_{\pi/2}^{\pi} \int_{5\pi/6}^{\pi/6} \int_{0}^{2} \rho^2 \sin \varphi\, d\rho\, d\varphi\, d\theta$. Find the volume V of the solid. Round your answer to three decimal places.

288. **[T]** Use a CAS to graph the solid whose volume is given by the iterated integral in spherical coordinates as $\int_{0}^{2\pi} \int_{3\pi/4}^{\pi/4} \int_{0}^{1} \rho^2 \sin \varphi\, d\rho\, d\varphi\, d\theta$. Find the volume V of the solid. Round your answer to three decimal places.

289. **[T]** Use a CAS to evaluate the integral $\iiint_E \left(x^2 + y^2\right) dV$ where E lies above the paraboloid $z = x^2 + y^2$ and below the plane $z = 3y$.

290. **[T]**

a. Evaluate the integral $\iiint_E e^{\sqrt{x^2 + y^2 + z^2}} dV$, where E is bounded by the spheres $4x^2 + 4y^2 + 4z^2 = 1$ and $x^2 + y^2 + z^2 = 1$.

b. Use a CAS to find an approximation of the previous integral. Round your answer to two decimal places.

291. Express the volume of the solid inside the sphere $x^2 + y^2 + z^2 = 16$ and outside the cylinder $x^2 + y^2 = 4$ as triple integrals in cylindrical coordinates and spherical coordinates, respectively.

292. Express the volume of the solid inside the sphere $x^2 + y^2 + z^2 = 16$ and outside the cylinder $x^2 + y^2 = 4$ that is located in the first octant as triple integrals in cylindrical coordinates and spherical coordinates, respectively.

293. The power emitted by an antenna has a power density per unit volume given in spherical coordinates by $p(\rho, \theta, \varphi) = \frac{P_0}{\rho^2} \cos^2 \theta \sin^4 \varphi$, where P_0 is a constant with units in watts. The total power within a sphere B of radius r meters is defined as $P = \iiint\limits_B p(\rho, \theta, \varphi) dV$. Find the total power P.

294. Use the preceding exercise to find the total power within a sphere B of radius 5 meters when the power density per unit volume is given by $p(\rho, \theta, \varphi) = \frac{30}{\rho^2} \cos^2 \theta \sin^4 \varphi$.

295. A charge cloud contained in a sphere B of radius r centimeters centered at the origin has its charge density given by $q(x, y, z) = k\sqrt{x^2 + y^2 + z^2} \frac{\mu \text{C}}{\text{cm}^3}$, where $k > 0$. The total charge contained in B is given by $Q = \iiint\limits_B q(x, y, z) dV$. Find the total charge Q.

296. Use the preceding exercise to find the total charge cloud contained in the unit sphere if the charge density is $q(x, y, z) = 20\sqrt{x^2 + y^2 + z^2} \frac{\mu \text{C}}{\text{cm}^3}$.

5.6 | Calculating Centers of Mass and Moments of Inertia

Learning Objectives

5.6.1 Use double integrals to locate the center of mass of a two-dimensional object.
5.6.2 Use double integrals to find the moment of inertia of a two-dimensional object.
5.6.3 Use triple integrals to locate the center of mass of a three-dimensional object.

We have already discussed a few applications of multiple integrals, such as finding areas, volumes, and the average value of a function over a bounded region. In this section we develop computational techniques for finding the center of mass and moments of inertia of several types of physical objects, using double integrals for a lamina (flat plate) and triple integrals for a three-dimensional object with variable density. The density is usually considered to be a constant number when the lamina or the object is homogeneous; that is, the object has uniform density.

Center of Mass in Two Dimensions

The center of mass is also known as the center of gravity if the object is in a uniform gravitational field. If the object has uniform density, the center of mass is the geometric center of the object, which is called the centroid. **Figure 5.64** shows a point P as the center of mass of a lamina. The lamina is perfectly balanced about its center of mass.

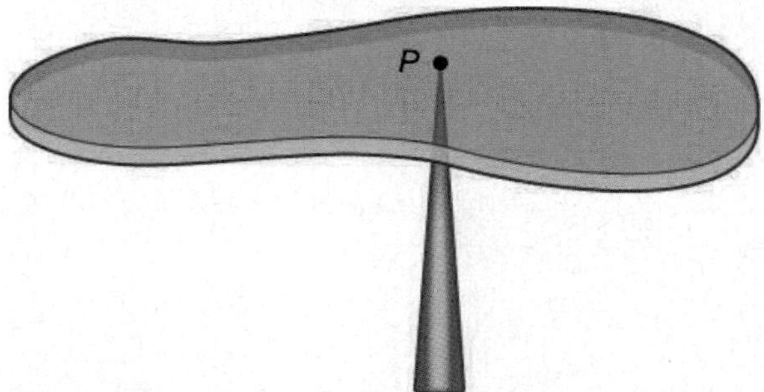

Figure 5.64 A lamina is perfectly balanced on a spindle if the lamina's center of mass sits on the spindle.

To find the coordinates of the center of mass $P(\bar{x}, \bar{y})$ of a lamina, we need to find the moment M_x of the lamina about the x-axis and the moment M_y about the y-axis. We also need to find the mass m of the lamina. Then

$$\bar{x} = \frac{M_y}{m} \text{ and } \bar{y} = \frac{M_x}{m}.$$

Refer to **Moments and Centers of Mass (http://cnx.org/content/m53649/latest/)** for the definitions and the methods of single integration to find the center of mass of a one-dimensional object (for example, a thin rod). We are going to use a similar idea here except that the object is a two-dimensional lamina and we use a double integral.

If we allow a constant density function, then $\bar{x} = \frac{M_y}{m}$ and $\bar{y} = \frac{M_x}{m}$ give the *centroid* of the lamina.

Suppose that the lamina occupies a region R in the xy-plane, and let $\rho(x, y)$ be its density (in units of mass per unit area) at any point (x, y). Hence, $\rho(x, y) = \lim_{\Delta A \to 0} \frac{\Delta m}{\Delta A}$, where Δm and ΔA are the mass and area of a small rectangle containing the point (x, y) and the limit is taken as the dimensions of the rectangle go to 0 (see the following figure).

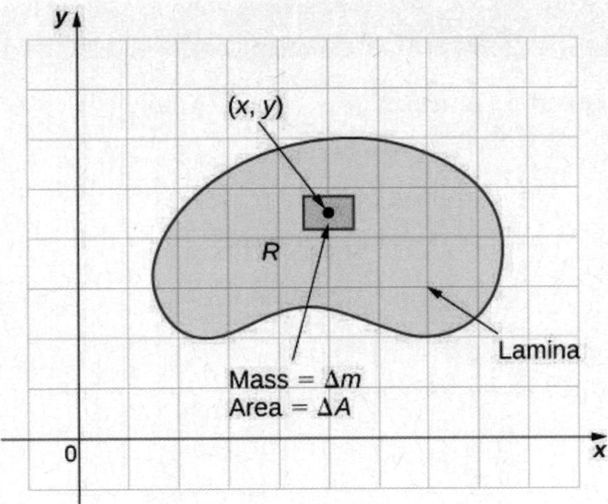

Figure 5.65 The density of a lamina at a point is the limit of its mass per area in a small rectangle about the point as the area goes to zero.

Just as before, we divide the region R into tiny rectangles R_{ij} with area ΔA and choose $\left(x_{ij}^*, y_{ij}^*\right)$ as sample points. Then the mass m_{ij} of each R_{ij} is equal to $\rho\left(x_{ij}^*, y_{ij}^*\right)\Delta A$ (**Figure 5.66**). Let k and l be the number of subintervals in x and $y,$ respectively. Also, note that the shape might not always be rectangular but the limit works anyway, as seen in previous sections.

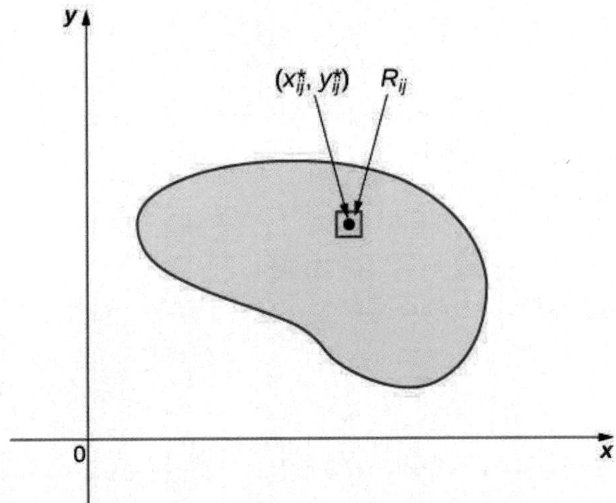

Figure 5.66 Subdividing the lamina into tiny rectangles $R_{ij},$ each containing a sample point (x_{ij}^*, y_{ij}^*).

Hence, the mass of the lamina is

$$m = \lim_{k,\, l \to \infty} \sum_{i=1}^{k} \sum_{j=1}^{l} m_{ij} = \lim_{k,\, l \to \infty} \sum_{i=1}^{k} \sum_{j=1}^{l} \rho(x_{ij}^*, y_{ij}^*)\Delta A = \iint_R \rho(x, y)dA. \tag{5.13}$$

Let’s see an example now of finding the total mass of a triangular lamina.

Example 5.55

Finding the Total Mass of a Lamina

Consider a triangular lamina R with vertices $(0, 0), (0, 3), (3, 0)$ and with density $\rho(x, y) = xy\,\text{kg/m}^2$. Find the total mass.

Solution

A sketch of the region R is always helpful, as shown in the following figure.

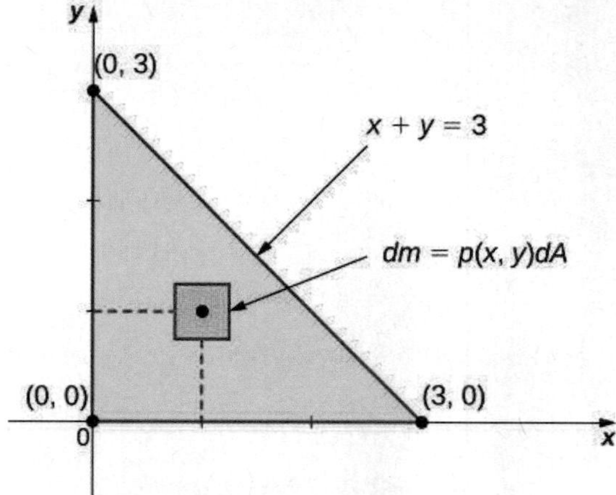

Figure 5.67 A lamina in the xy-plane with density $\rho(x, y) = xy$.

Using the expression developed for mass, we see that

$$\begin{aligned} m &= \iint_R dm = \iint_R \rho(x, y)dA = \int_{x=0}^{x=3}\int_{y=0}^{y=3-x} xy\,dy\,dx = \int_{x=0}^{x=3}\left[\left. x\frac{y^2}{2}\right|_{y=0}^{y=3-x}\right]dx \\ &= \int_{x=0}^{x=3}\frac{1}{2}x(3-x)^2\,dx = \left[\frac{9x^2}{4} - x^3 + \frac{x^4}{8}\right]\Bigg|_{x=0}^{x=3} \\ &= \frac{27}{8}. \end{aligned}$$

The computation is straightforward, giving the answer $m = \frac{27}{8}$ kg.

5.33 Consider the same region R as in the previous example, and use the density function $\rho(x, y) = \sqrt{xy}$. Find the total mass.

Now that we have established the expression for mass, we have the tools we need for calculating moments and centers of mass. The moment M_x about the x-axis for R is the limit of the sums of moments of the regions R_{ij} about the x-axis. Hence

$$M_x = \lim_{k,\,l\to\infty}\sum_{i=1}^{k}\sum_{j=1}^{l}\left(y_{ij}^*\right)m_{ij} = \lim_{k,\,l\to\infty}\sum_{i=1}^{k}\sum_{j=1}^{l}\left(y_{ij}^*\right)\rho\left(x_{ij}^*, y_{ij}^*\right)\Delta A = \iint_R y\rho(x, y)dA. \quad (5.14)$$

Similarly, the moment M_y about the y-axis for R is the limit of the sums of moments of the regions R_{ij} about the y-axis. Hence

$$M_y = \lim_{k,\, l \to \infty} \sum_{i=1}^{k} \sum_{j=1}^{l} \left(x_{ij}^*\right) m_{ij} = \lim_{k,\, l \to \infty} \sum_{i=1}^{k} \sum_{j=1}^{l} \left(y_{ij}^*\right) \rho\left(x_{ij}^*, y_{ij}^*\right) \Delta A = \iint_R x\rho(x, y)dA. \tag{5.15}$$

Example 5.56

Finding Moments

Consider the same triangular lamina R with vertices $(0, 0), (0, 3), (3, 0)$ and with density $\rho(x, y) = xy$. Find the moments M_x and M_y.

Solution

Use double integrals for each moment and compute their values:

$$M_x = \iint_R y\rho(x, y)dA = \int_{x=0}^{x=3} \int_{y=0}^{y=3-x} xy^2 \, dy \, dx = \frac{81}{20},$$

$$M_y = \iint_R x\rho(x, y)dA = \int_{x=0}^{x=3} \int_{y=0}^{y=3-x} x^2 y \, dy \, dx = \frac{81}{20}.$$

The computation is quite straightforward.

5.34 Consider the same lamina R as above, and use the density function $\rho(x, y) = \sqrt{xy}$. Find the moments M_x and M_y.

Finally we are ready to restate the expressions for the center of mass in terms of integrals. We denote the x-coordinate of the center of mass by $\bar{x}$ and the y-coordinate by $\bar{y}$. Specifically,

$$\bar{x} = \frac{M_y}{m} = \frac{\iint_R x\rho(x, y)dA}{\iint_R \rho(x, y)dA} \text{ and } \bar{y} = \frac{M_x}{m} = \frac{\iint_R y\rho(x, y)dA}{\iint_R \rho(x, y)dA}. \tag{5.16}$$

Example 5.57

Finding the Center of Mass

Again consider the same triangular region R with vertices $(0, 0), (0, 3), (3, 0)$ and with density function $\rho(x, y) = xy$. Find the center of mass.

Solution

Using the formulas we developed, we have

$$\bar{x} = \frac{M_y}{m} = \frac{\iint\limits_R x\rho(x, y)dA}{\iint\limits_R \rho(x, y)dA} = \frac{81/20}{27/8} = \frac{6}{5},$$

$$\bar{y} = \frac{M_x}{m} = \frac{\iint\limits_R y\rho(x, y)dA}{\iint\limits_R \rho(x, y)dA} = \frac{81/20}{27/8} = \frac{6}{5}.$$

Therefore, the center of mass is the point $\left(\frac{6}{5}, \frac{6}{5}\right)$.

Analysis

If we choose the density $\rho(x, y)$ instead to be uniform throughout the region (i.e., constant), such as the value 1 (any constant will do), then we can compute the centroid,

$$x_c = \frac{M_y}{m} = \frac{\iint\limits_R x\,dA}{\iint\limits_R dA} = \frac{9/2}{9/2} = 1,$$

$$y_c = \frac{M_x}{m} \frac{\iint\limits_R y\,dA}{\iint\limits_R dA} = \frac{9/2}{9/2} = 1.$$

Notice that the center of mass $\left(\frac{6}{5}, \frac{6}{5}\right)$ is not exactly the same as the centroid $(1, 1)$ of the triangular region. This is due to the variable density of R. If the density is constant, then we just use $\rho(x, y) = c$ (constant). This value cancels out from the formulas, so for a constant density, the center of mass coincides with the centroid of the lamina.

5.35 Again use the same region R as above and the density function $\rho(x, y) = \sqrt{xy}$. Find the center of mass.

Once again, based on the comments at the end of **Example 5.57**, we have expressions for the centroid of a region on the plane:

$$x_c = \frac{M_y}{m} = \frac{\iint\limits_R x\,dA}{\iint\limits_R dA} \text{ and } y_c = \frac{M_x}{m} \frac{\iint\limits_R y\,dA}{\iint\limits_R dA}.$$

We should use these formulas and verify the centroid of the triangular region R referred to in the last three examples.

Example 5.58

Finding Mass, Moments, and Center of Mass

Find the mass, moments, and the center of mass of the lamina of density $\rho(x, y) = x + y$ occupying the region R under the curve $y = x^2$ in the interval $0 \le x \le 2$ (see the following figure).

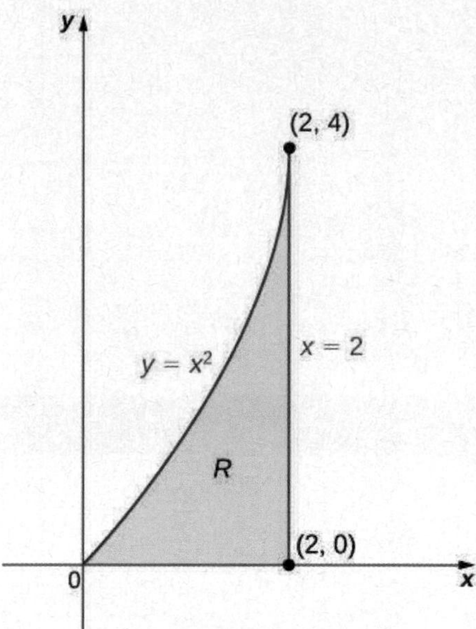

Figure 5.68 Locating the center of mass of a lamina R with density $\rho(x, y) = x + y$.

Solution

First we compute the mass m. We need to describe the region between the graph of $y = x^2$ and the vertical lines $x = 0$ and $x = 2$:

$$\begin{aligned} m &= \iint_R dm = \iint_R \rho(x, y)dA = \int_{x=0}^{x=2}\int_{y=0}^{y=x^2} (x + y)dy\,dx = \int_{x=0}^{x=2}\left[xy + \frac{y^2}{2}\Big|_{y=0}^{y=x^2}\right]dx \\ &= \int_{x=0}^{x=2}\left[x^3 + \frac{x^4}{2}\right]dx = \left[\frac{x^4}{4} + \frac{x^5}{10}\right]\Big|_{x=0}^{x=2} = \frac{36}{5}. \end{aligned}$$

Now compute the moments M_x and M_y:

$$M_x = \iint_R y\rho(x, y)dA = \int_{x=0}^{x=2}\int_{y=0}^{y=x^2} y(x + y)dy\,dx = \frac{80}{7},$$

$$M_y = \iint_R x\rho(x, y)dA = \int_{x=0}^{x=2}\int_{y=0}^{y=x^2} x(x + y)dy\,dx = \frac{176}{15}.$$

Finally, evaluate the center of mass,

$$\bar{x} = \frac{M_y}{m} = \frac{\iint_R x\rho(x, y)dA}{\iint_R \rho(x, y)dA} = \frac{176/15}{36/5} = \frac{44}{27},$$

$$\bar{y} = \frac{M_x}{m} = \frac{\iint_R y\rho(x, y)dA}{\iint_R \rho(x, y)dA} = \frac{80/7}{36/5} = \frac{100}{63}.$$

Hence the center of mass is $(\bar{x}, \bar{y}) = \left(\frac{44}{27}, \frac{100}{63}\right)$.

5.36 Calculate the mass, moments, and the center of mass of the region between the curves $y = x$ and $y = x^2$ with the density function $\rho(x, y) = x$ in the interval $0 \le x \le 1$.

Example 5.59

Finding a Centroid

Find the centroid of the region under the curve $y = e^x$ over the interval $1 \le x \le 3$ (see the following figure).

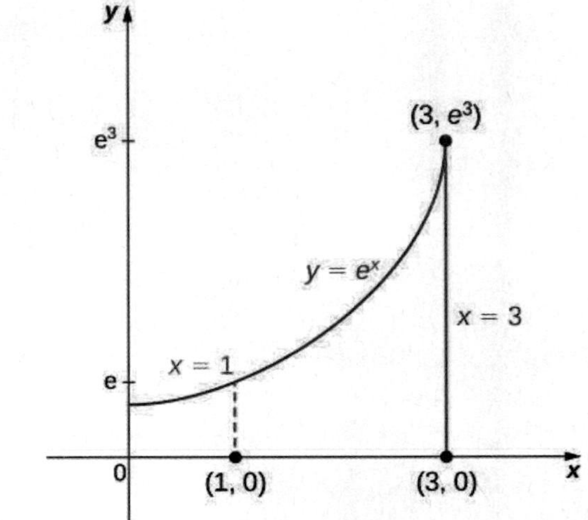

Figure 5.69 Finding a centroid of a region below the curve $y = e^x$.

Solution

To compute the centroid, we assume that the density function is constant and hence it cancels out:

$$x_c = \frac{M_y}{m} = \frac{\iint_R x\,dA}{\iint_R dA} \text{ and } y_c = \frac{M_x}{m} = \frac{\iint_R y\,dA}{\iint_R dA},$$

$$x_c = \frac{M_y}{m} = \frac{\iint_R x\,dA}{\iint_R dA} = \frac{\int_{x=1}^{x=3}\int_{y=0}^{y=e^x} x\,dy\,dx}{\int_{x=1}^{x=3}\int_{y=0}^{y=e^x} dy\,dx} = \frac{\int_{x=1}^{x=3} xe^x\,dx}{\int_{x=1}^{x=3} e^x\,dx} = \frac{2e^3}{e^3 - e} = \frac{2e^2}{e^2 - 1},$$

$$y_c = \frac{M_x}{m} = \frac{\iint_R y\,dA}{\iint_R dA} = \frac{\int_{x=1}^{x=3}\int_{y=0}^{y=e^x} y\,dy\,dx}{\int_{x=1}^{x=3}\int_{y=0}^{y=e^x} dy\,dx} = \frac{\int_{x=1}^{x=3} \frac{e^{2x}}{2}dx}{\int_{x=1}^{x=3} e^x\,dx} = \frac{\frac{1}{4}e^2\left(e^4 - 1\right)}{e\left(e^2 - 1\right)} = \frac{1}{4}e\left(e^2 + 1\right).$$

Thus the centroid of the region is

$$(x_c, y_c) = \left(\frac{2e^2}{e^2 - 1}, \frac{1}{4}e\left(e^2 + 1\right)\right).$$

5.37 Calculate the centroid of the region between the curves $y = x$ and $y = \sqrt{x}$ with uniform density in the interval $0 \le x \le 1$.

Moments of Inertia

For a clear understanding of how to calculate moments of inertia using double integrals, we need to go back to the general definition in Section 6.6. The moment of inertia of a particle of mass m about an axis is mr^2, where r is the distance of the particle from the axis. We can see from **Figure 5.66** that the moment of inertia of the subrectangle R_{ij} about the x-axis is $(y_{ij}^*)^2 \rho(x_{ij}^*, y_{ij}^*)\Delta A$. Similarly, the moment of inertia of the subrectangle R_{ij} about the y-axis is $(x_{ij}^*)^2 \rho(x_{ij}^*, y_{ij}^*)\Delta A$. The moment of inertia is related to the rotation of the mass; specifically, it measures the tendency of the mass to resist a change in rotational motion about an axis.

The moment of inertia I_x about the x-axis for the region R is the limit of the sum of moments of inertia of the regions R_{ij} about the x-axis. Hence

$$I_x = \lim_{k, l \to \infty} \sum_{i=1}^{k} \sum_{j=1}^{l} \left(y_{ij}^*\right)^2 m_{ij} = \lim_{k, l \to \infty} \sum_{i=1}^{k} \sum_{j=1}^{l} \left(y_{ij}^*\right)^2 \rho\left(x_{ij}^*, y_{ij}^*\right)\Delta A = \iint_R y^2 \rho(x, y)dA.$$

Similarly, the moment of inertia I_y about the y-axis for R is the limit of the sum of moments of inertia of the regions R_{ij} about the y-axis. Hence

$$I_y = \lim_{k, l \to \infty} \sum_{i=1}^{k} \sum_{j=1}^{l} \left(x_{ij}^*\right)^2 m_{ij} = \lim_{k, l \to \infty} \sum_{i=1}^{k} \sum_{j=1}^{l} \left(x_{ij}^*\right)^2 \rho\left(x_{ij}^*, y_{ij}^*\right)\Delta A = \iint_R x^2 \rho(x, y)dA.$$

Sometimes, we need to find the moment of inertia of an object about the origin, which is known as the polar moment of inertia. We denote this by I_0 and obtain it by adding the moments of inertia I_x and I_y. Hence

$$I_0 = I_x + I_y = \iint_R \left(x^2 + y^2\right)\rho(x, y)dA.$$

All these expressions can be written in polar coordinates by substituting $x = r\cos\theta,\quad y = r\sin\theta,$ and $dA = r\,dr\,d\theta.$ For example, $I_0 = \iint_R r^2\rho(r\cos\theta, r\sin\theta)dA.$

Example 5.60

Finding Moments of Inertia for a Triangular Lamina

Use the triangular region R with vertices $(0, 0), (2, 2),$ and $(2, 0)$ and with density $\rho(x, y) = xy$ as in previous examples. Find the moments of inertia.

Solution

Using the expressions established above for the moments of inertia, we have

$$\begin{aligned} I_x &= \iint_R y^2\rho(x, y)dA = \int_{x=0}^{x=2}\int_{y=0}^{y=x} xy^3\,dy\,dx = \frac{8}{3}, \\ I_y &= \iint_R x^2\rho(x, y)dA = \int_{x=0}^{x=2}\int_{y=0}^{y=x} x^3y\,dy\,dx = \frac{16}{3}, \\ I_0 &= \iint_R \left(x^2 + y^2\right)\rho(x, y)dA = \int_0^2\int_0^x \left(x^2 + y^2\right)xy\,dy\,dx \\ &= I_x + I_y = 8. \end{aligned}$$

5.38 Again use the same region R as above and the density function $\rho(x, y) = \sqrt{xy}$. Find the moments of inertia.

As mentioned earlier, the moment of inertia of a particle of mass m about an axis is mr^2 where r is the distance of the particle from the axis, also known as the **radius of gyration**.

Hence the radii of gyration with respect to the x-axis, the y-axis, and the origin are

$$R_x = \sqrt{\frac{I_x}{m}},\ R_y = \sqrt{\frac{I_y}{m}},\ \text{and } R_0 = \sqrt{\frac{I_0}{m}},$$

respectively. In each case, the radius of gyration tells us how far (perpendicular distance) from the axis of rotation the entire mass of an object might be concentrated. The moments of an object are useful for finding information on the balance and torque of the object about an axis, but radii of gyration are used to describe the distribution of mass around its centroidal axis. There are many applications in engineering and physics. Sometimes it is necessary to find the radius of gyration, as in the next example.

Example 5.61

Finding the Radius of Gyration for a Triangular Lamina

Consider the same triangular lamina R with vertices $(0, 0), (2, 2),$ and $(2, 0)$ and with density $\rho(x, y) = xy$ as in previous examples. Find the radii of gyration with respect to the x-axis, the y-axis, and the origin.

Solution

If we compute the mass of this region we find that $m = 2.$ We found the moments of inertia of this lamina in **Example 5.58**. From these data, the radii of gyration with respect to the x-axis, y-axis, and the origin are, respectively,

$$\begin{aligned} R_x &= \sqrt{\frac{I_x}{m}} = \sqrt{\frac{8/3}{2}} = \sqrt{\frac{8}{6}} = \frac{2\sqrt{3}}{3}, \\ R_y &= \sqrt{\frac{I_y}{m}} = \sqrt{\frac{16/3}{2}} = \sqrt{\frac{8}{3}} = \frac{2\sqrt{6}}{3}, \\ R_0 &= \sqrt{\frac{I_0}{m}} = \sqrt{\frac{8}{2}} = \sqrt{4} = 2. \end{aligned}$$

5.39 Use the same region R from **Example 5.61** and the density function $\rho(x, y) = \sqrt{xy}.$ Find the radii of gyration with respect to the x-axis, the y-axis, and the origin.

Center of Mass and Moments of Inertia in Three Dimensions

All the expressions of double integrals discussed so far can be modified to become triple integrals.

Definition

If we have a solid object Q with a density function $\rho(x, y, z)$ at any point (x, y, z) in space, then its mass is

$$m = \iiint_Q \rho(x, y, z)dV.$$

Its moments about the xy-plane, the xz-plane, and the yz-plane are

$$\begin{aligned} M_{xy} &= \iiint_Q z\rho(x, y, z)dV, \; M_{xz} = \iiint_Q y\rho(x, y, z)dV, \\ M_{yz} &= \iiint_Q x\rho(x, y, z)dV. \end{aligned}$$

If the center of mass of the object is the point $(\bar{x}, \bar{y}, \bar{z}),$ then

$$\bar{x} = \frac{M_{yz}}{m}, \; \bar{y} = \frac{M_{xz}}{m}, \; \bar{z} = \frac{M_{xy}}{m}.$$

Also, if the solid object is homogeneous (with constant density), then the center of mass becomes the centroid of the solid. Finally, the moments of inertia about the yz-plane, the xz-plane, and the xy-plane are

$$\begin{aligned} I_x &= \iiint_Q \left(y^2 + z^2\right)\rho(x, y, z)dV, \\ I_y &= \iiint_Q \left(x^2 + z^2\right)\rho(x, y, z)dV, \\ I_z &= \iiint_Q \left(x^2 + y^2\right)\rho(x, y, z)dV. \end{aligned}$$

Example 5.62

Finding the Mass of a Solid

Suppose that Q is a solid region bounded by $x+2y+3z=6$ and the coordinate planes and has density $\rho(x, y, z)=x^2yz$. Find the total mass.

Solution

The region Q is a tetrahedron (**Figure 5.70**) meeting the axes at the points $(6, 0, 0)$, $(0, 3, 0)$, and $(0, 0, 2)$. To find the limits of integration, let $z=0$ in the slanted plane $z=\frac{1}{3}(6-x-2y)$. Then for x and y find the projection of Q onto the xy-plane, which is bounded by the axes and the line $x+2y=6$. Hence the mass is

$$m=\iiint_Q \rho(x, y, z)dV=\int_{x=0}^{x=6}\int_{y=0}^{y=1/2(6-x)}\int_{z=0}^{z=1/3(6-x-2y)} x^2yz\,dz\,dy\,dx=\frac{108}{35}\approx 3.086.$$

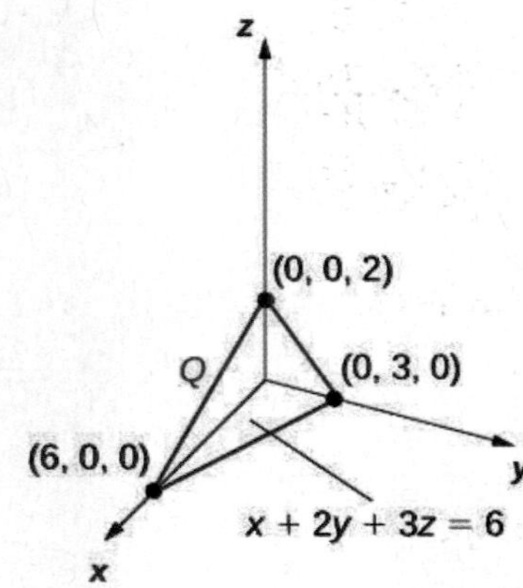

Figure 5.70 Finding the mass of a three-dimensional solid Q.

5.40 Consider the same region Q (**Figure 5.70**), and use the density function $\rho(x, y, z)=xy^2z$. Find the mass.

Example 5.63

Finding the Center of Mass of a Solid

Suppose Q is a solid region bounded by the plane $x+2y+3z=6$ and the coordinate planes with density $\rho(x, y, z)=x^2yz$ (see **Figure 5.70**). Find the center of mass using decimal approximation.

Solution

We have used this tetrahedron before and know the limits of integration, so we can proceed to the computations right away. First, we need to find the moments about the xy-plane, the xz-plane, and the yz-plane:

$$M_{xy} = \iiint_Q z\rho(x, y, z)dV = \int_{x=0}^{x=6} \int_{y=0}^{y=1/2(6-x)} \int_{z=0}^{z=1/3(6-x-2y)} x^2 yz^2 \, dz \, dy \, dx = \frac{54}{35} \approx 1.543,$$

$$M_{xz} = \iiint_Q y\rho(x, y, z)dV = \int_{x=0}^{x=6} \int_{y=0}^{y=1/2(6-x)} \int_{z=0}^{z=1/3(6-x-2y)} x^2 y^2 z \, dz \, dy \, dx = \frac{81}{35} \approx 2.314,$$

$$M_{yz} = \iiint_Q x\rho(x, y, z)dV = \int_{x=0}^{x=6} \int_{y=0}^{y=1/2(6-x)} \int_{z=0}^{z=1/3(6-x-2y)} x^3 yz \, dz \, dy \, dx = \frac{243}{35} \approx 6.943.$$

Hence the center of mass is

$$\bar{x} = \frac{M_{yz}}{m}, \; \bar{y} = \frac{M_{xz}}{m}, \; \bar{z} = \frac{M_{xy}}{m},$$

$$\bar{x} = \frac{M_{yz}}{m} = \frac{243/35}{108/35} = \frac{243}{108} = 2.25,$$

$$\bar{y} = \frac{M_{xz}}{m} = \frac{81/35}{108/35} = \frac{81}{108} = 0.75,$$

$$\bar{z} = \frac{M_{xy}}{m} = \frac{54/35}{108/35} = \frac{54}{108} = 0.5.$$

The center of mass for the tetrahedron Q is the point $(2.25, 0.75, 0.5)$.

5.41 Consider the same region Q (**Figure 5.70**) and use the density function $\rho(x, y, z) = xy^2 z$. Find the center of mass.

We conclude this section with an example of finding moments of inertia $I_x, I_y,$ and I_z.

Example 5.64

Finding the Moments of Inertia of a Solid

Suppose that Q is a solid region and is bounded by $x + 2y + 3z = 6$ and the coordinate planes with density $\rho(x, y, z) = x^2 yz$ (see **Figure 5.70**). Find the moments of inertia of the tetrahedron Q about the yz-plane, the xz-plane, and the xy-plane.

Solution

Once again, we can almost immediately write the limits of integration and hence we can quickly proceed to evaluating the moments of inertia. Using the formula stated before, the moments of inertia of the tetrahedron Q about the xy-plane, the xz-plane, and the yz-plane are

$$I_x = \iiint_Q \left(y^2 + z^2\right)\rho(x, y, z)dV,$$
$$I_y = \iiint_Q \left(x^2 + z^2\right)\rho(x, y, z)dV,$$

and

$$I_z = \iiint_Q \left(x^2 + y^2\right)\rho(x, y, z)dV \text{ with } \rho(x, y, z) = x^2 yz.$$

Proceeding with the computations, we have

$$I_x = \iiint_Q \left(y^2 + z^2\right)x^2 yz\, dV = \int_{x=0}^{x=6} \int_{y=0}^{y=\frac{1}{2}(6-x)} \int_{z=0}^{z=\frac{1}{3}(6-x-2y)} \left(y^2 + z^2\right)x^2 yz\, dz\, dy\, dx = \frac{117}{35} \approx 3.343,$$
$$I_y = \iiint_Q \left(x^2 + z^2\right)x^2 yz\, dV = \int_{x=0}^{x=6} \int_{y=0}^{y=\frac{1}{2}(6-x)} \int_{z=0}^{z=\frac{1}{3}(6-x-2y)} \left(x^2 + z^2\right)x^2 yz\, dz\, dy\, dx = \frac{684}{35} \approx 19.543,$$
$$I_z = \iiint_Q \left(x^2 + y^2\right)x^2 yz\, dV = \int_{x=0}^{x=6} \int_{y=0}^{y=\frac{1}{2}(6-x)} \int_{z=0}^{z=\frac{1}{3}(6-x-2y)} \left(x^2 + y^2\right)x^2 yz\, dz\, dy\, dx = \frac{729}{35} \approx 20.829.$$

Thus, the moments of inertia of the tetrahedron Q about the yz-plane, the xz-plane, and the xy-plane are $117/35$, $684/35$, and $729/35$, respectively.

5.42 Consider the same region Q (**Figure 5.70**), and use the density function $\rho(x, y, z) = xy^2 z$. Find the moments of inertia about the three coordinate planes.

5.6 EXERCISES

In the following exercises, the region R occupied by a lamina is shown in a graph. Find the mass of R with the density function ρ.

297. R is the triangular region with vertices $(0, 0), (0, 3),$ and $(6, 0)$; $\rho(x, y) = xy$.

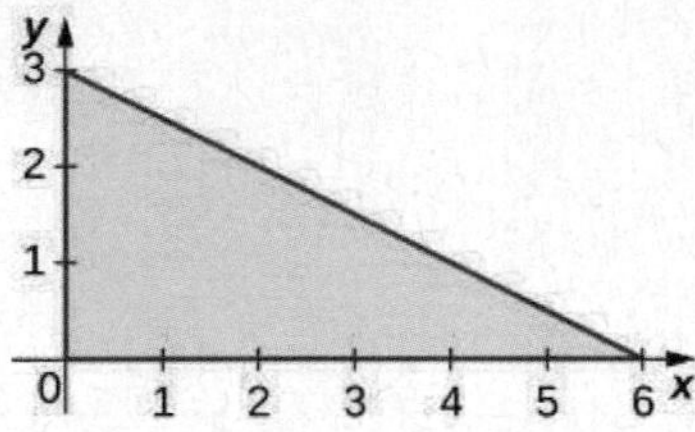

298. R is the triangular region with vertices $(0, 0), (1, 1),$ $(0, 5)$; $\rho(x, y) = x + y$.

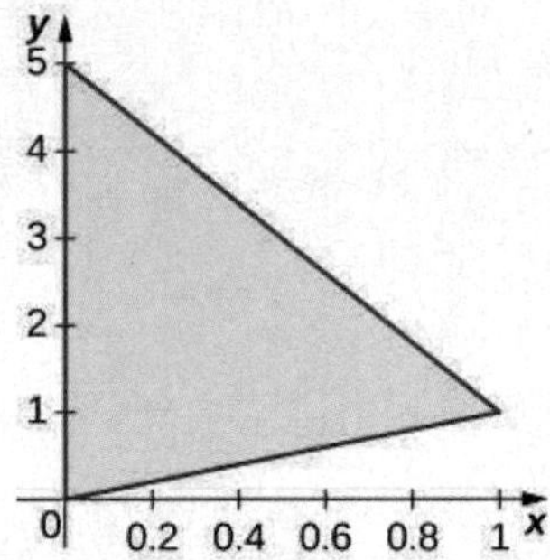

299. R is the rectangular region with vertices $(0, 0), (0, 3), (6, 3),$ and $(6, 0)$; $\rho(x, y) = \sqrt{xy}$.

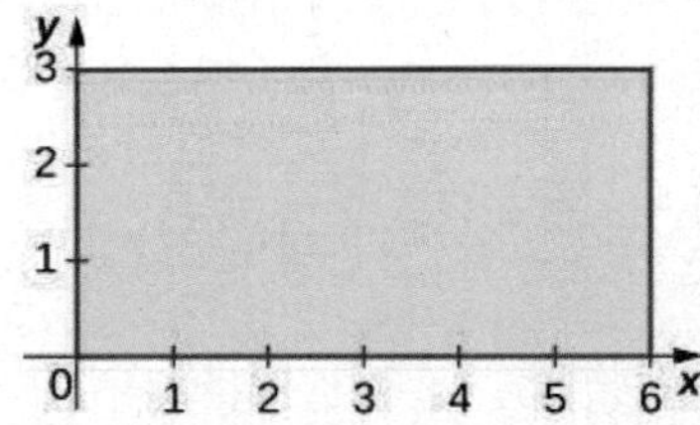

300. R is the rectangular region with vertices $(0, 1), (0, 3), (3, 3),$ and $(3, 1)$; $\rho(x, y) = x^2 y$.

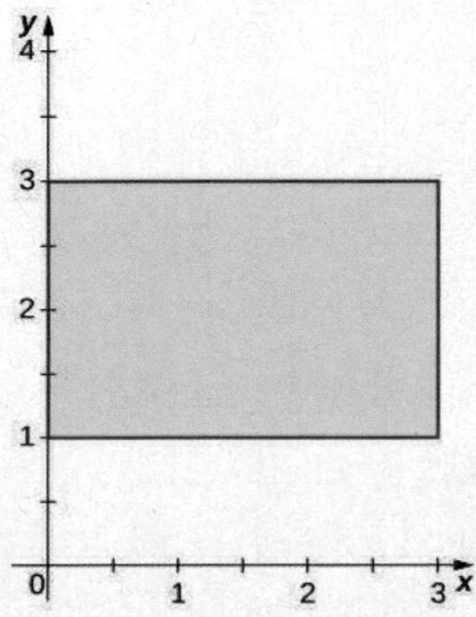

301. R is the trapezoidal region determined by the lines $y = -\frac{1}{4}x + \frac{5}{2}$, $y = 0$, $y = 2$, and $x = 0$; $\rho(x, y) = 3xy$.

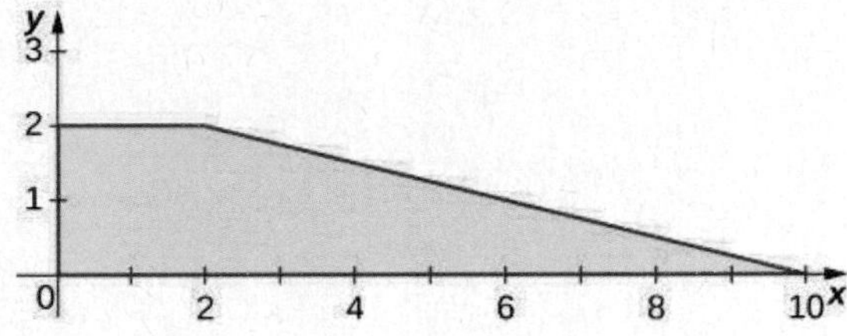

302. R is the trapezoidal region determined by the lines $y = 0$, $y = 1$, $y = x$, and $y = -x + 3$; $\rho(x, y) = 2x + y$.

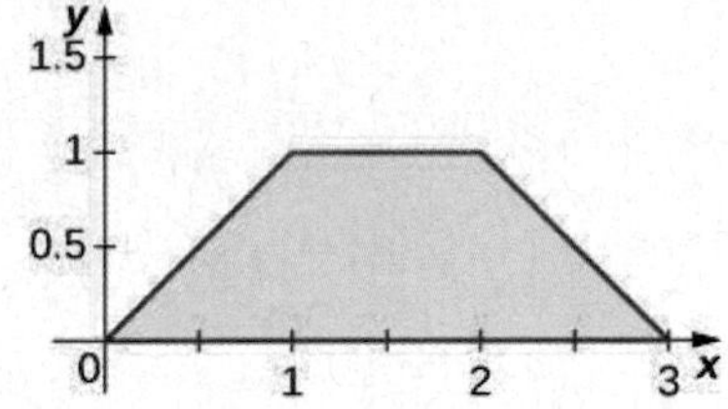

303. R is the disk of radius 2 centered at $(1, 2)$; $\rho(x, y) = x^2 + y^2 - 2x - 4y + 5$.

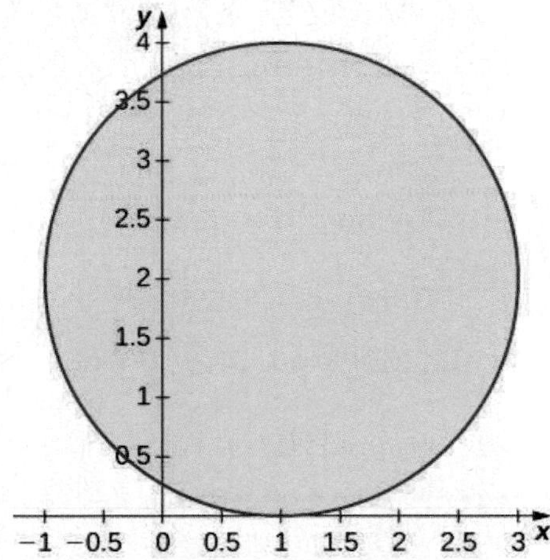

304. R is the unit disk; $\rho(x, y) = 3x^4 + 6x^2y^2 + 3y^4$.

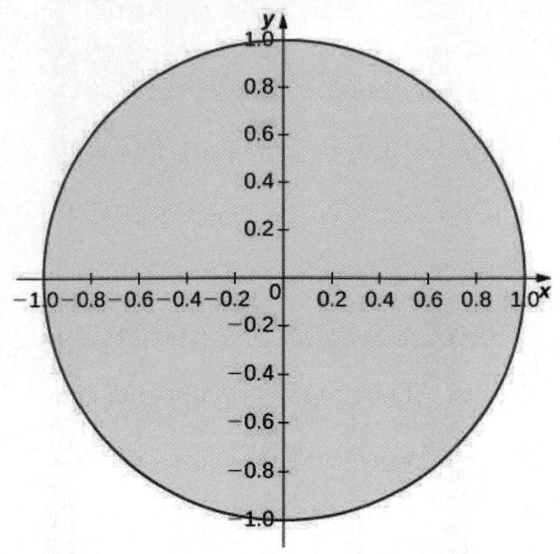

305. R is the region enclosed by the ellipse $x^2 + 4y^2 = 1$; $\rho(x, y) = 1$.

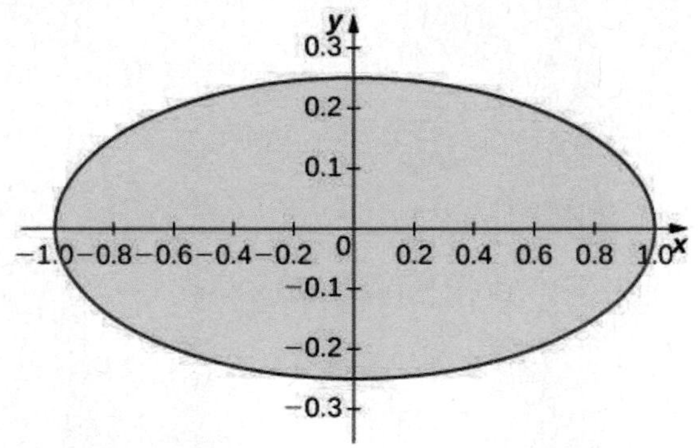

306. $R = \{(x, y) | 9x^2 + y^2 \le 1, x \ge 0, y \ge 0\}$; $\rho(x, y) = \sqrt{9x^2 + y^2}$.

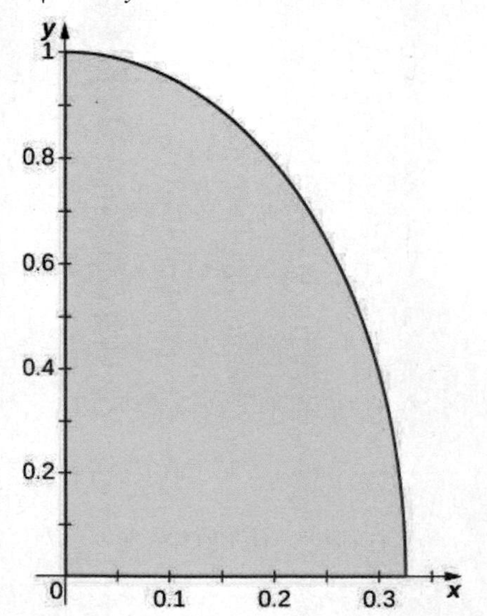

307. R is the region bounded by $y = x$, $y = -x$, $y = x + 2$, $y = -x + 2$; $\rho(x, y) = 1$.

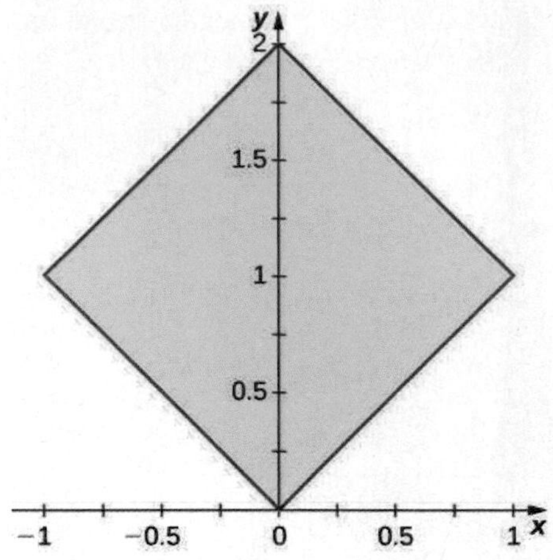

308. R is the region bounded by $y = \frac{1}{x}$, $y = \frac{2}{x}$, $y = 1$, and $y = 2$; $\rho(x, y) = 4(x + y)$.

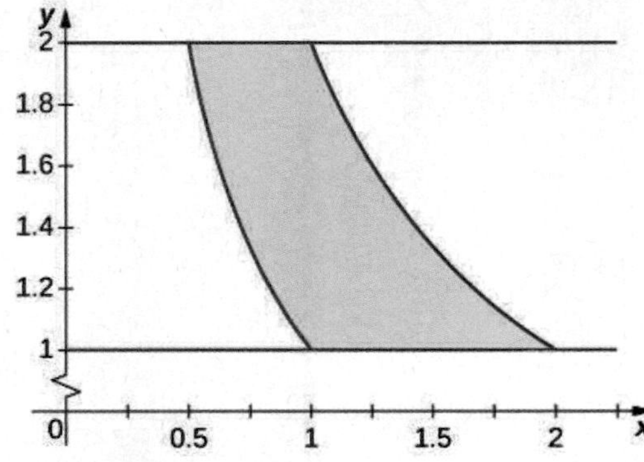

In the following exercises, consider a lamina occupying the region R and having the density function ρ given in the preceding group of exercises. Use a computer algebra system (CAS) to answer the following questions.

a. Find the moments M_x and M_y about the x-axis and y-axis, respectively.

b. Calculate and plot the center of mass of the lamina.

c. **[T]** Use a CAS to locate the center of mass on the graph of R.

309. **[T]** R is the triangular region with vertices $(0, 0)$, $(0, 3)$, and $(6, 0)$; $\rho(x, y) = xy$.

310. **[T]** R is the triangular region with vertices $(0, 0)$, $(1, 1)$, and $(0, 5)$; $\rho(x, y) = x + y$.

311. **[T]** R is the rectangular region with vertices $(0, 0)$, $(0, 3)$, $(6, 3)$, and $(6, 0)$; $\rho(x, y) = \sqrt{xy}$.

312. **[T]** R is the rectangular region with vertices $(0, 1)$, $(0, 3)$, $(3, 3)$, and $(3, 1)$; $\rho(x, y) = x^2y$.

313. **[T]** R is the trapezoidal region determined by the lines $y = -\frac{1}{4}x + \frac{5}{2}$, $y = 0$, $y = 2$, and $x = 0$; $\rho(x, y) = 3xy$.

314. **[T]** R is the trapezoidal region determined by the lines $y = 0$, $y = 1$, $y = x$, and $y = -x + 3$; $\rho(x, y) = 2x + y$.

315. **[T]** R is the disk of radius 2 centered at $(1, 2)$; $\rho(x, y) = x^2 + y^2 - 2x - 4y + 5$.

316. **[T]** R is the unit disk; $\rho(x, y) = 3x^4 + 6x^2y^2 + 3y^4$.

317. **[T]** R is the region enclosed by the ellipse $x^2 + 4y^2 = 1$; $\rho(x, y) = 1$.

318. **[T]** $R = \{(x, y) | 9x^2 + y^2 \le 1, x \ge 0, y \ge 0\}$; $\rho(x, y) = \sqrt{9x^2 + y^2}$.

319. **[T]** R is the region bounded by $y = x$, $y = -x$, $y = x + 2$, and $y = -x + 2$; $\rho(x, y) = 1$.

320. **[T]** R is the region bounded by $y = \frac{1}{x}$, $y = \frac{2}{x}$, $y = 1$, and $y = 2$; $\rho(x, y) = 4(x + y)$.

In the following exercises, consider a lamina occupying the region R and having the density function ρ given in the first two groups of Exercises.

a. Find the moments of inertia I_x, I_y, and I_0 about the x-axis, y-axis, and origin, respectively.

b. Find the radii of gyration with respect to the x-axis, y-axis, and origin, respectively.

321. R is the triangular region with vertices $(0, 0)$, $(0, 3)$, and $(6, 0)$; $\rho(x, y) = xy$.

322. R is the triangular region with vertices $(0, 0)$, $(1, 1)$, and $(0, 5)$; $\rho(x, y) = x + y$.

323. R is the rectangular region with vertices $(0, 0)$, $(0, 3)$, $(6, 3)$, and $(6, 0)$; $\rho(x, y) = \sqrt{xy}$.

324. R is the rectangular region with vertices $(0, 1)$, $(0, 3)$, $(3, 3)$, and $(3, 1)$; $\rho(x, y) = x^2 y$.

325. R is the trapezoidal region determined by the lines $y = -\frac{1}{4}x + \frac{5}{2}$, $y = 0$, $y = 2$, and $x = 0$; $\rho(x, y) = 3xy$.

326. R is the trapezoidal region determined by the lines $y = 0$, $y = 1$, $y = x$, and $y = -x + 3$; $\rho(x, y) = 2x + y$.

327. R is the disk of radius 2 centered at $(1, 2)$; $\rho(x, y) = x^2 + y^2 - 2x - 4y + 5$.

328. R is the unit disk; $\rho(x, y) = 3x^4 + 6x^2y^2 + 3y^4$.

329. R is the region enclosed by the ellipse $x^2 + 4y^2 = 1$; $\rho(x, y) = 1$.

330. $R = \{(x, y) | 9x^2 + y^2 \le 1, x \ge 0, y \ge 0\}$; $\rho(x, y) = \sqrt{9x^2 + y^2}$.

331. R is the region bounded by $y = x$, $y = -x$, $y = x + 2$, and $y = -x + 2$; $\rho(x, y) = 1$.

332. R is the region bounded by $y = \frac{1}{x}$, $y = \frac{2}{x}$, $y = 1$, and $y = 2$; $\rho(x, y) = 4(x + y)$.

333. Let Q be the solid unit cube. Find the mass of the solid if its density ρ is equal to the square of the distance of an arbitrary point of Q to the xy-plane.

334. Let Q be the solid unit hemisphere. Find the mass of the solid if its density ρ is proportional to the distance of an arbitrary point of Q to the origin.

335. The solid Q of constant density 1 is situated inside the sphere $x^2 + y^2 + z^2 = 16$ and outside the sphere $x^2 + y^2 + z^2 = 1$. Show that the center of mass of the solid is not located within the solid.

336. Find the mass of the solid $Q = \{(x, y, z) | 1 \le x^2 + z^2 \le 25, y \le 1 - x^2 - z^2\}$ whose density is $\rho(x, y, z) = k$, where $k > 0$.

337. **[T]** The solid $Q = \{(x, y, z) | x^2 + y^2 \le 9, 0 \le z \le 1, x \ge 0, y \ge 0\}$ has density equal to the distance to the xy-plane. Use a CAS to answer the following questions.

a. Find the mass of Q.
b. Find the moments M_{xy}, M_{xz}, and M_{yz} about the xy-plane, xz-plane, and yz-plane, respectively.
c. Find the center of mass of Q.
d. Graph Q and locate its center of mass.

338. Consider the solid $Q = \{(x, y, z) | 0 \le x \le 1, 0 \le y \le 2, 0 \le z \le 3\}$ with the density function $\rho(x, y, z) = x + y + 1$.

a. Find the mass of Q.
b. Find the moments M_{xy}, M_{xz}, and M_{yz} about the xy-plane, xz-plane, and yz-plane, respectively.
c. Find the center of mass of Q.

339. **[T]** The solid Q has the mass given by the triple integral $\int_{-1}^{1}\int_{0}^{\pi/4}\int_{0}^{1} r^2\,dr\,d\theta\,dz$. Use a CAS to answer the following questions.

a. Show that the center of mass of Q is located in the xy-plane.
b. Graph Q and locate its center of mass.

340. The solid Q is bounded by the planes $x + 4y + z = 8$, $x = 0$, $y = 0$, and $z = 0$. Its density at any point is equal to the distance to the xz-plane. Find the moments of inertia I_y of the solid about the xz-plane.

341. The solid Q is bounded by the planes $x + y + z = 3$, $x = 0$, $y = 0$, and $z = 0$. Its density is $\rho(x, y, z) = x + ay$, where $a > 0$. Show that the center of mass of the solid is located in the plane $z = \frac{3}{5}$ for any value of a.

342. Let Q be the solid situated outside the sphere $x^2 + y^2 + z^2 = z$ and inside the upper hemisphere $x^2 + y^2 + z^2 = R^2$, where $R > 1$. If the density of the solid is $\rho(x, y, z) = \frac{1}{\sqrt{x^2 + y^2 + z^2}}$, find R such that the mass of the solid is $\frac{7\pi}{2}$.

343. The mass of a solid Q is given by $\int_{0}^{2}\int_{0}^{\sqrt{4-x^2}}\int_{\sqrt{x^2+y^2}}^{\sqrt{16-x^2-y^2}} \left(x^2 + y^2 + z^2\right)^n dz\,dy\,dx$, where n is an integer. Determine n such the mass of the solid is $(2 - \sqrt{2})\pi$.

344. Let Q be the solid bounded above the cone $x^2 + y^2 = z^2$ and below the sphere $x^2 + y^2 + z^2 - 4z = 0$. Its density is a constant $k > 0$. Find k such that the center of mass of the solid is situated 7 units from the origin.

345. The solid $Q = \{(x, y, z) | 0 \le x^2 + y^2 \le 16, x \ge 0, y \ge 0, 0 \le z \le x\}$ has the density $\rho(x, y, z) = k$. Show that the moment M_{xy} about the xy-plane is half of the moment M_{yz} about the yz-plane.

346. The solid Q is bounded by the cylinder $x^2 + y^2 = a^2$, the paraboloid $b^2 - z = x^2 + y^2$, and the xy-plane, where $0 < a < b$. Find the mass of the solid if its density is given by $\rho(x, y, z) = \sqrt{x^2 + y^2}$.

347. Let Q be a solid of constant density k, where $k > 0$, that is located in the first octant, inside the circular cone $x^2 + y^2 = 9(z - 1)^2$, and above the plane $z = 0$. Show that the moment M_{xy} about the xy-plane is the same as the moment M_{yz} about the xz-plane.

348. The solid Q has the mass given by the triple integral $\int_{0}^{1}\int_{0}^{\pi/2}\int_{0}^{r^2} \left(r^4 + r\right) dz\,d\theta\,dr$.

a. Find the density of the solid in rectangular coordinates.
b. Find the moment M_{xy} about the xy-plane.

349. The solid Q has the moment of inertia I_x about the yz-plane given by the triple integral $\int_{0}^{2}\int_{-\sqrt{4-y^2}}^{\sqrt{4-y^2}}\int_{\frac{1}{2}(x^2+y^2)}^{\sqrt{x^2+y^2}} \left(y^2 + z^2\right)\left(x^2 + y^2\right) dz\,dx\,dy$.

a. Find the density of Q.
b. Find the moment of inertia I_z about the xy-plane.

350. The solid Q has the mass given by the triple integral

$$\int_0^{\pi/4}\int_0^{2\sec\theta}\int_0^1 \left(r^3\cos\theta\sin\theta + 2r\right)dz\,dr\,d\theta.$$

a. Find the density of the solid in rectangular coordinates.
b. Find the moment M_{xz} about the xz-plane.

351. Let Q be the solid bounded by the xy-plane, the cylinder $x^2 + y^2 = a^2$, and the plane $z = 1$, where $a > 1$ is a real number. Find the moment M_{xy} of the solid about the xy-plane if its density given in cylindrical coordinates is $\rho(r, \theta, z) = \frac{d^2 f}{dr^2}(r)$, where f is a differentiable function with the first and second derivatives continuous and differentiable on $(0, a)$.

352. A solid Q has a volume given by $\iint_D \int_a^b dA\,dz$, where D is the projection of the solid onto the xy-plane and $a < b$ are real numbers, and its density does not depend on the variable z. Show that its center of mass lies in the plane $z = \frac{a+b}{2}$.

353. Consider the solid enclosed by the cylinder $x^2 + z^2 = a^2$ and the planes $y = b$ and $y = c$, where $a > 0$ and $b < c$ are real numbers. The density of Q is given by $\rho(x, y, z) = f'(y)$, where f is a differential function whose derivative is continuous on (b, c). Show that if $f(b) = f(c)$, then the moment of inertia about the xz-plane of Q is null.

354. **[T]** The average density of a solid Q is defined as $\rho_{ave} = \frac{1}{V(Q)}\iiint_Q \rho(x, y, z)dV = \frac{m}{V(Q)}$, where $V(Q)$ and m are the volume and the mass of Q, respectively. If the density of the unit ball centered at the origin is $\rho(x, y, z) = e^{-x^2 - y^2 - z^2}$, use a CAS to find its average density. Round your answer to three decimal places.

355. Show that the moments of inertia I_x, I_y, and I_z about the yz-plane, xz-plane, and xy-plane, respectively, of the unit ball centered at the origin whose density is $\rho(x, y, z) = e^{-x^2 - y^2 - z^2}$ are the same. Round your answer to two decimal places.

5.7 | Change of Variables in Multiple Integrals

Learning Objectives

5.7.1 Determine the image of a region under a given transformation of variables.
5.7.2 Compute the Jacobian of a given transformation.
5.7.3 Evaluate a double integral using a change of variables.
5.7.4 Evaluate a triple integral using a change of variables.

Recall from **Substitution Rule (http://cnx.org/content/m53634/latest/)** the method of integration by substitution. When evaluating an integral such as $\int_2^3 x(x^2-4)^5\,dx,$ we substitute $u = g(x) = x^2 - 4.$ Then $du = 2x\,dx$ or $x\,dx = \frac{1}{2}du$ and the limits change to $u = g(2) = 2^2 - 4 = 0$ and $u = g(3) = 9 - 4 = 5.$ Thus the integral becomes $\int_0^5 \frac{1}{2}u^5\,du$ and this integral is much simpler to evaluate. In other words, when solving integration problems, we make appropriate substitutions to obtain an integral that becomes much simpler than the original integral.

We also used this idea when we transformed double integrals in rectangular coordinates to polar coordinates and transformed triple integrals in rectangular coordinates to cylindrical or spherical coordinates to make the computations simpler. More generally,

$$\int_a^b f(x)dx = \int_c^d f(g(u))g'(u)du,$$

Where $x = g(u),\ dx = g'(u)du,$ and $u = c$ and $u = d$ satisfy $c = g(a)$ and $d = g(b).$

A similar result occurs in double integrals when we substitute $x = f(r, \theta) = r\cos\theta,$ $y = g(r, \theta) = r\sin\theta,$ and $dA = dx\,dy = r\,dr\,d\theta.$ Then we get

$$\iint_R f(x, y)dA = \iint_S f(r\cos\theta, r\sin\theta)r\,dr\,d\theta$$

where the domain R is replaced by the domain S in polar coordinates. Generally, the function that we use to change the variables to make the integration simpler is called a **transformation** or mapping.

Planar Transformations

A **planar transformation** T is a function that transforms a region G in one plane into a region R in another plane by a change of variables. Both G and R are subsets of $R^2.$ For example, **Figure 5.71** shows a region G in the uv-plane transformed into a region R in the xy-plane by the change of variables $x = g(u, v)$ and $y = h(u, v),$ or sometimes we write $x = x(u, v)$ and $y = y(u, v).$ We shall typically assume that each of these functions has continuous first partial derivatives, which means $g_u, g_v, h_u,$ and h_v exist and are also continuous. The need for this requirement will become clear soon.

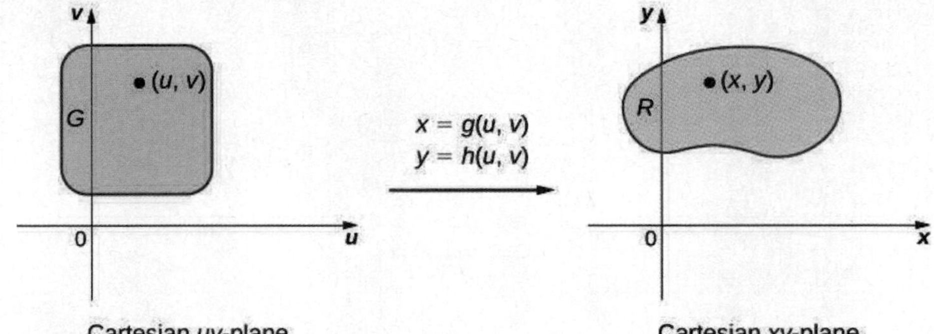

Figure 5.71 The transformation of a region G in the uv-plane into a region R in the xy-plane.

Definition

A transformation $T: G \to R,$ defined as $T(u, v) = (x, y),$ is said to be a **one-to-one transformation** if no two points map to the same image point.

To show that T is a one-to-one transformation, we assume $T(u_1, v_1) = T(u_2, v_2)$ and show that as a consequence we obtain $(u_1, v_1) = (u_2, v_2).$ If the transformation T is one-to-one in the domain $G,$ then the inverse T^{-1} exists with the domain R such that $T^{-1} \circ T$ and $T \circ T^{-1}$ are identity functions.

Figure 5.71 shows the mapping $T(u, v) = (x, y)$ where x and y are related to u and v by the equations $x = g(u, v)$ and $y = h(u, v).$ The region G is the domain of T and the region R is the range of $T,$ also known as the *image* of G under the transformation $T.$

Example 5.65

Determining How the Transformation Works

Suppose a transformation T is defined as $T(r, \theta) = (x, y)$ where $x = r\cos\theta,\ y = r\sin\theta.$ Find the image of the polar rectangle $G = \{(r, \theta) | 0 < r \le 1, 0 \le \theta \le \pi/2\}$ in the $r\theta$-plane to a region R in the xy-plane. Show that T is a one-to-one transformation in G and find $T^{-1}(x, y).$

Solution

Since r varies from 0 to 1 in the $r\theta$-plane, we have a circular disc of radius 0 to 1 in the xy-plane. Because θ varies from 0 to $\pi/2$ in the $r\theta$-plane, we end up getting a quarter circle of radius 1 in the first quadrant of the xy-plane (**Figure 5.72**). Hence R is a quarter circle bounded by $x^2 + y^2 = 1$ in the first quadrant.

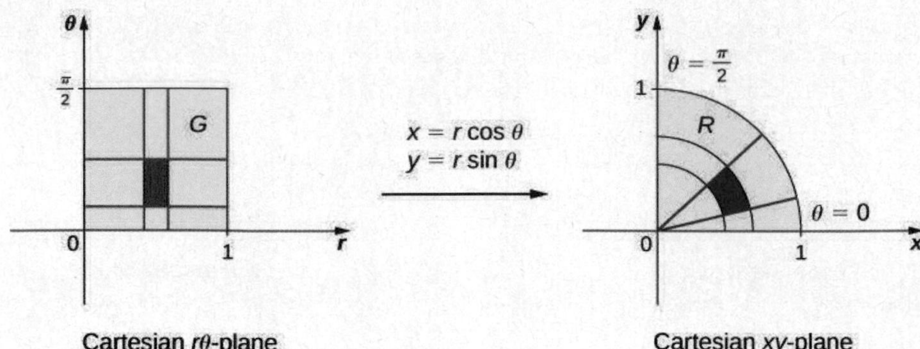

Figure 5.72 A rectangle in the $r\theta$-plane is mapped into a quarter circle in the xy-plane.

In order to show that T is a one-to-one transformation, assume $T(r_1, \theta_1) = T(r_2, \theta_2)$ and show as a consequence that $(r_1, \theta_1) = (r_2, \theta_2)$. In this case, we have

$$\begin{aligned} T(r_1, \theta_1) &= T(r_2, \theta_2), \\ (x_1, y_1) &= (x_1, y_1), \\ (r_1 \cos\theta_1, r_1 \sin\theta_1) &= (r_2 \cos\theta_2, r_2 \sin\theta_2), \\ r_1 \cos\theta_1 &= r_2 \cos\theta_2, \, r_1 \sin\theta_1 = r_2 \sin\theta_2. \end{aligned}$$

Dividing, we obtain

$$\begin{aligned} \frac{r_1 \cos\theta_1}{r_1 \sin\theta_1} &= \frac{r_2 \cos\theta_2}{r_2 \sin\theta_2} \\ \frac{\cos\theta_1}{\sin\theta_1} &= \frac{\cos\theta_2}{\sin\theta_2} \\ \tan\theta_1 &= \tan\theta_2 \\ \theta_1 &= \theta_2 \end{aligned}$$

since the tangent function is one-one function in the interval $0 \le \theta \le \pi/2$. Also, since $0 < r \le 1$, we have $r_1 = r_2, \theta_1 = \theta_2$. Therefore, $(r_1, \theta_1) = (r_2, \theta_2)$ and T is a one-to-one transformation from G into R.

To find $T^{-1}(x, y)$ solve for r, θ in terms of x, y. We already know that $r^2 = x^2 + y^2$ and $\tan\theta = \frac{y}{x}$. Thus $T^{-1}(x, y) = (r, \theta)$ is defined as $r = \sqrt{x^2 + y^2}$ and $\theta = \tan^{-1}\left(\frac{y}{x}\right)$.

Example 5.66

Finding the Image under T

Let the transformation T be defined by $T(u, v) = (x, y)$ where $x = u^2 - v^2$ and $y = uv$. Find the image of the triangle in the uv-plane with vertices $(0, 0)$, $(0, 1)$, and $(1, 1)$.

Solution

The triangle and its image are shown in **Figure 5.73**. To understand how the sides of the triangle transform, call the side that joins $(0, 0)$ and $(0, 1)$ side $A,$ the side that joins $(0, 0)$ and $(1, 1)$ side $B,$ and the side that joins $(1, 1)$ and $(0, 1)$ side $C.$

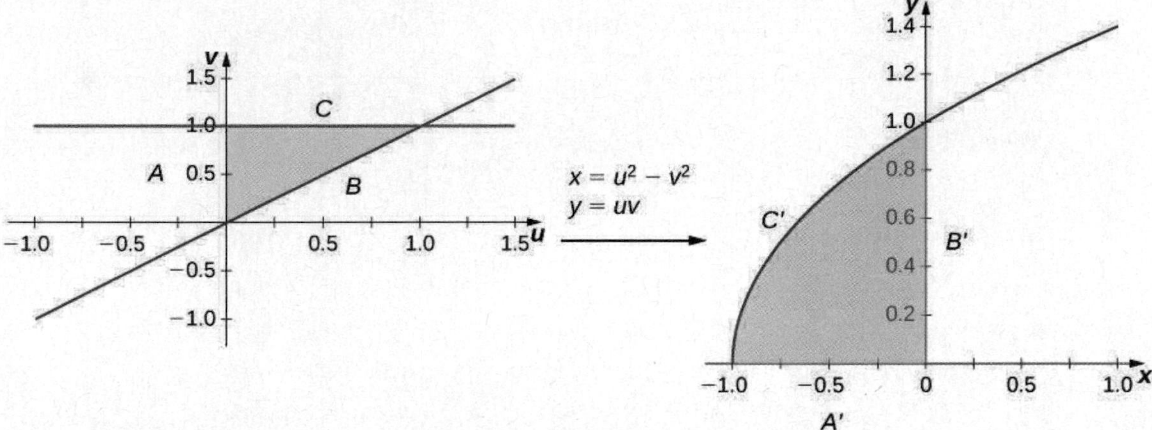

Figure 5.73 A triangular region in the uv-plane is transformed into an image in the xy-plane.

For the side $A: u = 0,\ 0 \leq v \leq 1$ transforms to $x = -v^2,\ y = 0$ so this is the side A' that joins $(-1, 0)$ and $(0, 0)$.

For the side $B: u = v,\ 0 \leq u \leq 1$ transforms to $x = 0,\ y = u^2$ so this is the side B' that joins $(0, 0)$ and $(0, 1)$.

For the side $C: 0 \leq u \leq 1,\ v = 1$ transforms to $x = u^2 - 1,\ y = u$ (hence $x = y^2 - 1$) so this is the side C' that makes the upper half of the parabolic arc joining $(-1, 0)$ and $(0, 1)$.

All the points in the entire region of the triangle in the uv-plane are mapped inside the parabolic region in the xy-plane.

5.43 Let a transformation T be defined as $T(u, v) = (x, y)$ where $x = u + v,\ y = 3v$. Find the image of the rectangle $G = \{(u, v): 0 \leq u \leq 1,\ 0 \leq v \leq 2\}$ from the uv-plane after the transformation into a region R in the xy-plane. Show that T is a one-to-one transformation and find $T^{-1}(x, y)$.

Jacobians

Recall that we mentioned near the beginning of this section that each of the component functions must have continuous first partial derivatives, which means that $g_u,\ g_v,\ h_u,$ and h_v exist and are also continuous. A transformation that has this property is called a C^1 transformation (here C denotes continuous). Let $T(u, v) = (g(u, v), h(u, v)),$ where $x = g(u, v)$ and $y = h(u, v),$ be a one-to-one C^1 transformation. We want to see how it transforms a small rectangular region $S,$ Δu units by Δv units, in the uv-plane (see the following figure).

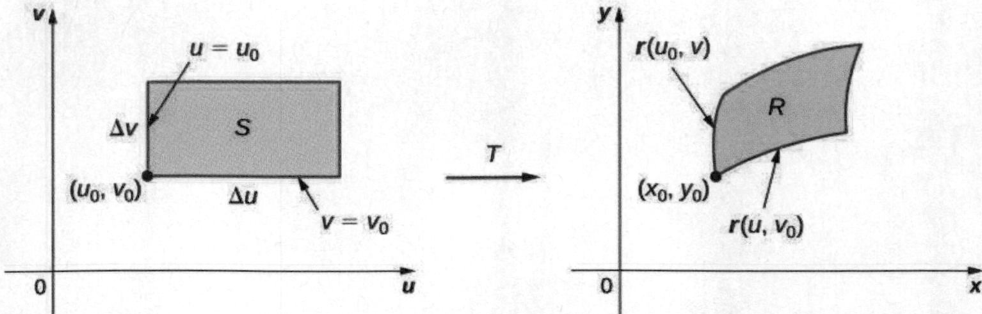

Figure 5.74 A small rectangle S in the uv-plane is transformed into a region R in the xy-plane.

Since $x = g(u, v)$ and $y = h(u, v)$, we have the position vector $\mathbf{r}(u, v) = g(u, v)\mathbf{i} + h(u, v)\mathbf{j}$ of the image of the point (u, v). Suppose that (u_0, v_0) is the coordinate of the point at the lower left corner that mapped to $(x_0, y_0) = T(u_0, v_0)$. The line $v = v_0$ maps to the image curve with vector function $\text{r}(u, v_0)$, and the tangent vector at (x_0, y_0) to the image curve is

$$\mathbf{r}_u = g_u(u_0, v_0)\mathbf{i} + h_u(u_0, v_0)\mathbf{j} = \frac{\partial x}{\partial u}\mathbf{i} + \frac{\partial y}{\partial u}\mathbf{j}.$$

Similarly, the line $u = u_0$ maps to the image curve with vector function $\mathbf{r}(u_0, v)$, and the tangent vector at (x_0, y_0) to the image curve is

$$\mathbf{r}_v = g_v(u_0, v_0)\mathbf{i} + h_v(u_0, v_0)\mathbf{j} = \frac{\partial x}{\partial v}\mathbf{i} + \frac{\partial y}{\partial v}\mathbf{j}.$$

Now, note that

$$\mathbf{r}_u = \lim_{\Delta u \to 0} \frac{\mathbf{r}(u_0 + \Delta u, v_0) - \mathbf{r}(u_0, v_0)}{\Delta u} \text{ so } \mathbf{r}(u_0 + \Delta u, v_0) - \mathbf{r}(u_0, v_0) \approx \Delta u \mathbf{r}_u.$$

Similarly,

$$\mathbf{r}_v = \lim_{\Delta v \to 0} \frac{\mathbf{r}(u_0, v_0 + \Delta v) - \mathbf{r}(u_0, v_0)}{\Delta v} \text{ so } \mathbf{r}(u_0, v_0 + \Delta v) - \mathbf{r}(u_0, v_0) \approx \Delta v \mathbf{r}_v.$$

This allows us to estimate the area ΔA of the image R by finding the area of the parallelogram formed by the sides $\Delta v \mathbf{r}_v$ and $\Delta u \mathbf{r}_u$. By using the cross product of these two vectors by adding the **k**th component as 0, the area ΔA of the image R (refer to **The Cross Product**) is approximately $|\Delta u \mathbf{r}_u \times \Delta v \mathbf{r}_v| = |\mathbf{r}_u \times \mathbf{r}_v| \Delta u \Delta v$. In determinant form, the cross product is

$$\mathbf{r}_u \times \mathbf{r}_v = \begin{vmatrix} \mathbf{i} & \mathbf{j} & \mathbf{k} \\ \frac{\partial x}{\partial u} & \frac{\partial y}{\partial u} & 0 \\ \frac{\partial x}{\partial v} & \frac{\partial y}{\partial v} & 0 \end{vmatrix} = \begin{vmatrix} \frac{\partial x}{\partial u} & \frac{\partial y}{\partial u} \\ \frac{\partial x}{\partial v} & \frac{\partial y}{\partial v} \end{vmatrix} \mathbf{k} = \left(\frac{\partial x}{\partial u}\frac{\partial y}{\partial v} - \frac{\partial x}{\partial v}\frac{\partial y}{\partial u} \right) \mathbf{k}.$$

Since $|\mathbf{k}| = 1$, we have $\Delta A \approx |\mathbf{r}_u \times \mathbf{r}_v| \Delta u \Delta v = \left(\frac{\partial x}{\partial u}\frac{\partial y}{\partial v} - \frac{\partial x}{\partial v}\frac{\partial y}{\partial u} \right) \Delta u \Delta v.$

Definition

The **Jacobian** of the C^1 transformation $T(u, v) = (g(u, v), h(u, v))$ is denoted by $J(u, v)$ and is defined by the 2×2 determinant

$$J(u, v) = \left|\frac{\partial(x, y)}{\partial(u, v)}\right| = \begin{vmatrix} \frac{\partial x}{\partial u} & \frac{\partial y}{\partial u} \\ \frac{\partial x}{\partial v} & \frac{\partial y}{\partial v} \end{vmatrix} = \left(\frac{\partial x}{\partial u}\frac{\partial y}{\partial v} - \frac{\partial x}{\partial v}\frac{\partial y}{\partial u}\right).$$

Using the definition, we have

$$\Delta A \approx J(u, v)\Delta u \Delta v = \left|\frac{\partial(x, y)}{\partial(u, v)}\right|\Delta u \Delta v.$$

Note that the Jacobian is frequently denoted simply by

$$J(u, v) = \frac{\partial(x, y)}{\partial(u, v)}.$$

Note also that

$$\begin{vmatrix} \frac{\partial x}{\partial u} & \frac{\partial y}{\partial u} \\ \frac{\partial x}{\partial v} & \frac{\partial y}{\partial v} \end{vmatrix} = \left(\frac{\partial x}{\partial u}\frac{\partial y}{\partial v} - \frac{\partial x}{\partial v}\frac{\partial y}{\partial u}\right) = \begin{vmatrix} \frac{\partial x}{\partial u} & \frac{\partial x}{\partial v} \\ \frac{\partial y}{\partial u} & \frac{\partial y}{\partial v} \end{vmatrix}.$$

Hence the notation $J(u, v) = \frac{\partial(x, y)}{\partial(u, v)}$ suggests that we can write the Jacobian determinant with partials of x in the first row and partials of y in the second row.

Example 5.67

Finding the Jacobian

Find the Jacobian of the transformation given in **Example 5.65**.

Solution

The transformation in the example is $T(r, \theta) = (r\cos\theta, r\sin\theta)$ where $x = r\cos\theta$ and $y = r\sin\theta$. Thus the Jacobian is

$$\begin{aligned} J(r, \theta) &= \frac{\partial(x, y)}{\partial(r, \theta)} = \begin{vmatrix} \frac{\partial x}{\partial r} & \frac{\partial x}{\partial \theta} \\ \frac{\partial y}{\partial r} & \frac{\partial y}{\partial \theta} \end{vmatrix} = \begin{vmatrix} \cos\theta & -r\sin\theta \\ \sin\theta & r\cos\theta \end{vmatrix} \\ &= r\cos^2\theta + r\sin^2\theta = r\left(\cos^2\theta + \sin^2\theta\right) = r. \end{aligned}$$

Example 5.68

Finding the Jacobian

Find the Jacobian of the transformation given in **Example 5.66**.

Solution

The transformation in the example is $T(u, v) = \left(u^2 - v^2, uv\right)$ where $x = u^2 - v^2$ and $y = uv$. Thus the Jacobian is

$$J(u, v) = \frac{\partial(x, y)}{\partial(u, v)} = \begin{vmatrix} \frac{\partial x}{\partial u} & \frac{\partial x}{\partial v} \\ \frac{\partial y}{\partial u} & \frac{\partial y}{\partial v} \end{vmatrix} = \begin{vmatrix} 2u & v \\ -2v & u \end{vmatrix} = 2u^2 + 2v^2.$$

5.44 Find the Jacobian of the transformation given in the previous checkpoint: $T(u, v) = (u + v, 2v)$.

Change of Variables for Double Integrals

We have already seen that, under the change of variables $T(u, v) = (x, y)$ where $x = g(u, v)$ and $y = h(u, v)$, a small region ΔA in the xy-plane is related to the area formed by the product $\Delta u \Delta v$ in the uv-plane by the approximation

$$\Delta A \approx J(u, v)\Delta u, \Delta v.$$

Now let's go back to the definition of double integral for a minute:

$$\iint_R f(x, y)dA = \lim_{m, n \to \infty} \sum_{i=1}^{m} \sum_{j=1}^{n} f(x_{ij}, y_{ij})\Delta A.$$

Referring to **Figure 5.75**, observe that we divided the region S in the uv-plane into small subrectangles S_{ij} and we let the subrectangles R_{ij} in the xy-plane be the images of S_{ij} under the transformation $T(u, v) = (x, y)$.

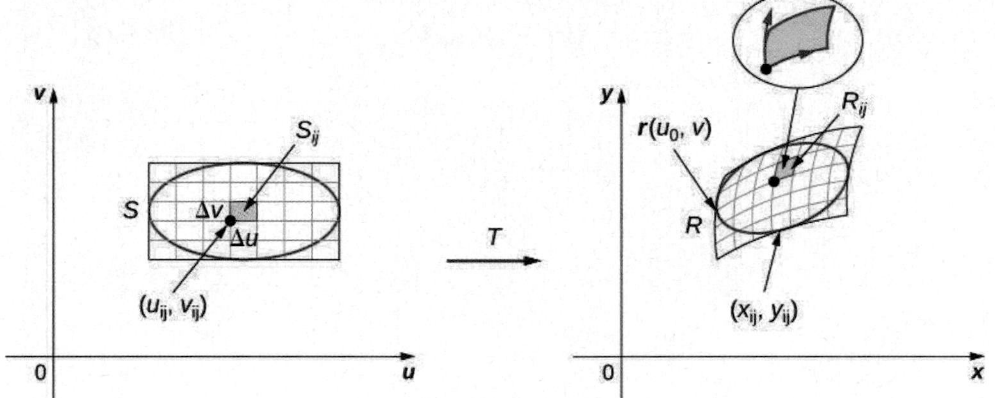

Figure 5.75 The subrectangles S_{ij} in the uv-plane transform into subrectangles R_{ij} in the xy-plane.

Then the double integral becomes

$$\iint_R f(x, y)dA = \lim_{m, n \to \infty} \sum_{i=1}^{m} \sum_{j=1}^{n} f(x_{ij}, y_{ij})\Delta A = \lim_{m, n \to \infty} \sum_{i=1}^{m} \sum_{j=1}^{n} f(g(u_{ij}, v_{ij}), h(u_{ij}, v_{ij}))|J(u_{ij}, v_{ij})|\Delta u \Delta v.$$

Notice this is exactly the double Riemann sum for the integral

$$\iint_S f(g(u, v), h(u, v))\left|\frac{\partial(x, y)}{\partial(u, v)}\right| du\, dv.$$

Theorem 5.14: Change of Variables for Double Integrals

Let $T(u, v) = (x, y)$ where $x = g(u, v)$ and $y = h(u, v)$ be a one-to-one C^1 transformation, with a nonzero Jacobian on the interior of the region S in the uv-plane; it maps S into the region R in the xy-plane. If f is continuous on R, then

$$\iint\limits_R f(x, y)dA = \iint\limits_S f(g(u, v), h(u, v))\left|\frac{\partial(x, y)}{\partial(u, v)}\right|du\,dv.$$

With this theorem for double integrals, we can change the variables from (x, y) to (u, v) in a double integral simply by replacing

$$dA = dx\,dy = \left|\frac{\partial(x, y)}{\partial(u, v)}\right|du\,dv$$

when we use the substitutions $x = g(u, v)$ and $y = h(u, v)$ and then change the limits of integration accordingly. This change of variables often makes any computations much simpler.

Example 5.69

Changing Variables from Rectangular to Polar Coordinates

Consider the integral

$$\int_0^2 \int_0^{\sqrt{2x - x^2}} \sqrt{x^2 + y^2}\,dy\,dx.$$

Use the change of variables $x = r\cos\theta$ and $y = r\sin\theta$, and find the resulting integral.

Solution

First we need to find the region of integration. This region is bounded below by $y = 0$ and above by $y = \sqrt{2x - x^2}$ (see the following figure).

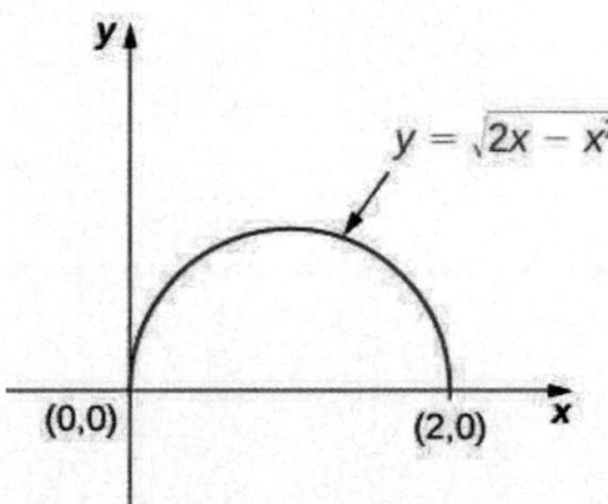

Figure 5.76 Changing a region from rectangular to polar coordinates.

Squaring and collecting terms, we find that the region is the upper half of the circle $x^2 + y^2 - 2x = 0$, that is, $y^2 + (x - 1)^2 = 1$. In polar coordinates, the circle is $r = 2\cos\theta$ so the region of integration in polar coordinates is bounded by $0 \leq r \leq \cos\theta$ and $0 \leq \theta \leq \frac{\pi}{2}$.

The Jacobian is $J(r, \theta) = r,$ as shown in **Example 5.67**. Since $r \geq 0,$ we have $|J(r, \theta)| = r.$

The integrand $\sqrt{x^2 + y^2}$ changes to r in polar coordinates, so the double iterated integral is

$$\int_0^2 \int_0^{\sqrt{2x - x^2}} \sqrt{x^2 + y^2}\,dy\,dx = \int_0^{\pi/2} \int_0^{2\cos\theta} r|J(r, \theta)|dr\,d\theta = \int_0^{\pi/2} \int_0^{2\cos\theta} r^2 dr\,d\theta.$$

5.45 Considering the integral $\int_0^1 \int_0^{\sqrt{1 - x^2}} \left(x^2 + y^2\right) dy\,dx,$ use the change of variables $x = r\cos\theta$ and $y = r\sin\theta,$ and find the resulting integral.

Notice in the next example that the region over which we are to integrate may suggest a suitable transformation for the integration. This is a common and important situation.

Example 5.70

Changing Variables

Consider the integral $\iint\limits_R (x - y)dy\,dx,$ where R is the parallelogram joining the points $(1, 2),$ $(3, 4), (4, 3),$ and $(6, 5)$ (**Figure 5.77**). Make appropriate changes of variables, and write the resulting integral.

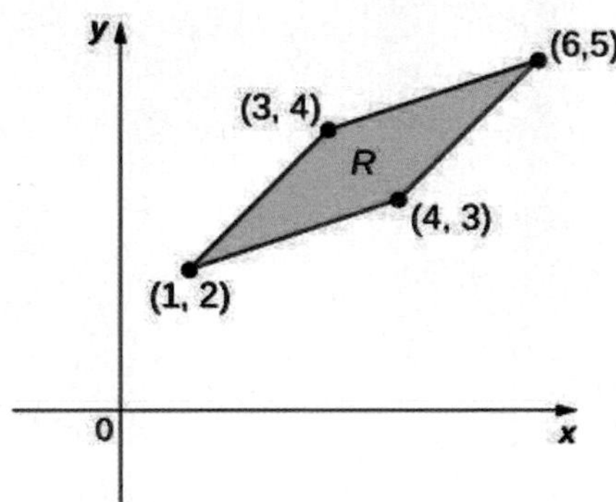

Figure 5.77 The region of integration for the given integral.

Solution

First, we need to understand the region over which we are to integrate. The sides of the parallelogram are $x - y + 1 = 0,$ $x - y - 1 = 0,$ $x - 3y + 5 = 0,$ and $x - 3y + 9 = 0$ (**Figure 5.78**). Another way to look at them is $x - y = -1,$ $x - y = 1,$ $x - 3y = -5,$ and $x - 3y = 9.$

Clearly the parallelogram is bounded by the lines $y = x + 1,$ $y = x - 1,$ $y = \frac{1}{3}(x + 5),$ and $y = \frac{1}{3}(x + 9).$

Notice that if we were to make $u = x - y$ and $v = x - 3y,$ then the limits on the integral would be

$-1 \leq u \leq 1$ and $-9 \leq v \leq -5$.

To solve for x and y, we multiply the first equation by 3 and subtract the second equation, $3u - v = (3x - 3y) - (x - 3y) = 2x$. Then we have $x = \frac{3u - v}{2}$. Moreover, if we simply subtract the second equation from the first, we get $u - v = (x - y) - (x - 3y) = 2y$ and $y = \frac{u - v}{2}$.

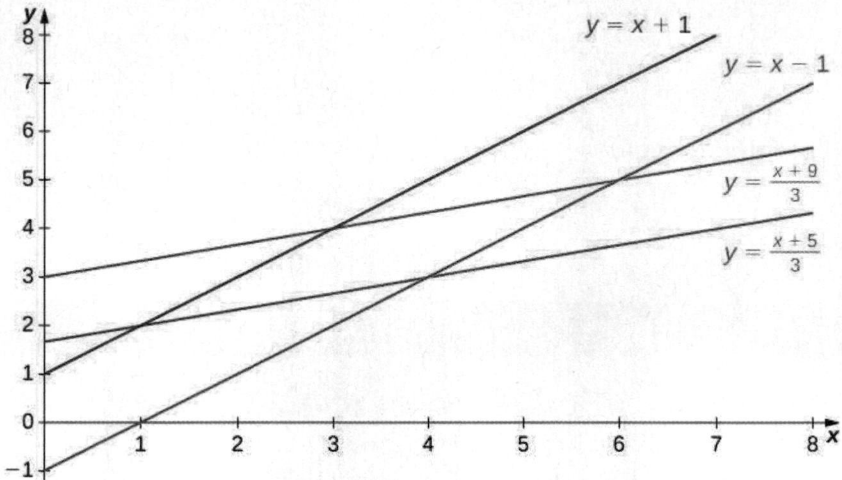

Figure 5.78 A parallelogram in the xy-plane that we want to transform by a change in variables.

Thus, we can choose the transformation

$$T(u, v) = \left(\frac{3u - v}{2}, \frac{u - v}{2}\right)$$

and compute the Jacobian $J(u, v)$. We have

$$J(u, v) = \frac{\partial(x, y)}{\partial(u, v)} = \begin{vmatrix} \frac{\partial x}{\partial u} & \frac{\partial x}{\partial v} \\ \frac{\partial y}{\partial u} & \frac{\partial y}{\partial v} \end{vmatrix} = \begin{vmatrix} 3/2 & -1/2 \\ 1/2 & -1/2 \end{vmatrix} = -\frac{3}{4} + \frac{1}{4} = -\frac{1}{2}.$$

Therefore, $|J(u, v)| = \frac{1}{2}$. Also, the original integrand becomes

$$x - y = \frac{1}{2}[3u - v - u + v] = \frac{1}{2}[3u - u] = \frac{1}{2}[2u] = u.$$

Therefore, by the use of the transformation T, the integral changes to

$$\iint_R (x - y)dy\,dx = \int_{-9}^{-5} \int_{-1}^{1} J(u, v)u\,du\,dv = \int_{-9}^{-5} \int_{-1}^{1} \left(\frac{1}{2}\right)u\,du\,dv,$$

which is much simpler to compute.

5.46 Make appropriate changes of variables in the integral $\iint_R \frac{4}{(x - y)^2}dy\,dx$, where R is the trapezoid bounded by the lines $x - y = 2$, $x - y = 4$, $x = 0$, and $y = 0$. Write the resulting integral.

We are ready to give a problem-solving strategy for change of variables.

Problem-Solving Strategy: Change of Variables

1. Sketch the region given by the problem in the xy-plane and then write the equations of the curves that form the boundary.
2. Depending on the region or the integrand, choose the transformations $x = g(u, v)$ and $y = h(u, v)$.
3. Determine the new limits of integration in the uv-plane.
4. Find the Jacobian $J(u, v)$.
5. In the integrand, replace the variables to obtain the new integrand.
6. Replace $dy\,dx$ or $dx\,dy$, whichever occurs, by $J(u, v)du\,dv$.

In the next example, we find a substitution that makes the integrand much simpler to compute.

Example 5.71

Evaluating an Integral

Using the change of variables $u = x - y$ and $v = x + y$, evaluate the integral

$$\iint_R (x - y)e^{x^2 - y^2}\, dA,$$

where R is the region bounded by the lines $x + y = 1$ and $x + y = 3$ and the curves $x^2 - y^2 = -1$ and $x^2 - y^2 = 1$ (see the first region in **Figure 5.79**).

Solution

As before, first find the region R and picture the transformation so it becomes easier to obtain the limits of integration after the transformations are made (**Figure 5.79**).

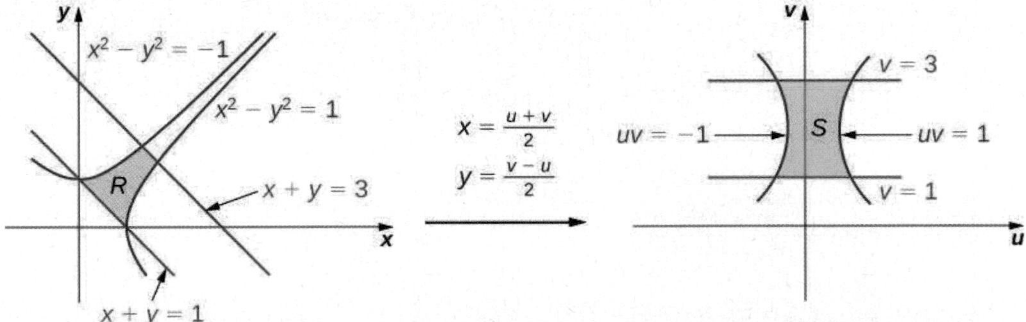

Figure 5.79 Transforming the region R into the region S to simplify the computation of an integral.

Given $u = x - y$ and $v = x + y$, we have $x = \frac{u + v}{2}$ and $y = \frac{v - u}{2}$ and hence the transformation to use is $T(u, v) = \left(\frac{u + v}{2}, \frac{v - u}{2}\right)$. The lines $x + y = 1$ and $x + y = 3$ become $v = 1$ and $v = 3$, respectively. The curves $x^2 - y^2 = 1$ and $x^2 - y^2 = -1$ become $uv = 1$ and $uv = -1,$ respectively.

Thus we can describe the region S (see the second region **Figure 5.79**) as

$$S = \left\{(u, v) | 1 \le v \le 3, \frac{-1}{v} \le u \le \frac{1}{v}\right\}.$$

The Jacobian for this transformation is

$$J(u, v) = \frac{\partial(x, y)}{\partial(u, v)} = \begin{vmatrix} \frac{\partial x}{\partial u} & \frac{\partial x}{\partial v} \\ \frac{\partial y}{\partial u} & \frac{\partial y}{\partial v} \end{vmatrix} = \begin{vmatrix} 1/2 & -1/2 \\ 1/2 & 1/2 \end{vmatrix} = \frac{1}{2}.$$

Therefore, by using the transformation $T,$ the integral changes to

$$\iint_R (x - y)e^{x^2 - y^2} dA = \frac{1}{2}\int_1^3 \int_{-1/v}^{1/v} ue^{uv} \, du \, dv.$$

Doing the evaluation, we have

$$\frac{1}{2}\int_1^3 \int_{-1/v}^{1/v} ue^{uv} \, du \, dv = \frac{4}{3e} \approx 0.490.$$

5.47 Using the substitutions $x = v$ and $y = \sqrt{u + v},$ evaluate the integral $\iint_R y \sin\left(y^2 - x\right) dA$ where R is the region bounded by the lines $y = \sqrt{x}, \ x = 2,$ and $y = 0.$

Change of Variables for Triple Integrals

Changing variables in triple integrals works in exactly the same way. Cylindrical and spherical coordinate substitutions are special cases of this method, which we demonstrate here.

Suppose that G is a region in uvw-space and is mapped to D in xyz-space (**Figure 5.80**) by a one-to-one C^1 transformation $T(u, v, w) = (x, y, z)$ where $x = g(u, v, w), \quad y = h(u, v, w),$ and $z = k(u, v, w).$

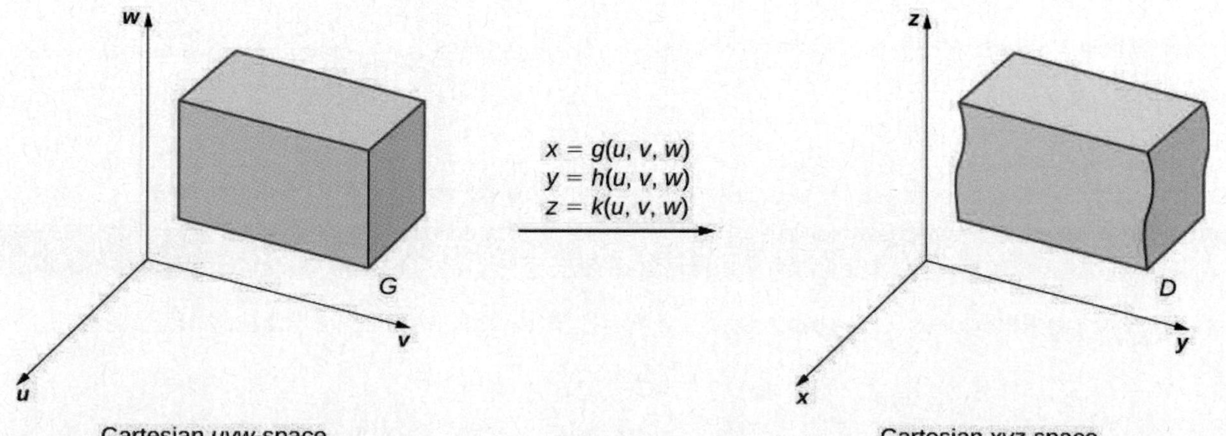

Figure 5.80 A region G in uvw-space mapped to a region D in xyz-space.

Then any function $F(x, y, z)$ defined on D can be thought of as another function $H(u, v, w)$ that is defined on G:

$$F(x, y, z) = F(g(u, v, w), h(u, v, w), k(u, v, w)) = H(u, v, w).$$

Now we need to define the Jacobian for three variables.

Definition

The Jacobian determinant $J(u, v, w)$ in three variables is defined as follows:

$$J(u, v, w) = \begin{vmatrix} \frac{\partial x}{\partial u} & \frac{\partial y}{\partial u} & \frac{\partial z}{\partial u} \\ \frac{\partial x}{\partial v} & \frac{\partial y}{\partial v} & \frac{\partial z}{\partial v} \\ \frac{\partial x}{\partial w} & \frac{\partial y}{\partial w} & \frac{\partial z}{\partial w} \end{vmatrix}.$$

This is also the same as

$$J(u, v, w) = \begin{vmatrix} \frac{\partial x}{\partial u} & \frac{\partial x}{\partial v} & \frac{\partial x}{\partial w} \\ \frac{\partial y}{\partial u} & \frac{\partial y}{\partial v} & \frac{\partial y}{\partial w} \\ \frac{\partial z}{\partial u} & \frac{\partial z}{\partial v} & \frac{\partial z}{\partial w} \end{vmatrix}.$$

The Jacobian can also be simply denoted as $\frac{\partial(x, y, z)}{\partial(u, v, w)}$.

With the transformations and the Jacobian for three variables, we are ready to establish the theorem that describes change of variables for triple integrals.

Theorem 5.15: Change of Variables for Triple Integrals

Let $T(u, v, w) = (x, y, z)$ where $x = g(u, v, w), y = h(u, v, w),$ and $z = k(u, v, w),$ be a one-to-one C^1 transformation, with a nonzero Jacobian, that maps the region G in the uvw-plane into the region D in the xyz-plane. As in the two-dimensional case, if F is continuous on $D,$ then

$$\begin{aligned} \iiint_R F(x, y, z)dV &= \iiint_G F(g(u, v, w), h(u, v, w), k(u, v, w))\left|\frac{\partial(x, y, z)}{\partial(u, v, w)}\right|du\,dv\,dw \\ &= \iiint_G H(u, v, w)|J(u, v, w)|du\,dv\,dw. \end{aligned}$$

Let us now see how changes in triple integrals for cylindrical and spherical coordinates are affected by this theorem. We expect to obtain the same formulas as in **Triple Integrals in Cylindrical and Spherical Coordinates**.

Example 5.72

Obtaining Formulas in Triple Integrals for Cylindrical and Spherical Coordinates

Derive the formula in triple integrals for

a. cylindrical and

b. spherical coordinates.

Solution

a. For cylindrical coordinates, the transformation is $T(r, \theta, z) = (x, y, z)$ from the Cartesian $r\theta z$-plane to the Cartesian xyz-plane (**Figure 5.81**). Here $x = r\cos\theta$, $y = r\sin\theta$, and $z = z$. The Jacobian for the transformation is

$$J(r, \theta, z) = \frac{\partial(x, y, z)}{\partial(r, \theta, z)} = \begin{vmatrix} \frac{\partial x}{\partial r} & \frac{\partial x}{\partial \theta} & \frac{\partial x}{\partial z} \\ \frac{\partial y}{\partial r} & \frac{\partial y}{\partial \theta} & \frac{\partial y}{\partial z} \\ \frac{\partial z}{\partial r} & \frac{\partial z}{\partial \theta} & \frac{\partial z}{\partial z} \end{vmatrix}$$

$$= \begin{vmatrix} \cos\theta & -r\sin\theta & 0 \\ \sin\theta & r\cos\theta & 0 \\ 0 & 0 & 1 \end{vmatrix} = r\cos^2\theta + r\sin^2\theta = r\left(\cos^2\theta + \sin^2\theta\right) = r.$$

We know that $r \geq 0$, so $|J(r, \theta, z)| = r$. Then the triple integral is

$$\iiint\limits_D f(x, y, z)dV = \iiint\limits_G f(r\cos\theta, r\sin\theta, z)r\,dr\,d\theta\,dz.$$

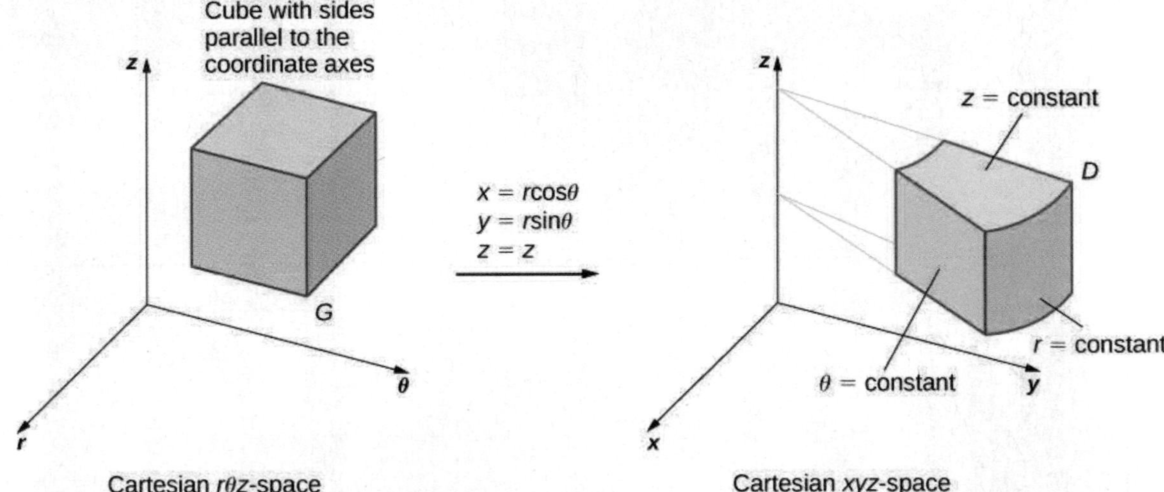

Figure 5.81 The transformation from rectangular coordinates to cylindrical coordinates can be treated as a change of variables from region G in $r\theta z$-space to region D in xyz-space.

b. For spherical coordinates, the transformation is $T(\rho, \theta, \varphi) = (x, y, z)$ from the Cartesian $p\theta\varphi$-plane to the Cartesian xyz-plane (**Figure 5.82**). Here $x = \rho\sin\varphi\cos\theta$, $y = \rho\sin\varphi\sin\theta$, and $z = \rho\cos\varphi$. The Jacobian for the transformation is

$$J(\rho, \theta, \varphi) = \frac{\partial(x, y, z)}{\partial(\rho, \theta, \varphi)} = \begin{vmatrix} \frac{\partial x}{\partial \rho} & \frac{\partial x}{\partial \theta} & \frac{\partial x}{\partial \varphi} \\ \frac{\partial y}{\partial \rho} & \frac{\partial y}{\partial \theta} & \frac{\partial y}{\partial \varphi} \\ \frac{\partial z}{\partial \rho} & \frac{\partial z}{\partial \theta} & \frac{\partial z}{\partial \varphi} \end{vmatrix} = \begin{vmatrix} \sin\varphi\cos\theta & -\rho\sin\varphi\sin\theta & \rho\cos\varphi\cos\theta \\ \sin\varphi\sin\theta & -\rho\sin\varphi\cos\theta & \rho\cos\varphi\sin\theta \\ \cos\theta & 0 & -\rho\sin\varphi \end{vmatrix}.$$

Expanding the determinant with respect to the third row:

$$= \cos\varphi \begin{vmatrix} -\rho\sin\varphi\sin\theta & \rho\cos\varphi\cos\theta \\ \rho\sin\varphi\sin\theta & \rho\cos\varphi\sin\theta \end{vmatrix} - \rho\sin\varphi \begin{vmatrix} \sin\varphi\cos\theta & -\rho\sin\varphi\sin\theta \\ \sin\varphi\sin\theta & \rho\sin\varphi\cos\theta \end{vmatrix}$$

$$= \cos\varphi\left(-\rho^2\sin\varphi\cos\varphi\sin^2\theta - \rho^2\sin\varphi\cos\varphi\cos^2\theta\right)$$
$$-\rho\sin\varphi\left(\rho\sin^2\varphi\cos^2\theta + \rho\sin^2\varphi\sin^2\theta\right)$$

$$= -\rho^2\sin\varphi\cos^2\varphi\left(\sin^2\theta + \cos^2\theta\right) - \rho^2\sin\varphi\sin^2\varphi\left(\sin^2\theta + \cos^2\theta\right)$$
$$= -\rho^2\sin\varphi\cos^2\varphi - \rho^2\sin\varphi\sin^2\varphi$$
$$= -\rho^2\sin\varphi\left(\cos^2\varphi + \sin^2\varphi\right) = -\rho^2\sin\varphi.$$

Since $0 \le \varphi \le \pi$, we must have $\sin\varphi \ge 0$. Thus $|J(\rho, \theta, \varphi)| = \left|-\rho^2\sin\varphi\right| = \rho^2\sin\varphi$.

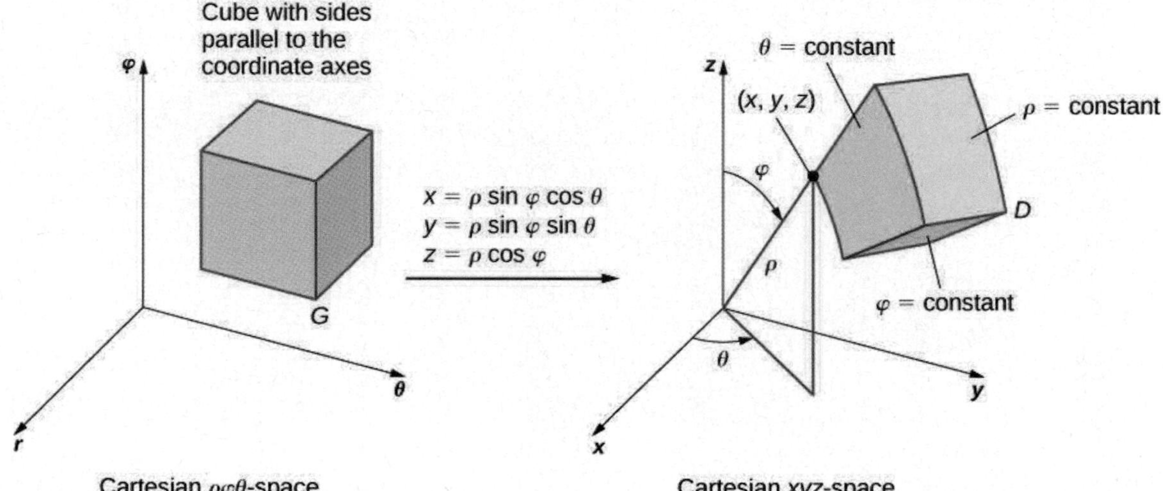

Figure 5.82 The transformation from rectangular coordinates to spherical coordinates can be treated as a change of variables from region G in $\rho\theta\varphi$-space to region D in xyz-space.

Then the triple integral becomes

$$\iiint_D f(x, y, z)dV = \iiint_G f(\rho\sin\varphi\cos\theta, \rho\sin\varphi\sin\theta, \rho\cos\varphi)\rho^2\sin\varphi\, d\rho\, d\varphi\, d\theta.$$

Let's try another example with a different substitution.

Example 5.73

Evaluating a Triple Integral with a Change of Variables

Evaluate the triple integral

$$\int_0^3 \int_0^4 \int_{y/2}^{(y/2)+1} \left(x + \frac{z}{3}\right) dx\, dy\, dz$$

in xyz-space by using the transformation

$$u = (2x - y)/2, \ v = y/2, \text{ and } w = z/3.$$

Then integrate over an appropriate region in uvw-space.

Solution

As before, some kind of sketch of the region G in xyz-space over which we have to perform the integration can help identify the region D in uvw-space (**Figure 5.83**). Clearly G in xyz-space is bounded by the planes $x = y/2$, $x = (y/2) + 1$, $y = 0$, $y = 4$, $z = 0$, and $z = 4$. We also know that we have to use $u = (2x - y)/2$, $v = y/2$, and $w = z/3$ for the transformations. We need to solve for x, y, and z. Here we find that $x = u + v$, $y = 2v$, and $z = 3w$.

Using elementary algebra, we can find the corresponding surfaces for the region G and the limits of integration in uvw-space. It is convenient to list these equations in a table.

Equations in xyz for the region D	**Corresponding equations in uvw for the region G**	**Limits for the integration in uvw**
$x = y/2$	$u + v = 2v/2 = v$	$u = 0$
$x = y/2$	$u + v = (2v/2) + 1 = v + 1$	$u = 1$
$y = 0$	$2v = 0$	$v = 0$
$y = 4$	$2v = 4$	$v = 2$
$z = 0$	$3w = 0$	$w = 0$
$z = 3$	$3w = 3$	$w = 1$

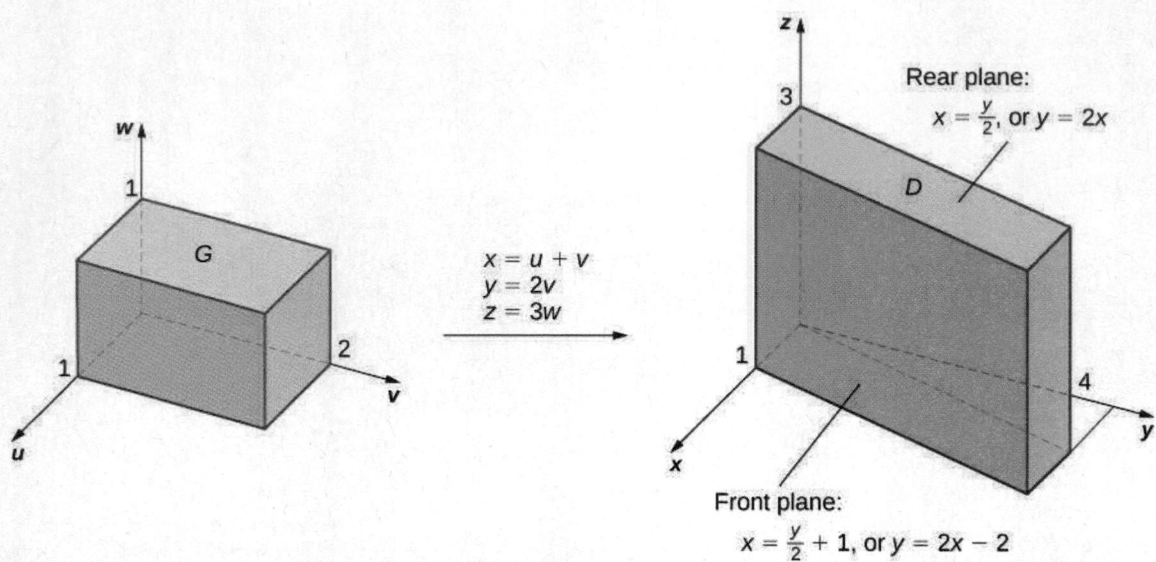

Figure 5.83 The region G in uvw-space is transformed to region D in xyz-space.

Now we can calculate the Jacobian for the transformation:

$$J(u, v, w) = \begin{vmatrix} \frac{\partial x}{\partial u} & \frac{\partial x}{\partial v} & \frac{\partial x}{\partial w} \\ \frac{\partial y}{\partial u} & \frac{\partial y}{\partial v} & \frac{\partial y}{\partial w} \\ \frac{\partial z}{\partial u} & \frac{\partial z}{\partial v} & \frac{\partial z}{\partial w} \end{vmatrix} = \begin{vmatrix} 1 & 1 & 0 \\ 0 & 2 & 0 \\ 0 & 0 & 3 \end{vmatrix} = 6.$$

The function to be integrated becomes

$$f(x, y, z) = x + \frac{z}{3} = u + v + \frac{3w}{3} = u + v + w.$$

We are now ready to put everything together and complete the problem.

$$\int_0^3 \int_0^4 \int_{y/2}^{(y/2)+1} \left(x + \frac{z}{3}\right) dx\, dy\, dz$$

$$\begin{aligned}
&= \int_0^1 \int_0^2 \int_0^1 (u + v + w)|J(u, v, w)|du\, dv\, dw = \int_0^1 \int_0^2 \int_0^1 (u + v + w)|6|du\, dv\, dw \\
&= 6\int_0^1 \int_0^2 \int_0^1 (u + v + w)du\, dv\, dw = 6\int_0^1 \int_0^2 \left[\frac{u^2}{2} + vu + wu\right]_0^1 dv\, dw \\
&= 6\int_0^1 \int_0^2 \left(\frac{1}{2} + v + w\right)dv\, dw = 6\int_0^1 \left[\frac{1}{2}v + \frac{v^2}{2} + wv\right]_0^2 dw \\
&= 6\int_0^1 (3 + 2w)dw = 6\left[3w + w^2\right]_0^1 = 24.
\end{aligned}$$

5.48 Let D be the region in xyz-space defined by $1 \le x \le 2$, $0 \le xy \le 2$, and $0 \le z \le 1$.

Evaluate $\iiint\limits_D (x^2 y + 3xyz)\,dx\,dy\,dz$ by using the transformation $u = x$, $v = xy$, and $w = 3z$.

5.7 EXERCISES

In the following exercises, the function $T : S \to R,\ T(u, v) = (x, y)$ on the region $S = \{(u, v) | 0 \le u \le 1, 0 \le v \le 1\}$ bounded by the unit square is given, where $R \subset \mathbb{R}^2$ is the image of S under T.

a. Justify that the function T is a C^1 transformation.

b. Find the images of the vertices of the unit square S through the function T.

c. Determine the image R of the unit square S and graph it.

356. $x = 2u,\ y = 3v$

357. $x = \frac{u}{2},\ y = \frac{v}{3}$

358. $x = u - v,\ y = u + v$

359. $x = 2u - v,\ y = u + 2v$

360. $x = u^2,\ y = v^2$

361. $x = u^3,\ y = v^3$

In the following exercises, determine whether the transformations $T : S \to R$ are one-to-one or not.

362. $x = u^2,\ y = v^2$, where S is the rectangle of vertices $(-1, 0), (1, 0), (1, 1)$, and $(-1, 1)$.

363. $x = u^4,\ y = u^2 + v$, where S is the triangle of vertices $(-2, 0), (2, 0)$, and $(0, 2)$.

364. $x = 2u,\ y = 3v$, where S is the square of vertices $(-1, 1), (-1, -1), (1, -1)$, and $(1, 1)$.

365. $T(u, v) = (2u - v, u)$, where S is the triangle of vertices $(-1, 1), (-1, -1)$, and $(1, -1)$.

366. $x = u + v + w,\ y = u + v,\ z = w$, where $S = R = \mathbb{R}^3$.

367. $x = u^2 + v + w,\ y = u^2 + v,\ z = w$, where $S = R = \mathbb{R}^3$.

In the following exercises, the transformations $T : S \to R$ are one-to-one. Find their related inverse transformations $T^{-1} : R \to S$.

368. $x = 4u,\ y = 5v$, where $S = R = \mathbb{R}^2$.

369. $x = u + 2v,\ y = -u + v$, where $S = R = \mathbb{R}^2$.

370. $x = e^{2u + v},\ y = e^{u - v}$, where $S = \mathbb{R}^2$ and $R = \{(x, y) | x > 0, y > 0\}$

371. $x = \ln u,\ y = \ln(uv)$, where $S = \{(u, v) | u > 0, v > 0\}$ and $R = \mathbb{R}^2$.

372. $x = u + v + w,\ y = 3v,\ z = 2w$, where $S = R = \mathbb{R}^3$.

373. $x = u + v,\ y = v + w,\ z = u + w$, where $S = R = \mathbb{R}^3$.

In the following exercises, the transformation $T : S \to R,\ T(u, v) = (x, y)$ and the region $R \subset \mathbb{R}^2$ are given. Find the region $S \subset \mathbb{R}^2$.

374. $x = au,\ y = bv,\ R = \{(x, y) | x^2 + y^2 \le a^2 b^2\}$, where $a, b > 0$

375. $x = au,\ y = bv,\ R = \left\{(x, y) | \frac{x^2}{a^2} + \frac{y^2}{b^2} \le 1\right\}$, where $a, b > 0$

376. $x = \frac{u}{a},\ y = \frac{v}{b},\ z = \frac{w}{c}$, $R = \{(x, y) | x^2 + y^2 + z^2 \le 1\}$, where $a, b, c > 0$

377. $x = au,\ y = bv,\ z = cw,\ R = \left\{(x, y) | \frac{x^2}{a^2} - \frac{y^2}{b^2} - \frac{z^2}{c^2} \le 1, z > 0\right\}$, where $a, b, c > 0$

In the following exercises, find the Jacobian J of the transformation.

378. $x = u + 2v,\ y = -u + v$

379. $x = \frac{u^3}{2},\ y = \frac{v}{u^2}$

380. $x = e^{2u - v},\ y = e^{u + v}$

381. $x = ue^v,\ y = e^{-v}$

382. $x = u\cos(e^v),\ y = u\sin(e^v)$

383. $x = v\sin\left(u^2\right),\ y = v\cos\left(u^2\right)$

384. $x = u\cosh v,\ y = u\sinh v,\ z = w$

385. $x = v\cosh\left(\frac{1}{u}\right),\ y = v\sinh\left(\frac{1}{u}\right),\ z = u + w^2$

386. $x = u + v,\ y = v + w,\ z = u$

387. $x = u - v,\ y = u + v,\ z = u + v + w$

388. The triangular region R with the vertices $(0, 0), (1, 1)$, and $(1, 2)$ is shown in the following figure.

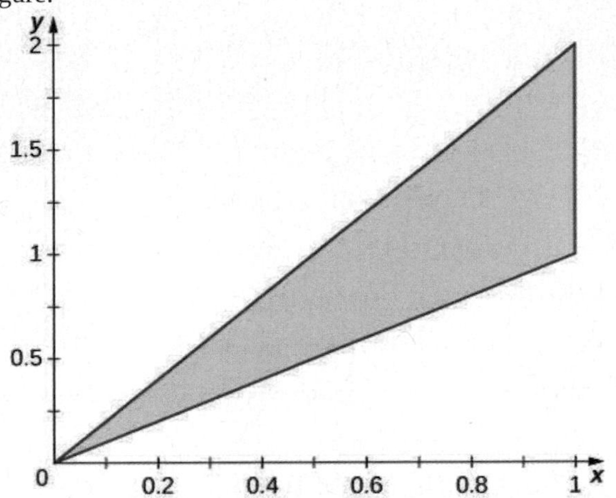

a. Find a transformation $T : S \to R$, $T(u, v) = (x, y) = (au + bv, cu + dv)$, where $a, b, c,$ and d are real numbers with $ad - bc \neq 0$ such that $T^{-1}(0, 0) = (0, 0), T^{-1}(1, 1) = (1, 0)$, and $T^{-1}(1, 2) = (0, 1)$.

b. Use the transformation T to find the area $A(R)$ of the region R.

389. The triangular region R with the vertices $(0, 0), (2, 0)$, and $(1, 3)$ is shown in the following figure.

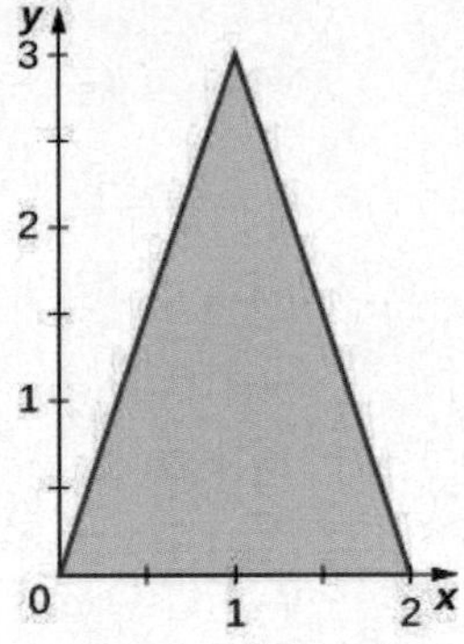

a. Find a transformation $T : S \to R$, $T(u, v) = (x, y) = (au + bv, cu + dv)$, where a, b, c and d are real numbers with $ad - bc \neq 0$ such that $T^{-1}(0, 0) = (0, 0)$, $T^{-1}(2, 0) = (1, 0)$, and $T^{-1}(1, 3) = (0, 1)$.

b. Use the transformation T to find the area $A(R)$ of the region R.

In the following exercises, use the transformation $u = y - x,\ v = y$, to evaluate the integrals on the parallelogram R of vertices $(0, 0), (1, 0), (2, 1)$, and $(1, 1)$ shown in the following figure.

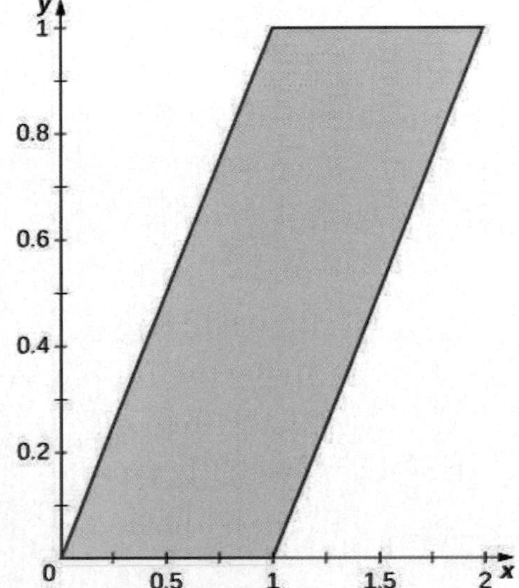

390. $\iint\limits_R (y - x)dA$

391. $\iint\limits_R \left(y^2 - xy\right)dA$

In the following exercises, use the transformation

$y - x = u,\ x + y = v$ to evaluate the integrals on the square R determined by the lines $y = x,\ y = -x + 2,\ y = x + 2,$ and $y = -x$ shown in the following figure.

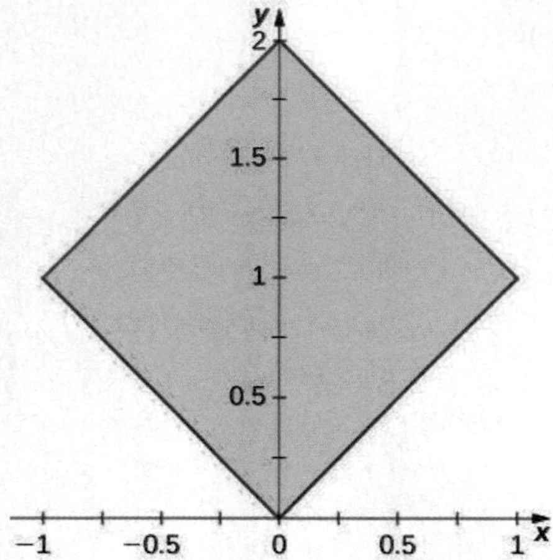

392. $\iint\limits_R e^{x+y} dA$

393. $\iint\limits_R \sin(x - y)dA$

In the following exercises, use the transformation $x = u,\ 5y = v$ to evaluate the integrals on the region R bounded by the ellipse $x^2 + 25y^2 = 1$ shown in the following figure.

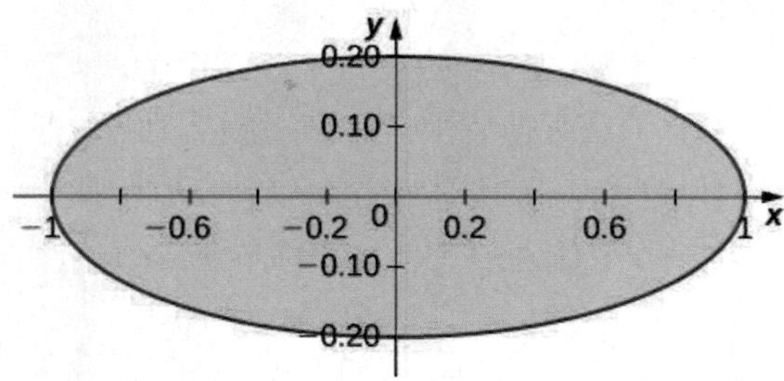

394. $\iint\limits_R \sqrt{x^2 + 25y^2}\, dA$

395. $\iint\limits_R \left(x^2 + 25y^2\right)^2 dA$

In the following exercises, use the transformation $u = x + y,\ v = x - y$ to evaluate the integrals on the trapezoidal region R determined by the points $(1, 0), (2, 0), (0, 2),$ and $(0, 1)$ shown in the following figure.

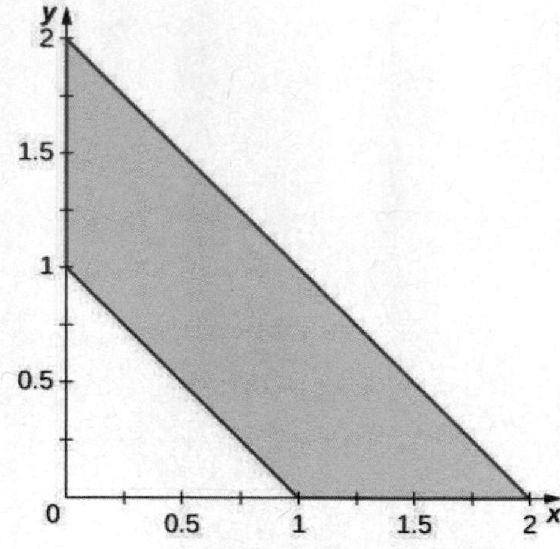

396. $\iint\limits_R \left(x^2 - 2xy + y^2\right)e^{x+y} dA$

397. $\iint\limits_R \left(x^3 + 3x^2 y + 3xy^2 + y^3\right)dA$

398. The circular annulus sector R bounded by the circles $4x^2 + 4y^2 = 1$ and $9x^2 + 9y^2 = 64,$ the line $x = y\sqrt{3},$ and the y-axis is shown in the following figure. Find a transformation T from a rectangular region S in the $r\theta$-plane to the region R in the xy-plane. Graph S.

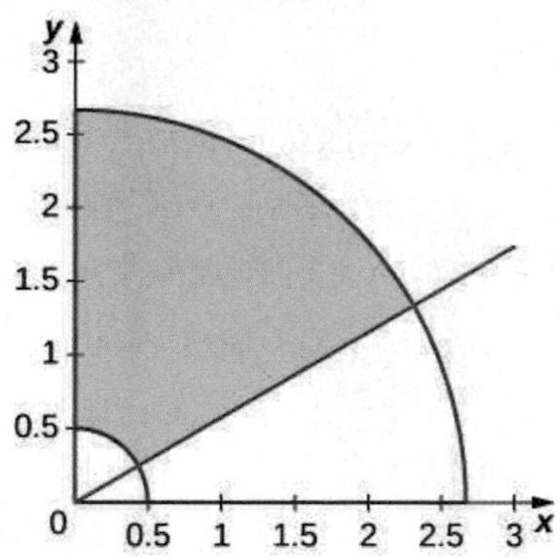

399. The solid R bounded by the circular cylinder $x^2 + y^2 = 9$ and the planes $z = 0, z = 1,$ $x = 0,$ and $y = 0$ is shown in the following figure. Find a transformation T from a cylindrical box S in $r\theta z$-space to the solid R in xyz-space.

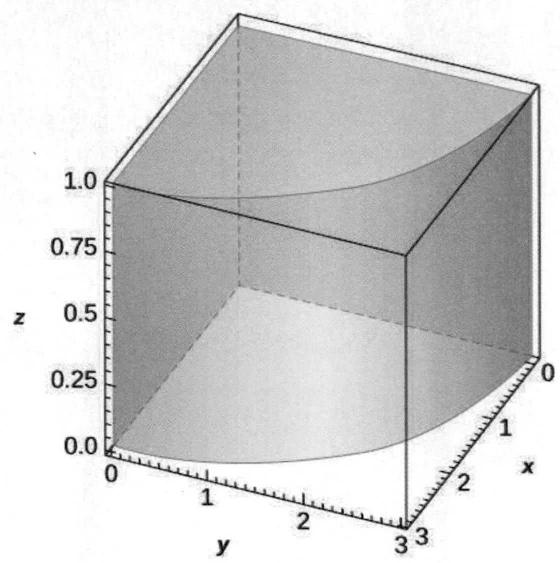

400. Show that $\iint\limits_R f\left(\sqrt{\frac{x^2}{3} + \frac{y^2}{3}}\right) dA = 2\pi\sqrt{15}\int_0^1 f(\rho)\rho\, d\rho,$ where f is a continuous function on $[0, 1]$ and R is the region bounded by the ellipse $5x^2 + 3y^2 = 15.$

401. Show that $\iiint\limits_R f\left(\sqrt{16x^2 + 4y^2 + z^2}\right) dV = \frac{\pi}{2}\int_0^1 f(\rho)\rho^2\, d\rho,$ where f is a continuous function on $[0, 1]$ and R is the region bounded by the ellipsoid $16x^2 + 4y^2 + z^2 = 1.$

402. **[T]** Find the area of the region bounded by the curves $xy = 1, xy = 3, y = 2x,$ and $y = 3x$ by using the transformation $u = xy$ and $v = \frac{y}{x}.$ Use a computer algebra system (CAS) to graph the boundary curves of the region $R.$

403. **[T]** Find the area of the region bounded by the curves $x^2 y = 2, x^2 y = 3, y = x,$ and $y = 2x$ by using the transformation $u = x^2 y$ and $v = \frac{y}{x}.$ Use a CAS to graph the boundary curves of the region $R.$

404. Evaluate the triple integral $\int_0^1 \int_1^2 \int_z^{z+1} (y + 1)dx\, dy\, dz$ by using the transformation $u = x - z,$ $v = 3y,$ and $w = \frac{z}{2}.$

405. Evaluate the triple integral $\int_0^2 \int_4^6 \int_{3z}^{3z+2} (5 - 4y)dx\, dz\, dy$ by using the transformation $u = x - 3z,\ v = 4y,$ and $w = z.$

406. A transformation $T : \mathrm{R}^2 \to \mathrm{R}^2,\ T(u, v) = (x, y)$ of the form $x = au + bv,\ y = cu + dv,$ where $a, b, c,$ and d are real numbers, is called linear. Show that a linear transformation for which $ad - bc \neq 0$ maps parallelograms to parallelograms.

407. The transformation $T_\theta : \mathrm{R}^2 \to \mathrm{R}^2,\ T_\theta(u, v) = (x, y),$ where $x = u\cos\theta - v\sin\theta,\quad y = u\sin\theta + v\cos\theta,$ is called a rotation of angle $\theta.$ Show that the inverse transformation of T_θ satisfies $T_\theta{}^{-1} = T_{-\theta},$ where $T_{-\theta}$ is the rotation of angle $-\theta.$

408. **[T]** Find the region S in the uv-plane whose image through a rotation of angle $\frac{\pi}{4}$ is the region R enclosed by the ellipse $x^2 + 4y^2 = 1.$ Use a CAS to answer the following questions.

a. Graph the region $S.$
b. Evaluate the integral $\iint\limits_S e^{-2uv} du\, dv.$ Round your answer to two decimal places.

409. **[T]** The transformations $T_i : \mathbb{R}^2 \to \mathbb{R}^2,$ $i = 1,\ldots, 4,$ defined by $T_1(u, v) = (u, -v),$ $T_2(u, v) = (-u, v),\ T_3(u, v) = (-u, -v),$ and $T_4(u, v) = (v, u)$ are called reflections about the x-axis, y-axis, origin, and the line $y = x,$ respectively.

a. Find the image of the region $S = \left\{(u, v)\middle| u^2 + v^2 - 2u - 4v + 1 \leq 0\right\}$ in the xy-plane through the transformation $T_1 \circ T_2 \circ T_3 \circ T_4.$
b. Use a CAS to graph $R.$
c. Evaluate the integral $\iint\limits_S \sin(u^2)du\, dv$ by using a CAS. Round your answer to two decimal places.

410. **[T]** The transformation $T_{k,\,1,\,1} : \mathbb{R}^3 \to \mathbb{R}^3,\ T_{k,\,1,\,1}(u,\ v,\ w) = (x,\ y,\ z)$ of the form $x = ku,\quad y = v,\ z = w,$ where $k \neq 1$ is a positive real number, is called a stretch if $k > 1$ and a compression if $0 < k < 1$ in the x-direction. Use a CAS to evaluate the integral $\iiint\limits_S e^{-\left(4x^2 + 9y^2 + 25z^2\right)} dx\,dy\,dz$ on the solid $S = \left\{(x,\ y,\ z) | 4x^2 + 9y^2 + 25z^2 \leq 1\right\}$ by considering the compression $T_{2,\,3,\,5}(u,\ v,\ w) = (x,\ y,\ z)$ defined by $x = \frac{u}{2},\ y = \frac{v}{3},$ and $z = \frac{w}{5}$. Round your answer to four decimal places.

411. **[T]** The transformation $T_{a,\,0} : \mathbb{R}^2 \to \mathbb{R}^2,\ T_{a,\,0}(u,\ v) = (u + av,\ v),$ where $a \neq 0$ is a real number, is called a shear in the x-direction. The transformation, $T_{b,\,0} : \text{R}^2 \to \text{R}^2,\ T_{o,\,b}(u,\ v) = (u,\ bu + v),$ where $b \neq 0$ is a real number, is called a shear in the y-direction.

a. Find transformations $T_{0,\,2} \circ T_{3,\,0}$.
b. Find the image R of the trapezoidal region S bounded by $u = 0,\ v = 0,\ v = 1,$ and $v = 2 - u$ through the transformation $T_{0,\,2} \circ T_{3,\,0}$.
c. Use a CAS to graph the image R in the xy-plane.
d. Find the area of the region R by using the area of region S.

412. Use the transformation, $x = au,\ y = av,\ z = cw$ and spherical coordinates to show that the volume of a region bounded by the spheroid $\frac{x^2 + y^2}{a^2} + \frac{z^2}{c^2} = 1$ is $\frac{4\pi a^2 c}{3}$.

413. Find the volume of a football whose shape is a spheroid $\frac{x^2 + y^2}{a^2} + \frac{z^2}{c^2} = 1$ whose length from tip to tip is 11 inches and circumference at the center is 22 inches. Round your answer to two decimal places.

414. **[T]** Lamé ovals (or superellipses) are plane curves of equations $\left(\frac{x}{a}\right)^n + \left(\frac{y}{b}\right)^n = 1,$ where *a*, *b*, and *n* are positive real numbers.

a. Use a CAS to graph the regions R bounded by Lamé ovals for $a = 1,\ b = 2,\ n = 4$ and $n = 6,$ respectively.
b. Find the transformations that map the region R bounded by the Lamé oval $x^4 + y^4 = 1,$ also called a squircle and graphed in the following figure, into the unit disk.

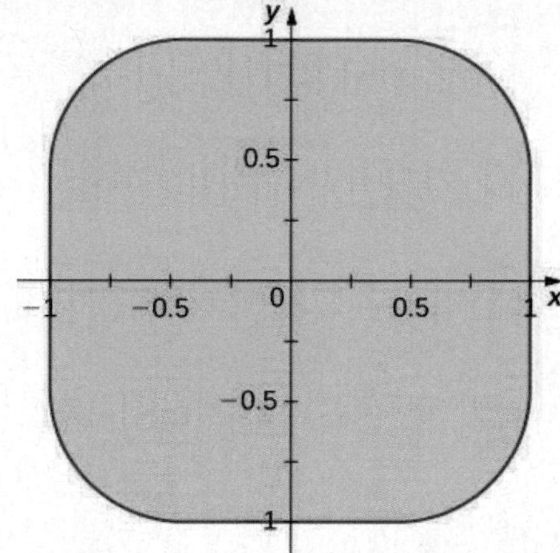

c. Use a CAS to find an approximation of the area $A(R)$ of the region R bounded by $x^4 + y^4 = 1$. Round your answer to two decimal places.

415. **[T]** Lamé ovals have been consistently used by designers and architects. For instance, Gerald Robinson, a Canadian architect, has designed a parking garage in a shopping center in Peterborough, Ontario, in the shape of a superellipse of the equation $\left(\frac{x}{a}\right)^n + \left(\frac{y}{b}\right)^n = 1$ with $\frac{a}{b} = \frac{9}{7}$ and $n = e$. Use a CAS to find an approximation of the area of the parking garage in the case $a = 900$ yards, $b = 700$ yards, and $n = 2.72$ yards.

CHAPTER 5 REVIEW

KEY TERMS

double integral of the function $f(x, y)$ over the region R in the xy-plane is defined as the limit of a double Riemann sum, $\iint_R f(x, y)dA = \lim_{m, n \to \infty} \sum_{i=1}^{m} \sum_{j=1}^{n} f(x_{ij}^*, y_{ij}^*)\Delta A.$

double Riemann sum of the function $f(x, y)$ over a rectangular region R is $\sum_{i=1}^{m} \sum_{j=1}^{n} f(x_{ij}^*, y_{ij}^*)\Delta A$ where R is divided into smaller subrectangles R_{ij} and (x_{ij}^*, y_{ij}^*) is an arbitrary point in R_{ij}

Fubini's theorem if $f(x, y)$ is a function of two variables that is continuous over a rectangular region $R = \{(x, y) \in \mathbb{R}^2 | a \le x \le b, c \le y \le d\}$, then the double integral of f over the region equals an iterated integral,

$$\iint_R f(x, y)dy\,dx = \int_a^b \int_c^d f(x, y)dx\,dy = \int_c^d \int_a^b f(x, y)dx\,dy$$

improper double integral a double integral over an unbounded region or of an unbounded function

iterated integral for a function $f(x, y)$ over the region R is

a. $\int_a^b \int_c^d f(x, y)dx\,dy = \int_a^b \left[\int_c^d f(x, y)dy\right]dx,$

b. $\int_c^d \int_b^a f(x, y)dx\,dy = \int_c^d \left[\int_a^b f(x, y)dx\right]dy,$

where $a, b, c,$ and d are any real numbers and $R = [a, b] \times [c, d]$

Jacobian the Jacobian $J(u, v)$ in two variables is a 2×2 determinant:

$$J(u, v) = \begin{vmatrix} \frac{\partial x}{\partial u} & \frac{\partial y}{\partial u} \\ \frac{\partial x}{\partial v} & \frac{\partial y}{\partial v} \end{vmatrix};$$

the Jacobian $J(u, v, w)$ in three variables is a 3×3 determinant:

$$J(u, v, w) = \begin{vmatrix} \frac{\partial x}{\partial u} & \frac{\partial y}{\partial u} & \frac{\partial z}{\partial u} \\ \frac{\partial x}{\partial v} & \frac{\partial y}{\partial v} & \frac{\partial z}{\partial v} \\ \frac{\partial x}{\partial w} & \frac{\partial y}{\partial w} & \frac{\partial z}{\partial w} \end{vmatrix}$$

one-to-one transformation a transformation $T : G \to R$ defined as $T(u, v) = (x, y)$ is said to be one-to-one if no two points map to the same image point

planar transformation a function T that transforms a region G in one plane into a region R in another plane by a change of variables

polar rectangle the region enclosed between the circles $r = a$ and $r = b$ and the angles $\theta = \alpha$ and $\theta = \beta$; it is described as $R = \{(r, \theta) | a \le r \le b, \alpha \le \theta \le \beta\}$

radius of gyration the distance from an object's center of mass to its axis of rotation

transformation a function that transforms a region G in one plane into a region R in another plane by a change of variables

triple integral the triple integral of a continuous function $f(x, y, z)$ over a rectangular solid box B is the limit of a Riemann sum for a function of three variables, if this limit exists

triple integral in cylindrical coordinates the limit of a triple Riemann sum, provided the following limit exists:

$$\lim_{l, m, n \to \infty} \sum_{i=1}^{l} \sum_{j=1}^{m} \sum_{k=1}^{n} f(r_{ijk}^*, \theta_{ijk}^*, z_{ijk}^*) r_{ijk}^* \Delta r \Delta\theta \Delta z$$

triple integral in spherical coordinates the limit of a triple Riemann sum, provided the following limit exists:

$$\lim_{l, m, n \to \infty} \sum_{i=1}^{l} \sum_{j=1}^{m} \sum_{k=1}^{n} f(\rho_{ijk}^*, \theta_{ijk}^*, \varphi_{ijk}^*)(\rho_{ijk}^*)^2 \sin\varphi \Delta\rho \Delta\theta \Delta\varphi$$

Type I a region D in the xy-plane is Type I if it lies between two vertical lines and the graphs of two continuous functions $g_1(x)$ and $g_2(x)$

Type II a region D in the xy-plane is Type II if it lies between two horizontal lines and the graphs of two continuous functions $h_1(y)$ and $h_2(y)$

KEY EQUATIONS

- **Double integral**

  $$\iint_R f(x, y)dA = \lim_{m, n \to \infty} \sum_{i=1}^{m} \sum_{j=1}^{n} f(x_{ij}^*, y_{ij}^*)\Delta A$$

- **Iterated integral**

  $$\int_a^b \int_c^d f(x, y)dx\,dy = \int_a^b \left[\int_c^d f(x, y)dy\right]dx$$

  or

  $$\int_c^d \int_b^a f(x, y)dx\,dy = \int_c^d \left[\int_a^b f(x, y)dx\right]dy$$

- **Average value of a function of two variables**

  $$f_{\text{ave}} = \frac{1}{\text{Area } R} \iint_R f(x, y)dx\,dy$$

- **Iterated integral over a Type I region**

  $$\iint_D f(x, y)dA = \iint_D f(x, y)dy\,dx = \int_a^b \left[\int_{g_1(x)}^{g_2(x)} f(x, y)dy\right]dx$$

- **Iterated integral over a Type II region**

  $$\iint_D f(x, y)dA = \iint_D f(x, y)dx\,dy = \int_c^d \left[\int_{h_1(y)}^{h_2(y)} f(x, y)dx\right]dy$$

- **Double integral over a polar rectangular region R**

  $$\iint_R f(r, \theta)dA = \lim_{m, n \to \infty} \sum_{i=1}^{m} \sum_{j=1}^{n} f\left(r_{ij}^*, \theta_{ij}^*\right)\Delta A = \lim_{m, n \to \infty} \sum_{i=1}^{m} \sum_{j=1}^{n} f\left(r_{ij}^*, \theta_{ij}^*\right)r_{ij}^* \Delta r \Delta\theta$$

- **Double integral over a general polar region**

$$\iint_D f(r,\theta)r\,dr\,d\theta = \int_{\theta=\alpha}^{\theta=\beta}\int_{r=h_1(\theta)}^{r=h_2(\theta)} f(r,\theta)r\,dr\,d\theta$$

- **Triple integral**

$$\lim_{l,m,n\to\infty}\sum_{i=1}^{l}\sum_{j=1}^{m}\sum_{k=1}^{n} f(x_{ijk}^*, y_{ijk}^*, z_{ijk}^*)\Delta x\Delta y\Delta z = \iiint_B f(x,y,z)dV$$

- **Triple integral in cylindrical coordinates**

$$\iiint_B g(x,y,z)dV = \iiint_B g(r\cos\theta, r\sin\theta, z)r\,dr\,d\theta\,dz = \iiint_B f(r,\theta,z)r\,dr\,d\theta\,dz$$

- **Triple integral in spherical coordinates**

$$\iiint_B f(\rho,\theta,\varphi)\rho^2\sin\varphi\,d\rho\,d\varphi\,d\theta = \int_{\varphi=\gamma}^{\varphi=\psi}\int_{\theta=\alpha}^{\theta=\beta}\int_{\rho=a}^{\rho=b} f(\rho,\theta,\varphi)\rho^2\sin\varphi\,d\rho\,d\varphi\,d\theta$$

- **Mass of a lamina**

$$m = \lim_{k,l\to\infty}\sum_{i=1}^{k}\sum_{j=1}^{l} m_{ij} = \lim_{k,l\to\infty}\sum_{i=1}^{k}\sum_{j=1}^{l}\rho(x_{ij}^*, y_{ij}^*)\Delta A = \iint_R \rho(x,y)dA$$

- **Moment about the** x**-axis**

$$M_x = \lim_{k,l\to\infty}\sum_{i=1}^{k}\sum_{j=1}^{l}\left(y_{ij}^*\right)m_{ij} = \lim_{k,l\to\infty}\sum_{i=1}^{k}\sum_{j=1}^{l}\left(y_{ij}^*\right)\rho(x_{ij}^*, y_{ij}^*)\Delta A = \iint_R y\rho(x,y)dA$$

- **Moment about the** y**-axis**

$$M_y = \lim_{k,l\to\infty}\sum_{i=1}^{k}\sum_{j=1}^{l}\left(x_{ij}^*\right)m_{ij} = \lim_{k,l\to\infty}\sum_{i=1}^{k}\sum_{j=1}^{l}\left(x_{ij}^*\right)\rho(x_{ij}^*, y_{ij}^*)\Delta A = \iint_R x\rho(x,y)dA$$

- **Center of mass of a lamina**

$$\bar{x} = \frac{M_y}{m} = \frac{\iint_R x\rho(x,y)dA}{\iint_R \rho(x,y)dA} \text{ and } \bar{y} = \frac{M_x}{m} = \frac{\iint_R y\rho(x,y)dA}{\iint_R \rho(x,y)dA}$$

KEY CONCEPTS

5.1 Double Integrals over Rectangular Regions

- We can use a double Riemann sum to approximate the volume of a solid bounded above by a function of two variables over a rectangular region. By taking the limit, this becomes a double integral representing the volume of the solid.
- Properties of double integral are useful to simplify computation and find bounds on their values.
- We can use Fubini's theorem to write and evaluate a double integral as an iterated integral.
- Double integrals are used to calculate the area of a region, the volume under a surface, and the average value of a function of two variables over a rectangular region.

5.2 Double Integrals over General Regions

- A general bounded region D on the plane is a region that can be enclosed inside a rectangular region. We can use this idea to define a double integral over a general bounded region.
- To evaluate an iterated integral of a function over a general nonrectangular region, we sketch the region and express it as a Type I or as a Type II region or as a union of several Type I or Type II regions that overlap only on their boundaries.

- We can use double integrals to find volumes, areas, and average values of a function over general regions, similarly to calculations over rectangular regions.
- We can use Fubini's theorem for improper integrals to evaluate some types of improper integrals.

5.3 Double Integrals in Polar Coordinates

- To apply a double integral to a situation with circular symmetry, it is often convenient to use a double integral in polar coordinates. We can apply these double integrals over a polar rectangular region or a general polar region, using an iterated integral similar to those used with rectangular double integrals.
- The area dA in polar coordinates becomes $r\,dr\,d\theta$.
- Use $x = r\cos\theta$, $y = r\sin\theta$, and $dA = r\,dr\,d\theta$ to convert an integral in rectangular coordinates to an integral in polar coordinates.
- Use $r^2 = x^2 + y^2$ and $\theta = \tan^{-1}\left(\frac{y}{x}\right)$ to convert an integral in polar coordinates to an integral in rectangular coordinates, if needed.
- To find the volume in polar coordinates bounded above by a surface $z = f(r, \theta)$ over a region on the xy-plane, use a double integral in polar coordinates.

5.4 Triple Integrals

- To compute a triple integral we use Fubini's theorem, which states that if $f(x, y, z)$ is continuous on a rectangular box $B = [a, b] \times [c, d] \times [e, f]$, then

$$\iiint_B f(x, y, z)dV = \int_e^f \int_c^d \int_a^b f(x, y, z)dx\,dy\,dz$$

  and is also equal to any of the other five possible orderings for the iterated triple integral.
- To compute the volume of a general solid bounded region E we use the triple integral

$$V(E) = \iiint_E 1dV.$$

- Interchanging the order of the iterated integrals does not change the answer. As a matter of fact, interchanging the order of integration can help simplify the computation.
- To compute the average value of a function over a general three-dimensional region, we use

$$f_{\text{ave}} = \frac{1}{V(E)} \iiint_E f(x, y, z)dV.$$

5.5 Triple Integrals in Cylindrical and Spherical Coordinates

- To evaluate a triple integral in cylindrical coordinates, use the iterated integral

$$\int_{\theta=\alpha}^{\theta=\beta} \int_{r=g_1(\theta)}^{r=g_2(\theta)} \int_{z=u_1(r,\theta)}^{z=u_2(r,\theta)} f(r, \theta, z)r\,dz\,dr\,d\theta.$$

- To evaluate a triple integral in spherical coordinates, use the iterated integral

$$\int_{\theta=\alpha}^{\theta=\beta} \int_{\rho=g_1(\theta)}^{\rho=g_2(\theta)} \int_{\varphi=u_1(r,\theta)}^{\varphi=u_2(r,\theta)} f(\rho, \theta, \varphi)\rho^2 \sin\varphi\,d\varphi\,d\rho\,d\theta.$$

5.6 Calculating Centers of Mass and Moments of Inertia

Finding the mass, center of mass, moments, and moments of inertia in double integrals:

- For a lamina R with a density function $\rho(x, y)$ at any point (x, y) in the plane, the mass is $m = \iint_R \rho(x, y)dA$.
- The moments about the x-axis and y-axis are

$$M_x = \iint_R y\rho(x, y)dA \text{ and } M_y = \iint_R x\rho(x, y)dA.$$

- The center of mass is given by $\bar{x} = \frac{M_y}{m}$, $\bar{y} = \frac{M_x}{m}$.
- The center of mass becomes the centroid of the plane when the density is constant.
- The moments of inertia about the $x-$ axis, $y-$ axis, and the origin are

$$I_x = \iint_R y^2 \rho(x, y)dA, \quad I_y = \iint_R x^2 \rho(x, y)dA, \quad \text{and } I_0 = I_x + I_y = \iint_R \left(x^2 + y^2\right)\rho(x, y)dA.$$

Finding the mass, center of mass, moments, and moments of inertia in triple integrals:

- For a solid object Q with a density function $\rho(x, y, z)$ at any point (x, y, z) in space, the mass is $m = \iiint_Q \rho(x, y, z)dV$.
- The moments about the xy-plane, the xz-plane, and the yz-plane are

$$M_{xy} = \iiint_Q z\rho(x, y, z)dV, \; M_{xz} = \iiint_Q y\rho(x, y, z)dV, \; M_{yz} = \iiint_Q x\rho(x, y, z)dV.$$

- The center of mass is given by $\bar{x} = \frac{M_{yz}}{m}$, $\bar{y} = \frac{M_{xz}}{m}$, $\bar{z} = \frac{M_{xy}}{m}$.
- The center of mass becomes the centroid of the solid when the density is constant.
- The moments of inertia about the yz-plane, the xz-plane, and the xy-plane are

$$I_x = \iiint_Q \left(y^2 + z^2\right)\rho(x, y, z)dV, \; I_y = \iiint_Q \left(x^2 + z^2\right)\rho(x, y, z)dV,$$
$$I_z = \iiint_Q \left(x^2 + y^2\right)\rho(x, y, z)dV.$$

5.7 Change of Variables in Multiple Integrals

- A transformation T is a function that transforms a region G in one plane (space) into a region R in another plane (space) by a change of variables.
- A transformation $T : G \to R$ defined as $T(u, v) = (x, y)$ (or $T(u, v, w) = (x, y, z)$) is said to be a one-to-one transformation if no two points map to the same image point.
- If f is continuous on R, then $\iint_R f(x, y)dA = \iint_S f(g(u, v), h(u, v))\left|\frac{\partial(x, y)}{\partial(u, v)}\right|du\,dv.$
- If F is continuous on R, then

$$\begin{aligned}\iiint_R F(x, y, z)dV &= \iiint_G F(g(u, v, w), h(u, v, w), k(u, v, w))\left|\frac{\partial(x, y, z)}{\partial(u, v, w)}\right|du\,dv\,dw \\ &= \iiint_G H(u, v, w)|J(u, v, w)|du\,dv\,dw.\end{aligned}$$

CHAPTER 5 REVIEW EXERCISES

True or False? Justify your answer with a proof or a counterexample.

416. $\int_a^b \int_c^d f(x, y)dy\,dx = \int_c^d \int_a^b f(x, y)dy\,dx$

417. Fubini's theorem can be extended to three dimensions, as long as f is continuous in all variables.

418. The integral $\int_0^{2\pi}\int_0^1\int_r^1 dz\,dr\,d\theta$ represents the volume of a right cone.

419. The Jacobian of the transformation for $x = u^2 - 2v,\ y = 3v - 2uv$ is given by $-4u^2 + 6u + 4v$.

Evaluate the following integrals.

420.
$\iint_R \left(5x^3y^2 - y^2\right)dA,\ R = \{(x, y)|0 \le x \le 2,\ 1 \le y \le 4\}$

421.
$\iint_D \frac{y}{3x^2 + 1}dA,\ D = \{(x, y)|0 \le x \le 1,\ -x \le y \le x\}$

422. $\iint_D \sin\left(x^2 + y^2\right)dA$ where D is a disk of radius 2 centered at the origin

423. $\int_0^1\int_y^1 xye^{x^2}\,dx\,dy$

424. $\int_{-1}^1\int_0^z\int_0^{x-z} 6dy\,dx\,dz$

425. $\iiint_R 3y\,dV,$ where $R = \left\{(x, y, z)|0 \le x \le 1,\ 0 \le y \le x,\ 0 \le z \le \sqrt{9 - y^2}\right\}$

426. $\int_0^2\int_0^{2\pi}\int_r^1 r\,dz\,d\theta\,dr$

427. $\int_0^{2\pi}\int_0^{\pi/2}\int_1^3 \rho^2\sin(\varphi)d\rho\,d\varphi\,d\theta$

428. $\int_0^1\int_{-\sqrt{1-x^2}}^{\sqrt{1-x^2}}\int_{-\sqrt{1-x^2-y^2}}^{\sqrt{1-x^2-y^2}} dz\,dy\,dx$

For the following problems, find the specified area or volume.

429. The area of region enclosed by one petal of $r = \cos(4\theta)$.

430. The volume of the solid that lies between the paraboloid $z = 2x^2 + 2y^2$ and the plane $z = 8$.

431. The volume of the solid bounded by the cylinder $x^2 + y^2 = 16$ and from $z = 1$ to $z + x = 2$.

432. The volume of the intersection between two spheres of radius 1, the top whose center is $(0, 0, 0.25)$ and the bottom, which is centered at $(0, 0, 0)$.

For the following problems, find the center of mass of the region.

433. $\rho(x, y) = xy$ on the circle with radius 1 in the first quadrant only.

434. $\rho(x, y) = (y + 1)\sqrt{x}$ in the region bounded by $y = e^x$, $y = 0$, and $x = 1$.

435. $\rho(x, y, z) = z$ on the inverted cone with radius 2 and height 2.

436. The volume an ice cream cone that is given by the solid above $z = \sqrt{\left(x^2 + y^2\right)}$ and below $z^2 + x^2 + y^2 = z$.

The following problems examine Mount Holly in the state of Michigan. Mount Holly is a landfill that was converted into a ski resort. The shape of Mount Holly can be approximated by a right circular cone of height 1100 ft and radius 6000 ft.

437. If the compacted trash used to build Mount Holly on average has a density $400\ \text{lb/ft}^3$, find the amount of work required to build the mountain.

438. In reality, it is very likely that the trash at the bottom of Mount Holly has become more compacted with all the weight of the above trash. Consider a density function with respect to height: the density at the top of the mountain is still density $400\ \text{lb/ft}^3$ and the density increases. Every 100 feet deeper, the density doubles. What is the total weight of Mount Holly?

The following problems consider the temperature and density of Earth's layers.

439. **[T]** The temperature of Earth's layers is exhibited in the table below. Use your calculator to fit a polynomial of degree 3 to the temperature along the radius of the Earth. Then find the average temperature of Earth. (*Hint*: begin at 0 in the inner core and increase outward toward the surface)

Layer	Depth from center (km)	Temperature °C
Rocky Crust	0 to 40	0
Upper Mantle	40 to 150	870
Mantle	400 to 650	870
Inner Mantel	650 to 2700	870
Molten Outer Core	2890 to 5150	4300
Inner Core	5150 to 6378	7200

Source: http://www.enchantedlearning.com/subjects/astronomy/planets/earth/Inside.shtml

440. **[T]** The density of Earth's layers is displayed in the table below. Using your calculator or a computer program, find the best-fit quadratic equation to the density. Using this equation, find the total mass of Earth.

Layer	Depth from center (km)	Density (g/cm3)
Inner Core	0	12.95
Outer Core	1228	11.05
Mantle	3488	5.00
Upper Mantle	6338	3.90
Crust	6378	2.55

Source: http://hyperphysics.phy-astr.gsu.edu/hbase/geophys/earthstruct.html

The following problems concern the Theorem of Pappus (see **Moments and Centers of Mass (http://cnx.org/content/m53649/latest/)** for a refresher), a method for calculating volume using centroids. Assuming a region R, when you revolve around the x-axis the volume is given by $V_x = 2\pi A\,\overline{y}$, and when you revolve around the y-axis the volume is given by $V_y = 2\pi A\,\overline{x}$, where A is the area of R. Consider the region bounded by $x^2 + y^2 = 1$ and above $y = x + 1$.

441. Find the volume when you revolve the region around the x-axis.

442. Find the volume when you revolve the region around the y-axis.

6 | VECTOR CALCULUS

Figure 6.1 Hurricanes form from rotating winds driven by warm temperatures over the ocean. Meteorologists forecast the motion of hurricanes by studying the rotating vector fields of their wind velocity. Shown is Cyclone Catarina in the South Atlantic Ocean in 2004, as seen from the International Space Station. (credit: modification of work by NASA)

Chapter Outline

Introduction

Hurricanes are huge storms that can produce tremendous amounts of damage to life and property, especially when they reach land. Predicting where and when they will strike and how strong the winds will be is of great importance for preparing for protection or evacuation. Scientists rely on studies of rotational vector fields for their forecasts (see **Example 6.3**).

In this chapter, we learn to model new kinds of integrals over fields such as magnetic fields, gravitational fields, or velocity fields. We also learn how to calculate the work done on a charged particle traveling through a magnetic field, the work done on a particle with mass traveling through a gravitational field, and the volume per unit time of water flowing through a net dropped in a river.

All these applications are based on the concept of a vector field, which we explore in this chapter. Vector fields have many applications because they can be used to model real fields such as electromagnetic or gravitational fields. A deep understanding of physics or engineering is impossible without an understanding of vector fields. Furthermore, vector fields have mathematical properties that are worthy of study in their own right. In particular, vector fields can be used to develop several higher-dimensional versions of the Fundamental Theorem of Calculus.

6.1 | Vector Fields

Learning Objectives

6.1.1 Recognize a vector field in a plane or in space.
6.1.2 Sketch a vector field from a given equation.
6.1.3 Identify a conservative field and its associated potential function.

Vector fields are an important tool for describing many physical concepts, such as gravitation and electromagnetism, which affect the behavior of objects over a large region of a plane or of space. They are also useful for dealing with large-scale behavior such as atmospheric storms or deep-sea ocean currents. In this section, we examine the basic definitions and graphs of vector fields so we can study them in more detail in the rest of this chapter.

Examples of Vector Fields

How can we model the gravitational force exerted by multiple astronomical objects? How can we model the velocity of water particles on the surface of a river? **Figure 6.2** gives visual representations of such phenomena.

Figure 6.2(a) shows a gravitational field exerted by two astronomical objects, such as a star and a planet or a planet and a moon. At any point in the figure, the vector associated with a point gives the net gravitational force exerted by the two objects on an object of unit mass. The vectors of largest magnitude in the figure are the vectors closest to the larger object. The larger object has greater mass, so it exerts a gravitational force of greater magnitude than the smaller object.

Figure 6.2(b) shows the velocity of a river at points on its surface. The vector associated with a given point on the river's surface gives the velocity of the water at that point. Since the vectors to the left of the figure are small in magnitude, the water is flowing slowly on that part of the surface. As the water moves from left to right, it encounters some rapids around a rock. The speed of the water increases, and a whirlpool occurs in part of the rapids.

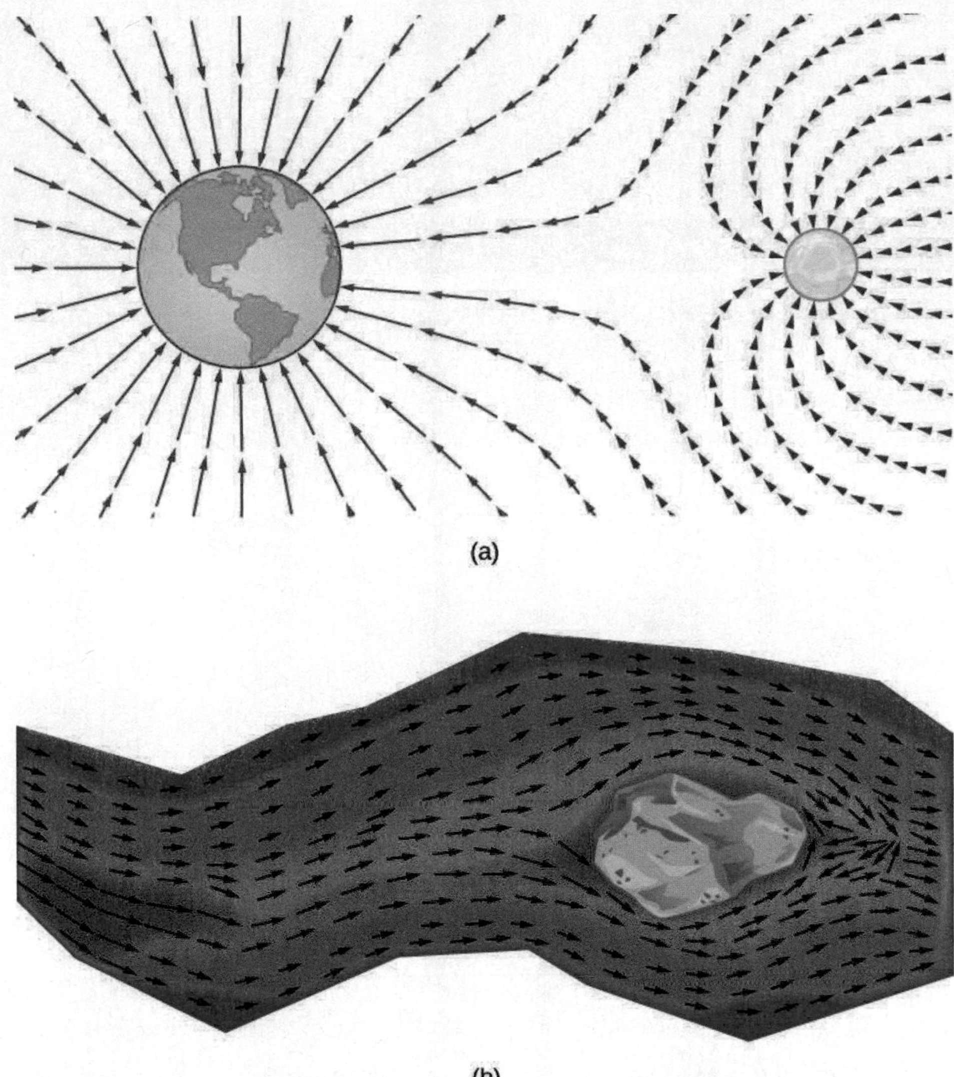

Figure 6.2 (a) The gravitational field exerted by two astronomical bodies on a small object. (b) The vector velocity field of water on the surface of a river shows the varied speeds of water. Red indicates that the magnitude of the vector is greater, so the water flows more quickly; blue indicates a lesser magnitude and a slower speed of water flow.

Each figure illustrates an example of a vector field. Intuitively, a vector field is a map of vectors. In this section, we study vector fields in $\mathbb{R}^2$ and $\mathbb{R}^3$.

Definition

A **vector field F** in $\mathbb{R}^2$ is an assignment of a two-dimensional vector $\mathbf{F}(x, y)$ to each point (x, y) of a subset D of $\mathbb{R}^2$. The subset D is the domain of the vector field.

A vector field **F** in $\mathbb{R}^3$ is an assignment of a three-dimensional vector $\mathbf{F}(x, y, z)$ to each point (x, y, z) of a subset D of $\mathbb{R}^3$. The subset D is the domain of the vector field.

Vector Fields in $\mathbb{R}^2$

A vector field in $\mathbb{R}^2$ can be represented in either of two equivalent ways. The first way is to use a vector with components that are two-variable functions:

$$\mathbf{F}(x, y) = \langle P(x, y), Q(x, y) \rangle. \tag{6.1}$$

The second way is to use the standard unit vectors:

$$\mathbf{F}(x, y) = P(x, y)\mathbf{i} + Q(x, y)\mathbf{j}. \tag{6.2}$$

A vector field is said to be *continuous* if its component functions are continuous.

Example 6.1

Finding a Vector Associated with a Given Point

Let $\mathbf{F}(x, y) = (2y^2 + x - 4)\mathbf{i} + \cos(x)\mathbf{j}$ be a vector field in $\mathbb{R}^2$. Note that this is an example of a continuous vector field since both component functions are continuous. What vector is associated with point $(0, -1)$?

Solution

Substitute the point values for x and y:

$$\begin{aligned}\mathbf{F}(0, 1) &= (2(-1)^2 + 0 - 4)\mathbf{i} + \cos(0)\mathbf{j} \\ &= -2\mathbf{i} + \mathbf{j}.\end{aligned}$$

6.1 Let $\mathbf{G}(x, y) = x^2 y\mathbf{i} - (x + y)\mathbf{j}$ be a vector field in $\mathbb{R}^2$. What vector is associated with the point $(-2, 3)$?

Drawing a Vector Field

We can now represent a vector field in terms of its components of functions or unit vectors, but representing it visually by sketching it is more complex because the domain of a vector field is in $\mathbb{R}^2$, as is the range. Therefore the "graph" of a vector field in $\mathbb{R}^2$ lives in four-dimensional space. Since we cannot represent four-dimensional space visually, we instead draw vector fields in $\mathbb{R}^2$ in a plane itself. To do this, draw the vector associated with a given point at the point in a plane. For example, suppose the vector associated with point $(4, -1)$ is $\langle 3, 1 \rangle$. Then, we would draw vector $\langle 3, 1 \rangle$ at point $(4, -1)$.

We should plot enough vectors to see the general shape, but not so many that the sketch becomes a jumbled mess. If we were to plot the image vector at each point in the region, it would fill the region completely and is useless. Instead, we can choose points at the intersections of grid lines and plot a sample of several vectors from each quadrant of a rectangular coordinate system in $\mathbb{R}^2$.

There are two types of vector fields in $\mathbb{R}^2$ on which this chapter focuses: radial fields and rotational fields. Radial fields model certain gravitational fields and energy source fields, and rotational fields model the movement of a fluid in a vortex. In a **radial field**, all vectors either point directly toward or directly away from the origin. Furthermore, the magnitude of any vector depends only on its distance from the origin. In a radial field, the vector located at point (x, y) is perpendicular to the circle centered at the origin that contains point (x, y), and all other vectors on this circle have the same magnitude.

Example 6.2

Drawing a Radial Vector Field

Sketch the vector field $\mathbf{F}(x, y) = \frac{x}{2}\mathbf{i} + \frac{y}{2}\mathbf{j}$.

Solution

To sketch this vector field, choose a sample of points from each quadrant and compute the corresponding vector. The following table gives a representative sample of points in a plane and the corresponding vectors.

(x, y)	$\mathbf{F}(x, y)$	(x, y)	$\mathbf{F}(x, y)$	(x, y)	$\mathbf{F}(x, y)$
$(1, 0)$	$\langle \frac{1}{2}, 0 \rangle$	$(2, 0)$	$\langle 1, 0 \rangle$	$(1, 1)$	$\langle \frac{1}{2}, \frac{1}{2} \rangle$
$(0, 1)$	$\langle 0, \frac{1}{2} \rangle$	$(0, 2)$	$\langle 0, 1 \rangle$	$(-1, 1)$	$\langle -\frac{1}{2}, \frac{1}{2} \rangle$
$(-1, 0)$	$\langle -\frac{1}{2}, 0 \rangle$	$(-2, 0)$	$\langle -1, 0 \rangle$	$(-1, -1)$	$\langle -\frac{1}{2}, -\frac{1}{2} \rangle$
$(0, -1)$	$\langle 0, -\frac{1}{2} \rangle$	$(0, -2)$	$\langle 0, -1 \rangle$	$(1, -1)$	$\langle \frac{1}{2}, -\frac{1}{2} \rangle$

Figure 6.3(a) shows the vector field. To see that each vector is perpendicular to the corresponding circle, **Figure 6.3**(b) shows circles overlain on the vector field.

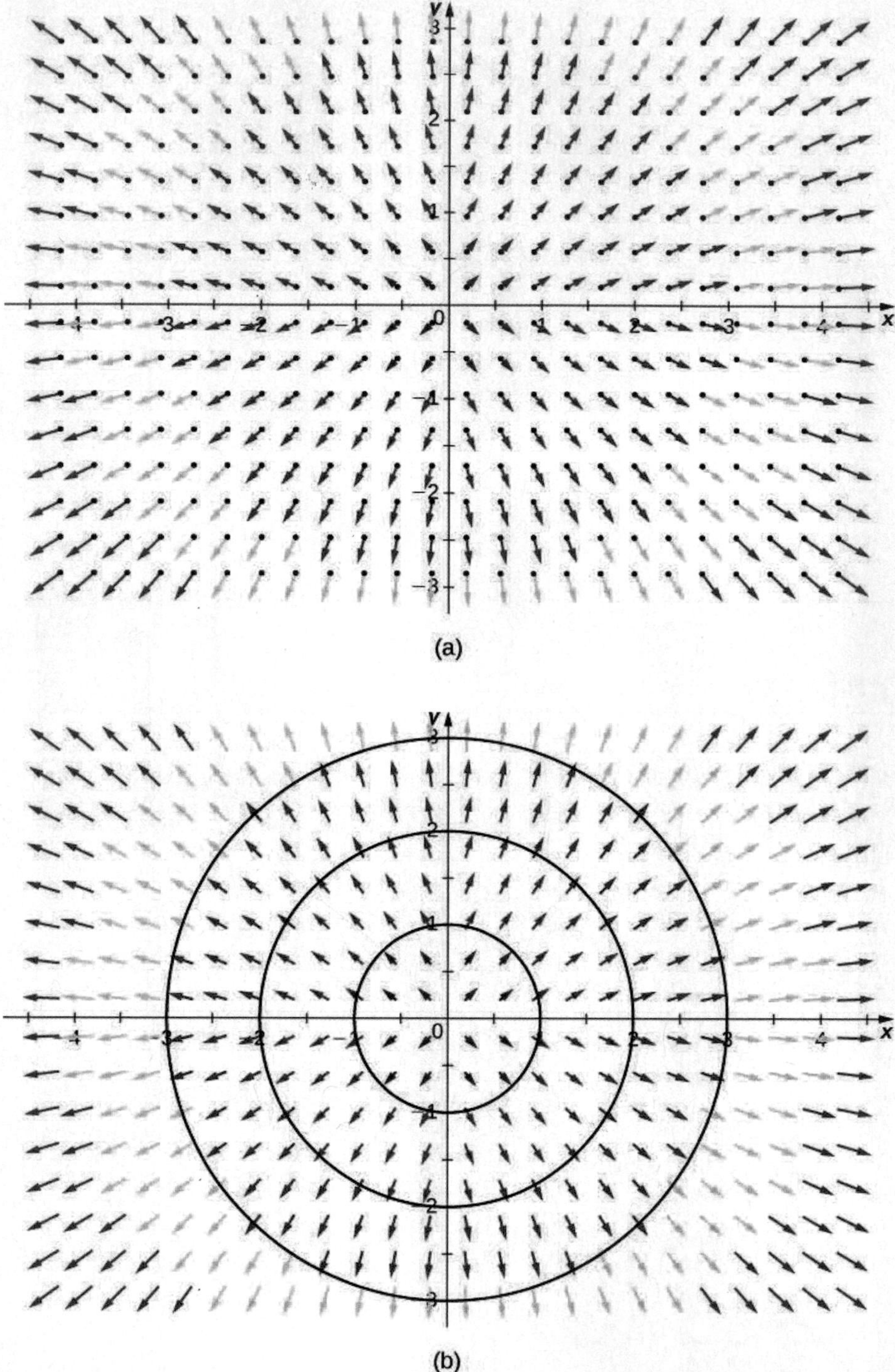

Figure 6.3 (a) A visual representation of the radial vector field $\mathbf{F}(x,\ y) = \frac{x}{2}\mathbf{i} + \frac{y}{2}\mathbf{j}$. (b) The radial vector field $\mathbf{F}(x,\ y) = \frac{x}{2}\mathbf{i} + \frac{y}{2}\mathbf{j}$ with overlaid circles. Notice that each vector is perpendicular to the circle on which it is located.

6.2 Draw the radial field $\mathbf{F}(x, y) = -\frac{x}{3}\mathbf{i} - \frac{y}{3}\mathbf{j}$.

In contrast to radial fields, in a **rotational field**, the vector at point (x, y) is tangent (not perpendicular) to a circle with radius $r = \sqrt{x^2 + y^2}$. In a standard rotational field, all vectors point either in a clockwise direction or in a counterclockwise direction, and the magnitude of a vector depends only on its distance from the origin. Both of the following examples are clockwise rotational fields, and we see from their visual representations that the vectors appear to rotate around the origin.

Example 6.3

Chapter Opener: Drawing a Rotational Vector Field

Figure 6.4 (credit: modification of work by NASA)

Sketch the vector field $\mathbf{F}(x, y) = \langle y, -x \rangle$.

Solution

Create a table (see the one that follows) using a representative sample of points in a plane and their corresponding vectors. **Figure 6.6** shows the resulting vector field.

(x, y)	$\mathbf{F}(x, y)$	(x, y)	$\mathbf{F}(x, y)$	(x, y)	$\mathbf{F}(x, y)$
$(1, 0)$	$\langle 0, -1 \rangle$	$(2, 0)$	$\langle 0, -2 \rangle$	$(1, 1)$	$\langle 1, -1 \rangle$
$(0, 1)$	$\langle 1, 0 \rangle$	$(0, 2)$	$\langle 2, 0 \rangle$	$(-1, 1)$	$\langle 1, 1 \rangle$
$(-1, 0)$	$\langle 0, 1 \rangle$	$(-2, 0)$	$\langle 0, 2 \rangle$	$(-1, -1)$	$\langle -1, 1 \rangle$
$(0, -1)$	$\langle -1, 0 \rangle$	$(0, -2)$	$\langle -2, 0 \rangle$	$(1, -1)$	$\langle -1, -1 \rangle$

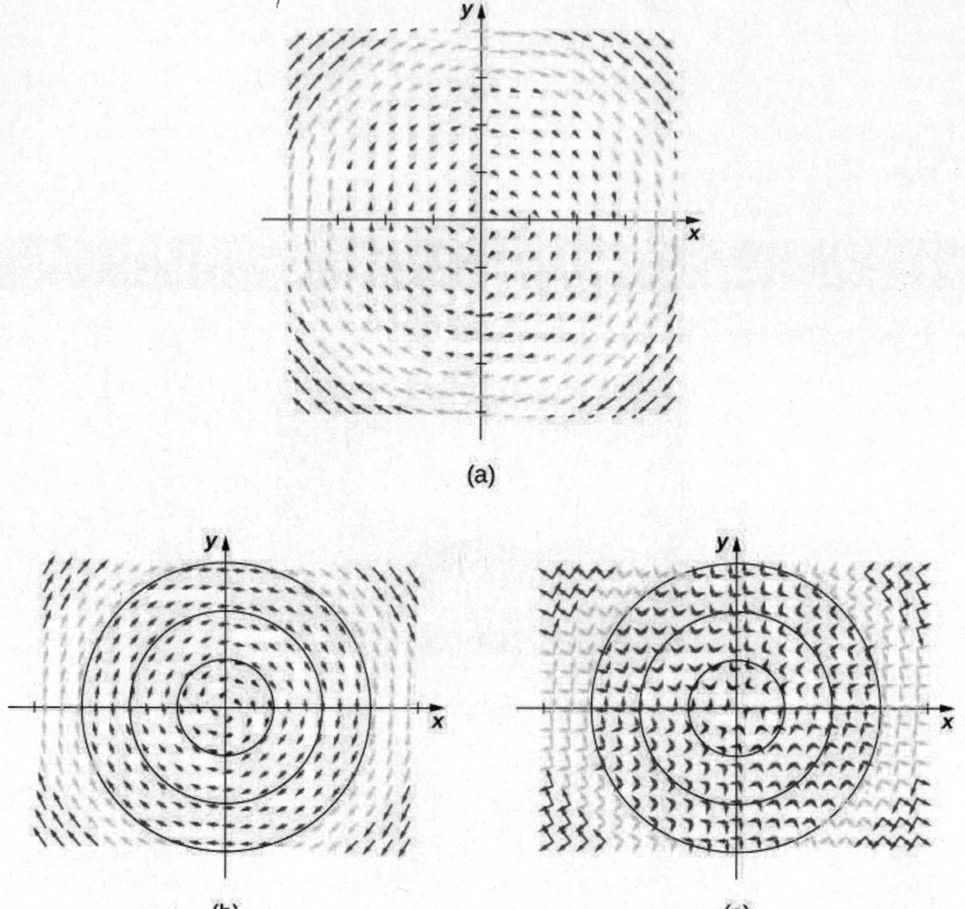

Figure 6.5 (a) A visual representation of vector field $\mathbf{F}(x, y) = \langle y, -x \rangle$. (b) Vector field $\mathbf{F}(x, y) = \langle y, -x \rangle$ with circles centered at the origin. (c) Vector $\mathbf{F}(a, b)$ is perpendicular to radial vector $\langle a, b \rangle$ at point (a, b).

Analysis

Note that vector $\mathbf{F}(a, b) = \langle b, -a \rangle$ points clockwise and is perpendicular to radial vector $\langle a, b \rangle$. (We can verify this assertion by computing the dot product of the two vectors: $\langle a, b \rangle \cdot \langle -b, a \rangle = -ab + ab = 0$.) Furthermore, vector $\langle b, -a \rangle$ has length $r = \sqrt{a^2 + b^2}$. Thus, we have a complete description of this rotational vector field: the vector associated with point (a, b) is the vector with length r tangent to the circle with radius r, and it points in the clockwise direction.

Sketches such as that in **Figure 6.6** are often used to analyze major storm systems, including hurricanes and cyclones. In the northern hemisphere, storms rotate counterclockwise; in the southern hemisphere, storms rotate clockwise. (This is an effect caused by Earth's rotation about its axis and is called the Coriolis Effect.)

Example 6.4

Sketching a Vector Field

Sketch vector field $\mathbf{F}(x, y) = \frac{y}{x^2 + y^2}\mathbf{i} - \frac{x}{x^2 + y^2}\mathbf{j}$.

Solution

To visualize this vector field, first note that the dot product $\mathbf{F}(a, b) \cdot (a\mathbf{i} + b\mathbf{j})$ is zero for any point (a, b). Therefore, each vector is tangent to the circle on which it is located. Also, as $(a, b) \to (0, 0)$, the magnitude of $\mathbf{F}(a, b)$ goes to infinity. To see this, note that

$$\|\mathbf{F}(a, b)\| = \sqrt{\frac{a^2 + b^2}{(a^2 + b^2)^2}} = \sqrt{\frac{1}{a^2 + b^2}}.$$

Since $\frac{1}{a^2 + b^2} \to \infty$ as $(a, b) \to (0, 0)$, then $\|\mathbf{F}(a, b)\| \to \infty$ as $(a, b) \to (0, 0)$. This vector field looks similar to the vector field in **Example 6.3**, but in this case the magnitudes of the vectors close to the origin are large. **Table 6.3** shows a sample of points and the corresponding vectors, and **Figure 6.6** shows the vector field. Note that this vector field models the whirlpool motion of the river in **Figure 6.2**(b). The domain of this vector field is all of $\mathbb{R}^2$ except for point $(0, 0)$.

(x, y)	$\mathbf{F}(x, y)$	(x, y)	$\mathbf{F}(x, y)$	(x, y)	$\mathbf{F}(x, y)$
$(1, 0)$	$\langle 0, -1 \rangle$	$(2, 0)$	$\langle 0, -\frac{1}{2} \rangle$	$(1, 1)$	$\langle \frac{1}{2}, -\frac{1}{2} \rangle$
$(0, 1)$	$\langle 1, 0 \rangle$	$(0, 2)$	$\langle \frac{1}{2}, 0 \rangle$	$(-1, 1)$	$\langle \frac{1}{2}, \frac{1}{2} \rangle$
$(-1, 0)$	$\langle 0, 1 \rangle$	$(-2, 0)$	$\langle 0, \frac{1}{2} \rangle$	$(-1, -1)$	$\langle -\frac{1}{2}, \frac{1}{2} \rangle$
$(0, -1)$	$\langle -1, 0 \rangle$	$(0, -2)$	$\langle -\frac{1}{2}, 0 \rangle$	$(1, -1)$	$\langle -\frac{1}{2}, -\frac{1}{2} \rangle$

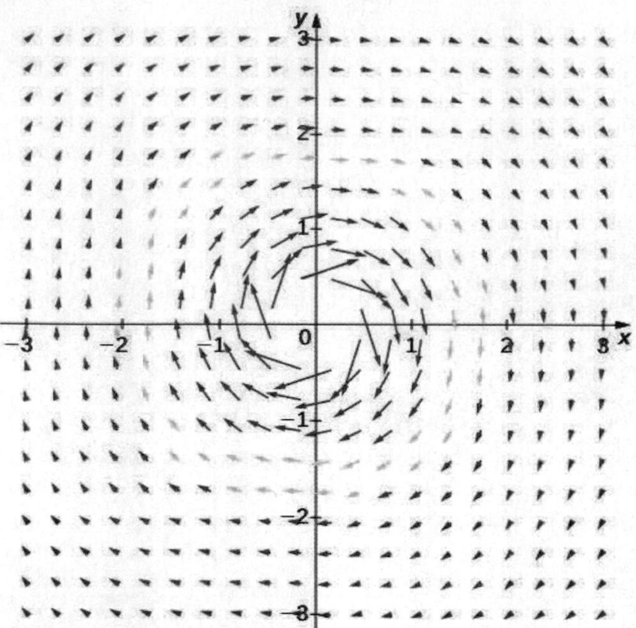

Figure 6.6 A visual representation of vector field $\mathbf{F}(x, y) = \frac{y}{x^2 + y^2}\mathbf{i} - \frac{x}{x^2 + y^2}\mathbf{j}$. This vector field could be used to model whirlpool motion of a fluid.

6.3 Sketch vector field $\mathbf{F}(x, y) = \langle -2y, 2x \rangle$. Is the vector field radial, rotational, or neither?

Example 6.5

Velocity Field of a Fluid

Suppose that $\mathbf{v}(x, y) = -\frac{2y}{x^2 + y^2}\mathbf{i} + \frac{2x}{x^2 + y^2}\mathbf{j}$ is the velocity field of a fluid. How fast is the fluid moving at point $(1, -1)$? (Assume the units of speed are meters per second.)

Solution

To find the velocity of the fluid at point $(1, -1)$, substitute the point into $\mathbf{v}$:

$$\mathbf{v}(1, -1) = -\frac{2(-1)}{1+1}\mathbf{i} + \frac{2(1)}{1+1}\mathbf{j} = \mathbf{i} + \mathbf{j}.$$

The speed of the fluid at $(1, -1)$ is the magnitude of this vector. Therefore, the speed is $\|\mathbf{i} + \mathbf{j}\| = \sqrt{2}$ m/sec.

6.4 Vector field $v(x, y) = \langle 4|x|, 1 \rangle$ models the velocity of water on the surface of a river. What is the speed of the water at point $(2, 3)$? Use meters per second as the units.

We have examined vector fields that contain vectors of various magnitudes, but just as we have unit vectors, we can also have a unit vector field. A vector field **F** is a **unit vector field** if the magnitude of each vector in the field is 1. In a unit vector field, the only relevant information is the direction of each vector.

Example 6.6

A Unit Vector Field

Show that vector field $\mathbf{F}(x, y) = \left\langle \frac{y}{\sqrt{x^2 + y^2}}, -\frac{x}{\sqrt{x^2 + y^2}} \right\rangle$ is a unit vector field.

Solution

To show that **F** is a unit field, we must show that the magnitude of each vector is 1. Note that

$$\begin{aligned} \sqrt{\left(\frac{y}{\sqrt{x^2+y^2}}\right)^2 + \left(-\frac{x}{\sqrt{x^2+y^2}}\right)^2} &= \sqrt{\frac{y^2}{x^2+y^2} + \frac{x^2}{x^2+y^2}} \\ &= \sqrt{\frac{x^2+y^2}{x^2+y^2}} \\ &= 1. \end{aligned}$$

Therefore, **F** is a unit vector field.

6.5 Is vector field $\mathbf{F}(x, y) = \langle -y, x \rangle$ a unit vector field?

Why are unit vector fields important? Suppose we are studying the flow of a fluid, and we care only about the direction in which the fluid is flowing at a given point. In this case, the speed of the fluid (which is the magnitude of the corresponding velocity vector) is irrelevant, because all we care about is the direction of each vector. Therefore, the unit vector field associated with velocity is the field we would study.

If $\mathbf{F} = \langle P, Q, R \rangle$ is a vector field, then the corresponding unit vector field is $\left\langle \frac{P}{\|\mathbf{F}\|}, \frac{Q}{\|\mathbf{F}\|}, \frac{R}{\|\mathbf{F}\|} \right\rangle$. Notice that if $\mathbf{F}(x, y) = \langle y, -x \rangle$ is the vector field from **Example 6.3**, then the magnitude of **F** is $\sqrt{x^2 + y^2}$, and therefore the corresponding unit vector field is the field **G** from the previous example.

If **F** is a vector field, then the process of dividing **F** by its magnitude to form unit vector field $\mathbf{F}/\|\mathbf{F}\|$ is called *normalizing* the field **F**.

Vector Fields in $\mathbb{R}^3$

We have seen several examples of vector fields in $\mathbb{R}^2$; let's now turn our attention to vector fields in $\mathbb{R}^3$. These vector fields can be used to model gravitational or electromagnetic fields, and they can also be used to model fluid flow or heat flow in three dimensions. A two-dimensional vector field can really only model the movement of water on a two-dimensional slice of a river (such as the river's surface). Since a river flows through three spatial dimensions, to model the flow of the entire depth of the river, we need a vector field in three dimensions.

The extra dimension of a three-dimensional field can make vector fields in $\mathbb{R}^3$ more difficult to visualize, but the idea is the same. To visualize a vector field in $\mathbb{R}^3$, plot enough vectors to show the overall shape. We can use a similar method to visualizing a vector field in $\mathbb{R}^2$ by choosing points in each octant.

Just as with vector fields in $\mathbb{R}^2$, we can represent vector fields in $\mathbb{R}^3$ with component functions. We simply need an extra component function for the extra dimension. We write either

$$\mathbf{F}(x, y, z) = \langle P(x, y, z), Q(x, y, z), R(x, y, z) \rangle \tag{6.3}$$

or

$$\mathbf{F}(x, y, z) = P(x, y, z)\mathbf{i} + Q(x, y, z)\mathbf{j} + R(x, y, z)\mathbf{k}. \tag{6.4}$$

Example 6.7

Sketching a Vector Field in Three Dimensions

Describe vector field $\mathbf{F}(x, y, z) = \langle 1, 1, z \rangle$.

Solution

For this vector field, the *x* and *y* components are constant, so every point in $\mathbb{R}^3$ has an associated vector with *x* and *y* components equal to one. To visualize **F**, we first consider what the field looks like in the *xy*-plane. In the *xy*-plane, $z = 0$. Hence, each point of the form $(a, b, 0)$ has vector $\langle 1, 1, 0 \rangle$ associated with it. For points not in the *xy*-plane but slightly above it, the associated vector has a small but positive *z* component, and therefore the associated vector points slightly upward. For points that are far above the *xy*-plane, the *z* component is large, so the vector is almost vertical. **Figure 6.7** shows this vector field.

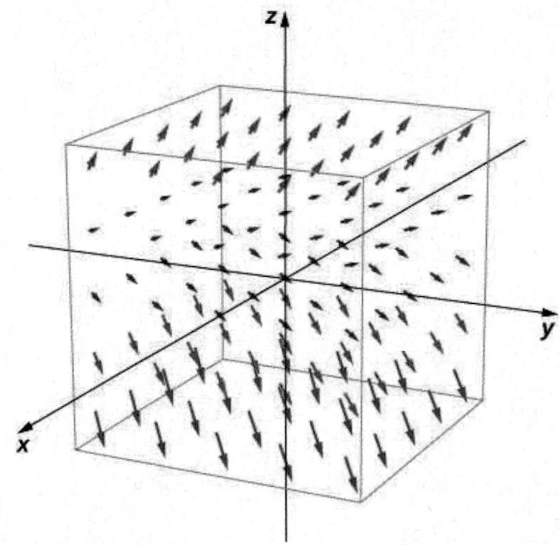

Figure 6.7 A visual representation of vector field $\mathbf{F}(x, y, z) = \langle 1, 1, z \rangle$.

6.6 Sketch vector field $\mathbf{G}(x, y, z) = \langle 2, \frac{z}{2}, 1 \rangle$.

In the next example, we explore one of the classic cases of a three-dimensional vector field: a gravitational field.

Example 6.8

Describing a Gravitational Vector Field

Newton's law of gravitation states that $\mathbf{F} = -G\frac{m_1 m_2}{r^2}\hat{\mathbf{r}},$ where G is the universal gravitational constant. It describes the gravitational field exerted by an object (object 1) of mass m_1 located at the origin on another object (object 2) of mass m_2 located at point (x, y, z). Field $\mathbf{F}$ denotes the gravitational force that object 1 exerts on object 2, r is the distance between the two objects, and $\hat{\mathbf{r}}$ indicates the unit vector from the first object to the second. The minus sign shows that the gravitational force attracts toward the origin; that is, the force of object 1 is attractive. Sketch the vector field associated with this equation.

Solution

Since object 1 is located at the origin, the distance between the objects is given by $r = \sqrt{x^2 + y^2 + z^2}$. The unit vector from object 1 to object 2 is $\hat{\mathbf{r}} = \frac{\langle x, y, z \rangle}{\| \langle x, y, z \rangle \|},$ and hence $\hat{\mathbf{r}} = \langle \frac{x}{r}, \frac{y}{r}, \frac{z}{r} \rangle$. Therefore, gravitational vector field $\mathbf{F}$ exerted by object 1 on object 2 is

$$\mathbf{F} = -Gm_1 m_2 \langle \frac{x}{r^3}, \frac{y}{r^3}, \frac{z}{r^3} \rangle.$$

This is an example of a radial vector field in $\mathbb{R}^3$.

Figure 6.8 shows what this gravitational field looks like for a large mass at the origin. Note that the magnitudes of the vectors increase as the vectors get closer to the origin.

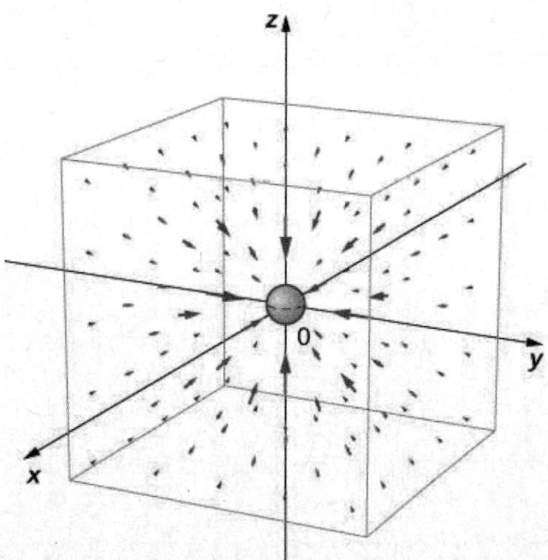

Figure 6.8 A visual representation of gravitational vector field $\mathbf{F} = -Gm_1 m_2 \langle \frac{x}{r^3}, \frac{y}{r^3}, \frac{z}{r^3} \rangle$ for a large mass at the origin.

6.7 The mass of asteroid 1 is 750,000 kg and the mass of asteroid 2 is 130,000 kg. Assume asteroid 1 is located at the origin, and asteroid 2 is located at $(15, -5, 10)$, measured in units of 10 to the eighth power kilometers. Given that the universal gravitational constant is $G = 6.67384 \times 10^{-11}\ \text{m}^3\text{kg}^{-1}\text{s}^{-2}$, find the gravitational force vector that asteroid 1 exerts on asteroid 2.

Gradient Fields

In this section, we study a special kind of vector field called a gradient field or a **conservative field**. These vector fields are extremely important in physics because they can be used to model physical systems in which energy is conserved. Gravitational fields and electric fields associated with a static charge are examples of gradient fields.

Recall that if f is a (scalar) function of x and y, then the gradient of f is

$$\text{grad } f = \nabla f = f_x(x, y)\mathbf{i} + f_y(x, y)\mathbf{j}.$$

We can see from the form in which the gradient is written that ∇f is a vector field in $\mathbb{R}^2$. Similarly, if f is a function of x, y, and z, then the gradient of f is

$$\text{grad } f = \nabla f = f_x(x, y, z)\mathbf{i} + f_y(x, y, z)\mathbf{j} + f_z(x, y, z)\mathbf{k}.$$

The gradient of a three-variable function is a vector field in $\mathbb{R}^3$.

A gradient field is a vector field that can be written as the gradient of a function, and we have the following definition.

Definition

A vector field $\mathbf{F}$ in $\mathbb{R}^2$ or in $\mathbb{R}^3$ is a **gradient field** if there exists a scalar function f such that $\nabla f = \mathbf{F}$.

Example 6.9

Sketching a Gradient Vector Field

Use technology to plot the gradient vector field of $f(x, y) = x^2y^2$ $f(x, y) = x^2y^2$.

Solution

The gradient of f is $\nabla f = \langle 2xy^2, 2x^2y \rangle$ $\nabla f = \langle 2xy^2, 2x^2y \rangle$. To sketch the vector field, use a computer algebra system such as Mathematica. **Figure 6.9** shows ∇f.

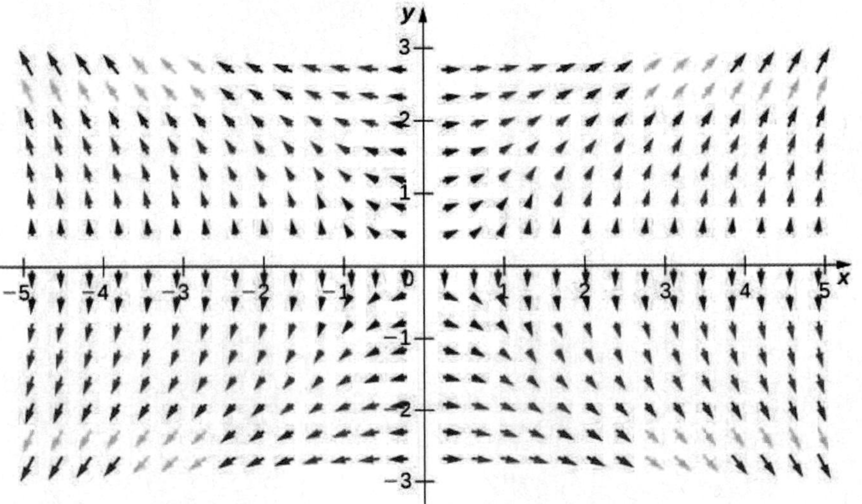

Figure 6.9 The gradient vector field is ∇f, where $f(x, y) = x^2y^2$.

6.8 Use technology to plot the gradient vector field of $f(x, y) = \sin x \cos y$.

Consider the function $f(x, y) = x^2 y^2$ from **Example 6.9**. **Figure 6.11** shows the level curves of this function overlaid on the function's gradient vector field. The gradient vectors are perpendicular to the level curves, and the magnitudes of the vectors get larger as the level curves get closer together, because closely grouped level curves indicate the graph is steep, and the magnitude of the gradient vector is the largest value of the directional derivative. Therefore, you can see the local steepness of a graph by investigating the corresponding function's gradient field.

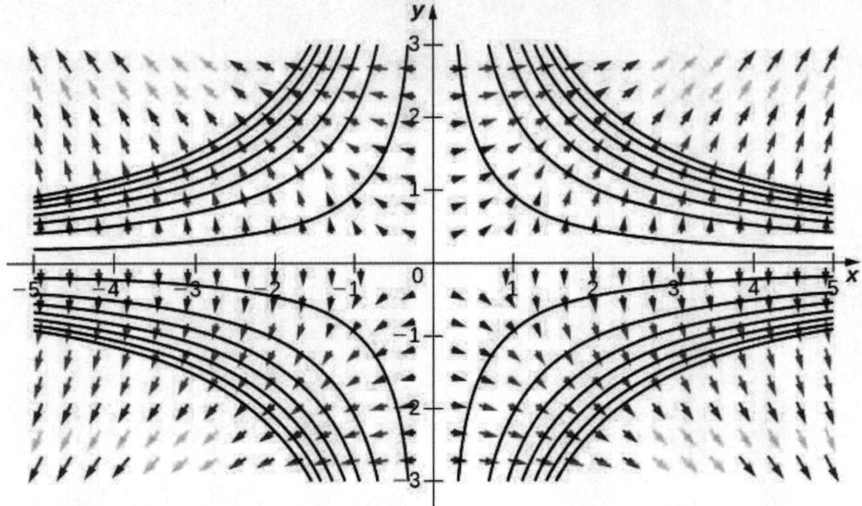

Figure 6.10 The gradient field of $f(x, y) = x^2 y^2$ and several level curves of f. Notice that as the level curves get closer together, the magnitude of the gradient vectors increases.

As we learned earlier, a vector field $\mathbf{F}$ is a conservative vector field, or a gradient field if there exists a scalar function f such that $\nabla f = \mathbf{F}$. In this situation, f is called a **potential function** for $\mathbf{F}$. Conservative vector fields arise in many applications, particularly in physics. The reason such fields are called *conservative* is that they model forces of physical systems in which energy is conserved. We study conservative vector fields in more detail later in this chapter.

You might notice that, in some applications, a potential function f for $\mathbf{F}$ is defined instead as a function such that $-\nabla f = \mathbf{F}$. This is the case for certain contexts in physics, for example.

Example 6.10

Verifying a Potential Function

Is $f(x, y, z) = x^2 yz - \sin(xy)$ a potential function for vector field

$$\mathbf{F}(x, y, z) = \langle 2xyz - y\cos(xy), x^2 z - x\cos(xy), x^2 y \rangle ?$$

Solution

We need to confirm whether $\nabla f = \mathbf{F}$. We have

$$f_x = 2xyz - y\cos(xy), \; f_y = x^2 z - x\cos(xy), \; \text{and } f_z = x^2 y.$$

Therefore, $\nabla f = \mathbf{F}$ and f is a potential function for $\mathbf{F}$.

6.9 Is $f(x, y, z) = x^2 \cos(yz) + y^2 z^2$ a potential function for $\mathbf{F}(x, y, z) = \langle 2x\cos(yz), -x^2 z\sin(yz) + 2yz^2, y^2 \rangle$?

Example 6.11

Verifying a Potential Function

The velocity of a fluid is modeled by field $\mathbf{v}(x, y) = \langle xy, \frac{x^2}{2} - y \rangle$. Verify that $f(x, y) = \frac{x^2 y}{2} - \frac{y^2}{2}$ is a potential function for $\mathbf{v}$.

Solution

To show that f is a potential function, we must show that $\nabla f = \mathbf{v}$. Note that $f_x = xy$ and $f_x = \frac{x^2}{2} - y$.

Therefore, $\nabla f = \langle xy, \frac{x^2}{2} - y \rangle$ and f is a potential function for v (**Figure 6.11**).

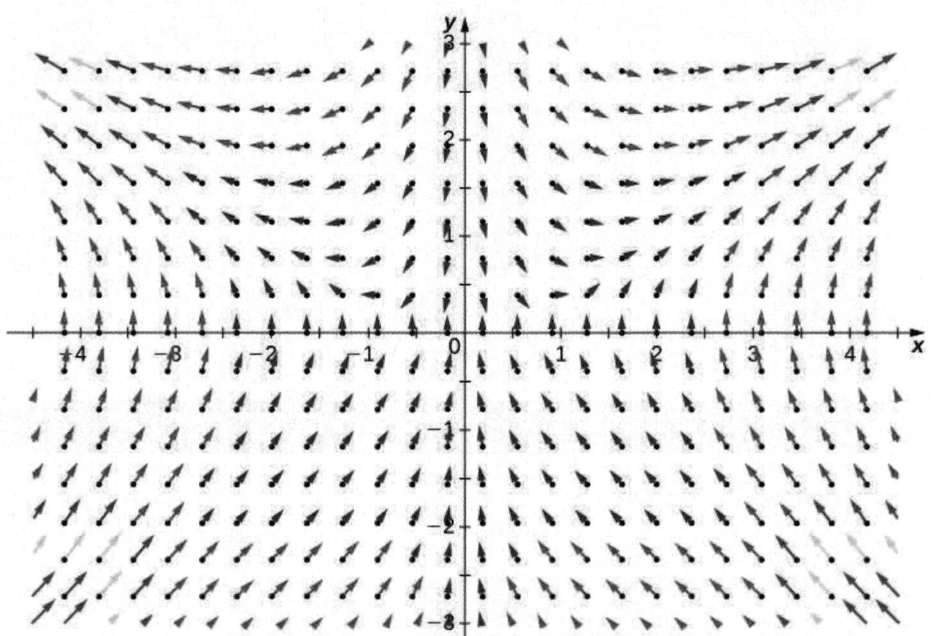

Figure 6.11 Velocity field $\mathbf{v}(x, y)$ has a potential function and is a conservative field.

6.10 Verify that $f(x, y) = x^2 y^2 + x$ is a potential function for velocity field $\mathbf{v}(x, y) = \langle 3x^2 y^2 + 1, 2x^3 y \rangle$.

If **F** is a conservative vector field, then there is at least one potential function f such that $\nabla f = \mathbf{F}$. But, could there be more than one potential function? If so, is there any relationship between two potential functions for the same vector field? Before answering these questions, let's recall some facts from single-variable calculus to guide our intuition. Recall that if $k(x)$ is an integrable function, then k has infinitely many antiderivatives. Furthermore, if F and G are both antiderivatives of k, then F and G differ only by a constant. That is, there is some number C such that $F(x) = G(x) + C$.

Now let **F** be a conservative vector field and let f and g be potential functions for **F**. Since the gradient is like a derivative, **F** being conservative means that **F** is "integrable" with "antiderivatives" f and g. Therefore, if the analogy with single-variable calculus is valid, we expect there is some constant C such that $f(x) = g(x) + C$. The next theorem says that this is indeed the case.

To state the next theorem with precision, we need to assume the domain of the vector field is connected and open. To be connected means if P_1 and P_2 are any two points in the domain, then you can walk from P_1 to P_2 along a path that stays entirely inside the domain.

Theorem 6.1: Uniqueness of Potential Functions

Let **F** be a conservative vector field on an open and connected domain and let f and g be functions such that $\nabla f = \mathbf{F}$ and $\nabla g = \mathbf{F}$. Then, there is a constant C such that $f = g + C$.

Proof

Since f and g are both potential functions for **F**, then $\nabla f = (f - g) = \nabla f - \nabla g = \mathbf{F} - \mathbf{F} = 0$. Let $h = f - g$, then we have $\nabla h = 0$. We would like to show that h is a constant function.

Assume h is a function of x and y (the logic of this proof extends to any number of independent variables). Since $\nabla h = 0$, we have $h_x = 0$ and $h_y = 0$. The expression $h_x = 0$ implies that h is a constant function with respect to x—that is, $h(x, y) = k_1(y)$ for some function k_1. Similarly, $h_y = 0$ implies $h(x, y) = k_2(x)$ for some function k_2. Therefore, function h depends only on y and also depends only on x. Thus, $h(x, y) = C$ for some constant C on the connected domain of **F**. Note that we really do need connectedness at this point; if the domain of **F** came in two separate pieces, then k could be a constant C_1 on one piece but could be a different constant C_2 on the other piece. Since $f - g = h = C$, we have that $f - g + C$, as desired.

□

Conservative vector fields also have a special property called the *cross-partial property*. This property helps test whether a given vector field is conservative.

Theorem 6.2: The Cross-Partial Property of Conservative Vector Fields

Let **F** be a vector field in two or three dimensions such that the component functions of **F** have continuous second-order mixed-partial derivatives on the domain of **F**.

If $\mathbf{F}(x, y) = \langle P(x, y), Q(x, y) \rangle$ is a conservative vector field in $\mathbb{R}^2$, then $\frac{\partial P}{\partial y} = \frac{\partial Q}{\partial x}$. If $\mathbf{F}(x, y, z) = \langle P(x, y, z), Q(x, y, z), R(x, y, z) \rangle$ is a conservative vector field in $\mathbb{R}^3$, then

$$\frac{\partial P}{\partial y} = \frac{\partial Q}{\partial x}, \frac{\partial Q}{\partial z} = \frac{\partial R}{\partial y}, \text{ and } \frac{\partial R}{\partial x} = \frac{\partial P}{\partial z}.$$

Proof

Since **F** is conservative, there is a function $f(x, y)$ such that $\nabla f = \mathbf{F}$. Therefore, by the definition of the gradient, $f_x = P$

and $f_y = Q$. By Clairaut's theorem, $f_{xy} = f_{yx}$. But, $f_{xy} = P_y$ and $f_{yx} = Q_x$, and thus $P_y = Q_x$.

□

Clairaut's theorem gives a fast proof of the cross-partial property of conservative vector fields in $\mathbb{R}^3$, just as it did for vector fields in $\mathbb{R}^2$.

The Cross-Partial Property of Conservative Vector Fields shows that most vector fields are not conservative. The cross-partial property is difficult to satisfy in general, so most vector fields won't have equal cross-partials.

Example 6.12

Showing a Vector Field Is Not Conservative

Show that rotational vector field $\mathbf{F}(x, y) = \langle y, -x \rangle$ is not conservative.

Solution

Let $P(x, y) = y$ and $Q(x, y) = -x$. If $\mathbf{F}$ is conservative, then the cross-partials would be equal—that is, P_y would equal Q_x. Therefore, to show that $\mathbf{F}$ is not conservative, check that $P_y \neq Q_x$. Since $P_y = 1$ and $Q_x = -1$, the vector field is not conservative.

6.11 Show that vector field $\mathbf{F}(x, y)xy\mathbf{i} - x^2 y\mathbf{j}$ is not conservative.

Example 6.13

Showing a Vector Field Is Not Conservative

Is vector field $\mathbf{F}(x, y, z) = \langle 7, -2, x^3 \rangle$ conservative?

Solution

Let $P(x, y, z) = 7$, $Q(x, y, z) = -2$, and $R(x, y, z) = x^3$. If $\mathbf{F}$ is conservative, then all three cross-partial equations will be satisfied—that is, if $\mathbf{F}$ is conservative, then P_y would equal Q_x, Q_z would equal R_y, and R_x would equal P_z. Note that $P_y = Q_x = R_y = Q_z = 0$, so the first two necessary equalities hold. However, $R_x = 3x^3$ and $P_z = 0$ so $R_x \neq P_z$. Therefore, $\mathbf{F}$ is not conservative.

6.12 Is vector field $G(x, y, z) = \langle y, x, xyz \rangle$ conservative?

We conclude this section with a word of warning: **The Cross-Partial Property of Conservative Vector Fields** says that if $\mathbf{F}$ is conservative, then $\mathbf{F}$ has the cross-partial property. The theorem does *not* say that, if $\mathbf{F}$ has the cross-partial property, then $\mathbf{F}$ is conservative (the converse of an implication is not logically equivalent to the original implication). In other words, **The Cross-Partial Property of Conservative Vector Fields** can only help determine that a field is not conservative; it does not let you conclude that a vector field is conservative. For example, consider vector field

$\mathbf{F}(x, y) = \langle x^2 y, \frac{x^3}{3} \rangle$. This field has the cross-partial property, so it is natural to try to use **The Cross-Partial Property of Conservative Vector Fields** to conclude this vector field is conservative. However, this is a misapplication of the theorem. We learn later how to conclude that **F** is conservative.

6.1 EXERCISES

1. The domain of vector field $\mathbf{F} = \mathbf{F}(x, y)$ is a set of points (x, y) in a plane, and the range of $\mathbf{F}$ is a set of *what* in the plane?

For the following exercises, determine whether the statement is *true or false*.

2. Vector field $\mathbf{F} = \langle 3x^2, 1 \rangle$ is a gradient field for both $\phi_1(x, y) = x^3 + y$ and $\phi_2(x, y) = y + x^3 + 100$.

3. Vector field $\mathbf{F} = \dfrac{\langle y, x \rangle}{\sqrt{x^2 + y^2}}$ is constant in direction and magnitude on a unit circle.

4. Vector field $\mathbf{F} = \dfrac{\langle y, x \rangle}{\sqrt{x^2 + y^2}}$ is neither a radial field nor a rotation.

For the following exercises, describe each vector field by drawing some of its vectors.

5. **[T]** $\mathbf{F}(x, y) = x\mathbf{i} + y\mathbf{j}$

6. **[T]** $\mathbf{F}(x, y) = -y\mathbf{i} + x\mathbf{j}$

7. **[T]** $\mathbf{F}(x, y) = x\mathbf{i} - y\mathbf{j}$

8. **[T]** $\mathbf{F}(x, y) = \mathbf{i} + \mathbf{j}$

9. **[T]** $\mathbf{F}(x, y) = 2x\mathbf{i} + 3y\mathbf{j}$

10. **[T]** $\mathbf{F}(x, y) = 3\mathbf{i} + x\mathbf{j}$

11. **[T]** $\mathbf{F}(x, y) = y\mathbf{i} + \sin x\mathbf{j}$

12. **[T]** $\mathbf{F}(x, y, z) = x\mathbf{i} + y\mathbf{j} + z\mathbf{k}$

13. **[T]** $\mathbf{F}(x, y, z) = 2x\mathbf{i} - 2y\mathbf{j} - 2z\mathbf{k}$

14. **[T]** $\mathbf{F}(x, y, z) = \frac{y}{z}\mathbf{i} - \frac{x}{z}\mathbf{j}$

For the following exercises, find the gradient vector field of each function f.

15. $f(x, y) = x\sin y + \cos y$

16. $f(x, y, z) = ze^{-xy}$

17. $f(x, y, z) = x^2y + xy + y^2z$

18. $f(x, y) = x^2\sin(5y)$

19. $f(x, y) = \ln\left(1 + x^2 + 2y^2\right)$

20. $f(x, y, z) = x\cos\left(\frac{y}{z}\right)$

21. What is vector field $\mathbf{F}(x, y)$ with a value at (x, y) that is of unit length and points toward $(1, 0)$?

For the following exercises, write formulas for the vector fields with the given properties.

22. All vectors are parallel to the x-axis and all vectors on a vertical line have the same magnitude.

23. All vectors point toward the origin and have constant length.

24. All vectors are of unit length and are perpendicular to the position vector at that point.

25. Give a formula $\mathbf{F}(x, y) = M(x, y)\mathbf{i} + N(x, y)\mathbf{j}$ for the vector field in a plane that has the properties that $\mathbf{F} = 0$ at $(0, 0)$ and that at any other point (a, b), $\mathbf{F}$ is tangent to circle $x^2 + y^2 = a^2 + b^2$ and points in the clockwise direction with magnitude $|\mathbf{F}| = \sqrt{a^2 + b^2}$.

26. Is vector field $\mathbf{F}(x, y) = (P(x, y), Q(x, y)) = (\sin x + y)\mathbf{i} + (\cos y + x)\mathbf{j}$ a gradient field?

27. Find a formula for vector field $\mathbf{F}(x, y) = \mathrm{M}(x, y)\mathbf{i} + N(x, y)\mathbf{j}$ given the fact that for all points (x, y), $\mathbf{F}$ points toward the origin and $|\mathbf{F}| = \dfrac{10}{x^2 + y^2}$.

For the following exercises, assume that an electric field in the xy-plane caused by an infinite line of charge along the x-axis is a gradient field with potential function $V(x, y) = c\ln\left(\dfrac{r_0}{\sqrt{x^2 + y^2}}\right)$, where $c > 0$ is a constant and r_0 is a reference distance at which the potential is assumed to be zero.

28. Find the components of the electric field in the x- and y-directions, where $\mathbf{E}(x, y) = -\nabla V(x, y)$.

29. Show that the electric field at a point in the xy-plane is directed outward from the origin and has magnitude $\mathbf{E}| = \frac{c}{r}$, where $r = \sqrt{x^2 = y^2}$.

A *flow line* (or *streamline*) of a vector field $\mathbf{F}$ is a curve $\mathbf{r}(t)$ such that $d\mathbf{r}/dt = \mathbf{F}(\mathbf{r}(t))$. If $\mathbf{F}$ represents the velocity field of a moving particle, then the flow lines are paths taken by the particle. Therefore, flow lines are tangent to the vector field. For the following exercises, show that the given curve $\mathbf{c}(t)$ is a flow line of the given velocity vector field $\mathbf{F}(x, y, z)$.

30. $\mathbf{c}(t) = \left(e^{2t}, \ln|t|, \frac{1}{t}\right), t \neq 0; \mathbf{F}(x, y, z) = \langle 2x, z, -z^2 \rangle$

31. $\mathbf{c}(t) = (\sin t, \cos t, e^t); \mathbf{F}(x, y, z) = \langle y, -x, z \rangle$

For the following exercises, let $\mathbf{F} = x\mathbf{i} + y\mathbf{j}$, $\mathbf{G} = -y\mathbf{i} + x\mathbf{j}$, and $\mathbf{H} = x\mathbf{i} - y\mathbf{j}$. Match $\mathbf{F}$, $\mathbf{G}$, and $\mathbf{H}$ with their graphs.

32.

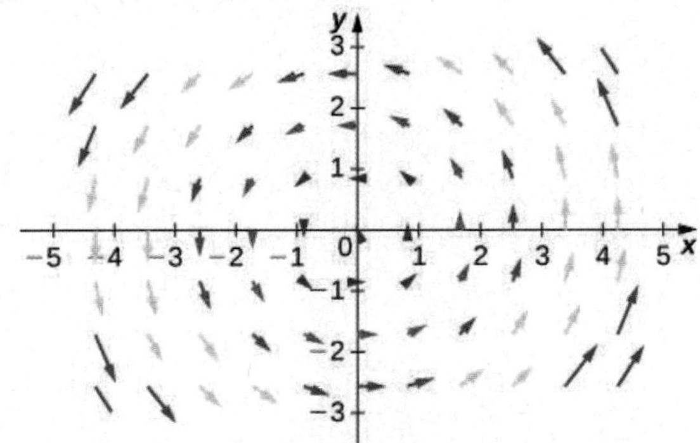

33.

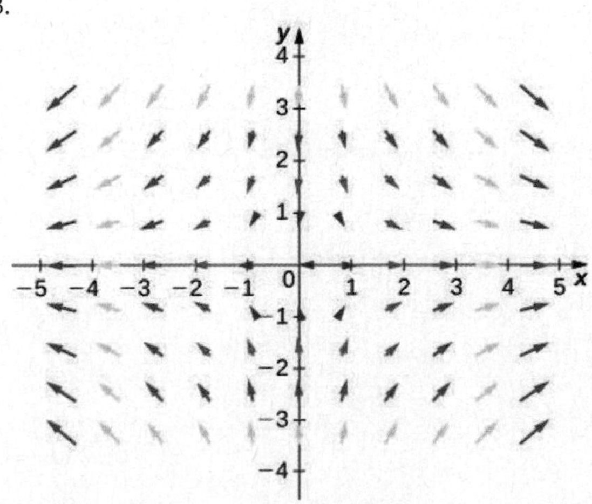

34.

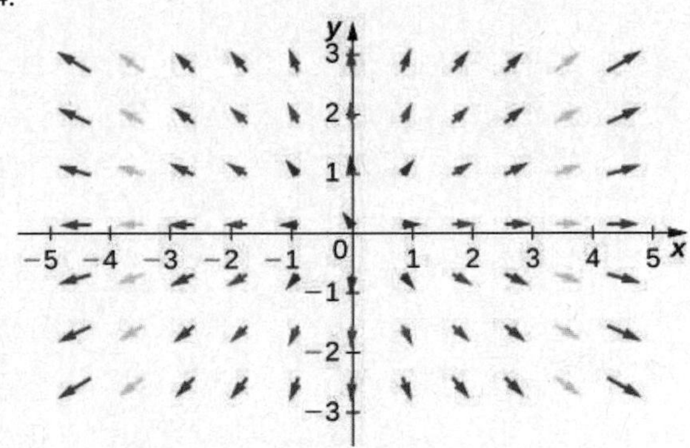

For the following exercises, let $\mathbf{F} = x\mathbf{i} + y\mathbf{j}$, $\mathbf{G} = -y\mathbf{i} + x\mathbf{j}$, and $\mathbf{H} = -x\mathbf{j} + y\mathbf{j}$. Match the vector fields with their graphs in (I) – (IV).

a. $\mathbf{F} + \mathbf{G}$

b. $\mathbf{F} + \mathbf{H}$

c. $\mathbf{G} + \mathbf{H}$

d. $-\mathbf{F} + \mathbf{G}$

35.

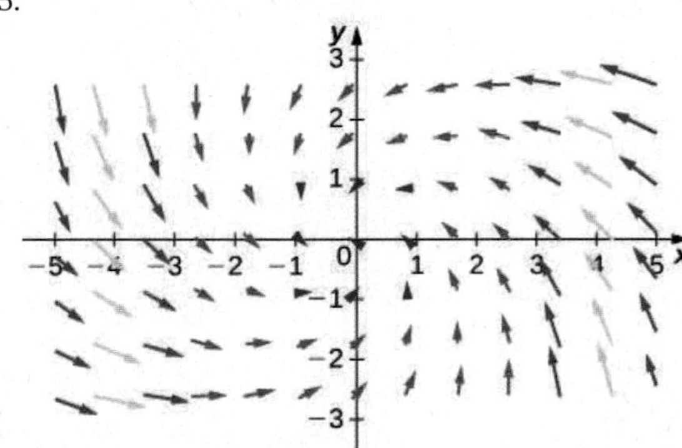

36.

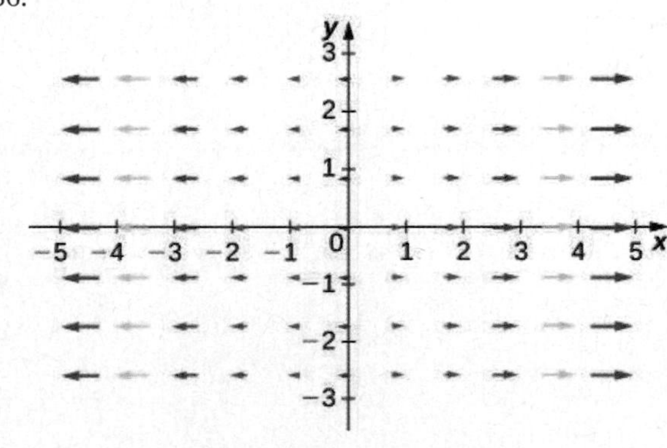

37.

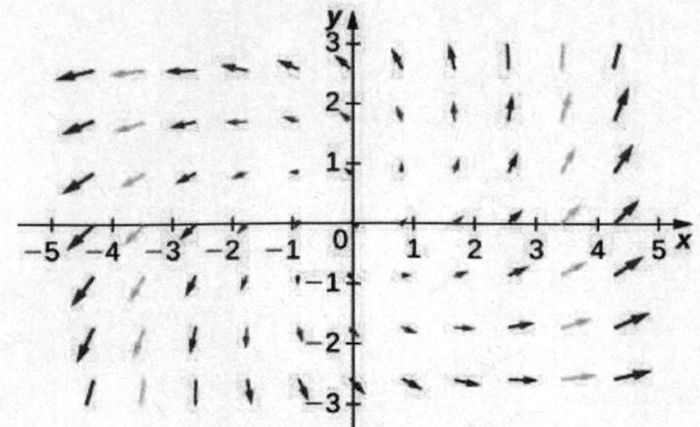

38.

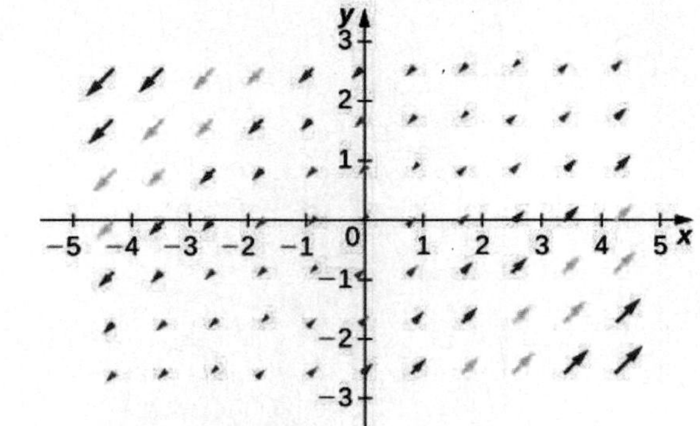

6.2 | Line Integrals

Learning Objectives

- **6.2.1** Calculate a scalar line integral along a curve.
- **6.2.2** Calculate a vector line integral along an oriented curve in space.
- **6.2.3** Use a line integral to compute the work done in moving an object along a curve in a vector field.
- **6.2.4** Describe the flux and circulation of a vector field.

We are familiar with single-variable integrals of the form $\int_a^b f(x)dx,$ where the domain of integration is an interval $[a, b]$. Such an interval can be thought of as a curve in the *xy*-plane, since the interval defines a line segment with endpoints $(a, 0)$ and $(b, 0)$—in other words, a line segment located on the *x*-axis. Suppose we want to integrate over *any* curve in the plane, not just over a line segment on the *x*-axis. Such a task requires a new kind of integral, called a *line integral.*

Line integrals have many applications to engineering and physics. They also allow us to make several useful generalizations of the Fundamental Theorem of Calculus. And, they are closely connected to the properties of vector fields, as we shall see.

Scalar Line Integrals

A **line integral** gives us the ability to integrate multivariable functions and vector fields over arbitrary curves in a plane or in space. There are two types of line integrals: scalar line integrals and vector line integrals. Scalar line integrals are integrals of a scalar function over a curve in a plane or in space. Vector line integrals are integrals of a vector field over a curve in a plane or in space. Let's look at scalar line integrals first.

A scalar line integral is defined just as a single-variable integral is defined, except that for a scalar line integral, the integrand is a function of more than one variable and the domain of integration is a curve in a plane or in space, as opposed to a curve on the *x*-axis.

For a scalar line integral, we let C be a smooth curve in a plane or in space and let f be a function with a domain that includes C. We chop the curve into small pieces. For each piece, we choose point P in that piece and evaluate f at P. (We can do this because all the points in the curve are in the domain of f.) We multiply $f(P)$ by the arc length of the piece $\Delta s,$ add the product $f(P)\Delta s$ over all the pieces, and then let the arc length of the pieces shrink to zero by taking a limit. The result is the scalar line integral of the function over the curve.

For a formal description of a scalar line integral, let C be a smooth curve in space given by the parameterization $\mathbf{r}(t) = \langle x(t), y(t), z(t) \rangle, \quad a \le t \le b.$ Let $f(x, y, z)$ be a function with a domain that includes curve $C.$ To define the line integral of the function f over $C,$ we begin as most definitions of an integral begin: we chop the curve into small pieces. Partition the parameter interval $[a, b]$ into n subintervals $[t_{i-1}, t_i]$ of equal width for $1 \le i \le n,$ where $t_0 = a$ and $t_n = b$ (**Figure 6.12**). Let t_i^* be a value in the ith interval $[t_{i-1}, t_i]$. Denote the endpoints of $\mathbf{r}(t_0), \mathbf{r}(t_1),\ldots, \mathbf{r}(t_n)$ by $P_0,\ldots, P_n$. Points P_i divide curve C into n pieces $C_1, C_2,\ldots, C_n,$ with lengths $\Delta s_1, \Delta s_2,\ldots, \Delta s_n,$ respectively. Let P_i^* denote the endpoint of $\mathbf{r}(t_i^*)$ for $1 \le i \le n.$ Now, we evaluate the function f at point P_i^* for $1 \le i \le n.$ Note that P_i^* is in piece $C_1,$ and therefore P_i^* is in the domain of $f.$ Multiply $f(P_i^*)$ by the length Δs_1 of $C_1,$ which gives the area of the "sheet" with base $C_1,$ and height $f(P_i^*)$. This is analogous to using rectangles to approximate area in a single-variable integral. Now, we form the sum $\sum_{i=1}^{n} f(P_i^*)\Delta s_i.$ Note the similarity of this sum versus a Riemann sum; in fact, this definition is a generalization of a Riemann sum to arbitrary curves in space. Just as with Riemann sums and integrals of form $\int_a^b g(x)dx,$ we define an integral by letting the width of the pieces of the curve shrink to zero by taking a limit. The result is the scalar line integral of f along $C.$

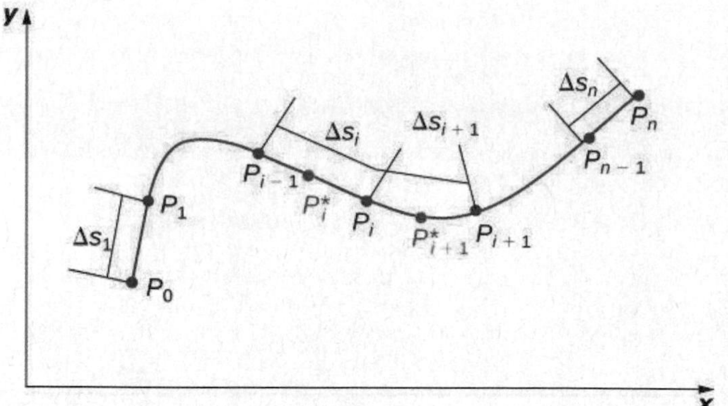

Figure 6.12 Curve C has been divided into n pieces, and a point inside each piece has been chosen.

You may have noticed a difference between this definition of a scalar line integral and a single-variable integral. In this definition, the arc lengths $\Delta s_1, \Delta s_2, \ldots, \Delta s_n$ aren't necessarily the same; in the definition of a single-variable integral, the curve in the x-axis is partitioned into pieces of equal length. This difference does not have any effect in the limit. As we shrink the arc lengths to zero, their values become close enough that any small difference becomes irrelevant.

Definition

Let f be a function with a domain that includes the smooth curve C that is parameterized by $\mathbf{r}(t) = \langle x(t), y(t), z(t) \rangle, \quad a \le t \le b.$ The **scalar line integral** of f along C is

$$\int_C f(x, y, z)ds = \lim_{n \to \infty} \sum_{i=1}^{n} f(P_i^*)\Delta s_i \tag{6.5}$$

if this limit exists (t_i^* and Δs_i are defined as in the previous paragraphs). If C is a planar curve, then C can be represented by the parametric equations $x = x(t),\ y = y(t),$ and $a \le t \le b.$ If C is smooth and $f(x, y)$ is a function of two variables, then the scalar line integral of f along C is defined similarly as

$$\int_C f(x, y)ds = \lim_{n \to \infty} \sum_{i=1}^{n} f(P_i^*)\Delta s_i,$$

if this limit exists.

If f is a continuous function on a smooth curve C, then $\int_C f ds$ always exists. Since $\int_C f ds$ is defined as a limit of Riemann sums, the continuity of f is enough to guarantee the existence of the limit, just as the integral $\int_a^b g(x)dx$ exists if g is continuous over $[a, b]$.

Before looking at how to compute a line integral, we need to examine the geometry captured by these integrals. Suppose that $f(x, y) \ge 0$ for all points (x, y) on a smooth planar curve C. Imagine taking curve C and projecting it "up" to the surface defined by $f(x, y),$ thereby creating a new curve C' that lies in the graph of $f(x, y)$ (**Figure 6.13**). Now we drop a "sheet" from C' down to the xy-plane. The area of this sheet is $\int_C f(x, y)ds.$ If $f(x, y) \le 0$ for some points in $C,$ then the value of $\int_C f(x, y)ds$ is the area above the xy-plane less the area below the xy-plane. (Note the similarity with integrals of the form $\int_a^b g(x)dx.$)

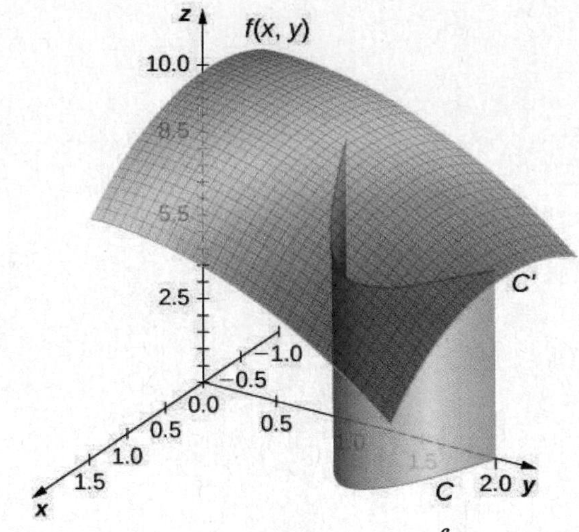

Figure 6.13 The area of the blue sheet is $\int_C f(x, y)ds$.

From this geometry, we can see that line integral $\int_C f(x, y)ds$ does not depend on the parameterization $\mathbf{r}(t)$ of C. As long as the curve is traversed exactly once by the parameterization, the area of the sheet formed by the function and the curve is the same. This same kind of geometric argument can be extended to show that the line integral of a three-variable function over a curve in space does not depend on the parameterization of the curve.

Example 6.14

Finding the Value of a Line Integral

Find the value of integral $\int_C 2ds$, where C is the upper half of the unit circle.

Solution

The integrand is $f(x, y) = 2$. **Figure 6.14** shows the graph of $f(x, y) = 2$, curve C, and the sheet formed by them. Notice that this sheet has the same area as a rectangle with width π and length 2. Therefore, $\int_C 2ds = 2\pi$.

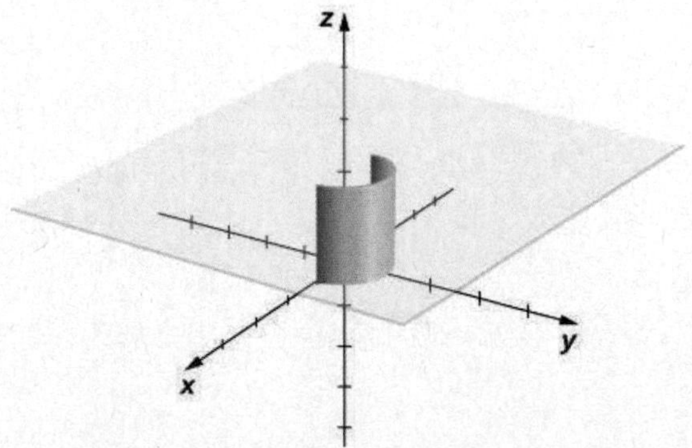

Figure 6.14 The sheet that is formed by the upper half of the unit circle in a plane and the graph of $f(x, y) = 2$.

To see that $\int_C 2ds = 2\pi$ using the definition of line integral, we let $\mathbf{r}(t)$ be a parameterization of C. Then, $f(\mathbf{r}(t_i)) = 2$ for any number t_i in the domain of $\mathbf{r}$. Therefore,

$$\begin{aligned}\int_C f\,ds &= \lim_{n \to \infty} \sum_{i=1}^{n} f(\mathbf{r}(t_i^*))\Delta s_i \\ &= \lim_{n \to \infty} \sum_{i=1}^{n} 2\Delta s_i \\ &= 2 \lim_{n \to \infty} \sum_{i=1}^{n} 2\Delta s_i \\ &= 2(\text{length of C}) \\ &= 2\pi.\end{aligned}$$

6.13 Find the value of $\int_C (x+y)ds$, where C is the curve parameterized by $x = t$, $y = t$, $0 \le t \le 1$.

Note that in a scalar line integral, the integration is done with respect to arc length s, which can make a scalar line integral difficult to calculate. To make the calculations easier, we can translate $\int_C f\,ds$ to an integral with a variable of integration that is t.

Let $\mathbf{r}(t) = \langle x(t), y(t), z(t) \rangle$ for $a \le t \le b$ be a parameterization of C. Since we are assuming that C is smooth, $\mathbf{r}'(t) = \langle x'(t), y'(t), z'(t) \rangle$ is continuous for all t in $[a, b]$. In particular, $x'(t), y'(t),$ and $z'(t)$ exist for all t in $[a, b]$. According to the arc length formula, we have

$$\text{length}(C_i) = \Delta s_i = \int_{t_{i-1}}^{t_i} \| \mathbf{r}'(t) \| \, dt.$$

If width $\Delta t_i = t_i - t_{i-1}$ is small, then function $\int_{t_{i-1}}^{t_i} \| \mathbf{r}'(t) \| \, dt \approx \| r'(t_i^*) \| \Delta t_i$, $\| \mathbf{r}'(t) \|$ is almost constant over the interval $[t_{i-1}, t_i]$. Therefore,

$$\int_{t_{i-1}}^{t_i} \| \mathbf{r}'(t) \| \, dt \approx \| \mathbf{r}'(t_i^*) \| \Delta t_i,$$

and we have

$$\sum_{i=1}^{n} f(\mathbf{r}(t_i^*))\Delta s_i = \sum_{i=1}^{n} f(\mathbf{r}(t_i^*)) \| \mathbf{r}'(t_i^*) \| \Delta t_i. \tag{6.6}$$

See **Figure 6.15**.

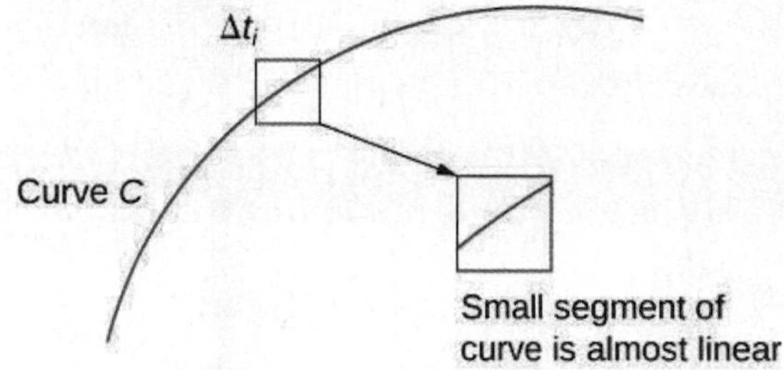

Figure 6.15 If we zoom in on the curve enough by making Δt_i very small, then the corresponding piece of the curve is approximately linear.

Note that

$$\lim_{n \to \infty} \sum_{i=1}^{n} f(\mathbf{r}(t_i^*)) \, \| \mathbf{r}'(t_i^*) \| \, \Delta t_i = \int_a^b f(\mathbf{r}(t)) \, \| \mathbf{r}'(t) \| \, dt.$$

In other words, as the widths of intervals $[t_{i-1}, t_i]$ shrink to zero, the sum $\sum_{i=1}^{n} f(\mathbf{r}(t_i^*)) \, \| \mathbf{r}'(t_i^*) \| \, \Delta t_i$ converges to the integral $\int_a^b f(\mathbf{r}(t)) \, \| \mathbf{r}'(t) \| \, dt$. Therefore, we have the following theorem.

Theorem 6.3: Evaluating a Scalar Line Integral

Let f be a continuous function with a domain that includes the smooth curve C with parameterization $\mathbf{r}(t)$, $a \le t \le b$. Then

$$\int_C f \, ds = \int_a^b f(\mathbf{r}(t)) \, \| \mathbf{r}'(t) \| \, dt. \tag{6.7}$$

Although we have labeled **Equation 6.6** as an equation, it is more accurately considered an approximation because we can show that the left-hand side of **Equation 6.6** approaches the right-hand side as $n \to \infty$. In other words, letting the widths of the pieces shrink to zero makes the right-hand sum arbitrarily close to the left-hand sum. Since

$$\| \mathbf{r}'(t) \| = \sqrt{(x'(t))^2 + (y'(t))^2 + (z'(t))^2},$$

we obtain the following theorem, which we use to compute scalar line integrals.

Theorem 6.4: Scalar Line Integral Calculation

Let f be a continuous function with a domain that includes the smooth curve C with parameterization $\mathbf{r}(t) = \langle x(t), y(t), z(t) \rangle$, $a \le t \le b$. Then

$$\int_C f(x, y, z) ds = \int_a^b f(\mathbf{r}(t)) \sqrt{(x'(t))^2 + (y'(t))^2 + (z'(t))^2} dt. \tag{6.8}$$

Similarly,

$$\int_C f(x, y) ds = \int_a^b f(\mathbf{r}(t)) \sqrt{(x'(t))^2 + (y'(t))^2} dt$$

if C is a planar curve and f is a function of two variables.

Note that a consequence of this theorem is the equation $ds = \| \mathbf{r}'(t) \| dt$. In other words, the change in arc length can be viewed as a change in the t domain, scaled by the magnitude of vector $\mathbf{r}'(t)$.

Example 6.15

Evaluating a Line Integral

Find the value of integral $\int_C (x^2 + y^2 + z) ds$, where C is part of the helix parameterized by $\mathbf{r}(t) = \langle \cos t, \sin t, t \rangle$, $0 \le t \le 2\pi$.

Solution

To compute a scalar line integral, we start by converting the variable of integration from arc length s to t. Then, we can use **Equation 6.8** to compute the integral with respect to t. Note that $f(\mathbf{r}(t)) = \cos^2 t + \sin^2 t + t = 1 + t$ and

$$\begin{aligned} \sqrt{(x'(t))^2 + (y'(t))^2 + (z'(t))^2} &= \sqrt{(-\sin(t))^2 + \cos^2(t) + 1} \\ &= \sqrt{2}. \end{aligned}$$

Therefore,

$$\int_C (x^2 + y^2 + z) ds = \int_0^{2\pi} (1 + t)\sqrt{2} dt.$$

Notice that **Equation 6.8** translated the original difficult line integral into a manageable single-variable integral. Since

$$\begin{aligned} \int_0^{2\pi} (1 + t)\sqrt{2} dt &= \left[\sqrt{2}t + \frac{\sqrt{2}t^2}{2} \right]_0^{2\pi} \\ &= 2\sqrt{2}\pi + 2\sqrt{2}\pi^2, \end{aligned}$$

we have

$$\int_C (x^2 + y^2 + z) ds = 2\sqrt{2}\pi + 2\sqrt{2}\pi^2.$$

 **6.14** Evaluate $\int_C (x^2 + y^2 + z) ds$, where C is the curve with parameterization $\mathbf{r}(t) = \langle \sin(3t), \cos(3t) \rangle$, $0 \le t \le \frac{\pi}{4}$.

Example 6.16

Independence of Parameterization

Find the value of integral $\int_C (x^2 + y^2 + z) ds$, where C is part of the helix parameterized by $\mathbf{r}(t) = \langle \cos(2t), \sin(2t), 2t \rangle$, $0 \le t \le \pi$. Notice that this function and curve are the same as in the previous example; the only difference is that the curve has been reparameterized so that time runs twice as fast.

Solution

As with the previous example, we use **Equation 6.8** to compute the integral with respect to t. Note that $f(\mathbf{r}(t)) = \cos^2(2t) + \sin^2(2t) + 2t = 2t + 1$ and

$$\begin{aligned}\sqrt{(x'(t))^2 + (y'(t))^2 + (z'(t))^2} &= \sqrt{(-\sin t + \cos t + 4)}\\ &= 2\sqrt{2}\end{aligned}$$

so we have

$$\begin{aligned}\int_C \left(x^2 + y^2 + z\right)ds &= 2\sqrt{2}\int_0^{\pi}(1 + 2t)dt\\ &= 2\sqrt{2}\left[t + t^2\right]_0^{\pi}\\ &= 2\sqrt{2}\left(\pi + \pi^2\right).\end{aligned}$$

Notice that this agrees with the answer in the previous example. Changing the parameterization did not change the value of the line integral. Scalar line integrals are independent of parameterization, as long as the curve is traversed exactly once by the parameterization.

6.15 Evaluate line integral $\int_C \left(x^2 + yz\right)ds$, where C is the line with parameterization $\mathbf{r}(t) = \langle 2t, 5t, -t \rangle, 0 \le t \le 10$. Reparameterize C with parameterization $\mathbf{s}(t) = \langle 4t, 10t, -2t \rangle, 0 \le t \le 5$, recalculate line integral $\int_C \left(x^2 + yz\right)ds$, and notice that the change of parameterization had no effect on the value of the integral.

Now that we can evaluate line integrals, we can use them to calculate arc length. If $f(x, y, z) = 1$, then

$$\begin{aligned}\int_C f(x, y, z)ds &= \lim_{n \to \infty}\sum_{i=1}^{n} f(t_i^*)\Delta s_i\\ &= \lim_{n \to \infty}\sum_{i=1}^{n}\Delta s_i\\ &= \lim_{n \to \infty}\text{length}(C)\\ &= \text{length}(C).\end{aligned}$$

Therefore, $\int_C 1ds$ is the arc length of C.

Example 6.17

Calculating Arc Length

A wire has a shape that can be modeled with the parameterization $\mathbf{r}(t) = \langle \cos t, \sin t, \sqrt{t} \rangle, 0 \le t \le 4\pi$. Find the length of the wire.

Solution

The length of the wire is given by $\int_C 1ds,$ where C is the curve with parameterization $\mathbf{r}$. Therefore,

$$\begin{aligned}\text{The length of the wire } &= \int_C 1ds \\ &= \int_0^{4\pi} \| \mathbf{r}'(t) \| \, dt \\ &= \int_0^{4\pi} \sqrt{(-\sin t)^2 + \cos^2 t + t}dt \\ &= \int_0^{4\pi} \sqrt{1 + t}dt \\ &= \left[\frac{2(1+t)^{3/2}}{3}\right]_0^{4\pi} \\ &= \frac{2}{3}\left((1+4\pi)^{3/2} - 1\right).\end{aligned}$$

6.16 Find the length of a wire with parameterization $\mathbf{r}(t) = \langle 3t + 1, 4 - 2t, 5 + 2t \rangle, 0 \le t \le 4.$

Vector Line Integrals

The second type of line integrals are vector line integrals, in which we integrate along a curve through a vector field. For example, let

$$\mathbf{F}(x, y, z) = P(x, y, z)\mathbf{i} + Q(x, y, z)\mathbf{j} + R(x, y, z)\mathbf{k}$$

be a continuous vector field in $\mathbb{R}^3$ that represents a force on a particle, and let C be a smooth curve in $\mathbb{R}^3$ contained in the domain of $\mathbf{F}$. How would we compute the work done by $\mathbf{F}$ in moving a particle along C?

To answer this question, first note that a particle could travel in two directions along a curve: a forward direction and a backward direction. The work done by the vector field depends on the direction in which the particle is moving. Therefore, we must specify a direction along curve C; such a specified direction is called an **orientation of a curve**. The specified direction is the *positive* direction along C; the opposite direction is the *negative* direction along C. When C has been given an orientation, C is called an *oriented curve* (**Figure 6.16**). The work done on the particle depends on the direction along the curve in which the particle is moving.

A **closed curve** is one for which there exists a parameterization $\mathbf{r}(t),\ \ a \le t \le b,$ such that $\mathbf{r}(a) = \mathbf{r}(b),$ and the curve is traversed exactly once. In other words, the parameterization is one-to-one on the domain (a, b).

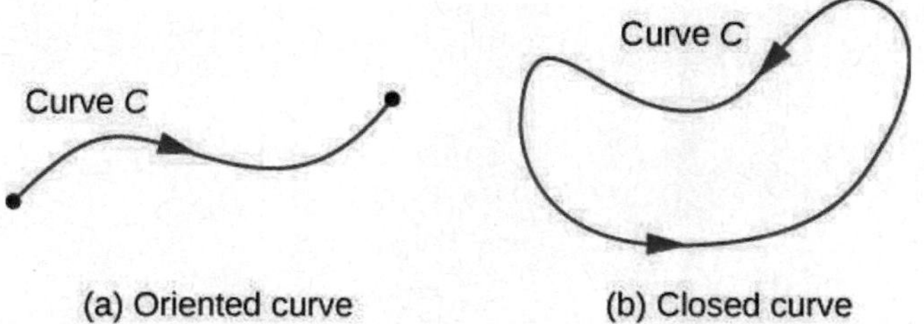

Figure 6.16 (a) An oriented curve between two points. (b) A closed oriented curve.

Let $\mathbf{r}(t)$ be a parameterization of C for $a \le t \le b$ such that the curve is traversed exactly once by the particle and the particle moves in the positive direction along C. Divide the parameter interval $[a, b]$ into n subintervals $[t_{i-1}, t_i]$, $0 \leq i \leq n$, of equal width. Denote the endpoints of $\mathbf{r}(t_0), \mathbf{r}(t_1), \ldots, \mathbf{r}(t_n)$ by $P_0, \ldots, P_n$. Points P_i divide C into n pieces. Denote the length of the piece from P_{i-1} to P_i by Δs_i. For each i, choose a value t_i^* in the subinterval $[t_{i-1}, t_i]$. Then, the endpoint of $\mathbf{r}(t_i^*)$ is a point in the piece of C between P_{i-1} and P_i (**Figure 6.17**). If Δs_i is small, then as the particle moves from P_{i-1} to P_i along C, it moves approximately in the direction of $\mathbf{T}(P_i)$, the unit tangent vector at the endpoint of $\mathbf{r}(t_i^*)$. Let P_i^* denote the endpoint of $\mathbf{r}(t_i^*)$. Then, the work done by the force vector field in moving the particle from P_{i-1} to P_i is $\mathbf{F}(P_i^*) \cdot (\Delta s_i \mathbf{T}(P_i^*))$, so the total work done along C is

$$\sum_{i=1}^{n} \mathbf{F}(P_i^*) \cdot (\Delta s_i \mathbf{T}(P_i^*)) = \sum_{i=1}^{n} \mathbf{F}(P_i^*) \cdot \mathbf{T}(P_i^*) \Delta s_i.$$

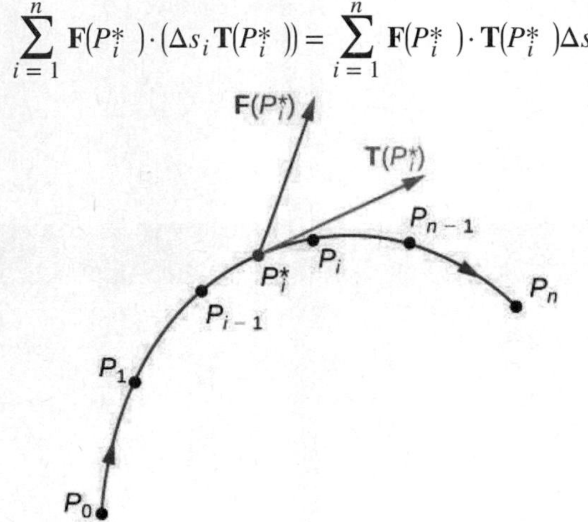

Figure 6.17 Curve C is divided into n pieces, and a point inside each piece is chosen. The dot product of any tangent vector in the ith piece with the corresponding vector $\mathbf{F}$ is approximated by $\mathbf{F}(P_i^*) \cdot \mathbf{T}(P_i^*)$.

Letting the arc length of the pieces of C get arbitrarily small by taking a limit as $n \to \infty$ gives us the work done by the field in moving the particle along C. Therefore, the work done by $\mathbf{F}$ in moving the particle in the positive direction along C is defined as

$$W = \int_C \mathbf{f} \cdot \leq \mathbf{T} ds,$$

which gives us the concept of a vector line integral.

Definition

The **vector line integral** of vector field $\mathbf{F}$ along oriented smooth curve C is

$$\int_C \mathbf{F} \cdot \mathbf{T} ds = \lim_{n \to \infty} \sum_{i=1}^{n} \mathbf{F}(P_i^*) \cdot \mathbf{T}(P_i^*) \Delta s_i$$

if that limit exists.

With scalar line integrals, neither the orientation nor the parameterization of the curve matters. As long as the curve is traversed exactly once by the parameterization, the value of the line integral is unchanged. With vector line integrals, the orientation of the curve does matter. If we think of the line integral as computing work, then this makes sense: if you hike up a mountain, then the gravitational force of Earth does negative work on you. If you walk down the mountain by the exact same path, then Earth's gravitational force does positive work on you. In other words, reversing the path changes the work value from negative to positive in this case. Note that if C is an oriented curve, then we let $-C$ represent the same curve but with opposite orientation.

As with scalar line integrals, it is easier to compute a vector line integral if we express it in terms of the parameterization function $\mathbf{r}$ and the variable t. To translate the integral $\int_C \mathbf{F} \cdot \mathbf{T} ds$ in terms of t, note that unit tangent vector $\mathbf{T}$ along C is given by $\mathbf{T} = \frac{\mathbf{r}'(t)}{\| \mathbf{r}'(t) \|}$ (assuming $\| \mathbf{r}'(t) \| \neq 0$). Since $ds = \| \mathbf{r}'(t) \| dt,$ as we saw when discussing scalar line integrals, we have

$$\mathbf{F} \cdot \mathbf{T} ds = \mathbf{F}(\mathbf{r}(t)) \cdot \frac{\mathbf{r}'(t)}{\| \mathbf{r}'(t) \|} \| \mathbf{r}'(t) \| dt = \mathbf{F}(\mathbf{r}(t)) \cdot \mathbf{r}'(t) dt.$$

Thus, we have the following formula for computing vector line integrals:

$$\int_C \mathbf{F} \cdot \mathbf{T} ds = \int_a^b \mathbf{F}(\mathbf{r}(t)) \cdot \mathbf{r}'(t) dt. \tag{6.9}$$

Because of **Equation 6.9**, we often use the notation $\int_C \mathbf{F} \cdot d\mathbf{r}$ for the line integral $\int_C \mathbf{F} \cdot \mathbf{T} ds.$

If $\mathbf{r}(t) = \langle x(t), y(t), z(t) \rangle,$ then $d\mathbf{r}$ denotes vector $\langle x'(t), y'(t), z'(t) \rangle.$

Example 6.18

Evaluating a Vector Line Integral

Find the value of integral $\int_C \mathbf{F} \cdot d\mathbf{r},$ where C is the semicircle parameterized by $\mathbf{r}(t) = \langle \cos t, \sin t \rangle,$ $0 \leq t \leq \pi$ and $\mathbf{F} = \langle -y, x \rangle.$

Solution

We can use **Equation 6.9** to convert the variable of integration from s to t. We then have

$$\mathbf{F}(\mathbf{r}(t)) = \langle -\sin t, \cos t \rangle \text{ and } \mathbf{r}'(t) = \langle -\sin t, \cos t \rangle.$$

Therefore,

$$\begin{aligned} \int_C \mathbf{F} \cdot d\mathbf{r} &= \int_0^\pi \langle -\sin t, \cos t \rangle \cdot \langle -\sin t, \cos t \rangle dt \\ &= \int_0^\pi \sin^2 t + \cos^2 t dt \\ &= \int_0^\pi 1 dt = \pi. \end{aligned}$$

See **Figure 6.18**.

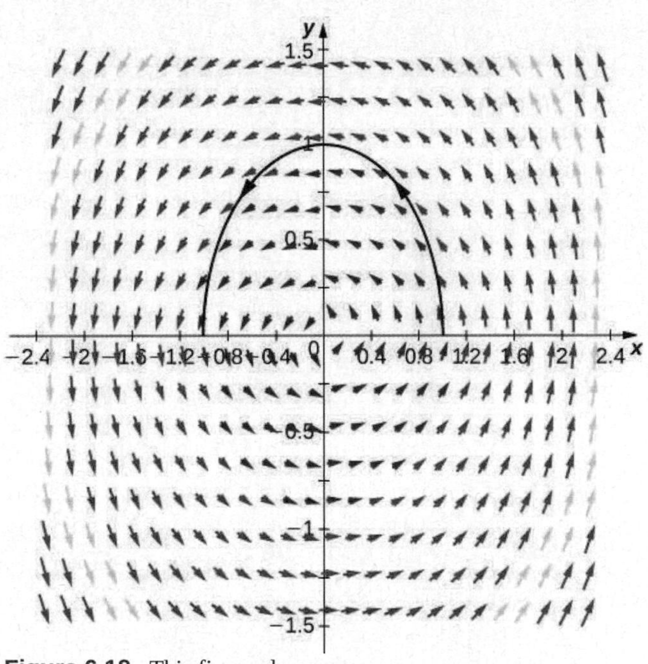

Figure 6.18 This figure shows curve $\mathbf{r}(t) = \langle \cos t, \sin t \rangle, 0 \le t \le \pi$ in vector field $\mathbf{F} = \langle -y, x \rangle$.

Example 6.19

Reversing Orientation

Find the value of integral $\int_C \mathbf{F} \cdot d\mathbf{r}$, where C is the semicircle parameterized by $\mathbf{r}(t) = \langle \cos t + \pi, \sin t \rangle, 0 \le t \le \pi$ and $\mathbf{F} = \langle -y, x \rangle$.

Solution

Notice that this is the same problem as **Example 6.18**, except the orientation of the curve has been traversed. In this example, the parameterization starts at $\mathbf{r}(0) = \langle \pi, 0 \rangle$ and ends at $\mathbf{r}(\pi) = \langle 0, 0 \rangle$. By **Equation 6.9**,

$$\begin{aligned}\int_C \mathbf{F} \cdot d\mathbf{r} &= \int_0^\pi \langle -\sin t, \cos t + \pi \rangle \cdot \langle -\sin t + \pi, \cos t \rangle \, dt \\ &= \int_0^\pi \langle -\sin t, -\cos t \rangle \cdot \langle \sin t, \cos t \rangle \, dt \\ &= \int_0^\pi \left(-\sin^2 t - \cos^2 t\right) dt \\ &= \int_0^\pi -1 dt \\ &= -\pi.\end{aligned}$$

Notice that this is the negative of the answer in **Example 6.18**. It makes sense that this answer is negative because the orientation of the curve goes against the "flow" of the vector field.

Let C be an oriented curve and let $-C$ denote the same curve but with the orientation reversed. Then, the previous two examples illustrate the following fact:

$$\int_{-C} \mathbf{F} \cdot d\mathbf{r} = -\int_{C} \mathbf{F} \cdot d\mathbf{r}.$$

That is, reversing the orientation of a curve changes the sign of a line integral.

6.17 Let $\mathbf{F} = x\mathbf{i} + y\mathbf{j}$ be a vector field and let C be the curve with parameterization $\langle t, t^2 \rangle$ for $0 \le t \le 2$. Which is greater: $\int_C \mathbf{F} \cdot \mathbf{T} ds$ or $\int_{-C} \mathbf{F} \cdot \mathbf{T} ds$?

Another standard notation for integral $\int_C \mathbf{F} \cdot d\mathbf{r}$ is $\int_C P dx + Q dy + R dz$. In this notation, P, Q, and R are functions, and we think of $d\mathbf{r}$ as vector $\langle dx, dy, dz \rangle$. To justify this convention, recall that $d\mathbf{r} = \mathbf{T} ds = \mathbf{r}'(t) dt = \langle \frac{dx}{dt}, \frac{dy}{dt}, \frac{dz}{dt} \rangle dt$. Therefore,

$$\mathbf{F} \cdot d\mathbf{r} = \langle P, Q, R \rangle \cdot \langle dx, dy, dz \rangle = P dx + Q dy + R dz.$$

If $d\mathbf{r} = \langle dx, dy, dz \rangle$, then $\frac{d\mathbf{r}}{dt} = \langle \frac{dx}{dt}, \frac{dy}{dt}, \frac{dz}{dt} \rangle$, which implies that $\frac{d\mathbf{r}}{dt} = \langle \frac{dx}{dt}, \frac{dy}{dt}, \frac{dz}{dt} \rangle dt$. Therefore

$$\begin{aligned} \int_C \mathbf{F} \cdot d\mathbf{r} &= \int_C P dx + Q dy + R dz \\ &= \int \left(P(\mathbf{r}(t)) \frac{dx}{dt} + Q(\mathbf{r}(t)) \frac{dy}{dt} + R(\mathbf{r}(t)) \frac{dz}{dt} \right) dt. \end{aligned} \quad \textbf{(6.10)}$$

Example 6.20

Finding the Value of an Integral of the Form $\int_C P dx + Q dy + R dz$

Find the value of integral $\int_C z dx + x dy + y dz,$ where C is the curve parameterized by $\mathbf{r}(t) = \langle t^2, \sqrt{t}, t \rangle, 1 \le t \le 4.$

Solution

As with our previous examples, to compute this line integral we should perform a change of variables to write everything in terms of t. In this case, **Equation 6.10** allows us to make this change:

$$\begin{aligned}\int_C zdx + xdy + ydz &= \int_1^4 \left(t(2t) + t^2\left(\frac{1}{2\sqrt{t}}\right) + \sqrt{t}\right)dt \\ &= \int_1^4 \left(2t^2 + \frac{t^{3/2}}{2} + \sqrt{t}\right)dt \\ &= \left[\frac{2t^3}{3} + \frac{t^{5/2}}{5} + \frac{2t^{3/2}}{3}\right]_{t=1}^{t=4} \\ &= \frac{793}{15}.\end{aligned}$$

6.18 Find the value of $\int_C 4xdx + zdy + 4y^2 dz,$ where C is the curve parameterized by $\mathbf{r}(t) = \langle 4\cos(2t), 2\sin(2t), 3\rangle, 0 \le t \le \frac{\pi}{4}.$

We have learned how to integrate smooth oriented curves. Now, suppose that C is an oriented curve that is not smooth, but can be written as the union of finitely many smooth curves. In this case, we say that C is a **piecewise smooth curve**. To be precise, curve C is piecewise smooth if C can be written as a union of n smooth curves $C_1, C_2,\ldots, C_n$ such that the endpoint of C_i is the starting point of C_{i+1} (**Figure 6.19**). When curves C_i satisfy the condition that the endpoint of C_i is the starting point of $C_{i+1},$ we write their union as $C_1 + C_2 + \cdots + C_n.$

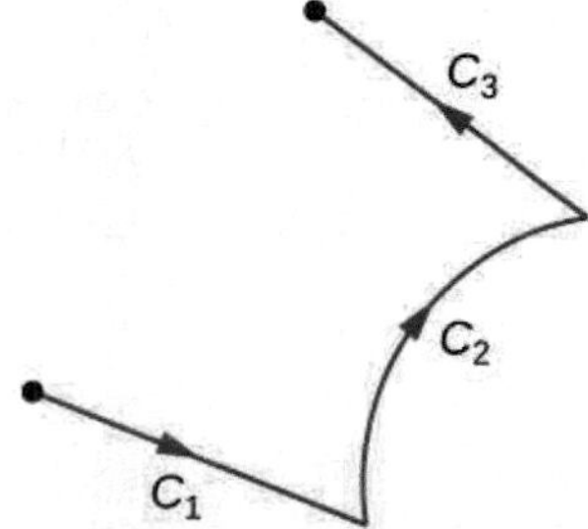

Figure 6.19 The union of C_1, C_2, C_3 is a piecewise smooth curve.

The next theorem summarizes several key properties of vector line integrals.

Theorem 6.5: Properties of Vector Line Integrals

Let **F** and **G** be continuous vector fields with domains that include the oriented smooth curve C. Then

i. $\int_C (\mathbf{F} + \mathbf{G}) \cdot d\mathbf{r} = \int_C \mathbf{F} \cdot d\mathbf{r} + \int_C \mathbf{G} \cdot d\mathbf{r}$

ii. $\int_C k\mathbf{F} \cdot d\mathbf{r} = k\int_C \mathbf{F} \cdot d\mathbf{r},$ where k is a constant

iii. $\int_{-C} \mathbf{F} \cdot d\mathbf{r} = -\int_C \mathbf{F} \cdot d\mathbf{r}$

iv. Suppose instead that C is a piecewise smooth curve in the domains of **F** and **G**, where $C = C_1 + C_2 + \cdots + C_n$ and $C_1, C_2,\ldots, C_n$ are smooth curves such that the endpoint of C_i is the starting point of C_{i+1}. Then

$$\int_C \mathbf{F} \cdot d\mathbf{s} = \int_{C_1} \mathbf{F} \cdot d\mathbf{s} + \int_{C_2} \mathbf{F} \cdot d\mathbf{s} + \cdots + \int_{C_n} \mathbf{F} \cdot d\mathbf{s}.$$

Notice the similarities between these items and the properties of single-variable integrals. Properties i. and ii. say that line integrals are linear, which is true of single-variable integrals as well. Property iii. says that reversing the orientation of a curve changes the sign of the integral. If we think of the integral as computing the work done on a particle traveling along C, then this makes sense. If the particle moves backward rather than forward, then the value of the work done has the opposite sign. This is analogous to the equation $\int_a^b f(x)dx = -\int_b^a f(x)dx$. Finally, if $[a_1, a_2], [a_2, a_3], \ldots, [a_{n-1}, a_n]$ are intervals, then

$$\int_{a_1}^{a_n} f(x)dx = \int_{a_1}^{a_2} f(x)dx + \int_{a_1}^{a_3} f(x)dx + \cdots + \int_{a_{n-1}}^{a_n} f(x)dx,$$

which is analogous to property iv.

Example 6.21

Using Properties to Compute a Vector Line Integral

Find the value of integral $\int_C \mathbf{F} \cdot \mathbf{T}ds,$ where C is the rectangle (oriented counterclockwise) in a plane with vertices $(0, 0), (2, 0), (2, 1),$ and $(0, 1),$ and where $\mathbf{F} = \langle x - 2y, y - x \rangle$ (**Figure 6.20**).

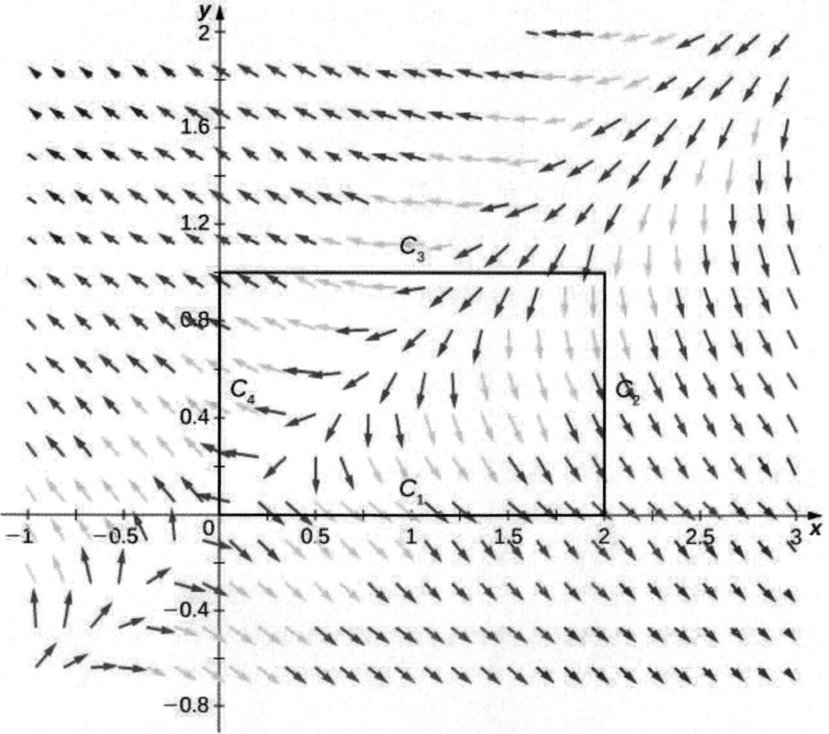

Figure 6.20 Rectangle and vector field for **Example 6.21**.

Solution

Note that curve C is the union of its four sides, and each side is smooth. Therefore C is piecewise smooth. Let C_1 represent the side from $(0, 0)$ to $(2, 0)$, let C_2 represent the side from $(2, 0)$ to $(2, 1)$, let C_3 represent the side from $(2, 1)$ to $(0, 1)$, and let C_4 represent the side from $(0, 1)$ to $(0, 0)$ (**Figure 6.20**). Then,

$$\int_C \mathbf{F} \cdot \mathbf{T}d\mathbf{r} = \int_{C_1} \mathbf{F} \cdot \mathbf{T}d\mathbf{r} + \int_{C_2} \mathbf{F} \cdot \mathbf{T}d\mathbf{r} + \int_{C_3} \mathbf{F} \cdot \mathbf{T}d\mathbf{r} + \int_{C_4} \mathbf{F} \cdot \mathbf{T}d\mathbf{r}.$$

We want to compute each of the four integrals on the right-hand side using **Equation 6.8**. Before doing this, we need a parameterization of each side of the rectangle. Here are four parameterizations (note that they traverse C counterclockwise):

$$\begin{aligned} C_1 &: \langle t, 0 \rangle, 0 \le t \le 2 \\ C_2 &: \langle 2, t \rangle, 0 \le t \le 1 \\ C_3 &: \langle 2 - t, 1 \rangle, 0 \le t \le 2 \\ C_4 &: \langle 0, 1 - t \rangle, 0 \le t \le 1. \end{aligned}$$

Therefore,

$$\begin{aligned} \int_{C_1} \mathbf{F} \cdot \mathbf{T}d\mathbf{r} &= \int_0^2 \mathbf{F}(\mathbf{r}(t)) \cdot \mathbf{r}'(t)dt \\ &= \int_0^2 \langle t - 2(0), 0 - t \rangle \cdot \langle 1, 0 \rangle \, dt = \int_0^1 tdt \\ &= \left[\frac{t^2}{2}\right]_0^2 = 2. \end{aligned}$$

Notice that the value of this integral is positive, which should not be surprising. As we move along curve C_1 from left to right, our movement flows in the general direction of the vector field itself. At any point along C_1, the tangent vector to the curve and the corresponding vector in the field form an angle that is less than 90°. Therefore, the tangent vector and the force vector have a positive dot product all along C_1, and the line integral will have positive value.

The calculations for the three other line integrals are done similarly:

$$\begin{aligned} \int_{C_2} \mathbf{F} \cdot d\mathbf{r} &= \int_0^1 \langle 2 - 2t, t - 2 \rangle \cdot \langle 0, 1 \rangle \, dt \\ &= \int_0^1 (t - 2)dt \\ &= \left[\frac{t^2}{2} - 2t\right]_0^1 = -\frac{3}{2}, \end{aligned}$$

$$\begin{aligned} \int_{C_3} \mathbf{F} \cdot \mathbf{T}ds &= \int_0^2 \langle (2 - t) - 2, 1 - (2 - t) \rangle \cdot \langle -1, 0 \rangle \, dt \\ &= \int_0^2 tdt = 2, \end{aligned}$$

and

$$\begin{aligned}\int_{C_4} \mathbf{F} \cdot d\mathbf{r} &= \int_0^1 \langle -2(1-t), 1-t \rangle \cdot \langle 0, -1 \rangle \, dt \\ &= \int_0^1 (t-1)dt \\ &= \left[\frac{t^2}{2} - t\right]_0^1 = -\frac{1}{2}.\end{aligned}$$

Thus, we have $\int_C \mathbf{F} \cdot d\mathbf{r} = 2.$

6.19 Calculate line integral $\int_C \mathbf{F} \cdot d\mathbf{r},$ where $\mathbf{F}$ is vector field $\langle y^2, 2xy + 1 \rangle$ and C is a triangle with vertices $(0, 0),$ $(4, 0),$ and $(0, 5),$ oriented counterclockwise.

Applications of Line Integrals

Scalar line integrals have many applications. They can be used to calculate the length or mass of a wire, the surface area of a sheet of a given height, or the electric potential of a charged wire given a linear charge density. Vector line integrals are extremely useful in physics. They can be used to calculate the work done on a particle as it moves through a force field, or the flow rate of a fluid across a curve. Here, we calculate the mass of a wire using a scalar line integral and the work done by a force using a vector line integral.

Suppose that a piece of wire is modeled by curve C in space. The mass per unit length (the linear density) of the wire is a continuous function $\rho(x, y, z).$ We can calculate the total mass of the wire using the scalar line integral $\int_C \rho(x, y, z)ds.$

The reason is that mass is density multiplied by length, and therefore the density of a small piece of the wire can be approximated by $\rho(x^*, y^*, z^*)\Delta s$ for some point (x^*, y^*, z^*) in the piece. Letting the length of the pieces shrink to zero with a limit yields the line integral $\int_C \rho(x, y, z)ds.$

Example 6.22

Calculating the Mass of a Wire

Calculate the mass of a spring in the shape of a curve parameterized by $\langle t, 2\cos t, 2\sin t \rangle,$ $0 \le t \le \frac{\pi}{2},$ with a density function given by $\rho(x, y, z) = e^x + yz$ kg/m (**Figure 6.21**).

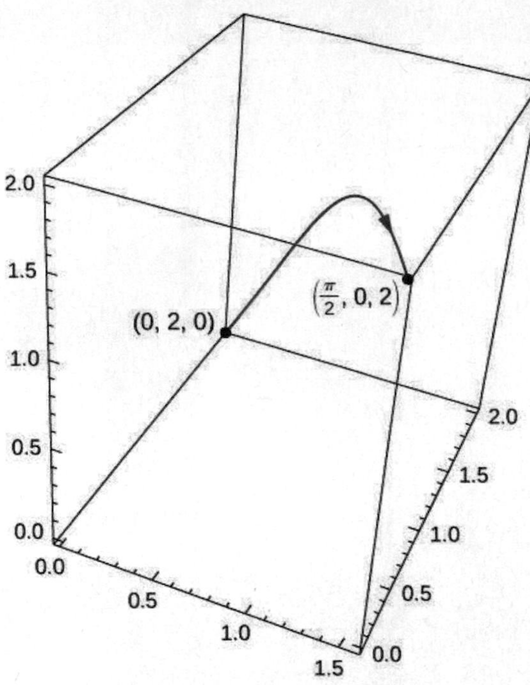

Figure 6.21 The wire from **Example 6.22**.

Solution

To calculate the mass of the spring, we must find the value of the scalar line integral $\int_C (e^x + yz)ds,$ where C is the given helix. To calculate this integral, we write it in terms of t using **Equation 6.8**:

$$\begin{aligned}\int_C e^x + yzds &= \int_0^{\pi/2} \left((e^t + 4\cos t\sin t)\sqrt{1 + (-2\cos t)^2 + (2\sin t)^2}\right)dt \\ &= \int_0^{\pi/2} \left((e^t + 4\cos t\sin t)\sqrt{5}\right)dt \\ &= \sqrt{5}\left[e^t + 2\sin^2 t\right]_{t=0}^{t=\pi/2} \\ &= \sqrt{5\left(e^{\pi/2} + 1\right)}.\end{aligned}$$

Therefore, the mass is $\sqrt{5}\left(e^{\pi/2} + 1\right)$ kg.

6.20 Calculate the mass of a spring in the shape of a helix parameterized by $\mathbf{r}(t) = \langle \cos t, \sin t, t \rangle, 0 \le t \le 6\pi,$ with a density function given by $\rho(x, y, z) = x + y + z$ kg/m.

When we first defined vector line integrals, we used the concept of work to motivate the definition. Therefore, it is not surprising that calculating the work done by a vector field representing a force is a standard use of vector line integrals. Recall that if an object moves along curve C in force field $\mathbf{F}$, then the work required to move the object is given by $\int_C \mathbf{F} \cdot d\mathbf{r}$.

Example 6.23

Calculating Work

How much work is required to move an object in vector force field $\mathbf{F} = \langle yz, xy, xz \rangle$ along path $\mathbf{r}(t) = \langle t^2, t, t^4 \rangle, \quad 0 \le t \le 1$? See **Figure 6.22**.

Solution

Let C denote the given path. We need to find the value of $\int_C \mathbf{F} \cdot d\mathbf{r}$. To do this, we use **Equation 6.9**:

$$\begin{aligned}\int_C \mathbf{F} \cdot d\mathbf{r} &= \int_0^1 \left(\langle t^5, t^3, t^6 \rangle \cdot \langle 2t, 1, 4t^3 \rangle \right) dt \\ &= \int_0^1 \left(2t^6 + t^3 + 4t^9 \right) dt \\ &= \left[\frac{2t^7}{7} + \frac{t^4}{4} + \frac{2t^{10}}{5} \right]_{t=0}^{t=1} = \frac{131}{140}.\end{aligned}$$

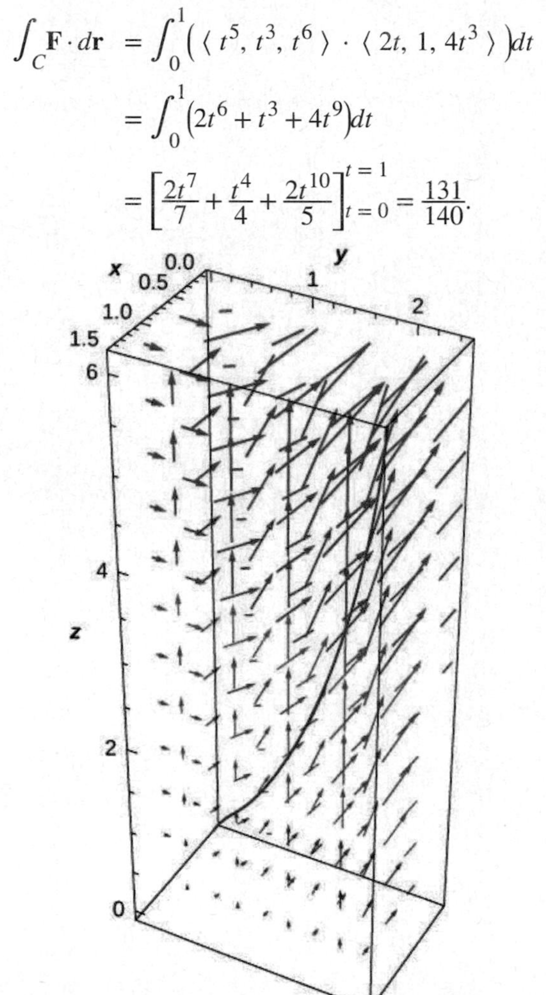

Figure 6.22 The curve and vector field for **Example 6.23**.

Flux and Circulation

We close this section by discussing two key concepts related to line integrals: flux across a plane curve and circulation along a plane curve. Flux is used in applications to calculate fluid flow across a curve, and the concept of circulation is important for characterizing conservative gradient fields in terms of line integrals. Both these concepts are used heavily throughout the rest of this chapter. The idea of flux is especially important for Green's theorem, and in higher dimensions for Stokes' theorem and the divergence theorem.

Let C be a plane curve and let $\mathbf{F}$ be a vector field in the plane. Imagine C is a membrane across which fluid flows, but C does not impede the flow of the fluid. In other words, C is an idealized membrane invisible to the fluid. Suppose $\mathbf{F}$ represents the velocity field of the fluid. How could we quantify the rate at which the fluid is crossing C?

Recall that the line integral of $\mathbf{F}$ along C is $\int_C \mathbf{F} \cdot \mathbf{T}ds$—in other words, the line integral is the dot product of the vector field with the unit tangential vector with respect to arc length. If we replace the unit tangential vector with unit normal vector $\mathbf{N}(t)$ and instead compute integral $\int_C \mathbf{F} \cdot \mathbf{N}ds,$ we determine the flux across C. To be precise, the definition of integral $\int_C \mathbf{F} \cdot \mathbf{N}ds$ is the same as integral $\int_C \mathbf{F} \cdot \mathbf{T}ds,$ except the $\mathbf{T}$ in the Riemann sum is replaced with $\mathbf{N}$. Therefore, the flux across C is defined as

$$\int_C \mathbf{F} \cdot \mathbf{N}ds = \lim_{n \to \infty} \sum_{i=1}^{n} \mathbf{F}(P_i^*) \cdot \mathbf{N}(P_i^*)\Delta s_i,$$

where P_i^* and Δs_i are defined as they were for integral $\int_C \mathbf{F} \cdot \mathbf{T}ds$. Therefore, a flux integral is an integral that is *perpendicular* to a vector line integral, because $\mathbf{N}$ and $\mathbf{T}$ are perpendicular vectors.

If $\mathbf{F}$ is a velocity field of a fluid and C is a curve that represents a membrane, then the flux of $\mathbf{F}$ across C is the quantity of fluid flowing across C per unit time, or the rate of flow.

More formally, let C be a plane curve parameterized by $\mathbf{r}(t) = \langle x(t), y(t) \rangle$, $a \le t \le b$. Let $\mathbf{n}(t) = \langle y'(t), -x'(t) \rangle$ be the vector that is normal to C at the endpoint of $\mathbf{r}(t)$ and points to the right as we traverse C in the positive direction (**Figure 6.23**). Then, $\mathbf{N}(t) = \frac{\mathbf{n}(t)}{\|\mathbf{n}(t)\|}$ is the unit normal vector to C at the endpoint of $\mathbf{r}(t)$ that points to the right as we traverse C.

Definition

The **flux** of $\mathbf{F}$ across C is line integral $\int_C \mathbf{F} \cdot \frac{\mathbf{n}(t)}{\|\mathbf{n}(t)\|}ds.$

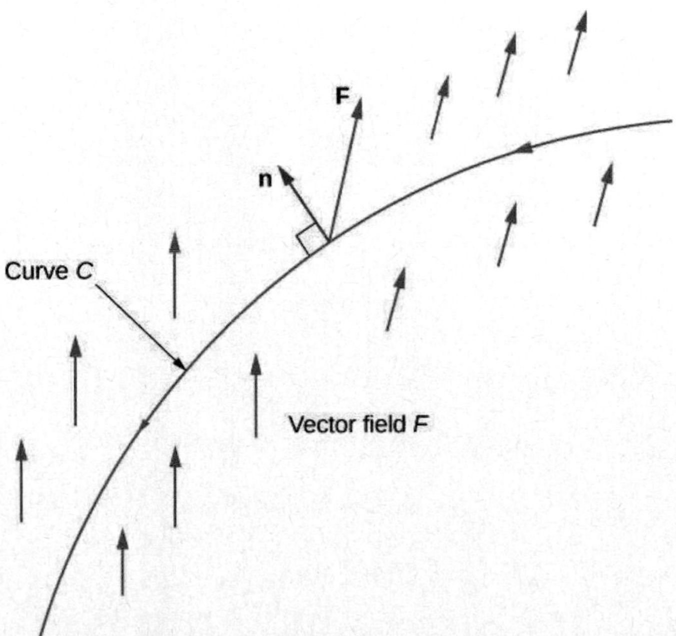

Figure 6.23 The flux of vector field $\mathbf{F}$ across curve C is computed by an integral similar to a vector line integral.

We now give a formula for calculating the flux across a curve. This formula is analogous to the formula used to calculate a vector line integral (see **Equation 6.9**).

Theorem 6.6: Calculating Flux across a Curve

Let $\mathbf{F}$ be a vector field and let C be a smooth curve with parameterization $\mathbf{r}(t) = \langle x(t), y(t) \rangle$, $a \le t \le b$. Let $\mathbf{n}(t) = \langle y'(t), -x'(t) \rangle$. The flux of $\mathbf{F}$ across C is

$$\int_C \mathbf{F} \cdot \mathbf{N} ds = \int_a^b \mathbf{F}(\mathbf{r}(t)) \cdot \mathbf{n}(t) dt \tag{6.11}$$

Proof

The proof of **Equation 6.11** is similar to the proof of **Equation 6.8**. Before deriving the formula, note that $\| \mathbf{n}(t) \| = \| \langle y'(t), -x'(t) \rangle \| = \sqrt{(y'(t))^2 + (x'(t))^2} = \| \mathbf{r}'(t) \|$. Therefore,

$$\begin{aligned} \int_C \mathbf{F} \cdot \mathbf{N} ds &= \int_C \mathbf{F} \cdot \frac{\mathbf{n}(t)}{\| \mathbf{n}(t) \|} ds \\ &= \int_a^b \mathbf{F} \cdot \frac{\mathbf{n}(t)}{\| \mathbf{n}(t) \|} \| \mathbf{r}'(t) \| dt \\ &= \int_a^b \mathbf{F}(\mathbf{r}(t)) \cdot \mathbf{n}(t) dt. \end{aligned}$$

□

Example 6.24

Flux across a Curve

Calculate the flux of $\mathbf{F} = \langle 2x, 2y \rangle$ across a unit circle oriented counterclockwise (**Figure 6.24**).

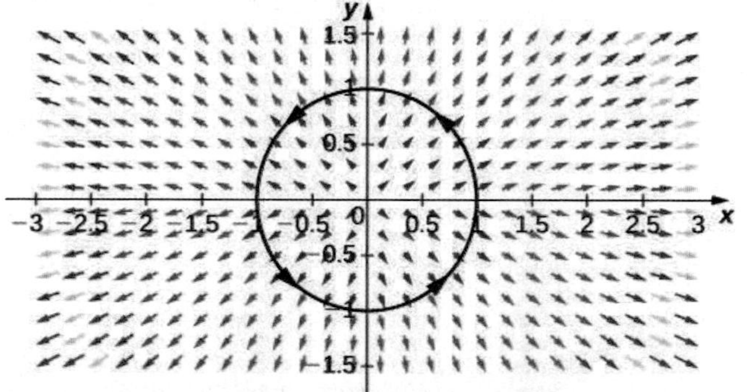

Figure 6.24 A unit circle in vector field $\mathbf{F} = \langle 2x, 2y \rangle$.

Solution

To compute the flux, we first need a parameterization of the unit circle. We can use the standard parameterization $\mathbf{r}(t) = \langle \cos t, \sin t \rangle$, $0 \le t \le 2\pi$. The normal vector to a unit circle is $\langle \cos t, \sin t \rangle$. Therefore, the flux is

$$\begin{aligned}\int_C \mathbf{F}\cdot\mathbf{N}ds &= \int_0^{2\pi} \langle 2\cos t, 2\sin t\rangle \cdot \langle \cos t, \sin t\rangle \, dt \\ &= \int_0^{2\pi} \left(2\cos^2 t + 2\sin^2 t\right) dt = 2\int_0^{2\pi} \left(\cos^2 t + \sin^2 t\right) dt \\ &= 2\int_0^{2\pi} dt = 4\pi.\end{aligned}$$

6.21 Calculate the flux of $\mathbf{F} = \langle x + y, 2y \rangle$ across the line segment from $(0, 0)$ to $(2, 3)$, where the curve is oriented from left to right.

Let $\mathbf{F}(x, y) = \langle P(x, y), Q(x, y) \rangle$ be a two-dimensional vector field. Recall that integral $\int_C \mathbf{F}\cdot\mathbf{T}ds$ is sometimes written as $\int_C Pdx + Qdy$. Analogously, flux $\int_C \mathbf{F}\cdot\mathbf{N}ds$ is sometimes written in the notation $\int_C -Qdx + Pdy$, because the unit normal vector **N** is perpendicular to the unit tangent **T**. Rotating the vector $d\mathbf{r} = \langle dx, dy \rangle$ by 90° results in vector $\langle dy, -dx \rangle$. Therefore, the line integral in **Example 6.21** can be written as $\int_C -2ydx + 2xdy$.

Now that we have defined flux, we can turn our attention to circulation. The line integral of vector field **F** along an oriented closed curve is called the **circulation** of **F** along *C*. Circulation line integrals have their own notation: $\oint_C \mathbf{F}\cdot\mathbf{T}ds$. The circle on the integral symbol denotes that *C* is "circular" in that it has no endpoints. **Example 6.18** shows a calculation of circulation.

To see where the term *circulation* comes from and what it measures, let **v** represent the velocity field of a fluid and let *C* be an oriented closed curve. At a particular point *P*, the closer the direction of $\mathbf{v}(P)$ is to the direction of $\mathbf{T}(P)$, the larger the value of the dot product $\mathbf{v}(P)\cdot\mathbf{T}(P)$. The maximum value of $\mathbf{v}(P)\cdot\mathbf{T}(P)$ occurs when the two vectors are pointing in the exact same direction; the minimum value of $\mathbf{v}(P)\cdot\mathbf{T}(P)$ occurs when the two vectors are pointing in opposite directions. Thus, the value of the circulation $\oint_C \mathbf{v}\cdot\mathbf{T}ds$ measures the tendency of the fluid to move in the direction of *C*.

Example 6.25

Calculating Circulation

Let $\mathbf{F} = \langle -y, x \rangle$ be the vector field from **Example 6.16** and let *C* represent the unit circle oriented counterclockwise. Calculate the circulation of **F** along *C*.

Solution

We use the standard parameterization of the unit circle: $\mathbf{r}(t) = \langle \cos t, \sin t \rangle, 0 \le t \le 2\pi$. Then, $\mathbf{F}(\mathbf{r}(t)) = \langle -\sin t, \cos t \rangle$ and $\mathbf{r}'(t) = \langle -\sin t, \cos t \rangle$. Therefore, the circulation of **F** along *C* is

$$\begin{aligned}\oint_C \mathbf{F}\cdot\mathbf{T}ds &= \int_0^{2\pi} \langle -\sin t, \cos t\rangle \cdot \langle -\sin t, \cos t\rangle\, dt \\ &= \int_0^{2\pi} \left(\sin^2 t + \cos^2 t\right) dt \\ &= \int_0^{2\pi} dt = 2\pi.\end{aligned}$$

Notice that the circulation is positive. The reason for this is that the orientation of C "flows" with the direction of $\mathbf{F}$. At any point along the circle, the tangent vector and the vector from $\mathbf{F}$ form an angle of less than 90°, and therefore the corresponding dot product is positive.

In **Example 6.25**, what if we had oriented the unit circle clockwise? We denote the unit circle oriented clockwise by $-C$. Then

$$\oint_{-C} \mathbf{F}\cdot\mathbf{T}ds = -\oint_C \mathbf{F}\cdot\mathbf{T}ds = -2\pi.$$

Notice that the circulation is negative in this case. The reason for this is that the orientation of the curve flows against the direction of $\mathbf{F}$.

6.22 Calculate the circulation of $\mathbf{F}(x, y) = \left\langle -\frac{y}{x^2+y^2}, \frac{x}{x^2+y^2} \right\rangle$ along a unit circle oriented counterclockwise.

Example 6.26

Calculating Work

Calculate the work done on a particle that traverses circle C of radius 2 centered at the origin, oriented counterclockwise, by field $\mathbf{F}(x, y) = \langle -2, y\rangle$. Assume the particle starts its movement at $(1, 0)$.

Solution

The work done by $\mathbf{F}$ on the particle is the circulation of $\mathbf{F}$ along C: $\oint_C \mathbf{F}\cdot\mathbf{T}ds$. We use the parameterization $\mathbf{r}(t) = \langle 2\cos t, 2\sin t\rangle, 0 \le t \le 2\pi$ for C. Then, $\mathbf{r}'(t) = \langle -2\sin t, 2\cos t\rangle$ and $\mathbf{F}(\mathbf{r}(t)) = \langle -2, 2\sin t\rangle$. Therefore, the circulation of $\mathbf{F}$ along C is

$$\begin{aligned}\oint_C \mathbf{F}\cdot\mathbf{T}ds &= \int_0^{2\pi} \langle -2, 2\sin t\rangle \cdot \langle -2\sin t, 2\cos t\rangle\, dt \\ &= \int_0^{2\pi} (4\sin t + 4\sin t\cos t)dt \\ &= \left[-4\cos t + 4\sin^2 t\right]_0^{2\pi} \\ &= \left(-4\cos(2\pi) + 2\sin^2(2\pi)\right) - \left(-4\cos(0) + 4\sin^2(0)\right) \\ &= -4 + 4 = 0.\end{aligned}$$

The force field does zero work on the particle.

Notice that the circulation of **F** along C is zero. Furthermore, notice that since **F** is the gradient of $f(x, y) = -2x + \frac{y^2}{2}$, **F** is conservative. We prove in a later section that under certain broad conditions, the circulation of a conservative vector field along a closed curve is zero.

6.23 Calculate the work done by field $\mathbf{F}(x, y) = \langle 2x, 3y \rangle$ on a particle that traverses the unit circle. Assume the particle begins its movement at $(-1, 0)$.

6.2 EXERCISES

39. *True or False?* Line integral $\int_C f(x, y)ds$ is equal to a definite integral if C is a smooth curve defined on $[a, b]$ and if function f is continuous on some region that contains curve C.

40. *True or False?* Vector functions $\mathbf{r}_1 = t\mathbf{i} + t^2\mathbf{j}$, $0 \le t \le 1$, and $\mathbf{r}_2 = (1-t)\mathbf{i} + (1-t)^2\mathbf{j}$, $0 \le t \le 1$, define the same oriented curve.

41. *True or False?* $\int_{-C}(Pdx + Qdy) = \int_C(Pdx - Qdy)$

42. *True or False?* A piecewise smooth curve C consists of a finite number of smooth curves that are joined together end to end.

43. *True or False?* If C is given by $x(t) = t, y(t) = t, 0 \le t \le 1$, then $\int_C xyds = \int_0^1 t^2 dt$.

For the following exercises, use a computer algebra system (CAS) to evaluate the line integrals over the indicated path.

44. **[T]** $\int_C (x + y)ds$ $C: x = t,\ y = (1-t), z = 0$ from $(0, 1, 0)$ to $(1, 0, 0)$

45. **[T]** $\int_C (x - y)ds$ $C: \mathbf{r}(t) = 4t\mathbf{i} + 3t\mathbf{j}$ when $0 \le t \le 2$

46. **[T]** $\int_C (x^2 + y^2 + z^2)ds$ $C: \mathbf{r}(t) = \sin t\mathbf{i} + \cos t\mathbf{j} + 8t\mathbf{k}$ when $0 \le t \le \frac{\pi}{2}$

47. **[T]** Evaluate $\int_C xy^4 ds$, where C is the right half of circle $x^2 + y^2 = 16$ and is traversed in the clockwise direction.

48. **[T]** Evaluate $\int_C 4x^3 ds$, where C is the line segment from $(-2, -1)$ to $(1, 2)$.

For the following exercises, find the work done.

49. Find the work done by vector field $\mathbf{F}(x, y, z) = x\mathbf{i} + 3xy\mathbf{j} - (x + z)\mathbf{k}$ on a particle moving along a line segment that goes from $(1, 4, 2)$ to $(0, 5, 1)$.

50. Find the work done by a person weighing 150 lb walking exactly one revolution up a circular, spiral staircase of radius 3 ft if the person rises 10 ft.

51. Find the work done by force field $\mathbf{F}(x, y, z) = -\frac{1}{2}x\mathbf{i} - \frac{1}{2}y\mathbf{j} + \frac{1}{4}\mathbf{k}$ on a particle as it moves along the helix $\mathbf{r}(t) = \cos t\mathbf{i} + \sin t\mathbf{j} + t\mathbf{k}$ from point $(1, 0, 0)$ to point $(-1, 0, 3\pi)$.

52. Find the work done by vector field $\mathbf{F}(x, y) = y\mathbf{i} + 2x\mathbf{j}$ in moving an object along path C, which joins points (1, 0) and (0, 1).

53. Find the work done by force $\mathbf{F}(x, y) = 2y\mathbf{i} + 3x\mathbf{j} + (x + y)\mathbf{k}$ in moving an object along curve $\mathbf{r}(t) = \cos(t)\mathbf{i} + \sin(t)\mathbf{j} + \frac{1}{6}\mathbf{k}$, where $0 \le t \le 2\pi$.

54. Find the mass of a wire in the shape of a circle of radius 2 centered at (3, 4) with linear mass density $\rho(x, y) = y^2$.

For the following exercises, evaluate the line integrals.

55. Evaluate $\int_C \mathbf{F} \cdot d\mathbf{r}$, where $\mathbf{F}(x, y) = -1\mathbf{j}$, and C is the part of the graph of $y = \frac{1}{2}x^3 - x$ from (2, 2) to (−2, −2).

56. Evaluate $\int_\gamma \left(x^2 + y^2 + z^2\right)^{-1} ds$, where γ is the helix $x = \cos t,\ y = \sin t,\ z = t(0 \le t \le T)$.

57. Evaluate $\int_C yzdx + xzdy + xydz$ over the line segment from $(1, 1, 1)$ to $(3, 2, 0)$.

58. Let C be the line segment from point (0, 1, 1) to point (2, 2, 3). Evaluate line integral $\int_C yds$.

59. **[T]** Use a computer algebra system to evaluate the line integral $\int_C y^2 dx + xdy$, where C is the arc of the parabola $x = 4 - y^2$ from (−5, −3) to (0, 2).

60. **[T]** Use a computer algebra system to evaluate the line integral $\int_C (x + 3y^2)dy$ over the path C given by $x = 2t, y = 10t,$ where $0 \le t \le 1.$

61. **[T]** Use a CAS to evaluate line integral $\int_C xydx + ydy$ over path C given by $x = 2t, y = 10t,$ where $0 \le t \le 1.$

62. Evaluate line integral $\int_C (2x - y)dx + (x + 3y)dy,$ where C lies along the x-axis from $x = 0$ to $x = 5.$

63. **[T]** Use a CAS to evaluate $\int_C \frac{y}{2x^2 - y^2}ds,$ where C is $x = t, y = t, 1 \le t \le 5.$

64. **[T]** Use a CAS to evaluate $\int_C xyds,$ where C is $x = t^2, y = 4t, 0 \le t \le 1.$

In the following exercises, find the work done by force field **F** on an object moving along the indicated path.

65. $\mathbf{F}(x, y) = -x\mathbf{i} - 2y\mathbf{j}$

$C: y = x^3$ from $(0, 0)$ to $(2, 8)$

66. $\mathbf{F}(x, y) = 2xi + y\mathbf{j}$ C: counterclockwise around the triangle with vertices (0, 0), (1, 0), and (1, 1)

67. $\mathbf{F}(x, y, z) = x\mathbf{i} + y\mathbf{j} - 5z\mathbf{k}$

$C: \mathbf{r}(t) = 2\cos t\mathbf{i} + 2\sin t\mathbf{j} + t\mathbf{k}, 0 \le t \le 2\pi$

68. Let **F** be vector field $\mathbf{F}(x, y) = (y^2 + 2xe^y + 1)\mathbf{i} + (2xy + x^2e^y + 2y)\mathbf{j}.$ Compute the work of integral $\int_C \mathbf{F} \cdot d\mathbf{r},$ where C is the path $\mathbf{r}(t) = \sin t\mathbf{i} + \cos t\mathbf{j}, 0 \le t \le \frac{\pi}{2}.$

69. Compute the work done by force $\mathbf{F}(x, y, z) = 2x\mathbf{i} + 3y\mathbf{j} - z\mathbf{k}$ along path $\mathbf{r}(t) = t\mathbf{i} + t^2\mathbf{j} + t^3\mathbf{k},$ where $0 \le t \le 1.$

70. Evaluate $\int_C \mathbf{F} \cdot d\mathbf{r},$ where $\mathbf{F}(x, y) = \frac{1}{x + y}\mathbf{i} + \frac{1}{x + y}\mathbf{j}$ and C is the segment of the unit circle going counterclockwise from $(1, 0)$ to $(0, 1).$

71. Force $\mathbf{F}(x, y, z) = zy\mathbf{i} + x\mathbf{j} + z^2x\mathbf{k}$ acts on a particle that travels from the origin to point (1, 2, 3). Calculate the work done if the particle travels:

a. along the path $(0, 0, 0) \to (1, 0, 0) \to (1, 2, 0) \to (1, 2, 3)$ along straight-line segments joining each pair of endpoints;

b. along the straight line joining the initial and final points.

c. Is the work the same along the two paths?

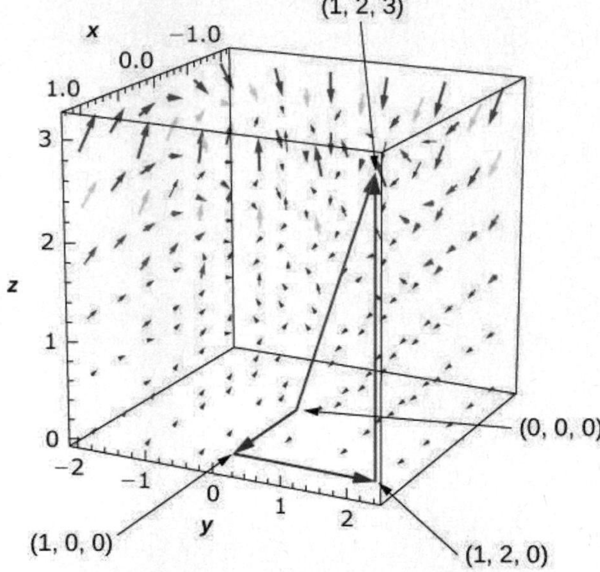

72. Find the work done by vector field $\mathbf{F}(x, y, z) = x\mathbf{i} + 3xy\mathbf{j} - (x + z)\mathbf{k}$ on a particle moving along a line segment that goes from (1, 4, 2) to (0, 5, 1).

73. How much work is required to move an object in vector field $\mathbf{F}(x, y) = y\mathbf{i} + 3x\mathbf{j}$ along the upper part of ellipse $\frac{x^2}{4} + y^2 = 1$ from (2, 0) to $(-2, 0)$?

74. A vector field is given by $\mathbf{F}(x, y) = (2x + 3y)\mathbf{i} + (3x + 2y)\mathbf{j}.$ Evaluate the line integral of the field around a circle of unit radius traversed in a clockwise fashion.

75. Evaluate the line integral of scalar function xy along parabolic path $y = x^2$ connecting the origin to point (1, 1).

76. Find $\int_C y^2 dx + (xy - x^2)dy$ along C: $y = 3x$ from (0, 0) to (1, 3).

77. Find $\int_C y^2 dx + (xy - x^2)dy$ along C: $y^2 = 9x$ from (0, 0) to (1, 3).

For the following exercises, use a CAS to evaluate the

given line integrals.

78. **[T]** Evaluate $\mathbf{F}(x, y, z) = x^2 z\mathbf{i} + 6y\mathbf{j} + yz^2\mathbf{k}$, where C is represented by $\mathbf{r}(t) = t\mathbf{i} + t^2\mathbf{j} + \ln t\mathbf{k}, 1 \le t \le 3$.

79. **[T]** Evaluate line integral $\int_\gamma xe^y\, ds$ where, γ is the arc of curve $x = e^y$ from $(1, 0)$ to $(e, 1)$.

80. **[T]** Evaluate the integral $\int_\gamma xy^2\, ds$, where γ is a triangle with vertices (0, 1, 2), (1, 0, 3), and $(0, -1, 0)$.

81. **[T]** Evaluate line integral $\int_\gamma \left(y^2 - xy\right)dx$, where γ is curve $y = \ln x$ from (1, 0) toward $(e, 1)$.

82. **[T]** Evaluate line integral $\int_\gamma xy^4\, ds$, where γ is the right half of circle $x^2 + y^2 = 16$.

83. **[T]** Evaluate $\int_C \mathbf{F} \cdot d\mathbf{r}$, where $\mathbf{F}(x, y, z) = x^2 y\mathbf{i} + (x - z)\mathbf{j} + xyz\mathbf{k}$ and C: $\mathbf{r}(t) = t\mathbf{i} + t^2\mathbf{j} + 2\mathbf{k}, 0 \le t \le 1$.

84. Evaluate $\int_C \mathbf{F} \cdot d\mathbf{r}$, where $\mathbf{F}(x, y) = 2x\sin(y)\mathbf{i} + \left(x^2\cos(y) - 3y^2\right)\mathbf{j}$ and C is any path from $(-1, 0)$ to $(5, 1)$.

85. Find the line integral of $\mathbf{F}(x, y, z) = 12x^2\mathbf{i} - 5xy\mathbf{j} + xz\mathbf{k}$ over path C defined by $y = x^2$, $z = x^3$ from point (0, 0, 0) to point (2, 4, 8).

86. Find the line integral of $\int_C \left(1 + x^2 y\right)ds$, where C is ellipse $\mathbf{r}(t) = 2\cos t\mathbf{i} + 3\sin t\mathbf{j}$ from $0 \le t \le \pi$.

For the following exercises, find the flux.

87. Compute the flux of $\mathbf{F} = x^2\mathbf{i} + y\mathbf{j}$ across a line segment from (0, 0) to (1, 2).

88. Let $\mathbf{F} = 5\mathbf{i}$ and let C be curve $y = 0, 0 \le x \le 4$. Find the flux across C.

89. Let $\mathbf{F} = 5\mathbf{j}$ and let C be curve $y = 0, 0 \le x \le 4$. Find the flux across C.

90. Let $\mathbf{F} = -y\mathbf{i} + x\mathbf{j}$ and let C: $\mathbf{r}(t) = \cos t\mathbf{i} + \sin t\mathbf{j}$ $(0 \le t \le 2\pi)$. Calculate the flux across C.

91. Let $\mathbf{F} = \left(x^2 + y^3\right)\mathbf{i} + (2xy)\mathbf{j}$. Calculate flux $\mathbf{F}$ orientated counterclockwise across curve C: $x^2 + y^2 = 9$.

92. Find the line integral of $\int_C z^2\, dx + y dy + 2y dz$, where C consists of two parts: C_1 and C_2. C_1 is the intersection of cylinder $x^2 + y^2 = 16$ and plane $z = 3$ from (0, 4, 3) to $(-4, 0, 3)$. C_2 is a line segment from $(-4, 0, 3)$ to (0, 1, 5).

93. A spring is made of a thin wire twisted into the shape of a circular helix $x = 2\cos t, y = 2\sin t, z = t$. Find the mass of two turns of the spring if the wire has constant mass density.

94. A thin wire is bent into the shape of a semicircle of radius a. If the linear mass density at point P is directly proportional to its distance from the line through the endpoints, find the mass of the wire.

95. An object moves in force field $\mathbf{F}(x, y, z) = y^2\mathbf{i} + 2(x + 1)y\mathbf{j}$ counterclockwise from point (2, 0) along elliptical path $x^2 + 4y^2 = 4$ to $(-2, 0)$, and back to point (2, 0) along the x-axis. How much work is done by the force field on the object?

96. Find the work done when an object moves in force field $\mathbf{F}(x, y, z) = 2x\mathbf{i} - (x + z)\mathbf{j} + (y - x)\mathbf{k}$ along the path given by $\mathbf{r}(t) = t^2\mathbf{i} + \left(t^2 - t\right)\mathbf{j} + 3\mathbf{k}$, $0 \le t \le 1$.

97. If an inverse force field $\mathbf{F}$ is given by $\mathbf{F}(x, y, z) = \dfrac{\mathbf{k}}{\| \mathbf{r} \|^3}\mathbf{r}$, where k is a constant, find the work done by $\mathbf{F}$ as its point of application moves along the x-axis from $A(1, 0, 0)$ to $B(2, 0, 0)$.

98. David and Sandra plan to evaluate line integral $\int_C \mathbf{F} \cdot d\mathbf{r}$ along a path in the xy-plane from (0, 0) to (1, 1). The force field is $\mathbf{F}(x, y) = (x + 2y)\mathbf{i} + (-x + y^2)\mathbf{j}$. David chooses the path that runs along the x-axis from (0, 0) to (1, 0) and then runs along the vertical line $x = 1$ from (1, 0) to the final point (1, 1). Sandra chooses the direct path along the diagonal line $y = x$ from (0, 0) to (1, 1). Whose line integral is larger and by how much?

6.3 | Conservative Vector Fields

Learning Objectives

6.3.1 Describe simple and closed curves; define connected and simply connected regions.
6.3.2 Explain how to find a potential function for a conservative vector field.
6.3.3 Use the Fundamental Theorem for Line Integrals to evaluate a line integral in a vector field.
6.3.4 Explain how to test a vector field to determine whether it is conservative.

In this section, we continue the study of conservative vector fields. We examine the Fundamental Theorem for Line Integrals, which is a useful generalization of the Fundamental Theorem of Calculus to line integrals of conservative vector fields. We also discover show how to test whether a given vector field is conservative, and determine how to build a potential function for a vector field known to be conservative.

Curves and Regions

Before continuing our study of conservative vector fields, we need some geometric definitions. The theorems in the subsequent sections all rely on integrating over certain kinds of curves and regions, so we develop the definitions of those curves and regions here.

We first define two special kinds of curves: closed curves and simple curves. As we have learned, a closed curve is one that begins and ends at the same point. A simple curve is one that does not cross itself. A curve that is both closed and simple is a simple closed curve (**Figure 6.25**).

Definition

Curve C is a **closed curve** if there is a parameterization $\mathbf{r}(t),\ a \le t \le b$ of C such that the parameterization traverses the curve exactly once and $\mathbf{r}(a) = \mathbf{r}(b)$. Curve C is a **simple curve** if C does not cross itself. That is, C is simple if there exists a parameterization $\mathbf{r}(t),\ a \le t \le b$ of C such that $\mathbf{r}$ is one-to-one over (a, b). It is possible for $\mathbf{r}(a) = \mathbf{r}(b)$, meaning that the simple curve is also closed.

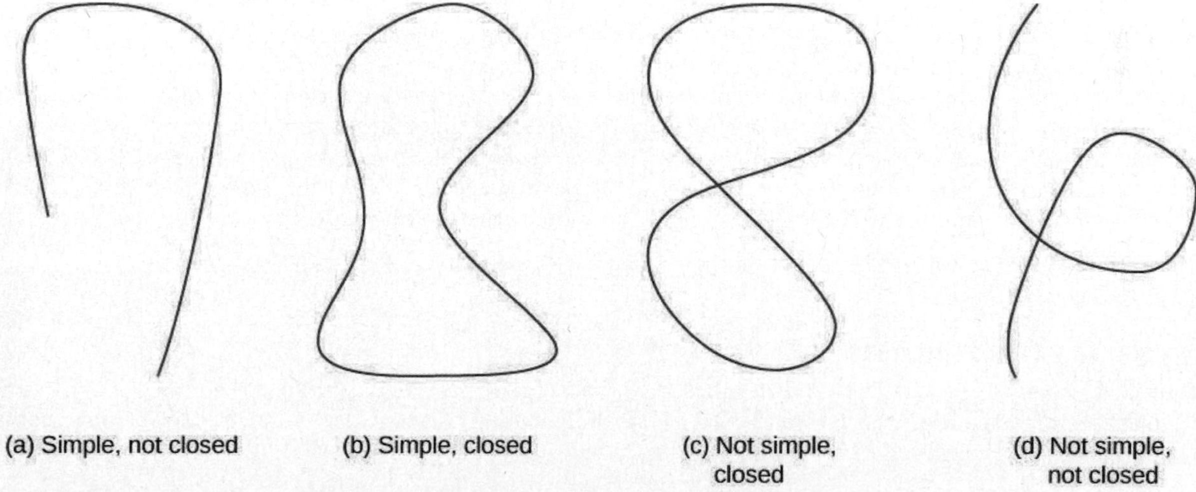

Figure 6.25 Types of curves that are simple or not simple and closed or not closed.

Example 6.27

Determining Whether a Curve Is Simple and Closed

Is the curve with parameterization $\mathbf{r}(t) = \langle \cos t, \frac{\sin(2t)}{2} \rangle, \ 0 \leq t \leq 2\pi$ a simple closed curve?

Solution

Note that $\mathbf{r}(0) = \langle 1, 0 \rangle = \mathbf{r}(2\pi)$; therefore, the curve is closed. The curve is not simple, however. To see this, note that $\mathbf{r}\left(\frac{\pi}{2}\right) = \langle 0, 0 \rangle = \mathbf{r}\left(\frac{3\pi}{2}\right)$, and therefore the curve crosses itself at the origin (**Figure 6.26**).

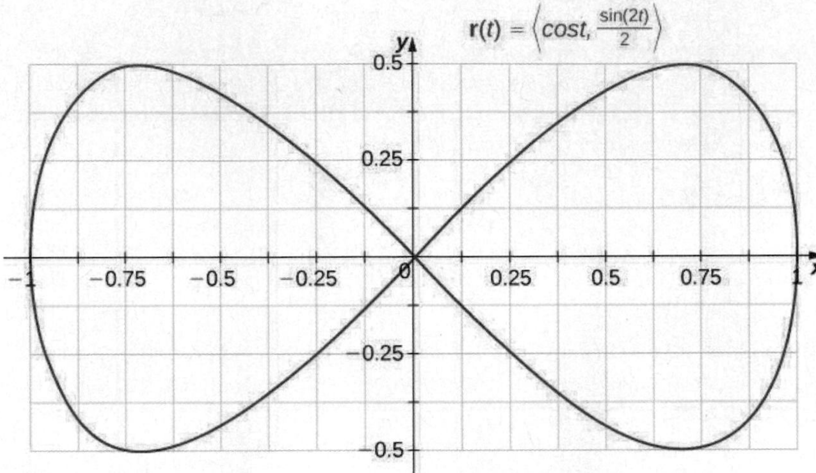

Figure 6.26 A curve that is closed but not simple.

6.24 Is the curve given by parameterization $\mathbf{r}(t) = \langle 2\cos t, 3\sin t \rangle, \ 0 \leq t \leq 6\pi,$ a simple closed curve?

Many of the theorems in this chapter relate an integral over a region to an integral over the boundary of the region, where the region's boundary is a simple closed curve or a union of simple closed curves. To develop these theorems, we need two geometric definitions for regions: that of a connected region and that of a simply connected region. A connected region is one in which there is a path in the region that connects any two points that lie within that region. A simply connected region is a connected region that does not have any holes in it. These two notions, along with the notion of a simple closed curve, allow us to state several generalizations of the Fundamental Theorem of Calculus later in the chapter. These two definitions are valid for regions in any number of dimensions, but we are only concerned with regions in two or three dimensions.

Definition

A region D is a **connected region** if, for any two points P_1 and $P_2,$ there is a path from P_1 to P_2 with a trace contained entirely inside D. A region D is a **simply connected region** if D is connected for any simple closed curve C that lies inside D, and curve C can be shrunk continuously to a point while staying entirely inside D. In two dimensions, a region is simply connected if it is connected and has no holes.

All simply connected regions are connected, but not all connected regions are simply connected (**Figure 6.27**).

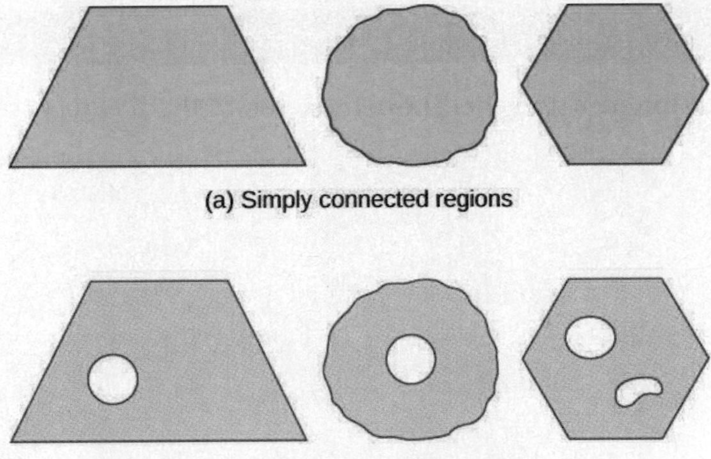

(b) Connected regions that are not simply connected

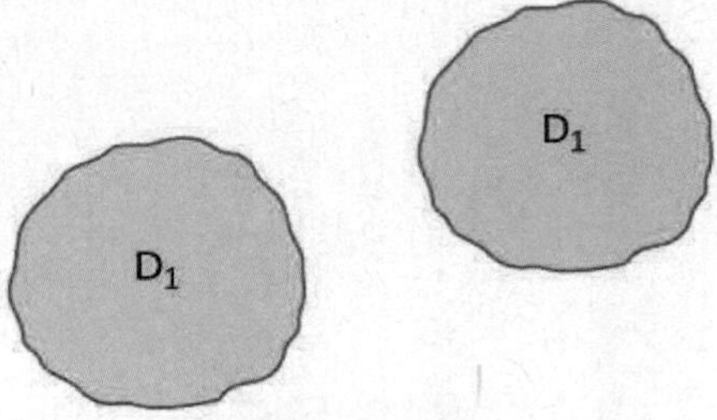

(c) A region that is not connected

Figure 6.27 Not all connected regions are simply connected. (a) Simply connected regions have no holes. (b) Connected regions that are not simply connected may have holes but you can still find a path in the region between any two points. (c) A region that is not connected has some points that cannot be connected by a path in the region.

6.25 Is the region in the below image connected? Is the region simply connected?

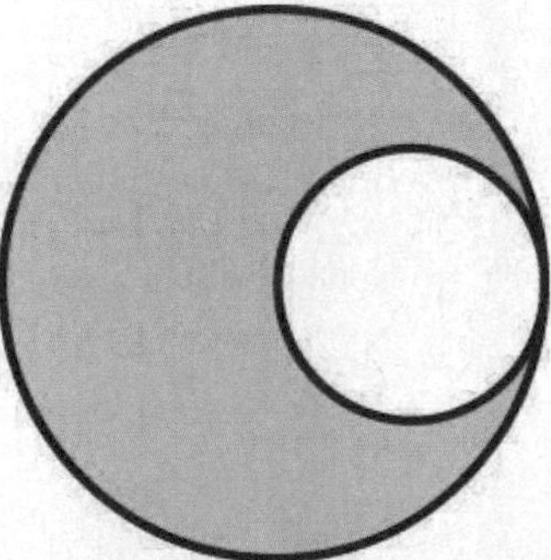

Fundamental Theorem for Line Integrals

Now that we understand some basic curves and regions, let's generalize the Fundamental Theorem of Calculus to line integrals. Recall that the Fundamental Theorem of Calculus says that if a function f has an antiderivative F, then the integral of f from a to b depends only on the values of F at a and at b—that is,

$$\int_a^b f(x)dx = \mathrm{F}(b) - \mathrm{F}(a).$$

If we think of the gradient as a derivative, then the same theorem holds for vector line integrals. We show how this works using a motivational example.

Example 6.28

Evaluating a Line Integral and the Antiderivatives of the Endpoints

Let $\mathbf{F}(x, y) = \langle 2x, 4y \rangle$. Calculate $\int_C \mathbf{F} \cdot d\mathbf{r}$, where C is the line segment from (0,0) to (2,2)(**Figure 6.28**).

Solution

We use **Equation 6.9** to calculate $\int_C \mathbf{F} \cdot d\mathbf{r}$. Curve C can be parameterized by $\mathbf{r}(t) = \langle 2t, 2t \rangle, 0 \le t \le 1$. Then, $\mathbf{F}(\mathbf{r}(t)) = \langle 4t, 8t \rangle$ and $\mathbf{r}'(t) = \langle 2, 2 \rangle$, which implies that

$$\begin{aligned}\int_C \mathbf{F} \cdot d\mathbf{r} &= \int_0^1 \langle 4t, 8t \rangle \cdot \langle 2, 2 \rangle \, dt \\ &= \int_0^1 (8t + 16t)dt = \int_0^1 24t \, dt \\ &= \left[12t^2\right]_0^1 = 12.\end{aligned}$$

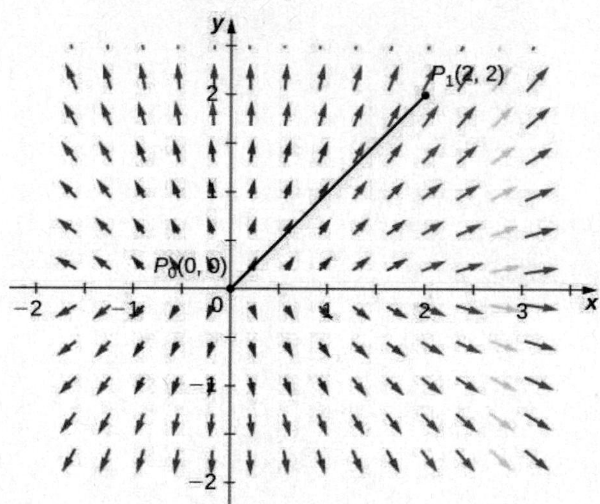

Figure 6.28 The value of line integral $\int_C \mathbf{F} \cdot d\mathbf{r}$ depends only on the value of the potential function of **F** at the endpoints of the curve.

Notice that $F = \nabla f$, where $f(x, y) = x^2 + 2y^2$. If we think of the gradient as a derivative, then f is an "antiderivative" of **F**. In the case of single-variable integrals, the integral of derivative $g'(x)$ is $g(b) - g(a)$, where a is the start point of the interval of integration and b is the endpoint. If vector line integrals work like single-variable integrals, then we would expect integral **F** to be $f(P_1) - f(P_0)$, where P_1 is the endpoint of the curve of integration and P_0 is the start point. Notice that this is the case for this example:

$$\int_C \mathbf{F} \cdot d\mathbf{r} = \int_C \nabla f \cdot d\mathbf{r} = 12$$

and

$$f(2, 2) - f(0, 0) = 4 + 8 - 0 = 12.$$

In other words, the integral of a “derivative” can be calculated by evaluating an “antiderivative” at the endpoints of the curve and subtracting, just as for single-variable integrals.

The following theorem says that, under certain conditions, what happened in the previous example holds for any gradient field. The same theorem holds for vector line integrals, which we call the **Fundamental Theorem for Line Integrals.**

Theorem 6.7: The Fundamental Theorem for Line Integrals

Let C be a piecewise smooth curve with parameterization $\mathbf{r}(t)$, $a \le t \le b$. Let f be a function of two or three variables with first-order partial derivatives that exist and are continuous on C. Then,

$$\int_C \nabla f \bullet d\mathbf{r} = f(\mathbf{r}(b)) - f(\mathbf{r}(a)). \tag{6.12}$$

Proof

By **Equation 6.9**,

$$\int_C \nabla f \bullet d\mathbf{r} = \int_a^b \nabla f(\mathbf{r}(t)) \bullet \mathbf{r}'(t)dt.$$

By the chain rule,

$$\frac{d}{dt}(f(\mathbf{r}(t)) = \nabla f(\mathbf{r}(t)) \bullet \mathbf{r}'(t).$$

Therefore, by the Fundamental Theorem of Calculus,

$$\begin{aligned}\int_C \nabla f \bullet d\mathbf{r} &= \int_a^b \nabla f(\mathbf{r}(t)) \bullet \mathbf{r}'(t)dt \\ &= \int_a^b \frac{d}{dt}(f(\mathbf{r}(t))dt \\ &= [f(\mathbf{r}(t))]_{t=a}^{t=b} \\ &= f(\mathbf{r}(b)) - f(\mathbf{r}(a)).\end{aligned}$$

□

We know that if $\mathbf{F}$ is a conservative vector field, there are potential functions f such that $\nabla f = \mathbf{F}$. Therefore $\int_C \mathbf{F} \cdot d\mathbf{r} = \int_C \nabla f \cdot d\mathbf{r} = f(\mathbf{r}(b)) - f(\mathbf{r}(a))$. In other words, just as with the Fundamental Theorem of Calculus, computing the line integral $\int_C \mathbf{F} \cdot d\mathbf{r}$, where $\mathbf{F}$ is conservative, is a two-step process: (1) find a potential function (“antiderivative”) f for $\mathbf{F}$ and (2) compute the value of f at the endpoints of C and calculate their difference $f(\mathbf{r}(b)) - f(\mathbf{r}(a))$. Keep in mind, however, there is one major difference between the Fundamental Theorem of Calculus and the Fundamental Theorem for Line Integrals. *A function of one variable that is continuous must have an antiderivative. However, a vector field, even if it is continuous, does not need to have a potential function.*

Example 6.29

Applying the Fundamental Theorem

Calculate integral $\int_C \mathbf{F} \bullet d\mathbf{r}$, where $\mathbf{F}(x, y, z) = \langle 2x \ln y, \frac{x^2}{y} + z^2, 2yz \rangle$ and C is a curve with parameterization $\mathbf{r}(t) = \langle t^2, t, t \rangle, 1 \le t \le e$

a. without using the Fundamental Theorem of Line Integrals and

b. using the Fundamental Theorem of Line Integrals.

Solution

a. First, let's calculate the integral without the Fundamental Theorem for Line Integrals and instead use **Equation 6.9**:

$$\begin{aligned}\int_C \mathbf{F} \bullet dr &= \int_1^e \mathbf{F}(r(t)) \bullet r'(t)dt \\ &= \int_1^e \langle 2t^2 \ln t, \frac{t^4}{t} + t^2, 2t^2 \rangle \bullet \langle 2t, 1, 1 \rangle dt \\ &= \int_1^e \left(4t^3 \ln t + t^3 + 3t^2\right)dt \\ &= \int_1^e 4t^3 \ln t dt + \int_1^e \left(t^3 + 3t^2\right)dt \\ &= \int_1^e 4t^3 \ln t dt + \left[\frac{t^4}{4} + t^3\right]_1^e \\ &= r\int_1^e t^3 \ln t dt + \frac{e^4}{4} + e^3 - \frac{5}{4}.\end{aligned}$$

Integral $\int_1^e t^3 \ln t dt$ requires integration by parts. Let $u = \ln t$ and $dv = t^3$. Then $u = \ln t, dv = t^3$ and

$$du = \frac{1}{t}dt, v = \frac{t^4}{4}.$$

Therefore,

$$\begin{aligned}\int_1^e t^3 \ln t dt &= \left[\frac{t^4}{4} \ln t\right]_1^e - \frac{1}{4}\int_1^e t^3 dt \\ &= \frac{e^4}{4} - \frac{1}{r}\left(\frac{e^4}{4} - \frac{1}{4}\right).\end{aligned}$$

Thus,

$$\begin{aligned}\int_C \mathbf{F} \bullet dr &= 4\int_1^e t^3 \ln t dt + \frac{e^4}{4} + e^3 - \frac{5}{4} \\ &= 4\left(\frac{e^4}{4} - \frac{1}{4}\left(\frac{e^4}{4} - \frac{1}{4}\right)\right) + \frac{e^4}{4} + e^3 - \frac{5}{4} \\ &= e^4 - \frac{e^4}{4} + \frac{1}{4} + \frac{e^4}{4} + e^3 - \frac{5}{4} \\ &= e^4 + e^3 - 1.\end{aligned}$$

b. Given that $f(x, y, z) = x^2 \ln y + yz^2$ is a potential function for $\mathbf{F}$, let's use the Fundamental Theorem for Line Integrals to calculate the integral. Note that

$$\begin{aligned}\int_C \mathbf{F} \bullet d\mathbf{r} &= \int_C \nabla f \bullet d\mathbf{r} \\ &= f(\mathbf{r}(e)) - f(\mathbf{r}(1)) \\ &= f\left(e^2, e, e\right) - f(1, 1, 1) \\ &= e^4 + e^3 - 1.\end{aligned}$$

This calculation is much more straightforward than the calculation we did in (a). As long as we have a potential function, calculating a line integral using the Fundamental Theorem for Line Integrals is much easier than calculating without the theorem.

Example 6.29 illustrates a nice feature of the Fundamental Theorem of Line Integrals: it allows us to calculate more easily many vector line integrals. As long as we have a potential function, calculating the line integral is only a matter of evaluating the potential function at the endpoints and subtracting.

6.26 Given that $f(x, y) = (x-1)^2 y + (y+1)^2 x$ is a potential function for $\mathbf{F} = \langle 2xy - 2y + (y+1)^2, (x-1)^2 + 2yx + 2x \rangle$, calculate integral $\int_C \mathbf{F} \cdot d\mathbf{r}$, where C is the lower half of the unit circle oriented counterclockwise.

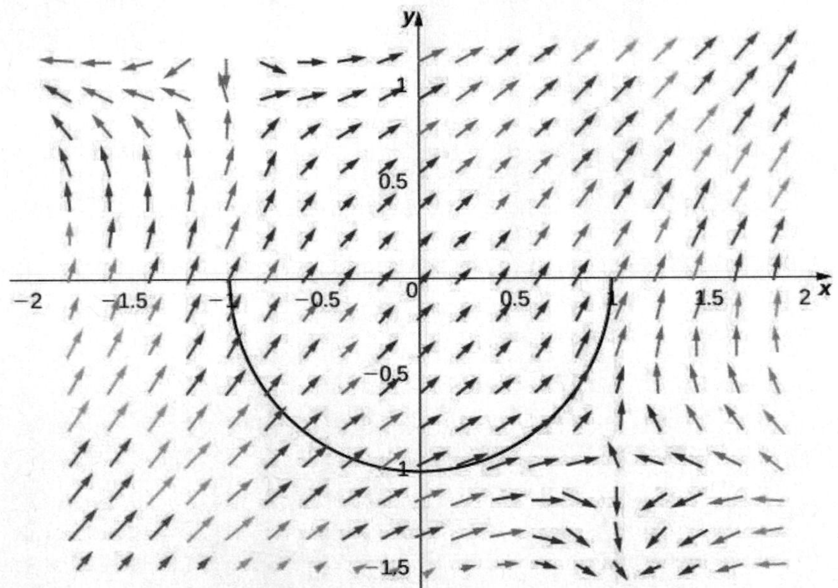

The Fundamental Theorem for Line Integrals has two important consequences. The first consequence is that if **F** is conservative and C is a closed curve, then the circulation of **F** along C is zero—that is, $\int_C \mathbf{F} \cdot d\mathbf{r} = 0$. To see why this is true, let f be a potential function for **F**. Since C is a closed curve, the terminal point **r**(b) of C is the same as the initial point **r**(a) of C—that is, $\mathbf{r}(a) = \mathbf{r}(b)$. Therefore, by the Fundamental Theorem for Line Integrals,

$$\begin{aligned}\oint_C \mathbf{F} \cdot d\mathbf{r} &= \oint_C \nabla f \cdot d\mathbf{r} \\ &= f(\mathbf{r}(b)) - f(\mathbf{r}(a)) \\ &= f(\mathbf{r}(b)) - f(\mathbf{r}(b)) \\ &= 0.\end{aligned}$$

Recall that the reason a conservative vector field **F** is called "conservative" is because such vector fields model forces in which energy is conserved. We have shown gravity to be an example of such a force. If we think of vector field **F** in integral $\oint_C \mathbf{F} \cdot d\mathbf{r}$ as a gravitational field, then the equation $\oint_C \mathbf{F} \cdot d\mathbf{r} = 0$ follows. If a particle travels along a path that starts and ends at the same place, then the work done by gravity on the particle is zero.

The second important consequence of the Fundamental Theorem for Line Integrals is that line integrals of conservative vector fields are independent of path—meaning, they depend only on the endpoints of the given curve, and do not depend on the path between the endpoints.

Definition

Let **F** be a vector field with domain *D*. The vector field **F** is **independent of path** (or **path independent**) if $\int_{C_1} \mathbf{F} \cdot d\mathbf{r} = \int_{C_2} \mathbf{F} \cdot d\mathbf{r}$ for any paths C_1 and C_2 in *D* with the same initial and terminal points.

The second consequence is stated formally in the following theorem.

Theorem 6.8: Path Independence of Conservative Fields

If **F** is a conservative vector field, then **F** is independent of path.

Proof

Let *D* denote the domain of **F** and let C_1 and C_2 be two paths in *D* with the same initial and terminal points (**Figure 6.29**). Call the initial point P_1 and the terminal point P_2. Since **F** is conservative, there is a potential function f for **F**. By the Fundamental Theorem for Line Integrals,

$$\int_{C_1} \mathbf{F} \cdot d\mathbf{r} = f(P_2) - f(P_1) = \int_{C_2} \mathbf{F} \cdot d\mathbf{r}.$$

Therefore, $\int_{C_1} \mathbf{F} \cdot d\mathbf{r} = \int_{C_2} \mathbf{F} \cdot d\mathbf{r}$ and **F** is independent of path.

□

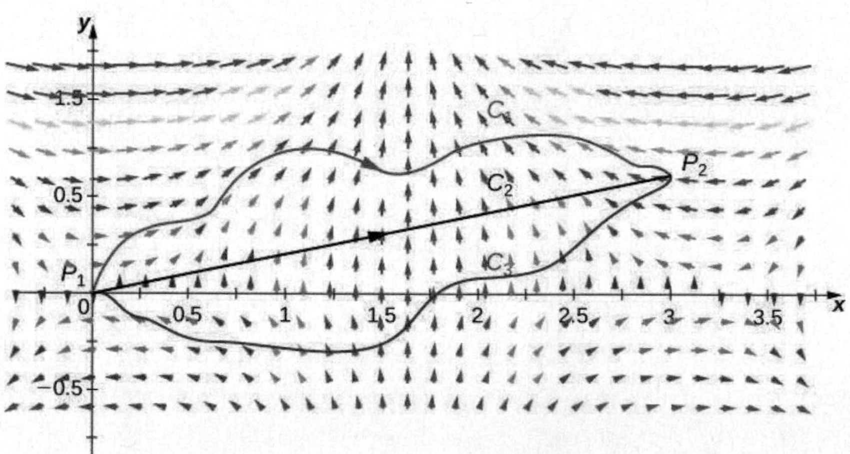

Figure 6.29 The vector field is conservative, and therefore independent of path.

To visualize what independence of path means, imagine three hikers climbing from base camp to the top of a mountain. Hiker 1 takes a steep route directly from camp to the top. Hiker 2 takes a winding route that is not steep from camp to the top. Hiker 3 starts by taking the steep route but halfway to the top decides it is too difficult for him. Therefore he returns to camp and takes the non-steep path to the top. All three hikers are traveling along paths in a gravitational field. Since gravity is a force in which energy is conserved, the gravitational field is conservative. By independence of path, the total amount of work done by gravity on each of the hikers is the same because they all started in the same place and ended in the same place. The work done by the hikers includes other factors such as friction and muscle movement, so the total amount of energy each one expended is not the same, but the net energy expended against gravity is the same for all three hikers.

We have shown that if **F** is conservative, then **F** is independent of path. It turns out that if the domain of **F** is open and connected, then the converse is also true. That is, if **F** is independent of path and the domain of **F** is open and connected, then **F** is conservative. Therefore, the set of conservative vector fields on open and connected domains is precisely the set of vector fields independent of path.

Theorem 6.9: The Path Independence Test for Conservative Fields

If **F** is a continuous vector field that is independent of path and the domain *D* of **F** is open and connected, then **F** is conservative.

Proof

We prove the theorem for vector fields in $\mathbb{R}^2$. The proof for vector fields in $\mathbb{R}^3$ is similar. To show that $\mathbf{F} = \langle P, Q \rangle$ is conservative, we must find a potential function f for **F**. To that end, let *X* be a fixed point in *D*. For any point (x, y) in *D*, let *C* be a path from *X* to (x, y). Define $f\,(x, y)$ by $f(x, y) = \int_C \mathbf{F} \cdot d\mathbf{r}$. (Note that this definition of f makes sense only because **F** is independent of path. If **F** was not independent of path, then it might be possible to find another path C' from *X* to (x, y) such that $\int_C \mathbf{F} \cdot d\mathbf{r} \neq \int_{C'} \mathbf{F} \cdot d\mathbf{r}$, and in such a case $f\,(x, y)$ would not be a function.) We want to show that f has the property $\nabla f = \mathbf{F}$.

Since domain *D* is open, it is possible to find a disk centered at (x, y) such that the disk is contained entirely inside *D*. Let (a, y) with $a < x$ be a point in that disk. Let *C* be a path from *X* to (x, y) that consists of two pieces: C_1 and C_2. The first piece, C_1, is any path from *C* to (a, y) that stays inside *D*; C_2 is the horizontal line segment from (a, y) to (x, y) (**Figure 6.30**). Then

$$f(x, y) = \int_{C_1} \mathbf{F} \cdot d\mathbf{r} + \int_{C_2} \mathbf{F} \cdot d\mathbf{r}.$$

The first integral does not depend on *x*, so

$$f_x = \frac{\partial}{\partial x} \int_{C_2} \mathbf{F} \bullet d\mathbf{r}.$$

If we parameterize C_2 by $\mathbf{r}(t) = \langle t, y \rangle,\ a \le t \le x,$ then

$$\begin{aligned} f_x &= \frac{\partial}{\partial x} \int_{C2} \mathbf{F} \bullet d\mathbf{r} \\ &= \frac{\partial}{\partial x} \int_a^x \mathbf{F}(\mathbf{r}(t)) \bullet \mathbf{r}'(t) dt \\ &= \frac{\partial}{\partial x} \int_a^x \mathbf{F}(\mathbf{r}(t)) \bullet \frac{d}{dt}(\langle t, y \rangle) dt \\ &= \frac{\partial}{\partial x} \int_a^x \mathbf{F}(r(t)) \bullet \langle 1, 0 \rangle\, dt \\ &= \frac{\partial}{\partial x} \int_a^x P(t, y) dt. \end{aligned}$$

By the Fundamental Theorem of Calculus (part 1),

$$f_x = \frac{\partial}{\partial x} \int_a^x P(t, y) dt = P(x, y).$$

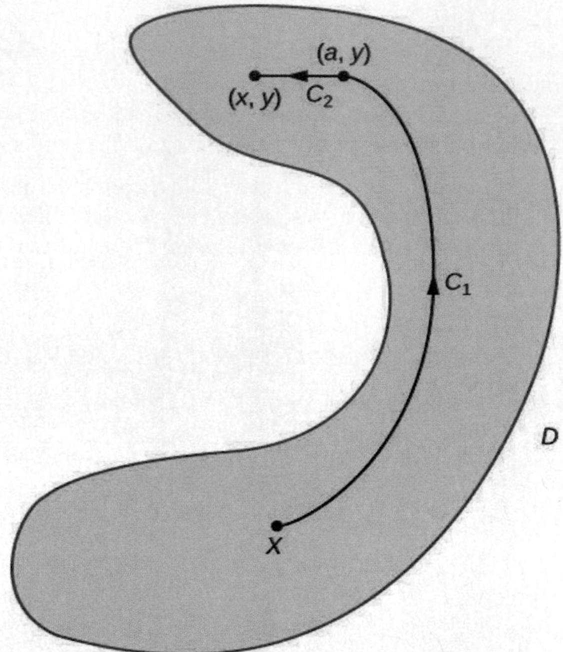

Figure 6.30 Here, C_1 is any path from C to (a, y) that stays inside D, and C_2 is the horizontal line segment from (a, y) to (x, y).

A similar argument using a vertical line segment rather than a horizontal line segment shows that $f_y = Q(x, y)$.

Therefore $\nabla f = \mathbf{F}$ and **F** is conservative.

□

We have spent a lot of time discussing and proving **Path Independence of Conservative Fields** and **The Path Independence Test for Conservative Fields**, but we can summarize them simply: a vector field **F** on an open and connected domain is conservative if and only if it is independent of path. This is important to know because conservative vector fields are extremely important in applications, and these theorems give us a different way of viewing what it means to be conservative using path independence.

Example 6.30

Showing That a Vector Field Is Not Conservative

Use path independence to show that vector field $\mathbf{F}(x, y) = \langle x^2 y, y + 5 \rangle$ is not conservative.

Solution

We can indicate that **F** is not conservative by showing that **F** is not path independent. We do so by giving two different paths, C_1 and C_2, that both start at $(0, 0)$ and end at $(1, 1)$, and yet $\int_{C_1} \mathbf{F} \cdot d\mathbf{r} \neq \int_{C_2} \mathbf{F} \cdot d\mathbf{r}$.

Let C_1 be the curve with parameterization $r_1(t) = \langle t, t \rangle, 0 \leq t \leq 1$ and let C_2 be the curve with parameterization $r_2(t) = \langle t, t^2 \rangle, 0 \leq t \leq 1$ (**Figure 6.31**). Then

$$\begin{aligned}\int_{C_1} \mathbf{F}\cdot dr &= \int_0^1 \mathbf{F}(r_1(t))\cdot r_1{}'(t)dt \\ &= \int_0^1 \langle t^3, t+5 \rangle \cdot \langle 1, 1 \rangle\, dt = \int_0^1 \left(t^3 + t + 5\right)dt \\ &= \left[\frac{t^4}{4} + \frac{t^2}{2} + 5t\right]_0^1 = \frac{23}{4}\end{aligned}$$

and

$$\begin{aligned}\int_{C_2} \mathbf{F}\cdot dr &= \int_0^1 \mathbf{F}(r_2(t))\cdot r_2{}'(t)dt \\ &= \int_0^1 \langle t^4, t^2+5 \rangle \cdot \langle 1, 2t \rangle\, dt = \int_0^1 \left(t^4 + 2t^3 + 10t\right)dt \\ &= \left[\frac{t^5}{5} + \frac{t^4}{2} + 5t^2\right]_0^1 = \frac{57}{10}.\end{aligned}$$

Since $\int_{C_1} \mathbf{F} \bullet d\mathbf{r} \neq \int_{C_2} \mathbf{F} \bullet d\mathbf{r},$ the value of a line integral of **F** depends on the path between two given points. Therefore, **F** is not independent of path, and **F** is not conservative.

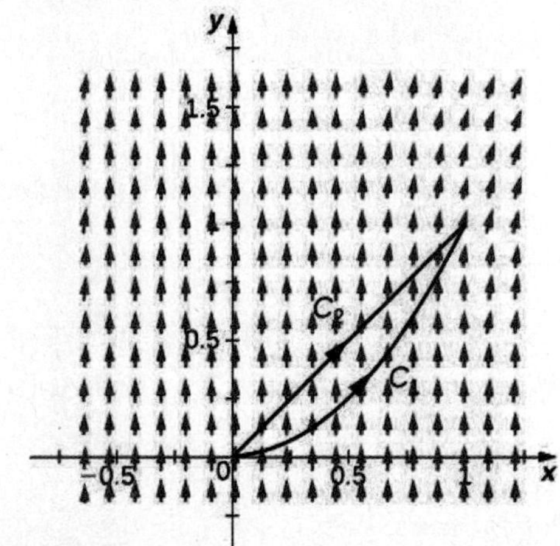

Figure 6.31 Curves C_1 and C_2 are both oriented from left to right.

6.27 Show that $\mathbf{F}(x, y) = \langle xy, x^2y^2 \rangle$ is not path independent by considering the line segment from $(0, 0)$ to $(0, 2)$ and the piece of the graph of $y = \frac{x^2}{2}$ that goes from $(0, 0)$ to $(0, 2)$.

Conservative Vector Fields and Potential Functions

As we have learned, the Fundamental Theorem for Line Integrals says that if **F** is conservative, then calculating $\int_C \mathbf{F}\cdot dr$ has two steps: first, find a potential function f for **F** and, second, calculate $f(P_1) - f(P_0)$, where P_1 is the endpoint of C and P_0 is the starting point. To use this theorem for a conservative field **F**, we must be able to find a potential function f for **F**. Therefore, we must answer the following question: Given a conservative vector field **F**, how do we find a function

f such that $\nabla f = \mathbf{F}$? Before giving a general method for finding a potential function, let's motivate the method with an example.

Example 6.31

Finding a Potential Function

Find a potential function for $\mathbf{F}(x, y) = \langle 2xy^3, 3x^2y^2 + \cos(y) \rangle$, thereby showing that $\mathbf{F}$ is conservative.

Solution

Suppose that $f(x, y)$ is a potential function for $\mathbf{F}$. Then, $\nabla f = \mathbf{F}$, and therefore

$$f_x = 2xy^3 \text{ and } f_y = 3x^2y^2 + \cos y.$$

Integrating the equation $f_x = 2xy^3$ with respect to x yields the equation

$$f(x, y) = x^2y^3 + h(y).$$

Notice that since we are integrating a two-variable function with respect to x, we must add a constant of integration that is a constant with respect to x, but may still be a function of y. The equation $f(x, y) = x^2y^3 + h(y)$ can be confirmed by taking the partial derivative with respect to x:

$$\frac{\partial f}{\partial x} = \frac{\partial}{\partial x}\left(x^2y^3\right) + \frac{\partial}{\partial x}(h(y)) = 2xy^3 + 0 = 2xy^3.$$

Since f is a potential function for $\mathbf{F}$,

$$f_y = 3x^2y^2 + \cos(y),$$

and therefore

$$3x^2y^2 + g'(y) = 3x^2y^2 + \cos(y).$$

This implies that $h'(y) = \cos y$, so $h(y) = \sin y + C$. Therefore, *any* function of the form $f(x, y) = x^2y^3 + \sin(y) + C$ is a potential function. Taking, in particular, $C = 0$ gives the potential function $f(x, y) = x^2y^3 + \sin(y)$.

To verify that f is a potential function, note that $\nabla f = \langle 2xy^3, 3x^2y^2 + \cos y \rangle = \mathbf{F}$.

 **6.28** Find a potential function for $\mathbf{F}(x, y) = \langle e^xy^3 + y, 3e^xy^2 + x \rangle$.

The logic of the previous example extends to finding the potential function for any conservative vector field in $\mathbb{R}^2$. Thus, we have the following problem-solving strategy for finding potential functions:

Problem-Solving Stragegy: Finding a Potential Function for a Conservative Vector Field $\mathbf{F}(x, y) = \langle P(x, y), Q(x, y) \rangle$

1. Integrate P with respect to x. This results in a function of the form $g(x, y) + h(y)$, where $h(y)$ is unknown.

2. Take the partial derivative of $g(x, y) + h(y)$ with respect to y, which results in the function $g_y(x, y) + h'(y)$.
3. Use the equation $g_y(x, y) + h'(y) = Q(x, y)$ to find $h'(y)$.
4. Integrate $h'(y)$ to find $h(y)$.
5. Any function of the form $f(x, y) = g(x, y) + h(y) + C$, where C is a constant, is a potential function for **F**.

We can adapt this strategy to find potential functions for vector fields in $\mathbb{R}^3$, as shown in the next example.

Example 6.32

Finding a Potential Function in $\mathbb{R}^3$

Find a potential function for $\mathbf{F}(x, y) = \langle 2xy, x^2 + 2yz^3, 3y^2z^2 + 2z \rangle$, thereby showing that **F** is conservative.

Solution

Suppose that f is a potential function. Then, $\nabla f = \mathbf{F}$ and therefore $f_x = 2xy$. Integrating this equation with respect to x yields the equation $f(x, y, z) = x^2y + g(y, z)$ for some function g. Notice that, in this case, the constant of integration with respect to x is a function of y and z.

Since f is a potential function,

$$x^2 + 2yz^3 = f_y = x^2 + g_y.$$

Therefore,

$$g_y = 2yz^3.$$

Integrating this function with respect to y yields

$$g(y, z) = y^2z^3 + h(z)$$

for some function $h(z)$ of z alone. (Notice that, because we know that g is a function of only y and z, we do not need to write $g(y, z) = y^2z^3 + h(x, z)$.) Therefore,

$$f(x, y, z) = x^2y + g(y, z) = x^2y + y^2z^3 + h(z).$$

To find f, we now must only find h. Since f is a potential function,

$$3y^2z^2 + 2z = g_z = 3y^2z^2 + h'(z).$$

This implies that $h'(z) = 2z$, so $h(z) = z^2 + C$. Letting $C = 0$ gives the potential function

$$f(x, y, z) = x^2y + y^2z^3 + z^2.$$

To verify that f is a potential function, note that $\nabla f = \langle 2xy, x^2 + 2yz^3, 3y^2z^2 + 2z \rangle = \mathbf{F}$.

6.29 Find a potential function for $\mathbf{F}(x, y, z) = \langle 12x^2, \cos y \cos z, 1 - \sin y \sin z \rangle$.

We can apply the process of finding a potential function to a gravitational force. Recall that, if an object has unit mass and is located at the origin, then the gravitational force in $\mathbb{R}^2$ that the object exerts on another object of unit mass at the point (x, y) is given by vector field

$$\mathbf{F}(x, y) = -G \left\langle \frac{x}{\left(x^2 + y^2\right)^{3/2}}, \frac{y}{\left(x^2 + y^2\right)^{3/2}} \right\rangle,$$

where G is the universal gravitational constant. In the next example, we build a potential function for **F**, thus confirming what we already know: that gravity is conservative.

Example 6.33

Finding a Potential Function

Find a potential function f for $\mathbf{F}(x, y) = -G \left\langle \frac{x}{\left(x^2 + y^2\right)^{3/2}}, \frac{y}{\left(x^2 + y^2\right)^{3/2}} \right\rangle.$

Solution

Suppose that f is a potential function. Then, $\nabla f = \mathbf{F}$ and therefore

$$f_x = \frac{-Gx}{\left(x^2 + y^2\right)^{3/2}}.$$

To integrate this function with respect to x, we can use u-substitution. If $u = x^2 + y^2,$ then $\frac{du}{2} = xdx,$ so

$$\begin{aligned} \int \frac{-Gx}{\left(x^2 + y^2\right)^{3/2}} dx &= \int \frac{-G}{2u^{3/2}} du \\ &= \frac{G}{\sqrt{u}} + h(y) \\ &= \frac{G}{\sqrt{x^2 + y^2}} + h(y) \end{aligned}$$

for some function $h(y)$. Therefore,

$$f(x, y) = \frac{G}{\sqrt{x^2 + y^2}} + h(y).$$

Since f is a potential function for **F**,

$$f_y = \frac{-Gy}{\left(x^2 + y^2\right)^{3/2}}.$$

Since $f(x, y) = \frac{G}{\sqrt{x^2 + y^2}} + h(y),$ f_y also equals $\frac{-Gy}{\left(x^2 + y^2\right)^{3/2}} + h'(y).$

Therefore,

$$\frac{-Gy}{\left(x^2 + y^2\right)^{3/2}} + h'(y) = \frac{-Gy}{\left(x^2 + y^2\right)^{3/2}},$$

which implies that $h'(y) = 0.$ Thus, we can take $h(y)$ to be any constant; in particular, we can let $h(y) = 0.$

The function

$$f(x, y) = \frac{G}{\sqrt{x^2 + y^2}}$$

is a potential function for the gravitational field **F**. To confirm that f is a potential function, note that

$$\begin{aligned} \nabla f &= \langle -\frac{1}{2} \frac{G}{\left(x^2 + y^2\right)^{3/2}}(2x), -\frac{1}{2} \frac{G}{\left(x^2 + y^2\right)^{3/2}}(2y) \rangle \\ &= \langle \frac{-Gx}{\left(x^2 + y^2\right)^{3/2}}, \frac{-Gy}{\left(x^2 + y^2\right)^{3/2}} \rangle \\ &= \mathbf{F}. \end{aligned}$$

 **6.30** Find a potential function f for the three-dimensional gravitational force $\mathbf{F}(x, y, z) = \langle \frac{-Gx}{\left(x^2 + y^2 + z^2\right)^{3/2}}, \frac{-Gy}{\left(x^2 + y^2 + z^2\right)^{3/2}}, \frac{-Gz}{\left(x^2 + y^2 + z^2\right)^{3/2}} \rangle$.

Testing a Vector Field

Until now, we have worked with vector fields that we know are conservative, but if we are not told that a vector field is conservative, we need to be able to test whether it is conservative. Recall that, if **F** is conservative, then **F** has the cross-partial property (see **The Cross-Partial Property of Conservative Vector Fields**). That is, if $\mathbf{F} = \langle P, Q, R \rangle$ is conservative, then $P_y = Q_x$, $P_z = R_x$, and $Q_z = R_y$. So, if **F** has the cross-partial property, then is **F** conservative? If the domain of **F** is open and simply connected, then the answer is yes.

Theorem 6.10: The Cross-Partial Test for Conservative Fields

If $\mathbf{F} = \langle P, Q, R \rangle$ is a vector field on an open, simply connected region D and $P_y = Q_x$, $P_z = R_x$, and $Q_z = R_y$ throughout D, then **F** is conservative.

Although a proof of this theorem is beyond the scope of the text, we can discover its power with some examples. Later, we see why it is necessary for the region to be simply connected.

Combining this theorem with the cross-partial property, we can determine whether a given vector field is conservative:

Theorem 6.11: Cross-Partial Property of Conservative Fields

Let $\mathbf{F} = \langle P, Q, R \rangle$ be a vector field on an open, simply connected region D. Then $P_y = Q_x$, $P_z = R_x$, and $Q_z = R_y$ throughout D if and only if **F** is conservative.

The version of this theorem in $\mathbb{R}^2$ is also true. If $\mathbf{F} = \langle P, Q \rangle$ is a vector field on an open, simply connected domain in $\mathbb{R}^2$, then **F** is conservative if and only if $P_y = Q_x$.

Example 6.34

Determining Whether a Vector Field Is Conservative

Determine whether vector field $\mathbf{F}(x, y, z) = \langle xy^2 z, x^2 yz, z^2 \rangle$ is conservative.

Solution

Note that the domain of **F** is all of $\mathbb{R}^2$ and $\mathbb{R}^3$ is simply connected. Therefore, we can use **Cross-Partial Property of Conservative Fields** to determine whether **F** is conservative. Let

$$P(x, y, z) = xy^2 z,\ Q(x, y, z) = x^2 yz,\ \text{and } R(x, y, z) = z^2.$$

Since $Q_z = x^2 y$ and $R_y = 0,$ the vector field is not conservative.

Example 6.35

Determining Whether a Vector Field Is Conservative

Determine vector field $\mathbf{F}(x, y) = \langle x\ln(y), \frac{x^2}{2y} \rangle$ is conservative.

Solution

Note that the domain of **F** is the part of $\mathbb{R}^2$ in which $y > 0.$ Thus, the domain of **F** is part of a plane above the x-axis, and this domain is simply connected (there are no holes in this region and this region is connected). Therefore, we can use **Cross-Partial Property of Conservative Fields** to determine whether **F** is conservative. Let

$$P(x, y) = x\ln(y) \text{ and } Q(x, y) = \frac{x^2}{2y}.$$

Then $P_y = \frac{x}{y} = Q_x$ and thus **F** is conservative.

6.31 Determine whether $\mathbf{F}(x, y) = \langle \sin x \cos y, \cos x \sin y \rangle$ is conservative.

When using **Cross-Partial Property of Conservative Fields**, it is important to remember that a theorem is a tool, and like any tool, it can be applied only under the right conditions. In the case of **Cross-Partial Property of Conservative Fields**, the theorem can be applied only if the domain of the vector field is simply connected.

To see what can go wrong when misapplying the theorem, consider the vector field from **Example 6.30**:

$$\mathbf{F}(x, y) = \frac{y}{x^2 + y^2}\mathbf{i} + \frac{-x}{x^2 + y^2}\mathbf{j}.$$

This vector field satisfies the cross-partial property, since

$$\frac{\partial}{\partial y}\left(\frac{y}{x^2+y^2}\right) = \frac{\left(x^2+y^2\right) - y(2y)}{\left(x^2+y^2\right)^2} = \frac{x^2-y^2}{\left(x^2+y^2\right)^2}$$

and

$$\frac{\partial}{\partial x}\left(\frac{-x}{x^2+y^2}\right) = \frac{-\left(x^2+y^2\right) + x(2x)}{\left(x^2+y^2\right)^2} = \frac{x^2-y^2}{\left(x^2+y^2\right)^2}.$$

Since **F** satisfies the cross-partial property, we might be tempted to conclude that **F** is conservative. However, **F** is not conservative. To see this, let

$$\mathbf{r}(t) = \langle \cos t, \sin t \rangle, \ 0 \le t \le \pi$$

be a parameterization of the upper half of a unit circle oriented counterclockwise (denote this C_1) and let

$$\mathrm{s}(t) = \langle \cos t, -\sin t \rangle, \ 0 \le t \le \pi$$

be a parameterization of the lower half of a unit circle oriented clockwise (denote this C_2). Notice that C_1 and C_2 have the same starting point and endpoint. Since $\sin^2 t + \cos^2 t = 1$,

$$\mathbf{F}(\mathbf{r}(t)) \bullet \mathbf{r}'(t) = \langle \sin(t), -\cos(t) \rangle \bullet \langle -\sin(t), \cos(t) \rangle = -1$$

and

$$\begin{aligned} \mathbf{F}(s(t)) \cdot \mathbf{s}'(t) &= \langle -\sin t, -\cos t \rangle \cdot \langle -\sin t, -\cos t \rangle \\ &= \sin^2 t + \cos^2 t \\ &= 1. \end{aligned}$$

Therefore,

$$\int_{C_1} \mathbf{F} \cdot d\mathbf{r} = \int_0^{\pi} -1 dt = -\pi \text{ and } \int_{C_2} \mathbf{F} \cdot dr = \int_0^{\pi} 1 dt = \pi.$$

Thus, C_1 and C_2 have the same starting point and endpoint, but $\int_{C_1} \mathbf{F} \cdot d\mathbf{r} \ne \int_{C_2} \mathbf{F} \cdot d\mathbf{r}$. Therefore, **F** is not independent of path and **F** is not conservative.

To summarize: **F** satisfies the cross-partial property and yet **F** is not conservative. What went wrong? Does this contradict **Cross-Partial Property of Conservative Fields**? The issue is that the domain of **F** is all of $\mathbb{R}^2$ except for the origin. In other words, the domain of **F** has a hole at the origin, and therefore the domain is not simply connected. Since the domain is not simply connected, **Cross-Partial Property of Conservative Fields** does not apply to **F**.

We close this section by looking at an example of the usefulness of the Fundamental Theorem for Line Integrals. Now that we can test whether a vector field is conservative, we can always decide whether the Fundamental Theorem for Line Integrals can be used to calculate a vector line integral. If we are asked to calculate an integral of the form $\int_C \mathbf{F} \cdot d\mathbf{r}$, then our first question should be: Is **F** conservative? If the answer is yes, then we should find a potential function and use the Fundamental Theorem for Line Integrals to calculate the integral. If the answer is no, then the Fundamental Theorem for Line Integrals can't help us and we have to use other methods, such as using **Equation 6.9**.

Example 6.36

Using the Fundamental Theorem for Line Integrals

Calculate line integral $\int_C \mathbf{F} \cdot dr$, where $\mathbf{F}(x, y, z) = \langle 2xe^y z + e^x z, x^2 e^y z, x^2 e^y + e^x \rangle$ and C is any smooth curve that goes from the origin to $(1, 1, 1)$.

Solution

Before trying to compute the integral, we need to determine whether **F** is conservative and whether the domain of **F** is simply connected. The domain of **F** is all of $\mathbb{R}^3$, which is connected and has no holes. Therefore, the domain of **F** is simply connected. Let

$$P(x, y, z) = 2xe^y z + e^x z,\ Q(x, y, z) = x^2 e^y z,\ \text{and}\ R(x, y, z) = x^2 e^y + e^x$$

so that $\mathbf{F} = \langle P, Q, R \rangle$. Since the domain of **F** is simply connected, we can check the cross partials to determine whether **F** is conservative. Note that

$$\begin{aligned} P_y &= 2xe^y z = Q_x \\ P_z &= 2xe^y + e^x = R_x \\ Q_z &= x^2 e^y = R_y. \end{aligned}$$

Therefore, **F** is conservative.

To evaluate $\int_C \mathbf{F} \cdot dr$ using the Fundamental Theorem for Line Integrals, we need to find a potential function f for **F**. Let f be a potential function for **F**. Then, $\nabla f = \mathbf{F}$, and therefore $f_x = 2xe^y z + e^x z$. Integrating this equation with respect to x gives $f(x, y, z) = x^2 e^y z + e^x z + h(y, z)$ for some function h. Differentiating this equation with respect to y gives $x^2 e^y z + h_y = Q = x^2 e^y z$, which implies that $h_y = 0$. Therefore, h is a function of z only, and $f(x, y, z) = x^2 e^y z + e^x z + h(z)$. To find h, note that $f_z = x^2 e^y + e^x + h'(z) = R = x^2 e^y + e^x$. Therefore, $h'(z) = 0$ and we can take $h(z) = 0$. A potential function for **F** is $f(x, y, z) = x^2 e^y z + e^x z$.

Now that we have a potential function, we can use the Fundamental Theorem for Line Integrals to evaluate the integral. By the theorem,

$$\begin{aligned} \int_C \mathbf{F} \cdot d\mathbf{r} &= \int_C \nabla f \cdot d\mathbf{r} \\ &= f(1, 1, 1) - f(0, 0, 0) \\ &= 2e. \end{aligned}$$

Analysis

Notice that if we hadn't recognized that **F** is conservative, we would have had to parameterize C and use **Equation 6.9**. Since curve C is unknown, using the Fundamental Theorem for Line Integrals is much simpler.

6.32 Calculate integral $\int_C \mathbf{F} \cdot d\mathbf{r}$, where $\mathbf{F}(x, y) = \langle \sin x \sin y, 5 - \cos x \cos y \rangle$ and C is a semicircle with starting point $(0, \pi)$ and endpoint $(0, -\pi)$.

Example 6.37

Work Done on a Particle

Let $\mathbf{F}(x, y) = \langle 2xy^2, 2x^2 y \rangle$ be a force field. Suppose that a particle begins its motion at the origin and ends its movement at any point in a plane that is not on the *x*-axis or the *y*-axis. Furthermore, the particle's motion can be modeled with a smooth parameterization. Show that **F** does positive work on the particle.

Solution

We show that **F** does positive work on the particle by showing that **F** is conservative and then by using the Fundamental Theorem for Line Integrals.

To show that **F** is conservative, suppose $f(x, y)$ were a potential function for **F**. Then, $\nabla f = \mathbf{F} = \langle 2xy^2, 2x^2 y \rangle$ and therefore $f_x = 2xy^2$ and $f_y = 2x^2 y$. Equation $f_x = 2xy^2$ implies that $f(x, y) = x^2 y^2 + h(y)$. Deriving both sides with respect to *y* yields $f_y = 2x^2 y + h'(y)$. Therefore, $h'(y) = 0$ and we can take $h(y) = 0$.

If $f(x, y) = x^2 y^2$, then note that $\nabla f = \langle 2xy^2, 2x^2 y \rangle = \mathbf{F}$, and therefore f is a potential function for **F**.

Let (a, b) be the point at which the particle stops is motion, and let *C* denote the curve that models the particle's motion. The work done by **F** on the particle is $\int_C \mathbf{F} \cdot d\mathbf{r}$. By the Fundamental Theorem for Line Integrals,

$$\begin{aligned} \int_C \mathbf{F} \cdot d\mathbf{r} &= \int_C \nabla f \cdot d\mathbf{r} \\ &= f(a, b) - f(0, 0) \\ &= a^2 b^2. \end{aligned}$$

Since $a \neq 0$ and $b \neq 0$, by assumption, $a^2 b^2 > 0$. Therefore, $\int_C \mathbf{F} \cdot d\mathbf{r} > 0$, and **F** does positive work on the particle.

Analysis

Notice that this problem would be much more difficult without using the Fundamental Theorem for Line Integrals. To apply the tools we have learned, we would need to give a curve parameterization and use **Equation 6.9**. Since the path of motion *C* can be as exotic as we wish (as long as it is smooth), it can be very difficult to parameterize the motion of the particle.

6.33 Let $\mathbf{F}(x, y) = \langle 4x^3 y^4, 4x^4 y^3 \rangle$, and suppose that a particle moves from point $(4, 4)$ to $(1, 1)$ along any smooth curve. Is the work done by **F** on the particle positive, negative, or zero?

6.3 EXERCISES

99. *True* or *False?* If vector field **F** is conservative on the open and connected region *D*, then line integrals of **F** are path independent on *D*, regardless of the shape of *D*.

100. *True* or *False?* Function $\mathbf{r}(t) = \mathbf{a} + t(\mathbf{b} - \mathbf{a})$, where $0 \le t \le 1$, parameterizes the straight-line segment from $\mathbf{a}$ to $\mathbf{b}$.

101. *True* or *False?* Vector field $\mathbf{F}(x, y, z) = (y \sin z)\mathbf{i} + (x \sin z)\mathbf{j} + (xy \cos z)\mathbf{k}$ is conservative.

102. *True* or *False?* Vector field $\mathbf{F}(x, y, z) = y\mathbf{i} + (x + z)\mathbf{j} - y\mathbf{k}$ is conservative.

103. Justify the Fundamental Theorem of Line Integrals for $\int_C \mathbf{F} \cdot d\mathbf{r}$ in the case when $\mathbf{F}(x, y) = (2x + 2y)\mathbf{i} + (2x + 2y)\mathbf{j}$ and *C* is a portion of the positively oriented circle $x^2 + y^2 = 25$ from (5, 0) to (3, 4).

104. **[T]** Find $\int_C \mathbf{F} \cdot d\mathbf{r},$,] where $\mathbf{F}(x, y) = \left(ye^{xy} + \cos x\right)\mathbf{i} + \left(xe^{xy} + \frac{1}{y^2 + 1}\right)\mathbf{j}$ and *C* is a portion of curve $y = \sin x$ from $x = 0$ to $x = \frac{\pi}{2}$.

105. **[T]** Evaluate line integral $\int_C \mathbf{F} \cdot d\mathbf{r}$, where $\mathbf{F}(x, y) = (e^x \sin y - y)\mathbf{i} + (e^x \cos y - x - 2)\mathbf{j}$, and *C* is the path given by $r(t) = \left[t^3 \sin \frac{\pi t}{2}\right]\mathbf{i} - \left[\frac{\pi}{2}\cos\left(\frac{\pi t}{2} + \frac{\pi}{2}\right)\right]\mathbf{j}$ for $0 \le t \le 1$.

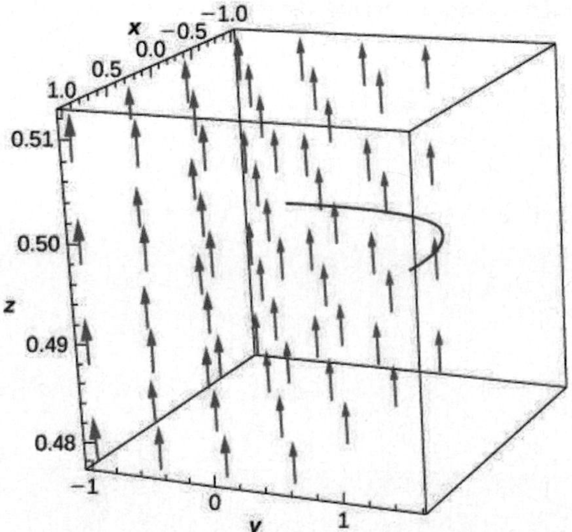

For the following exercises, determine whether the vector field is conservative and, if it is, find the potential function.

106. $\mathbf{F}(x, y) = 2xy^3\,\mathbf{i} + 3y^2x^2\,\mathbf{j}$

107. $\mathbf{F}(x, y) = (-y + e^x \sin y)\mathbf{i} + [(x + 2)e^x \cos y]\mathbf{j}$

108. $\mathbf{F}(x, y) = \left(e^{2x} \sin y\right)\mathbf{i} + \left[e^{2x} \cos y\right]\mathbf{j}$

109. $\mathbf{F}(x, y) = (6x + 5y)\mathbf{i} + (5x + 4y)\mathbf{j}$

110. $\mathbf{F}(x, y) = [2x\cos(y) - y\cos(x)]\mathbf{i} + \left[-x^2\sin(y) - \sin(x)\right]\mathbf{j}$

111. $\mathbf{F}(x, y) = [ye^x + \sin(y)]\mathbf{i} + [e^x + x\cos(y)]\mathbf{j}$

For the following exercises, evaluate the line integrals using the Fundamental Theorem of Line Integrals.

112. $\oint_C (y\mathbf{i} + x\mathbf{j}) \cdot d\mathbf{r}$, where *C* is any path from (0, 0) to (2, 4)

113. $\oint_C (2y\,dx + 2x\,dy)$, where *C* is the line segment from (0, 0) to (4, 4)

114. **[T]** $\oint_C \left[\arctan\frac{y}{x} - \frac{xy}{x^2 + y^2}\right]dx + \left[\frac{x^2}{x^2 + y^2} + e^{-y}(1 - y)\right]dy$, where *C* is any smooth curve from (1, 1) to (−1, 2)

115. Find the conservative vector field for the potential function

$$f(x, y) = 5x^2 + 3xy + 10y^2.$$

For the following exercises, determine whether the vector field is conservative and, if so, find a potential function.

116. $\mathbf{F}(x, y) = (12xy)\mathbf{i} + 6\left(x^2 + y^2\right)\mathbf{j}$

117. $\mathbf{F}(x, y) = (e^x \cos y)\mathbf{i} + 6(e^x \sin y)\mathbf{j}$

118. $\mathbf{F}(x, y) = \left(2xye^{x^2 y}\right)\mathbf{i} + 6\left(x^2 e^{x^2 y}\right)\mathbf{j}$

119. $\mathbf{F}(x, y, z) = (ye^z)\mathbf{i} + (xe^z)\mathbf{j} + (xye^z)\mathbf{k}$

120. $\mathbf{F}(x, y, z) = (\sin y)\mathbf{i} - (x\cos y)\mathbf{j} + \mathbf{k}$

121. $\mathbf{F}(x, y, z) = \left(\frac{1}{y}\right)\mathbf{i} + \left(\frac{x}{y^2}\right)\mathbf{j} + (2z - 1)\mathbf{k}$

122. $\mathbf{F}(x, y, z) = 3z^2\mathbf{i} - \cos y\mathbf{j} + 2xz\mathbf{k}$

123. $\mathbf{F}(x, y, z) = (2xy)\mathbf{i} + \left(x^2 + 2yz\right)\mathbf{j} + y^2\mathbf{k}$

For the following exercises, determine whether the given vector field is conservative and find a potential function.

124. $\mathbf{F}(x, y) = (e^x \cos y)\mathbf{i} + 6(e^x \sin y)\mathbf{j}$

125. $\mathbf{F}(x, y) = \left(2xye^{x^2 y}\right)\mathbf{i} + 6\left(x^2 e^{x^2 y}\right)\mathbf{j}$

For the following exercises, evaluate the integral using the Fundamental Theorem of Line Integrals.

126. Evaluate $\int_C \nabla f \cdot d\mathbf{r}$, where $f(x, y, z) = \cos(\pi x) + \sin(\pi y) - xyz$ and C is any path that starts at $\left(1, \frac{1}{2}, 2\right)$ and ends at $(2, 1, -1)$.

127. **[T]** Evaluate $\int_C \nabla f \cdot d\mathbf{r}$, where $f(x, y) = xy + e^x$ and C is a straight line from $(0, 0)$ to $(2, 1)$.

128. **[T]** Evaluate $\int_C \nabla f \cdot d\mathbf{r}$, where $f(x, y) = x^2 y - x$ and C is any path in a plane from (1, 2) to (3, 2).

129. Evaluate $\int_C \nabla f \cdot d\mathbf{r}$, where $f(x, y, z) = xyz^2 - yz$ and C has initial point (1, 2) and terminal point (3, 5).

For the following exercises, let $\mathbf{F}(x, y) = 2xy^2\mathbf{i} + \left(2yx^2 + 2y\right)\mathbf{j}$ and $G(x, y) = (y + x)\mathbf{i} + (y - x)\mathbf{j}$, and let C_1 be the curve consisting of the circle of radius 2, centered at the origin and oriented counterclockwise, and C_2 be the curve consisting of a line segment from (0, 0) to (1, 1) followed by a line segment from (1, 1) to (3, 1).

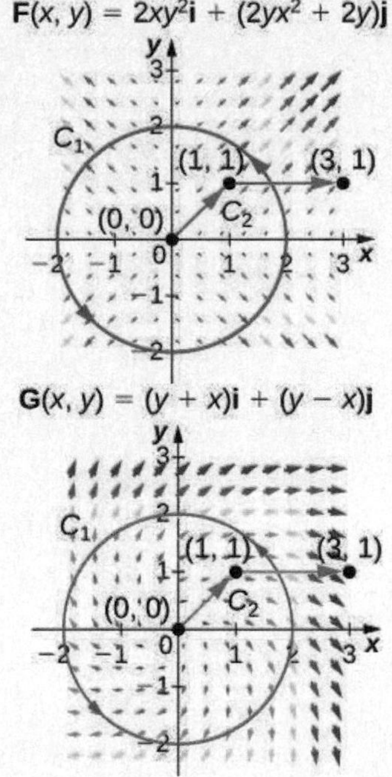

130. Calculate the line integral of $\mathbf{F}$ over C_1.

131. Calculate the line integral of $\mathbf{G}$ over C_1.

132. Calculate the line integral of $\mathbf{F}$ over C_2.

133. Calculate the line integral of $\mathbf{G}$ over C_2.

134. **[T]** Let $\mathbf{F}(x, y, z) = x^2\mathbf{i} + z\sin(yz)\mathbf{j} + y\sin(yz)\mathbf{k}$. Calculate $\oint_C \mathbf{F} \cdot dr$, where C is a path from $A = (0, 0, 1)$ to $B = (3, 1, 2)$.

135. **[T]** Find line integral $\oint_C \mathbf{F} \cdot dr$ of vector field $\mathbf{F}(x, y, z) = 3x^2 z\mathbf{i} + z^2\mathbf{j} + \left(x^3 + 2yz\right)\mathbf{k}$ along curve C parameterized by $r(t) = \left(\frac{\ln t}{\ln 2}\right)\mathbf{i} + t^{3/2}\mathbf{j} + t\cos(\pi t), 1 \le t \le 4$.

For the following exercises, show that the following vector fields are conservative by using a computer. Calculate $\int_C \mathbf{F} \cdot d\mathbf{r}$ for the given curve.

136. $\mathbf{F} = \left(xy^2 + 3x^2 y\right)\mathbf{i} + (x + y)x^2\mathbf{j}$; C is the curve consisting of line segments from $(1, 1)$ to $(0, 2)$ to $(3, 0)$.

137. $\mathbf{F} = \frac{2x}{y^2+1}\mathbf{i} - \frac{2y(x^2+1)}{(y^2+1)^2}\mathbf{j}$; C is parameterized by $x = t^3 - 1,\ y = t^6 - t,\ 0 \le t \le 1$.

138. **[T]** $\mathbf{F} = [\cos(xy^2) - xy^2\sin(xy^2)]\mathbf{i} - 2x^2y\sin(xy^2)\mathbf{j}$; C is curve $(e^t, e^{t+1}),\ -1 \le t \le 0$.

139. The mass of Earth is approximately 6×10^{27} g and that of the Sun is 330,000 times as much. The gravitational constant is $6.7 \times 10^{-8}\,\text{cm}^3/\text{s}^2 \cdot \text{g}$. The distance of Earth from the Sun is about 1.5×10^{12} cm. Compute, approximately, the work necessary to increase the distance of Earth from the Sun by 1 cm.

140. **[T]** Let $\mathbf{F} = (x, y, z) = (e^x \sin y)\mathbf{i} + (e^x \cos y)\mathbf{j} + z^2\mathbf{k}$. Evaluate the integral $\int_C \mathbf{F} \cdot ds$, where $\mathbf{c}(t) = (\sqrt{t}, t^3, e^{\sqrt{t}}),\ 0 \le t \le 1$.

141. **[T]** Let $\mathbf{c} : [1, 2] \to \mathbb{R}^2$ be given by $x = e^{t-1},\ y = \sin\left(\frac{\pi}{t}\right)$. Use a computer to compute the integral $\int_C \mathbf{F} \cdot d\mathbf{s} = \int_C 2x\cos y\,dx - x^2 \sin y\,dy$, where $\mathbf{F} = (2x\cos y)\mathbf{i} - (x^2 \sin y)\mathbf{j}$.

142. **[T]** Use a computer algebra system to find the mass of a wire that lies along curve $\mathbf{r}(t) = (t^2 - 1)\mathbf{j} + 2t\mathbf{k},\ 0 \le t \le 1$, if the density is $\frac{3}{2}t$.

143. Find the circulation and flux of field $\mathbf{F} = -y\mathbf{i} + x\mathbf{j}$ around and across the closed semicircular path that consists of semicircular arch $\mathbf{r}_1(t) = (a\cos t)\mathbf{i} + (a\sin t)\mathbf{j},\ 0 \le t \le \pi$, followed by line segment $\mathbf{r}_2(t) = t\mathbf{i},\ -a \le t \le a$.

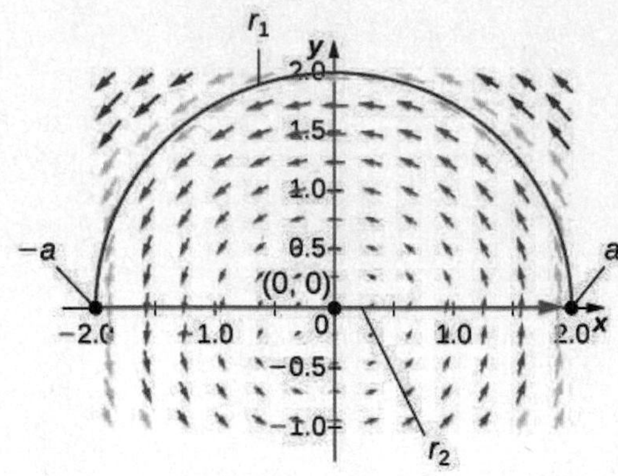

144. Compute $\int_C \cos x \cos y\,dx - \sin x \sin y\,dy$, where $\mathbf{c}(t) = (t, t^2),\ 0 \le t \le 1$.

145. Complete the proof of **The Path Independence Test for Conservative Fields** by showing that $f_y = Q(x, y)$.

6.4 | Green's Theorem

Learning Objectives

6.4.1 Apply the circulation form of Green's theorem.
6.4.2 Apply the flux form of Green's theorem.
6.4.3 Calculate circulation and flux on more general regions.

In this section, we examine Green's theorem, which is an extension of the Fundamental Theorem of Calculus to two dimensions. Green's theorem has two forms: a circulation form and a flux form, both of which require region D in the double integral to be simply connected. However, we will extend Green's theorem to regions that are not simply connected.

Put simply, Green's theorem relates a line integral around a simply closed plane curve C and a double integral over the region enclosed by C. The theorem is useful because it allows us to translate difficult line integrals into more simple double integrals, or difficult double integrals into more simple line integrals.

Extending the Fundamental Theorem of Calculus

Recall that the Fundamental Theorem of Calculus says that

$$\int_a^b F'(x)dx = F(b) - F(a).$$

As a geometric statement, this equation says that the integral over the region below the graph of $F'(x)$ and above the line segment $[a, b]$ depends only on the value of F at the endpoints a and b of that segment. Since the numbers a and b are the boundary of the line segment $[a, b]$, the theorem says we can calculate integral $\int_a^b F'(x)dx$ based on information about the boundary of line segment $[a, b]$ (**Figure 6.32**). The same idea is true of the Fundamental Theorem for Line Integrals:

$$\int_C \nabla f \cdot d\mathbf{r} = f(\mathbf{r}(b)) - f(\mathbf{r}(a)).$$

When we have a potential function (an "antiderivative"), we can calculate the line integral based solely on information about the boundary of curve C.

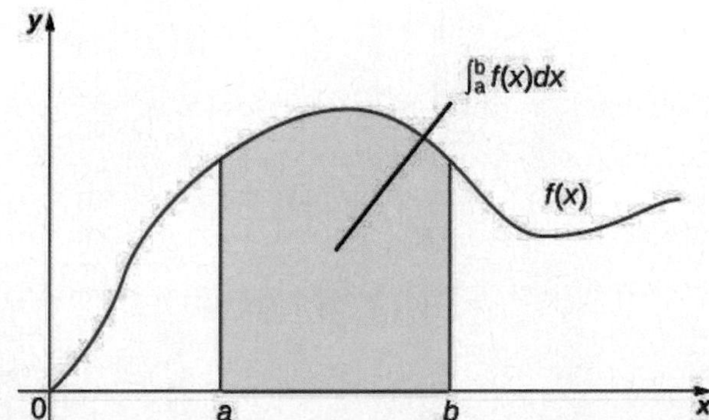

Figure 6.32 The Fundamental Theorem of Calculus says that the integral over line segment $[a, b]$ depends only on the values of the antiderivative at the endpoints of $[a, b]$.

Green's theorem takes this idea and extends it to calculating double integrals. Green's theorem says that we can calculate a double integral over region D based solely on information about the boundary of D. Green's theorem also says we can calculate a line integral over a simple closed curve C based solely on information about the region that C encloses. In particular, Green's theorem connects a double integral over region D to a line integral around the boundary of D.

Circulation Form of Green's Theorem

The first form of Green's theorem that we examine is the circulation form. This form of the theorem relates the vector line integral over a simple, closed plane curve C to a double integral over the region enclosed by C. Therefore, the circulation of a vector field along a simple closed curve can be transformed into a double integral and vice versa.

Theorem 6.12: Green's Theorem, Circulation Form

Let D be an open, simply connected region with a boundary curve C that is a piecewise smooth, simple closed curve oriented counterclockwise (**Figure 6.33**). Let $\mathbf{F} = \langle P, Q \rangle$ be a vector field with component functions that have continuous partial derivatives on D. Then,

$$\oint_C \mathbf{F} \cdot d\mathbf{r} = \oint_C Pdx + Qdy = \iint_D (Q_x - P_y)dA. \tag{6.13}$$

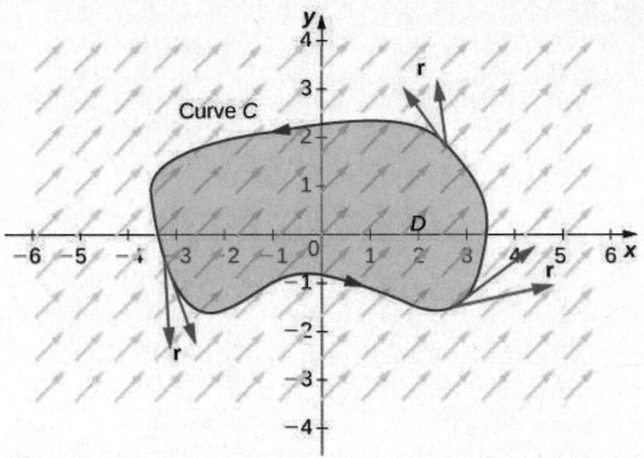

Figure 6.33 The circulation form of Green's theorem relates a line integral over curve C to a double integral over region D.

Notice that Green's theorem can be used only for a two-dimensional vector field $\mathbf{F}$. If $\mathbf{F}$ is a three-dimensional field, then Green's theorem does not apply. Since

$$\int_C Pdx + Qdy = \int_C \mathbf{F} \cdot \mathbf{T}ds,$$

this version of Green's theorem is sometimes referred to as the *tangential form* of Green's theorem.

The proof of Green's theorem is rather technical, and beyond the scope of this text. Here we examine a proof of the theorem in the special case that D is a rectangle. For now, notice that we can quickly confirm that the theorem is true for the special case in which $\mathbf{F} = \langle P, Q \rangle$ is conservative. In this case,

$$\oint_C Pdx + Qdy = 0$$

because the circulation is zero in conservative vector fields. By **Cross-Partial Property of Conservative Fields**, $\mathbf{F}$ satisfies the cross-partial condition, so $P_y = Q_x$. Therefore,

$$\iint_D (Q_x - P_y)dA = \iint_D 0dA = 0 = \oint_C Pdx + Qdy,$$

which confirms Green's theorem in the case of conservative vector fields.

Proof

Let's now prove that the circulation form of Green's theorem is true when the region D is a rectangle. Let D be the rectangle $[a, b] \times [c, d]$ oriented counterclockwise. Then, the boundary C of D consists of four piecewise smooth pieces C_1, C_2, C_3, and C_4 (**Figure 6.34**). We parameterize each side of D as follows:

$$\begin{aligned} C_1 : \mathbf{r}_1(t) &= \langle t, c \rangle, a \le t \le b \\ C_2 : \mathbf{r}_2(t) &= \langle b, t \rangle, c \le t \le d \\ -C_3 : \mathbf{r}_3(t) &= \langle t, d \rangle, a \le t \le b \\ -C_4 : \mathbf{r}_4(t) &= \langle a, t \rangle, c \le t \le d. \end{aligned}$$

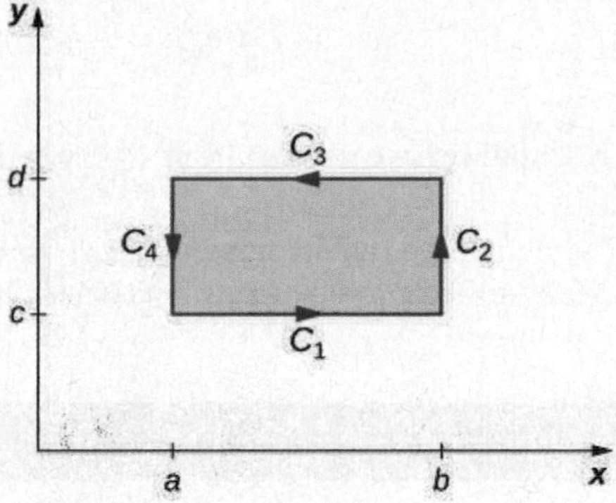

Figure 6.34 Rectangle D is oriented counterclockwise.

Then,

$$\begin{aligned} \int_C \mathbf{F} \bullet d\mathbf{r} &= \int_{C_1} \mathbf{F} \bullet d\mathbf{r} + \int_{C_2} \mathbf{F} \bullet d\mathbf{r} + \int_{C_3} \mathbf{F} \bullet d\mathbf{r} + \int_{C_4} \mathbf{F} \bullet d\mathbf{r} \\ &= \int_{C_1} \mathbf{F} \bullet d\mathbf{r} + \int_{C_2} \mathbf{F} \bullet d\mathbf{r} - \int_{-C_3} \mathbf{F} \bullet d\mathbf{r} - \int_{-C_4} \mathbf{F} \bullet d\mathbf{r} \\ &= \int_a^b \mathbf{F}(\mathbf{r}_1(t)) \bullet \mathbf{r}_1(t)dt + \int_c^d \mathbf{F}(\mathbf{r}_2(t)) \bullet \mathbf{r}_2(t)dt \\ &\quad - \int_a^b \mathbf{F}(\mathbf{r}_3(t)) \bullet \mathbf{r}_3(t)dt - \int_c^d \mathbf{F}(\mathbf{r}_4(t)) \bullet \mathbf{r}_4(t)dt \\ &= \int_a^b P(t, c)dt + \int_c^d Q(b, t)dt - \int_a^b P(t, d)dt - \int_c^d Q(a, t)dt \\ &= \int_a^b (P(t, c) - P(t, d))dt + \int_c^d (Q(b, t) - Q(a, t))dt \\ &= -\int_a^b (P(t, d) - P(t, c))dt + \int_c^d (Q(b, t) - Q(a, t))dt. \end{aligned}$$

By the Fundamental Theorem of Calculus,

$$P(t, d) - P(t, c) = \int_c^d \frac{\partial}{\partial y} P(t, y)dy \text{ and } Q(b, t) - Q(a, t) = \int_a^b \frac{\partial}{\partial x} Q(x, t)dx.$$

Therefore,

$$\begin{aligned} &-\int_a^b (P(t, d) - P(t, c))dt + \int_c^d (Q(b, t) - Q(a, t))dt \\ &= -\int_a^b \int_c^d \frac{\partial}{\partial y} P(t, y)dydt + \int_c^d \int_a^b \frac{\partial}{\partial x} Q(x, t)dxdt. \end{aligned}$$

But,

$$-\int_a^b \int_c^d \frac{\partial}{\partial y} P(t, y) dy dt + \int_c^d \int_a^b \frac{\partial}{\partial x} Q(x, t) dx dt = -\int_a^b \int_c^d \frac{\partial}{\partial y} P(x, y) dy dx + \int_c^d \int_a^b \frac{\partial}{\partial x} Q(x, y) dx dy$$

$$= \int_a^b \int_c^d (Q_x - P_y) dy dx$$

$$= \iint_D (Q_x - P_y) dA.$$

Therefore, $\int_C \mathbf{F} \cdot d\mathbf{r} = \iint_D (Q_x - P_y) dA$ and we have proved Green's theorem in the case of a rectangle.

To prove Green's theorem over a general region D, we can decompose D into many tiny rectangles and use the proof that the theorem works over rectangles. The details are technical, however, and beyond the scope of this text.

□

Example 6.38

Applying Green's Theorem over a Rectangle

Calculate the line integral

$$\oint_C x^2 y dx + (y - 3) dy,$$

where C is a rectangle with vertices $(1, 1)$, $(4, 1)$, $(4, 5)$, and $(1, 5)$ oriented counterclockwise.

Solution

Let $\mathbf{F}(x, y) = \langle P(x, y), Q(x, y) \rangle = \langle x^2 y, y - 3 \rangle$. Then, $Q_x = 0$ and $P_y = x^2$. Therefore, $Q_x - P_y = -x^2$.

Let D be the rectangular region enclosed by C (**Figure 6.35**). By Green's theorem,

$$\oint_C x^2 y dx + (y - 3) dy = \iint_D (Q_x - P_y) dA$$

$$= \iint_D -x^2 dA = \int_1^5 \int_1^4 -x^2 dx dy$$

$$= \int_1^5 -21 dy = -84.$$

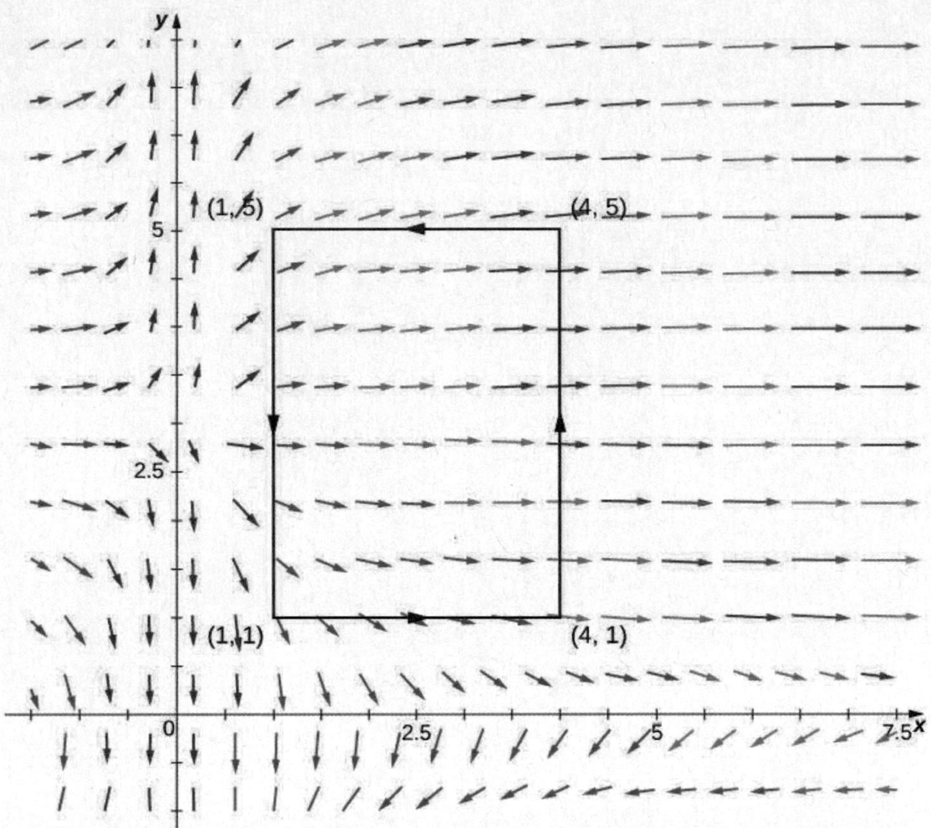

Figure 6.35 The line integral over the boundary of the rectangle can be transformed into a double integral over the rectangle.

Analysis

If we were to evaluate this line integral without using Green's theorem, we would need to parameterize each side of the rectangle, break the line integral into four separate line integrals, and use the methods from **Line Integrals** to evaluate each integral. Furthermore, since the vector field here is not conservative, we cannot apply the Fundamental Theorem for Line Integrals. Green's theorem makes the calculation much simpler.

Example 6.39

Applying Green's Theorem to Calculate Work

Calculate the work done on a particle by force field

$$\mathbf{F}(x, y) = \langle\, y + \sin x,\ e^y - x \,\rangle$$

as the particle traverses circle $x^2 + y^2 = 4$ exactly once in the counterclockwise direction, starting and ending at point $(2, 0)$.

Solution

Let C denote the circle and let D be the disk enclosed by C. The work done on the particle is

$$W = \oint_C (y + \sin x)dx + (e^y - x)dy.$$

As with **Example 6.38**, this integral can be calculated using tools we have learned, but it is easier to use the double integral given by Green's theorem (**Figure 6.36**).

Let $\mathbf{F}(x, y) = \langle P(x, y), Q(x, y) \rangle = \langle y + \sin x, e^y - x \rangle$. Then, $Q_x = -1$ and $P_y = 1$. Therefore, $Q_x - P_y = -2$.

By Green's theorem,

$$\begin{aligned} W &= \oint_C (y + \sin(x))dx + (e^y - x)dy \\ &= \iint_D (Q_x - P_y)dA = \iint_D -2dA \\ &= -2(\text{area}(D)) = -2\pi(2^2) = -8\pi. \end{aligned}$$

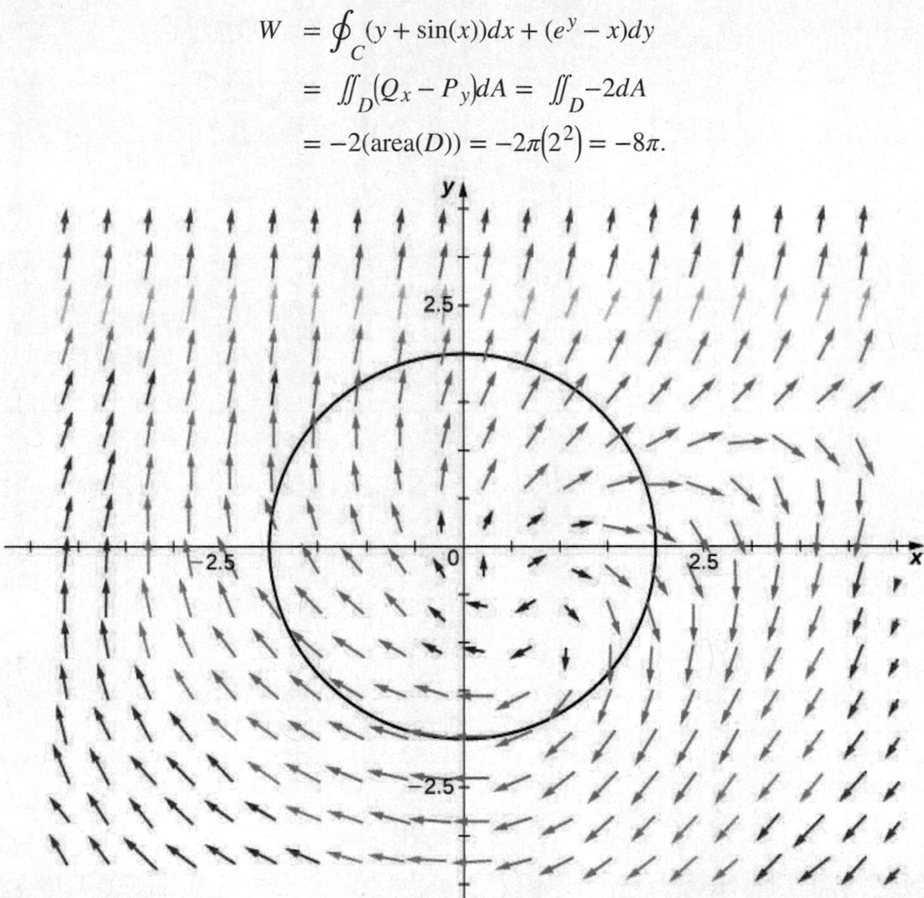

Figure 6.36 The line integral over the boundary circle can be transformed into a double integral over the disk enclosed by the circle.

6.34 Use Green's theorem to calculate line integral

$$\oint_C \sin(x^2)dx + (3x - y)dy,$$

where C is a right triangle with vertices $(-1, 2)$, $(4, 2)$, and $(4, 5)$ oriented counterclockwise.

In the preceding two examples, the double integral in Green's theorem was easier to calculate than the line integral, so we used the theorem to calculate the line integral. In the next example, the double integral is more difficult to calculate than the line integral, so we use Green's theorem to translate a double integral into a line integral.

Example 6.40

Applying Green's Theorem over an Ellipse

Calculate the area enclosed by ellipse $\frac{x^2}{a^2} + \frac{y^2}{b^2} = 1$ (**Figure 6.37**).

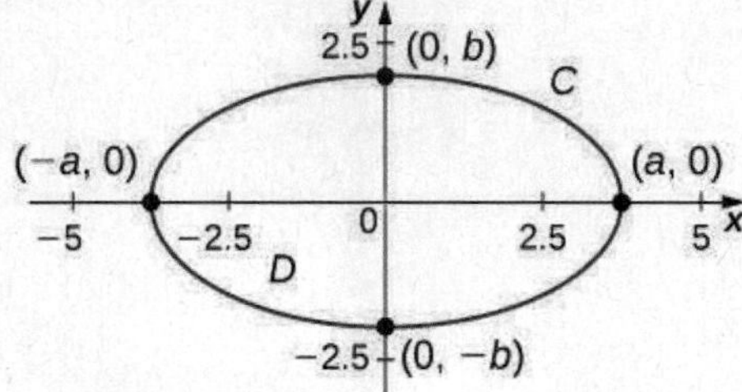

Figure 6.37 Ellipse $\frac{x^2}{a^2} + \frac{y^2}{b^2} = 1$ is denoted by C.

Solution

Let C denote the ellipse and let D be the region enclosed by C. Recall that ellipse C can be parameterized by

$$x = a \cos t, \; y = b \sin t, \; 0 \le t \le 2\pi.$$

Calculating the area of D is equivalent to computing double integral $\iint_D dA$. To calculate this integral without Green's theorem, we would need to divide D into two regions: the region above the x-axis and the region below. The area of the ellipse is

$$\int_{-a}^{a} \int_{0}^{\sqrt{b^2 - (bx/a)^2}} dy dx + \int_{-a}^{a} \int_{-\sqrt{b^2 - (bx/a)^2}}^{0} dy dx.$$

These two integrals are not straightforward to calculate (although when we know the value of the first integral, we know the value of the second by symmetry). Instead of trying to calculate them, we use Green's theorem to transform $\iint_D dA$ into a line integral around the boundary C.

Consider vector field

$$\mathbf{F}(x, y) = \langle P, Q \rangle = \langle -\frac{y}{2}, \frac{x}{2} \rangle.$$

Then, $Q_x = \frac{1}{2}$ and $P_y = -\frac{1}{2}$, and therefore $Q_x - P_y = 1$. Notice that $\mathbf{F}$ was chosen to have the property that $Q_x - P_y = 1$. Since this is the case, Green's theorem transforms the line integral of $\mathbf{F}$ over C into the double integral of 1 over D.

By Green's theorem,

$$\begin{aligned}\iint_D dA &= \iint_D (Q_x - P_y) dA \\ &= \int_C \mathbf{F} \bullet d\mathbf{r} = \frac{1}{2}\int_C -ydx + xdy \\ &= \frac{1}{2}\int_0^{2\pi} -b \sin t(-a \sin t) + a(\cos t)b \cos t dt \\ &= \frac{1}{2}\int_0^{2\pi} ab \cos^2 t + ab \sin^2 t dt = \frac{1}{2}\int_0^{2\pi} ab dt = \pi ab.\end{aligned}$$

Therefore, the area of the ellipse is πab.

In **Example 6.40**, we used vector field $\mathbf{F}(x, y) = \langle P, Q \rangle = \langle -\frac{y}{2}, \frac{x}{2} \rangle$ to find the area of any ellipse. The logic of the previous example can be extended to derive a formula for the area of any region D. Let D be any region with a boundary that is a simple closed curve C oriented counterclockwise. If $\mathbf{F}(x, y) = \langle P, Q \rangle = \langle -\frac{y}{2}, \frac{x}{2} \rangle$, then $Q_x - P_y = 1$. Therefore, by the same logic as in **Example 6.40**,

$$\text{area of } D = \iint_D dA = \frac{1}{2}\oint_C -ydx + xdy. \quad \textbf{(6.14)}$$

It's worth noting that if $\mathbf{F} = \langle P, Q \rangle$ is any vector field with $Q_x - P_y = 1$, then the logic of the previous paragraph works. So. **Equation 6.14** is not the only equation that uses a vector field's mixed partials to get the area of a region.

6.35 Find the area of the region enclosed by the curve with parameterization $\mathbf{r}(t) = \langle \sin t \cos t, \sin t \rangle, 0 \le t \le \pi$.

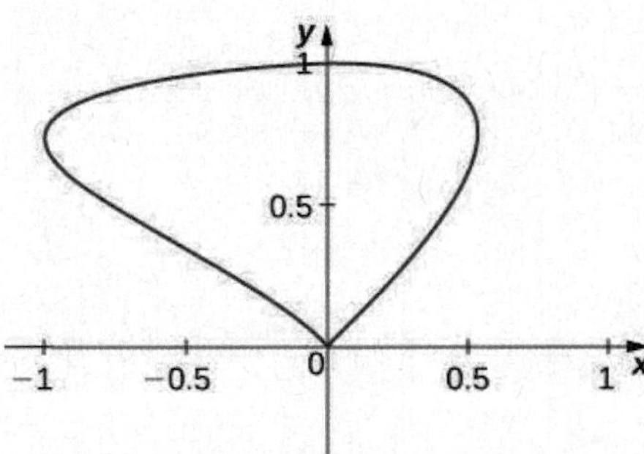

Flux Form of Green's Theorem

The circulation form of Green's theorem relates a double integral over region D to line integral $\oint_C \mathbf{F} \cdot \mathbf{T} ds$, where C is the boundary of D. The flux form of Green's theorem relates a double integral over region D to the flux across boundary C. The flux of a fluid across a curve can be difficult to calculate using the flux line integral. This form of Green's theorem allows us to translate a difficult flux integral into a double integral that is often easier to calculate.

Theorem 6.13: Green's Theorem, Flux Form

Let D be an open, simply connected region with a boundary curve C that is a piecewise smooth, simple closed curve that is oriented counterclockwise (**Figure 6.38**). Let $\mathbf{F} = \langle P, Q \rangle$ be a vector field with component functions that have continuous partial derivatives on an open region containing D. Then,

$$\oint_C \mathbf{F} \cdot \mathbf{N} ds = \iint_D P_x + Q_y dA. \tag{6.15}$$

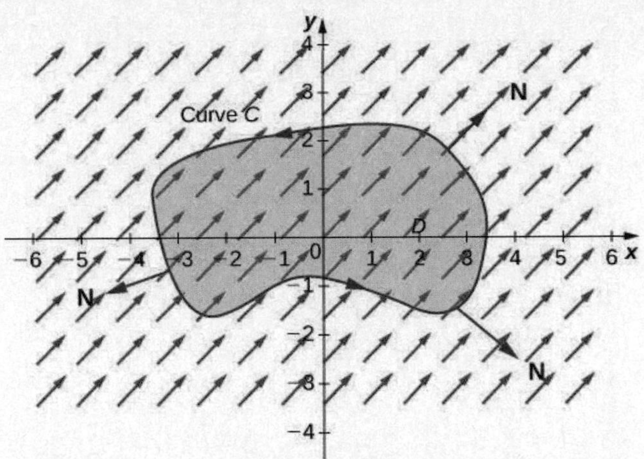

Figure 6.38 The flux form of Green's theorem relates a double integral over region D to the flux across curve C.

Because this form of Green's theorem contains unit normal vector **N**, it is sometimes referred to as the *normal form* of Green's theorem.

Proof

Recall that $\oint_C \mathbf{F} \cdot \mathbf{N} ds = \oint_C -Q dx + P dy$. Let $M = -Q$ and $N = P$. By the circulation form of Green's theorem,

$$\begin{aligned} \oint_C -Q dx + P dy &= \oint_C M dx + N dy \\ &= \iint_D N_x - M_y dA \\ &= \iint_D P_x - (-Q)_y dA \\ &= \iint_D P_x + Q_y dA. \end{aligned}$$

□

Example 6.41

Applying Green's Theorem for Flux across a Circle

Let C be a circle of radius r centered at the origin (**Figure 6.39**) and let $\mathbf{F}(x, y) = \langle x, y \rangle$. Calculate the flux across C.

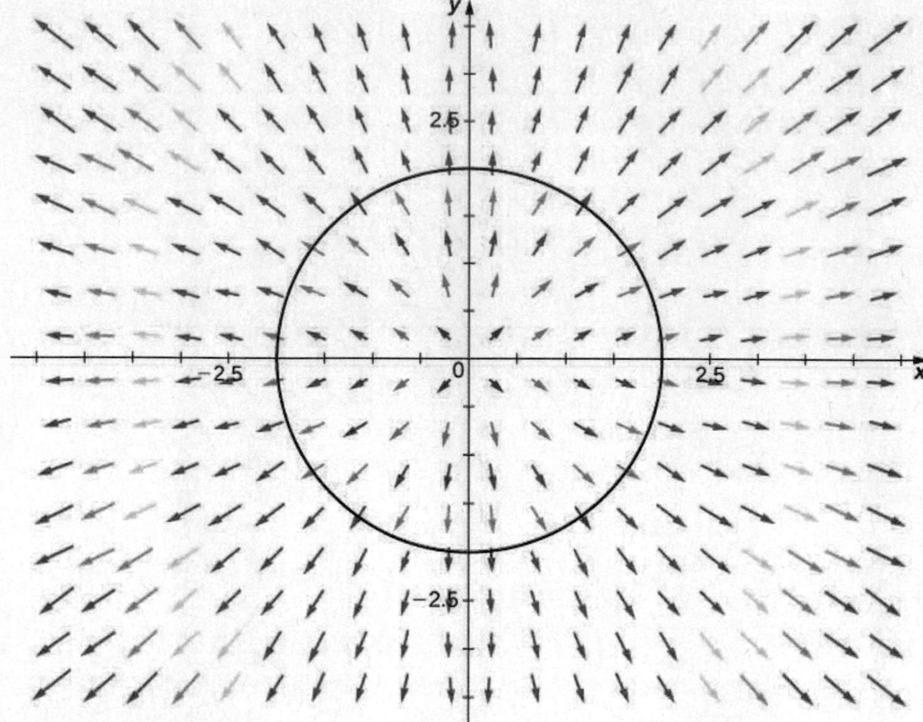

Figure 6.39 Curve C is a circle of radius r centered at the origin.

Solution

Let D be the disk enclosed by C. The flux across C is $\oint_C \mathbf{F} \cdot \mathbf{N} ds$. We could evaluate this integral using tools we have learned, but Green's theorem makes the calculation much more simple. Let $P(x, y) = x$ and $Q(x, y) = y$ so that $\mathbf{F} = \langle P, Q \rangle$. Note that $P_x = 1 = Q_y$, and therefore $P_x + Q_y = 2$. By Green's theorem,

$$\int_C \mathbf{F} \bullet \mathbf{N} ds = \iint_D 2dA = 2\iint_D dA.$$

Since $\iint_D dA$ is the area of the circle, $\iint_D dA = \pi r^2$. Therefore, the flux across C is $2\pi r^2$.

Example 6.42

Applying Green's Theorem for Flux across a Triangle

Let S be the triangle with vertices $(0, 0)$, $(1, 0)$, and $(0, 3)$ oriented clockwise (**Figure 6.40**). Calculate the flux of $\mathbf{F}(x, y) = \langle P(x, y), Q(x, y) \rangle = \langle x^2 + e^y, x + y \rangle$ across S.

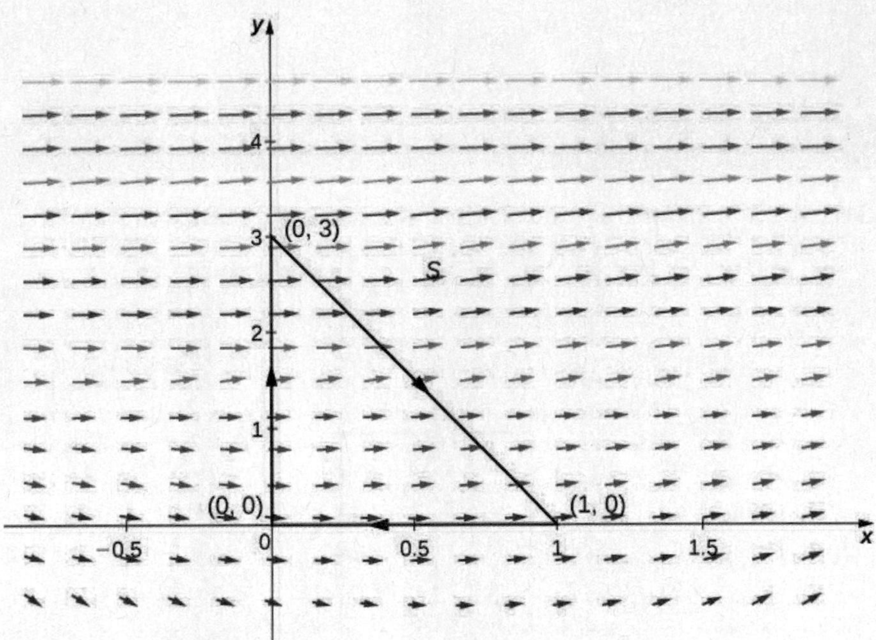

Figure 6.40 Curve S is a triangle with vertices $(0, 0)$, $(1, 0)$, and $(0, 3)$ oriented clockwise.

Solution

To calculate the flux without Green's theorem, we would need to break the flux integral into three line integrals, one integral for each side of the triangle. Using Green's theorem to translate the flux line integral into a single double integral is much more simple.

Let D be the region enclosed by S. Note that $P_x = 2x$ and $Q_y = 1$; therefore, $P_x + Q_y = 2x + 1$. Green's theorem applies only to simple closed curves oriented counterclockwise, but we can still apply the theorem because $\oint_C \mathbf{F} \cdot \mathbf{N} ds = -\oint_{-S} \mathbf{F} \cdot \mathbf{N} ds$ and $-S$ is oriented counterclockwise. By Green's theorem, the flux is

$$\begin{aligned}\oint_C \mathbf{F} \cdot \mathbf{N} ds &= \oint_{-S} \mathbf{F} \cdot \mathbf{N} ds \\ &= -\iint_D (P_x + Q_y) dA \\ &= -\iint_D (2x + 1) dA.\end{aligned}$$

Notice that the top edge of the triangle is the line $y = -3x + 3$. Therefore, in the iterated double integral, the y-values run from $y = 0$ to $y = -3x + 3$, and we have

$$\begin{aligned}-\iint_D (2x + 1) dA &= -\int_0^1 \int_0^{-3x+3} (2x + 1) dy dx \\ &= -\int_0^1 (2x + 1)(-3x + 3) dx = -\int_0^1 \left(-6x^2 + 3x + 3\right) dx \\ &= -\left[-2x^3 + \frac{3x^2}{2} + 3x\right]_0^1 = -\frac{5}{2}.\end{aligned}$$

6.36 Calculate the flux of $\mathbf{F}(x, y) = \langle x^3, y^3 \rangle$ across a unit circle oriented counterclockwise.

Example 6.43

Applying Green's Theorem for Water Flow across a Rectangle

Water flows from a spring located at the origin. The velocity of the water is modeled by vector field $\mathbf{v}(x, y) = \langle 5x + y, x + 3y \rangle$ m/sec. Find the amount of water per second that flows across the rectangle with vertices $(-1, -2), (1, -2), (1, 3),$ and $(-1, 3),$ oriented counterclockwise (**Figure 6.41**).

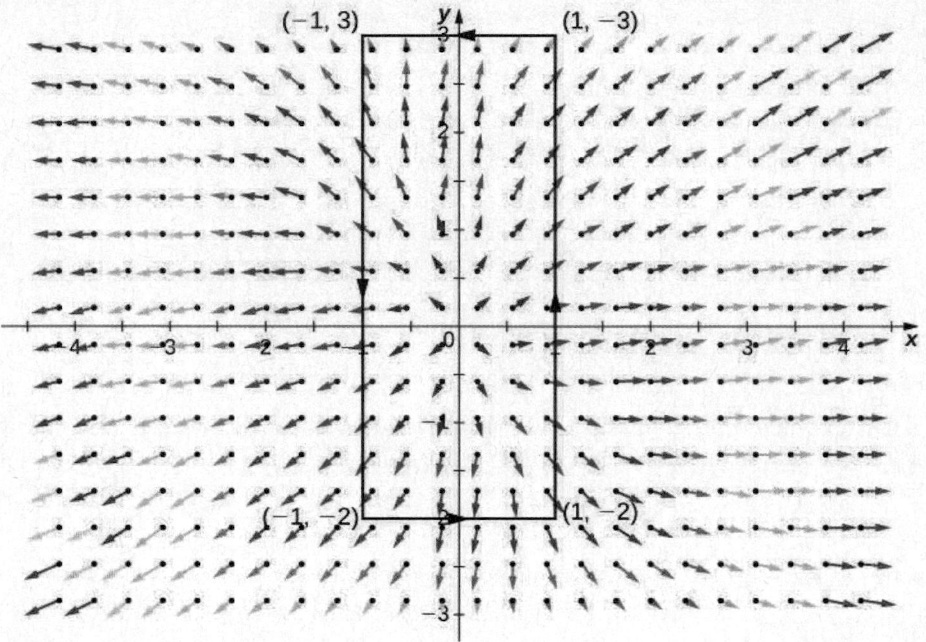

Figure 6.41 Water flows across the rectangle with vertices $(-1, -2), (1, -2), (1, 3),$ and $(-1, 3),$ oriented counterclockwise.

Solution

Let C represent the given rectangle and let D be the rectangular region enclosed by C. To find the amount of water flowing across C, we calculate flux $\int_C \mathbf{v} \cdot d\mathbf{r}$. Let $P(x, y) = 5x + y$ and $Q(x, y) = x + 3y$ so that $\mathbf{v} = (P, Q)$. Then, $P_x = 5$ and $Q_y = 3$. By Green's theorem,

$$\begin{aligned} \int_C \mathbf{v} \cdot d\mathbf{r} &= \iint_D (P_x + Q_y) dA \\ &= \iint_D 8 dA \\ &= 8(\text{area of } D) = 80. \end{aligned}$$

Therefore, the water flux is 80 m^2/sec.

Recall that if vector field $\mathbf{F}$ is conservative, then $\mathbf{F}$ does no work around closed curves—that is, the circulation of $\mathbf{F}$ around a closed curve is zero. In fact, if the domain of $\mathbf{F}$ is simply connected, then $\mathbf{F}$ is conservative if and only if the circulation of $\mathbf{F}$ around any closed curve is zero. If we replace "circulation of $\mathbf{F}$" with "flux of $\mathbf{F}$," then we get a definition of a source-free vector field. The following statements are all equivalent ways of defining a source-free field $\mathbf{F} = \langle P, Q \rangle$ on a simply connected domain (note the similarities with properties of conservative vector fields):

1. The flux $\oint_C \mathbf{F} \cdot \mathbf{N} ds$ across any closed curve C is zero.
2. If C_1 and C_2 are curves in the domain of $\mathbf{F}$ with the same starting points and endpoints, then $\int_{C_1} \mathbf{F} \cdot \mathbf{N} ds = \int_{C_2} \mathbf{F} \cdot \mathbf{N} ds$. In other words, flux is independent of path.
3. There is a **stream function** $g(x, y)$ for $\mathbf{F}$. A stream function for $\mathbf{F} = \langle P, Q \rangle$ is a function g such that $P = g_y$ and $Q = -g_x$. Geometrically, $\mathbf{F} = (a, b)$ is tangential to the level curve of g at (a, b). Since the gradient of g is perpendicular to the level curve of g at (a, b), stream function g has the property $\mathbf{F}(a, b) \bullet \nabla g(a, b) = 0$ for any point (a, b) in the domain of g. (Stream functions play the same role for source-free fields that potential functions play for conservative fields.)
4. $P_x + Q_y = 0$

Example 6.44

Finding a Stream Function

Verify that rotation vector field $\mathbf{F}(x, y) = \langle y, -x \rangle$ is source free, and find a stream function for $\mathbf{F}$.

Solution

Note that the domain of $\mathbf{F}$ is all of $\mathbb{R}^2$, which is simply connected. Therefore, to show that $\mathbf{F}$ is source free, we can show any of items 1 through 4 from the previous list to be true. In this example, we show that item 4 is true. Let $P(x, y) = y$ and $Q(x, y) = -x$. Then $P_x + 0 = Q_y$, and therefore $P_x + Q_y = 0$. Thus, $\mathbf{F}$ is source free.

To find a stream function for $\mathbf{F}$, proceed in the same manner as finding a potential function for a conservative field. Let g be a stream function for $\mathbf{F}$. Then $g_y = y$, which implies that

$$g(x, y) = \frac{y^2}{2} + h(x).$$

Since $-g_x = Q = -x$, we have $h'(x) = x$. Therefore,

$$h(x) = \frac{x^2}{2} + C.$$

Letting $C = 0$ gives stream function

$$g(x, y) = \frac{x^2}{2} + \frac{y^2}{2}.$$

To confirm that g is a stream function for $\mathbf{F}$, note that $g_y = y = P$ and $-g_x = -x = Q$.

Notice that source-free rotation vector field $\mathbf{F}(x, y) = \langle y, -x \rangle$ is perpendicular to conservative radial vector field $\nabla g = \langle x, y \rangle$ (**Figure 6.42**).

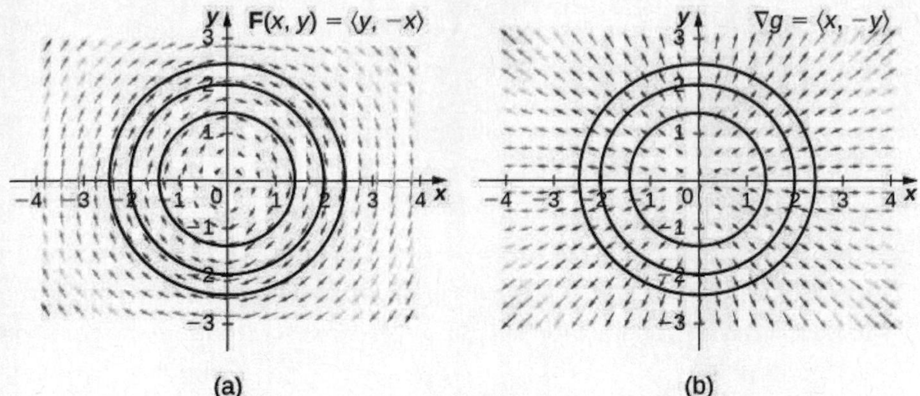

Figure 6.42 (a) In this image, we see the three-level curves of g and vector field **F**. Note that the **F** vectors on a given level curve are tangent to the level curve. (b) In this image, we see the three-level curves of g and vector field ∇g. The gradient vectors are perpendicular to the corresponding level curve. Therefore, $\mathbf{F}(a, b) \bullet \nabla g(a, b) = 0$ for any point in the domain of g.

6.37 Find a stream function for vector field $\mathbf{F}(x, y) = \langle x \sin y, \cos y \rangle$.

Vector fields that are both conservative and source free are important vector fields. One important feature of conservative and source-free vector fields on a simply connected domain is that any potential function f of such a field satisfies Laplace's equation $f_{xx} + f_{yy} = 0$. Laplace's equation is foundational in the field of partial differential equations because it models such phenomena as gravitational and magnetic potentials in space, and the velocity potential of an ideal fluid. A function that satisfies Laplace's equation is called a *harmonic* function. Therefore any potential function of a conservative and source-free vector field is harmonic.

To see that any potential function of a conservative and source-free vector field on a simply connected domain is harmonic, let f be such a potential function of vector field $\mathbf{F} = \langle P, Q \rangle$. Then, $f_x = P$ and $f_x = Q$ because $\nabla f = \mathbf{F}$. Therefore, $f_{xx} = P_x$ and $f_{yy} = Q_y$. Since **F** is source free, $f_{xx} + f_{yy} = P_x + Q_y = 0,$ and we have that f is harmonic.

Example 6.45

Satisfying Laplace's Equation

For vector field $\mathbf{F}(x, y) = \langle e^x \sin y, e^x \cos y \rangle$, verify that the field is both conservative and source free, find a potential function for **F**, and verify that the potential function is harmonic.

Solution

Let $P(x, y) = e^x \sin y$ and $Q(x, y) = e^x \cos y$. Notice that the domain of **F** is all of two-space, which is simply connected. Therefore, we can check the cross-partials of **F** to determine whether **F** is conservative. Note that $P_y = e^x \cos y = Q_x,$ so **F** is conservative. Since $P_x = e^x \sin y$ and $Q_y = e^x \sin y, P_x + Q_y = 0$ and the field is source free.

To find a potential function for **F**, let f be a potential function. Then, $\nabla f = \mathbf{F}$, so $f_x = e^x \sin y$. Integrating this equation with respect to x gives $f(x, y) = e^x \sin y + h(y)$. Since $f_y = e^x \cos y$, differentiating f with respect to y gives $e^x \cos y = e^x \cos y + h'(y)$. Therefore, we can take $h(y) = 0$, and $f(x, y) = e^x \sin y$ is a potential function for f.

To verify that f is a harmonic function, note that $f_{xx} = \frac{\partial}{\partial x}(e^x \sin y) = e^x \sin y$ and

$f_{yy} = \frac{\partial}{\partial x}(e^x \cos y) = -e^x \sin y$. Therefore, $f_{xx} + f_{yy} = 0$, and f satisfies Laplace's equation.

6.38 Is the function $f(x, y) = e^{x + 5y}$ harmonic?

Green's Theorem on General Regions

Green's theorem, as stated, applies only to regions that are simply connected—that is, Green's theorem as stated so far cannot handle regions with holes. Here, we extend Green's theorem so that it does work on regions with finitely many holes (**Figure 6.43**).

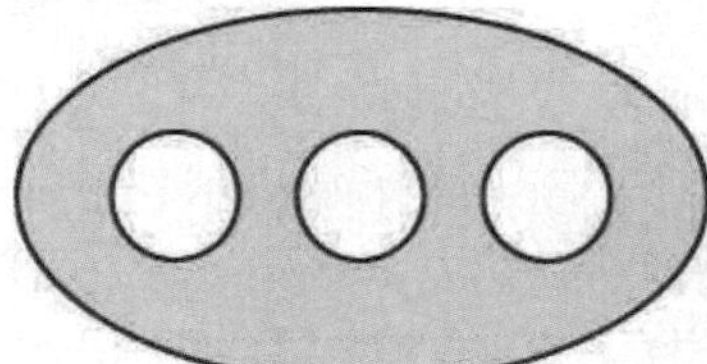

Figure 6.43 Green's theorem, as stated, does not apply to a nonsimply connected region with three holes like this one.

Before discussing extensions of Green's theorem, we need to go over some terminology regarding the boundary of a region. Let D be a region and let C be a component of the boundary of D. We say that C is *positively oriented* if, as we walk along C in the direction of orientation, region D is always on our left. Therefore, the counterclockwise orientation of the boundary of a disk is a positive orientation, for example. Curve C is *negatively oriented* if, as we walk along C in the direction of orientation, region D is always on our right. The clockwise orientation of the boundary of a disk is a negative orientation, for example.

Let D be a region with finitely many holes (so that D has finitely many boundary curves), and denote the boundary of D by ∂D (**Figure 6.44**). To extend Green's theorem so it can handle D, we divide region D into two regions, D_1 and D_2 (with respective boundaries ∂D_1 and ∂D_2), in such a way that $D = D_1 \cup D_2$ and neither D_1 nor D_2 has any holes (**Figure 6.44**).

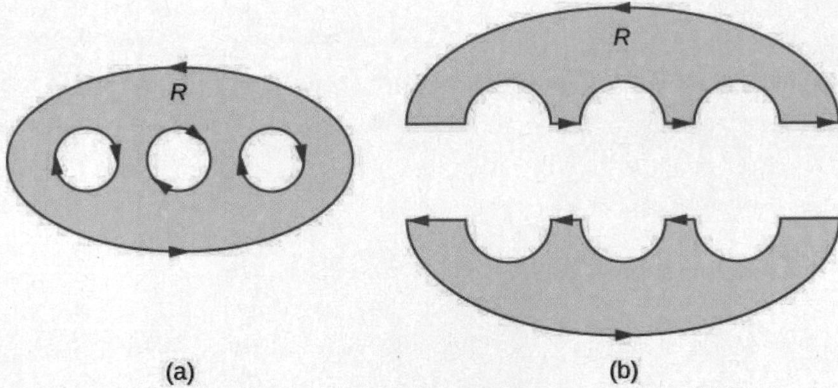

Figure 6.44 (a) Region D with an oriented boundary has three holes. (b) Region D split into two simply connected regions has no holes.

Assume the boundary of D is oriented as in the figure, with the inner holes given a negative orientation and the outer boundary given a positive orientation. The boundary of each simply connected region D_1 and D_2 is positively oriented. If **F** is a vector field defined on D, then Green's theorem says that

$$\begin{aligned}\oint_{\partial D} \mathbf{F} \cdot d\mathbf{r} &= \oint_{\partial D_1} \mathbf{F} \cdot d\mathbf{r} + \oint_{\partial D_2} \mathbf{F} \cdot d\mathbf{r} \\ &= \iint_{D_1} Q_x - P_y dA + \iint_{D_2} Q_x - P_y dA \\ &= \iint_D (Q_x - P_y) dA.\end{aligned}$$

Therefore, Green's theorem still works on a region with holes.

To see how this works in practice, consider annulus D in **Figure 6.45** and suppose that $\mathbf{F} = \langle P, Q \rangle$ is a vector field defined on this annulus. Region D has a hole, so it is not simply connected. Orient the outer circle of the annulus counterclockwise and the inner circle clockwise (**Figure 6.45**) so that, when we divide the region into D_1 and D_2, we are able to keep the region on our left as we walk along a path that traverses the boundary. Let D_1 be the upper half of the annulus and D_2 be the lower half. Neither of these regions has holes, so we have divided D into two simply connected regions.

We label each piece of these new boundaries as P_i for some i, as in **Figure 6.45**. If we begin at P and travel along the oriented boundary, the first segment is P_1, then P_2, P_3, and P_4. Now we have traversed D_1 and returned to P. Next, we start at P again and traverse D_2. Since the first piece of the boundary is the same as P_4 in D_1, but oriented in the opposite direction, the first piece of D_2 is $-P_4$. Next, we have P_5, then $-P_2$, and finally P_6.

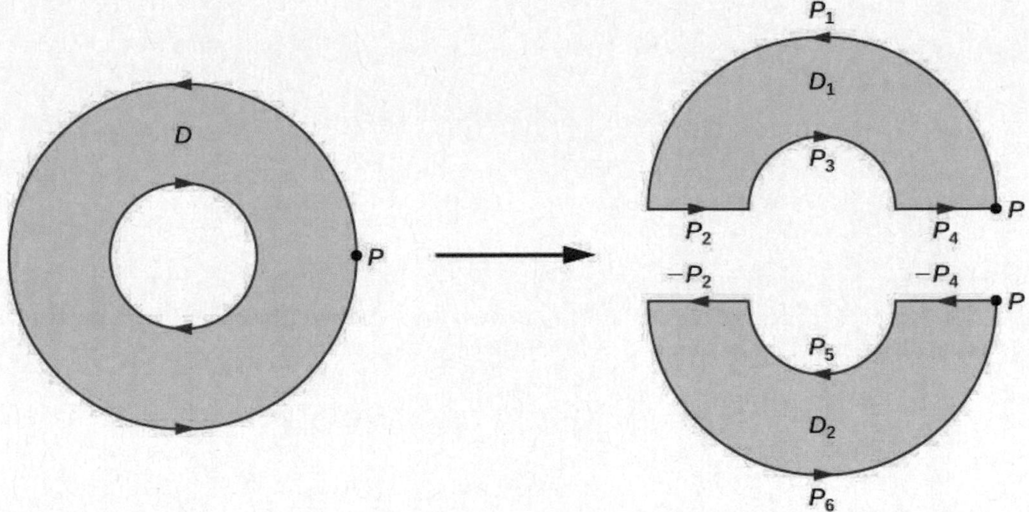

Figure 6.45 Breaking the annulus into two separate regions gives us two simply connected regions. The line integrals over the common boundaries cancel out.

Figure 6.45 shows a path that traverses the boundary of *D*. Notice that this path traverses the boundary of region D_1, returns to the starting point, and then traverses the boundary of region D_2. Furthermore, as we walk along the path, the region is always on our left. Notice that this traversal of the P_i paths covers the entire boundary of region *D*. If we had only traversed one portion of the boundary of *D*, then we cannot apply Green's theorem to *D*.

The boundary of the upper half of the annulus, therefore, is $P_1 \cup P_2 \cup P_3 \cup P_4$ and the boundary of the lower half of the annulus is $-P_4 \cup P_5 \cup -P_2 \cup P_6$. Then, Green's theorem implies

$$\begin{aligned}
\int_{\partial D} \mathbf{F} \cdot d\mathbf{r} &= \int_{P_1} \mathbf{F} \cdot d\mathbf{r} + \int_{P_2} \mathbf{F} \cdot d\mathbf{r} + \int_{P_3} \mathbf{F} \cdot d\mathbf{r} + \int_{P_4} \mathbf{F} \cdot d\mathbf{r} + \int_{-P_4} \mathbf{F} \cdot d\mathbf{r} + \int_{P_5} \mathbf{F} \cdot d\mathbf{r} - \int_{P_2} \mathbf{F} \cdot d\mathbf{r} + \int_{P_6} \mathbf{F} \cdot d\mathbf{r} \\
&= \int_{P_1} \mathbf{F} \cdot d\mathbf{r} + \int_{P_2} \mathbf{F} \cdot d\mathbf{r} + \int_{P_3} \mathbf{F} \cdot d\mathbf{r} + \int_{P_4} \mathbf{F} \cdot d\mathbf{r} - \int_{P_4} \mathbf{F} \cdot d\mathbf{r} + \int_{P_5} \mathbf{F} \cdot d\mathbf{r} - \int_{P_2} \mathbf{F} \cdot d\mathbf{r} + \int_{P_6} \mathbf{F} \cdot d\mathbf{r} \\
&= \int_{P_1} \mathbf{F} \cdot d\mathbf{r} + \int_{P_3} \mathbf{F} \cdot d\mathbf{r} + \int_{P_5} \mathbf{F} \cdot d\mathbf{r} + \int_{P_6} \mathbf{F} \cdot d\mathbf{r} \\
&= \int_{\partial D_1} \mathbf{F} \cdot d\mathbf{r} + \int_{\partial D_2} \mathbf{F} \cdot d\mathbf{r} \\
&= \iint_{D_1} (Q_x - P_y) dA + \iint_{D_2} (Q_x - P_y) dA \\
&= \iint_{D} (Q_x - P_y) dA.
\end{aligned}$$

Therefore, we arrive at the equation found in Green's theorem—namely,

$$\oint_{\partial D} \mathbf{F} \cdot d\mathbf{r} = \iint_D (Q_x - P_y) dA.$$

The same logic implies that the flux form of Green's theorem can also be extended to a region with finitely many holes:

$$\oint_C \mathbf{F} \cdot \mathbf{N} ds = \iint_D (P_x + Q_y) dA.$$

Example 6.46

Using Green's Theorem on a Region with Holes

Calculate integral

$$\oint_{\partial D} \left(\sin x - \frac{y^3}{3}\right)dx + \left(\frac{y^3}{3} + \sin y\right)dy,$$

where D is the annulus given by the polar inequalities $1 \le \mathbf{r} \le 2, \quad 0 \le \theta \le 2\pi$.

Solution

Although D is not simply connected, we can use the extended form of Green's theorem to calculate the integral. Since the integration occurs over an annulus, we convert to polar coordinates:

$$\begin{aligned} \oint_{\partial D} \left(\sin x - \frac{y^3}{3}\right)dx + \left(\frac{x^3}{3} + \sin y\right)dy &= \iint_D (Q_x - P_y)dA \\ &= \iint_D (x^2 + y^2)dA \\ &= \int_0^{2\pi} \int_1^2 r^3\, dr d\theta = \int_0^{2\pi} \frac{15}{4} d\theta \\ &= \frac{15\pi}{2}. \end{aligned}$$

Example 6.47

Using the Extended Form of Green's Theorem

Let $\mathbf{F} = \langle P, Q \rangle = \langle \frac{y}{x^2 + y^2}, -\frac{x}{x^2 + y^2} \rangle$ and let C be any simple closed curve in a plane oriented counterclockwise. What are the possible values of $\oint_C \mathbf{F} \cdot d\mathbf{r}$?

Solution

We use the extended form of Green's theorem to show that $\oint_C \mathbf{F} \cdot d\mathbf{r}$ is either 0 or -2π—that is, no matter how crazy curve C is, the line integral of $\mathbf{F}$ along C can have only one of two possible values. We consider two cases: the case when C encompasses the origin and the case when C does not encompass the origin.

Case 1: C Does Not Encompass the Origin

In this case, the region enclosed by C is simply connected because the only hole in the domain of $\mathbf{F}$ is at the origin. We showed in our discussion of cross-partials that $\mathbf{F}$ satisfies the cross-partial condition. If we restrict the domain of $\mathbf{F}$ just to C and the region it encloses, then $\mathbf{F}$ with this restricted domain is now defined on a simply connected domain. Since $\mathbf{F}$ satisfies the cross-partial property on its restricted domain, the field $\mathbf{F}$ is conservative on this simply connected region and hence the circulation $\oint_C \mathbf{F} \cdot d\mathbf{r}$ is zero.

Case 2: C Does Encompass the Origin

In this case, the region enclosed by C is not simply connected because this region contains a hole at the origin. Let C_1 be a circle of radius a centered at the origin so that C_1 is entirely inside the region enclosed by C (**Figure 6.46**). Give C_1 a clockwise orientation.

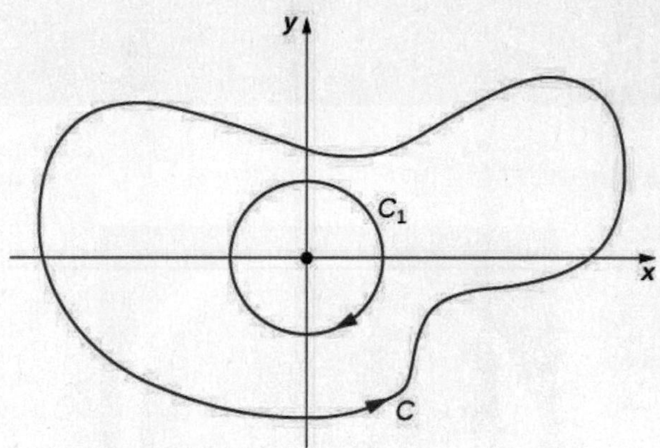

Figure 6.46 Choose circle C_1 centered at the origin that is contained entirely inside *C*.

Let *D* be the region between C_1 and *C*, and *C* is orientated counterclockwise. By the extended version of Green's theorem,

$$\begin{aligned}\int_C \mathbf{F}\cdot d\mathbf{r} + \int_{C_1} \mathbf{F}\cdot d\mathbf{r} &= \iint_D Q_x - P_y dA \\ &= \iint_D -\frac{y^2 - x^2}{(x^2+y^2)^2} + \frac{y^2 - x^2}{(x^2+y^2)^2} dA \\ &= 0,\end{aligned}$$

and therefore

$$\int_C \mathbf{F}\cdot d\mathbf{r} = -\int_{C_1} \mathbf{F}\cdot d\mathbf{r}.$$

Since C_1 is a specific curve, we can evaluate $\int_{C_1} \mathbf{F}\cdot d\mathbf{r}$. Let

$$x = a\cos t,\ y = a\sin t,\ 0 \le t \le 2\pi$$

be a parameterization of C_1. Then,

$$\begin{aligned}\int_{C_1} \mathbf{F}\cdot d\mathbf{r} &= \int_0^{2\pi} \mathbf{F}(\mathbf{r}(t))\cdot \mathbf{r}'(t)dt \\ &= \int_0^{2\pi} \langle -\frac{\sin(t)}{a},\ -\frac{\cos(t)}{a} \rangle \cdot \langle -a\sin(t),\ -a\cos(t) \rangle\ dt \\ &= \int_0^{2\pi} \sin^2(t) + \cos^2(t)dt = \int_0^{2\pi} dt = 2\pi.\end{aligned}$$

Therefore, $\int_C \mathbf{F}\cdot ds = -2\pi.$

6.39 Calculate integral $\oint_{\partial D} \mathbf{F}\cdot d\mathbf{r},$ where *D* is the annulus given by the polar inequalities $2 \le r \le 5,\ 0 \le \theta \le 2\pi,$ and $\mathbf{F}(x, y) = \langle x^3,\ 5x + e^y \sin y \rangle$.

Student PROJECT

Measuring Area from a Boundary: The Planimeter

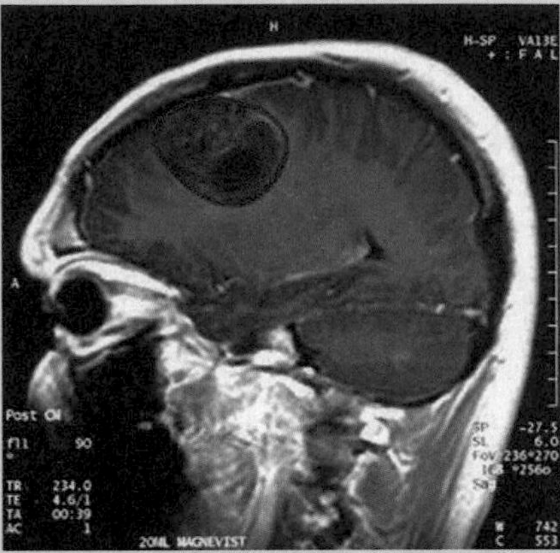

Figure 6.47 This magnetic resonance image of a patient's brain shows a tumor, which is highlighted in red. (credit: modification of work by Christaras A, Wikimedia Commons)

Imagine you are a doctor who has just received a magnetic resonance image of your patient's brain. The brain has a tumor (Figure 6.47). How large is the tumor? To be precise, what is the area of the red region? The red cross-section of the tumor has an irregular shape, and therefore it is unlikely that you would be able to find a set of equations or inequalities for the region and then be able to calculate its area by conventional means. You could approximate the area by chopping the region into tiny squares (a Riemann sum approach), but this method always gives an answer with some error.

Instead of trying to measure the area of the region directly, we can use a device called a *rolling planimeter* to calculate the area of the region exactly, simply by measuring its boundary. In this project you investigate how a planimeter works, and you use Green's theorem to show the device calculates area correctly.

A rolling planimeter is a device that measures the area of a planar region by tracing out the boundary of that region (Figure 6.48). To measure the area of a region, we simply run the tracer of the planimeter around the boundary of the region. The planimeter measures the number of turns through which the wheel rotates as we trace the boundary; the area of the shape is proportional to this number of wheel turns. We can derive the precise proportionality equation using Green's theorem. As the tracer moves around the boundary of the region, the tracer arm rotates and the roller moves back and forth (but does not rotate).

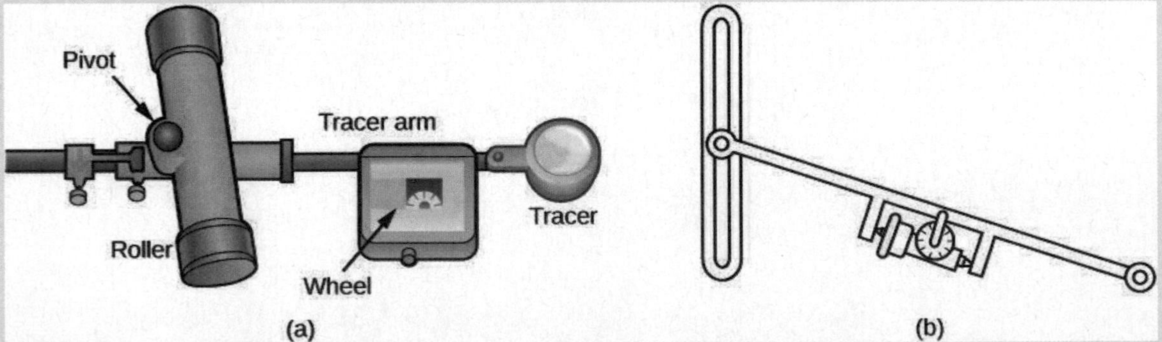

Figure 6.48 (a) A rolling planimeter. The pivot allows the tracer arm to rotate. The roller itself does not rotate; it only moves back and forth. (b) An interior view of a rolling planimeter. Notice that the wheel cannot turn if the planimeter is moving back and forth with the tracer arm perpendicular to the roller.

Let C denote the boundary of region D, the area to be calculated. As the tracer traverses curve C, assume the roller moves along the y-axis (since the roller does not rotate, one can assume it moves along a straight line). Use the coordinates (x, y) to represent points on boundary C, and coordinates $(0, Y)$ to represent the position of the pivot. As the planimeter traces C, the pivot moves along the y-axis while the tracer arm rotates on the pivot.

Watch a **short animation (http://www.openstaxcollege.org/l/20_planimeter)** of a planimeter in action.

Begin the analysis by considering the motion of the tracer as it moves from point (x, y) counterclockwise to point $(x + dx, y + dy)$ that is close to (x, y) (**Figure 6.49**). The pivot also moves, from point $(0, Y)$ to nearby point $(0, Y + dY)$. How much does the wheel turn as a result of this motion? To answer this question, break the motion into two parts. First, roll the pivot along the y-axis from $(0, Y)$ to $(0, Y + dY)$ without rotating the tracer arm. The tracer arm then ends up at point $(x, y + dY)$ while maintaining a constant angle ϕ with the x-axis. Second, rotate the tracer arm by an angle $d\theta$ without moving the roller. Now the tracer is at point $(x + dx, y + dy)$. Let l be the distance from the pivot to the wheel and let L be the distance from the pivot to the tracer (the length of the tracer arm).

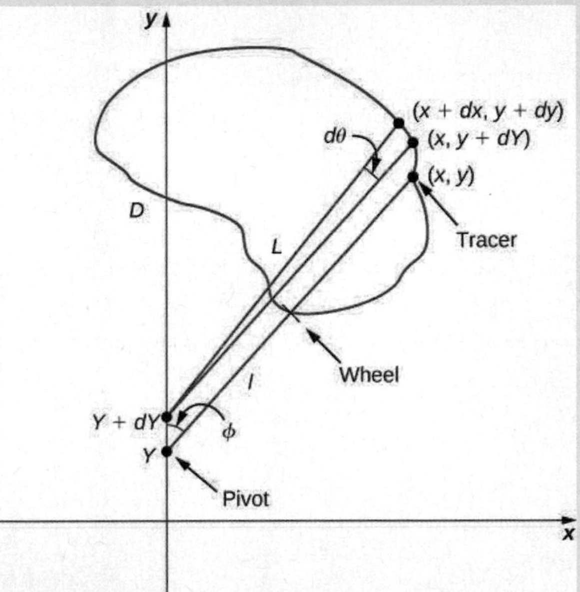

Figure 6.49 Mathematical analysis of the motion of the planimeter.

1. Explain why the total distance through which the wheel rolls the small motion just described is $\sin \phi dY + l d\theta = \frac{x}{L} dY + l d\theta$.

2. Show that $\oint_C d\theta = 0$.

3. Use step 2 to show that the total rolling distance of the wheel as the tracer traverses curve C is
Total wheel roll $= \frac{1}{L} \oint_C x dY$.

   Now that you have an equation for the total rolling distance of the wheel, connect this equation to Green's theorem to calculate area D enclosed by C.

4. Show that $x^2 + (y - Y)^2 = L^2$.

5. Assume the orientation of the planimeter is as shown in **Figure 6.49**. Explain why $Y \le y$, and use this inequality to show there is a unique value of Y for each point (x, y): $Y = y = \sqrt{L^2 - x^2}$.

6. Use step 5 to show that $dY = dy + \frac{x}{\sqrt{L^2 - x^2}}dx.$

7. Use Green's theorem to show that $\oint_C \frac{x}{\sqrt{L^2 - x^2}}dx = 0.$

8. Use step 7 to show that the total wheel roll is
   Total wheel roll $= \frac{1}{L}\oint_C xdy.$

   It took a bit of work, but this equation says that the variable of integration Y in step 3 can be replaced with y.

9. Use Green's theorem to show that the area of D is $\oint_C xdy$. The logic is similar to the logic used to show that the area of $D = \frac{1}{2}\oint_C -ydx + xdy.$

10. Conclude that the area of D equals the length of the tracer arm multiplied by the total rolling distance of the wheel.
    You now know how a planimeter works and you have used Green's theorem to justify that it works. To calculate the area of a planar region D, use a planimeter to trace the boundary of the region. The area of the region is the length of the tracer arm multiplied by the distance the wheel rolled.

6.4 EXERCISES

For the following exercises, evaluate the line integrals by applying Green's theorem.

146. $\int_C 2xy dx + (x + y) dy,$ where C is the path from $(0, 0)$ to $(1, 1)$ along the graph of $y = x^3$ and from $(1, 1)$ to $(0, 0)$ along the graph of $y = x$ oriented in the counterclockwise direction

147. $\int_C 2xy dx + (x + y) dy,$ where C is the boundary of the region lying between the graphs of $y = 0$ and $y = 4 - x^2$ oriented in the counterclockwise direction

148. $\int_C 2\arctan\left(\frac{y}{x}\right) dx + \ln\left(x^2 + y^2\right) dy,$ where C is defined by $x = 4 + 2\cos\theta,\ y = 4\sin\theta$ oriented in the counterclockwise direction

149. $\int_C \sin x \cos y dx + (xy + \cos x \sin y) dy,$ where C is the boundary of the region lying between the graphs of $y = x$ and $y = \sqrt{x}$ oriented in the counterclockwise direction

150. $\int_C xy dx + (x + y) dy,$ where C is the boundary of the region lying between the graphs of $x^2 + y^2 = 1$ and $x^2 + y^2 = 9$ oriented in the counterclockwise direction

151. $\oint_C (-y dx + x dy),$ where C consists of line segment C_1 from $(-1, 0)$ to $(1, 0)$, followed by the semicircular arc C_2 from $(1, 0)$ back to $(1, 0)$

For the following exercises, use Green's theorem.

152. Let C be the curve consisting of line segments from $(0, 0)$ to $(1, 1)$ to $(0, 1)$ and back to $(0, 0)$. Find the value of $\int_C xy dx + \sqrt{y^2 + 1} dy.$

153. Evaluate line integral $\int_C xe^{-2x} dx + \left(x^4 + 2x^2 y^2\right) dy,$ where C is the boundary of the region between circles $x^2 + y^2 = 1$ and $x^2 + y^2 = 4,$ and is a positively oriented curve.

154. Find the counterclockwise circulation of field $\mathbf{F}(x, y) = xy\mathbf{i} + y^2\mathbf{j}$ around and over the boundary of the region enclosed by curves $y = x^2$ and $y = x$ in the first quadrant and oriented in the counterclockwise direction.

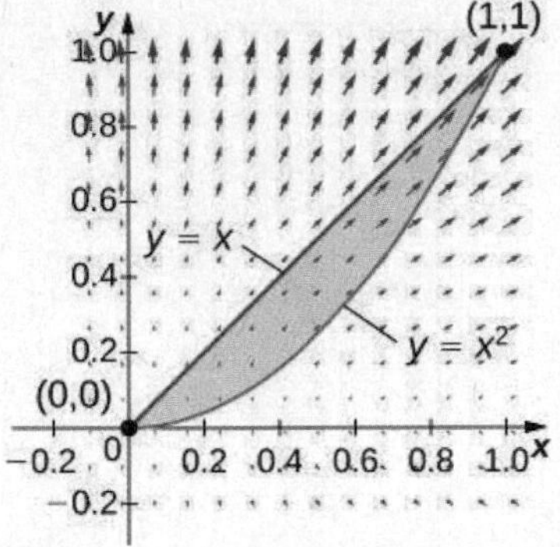

155. Evaluate $\oint_C y^3 dx - x^3 y^2 dy,$ where C is the positively oriented circle of radius 2 centered at the origin.

156. Evaluate $\oint_C y^3 dx - x^3 dy,$ where C includes the two circles of radius 2 and radius 1 centered at the origin, both with positive orientation.

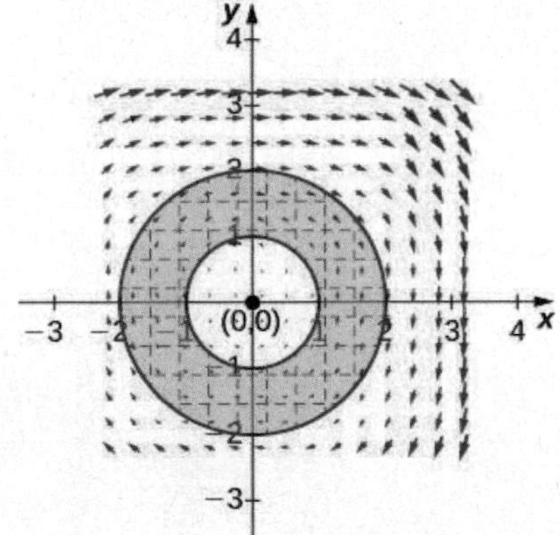

157. Calculate $\oint_C -x^2 y dx + xy^2 dy,$ where C is a circle of radius 2 centered at the origin and oriented in the counterclockwise direction.

158. Calculate integral $\oint_C 2[y + x\sin(y)] dx + \left[x^2\cos(y) - 3y^2\right] dy$ along triangle C with vertices $(0, 0)$, $(1, 0)$ and $(1, 1)$, oriented counterclockwise, using Green's theorem.

159. Evaluate integral $\oint_C (x^2 + y^2)dx + 2xydy,$ where C is the curve that follows parabola $y = x^2$ from (0, 0)(2, 4), then the line from (2, 4) to (2, 0), and finally the line from (2, 0) to (0, 0).

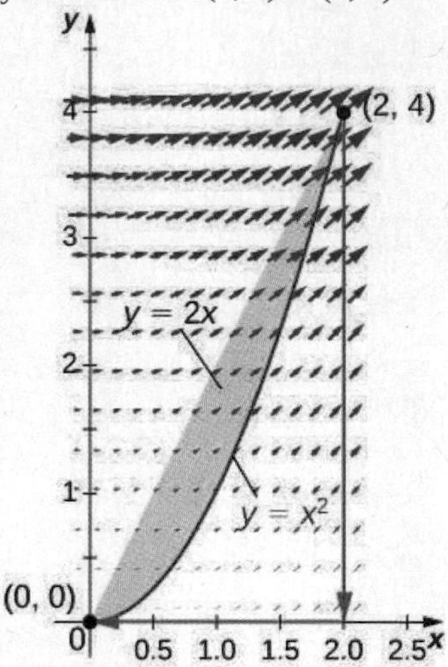

160. Evaluate line integral $\oint_C (y - \sin(y)\cos(y))dx + 2x\sin^2(y)dy,$ where C is oriented in a counterclockwise path around the region bounded by $x = -1,\ x = 2,\ y = 4 - x^2,$ and $y = x - 2.$

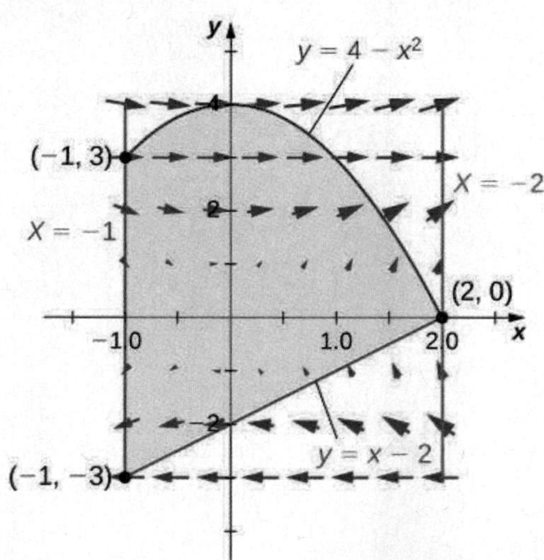

For the following exercises, use Green's theorem to find the area.

161. Find the area between ellipse $\frac{x^2}{9} + \frac{y^2}{4} = 1$ and circle $x^2 + y^2 = 25.$

162. Find the area of the region enclosed by parametric equation $p(\theta) = (\cos(\theta) - \cos^2(\theta))\mathbf{i} + (\sin(\theta) - \cos(\theta)\sin(\theta))\mathbf{j}$ for $0 \le \theta \le 2\pi.$

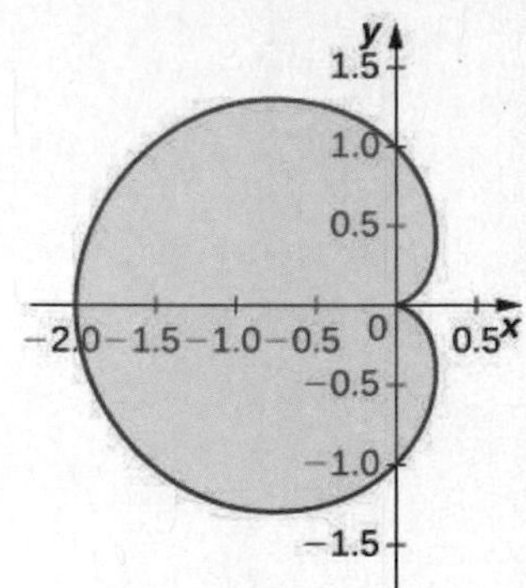

163. Find the area of the region bounded by hypocycloid $\mathbf{r}(t) = \cos^3(t)\mathbf{i} + \sin^3(t)\mathbf{j}.$ The curve is parameterized by $t \in [0, 2\pi].$

164. Find the area of a pentagon with vertices $(0, 4), (4, 1), (3, 0), (-1, -1),$ and $(-2, 2).$

165. Use Green's theorem to evaluate $\int_{C+} (y^2 + x^3)dx + x^4 dy,$ where C^+ is the perimeter of square $[0, 1] \times [0, 1]$ oriented counterclockwise.

166. Use Green's theorem to prove the area of a disk with radius a is $A = \pi a^2.$

167. Use Green's theorem to find the area of one loop of a four-leaf rose $r = 3\sin 2\theta.$ (*Hint*: $xdy - ydx = \mathbf{r}^2 d\theta$).

168. Use Green's theorem to find the area under one arch of the cycloid given by parametric plane $x = t - \sin t,\ y = 1 - \cos t,\ t \ge 0.$

169. Use Green's theorem to find the area of the region enclosed by curve

$$\mathbf{r}(t) = t^2\mathbf{i} + \left(\frac{t^3}{3} - t\right)\mathbf{j},\ -\sqrt{3} \le t\sqrt{3}.$$

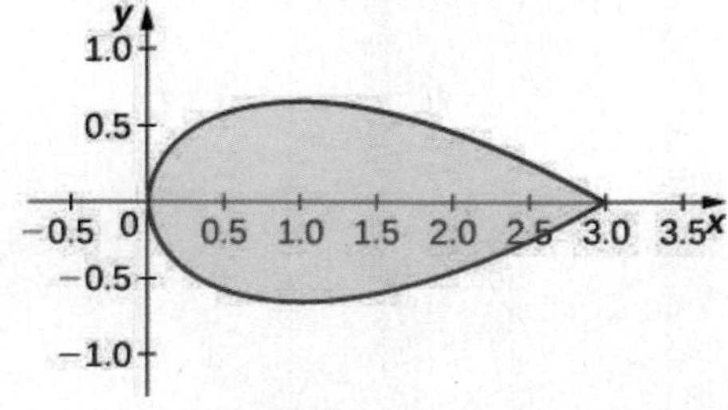

170. **[T]** Evaluate Green's theorem using a computer algebra system to evaluate the integral $\int_C xe^y\,dx + e^x\,dy,$ where C is the circle given by $x^2 + y^2 = 4$ and is oriented in the counterclockwise direction.

171. Evaluate $\int_C \left(x^2 y - 2xy + y^2\right) ds,$ where C is the boundary of the unit square $0 \le x \le 1, 0 \le y \le 1,$ traversed counterclockwise.

172. Evaluate $\int_C \frac{-(y+2)dx + (x-1)dy}{(x-1)^2 + (y+2)^2},$ where C is any simple closed curve with an interior that does not contain point $(1, -2)$ traversed counterclockwise.

173. Evaluate $\int_C \frac{xdx + ydy}{x^2 + y^2},$ where C is any piecewise, smooth simple closed curve enclosing the origin, traversed counterclockwise.

For the following exercises, use Green's theorem to calculate the work done by force **F** on a particle that is moving counterclockwise around closed path C.

174. $\mathbf{F}(x, y) = xy\mathbf{i} + (x + y)\mathbf{j}, \quad C: x^2 + y^2 = 4$

175. $\mathbf{F}(x, y) = \left(x^{3/2} - 3y\right)\mathbf{i} + \left(6x + 5\sqrt{y}\right)\mathbf{j}, \quad C:$ boundary of a triangle with vertices (0, 0), (5, 0), and (0, 5)

176. Evaluate $\int_C \left(2x^3 - y^3\right)dx + \left(x^3 + y^3\right)dy,$ where C is a unit circle oriented in the counterclockwise direction.

177. A particle starts at point $(-2, 0),$ moves along the x-axis to $(2, 0),$ and then travels along semicircle $y = \sqrt{4 - x^2}$ to the starting point. Use Green's theorem to find the work done on this particle by force field $\mathbf{F}(x, y) = x\mathbf{i} + \left(x^3 + 3xy^2\right)\mathbf{j}.$

178. David and Sandra are skating on a frictionless pond in the wind. David skates on the inside, going along a circle of radius 2 in a counterclockwise direction. Sandra skates once around a circle of radius 3, also in the counterclockwise direction. Suppose the force of the wind at point (x, y) (x, y) (x, y) is $\mathbf{F}(x, y) = \left(x^2 y + 10y\right)\mathbf{i} + \left(x^3 + 2xy^2\right)\mathbf{j}.$ Use Green's theorem to determine who does more work.

179. Use Green's theorem to find the work done by force field $\mathbf{F}(x, y) = (3y - 4x)\mathbf{i} + (4x - y)\mathbf{j}$ when an object moves once counterclockwise around ellipse $4x^2 + y^2 = 4.$

180. Use Green's theorem to evaluate line integral $\oint_C e^{2x} \sin 2y dx + e^{2x} \cos 2y dy,$ where C is ellipse $9(x-1)^2 + 4(y-3)^2 = 36$ oriented counterclockwise.

181. Evaluate line integral $\oint_C y^2\,dx + x^2\,dy,$ where C is the boundary of a triangle with vertices $(0, 0), (1, 1),$ and $(1, 0),$ with the counterclockwise orientation.

182. Use Green's theorem to evaluate line integral $\int_C \mathbf{h} \cdot d\mathbf{r}$ if $\mathbf{h}(x, y) = e^y \mathbf{i} - \sin \pi x \mathbf{j},$ where C is a triangle with vertices (1, 0), (0, 1), and $(-1, 0)$ $(-1, 0)$ traversed counterclockwise.

183. Use Green's theorem to evaluate line integral $\int_C \sqrt{1 + x^3} dx + 2xydy$ where C is a triangle with vertices (0, 0), (1, 0), and (1, 3) oriented clockwise.

184. Use Green's theorem to evaluate line integral $\int_C x^2 ydx - xy^2 dy$ where C is a circle $x^2 + y^2 = 4$ oriented counterclockwise.

185. Use Green's theorem to evaluate line integral $\int_C \left(3y - e^{\sin x}\right)dx + \left(7x + \sqrt{y^4 + 1}\right)dy$ where C is circle $x^2 + y^2 = 9$ oriented in the counterclockwise direction.

186. Use Green's theorem to evaluate line integral $\int_C (3x - 5y)dx + (x - 6y)dy,$ where C is ellipse $\frac{x^2}{4} + y^2 = 1$ and is oriented in the counterclockwise direction.

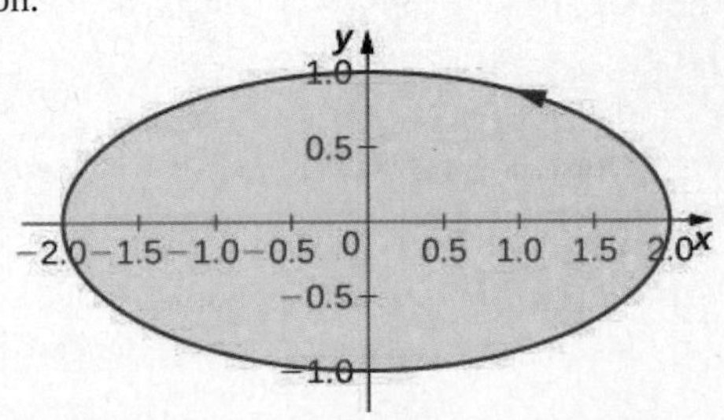

187. Let C be a triangular closed curve from (0, 0) to (1, 0) to (1, 1) and finally back to (0, 0). Let $\mathbf{F}(x, y) = 4y\mathbf{i} + 6x^2\mathbf{j}$. Use Green's theorem to evaluate $\oint_C \mathbf{F} \cdot d\mathbf{s}$.

188. Use Green's theorem to evaluate line integral $\oint_C ydx - xdy$, where C is circle $x^2 + y^2 = a^2$ oriented in the clockwise direction.

189. Use Green's theorem to evaluate line integral $\oint_C (y + x)dx + (x + \sin y)dy$, where C is any smooth simple closed curve joining the origin to itself oriented in the counterclockwise direction.

190. Use Green's theorem to evaluate line integral $\oint_C \left(y - \ln\left(x^2 + y^2\right)\right)dx + \left(2\arctan\frac{y}{x}\right)dy$, where C is the positively oriented circle $(x - 2)^2 + (y - 3)^2 = 1$.

191. Use Green's theorem to evaluate $\oint_C xydx + x^3y^3dy$, where C is a triangle with vertices (0, 0), (1, 0), and (1, 2) with positive orientation.

192. Use Green's theorem to evaluate line integral $\int_C \sin ydx + x\cos ydy$, where C is ellipse $x^2 + xy + y^2 = 1$ oriented in the counterclockwise direction.

193. Let $\mathbf{F}(x, y) = \left(\cos\left(x^5\right)\right) - \frac{1}{3}y^3\mathbf{i} + \frac{1}{3}x^3\mathbf{j}$. Find the counterclockwise circulation $\oint_C \mathbf{F} \cdot d\mathbf{r}$, where C is a curve consisting of the line segment joining (−2, 0) and (−1, 0), half circle $y = \sqrt{1 - x^2}$, the line segment joining (1, 0) and (2, 0), and half circle $y = \sqrt{4 - x^2}$.

194. Use Green's theorem to evaluate line integral $\int_C \sin\left(x^3\right)dx + 2ye^{x^2}dy$, where C is a triangular closed curve that connects the points (0, 0), (2, 2), and (0, 2) counterclockwise.

195. Let C be the boundary of square $0 \le x \le \pi, 0 \le y \le \pi$, traversed counterclockwise. Use Green's theorem to find $\int_C \sin(x + y)dx + \cos(x + y)dy$.

196. Use Green's theorem to evaluate line integral $\int_C \mathbf{F} \cdot d\mathbf{r}$, where $\mathbf{F}(x, y) = \left(y^2 - x^2\right)\mathbf{i} + \left(x^2 + y^2\right)\mathbf{j}$, and C is a triangle bounded by $y = 0, x = 3$, and $y = x$, oriented counterclockwise.

197. Use Green's Theorem to evaluate integral $\int_C \mathbf{F} \cdot d\mathbf{r}$, where $\mathbf{F}(x, y) = \left(xy^2\right)\mathbf{i} + x\mathbf{j}$, and C is a unit circle oriented in the counterclockwise direction.

198. Use Green's theorem in a plane to evaluate line integral $\oint_C \left(xy + y^2\right)dx + x^2dy$, where C is a closed curve of a region bounded by $y = x$ and $y = x^2$ oriented in the counterclockwise direction.

199. Calculate the outward flux of $\mathbf{F} = -x\mathbf{i} + 2y\mathbf{j}$ over a square with corners $(\pm 1, \pm 1)$, where the unit normal is outward pointing and oriented in the counterclockwise direction.

200. **[T]** Let C be circle $x^2 + y^2 = 4$ oriented in the counterclockwise direction. Evaluate $\oint_C \left[\left(3y - e^{\tan^{-1}x}\right)dx + \left(7x + \sqrt{y^4 + 1}\right)dy\right]$ using a computer algebra system.

201. Find the flux of field $\mathbf{F} = -x\mathbf{i} + y\mathbf{j}$ across $x^2 + y^2 = 16$ oriented in the counterclockwise direction.

202. Let $\mathbf{F} = \left(y^2 - x^2\right)\mathbf{i} + \left(x^2 + y^2\right)\mathbf{j}$, and let C be a triangle bounded by $y = 0$, $x = 3$, and $y = x$ oriented in the counterclockwise direction. Find the outward flux of **F** through C.

203. **[T]** Let C be unit circle $x^2 + y^2 = 1$ traversed once counterclockwise. Evaluate $\int_C \left[-y^3 + \sin(xy) + xy\cos(xy)\right]dx + \left[x^3 + x^2\cos(xy)\right]dy$ by using a computer algebra system.

204. **[T]** Find the outward flux of vector field $\mathbf{F} = xy^2\mathbf{i} + x^2y\mathbf{j}$ across the boundary of annulus $R = \left\{(x, y) : 1 \le x^2 + y^2 \le 4\right\} = \{(r, \theta) : 1 \le r \le 2, 0 \le \theta \le 2\pi\}$ using a computer algebra system.

205. Consider region R bounded by parabolas $y = x^2$ and $x = y^2$. Let C be the boundary of R oriented counterclockwise. Use Green's theorem to evaluate $\oint_C \left(y + e^{\sqrt{x}}\right)dx + \left(2x + \cos\left(y^2\right)\right)dy$.

6.5 | Divergence and Curl

Learning Objectives

6.5.1 Determine divergence from the formula for a given vector field.
6.5.2 Determine curl from the formula for a given vector field.
6.5.3 Use the properties of curl and divergence to determine whether a vector field is conservative.

In this section, we examine two important operations on a vector field: divergence and curl. They are important to the field of calculus for several reasons, including the use of curl and divergence to develop some higher-dimensional versions of the Fundamental Theorem of Calculus. In addition, curl and divergence appear in mathematical descriptions of fluid mechanics, electromagnetism, and elasticity theory, which are important concepts in physics and engineering. We can also apply curl and divergence to other concepts we already explored. For example, under certain conditions, a vector field is conservative if and only if its curl is zero.

In addition to defining curl and divergence, we look at some physical interpretations of them, and show their relationship to conservative and source-free vector fields.

Divergence

Divergence is an operation on a vector field that tells us how the field behaves toward or away from a point. Locally, the divergence of a vector field **F** in $\mathbb{R}^2$ or $\mathbb{R}^3$ at a particular point *P* is a measure of the "outflowing-ness" of the vector field at *P*. If **F** represents the velocity of a fluid, then the divergence of **F** at *P* measures the net rate of change with respect to time of the amount of fluid flowing away from *P* (the tendency of the fluid to flow "out of" *P*). In particular, if the amount of fluid flowing into *P* is the same as the amount flowing out, then the divergence at *P* is zero.

Definition

If $\mathbf{F} = \langle P, Q, R \rangle$ is a vector field in $\mathbb{R}^3$ and $P_x, Q_y,$ and R_z all exist, then the **divergence** of **F** is defined by

$$\text{div}\,\mathbf{F} = P_x + Q_y + R_z = \frac{\partial P}{\partial x} + \frac{\partial Q}{\partial y} + \frac{\partial R}{\partial z}. \tag{6.16}$$

Note the divergence of a vector field is not a vector field, but a scalar function. In terms of the gradient operator $\nabla = \langle \frac{\partial}{\partial x}, \frac{\partial}{\partial y}, \frac{\partial}{\partial z} \rangle$, divergence can be written symbolically as the dot product

$$\text{div}\,\mathbf{F} = \nabla \cdot \mathbf{F}.$$

Note this is merely helpful notation, because the dot product of a vector of operators and a vector of functions is not meaningfully defined given our current definition of dot product.

If $\mathbf{F} = \langle P, Q \rangle$ is a vector field in $\mathbb{R}^2$, and P_x and Q_y both exist, then the divergence of **F** is defined similarly as

$$\text{div}\,\mathbf{F} = P_x + Q_y = \frac{\partial P}{\partial x} + \frac{\partial Q}{\partial y} = \nabla \cdot \mathbf{F}.$$

To illustrate this point, consider the two vector fields in **Figure 6.50**. At any particular point, the amount flowing in is the same as the amount flowing out, so at every point the "outflowing-ness" of the field is zero. Therefore, we expect the divergence of both fields to be zero, and this is indeed the case, as

$$\text{div}(\langle 1, 2 \rangle) = \frac{\partial}{\partial x}(1) + \frac{\partial}{\partial y}(2) = 0 \text{ and } \text{div}(\langle -y, x \rangle) = \frac{\partial}{\partial x}(-y) + \frac{\partial}{\partial y}(x) = 0.$$

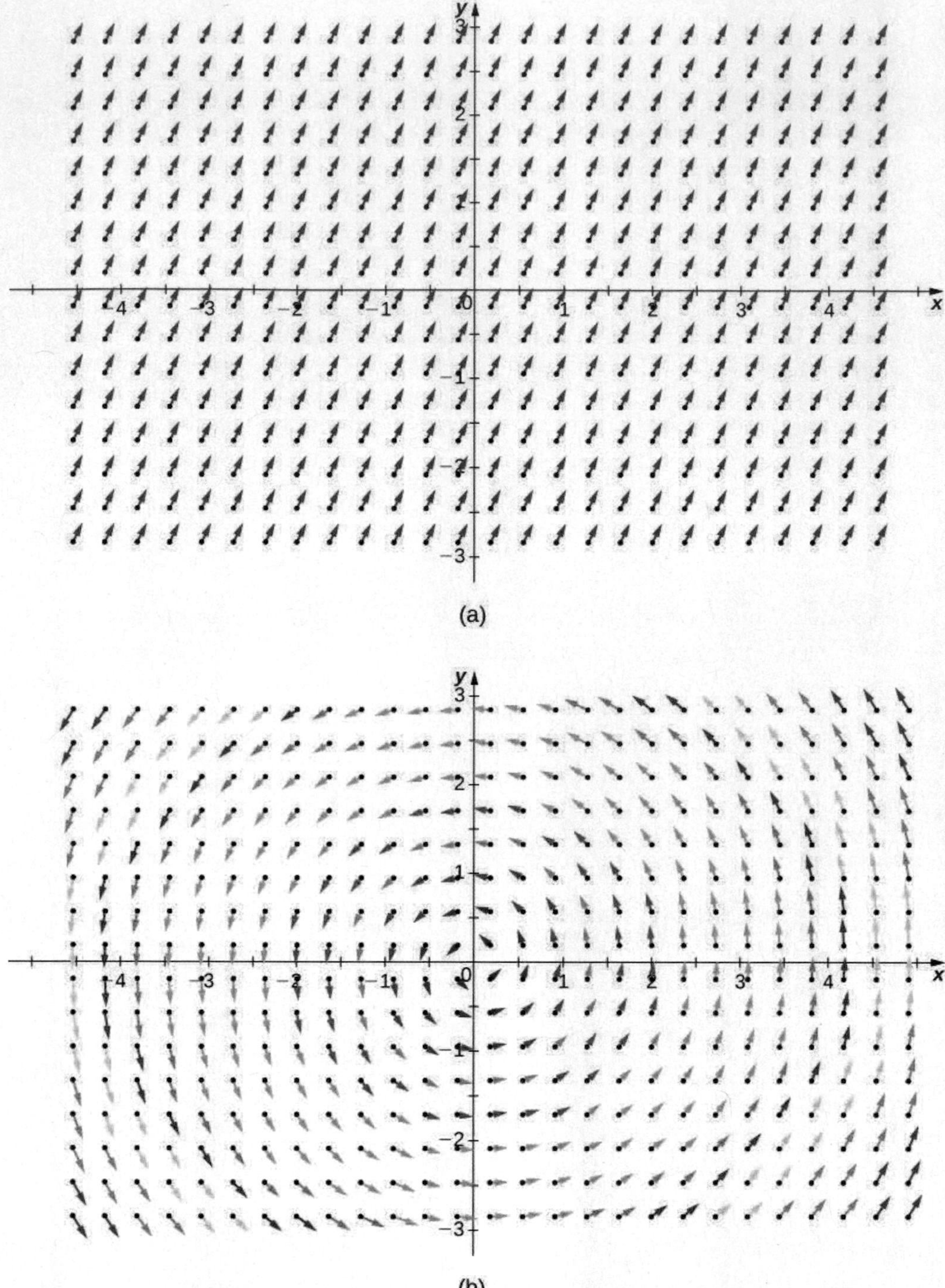

Figure 6.50 (a) Vector field $\langle 1, 2 \rangle$ has zero divergence. (b) Vector field $\langle -y, x \rangle$ also has zero divergence.

By contrast, consider radial vector field $\mathbf{R}(x, y) = \langle -x, -y \rangle$ in **Figure 6.51**. At any given point, more fluid is flowing in than is flowing out, and therefore the "outgoingness" of the field is negative. We expect the divergence of this field to be negative, and this is indeed the case, as $\text{div}(\mathbf{R}) = \frac{\partial}{\partial x}(-x) + \frac{\partial}{\partial y}(-y) = -2$.

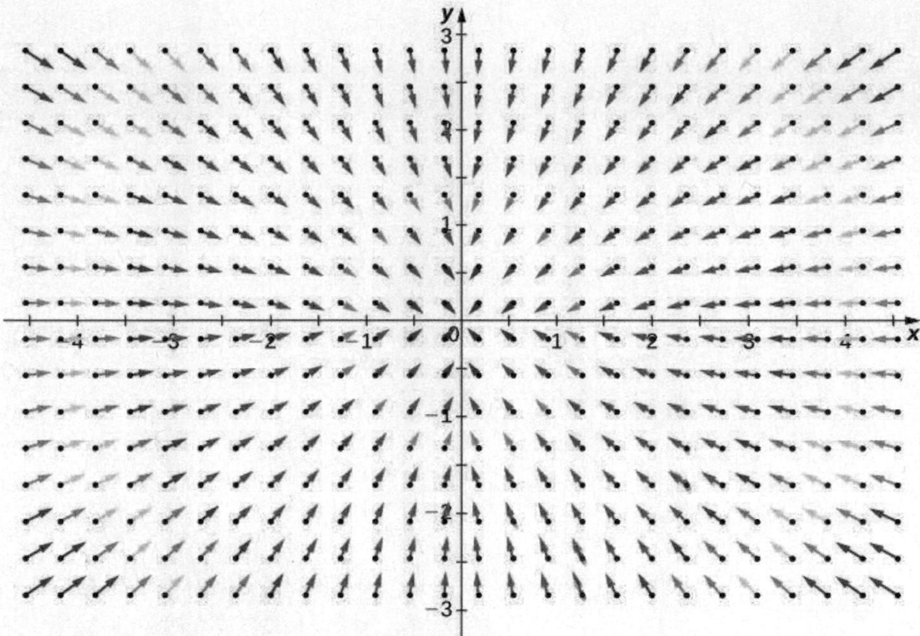

Figure 6.51 This vector field has negative divergence.

To get a global sense of what divergence is telling us, suppose that a vector field in $\mathbb{R}^2$ represents the velocity of a fluid. Imagine taking an elastic circle (a circle with a shape that can be changed by the vector field) and dropping it into a fluid. If the circle maintains its exact area as it flows through the fluid, then the divergence is zero. This would occur for both vector fields in **Figure 6.50**. On the other hand, if the circle's shape is distorted so that its area shrinks or expands, then the divergence is not zero. Imagine dropping such an elastic circle into the radial vector field in **Figure 6.51** so that the center of the circle lands at point (3, 3). The circle would flow toward the origin, and as it did so the front of the circle would travel more slowly than the back, causing the circle to "scrunch" and lose area. This is how you can see a negative divergence.

Example 6.48

Calculating Divergence at a Point

If $\mathbf{F}(x, y, z) = e^x\mathbf{i} + yz\mathbf{j} - y^2\mathbf{k},$ then find the divergence of $\mathbf{F}$ at $(0, 2, -1)$.

Solution

The divergence of $\mathbf{F}$ is

$$\frac{\partial}{\partial x}(e^x) + \frac{\partial}{\partial y}(yz) - \frac{\partial}{\partial z}(yz^2) = e^x + z - 2yz.$$

Therefore, the divergence at $(0, 2, -1)$ is $e^0 - 1 + 4 = 4.$ If $\mathbf{F}$ represents the velocity of a fluid, then more fluid is flowing out than flowing in at point $(0, 2, -1)$.

 **6.40** Find div $\mathbf{F}$ for $\mathbf{F}(x, y, z) = \langle xy, 5 - z^2y, x^2 + y^2 \rangle$.

One application for divergence occurs in physics, when working with magnetic fields. A magnetic field is a vector field that models the influence of electric currents and magnetic materials. Physicists use divergence in Gauss's law for magnetism, which states that if $\mathbf{B}$ is a magnetic field, then $\nabla \cdot \mathbf{B} = 0$; in other words, the divergence of a magnetic field is zero.

Example 6.49

Determining Whether a Field Is Magnetic

Is it possible for $\mathbf{F}(x, y) = \langle x^2 y, y - xy^2 \rangle$ to be a magnetic field?

Solution

If $\mathbf{F}$ were magnetic, then its divergence would be zero. The divergence of $\mathbf{F}$ is

$$\frac{\partial}{\partial x}(x^2 y) + \frac{\partial}{\partial y}(y - xy^2) = 2xy + 1 - 2xy = 1$$

and therefore $\mathbf{F}$ cannot model a magnetic field (**Figure 6.52**).

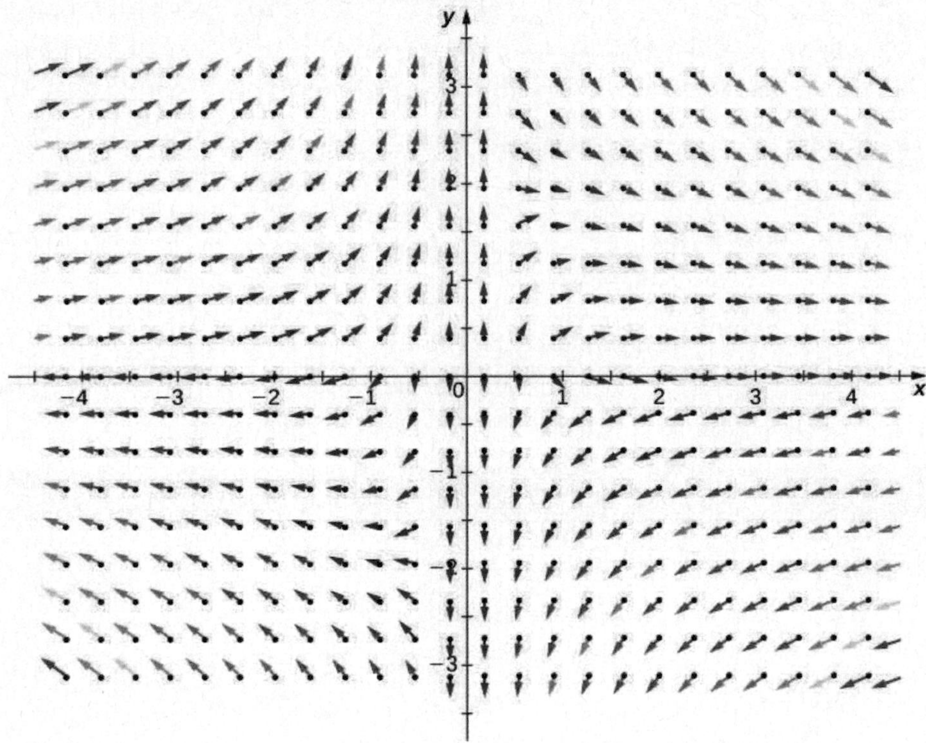

Figure 6.52 The divergence of vector field $\mathbf{F}(x, y) = \langle x^2 y, y - xy^2 \rangle$ is one, so it cannot model a magnetic field.

Another application for divergence is detecting whether a field is source free. Recall that a source-free field is a vector field that has a stream function; equivalently, a source-free field is a field with a flux that is zero along any closed curve. The next two theorems say that, under certain conditions, source-free vector fields are precisely the vector fields with zero divergence.

Theorem 6.14: Divergence of a Source-Free Vector Field

If $\mathbf{F} = \langle P, Q \rangle$ is a source-free continuous vector field with differentiable component functions, then $\text{div}\,\mathbf{F} = 0$.

Proof

Since **F** is source free, there is a function $g(x, y)$ with $g_y = P$ and $-g_x = Q$. Therefore, $\mathbf{F} = \langle g_y, -g_x \rangle$ and $\text{div } \mathbf{F} = g_{yx} - g_{xy} = 0$ by Clairaut's theorem.

□

The converse of **Divergence of a Source-Free Vector Field** is true on simply connected regions, but the proof is too technical to include here. Thus, we have the following theorem, which can test whether a vector field in $\mathbb{R}^2$ is source free.

Theorem 6.15: Divergence Test for Source-Free Vector Fields

Let $\mathbf{F} = \langle P, Q \rangle$ be a continuous vector field with differentiable component functions with a domain that is simply connected. Then, $\text{div } \mathbf{F} = 0$ if and only if **F** is source free.

Example 6.50

Determining Whether a Field Is Source Free

Is field $\mathbf{F}(x, y) = \langle x^2 y, 5 - xy^2 \rangle$ source free?

Solution

Note the domain of **F** is $\mathbb{R}^2$, which is simply connected. Furthermore, **F** is continuous with differentiable component functions. Therefore, we can use **Divergence Test for Source-Free Vector Fields** to analyze **F**. The divergence of **F** is

$$\frac{\partial}{\partial x}(x^2 y) + \frac{\partial}{\partial y}(5 - xy^2) = 2xy - 2xy = 0.$$

Therefore, **F** is source free by **Divergence Test for Source-Free Vector Fields**.

 **6.41** Let $\mathbf{F}(x, y) = \langle -ay, bx \rangle$ be a rotational field where a and b are positive constants. Is **F** source free?

Recall that the flux form of Green's theorem says that

$$\oint_C \mathbf{F} \cdot \mathbf{N} ds = \iint_D P_x + Q_y dA,$$

where C is a simple closed curve and D is the region enclosed by C. Since $P_x + Q_y = \text{div } \mathbf{F}$, Green's theorem is sometimes written as

$$\oint_C \mathbf{F} \cdot \mathbf{N} ds = \iint_D \text{div } \mathbf{F} dA.$$

Therefore, Green's theorem can be written in terms of divergence. If we think of divergence as a derivative of sorts, then Green's theorem says the "derivative" of **F** on a region can be translated into a line integral of **F** along the boundary of the region. This is analogous to the Fundamental Theorem of Calculus, in which the derivative of a function f on a line segment $[a, b]$ can be translated into a statement about f on the boundary of $[a, b]$. Using divergence, we can see that Green's theorem is a higher-dimensional analog of the Fundamental Theorem of Calculus.

We can use all of what we have learned in the application of divergence. Let **v** be a vector field modeling the velocity of a fluid. Since the divergence of **v** at point P measures the "outflowing-ness" of the fluid at P, $\text{div}\,\mathbf{v}(P) > 0$ implies that more fluid is flowing out of P than flowing in. Similarly, $\text{div}\,\mathbf{v}(P) < 0$ implies the more fluid is flowing in to P than is flowing out, and $\text{div}\,\mathbf{v}(P) = 0$ implies the same amount of fluid is flowing in as flowing out.

Example 6.51

Determining Flow of a Fluid

Suppose $\mathbf{v}(x, y) = \langle -xy, y \rangle,\ y > 0$ models the flow of a fluid. Is more fluid flowing into point $(1, 4)$ than flowing out?

Solution

To determine whether more fluid is flowing into $(1, 4)$ than is flowing out, we calculate the divergence of **v** at $(1, 4)$:

$$\text{div}(\mathbf{v}) = \frac{\partial}{\partial x}(-xy) + \frac{\partial}{\partial y}(y) = -y + 1.$$

To find the divergence at $(1, 4)$, substitute the point into the divergence: $-4 + 1 = -3$. Since the divergence of **v** at $(1, 4)$ is negative, more fluid is flowing in than flowing out (**Figure 6.53**).

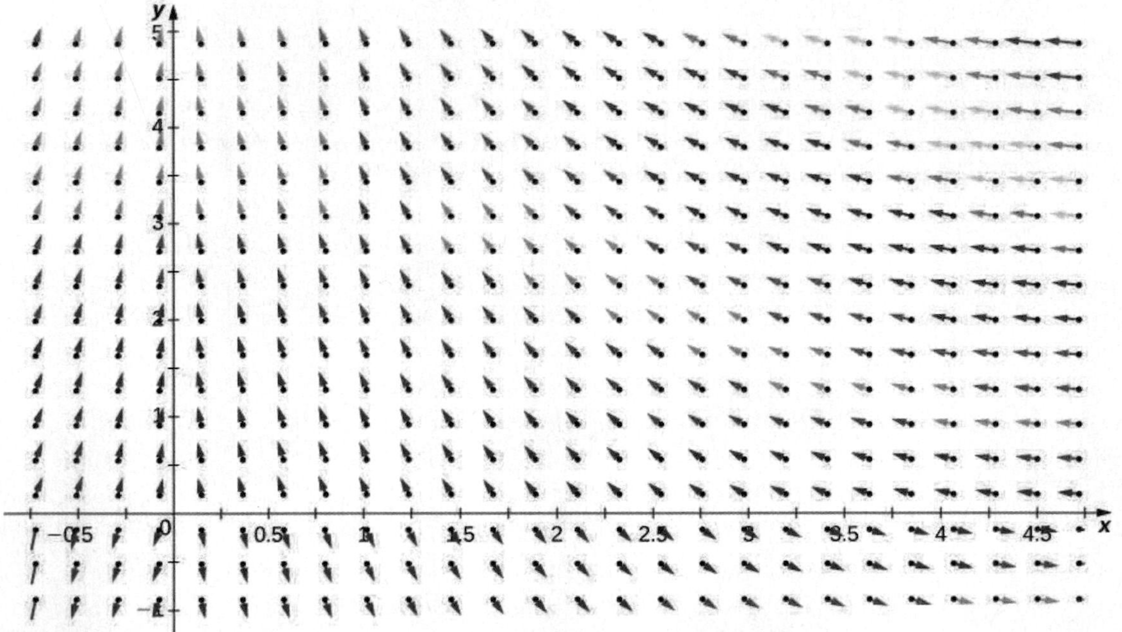

Figure 6.53 Vector field $\mathbf{v}(x, y) = \langle -xy, y \rangle$ has negative divergence at $(1, 4)$.

6.42 For vector field $\mathbf{v}(x, y) = \langle -xy, y \rangle,\ y > 0,$ find all points P such that the amount of fluid flowing in to P equals the amount of fluid flowing out of P.

Curl

The second operation on a vector field that we examine is the curl, which measures the extent of rotation of the field about a point. Suppose that **F** represents the velocity field of a fluid. Then, the curl of **F** at point P is a vector that measures the tendency of particles near P to rotate about the axis that points in the direction of this vector. The magnitude of the curl vector at P measures how quickly the particles rotate around this axis. In other words, the curl at a point is a measure of the vector field's "spin" at that point. Visually, imagine placing a paddlewheel into a fluid at P, with the axis of the paddlewheel aligned with the curl vector (**Figure 6.54**). The curl measures the tendency of the paddlewheel to rotate.

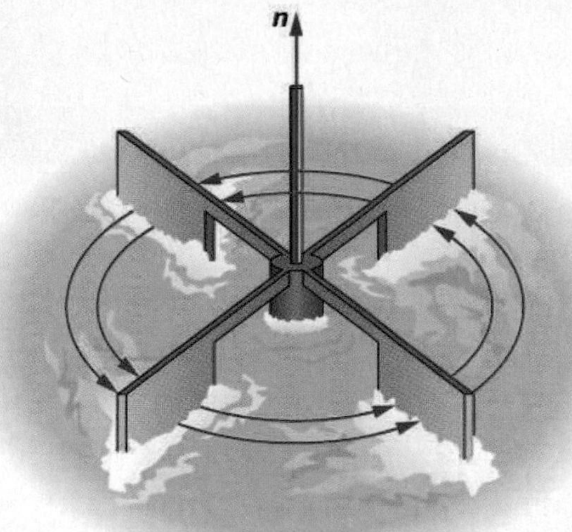

Figure 6.54 To visualize curl at a point, imagine placing a small paddlewheel into the vector field at a point.

Consider the vector fields in **Figure 6.50**. In part (a), the vector field is constant and there is no spin at any point. Therefore, we expect the curl of the field to be zero, and this is indeed the case. Part (b) shows a rotational field, so the field has spin. In particular, if you place a paddlewheel into a field at any point so that the axis of the wheel is perpendicular to a plane, the wheel rotates counterclockwise. Therefore, we expect the curl of the field to be nonzero, and this is indeed the case (the curl is $2\mathbf{k}$).

To see what curl is measuring globally, imagine dropping a leaf into the fluid. As the leaf moves along with the fluid flow, the curl measures the tendency of the leaf to rotate. If the curl is zero, then the leaf doesn't rotate as it moves through the fluid.

Definition

If $\mathbf{F} = \langle P, Q, R \rangle$ is a vector field in $\mathbb{R}^3$, and P_x, Q_y, and R_z all exist, then the **curl** of **F** is defined by

$$\begin{aligned}\text{curl}\,\mathbf{F} &= (R_y - Q_z)\mathbf{i} + (P_z - R_x)\mathbf{j} + (Q_x - P_y)\mathbf{k} \\ &= \left(\frac{\partial R}{\partial y} - \frac{\partial Q}{\partial z}\right)\mathbf{i} + \left(\frac{\partial P}{\partial z} - \frac{\partial R}{\partial x}\right)\mathbf{j} + \left(\frac{\partial Q}{\partial x} - \frac{\partial P}{\partial y}\right)\mathbf{k}.\end{aligned} \quad \textbf{(6.17)}$$

Note that the curl of a vector field is a vector field, in contrast to divergence.

The definition of curl can be difficult to remember. To help with remembering, we use the notation $\nabla \times \mathbf{F}$ to stand for a "determinant" that gives the curl formula:

$$\begin{vmatrix} \mathbf{i} & \mathbf{j} & \mathbf{k} \\ \frac{\partial}{\partial x} & \frac{\partial}{\partial y} & \frac{\partial}{\partial z} \\ P & Q & R \end{vmatrix}.$$

The determinant of this matrix is

$$(R_y - Q_z)\mathbf{i} - (R_x - P_z)\mathbf{j} + (Q_x - P_y)\mathbf{k} = (R_y - Q_z)\mathbf{i} + (P_z - R_x)\mathbf{j} + (Q_x - P_y)\mathbf{k} = \text{curl}\,\mathbf{F}.$$

Thus, this matrix is a way to help remember the formula for curl. Keep in mind, though, that the word *determinant* is used very loosely. A determinant is not really defined on a matrix with entries that are three vectors, three operators, and three functions.

If $\mathbf{F} = \langle P, Q \rangle$ is a vector field in $\mathbb{R}^2$, then the curl of **F**, by definition, is

$$\text{curl } \mathbf{F} = (Q_x - P_y)\mathbf{k} = \left(\frac{\partial Q}{\partial x} - \frac{\partial P}{\partial y}\right)\mathbf{k}.$$

Example 6.52

Finding the Curl of a Three-Dimensional Vector Field

Find the curl of $\mathbf{F}(P, Q, R) = \langle x^2 z, e^y + xz, xyz \rangle$.

Solution

The curl is

$$\begin{aligned} \text{curl } \mathbf{F} &= \nabla \times \mathbf{F} \\ &= \begin{vmatrix} \mathbf{i} & \mathbf{j} & \mathbf{k} \\ \partial/\partial x & \partial/\partial y & \partial/\partial z \\ P & Q & R \end{vmatrix} \\ &= (R_y - Q_z)\mathbf{i} + (P_z - R_x)\mathbf{j} + (Q_x - P_y)\mathbf{k} \\ &= (xz - x)\mathbf{i} + (x^2 - yz)\mathbf{j} + z\mathbf{k}. \end{aligned}$$

6.43 Find the curl of $\mathbf{F} = \langle \sin x \cos z, \sin y \sin z, \cos x \cos y \rangle$ at point $\left(0, \frac{\pi}{2}, \frac{\pi}{2}\right)$.

Example 6.53

Finding the Curl of a Two-Dimensional Vector Field

Find the curl of $\mathbf{F} = \langle P, Q \rangle = \langle y, 0 \rangle$.

Solution

Notice that this vector field consists of vectors that are all parallel. In fact, each vector in the field is parallel to the *x*-axis. This fact might lead us to the conclusion that the field has no spin and that the curl is zero. To test this theory, note that

$$\text{curl } \mathbf{F} = (Q_x - P_y)\mathbf{k} = -\mathbf{k} \neq 0.$$

Therefore, this vector field does have spin. To see why, imagine placing a paddlewheel at any point in the first quadrant (**Figure 6.55**). The larger magnitudes of the vectors at the top of the wheel cause the wheel to rotate. The wheel rotates in the clockwise (negative) direction, causing the coefficient of the curl to be negative.

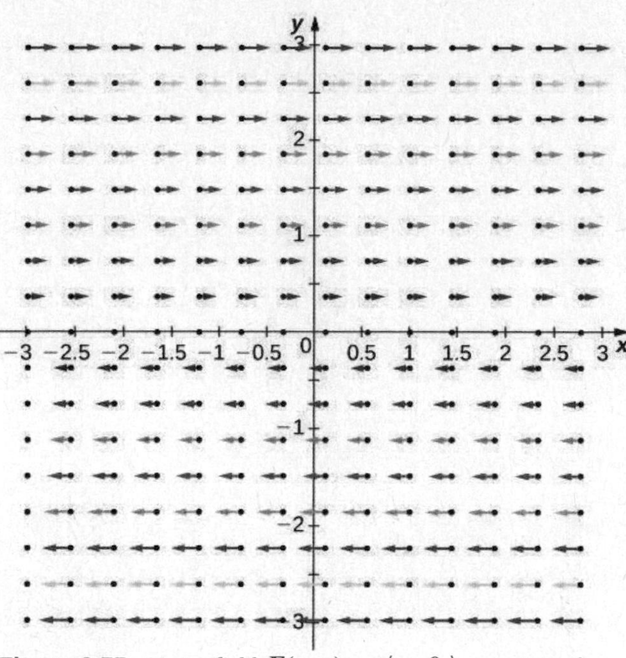

Figure 6.55 Vector field $\mathbf{F}(x, y) = \langle y, 0 \rangle$ consists of vectors that are all parallel.

Note that if $\mathbf{F} = \langle P, Q \rangle$ is a vector field in a plane, then $\text{curl}\,\mathbf{F} \cdot \mathbf{k} = (Q_x - P_y)\mathbf{k} \cdot \mathbf{k} = Q_x - P_y$. Therefore, the circulation form of Green's theorem is sometimes written as

$$\oint_C \mathbf{F} \cdot d\mathbf{r} = \iint_D \text{curl}\,\mathbf{F} \cdot \mathbf{k}\,dA,$$

where C is a simple closed curve and D is the region enclosed by C. Therefore, the circulation form of Green's theorem can be written in terms of the curl. If we think of curl as a derivative of sorts, then Green's theorem says that the "derivative" of $\mathbf{F}$ on a region can be translated into a line integral of $\mathbf{F}$ along the boundary of the region. This is analogous to the Fundamental Theorem of Calculus, in which the derivative of a function f on line segment $[a, b]$ can be translated into a statement about f on the boundary of $[a, b]$. Using curl, we can see the circulation form of Green's theorem is a higher-dimensional analog of the Fundamental Theorem of Calculus.

We can now use what we have learned about curl to show that gravitational fields have no "spin." Suppose there is an object at the origin with mass m_1 at the origin and an object with mass m_2. Recall that the gravitational force that object 1 exerts on object 2 is given by field

$$\mathbf{F}(x, y, z) = -Gm_2m_2 \left\langle \frac{x}{(x^2+y^2+z^2)^{3/2}}, \frac{y}{(x^2+y^2+z^2)^{3/2}}, \frac{z}{(x^2+y^2+z^2)^{3/2}} \right\rangle.$$

Example 6.54

Determining the Spin of a Gravitational Field

Show that a gravitational field has no spin.

Solution

To show that $\mathbf{F}$ has no spin, we calculate its curl. Let $P(x, y, z) = \frac{x}{\left(x^2+y^2+z^2\right)^{3/2}}$, $Q(x, y, z) = \frac{y}{\left(x^2+y^2+z^2\right)^{3/2}}$, and $R(x, y, z) = \frac{z}{\left(x^2+y^2+z^2\right)^{3/2}}$. Then,

$$\begin{aligned} \text{curl } \mathbf{F} &= -Gm_1m_2\left[\left(R_y - Q_z\right)\mathbf{i} + \left(P_z - R_x\right)\mathbf{j} + \left(Q_x - P_y\right)\mathbf{k}\right] \\ &= -Gm_1m_2\left[\begin{array}{l} \left(\frac{-3yz}{\left(x^2+y^2+z^2\right)^{5/2}} - \left(\frac{-3yz}{\left(x^2+y^2+z^2\right)^{5/2}}\right)\right)\mathbf{i} \\ +\left(\frac{-3xz}{\left(x^2+y^2+z^2\right)^{5/2}} - \left(\frac{-3xz}{\left(x^2+y^2+z^2\right)^{5/2}}\right)\right)\mathbf{j} \\ +\left(\frac{-3xy}{\left(x^2+y^2+z^2\right)^{5/2}} - \left(\frac{-3xy}{\left(x^2+y^2+z^2\right)^{5/2}}\right)\right)\mathbf{k} \end{array}\right] \\ &= 0. \end{aligned}$$

Since the curl of the gravitational field is zero, the field has no spin.

6.44 Field $\mathbf{v}(x, y) = \left\langle -\frac{y}{x^2+y^2}, \frac{x}{x^2+y^2} \right\rangle$ models the flow of a fluid. Show that if you drop a leaf into this fluid, as the leaf moves over time, the leaf does not rotate.

Using Divergence and Curl

Now that we understand the basic concepts of divergence and curl, we can discuss their properties and establish relationships between them and conservative vector fields.

If $\mathbf{F}$ is a vector field in $\mathbb{R}^3$, then the curl of $\mathbf{F}$ is also a vector field in $\mathbb{R}^3$. Therefore, we can take the divergence of a curl. The next theorem says that the result is always zero. This result is useful because it gives us a way to show that some vector fields are not the curl of any other field. To give this result a physical interpretation, recall that divergence of a velocity field $\mathbf{v}$ at point P measures the tendency of the corresponding fluid to flow out of P. Since $\text{div curl}\,(\mathbf{v}) = 0$, the net rate of flow in vector field curl($\mathbf{v}$) at any point is zero. Taking the curl of vector field $\mathbf{F}$ eliminates whatever divergence was present in $\mathbf{F}$.

Theorem 6.16: Divergence of the Curl

Let $\mathbf{F} = \langle P, Q, R \rangle$ be a vector field in $\mathbb{R}^3$ such that the component functions all have continuous second-order partial derivatives. Then, $\text{div curl}\,(\mathbf{F}) = \nabla \cdot (\nabla \times \mathbf{F}) = 0$.

Proof

By the definitions of divergence and curl, and by Clairaut's theorem,

$$\begin{aligned}\text{div curl } \mathbf{F} &= \text{div}[(R_y - Q_z)\mathbf{i} + (P_z - R_x)\mathbf{j} + (Q_x - P_y)\mathbf{k}] \\ &= R_{yx} - Q_{xz} + P_{yz} - R_{yx} + Q_{zx} - P_{zy} \\ &= 0.\end{aligned}$$

□

Example 6.55

Showing That a Vector Field Is Not the Curl of Another

Show that $\mathbf{F}(x, y, z) = e^x\mathbf{i} + yz\mathbf{j} + xz^2\mathbf{k}$ is not the curl of another vector field. That is, show that there is no other vector **G** with $\text{curl } \mathbf{G} = \mathbf{F}$.

Solution

Notice that the domain of **F** is all of $\mathbb{R}^3$ and the second-order partials of **F** are all continuous. Therefore, we can apply the previous theorem to **F**.

The divergence of **F** is $e^x + z + 2xz$. If **F** were the curl of vector field **G**, then $\text{div } \mathbf{F} = \text{div curl } \mathbf{G} = 0$. But, the divergence of **F** is not zero, and therefore **F** is not the curl of any other vector field.

 **6.45** Is it possible for $\mathbf{G}(x, y, z) = \langle \sin x, \cos y, \sin(xyz) \rangle$ to be the curl of a vector field?

With the next two theorems, we show that if **F** is a conservative vector field then its curl is zero, and if the domain of **F** is simply connected then the converse is also true. This gives us another way to test whether a vector field is conservative.

Theorem 6.17: Curl of a Conservative Vector Field

If $\mathbf{F} = \langle P, Q, R \rangle$ is conservative, then $\text{curl } \mathbf{F} = 0$.

Proof

Since conservative vector fields satisfy the cross-partials property, all the cross-partials of **F** are equal. Therefore,

$$\begin{aligned}\text{curl } \mathbf{F} &= (R_y - Q_z)\mathbf{i} + (P_z - R_x)\mathbf{j} + (Q_x - P_y)\mathbf{k} \\ &= 0.\end{aligned}$$

□

The same theorem is true for vector fields in a plane.

Since a conservative vector field is the gradient of a scalar function, the previous theorem says that $\text{curl } (\nabla f) = 0$ for any scalar function f. In terms of our curl notation, $\nabla \times \nabla(f) = 0$. This equation makes sense because the cross product of a vector with itself is always the zero vector. Sometimes equation $\nabla \times \nabla(f) = 0$ is simplified as $\nabla \times \nabla = 0$.

Theorem 6.18: Curl Test for a Conservative Field

Let $\mathbf{F} = \langle P, Q, R \rangle$ be a vector field in space on a simply connected domain. If $\text{curl } \mathbf{F} = 0$, then **F** is conservative.

Proof

Since $\text{curl}\,\mathbf{F} = 0,$ we have that $R_y = Q_z, P_z = R_x,$ and $Q_x = P_y.$ Therefore, **F** satisfies the cross-partials property on a simply connected domain, and **Cross-Partial Property of Conservative Fields** implies that **F** is conservative.

□

The same theorem is also true in a plane. Therefore, if **F** is a vector field in a plane or in space and the domain is simply connected, then **F** is conservative if and only if $\text{curl}\,\mathbf{F} = 0.$

Example 6.56

Testing Whether a Vector Field Is Conservative

Use the curl to determine whether $\mathbf{F}(x, y, z) = \langle yz, xz, xy \rangle$ is conservative.

Solution

Note that the domain of **F** is all of $\mathbb{R}^3,$ which is simply connected (**Figure 6.56**). Therefore, we can test whether **F** is conservative by calculating its curl.

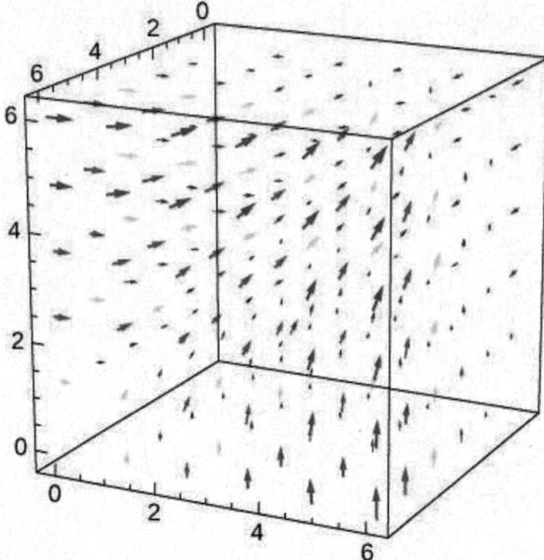

Figure 6.56 The curl of vector field $\mathbf{F}(x, y, z) = \langle yz, xz, xy \rangle$ is zero.

The curl of **F** is

$$\left(\frac{\partial}{\partial y}xy - \frac{\partial}{\partial z}xz\right)\mathbf{i} + \left(\frac{\partial}{\partial y}yz - \frac{\partial}{\partial z}xy\right)\mathbf{j} + \left(\frac{\partial}{\partial y}xz - \frac{\partial}{\partial z}yz\right)\mathbf{k} = (x - x)\mathbf{i} + (y - y)\mathbf{j} + (z - z)\mathbf{k} = 0.$$

Thus, **F** is conservative.

We have seen that the curl of a gradient is zero. What is the divergence of a gradient? If f is a function of two variables, then $\text{div}(\nabla f) = \nabla \cdot (\nabla f) = f_{xx} + f_{yy}.$ We abbreviate this "double dot product" as $\nabla^2.$ This operator is called the *Laplace operator*, and in this notation Laplace's equation becomes $\nabla^2 f = 0.$ Therefore, a harmonic function is a function that becomes zero after taking the divergence of a gradient.

Similarly, if f is a function of three variables then

$$\text{div}(\nabla f) = \nabla \cdot (\nabla f) = f_{xx} + f_{yy} + f_{zz}.$$

Using this notation we get Laplace's equation for harmonic functions of three variables:

$$\nabla^2 f = 0.$$

Harmonic functions arise in many applications. For example, the potential function of an electrostatic field in a region of space that has no static charge is harmonic.

Example 6.57

Analyzing a Function

Is it possible for $f(x, y) = x^2 + x - y$ to be the potential function of an electrostatic field that is located in a region of $\mathbb{R}^2$ free of static charge?

Solution

If f were such a potential function, then f would be harmonic. Note that $f_{xx} = 2$ and $f_{yy} = 0,$ and so $f_{xx} + f_{yy} \neq 0.$ Therefore, f is not harmonic and f cannot represent an electrostatic potential.

6.46 Is it possible for function $f(x, y) = x^2 - y^2 + x$ to be the potential function of an electrostatic field located in a region of $\mathbb{R}^2$ free of static charge?

6.5 EXERCISES

For the following exercises, determine whether the statement is *true or false*.

206. If the coordinate functions of $\mathbf{F} : \mathbb{R}^3 \to \mathbb{R}^3$ have continuous second partial derivatives, then $\text{curl}\,(\text{div}(\mathbf{F}))$ equals zero.

207. $\nabla \cdot (x\mathbf{i} + y\mathbf{j} + z\mathbf{k}) = 1.$

208. All vector fields of the form $\mathbf{F}(x, y, z) = f(x)\mathbf{i} + g(y)\mathbf{j} + h(z)\mathbf{k}$ are conservative.

209. If $\text{curl}\,\mathbf{F} = 0,$ then $\mathbf{F}$ is conservative.

210. If $\mathbf{F}$ is a constant vector field then $\text{div}\,\mathbf{F} = 0.$

211. If $\mathbf{F}$ is a constant vector field then $\text{curl}\,\mathbf{F} = 0.$

For the following exercises, find the curl of $\mathbf{F}$.

212. $\mathbf{F}(x, y, z) = xy^2z^4\mathbf{i} + \left(2x^2y + z\right)\mathbf{j} + y^3z^2\mathbf{k}$

213. $\mathbf{F}(x, y, z) = x^2z\mathbf{i} + y^2x\mathbf{j} + (y + 2z)\mathbf{k}$

214. $\mathbf{F}(x, y, z) = 3xyz^2\mathbf{i} + y^2\sin z\mathbf{j} + xe^{2z}\mathbf{k}$

215. $\mathbf{F}(x, y, z) = x^2yz\mathbf{i} + xy^2z\mathbf{j} + xyz^2\mathbf{k}$

216. $\mathbf{F}(x, y, z) = (x\cos y)\mathbf{i} + xy^2\mathbf{j}$

217. $\mathbf{F}(x, y, z) = (x - y)\mathbf{i} + (y - z)\mathbf{j} + (z - x)\mathbf{k}$

218. $\mathbf{F}(x, y, z) = xyz\mathbf{i} + x^2y^2z^2\mathbf{j} + y^2z^3\mathbf{k}$

219. $\mathbf{F}(x, y, z) = xy\mathbf{i} + yz\mathbf{j} + xz\mathbf{k}$

220. $\mathbf{F}(x, y, z) = x^2\mathbf{i} + y^2\mathbf{j} + z^2\mathbf{k}$

221. $\mathbf{F}(x, y, z) = ax\mathbf{i} + by\mathbf{j} + c\mathbf{k}$ for constants a, b, c

For the following exercises, find the divergence of $\mathbf{F}$.

222. $\mathbf{F}(x, y, z) = x^2z\mathbf{i} + y^2x\mathbf{j} + (y + 2z)\mathbf{k}$

223. $\mathbf{F}(x, y, z) = 3xyz^2\mathbf{i} + y^2\sin z\mathbf{j} + xe^{2z}\mathbf{k}$

224. $\mathbf{F}(x, y) = (\sin x)\mathbf{i} + (\cos y)\mathbf{j}$

225. $\mathbf{F}(x, y, z) = x^2\mathbf{i} + y^2\mathbf{j} + z^2\mathbf{k}$

226. $\mathbf{F}(x, y, z) = (x - y)\mathbf{i} + (y - z)\mathbf{j} + (z - x)\mathbf{k}$

227. $\mathbf{F}(x, y) = \dfrac{x}{\sqrt{x^2 + y^2}}\mathbf{i} + \dfrac{y}{\sqrt{x^2 + y^2}}\mathbf{j}$

228. $\mathbf{F}(x, y) = x\mathbf{i} - y\mathbf{j}$

229. $\mathbf{F}(x, y, z) = ax\mathbf{i} + by\mathbf{j} + c\mathbf{k}$ for constants a, b, c

230. $\mathbf{F}(x, y, z) = xyz\mathbf{i} + x^2y^2z^2\mathbf{j} + y^2z^3\mathbf{k}$

231. $\mathbf{F}(x, y, z) = xy\mathbf{i} + yz\mathbf{j} + xz\mathbf{k}$

For the following exercises, determine whether each of the given scalar functions is harmonic.

232. $u(x, y, z) = e^{-x}(\cos y - \sin y)$

233. $w(x, y, z) = \left(x^2 + y^2 + z^2\right)^{-1/2}$

234. If $\mathbf{F}(x, y, z) = 2\mathbf{i} + 2x\mathbf{j} + 3y\mathbf{k}$ and $\mathbf{G}(x, y, z) = x\mathbf{i} - y\mathbf{j} + z\mathbf{k},$ find $\text{curl}\,(\mathbf{F} \times \mathbf{G}).$

235. If $\mathbf{F}(x, y, z) = 2\mathbf{i} + 2x\mathbf{j} + 3y\mathbf{k}$ and $\mathbf{G}(x, y, z) = x\mathbf{i} - y\mathbf{j} + z\mathbf{k},$ find $\text{div}\,(\mathbf{F} \times \mathbf{G}).$

236. Find $\text{div}\,\mathbf{F},$ given that $\mathbf{F} = \nabla f,$ where $f(x, y, z) = xy^3z^2.$

237. Find the divergence of $\mathbf{F}$ for vector field $\mathbf{F}(x, y, z) = \left(y^2 + z^2\right)(x + y)\mathbf{i} + \left(z^2 + x^2\right)(y + z)\mathbf{j} + \left(x^2 + y^2\right)(z + x)\mathbf{k}.$

238. Find the divergence of $\mathbf{F}$ for vector field $\mathbf{F}(x, y, z) = f_1(y, z)\mathbf{i} + f_2(x, z)\mathbf{j} + f_3(x, y)\mathbf{k}.$

For the following exercises, use $r = |\mathbf{r}|$ and $\mathbf{r} = (x, y, z).$

239. Find the $\text{curl}\,\mathbf{r}.$

240. Find the $\text{curl}\,\dfrac{\mathbf{r}}{r}.$

241. Find the $\text{curl}\,\dfrac{\mathbf{r}}{r^3}.$

242. Let $\mathbf{F}(x, y) = \dfrac{-y\mathbf{i} + x\mathbf{j}}{x^2 + y^2},$ where $\mathbf{F}$ is defined on $\{(x, y) \in \mathbb{R} \,|\, (x, y) \neq (0, 0)\}.$ Find $\text{curl}\,\mathbf{F}.$

For the following exercises, use a computer algebra system

to find the curl of the given vector fields.

243. **[T]** $\mathbf{F}(x, y, z) = \arctan\left(\frac{x}{y}\right)\mathbf{i} + \ln\sqrt{x^2 + y^2}\mathbf{j} + \mathbf{k}$

244. **[T]** $\mathbf{F}(x, y, z) = \sin(x - y)\mathbf{i} + \sin(y - z)\mathbf{j} + \sin(z - x)\mathbf{k}$

For the following exercises, find the divergence of **F** at the given point.

245. $\mathbf{F}(x, y, z) = \mathbf{i} + \mathbf{j} + \mathbf{k}$ at $(2, -1, 3)$

246. $\mathbf{F}(x, y, z) = xyz\mathbf{i} + y\mathbf{j} + z\mathbf{k}$ at $(1, 2, 3)$

247. $\mathbf{F}(x, y, z) = e^{-xy}\mathbf{i} + e^{xz}\mathbf{j} + e^{yz}\mathbf{k}$ at $(3, 2, 0)$

248. $\mathbf{F}(x, y, z) = xyz\mathbf{i} + y\mathbf{j} + z\mathbf{k}$ at $(1, 2, 1)$

249. $\mathbf{F}(x, y, z) = e^x \sin y\mathbf{i} - e^x \cos y\mathbf{j}$ at $(0, 0, 3)$

For the following exercises, find the curl of **F** at the given point.

250. $\mathbf{F}(x, y, z) = \mathbf{i} + \mathbf{j} + \mathbf{k}$ at $(2, -1, 3)$

251. $\mathbf{F}(x, y, z) = xyz\mathbf{i} + y\mathbf{j} + x\mathbf{k}$ at $(1, 2, 3)$

252. $\mathbf{F}(x, y, z) = e^{-xy}\mathbf{i} + e^{xz}\mathbf{j} + e^{yz}\mathbf{k}$ at $(3, 2, 0)$

253. $\mathbf{F}(x, y, z) = xyz\mathbf{i} + y\mathbf{j} + z\mathbf{k}$ at $(1, 2, 1)$

254. $\mathbf{F}(x, y, z) = e^x \sin y\mathbf{i} - e^x \cos y\mathbf{j}$ at $(0, 0, 3)$

255. Let $\mathbf{F}(x, y, z) = \left(3x^2 y + az\right)\mathbf{i} + x^3\mathbf{j} + \left(3x + 3z^2\right)\mathbf{k}$. For what value of a is **F** conservative?

256. Given vector field $\mathbf{F}(x, y) = \frac{1}{x^2 + y^2}(-y, x)$ on domain $D = \frac{\mathbb{R}^2}{\{(0, 0)\}} = \left\{(x, y) \in \mathbb{R}^2 \,|\, (x, y) \neq (0, 0)\right\}$, is **F** conservative?

257. Given vector field $\mathbf{F}(x, y) = \frac{1}{x^2 + y^2}(x, y)$ on domain $D = \frac{\mathbb{R}^2}{\{(0, 0)\}}$, is **F** conservative?

258. Find the work done by force field $\mathbf{F}(x, y) = e^{-y}\mathbf{i} - xe^{-y}\mathbf{j}$ in moving an object from $P(0, 1)$ to $Q(2, 0)$. Is the force field conservative?

259. Compute divergence $\mathbf{F} = (\sinh x)\mathbf{i} + (\cosh y)\mathbf{j} - xyz\mathbf{k}$.

260. Compute curl $\mathbf{F} = (\sinh x)\mathbf{i} + (\cosh y)\mathbf{j} - xyz\mathbf{k}$.

For the following exercises, consider a rigid body that is rotating about the x-axis counterclockwise with constant angular velocity $\omega = \langle a, b, c \rangle$. If P is a point in the body located at $\mathbf{r} = x\mathbf{i} + y\mathbf{j} + z\mathbf{k}$, the velocity at P is given by vector field $\mathbf{F} = \omega \times \mathbf{r}$.

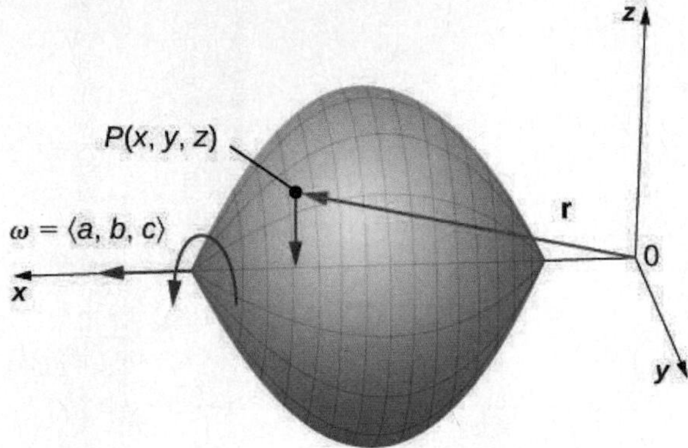

261. Express **F** in terms of **i**, **j**, and **k** vectors.

262. Find div **F**.

263. Find curl **F**

In the following exercises, suppose that $\nabla \cdot \mathbf{F} = 0$ and $\nabla \cdot \mathbf{G} = 0$.

264. Does $\mathbf{F} + \mathbf{G}$ necessarily have zero divergence?

265. Does $\mathbf{F} \times \mathbf{G}$ necessarily have zero divergence?

In the following exercises, suppose a solid object in $\mathbb{R}^3$ has a temperature distribution given by $T(x, y, z)$. The heat flow vector field in the object is $\mathbf{F} = -k\nabla T$, where $k > 0$ is a property of the material. The heat flow vector points in the direction opposite to that of the gradient, which is the direction of greatest temperature decrease. The divergence of the heat flow vector is $\nabla \cdot \mathbf{F} = -k\nabla \cdot \nabla T = -k\nabla^2 T$.

266. Compute the heat flow vector field.

267. Compute the divergence.

268. **[T]** Consider rotational velocity field $\mathbf{v} = \langle 0, 10z, -10y \rangle$. If a paddlewheel is placed in plane $x + y + z = 1$ with its axis normal to this plane, using a computer algebra system, calculate how fast the paddlewheel spins in revolutions per unit time.

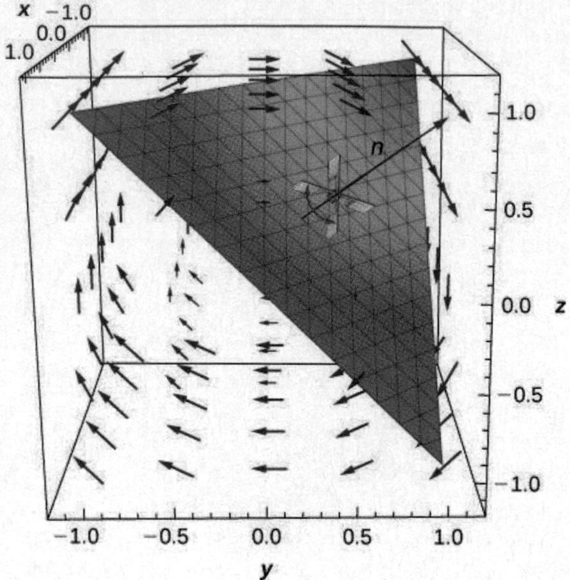

6.6 | Surface Integrals

Learning Objectives

6.6.1 Find the parametric representations of a cylinder, a cone, and a sphere.
6.6.2 Describe the surface integral of a scalar-valued function over a parametric surface.
6.6.3 Use a surface integral to calculate the area of a given surface.
6.6.4 Explain the meaning of an oriented surface, giving an example.
6.6.5 Describe the surface integral of a vector field.
6.6.6 Use surface integrals to solve applied problems.

We have seen that a line integral is an integral over a path in a plane or in space. However, if we wish to integrate over a surface (a two-dimensional object) rather than a path (a one-dimensional object) in space, then we need a new kind of integral that can handle integration over objects in higher dimensions. We can extend the concept of a line integral to a surface integral to allow us to perform this integration.

Surface integrals are important for the same reasons that line integrals are important. They have many applications to physics and engineering, and they allow us to develop higher dimensional versions of the Fundamental Theorem of Calculus. In particular, surface integrals allow us to generalize Green's theorem to higher dimensions, and they appear in some important theorems we discuss in later sections.

Parametric Surfaces

A surface integral is similar to a line integral, except the integration is done over a surface rather than a path. In this sense, surface integrals expand on our study of line integrals. Just as with line integrals, there are two kinds of surface integrals: a surface integral of a scalar-valued function and a surface integral of a vector field.

However, before we can integrate over a surface, we need to consider the surface itself. Recall that to calculate a scalar or vector line integral over curve C, we first need to parameterize C. In a similar way, to calculate a surface integral over surface S, we need to parameterize S. That is, we need a working concept of a **parameterized surface** (or a **parametric surface**), in the same way that we already have a concept of a parameterized curve.

A parameterized surface is given by a description of the form

$$\mathbf{r}(u, v) = \langle x(u, v), y(u, v), z(u, v) \rangle .$$

Notice that this parameterization involves two parameters, u and v, because a surface is two-dimensional, and therefore two variables are needed to trace out the surface. The parameters u and v vary over a region called the parameter domain, or **parameter space**—the set of points in the uv-plane that can be substituted into $\mathbf{r}$. Each choice of u and v in the parameter domain gives a point on the surface, just as each choice of a parameter t gives a point on a parameterized curve. The entire surface is created by making all possible choices of u and v over the parameter domain.

Definition

Given a parameterization of surface $\mathbf{r}(u, v) = \langle x(u, v), y(u, v), z(u, v) \rangle$, the **parameter domain** of the parameterization is the set of points in the uv-plane that can be substituted into $\mathbf{r}$.

Example 6.58

Parameterizing a Cylinder

Describe surface S parameterized by

$$\mathbf{r}(u, v) = \langle \cos u, \sin u, v \rangle, -\infty < u < \infty, -\infty < v < \infty.$$

Solution

To get an idea of the shape of the surface, we first plot some points. Since the parameter domain is all of $\mathbb{R}^2$, we can choose any value for u and v and plot the corresponding point. If $u = v = 0$, then $\mathbf{r}(0, 0) = \langle 1, 0, 0 \rangle$, so point $(1, 0, 0)$ is on S. Similarly, points $\mathbf{r}(\pi, 2) = (-1, 0, 2)$ and $\mathbf{r}\left(\frac{\pi}{2}, 4\right) = (0, 1, 4)$ are on S.

Although plotting points may give us an idea of the shape of the surface, we usually need quite a few points to see the shape. Since it is time-consuming to plot dozens or hundreds of points, we use another strategy. To visualize S, we visualize two families of curves that lie on S. In the first family of curves we hold u constant; in the second family of curves we hold v constant. This allows us to build a "skeleton" of the surface, thereby getting an idea of its shape.

First, suppose that u is a constant K. Then the curve traced out by the parameterization is $\langle \cos K, \sin K, v \rangle$, which gives a vertical line that goes through point $(\cos K, \sin K, v)$ in the xy-plane.

Now suppose that v is a constant K. Then the curve traced out by the parameterization is $\langle \cos u, \sin u, K \rangle$, which gives a circle in plane $z = K$ with radius 1 and center $(0, 0, K)$.

If u is held constant, then we get vertical lines; if v is held constant, then we get circles of radius 1 centered around the vertical line that goes through the origin. Therefore the surface traced out by the parameterization is cylinder $x^2 + y^2 = 1$ (**Figure 6.57**).

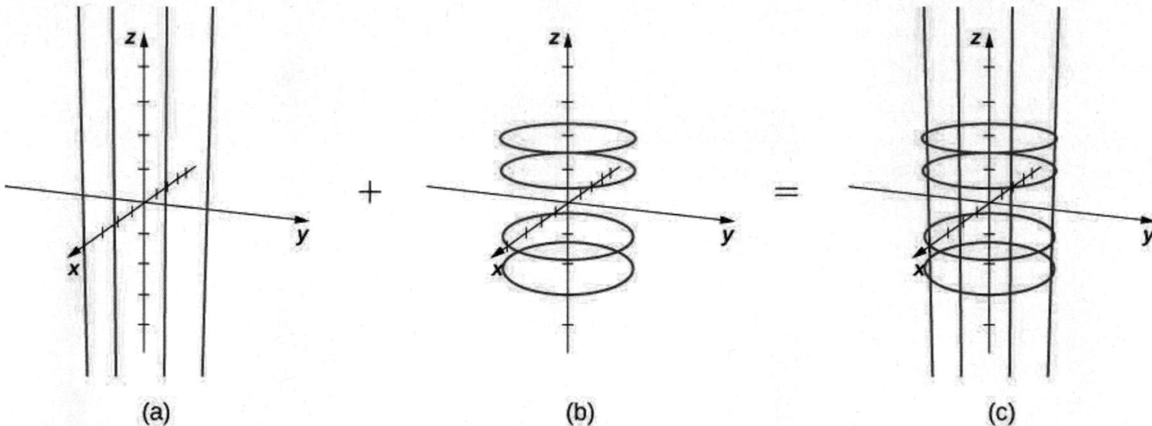

Figure 6.57 (a) Lines $\langle \cos K, \sin K, v \rangle$ for $K = 0, \frac{\pi}{2}, \pi,$ and $\frac{3\pi}{2}$. (b) Circles $\langle \cos u, \sin u, K \rangle$ for $K = -2, -1, 1,$ and 2. (c) The lines and circles together. As u and v vary, they describe a cylinder.

Notice that if $x = \cos u$ and $y = \sin u$, then $x^2 + y^2 = 1$, so points from S do indeed lie on the cylinder. Conversely, each point on the cylinder is contained in some circle $\langle \cos u, \sin u, k \rangle$ for some k, and therefore each point on the cylinder is contained in the parameterized surface (**Figure 6.58**).

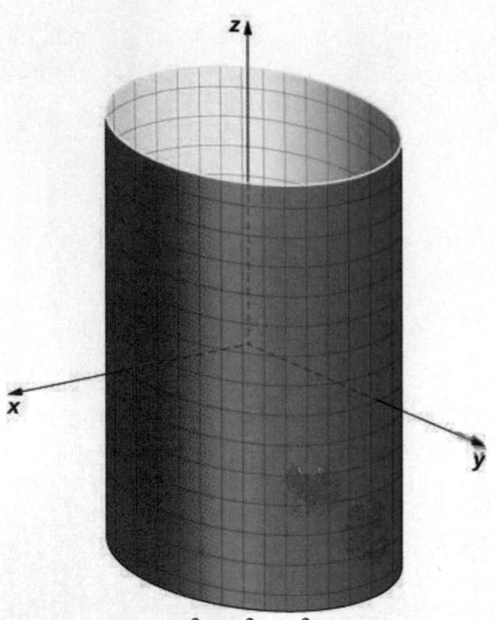

Figure 6.58 Cylinder $x^2 + y^2 = r^2$ has parameterization $\mathbf{r}(u, v) = \langle r\cos u, r\sin u, v \rangle$, $0 \le u \le 2\pi, -\infty < v < \infty.$

Analysis

Notice that if we change the parameter domain, we could get a different surface. For example, if we restricted the domain to $0 \le u \le \pi, 0 < v < 6,$ then the surface would be a half-cylinder of height 6.

6.47 Describe the surface with parameterization $\mathbf{r}(u, v) = \langle 2\cos u, 2\sin u, v \rangle, 0 \le u < 2\pi, -\infty < v < \infty.$

It follows from **Example 6.58** that we can parameterize all cylinders of the form $x^2 + y^2 = R^2$. If *S* is a cylinder given by equation $x^2 + y^2 = R^2,$ then a parameterization of *S* is

$$\mathbf{r}(u, v) = \langle R\cos u, R\sin u, v \rangle, 0 \le u < 2\pi, -\infty < v < \infty.$$

We can also find different types of surfaces given their parameterization, or we can find a parameterization when we are given a surface.

Example 6.59

Describing a Surface

Describe surface *S* parameterized by

$$\mathbf{r}(u, v) = \langle u\cos v, u\sin v, u^2 \rangle, 0 \le u < \infty, 0 \le v < 2\pi.$$

Solution

Notice that if u is held constant, then the resulting curve is a circle of radius u in plane $z = u$. Therefore, as u increases, the radius of the resulting circle increases. If v is held constant, then the resulting curve is a vertical parabola. Therefore, we expect the surface to be an elliptic paraboloid. To confirm this, notice that

$$\begin{aligned} x^2 + y^2 &= (u \cos v)^2 + (u \sin v)^2 \\ &= u^2 \cos^2 v + u^2 \sin^2 v \\ &= u^2 \\ &= z. \end{aligned}$$

Therefore, the surface is elliptic paraboloid $x^2 + y^2 = z$ (**Figure 6.59**).

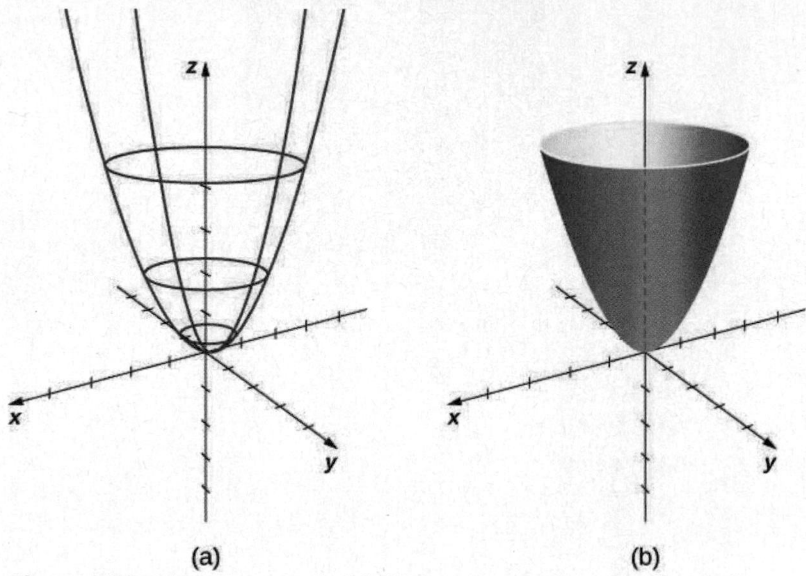

Figure 6.59 (a) Circles arise from holding u constant; the vertical parabolas arise from holding v constant. (b) An elliptic paraboloid results from all choices of u and v in the parameter domain.

6.48 Describe the surface parameterized by $\mathbf{r}(u, v) = \langle u \cos v, u \sin v, u \rangle$, $-\infty < u < \infty$, $0 \le v < 2\pi$.

Example 6.60

Finding a Parameterization

Give a parameterization of the cone $x^2 + y^2 = z^2$ lying on or above the plane $z = -2$.

Solution

The horizontal cross-section of the cone at height $z = u$ is circle $x^2 + y^2 = u^2$. Therefore, a point on the cone at height u has coordinates $(u \cos v, u \sin v, u)$ for angle v. Hence, a parameterization of the cone is $\mathbf{r}(u, v) = \langle u \cos v, u \sin v, u \rangle$. Since we are not interested in the entire cone, only the portion on or above plane $z = -2$, the parameter domain is given by $-2 \le u < \infty,\ 0 \le v < 2\pi$ (**Figure 6.60**).

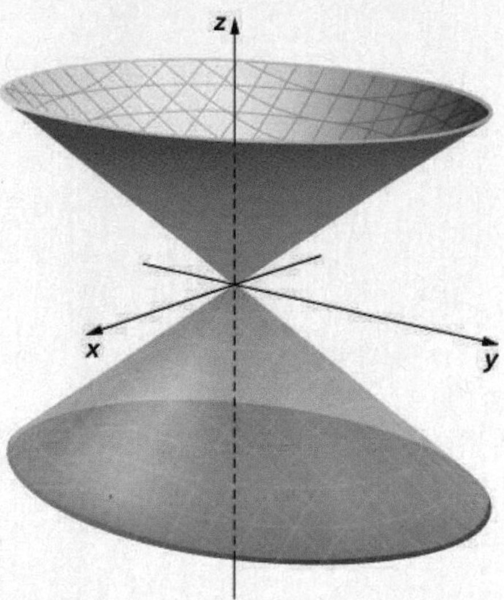

Figure 6.60 Cone $x^2 + y^2 = z^2$ has parameterization $r(u, v) = \langle u \cos v, u \sin v, u \rangle,\ -\infty < u < \infty,\ 0 \le v \le 2\pi$.

6.49 Give a parameterization for the portion of cone $x^2 + y^2 = z^2$ lying in the first octant.

We have discussed parameterizations of various surfaces, but two important types of surfaces need a separate discussion: spheres and graphs of two-variable functions. To parameterize a sphere, it is easiest to use spherical coordinates. The sphere of radius ρ centered at the origin is given by the parameterization

$$\mathbf{r}(\phi, \theta) = \langle \rho \cos \theta \sin \phi, \rho \sin \theta \sin \phi, \rho \cos \phi \rangle,\ 0 \le \theta \le 2\pi,\ 0 \le \phi \le \pi.$$

The idea of this parameterization is that as ϕ sweeps downward from the positive z-axis, a circle of radius $\rho \sin \phi$ is traced out by letting θ run from 0 to 2π. To see this, let ϕ be fixed. Then

$$\begin{aligned} x^2 + y^2 &= (\rho \cos \theta \sin \phi)^2 + (\rho \sin \theta \sin \phi)^2 \\ &= \rho^2 \sin^2 \phi \left(\cos^2 \theta + \sin^2 \theta\right) \\ &= \rho^2 \sin^2 \phi \\ &= (\rho \sin \phi)^2. \end{aligned}$$

This results in the desired circle (**Figure 6.61**).

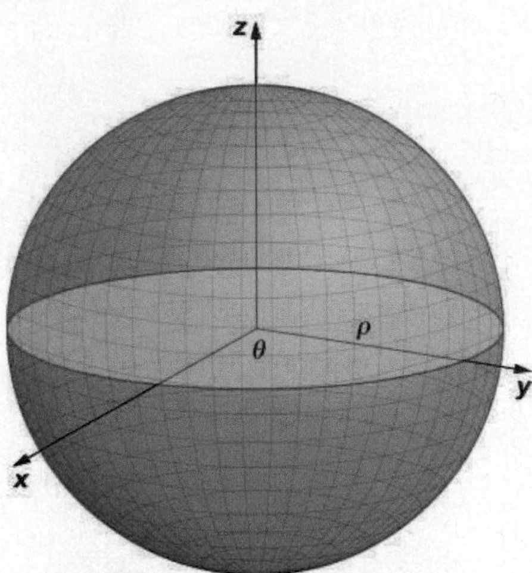

Figure 6.61 The sphere of radius ρ has parameterization $\mathbf{r}(\phi, \theta) = \langle \rho \cos \theta \sin \phi, \rho \sin \theta \sin \phi, \rho \cos \phi \rangle$, $0 \le \theta \le 2\pi, 0 \le \phi \le \pi.$

Finally, to parameterize the graph of a two-variable function, we first let $z = f(x, y)$ be a function of two variables. The simplest parameterization of the graph of f is $\mathbf{r}(x, y) = \langle x, y, f(x, y) \rangle$, where x and y vary over the domain of f (**Figure 6.62**). For example, the graph of $f(x, y) = x^2 y$ can be parameterized by $\mathbf{r}(x, y) = \langle x, y, x^2 y \rangle$, where the parameters x and y vary over the domain of f. If we only care about a piece of the graph of f—say, the piece of the graph over rectangle $[1, 3] \times [2, 5]$—then we can restrict the parameter domain to give this piece of the surface:

$$\mathbf{r}(x, y) = \langle x, y, x^2 y \rangle, 1 \le x \le 3, 2 \le y \le 5.$$

Similarly, if S is a surface given by equation $x = g(y, z)$ or equation $y = h(x, z)$, then a parameterization of S is $\mathbf{r}(y, z) = \langle g(y, z), y, z \rangle$ or $\mathbf{r}(x, z) = \langle x, h(x, z), z \rangle$, respectively. For example, the graph of paraboloid $2y = x^2 + z^2$ can be parameterized by $\mathbf{r}(x, z) = \langle x, \frac{x^2 + z^2}{2}, z \rangle, 0 \le x < \infty, 0 \le z < \infty$. Notice that we do not need to vary over the entire domain of y because x and z are squared.

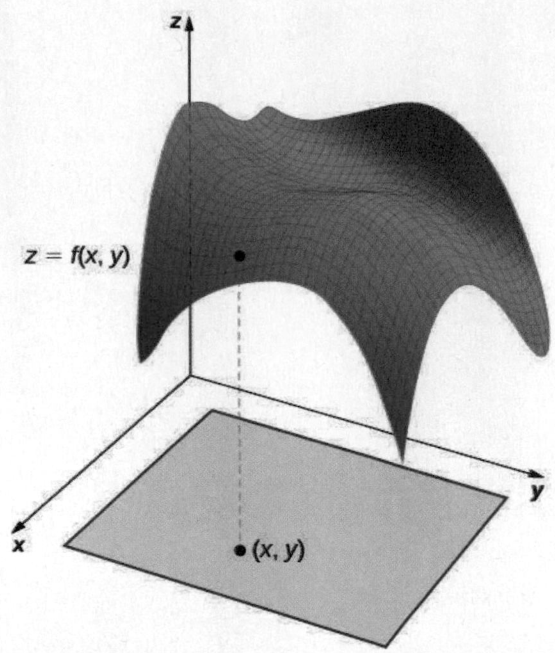

Figure 6.62 The simplest parameterization of the graph of a function is $\mathbf{r}(x, y) = \langle x, y, f(x, y) \rangle$.

Let's now generalize the notions of smoothness and regularity to a parametric surface. Recall that curve parameterization $\mathbf{r}(t), a \le t \le b$ is regular if $\mathbf{r}'(t) \ne 0$ for all t in $[a, b]$. For a curve, this condition ensures that the image of $\mathbf{r}$ really is a curve, and not just a point. For example, consider curve parameterization $\mathbf{r}(t) = \langle 1, 2 \rangle, 0 \le t \le 5$. The image of this parameterization is simply point $(1, 2),$ which is not a curve. Notice also that $\mathbf{r}'(t) = 0$. The fact that the derivative is zero indicates we are not actually looking at a curve.

Analogously, we would like a notion of regularity for surfaces so that a surface parameterization really does trace out a surface. To motivate the definition of regularity of a surface parameterization, consider parameterization

$$\mathbf{r}(u, v) = \langle 0, \cos v, 1 \rangle, 0 \le u \le 1, 0 \le v \le \pi.$$

Although this parameterization appears to be the parameterization of a surface, notice that the image is actually a line (**Figure 6.63**). How could we avoid parameterizations such as this? Parameterizations that do not give an actual surface? Notice that $\mathbf{r}_u = \langle 0, 0, 0 \rangle$ and $\mathbf{r}_v = \langle 0, -\sin v, 0 \rangle,$ and the corresponding cross product is zero. The analog of the condition $\mathbf{r}'(t) = 0$ is that $\mathbf{r}_u \times \mathbf{r}_v$ is not zero for point (u, v) in the parameter domain, which is a regular parameterization.

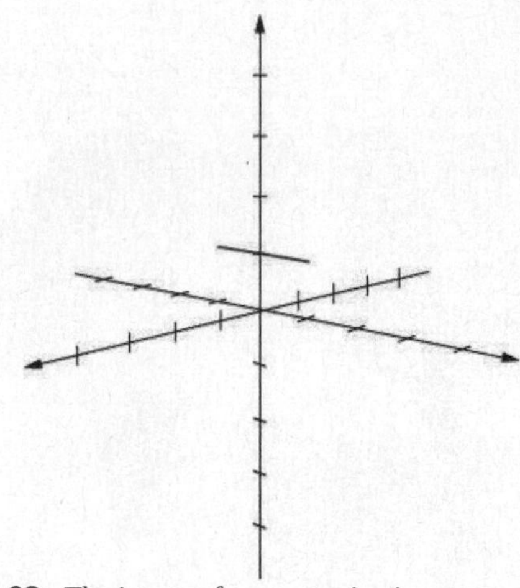

Figure 6.63 The image of parameterization $\mathbf{r}(u, v) = \langle 0, \cos v, 1 \rangle,\ 0 \le u \le 1,\ 0 \le v \le \pi$ is a line.

Definition

Parameterization $\mathbf{r}(u, v) = \langle x(u, v), y(u, v), z(u, v) \rangle$ is a **regular parameterization** if $\mathbf{r}_u \times \mathbf{r}_v$ is not zero for point (u, v) in the parameter domain.

If parameterization $\mathbf{r}$ is regular, then the image of $\mathbf{r}$ is a two-dimensional object, as a surface should be. Throughout this chapter, parameterizations $\mathbf{r}(u, v) = \langle x(u, v), y(u, v), z(u, v) \rangle$ are assumed to be regular.

Recall that curve parameterization $\mathbf{r}(t),\ a \le t \le b$ is smooth if $\mathbf{r}'(t)$ is continuous and $\mathbf{r}'(t) \ne 0$ for all t in $[a, b]$. Informally, a curve parameterization is smooth if the resulting curve has no sharp corners. The definition of a smooth surface parameterization is similar. Informally, a surface parameterization is *smooth* if the resulting surface has no sharp corners.

Definition

A surface parameterization $\mathbf{r}(u, v) = \langle x(u, v), y(u, v), z(u, v) \rangle$ is *smooth* if vector $\mathbf{r}_u \times \mathbf{r}_v$ is not zero for any choice of u and v in the parameter domain.

A surface may also be *piecewise smooth* if it has smooth faces but also has locations where the directional derivatives do not exist.

Example 6.61

Identifying Smooth and Nonsmooth Surfaces

Which of the figures in **Figure 6.64** is smooth?

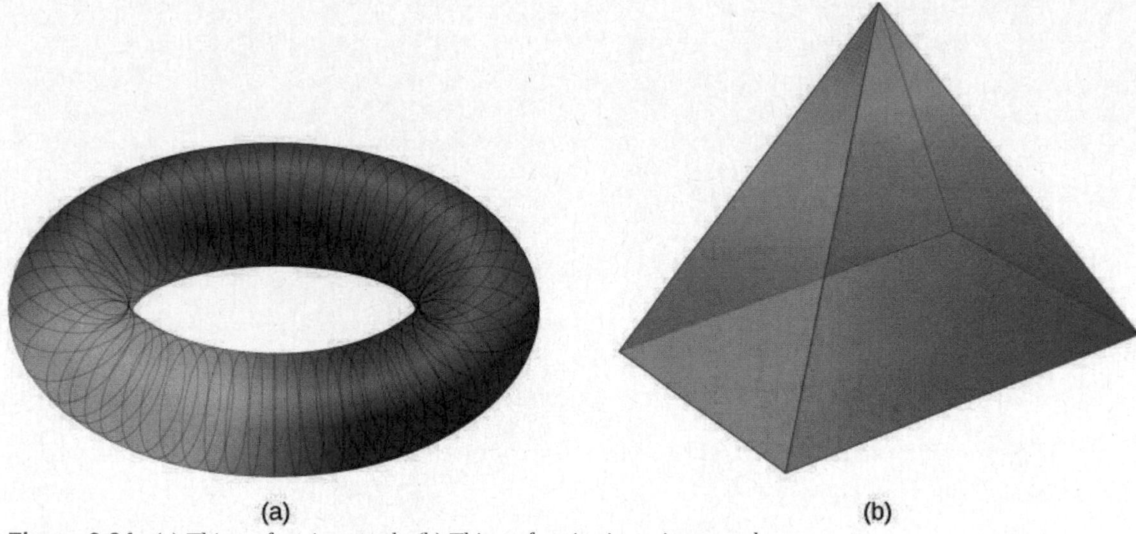

Figure 6.64 (a) This surface is smooth. (b) This surface is piecewise smooth.

Solution

The surface in **Figure 6.64**(a) can be parameterized by

$$\mathbf{r}(u, v) = \langle (2+\cos v)\cos u, (2+\cos v)\sin u, \sin v \rangle, \; 0 \le u < 2\pi, \; 0 \le v < 2\pi$$

(we can use technology to verify). Notice that vectors

$$\mathbf{r}_u = \langle -(2+\cos v)\sin u, (2+\cos v)\cos u, 0 \rangle \text{ and } \mathbf{r}_v = \langle -\sin v \cos u, -\sin v \sin u, \cos v \rangle$$

exist for any choice of u and v in the parameter domain, and

$$\begin{aligned}\mathbf{r}_u \times \mathbf{r}_v &= \begin{vmatrix} \mathbf{i} & \mathbf{j} & \mathbf{k} \\ -(2+\cos v)\sin u & (2+\cos v)\cos u & 0 \\ -\sin v \cos u & -\sin v \sin u & \cos v \end{vmatrix} \\ &= [(2+\cos v)\cos u \cos v]\mathbf{i} + [(2+\cos v)\sin u \cos v]\mathbf{j} \\ &\quad + \left[(2+\cos v)\sin v \sin^2 u + (2+\cos v)\sin v \cos^2 u\right]\mathbf{k} \\ &= [(2+\cos v)\cos u \cos v]\mathbf{i} + [(2+\cos v)\sin u \cos v]\mathbf{j} + [(2+\cos v)\sin v]\mathbf{k}.\end{aligned}$$

The $\mathbf{k}$ component of this vector is zero only if $v = 0$ or $v = \pi$. If $v = 0$ or $v = \pi$, then the only choices for u that make the $\mathbf{j}$ component zero are $u = 0$ or $u = \pi$. But, these choices of u do not make the $\mathbf{i}$ component zero. Therefore, $\mathbf{r}_u \times \mathbf{r}_v$ is not zero for any choice of u and v in the parameter domain, and the parameterization is smooth. Notice that the corresponding surface has no sharp corners.

In the pyramid in **Figure 6.64**(b), the sharpness of the corners ensures that directional derivatives do not exist at those locations. Therefore, the pyramid has no smooth parameterization. However, the pyramid consists of four smooth faces, and thus this surface is piecewise smooth.

6.50 Is the surface parameterization $\mathbf{r}(u, v) = \langle u^{2v}, v+1, \sin u \rangle, \; 0 \le u \le 2, \; 0 \le v \le 3$ smooth?

Surface Area of a Parametric Surface

Our goal is to define a surface integral, and as a first step we have examined how to parameterize a surface. The second step is to define the surface area of a parametric surface. The notation needed to develop this definition is used throughout the rest of this chapter.

Let S be a surface with parameterization $\mathbf{r}(u, v) = \langle x(u, v), y(u, v), z(u, v) \rangle$ over some parameter domain D. We assume here and throughout that the surface parameterization $\mathbf{r}(u, v) = \langle x(u, v), y(u, v), z(u, v) \rangle$ is continuously differentiable—meaning, each component function has continuous partial derivatives. Assume for the sake of simplicity that D is a rectangle (although the following material can be extended to handle nonrectangular parameter domains). Divide rectangle D into subrectangles D_{ij} with horizontal width Δu and vertical length Δv. Suppose that i ranges from 1 to m and j ranges from 1 to n so that D is subdivided into mn rectangles. This division of D into subrectangles gives a corresponding division of surface S into pieces S_{ij}. Choose point P_{ij} in each piece S_{ij}. Point P_{ij} corresponds to point (u_i, v_j) in the parameter domain.

Note that we can form a grid with lines that are parallel to the u-axis and the v-axis in the uv-plane. These grid lines correspond to a set of **grid curves** on surface S that is parameterized by $\mathbf{r}(u, v)$. Without loss of generality, we assume that P_{ij} is located at the corner of two grid curves, as in **Figure 6.65**. If we think of $\mathbf{r}$ as a mapping from the uv-plane to $\mathbb{R}^3$, the grid curves are the image of the grid lines under $\mathbf{r}$. To be precise, consider the grid lines that go through point (u_i, v_j). One line is given by $x = u_i, y = v$; the other is given by $x = u, y = v_j$. In the first grid line, the horizontal component is held constant, yielding a vertical line through (u_i, v_j). In the second grid line, the vertical component is held constant, yielding a horizontal line through (u_i, v_j). The corresponding grid curves are $\mathbf{r}(u_i, v)$ and $\mathbf{r}(u, v_j)$, and these curves intersect at point P_{ij}.

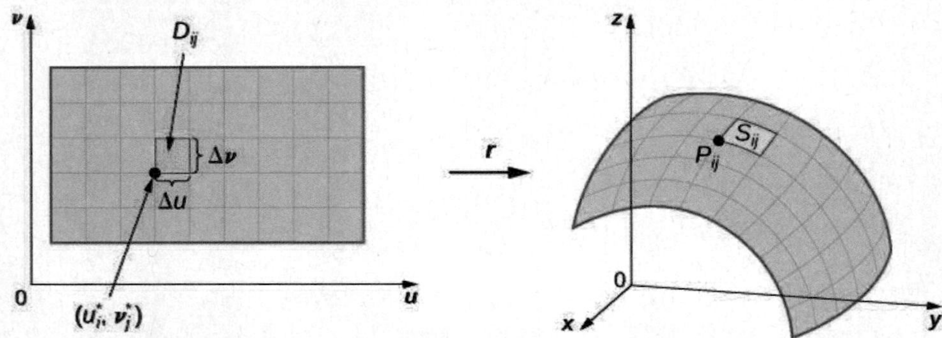

Figure 6.65 Grid lines on a parameter domain correspond to grid curves on a surface.

Now consider the vectors that are tangent to these grid curves. For grid curve $\mathbf{r}(u_i, v)$, the tangent vector at P_{ij} is

$$\mathbf{t}_v(P_{ij}) = \mathbf{r}_v(u_i, v_j) = \langle x_v(u_i, v_j), y_v(u_i, v_j), z_v(u_i, v_j) \rangle.$$

For grid curve $\mathbf{r}(u, v_j)$, the tangent vector at P_{ij} is

$$\mathbf{t}_u(P_{ij}) = \mathbf{r}_u(u_i, v_j) = \langle x_u(u_i, v_j), y_u(u_i, v_j), z_u(u_i, v_j) \rangle.$$

If vector $\mathbf{N} = \mathbf{t}_u(P_{ij}) \times \mathbf{t}_v(P_{ij})$ exists and is not zero, then the tangent plane at P_{ij} exists (**Figure 6.66**). If piece S_{ij} is small enough, then the tangent plane at point P_{ij} is a good approximation of piece S_{ij}.

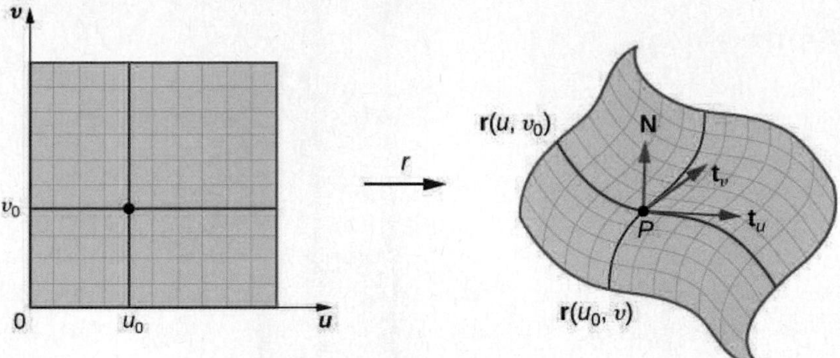

Figure 6.66 If the cross product of vectors $\mathbf{t}_u$ and $\mathbf{t}_v$ exists, then there is a tangent plane.

The tangent plane at P_{ij} contains vectors $\mathbf{t}_u(P_{ij})$ and $\mathbf{t}_v(P_{ij}),$ and therefore the parallelogram spanned by $\mathbf{t}_u(P_{ij})$ and $\mathbf{t}_v(P_{ij})$ is in the tangent plane. Since the original rectangle in the uv-plane corresponding to S_{ij} has width Δu and length $\Delta v,$ the parallelogram that we use to approximate S_{ij} is the parallelogram spanned by $\Delta u \mathbf{t}_u(P_{ij})$ and $\Delta v \mathbf{t}_v(P_{ij})$. In other words, we scale the tangent vectors by the constants Δu and Δv to match the scale of the original division of rectangles in the parameter domain. Therefore, the area of the parallelogram used to approximate the area of S_{ij} is

$$\Delta S_{ij} \approx \| (\Delta u \mathbf{t}_u(P_{ij})) \times (\Delta v \mathbf{t}_v(P_{ij})) \| = \| \mathbf{t}_u(P_{ij}) \times \mathbf{t}_v(P_{ij}) \| \Delta u \Delta v.$$

Varying point P_{ij} over all pieces S_{ij} and the previous approximation leads to the following definition of surface area of a parametric surface (**Figure 6.67**).

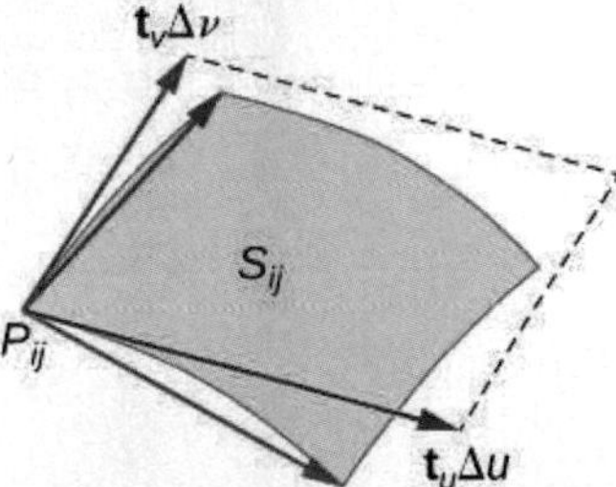

Figure 6.67 The parallelogram spanned by $\mathbf{t}_u$ and $\mathbf{t}_v$ approximates the piece of surface S_{ij}.

Definition

Let $\mathbf{r}(u, v) = \langle x(u, v), y(u, v), z(u, v) \rangle$ with parameter domain D be a smooth parameterization of surface S. Furthermore, assume that S is traced out only once as (u, v) varies over D. The **surface area** of S is

$$\iint_D \| \mathbf{t}_u \times \mathbf{t}_v \| \, dA, \tag{6.18}$$

where $\mathbf{t}_u = \langle \frac{\partial x}{\partial u}, \frac{\partial y}{\partial u}, \frac{\partial z}{\partial u} \rangle$ and $\mathbf{t}_v = \langle \frac{\partial x}{\partial v}, \frac{\partial y}{\partial v}, \frac{\partial z}{\partial v} \rangle$.

Example 6.62

Calculating Surface Area

Calculate the lateral surface area (the area of the "side," not including the base) of the right circular cone with height h and radius r.

Solution

Before calculating the surface area of this cone using **Equation 6.18**, we need a parameterization. We assume this cone is in $\mathbb{R}^3$ with its vertex at the origin (**Figure 6.68**). To obtain a parameterization, let α be the angle that is swept out by starting at the positive z-axis and ending at the cone, and let $k = \tan \alpha$. For a height value v with $0 \leq v \leq h$, the radius of the circle formed by intersecting the cone with plane $z = v$ is kv. Therefore, a parameterization of this cone is

$$\mathbf{s}(u, v) = \langle kv \cos u, kv \sin u, v \rangle, 0 \leq u < 2\pi, 0 \leq v \leq h.$$

The idea behind this parameterization is that for a fixed v value, the circle swept out by letting u vary is the circle at height v and radius kv. As v increases, the parameterization sweeps out a "stack" of circles, resulting in the desired cone.

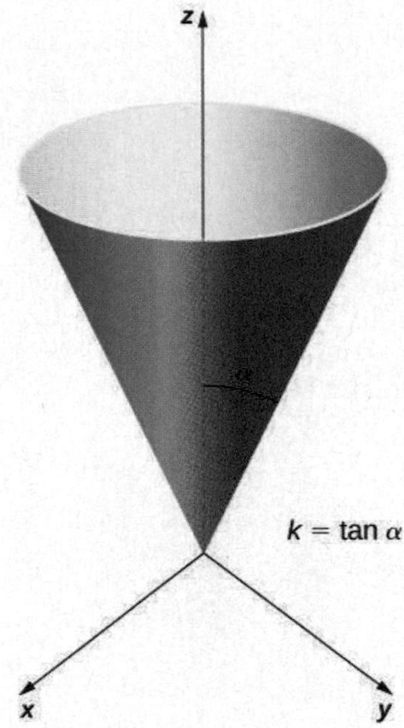

Figure 6.68 The right circular cone with radius $r = kh$ and height h has parameterization $\mathbf{s}(u, v) = \langle kv \cos u, kv \sin u, v \rangle, 0 \leq u < 2\pi, 0 \leq v \leq h.$

With a parameterization in hand, we can calculate the surface area of the cone using **Equation 6.18**. The tangent vectors are $\mathbf{t}_u = \langle -kv \sin u, kv \cos u, 0 \rangle$ and $\mathbf{t}_v = \langle k \cos u, k \sin u, 1 \rangle$. Therefore,

$$\begin{aligned} \mathbf{t}_u \times \mathbf{t}_v &= \begin{vmatrix} \mathbf{i} & \mathbf{j} & \mathbf{k} \\ -kv \sin u & kv \cos u & 0 \\ k \cos u & k \sin u & 1 \end{vmatrix} \\ &= \langle kv \cos u, kv \sin u, -k^2 v \sin^2 u - k^2 v \cos^2 u \rangle \\ &= \langle kv \cos u, kv \sin u, -k^2 v \rangle. \end{aligned}$$

The magnitude of this vector is

$$\| \langle kv\cos u,\ kv\sin u,\ -k^2 v \rangle \| = \sqrt{k^2 v^2 \cos^2 u + k^2 v^2 \sin^2 u + k^4 v^2}$$
$$= \sqrt{k^2 v^2 + k^4 v^2}$$
$$= kv\sqrt{1 + k^2}.$$

By **Equation 6.18**, the surface area of the cone is

$$\iint_D \| \mathbf{t}_u \times \mathbf{t}_v \| \, dA = \int_0^h \int_0^{2\pi} kv\sqrt{1 + k^2} du dv$$
$$= 2\pi k\sqrt{1 + k^2} \int_0^h v dv$$
$$= 2\pi k\sqrt{1 + k^2} \left[\frac{v^2}{2} \right]_0^h$$
$$= \pi k h^2 \sqrt{1 + k^2}.$$

Since $k = \tan \alpha = r/h$,

$$\pi k h^2 \sqrt{1 + k^2} = \pi \frac{r}{h} h^2 \sqrt{1 + \frac{r^2}{h^2}}$$
$$= \pi r h \sqrt{1 + \frac{r^2}{h^2}}$$
$$= \pi r \sqrt{h^2 + h^2 \left(\frac{r^2}{h^2} \right)}$$
$$= \pi r \sqrt{h^2 + r^2}.$$

Therefore, the lateral surface area of the cone is $\pi r \sqrt{h^2 + r^2}$.

Analysis

The surface area of a right circular cone with radius r and height h is usually given as $\pi r^2 + \pi r \sqrt{h^2 + r^2}$. The reason for this is that the circular base is included as part of the cone, and therefore the area of the base πr^2 is added to the lateral surface area $\pi r \sqrt{h^2 + r^2}$ that we found.

6.51 Find the surface area of the surface with parameterization $\mathbf{r}(u, v) = \langle u + v, u^2, 2v \rangle$, $0 \le u \le 3$, $0 \le v \le 2$.

Example 6.63

Calculating Surface Area

Show that the surface area of the sphere $x^2 + y^2 + z^2 = r^2$ is $4\pi r^2$.

Solution

The sphere has parameterization

$$\langle\, r\cos\theta\sin\phi,\ r\sin\theta\sin\phi,\ r\cos\phi\,\rangle,\ 0\le\theta<2\pi,\ 0\le\phi\le\pi.$$

The tangent vectors are

$$\mathbf{t}_\theta = \langle -r\sin\theta\sin\phi,\ r\cos\theta\sin\phi,\ 0\rangle \text{ and } \mathbf{t}_\phi = \langle\, r\cos\theta\cos\phi,\ r\sin\theta\cos\phi,\ -r\sin\phi\,\rangle.$$

Therefore,

$$\begin{aligned}\mathbf{t}_\phi\times\mathbf{t}_\theta &= \langle\, r^2\cos\theta\sin^2\phi,\ r^2\sin\theta\sin^2\phi,\ r^2\sin^2\theta\sin\phi\cos\phi + r^2\cos^2\theta\sin\phi\cos\phi\,\rangle\\ &= \langle\, r^2\cos\theta\sin^2\phi,\ r^2\sin\theta\sin^2\phi,\ r^2\sin\phi\cos\phi\,\rangle.\end{aligned}$$

Now,

$$\begin{aligned}\|\,\mathbf{t}_\phi\times\mathbf{t}_\theta &= \sqrt{r^4\sin^4\phi\cos^2\theta + r^4\sin^4\phi\sin^2\theta + r^4\sin^2\phi\cos^2\phi}\\ &= \sqrt{r^4\sin^4\phi + r^4\sin^2\phi\cos^2\phi}\\ &= r^2\sqrt{\sin^2\phi}\\ &= r\sin\phi.\end{aligned}$$

Notice that $\sin\phi\ge 0$ on the parameter domain because $0\le\phi<\pi,$ and this justifies equation $\sqrt{\sin^2\phi}=\sin\phi.$ The surface area of the sphere is

$$\int_0^{2\pi}\int_0^{\pi} r^2\sin\phi\, d\phi\, d\theta = r^2\int_0^{2\pi} 2\,d\theta = 4\pi r^2.$$

We have derived the familiar formula for the surface area of a sphere using surface integrals.

6.52 Show that the surface area of cylinder $x^2+y^2=r^2,\ 0\le z\le h$ is $2\pi rh.$ Notice that this cylinder does not include the top and bottom circles.

In addition to parameterizing surfaces given by equations or standard geometric shapes such as cones and spheres, we can also parameterize surfaces of revolution. Therefore, we can calculate the surface area of a surface of revolution by using the same techniques. Let $y=f(x)\ge 0$ be a positive single-variable function on the domain $a\le x\le b$ and let S be the surface obtained by rotating f about the x-axis (**Figure 6.69**). Let θ be the angle of rotation. Then, S can be parameterized with parameters x and θ by

$$\mathbf{r}(x,\theta) = \langle\, x,\ f(x)\cos\theta,\ f(x)\sin\theta\,\rangle,\ a\le x\le b,\ 0\le x<2\pi.$$

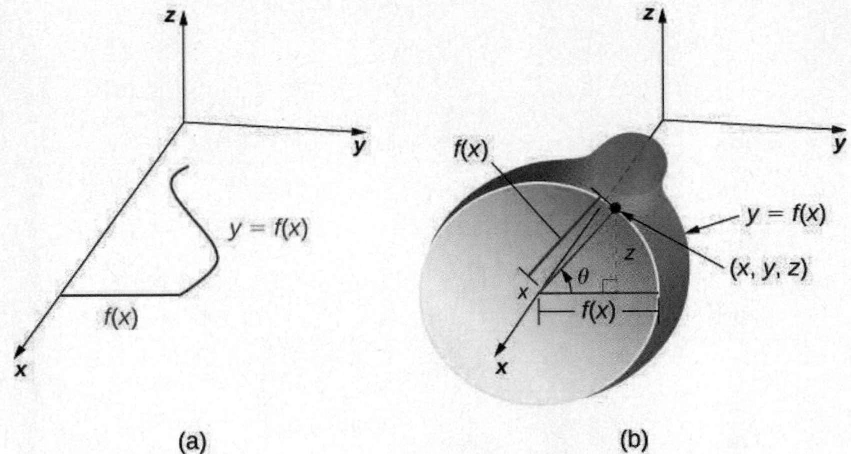

Figure 6.69 We can parameterize a surface of revolution by $\mathbf{r}(x, \theta) = \langle x, f(x)\cos\theta, f(x)\sin\theta \rangle, \; a \le x \le b, 0 \le x < 2\pi.$

Example 6.64

Calculating Surface Area

Find the area of the surface of revolution obtained by rotating $y = x^2, 0 \le x \le b$ about the x-axis (**Figure 6.70**).

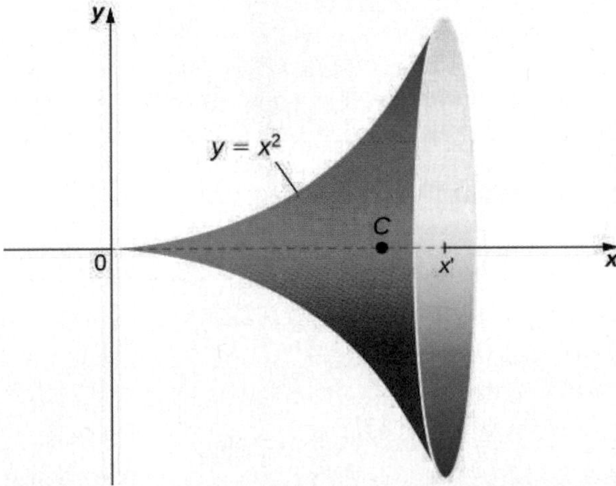

Figure 6.70 A surface integral can be used to calculate the surface area of this solid of revolution.

Solution

This surface has parameterization

$$\mathbf{r}(x, \theta) = \langle x, x^2\cos\theta, x^2\sin\theta \rangle, 0 \le x \le b, 0 \le x < 2\pi.$$

The tangent vectors are $\mathbf{t}_x = \langle 1, 2x\cos\theta, 2x\sin\theta \rangle$ and $\mathbf{t}_\theta = \langle 0, -x^2\sin\theta, -x^2\cos\theta \rangle$. Therefore,

$$\begin{aligned}\mathbf{t}_x \times \mathbf{t}_\theta &= \langle 2x^3\cos^2\theta + 2x^3\sin^2\theta, -x^2\cos\theta, -x^2\sin\theta \rangle \\ &= \langle 2x^3, -x^2\cos\theta, -x^2\sin\theta \rangle\end{aligned}$$

and

$$\begin{aligned} \mathbf{t}_x \times \mathbf{t}_\theta &= \sqrt{4x^6 + x^4 \cos^2\theta + x^4 \sin^2\theta} \\ &= \sqrt{4x^6 + x^4} \\ &= x^2\sqrt{4x^2 + 1}. \end{aligned}$$

The area of the surface of revolution is

$$\begin{aligned} \int_0^b \int_0^\pi x^2\sqrt{4x^2 + 1}\,d\theta dx &= 2\pi \int_0^b x^2\sqrt{4x^2 + 1}\,dx \\ &= 2\pi\left[\frac{1}{64}\left(2\sqrt{4x^2 + 1}\left(8x^3 + x\right)\sinh^{-1}(2x)\right)\right]_0^b \\ &= 2\pi\left[\frac{1}{64}\left(2\sqrt{4b^2 + 1}\left(8b^3 + b\right)\sinh^{-1}(2b)\right)\right]. \end{aligned}$$

6.53 Use **Equation 6.18** to find the area of the surface of revolution obtained by rotating curve $y = \sin x,\ 0 \le x \le \pi$ about the x-axis.

Surface Integral of a Scalar-Valued Function

Now that we can parameterize surfaces and we can calculate their surface areas, we are able to define surface integrals. First, let's look at the surface integral of a scalar-valued function. Informally, the surface integral of a scalar-valued function is an analog of a scalar line integral in one higher dimension. The domain of integration of a scalar line integral is a parameterized curve (a one-dimensional object); the domain of integration of a scalar surface integral is a parameterized surface (a two-dimensional object). Therefore, the definition of a surface integral follows the definition of a line integral quite closely. For scalar line integrals, we chopped the domain curve into tiny pieces, chose a point in each piece, computed the function at that point, and took a limit of the corresponding Riemann sum. For scalar surface integrals, we chop the domain *region* (no longer a curve) into tiny pieces and proceed in the same fashion.

Let S be a piecewise smooth surface with parameterization $\mathbf{r}(u, v) = \langle x(u, v), y(u, v), z(u, v) \rangle$ with parameter domain D and let $f(x, y, z)$ be a function with a domain that contains S. For now, assume the parameter domain D is a rectangle, but we can extend the basic logic of how we proceed to any parameter domain (the choice of a rectangle is simply to make the notation more manageable). Divide rectangle D into subrectangles D_{ij} with horizontal width Δu and vertical length Δv. Suppose that i ranges from 1 to m and j ranges from 1 to n so that D is subdivided into mn rectangles. This division of D into subrectangles gives a corresponding division of S into pieces S_{ij}. Choose point P_{ij} in each piece S_{ij}, evaluate P_{ij} at f, and multiply by area ΔS_{ij} to form the Riemann sum

$$\sum_{i=1}^{m} \sum_{j=1}^{n} f(P_{ij})\Delta S_{ij}.$$

To define a surface integral of a scalar-valued function, we let the areas of the pieces of S shrink to zero by taking a limit.

Definition

The **surface integral of a scalar-valued function** of f over a piecewise smooth surface S is

$$\iint_S f(x, y, z)dS = \lim_{m, n \to \infty} \sum_{i=1}^{m} \sum_{j=1}^{n} f(P_{ij})\Delta S_{ij}.$$

Again, notice the similarities between this definition and the definition of a scalar line integral. In the definition of a line integral we chop a curve into pieces, evaluate a function at a point in each piece, and let the length of the pieces shrink to zero by taking the limit of the corresponding Riemann sum. In the definition of a surface integral, we chop a surface into pieces, evaluate a function at a point in each piece, and let the area of the pieces shrink to zero by taking the limit of the corresponding Riemann sum. Thus, a surface integral is similar to a line integral but in one higher dimension.

The definition of a scalar line integral can be extended to parameter domains that are not rectangles by using the same logic used earlier. The basic idea is to chop the parameter domain into small pieces, choose a sample point in each piece, and so on. The exact shape of each piece in the sample domain becomes irrelevant as the areas of the pieces shrink to zero.

Scalar surface integrals are difficult to compute from the definition, just as scalar line integrals are. To develop a method that makes surface integrals easier to compute, we approximate surface areas ΔS_{ij} with small pieces of a tangent plane, just as we did in the previous subsection. Recall the definition of vectors $\mathbf{t}_u$ and $\mathbf{t}_v$:

$$\mathbf{t}_u = \langle \frac{\partial x}{\partial u}, \frac{\partial y}{\partial u}, \frac{\partial z}{\partial u} \rangle \text{ and } \mathbf{t}_v = \langle \frac{\partial x}{\partial v}, \frac{\partial y}{\partial v}, \frac{\partial z}{\partial v} \rangle .$$

From the material we have already studied, we know that

$$\Delta S_{ij} \approx \| \mathbf{t}_u(P_{ij}) \times \mathbf{t}_v(P_{ij}) \| \Delta u \Delta v.$$

Therefore,

$$\iint_S f(x, y, z)dS \approx \lim_{m, n \to \infty} \sum_{i=1}^{m} \sum_{j=1}^{n} f(P_{ij}) \| \mathbf{t}_u(P_{ij}) \times \mathbf{t}_v(P_{ij}) \| \Delta u \Delta v.$$

This approximation becomes arbitrarily close to $\lim_{m, n \to \infty} \sum_{i=1}^{m} \sum_{j=1}^{n} f(P_{ij})\Delta S_{ij}$ as we increase the number of pieces S_{ij} by letting m and n go to infinity. Therefore, we have the following equation to calculate scalar surface integrals:

$$\iint_S f(x, y, z)dS = \iint_D f(\mathbf{r}(u, v)) \| \mathbf{t}_u \times \mathbf{t}_v \| dA. \tag{6.19}$$

Equation 6.19 allows us to calculate a surface integral by transforming it into a double integral. This equation for surface integrals is analogous to **Equation 6.20** for line integrals:

$$\iint_C f(x, y, z)ds = \int_a^b f(\mathbf{r}(t)) \| \mathbf{r}'(t) \| dt.$$

In this case, vector $\mathbf{t}_u \times \mathbf{t}_v$ is perpendicular to the surface, whereas vector $\mathbf{r}'(t)$ is tangent to the curve.

Example 6.65

Calculating a Surface Integral

Calculate surface integral $\iint_S 5dS,$ where S is the surface with parameterization $\mathbf{r}(u, v) = \langle u, u^2, v \rangle$ for $0 \leq u \leq 2$ and $0 \leq v \leq u.$

Solution

Notice that this parameter domain D is a triangle, and therefore the parameter domain is not rectangular. This is not an issue though, because **Equation 6.19** does not place any restrictions on the shape of the parameter domain.

To use **Equation 6.19** to calculate the surface integral, we first find vector $\mathbf{t}_u$ and $\mathbf{t}_v$. Note that $\mathbf{t}_u = \langle 1, 2u, 0 \rangle$ and $\mathbf{t}_v = \langle 0, 0, 1 \rangle$. Therefore,

$$\mathbf{t}_u \times \mathbf{t}_v = \begin{vmatrix} \mathbf{i} & \mathbf{j} & \mathbf{k} \\ 1 & 2u & 0 \\ 0 & 0 & 1 \end{vmatrix} = \langle 2u, -1, 0 \rangle$$

and

$$\| \mathbf{t}_u \times \mathbf{t}_v \| = \sqrt{1+4u^2}.$$

By **Equation 6.19**,

$$\begin{aligned} \iint_S 5\,dS &= 5 \iint_D u\sqrt{1+4u^2}\,dA \\ &= 5\int_0^2 \int_0^u \sqrt{1+4u^2}\,dv\,du = 5\int_0^2 u\sqrt{1+4u^2}\,du \\ &= 5\left[\frac{\left(1+4u^2\right)^{3/2}}{3}\right]_0^2 = \frac{5\left(17^{3/2}-1\right)}{3} \approx 115.15. \end{aligned}$$

Example 6.66

Calculating the Surface Integral of a Cylinder

Calculate surface integral $\iint_S \left(x+y^2\right) dS,$ where S is cylinder $x^2+y^2=4,\ 0 \le z \le 3$ (**Figure 6.71**).

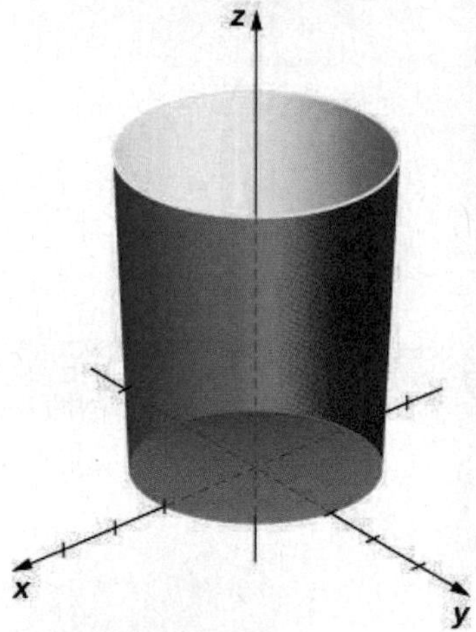

Figure 6.71 Integrating function $f(x, y, z) = x + y^2$ over a cylinder.

Solution

To calculate the surface integral, we first need a parameterization of the cylinder. Following **Example 6.58**, a parameterization is

$$\mathbf{r}(u, v) = \langle \cos u, \sin u, v \rangle,\ 0 \le u \le 2\pi,\ 0 \le v \le 3.$$

The tangent vectors are $\mathbf{t}_u = \langle \sin u, \cos u, 0 \rangle$ and $\mathbf{t}_v = \langle 0, 0, 1 \rangle$. Then,

$$\mathbf{t}_u \times \mathbf{t}_v = \begin{vmatrix} \mathbf{i} & \mathbf{j} & \mathbf{k} \\ -\sin u & \cos u & 0 \\ 0 & 0 & 1 \end{vmatrix} = \langle \cos u, \sin u, 0 \rangle$$

and $\| \mathbf{t}_u \times \mathbf{t}_v \| = \sqrt{\cos^2 u + \sin^2 u} = 1$. By **Equation 6.19**,

$$\begin{aligned} \iint_S f(x, y, z)dS &= \iint_D f(\mathbf{r}(u, v)) \| \mathbf{t}_u \times \mathbf{t}_v \| \, dA \\ &= \int_0^3 \int_0^{2\pi} \left(\cos u + \sin^2 u\right) du dv \\ &= \int_0^3 \left[\sin u + \frac{u}{2} - \frac{\sin(2u)}{4}\right]_0^{2\pi} dv = \int_0^3 \pi dv = 3\pi. \end{aligned}$$

6.54 Calculate $\iint_S \left(x^2 - z\right) dS$, where S is the surface with parameterization $\mathbf{r}(u, v) = \langle v, u^2 + v^2, 1 \rangle, \; 0 \le u \le 2, \; 0 \le v \le 3$.

Example 6.67

Calculating the Surface Integral of a Piece of a Sphere

Calculate surface integral $\iint_S f(x, y, z)dS$, where $f(x, y, z) = z^2$ and S is the surface that consists of the piece of sphere $x^2 + y^2 + z^2 = 4$ that lies on or above plane $z = 1$ and the disk that is enclosed by intersection plane $z = 1$ and the given sphere (**Figure 6.72**).

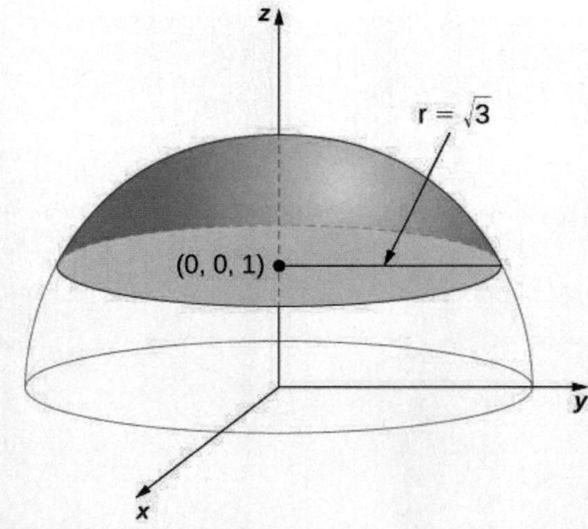

Figure 6.72 Calculating a surface integral over surface S.

Solution

Notice that S is not smooth but is piecewise smooth; S can be written as the union of its base S_1 and its spherical top S_2, and both S_1 and S_2 are smooth. Therefore, to calculate $\iint_S z^2\,dS$, we write this integral as $\iint_{S_1} z^2\,dS + \iint_{S_2} z^2\,dS$ and we calculate integrals $\iint_{S_1} z^2\,dS$ and $\iint_{S_2} z^2\,dS$.

First, we calculate $\iint_{S_1} z^2\,dS$. To calculate this integral we need a parameterization of S_1. This surface is a disk in plane $z = 1$ centered at $(0, 0, 1)$. To parameterize this disk, we need to know its radius. Since the disk is formed where plane $z = 1$ intersects sphere $x^2 + y^2 + z^2 = 4$, we can substitute $z = 1$ into equation $x^2 + y^2 + z^2 = 4$:

$$x^2 + y^2 + 1 = 4 \Rightarrow x^2 + y^2 = 3.$$

Therefore, the radius of the disk is $\sqrt{3}$ and a parameterization of S_1 is $\mathbf{r}(u, v) = \langle u\cos v, u\sin v, 1 \rangle, 0 \le u \le \sqrt{3}, 0 \le v \le 2\pi$. The tangent vectors are $\mathbf{t}_u = \langle \cos v, \sin v, 0 \rangle$ and $\mathbf{t}_v = \langle -u\sin v, u\cos v, 0 \rangle$, and thus

$$\mathbf{t}_u \times \mathbf{t}_v = \begin{vmatrix} \mathbf{i} & \mathbf{j} & \mathbf{k} \\ \cos v & \sin v & 0 \\ -u\sin v & u\cos v & 0 \end{vmatrix} = \langle 0, 0, u\cos^2 v + u\sin^2 v \rangle = \langle 0, 0, u \rangle.$$

The magnitude of this vector is u. Therefore,

$$\begin{aligned} \iint_{S_1} z^2\,dS &= \int_0^{\sqrt{3}} \int_0^{2\pi} f(\mathbf{r}(u, v))\, \|\mathbf{t}_u \times \mathbf{t}_v\|\, dv\, du \\ &= \int_0^{\sqrt{3}} \int_0^{2\pi} u\, dv\, du \\ &= 2\pi \int_0^{\sqrt{3}} u du \\ &= 2\pi\sqrt{3}. \end{aligned}$$

Now we calculate $\iint_{S_2} dS$. To calculate this integral, we need a parameterization of S_2. The parameterization of full sphere $x^2 + y^2 + z^2 = 4$ is

$$\mathbf{r}(\phi, \theta) = \langle 2\cos\theta\sin\phi, 2\sin\theta\sin\phi, 2\cos\phi \rangle, 0 \le \theta \le 2\pi, 0 \le \phi \le \pi.$$

Since we are only taking the piece of the sphere on or above plane $z = 1$, we have to restrict the domain of ϕ. To see how far this angle sweeps, notice that the angle can be located in a right triangle, as shown in **Figure 6.73** (the $\sqrt{3}$ comes from the fact that the base of S is a disk with radius $\sqrt{3}$). Therefore, the tangent of ϕ is $\sqrt{3}$, which implies that ϕ is $\pi/6$. We now have a parameterization of S_2:

$$\mathbf{r}(\phi, \theta) = \langle 2\cos\theta\sin\phi, 2\sin\theta\sin\phi, 2\cos\phi \rangle, 0 \le \theta \le 2\pi, 0 \le \phi \le \pi/3.$$

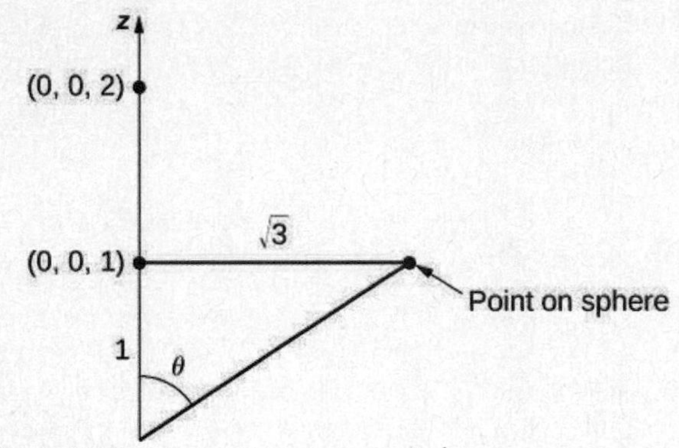

Figure 6.73 The maximum value of ϕ has a tangent value of $\sqrt{3}$.

The tangent vectors are

$$\mathbf{t}_\phi = \langle 2\cos\theta\cos\phi, 2\sin\theta\cos\phi, -2\sin\phi \rangle \text{ and } \mathbf{t}_\theta = \langle -2\sin\theta\sin\phi, u\cos\theta\sin\phi, 0 \rangle,$$

and thus

$$\begin{aligned} \mathbf{t}_\phi \times \mathbf{t}_\theta &= \begin{vmatrix} \mathbf{i} & \mathbf{j} & \mathbf{k} \\ 2\cos\theta\cos\phi & 2\sin\theta\cos\phi & -2\sin\phi \\ -2\sin\theta\sin\phi & 2\cos\theta\sin\phi & 0 \end{vmatrix} \\ &= \langle 4\cos\theta\sin^2\phi, 4\sin\theta\sin^2\phi, 4\cos^2\theta\cos\phi\sin\phi + 4\sin^2\theta\cos\phi\sin\phi \rangle \\ &= \langle 4\cos\theta\sin^2\phi, 4\sin\theta\sin^2\phi, 4\cos\phi\sin\phi \rangle. \end{aligned}$$

The magnitude of this vector is

$$\begin{aligned} \|\mathbf{t}_\phi \times \mathbf{t}_\theta\| &= \sqrt{16\cos^2\theta\sin^4\phi + 16\sin^2\theta\sin^4\phi + 16\cos^2\phi\sin^2\phi} \\ &= 4\sqrt{\sin^4\phi + \cos^2\phi\sin^2\phi}. \end{aligned}$$

Therefore,

$$\begin{aligned} \iint_{S_2} z\,dS &= \int_0^{\pi/6}\int_0^{2\pi} f(\mathbf{r}(\phi, \theta))\,\|\mathbf{t}_\phi \times \mathbf{t}_\theta\|\,d\theta\,d\phi \\ &= \int_0^{\pi/6}\int_0^{2\pi} 16\cos^2\phi\sqrt{\sin^4\phi + \cos^2\phi\sin^2\phi}\,d\theta\,d\phi \\ &= 32\pi\int_0^{\pi/6} \cos^2\phi\sqrt{\sin^4\phi + \cos^2\phi\sin^2\phi}\,d\phi \\ &= 32\pi\int_0^{\pi/6} \cos^2\phi\sin\phi\sqrt{\sin^2\phi + \cos^2\phi}\,d\phi \\ &= 32\pi\int_0^{\pi/6} \cos^2\phi\sin\phi\,d\phi \\ &= 32\pi\left[-\frac{\cos^3\phi}{3}\right]_0^{\pi/6} = 32\pi\left[\frac{1}{3} - \frac{\sqrt{3}}{8}\right] = \frac{32\pi}{3} - 4\sqrt{3}. \end{aligned}$$

Since $\iint_S z^2\,dS = \iint_{S_1} z^2\,dS + \iint_{S_2} z^2\,dS$, we have $\iint_S z^2\,dS = (2\pi - 4)\sqrt{3} + \frac{32\pi}{3}$.

Analysis

In this example we broke a surface integral over a piecewise surface into the addition of surface integrals over smooth subsurfaces. There were only two smooth subsurfaces in this example, but this technique extends to finitely many smooth subsurfaces.

6.55 Calculate line integral $\iint_S (x - y)dS,$ where S is cylinder $x^2 + y^2 = 1, 0 \leq z \leq 2,$ including the circular top and bottom.

Scalar surface integrals have several real-world applications. Recall that scalar line integrals can be used to compute the mass of a wire given its density function. In a similar fashion, we can use scalar surface integrals to compute the mass of a sheet given its density function. If a thin sheet of metal has the shape of surface S and the density of the sheet at point (x, y, z) is $\rho(x, y, z),$ then mass m of the sheet is $m = \iint_S \rho(x, y, z)dS.$

Example 6.68

Calculating the Mass of a Sheet

A flat sheet of metal has the shape of surface $z = 1 + x + 2y$ that lies above rectangle $0 \leq x \leq 4$ and $0 \leq y \leq 2.$ If the density of the sheet is given by $\rho(x, y, z) = x^2 yz,$ what is the mass of the sheet?

Solution

Let S be the surface that describes the sheet. Then, the mass of the sheet is given by $m = \iint_S x^2 yzdS.$

To compute this surface integral, we first need a parameterization of S. Since S is given by the function $f(x, y) = 1 + x + 2y,$ a parameterization of S is $\mathbf{r}(x, y) = \langle x, y, 1 + x + 2y \rangle, 0 \leq x \leq 4, 0 \leq y \leq 2.$

The tangent vectors are $\mathbf{t}_x = \langle 1, 0, 1 \rangle$ and $\mathbf{t}_y = \langle 1, 0, 2 \rangle.$ Therefore, $\mathbf{t}_x \times \mathbf{t}_y = \langle -1, -2, 1 \rangle$ and $\| \mathbf{t}_x \times \mathbf{t}_y \| = \sqrt{6}.$ By **Equation 6.5**,

$$\begin{aligned} m &= \iint_S x^2 yz\, dS \\ &= \sqrt{6} \int_0^4 \int_0^2 x^2 y(1 + x + 2y)dydx \\ &= \sqrt{6} \int_0^4 \frac{22x^2}{3} + 2x^3\, dx \\ &= \frac{2560\sqrt{6}}{9} \\ &\approx 696.74. \end{aligned}$$

6.56 A piece of metal has a shape that is modeled by paraboloid $z = x^2 + y^2, 0 \leq z \leq 4,$ and the density of the metal is given by $\rho(x, y, z) = z + 1.$ Find the mass of the piece of metal.

Orientation of a Surface

Recall that when we defined a scalar line integral, we did not need to worry about an orientation of the curve of integration. The same was true for scalar surface integrals: we did not need to worry about an "orientation" of the surface of integration.

On the other hand, when we defined vector line integrals, the curve of integration needed an orientation. That is, we needed the notion of an oriented curve to define a vector line integral without ambiguity. Similarly, when we define a surface integral of a vector field, we need the notion of an oriented surface. An oriented surface is given an "upward" or "downward" orientation or, in the case of surfaces such as a sphere or cylinder, an "outward" or "inward" orientation.

Let S be a smooth surface. For any point (x, y, z) on S, we can identify two unit normal vectors $\mathbf{N}$ and $-\mathbf{N}$. If it is possible to choose a unit normal vector $\mathbf{N}$ at every point (x, y, z) on S so that $\mathbf{N}$ varies continuously over S, then S is "*orientable*." Such a choice of unit normal vector at each point gives the **orientation of a surface** S. If you think of the normal field as describing water flow, then the side of the surface that water flows toward is the "negative" side and the side of the surface at which the water flows away is the "positive" side. Informally, a choice of orientation gives S an "outer" side and an "inner" side (or an "upward" side and a "downward" side), just as a choice of orientation of a curve gives the curve "forward" and "backward" directions.

Closed surfaces such as spheres are orientable: if we choose the outward normal vector at each point on the surface of the sphere, then the unit normal vectors vary continuously. This is called the *positive orientation of the closed surface* (**Figure 6.74**). We also could choose the inward normal vector at each point to give an "inward" orientation, which is the negative orientation of the surface.

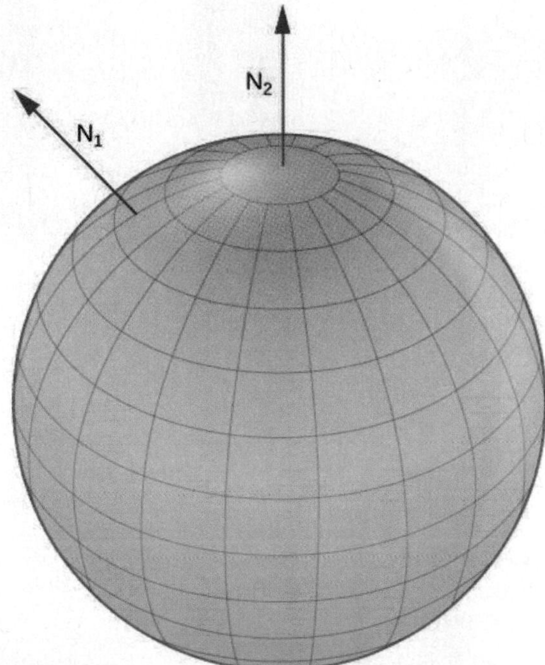

Figure 6.74 An oriented sphere with positive orientation.

A portion of the graph of any smooth function $z = f(x, y)$ is also orientable. If we choose the unit normal vector that points "above" the surface at each point, then the unit normal vectors vary continuously over the surface. We could also choose the unit normal vector that points "below" the surface at each point. To get such an orientation, we parameterize the graph of f in the standard way: $\mathbf{r}(x, y) = \langle x, y, f(x, y) \rangle$, where x and y vary over the domain of f. Then, $\mathbf{t}_x = \langle 1, 0, f_x \rangle$ and $\mathbf{t}_y = \langle 0, 1, f_y \rangle$, and therefore the cross product $\mathbf{t}_x \times \mathbf{t}_y$ (which is normal to the surface at any point on the surface) is $\langle -f_x, -f_y, 1 \rangle$. Since the z component of this vector is one, the corresponding unit normal vector points "upward," and the upward side of the surface is chosen to be the "positive" side.

Let S be a smooth orientable surface with parameterization $\mathbf{r}(u, v)$. For each point $\mathbf{r}(a, b)$ on the surface, vectors $\mathbf{t}_u$ and $\mathbf{t}_v$ lie in the tangent plane at that point. Vector $\mathbf{t}_u \times \mathbf{t}_v$ is normal to the tangent plane at $\mathbf{r}(a, b)$ and is therefore normal to S at that point. Therefore, the choice of unit normal vector

$$\mathbf{N} = \frac{\mathbf{t}_u \times \mathbf{t}_v}{\| \mathbf{t}_u \times \mathbf{t}_v \|}$$

gives an orientation of surface S.

Example 6.69

Choosing an Orientation

Give an orientation of cylinder $x^2 + y^2 = r^2, 0 \le z \le h$.

Solution

This surface has parameterization

$$\mathbf{r}(u, v) = \langle r\cos u, r\sin u, v \rangle, 0 \le u < 2\pi, 0 \le v \le h.$$

The tangent vectors are $\mathbf{t}_u = \langle -r\sin u, r\cos u, 0 \rangle$ and $\mathbf{t}_v = \langle 0, 0, 1 \rangle$. To get an orientation of the surface, we compute the unit normal vector

$$\mathbf{N} = \frac{\mathbf{t}_u \times \mathbf{t}_v}{\| \mathbf{t}_u \times \mathbf{t}_v \|}.$$

In this case, $\mathbf{t}_u \times \mathbf{t}_v = \langle r\cos u, r\sin u, 0 \rangle$ and therefore

$$\| \mathbf{t}_u \times \mathbf{t}_v \| = \sqrt{r^2\cos^2 u + r^2\sin^2 u} = r.$$

An orientation of the cylinder is

$$\mathbf{N}(u, v) = \frac{\langle r\cos u, r\sin u, 0 \rangle}{r} = \langle \cos u, \sin u, 0 \rangle.$$

Notice that all vectors are parallel to the *xy*-plane, which should be the case with vectors that are normal to the cylinder. Furthermore, all the vectors point outward, and therefore this is an outward orientation of the cylinder (**Figure 6.75**).

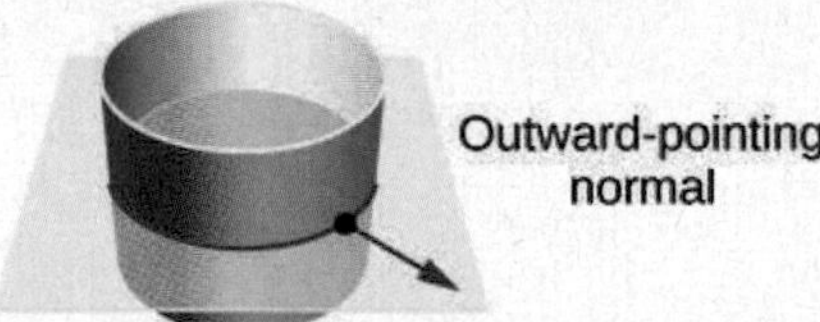

Figure 6.75 If all the vectors normal to a cylinder point outward, then this is an outward orientation of the cylinder.

6.57 Give the "upward" orientation of the graph of $f(x, y) = xy$.

Since every curve has a "forward" and "backward" direction (or, in the case of a closed curve, a clockwise and counterclockwise direction), it is possible to give an orientation to any curve. Hence, it is possible to think of every curve as an oriented curve. This is not the case with surfaces, however. Some surfaces cannot be oriented; such surfaces are called *nonorientable*. Essentially, a surface can be oriented if the surface has an "inner" side and an "outer" side, or an "upward" side and a "downward" side. Some surfaces are twisted in such a fashion that there is no well-defined notion of an "inner" or "outer" side.

The classic example of a nonorientable surface is the Möbius strip. To create a Möbius strip, take a rectangular strip of paper, give the piece of paper a half-twist, and the glue the ends together (**Figure 6.76**). Because of the half-twist in the strip, the surface has no "outer" side or "inner" side. If you imagine placing a normal vector at a point on the strip and having the vector travel all the way around the band, then (because of the half-twist) the vector points in the opposite direction when it gets back to its original position. Therefore, the strip really only has one side.

Figure 6.76 The construction of a Möbius strip.

Since some surfaces are nonorientable, it is not possible to define a vector surface integral on all piecewise smooth surfaces. This is in contrast to vector line integrals, which can be defined on any piecewise smooth curve.

Surface Integral of a Vector Field

With the idea of orientable surfaces in place, we are now ready to define a **surface integral of a vector field**. The definition is analogous to the definition of the flux of a vector field along a plane curve. Recall that if **F** is a two-dimensional vector field and *C* is a plane curve, then the definition of the flux of **F** along *C* involved chopping *C* into small pieces, choosing a point inside each piece, and calculating $\mathbf{F} \cdot \mathbf{N}$ at the point (where **N** is the unit normal vector at the point). The definition of a surface integral of a vector field proceeds in the same fashion, except now we chop surface *S* into small pieces, choose a point in the small (two-dimensional) piece, and calculate $\mathbf{F} \cdot \mathbf{N}$ at the point.

To place this definition in a real-world setting, let *S* be an oriented surface with unit normal vector **N**. Let **v** be a velocity field of a fluid flowing through *S*, and suppose the fluid has density $\rho(x, y, z)$. Imagine the fluid flows through *S*, but *S* is completely permeable so that it does not impede the fluid flow (**Figure 6.77**). The **mass flux** of the fluid is the rate of mass flow per unit area. The mass flux is measured in mass per unit time per unit area. How could we calculate the mass flux of the fluid across *S*?

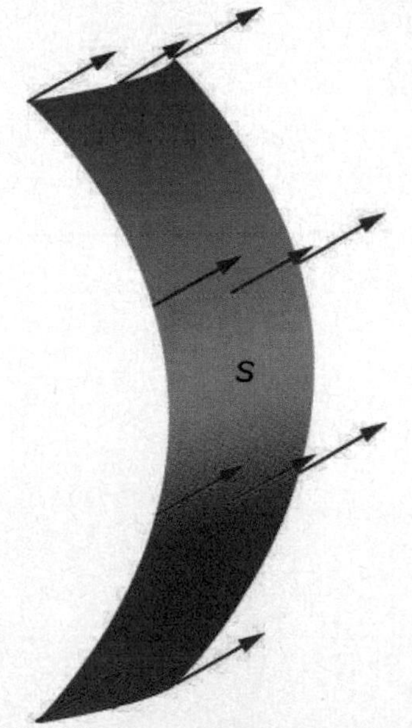

Figure 6.77 Fluid flows across a completely permeable surface *S*.

The rate of flow, measured in mass per unit time per unit area, is $\rho\mathbf{N}$. To calculate the mass flux across *S*, chop *S* into small pieces S_{ij}. If S_{ij} is small enough, then it can be approximated by a tangent plane at some point *P* in S_{ij}. Therefore, the unit normal vector at *P* can be used to approximate $\mathbf{N}(x, y, z)$ across the entire piece S_{ij}, because the normal vector to a plane does not change as we move across the plane. The component of the vector $\rho\mathbf{v}$ at *P* in the direction of **N** is $\rho\mathbf{v} \cdot \mathbf{N}$ at *P*. Since S_{ij} is small, the dot product $\rho\mathbf{v} \cdot \mathbf{N}$ changes very little as we vary across S_{ij}, and therefore $\rho\mathbf{v} \cdot \mathbf{N}$ can be taken as approximately constant across S_{ij}. To approximate the mass of fluid per unit time flowing across S_{ij} (and not just locally at point *P*), we need to multiply $(\rho\mathbf{v} \cdot \mathbf{N})(P)$ by the area of S_{ij}. Therefore, the mass of fluid per unit time flowing across S_{ij} in the direction of **N** can be approximated by $(\rho \mathbf{v} \cdot \mathbf{N})\Delta S_{ij}$, where **N**, ρ, and **v** are all evaluated at P (**Figure 6.78**). This is analogous to the flux of two-dimensional vector field **F** across plane curve C, in which we approximated flux across a small piece of C with the expression $(\mathbf{F} \cdot \mathbf{N})\Delta s$. To approximate the mass flux across S, form the sum $\sum_{i=1}^{m} \sum_{j=1}^{n} (\rho \mathbf{v} \cdot \mathbf{N})\Delta \mathbf{S}_{ij}$. As pieces S_{ij} get smaller, the sum $\sum_{i=1}^{m} \sum_{j=1}^{n} (\rho \mathbf{v} \cdot \mathbf{N})\Delta \mathbf{S}_{ij}$ gets arbitrarily close to the mass flux. Therefore, the mass flux is

$$\iint_S \rho \mathbf{v} \cdot \mathbf{N} dS = \lim_{m, n \to \infty} \sum_{i=1}^{m} \sum_{j=1}^{n} (\rho \mathbf{v} \cdot \mathbf{N})\Delta \mathbf{S}_{ij}.$$

This is a surface integral of a vector field. Letting the vector field $\rho \mathbf{v}$ be an arbitrary vector field **F** leads to the following definition.

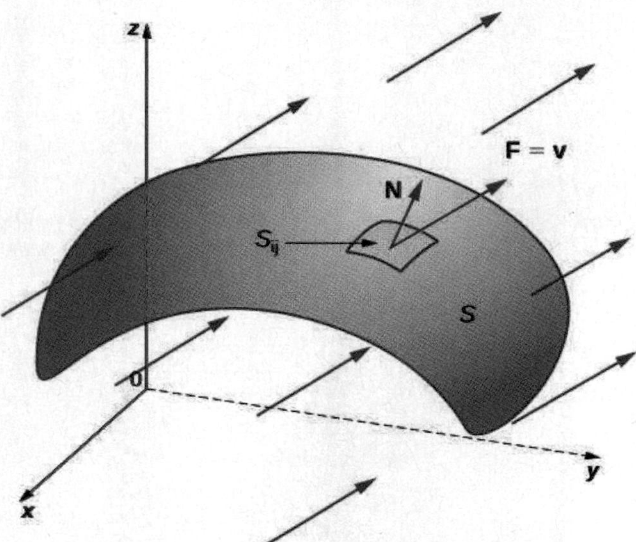

Figure 6.78 The mass of fluid per unit time flowing across S_{ij} in the direction of **N** can be approximated by $(\rho \mathbf{v} \cdot \mathbf{N})\Delta S_{ij}$.

Definition

Let **F** be a continuous vector field with a domain that contains oriented surface S with unit normal vector **N**. The **surface integral** of **F** over S is

$$\iint_S \mathbf{F} \cdot d\mathbf{S} = \iint_S \mathbf{F} \cdot \mathbf{N} dS. \qquad \textbf{(6.20)}$$

Notice the parallel between this definition and the definition of vector line integral $\int_C \mathbf{F} \cdot \mathbf{N} ds$. A surface integral of a vector field is defined in a similar way to a flux line integral across a curve, except the domain of integration is a surface (a two-dimensional object) rather than a curve (a one-dimensional object). Integral $\iint_S \mathbf{F} \cdot \mathbf{N} dS$ is called the *flux of F across S*, just as integral $\int_C \mathbf{F} \cdot \mathbf{N} ds$ is the flux of **F** across curve C. A surface integral over a vector field is also called a **flux integral**.

Just as with vector line integrals, surface integral $\iint_S \mathbf{F} \cdot \mathbf{N} d\mathbf{S}$ is easier to compute after surface S has been parameterized. Let $\mathbf{r}(u, v)$ be a parameterization of S with parameter domain D. Then, the unit normal vector is given by

$\mathbf{N} = \dfrac{\mathbf{t}_u \times \mathbf{t}_v}{\| \mathbf{t}_u \times \mathbf{t}_v \|}$ and, from **Equation 6.20**, we have

$$\begin{aligned}\iint_S \mathbf{F} \cdot \mathbf{N} d\mathbf{S} &= \iint_S \mathbf{F} \cdot \mathbf{N} dS \\ &= \iint_S \mathbf{F} \cdot \frac{\mathbf{t}_u \times \mathbf{t}_v}{\| \mathbf{t}_u \times \mathbf{t}_v \|} dS \\ &= \iint_D \left(\mathbf{F}(\mathbf{r}(u, v)) \cdot \frac{\mathbf{t}_u \times \mathbf{t}_v}{\| \mathbf{t}_u \times \mathbf{t}_v \|} \right) \| \mathbf{t}_u \times \mathbf{t}_v \| \, dA \\ &= \iint_D (\mathbf{F}(\mathbf{r}(u, v)) \cdot (\mathbf{t}_u \times \mathbf{t}_v)) dA.\end{aligned}$$

Therefore, to compute a surface integral over a vector field we can use the equation

$$\iint_S \mathbf{F} \cdot \mathbf{N} d\mathbf{S} = \iint_D (\mathbf{F}(\mathbf{r}(u, v)) \cdot (\mathbf{t}_u \times \mathbf{t}_v)) dA. \qquad \textbf{(6.21)}$$

Example 6.70

Calculating a Surface Integral

Calculate the surface integral $\iint_S \mathbf{F} \cdot \mathbf{N} dS$, where $\mathbf{F} = \langle -y, x, 0 \rangle$ and S is the surface with parameterization $\mathbf{r}(u, v) = \langle u, v^2 - u, u + v \rangle, \, 0 \le u < 3, \, 0 \le v \le 4.$

Solution

The tangent vectors are $\mathbf{t}_u = \langle 1, -1, 1 \rangle$ and $\mathbf{t}_v = \langle 0, 2v, 1 \rangle$. Therefore,

$$\mathbf{t}_u \times \mathbf{t}_v = \langle -1 - 2v, -1, 2v \rangle.$$

By **Equation 6.21**,

$$\begin{aligned}\iint_S \mathbf{F} \cdot d\mathbf{S} &= \int_0^4 \int_0^3 \mathbf{F}(\mathbf{r}(u, v)) \cdot (\mathbf{t}_u \times \mathbf{t}_v) du dv \\ &= \int_0^4 \int_0^3 \langle u - v^2, u, 0 \rangle \cdot \langle -1 - 2v, -1, 2v \rangle \, du dv \\ &= \int_0^4 \int_0^3 \left[(u - v^2)(-1 - 2v) - u \right] du dv \\ &= \int_0^4 \int_0^3 \left(2v^3 + v^2 - 2uv - 2u \right) du dv \\ &= \int_0^4 \left[2v^3 u + v^2 u - vu^2 - u^2 \right]_0^3 dv \\ &= \int_0^4 \left(6v^3 + 3v^2 - 9v - 9 \right) dv \\ &= \left[\frac{3v^4}{2} + v^3 - \frac{9v^2}{2} - 9v \right]_0^4 \\ &= 340.\end{aligned}$$

Therefore, the flux of $\mathbf{F}$ across S is 340.

6.58 Calculate surface integral $\iint_S \mathbf{F} \cdot d\mathbf{S}$, where $\mathbf{F} = \langle 0, -z, y \rangle$ and S is the portion of the unit sphere in the first octant with outward orientation.

Example 6.71

Calculating Mass Flow Rate

Let $\mathbf{v}(x, y, z) = \langle 2x, 2y, z \rangle$ represent a velocity field (with units of meters per second) of a fluid with constant density 80 kg/m^3. Let S be hemisphere $x^2 + y^2 + z^2 = 9$ with $z \geq 0$ such that S is oriented outward. Find the mass flow rate of the fluid across S.

Solution

A parameterization of the surface is

$$\mathbf{r}(\phi, \theta) = \langle 3 \cos\theta \sin\phi, 3 \sin\theta \sin\phi, 3 \cos\phi \rangle, 0 \leq \theta \leq 2\pi, 0 \leq \phi \leq \pi/2.$$

As in **Example 6.64**, the tangent vectors are

$$\mathbf{t}_\theta \langle -3 \sin\theta \sin\phi, 3 \cos\theta \sin\phi, 0 \rangle \text{ and } \mathbf{t}_\phi \langle 3 \cos\theta \cos\phi, 3 \sin\theta \cos\phi, -3 \sin\phi \rangle,$$

and their cross product is

$$\mathbf{t}_\phi \times \mathbf{t}_\theta = \langle 9 \cos\theta \sin^2\phi, 9 \sin\theta \sin^2\phi, 9 \sin\phi \cos\phi \rangle.$$

Notice that each component of the cross product is positive, and therefore this vector gives the outward orientation. Therefore we use the orientation $\mathbf{N} = \langle 9 \cos\theta \sin^2\phi, 9 \sin\theta \sin^2\phi, 9 \sin\phi \cos\phi \rangle$ for the sphere.

By **Equation 6.20**,

$$\begin{aligned}
\iint_S \rho \mathbf{v} \cdot d\mathbf{S} &= 80 \int_0^{2\pi} \int_0^{\pi/2} \mathbf{v}(\mathbf{r}(\phi, \theta)) \cdot \left(\mathbf{t}_\phi \times \mathbf{t}_\theta\right) d\phi d\theta \\
&= 80 \int_0^{2\pi} \int_0^{\pi/2} \\
&= 80 \int_0^{2\pi} \int_o^{\pi/2} \langle 6 \cos\theta \sin\phi, 6 \sin\theta \sin\phi, 3 \cos\phi \rangle \\
&\qquad \cdot \langle 9 \cos\theta \sin^2\phi, 9 \sin\theta \sin^2\phi, 9 \sin\phi \cos\phi \rangle \, d\phi d\theta \\
&= 80 \int_0^{2\pi} \int_0^{\pi/2} 54 \sin^3\phi + 27 \cos^2\phi \sin\phi d\phi d\theta \\
&= 80 \int_0^{2\pi} \int_0^{\pi/2} 54\left(1 - \cos^2\phi\right) \sin\phi + 27 \cos^2\phi \sin\phi d\phi d\theta \\
&= 80 \int_0^{2\pi} \int_0^{\pi/2} 54 \sin\phi - 27 \cos^2\phi \sin\phi d\phi d\theta \\
&= 80 \int_0^{2\pi} \left[-54 \cos\phi + 9 \cos^3\phi\right]_{\phi=0}^{\phi=2\pi} d\theta \\
&= 80 \int_0^{2\pi} 45 d\theta = 7200\pi.
\end{aligned}$$

Therefore, the mass flow rate is 7200π kg/sec/m^2.

6.59 Let $\mathbf{v}(x, y, z) = \langle x^2 + y^2, z, 4y \rangle$ m/sec represent a velocity field of a fluid with constant density 100 kg/m^3. Let S be the half-cylinder $\mathbf{r}(u, v) = \langle \cos u, \sin u, v \rangle$, $0 \leq u \leq \pi$, $0 \leq v \leq 2$ oriented outward. Calculate the mass flux of the fluid across S.

In **Example 6.70**, we computed the mass flux, which is the rate of mass flow per unit area. If we want to find the flow rate (measured in volume per time) instead, we can use flux integral $\iint_S \mathbf{v} \bullet \mathbf{N}dS,$ which leaves out the density. Since the flow rate of a fluid is measured in volume per unit time, flow rate does not take mass into account. Therefore, we have the following characterization of the flow rate of a fluid with velocity **v** across a surface *S*:

$$\text{Flow rate of fluid across } S = \iint_S \mathbf{v} \bullet d\mathbf{S}.$$

To compute the flow rate of the fluid in **Example 6.68**, we simply remove the density constant, which gives a flow rate of $90\pi \text{ m}^3/\text{sec}$.

Both mass flux and flow rate are important in physics and engineering. Mass flux measures how much mass is flowing across a surface; flow rate measures how much volume of fluid is flowing across a surface.

In addition to modeling fluid flow, surface integrals can be used to model heat flow. Suppose that the temperature at point (x, y, z) in an object is $T(x, y, z)$. Then the **heat flow** is a vector field proportional to the negative temperature gradient in the object. To be precise, the heat flow is defined as vector field $\mathbf{F} = -k\nabla T,$ where the constant *k* is the *thermal conductivity* of the substance from which the object is made (this constant is determined experimentally). The rate of heat flow across surface *S* in the object is given by the flux integral

$$\iint_S \mathbf{F} \cdot d\mathbf{S} = \iint_S -k\nabla T \cdot d\mathbf{S}.$$

Example 6.72

Calculating Heat Flow

A cast-iron solid cylinder is given by inequalities $x^2 + y^2 \le 1, \quad 1 \le z \le 4$. The temperature at point (x, y, z) in a region containing the cylinder is $T(x, y, z) = (x^2 + y^2)z$. Given that the thermal conductivity of cast iron is 55, find the heat flow across the boundary of the solid if this boundary is oriented outward.

Solution

Let *S* denote the boundary of the object. To find the heat flow, we need to calculate flux integral $\iint_S -k\nabla T \cdot d\mathbf{S}$.

Notice that *S* is not a smooth surface but is piecewise smooth, since *S* is the union of three smooth surfaces (the circular top and bottom, and the cylindrical side). Therefore, we calculate three separate integrals, one for each smooth piece of *S*. Before calculating any integrals, note that the gradient of the temperature is $\nabla T = \langle 2xz, 2yz, x^2 + y^2 \rangle$.

First we consider the circular bottom of the object, which we denote S_1. We can see that S_1 is a circle of radius 1 centered at point $(0, 0, 1),$ sitting in plane $z = 1$. This surface has parameterization $\mathbf{r}(u, v) = \langle v\cos u, v\sin u, 1 \rangle, 0 \le u < 2\pi, 0 \le v \le 1$. Therefore,

$$\mathbf{t}_u = \langle -v\sin u, v\cos u, 0 \rangle \text{ and } \mathbf{t}_v = \langle \cos u, v\sin u, 0 \rangle,$$

and

$$\mathbf{t}_u \times \mathbf{t}_v = \langle 0, 0, -v\sin^2 u - v\cos^2 u \rangle = \langle 0, 0, -v \rangle.$$

Since the surface is oriented outward and S_1 is the bottom of the object, it makes sense that this vector points downward. By **Equation 6.21**, the heat flow across S_1 is

$$\begin{aligned}\iint_{S_1} -k\nabla T \cdot d\mathbf{S} &= -55\int_0^{2\pi}\int_0^1 \nabla T(u, v) \cdot (\mathbf{t}_u \times \mathbf{t}_v) dvdu \\ &= -55\int_0^{2\pi}\int_0^1 \langle\, 2v\cos u,\, 2v\sin u,\, v^2\cos^2 u + v^2\sin^2 u \,\rangle \cdot \langle\, 0, 0, -v \,\rangle\, dvdu \\ &= -55\int_0^{2\pi}\int_0^1 \langle\, 2v\cos u,\, 2v\sin u,\, v^2 \,\rangle \cdot \langle\, 0, 0, -v \,\rangle\, dvdu \\ &= -55\int_0^{2\pi}\int_0^1 -v^3 dvdu = -55\int_0^{2\pi} -\frac{1}{4}du = \frac{55\pi}{2}.\end{aligned}$$

Now let's consider the circular top of the object, which we denote S_2. We see that S_2 is a circle of radius 1 centered at point $(0, 0, 4)$, sitting in plane $z = 4$. This surface has parameterization $\mathbf{r}(u, v) = \langle\, v\cos u, v\sin u, 4 \,\rangle$, $0 \le u < 2\pi$, $0 \le v \le 1$. Therefore,

$$\mathbf{t}_u = \langle\, -v\sin u, v\cos u, 0 \,\rangle \text{ and } \mathbf{t}_v = \langle\, \cos u, v\sin u, 0 \,\rangle,$$

and

$$\mathbf{t}_u \times \mathbf{t}_v = \langle\, 0, 0, -v\sin^2 u - v\cos^2 u \,\rangle = \langle\, 0, 0, -v \,\rangle.$$

Since the surface is oriented outward and S_1 is the top of the object, we instead take vector $\mathbf{t}_v \times \mathbf{t}_u = \langle\, 0, 0, v \,\rangle$. By **Equation 6.21**, the heat flow across S_1 is

$$\begin{aligned}\iint_{S_2} -k\nabla T \bullet d\mathbf{S} &= -55\int_0^{2\pi}\int_0^1 \nabla T(u, v) \bullet (\mathbf{t}_v \times \mathbf{t}_u) dvdu \\ &= -55\int_0^{2\pi}\int_0^1 \langle\, 8v\cos u,\, 8v\sin u,\, v^2\cos^2 u + v^2\sin^2 u \,\rangle \bullet \langle\, 0, 0, v \,\rangle\, dvdu \\ &= -55\int_0^{2\pi}\int_0^1 \langle\, 8v\cos u,\, 8v\sin u,\, v^2 \,\rangle \bullet \langle\, 0, 0, v \,\rangle\, dvdu \\ &= -55\int_0^{2\pi}\int_0^1 v^3\, dvdu = -\frac{55\pi}{2}.\end{aligned}$$

Last, let's consider the cylindrical side of the object. This surface has parameterization $\mathbf{r}(u, v) = \langle\, \cos u, \sin u, v \,\rangle$, $0 \le u < 2\pi$, $1 \le v \le 4$. By **Example 6.66**, we know that $\mathbf{t}_u \times \mathbf{t}_v = \langle\, \cos u, \sin u, 0 \,\rangle$. By **Equation 6.21**,

$$\begin{aligned}\iint_{S_3} -k\nabla T \bullet d\mathbf{S} &= -55\int_0^{2\pi}\int_1^4 \nabla T(u, v) \bullet (\mathbf{t}_v \times \mathbf{t}_u) dvdu \\ &= -55\int_0^{2\pi}\int_1^4 \langle\, 2v\cos u,\, 2v\sin u,\, \cos^2 u + \sin^2 u \,\rangle \bullet \langle\, \cos u, \sin u, 0 \,\rangle\, dvdu \\ &= -55\int_0^{2\pi}\int_0^1 \langle\, 2v\cos u,\, 2v\sin u,\, 1 \,\rangle \bullet \langle\, \cos u, \sin u, 0 \,\rangle\, dvdu \\ &= -55\int_0^{2\pi}\int_0^1 \left(2v\cos^2 u + 2v\sin^2 u\right) dvdu \\ &= -55\int_0^{2\pi}\int_0^1 2v dvdu = -55\int_0^{2\pi} du = -110\pi.\end{aligned}$$

Therefore, the rate of heat flow across S is $\frac{55\pi}{2} - \frac{55\pi}{2} - 110\pi = -110\pi$.

6.60 A cast-iron solid ball is given by inequality $x^2 + y^2 + z^2 \leq 1$. The temperature at a point in a region containing the ball is $T(x, y, z) = \frac{1}{3}(x^2 + y^2 + z^2)$. Find the heat flow across the boundary of the solid if this boundary is oriented outward.

6.6 EXERCISES

For the following exercises, determine whether the statements are *true or false*.

269. If surface S is given by $\{(x, y, z) : 0 \le x \le 1, 0 \le y \le 1, z = 10\}$, then $\iint_S f(x, y, z)dS = \int_0^1 \int_0^1 f(x, y, 10)dxdy.$

270. If surface S is given by $\{(x, y, z) : 0 \le x \le 1, 0 \le y \le 1, z = x\}$, then $\iint_S f(x, y, z)dS = \int_0^1 \int_0^1 f(x, y, x)dxdy.$

271. Surface $\mathbf{r} = \langle v\cos u, v\sin u, v^2 \rangle$, for $0 \le u \le \pi, 0 \le v \le 2$, is the same as surface $\mathbf{r} = \langle \sqrt{v}\cos 2u, \sqrt{v}\sin 2u, v \rangle$, for $0 \le u \le \frac{\pi}{2}, 0 \le v \le 4$.

272. Given the standard parameterization of a sphere, normal vectors $\mathrm{t}_u \times \mathrm{t}_v$ are outward normal vectors.

For the following exercises, find parametric descriptions for the following surfaces.

273. Plane $3x - 2y + z = 2$

274. Paraboloid $z = x^2 + y^2$, for $0 \le z \le 9$.

275. Plane $2x - 4y + 3z = 16$

276. The frustum of cone $z^2 = x^2 + y^2$, for $2 \le z \le 8$

277. The portion of cylinder $x^2 + y^2 = 9$ in the first octant, for $0 \le z \le 3$

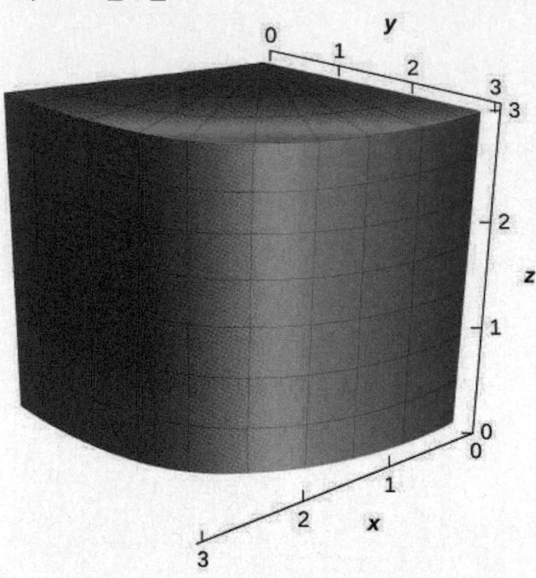

278. A cone with base radius r and height h, where r and h are positive constants

For the following exercises, use a computer algebra system to approximate the area of the following surfaces using a parametric description of the surface.

279. **[T]** Half cylinder $\{(r, \theta, z) : r = 4, 0 \le \theta \le \pi, 0 \le z \le 7\}$

280. **[T]** Plane $z = 10 - x - y$ above square $|x| \le 2, |y| \le 2$

For the following exercises, let S be the hemisphere $x^2 + y^2 + z^2 = 4$, with $z \ge 0$, and evaluate each surface integral, in the counterclockwise direction.

281. $\iint_S zdS$

282. $\iint_S (x - 2y)dS$

283. $\iint_S (x^2 + y^2)zdS$

For the following exercises, evaluate $\int\int_S \mathbf{F} \cdot \mathbf{N}ds$ for vector field $\mathbf{F}$, where $\mathbf{N}$ is an outward normal vector to surface S.

284. $\mathbf{F}(x, y, z) = x\mathbf{i} + 2y\mathbf{j} - 3z\mathbf{k},$ and S is that part of plane $15x - 12y + 3z = 6$ that lies above unit square $0 \le x \le 1, 0 \le y \le 1.$

285. $\mathbf{F}(x, y, z) = x\mathbf{i} + y\mathbf{j},$ and S is hemisphere $z = \sqrt{1 - x^2 - y^2}.$

286. $\mathbf{F}(x, y, z) = x^2\mathbf{i} + y^2\mathbf{j} + z^2\mathbf{k},$ and S is the portion of plane $z = y + 1$ that lies inside cylinder $x^2 + y^2 = 1.$

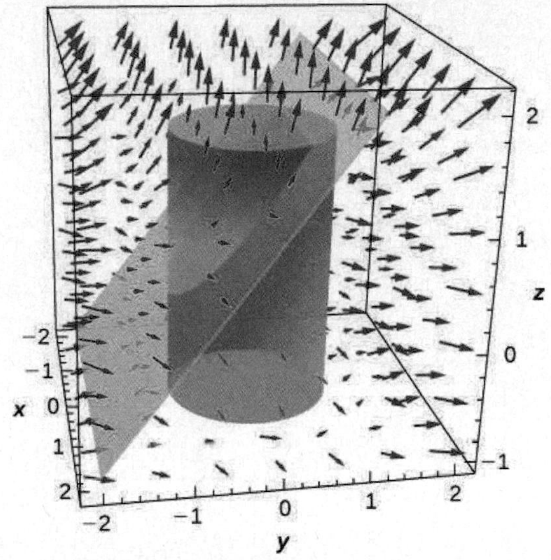

For the following exercises, approximate the mass of the homogeneous lamina that has the shape of given surface S. Round to four decimal places.

287. **[T]** S is surface $z = 4 - x - 2y,$ with $z \ge 0, x \ge 0, y \ge 0; \xi = x.$

288. **[T]** S is surface $z = x^2 + y^2,$ with $z \le 1; \xi = z.$

289. **[T]** S is surface $x^2 + y^2 + x^2 = 5,$ with $z \ge 1; \xi = \theta^2.$

290. Evaluate $\iint_S \left(y^2 z\mathbf{i} + y^3\mathbf{j} + xz\mathbf{k}\right) \cdot d\mathbf{S},$ where S is the surface of cube $-1 \le x \le 1, -1 \le y \le 1,$ and $0 \le z \le 2.$ in a counterclockwise direction.

291. Evaluate surface integral $\iint_S g dS,$ where $g(x, y, z) = xz + 2x^2 - 3xy$ and S is the portion of plane $2x - 3y + z = 6$ that lies over unit square R: $0 \le x \le 1, 0 \le y \le 1.$

292. Evaluate $\iint_S (x + y + z)d\mathbf{S},$ where S is the surface defined parametrically by $\mathbf{R}(u, v) = (2u + v)\mathbf{i} + (u - 2v)\mathbf{j} + (u + 3v)\mathbf{k}$ for $0 \le u \le 1,$ and $0 \le v \le 2.$

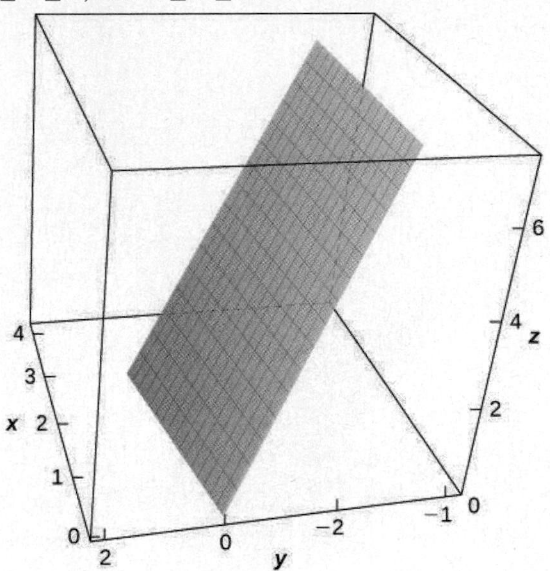

293. **[T]** Evaluate $\iint_S (x - y^2 + z)d\mathbf{S},$ where S is the surface defined by $\mathbf{R}(u, v) = u^2\mathbf{i} + v\mathbf{j} + u\mathbf{k}, 0 \le u \le 1, 0 \le v \le 1.$

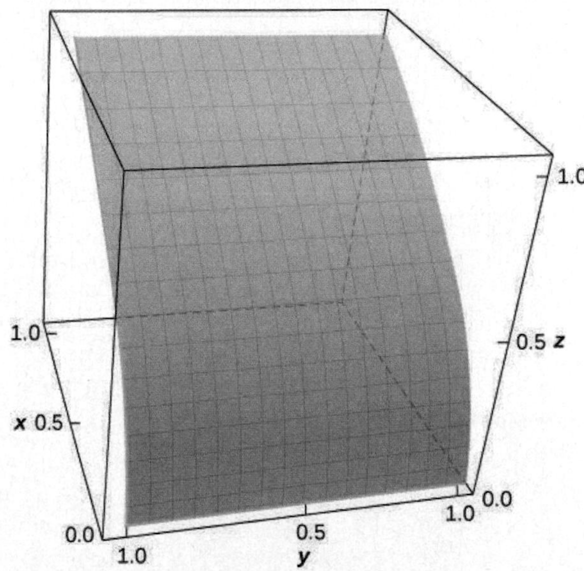

294. **[T]** Evaluate where S is the surface defined by $\mathbf{R}(u, v) = u\mathbf{i} - u^2\mathbf{j} + v\mathbf{k}, 0 \le u \le 2, 0 \le v \le 1.$ for $0 \le u \le 1, 0 \le v \le 2.$

295. Evaluate $\iint_S (x^2 + y^2)d\mathbf{S},$ where S is the surface bounded above hemisphere $z = \sqrt{1 - x^2 - y^2},$ and below by plane $z = 0.$

296. Evaluate $\iint_S (x^2 + y^2 + z^2) d\mathbf{S}$, where S is the portion of plane $z = x + 1$ that lies inside cylinder $x^2 + y^2 = 1$.

297. **[T]** Evaluate $\iint_S x^2 z dS$, where S is the portion of cone $z^2 = x^2 + y^2$ that lies between planes $z = 1$ and $z = 4$.

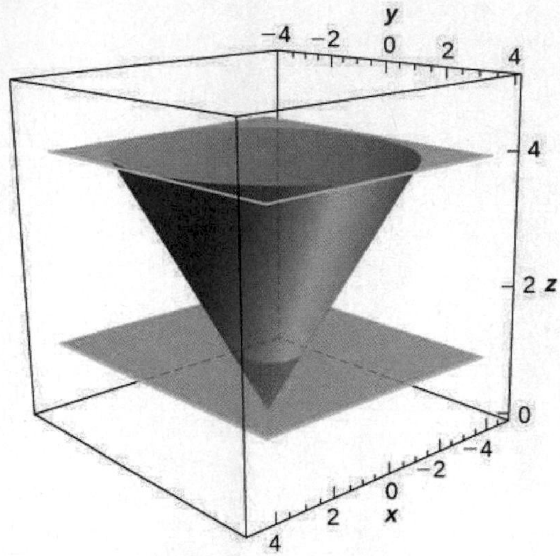

298. **[T]** Evaluate $\iint_S (xz/y) dS$, where S is the portion of cylinder $x = y^2$ that lies in the first octant between planes $z = 0$, $z = 5$, $y = 1$, and $y = 4$.

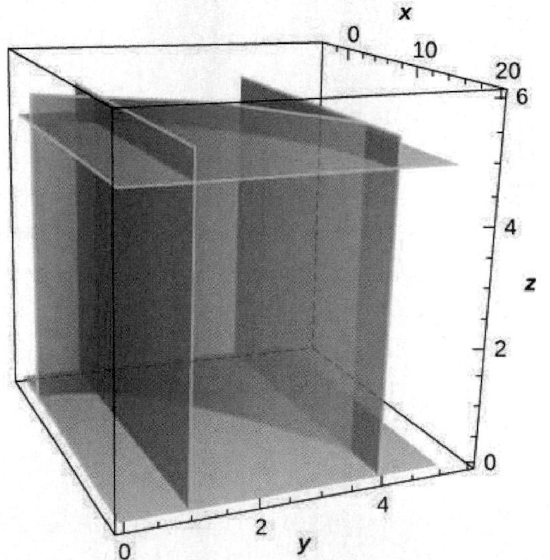

299. **[T]** Evaluate $\iint_S (z + y) dS$, where S is the part of the graph of $z = \sqrt{1 - x^2}$ in the first octant between the xz-plane and plane $y = 3$.

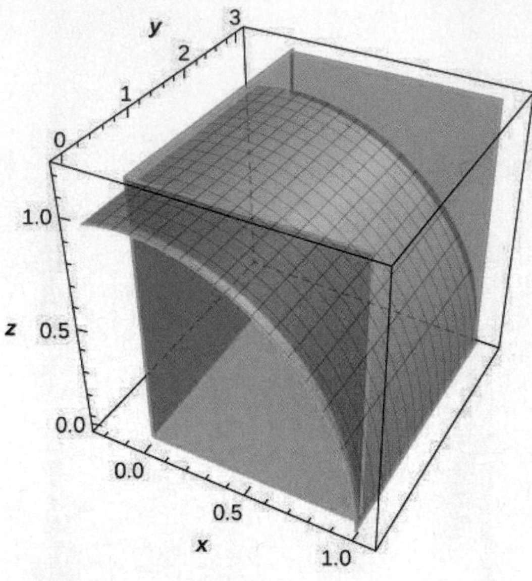

300. Evaluate $\iint_S xyz dS$ if S is the part of plane $z = x + y$ that lies over the triangular region in the xy-plane with vertices (0, 0, 0), (1, 0, 0), and (0, 2, 0).

301. Find the mass of a lamina of density $\xi(x, y, z) = z$ in the shape of hemisphere $z = (a^2 - x^2 - y^2)^{1/2}$.

302. Compute $\int\int_S \mathbf{F} \cdot \mathbf{N} dS$, where $\mathbf{F}(x, y, z) = x\mathbf{i} - 5y\mathbf{j} + 4z\mathbf{k}$ and $\mathbf{N}$ is an outward normal vector S, where S is the union of two squares $S_1 : x = 0, 0 \le y \le 1, 0 \le z \le 1$ and $S_2 : z = 1, 0 \le x \le 1, 0 \le y \le 1$.

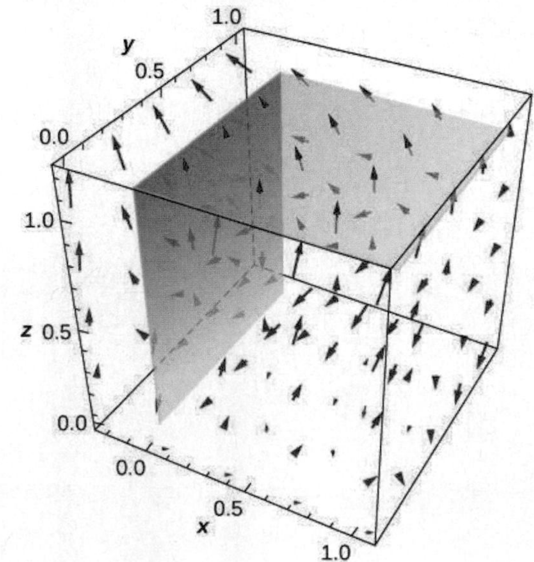

303. Compute $\int\int_S \mathbf{F} \cdot \mathbf{N} dS,$ where $\mathbf{F}(x, y, z) = xy\mathbf{i} + z\mathbf{j} + (x + y)\mathbf{k}$ and $\mathbf{N}$ is an outward normal vector S, where S is the triangular region cut off from plane $x + y + z = 1$ by the positive coordinate axes.

304. Compute $\int\int_S \mathbf{F} \cdot \mathbf{N} dS,$ where $\mathbf{F}(x, y, z) = 2yz\mathbf{i} + \left(\tan^{-1} xz\right)\mathbf{j} + e^{xy}\mathbf{k}$ and $\mathbf{N}$ is an outward normal vector *S*, where *S* is the surface of sphere $x^2 + y^2 + z^2 = 1.$

305. Compute $\int\int_S \mathbf{F} \cdot \mathbf{N} dS,$ where $\mathbf{F}(x, y, z) = xyz\mathbf{i} + xyz\mathbf{j} + xyz\mathbf{k}$ and $\mathbf{N}$ is an outward normal vector *S*, where *S* is the surface of the five faces of the unit cube $0 \le x \le 1, 0 \le y \le 1, 0 \le z \le 1$ missing $z = 0.$

For the following exercises, express the surface integral as an iterated double integral by using a projection on *S* on the *yz*-plane.

306. $\iint_S xy^2 z^3\, dS;$ *S* is the first-octant portion of plane $2x + 3y + 4z = 12.$

307. $\iint_S \left(x^2 - 2y + z\right) dS;$ *S* is the portion of the graph of $4x + y = 8$ bounded by the coordinate planes and plane $z = 6.$

For the following exercises, express the surface integral as an iterated double integral by using a projection on *S* on the *xz*-plane

308. $\iint_S xy^2 z^3\, dS;$ *S* is the first-octant portion of plane $2x + 3y + 4z = 12.$

309. $\iint_S \left(x^2 - 2y + z\right) dS;$ *S* is the portion of the graph of $4x + y = 8$ bounded by the coordinate planes and plane $z = 6.$

310. Evaluate surface integral $\iint_S yz dS,$ where *S* is the first-octant part of plane $x + y + z = \lambda,$ where λ is a positive constant.

311. Evaluate surface integral $\iint_S \left(x^2 z + y^2 z\right) dS,$ where *S* is hemisphere $x^2 + y^2 + z^2 = a^2,\ z \ge 0.$

312. Evaluate surface integral $\iint_S z dA,$ where *S* is surface $z = \sqrt{x^2 + y^2},\ 0 \le z \le 2.$

313. Evaluate surface integral $\iint_S x^2 yz dS,$ where *S* is the part of plane $z = 1 + 2x + 3y$ that lies above rectangle $0 \le x \le 3$ and $0 \le y \le 2.$

314. Evaluate surface integral $\iint_S yz dS,$ where *S* is plane $x + y + z = 1$ that lies in the first octant.

315. Evaluate surface integral $\iint_S yz dS,$ where *S* is the part of plane $z = y + 3$ that lies inside cylinder $x^2 + y^2 = 1.$

For the following exercises, use geometric reasoning to evaluate the given surface integrals.

316. $\iint_S \sqrt{x^2 + y^2 + z^2} dS,$ where *S* is surface $x^2 + y^2 + z^2 = 4,\ z \ge 0$

317. $\iint_S (x\mathbf{i} + y\mathbf{j}) \cdot d\mathbf{S},$ where *S* is surface $x^2 + y^2 = 4,\ 1 \le z \le 3,$ oriented with unit normal vectors pointing outward

318. $\iint_S (z\mathbf{k}) \cdot d\mathbf{S},$ where *S* is disc $x^2 + y^2 \le 9$ on plane $z = 4,$ oriented with unit normal vectors pointing upward

319. A lamina has the shape of a portion of sphere $x^2 + y^2 + z^2 = a^2$ that lies within cone $z = \sqrt{x^2 + y^2}$. Let S be the spherical shell centered at the origin with radius a, and let C be the right circular cone with a vertex at the origin and an axis of symmetry that coincides with the z-axis. Determine the mass of the lamina if $\delta(x, y, z) = x^2 y^2 z$.

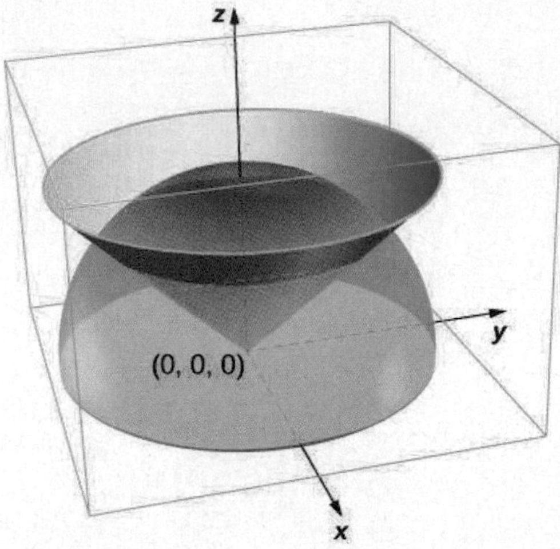

320. A lamina has the shape of a portion of sphere $x^2 + y^2 + z^2 = a^2$ that lies within cone $z = \sqrt{x^2 + y^2}$. Let S be the spherical shell centered at the origin with radius a, and let C be the right circular cone with a vertex at the origin and an axis of symmetry that coincides with the z-axis. Suppose the vertex angle of the cone is ϕ_0, with $0 \le \phi_0 < \frac{\pi}{2}$. Determine the mass of that portion of the shape enclosed in the intersection of S and C. Assume $\delta(x, y, z) = x^2 y^2 z$.

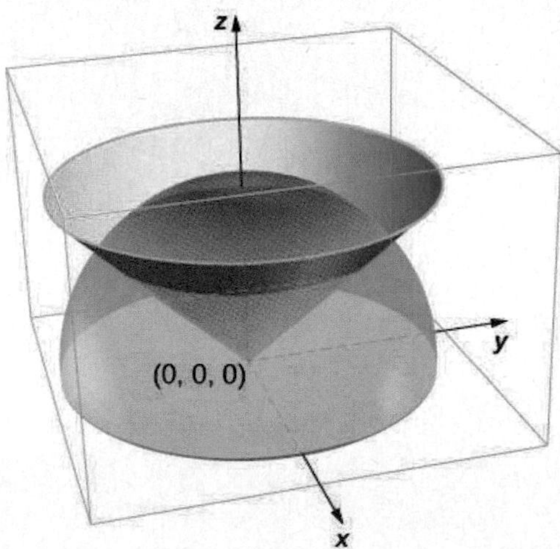

321. A paper cup has the shape of an inverted right circular cone of height 6 in. and radius of top 3 in. If the cup is full of water weighing 62.5 lb/ft^3, find the total force exerted by the water on the inside surface of the cup.

For the following exercises, the heat flow vector field for conducting objects i $\mathbf{F} = -k\nabla T$, where $T(x, y, z)$ is the temperature in the object and $k > 0$ is a constant that depends on the material. Find the outward flux of $\mathbf{F}$ across the following surfaces S for the given temperature distributions and assume $k = 1$.

322. $T(x, y, z) = 100e^{-x-y}$; S consists of the faces of cube $|x| \le 1$, $|y| \le 1$, $|z| \le 1$.

323. $T(x, y, z) = -\ln(x^2 + y^2 + z^2)$; S is sphere $x^2 + y^2 + z^2 = a^2$.

For the following exercises, consider the radial fields $\mathbf{F} = \dfrac{\langle x, y, z \rangle}{(x^2 + y^2 + z^2)^{\frac{p}{2}}} = \dfrac{\mathbf{r}}{|\mathbf{r}|^p}$, where p is a real number. Let S consist of spheres A and B centered at the origin with radii $0 < a < b$. The total outward flux across S consists of the outward flux across the outer sphere B less the flux into S across inner sphere A.

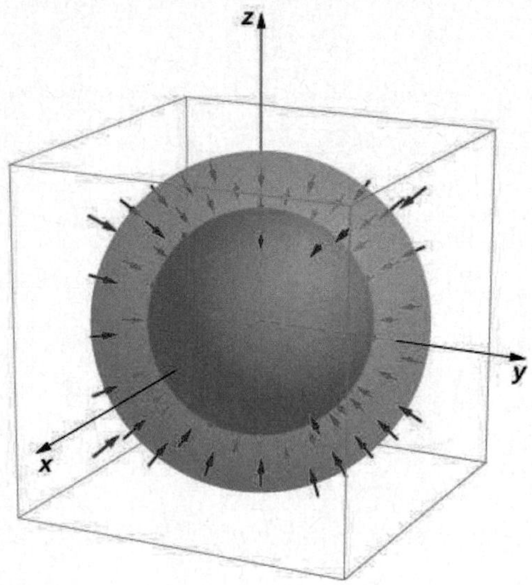

324. Find the total flux across S with $p = 0$.

325. Show that for $p = 3$ the flux across S is independent of a and b.

6.7 | Stokes' Theorem

Learning Objectives

6.7.1 Explain the meaning of Stokes' theorem.
6.7.2 Use Stokes' theorem to evaluate a line integral.
6.7.3 Use Stokes' theorem to calculate a surface integral.
6.7.4 Use Stokes' theorem to calculate a curl.

In this section, we study Stokes' theorem, a higher-dimensional generalization of Green's theorem. This theorem, like the Fundamental Theorem for Line Integrals and Green's theorem, is a generalization of the Fundamental Theorem of Calculus to higher dimensions. Stokes' theorem relates a vector surface integral over surface S in space to a line integral around the boundary of S. Therefore, just as the theorems before it, Stokes' theorem can be used to reduce an integral over a geometric object S to an integral over the boundary of S.

In addition to allowing us to translate between line integrals and surface integrals, Stokes' theorem connects the concepts of curl and circulation. Furthermore, the theorem has applications in fluid mechanics and electromagnetism. We use Stokes' theorem to derive Faraday's law, an important result involving electric fields.

Stokes' Theorem

Stokes' theorem says we can calculate the flux of curl $\mathbf{F}$ across surface S by knowing information only about the values of $\mathbf{F}$ along the boundary of S. Conversely, we can calculate the line integral of vector field $\mathbf{F}$ along the boundary of surface S by translating to a double integral of the curl of $\mathbf{F}$ over S.

Let S be an oriented smooth surface with unit normal vector $\mathbf{N}$. Furthermore, suppose the boundary of S is a simple closed curve C. The orientation of S induces the positive orientation of C if, as you walk in the positive direction around C with your head pointing in the direction of $\mathbf{N}$, the surface is always on your left. With this definition in place, we can state Stokes' theorem.

Theorem 6.19: Stokes' Theorem

Let S be a piecewise smooth oriented surface with a boundary that is a simple closed curve C with positive orientation (**Figure 6.79**). If $\mathbf{F}$ is a vector field with component functions that have continuous partial derivatives on an open region containing S, then

$$\int_C \mathbf{F} \cdot d\mathbf{r} = \iint_S \text{curl } \mathbf{F} \cdot d\mathbf{S}.$$

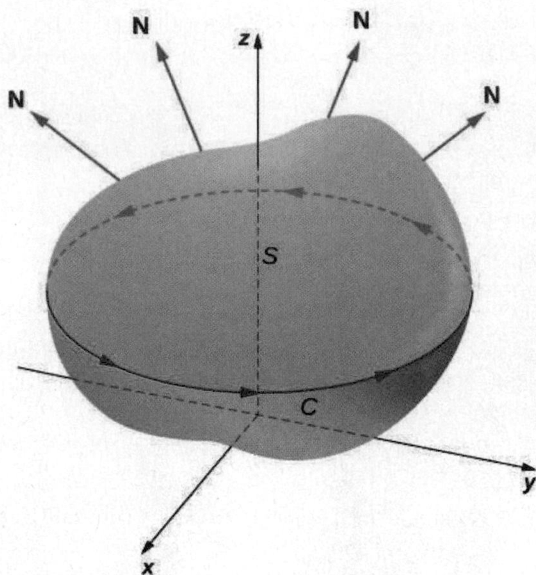

Figure 6.79 Stokes' theorem relates the flux integral over the surface to a line integral around the boundary of the surface. Note that the orientation of the curve is positive.

Suppose surface S is a flat region in the xy-plane with upward orientation. Then the unit normal vector is $\mathbf{k}$ and surface integral $\iint_S \text{curl}\,\mathbf{F}\cdot d\mathbf{S}$ is actually the double integral $\iint_S \text{curl}\,\mathbf{F}\cdot\mathbf{k}dA$. In this special case, Stokes' theorem gives $\int_C \mathbf{F}\cdot d\mathbf{r} = \iint_S \text{curl}\,\mathbf{F}\cdot\mathbf{k}dA$. However, this is the flux form of Green's theorem, which shows us that Green's theorem is a special case of Stokes' theorem. Green's theorem can only handle surfaces in a plane, but Stokes' theorem can handle surfaces in a plane or in space.

The complete proof of Stokes' theorem is beyond the scope of this text. We look at an intuitive explanation for the truth of the theorem and then see proof of the theorem in the special case that surface S is a portion of a graph of a function, and S, the boundary of S, and $\mathbf{F}$ are all fairly tame.

Proof

First, we look at an informal proof of the theorem. This proof is not rigorous, but it is meant to give a general feeling for why the theorem is true. Let S be a surface and let D be a small piece of the surface so that D does not share any points with the boundary of S. We choose D to be small enough so that it can be approximated by an oriented square E. Let D inherit its orientation from S, and give E the same orientation. This square has four sides; denote them E_l, E_r, E_u, and E_d for the left, right, up, and down sides, respectively. On the square, we can use the flux form of Green's theorem:

$$\int_{E_l+E_d+E_r+E_u} \mathbf{F}\cdot d\mathbf{r} = \iint_E \text{curl}\,\mathbf{F}\cdot\mathbf{N}dS = \iint_E \text{curl}\,\mathbf{F}\cdot d\mathbf{S}.$$

To approximate the flux over the entire surface, we add the values of the flux on the small squares approximating small pieces of the surface (**Figure 6.80**). By Green's theorem, the flux across each approximating square is a line integral over its boundary. Let F be an approximating square with an orientation inherited from S and with a right side E_l (so F is to the left of E). Let F_r denote the right side of F; then, $E_l = -F_r$. In other words, the right side of F is the same curve as the left side of E, just oriented in the opposite direction. Therefore,

$$\int_{E_l} \mathbf{F}\cdot d\mathbf{r} = -\int_{F_r} \mathbf{F}\cdot d\mathbf{r}.$$

As we add up all the fluxes over all the squares approximating surface S, line integrals $\int_{E_l} \mathbf{F}\cdot d\mathbf{r}$ and $\int_{F_r} \mathbf{F}\cdot d\mathbf{r}$ cancel each other out. The same goes for the line integrals over the other three sides of E. These three line integrals cancel out with the line integral of the lower side of the square above E, the line integral over the left side of the square to the right of E, and the line integral over the upper side of the square below E (**Figure 6.81**). After all this cancelation occurs over all the approximating squares, the only line integrals that survive are the line integrals over sides approximating the boundary of S. Therefore, the sum of all the fluxes (which, by Green's theorem, is the sum of all the line integrals around the boundaries of approximating squares) can be approximated by a line integral over the boundary of S. In the limit, as the areas of the approximating squares go to zero, this approximation gets arbitrarily close to the flux.

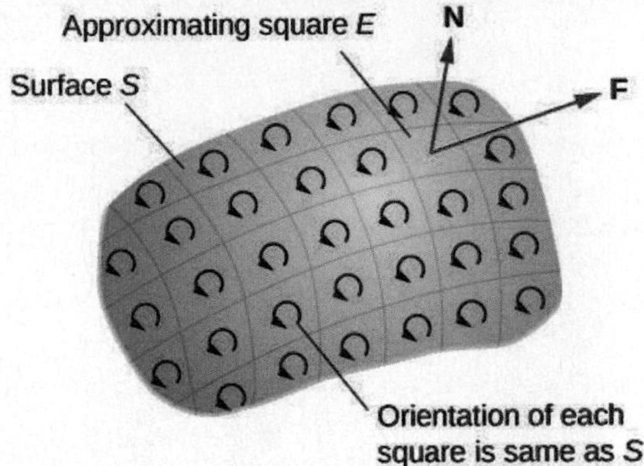

Figure 6.80 Chop the surface into small pieces. The pieces should be small enough that they can be approximated by a square.

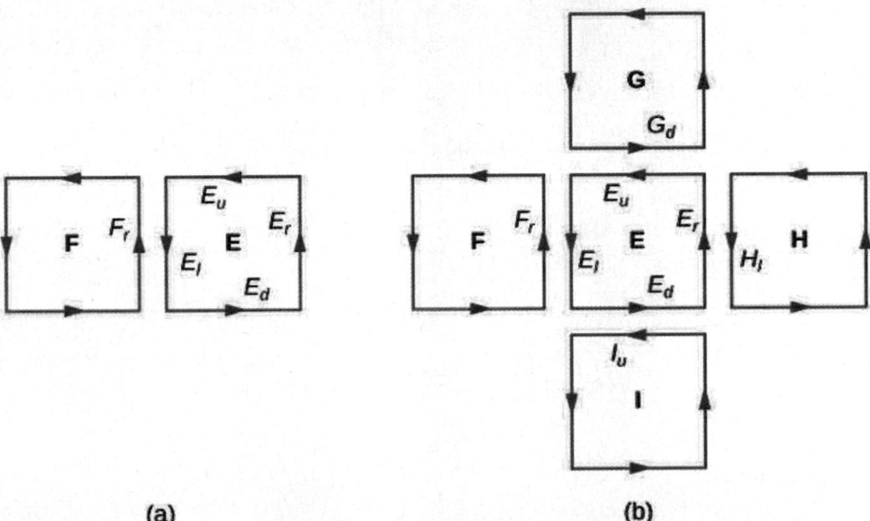

Figure 6.81 (a) The line integral along E_l cancels out the line integral along F_r because $E_l = -F_r$. (b) The line integral along any of the sides of E cancels out with the line integral along a side of an adjacent approximating square.

Let's now look at a rigorous proof of the theorem in the special case that S is the graph of function $z = f(x, y)$, where x and y vary over a bounded, simply connected region D of finite area (**Figure 6.82**). Furthermore, assume that f has continuous second-order partial derivatives. Let C denote the boundary of S and let C' denote the boundary of D. Then, D is the "shadow" of S in the plane and C' is the "shadow" of C. Suppose that S is oriented upward. The counterclockwise orientation of C is positive, as is the counterclockwise orientation of C'. Let $\mathbf{F}(x, y, z) = \langle P, Q, R \rangle$ be a vector field with component functions that have continuous partial derivatives.

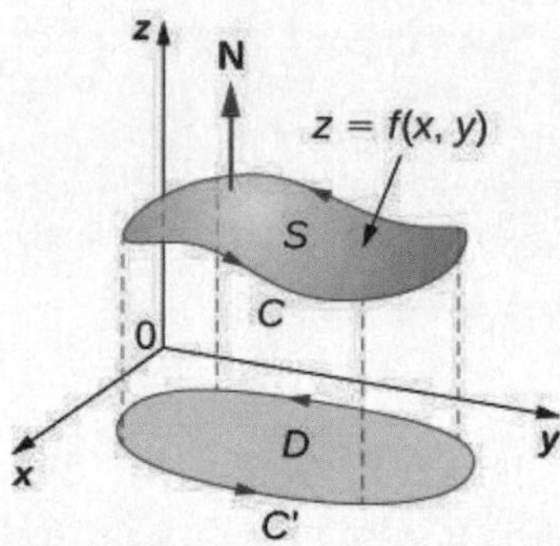

Figure 6.82 D is the "shadow," or projection, of S in the plane and C' is the projection of C.

We take the standard parameterization of $S : x = x,\ y = y,\ z = g(x, y)$. The tangent vectors are $\mathbf{t}_x = \langle 1, 0, g_x \rangle$ and $\mathbf{t}_y = \langle 0, 1, g_y \rangle$, and therefore, $\mathbf{t}_x \cdot \mathbf{t}_y = \langle -g_x, -g_y, 1 \rangle$. By **Equation 6.19**,

$$\iint_S \text{curl}\,\mathbf{F} \cdot d\mathbf{S} = \iint_D \left[-(R_y - Q_z)z_x - (P_z - R_x)z_y + (Q_x - P_y)\right]dA,$$

where the partial derivatives are all evaluated at $(x, y, g(x, y))$, making the integrand depend on x and y only. Suppose $\langle x(t), y(t) \rangle,\ a \le t \le b$ is a parameterization of C'. Then, a parameterization of C is $\langle x(t), y(t), g(x(t), y(t)) \rangle,\ a \le t \le b$. Armed with these parameterizations, the Chain rule, and Green's theorem, and keeping in mind that P, Q, and R are all functions of x and y, we can evaluate line integral $\int_C \mathbf{F} \cdot d\mathbf{r}$:

$$\begin{aligned}
\int_C \mathbf{F} \cdot d\mathbf{r} &= \int_a^b (Px'(t) + Qy'(t) + Rz'(t))dt \\
&= \int_a^b \left[Px'(t) + Qy'(t) + R\left(\frac{\partial z}{\partial x}\frac{dx}{dt} + \frac{\partial z}{\partial y}\frac{dy}{dt}\right)\right]dt \\
&= \int_a^b \left[\left(P + R\frac{\partial z}{\partial x}\right)x'(t) + \left(Q + R\frac{\partial z}{\partial y}\right)y'(t)\right]dt \\
&= \int_{C'} \left(P + R\frac{\partial z}{\partial x}\right)dx + \left(Q + R\frac{\partial z}{\partial y}\right)dy \\
&= \iint_D \left[\frac{\partial}{\partial x}\left(Q + R\frac{\partial z}{\partial y}\right) - \frac{\partial}{\partial y}\left(P + R\frac{\partial z}{\partial x}\right)\right]dA \\
&= \iint_D \begin{pmatrix} \left(\dfrac{\partial Q}{\partial x} + \dfrac{\partial Q}{\partial z}\dfrac{\partial z}{\partial x} + \dfrac{\partial R}{\partial x}\dfrac{\partial z}{\partial y} + \dfrac{\partial R}{\partial z}\dfrac{\partial z}{\partial x}\dfrac{\partial z}{\partial y} + R\dfrac{\partial^2 z}{\partial x \partial y}\right) \\ -\left(\dfrac{\partial P}{\partial y} + \dfrac{\partial P}{\partial z}\dfrac{\partial z}{\partial y} + \dfrac{\partial R}{\partial z}\dfrac{\partial z}{\partial y}\dfrac{\partial z}{\partial x} + R\dfrac{\partial^2 z}{\partial y \partial x}\right) \end{pmatrix} dA.
\end{aligned}$$

By Clairaut's theorem, $\frac{\partial^2 z}{\partial x \partial y} = \frac{\partial^2 z}{\partial y \partial x}$. Therefore, four of the terms disappear from this double integral, and we are left with

$$\iint_D \left[-(R_y - Q_z)z_x - (P_z - R_x)z_y + (Q_x - P_y)\right]dA,$$

which equals $\iint_S \text{curl}\,\mathbf{F} \cdot d\mathbf{S}$.

□

We have shown that Stokes' theorem is true in the case of a function with a domain that is a simply connected region of finite area. We can quickly confirm this theorem for another important case: when vector field **F** is conservative. If **F** is conservative, the curl of **F** is zero, so $\iint_S \text{curl } \mathbf{F} \cdot d\mathbf{S} = 0$. Since the boundary of S is a closed curve, $\int_C \mathbf{F} \cdot d\mathbf{r}$ is also zero.

Example 6.73

Verifying Stokes' Theorem for a Specific Case

Verify that Stokes' theorem is true for vector field $\mathbf{F}(x, y, z) = \langle y, 2z, x^2 \rangle$ and surface S, where S is the paravbolid $z = 4 - x^2 - y^2$.

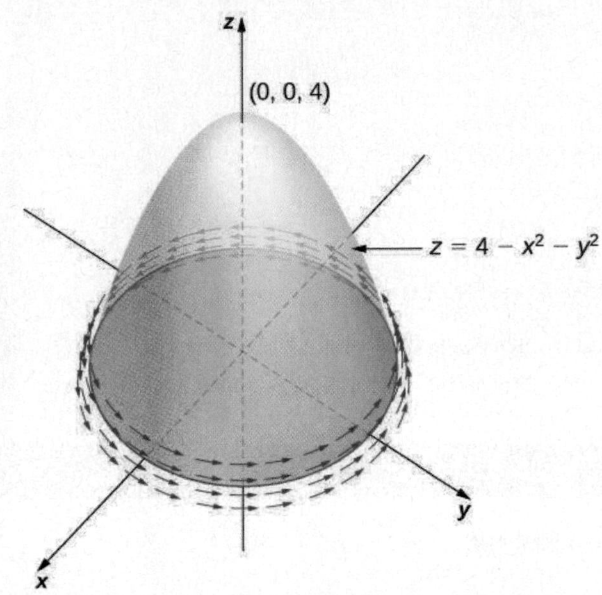

Figure 6.83 Verifying Stokes' theorem for a hemisphere in a vector field.

Solution

As a surface integral, you have $g(x, y) = 4 - x^2 - y^2$, $g_x = -2y$ and

$$\text{curl } \mathbf{F} = \begin{vmatrix} \mathbf{i} & \mathbf{j} & \mathbf{k} \\ \frac{\partial}{\partial x} & \frac{\partial}{\partial y} & \frac{\partial}{\partial z} \\ y & 2z & x^2 \end{vmatrix} = \langle -2, -2x, -1 \rangle.$$

By **Equation 6.19**,

$$\begin{aligned}
\iint_S \text{curl } \mathbf{F} \cdot d\mathbf{S} &= \iint_D \text{curl } \mathbf{F}(\mathbf{r}(\phi, \theta)) \cdot (\mathbf{t}_\phi \times \mathbf{t}_\theta) dA \\
&= \iint_D \langle -2, -2x, -1 \rangle \cdot \langle 2x, 2y, 1 \rangle \, dA \\
&= \int_{-2}^{2} \int_{\sqrt{4 - x^2}}^{\sqrt{4 - x^2}} (-4x - 4xy - 1) dy dx \\
&= \int_{-2}^{2} \left(-8x\sqrt{4 - x^2} - 2\sqrt{4 - x^2}\right) dx \\
&= -4\pi
\end{aligned}$$

As a line integral, you can parameterize C by $\mathbf{r}(t) = \langle 2\cos t, 2\sin t, 0 \rangle$ $0 \le t \le 2\pi$. By **Equation 6.19**,

$$\begin{aligned}\int_C \mathbf{F} \cdot d\mathbf{r} &= \int_0^{2\pi} \langle 2\sin t, 0, 4\cos^2 t \rangle \cdot \langle -2\sin t, 2\cos t, 0 \rangle \, dt \\ &= \int_0^{2\pi} -4\sin^2 t dt = -4\pi\end{aligned} \tag{6.22}$$

Therefore, we have verified Stokes' theorem for this example.

6.61 Verify that Stokes' theorem is true for vector field $\mathbf{F}(x, y, z) = \langle y, x, -z \rangle$ and surface S, where S is the upwardly oriented portion of the graph of $f(x, y) = x^2 y$ over a triangle in the xy-plane with vertices $(0, 0)$, $(2, 0)$, and $(0, 2)$.

Applying Stokes' Theorem

Stokes' theorem translates between the flux integral of surface S to a line integral around the boundary of S. Therefore, the theorem allows us to compute surface integrals or line integrals that would ordinarily be quite difficult by translating the line integral into a surface integral or vice versa. We now study some examples of each kind of translation.

Example 6.74

Calculating a Surface Integral

Calculate surface integral $\iint_S \text{curl } \mathbf{F} \cdot d\mathbf{S}$, where S is the surface, oriented outward, in **Figure 6.84** and $\mathbf{F} = \langle z, 2xy, x + y \rangle$.

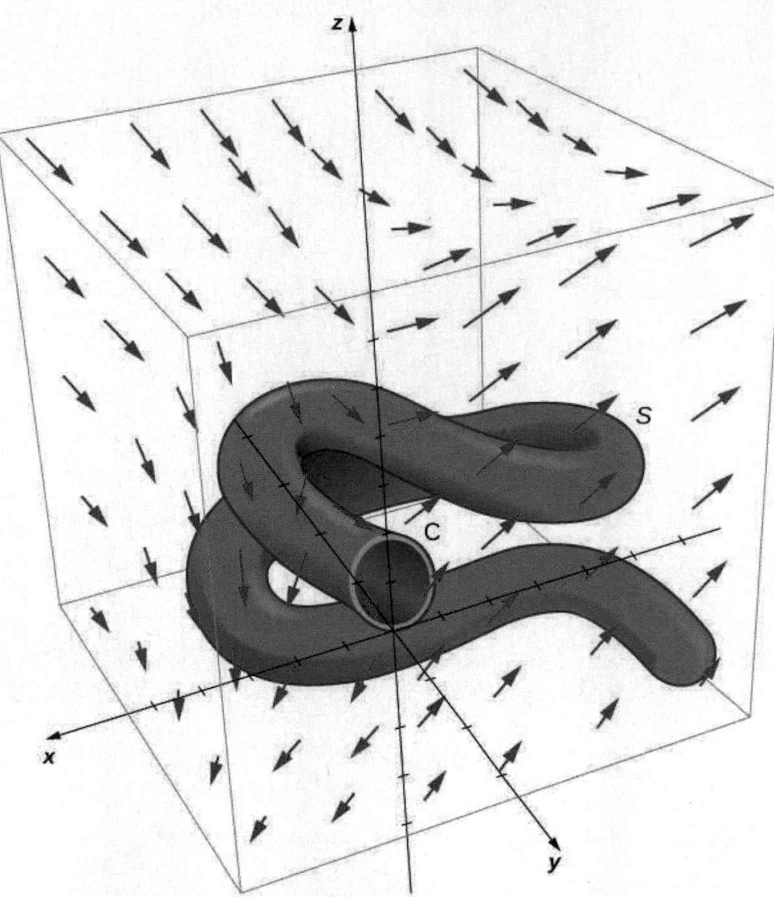

Figure 6.84 A complicated surface in a vector field.

Solution

Note that to calculate $\iint_S \text{curl } \mathbf{F} \cdot d\mathbf{S}$ without using Stokes' theorem, we would need to use **Equation 6.19**. Use of this equation requires a parameterization of S. Surface S is complicated enough that it would be extremely difficult to find a parameterization. Therefore, the methods we have learned in previous sections are not useful for this problem. Instead, we use Stokes' theorem, noting that the boundary C of the surface is merely a single circle with radius 1.

The curl of $\mathbf{F}$ is $\langle 1, 1, 2y \rangle$. By Stokes' theorem,

$$\iint_S \text{curl } \mathbf{F} \cdot d\mathbf{S} = \int_C \mathbf{F} \cdot d\mathbf{r},$$

where C has parameterization $\mathbf{r}(t) = \langle -\sin t, 0, 1 - \cos t \rangle, \ 0 \le t < 2\pi$. By **Equation 6.9**,

$$\begin{aligned}
\iint_S \text{curl}\, \mathbf{F} \cdot d\mathbf{S} &= \int_C \mathbf{F} \cdot d\mathbf{r} \\
&= \int_0^{2\pi} \langle 1 - \cos t, 0, -\sin t \rangle \cdot \langle -\cos t, 0, \sin t \rangle \, dt \\
&= \int_0^{2\pi} \left(-\cos t + \cos^2 t - \sin^2 t\right) dt \\
&= \left[-\sin t + \frac{1}{2}\sin(2t)\right]_0^{2\pi} \\
&= (-\sin(2\pi) + \frac{1}{2}\sin(4\pi)) - (-\sin 0 + \frac{1}{2}\sin 0) \\
&= 0.
\end{aligned}$$

An amazing consequence of Stokes' theorem is that if S' is any other smooth surface with boundary C and the same orientation as S, then $\iint_S \text{curl}\, \mathbf{F} \cdot d\mathbf{S} = \int_C \mathbf{F} \cdot d\mathbf{r} = 0$ because Stokes' theorem says the surface integral depends on the line integral around the boundary only.

In **Example 6.74**, we calculated a surface integral simply by using information about the boundary of the surface. In general, let S_1 and S_2 be smooth surfaces with the same boundary C and the same orientation. By Stokes' theorem,

$$\iint_{S_1} \text{curl}\, \mathbf{F} \cdot d\mathbf{S} = \int_C \mathbf{F} \cdot d\mathbf{r} = \iint_{S_2} \text{curl}\, \mathbf{F} \cdot d\mathbf{S}. \tag{6.23}$$

Therefore, if $\iint_{S_1} \text{curl}\, \mathbf{F} \cdot d\mathbf{S}$ is difficult to calculate but $\iint_{S_2} \text{curl}\, \mathbf{F} \cdot d\mathbf{S}$ is easy to calculate, Stokes' theorem allows us to calculate the easier surface integral. In **Example 6.74**, we could have calculated $\iint_S \text{curl}\, \mathbf{F} \cdot d\mathbf{S}$ by calculating $\iint_{S'} \text{curl}\, \mathbf{F} \cdot d\mathbf{S},$ where S' is the disk enclosed by boundary curve C (a much more simple surface with which to work).

Equation 6.23 shows that flux integrals of curl vector fields are **surface independent** in the same way that line integrals of gradient fields are path independent. Recall that if **F** is a two-dimensional conservative vector field defined on a simply connected domain, f is a potential function for **F**, and C is a curve in the domain of **F**, then $\int_C \mathbf{F} \cdot d\mathbf{r}$ depends only on the endpoints of C. Therefore if C' is any other curve with the same starting point and endpoint as C (that is, C' has the same orientation as C), then $\int_C \mathbf{F} \cdot d\mathbf{r} = \int_{C'} \mathbf{F} \cdot d\mathbf{r}$. In other words, the value of the integral depends on the boundary of the path only; it does not really depend on the path itself.

Analogously, suppose that S and S' are surfaces with the same boundary and same orientation, and suppose that **G** is a three-dimensional vector field that can be written as the curl of another vector field **F** (so that **F** is like a "potential field" of **G**). By **Equation 6.23**,

$$\iint_S \mathbf{G} \cdot d\mathbf{S} = \iint_S \text{curl}\, \mathbf{F} \cdot d\mathbf{S} = \int_C \mathbf{F} \cdot d\mathbf{r} = \iint_{S'} \text{curl}\, \mathbf{F} \cdot d\mathbf{S} = \iint_{S'} \mathbf{G} \cdot d\mathbf{S}.$$

Therefore, the flux integral of **G** does not depend on the surface, only on the boundary of the surface. Flux integrals of vector fields that can be written as the curl of a vector field are surface independent in the same way that line integrals of vector fields that can be written as the gradient of a scalar function are path independent.

6.62 Use Stokes' theorem to calculate surface integral $\iint_S \text{curl } \mathbf{F} \cdot d\mathbf{S}$, where $\mathbf{F} = \langle z, x, y \rangle$ and S is the surface as shown in the following figure. The boundary curve, C, is oriented clockwise.

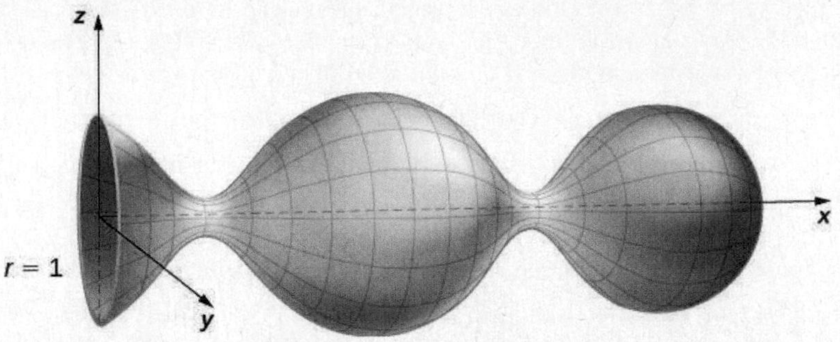

Example 6.75

Calculating a Line Integral

Calculate the line integral $\int_C \mathbf{F} \cdot d\mathbf{r}$, where $\mathbf{F} = \langle xy, x^2 + y^2 + z^2, yz \rangle$ and C is the boundary of the parallelogram with vertices $(0, 0, 1)$, $(0, 1, 0)$, $(2, 0, -1)$, and $(2, 1, -2)$.

Solution

To calculate the line integral directly, we need to parameterize each side of the parallelogram separately, calculate four separate line integrals, and add the result. This is not overly complicated, but it is time-consuming.

By contrast, let's calculate the line integral using Stokes' theorem. Let S denote the surface of the parallelogram. Note that S is the portion of the graph of $z = 1 - x - y$ for (x, y) varying over the rectangular region with vertices $(0, 0)$, $(0, 1)$, $(2, 0)$, and $(2, 1)$ in the xy-plane. Therefore, a parameterization of S is $\langle x, y, 1 - x - y \rangle$, $0 \le x \le 2$, $0 \le y \le 1$. The curl of $\mathbf{F}$ is $-\langle z, 0, x \rangle$, and Stokes' theorem and **Equation 6.19** give

$$\begin{aligned}
\int_C \mathbf{F} \cdot d\mathbf{r} &= \iint_S \text{curl } \mathbf{F} \cdot d\mathbf{S} \\
&= \int_0^2 \int_0^1 \text{curl } \mathbf{F}(x, y) \cdot (\mathbf{t}_x \times \mathbf{t}_y) dy dx \\
&= \int_0^2 \int_0^1 \langle -(1 - x - y), 0, x \rangle \cdot (\langle 1, 0, -1 \rangle \times \langle 0, 1, -1 \rangle) dy dx \\
&= \int_0^2 \int_0^1 \langle x + y - 1, 0, x \rangle \cdot \langle 1, 1, 1 \rangle \, dy dx \\
& \int_0^2 \int_0^1 2x + y - 1 dy dx \\
&= 3.
\end{aligned}$$

6.63 Use Stokes' theorem to calculate line integral $\int_C \mathbf{F} \cdot d\mathbf{r}$, where $\mathbf{F} = \langle z, x, y \rangle$ and C is oriented clockwise and is the boundary of a triangle with vertices $(0, 0, 1)$, $(3, 0, -2)$, and $(0, 1, 2)$.

Interpretation of Curl

In addition to translating between line integrals and flux integrals, Stokes' theorem can be used to justify the physical interpretation of curl that we have learned. Here we investigate the relationship between curl and circulation, and we use Stokes' theorem to state Faraday's law—an important law in electricity and magnetism that relates the curl of an electric field to the rate of change of a magnetic field.

Recall that if C is a closed curve and $\mathbf{F}$ is a vector field defined on C, then the circulation of $\mathbf{F}$ around C is line integral $\int_C \mathbf{F} \cdot d\mathbf{r}$. If $\mathbf{F}$ represents the velocity field of a fluid in space, then the circulation measures the tendency of the fluid to move in the direction of C.

Let $\mathbf{F}$ be a continuous vector field and let D_r be a small disk of radius r with center P_0 (**Figure 6.85**). If D_r is small enough, then $(\text{curl}\,\mathbf{F})(P) \approx (\text{curl}\,\mathbf{F})(P_0)$ for all points P in D_r because the curl is continuous. Let C_r be the boundary circle of D_r. By Stokes' theorem,

$$\int_{C_r} \mathbf{F} \cdot d\mathbf{r} = \iint_{D_r} \text{curl}\,\mathbf{F} \cdot \mathbf{N}dS \approx \iint_{D_r} (\text{curl}\,\mathbf{F})(P_0) \cdot \mathbf{N}(P_0)dS.$$

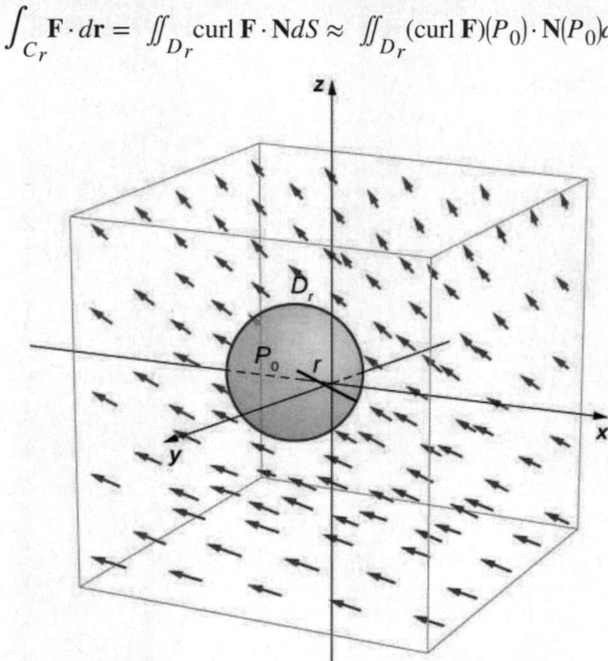

Figure 6.85 Disk D_r is a small disk in a continuous vector field.

The quantity $(\text{curl}\,\mathbf{F})(P_0) \cdot \mathbf{N}(P_0)$ is constant, and therefore

$$\iint_{D_r} (\text{curl}\,\mathbf{F})(P_0) \cdot \mathbf{N}(P_0)dS = \pi r^2 [(\text{curl}\,\mathbf{F})(P_0) \cdot \mathbf{N}(P_0)].$$

Thus

$$\int_{C_r} \mathbf{F} \cdot d\mathbf{r} \approx \pi r^2 [(\text{curl}\,\mathbf{F})(P_0) \cdot \mathbf{N}(P_0)],$$

and the approximation gets arbitrarily close as the radius shrinks to zero. Therefore Stokes' theorem implies that

$$(\text{curl}\,\mathbf{F})(P_0) \cdot \mathbf{N}(P_0) = \lim_{r \to 0^+} \frac{1}{\pi r^2} \int_{C_r} \mathbf{F} \cdot d\mathbf{r}.$$

This equation relates the curl of a vector field to the circulation. Since the area of the disk is πr^2, this equation says we can view the curl (in the limit) as the circulation per unit area. Recall that if $\mathbf{F}$ is the velocity field of a fluid, then circulation

$\oint_{C_r} \mathbf{F} \cdot d\mathbf{r} = \oint_{C_r} \mathbf{F} \cdot \mathbf{T} ds$ is a measure of the tendency of the fluid to move around C_r. The reason for this is that $\mathbf{F} \cdot \mathbf{T}$ is a component of **F** in the direction of **T**, and the closer the direction of **F** is to **T**, the larger the value of $\mathbf{F} \cdot \mathbf{T}$ (remember that if **a** and **b** are vectors and **b** is fixed, then the dot product $\mathbf{a} \cdot \mathbf{b}$ is maximal when **a** points in the same direction as **b**). Therefore, if **F** is the velocity field of a fluid, then $\text{curl}\, \mathbf{F} \cdot \mathbf{N}$ is a measure of how the fluid rotates about axis **N**. The effect of the curl is largest about the axis that points in the direction of **N**, because in this case $\text{curl}\, \mathbf{F} \cdot \mathbf{N}$ is as large as possible.

To see this effect in a more concrete fashion, imagine placing a tiny paddlewheel at point P_0 (**Figure 6.86**). The paddlewheel achieves its maximum speed when the axis of the wheel points in the direction of curl**F**. This justifies the interpretation of the curl we have learned: curl is a measure of the rotation in the vector field about the axis that points in the direction of the normal vector **N**, and Stokes' theorem justifies this interpretation.

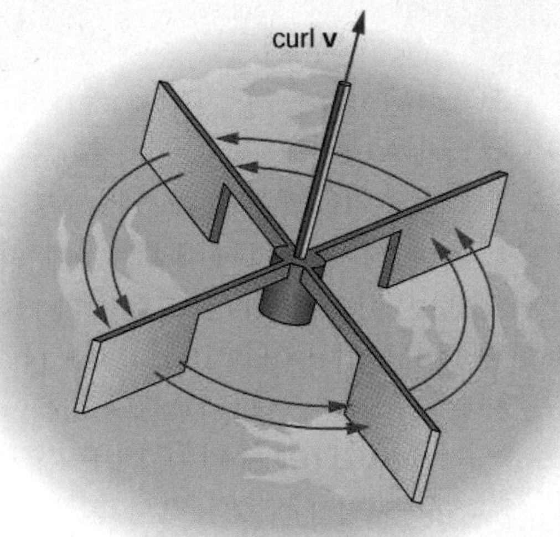

Figure 6.86 To visualize curl at a point, imagine placing a tiny paddlewheel at that point in the vector field.

Now that we have learned about Stokes' theorem, we can discuss applications in the area of electromagnetism. In particular, we examine how we can use Stokes' theorem to translate between two equivalent forms of Faraday's law. Before stating the two forms of Faraday's law, we need some background terminology.

Let C be a closed curve that models a thin wire. In the context of electric fields, the wire may be moving over time, so we write $C(t)$ to represent the wire. At a given time t, curve $C(t)$ may be different from original curve C because of the movement of the wire, but we assume that $C(t)$ is a closed curve for all times t. Let $D(t)$ be a surface with $C(t)$ as its boundary, and orient $C(t)$ so that $D(t)$ has positive orientation. Suppose that $C(t)$ is in a magnetic field $\mathbf{B}(t)$ that can also change over time. In other words, **B** has the form

$$\mathbf{B}(x, y, z) = \langle P(x, y, z), Q(x, y, z), R(x, y, z) \rangle,$$

where P, Q, and R can all vary continuously over time. We can produce current along the wire by changing field $\mathbf{B}(t)$ (this is a consequence of Ampere's law). Flux $\phi(t) = \iint_{D(t)} \mathbf{B}(t) \cdot d\mathbf{S}$ creates electric field $\mathbf{E}(t)$ that does work. The integral form of Faraday's law states that

$$\text{Work} = \int_{C(t)} \mathbf{E}(t) \cdot d\mathbf{r} = -\frac{\partial \phi}{\partial t}.$$

In other words, the work done by **E** is the line integral around the boundary, which is also equal to the rate of change of the flux with respect to time. The differential form of Faraday's law states that

$$\text{curl}\, \mathbf{E} = -\frac{\partial \mathbf{B}}{\partial t}.$$

Using Stokes' theorem, we can show that the differential form of Faraday's law is a consequence of the integral form. By Stokes' theorem, we can convert the line integral in the integral form into surface integral

$$-\frac{\partial \phi}{\partial t} = \int_{C(t)} \mathbf{E}(t) \cdot d\mathbf{r} = \iint_{D(t)} \text{curl } \mathbf{E}(t) \cdot d\mathbf{S}.$$

Since $\phi(t) = \iint_{D(t)} \mathbf{B}(t) \cdot d\mathbf{S},$ then as long as the integration of the surface does not vary with time we also have

$$-\frac{\partial \phi}{\partial t} = \iint_{D(t)} -\frac{\partial \mathbf{B}}{\partial t} \cdot d\mathbf{S}.$$

Therefore,

$$\iint_{D(t)} -\frac{\partial \mathbf{B}}{\partial t} \cdot d\mathbf{S} = \iint_{D(t)} \text{curl } \mathbf{E} \cdot d\mathbf{S}.$$

To derive the differential form of Faraday's law, we would like to conclude that $\text{curl } \mathbf{E} = -\frac{\partial \mathbf{B}}{\partial t}$. In general, the equation

$$\iint_{D(t)} -\frac{\partial \mathbf{B}}{\partial t} \cdot d\mathbf{S} = \iint_{D(t)} \text{curl } \mathbf{E} \cdot d\mathbf{S}$$

is not enough to conclude that $\text{curl } \mathbf{E} = -\frac{\partial \mathbf{B}}{\partial t}$. The integral symbols do not simply "cancel out," leaving equality of the integrands. To see why the integral symbol does not just cancel out in general, consider the two single-variable integrals $\int_0^1 x dx$ and $\int_0^1 f(x) dx,$ where

$$f(x) = \begin{cases} 1, & 0 \le x \le 1/2 \\ 0, & 1/2 \le x \le 1. \end{cases}$$

Both of these integrals equal $\frac{1}{2},$ so $\int_0^1 x dx = \int_0^1 f(x) dx$. However, $x \neq f(x)$. Analogously, with our equation $\iint_{D(t)} -\frac{\partial \mathbf{B}}{\partial t} \cdot d\mathbf{S} = \iint_{D(t)} \text{curl } \mathbf{E} \cdot d\mathbf{S},$ we cannot simply conclude that $\text{curl } \mathbf{E} = -\frac{\partial \mathbf{B}}{\partial t}$ just because their integrals are equal. However, in our context, equation $\iint_{D(t)} -\frac{\partial \mathbf{B}}{\partial t} \cdot d\mathbf{S} = \iint_{D(t)} \text{curl } \mathbf{E} \cdot d\mathbf{S}$ is true for *any* region, however small (this is in contrast to the single-variable integrals just discussed). If $\mathbf{F}$ and $\mathbf{G}$ are three-dimensional vector fields such that $\iint_S \mathbf{F} \cdot d\mathbf{S} = \iint_S \mathbf{G} \cdot d\mathbf{S}$ for any surface S, then it is possible to show that $\mathbf{F} = \mathbf{G}$ by shrinking the area of S to zero by taking a limit (the smaller the area of S, the closer the value of $\iint_S \mathbf{F} \cdot d\mathbf{S}$ to the value of $\mathbf{F}$ at a point inside S). Therefore, we can let area $D(t)$ shrink to zero by taking a limit and obtain the differential form of Faraday's law:

$$\text{curl } \mathbf{E} = -\frac{\partial \mathbf{B}}{\partial t}.$$

In the context of electric fields, the curl of the electric field can be interpreted as the negative of the rate of change of the corresponding magnetic field with respect to time.

Example 6.76

Using Faraday's Law

Calculate the curl of electric field $\mathbf{E}$ if the corresponding magnetic field is constant field $\mathbf{B}(t) = \langle 1, -4, 2 \rangle$.

Solution

Since the magnetic field does not change with respect to time, $-\frac{\partial \mathbf{B}}{\partial t} = \mathbf{0}$. By Faraday's law, the curl of the electric field is therefore also zero.

Analysis

A consequence of Faraday's law is that the curl of the electric field corresponding to a constant magnetic field is always zero.

6.64 Calculate the curl of electric field **E** if the corresponding magnetic field is $\mathbf{B}(t) = \langle tx, ty, -2tz \rangle$, $0 \le t < \infty$.

Notice that the curl of the electric field does not change over time, although the magnetic field does change over time.

6.7 EXERCISES

For the following exercises, without using Stokes' theorem, calculate directly both the flux of $\text{curl}\,\mathbf{F} \cdot \mathbf{N}$ over the given surface and the circulation integral around its boundary, assuming all boundaries are oriented clockwise as viewed from above.

326. $\mathbf{F}(x, y, z) = y^2\mathbf{i} + z^2\mathbf{j} + x^2\mathbf{k};$ S is the first-octant portion of plane $x + y + z = 1.$

327. $\mathbf{F}(x, y, z) = z\mathbf{i} + x\mathbf{j} + y\mathbf{k};$ S is hemisphere $z = \left(a^2 - x^2 - y^2\right)^{1/2}.$

328. $\mathbf{F}(x, y, z) = y^2\mathbf{i} + 2x\mathbf{j} + 5\mathbf{k};$ S is hemisphere $z = \left(4 - x^2 - y^2\right)^{1/2}.$

329. $\mathbf{F}(x, y, z) = z\mathbf{i} + 2x\mathbf{j} + 3y\mathbf{k};$ S is upper hemisphere $z = \sqrt{9 - x^2 - y^2}.$

330. $\mathbf{F}(x, y, z) = (x + 2z)\mathbf{i} + (y - x)\mathbf{j} + (z - y)\mathbf{k};$ S is a triangular region with vertices (3, 0, 0), (0, 3/2, 0), and (0, 0, 3).

331. $\mathbf{F}(x, y, z) = 2y\mathbf{i} - 6z\mathbf{j} + 3x\mathbf{k};$ S is a portion of paraboloid $z = 4 - x^2 - y^2$ and is above the xy-plane.

For the following exercises, use Stokes' theorem to evaluate $\iint_S (\text{curl}\,\mathbf{F} \cdot \mathbf{N})dS$ for the vector fields and surface.

332. $\mathbf{F}(x, y, z) = xy\mathbf{i} - z\mathbf{j}$ and S is the surface of the cube $0 \le x \le 1, 0 \le y \le 1, 0 \le z \le 1,$ except for the face where $z = 0,$ and using the outward unit normal vector.

333. $\mathbf{F}(x, y, z) = xy\mathbf{i} + x^2\mathbf{j} + z^2\mathbf{k};$ and C is the intersection of paraboloid $z = x^2 + y^2$ and plane $z = y,$ and using the outward normal vector.

334. $\mathbf{F}(x, y, z) = 4y\mathbf{i} + z\mathbf{j} + 2y\mathbf{k}$ and C is the intersection of sphere $x^2 + y^2 + z^2 = 4$ with plane $z = 0,$ and using the outward normal vector

335. Use Stokes' theorem to evaluate $\int_C \left[2xy^2 z\,dx + 2x^2 yz\,dy + \left(x^2 y^2 - 2z\right)dz\right],$ where C is the curve given by $x = \cos t,\ y = \sin t,\ z = \sin t,\ 0 \le t \le 2\pi,$ traversed in the direction of increasing t.

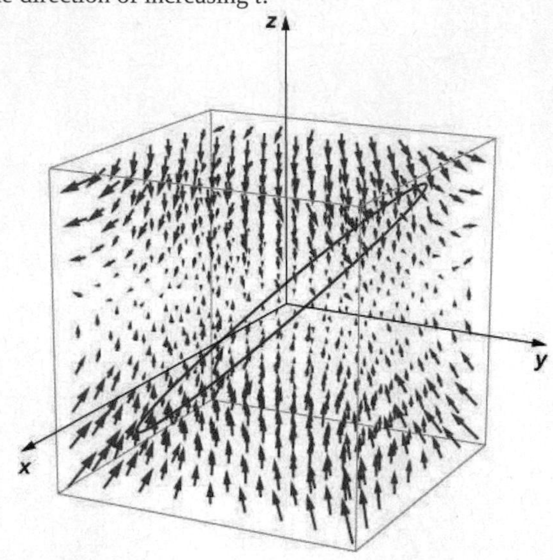

336. **[T]** Use a computer algebraic system (CAS) and Stokes' theorem to approximate line integral $\int_C (y\,dx + z\,dy + x\,dz),$ where C is the intersection of plane $x + y = 2$ and surface $x^2 + y^2 + z^2 = 2(x + y),$ traversed counterclockwise viewed from the origin.

337. **[T]** Use a CAS and Stokes' theorem to approximate line integral $\int_C (3y\,dx + 2z\,dy - 5x\,dz),$ where C is the intersection of the xy-plane and hemisphere $z = \sqrt{1 - x^2 - y^2},$ traversed counterclockwise viewed from the top—that is, from the positive z-axis toward the xy-plane.

338. **[T]** Use a CAS and Stokes' theorem to approximate line integral $\int_C [(1 + y)z\,dx + (1 + z)x\,dy + (1 + x)y\,dz],$ where C is a triangle with vertices $(1, 0, 0),$ $(0, 1, 0),$ and $(0, 0, 1)$ oriented counterclockwise.

339. Use Stokes' theorem to evaluate $\iint_S \text{curl}\,\mathbf{F} \cdot d\mathbf{S},$ where $\mathbf{F}(x, y, z) = e^{xy}\cos z\mathbf{i} + x^2 z\mathbf{j} + xy\mathbf{k},$ and S is half of sphere $x = \sqrt{1 - y^2 - z^2},$ oriented out toward the positive x-axis.

340. **[T]** Use a CAS and Stokes' theorem to evaluate $\iint_S (\text{curl } \mathbf{F} \cdot \mathbf{N})dS,$ where $\mathbf{F}(x, y, z) = x^2 y\mathbf{i} + xy^2 \mathbf{j} + z^3 \mathbf{k}$ and C is the curve of the intersection of plane $3x + 2y + z = 6$ and cylinder $x^2 + y^2 = 4,$ oriented clockwise when viewed from above.

341. **[T]** Use a CAS and Stokes' theorem to evaluate $\iint\limits_S \text{curl } \mathbf{F} \cdot d\mathbf{S},$ where $\mathbf{F}(x, y, z) = \left(\sin(y + z) - yx^2 - \frac{y^3}{3}\right)\mathbf{i} + x\cos(y + z)\mathbf{j} + \cos(2y)\mathbf{k}$ and S consists of the top and the four sides but not the bottom of the cube with vertices $(\pm 1, \pm 1, \pm 1),$ oriented outward.

342. **[T]** Use a CAS and Stokes' theorem to evaluate $\iint\limits_S \text{curl } \mathbf{F} \cdot d\mathbf{S},$ where $\mathbf{F}(x, y, z) = z^2 \mathbf{i} - 3xy\mathbf{j} + x^3 y^3 \mathbf{k}$ and S is the top part of $z = 5 - x^2 - y^2$ above plane $z = 1,$ and S is oriented upward.

343. Use Stokes' theorem to evaluate $\iint_S (\text{curl } \mathbf{F} \cdot \mathbf{N})dS,$ where $\mathbf{F}(x, y, z) = z^2 \mathbf{i} + y^2 \mathbf{j} + x\mathbf{k}$ and S is a triangle with vertices (1, 0, 0), (0, 1, 0) and (0, 0, 1) with counterclockwise orientation.

344. Use Stokes' theorem to evaluate line integral $\int\limits_C (zdx + xdy + ydz),$ where C is a triangle with vertices (3, 0, 0), (0, 0, 2), and (0, 6, 0) traversed in the given order.

345. Use Stokes' theorem to evaluate $\int\limits_C \left(\frac{1}{2}y^2\, dx + zdy + xdz\right),$ where C is the curve of intersection of plane $x + z = 1$ and ellipsoid $x^2 + 2y^2 + z^2 = 1,$ oriented clockwise from the origin.

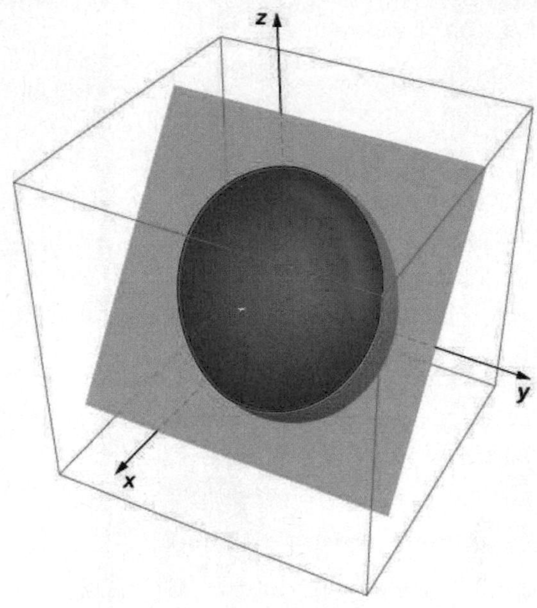

346. Use Stokes' theorem to evaluate $\iint_S (\text{curl } \mathbf{F} \cdot \mathbf{N})dS,$ where $\mathbf{F}(x, y, z) = x\mathbf{i} + y^2 \mathbf{j} + ze^{xy} \mathbf{k}$ and S is the part of surface $z = 1 - x^2 - 2y^2$ with $z \geq 0,$ oriented counterclockwise.

347. Use Stokes' theorem for vector field $\mathbf{F}(x, y, z) = z\mathbf{i} + 3x\mathbf{j} + 2z\mathbf{k}$ where S is surface $z = 1 - x^2 - 2y^2, z \geq 0,$ C is boundary circle $x^2 + y^2 = 1,$ and S is oriented in the positive z-direction.

348. Use Stokes' theorem for vector field $\mathbf{F}(x, y, z) = -\frac{3}{2}y^2 \mathbf{i} - 2xy\mathbf{j} + yz\mathbf{k},$ where S is that part of the surface of plane $x + y + z = 1$ contained within triangle C with vertices (1, 0, 0), (0, 1, 0), and (0, 0, 1), traversed counterclockwise as viewed from above.

349. A certain closed path C in plane $2x + 2y + z = 1$ is known to project onto unit circle $x^2 + y^2 = 1$ in the xy-plane. Let c be a constant and let $\mathbf{R}(x, y, z) = x\mathbf{i} + y\mathbf{j} + z\mathbf{k}.$ Use Stokes' theorem to evaluate $\int_C (c\mathbf{k} \times \mathbf{R}) \cdot d\mathbf{S}.$

350. Use Stokes' theorem and let C be the boundary of surface $z = x^2 + y^2$ with $0 \le x \le 2$ and $0 \le y \le 1$, oriented with upward facing normal. Define $\mathbf{F}(x, y, z) = \left[\sin(x^3) + xz\right]\mathbf{i} + (x - yz)\mathbf{j} + \cos(z^4)\mathbf{k}$ and evaluate $\int_C \mathbf{F} \cdot d\mathbf{S}$.

351. Let S be hemisphere $x^2 + y^2 + z^2 = 4$ with $z \ge 0$, oriented upward. Let $\mathbf{F}(x, y, z) = x^2 e^{yz}\mathbf{i} + y^2 e^{xz}\mathbf{j} + z^2 e^{xy}\mathbf{k}$ be a vector field. Use Stokes' theorem to evaluate $\iint_S \text{curl}\, \mathbf{F} \cdot d\mathbf{S}$.

352. Let $\mathbf{F}(x, y, z) = xy\mathbf{i} + \left(e^{z^2} + y\right)\mathbf{j} + (x + y)\mathbf{k}$ and let S be the graph of function $y = \frac{x^2}{9} + \frac{z^2}{9} - 1$ with $z \le 0$ oriented so that the normal vector S has a positive y component. Use Stokes' theorem to compute integral $\iint_S \text{curl}\, \mathbf{F} \cdot d\mathbf{S}$.

353. Use Stokes' theorem to evaluate $\oint \mathbf{F} \cdot d\mathbf{S}$, where $\mathbf{F}(x, y, z) = y\mathbf{i} + z\mathbf{j} + x\mathbf{k}$ and C is a triangle with vertices $(0, 0, 0)$, $(2, 0, 0)$ and $(0, -2, 2)$ oriented counterclockwise when viewed from above.

354. Use the surface integral in Stokes' theorem to calculate the circulation of field $\mathbf{F}$, $\mathbf{F}(x, y, z) = x^2 y^3\mathbf{i} + \mathbf{j} + z\mathbf{k}$ around C, which is the intersection of cylinder $x^2 + y^2 = 4$ and hemisphere $x^2 + y^2 + z^2 = 16$, $z \ge 0$, oriented counterclockwise when viewed from above.

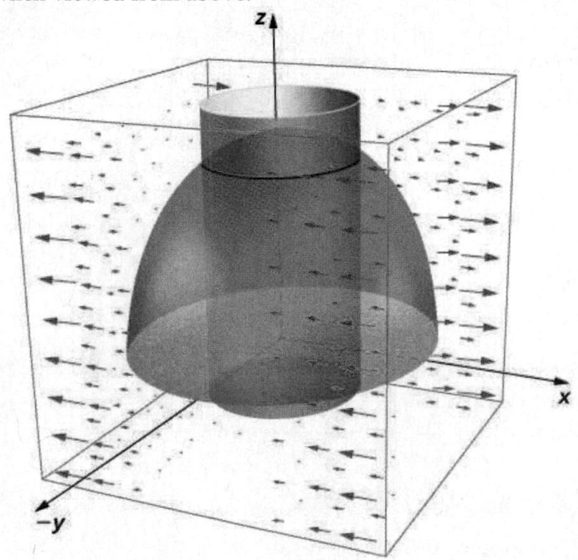

355. Use Stokes' theorem to compute $\iint_S \text{curl}\, \mathbf{F} \cdot d\mathbf{S}$, where $\mathbf{F}(x, y, z) = \mathbf{i} + xy^2\mathbf{j} + xy^2\mathbf{k}$ and S is a part of plane $y + z = 2$ inside cylinder $x^2 + y^2 = 1$ and oriented counterclockwise.

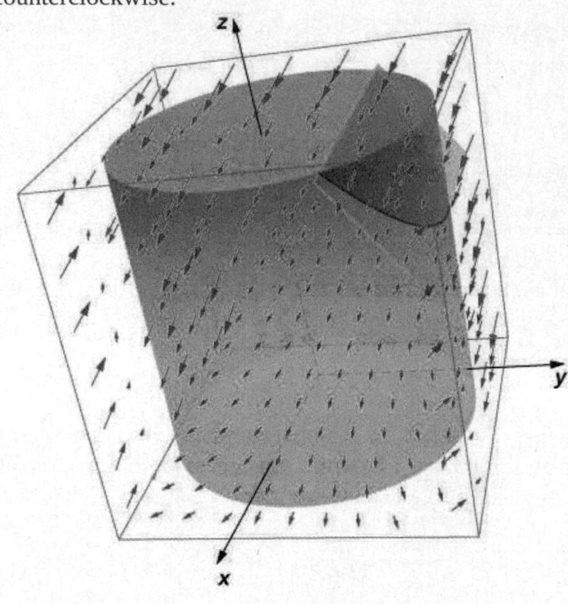

356. Use Stokes' theorem to evaluate $\iint_S \text{curl}\, \mathbf{F} \cdot d\mathbf{S}$, where $\mathbf{F}(x, y, z) = -y^2\mathbf{i} + x\mathbf{j} + z^2\mathbf{k}$ and S is the part of plane $x + y + z = 1$ in the positive octant and oriented counterclockwise $x \ge 0, y \ge 0, z \ge 0$.

357. Let $\mathbf{F}(x, y, z) = xy\mathbf{i} + 2z\mathbf{j} - 2y\mathbf{k}$ and let C be the intersection of plane $x + z = 5$ and cylinder $x^2 + y^2 = 9$, which is oriented counterclockwise when viewed from the top. Compute the line integral of $\mathbf{F}$ over C using Stokes' theorem.

358. **[T]** Use a CAS and let $\mathbf{F}(x, y, z) = xy^2\mathbf{i} + (yz - x)\mathbf{j} + e^{yxz}\mathbf{k}$. Use Stokes' theorem to compute the surface integral of curl $\mathbf{F}$ over surface S with inward orientation consisting of cube $[0, 1] \times [0, 1] \times [0, 1]$ with the right side missing.

359. Let S be ellipsoid $\frac{x^2}{4} + \frac{y^2}{9} + z^2 = 1$ oriented counterclockwise and let $\mathbf{F}$ be a vector field with component functions that have continuous partial derivatives.

360. Let S be the part of paraboloid $z = 9 - x^2 - y^2$ with $z \ge 0$. Verify Stokes' theorem for vector field $\mathbf{F}(x, y, z) = 3z\mathbf{i} + 4x\mathbf{j} + 2y\mathbf{k}$.

361. **[T]** Use a CAS and Stokes' theorem to evaluate $\oint_C \mathbf{F} \cdot d\mathbf{S}$, if $\mathbf{F}(x, y, z) = (3z - \sin x)\mathbf{i} + (x^2 + e^y)\mathbf{j} + (y^3 - \cos z)\mathbf{k}$, where C is the curve given by $x = \cos t,\ y = \sin t,\ z = 1;\ 0 \le t \le 2\pi$.

362. **[T]** Use a CAS and Stokes' theorem to evaluate $\mathbf{F}(x, y, z) = 2y\mathbf{i} + e^z\mathbf{j} - \arctan x\mathbf{k}$ with S as a portion of paraboloid $z = 4 - x^2 - y^2$ cut off by the xy-plane oriented counterclockwise.

363. **[T]** Use a CAS to evaluate $\iint_S \text{curl}(\mathbf{F}) \cdot d\mathbf{S}$, where $\mathbf{F}(x, y, z) = 2z\mathbf{i} + 3x\mathbf{j} + 5y\mathbf{k}$ and **S** is the surface parametrically by $\mathbf{r}(r, \theta) = r\cos\theta\mathbf{i} + r\sin\theta\mathbf{j} + (4 - r^2)\mathbf{k}$ $(0 \le \theta \le 2\pi, 0 \le r \le 3)$.

364. Let S be paraboloid $z = a(1 - x^2 - y^2)$, for $z \ge 0$, where $a > 0$ is a real number. Let $\mathbf{F} = \langle x - y, y + z, z - x \rangle$. For what value(s) of a (if any) does $\iint_S (\nabla \times \mathbf{F}) \cdot \mathbf{n}dS$ have its maximum value?

For the following application exercises, the goal is to evaluate $A = \iint_S (\nabla \times \mathbf{F}) \cdot \mathbf{n}dS$, where $\mathbf{F} = \langle xz, -xz, xy \rangle$ and S is the upper half of ellipsoid $x^2 + y^2 + 8z^2 = 1$, where $z \ge 0$.

365. Evaluate a surface integral over a more convenient surface to find the value of A.

366. Evaluate A using a line integral.

367. Take paraboloid $z = x^2 + y^2$, for $0 \le z \le 4$, and slice it with plane $y = 0$. Let S be the surface that remains for $y \ge 0$, including the planar surface in the xz-plane. Let C be the semicircle and line segment that bounded the cap of S in plane $z = 4$ with counterclockwise orientation. Let $\mathbf{F} = \langle 2z + y, 2x + z, 2y + x \rangle$. Evaluate $\iint_S (\nabla \times \mathbf{F}) \cdot \mathbf{n}dS$.

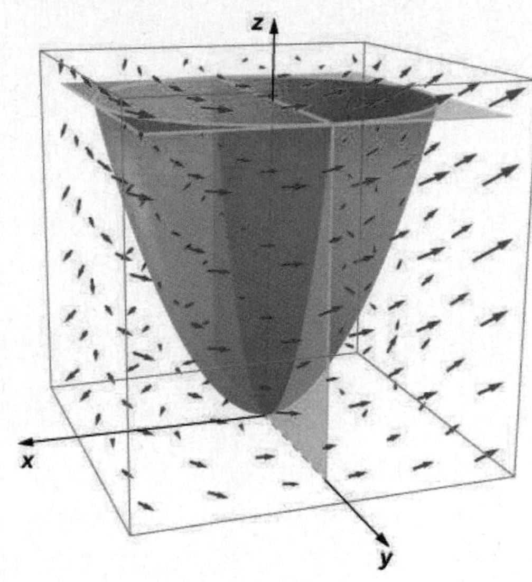

For the following exercises, let S be the disk enclosed by curve $C : \mathbf{r}(t) = \langle \cos\varphi\cos t, \sin t, \sin\varphi\cos t \rangle$, for $0 \le t \le 2\pi$, where $0 \le \varphi \le \frac{\pi}{2}$ is a fixed angle.

368. What is the length of C in terms of φ?

369. What is the circulation of C of vector field $\mathbf{F} = \langle -y, -z, x \rangle$ as a function of φ?

370. For what value of φ is the circulation a maximum?

371. Circle C in plane $x + y + z = 8$ has radius 4 and center (2, 3, 3). Evaluate $\oint_C \mathbf{F} \cdot d\mathbf{r}$ for $F = \langle 0, -z, 2y \rangle$, where C has a counterclockwise orientation when viewed from above.

372. Velocity field $\mathbf{v} = \langle 0, 1 - x^2, 0 \rangle$, for $|x| \le 1$ and $|z| \le 1$, represents a horizontal flow in the y-direction. Compute the curl of **v** in a clockwise rotation.

373. Evaluate integral $\iint_S (\nabla \times \mathbf{F}) \cdot \mathbf{n}dS$, where $\mathbf{F} = -xz\mathbf{i} + yz\mathbf{j} + xye^z\mathbf{k}$ and S is the cap of paraboloid $z = 5 - x^2 - y^2$ above plane $z = 3$, and **n** points in the positive z-direction on S.

For the following exercises, use Stokes' theorem to find the circulation of the following vector fields around any smooth, simple closed curve C.

374. $\mathbf{F} = \nabla(x \sin ye^z)$

375. $\mathbf{F} = \langle y^2 z^3, z2xyz^3, 3xy^2 z^2 \rangle$

6.8 | The Divergence Theorem

Learning Objectives

6.8.1 Explain the meaning of the divergence theorem.
6.8.2 Use the divergence theorem to calculate the flux of a vector field.
6.8.3 Apply the divergence theorem to an electrostatic field.

We have examined several versions of the Fundamental Theorem of Calculus in higher dimensions that relate the integral around an oriented boundary of a domain to a "derivative" of that entity on the oriented domain. In this section, we state the divergence theorem, which is the final theorem of this type that we will study. The divergence theorem has many uses in physics; in particular, the divergence theorem is used in the field of partial differential equations to derive equations modeling heat flow and conservation of mass. We use the theorem to calculate flux integrals and apply it to electrostatic fields.

Overview of Theorems

Before examining the divergence theorem, it is helpful to begin with an overview of the versions of the Fundamental Theorem of Calculus we have discussed:

1. **The Fundamental Theorem of Calculus**:

$$\int_a^b f'(x)dx = f(b) - f(a).$$

This theorem relates the integral of derivative f' over line segment $[a, b]$ along the x-axis to a difference of f evaluated on the boundary.

2. **The Fundamental Theorem for Line Integrals**:

$$\int_C \nabla f \cdot d\mathbf{r} = f(P_1) - f(P_0),$$

where P_0 is the initial point of C and P_1 is the terminal point of C. The Fundamental Theorem for Line Integrals allows path C to be a path in a plane or in space, not just a line segment on the x-axis. If we think of the gradient as a derivative, then this theorem relates an integral of derivative ∇f over path C to a difference of f evaluated on the boundary of C.

3. **Green's theorem, circulation form**:

$$\iint_D (Q_x - P_y)dA = \int_C \mathbf{F} \cdot d\mathbf{r}.$$

Since $Q_x - P_y = \text{curl}\,\mathbf{F} \cdot \mathbf{k}$ and curl is a derivative of sorts, Green's theorem relates the integral of derivative curl**F** over planar region D to an integral of **F** over the boundary of D.

4. **Green's theorem, flux form**:

$$\iint_D (P_x + Q_y)dA = \int_C \mathbf{F} \cdot \mathbf{N}ds.$$

Since $P_x + Q_y = \text{div}\,\mathbf{F}$ and divergence is a derivative of sorts, the flux form of Green's theorem relates the integral of derivative div**F** over planar region D to an integral of **F** over the boundary of D.

5. **Stokes' theorem**:

$$\iint_S \text{curl}\,\mathbf{F} \cdot d\mathbf{S} = \int_C \mathbf{F} \cdot d\mathbf{r}.$$

If we think of the curl as a derivative of sorts, then Stokes' theorem relates the integral of derivative curl**F** over surface S (not necessarily planar) to an integral of $\mathbf{F}$ over the boundary of S.

Stating the Divergence Theorem

The divergence theorem follows the general pattern of these other theorems. If we think of divergence as a derivative of sorts, then the **divergence theorem** relates a triple integral of derivative div$\mathbf{F}$ over a solid to a flux integral of $\mathbf{F}$ over the boundary of the solid. More specifically, the divergence theorem relates a flux integral of vector field $\mathbf{F}$ over a closed surface S to a triple integral of the divergence of $\mathbf{F}$ over the solid enclosed by S.

Theorem 6.20: The Divergence Theorem

Let S be a piecewise, smooth closed surface that encloses solid E in space. Assume that S is oriented outward, and let $\mathbf{F}$ be a vector field with continuous partial derivatives on an open region containing E (**Figure 6.87**). Then

$$\iiint_E \text{div}\,\mathbf{F}dV = \iint_S \mathbf{F}\cdot d\mathbf{S}. \tag{6.24}$$

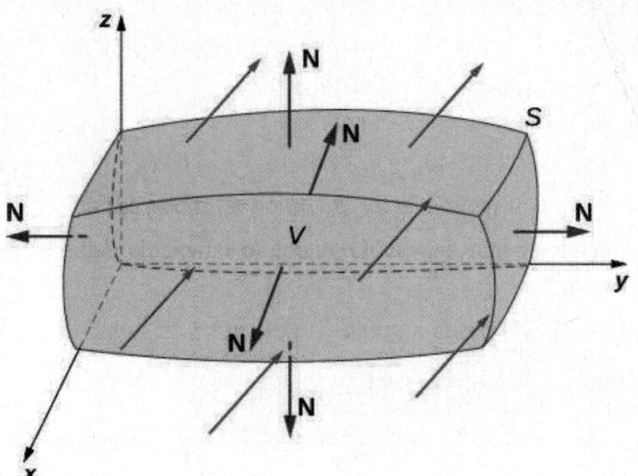

Figure 6.87 The divergence theorem relates a flux integral across a closed surface S to a triple integral over solid E enclosed by the surface.

Recall that the flux form of Green's theorem states that $\iint_D \text{div}\,\mathbf{F}dA = \int_C \mathbf{F}\cdot\mathbf{N}ds.$ Therefore, the divergence theorem is a version of Green's theorem in one higher dimension.

The proof of the divergence theorem is beyond the scope of this text. However, we look at an informal proof that gives a general feel for why the theorem is true, but does not prove the theorem with full rigor. This explanation follows the informal explanation given for why Stokes' theorem is true.

Proof

Let B be a small box with sides parallel to the coordinate planes inside E (**Figure 6.88**). Let the center of B have coordinates (x, y, z) and suppose the edge lengths are $\Delta x, \Delta y,$ and Δz (**Figure 6.88**(b)). The normal vector out of the top of the box is $\mathbf{k}$ and the normal vector out of the bottom of the box is $-\mathbf{k}$. The dot product of $\mathbf{F} = \langle P, Q, R \rangle$ with $\mathbf{k}$ is R and the dot product with $-\mathbf{k}$ is $-R$. The area of the top of the box (and the bottom of the box) ΔS is $\Delta x\Delta y$.

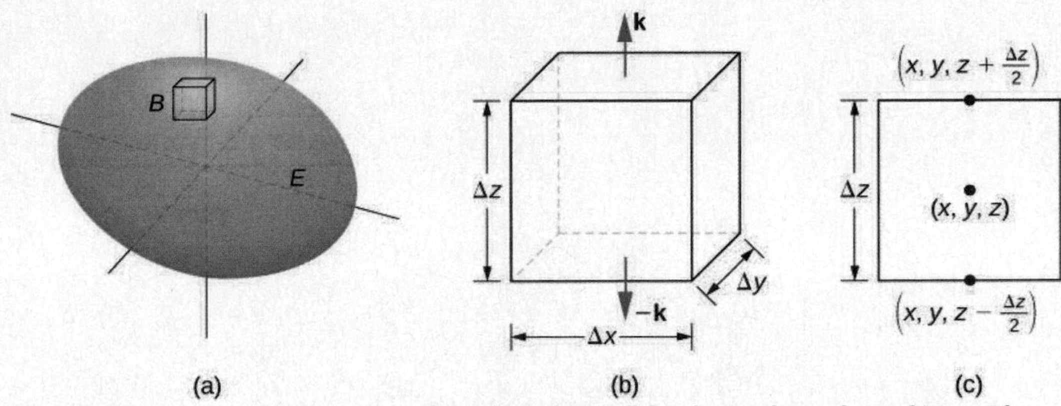

Figure 6.88 (a) A small box B inside surface E has sides parallel to the coordinate planes. (b) Box B has side lengths $\Delta x,\ \Delta y,$ and Δz (c) If we look at the side view of B, we see that, since $(x,\ y,\ z)$ is the center of the box, to get to the top of the box we must travel a vertical distance of $\Delta z/2$ up from $(x,\ y,\ z)$. Similarly, to get to the bottom of the box we must travel a distance $\Delta z/2$ down from $(x,\ y,\ z)$.

The flux out of the top of the box can be approximated by $R\left(x,\ y,\ z+\frac{\Delta z}{2}\right)\Delta x\Delta y$ (**Figure 6.88**(c)) and the flux out of the bottom of the box is $-R\left(x,\ y,\ z-\frac{\Delta z}{2}\right)\Delta x\Delta y.$ If we denote the difference between these values as $\Delta R,$ then the net flux in the vertical direction can be approximated by $\Delta R\Delta x\Delta y.$ However,

$$\Delta R\Delta x\Delta y=\left(\frac{\Delta R}{\Delta z}\right)\Delta x\Delta y\Delta z\approx\left(\frac{\partial R}{\partial z}\right)\Delta V.$$

Therefore, the net flux in the vertical direction can be approximated by $\left(\frac{\partial R}{\partial z}\right)\Delta V.$ Similarly, the net flux in the x-direction can be approximated by $\left(\frac{\partial P}{\partial x}\right)\Delta V$ and the net flux in the y-direction can be approximated by $\left(\frac{\partial Q}{\partial y}\right)\Delta V.$ Adding the fluxes in all three directions gives an approximation of the total flux out of the box:

$$\text{Total flux}\approx\left(\frac{\partial P}{\partial x}+\frac{\partial Q}{\partial y}+\frac{\partial R}{\partial z}\right)\Delta V=\text{div}\,\mathbf{F}\Delta V.$$

This approximation becomes arbitrarily close to the value of the total flux as the volume of the box shrinks to zero.

The sum of $\text{div}\,\mathbf{F}\Delta V$ over all the small boxes approximating E is approximately $\iiint_E \text{div}\,\mathbf{F}dV.$ On the other hand, the sum of $\text{div}\,\mathbf{F}\Delta V$ over all the small boxes approximating E is the sum of the fluxes over all these boxes. Just as in the informal proof of Stokes' theorem, adding these fluxes over all the boxes results in the cancelation of a lot of the terms. If an approximating box shares a face with another approximating box, then the flux over one face is the negative of the flux over the shared face of the adjacent box. These two integrals cancel out. When adding up all the fluxes, the only flux integrals that survive are the integrals over the faces approximating the boundary of E. As the volumes of the approximating boxes shrink to zero, this approximation becomes arbitrarily close to the flux over S.

□

Example 6.77

Verifying the Divergence Theorem

Verify the divergence theorem for vector field $\mathbf{F}=\langle x-y,\ x+z,\ z-y\rangle$ and surface S that consists of cone $x^2+y^2=z^2,\ 0\le z\le 1,$ and the circular top of the cone (see the following figure). Assume this surface is positively oriented.

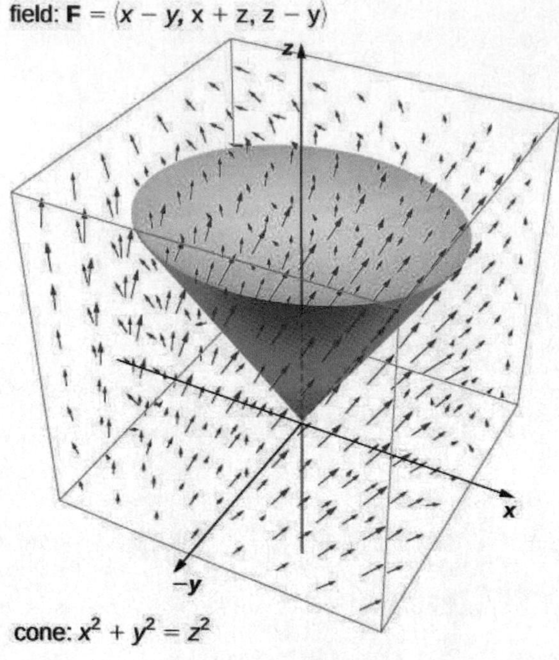

Solution

Let E be the solid cone enclosed by S. To verify the theorem for this example, we show that $\iiint_E \text{div}\,\mathbf{F}dV = \iint_S \mathbf{F}\cdot d\mathbf{S}$ by calculating each integral separately.

To compute the triple integral, note that $\text{div}\,\mathbf{F} = P_x + Q_y + R_z = 2,$ and therefore the triple integral is

$$\begin{aligned}\iiint_E \text{div}\,\mathbf{F}dV &= 2\iiint_E dV \\ &= 2(\text{volume of } E).\end{aligned}$$

The volume of a right circular cone is given by $\pi r^2\frac{h}{3}$. In this case, $h = r = 1$. Therefore,

$$\iiint_E \text{div}\,\mathbf{F}dV = 2(\text{volume of } E) = \frac{2\pi}{3}.$$

To compute the flux integral, first note that S is piecewise smooth; S can be written as a union of smooth surfaces. Therefore, we break the flux integral into two pieces: one flux integral across the circular top of the cone and one flux integral across the remaining portion of the cone. Call the circular top S_1 and the portion under the top S_2.

We start by calculating the flux across the circular top of the cone. Notice that S_1 has parameterization

$$\mathbf{r}(u, v) = \langle u\cos v, u\sin v, 1\rangle, 0 \le u \le 1, 0 \le v \le 2\pi.$$

Then, the tangent vectors are $\mathbf{t}_u = \langle \cos v, \sin v, 0\rangle$ and $\mathbf{t}_v = \langle -u\cos v, u\sin v, 0\rangle$. Therefore, the flux across S_1 is

$$\begin{aligned}\iint_{S_1} \mathbf{F} \cdot d\mathbf{S} &= \int_0^1 \int_0^{2\pi} \mathbf{F}(\mathbf{r}(u,\, v)) \cdot (\mathbf{t}_u \times \mathbf{t}_v) dA \\ &= \int_0^1 \int_0^{2\pi} \langle\, u \cos v - u \sin v,\, u \cos v + 1,\, 1 - u \sin v \,\rangle \cdot \langle\, 0,\, 0,\, u \,\rangle\, dvdu \\ &= \int_0^1 \int_0^{2\pi} u - u^2 \sin v\, dvdu = \pi.\end{aligned}$$

We now calculate the flux over S_2. A parameterization of this surface is

$$\mathbf{r}(u,\, v) = \langle\, u \cos v,\, u \sin v,\, u \,\rangle,\ 0 \le u \le 1,\ 0 \le v \le 2\pi.$$

The tangent vectors are $\mathbf{t}_u = \langle\, \cos v,\, \sin v,\, 1 \,\rangle$ and $\mathbf{t}_v = \langle\, -u \sin v,\, u \cos v,\, 0 \,\rangle$, so the cross product is

$$\mathbf{t}_u \times \mathbf{t}_v = \langle\, -u \cos v,\, -u \sin v,\, u \,\rangle.$$

Notice that the negative signs on the x and y components induce the negative (or inward) orientation of the cone. Since the surface is positively oriented, we use vector $\mathbf{t}_v \times \mathbf{t}_u = \langle\, u \cos v,\, u \sin v,\, -u \,\rangle$ in the flux integral. The flux across S_2 is then

$$\begin{aligned}\iint_{S_2} \mathbf{F} \cdot d\mathbf{S} &= \int_0^1 \int_0^{2\pi} \mathbf{F}(\mathbf{r}(u,\, v)) \cdot (\mathbf{t}_v \times \mathbf{t}_u) dA \\ &= \int_0^1 \int_0^{2\pi} \langle\, u \cos v - u \sin v,\, u \cos v + u,\, u - \sin v \,\rangle \cdot \langle\, u \cos v,\, u \sin v,\, -u \,\rangle \\ &= \int_0^1 \int_0^{2\pi} u^2 \cos^2 v + 2u^2 \sin v - u^2\, dvdu = -\tfrac{\pi}{3}.\end{aligned}$$

The total flux across S is

$$\iint_{S_2} \mathbf{F} \cdot d\mathbf{S} = \iint_{S_1} \mathbf{F} \cdot d\mathbf{S} + \iint_{S_2} \mathbf{F} \cdot d\mathbf{S} = \tfrac{2\pi}{3} = \iiint_E \text{div}\, \mathbf{F} dV,$$

and we have verified the divergence theorem for this example.

6.65 Verify the divergence theorem for vector field $\mathbf{F}(x,\, y,\, z) = \langle\, x + y + z,\, y,\, 2x - y \,\rangle$ and surface S given by the cylinder $x^2 + y^2 = 1,\ 0 \le z \le 3$ plus the circular top and bottom of the cylinder. Assume that S is positively oriented.

Recall that the divergence of continuous field $\mathbf{F}$ at point P is a measure of the "outflowing-ness" of the field at P. If $\mathbf{F}$ represents the velocity field of a fluid, then the divergence can be thought of as the rate per unit volume of the fluid flowing out less the rate per unit volume flowing in. The divergence theorem confirms this interpretation. To see this, let P be a point and let B_r be a ball of small radius r centered at P (**Figure 6.89**). Let S_r be the boundary sphere of B_r. Since the radius is small and $\mathbf{F}$ is continuous, $\text{div}\, \mathbf{F}(Q) \approx \text{div}\, \mathbf{F}(P)$ for all other points Q in the ball. Therefore, the flux across S_r can be approximated using the divergence theorem:

$$\iint_{S_r} \mathbf{F} \cdot d\mathbf{S} = \iiint_{B_r} \text{div}\, \mathbf{F} dV \approx \iiint_{B_r} \text{div}\, \mathbf{F}(P) dV.$$

Since $\text{div}\, \mathbf{F}(P)$ is a constant,

$$\iiint_{B_r} \text{div}\, \mathbf{F}(P) dV = \text{div}\, \mathbf{F}(P) V(B_r).$$

Therefore, flux $\iint_{S_r} \mathbf{F} \cdot d\mathbf{S}$ can be approximated by $\text{div}\,\mathbf{F}(P)V(B_r)$. This approximation gets better as the radius shrinks to zero, and therefore

$$\text{div}\,\mathbf{F}(P) = \lim_{r \to 0} \frac{1}{V(B_r)} \iint_{S_r} \mathbf{F} \cdot d\mathbf{S}.$$

This equation says that the divergence at *P* is the net rate of outward flux of the fluid per unit volume.

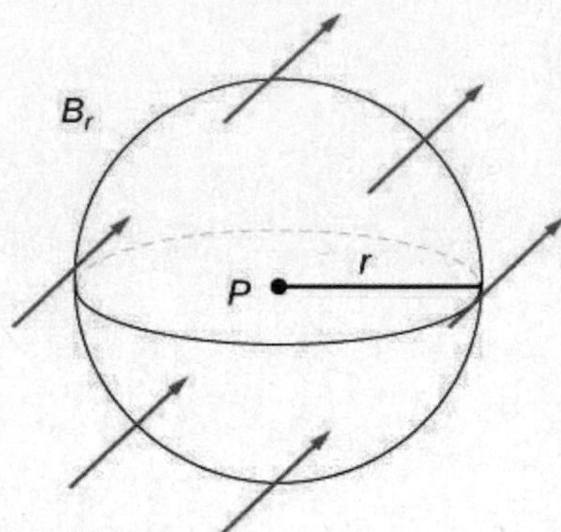

Figure 6.89 Ball B_r of small radius *r* centered at *P*.

Using the Divergence Theorem

The divergence theorem translates between the flux integral of closed surface *S* and a triple integral over the solid enclosed by *S*. Therefore, the theorem allows us to compute flux integrals or triple integrals that would ordinarily be difficult to compute by translating the flux integral into a triple integral and vice versa.

Example 6.78

Applying the Divergence Theorem

Calculate the surface integral $\iint_S \mathbf{F} \cdot d\mathbf{S}$, where *S* is cylinder $x^2 + y^2 = 1,\ 0 \le z \le 2$, including the circular top and bottom, and $\mathbf{F} = \left\langle \frac{x^3}{3} + yz,\ \frac{y^3}{3} - \sin(xz),\ z - x - y \right\rangle$.

Solution

We could calculate this integral without the divergence theorem, but the calculation is not straightforward because we would have to break the flux integral into three separate integrals: one for the top of the cylinder, one for the bottom, and one for the side. Furthermore, each integral would require parameterizing the corresponding surface, calculating tangent vectors and their cross product, and using **Equation 6.19**.

By contrast, the divergence theorem allows us to calculate the single triple integral $\iiint_E \text{div}\,\mathbf{F}dV$, where *E* is the solid enclosed by the cylinder. Using the divergence theorem and converting to cylindrical coordinates, we have

$$\begin{aligned} \iint_S \mathbf{F} \cdot d\mathbf{S} &= \iiint_E \text{div}\,\mathbf{F}\,dV \\ &= \iiint_E \left(x^2 + y^2 + 1\right) dV \\ &= \int_0^{2\pi} \int_0^1 \int_0^2 \left(r^2 + 1\right) r\,dz\,dr\,d\theta \\ &= \frac{3}{2} \int_0^{2\pi} d\theta = 3\pi. \end{aligned}$$

6.66 Use the divergence theorem to calculate flux integral $\iint_S \mathbf{F} \cdot d\mathbf{S},$ where S is the boundary of the box given by $0 \le x \le 2, 1 \le y \le 4, 0 \le z \le 1,$ and $\mathbf{F} = \langle x^2 + yz, y - z, 2x + 2y + 2z \rangle$ (see the following figure).

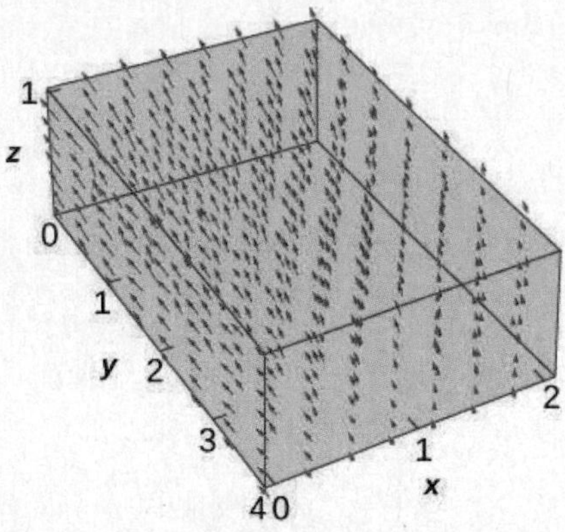

Example 6.79

Applying the Divergence Theorem

Let $\mathbf{v} = \langle -\frac{y}{z}, \frac{x}{z}, 0 \rangle$ be the velocity field of a fluid. Let C be the solid cube given by $1 \le x \le 4, 2 \le y \le 5, 1 \le z \le 4,$ and let S be the boundary of this cube (see the following figure). Find the flow rate of the fluid across S.

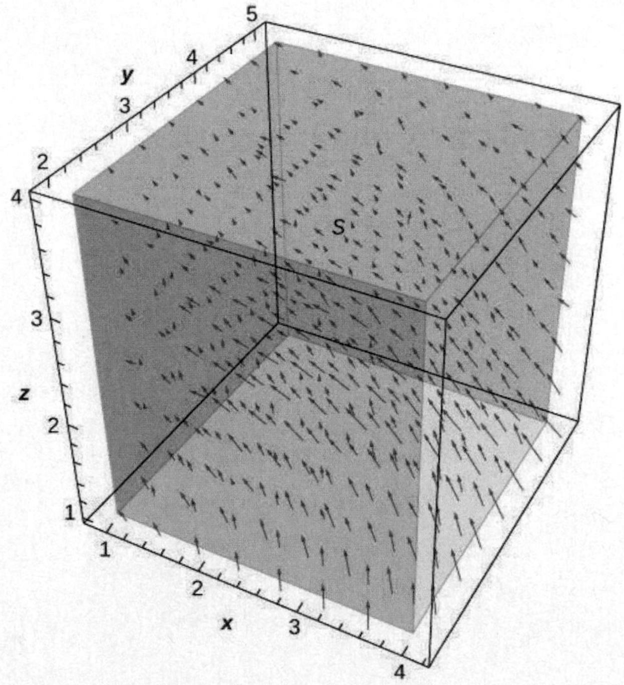

Figure 6.90 Vector field $\mathbf{v} = \langle -\frac{y}{z}, \frac{x}{z}, 0 \rangle$.

Solution

The flow rate of the fluid across S is $\iint_S \mathbf{v} \cdot d\mathbf{S}$. Before calculating this flux integral, let's discuss what the value of the integral should be. Based on **Figure 6.90**, we see that if we place this cube in the fluid (as long as the cube doesn't encompass the origin), then the rate of fluid entering the cube is the same as the rate of fluid exiting the cube. The field is rotational in nature and, for a given circle parallel to the *xy*-plane that has a center on the *z*-axis, the vectors along that circle are all the same magnitude. That is how we can see that the flow rate is the same entering and exiting the cube. The flow into the cube cancels with the flow out of the cube, and therefore the flow rate of the fluid across the cube should be zero.

To verify this intuition, we need to calculate the flux integral. Calculating the flux integral directly requires breaking the flux integral into six separate flux integrals, one for each face of the cube. We also need to find tangent vectors, compute their cross product, and use **Equation 6.19**. However, using the divergence theorem makes this calculation go much more quickly:

$$\begin{aligned}\iint_S \mathbf{v} \cdot d\mathbf{S} &= \iiint_C \operatorname{div}(\mathbf{v})dV \\ &= \iiint_C 0\, dV = 0.\end{aligned}$$

Therefore the flux is zero, as expected.

6.67 Let $\mathbf{v} = \langle \frac{x}{z}, \frac{y}{z}, 0 \rangle$ be the velocity field of a fluid. Let C be the solid cube given by $1 \le x \le 4,\ 2 \le y \le 5,\ 1 \le z \le 4,$ and let S be the boundary of this cube (see the following figure). Find the flow rate of the fluid across S.

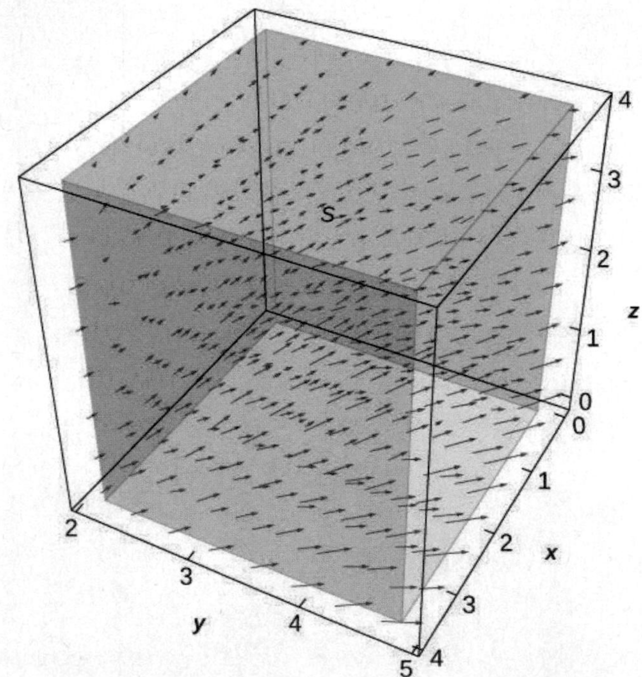

Example 6.79 illustrates a remarkable consequence of the divergence theorem. Let S be a piecewise, smooth closed surface and let $\mathbf{F}$ be a vector field defined on an open region containing the surface enclosed by S. If $\mathbf{F}$ has the form $\mathbf{F} = \langle f(y, z), g(x, z), h(x, y) \rangle$, then the divergence of $\mathbf{F}$ is zero. By the divergence theorem, the flux of $\mathbf{F}$ across S is also zero. This makes certain flux integrals incredibly easy to calculate. For example, suppose we wanted to calculate the flux integral $\iint_S \mathbf{F} \cdot d\mathbf{S}$ where S is a cube and

$$\mathbf{F} = \langle \sin(y)e^{yz}, x^2z^2, \cos(xy)e^{\sin x} \rangle .$$

Calculating the flux integral directly would be difficult, if not impossible, using techniques we studied previously. At the very least, we would have to break the flux integral into six integrals, one for each face of the cube. But, because the divergence of this field is zero, the divergence theorem immediately shows that the flux integral is zero.

We can now use the divergence theorem to justify the physical interpretation of divergence that we discussed earlier. Recall that if **F** is a continuous three-dimensional vector field and P is a point in the domain of **F**, then the divergence of **F** at P is a measure of the "outflowing-ness" of **F** at P. If **F** represents the velocity field of a fluid, then the divergence of **F** at P is a measure of the net flow rate out of point P (the flow of fluid out of P less the flow of fluid in to P). To see how the divergence theorem justifies this interpretation, let B_r be a ball of very small radius r with center P, and assume that B_r is in the domain of **F**. Furthermore, assume that B_r has a positive, outward orientation. Since the radius of B_r is small and **F** is continuous, the divergence of **F** is approximately constant on B_r. That is, if P' is any point in B_r, then $\text{div}\,\mathbf{F}(P) \approx \text{div}\,\mathbf{F}(P')$. Let S_r denote the boundary sphere of B_r. We can approximate the flux across S_r using the divergence theorem as follows:

$$\begin{aligned} \iint_{S_r} \mathbf{F} \cdot d\mathbf{S} &= \iiint_{B_r} \text{div}\,\mathbf{F}\,dV \\ &\approx \iiint_{B_r} \text{div}\,\mathbf{F}(P)dV \\ &= \text{div}\,\mathbf{F}(P)V(B_r). \end{aligned}$$

As we shrink the radius r to zero via a limit, the quantity $\text{div}\,\mathbf{F}(P)V(B_r)$ gets arbitrarily close to the flux. Therefore,

$$\text{div}\,\mathbf{F}(P) = \lim_{r \to 0} \frac{1}{V(B_r)} \iint_{S_r} \mathbf{F} \cdot d\mathbf{S}$$

and we can consider the divergence at P as measuring the net rate of outward flux per unit volume at P. Since "outflowing-ness" is an informal term for the net rate of outward flux per unit volume, we have justified the physical interpretation of divergence we discussed earlier, and we have used the divergence theorem to give this justification.

Application to Electrostatic Fields

The divergence theorem has many applications in physics and engineering. It allows us to write many physical laws in both an integral form and a differential form (in much the same way that Stokes' theorem allowed us to translate between an integral and differential form of Faraday's law). Areas of study such as fluid dynamics, electromagnetism, and quantum mechanics have equations that describe the conservation of mass, momentum, or energy, and the divergence theorem allows us to give these equations in both integral and differential forms.

One of the most common applications of the divergence theorem is to electrostatic fields. An important result in this subject is **Gauss' law**. This law states that if S is a closed surface in electrostatic field **E**, then the flux of **E** across S is the total charge enclosed by S (divided by an electric constant). We now use the divergence theorem to justify the special case of this law in which the electrostatic field is generated by a stationary point charge at the origin.

If (x, y, z) is a point in space, then the distance from the point to the origin is $r = \sqrt{x^2 + y^2 + z^2}$. Let $\mathbf{F}_r$ denote radial vector field $\mathbf{F}_r = \frac{1}{r^2} \langle \frac{x}{r}, \frac{y}{r}, \frac{z}{r} \rangle$. The vector at a given position in space points in the direction of unit radial vector $\langle \frac{x}{r}, \frac{y}{r}, \frac{z}{r} \rangle$ and is scaled by the quantity $1/r^2$. Therefore, the magnitude of a vector at a given point is inversely proportional to the square of the vector's distance from the origin. Suppose we have a stationary charge of q Coulombs at the origin, existing in a vacuum. The charge generates electrostatic field **E** given by

$$\mathbf{E} = \frac{q}{4\pi\varepsilon_0}\mathbf{F}_r,$$

where the approximation $\varepsilon_0 = 8.854 \times 10^{-12}$ farad (F)/m is an electric constant. (The constant ε_0 is a measure of the resistance encountered when forming an electric field in a vacuum.) Notice that **E** is a radial vector field similar to the gravitational field described in **Example 6.6**. The difference is that this field points outward whereas the gravitational field points inward. Because

$$\mathbf{E} = \frac{q}{4\pi\varepsilon_0}\mathbf{F}_r = \frac{q}{4\pi\varepsilon_0}\left(\frac{1}{r^2} \langle \frac{x}{r}, \frac{y}{r}, \frac{z}{r} \rangle\right),$$

we say that electrostatic fields obey an **inverse-square law**. That is, the electrostatic force at a given point is inversely proportional to the square of the distance from the source of the charge (which in this case is at the origin). Given this vector field, we show that the flux across closed surface S is zero if the charge is outside of S, and that the flux is q/ε_0 if the charge is inside of S. In other words, the flux across S is the charge inside the surface divided by constant ε_0. This is a special case of Gauss' law, and here we use the divergence theorem to justify this special case.

To show that the flux across S is the charge inside the surface divided by constant ε_0, we need two intermediate steps. First we show that the divergence of $\mathbf{F}_r$ is zero and then we show that the flux of $\mathbf{F}_r$ across any smooth surface S is either zero or 4π. We can then justify this special case of Gauss' law.

Example 6.80

The Divergence of $\mathbf{F}_r$ Is Zero

Verify that the divergence of $\mathbf{F}_r$ is zero where $\mathbf{F}_r$ is defined (away from the origin).

Solution

Since $r = \sqrt{x^2 + y^2 + z^2}$, the quotient rule gives us

$$\begin{aligned}\frac{\partial}{\partial x}\left(\frac{x}{r^3}\right) &= \frac{\partial}{\partial x}\left(\frac{x}{\left(x^2+y^2+z^2\right)^{3/2}}\right) \\ &= \frac{\left(x^2+y^2+z^2\right)^{3/2} - x\left[\frac{3}{2}\left(x^2+y^2+z^2\right)^{1/2} 2x\right]}{\left(x^2+y^2+z^2\right)^3} \\ &= \frac{r^3 - 3x^2 r}{r^6} = \frac{r^2 - 3x^2}{r^5}.\end{aligned}$$

Similarly,

$$\frac{\partial}{\partial y}\left(\frac{y}{r^3}\right) = \frac{r^2 - 3y^2}{r^5} \text{ and } \frac{\partial}{\partial z}\left(\frac{z}{r^3}\right) = \frac{r^2 - 3z^2}{r^5}.$$

Therefore,

$$\begin{aligned}\text{div}\,\mathbf{F}_r &= \frac{r^2 - 3x^2}{r^5} + \frac{r^2 - 3y^2}{r^5} + \frac{r^2 - 3z^2}{r^5} \\ &= \frac{3r^2 - 3\left(x^2+y^2+z^2\right)}{r^5} \\ &= \frac{3r^2 - 3r^2}{r^5} = 0.\end{aligned}$$

Notice that since the divergence of $\mathbf{F}_r$ is zero and $\mathbf{E}$ is $\mathbf{F}_r$ scaled by a constant, the divergence of electrostatic field $\mathbf{E}$ is also zero (except at the origin).

Theorem 6.21: Flux across a Smooth Surface

Let S be a connected, piecewise smooth closed surface and let $\mathbf{F}_r = \frac{1}{r^2}\left\langle \frac{x}{r}, \frac{y}{r}, \frac{z}{r}\right\rangle$. Then,

$$\iint_S \mathbf{F}_r \cdot d\mathbf{S} = \begin{cases} 0 & \text{if } S \text{ does not encompass the origin} \\ 4\pi & \text{if } S \text{ encompasses the origin.} \end{cases}$$

In other words, this theorem says that the flux of $\mathbf{F}_r$ across any piecewise smooth closed surface S depends only on whether the origin is inside of S.

Proof

The logic of this proof follows the logic of **Example 6.46**, only we use the divergence theorem rather than Green's theorem.

First, suppose that S does not encompass the origin. In this case, the solid enclosed by S is in the domain of $\mathbf{F}_r$, and since the divergence of $\mathbf{F}_r$ is zero, we can immediately apply the divergence theorem and find that $\iint_S \mathbf{F} \cdot d\mathbf{S}$ is zero.

Now suppose that S does encompass the origin. We cannot just use the divergence theorem to calculate the flux, because the field is not defined at the origin. Let S_a be a sphere of radius a inside of S centered at the origin. The outward normal vector field on the sphere, in spherical coordinates, is

$$\mathbf{t}_\phi \times \mathbf{t}_\theta = \langle a^2 \cos\theta \sin^2\phi, a^2 \sin\theta \sin^2\phi, a^2 \sin\phi \cos\phi \rangle$$

(see **Example 6.64**). Therefore, on the surface of the sphere, the dot product $\mathbf{F}_r \cdot \mathbf{N}$ (in spherical coordinates) is

$$\begin{aligned} \mathbf{F}_r \cdot \mathbf{N} &= \langle \frac{\sin\phi\cos\theta}{a^2}, \frac{\sin\phi\sin\theta}{a^2}, \frac{\cos\phi}{a^2} \rangle \cdot \langle a^2\cos\theta\sin^2\phi, a^2\sin\theta\sin^2\phi, a^2\sin\phi\cos\phi \rangle \\ &= \sin\phi(\langle \sin\phi\cos\theta, \sin\phi\sin\theta, \cos\phi \rangle \cdot \langle \sin\phi\cos\theta, \sin\phi\sin\theta, \cos\phi \rangle) \\ &= \sin\phi. \end{aligned}$$

The flux of $\mathbf{F}_r$ across S_a is

$$\iint_{S_a} \mathbf{F}_r \cdot \mathbf{N} dS = \int_0^{2\pi} \int_0^{\pi} \sin\phi \, d\phi \, d\theta = 4\pi.$$

Now, remember that we are interested in the flux across S, not necessarily the flux across S_a. To calculate the flux across S, let E be the solid between surfaces S_a and S. Then, the boundary of E consists of S_a and S. Denote this boundary by $S - S_a$ to indicate that S is oriented outward but now S_a is oriented inward. We would like to apply the divergence theorem to solid E. Notice that the divergence theorem, as stated, can't handle a solid such as E because E has a hole. However, the divergence theorem can be extended to handle solids with holes, just as Green's theorem can be extended to handle regions with holes. This allows us to use the divergence theorem in the following way. By the divergence theorem,

$$\begin{aligned} \iint_{S - S_a} \mathbf{F}_r \cdot d\mathbf{S} &= \iint_S \mathbf{F}_r \cdot d\mathbf{S} - \iint_{S_a} \mathbf{F}_r \cdot d\mathbf{S} \\ &= \iiint_E \operatorname{div}\mathbf{F}_r \, dV \\ &= \iiint_E 0 dV = 0. \end{aligned}$$

Therefore,

$$\iint_S \mathbf{F}_r \cdot d\mathbf{S} = \iint_{S_a} \mathbf{F}_r \cdot d\mathbf{S} = 4\pi,$$

and we have our desired result.

□

Now we return to calculating the flux across a smooth surface in the context of electrostatic field $\mathbf{E} = \frac{q}{4\pi\varepsilon_0}\mathbf{F}_r$ of a point charge at the origin. Let S be a piecewise smooth closed surface that encompasses the origin. Then

$$\begin{aligned}\iint_S \mathbf{E} \cdot d\mathbf{S} &= \iint_S \frac{q}{4\pi\varepsilon_0} \mathbf{F}_r \cdot d\mathbf{S} \\ &= \frac{q}{4\pi\varepsilon_0} \iint_S \mathbf{F}_r \cdot d\mathbf{S} \\ &= \frac{q}{\varepsilon_0}.\end{aligned}$$

If S does not encompass the origin, then

$$\iint_S \mathbf{E} \cdot d\mathbf{S} = \frac{q}{4\pi\varepsilon_0} \iint_S \mathbf{F}_r \cdot d\mathbf{S} = 0.$$

Therefore, we have justified the claim that we set out to justify: the flux across closed surface S is zero if the charge is outside of S, and the flux is q/ε_0 if the charge is inside of S.

This analysis works only if there is a single point charge at the origin. In this case, Gauss' law says that the flux of **E** across S is the total charge enclosed by S. Gauss' law can be extended to handle multiple charged solids in space, not just a single point charge at the origin. The logic is similar to the previous analysis, but beyond the scope of this text. In full generality, Gauss' law states that if S is a piecewise smooth closed surface and Q is the total amount of charge inside of S, then the flux of **E** across S is Q/ε_0.

Example 6.81

Using Gauss' law

Suppose we have four stationary point charges in space, all with a charge of 0.002 Coulombs (C). The charges are located at $(0, 1, 1)$, $(1, 1, 4)$, $(-1, 0, 0)$, and $(-2, -2, 2)$. Let **E** denote the electrostatic field generated by these point charges. If S is the sphere of radius 2 oriented outward and centered at the origin, then find $\iint_S \mathbf{E} \cdot d\mathbf{S}$.

Solution

According to Gauss' law, the flux of **E** across S is the total charge inside of S divided by the electric constant. Since S has radius 2, notice that only two of the charges are inside of S: the charge at $(0, 1, 1)$ and the charge at $(-1, 0, 0)$. Therefore, the total charge encompassed by S is 0.004 and, by Gauss' law,

$$\iint_S \mathbf{E} \cdot d\mathbf{S} = \frac{0.004}{8.854 \times 10^{-12}} \approx 4.518 \times 10^9 \text{ V-m}.$$

6.68 Work the previous example for surface S that is a sphere of radius 4 centered at the origin, oriented outward.

6.8 EXERCISES

For the following exercises, use a computer algebraic system (CAS) and the divergence theorem to evaluate surface integral $\int_S \mathbf{F} \cdot \mathbf{n}ds$ for the given choice of $\mathbf{F}$ and the boundary surface S. For each closed surface, assume $\mathbf{N}$ is the outward unit normal vector.

376. **[T]** $\mathbf{F}(x, y, z) = x\mathbf{i} + y\mathbf{j} + z\mathbf{k}$; S is the surface of cube $0 \le x \le 1, 0 \le y \le 1, 0 < z \le 1$.

377. **[T]** $\mathbf{F}(x, y, z) = (\cos yz)\mathbf{i} + e^{xz}\mathbf{j} + 3z^2\mathbf{k}$; S is the surface of hemisphere $z = \sqrt{4 - x^2 - y^2}$ together with disk $x^2 + y^2 \le 4$ in the xy-plane.

378. **[T]** $\mathbf{F}(x, y, z) = \left(x^2 + y^2 - x^2\right)\mathbf{i} + x^2 y\mathbf{j} + 3z\mathbf{k}$; S is the surface of the five faces of unit cube $0 \le x \le 1, 0 \le y \le 1, 0 < z \le 1$.

379. **[T]** $\mathbf{F}(x, y, z) = x\mathbf{i} + y\mathbf{j} + z\mathbf{k}$; S is the surface of paraboloid $z = x^2 + y^2$ for $0 \le z \le 9$.

380. **[T]** $\mathbf{F}(x, y, z) = x^2\mathbf{i} + y^2\mathbf{j} + z^2\mathbf{k}$; S is the surface of sphere $x^2 + y^2 + z^2 = 4$.

381. **[T]** $\mathbf{F}(x, y, z) = x\mathbf{i} + y\mathbf{j} + \left(z^2 - 1\right)\mathbf{k}$; S is the surface of the solid bounded by cylinder $x^2 + y^2 = 4$ and planes $z = 0$ and $z = 1$.

382. **[T]** $\mathbf{F}(x, y, z) = xy^2\mathbf{i} + yz^2\mathbf{j} + x^2 z\mathbf{k}$; S is the surface bounded above by sphere $\rho = 2$ and below by cone $\varphi = \frac{\pi}{4}$ in spherical coordinates. (Think of S as the surface of an "ice cream cone.")

383. **[T]** $\mathbf{F}(x, y, z) = x^3\mathbf{i} + y^3\mathbf{j} + 3a^2 z\mathbf{k}$ (constant $a > 0$); S is the surface bounded by cylinder $x^2 + y^2 = a^2$ and planes $z = 0$ and $z = 1$.

384. **[T]** Surface integral $\iint_S \mathbf{F} \cdot d\mathbf{S}$, where S is the solid bounded by paraboloid $z = x^2 + y^2$ and plane $z = 4$, and $\mathbf{F}(x, y, z) = \left(x + y^2 z^2\right)\mathbf{i} + \left(y + z^2 x^2\right)\mathbf{j} + \left(z + x^2 y^2\right)\mathbf{k}$

385. Use the divergence theorem to calculate surface integral $\iint_S \mathbf{F} \cdot d\mathbf{S}$, where $\mathbf{F}(x, y, z) = \left(e^{y^2}\right)\mathbf{i} + \left(y + \sin\left(z^2\right)\right)\mathbf{j} + (z - 1)\mathbf{k}$ and S is upper hemisphere $x^2 + y^2 + z^2 = 1, z \ge 0$, oriented upward.

386. Use the divergence theorem to calculate surface integral $\iint_S \mathbf{F} \cdot d\mathbf{S}$, where $\mathbf{F}(x, y, z) = x^4\mathbf{i} - x^3 z^2\mathbf{j} + 4xy^2 z\mathbf{k}$ and S is the surface bounded by cylinder $x^2 + y^2 = 1$ and planes $z = x + 2$ and $z = 0$.

387. Use the divergence theorem to calculate surface integral $\iint_S \mathbf{F} \cdot d\mathbf{S}$ when $\mathbf{F}(x, y, z) = x^2 z^3\mathbf{i} + 2xyz^3\mathbf{j} + xz^4\mathbf{k}$ and S is the surface of the box with vertices $(\pm 1, \pm 2, \pm 3)$.

388. Use the divergence theorem to calculate surface integral $\iint_S \mathbf{F} \cdot d\mathbf{S}$ when $\mathbf{F}(x, y, z) = z\tan^{-1}\left(y^2\right)\mathbf{i} + z^3\ln\left(x^2 + 1\right)\mathbf{j} + z\mathbf{k}$ and S is a part of paraboloid $x^2 + y^2 + z = 2$ that lies above plane $z = 1$ and is oriented upward.

389. **[T]** Use a CAS and the divergence theorem to calculate flux $\iint_S \mathbf{F} \cdot d\mathbf{S}$, where $\mathbf{F}(x, y, z) = \left(x^3 + y^3\right)\mathbf{i} + \left(y^3 + z^3\right)\mathbf{j} + \left(z^3 + x^3\right)\mathbf{k}$ and S is a sphere with center (0, 0) and radius 2.

390. Use the divergence theorem to compute the value of flux integral $\iint_S \mathbf{F} \cdot d\mathbf{S}$, where $\mathbf{F}(x, y, z) = (y^3 + 3x)\mathbf{i} + (xz + y)\mathbf{j} + [z + x^4 \cos(x^2 y)]\mathbf{k}$ and S is the area of the region bounded by $x^2 + y^2 = 1,\ x \geq 0,\ y \geq 0,$ and $0 \leq z \leq 1$.

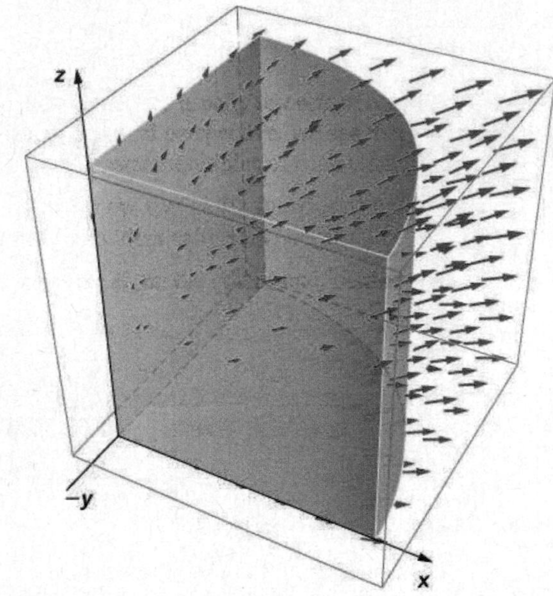

391. Use the divergence theorem to compute flux integral $\iint_S \mathbf{F} \cdot d\mathbf{S}$, where $\mathbf{F}(x, y, z) = y\mathbf{j} - z\mathbf{k}$ and S consists of the union of paraboloid $y = x^2 + z^2,\ 0 \leq y \leq 1,$ and disk $x^2 + z^2 \leq 1,\ y = 1,$ oriented outward. What is the flux through just the paraboloid?

392. Use the divergence theorem to compute flux integral $\iint_S \mathbf{F} \cdot d\mathbf{S}$, where $\mathbf{F}(x, y, z) = x + y\mathbf{j} + z^4\mathbf{k}$ and S is a part of cone $z = \sqrt{x^2 + y^2}$ beneath top plane $z = 1$, oriented downward.

393. Use the divergence theorem to calculate surface integral $\iint_S \mathbf{F} \cdot d\mathbf{S}$ for $\mathbf{F}(x, y, z) = x^4\mathbf{i} - x^3 z^2\mathbf{j} + 4xy^2 z\mathbf{k}$, where S is the surface bounded by cylinder $x^2 + y^2 = 1$ and planes $z = x + 2$ and $z = 0$.

394. Consider $\mathbf{F}(x, y, z) = x^2\mathbf{i} + xy\mathbf{j} + (z + 1)\mathbf{k}$. Let E be the solid enclosed by paraboloid $z = 4 - x^2 - y^2$ and plane $z = 0$ with normal vectors pointing outside E. Compute flux $\boldsymbol{F}$ across the boundary of E using the divergence theorem.

For the following exercises, use a CAS along with the divergence theorem to compute the net outward flux for the fields across the given surfaces S.

395. **[T]** $\mathbf{F} = \langle x, -2y, 3z \rangle$; S is sphere $\{(x, y, z) : x^2 + y^2 + z^2 = 6\}$.

396. **[T]** $\mathbf{F} = \langle x, 2y, z \rangle$; S is the boundary of the tetrahedron in the first octant formed by plane $x + y + z = 1$.

397. **[T]** $\mathbf{F} = \langle y - 2x, x^3 - y, y^2 - z \rangle$; S is sphere $\{(x, y, z) : x^2 + y^2 + z^2 = 4\}$.

398. **[T]** $\mathbf{F} = \langle x, y, z \rangle$; S is the surface of paraboloid $z = 4 - x^2 - y^2$, for $z \geq 0$, plus its base in the xy-plane.

For the following exercises, use a CAS and the divergence theorem to compute the net outward flux for the vector fields across the boundary of the given regions D.

399. **[T]** $\mathbf{F} = \langle z - x, x - y, 2y - z \rangle$; D is the region between spheres of radius 2 and 4 centered at the origin.

400. **[T]** $\mathbf{F} = \frac{\mathbf{r}}{|\mathbf{r}|} = \frac{\langle x, y, z \rangle}{\sqrt{x^2 + y^2 + z^2}}$; D is the region between spheres of radius 1 and 2 centered at the origin.

401. **[T]** $\mathbf{F} = \langle x^2, -y^2, z^2 \rangle$; D is the region in the first octant between planes $z = 4 - x - y$ and $z = 2 - x - y$.

402. Let $\mathbf{F}(x, y, z) = 2x\mathbf{i} - 3xy\mathbf{j} + xz^2\mathbf{k}$. Use the divergence theorem to calculate $\iint_S \mathbf{F} \cdot d\mathbf{S}$, where S is the surface of the cube with corners at $(0, 0, 0), (1, 0, 0), (0, 1, 0),$ $(1, 1, 0), (0, 0, 1), (1, 0, 1), (0, 1, 1),$ and $(1, 1, 1)$, oriented outward.

403. Use the divergence theorem to find the outward flux of field $\mathbf{F}(x, y, z) = (x^3 - 3y)\mathbf{i} + (2yz + 1)\mathbf{j} + xyz\mathbf{k}$ through the cube bounded by planes $x = \pm 1,\ y = \pm 1,$ and $z = \pm 1$.

404. Let $\mathbf{F}(x, y, z) = 2x\mathbf{i} - 3y\mathbf{j} + 5z\mathbf{k}$ and let S be hemisphere $z = \sqrt{9 - x^2 - y^2}$ together with disk $x^2 + y^2 \leq 9$ in the xy-plane. Use the divergence theorem.

405. Evaluate $\iint_S \mathbf{F} \cdot \mathbf{N} dS,$ where $\mathbf{F}(x, y, z) = x^2 \mathbf{i} + xy\mathbf{j} + x^3 y^3 \mathbf{k}$ and S is the surface consisting of all faces except the tetrahedron bounded by plane $x + y + z = 1$ and the coordinate planes, with outward unit normal vector $\mathbf{N}$.

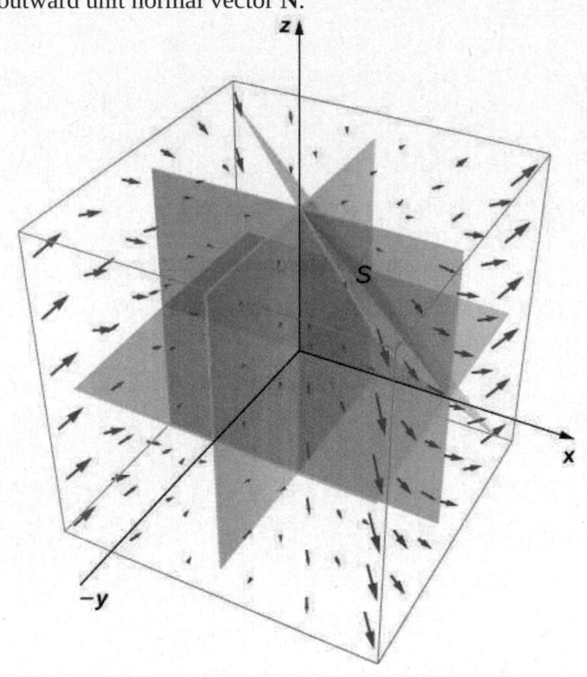

406. Find the net outward flux of field $\mathbf{F} = \langle bz - cy, cx - az, ay - bx \rangle$ across any smooth closed surface in $\mathbf{R}^3$, where a, b, and c are constants.

407. Use the divergence theorem to evaluate $\iint_S \| \mathbf{R} \| \mathbf{R} \cdot n ds,$ where $\mathbf{R}(x, y, z) = x\mathbf{i} + y\mathbf{j} + z\mathbf{k}$ and S is sphere $x^2 + y^2 + z^2 = a^2$, with constant $a > 0$.

408. Use the divergence theorem to evaluate $\iint_S \mathbf{F} \cdot d\mathbf{S},$ where $\mathbf{F}(x, y, z) = y^2 z\mathbf{i} + y^3 \mathbf{j} + xz\mathbf{k}$ and S is the boundary of the cube defined by $-1 \leq x \leq 1,\ -1 \leq y \leq 1,$ and $0 \leq z \leq 2.$

409. Let R be the region defined by $x^2 + y^2 + z^2 \leq 1.$ Use the divergence theorem to find $\iiint_R z^2 dV.$

410. Let E be the solid bounded by the xy-plane and paraboloid $z = 4 - x^2 - y^2$ so that S is the surface of the paraboloid piece together with the disk in the xy-plane that forms its bottom. If $\mathbf{F}(x, y, z) = \left(xz \sin(yz) + x^3\right)\mathbf{i} + \cos(yz)\mathbf{j} + \left(3zy^2 - e^{x^2 + y^2}\right)\mathbf{k},$ find $\iint_S \mathbf{F} \cdot d\mathbf{S}$ using the divergence theorem.

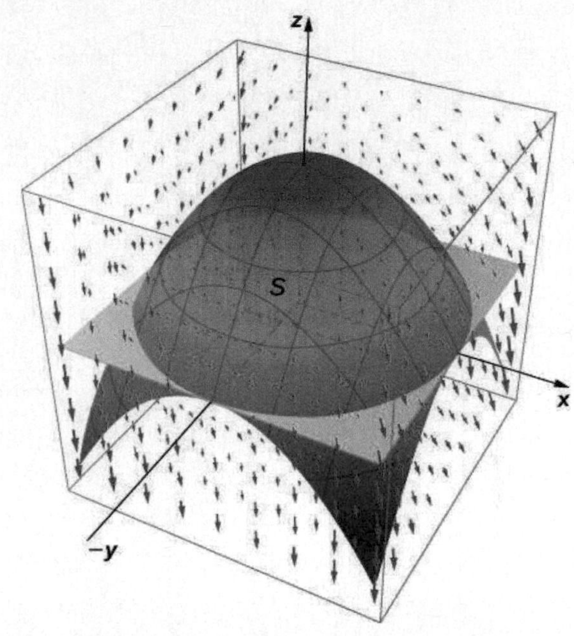

411. Let E be the solid unit cube with diagonally opposite corners at the origin and (1, 1, 1), and faces parallel to the coordinate planes. Let S be the surface of E, oriented with the outward-pointing normal. Use a CAS to find $\iint_S \mathbf{F} \cdot d\mathbf{S}$ using the divergence theorem if $\mathbf{F}(x, y, z) = 2xy\mathbf{i} + 3ye^z \mathbf{j} + x \sin z\mathbf{k}.$

412. Use the divergence theorem to calculate the flux of $\mathbf{F}(x, y, z) = x^3 \mathbf{i} + y^3 \mathbf{j} + z^3 \mathbf{k}$ through sphere $x^2 + y^2 + z^2 = 1.$

413. Find $\iint_S \mathbf{F} \cdot d\mathbf{S},$ where $\mathbf{F}(x, y, z) = x\mathbf{i} + y\mathbf{j} + z\mathbf{k}$ and S is the outwardly oriented surface obtained by removing cube $[1, 2] \times [1, 2] \times [1, 2]$ from cube $[0, 2] \times [0, 2] \times [0, 2].$

414. Consider radial vector field $\mathbf{F} = \dfrac{\mathbf{r}}{|\mathbf{r}|} = \dfrac{\langle x, y, z \rangle}{\left(x^2 + y^2 + z^2\right)^{1/2}}.$ Compute the surface integral, where S is the surface of a sphere of radius a centered at the origin.

415. Compute the flux of water through parabolic cylinder $S: y = x^2$, from $0 \le x \le 2$, $0 \le z \le 3$, if the velocity vector is $\mathbf{F}(x, y, z) = 3z^2\mathbf{i} + 6\mathbf{j} + 6xz\mathbf{k}$.

416. **[T]** Use a CAS to find the flux of vector field $\mathbf{F}(x, y, z) = z\mathbf{i} + z\mathbf{j} + \sqrt{x^2 + y^2}\mathbf{k}$ across the portion of hyperboloid $x^2 + y^2 = z^2 + 1$ between planes $z = 0$ and $z = \frac{\sqrt{3}}{3}$, oriented so the unit normal vector points away from the *z*-axis.

417. **[T]** Use a CAS to find the flux of vector field $\mathbf{F}(x, y, z) = (e^y + x)\mathbf{i} + (3\cos(xz) - y)\mathbf{j} + z\mathbf{k}$ through surface *S*, where *S* is given by $z^2 = 4x^2 + 4y^2$ from $0 \le z \le 4$, oriented so the unit normal vector points downward.

418. **[T]** Use a CAS to compute $\iint_S \mathbf{F} \cdot d\mathbf{S}$, where $\mathbf{F}(x, y, z) = x\mathbf{i} + y\mathbf{j} + 2z\mathbf{k}$ and *S* is a part of sphere $x^2 + y^2 + z^2 = 2$ with $0 \le z \le 1$.

419. Evaluate $\iint_S \mathbf{F} \cdot d\mathbf{S}$, where $\mathbf{F}(x, y, z) = bxy^2\mathbf{i} + bx^2y\mathbf{j} + \left(x^2 + y^2\right)z^2\mathbf{k}$ and *S* is a closed surface bounding the region and consisting of solid cylinder $x^2 + y^2 \le a^2$ and $0 \le z \le b$.

420. **[T]** Use a CAS to calculate the flux of $\mathbf{F}(x, y, z) = \left(x^3 + y\sin z\right)\mathbf{i} + \left(y^3 + z\sin x\right)\mathbf{j} + 3z\mathbf{k}$ across surface *S*, where *S* is the boundary of the solid bounded by hemispheres $z = \sqrt{4 - x^2 - y^2}$ and $z = \sqrt{1 - x^2 - y^2}$, and plane $z = 0$.

421. Use the divergence theorem to evaluate $\iint_S \mathbf{F} \cdot d\mathbf{S}$, where $\mathbf{F}(x, y, z) = xy\mathbf{i} - \frac{1}{2}y^2\mathbf{j} + z\mathbf{k}$ and *S* is the surface consisting of three pieces: $z = 4 - 3x^2 - 3y^2$, $1 \le z \le 4$ on the top; $x^2 + y^2 = 1$, $0 \le z \le 1$ on the sides; and $z = 0$ on the bottom.

422. **[T]** Use a CAS and the divergence theorem to evaluate $\iint_S \mathbf{F} \cdot d\mathbf{S}$, where $\mathbf{F}(x, y, z) = (2x + y\cos z)\mathbf{i} + \left(x^2 - y\right)\mathbf{j} + y^2z\mathbf{k}$ and *S* is sphere $x^2 + y^2 + z^2 = 4$ orientated outward.

423. Use the divergence theorem to evaluate $\iint_S \mathbf{F} \cdot d\mathbf{S}$, where $\mathbf{F}(x, y, z) = x\mathbf{i} + y\mathbf{j} + z\mathbf{k}$ and *S* is the boundary of the solid enclosed by paraboloid $y = x^2 + z^2 - 2$, cylinder $x^2 + z^2 = 1$, and plane $x + y = 2$, and *S* is oriented outward.

For the following exercises, Fourier's law of heat transfer states that the heat flow vector **F** at a point is proportional to the negative gradient of the temperature; that is, $\mathbf{F} = -k\nabla T$, which means that heat energy flows hot regions to cold regions. The constant $k > 0$ is called the *conductivity*, which has metric units of joules per meter per second-kelvin or watts per meter-kelvin. A temperature function for region *D* is given. Use the divergence theorem to find net outward heat flux $\iint_S \mathbf{F} \cdot \mathbf{N}dS = -k\iint_S \nabla T \cdot \mathbf{N}dS$ across the boundary *S* of *D*, where $k = 1$.

424. $T(x, y, z) = 100 + x + 2y + z$; $D = \{(x, y, z) : 0 \le x \le 1, 0 \le y \le 1, 0 \le z \le 1\}$

425. $T(x, y, z) = 100 + e^{-z}$; $D = \{(x, y, z) : 0 \le x \le 1, 0 \le y \le 1, 0 \le z \le 1\}$

426. $T(x, y, z) = 100e^{-x^2 - y^2 - z^2}$; *D* is the sphere of radius *a* centered at the origin.

CHAPTER 6 REVIEW

KEY TERMS

circulation the tendency of a fluid to move in the direction of curve C. If C is a closed curve, then the circulation of $\mathbf{F}$ along C is line integral $\int_C \mathbf{F} \cdot \mathbf{T} ds,$ which we also denote $\oint_C \mathbf{F} \cdot \mathbf{T} ds$

closed curve a curve for which there exists a parameterization $\mathbf{r}(t),\ \ a \le t \le b,$ such that $\mathbf{r}(a) = \mathbf{r}(b),$ and the curve is traversed exactly once

closed curve a curve that begins and ends at the same point

connected region a region in which any two points can be connected by a path with a trace contained entirely inside the region

conservative field a vector field for which there exists a scalar function f such that $\nabla f = \mathbf{F}$

curl the curl of vector field $\mathbf{F} = \langle P, Q, R \rangle,$ denoted $\nabla \times \mathbf{F},$ is the "determinant" of the matrix $\begin{vmatrix} \mathbf{i} & \mathbf{j} & \mathbf{k} \\ \frac{\partial}{\partial x} & \frac{\partial}{\partial y} & \frac{\partial}{\partial z} \\ P & Q & R \end{vmatrix}$ and is given by the expression $(R_y - Q_z)\mathbf{i} + (P_z - R_x)\mathbf{j} + (Q_x - P_y)\mathbf{k};$ it measures the tendency of particles at a point to rotate about the axis that points in the direction of the curl at the point

divergence the divergence of a vector field $\mathbf{F} = \langle P, Q, R \rangle,$ denoted $\nabla \times \mathbf{F},$ is $P_x + Q_y + R_z;$ it measures the "outflowing-ness" of a vector field

divergence theorem a theorem used to transform a difficult flux integral into an easier triple integral and vice versa

flux the rate of a fluid flowing across a curve in a vector field; the flux of vector field $\mathbf{F}$ across plane curve C is line integral $\int_C \mathbf{F} \cdot \frac{\mathbf{n}(t)}{\|\mathbf{n}(t)\|} ds$

flux integral another name for a surface integral of a vector field; the preferred term in physics and engineering

Fundamental Theorem for Line Integrals the value of line integral $\int_C \nabla f \cdot d\mathbf{r}$ depends only on the value of f at the endpoints of C: $\int_C \nabla f \cdot d\mathbf{r} = f(\mathbf{r}(b)) - f(\mathbf{r}(a))$

Gauss' law if S is a piecewise, smooth closed surface in a vacuum and Q is the total stationary charge inside of S, then the flux of electrostatic field $\mathbf{E}$ across S is Q/ε_0

gradient field a vector field $\mathbf{F}$ for which there exists a scalar function f such that $\nabla f = \mathbf{F};$ in other words, a vector field that is the gradient of a function; such vector fields are also called *conservative*

Green's theorem relates the integral over a connected region to an integral over the boundary of the region

grid curves curves on a surface that are parallel to grid lines in a coordinate plane

heat flow a vector field proportional to the negative temperature gradient in an object

independence of path a vector field $\mathbf{F}$ has path independence if $\int_{C_1} \mathbf{F} \cdot d\mathbf{r} = \int_{C_2} \mathbf{F} \cdot d\mathbf{r}$ for any curves C_1 and C_2 in the domain of $\mathbf{F}$ with the same initial points and terminal points

inverse-square law the electrostatic force at a given point is inversely proportional to the square of the distance from the source of the charge

line integral the integral of a function along a curve in a plane or in space

mass flux the rate of mass flow of a fluid per unit area, measured in mass per unit time per unit area

orientation of a curve the orientation of a curve C is a specified direction of C

orientation of a surface if a surface has an "inner" side and an "outer" side, then an orientation is a choice of the inner or the outer side; the surface could also have "upward" and "downward" orientations

parameter domain (parameter space) the region of the uv plane over which the parameters u and v vary for parameterization $\mathbf{r}(u, v) = \langle x(u, v), y(u, v), z(u, v) \rangle$

parameterized surface (parametric surface) a surface given by a description of the form $\mathbf{r}(u, v) = \langle x(u, v), y(u, v), z(u, v) \rangle$, where the parameters u and v vary over a parameter domain in the uv-plane

piecewise smooth curve an oriented curve that is not smooth, but can be written as the union of finitely many smooth curves

potential function a scalar function f such that $\nabla f = \mathbf{F}$

radial field a vector field in which all vectors either point directly toward or directly away from the origin; the magnitude of any vector depends only on its distance from the origin

regular parameterization parameterization $\mathbf{r}(u, v) = \langle x(u, v), y(u, v), z(u, v) \rangle$ such that $\mathbf{r}_u \times \mathbf{r}_v$ is not zero for point (u, v) in the parameter domain

rotational field a vector field in which the vector at point (x, y) is tangent to a circle with radius $r = \sqrt{x^2 + y^2}$; in a rotational field, all vectors flow either clockwise or counterclockwise, and the magnitude of a vector depends only on its distance from the origin

scalar line integral the scalar line integral of a function f along a curve C with respect to arc length is the integral $\int_C f ds$, it is the integral of a scalar function f along a curve in a plane or in space; such an integral is defined in terms of a Riemann sum, as is a single-variable integral

simple curve a curve that does not cross itself

simply connected region a region that is connected and has the property that any closed curve that lies entirely inside the region encompasses points that are entirely inside the region

Stokes' theorem relates the flux integral over a surface S to a line integral around the boundary C of the surface S

stream function if $\mathbf{F} = \langle P, Q \rangle$ is a source-free vector field, then stream function g is a function such that $P = g_y$ and $Q = -g_x$

surface area the area of surface S given by the surface integral $\iint_S dS$

surface independent flux integrals of curl vector fields are surface independent if their evaluation does not depend on the surface but only on the boundary of the surface

surface integral an integral of a function over a surface

surface integral of a scalar-valued function a surface integral in which the integrand is a scalar function

surface integral of a vector field a surface integral in which the integrand is a vector field

unit vector field a vector field in which the magnitude of every vector is 1

vector field measured in $\mathbb{R}^2$, an assignment of a vector $\mathbf{F}(x, y)$ to each point (x, y) of a subset D of $\mathbb{R}^2$; in $\mathbb{R}^3$, an assignment of a vector $\mathbf{F}(x, y, z)$ to each point (x, y, z) of a subset D of $\mathbb{R}^3$

vector line integral the vector line integral of vector field $\mathbf{F}$ along curve C is the integral of the dot product of $\mathbf{F}$ with unit tangent vector $\mathbf{T}$ of C with respect to arc length, $\int_C \mathbf{F} \cdot \mathbf{T} ds$; such an integral is defined in terms of a Riemann sum, similar to a single-variable integral

KEY EQUATIONS

- **Vector field in $\mathbb{R}^2$**
  $\mathbf{F}(x, y) = \langle P(x, y), Q(x, y) \rangle$
  or
  $\mathbf{F}(x, y) = P(x, y)\mathbf{i} + Q(x, y)\mathbf{j}$
- **Vector field in $\mathbb{R}^3$**
  $\mathbf{F}(x, y, z) = \langle P(x, y, z), Q(x, y, z), R(x, y, z) \rangle$
  or
  $\mathbf{F}(x, y, z) = P(x, y, z)\mathbf{i} + Q(x, y, z)\mathbf{j} + R(x, y, z)\mathbf{k}$
- **Calculating a scalar line integral**
  $\int_C f(x, y, z)ds = \int_a^b f(\mathbf{r}(t))\sqrt{(x'(t))^2 + (y'(t))^2 + (z'(t))^2}dt$
- **Calculating a vector line integral**
  $\int_C \mathbf{F} \cdot ds = \int_C \mathbf{F} \cdot \mathbf{T}ds = \int_a^b \mathbf{F}(\mathbf{r}(t)) \cdot \mathbf{r}'(t)dt$
  or
  $\int_C Pdx + Qdy + Rdz = \int_a^b \left(P(\mathbf{r}(t))\frac{dx}{dt} + Q(\mathbf{r}(t))\frac{dy}{dt} + R(\mathbf{r}(t))\frac{dz}{dt}\right)dt$
- **Calculating flux**
  $\int_C \mathbf{F} \cdot \frac{\mathbf{n}(t)}{\|\mathbf{n}(t)\|} ds = \int_a^b \mathbf{F}(\mathbf{r}(t)) \cdot \mathbf{n}(t)dt$
- **Fundamental Theorem for Line Integrals**
  $\int_C \nabla f \cdot d\mathbf{r} = f(\mathbf{r}(b)) - f(\mathbf{r}(a))$
- **Circulation of a conservative field over curve *C* that encloses a simply connected region**
  $\oint_C \nabla f \cdot d\mathbf{r} = 0$
- **Green's theorem, circulation form**
  $\oint_C Pdx + Qdy = \iint_D Q_x - P_y dA,$ where C is the boundary of D
- **Green's theorem, flux form**
  $\oint_C \mathbf{F} \cdot d\mathbf{r} = \iint_D Q_x - P_y dA,$ where C is the boundary of D
- **Green's theorem, extended version**
  $\oint_{\partial D} \mathbf{F} \cdot d\mathbf{r} = \iint_D Q_x - P_y dA$
- **Curl**
  $\nabla \times \mathbf{F} = (R_y - Q_z)\mathbf{i} + (P_z - R_x)\mathbf{j} + (Q_x - P_y)\mathbf{k}$
- **Divergence**
  $\nabla \cdot \mathbf{F} = P_x + Q_y + R_z$
- **Divergence of curl is zero**
  $\nabla \cdot (\nabla \times \mathbf{F}) = 0$
- **Curl of a gradient is the zero vector**

$\nabla \times (\nabla f) = 0$

- **Scalar surface integral**
  $\iint_S f(x, y, z)dS = \iint_D f(\mathbf{r}(u, v))\|\mathbf{t}_u \times \mathbf{t}_v\|dA$
- **Flux integral**
  $\iint_S \mathbf{F} \cdot \mathbf{N}dS = \iint_S \mathbf{F} \cdot d\mathbf{S} = \iint_D \mathbf{F}(\mathbf{r}(u, v)) \cdot (\mathbf{t}_u \times \mathbf{t}_v)dA$
- **Stokes' theorem**
  $\int_C \mathbf{F} \cdot d\mathbf{r} = \iint_S \text{curl } \mathbf{F} \cdot d\mathbf{S}$
- **Divergence theorem**
  $\iiint_E \text{div } \mathbf{F}dV = \iint_S \mathbf{F} \cdot d\mathbf{S}$

KEY CONCEPTS

6.1 Vector Fields

- A vector field assigns a vector $\mathbf{F}(x, y)$ to each point (x, y) in a subset D of $\mathbb{R}^2$ or $\mathbb{R}^3$. $\mathbf{F}(x, y, z)$ to each point (x, y, z) in a subset D of $\mathbb{R}^3$.
- Vector fields can describe the distribution of vector quantities such as forces or velocities over a region of the plane or of space. They are in common use in such areas as physics, engineering, meteorology, oceanography.
- We can sketch a vector field by examining its defining equation to determine relative magnitudes in various locations and then drawing enough vectors to determine a pattern.
- A vector field $\mathbf{F}$ is called conservative if there exists a scalar function f such that $\nabla f = \mathbf{F}$.

6.2 Line Integrals

- Line integrals generalize the notion of a single-variable integral to higher dimensions. The domain of integration in a single-variable integral is a line segment along the *x*-axis, but the domain of integration in a line integral is a curve in a plane or in space.
- If C is a curve, then the length of C is $\int_C ds$.
- There are two kinds of line integral: scalar line integrals and vector line integrals. Scalar line integrals can be used to calculate the mass of a wire; vector line integrals can be used to calculate the work done on a particle traveling through a field.
- Scalar line integrals can be calculated using **Equation 6.8**; vector line integrals can be calculated using **Equation 6.9**.
- Two key concepts expressed in terms of line integrals are flux and circulation. Flux measures the rate that a field crosses a given line; circulation measures the tendency of a field to move in the same direction as a given closed curve.

6.3 Conservative Vector Fields

- The theorems in this section require curves that are closed, simple, or both, and regions that are connected or simply connected.
- The line integral of a conservative vector field can be calculated using the Fundamental Theorem for Line Integrals. This theorem is a generalization of the Fundamental Theorem of Calculus in higher dimensions. Using this theorem usually makes the calculation of the line integral easier.
- Conservative fields are independent of path. The line integral of a conservative field depends only on the value of

the potential function at the endpoints of the domain curve.

- Given vector field **F**, we can test whether **F** is conservative by using the cross-partial property. If **F** has the cross-partial property and the domain is simply connected, then **F** is conservative (and thus has a potential function). If **F** is conservative, we can find a potential function by using the Problem-Solving Strategy.
- The circulation of a conservative vector field on a simply connected domain over a closed curve is zero.

6.4 Green's Theorem

- Green's theorem relates the integral over a connected region to an integral over the boundary of the region. Green's theorem is a version of the Fundamental Theorem of Calculus in one higher dimension.
- Green's Theorem comes in two forms: a circulation form and a flux form. In the circulation form, the integrand is $\mathbf{F} \cdot \mathbf{T}$. In the flux form, the integrand is $\mathbf{F} \cdot \mathbf{N}$.
- Green's theorem can be used to transform a difficult line integral into an easier double integral, or to transform a difficult double integral into an easier line integral.
- A vector field is source free if it has a stream function. The flux of a source-free vector field across a closed curve is zero, just as the circulation of a conservative vector field across a closed curve is zero.

6.5 Divergence and Curl

- The divergence of a vector field is a scalar function. Divergence measures the "outflowing-ness" of a vector field. If **v** is the velocity field of a fluid, then the divergence of **v** at a point is the outflow of the fluid less the inflow at the point.
- The curl of a vector field is a vector field. The curl of a vector field at point *P* measures the tendency of particles at *P* to rotate about the axis that points in the direction of the curl at *P*.
- A vector field with a simply connected domain is conservative if and only if its curl is zero.

6.6 Surface Integrals

- Surfaces can be parameterized, just as curves can be parameterized. In general, surfaces must be parameterized with two parameters.
- Surfaces can sometimes be oriented, just as curves can be oriented. Some surfaces, such as a Möbius strip, cannot be oriented.
- A surface integral is like a line integral in one higher dimension. The domain of integration of a surface integral is a surface in a plane or space, rather than a curve in a plane or space.
- The integrand of a surface integral can be a scalar function or a vector field. To calculate a surface integral with an integrand that is a function, use **Equation 6.19**. To calculate a surface integral with an integrand that is a vector field, use **Equation 6.20**.
- If S is a surface, then the area of S is $\iint_S dS.$

6.7 Stokes' Theorem

- Stokes' theorem relates a flux integral over a surface to a line integral around the boundary of the surface. Stokes' theorem is a higher dimensional version of Green's theorem, and therefore is another version of the Fundamental Theorem of Calculus in higher dimensions.
- Stokes' theorem can be used to transform a difficult surface integral into an easier line integral, or a difficult line integral into an easier surface integral.
- Through Stokes' theorem, line integrals can be evaluated using the simplest surface with boundary *C*.
- Faraday's law relates the curl of an electric field to the rate of change of the corresponding magnetic field. Stokes' theorem can be used to derive Faraday's law.

6.8 The Divergence Theorem

- The divergence theorem relates a surface integral across closed surface S to a triple integral over the solid enclosed by S. The divergence theorem is a higher dimensional version of the flux form of Green's theorem, and is therefore a higher dimensional version of the Fundamental Theorem of Calculus.
- The divergence theorem can be used to transform a difficult flux integral into an easier triple integral and vice versa.
- The divergence theorem can be used to derive Gauss' law, a fundamental law in electrostatics.

CHAPTER 6 REVIEW EXERCISES

True or False? Justify your answer with a proof or a counterexample.

427. Vector field $\mathbf{F}(x, y) = x^2 y\mathbf{i} + y^2 x\mathbf{j}$ is conservative.

428. For vector field $\mathbf{F}(x, y) = P(x, y)\mathbf{i} + Q(x, y)\mathbf{j}$, if $P_y(x, y) = Q_x(x, y)$ in open region D, then $\int_{\partial D} Pdx + Qdy = 0$.

429. The divergence of a vector field is a vector field.

430. If $\text{curl}\,\mathbf{F} = 0$, then $\mathbf{F}$ is a conservative vector field.

Draw the following vector fields.

431. $\mathbf{F}(x, y) = \frac{1}{2}\mathbf{i} + 2x\mathbf{j}$

432. $\mathbf{F}(x, y) = \sqrt{\dfrac{y\mathbf{i} + 3x\mathbf{j}}{x^2 + y^2}}$

Are the following the vector fields conservative? If so, find the potential function f such that $\mathbf{F} = \nabla f$.

433. $\mathbf{F}(x, y) = y\mathbf{i} + (x - 2e^y)\mathbf{j}$

434. $\mathbf{F}(x, y) = (6xy)\mathbf{i} + \left(3x^2 - ye^y\right)\mathbf{j}$

435. $\mathbf{F}(x, y, z) = \left(2xy + z^2\right)\mathbf{i} + \left(x^2 + 2yz\right)\mathbf{j} + \left(2xz + y^2\right)\mathbf{k}$

436. $\mathbf{F}(x, y, z) = (e^x y)\mathbf{i} + (e^x + z)\mathbf{j} + \left(e^x + y^2\right)\mathbf{k}$

Evaluate the following integrals.

437. $\int_C x^2 dy + (2x - 3xy)dx,$ along $C : y = \frac{1}{2}x$ from (0, 0) to (4, 2)

438. $\int_C ydx + xy^2 dy,$ where $C : x = \sqrt{t},\ y = t - 1,\ 0 \le t \le 1$

439. $\iint_S xy^2 dS,$ where S is surface $z = x^2 - y,\ 0 \le x \le 1,\ 0 \le y \le 4$

Find the divergence and curl for the following vector fields.

440. $\mathbf{F}(x, y, z) = 3xyz\mathbf{i} + xye^z\mathbf{j} - 3xy\mathbf{k}$

441. $\mathbf{F}(x, y, z) = e^x\mathbf{i} + e^{xy}\mathbf{j} + e^{xyz}\mathbf{k}$

Use Green's theorem to evaluate the following integrals.

442. $\int_C 3xydx + 2xy^2 dy,$ where C is a square with vertices (0, 0), (0, 2), (2, 2) and (2, 0)

443. $\oint_C 3ydx + (x + e^y)dy,$ where C is a circle centered at the origin with radius 3

Use Stokes' theorem to evaluate $\iint_S \text{curl}\,\mathbf{F} \cdot dS.$

444. $\mathbf{F}(x, y, z) = y\mathbf{i} - x\mathbf{j} + z\mathbf{k},$ where S is the upper half of the unit sphere

445. $\mathbf{F}(x, y, z) = y\mathbf{i} + xyz\mathbf{j} - 2zx\mathbf{k},$ where S is the upward-facing paraboloid $z = x^2 + y^2$ lying in cylinder $x^2 + y^2 = 1$

Use the divergence theorem to evaluate $\iint_S \mathbf{F} \cdot dS.$

446. $\mathbf{F}(x, y, z) = (x^3 y)\mathbf{i} + (3y - e^x)\mathbf{j} + (z + x)\mathbf{k}$, over cube S defined by $-1 \le x \le 1$, $0 \le y \le 2$, $0 \le z \le 2$

447. $\mathbf{F}(x, y, z) = (2xy)\mathbf{i} + (-y^2)\mathbf{j} + (2z^3)\mathbf{k}$, where S is bounded by paraboloid $z = x^2 + y^2$ and plane $z = 2$

448. Find the amount of work performed by a 50-kg woman ascending a helical staircase with radius 2 m and height 100 m. The woman completes five revolutions during the climb.

449. Find the total mass of a thin wire in the shape of a semicircle with radius $\sqrt{2}$, and a density function of $\rho(x, y) = y + x^2$.

450. Find the total mass of a thin sheet in the shape of a hemisphere with radius 2 for $z \ge 0$ with a density function $\rho(x, y, z) = x + y + z$.

451. Use the divergence theorem to compute the value of the flux integral over the unit sphere with $\mathbf{F}(x, y, z) = 3z\mathbf{i} + 2y\mathbf{j} + 2x\mathbf{k}$.

7 | SECOND-ORDER DIFFERENTIAL EQUATIONS

Figure 7.1 A motorcycle suspension system is an example of a damped spring-mass system. The spring absorbs bumps and keeps the tire in contact with the road. The shock absorber damps the motion so the motorcycle does not continue to bounce after going over each bump. (credit: nSeika, Flickr)

Chapter Outline

Introduction

We have already studied the basics of differential equations, including separable first-order equations. In this chapter, we go a little further and look at second-order equations, which are equations containing second derivatives of the dependent variable. The solution methods we examine are different from those discussed earlier, and the solutions tend to involve trigonometric functions as well as exponential functions. Here we concentrate primarily on second-order equations with constant coefficients.

Such equations have many practical applications. The operation of certain electrical circuits, known as resistor–inductor–capacitor (*RLC*) circuits, can be described by second-order differential equations with constant coefficients. These circuits are found in all kinds of modern electronic devices—from computers to smartphones to televisions. Such circuits can be used to select a range of frequencies from the entire radio wave spectrum, and are they commonly used for tuning AM/FM radios. We look at these circuits more closely in **Applications**.

Spring-mass systems, such as motorcycle shock absorbers, are a second common application of second-order differential equations. For motocross riders, the suspension systems on their motorcycles are very important. The off-road courses on which they ride often include jumps, and losing control of the motorcycle when landing could cost them the race. The movement of the shock absorber depends on the amount of damping in the system. In this chapter, we model forced and unforced spring-mass systems with varying amounts of damping.

7.1 | Second-Order Linear Equations

Learning Objectives

7.1.1 Recognize homogeneous and nonhomogeneous linear differential equations.
7.1.2 Determine the characteristic equation of a homogeneous linear equation.
7.1.3 Use the roots of the characteristic equation to find the solution to a homogeneous linear equation.
7.1.4 Solve initial-value and boundary-value problems involving linear differential equations.

When working with differential equations, usually the goal is to find a solution. In other words, we want to find a function (or functions) that satisfies the differential equation. The technique we use to find these solutions varies, depending on the form of the differential equation with which we are working. Second-order differential equations have several important characteristics that can help us determine which solution method to use. In this section, we examine some of these characteristics and the associated terminology.

Homogeneous Linear Equations

Consider the second-order differential equation

$$xy'' + 2x^2 y' + 5x^3 y = 0.$$

Notice that y and its derivatives appear in a relatively simple form. They are multiplied by functions of x, but are not raised to any powers themselves, nor are they multiplied together. As discussed in **Introduction to Differential Equations (http://cnx.org/content/m53696/latest/)** , first-order equations with similar characteristics are said to be linear. The same is true of second-order equations. Also note that all the terms in this differential equation involve either y or one of its derivatives. There are no terms involving only functions of x. Equations like this, in which every term contains y or one of its derivatives, are called homogeneous.

Not all differential equations are homogeneous. Consider the differential equation

$$xy'' + 2x^2 y' + 5x^3 y = x^2.$$

The x^2 term on the right side of the equal sign does not contain y or any of its derivatives. Therefore, this differential equation is nonhomogeneous.

Definition

A second-order differential equation is linear if it can be written in the form

$$a_2(x)y'' + a_1(x)y' + a_0(x)y = r(x), \tag{7.1}$$

where $a_2(x),\ a_1(x),\ a_0(x),$ and $r(x)$ are real-valued functions and $a_2(x)$ is not identically zero. If $r(x) \equiv 0$—in other words, if $r(x) = 0$ for every value of x—the equation is said to be a **homogeneous linear equation**. If $r(x) \neq 0$ for some value of $x,$ the equation is said to be a **nonhomogeneous linear equation**.

Visit this **website (http://www.openstaxcollege.org/l/20_Secondord)** to study more about second-order linear differential equations.

In linear differential equations, y and its derivatives can be raised only to the first power and they may not be multiplied by one another. Terms involving y^2 or $\sqrt{y'}$ make the equation nonlinear. Functions of y and its derivatives, such as $\sin y$ or $e^{y'}$, are similarly prohibited in linear differential equations.

Note that equations may not always be given in standard form (the form shown in the definition). It can be helpful to rewrite them in that form to decide whether they are linear, or whether a linear equation is homogeneous.

Example 7.1

Classifying Second-Order Equations

Classify each of the following equations as linear or nonlinear. If the equation is linear, determine further whether it is homogeneous or nonhomogeneous.

a. $y'' + 3x^4 y' + x^2 y^2 = x^3$

b. $(\sin x)y'' + (\cos x)y' + 3y = 0$

c. $4t^2 x'' + 3txx' + 4x = 0$

d. $5y'' + y = 4x^5$

e. $(\cos x)y'' - \sin y' + (\sin x)y - \cos x = 0$

f. $8ty'' - 6t^2 y' + 4ty - 3t^2 = 0$

g. $\sin(x^2)y'' - (\cos x)y' + x^2 y = y' - 3$

h. $y'' + 5xy' - 3y = \cos y$

Solution

a. This equation is nonlinear because of the y^2 term.

b. This equation is linear. There is no term involving a power or function of $y,$ and the coefficients are all functions of $x.$ The equation is already written in standard form, and $r(x)$ is identically zero, so the equation is homogeneous.

c. This equation is nonlinear. Note that, in this case, x is the dependent variable and t is the independent variable. The second term involves the product of x and $x',$ so the equation is nonlinear.

d. This equation is linear. Since $r(x) = 4x^5,$ the equation is nonhomogeneous.

e. This equation is nonlinear, because of the $\sin y'$ term.

f. This equation is linear. Rewriting it in standard form gives

$$8t^2 y'' - 6t^2 y' + 4ty = 3t^2.$$

With the equation in standard form, we can see that $r(t) = 3t^2,$ so the equation is nonhomogeneous.

g. This equation looks like it's linear, but we should rewrite it in standard form to be sure. We get

$$\sin(x^2)y'' - (\cos x + 1)y' + x^2 y = -3.$$

This equation is, indeed, linear. With $r(x) = -3,$ it is nonhomogeneous.

h. This equation is nonlinear because of the $\cos y$ term.

Visit this **website (http://www.openstaxcollege.org/l/20_Secondord2)** that discusses second-order differential equations.

7.1 Classify each of the following equations as linear or nonlinear. If the equation is linear, determine further whether it is homogeneous or nonhomogeneous.

a. $(y'')^2 - y' + 8x^3 y = 0$

b. $(\sin t)y'' + \cos t - 3ty' = 0$

Later in this section, we will see some techniques for solving specific types of differential equations. Before we get to that, however, let's get a feel for how solutions to linear differential equations behave. In many cases, solving differential equations depends on making educated guesses about what the solution might look like. Knowing how various types of solutions behave will be helpful.

Example 7.2

Verifying a Solution

Consider the linear, homogeneous differential equation

$$x^2 y'' - xy' - 3y = 0.$$

Looking at this equation, notice that the coefficient functions are polynomials, with higher powers of x associated with higher-order derivatives of y. Show that $y = x^3$ is a solution to this differential equation.

Solution

Let $y = x^3$. Then $y' = 3x^2$ and $y'' = 6x$. Substituting into the differential equation, we see that

$$\begin{aligned} x^2 y'' - xy' - 3y &= x^2(6x) - x\left(3x^2\right) - 3\left(x^3\right) \\ &= 6x^3 - 3x^3 - 3x^3 \\ &= 0. \end{aligned}$$

7.2 Show that $y = 2x^2$ is a solution to the differential equation

$$\frac{1}{2}x^2 y'' - xy' + y = 0.$$

Although simply finding any solution to a differential equation is important, mathematicians and engineers often want to go beyond finding *one* solution to a differential equation to finding *all* solutions to a differential equation. In other words, we want to find a general solution**.** Just as with first-order differential equations, a general solution (or family of solutions) gives the entire set of solutions to a differential equation. An important difference between first-order and second-order equations is that, with second-order equations, we typically need to find two different solutions to the equation to find the general solution. If we find two solutions, then any linear combination of these solutions is also a solution. We state this fact as the following theorem.

Theorem 7.1: Superposition Principle

If $y_1(x)$ and $y_2(x)$ are solutions to a linear homogeneous differential equation, then the function

$$y(x) = c_1 y_1(x) + c_2 y_2(x),$$

where c_1 and c_2 are constants, is also a solution.

The proof of this superposition principle theorem is left as an exercise.

Example 7.3

Verifying the Superposition Principle

Consider the differential equation

$$y'' - 4y' - 5y = 0.$$

Given that e^{-x} and e^{5x} are solutions to this differential equation, show that $4e^{-x} + e^{5x}$ is a solution.

Solution

We have

$$y(x) = 4e^{-x} + e^{5x}, \text{ so } y'(x) = -4e^{-x} + 5e^{5x} \text{ and } y''(x) = 4e^{-x} + 25e^{5x}.$$

Then

$$\begin{aligned} y'' - 4y' - 5y &= \left(4e^{-x} + 25e^{5x}\right) - 4\left(-4e^{-x} + 5e^{5x}\right) - 5\left(4e^{-x} + e^{5x}\right) \\ &= 4e^{-x} + 25e^{5x} + 16e^{-x} - 20e^{5x} - 20e^{-x} - 5e^{5x} \\ &= 0. \end{aligned}$$

Thus, $y(x) = 4e^{-x} + e^{5x}$ is a solution.

7.3 Consider the differential equation

$$y'' + 5y' + 6y = 0.$$

Given that e^{-2x} and e^{-3x} are solutions to this differential equation, show that $3e^{-2x} + 6e^{-3x}$ is a solution.

Unfortunately, to find the general solution to a second-order differential equation, it is not enough to find any two solutions and then combine them. Consider the differential equation

$$x'' + 7x' + 12x = 0.$$

Both e^{-3t} and $2e^{-3t}$ are solutions (check this). However, $x(t) = c_1 e^{-3t} + c_2\left(2e^{-3t}\right)$ is *not* the general solution. This expression does not account for all solutions to the differential equation. In particular, it fails to account for the function e^{-4t}, which is also a solution to the differential equation.

It turns out that to find the general solution to a second-order differential equation, we must find two linearly independent solutions. We define that terminology here.

Definition

A set of functions $f_1(x), f_2(x),\dots,f_n(x)$ is said to be **linearly dependent** if there are constants $c_1, c_2,\dots c_n,$ not all zero, such that $c_1 f_1(x) + c_2 f_2(x) + \cdots + c_n f_n(x) = 0$ for all *x* over the interval of interest. A set of functions that is not linearly dependent is said to be **linearly independent**.

In this chapter, we usually test sets of only two functions for linear independence, which allows us to simplify this definition. From a practical perspective, we see that two functions are linearly dependent if either one of them is identically zero or if they are constant multiples of each other.

First we show that if the functions meet the conditions given previously, then they are linearly dependent. If one of the functions is identically zero—say, $f_2(x) \equiv 0$—then choose $c_1 = 0$ and $c_2 = 1,$ and the condition for linear dependence is satisfied. If, on the other hand, neither $f_1(x)$ nor $f_2(x)$ is identically zero, but $f_1(x) = Cf_2(x)$ for some constant $C,$ then choose $c_1 = \frac{1}{C}$ and $c_2 = -1,$ and again, the condition is satisfied.

Next, we show that if two functions are linearly dependent, then either one is identically zero or they are constant multiples of one another. Assume $f_1(x)$ and $f_2(x)$ are linearly independent. Then, there are constants, c_1 and $c_2,$ not both zero, such that

$$c_1 f_1(x) + c_2 f_2(x) = 0$$

for all *x* over the interval of interest. Then,

$$c_1 f_1(x) = -c_2 f_2(x).$$

Now, since we stated that c_1 and c_2 can't both be zero, assume $c_2 \neq 0.$ Then, there are two cases: either $c_1 = 0$ or $c_1 \neq 0.$ If $c_1 = 0,$ then

$$0 = -c_2 f_2(x)$$
$$0 = f_2(x),$$

so one of the functions is identically zero. Now suppose $c_1 \neq 0.$ Then,

$$f_1(x) = \left(-\frac{c_2}{c_1}\right) f_2(x)$$

and we see that the functions are constant multiples of one another.

Theorem 7.2: Linear Dependence of Two Functions

Two functions, $f_1(x)$ and $f_2(x),$ are said to be linearly dependent if either one of them is identically zero or if $f_1(x) = Cf_2(x)$ for some constant *C* and for all *x* over the interval of interest. Functions that are not linearly dependent are said to be *linearly independent*.

Example 7.4

Testing for Linear Dependence

Determine whether the following pairs of functions are linearly dependent or linearly independent.

a. $f_1(x) = x^2, \quad f_2(x) = 5x^2$

b. $f_1(x) = \sin x, \quad f_2(x) = \cos x$

c. $f_1(x) = e^{3x}, \quad f_2(x) = e^{-3x}$

d. $f_1(x) = 3x, \quad f_2(x) = 3x + 1$

Solution

a. $f_2(x) = 5f_1(x),$ so the functions are linearly dependent.

b. There is no constant C such that $f_1(x) = Cf_2(x),$ so the functions are linearly independent.

c. There is no constant C such that $f_1(x) = Cf_2(x),$ so the functions are linearly independent. Don't get confused by the fact that the exponents are constant multiples of each other. With two exponential functions, unless the exponents are equal, the functions are linearly independent.

d. There is no constant C such that $f_1(x) = Cf_2(x),$ so the functions are linearly independent.

7.4 Determine whether the following pairs of functions are linearly dependent or linearly independent: $f_1(x) = e^x, \quad f_2(x) = 3e^{3x}.$

If we are able to find two linearly independent solutions to a second-order differential equation, then we can combine them to find the general solution. This result is formally stated in the following theorem.

Theorem 7.3: General Solution to a Homogeneous Equation

If $y_1(x)$ and $y_2(x)$ are linearly independent solutions to a second-order, linear, homogeneous differential equation, then the general solution is given by

$$y(x) = c_1 y_1(x) + c_2 y_2(x),$$

where c_1 and c_2 are constants.

When we say a family of functions is the general solution to a differential equation, we mean that (1) every expression of that form is a solution and (2) every solution to the differential equation can be written in that form, which makes this theorem extremely powerful. If we can find two linearly independent solutions to a differential equation, we have, effectively, found *all* solutions to the differential equation—quite a remarkable statement. The proof of this theorem is beyond the scope of this text.

Example 7.5

Writing the General Solution

If $y_1(t) = e^{3t}$ and $y_2(t) = e^{-3t}$ are solutions to $y'' - 9y = 0,$ what is the general solution?

Solution

Note that y_1 and y_2 are not constant multiples of one another, so they are linearly independent. Then, the general solution to the differential equation is $y(t) = c_1 e^{3t} + c_2 e^{-3t}$.

7.5 If $y_1(x) = e^{3x}$ and $y_2(x) = xe^{3x}$ are solutions to $y'' - 6y' + 9y = 0$, what is the general solution?

Second-Order Equations with Constant Coefficients

Now that we have a better feel for linear differential equations, we are going to concentrate on solving second-order equations of the form

$$ay'' + by' + cy = 0, \tag{7.2}$$

where a, b, and c are constants.

Since all the coefficients are constants, the solutions are probably going to be functions with derivatives that are constant multiples of themselves. We need all the terms to cancel out, and if taking a derivative introduces a term that is not a constant multiple of the original function, it is difficult to see how that term cancels out. Exponential functions have derivatives that are constant multiples of the original function, so let's see what happens when we try a solution of the form $y(x) = e^{\lambda x}$, where λ (the lowercase Greek letter lambda) is some constant.

If $y(x) = e^{\lambda x}$, then $y'(x) = \lambda e^{\lambda x}$ and $y'' = \lambda^2 e^{\lambda x}$. Substituting these expressions into **Equation 7.1**, we get

$$\begin{aligned} ay'' + by' + cy &= a(\lambda^2 e^{\lambda x}) + b(\lambda e^{\lambda x}) + ce^{\lambda x} \\ &= e^{\lambda x}(a\lambda^2 + b\lambda + c). \end{aligned}$$

Since $e^{\lambda x}$ is never zero, this expression can be equal to zero for all x only if

$$a\lambda^2 + b\lambda + c = 0.$$

We call this the characteristic equation of the differential equation.

Definition

The **characteristic equation** of the differential equation $ay'' + by' + cy = 0$ is $a\lambda^2 + b\lambda + c = 0$.

The characteristic equation is very important in finding solutions to differential equations of this form. We can solve the characteristic equation either by factoring or by using the quadratic formula

$$\lambda = \frac{-b \pm \sqrt{b^2 - 4ac}}{2a}.$$

This gives three cases. The characteristic equation has (1) distinct real roots; (2) a single, repeated real root; or (3) complex conjugate roots. We consider each of these cases separately.

Distinct Real Roots

If the characteristic equation has distinct real roots λ_1 and λ_2, then $e^{\lambda_1 x}$ and $e^{\lambda_2 x}$ are linearly independent solutions to **Example 7.1**, and the general solution is given by

$$y(x) = c_1 e^{\lambda_1 x} + c_2 e^{\lambda_2 x},$$

where c_1 and c_2 are constants.

For example, the differential equation $y'' + 9y' + 14y = 0$ has the associated characteristic equation $\lambda^2 + 9\lambda + 14 = 0$. This factors into $(\lambda + 2)(\lambda + 7) = 0$, which has roots $\lambda_1 = -2$ and $\lambda_2 = -7$. Therefore, the general solution to this differential equation is

$$y(x) = c_1 e^{-2x} + c_2 e^{-7x}.$$

Single Repeated Real Root

Things are a little more complicated if the characteristic equation has a repeated real root, λ. In this case, we know $e^{\lambda x}$ is a solution to **Equation 7.1**, but it is only one solution and we need two linearly independent solutions to determine the general solution. We might be tempted to try a function of the form $ke^{\lambda x}$, where k is some constant, but it would not be linearly independent of $e^{\lambda x}$. Therefore, let's try $xe^{\lambda x}$ as the second solution. First, note that by the quadratic formula,

$$\lambda = \frac{-b \pm \sqrt{b^2 - 4ac}}{2a}.$$

But, λ is a repeated root, so $b^2 - 4ac = 0$ and $\lambda = \frac{-b}{2a}$. Thus, if $y = xe^{\lambda x}$, we have

$$y' = e^{\lambda x} + \lambda xe^{\lambda x} \text{ and } y'' = 2\lambda e^{\lambda x} + \lambda^2 xe^{\lambda x}.$$

Substituting these expressions into **Equation 7.1**, we see that

$$\begin{aligned} ay'' + by' + cy &= a(2\lambda e^{\lambda x} + \lambda^2 xe^{\lambda x}) + b(e^{\lambda x} + \lambda xe^{\lambda x}) + cxe^{\lambda x} \\ &= xe^{\lambda x}(a\lambda^2 + b\lambda + c) + e^{\lambda x}(2a\lambda + b) \\ &= xe^{\lambda x}(0) + e^{\lambda x}\left(2a\left(\frac{-b}{2a}\right) + b\right) \\ &= 0 + e^{\lambda x}(0) \\ &= 0. \end{aligned}$$

This shows that $xe^{\lambda x}$ is a solution to **Equation 7.1**. Since $e^{\lambda x}$ and $xe^{\lambda x}$ are linearly independent, when the characteristic equation has a repeated root λ, the general solution to **Equation 7.1** is given by

$$y(x) = c_1 e^{\lambda x} + c_2 xe^{\lambda x},$$

where c_1 and c_2 are constants.

For example, the differential equation $y'' + 12y' + 36y = 0$ has the associated characteristic equation $\lambda^2 + 12\lambda + 36 = 0$. This factors into $(\lambda + 6)^2 = 0$, which has a repeated root $\lambda = -6$. Therefore, the general solution to this differential equation is

$$y(x) = c_1 e^{-6x} + c_2 xe^{-6x}.$$

Complex Conjugate Roots

The third case we must consider is when $b^2 - 4ac < 0$. In this case, when we apply the quadratic formula, we are taking the square root of a negative number. We must use the imaginary number $i = \sqrt{-1}$ to find the roots, which take the form $\lambda_1 = \alpha + \beta i$ and $\lambda_2 = \alpha - \beta i$. The complex number $\alpha + \beta i$ is called the *conjugate* of $\alpha - \beta i$. Thus, we see that when $b^2 - 4ac < 0$, the roots of our characteristic equation are always complex conjugates.

This creates a little bit of a problem for us. If we follow the same process we used for distinct real roots—using the roots of the characteristic equation as the coefficients in the exponents of exponential functions—we get the functions $e^{(\alpha + \beta i)x}$ and $e^{(\alpha - \beta i)x}$ as our solutions. However, there are problems with this approach. First, these functions take on complex (imaginary) values, and a complete discussion of such functions is beyond the scope of this text. Second, even if we were comfortable with complex-value functions, in this course we do not address the idea of a derivative for such functions. So, if possible, we'd like to find two linearly independent *real-value* solutions to the differential equation. For purposes of this development, we are going to manipulate and differentiate the functions $e^{(\alpha + \beta i)x}$ and $e^{(\alpha - \beta i)x}$ as if they were real-value functions. For these particular functions, this approach is valid mathematically, but be aware that there are other instances when complex-value functions do not follow the same rules as real-value functions. Those of you interested in a more in-depth discussion of complex-value functions should consult a complex analysis text.

Based on the roots $\alpha \pm \beta i$ of the characteristic equation, the functions $e^{(\alpha + \beta i)x}$ and $e^{(\alpha - \beta i)x}$ are linearly independent solutions to the differential equation. and the general solution is given by

$$y(x) = c_1 e^{(\alpha + \beta i)x} + c_2 e^{(\alpha - \beta i)x}.$$

Using some smart choices for c_1 and $c_2,$ and a little bit of algebraic manipulation, we can find two linearly independent, real-value solutions to **Equation 7.1** and express our general solution in those terms.

We encountered exponential functions with complex exponents earlier. One of the key tools we used to express these exponential functions in terms of sines and cosines was Euler's formula, which tells us that

$$e^{i\theta} = \cos\theta + i\sin\theta$$

for all real numbers θ.

Going back to the general solution, we have

$$\begin{aligned} y(x) &= c_1 e^{(\alpha + \beta i)x} + c_2 e^{(\alpha - \beta i)x} \\ &= c_1 e^{\alpha x} e^{\beta i x} + c_2 e^{\alpha x} e^{-\beta i x} \\ &= e^{\alpha x}\left(c_1 e^{\beta i x} + c_2 e^{-\beta i x}\right). \end{aligned}$$

Applying Euler's formula together with the identities $\cos(-x) = \cos x$ and $\sin(-x) = -\sin x,$ we get

$$\begin{aligned} y(x) &= e^{\alpha x}\left[c_1(\cos\beta x + i\sin\beta x) + c_2(\cos(-\beta x) + i\sin(-\beta x))\right] \\ &= e^{\alpha x}\left[(c_1 + c_2)\cos\beta x + (c_1 - c_2)i\sin\beta x\right]. \end{aligned}$$

Now, if we choose $c_1 = c_2 = \frac{1}{2},$ the second term is zero and we get

$$y(x) = e^{\alpha x}\cos\beta x$$

as a real-value solution to **Equation 7.1**. Similarly, if we choose $c_1 = -\frac{i}{2}$ and $c_2 = \frac{i}{2},$ the first term is zero and we get

$$y(x) = e^{\alpha x}\sin\beta x$$

as a second, linearly independent, real-value solution to **Equation 7.1**.

Based on this, we see that if the characteristic equation has complex conjugate roots $\alpha \pm \beta i,$ then the general solution to **Equation 7.1** is given by

$$\begin{aligned} y(x) &= c_1 e^{\alpha x}\cos\beta x + c_2 e^{\alpha x}\sin\beta x \\ &= e^{\alpha x}(c_1\cos\beta x + c_2\sin\beta x), \end{aligned}$$

where c_1 and c_2 are constants.

For example, the differential equation $y'' - 2y' + 5y = 0$ has the associated characteristic equation $\lambda^2 - 2\lambda + 5 = 0.$ By the quadratic formula, the roots of the characteristic equation are $1 \pm 2i.$ Therefore, the general solution to this differential equation is

$$y(x) = e^{x}(c_1\cos 2x + c_2\sin 2x).$$

Summary of Results

We can solve second-order, linear, homogeneous differential equations with constant coefficients by finding the roots of the associated characteristic equation. The form of the general solution varies, depending on whether the characteristic equation has distinct, real roots; a single, repeated real root; or complex conjugate roots. The three cases are summarized in **Table 7.1**.

Characteristic Equation Roots	General Solution to the Differential Equation
Distinct real roots, λ_1 and λ_2	$y(x) = c_1 e^{\lambda_1 x} + c_2 e^{\lambda_2 x}$
A repeated real root, λ	$y(x) = c_1 e^{\lambda x} + c_2 x e^{\lambda x}$
Complex conjugate roots $\alpha \pm \beta i$	$y(x) = e^{\alpha x}(c_1 \cos \beta x + c_2 \sin \beta x)$

Table 7.1 Summary of Characteristic Equation Cases

Problem-Solving Strategy: Using the Characteristic Equation to Solve Second-Order Differential Equations with Constant Coefficients

1. Write the differential equation in the form $ay'' + by' + cy = 0.$
2. Find the corresponding characteristic equation $a\lambda^2 + b\lambda + c = 0.$
3. Either factor the characteristic equation or use the quadratic formula to find the roots.
4. Determine the form of the general solution based on whether the characteristic equation has distinct, real roots; a single, repeated real root; or complex conjugate roots.

Example 7.6

Solving Second-Order Equations with Constant Coefficients

Find the general solution to the following differential equations. Give your answers as functions of x.

a. $y'' + 3y' - 4y = 0$

b. $y'' + 6y' + 13y = 0$

c. $y'' + 2y' + y = 0$

d. $y'' - 5y' = 0$

e. $y'' - 16y = 0$

f. $y'' + 16y = 0$

Solution

Note that all these equations are already given in standard form (step 1).

a. The characteristic equation is $\lambda^2 + 3\lambda - 4 = 0$ (step 2). This factors into $(\lambda + 4)(\lambda - 1) = 0,$ so the roots of the characteristic equation are $\lambda_1 = -4$ and $\lambda_2 = 1$ (step 3). Then the general solution to the differential equation is

$$y(x) = c_1 e^{-4x} + c_2 e^x \text{ (step 4).}$$

b. The characteristic equation is $\lambda^2 + 6\lambda + 13 = 0$ (step 2). Applying the quadratic formula, we see this equation has complex conjugate roots $-3 \pm 2i$ (step 3). Then the general solution to the differential equation is

$$y(t) = e^{-3t}(c_1 \cos 2t + c_2 \sin 2t) \text{(step 4).}$$

c. The characteristic equation is $\lambda^2 + 2\lambda + 1 = 0$ (step 2). This factors into $(\lambda + 1)^2 = 0,$ so the characteristic equation has a repeated real root $\lambda = -1$ (step 3). Then the general solution to the differential equation is

$$y(t) = c_1 e^{-t} + c_2 te^{-t} \text{ (step 4).}$$

d. The characteristic equation is $\lambda^2 - 5\lambda$ (step 2). This factors into $\lambda(\lambda - 5) = 0,$ so the roots of the characteristic equation are $\lambda_1 = 0$ and $\lambda_2 = 5$ (step 3). Note that $e^{0x} = e^0 = 1,$ so our first solution is just a constant. Then the general solution to the differential equation is

$$y(x) = c_1 + c_2 e^{5x} \text{ (step 4).}$$

e. The characteristic equation is $\lambda^2 - 16 = 0$ (step 2). This factors into $(\lambda + 4)(\lambda - 4) = 0,$ so the roots of the characteristic equation are $\lambda_1 = 4$ and $\lambda_2 = -4$ (step 3). Then the general solution to the differential equation is

$$y(x) = c_1 e^{4x} + c_2 e^{-4x} \text{ (step 4).}$$

f. The characteristic equation is $\lambda^2 + 16 = 0$ (step 2). This has complex conjugate roots $\pm 4i$ (step 3). Note that $e^{0x} = e^0 = 1,$ so the exponential term in our solution is just a constant. Then the general solution to the differential equation is

$$y(t) = c_1 \cos 4t + c_2 \sin 4t \text{ (step 4).}$$

7.6 Find the general solution to the following differential equations:

a. $y'' - 2y' + 10y = 0$

b. $y'' + 14y' + 49y = 0$

Initial-Value Problems and Boundary-Value Problems

So far, we have been finding general solutions to differential equations. However, differential equations are often used to describe physical systems, and the person studying that physical system usually knows something about the state of that system at one or more points in time. For example, if a constant-coefficient differential equation is representing how far a motorcycle shock absorber is compressed, we might know that the rider is sitting still on his motorcycle at the start of a race, time $t = t_0$. This means the system is at equilibrium, so $y(t_0) = 0,$ and the compression of the shock absorber is not changing, so $y'(t_0) = 0.$ With these two initial conditions and the general solution to the differential equation, we can find the *specific* solution to the differential equation that satisfies both initial conditions. This process is known as *solving an initial-value problem*. (Recall that we discussed initial-value problems in **Introduction to Differential Equations (http://cnx.org/content/m53696/latest/)** .) Note that second-order equations have two arbitrary constants in the general solution, and therefore we require two initial conditions to find the solution to the initial-value problem.

Sometimes we know the condition of the system at two different times. For example, we might know $y(t_0) = y_0$ and

$y(t_1) = y_1$. These conditions are called **boundary conditions**, and finding the solution to the differential equation that satisfies the boundary conditions is called solving a **boundary-value problem**.

Mathematicians, scientists, and engineers are interested in understanding the conditions under which an initial-value problem or a boundary-value problem has a unique solution. Although a complete treatment of this topic is beyond the scope of this text, it is useful to know that, within the context of constant-coefficient, second-order equations, initial-value problems are guaranteed to have a unique solution as long as two initial conditions are provided. Boundary-value problems, however, are not as well behaved. Even when two boundary conditions are known, we may encounter boundary-value problems with unique solutions, many solutions, or no solution at all.

Example 7.7

Solving an Initial-Value Problem

Solve the following initial-value problem: $y'' + 3y' - 4y = 0, \quad y(0) = 1, \quad y'(0) = -9.$

Solution

We already solved this differential equation in **Example 7.6**a. and found the general solution to be

$$y(x) = c_1 e^{-4x} + c_2 e^x.$$

Then

$$y'(x) = -4c_1 e^{-4x} + c_2 e^x.$$

When $x = 0,$ we have $y(0) = c_1 + c_2$ and $y'(0) = -4c_1 + c_2$. Applying the initial conditions, we have

$$\begin{aligned} c_1 + c_2 &= 1 \\ -4c_1 + c_2 &= -9. \end{aligned}$$

Then $c_1 = 1 - c_2$. Substituting this expression into the second equation, we see that

$$\begin{aligned} -4(1 - c_2) + c_2 &= -9 \\ -4 + 4c_2 + c_2 &= -9 \\ 5c_2 &= -5 \\ c_2 &= -1. \end{aligned}$$

So, $c_1 = 2$ and the solution to the initial-value problem is

$$y(x) = 2e^{-4x} - e^x.$$

7.7 Solve the initial-value problem $y'' - 3y' - 10y = 0, \quad y(0) = 0, \quad y'(0) = 7.$

Example 7.8

Solving an Initial-Value Problem and Graphing the Solution

Solve the following initial-value problem and graph the solution:

$$y'' + 6y' + 13y = 0, \; y(0) = 0, \; y'(0) = 2$$

Solution

We already solved this differential equation in **Example 7.6**b. and found the general solution to be

$$y(x) = e^{-3x}(c_1 \cos 2x + c_2 \sin 2x).$$

Then

$$y'(x) = e^{-3x}(-2c_1 \sin 2x + 2c_2 \cos 2x) - 3e^{-3x}(c_1 \cos 2x + c_2 \sin 2x).$$

When $x = 0,$ we have $y(0) = c_1$ and $y'(0) = 2c_2 - 3c_1$. Applying the initial conditions, we obtain

$$\begin{aligned} c_1 &= 0 \\ -3c_1 + 2c_2 &= 2. \end{aligned}$$

Therefore, $c_1 = 0,$ $c_2 = 1,$ and the solution to the initial value problem is shown in the following graph.

$$y = e^{-3x} \sin 2x.$$

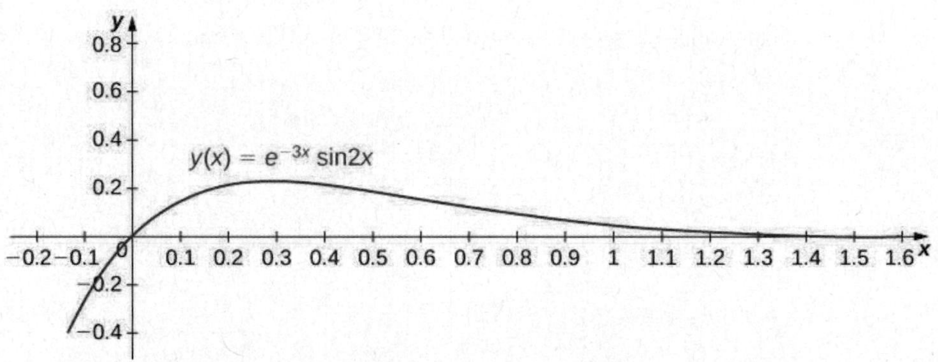

7.8 Solve the following initial-value problem and graph the solution: $y'' - 2y' + 10y = 0,\ y(0) = 2,\ y'(0) = -1$

Example 7.9

Initial-Value Problem Representing a Spring-Mass System

The following initial-value problem models the position of an object with mass attached to a spring. Spring-mass systems are examined in detail in **Applications**. The solution to the differential equation gives the position of the mass with respect to a neutral (equilibrium) position (in meters) at any given time. (Note that for spring-mass systems of this type, it is customary to define the downward direction as positive.)

$$y'' + 2y' + y = 0,\ y(0) = 1,\ y'(0) = 0$$

Solve the initial-value problem and graph the solution. What is the position of the mass at time $t = 2$ sec? How fast is the mass moving at time $t = 1$ sec? In what direction?

Solution

In **Example 7.6**c. we found the general solution to this differential equation to be

$$y(t) = c_1 e^{-t} + c_2 te^{-t}.$$

Then

$$y'(t) = -c_1 e^{-t} + c_2\left(-te^{-t} + e^{-t}\right).$$

When $t = 0,$ we have $y(0) = c_1$ and $y'(0) = -c_1 + c_2$. Applying the initial conditions, we obtain

$$\begin{aligned} c_1 &= 1 \\ -c_1 + c_2 &= 0. \end{aligned}$$

Thus, $c_1 = 1,$ $c_2 = 1,$ and the solution to the initial value problem is

$$y(t) = e^{-t} + te^{-t}.$$

This solution is represented in the following graph. At time $t = 2,$ the mass is at position $y(2) = e^{-2} + 2e^{-2} = 3e^{-2} \approx 0.406$ m below equilibrium.

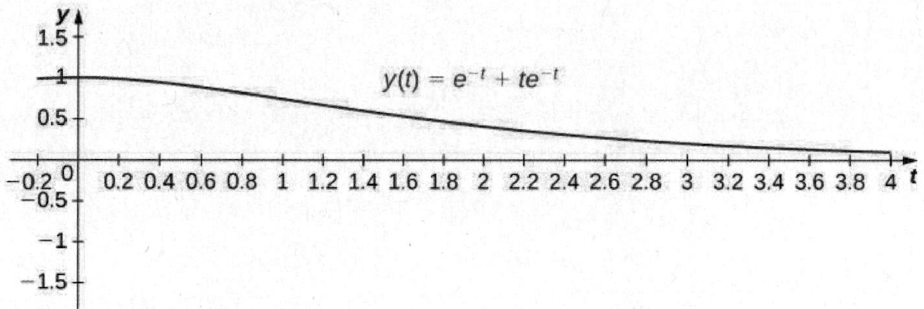

To calculate the velocity at time $t = 1,$ we need to find the derivative. We have $y(t) = e^{-t} + te^{-t},$ so

$$y'(t) = -e^{-t} + e^{-t} - te^{-t} = -te^{-t}.$$

Then $y'(1) = -e^{-1} \approx -0.3679.$ At time $t = 1,$ the mass is moving upward at 0.3679 m/sec.

7.9 Suppose the following initial-value problem models the position (in feet) of a mass in a spring-mass system at any given time. Solve the initial-value problem and graph the solution. What is the position of the mass at time $t = 0.3$ sec? How fast is it moving at time $t = 0.1$ sec? In what direction?

$$y'' + 14y' + 49y = 0,\ y(0) = 0,\ y'(0) = 1$$

Example 7.10

Solving a Boundary-Value Problem

In **Example 7.6**f. we solved the differential equation $y'' + 16y = 0$ and found the general solution to be $y(t) = c_1 \cos 4t + c_2 \sin 4t.$ If possible, solve the boundary-value problem if the boundary conditions are the following:

a. $y(0) = 0,\ \ y\left(\frac{\pi}{4}\right) = 0$

b. $y(0) = 1,\ \ y\left(\frac{\pi}{8}\right) = 0$

c. $y\left(\frac{\pi}{8}\right) = 0, \quad y\left(\frac{3\pi}{8}\right) = 2$

Solution

We have

$$y(x) = c_1 \cos 4t + c_2 \sin 4t.$$

a. Applying the first boundary condition given here, we get $y(0) = c_1 = 0.$ So the solution is of the form $y(t) = c_2 \sin 4t.$ When we apply the second boundary condition, though, we get $y\left(\frac{\pi}{4}\right) = c_2 \sin\left(4\left(\frac{\pi}{4}\right)\right) = c_2 \sin \pi = 0$ for all values of $c_2.$ The boundary conditions are not sufficient to determine a value for $c_2,$ so this boundary-value problem has infinitely many solutions. Thus, $y(t) = c_2 \sin 4t$ is a solution for any value of $c_2.$

b. Applying the first boundary condition given here, we get $y(0) = c_1 = 1.$ Applying the second boundary condition gives $y\left(\frac{\pi}{8}\right) = c_2 = 0,$ so $c_2 = 0.$ In this case, we have a unique solution: $y(t) = \cos 4t.$

c. Applying the first boundary condition given here, we get $y\left(\frac{\pi}{8}\right) = c_2 = 0.$ However, applying the second boundary condition gives $y\left(\frac{3\pi}{8}\right) = -c_2 = 2,$ so $c_2 = -2.$ We cannot have $c_2 = 0 = -2,$ so this boundary value problem has no solution.

7.1 EXERCISES

Classify each of the following equations as linear or nonlinear. If the equation is linear, determine whether it is homogeneous or nonhomogeneous.

1. $x^3 y'' + (x-1)y' - 8y = 0$

2. $\left(1+y^2\right)y'' + xy' - 3y = \cos x$

3. $xy'' + e^y y' = x$

4. $y'' + \frac{4}{x}y' - 8xy = 5x^2 + 1$

5. $y'' + (\sin x)y' - xy = 4y$

6. $y'' + \left(\frac{x+3}{y}\right)y' = 0$

For each of the following problems, verify that the given function is a solution to the differential equation. Use a graphing utility to graph the particular solutions for several values of c_1 and c_2. What do the solutions have in common?

7. **[T]** $y'' + 2y' - 3y = 0;\ \ y(x) = c_1 e^x + c_2 e^{-3x}$

8. **[T]** $x^2 y'' - 2y - 3x^2 + 1 = 0;$ $y(x) = c_1 x^2 + c_2 x^{-1} + x^2 \ln(x) + \frac{1}{2}$

9. **[T]** $y'' + 14y' + 49y = 0;\ \ y(x) = c_1 e^{-7x} + c_2 xe^{-7x}$

10. **[T]** $6y'' - 49y' + 8y = 0;\ \ y(x) = c_1 e^{x/6} + c_2 e^{8x}$

Find the general solution to the linear differential equation.

11. $y'' - 3y' - 10y = 0$

12. $y'' - 7y' + 12y = 0$

13. $y'' + 4y' + 4y = 0$

14. $4y'' - 12y' + 9y = 0$

15. $2y'' - 3y' - 5y = 0$

16. $3y'' - 14y' + 8y = 0$

17. $y'' + y' + y = 0$

18. $5y'' + 2y' + 4y = 0$

19. $y'' - 121y = 0$

20. $8y'' + 14y' - 15y = 0$

21. $y'' + 81y = 0$

22. $y'' - y' + 11y = 0$

23. $2y'' = 0$

24. $y'' - 6y' + 9y = 0$

25. $3y'' - 2y' - 7y = 0$

26. $4y'' - 10y' = 0$

27. $36\frac{d^2y}{dx^2} + 12\frac{dy}{dx} + y = 0$

28. $25\frac{d^2y}{dx^2} - 80\frac{dy}{dx} + 64y = 0$

29. $\frac{d^2y}{dx^2} - 9\frac{dy}{dx} = 0$

30. $4\frac{d^2y}{dx^2} + 8y = 0$

Solve the initial-value problem.

31. $y'' + 5y' + 6y = 0,\quad y(0) = 0,\ \ y'(0) = -2$

32. $y'' + 2y' - 8y = 0,\quad y(0) = 5,\ \ y'(0) = 4$

33. $y'' + 4y = 0,\quad y(0) = 3,\ \ y'(0) = 10$

34. $y'' - 18y' + 81y = 0,\quad y(0) = 1,\ \ y'(0) = 5$

35. $y'' - y' - 30y = 0,\quad y(0) = 1,\ \ y'(0) = -16$

36. $4y'' + 4y' - 8y = 0,\quad y(0) = 2,\ \ y'(0) = 1$

37. $25y'' + 10y' + y = 0,\quad y(0) = 2,\ \ y'(0) = 1$

38. $y'' + y = 0,\quad y(\pi) = 1,\ \ y'(\pi) = -5$

Solve the boundary-value problem, if possible.

39. $y'' + y' - 42y = 0,\quad y(0) = 0,\ \ y(1) = 2$

40. $9y'' + y = 0,\quad y\left(\frac{3\pi}{2}\right) = 6,\ \ y(0) = -8$

41. $y'' + 10y' + 34y = 0,\quad y(0) = 6,\ \ y(\pi) = 2$

42. $y'' + 7y' - 60y = 0, \quad y(0) = 4, \ y(2) = 0$

43. $y'' - 4y' + 4y = 0, \quad y(0) = 2, \ y(1) = -1$

44. $y'' - 5y' = 0, \quad y(0) = 3, \ y(-1) = 2$

45. $y'' + 9y = 0, \quad y(0) = 4, \ y\left(\frac{\pi}{3}\right) = -4$

46. $4y'' + 25y = 0, \quad y(0) = 2, \ y(2\pi) = -2$

47. Find a differential equation with a general solution that is $y = c_1 e^{x/5} + c_2 e^{-4x}$.

48. Find a differential equation with a general solution that is $y = c_1 e^{x} + c_2 e^{-4x/3}$.

For each of the following differential equations:

a. Solve the initial value problem.

b. **[T]** Use a graphing utility to graph the particular solution.

49. $y'' + 64y = 0; \quad y(0) = 3, \quad y'(0) = 16$

50. $y'' - 2y' + 10y = 0 \quad y(0) = 1, \quad y'(0) = 13$

51. $y'' + 5y' + 15y = 0 \quad y(0) = -2, \quad y'(0) = 7$

52. (Principle of superposition) Prove that if $y_1(x)$ and $y_2(x)$ are solutions to a linear homogeneous differential equation, $y'' + p(x)y' + q(x)y = 0,$ then the function $y(x) = c_1 y_1(x) + c_2 y_2(x),$ where c_1 and c_2 are constants, is also a solution.

53. Prove that if a, b, and c are positive constants, then all solutions to the second-order linear differential equation $ay'' + by' + cy = 0$ approach zero as $x \to \infty$. (*Hint:* Consider three cases: two distinct roots, repeated real roots, and complex conjugate roots.)

7.2 | Nonhomogeneous Linear Equations

Learning Objectives

7.2.1 Write the general solution to a nonhomogeneous differential equation.

7.2.2 Solve a nonhomogeneous differential equation by the method of undetermined coefficients.

7.2.3 Solve a nonhomogeneous differential equation by the method of variation of parameters.

In this section, we examine how to solve nonhomogeneous differential equations. The terminology and methods are different from those we used for homogeneous equations, so let's start by defining some new terms.

General Solution to a Nonhomogeneous Linear Equation

Consider the nonhomogeneous linear differential equation

$$a_2(x)y'' + a_1(x)y' + a_0(x)y = r(x).$$

The associated homogeneous equation

$$a_2(x)y'' + a_1(x)y' + a_0(x)y = 0 \quad \textbf{(7.3)}$$

is called the **complementary equation**. We will see that solving the complementary equation is an important step in solving a nonhomogeneous differential equation.

Definition

A solution $y_p(x)$ of a differential equation that contains no arbitrary constants is called a **particular solution** to the equation.

Theorem 7.4: General Solution to a Nonhomogeneous Equation

Let $y_p(x)$ be any particular solution to the nonhomogeneous linear differential equation

$$a_2(x)y'' + a_1(x)y' + a_0(x)y = r(x).$$

Also, let $c_1 y_1(x) + c_2 y_2(x)$ denote the general solution to the complementary equation. Then, the general solution to the nonhomogeneous equation is given by

$$y(x) = c_1 y_1(x) + c_2 y_2(x) + y_p(x). \quad \textbf{(7.4)}$$

Proof

To prove $y(x)$ is the general solution, we must first show that it solves the differential equation and, second, that any solution to the differential equation can be written in that form. Substituting $y(x)$ into the differential equation, we have

$$\begin{aligned} a_2(x)y'' + a_1(x)y' + a_0(x)y &= a_2(x)(c_1 y_1 + c_2 y_2 + y_p)'' + a_1(x)(c_1 y_1 + c_2 y_2 + y_p)' \\ &\quad + a_0(x)(c_1 y_1 + c_2 y_2 + y_p) \\ &= [a_2(x)(c_1 y_1 + c_2 y_2)'' + a_1(x)(c_1 y_1 + c_2 y_2)' + a_0(x)(c_1 y_1 + c_2 y_2)] \\ &\quad + a_2(x)y_p'' + a_1(x)y_p' + a_0(x)y_p \\ &= 0 + r(x) \\ &= r(x). \end{aligned}$$

So $y(x)$ is a solution.

Now, let $z(x)$ be any solution to $a_2(x)y'' + a_1(x)y' + a_0(x)y = r(x).$ Then

$$\begin{aligned} a_2(x)(z - y_p)'' + a_1(x)(z - y_p)' + a_0(x)(z - y_p) &= \left(a_2(x)z'' + a_1(x)z' + a_0(x)z\right) \\ &\quad - \left(a_2(x)y_p{}'' + a_1(x)y_p{}' + a_0(x)y_p\right) \\ &= r(x) - r(x) \\ &= 0, \end{aligned}$$

so $z(x) - y_p(x)$ is a solution to the complementary equation. But, $c_1 y_1(x) + c_2 y_2(x)$ is the general solution to the complementary equation, so there are constants c_1 and c_2 such that

$$z(x) - y_p(x) = c_1 y_1(x) + c_2 y_2(x).$$

Hence, we see that $z(x) = c_1 y_1(x) + c_2 y_2(x) + y_p(x).$

□

Example 7.11

Verifying the General Solution

Given that $y_p(x) = x$ is a particular solution to the differential equation $y'' + y = x,$ write the general solution and check by verifying that the solution satisfies the equation.

Solution

The complementary equation is $y'' + y = 0,$ which has the general solution $c_1 \cos x + c_2 \sin x.$ So, the general solution to the nonhomogeneous equation is

$$y(x) = c_1 \cos x + c_2 \sin x + x.$$

To verify that this is a solution, substitute it into the differential equation. We have

$$y'(x) = -c_1 \sin x + c_2 \cos x + 1 \text{ and } y''(x) = -c_1 \cos x - c_2 \sin x.$$

Then

$$\begin{aligned} y''(x) + y(x) &= -c_1 \cos x - c_2 \sin x + c_1 \cos x + c_2 \sin x + x \\ &= x. \end{aligned}$$

So, $y(x)$ is a solution to $y'' + y = x.$

 **7.10** Given that $y_p(x) = -2$ is a particular solution to $y'' - 3y' - 4y = 8,$ write the general solution and verify that the general solution satisfies the equation.

In the preceding section, we learned how to solve homogeneous equations with constant coefficients. Therefore, for nonhomogeneous equations of the form $ay'' + by' + cy = r(x),$ we already know how to solve the complementary equation, and the problem boils down to finding a particular solution for the nonhomogeneous equation. We now examine two techniques for this: the method of undetermined coefficients and the method of variation of parameters.

Undetermined Coefficients

The **method of undetermined coefficients** involves making educated guesses about the form of the particular solution based on the form of $r(x).$ When we take derivatives of polynomials, exponential functions, sines, and cosines, we get polynomials, exponential functions, sines, and cosines. So when $r(x)$ has one of these forms, it is possible that the solution to the nonhomogeneous differential equation might take that same form. Let's look at some examples to see how this works.

Example 7.12

Undetermined Coefficients When $r(x)$ Is a Polynomial

Find the general solution to $y'' + 4y' + 3y = 3x$.

Solution

The complementary equation is $y'' + 4y' + 3y = 0$, with general solution $c_1 e^{-x} + c_2 e^{-3x}$. Since $r(x) = 3x$, the particular solution might have the form $y_p(x) = Ax + B$. If this is the case, then we have $y_p{}'(x) = A$ and $y_p{}''(x) = 0$. For y_p to be a solution to the differential equation, we must find values for A and B such that

$$\begin{aligned} y'' + 4y' + 3y &= 3x \\ 0 + 4(A) + 3(Ax + B) &= 3x \\ 3Ax + (4A + 3B) &= 3x. \end{aligned}$$

Setting coefficients of like terms equal, we have

$$\begin{aligned} 3A &= 3 \\ 4A + 3B &= 0. \end{aligned}$$

Then, $A = 1$ and $B = -\frac{4}{3}$, so $y_p(x) = x - \frac{4}{3}$ and the general solution is

$$y(x) = c_1 e^{-x} + c_2 e^{-3x} + x - \frac{4}{3}.$$

In **Example 7.12**, notice that even though $r(x)$ did not include a constant term, it was necessary for us to include the constant term in our guess. If we had assumed a solution of the form $y_p = Ax$ (with no constant term), we would not have been able to find a solution. (Verify this!) If the function $r(x)$ is a polynomial, our guess for the particular solution should be a polynomial of the same degree, and it must include all lower-order terms, regardless of whether they are present in $r(x)$.

Example 7.13

Undetermined Coefficients When $r(x)$ Is an Exponential

Find the general solution to $y'' - y' - 2y = 2e^{3x}$.

Solution

The complementary equation is $y'' - y' - 2y = 0$, with the general solution $c_1 e^{-x} + c_2 e^{2x}$. Since $r(x) = 2e^{3x}$, the particular solution might have the form $y_p(x) = Ae^{3x}$. Then, we have $y_p{}'(x) = 3Ae^{3x}$ and $y_p{}''(x) = 9Ae^{3x}$. For y_p to be a solution to the differential equation, we must find a value for A such that

$$\begin{aligned} y'' - y' - 2y &= 2e^{3x} \\ 9Ae^{3x} - 3Ae^{3x} - 2Ae^{3x} &= 2e^{3x} \\ 4Ae^{3x} &= 2e^{3x}. \end{aligned}$$

So, $4A = 2$ and $A = 1/2$. Then, $y_p(x) = \left(\frac{1}{2}\right)e^{3x}$, and the general solution is

$$y(x) = c_1 e^{-x} + c_2 e^{2x} + \frac{1}{2}e^{3x}.$$

7.11 Find the general solution to $y'' - 4y' + 4y = 7\sin t - \cos t$.

In the previous checkpoint, $r(x)$ included both sine and cosine terms. However, even if $r(x)$ included a sine term only or a cosine term only, both terms must be present in the guess. The method of undetermined coefficients also works with products of polynomials, exponentials, sines, and cosines. Some of the key forms of $r(x)$ and the associated guesses for $y_p(x)$ are summarized in **Table 7.2**.

$r(x)$	**Initial guess for $y_p(x)$**
k (a constant)	A (a constant)
$ax + b$	$Ax + B$ (*Note*: The guess must include both terms even if $b = 0.$)
$ax^2 + bx + c$	$Ax^2 + Bx + C$ (*Note*: The guess must include all three terms even if b or c are zero.)
Higher-order polynomials	Polynomial of the same order as $r(x)$
$ae^{\lambda x}$	$Ae^{\lambda x}$
$a\cos\beta x + b\sin\beta x$	$A\cos\beta x + B\sin\beta x$ (*Note*: The guess must include both terms even if either $a = 0$ or $b = 0.$)
$ae^{\alpha x}\cos\beta x + be^{\alpha x}\sin\beta x$	$Ae^{\alpha x}\cos\beta x + Be^{\alpha x}\sin\beta x$
$(ax^2 + bx + c)e^{\lambda x}$	$(Ax^2 + Bx + C)e^{\lambda x}$
$(a_2x^2 + a_1x + a_0)\cos\beta x$ $+(b_2x^2 + b_1x + b_0)\sin\beta x$	$(A_2x^2 + A_1x + A_0)\cos\beta x$ $+(B_2x^2 + B_1x + B_0)\sin\beta x$
$(a_2x^2 + a_1x + a_0)e^{\alpha x}\cos\beta x$ $+(b_2x^2 + b_1x + b_0)e^{\alpha x}\sin\beta x$	$(A_2x^2 + A_1x + A_0)e^{\alpha x}\cos\beta x$ $+(B_2x^2 + B_1x + B_0)e^{\alpha x}\sin\beta x$

Table 7.2 Key Forms for the Method of Undetermined Coefficients

Keep in mind that there is a key pitfall to this method. Consider the differential equation $y'' + 5y' + 6y = 3e^{-2x}$. Based on the form of $r(x)$, we guess a particular solution of the form $y_p(x) = Ae^{-2x}$. But when we substitute this expression into the differential equation to find a value for A, we run into a problem. We have

$$y_p'(x) = -2Ae^{-2x}$$

and

$$y_p'' = 4Ae^{-2x},$$

so we want

$$\begin{aligned} y'' + 5y' + 6y &= 3e^{-2x} \\ 4Ae^{-2x} + 5\left(-2Ae^{-2x}\right) + 6Ae^{-2x} &= 3e^{-2x} \\ 4Ae^{-2x} - 10Ae^{-2x} + 6Ae^{-2x} &= 3e^{-2x} \\ 0 &= 3e^{-2x}, \end{aligned}$$

which is not possible.

Looking closely, we see that, in this case, the general solution to the complementary equation is $c_1 e^{-2x} + c_2 e^{-3x}$. The exponential function in $r(x)$ is actually a solution to the complementary equation, so, as we just saw, all the terms on the left side of the equation cancel out. We can still use the method of undetermined coefficients in this case, but we have to alter our guess by multiplying it by x. Using the new guess, $y_p(x) = Axe^{-2x}$, we have

$$y_p{}'(x) = A\left(e^{-2x} - 2xe^{-2x}\right)$$

and

$$y_p{}''(x) = -4Ae^{-2x} + 4Axe^{-2x}.$$

Substitution gives

$$\begin{aligned} y'' + 5y' + 6y &= 3e^{-2x} \\ \left(-4Ae^{-2x} + 4Axe^{-2x}\right) + 5\left(Ae^{-2x} - 2Axe^{-2x}\right) + 6Axe^{-2x} &= 3e^{-2x} \\ -4Ae^{-2x} + 4Axe^{-2x} + 5Ae^{-2x} - 10Axe^{-2x} + 6Axe^{-2x} &= 3e^{-2x} \\ Ae^{-2x} &= 3e^{-2x}. \end{aligned}$$

So, $A = 3$ and $y_p(x) = 3xe^{-2x}$. This gives us the following general solution

$$y(x) = c_1 e^{-2x} + c_2 e^{-3x} + 3xe^{-2x}.$$

Note that if xe^{-2x} were also a solution to the complementary equation, we would have to multiply by x again, and we would try $y_p(x) = Ax^2 e^{-2x}$.

Problem-Solving Strategy: Method of Undetermined Coefficients

1. Solve the complementary equation and write down the general solution.
2. Based on the form of $r(x)$, make an initial guess for $y_p(x)$.
3. Check whether any term in the guess for $y_p(x)$ is a solution to the complementary equation. If so, multiply the guess by x. Repeat this step until there are no terms in $y_p(x)$ that solve the complementary equation.
4. Substitute $y_p(x)$ into the differential equation and equate like terms to find values for the unknown coefficients in $y_p(x)$.
5. Add the general solution to the complementary equation and the particular solution you just found to obtain the general solution to the nonhomogeneous equation.

Example 7.14

Solving Nonhomogeneous Equations

Find the general solutions to the following differential equations.

a. $y'' - 9y = -6\cos 3x$

b. $x'' + 2x' + x = 4e^{-t}$

c. $y'' - 2y' + 5y = 10x^2 - 3x - 3$

d. $y'' - 3y' = -12t$

Solution

a. The complementary equation is $y'' - 9y = 0,$ which has the general solution $c_1 e^{3x} + c_2 e^{-3x}$ (step 1). Based on the form of $r(x) = -6\cos 3x,$ our initial guess for the particular solution is $y_p(x) = A\cos 3x + B\sin 3x$ (step 2). None of the terms in $y_p(x)$ solve the complementary equation, so this is a valid guess (step 3).
Now we want to find values for A and $B,$ so substitute y_p into the differential equation. We have

$$y_p{}'(x) = -3A\sin 3x + 3B\cos 3x \text{ and } y_p{}''(x) = -9A\cos 3x - 9B\sin 3x,$$

so we want to find values of A and B such that

$$\begin{aligned} y'' - 9y &= -6\cos 3x \\ -9A\cos 3x - 9B\sin 3x - 9(A\cos 3x + B\sin 3x) &= -6\cos 3x \\ -18A\cos 3x - 18B\sin 3x &= -6\cos 3x. \end{aligned}$$

Therefore,

$$\begin{aligned} -18A &= -6 \\ -18B &= 0. \end{aligned}$$

This gives $A = \frac{1}{3}$ and $B = 0,$ so $y_p(x) = \left(\frac{1}{3}\right)\cos 3x$ (step 4).
Putting everything together, we have the general solution

$$y(x) = c_1 e^{3x} + c_2 e^{-3x} + \frac{1}{3}\cos 3x.$$

b. The complementary equation is $x'' + 2x' + x = 0,$ which has the general solution $c_1 e^{-t} + c_2 te^{-t}$ (step 1). Based on the form $r(t) = 4e^{-t},$ our initial guess for the particular solution is $x_p(t) = Ae^{-t}$ (step 2). However, we see that this guess solves the complementary equation, so we must multiply by $t,$ which gives a new guess: $x_p(t) = Ate^{-t}$ (step 3). Checking this new guess, we see that it, too, solves the complementary equation, so we must multiply by t again, which gives $x_p(t) = At^2 e^{-t}$ (step 3 again). Now, checking this guess, we see that $x_p(t)$ does not solve the complementary equation, so this is a valid guess (step 3 yet again).
We now want to find a value for $A,$ so we substitute x_p into the differential equation. We have

$$\begin{aligned} x_p(t) &= At^2 e^{-t}, \text{ so} \\ x_p{}'(t) &= 2Ate^{-t} - At^2 e^{-t} \end{aligned}$$

and $x_p''(t) = 2Ae^{-t} - 2Ate^{-t} - \left(2Ate^{-t} - At^2 e^{-t}\right) = 2Ae^{-t} - 4Ate^{-t} + At^2 e^{-t}.$

Substituting into the differential equation, we want to find a value of A so that

$$\begin{aligned} x'' + 2x' + x &= 4e^{-t} \\ 2Ae^{-t} - 4Ate^{-t} + At^2 e^{-t} + 2\left(2Ate^{-t} - At^2 e^{-t}\right) + At^2 e^{-t} &= 4e^{-t} \\ 2Ae^{-t} &= 4e^{-t}. \end{aligned}$$

This gives $A = 2,$ so $x_p(t) = 2t^2 e^{-t}$ (step 4). Putting everything together, we have the general solution

$$x(t) = c_1 e^{-t} + c_2 te^{-t} + 2t^2 e^{-t}.$$

c. The complementary equation is $y'' - 2y' + 5y = 0,$ which has the general solution $c_1 e^x \cos 2x + c_2 e^x \sin 2x$ (step 1). Based on the form $r(x) = 10x^2 - 3x - 3,$ our initial guess for the particular solution is $y_p(x) = Ax^2 + Bx + C$ (step 2). None of the terms in $y_p(x)$ solve the complementary equation, so this is a valid guess (step 3). We now want to find values for $A,$ $B,$ and $C,$ so we substitute y_p into the differential equation. We have $y_p'(x) = 2Ax + B$ and $y_p''(x) = 2A,$ so we want to find values of $A,$ $B,$ and C such that

$$\begin{aligned} y'' - 2y' + 5y &= 10x^2 - 3x - 3 \\ 2A - 2(2Ax + B) + 5\left(Ax^2 + Bx + C\right) &= 10x^2 - 3x - 3 \\ 5Ax^2 + (5B - 4A)x + (5C - 2B + 2A) &= 10x^2 - 3x - 3. \end{aligned}$$

Therefore,

$$\begin{aligned} 5A &= 10 \\ 5B - 4A &= -3 \\ 5C - 2B + 2A &= -3. \end{aligned}$$

This gives $A = 2,$ $B = 1,$ and $C = -1,$ so $y_p(x) = 2x^2 + x - 1$ (step 4). Putting everything together, we have the general solution

$$y(x) = c_1 e^x \cos 2x + c_2 e^x \sin 2x + 2x^2 + x - 1.$$

d. The complementary equation is $y'' - 3y' = 0,$ which has the general solution $c_1 e^{3t} + c_2$ (step 1). Based on the form $r(t) = -12t,$ our initial guess for the particular solution is $y_p(t) = At + B$ (step 2). However, we see that the constant term in this guess solves the complementary equation, so we must multiply by $t,$ which gives a new guess: $y_p(t) = At^2 + Bt$ (step 3). Checking this new guess, we see that none of the terms in $y_p(t)$ solve the complementary equation, so this is a valid guess (step 3 again). We now want to find values for A and $B,$ so we substitute y_p into the differential equation. We have $y_p'(t) = 2At + B$ and $y_p''(t) = 2A,$ so we want to find values of A and B such that

$$\begin{aligned} y'' - 3y' &= -12t \\ 2A - 3(2At + B) &= -12t \\ -6At + (2A - 3B) &= -12t. \end{aligned}$$

Therefore,

$$\begin{aligned} -6A &= -12 \\ 2A - 3B &= 0. \end{aligned}$$

This gives $A = 2$ and $B = 4/3,$ so $y_p(t) = 2t^2 + (4/3)t$ (step 4). Putting everything together, we have the general solution

$$y(t) = c_1 e^{3t} + c_2 + 2t^2 + \frac{4}{3}t.$$

7.12 Find the general solution to the following differential equations.

a. $y'' - 5y' + 4y = 3e^x$

b. $y'' + y' - 6y = 52\cos 2t$

Variation of Parameters

Sometimes, $r(x)$ is not a combination of polynomials, exponentials, or sines and cosines. When this is the case, the method of undetermined coefficients does not work, and we have to use another approach to find a particular solution to the differential equation. We use an approach called the **method of variation of parameters**.

To simplify our calculations a little, we are going to divide the differential equation through by $a,$ so we have a leading coefficient of 1. Then the differential equation has the form

$$y'' + py' + qy = r(x),$$

where p and q are constants.

If the general solution to the complementary equation is given by $c_1 y_1(x) + c_2 y_2(x),$ we are going to look for a particular solution of the form $y_p(x) = u(x)y_1(x) + v(x)y_2(x).$ In this case, we use the two linearly independent solutions to the complementary equation to form our particular solution. However, we are assuming the coefficients are functions of $x,$ rather than constants. We want to find functions $u(x)$ and $v(x)$ such that $y_p(x)$ satisfies the differential equation. We have

$$\begin{aligned} y_p &= uy_1 + vy_2 \\ y_p' &= u'y_1 + uy_1' + v'y_2 + vy_2' \\ y_p'' &= (u'y_1 + v'y_2)' + u'y_1' + uy_1'' + v'y_2' + vy_2''. \end{aligned}$$

Substituting into the differential equation, we obtain

$$\begin{aligned} y_p'' + py_p' + qy_p &= [(u'y_1 + v'y_2)' + u'y_1' + uy_1'' + v'y_2' + vy_2''] \\ &\quad + p[u'y_1 + uy_1' + v'y_2 + vy_2'] + q[uy_1 + vy_2] \\ &= u[y_1'' + py_1' + qy_1] + v[y_2'' + py_2' + qy_2] \\ &\quad + (u'y_1 + v'y_2)' + p(u'y_1 + v'y_2) + (u'y_1' + v'y_2'). \end{aligned}$$

Note that y_1 and y_2 are solutions to the complementary equation, so the first two terms are zero. Thus, we have

$$(u'y_1 + v'y_2)' + p(u'y_1 + v'y_2) + (u'y_1' + v'y_2') = r(x).$$

If we simplify this equation by imposing the additional condition $u'y_1 + v'y_2 = 0,$ the first two terms are zero, and this reduces to $u'y_1' + v'y_2' = r(x).$ So, with this additional condition, we have a system of two equations in two unknowns:

$$\begin{aligned} u'y_1 + v'y_2 &= 0 \\ u'y_1' + v'y_2' &= r(x). \end{aligned}$$

Solving this system gives us u' and $v',$ which we can integrate to find u and v.

Then, $y_p(x) = u(x)y_1(x) + v(x)y_2(x)$ is a particular solution to the differential equation. Solving this system of equations is sometimes challenging, so let's take this opportunity to review Cramer's rule, which allows us to solve the system of equations using determinants.

Rule: Cramer's Rule

The system of equations

$$\begin{aligned} a_1 z_1 + b_1 z_2 &= r_1 \\ a_2 z_1 + b_2 z_2 &= r_2 \end{aligned}$$

has a unique solution if and only if the determinant of the coefficients is not zero. In this case, the solution is given by

$$z_1 = \frac{\begin{vmatrix} r_1 & b_1 \\ r_2 & b_2 \end{vmatrix}}{\begin{vmatrix} a_1 & b_1 \\ a_2 & b_2 \end{vmatrix}} \quad \text{and} \quad z_2 = \frac{\begin{vmatrix} a_1 & r_1 \\ a_2 & r_2 \end{vmatrix}}{\begin{vmatrix} a_1 & b_1 \\ a_2 & b_2 \end{vmatrix}}.$$

Example 7.15

Using Cramer's Rule

Use Cramer's rule to solve the following system of equations.

$$\begin{aligned} x^2 z_1 + 2xz_2 &= 0 \\ z_1 - 3x^2 z_2 &= 2x \end{aligned}$$

Solution

We have

$$\begin{aligned} a_1(x) &= x^2 \\ a_2(x) &= 1 \\ b_1(x) &= 2x \\ b_2(x) &= -3x^2 \\ r_1(x) &= 0 \\ r_2(x) &= 2x. \end{aligned}$$

Then,

$$\begin{vmatrix} a_1 & b_1 \\ a_2 & b_2 \end{vmatrix} = \begin{vmatrix} x^2 & 2x \\ 1 & -3x^2 \end{vmatrix} = -3x^4 - 2x$$

and

$$\begin{vmatrix} r_1 & b_1 \\ r_2 & b_2 \end{vmatrix} = \begin{vmatrix} 0 & 2x \\ 2x & -3x^2 \end{vmatrix} = 0 - 4x^2 = -4x^2.$$

Thus,

$$z_1 = \frac{\begin{vmatrix} r_1 & b_1 \\ r_2 & b_2 \end{vmatrix}}{\begin{vmatrix} a_1 & b_1 \\ a_2 & b_2 \end{vmatrix}} = \frac{-4x^2}{-3x^4 - 2x} = \frac{4x}{3x^3 + 2}.$$

In addition,

$$\begin{vmatrix} a_1 & r_1 \\ a_2 & r_2 \end{vmatrix} = \begin{vmatrix} x^2 & 0 \\ 1 & 2x \end{vmatrix} = 2x^3 - 0 = 2x^3.$$

Thus,

$$z_2 = \frac{\begin{vmatrix} a_1 & r_1 \\ a_2 & r_2 \end{vmatrix}}{\begin{vmatrix} a_1 & b_1 \\ a_2 & b_2 \end{vmatrix}} = \frac{2x^3}{-3x^4 - 2x} = \frac{-2x^2}{3x^3 + 2}.$$

7.13 Use Cramer's rule to solve the following system of equations.

$$\begin{aligned} 2xz_1 - 3z_2 &= 0 \\ x^2 z_1 + 4xz_2 &= x + 1 \end{aligned}$$

Problem-Solving Strategy: Method of Variation of Parameters

1. Solve the complementary equation and write down the general solution
$$c_1 y_1(x) + c_2 y_2(x).$$
2. Use Cramer's rule or another suitable technique to find functions $u'(x)$ and $v'(x)$ satisfying
$$\begin{aligned} u' y_1 + v' y_2 &= 0 \\ u' y_1{}' + v' y_2{}' &= r(x). \end{aligned}$$
3. Integrate u' and v' to find $u(x)$ and $v(x)$. Then, $y_p(x) = u(x)y_1(x) + v(x)y_2(x)$ is a particular solution to the equation.
4. Add the general solution to the complementary equation and the particular solution found in step 3 to obtain the general solution to the nonhomogeneous equation.

Example 7.16

Using the Method of Variation of Parameters

Find the general solution to the following differential equations.

a. $y'' - 2y' + y = \frac{e^t}{t^2}$

b. $y'' + y = 3\sin^2 x$

Solution

a. The complementary equation is $y'' - 2y' + y = 0$ with associated general solution $c_1 e^t + c_2 te^t$. Therefore, $y_1(t) = e^t$ and $y_2(t) = te^t$. Calculating the derivatives, we get $y_1{}'(t) = e^t$ and $y_2{}'(t) = e^t + te^t$ (step 1). Then, we want to find functions $u'(t)$ and $v'(t)$ so that

$$\begin{aligned} u'e^t + v'te^t &= 0 \\ u'e^t + v'\left(e^t + te^t\right) &= \frac{e^t}{t^2}. \end{aligned}$$

Applying Cramer's rule, we have

$$u' = \frac{\begin{vmatrix} 0 & te^t \\ \frac{e^t}{t^2} & e^t + te^t \end{vmatrix}}{\begin{vmatrix} e^t & te^t \\ e^t & e^t + te^t \end{vmatrix}} = \frac{0 - te^t\left(\frac{e^t}{t^2}\right)}{e^t\left(e^t + te^t\right) - e^t te^t} = \frac{-\frac{e^{2t}}{t}}{e^{2t}} = -\frac{1}{t}$$

and

$$v' = \frac{\begin{vmatrix} e^t & 0 \\ e^t & \frac{e^t}{t^2} \end{vmatrix}}{\begin{vmatrix} e^t & te^t \\ e^t & e^t + te^t \end{vmatrix}} = \frac{e^t\left(\frac{e^t}{t^2}\right)}{e^{2t}} = \frac{1}{t^2} \text{ (step 2).}$$

Integrating, we get

$$\begin{aligned} u &= -\int \frac{1}{t}dt = -\ln|t| \\ v &= \int \frac{1}{t^2}dt = -\frac{1}{t} \text{ (step 3).} \end{aligned}$$

Then we have

$$\begin{aligned} y_p &= -e^t \ln|t| - \frac{1}{t}te^t \\ &= -e^t \ln|t| - e^t \text{ (step 4).} \end{aligned}$$

The e^t term is a solution to the complementary equation, so we don't need to carry that term into our general solution explicitly. The general solution is

$$y(t) = c_1 e^t + c_2 te^t - e^t \ln|t| \text{ (step 5).}$$

b. The complementary equation is $y'' + y = 0$ with associated general solution $c_1 \cos x + c_2 \sin x$. So, $y_1(x) = \cos x$ and $y_2(x) = \sin x$ (step 1). Then, we want to find functions $u'(x)$ and $v'(x)$ such that

$$\begin{aligned} u' \cos x + v' \sin x &= 0 \\ -u' \sin x + v' \cos x &= 3 \sin x. \end{aligned}$$

Applying Cramer's rule, we have

$$u' = \frac{\begin{vmatrix} 0 & \sin x \\ 3\sin^2 x & \cos x \end{vmatrix}}{\begin{vmatrix} \cos x & \sin x \\ -\sin x & \cos x \end{vmatrix}} = \frac{0 - 3\sin^3 x}{\cos^2 x + \sin^2 x} = -3\sin^3 x$$

and

$$v' = \frac{\begin{vmatrix} \cos x & 0 \\ -\sin x & 3\sin^2 x \end{vmatrix}}{\begin{vmatrix} \cos x & \sin x \\ -\sin x & \cos x \end{vmatrix}} = \frac{3\sin^2 x \cos x}{1} = 3\sin^2 x \cos x \text{ (step 2).}$$

Integrating first to find u, we get

$$u = \int -3\sin^3 x dx = -3\left[-\tfrac{1}{3}\sin^2 x \cos x + \tfrac{2}{3}\int \sin x dx\right] = \sin^2 x \cos x + 2\cos x.$$

Now, we integrate to find v. Using substitution (with $w = \sin x$), we get

$$v = \int 3\sin^2 x \cos x dx = \int 3w^2 dw = w^3 = \sin^3 x.$$

Then,

$$\begin{aligned} y_p &= \left(\sin^2 x \cos x + 2\cos x\right)\cos x + \left(\sin^3 x\right)\sin x \\ &= \sin x \cos x + 2\cos x + \sin x \\ &= 2\cos x + \sin x\left(\cos^2 x + \sin^2 x\right) \qquad \text{(step 4).} \\ &= 2\cos x + \sin x \\ &= \cos x + 1 \end{aligned}$$

The general solution is

$$y(x) = c_1 \cos x + c_2 \sin x + 1 + \cos^2 x \text{ (step 5).}$$

7.14 Find the general solution to the following differential equations.

a. $y'' + y = \sec x$

b. $x'' - 2x' + x = \frac{e^t}{t}$

7.2 EXERCISES

Solve the following equations using the method of undetermined coefficients.

54. $2y'' - 5y' - 12y = 6$

55. $3y'' + y' - 4y = 8$

56. $y'' - 6y' + 5y = e^{-x}$

57. $y'' + 16y = e^{-2x}$

58. $y'' - 4y = x^2 + 1$

59. $y'' - 4y' + 4y = 8x^2 + 4x$

60. $y'' - 2y' - 3y = \sin 2x$

61. $y'' + 2y' + y = \sin x + \cos x$

62. $y'' + 9y = e^x \cos x$

63. $y'' + y = 3\sin 2x + x\cos 2x$

64. $y'' + 3y' - 28y = 10e^{4x}$

65. $y'' + 10y' + 25y = xe^{-5x} + 4$

In each of the following problems,

a. Write the form for the particular solution $y_p(x)$ for the method of undetermined coefficients.
b. **[T]** Use a computer algebra system to find a particular solution to the given equation.

66. $y'' - y' - y = x + e^{-x}$

67. $y'' - 3y = x^2 - 4x + 11$

68. $y'' - y' - 4y = e^x \cos 3x$

69. $2y'' - y' + y = \left(x^2 - 5x\right)e^{-x}$

70. $4y'' + 5y' - 2y = e^{2x} + x\sin x$

71. $y'' - y' - 2y = x^2 e^x \sin x$

Solve the differential equation using either the method of undetermined coefficients or the variation of parameters.

72. $y'' + 3y' - 4y = 2e^x$

73. $y'' + 2y' = e^{3x}$

74. $y'' + 6y' + 9y = e^{-x}$

75. $y'' + 2y' - 8y = 6e^{2x}$

Solve the differential equation using the method of variation of parameters.

76. $4y'' + y = 2\sin x$

77. $y'' - 9y = 8x$

78. $y'' + y = \sec x, \quad 0 < x < \pi/2$

79. $y'' + 4y = 3\csc 2x, \quad 0 < x < \pi/2$

Find the unique solution satisfying the differential equation and the initial conditions given, where $y_p(x)$ is the particular solution.

80. $y'' - 2y' + y = 12e^x, \quad y_p(x) = 6x^2 e^x,$ $y(0) = 6, \; y'(0) = 0$

81. $y'' - 7y' = 4xe^{7x}, \quad y_p(x) = \frac{2}{7}x^2 e^{7x} - \frac{4}{49}xe^{7x},$ $y(0) = -1, \; y'(0) = 0$

82. $y'' + y = \cos x - 4\sin x,$ $y_p(x) = 2x\cos x + \frac{1}{2}x\sin x, \; y(0) = 8, \; y'(0) = -4$

83. $y'' - 5y' = e^{5x} + 8e^{-5x},$ $y_p(x) = \frac{1}{5}xe^{5x} + \frac{4}{25}e^{-5x}, \; y(0) = -2, \; y'(0) = 0$

In each of the following problems, two linearly independent solutions— y_1 and y_2 —are given that satisfy the corresponding homogeneous equation. Use the method of variation of parameters to find a particular solution to the given nonhomogeneous equation. Assume $x > 0$ in each exercise.

84. $x^2 y'' + 2xy' - 2y = 3x,$ $y_1(x) = x, \quad y_2(x) = x^{-2}$

85. $x^2 y'' - 2y = 10x^2 - 1,$ $y_1(x) = x^2, \quad y_2(x) = x^{-1}$

7.3 | Applications

Learning Objectives

7.3.1 Solve a second-order differential equation representing simple harmonic motion.
7.3.2 Solve a second-order differential equation representing damped simple harmonic motion.
7.3.3 Solve a second-order differential equation representing forced simple harmonic motion.
7.3.4 Solve a second-order differential equation representing charge and current in an RLC series circuit.

We saw in the chapter introduction that second-order linear differential equations are used to model many situations in physics and engineering. In this section, we look at how this works for systems of an object with mass attached to a vertical spring and an electric circuit containing a resistor, an inductor, and a capacitor connected in series. Models such as these can be used to approximate other more complicated situations; for example, bonds between atoms or molecules are often modeled as springs that vibrate, as described by these same differential equations.

Simple Harmonic Motion

Consider a mass suspended from a spring attached to a rigid support. (This is commonly called a spring-mass system.) Gravity is pulling the mass downward and the restoring force of the spring is pulling the mass upward. As shown in **Figure 7.2**, when these two forces are equal, the mass is said to be at the equilibrium position. If the mass is displaced from equilibrium, it oscillates up and down. This behavior can be modeled by a second-order constant-coefficient differential equation.

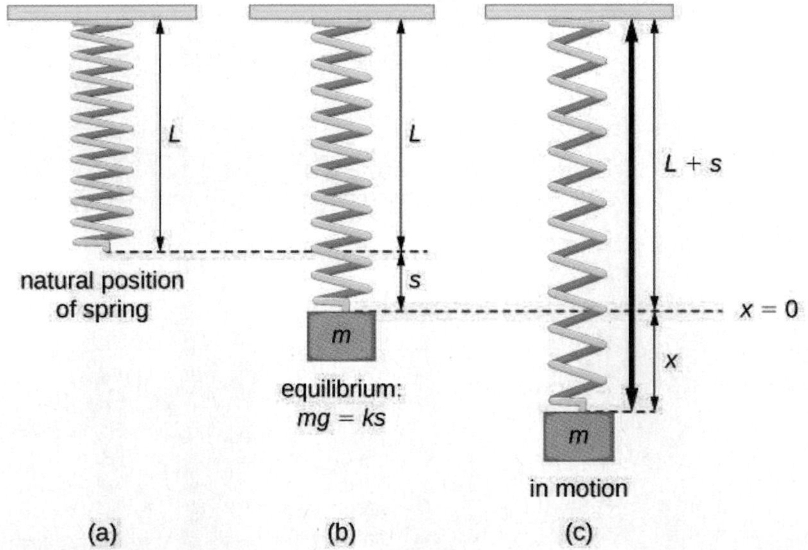

Figure 7.2 A spring in its natural position (a), at equilibrium with a mass m attached (b), and in oscillatory motion (c).

Let $x(t)$ denote the displacement of the mass from equilibrium. Note that for spring-mass systems of this type, it is customary to adopt the convention that down is positive. Thus, a positive displacement indicates the mass is *below* the equilibrium point, whereas a negative displacement indicates the mass is *above* equilibrium. Displacement is usually given in feet in the English system or meters in the metric system.

Consider the forces acting on the mass. The force of gravity is given by mg. In the English system, mass is in slugs and the acceleration resulting from gravity is in feet per second squared. The acceleration resulting from gravity is constant, so in the English system, $g = 32 \text{ ft/sec}^2$. Recall that 1 slug-foot/sec^2 is a pound, so the expression mg can be expressed in pounds. Metric system units are kilograms for mass and m/sec^2 for gravitational acceleration. In the metric system, we have $g = 9.8 \text{ m/sec}^2$.

According to Hooke's law, the restoring force of the spring is proportional to the displacement and acts in the opposite direction from the displacement, so the restoring force is given by $-k(s+x)$. The spring constant is given in pounds per foot in the English system and in newtons per meter in the metric system.

Now, by Newton's second law, the sum of the forces on the system (gravity plus the restoring force) is equal to mass times acceleration, so we have

$$\begin{aligned} mx'' &= -k(s+x)+mg \\ &= -ks-kx+mg. \end{aligned}$$

However, by the way we have defined our equilibrium position, $mg=ks$, the differential equation becomes

$$mx''+kx=0.$$

It is convenient to rearrange this equation and introduce a new variable, called the angular frequency, ω. Letting $\omega=\sqrt{k/m}$, we can write the equation as

$$x''+\omega^2 x=0. \tag{7.5}$$

This differential equation has the general solution

$$x(t)=c_1\cos\omega t+c_2\sin\omega t, \tag{7.6}$$

which gives the position of the mass at any point in time. The motion of the mass is called **simple harmonic motion**. The period of this motion (the time it takes to complete one oscillation) is $T=\frac{2\pi}{\omega}$ and the frequency is $f=\frac{1}{T}=\frac{\omega}{2\pi}$ (**Figure 7.3**).

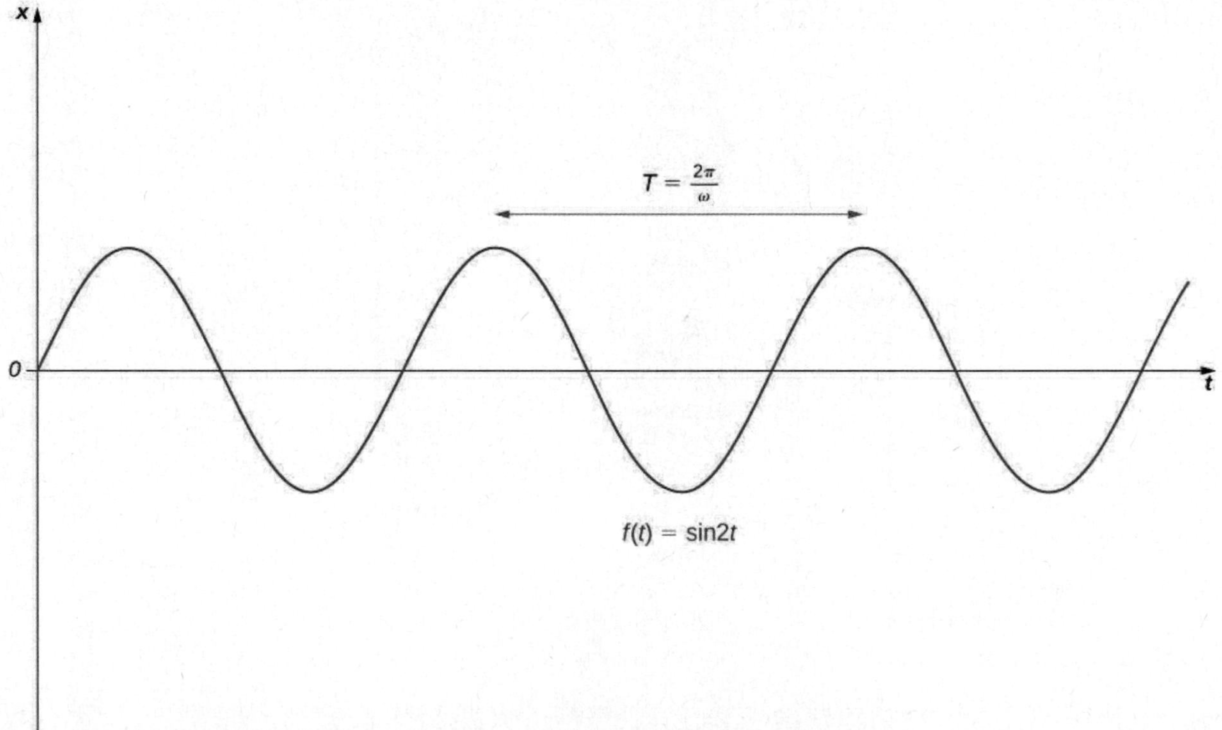

Figure 7.3 A graph of vertical displacement versus time for simple harmonic motion.

Example 7.17

Simple Harmonic Motion

Assume an object weighing 2 lb stretches a spring 6 in. Find the equation of motion if the spring is released from the equilibrium position with an upward velocity of 16 ft/sec. What is the period of the motion?

Solution

We first need to find the spring constant. We have

$$\begin{aligned} mg &= ks \\ 2 &= k\left(\frac{1}{2}\right) \\ k &= 4. \end{aligned}$$

We also know that weight W equals the product of mass m and the acceleration due to gravity g. In English units, the acceleration due to gravity is 32 ft/sec^2.

$$\begin{aligned} W &= mg \\ 2 &= m(32) \\ m &= \frac{1}{16} \end{aligned}$$

Thus, the differential equation representing this system is

$$\frac{1}{16}x'' + 4x = 0.$$

Multiplying through by 16, we get $x'' + 64x = 0,$ which can also be written in the form $x'' + (8^2)x = 0.$ This equation has the general solution

$$x(t) = c_1 \cos(8t) + c_2 \sin(8t).$$

The mass was released from the equilibrium position, so $x(0) = 0,$ and it had an initial upward velocity of 16 ft/sec, so $x'(0) = -16.$ Applying these initial conditions to solve for c_1 and $c_2.$ gives

$$x(t) = -2\sin 8t.$$

The period of this motion is $\frac{2\pi}{8} = \frac{\pi}{4}$ sec.

7.15 A 200-g mass stretches a spring 5 cm. Find the equation of motion of the mass if it is released from rest from a position 10 cm below the equilibrium position. What is the frequency of this motion?

Writing the general solution in the form $x(t) = c_1 \cos(\omega t) + c_2 \sin(\omega t)$ has some advantages. It is easy to see the link between the differential equation and the solution, and the period and frequency of motion are evident. This form of the function tells us very little about the amplitude of the motion, however. In some situations, we may prefer to write the solution in the form

$$x(t) = A\sin(\omega t + \phi). \tag{7.7}$$

Although the link to the differential equation is not as explicit in this case, the period and frequency of motion are still evident. Furthermore, the amplitude of the motion, A, is obvious in this form of the function. The constant ϕ is called a *phase shift* and has the effect of shifting the graph of the function to the left or right.

To convert the solution to this form, we want to find the values of A and ϕ such that

$$c_1 \cos(\omega t) + c_2 \sin(\omega t) = A\sin(\omega t + \phi).$$

We first apply the trigonometric identity

$$\sin(\alpha + \beta) = \sin\alpha\cos\beta + \cos\alpha\sin\beta$$

to get

$$\begin{aligned} c_1 \cos(\omega t) + c_2 \sin(\omega t) &= A(\sin(\omega t)\cos\phi + \cos(\omega t)\sin\phi) \\ &= A\sin\phi(\cos(\omega t)) + A\cos\phi(\sin(\omega t)). \end{aligned}$$

Thus,

$$c_1 = A\sin\phi \text{ and } c_2 = A\cos\phi.$$

If we square both of these equations and add them together, we get

$$\begin{aligned} c_1^2 + c_2^2 &= A^2 \sin\,\phi + A^2 \cos\,\phi \\ &= A^2\left(\sin^2\phi + \cos^2\phi\right) \\ &= A^2. \end{aligned}$$

Thus,

$$A = \sqrt{c_1^2 + c_2^2}.$$

Now, to find $\phi,$ go back to the equations for c_1 and $c_2,$ but this time, divide the first equation by the second equation to get

$$\begin{aligned} \frac{c_1}{c_2} &= \frac{A\sin\phi}{A\cos\phi} \\ &= \tan\phi. \end{aligned}$$

Then,

$$\tan\phi = \frac{c_1}{c_2}.$$

We summarize this finding in the following theorem.

Theorem 7.5: Solution to the Equation for Simple Harmonic Motion

The function $x(t) = c_1 \cos(\omega t) + c_2 \sin(\omega t)$ can be written in the form $x(t) = A\sin(\omega t + \phi),$ where $A = \sqrt{c_1^2 + c_2^2}$ and $\tan\phi = \frac{c_1}{c_2}.$

Note that when using the formula $\tan\phi = \frac{c_1}{c_2}$ to find $\phi,$ we must take care to ensure ϕ is in the right quadrant (**Figure 7.4**).

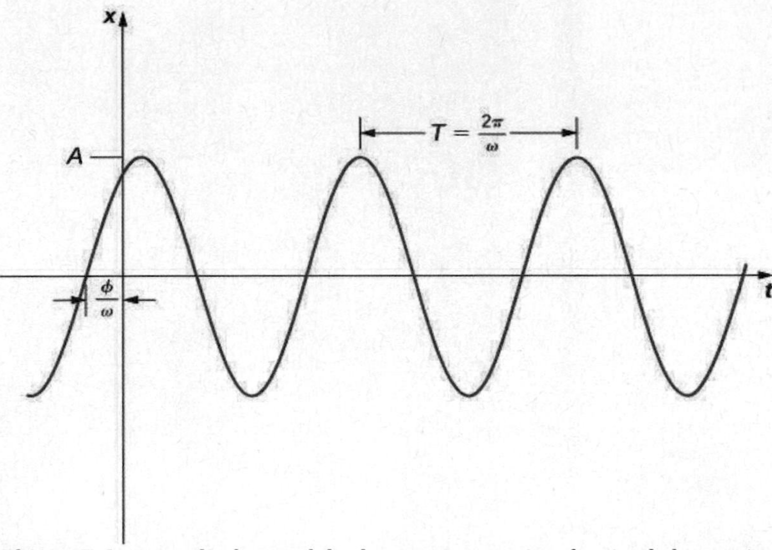

Figure 7.4 A graph of vertical displacement versus time for simple harmonic motion with a phase change.

Example 7.18

Expressing the Solution with a Phase Shift

Express the following functions in the form $A\sin(\omega t+\phi)$. What is the frequency of motion? The amplitude?

a. $x(t)=2\cos(3t)+\sin(3t)$

b. $x(t)=3\cos(2t)-2\sin(2t)$

Solution

a. We have

$$A=\sqrt{c_1^2+c_2^2}=\sqrt{2^2+1^2}=\sqrt{5}$$

and

$$\tan\phi=\frac{c_1}{c_2}=\frac{2}{1}=2.$$

Note that both c_1 and c_2 are positive, so ϕ is in the first quadrant. Thus,

$$\phi\approx 1.107\text{ rad},$$

so we have

$$x(t)=2\cos(3t)+\sin(3t)=\sqrt{5}\sin(3t+1.107).$$

The frequency is $\frac{\omega}{2\pi}=\frac{3}{2\pi}\approx 0.477$. The amplitude is $\sqrt{5}$.

b. We have

$$A=\sqrt{c_1^2+c_2^2}=\sqrt{3^2+2^2}=\sqrt{13}$$

and

$$\tan\phi = \frac{c_1}{c_2} = \frac{3}{-2} = -\frac{3}{2}.$$

Note that c_1 is positive but c_2 is negative, so ϕ is in the fourth quadrant. Thus,

$$\phi \approx -0.983 \text{ rad},$$

so we have

$$\begin{aligned} x(t) &= 3\cos(2t) - 2\sin(2t) \\ &= \sqrt{13}\sin(2t - 0.983). \end{aligned}$$

The frequency is $\frac{\omega}{2\pi} = \frac{2}{2\pi} \approx 0.318.$ The amplitude is $\sqrt{13}.$

7.16 Express the function $x(t) = \cos(4t) + 4\sin(4t)$ in the form $A\sin(\omega t + \phi)$. What is the frequency of motion? The amplitude?

Damped Vibrations

With the model just described, the motion of the mass continues indefinitely. Clearly, this doesn't happen in the real world. In the real world, there is almost always some friction in the system, which causes the oscillations to die off slowly—an effect called *damping*. So now let's look at how to incorporate that damping force into our differential equation.

Physical spring-mass systems almost always have some damping as a result of friction, air resistance, or a physical damper, called a *dashpot* (a pneumatic cylinder; see **Figure 7.5**).

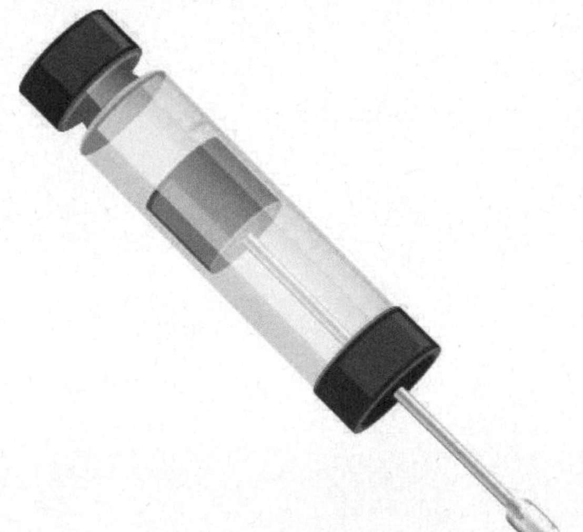

Figure 7.5 A dashpot is a pneumatic cylinder that dampens the motion of an oscillating system.

Because damping is primarily a friction force, we assume it is proportional to the velocity of the mass and acts in the opposite direction. So the damping force is given by $-bx'$ for some constant $b > 0$. Again applying Newton's second law, the differential equation becomes

$$mx'' + bx' + kx = 0.$$

Then the associated characteristic equation is

$$m\lambda^2 + b\lambda + k = 0.$$

Applying the quadratic formula, we have

$$\lambda = \frac{-b \pm \sqrt{b^2 - 4mk}}{2m}.$$

Just as in **Second-Order Linear Equations** we consider three cases, based on whether the characteristic equation has distinct real roots, a repeated real root, or complex conjugate roots.

Case 1: $b^2 > 4mk$

In this case, we say the system is *overdamped*. The general solution has the form

$$x(t) = c_1 e^{\lambda_1 t} + c_2 e^{\lambda_2 t},$$

where both λ_1 and λ_2 are less than zero. Because the exponents are negative, the displacement decays to zero over time, usually quite quickly. Overdamped systems do not oscillate (no more than one change of direction), but simply move back toward the equilibrium position. **Figure 7.6** shows what typical critically damped behavior looks like.

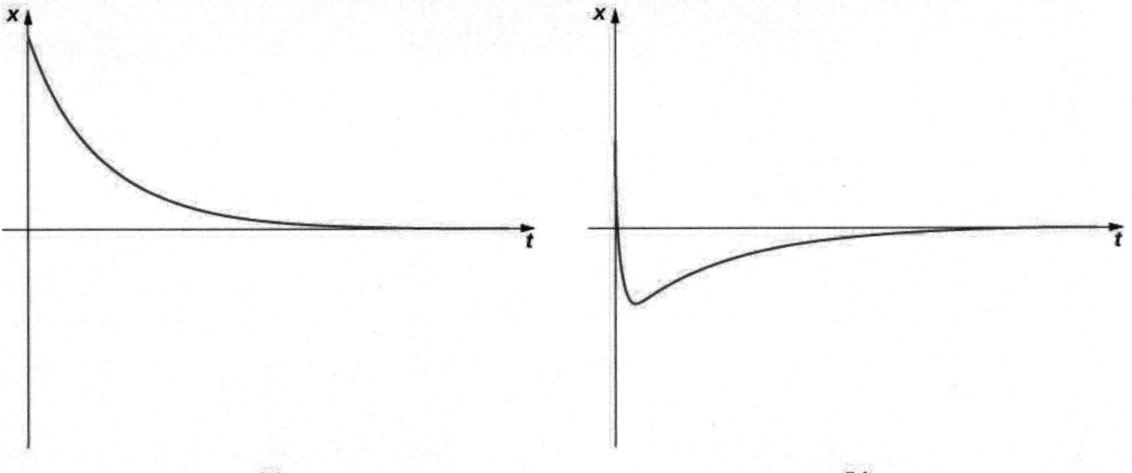

Figure 7.6 Behavior of an overdamped spring-mass system, with no change in direction (a) and only one change in direction (b).

Example 7.19

Overdamped Spring-Mass System

A 16-lb mass is attached to a 10-ft spring. When the mass comes to rest in the equilibrium position, the spring measures 15 ft 4 in. The system is immersed in a medium that imparts a damping force equal to $\frac{5}{2}$ times the instantaneous velocity of the mass. Find the equation of motion if the mass is pushed upward from the equilibrium position with an initial upward velocity of 5 ft/sec. What is the position of the mass after 10 sec? Its velocity?

Solution

The mass stretches the spring 5 ft 4 in., or $\frac{16}{3}$ ft. Thus, $16 = \left(\frac{16}{3}\right)k$, so $k = 3$. We also have $m = \frac{16}{32} = \frac{1}{2}$, so the differential equation is

$$\frac{1}{2}x'' + \frac{5}{2}x' + 3x = 0.$$

Multiplying through by 2 gives $x'' + 5x' + 6x = 0,$ which has the general solution

$$x(t) = c_1 e^{-2t} + c_2 e^{-3t}.$$

Applying the initial conditions, $x(0) = 0$ and $x'(0) = -5,$ we get

$$x(t) = -5e^{-2t} + 5e^{-3t}.$$

After 10 sec the mass is at position

$$x(10) = -5e^{-20} + 5e^{-30} \approx -1.0305 \times 10^{-8} \approx 0,$$

so it is, effectively, at the equilibrium position. We have $x'(t) = 10e^{-2t} - 15e^{-3t},$ so after 10 sec the mass is moving at a velocity of

$$x'(10) = 10e^{-20} - 15e^{-30} \approx 2.061 \times 10^{-8} \approx 0.$$

After only 10 sec, the mass is barely moving.

7.17 A 2-kg mass is attached to a spring with spring constant 24 N/m. The system is then immersed in a medium imparting a damping force equal to 16 times the instantaneous velocity of the mass. Find the equation of motion if it is released from rest at a point 40 cm below equilibrium.

Case 2: $b^2 = 4mk$

In this case, we say the system is *critically damped*. The general solution has the form

$$x(t) = c_1 e^{\lambda_1 t} + c_2 te^{\lambda_1 t},$$

where λ_1 is less than zero. The motion of a critically damped system is very similar to that of an overdamped system. It does not oscillate. However, with a critically damped system, if the damping is reduced even a little, oscillatory behavior results. From a practical perspective, physical systems are almost always either overdamped or underdamped (case 3, which we consider next). It is impossible to fine-tune the characteristics of a physical system so that b^2 and $4mk$ are exactly equal. **Figure 7.7** shows what typical critically damped behavior looks like.

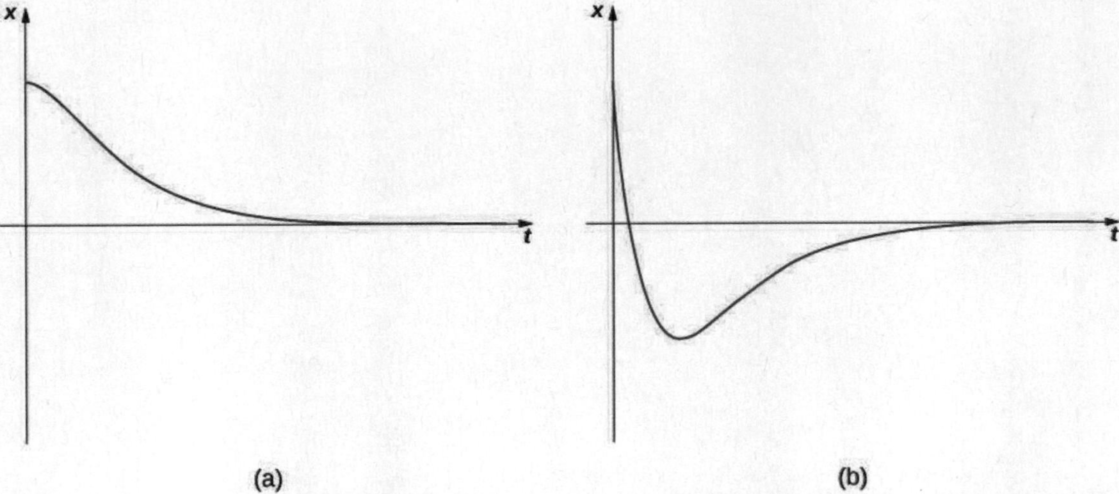

Figure 7.7 Behavior of a critically damped spring-mass system. The system graphed in part (a) has more damping than the system graphed in part (b).

Example 7.20

Critically Damped Spring-Mass System

A 1-kg mass stretches a spring 20 cm. The system is attached to a dashpot that imparts a damping force equal to 14 times the instantaneous velocity of the mass. Find the equation of motion if the mass is released from equilibrium with an upward velocity of 3 m/sec.

Solution

We have $mg = 1(9.8) = 0.2k$, so $k = 49$. Then, the differential equation is

$$x'' + 14x' + 49x = 0,$$

which has general solution

$$x(t) = c_1 e^{-7t} + c_2 te^{-7t}.$$

Applying the initial conditions $x(0) = 0$ and $x'(0) = -3$ gives

$$x(t) = -3te^{-7t}.$$

7.18 A 1-lb weight stretches a spring 6 in., and the system is attached to a dashpot that imparts a damping force equal to half the instantaneous velocity of the mass. Find the equation of motion if the mass is released from rest at a point 6 in. below equilibrium.

Case 3: $b^2 < 4mk$

In this case, we say the system is *underdamped*. The general solution has the form

$$x(t) = e^{\alpha t}(c_1 \cos(\beta t) + c_2 \sin(\beta t)),$$

where α is less than zero. Underdamped systems do oscillate because of the sine and cosine terms in the solution. However, the exponential term dominates eventually, so the amplitude of the oscillations decreases over time. **Figure 7.8** shows what typical underdamped behavior looks like.

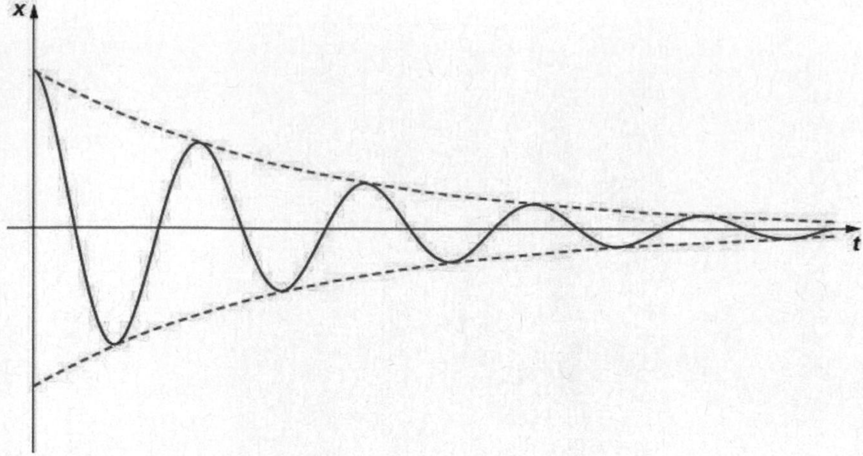

Figure 7.8 Behavior of an underdamped spring-mass system.

Note that for all damped systems, $\lim_{t \to \infty} x(t) = 0.$ The system always approaches the equilibrium position over time.

Example 7.21

Underdamped Spring-Mass System

A 16-lb weight stretches a spring 3.2 ft. Assume the damping force on the system is equal to the instantaneous velocity of the mass. Find the equation of motion if the mass is released from rest at a point 9 in. below equilibrium.

Solution

We have $k = \frac{16}{3.2} = 5$ and $m = \frac{16}{32} = \frac{1}{2},$ so the differential equation is

$$\frac{1}{2}x'' + x' + 5x = 0, \text{ or } x'' + 2x' + 10x = 0.$$

This equation has the general solution

$$x(t) = e^{-t}\left(c_1 \cos(3t) + c_2 \sin(3t)\right).$$

Applying the initial conditions, $x(0) = \frac{3}{4}$ and $x'(0) = 0,$ we get

$$x(t) = e^{-t}\left(\frac{3}{4}\cos(3t) + \frac{1}{4}\sin(3t)\right).$$

7.19 A 1-kg mass stretches a spring 49 cm. The system is immersed in a medium that imparts a damping force equal to four times the instantaneous velocity of the mass. Find the equation of motion if the mass is released from rest at a point 24 cm above equilibrium.

Example 7.22

Chapter Opener: Modeling a Motorcycle Suspension System

Figure 7.9 (credit: modification of work by nSeika, Flickr)

For motocross riders, the suspension systems on their motorcycles are very important. The off-road courses on which they ride often include jumps, and losing control of the motorcycle when they land could cost them the race.

This suspension system can be modeled as a damped spring-mass system. We define our frame of reference with respect to the frame of the motorcycle. Assume the end of the shock absorber attached to the motorcycle frame is fixed. Then, the "mass" in our spring-mass system is the motorcycle wheel. We measure the position of the wheel with respect to the motorcycle frame. This may seem counterintuitive, since, in many cases, it is actually the motorcycle frame that moves, but this frame of reference preserves the development of the differential equation that was done earlier. As with earlier development, we define the downward direction to be positive.

When the motorcycle is lifted by its frame, the wheel hangs freely and the spring is uncompressed. This is the spring's natural position. When the motorcycle is placed on the ground and the rider mounts the motorcycle, the spring compresses and the system is in the equilibrium position (**Figure 7.10**).

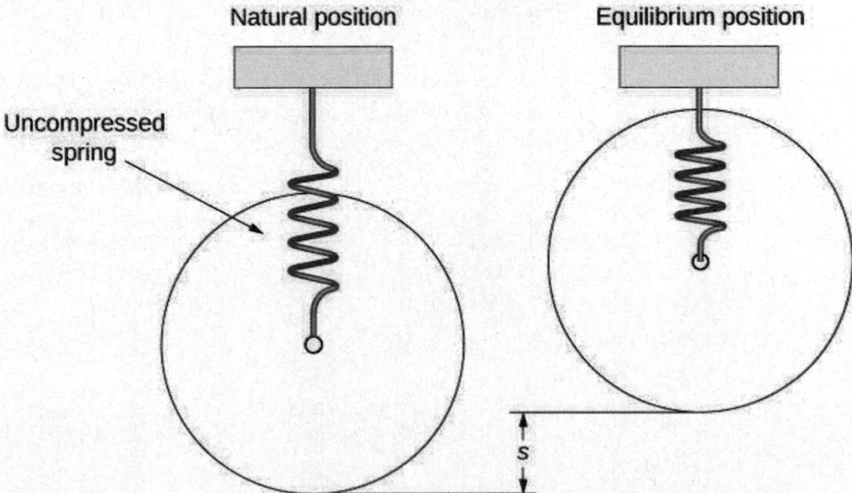

Figure 7.10 We can use a spring-mass system to model a motorcycle suspension.

This system can be modeled using the same differential equation we used before:

$$mx'' + bx' + kx = 0.$$

A motocross motorcycle weighs 204 lb, and we assume a rider weight of 180 lb. When the rider mounts the motorcycle, the suspension compresses 4 in., then comes to rest at equilibrium. The suspension system provides damping equal to 240 times the instantaneous vertical velocity of the motorcycle (and rider).

a. Set up the differential equation that models the behavior of the motorcycle suspension system.
b. We are interested in what happens when the motorcycle lands after taking a jump. Let time $t = 0$ denote the time when the motorcycle first contacts the ground. If the motorcycle hits the ground with a velocity of 10 ft/sec downward, find the equation of motion of the motorcycle after the jump.
c. Graph the equation of motion over the first second after the motorcycle hits the ground.

Solution

a. We have defined equilibrium to be the point where $mg = ks,$ so we have

$$\begin{aligned} mg &= ks \\ 384 &= k\left(\frac{1}{3}\right) \\ k &= 1152. \end{aligned}$$

We also have

$$\begin{aligned} W &= mg \\ 384 &= m(32) \\ m &= 12. \end{aligned}$$

Therefore, the differential equation that models the behavior of the motorcycle suspension is

$$12x'' + 240x' + 1152x = 0.$$

Dividing through by 12, we get

$$x'' + 20x' + 96x = 0.$$

b. The differential equation found in part a. has the general solution

$$x(t) = c_1 e^{-8t} + c_2 e^{-12t}.$$

Now, to determine our initial conditions, we consider the position and velocity of the motorcycle wheel when the wheel first contacts the ground. Since the motorcycle was in the air prior to contacting the ground, the wheel was hanging freely and the spring was uncompressed. Therefore the wheel is 4 in. $\left(\frac{1}{3}\text{ ft}\right)$ below the equilibrium position (with respect to the motorcycle frame), and we have $x(0) = \frac{1}{3}.$ According to the problem statement, the motorcycle has a velocity of 10 ft/sec downward when the motorcycle contacts the ground, so $x'(0) = 10.$ Applying these initial conditions, we get $c_1 = \frac{7}{2}$ and $c_2 = -\left(\frac{19}{6}\right),$ so the equation of motion is

$$x(t) = \frac{7}{2}e^{-8t} - \frac{19}{6}e^{-12t}.$$

c. The graph is shown in **Figure 7.11**.

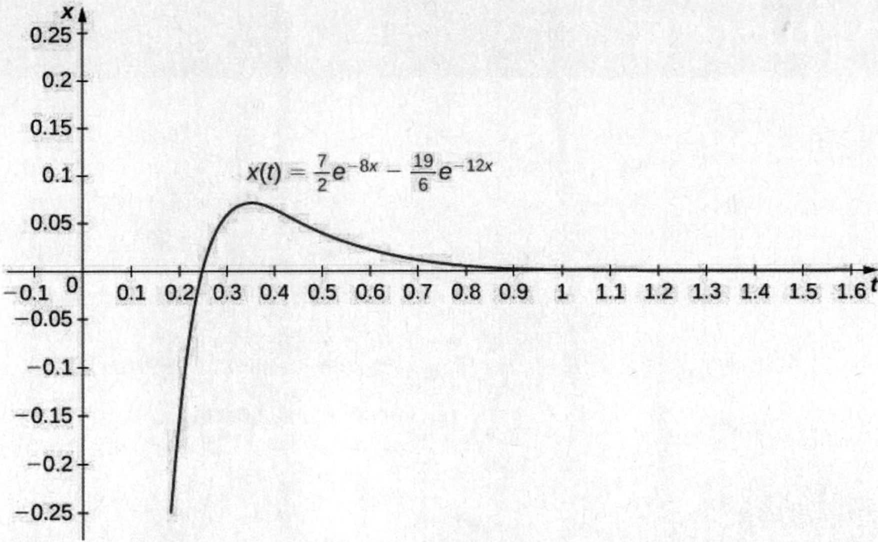

Figure 7.11 Graph of the equation of motion over a time of one second.

Student PROJECT

Landing Vehicle

NASA is planning a mission to Mars. To save money, engineers have decided to adapt one of the moon landing vehicles for the new mission. However, they are concerned about how the different gravitational forces will affect the suspension system that cushions the craft when it touches down. The acceleration resulting from gravity on the moon is 1.6 m/sec^2, whereas on Mars it is 3.7 m/sec^2.

The suspension system on the craft can be modeled as a damped spring-mass system. In this case, the spring is below the moon lander, so the spring is slightly compressed at equilibrium, as shown in **Figure 7.12**.

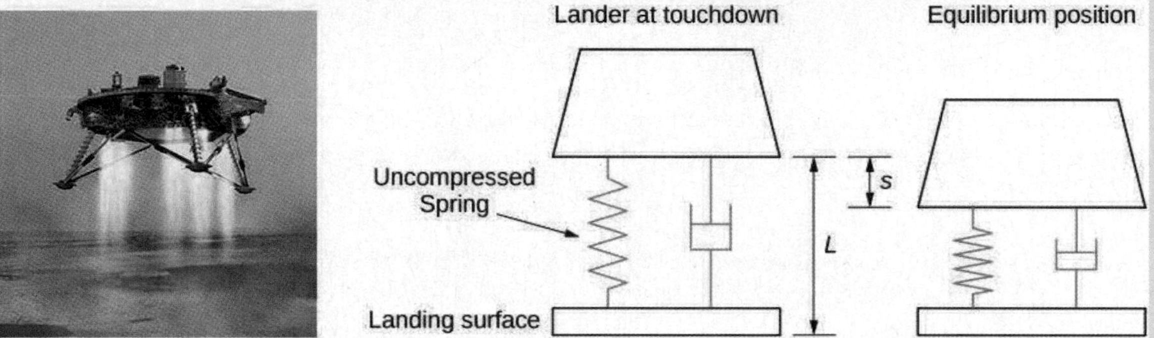

Figure 7.12 The landing craft suspension can be represented as a damped spring-mass system. (credit "lander": NASA)

We retain the convention that down is positive. Despite the new orientation, an examination of the forces affecting the lander shows that the same differential equation can be used to model the position of the landing craft relative to equilibrium:

$$mx'' + bx' + kx = 0,$$

where m is the mass of the lander, b is the damping coefficient, and k is the spring constant.

1. The lander has a mass of 15,000 kg and the spring is 2 m long when uncompressed. The lander is designed to compress the spring 0.5 m to reach the equilibrium position under lunar gravity. The dashpot imparts a damping force equal to 48,000 times the instantaneous velocity of the lander. Set up the differential equation that models the motion of the lander when the craft lands on the moon.
2. Let time $t = 0$ denote the instant the lander touches down. The rate of descent of the lander can be controlled by the crew, so that it is descending at a rate of 2 m/sec when it touches down. Find the equation of motion of the lander on the moon.
3. If the lander is traveling too fast when it touches down, it could fully compress the spring and "bottom out." Bottoming out could damage the landing craft and must be avoided at all costs. Graph the equation of motion found in part 2. If the spring is 0.5 m long when fully compressed, will the lander be in danger of bottoming out?
4. Assuming NASA engineers make no adjustments to the spring or the damper, how far does the lander compress the spring to reach the equilibrium position under Martian gravity?
5. If the lander crew uses the same procedures on Mars as on the moon, and keeps the rate of descent to 2 m/sec, will the lander bottom out when it lands on Mars?
6. What adjustments, if any, should the NASA engineers make to use the lander safely on Mars?

Forced Vibrations

The last case we consider is when an external force acts on the system. In the case of the motorcycle suspension system, for example, the bumps in the road act as an external force acting on the system. Another example is a spring hanging from a support; if the support is set in motion, that motion would be considered an external force on the system. We model these forced systems with the nonhomogeneous differential equation

$$mx'' + bx' + kx = f(t), \tag{7.8}$$

where the external force is represented by the $f(t)$ term. As we saw in **Nonhomogenous Linear Equations**, differential equations such as this have solutions of the form

$$x(t) = c_1 x_1(t) + c_2 x_2(t) + x_p(t),$$

where $c_1 x_1(t) + c_2 x_2(t)$ is the general solution to the complementary equation and $x_p(t)$ is a particular solution to the nonhomogeneous equation. If the system is damped, $\lim_{t \to \infty} c_1 x_1(t) + c_2 x_2(t) = 0.$ Since these terms do not affect the long-term behavior of the system, we call this part of the solution the *transient solution*. The long-term behavior of the system is determined by $x_p(t),$ so we call this part of the solution the **steady-state solution**.

This **website (http://www.openstaxcollege.org/l/20_Oscillations)** shows a simulation of forced vibrations.

Example 7.23

Forced Vibrations

A mass of 1 slug stretches a spring 2 ft and comes to rest at equilibrium. The system is attached to a dashpot that imparts a damping force equal to eight times the instantaneous velocity of the mass. Find the equation of motion if an external force equal to $f(t) = 8\sin(4t)$ is applied to the system beginning at time $t = 0.$ What is the transient solution? What is the steady-state solution?

Solution

We have $mg = 1(32) = 2k,$ so $k = 16$ and the differential equation is

$$x'' + 8x' + 16x = 8\sin(4t).$$

The general solution to the complementary equation is

$$c_1 e^{-4t} + c_2 te^{-4t}.$$

Assuming a particular solution of the form $x_p(t) = A\cos(4t) + B\sin(4t)$ and using the method of undetermined coefficients, we find $x_p(t) = -\frac{1}{4}\cos(4t),$ so

$$x(t) = c_1 e^{-4t} + c_2 te^{-4t} - \frac{1}{4}\cos(4t).$$

At $t = 0,$ the mass is at rest in the equilibrium position, so $x(0) = x'(0) = 0.$ Applying these initial conditions to solve for c_1 and $c_2,$ we get

$$x(t) = \frac{1}{4}e^{-4t} + te^{-4t} - \frac{1}{4}\cos(4t).$$

The transient solution is $\frac{1}{4}e^{-4t} + te^{-4t}.$ The steady-state solution is $-\frac{1}{4}\cos(4t).$

7.20 A mass of 2 kg is attached to a spring with constant 32 N/m and comes to rest in the equilibrium position. Beginning at time $t = 0,$ an external force equal to $f(t) = 68e^{-2t}\cos(4t)$ is applied to the system. Find the equation of motion if there is no damping. What is the transient solution? What is the steady-state solution?

Student PROJECT

Resonance

Consider an undamped system exhibiting simple harmonic motion. In the real world, we never truly have an undamped system; –some damping always occurs. For theoretical purposes, however, we could imagine a spring-mass system contained in a vacuum chamber. With no air resistance, the mass would continue to move up and down indefinitely.

The frequency of the resulting motion, given by $f = \frac{1}{T} = \frac{\omega}{2\pi}$, is called the *natural frequency of the system*. If an external force acting on the system has a frequency close to the natural frequency of the system, a phenomenon called *resonance* results. The external force reinforces and amplifies the natural motion of the system.

1. Consider the differential equation $x'' + x = 0$. Find the general solution. What is the natural frequency of the system?
2. Now suppose this system is subjected to an external force given by $f(t) = 5\cos t$. Solve the initial-value problem $x'' + x = 5\cos t$, $x(0) = 0$, $x'(0) = 1$.
3. Graph the solution. What happens to the behavior of the system over time?
4. In the real world, there is always some damping. However, if the damping force is weak, and the external force is strong enough, real-world systems can still exhibit resonance. One of the most famous examples of resonance is the collapse of the Tacoma Narrows Bridge on November 7, 1940. The bridge had exhibited strange behavior ever since it was built. The roadway had a strange "bounce" to it. On the day it collapsed, a strong windstorm caused the roadway to twist and ripple violently. The bridge was unable to withstand these forces and it ultimately collapsed. Experts believe the windstorm exerted forces on the bridge that were very close to its natural frequency, and the resulting resonance ultimately shook the bridge apart.

   This **website (http://www.openstaxcollege.org/l/20_TacomaNarrow)** contains more information about the collapse of the Tacoma Narrows Bridge.

   During the short time the Tacoma Narrows Bridge stood, it became quite a tourist attraction. Several people were on site the day the bridge collapsed, and one of them caught the collapse on film. Watch the **video (http://www.openstaxcollege.org/l/20_TacomaNarro2)** to see the collapse.

5. Another real-world example of resonance is a singer shattering a crystal wineglass when she sings just the right note. When someone taps a crystal wineglass or wets a finger and runs it around the rim, a tone can be heard. That note is created by the wineglass vibrating at its natural frequency. If a singer then sings that same note at a high enough volume, the glass shatters as a result of resonance.

   The TV show *Mythbusters* aired an episode on this phenomenon. Visit this **website (http://www.openstaxcollege.org/l/20_glass)** to learn more about it. Adam Savage also described the experience. Watch this **video (http://www.openstaxcollege.org/l/20_glass2)** for his account.

The *RLC* Series Circuit

Consider an electrical circuit containing a resistor, an inductor, and a capacitor, as shown in **Figure 7.10**. Such a circuit is called an ***RLC* series circuit**. *RLC* circuits are used in many electronic systems, most notably as tuners in AM/FM radios. The tuning knob varies the capacitance of the capacitor, which in turn tunes the radio. Such circuits can be modeled by second-order, constant-coefficient differential equations.

Let $I(t)$ denote the current in the *RLC* circuit and $q(t)$ denote the charge on the capacitor. Furthermore, let L denote inductance in henrys (H), R denote resistance in ohms (Ω), and C denote capacitance in farads (F). Last, let $E(t)$ denote electric potential in volts (V).

Kirchhoff's voltage rule states that the sum of the voltage drops around any closed loop must be zero. So, we need to consider the voltage drops across the inductor (denoted E_L), the resistor (denoted E_R), and the capacitor (denoted E_C). Because the *RLC* circuit shown in **Figure 7.10** includes a voltage source, $E(t)$, which adds voltage to the circuit, we have $E_L + E_R + E_C = E(t)$.

We present the formulas below without further development. Those of you interested in the derivation of these formulas should consult a physics text. Using Faraday's law and Lenz's law, the voltage drop across an inductor can be shown to be proportional to the instantaneous rate of change of current, with proportionality constant L. Thus,

$$E_L = L\frac{dI}{dt}.$$

Next, according to Ohm's law, the voltage drop across a resistor is proportional to the current passing through the resistor, with proportionality constant R. Therefore,

$$E_R = RI.$$

Last, the voltage drop across a capacitor is proportional to the charge, q, on the capacitor, with proportionality constant $1/C$. Thus,

$$E_C = \frac{1}{C}q.$$

Adding these terms together, we get

$$L\frac{dI}{dt} + RI + \frac{1}{C}q = E(t).$$

Noting that $I = (dq)/(dt)$, this becomes

$$L\frac{d^2q}{dt^2} + R\frac{dq}{dt} + \frac{1}{C}q = E(t). \quad (7.9)$$

Mathematically, this system is analogous to the spring-mass systems we have been examining in this section.

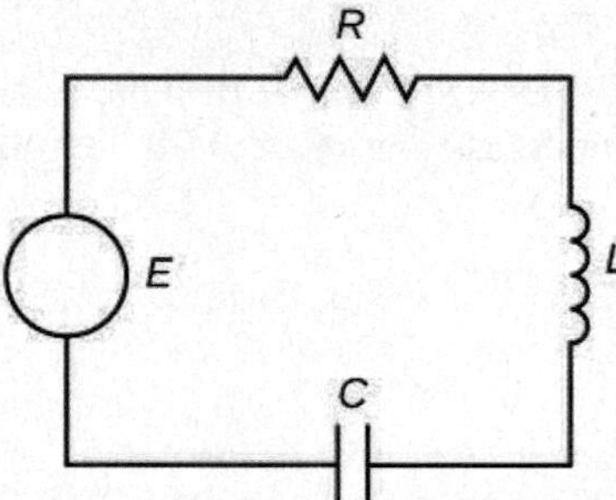

Figure 7.13 An *RLC* series circuit can be modeled by the same differential equation as a mass-spring system.

Example 7.24

The *RLC* Series Circuit

Find the charge on the capacitor in an *RLC* series circuit where $L = 5/3$ H, $R = 10\Omega$, $C = 1/30$ F, and $E(t) = 300$ V. Assume the initial charge on the capacitor is 0 C and the initial current is 9 A. What happens to the charge on the capacitor over time?

Solution

We have

$$\begin{aligned} L\frac{d^2q}{dt^2} + R\frac{dq}{dt} + \frac{1}{C}q &= E(t) \\ \frac{5}{3}\frac{d^2q}{dt^2} + 10\frac{dq}{dt} + 30q &= 300 \\ \frac{d^2q}{dt^2} + 6\frac{dq}{dt} + 18q &= 180. \end{aligned}$$

The general solution to the complementary equation is

$$e^{-3t}(c_1\cos(3t) + c_2\sin(3t)).$$

Assume a particular solution of the form $q_p = A,$ where A is a constant. Using the method of undetermined coefficients, we find $A = 10.$ So,

$$q(t) = e^{-3t}(c_1\cos(3t) + c_2\sin(3t)) + 10.$$

Applying the initial conditions $q(0) = 0$ and $i(0) = ((dq)/(dt))(0) = 9,$ we find $c_1 = -10$ and $c_2 = -7.$ So the charge on the capacitor is

$$q(t) = -10e^{-3t}\cos(3t) - 7e^{-3t}\sin(3t) + 10.$$

Looking closely at this function, we see the first two terms will decay over time (as a result of the negative exponent in the exponential function). Therefore, the capacitor eventually approaches a steady-state charge of 10 C.

7.21 Find the charge on the capacitor in an *RLC* series circuit where $L = 1/5$ H, $R = 2/5\Omega,$ $C = 1/2$ F, and $E(t) = 50$ V. Assume the initial charge on the capacitor is 0 C and the initial current is 4 A.

7.3 EXERCISES

86. A mass weighing 4 lb stretches a spring 8 in. Find the equation of motion if the spring is released from the equilibrium position with a downward velocity of 12 ft/sec. What is the period and frequency of the motion?

87. A mass weighing 2 lb stretches a spring 2 ft. Find the equation of motion if the spring is released from 2 in. below the equilibrium position with an upward velocity of 8 ft/sec. What is the period and frequency of the motion?

88. A 100-g mass stretches a spring 0.1 m. Find the equation of motion of the mass if it is released from rest from a position 20 cm below the equilibrium position. What is the frequency of this motion?

89. A 400-g mass stretches a spring 5 cm. Find the equation of motion of the mass if it is released from rest from a position 15 cm below the equilibrium position. What is the frequency of this motion?

90. A block has a mass of 9 kg and is attached to a vertical spring with a spring constant of 0.25 N/m. The block is stretched 0.75 m below its equilibrium position and released.

a. Find the position function $x(t)$ of the block.
b. Find the period and frequency of the vibration.
c. Sketch a graph of $x(t)$.
d. At what time does the block first pass through the equilibrium position?

91. A block has a mass of 5 kg and is attached to a vertical spring with a spring constant of 20 N/m. The block is released from the equilibrium position with a downward velocity of 10 m/sec.

a. Find the position function $x(t)$ of the block.
b. Find the period and frequency of the vibration.
c. Sketch a graph of $x(t)$.
d. At what time does the block first pass through the equilibrium position?

92. A 1-kg mass is attached to a vertical spring with a spring constant of 21 N/m. The resistance in the spring-mass system is equal to 10 times the instantaneous velocity of the mass.

a. Find the equation of motion if the mass is released from a position 2 m below its equilibrium position with a downward velocity of 2 m/sec.
b. Graph the solution and determine whether the motion is overdamped, critically damped, or underdamped.

93. An 800-lb weight (25 slugs) is attached to a vertical spring with a spring constant of 226 lb/ft. The system is immersed in a medium that imparts a damping force equal to 10 times the instantaneous velocity of the mass.

a. Find the equation of motion if it is released from a position 20 ft below its equilibrium position with a downward velocity of 41 ft/sec.
b. Graph the solution and determine whether the motion is overdamped, critically damped, or underdamped.

94. A 9-kg mass is attached to a vertical spring with a spring constant of 16 N/m. The system is immersed in a medium that imparts a damping force equal to 24 times the instantaneous velocity of the mass.

a. Find the equation of motion if it is released from its equilibrium position with an upward velocity of 4 m/sec.
b. Graph the solution and determine whether the motion is overdamped, critically damped, or underdamped.

95. A 1-kg mass stretches a spring 6.25 cm. The resistance in the spring-mass system is equal to eight times the instantaneous velocity of the mass.

a. Find the equation of motion if the mass is released from a position 5 m below its equilibrium position with an upward velocity of 10 m/sec.
b. Determine whether the motion is overdamped, critically damped, or underdamped.

96. A 32-lb weight (1 slug) stretches a vertical spring 4 in. The resistance in the spring-mass system is equal to four times the instantaneous velocity of the mass.

a. Find the equation of motion if it is released from its equilibrium position with a downward velocity of 12 ft/sec.
b. Determine whether the motion is overdamped, critically damped, or underdamped.

97. A 64-lb weight is attached to a vertical spring with a spring constant of 4.625 lb/ft. The resistance in the spring-mass system is equal to the instantaneous velocity. The weight is set in motion from a position 1 ft below its equilibrium position with an upward velocity of 2 ft/sec. Is the mass above or below the equation position at the end of π sec? By what distance?

98. A mass that weighs 8 lb stretches a spring 6 inches. The system is acted on by an external force of $8\sin 8t$ lb. If the mass is pulled down 3 inches and then released, determine the position of the mass at any time.

99. A mass that weighs 6 lb stretches a spring 3 in. The system is acted on by an external force of $8\sin(4t)$ lb. If the mass is pulled down 1 inch and then released, determine the position of the mass at any time.

100. Find the charge on the capacitor in an *RLC* series circuit where $L = 40$ H, $R = 30\Omega$, $C = 1/200$ F, and $E(t) = 200$ V. Assume the initial charge on the capacitor is 7 C and the initial current is 0 A.

101. Find the charge on the capacitor in an *RLC* series circuit where $L = 2$ H, $R = 24\Omega$, $C = 0.005$ F, and $E(t) = 12\sin 10t$ V. Assume the initial charge on the capacitor is 0.001 C and the initial current is 0 A.

102. A series circuit consists of a device where $L = 1$ H, $R = 20\Omega$, $C = 0.002$ F, and $E(t) = 12$ V. If the initial charge and current are both zero, find the charge and current at time *t*.

103. A series circuit consists of a device where $L = \frac{1}{2}$ H, $R = 10\Omega$, $C = \frac{1}{50}$ F, and $E(t) = 250$ V. If the initial charge on the capacitor is 0 C and the initial current is 18 A, find the charge and current at time *t*.

7.4 | Series Solutions of Differential Equations

Learning Objectives

7.4.1 Use power series to solve first-order and second-order differential equations.

In **Introduction to Power Series (http://cnx.org/content/m53760/latest/)** , we studied how functions can be represented as power series, $y(x) = \sum_{n=0}^{\infty} a_n x^n$. We also saw that we can find series representations of the derivatives of such functions by differentiating the power series term by term. This gives $y'(x) = \sum_{n=1}^{\infty} n a_n x^{n-1}$ and $y''(x) = \sum_{n=2}^{\infty} n(n-1) a_n x^{n-2}$. In some cases, these power series representations can be used to find solutions to differential equations.

Be aware that this subject is given only a very brief treatment in this text. Most introductory differential equations textbooks include an entire chapter on power series solutions. This text has only a single section on the topic, so several important issues are not addressed here, particularly issues related to existence of solutions. The examples and exercises in this section were chosen for which power solutions exist. However, it is not always the case that power solutions exist. Those of you interested in a more rigorous treatment of this topic should consult a differential equations text.

Problem-Solving Strategy: Finding Power Series Solutions to Differential Equations

1. Assume the differential equation has a solution of the form $y(x) = \sum_{n=0}^{\infty} a_n x^n$.
2. Differentiate the power series term by term to get $y'(x) = \sum_{n=1}^{\infty} n a_n x^{n-1}$ and $y''(x) = \sum_{n=2}^{\infty} n(n-1) a_n x^{n-2}$.
3. Substitute the power series expressions into the differential equation.
4. Re-index sums as necessary to combine terms and simplify the expression.
5. Equate coefficients of like powers of x to determine values for the coefficients a_n in the power series.
6. Substitute the coefficients back into the power series and write the solution.

Example 7.25

Series Solutions to Differential Equations

Find a power series solution for the following differential equations.

a. $y'' - y = 0$

b. $(x^2 - 1)y'' + 6xy' + 4y = -4$

Solution

a. Assume $y(x) = \sum_{n=0}^{\infty} a_n x^n$ (step 1). Then, $y'(x) = \sum_{n=1}^{\infty} n a_n x^{n-1}$ and $y''(x) = \sum_{n=2}^{\infty} n(n-1) a_n x^{n-2}$ (step 2). We want to find values for the coefficients a_n such that

$$\begin{aligned} y'' - y &= 0 \\ \sum_{n=2}^{\infty} n(n-1) a_n x^{n-2} - \sum_{n=0}^{\infty} a_n x^n &= 0 \text{ (step 3).} \end{aligned}$$

We want the indices on our sums to match so that we can express them using a single summation. That is, we want to rewrite the first summation so that it starts with $n = 0$.

To re-index the first term, replace n with $n + 2$ inside the sum, and change the lower summation limit to $n = 0.$ We get

$$\sum_{n=2}^{\infty} n(n-1) a_n x^{n-2} = \sum_{n=0}^{\infty} (n+2)(n+1) a_{n+2} x^n.$$

This gives

$$\begin{aligned} \sum_{n=0}^{\infty} (n+2)(n+1) a_{n+2} x^n - \sum_{n=0}^{\infty} a_n x^n &= 0 \\ \sum_{n=0}^{\infty} \left[(n+2)(n+1) a_{n+2} - a_n\right] x^n &= 0 \text{ (step 4).} \end{aligned}$$

Because power series expansions of functions are unique, this equation can be true only if the coefficients of each power of x are zero. So we have

$$(n+2)(n+1) a_{n+2} - a_n = 0 \text{ for } n = 0, 1, 2, \ldots.$$

This recurrence relationship allows us to express each coefficient a_n in terms of the coefficient two terms earlier. This yields one expression for even values of n and another expression for odd values of n. Looking first at the equations involving even values of n, we see that

$$\begin{aligned} a_2 &= \frac{a_0}{2} \\ a_4 &= \frac{a_2}{4 \cdot 3} = \frac{a_0}{4!} \\ a_6 &= \frac{a_4}{6 \cdot 5} = \frac{a_0}{6!} \\ &\vdots \end{aligned}$$

Thus, in general, when n is even, $a_n = \frac{a_0}{n!}$ (step 5).

For the equations involving odd values of n, we see that

$$\begin{aligned} a_3 &= \frac{a_1}{3 \cdot 2} = \frac{a_1}{3!} \\ a_5 &= \frac{a_3}{5 \cdot 4} = \frac{a_1}{5!} \\ a_7 &= \frac{a_5}{7 \cdot 6} = \frac{a_1}{7!} \\ &\vdots \end{aligned}$$

Therefore, in general, when n is odd, $a_n = \frac{a_1}{n!}$ (step 5 continued).

Putting this together, we have

$$\begin{aligned} y(x) &= \sum_{n=0}^{\infty} a_n x^n \\ &= a_0 + a_1 x + \frac{a_0}{2}x^2 + \frac{a_1}{3!}x^3 + \frac{a_0}{4!}x^4 + \frac{a_1}{5!}x^5 + \cdots. \end{aligned}$$

Re-indexing the sums to account for the even and odd values of n separately, we obtain

$$y(x) = a_0 \sum_{k=0}^{\infty} \frac{1}{(2k)!}x^{2k} + a_1 \sum_{k=0}^{\infty} \frac{1}{(2k+1)!}x^{2k+1} \text{ (step 6).}$$

Analysis for part a.

As expected for a second-order differential equation, this solution depends on two arbitrary constants. However, note that our differential equation is a constant-coefficient differential equation, yet the power series solution does not appear to have the familiar form (containing exponential functions) that we are used to seeing. Furthermore, since $y(x) = c_1 e^x + c_2 e^{-x}$ is the general solution to this equation, we must be able to write any solution in this form, and it is not clear whether the power series solution we just found can, in fact, be written in that form.

Fortunately, after writing the power series representations of e^x and e^{-x}, and doing some algebra, we find that if we choose

$$c_0 = \frac{(a_0 + a_1)}{2}, \quad c_1 = \frac{(a_0 - a_1)}{2},$$

we then have $a_0 = c_0 + c_1$ and $a_1 = c_0 - c_1$, and

$$\begin{aligned} y(x) &= a_0 + a_1 x + \frac{a_0}{2}x^2 + \frac{a_1}{3!}x^3 + \frac{a_0}{4!}x^4 + \frac{a_1}{5!}x^5 + \cdots \\ &= (c_0 + c_1) + (c_0 - c_1)x + \frac{(c_0 + c_1)}{2}x^2 + \frac{(c_0 - c_1)}{3!}x^3 + \frac{(c_0 + c_1)}{4!}x^4 + \frac{(c_0 - c_1)}{5!}x^5 + \cdots \\ &= c_0 \sum_{n=0}^{\infty} \frac{x^n}{n!} + c_1 \sum_{n=0}^{\infty} \frac{(-x)^n}{n!} \\ &= c_0 e^x + c_1 e^{-x}. \end{aligned}$$

So we have, in fact, found the same general solution. Note that this choice of c_1 and c_2 is not obvious. This is a case when we know what the answer should be, and have essentially "reverse-engineered" our choice of coefficients.

b. Assume $y(x) = \sum_{n=0}^{\infty} a_n x^n$ (step 1). Then, $y'(x) = \sum_{n=1}^{\infty} n a_n x^{n-1}$ and $y''(x) = \sum_{n=2}^{\infty} n(n-1) a_n x^{n-2}$ (step 2). We want to find values for the coefficients a_n such that

$$\begin{aligned}
(x^2-1)y''+6xy'+4y &= -4 \\
\left(x^2-1\right)\sum_{n=2}^{\infty} n(n-1)a_n x^{n-2}+6x\sum_{n=1}^{\infty} na_n x^{n-1}+4\sum_{n=0}^{\infty} a_n x^n &= -4 \\
x^2\sum_{n=2}^{\infty} n(n-1)a_n x^{n-2}-\sum_{n=2}^{\infty} n(n-1)a_n x^{n-2}+6x\sum_{n=1}^{\infty} na_n x^{n-1}+4\sum_{n=0}^{\infty} a_n x^n &= -4.
\end{aligned}$$

Taking the external factors inside the summations, we get

$$\sum_{n=2}^{\infty} n(n-1)a_n x^n-\sum_{n=2}^{\infty} n(n-1)a_n x^{n-2}+\sum_{n=1}^{\infty} 6na_n x^n+\sum_{n=0}^{\infty} 4a_n x^n=-4 \text{ (step 3)}.$$

Now, in the first summation, we see that when $n=0$ or $n=1$, the term evaluates to zero, so we can add these terms back into our sum to get

$$\sum_{n=2}^{\infty} n(n-1)a_n x^n=\sum_{n=0}^{\infty} n(n-1)a_n x^n.$$

Similarly, in the third term, we see that when $n=0$, the expression evaluates to zero, so we can add that term back in as well. We have

$$\sum_{n=1}^{\infty} 6na_n x^n=\sum_{n=0}^{\infty} 6na_n x^n.$$

Then, we need only shift the indices in our second term. We get

$$\sum_{n=2}^{\infty} n(n-1)a_n x^{n-2}=\sum_{n=0}^{\infty} (n+2)(n+1)a_{n+2} x^n.$$

Thus, we have

$$\begin{aligned}
\sum_{n=0}^{\infty} n(n-1)a_n x^n-\sum_{n=0}^{\infty} (n+2)(n+1)a_{n+2} x^n+\sum_{n=0}^{\infty} 6na_n x^n+\sum_{n=0}^{\infty} 4a_n x^n &= -4 \text{ (step 4)}. \\
\sum_{n=0}^{\infty}\left[n(n-1)a_n-(n+2)(n+1)a_{n+2}+6na_n+4a_n\right]x^n &= -4 \\
\sum_{n=0}^{\infty}\left[(n^2-n)a_n+6na_n+4a_n-(n+2)(n+1)a_{n+2}\right]x^n &= -4 \\
\sum_{n=0}^{\infty}\left[n^2a_n+5na_n+4a_n-(n+2)(n+1)a_{n+2}\right]x^n &= -4 \\
\sum_{n=0}^{\infty}\left[(n^2+5n+4)a_n-(n+2)(n+1)a_{n+2}\right]x^n &= -4 \\
\sum_{n=0}^{\infty}\left[(n+4)(n+1)a_n-(n+2)(n+1)a_{n+2}\right]x^n &= -4
\end{aligned}$$

Looking at the coefficients of each power of x, we see that the constant term must be equal to -4, and the coefficients of all other powers of x must be zero. Then, looking first at the constant term,

$$\begin{aligned} 4a_0 - 2a_2 &= -4 \\ a_2 &= 2a_0 + 2 \text{ (step 3).} \end{aligned}$$

For $n \geq 1,$ we have

$$\begin{aligned} (n+4)(n+1)a_n - (n+2)(n+1)a_{n+2} &= 0 \\ (n+1)\left[(n+4)a_n - (n+2)a_{n+2}\right] &= 0. \end{aligned}$$

Since $n \geq 1,$ $n + 1 \neq 0,$ we see that

$$(n+4)a_n - (n+2)a_{n+2} = 0$$

and thus

$$a_{n+2} = \frac{n+4}{n+2}a_n.$$

For even values of n, we have

$$\begin{aligned} a_4 &= \frac{6}{4}(2a_0 + 2) = 3a_0 + 3 \\ a_6 &= \frac{8}{6}(3a_0 + 3) = 4a_0 + 4 \\ &\vdots \end{aligned}$$

In general, $a_{2k} = (k+1)(a_0 + 1)$ (step 5).

For odd values of n, we have

$$\begin{aligned} a_3 &= \frac{5}{3}a_1 \\ a_5 &= \frac{7}{5}a_3 = \frac{7}{3}a_1 \\ a_7 &= \frac{9}{7}a_5 = \frac{9}{3}a_1 = 3a_1 \\ &\vdots \end{aligned}$$

In general, $a_{2k+1} = \frac{2k+3}{3}a_1$ (step 5 continued).

Putting this together, we have

$$y(x) = \sum_{k=0}^{\infty} (k+1)(a_0+1)x^{2k} + \sum_{k=0}^{\infty} \left(\frac{2k+3}{3}\right)a_1 x^{2k+1} \text{ (step 6).}$$

7.22 Find a power series solution for the following differential equations.

a. $y' + 2xy = 0$

b. $(x+1)y' = 3y$

We close this section with a brief introduction to Bessel functions. Complete treatment of Bessel functions is well beyond the scope of this course, but we get a little taste of the topic here so we can see how series solutions to differential equations are used in real-world applications. The Bessel equation of order n is given by

$$x^2 y'' + xy' + (x^2 - n^2)y = 0.$$

This equation arises in many physical applications, particularly those involving cylindrical coordinates, such as the vibration of a circular drum head and transient heating or cooling of a cylinder. In the next example, we find a power series solution to the Bessel equation of order 0.

Example 7.26

Power Series Solution to the Bessel Equation

Find a power series solution to the Bessel equation of order 0 and graph the solution.

Solution

The Bessel equation of order 0 is given by

$$x^2 y'' + xy' + x^2 y = 0.$$

We assume a solution of the form $y = \sum_{n=0}^{\infty} a_n x^n$. Then $y'(x) = \sum_{n=1}^{\infty} n a_n x^{n-1}$ and $y''(x) = \sum_{n=2}^{\infty} n(n-1) a_n x^{n-2}$. Substituting this into the differential equation, we get

$$\begin{aligned}
&x^2 \sum_{n=2}^{\infty} n(n-1) a_n x^{n-2} + x \sum_{n=1}^{\infty} n a_n x^{n-1} + x^2 \sum_{n=0}^{\infty} a_n x^n = 0 && \text{Substitution.} \\
&\sum_{n=2}^{\infty} n(n-1) a_n x^n + \sum_{n=1}^{\infty} n a_n x^n + \sum_{n=0}^{\infty} a_n x^{n+2} = 0 && \text{Bring external factors within sums.} \\
&\sum_{n=2}^{\infty} n(n-1) a_n x^n + \sum_{n=1}^{\infty} n a_n x^n + \sum_{n=2}^{\infty} a_{n-2} x^n = 0 && \text{Re-index third sum.} \\
&\sum_{n=2}^{\infty} n(n-1) a_n x^n + a_1 x + \sum_{n=2}^{\infty} n a_n x^n + \sum_{n=2}^{\infty} a_{n-2} x^n = 0 && \text{Separate } n = 1 \text{ term from second sum.} \\
&a_1 x + \sum_{n=2}^{\infty} \left[n(n-1) a_n + n a_n + a_{n-2} \right] x^n = 0 && \text{Collect summation terms.} \\
&a_1 x + \sum_{n=2}^{\infty} \left[(n^2 - n) a_n + n a_n + a_{n-2} \right] x^n = 0 && \text{Multiply through in first term.} \\
&a_1 x + \sum_{n=2}^{\infty} \left[n^2 a_n + a_{n-2} \right] x^n = 0. && \text{Simplify.}
\end{aligned}$$

Then, $a_1 = 0$, and for $n \geq 2$,

$$\begin{aligned}
n^2 a_n + a_{n-2} &= 0 \\
a_n &= -\frac{1}{n^2} a_{n-2}.
\end{aligned}$$

Because $a_1 = 0$, all odd terms are zero. Then, for even values of n, we have

$$\begin{aligned} a_2 &= -\frac{1}{2^2}a_0 \\ a_4 &= -\frac{1}{4^2}a_2 = \frac{1}{4^2 \cdot 2^2}a_0. \\ a_6 &= -\frac{1}{6^2}a_4 = -\frac{1}{6^2 \cdot 4^2 \cdot 2^2}a_0 \end{aligned}$$

In general,

$$a_{2k} = \frac{(-1)^k}{(2)^{2k}(k!)^2}a_0.$$

Thus, we have

$$y(x) = a_0 \sum_{k=0}^{\infty} \frac{(-1)^k}{(2)^{2k}(k!)^2}x^{2k}. \tag{7.10}$$

The graph appears below.

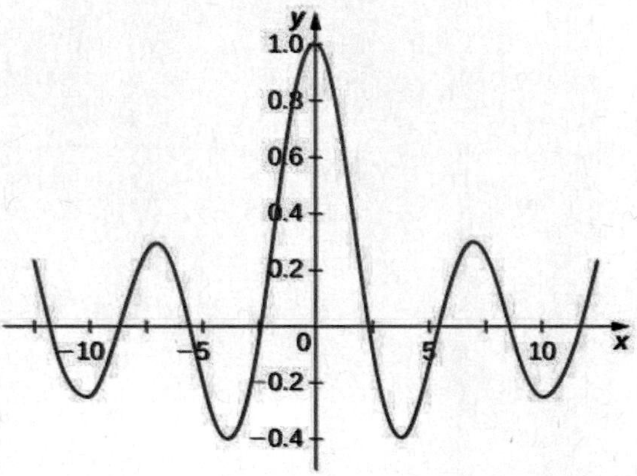

 **7.23** Verify that the expression found in **Example 7.26** is a solution to the Bessel equation of order 0.

7.4 EXERCISES

Find a power series solution for the following differential equations.

104. $y'' + 6y' = 0$

105. $5y'' + y' = 0$

106. $y'' + 25y = 0$

107. $y'' - y = 0$

108. $2y' + y = 0$

109. $y' - 2xy = 0$

110. $(x - 7)y' + 2y = 0$

111. $y'' - xy' - y = 0$

112. $\left(1 + x^2\right)y'' - 4xy' + 6y = 0$

113. $x^2 y'' - xy' - 3y = 0$

114. $y'' - 8y' = 0, \quad y(0) = -2, \quad y'(0) = 10$

115. $y'' - 2xy = 0, \quad y(0) = 1, \quad y'(0) = -3$

116. The differential equation $x^2 y'' + xy' + \left(x^2 - 1\right)y = 0$ is a Bessel equation of order 1. Use a power series of the form $y = \sum_{n=0}^{\infty} a_n x^n$ to find the solution.

CHAPTER 7 REVIEW

KEY TERMS

boundary conditions the conditions that give the state of a system at different times, such as the position of a spring-mass system at two different times

boundary-value problem a differential equation with associated boundary conditions

characteristic equation the equation $a\lambda^2 + b\lambda + c = 0$ for the differential equation $ay'' + by' + cy = 0$

complementary equation for the nonhomogeneous linear differential equation

$$a_2(x)y'' + a_1(x)y' + a_0(x)y = r(x),$$

the associated homogeneous equation, called the *complementary equation*, is

$$a_2(x)y'' + a_1(x)y' + a_0(x)y = 0$$

homogeneous linear equation a second-order differential equation that can be written in the form $a_2(x)y'' + a_1(x)y' + a_0(x)y = r(x)$, but $r(x) = 0$ for every value of x

linearly dependent a set of functions $f_1(x), f_2(x),\ldots,f_n(x)$ for which there are constants $c_1, c_2,\ldots c_n$, not all zero, such that $c_1 f_1(x) + c_2 f_2(x) + \cdots + c_n f_n(x) = 0$ for all x in the interval of interest

linearly independent a set of functions $f_1(x), f_2(x),\ldots,f_n(x)$ for which there are no constants $c_1, c_2,\ldots c_n$, such that $c_1 f_1(x) + c_2 f_2(x) + \cdots + c_n f_n(x) = 0$ for all x in the interval of interest

method of undetermined coefficients a method that involves making a guess about the form of the particular solution, then solving for the coefficients in the guess

method of variation of parameters a method that involves looking for particular solutions in the form $y_p(x) = u(x)y_1(x) + v(x)y_2(x)$, where y_1 and y_2 are linearly independent solutions to the complementary equations, and then solving a system of equations to find $u(x)$ and $v(x)$

nonhomogeneous linear equation a second-order differential equation that can be written in the form $a_2(x)y'' + a_1(x)y' + a_0(x)y = r(x)$, but $r(x) \neq 0$ for some value of x

particular solution a solution $y_p(x)$ of a differential equation that contains no arbitrary constants

***RLC* series circuit** a complete electrical path consisting of a resistor, an inductor, and a capacitor; a second-order, constant-coefficient differential equation can be used to model the charge on the capacitor in an *RLC* series circuit

simple harmonic motion motion described by the equation $x(t) = c_1 \cos(\omega t) + c_2 \sin(\omega t)$, as exhibited by an undamped spring-mass system in which the mass continues to oscillate indefinitely

steady-state solution a solution to a nonhomogeneous differential equation related to the forcing function; in the long term, the solution approaches the steady-state solution

KEY EQUATIONS

- **Linear second-order differential equation**
  $a_2(x)y'' + a_1(x)y' + a_0(x)y = r(x)$
- **Second-order equation with constant coefficients**
  $ay'' + by' + cy = 0$
- **Complementary equation**
  $a_2(x)y'' + a_1(x)y' + a_0(x)y = 0$

- **General solution to a nonhomogeneous linear differential equation**
  $y(x) = c_1 y_1(x) + c_2 y_2(x) + y_p(x)$
- **Equation of simple harmonic motion**
  $x'' + \omega^2 x = 0$
- **Solution for simple harmonic motion**
  $x(t) = c_1 \cos(\omega t) + c_2 \sin(\omega t)$
- **Alternative form of solution for SHM**
  $x(t) = A \sin(\omega t + \phi)$
- **Forced harmonic motion**
  $mx'' + bx' + kx = f(t)$
- **Charge in a *RLC* series circuit**
  $L\frac{d^2 q}{dt^2} + R\frac{dq}{dt} + \frac{1}{C}q = E(t)$

KEY CONCEPTS

7.1 Second-Order Linear Equations

- Second-order differential equations can be classified as linear or nonlinear, homogeneous or nonhomogeneous.
- To find a general solution for a homogeneous second-order differential equation, we must find two linearly independent solutions. If $y_1(x)$ and $y_2(x)$ are linearly independent solutions to a second-order, linear, homogeneous differential equation, then the general solution is given by
  $$y(x) = c_1 y_1(x) + c_2 y_2(x).$$
- To solve homogeneous second-order differential equations with constant coefficients, find the roots of the characteristic equation. The form of the general solution varies depending on whether the characteristic equation has distinct, real roots; a single, repeated real root; or complex conjugate roots.
- Initial conditions or boundary conditions can then be used to find the specific solution to a differential equation that satisfies those conditions, except when there is no solution or infinitely many solutions.

7.2 Nonhomogeneous Linear Equations

- To solve a nonhomogeneous linear second-order differential equation, first find the general solution to the complementary equation, then find a particular solution to the nonhomogeneous equation.
- Let $y_p(x)$ be any particular solution to the nonhomogeneous linear differential equation
  $$a_2(x)y'' + a_1(x)y' + a_0(x)y = r(x),$$
  and let $c_1 y_1(x) + c_2 y_2(x)$ denote the general solution to the complementary equation. Then, the general solution to the nonhomogeneous equation is given by
  $$y(x) = c_1 y_1(x) + c_2 y_2(x) + y_p(x).$$
- When $r(x)$ is a combination of polynomials, exponential functions, sines, and cosines, use the method of undetermined coefficients to find the particular solution. To use this method, assume a solution in the same form as $r(x)$, multiplying by x as necessary until the assumed solution is linearly independent of the general solution to the complementary equation. Then, substitute the assumed solution into the differential equation to find values for the coefficients.
- When $r(x)$ is *not* a combination of polynomials, exponential functions, or sines and cosines, use the method of variation of parameters to find the particular solution. This method involves using Cramer's rule or another suitable

technique to find functions $u'(x)$ and $v'(x)$ satisfying

$$\begin{aligned} u' y_1 + v' y_2 &= 0 \\ u' y_1{}' + v' y_2{}' &= r(x). \end{aligned}$$

Then, $y_p(x) = u(x)y_1(x) + v(x)y_2(x)$ is a particular solution to the differential equation.

7.3 Applications

- Second-order constant-coefficient differential equations can be used to model spring-mass systems.
- An examination of the forces on a spring-mass system results in a differential equation of the form

$$mx'' + bx' + kx = f(t),$$

  where m represents the mass, b is the coefficient of the damping force, k is the spring constant, and $f(t)$ represents any net external forces on the system.
- If $b = 0,$ there is no damping force acting on the system, and simple harmonic motion results. If $b \neq 0,$ the behavior of the system depends on whether $b^2 - 4mk > 0,$ $b^2 - 4mk = 0,$ or $b^2 - 4mk < 0.$
- If $b^2 - 4mk > 0,$ the system is overdamped and does not exhibit oscillatory behavior.
- If $b^2 - 4mk = 0,$ the system is critically damped. It does not exhibit oscillatory behavior, but any slight reduction in the damping would result in oscillatory behavior.
- If $b^2 - 4mk < 0,$ the system is underdamped. It exhibits oscillatory behavior, but the amplitude of the oscillations decreases over time.
- If $f(t) \neq 0,$ the solution to the differential equation is the sum of a transient solution and a steady-state solution. The steady-state solution governs the long-term behavior of the system.
- The charge on the capacitor in an *RLC* series circuit can also be modeled with a second-order constant-coefficient differential equation of the form

$$L\frac{d^2q}{dt^2} + R\frac{dq}{dt} + \frac{1}{C}q = E(t),$$

  where *L* is the inductance, *R* is the resistance, *C* is the capacitance, and $E(t)$ is the voltage source.

7.4 Series Solutions of Differential Equations

- Power series representations of functions can sometimes be used to find solutions to differential equations.
- Differentiate the power series term by term and substitute into the differential equation to find relationships between the power series coefficients.

CHAPTER 7 REVIEW EXERCISES

True or False? Justify your answer with a proof or a counterexample.

117. If y and z are both solutions to $y'' + 2y' + y = 0,$ then $y + z$ is also a solution.

118. The following system of algebraic equations has a unique solution:

$$6z_1 + 3z_2 = 8$$
$$4z_1 + 2z_2 = 4.$$

119. $y = e^x \cos(3x) + e^x \sin(2x)$ is a solution to the second-order differential equation $y'' + 2y' + 10 = 0.$

120. To find the particular solution to a second-order differential equation, you need one initial condition.

Classify the differential equation. Determine the order, whether it is linear and, if linear, whether the differential equation is homogeneous or nonhomogeneous. If the equation is second-order homogeneous and linear, find the characteristic equation.

121. $y'' - 2y = 0$

122. $y'' - 3y + 2y = \cos(t)$

123. $\left(\frac{dy}{dt}\right)^2 + yy' = 1$

124. $\frac{d^2y}{dt^2} + t\frac{dy}{dt} + \sin^2(t)y = e^t$

For the following problems, find the general solution.

125. $y'' + 9y = 0$

126. $y'' + 2y' + y = 0$

127. $y'' - 2y' + 10y = 4x$

128. $y'' = \cos(x) + 2y' + y$

129. $y'' + 5y + y = x + e^{2x}$

130. $y'' = 3y' + xe^{-x}$

131. $y'' - x^2 = -3y' - \frac{9}{4}y + 3x$

132. $y'' = 2\cos x + y' - y$

For the following problems, find the solution to the initial-value problem, if possible.

133. $y'' + 4y' + 6y = 0, \quad y(0) = 0, \quad y'(0) = \sqrt{2}$

134. $y'' = 3y - \cos(x), \quad y(0) = \frac{9}{4}, \quad y'(0) = 0$

For the following problems, find the solution to the boundary-value problem.

135. $4y' = -6y + 2y'', \quad y(0) = 0, \quad y(1) = 1$

136. $y'' = 3x - y - y', \quad y(0) = -3, \quad y(1) = 0$

For the following problem, set up and solve the differential equation.

137. The motion of a swinging pendulum for small angles θ can be approximated by $\frac{d^2\theta}{dt^2} + \frac{g}{L}\theta = 0,$ where θ is the angle the pendulum makes with respect to a vertical line, g is the acceleration resulting from gravity, and L is the length of the pendulum. Find the equation describing the angle of the pendulum at time $t,$ assuming an initial displacement of θ_0 and an initial velocity of zero.

The following problems consider the "beats" that occur when the forcing term of a differential equation causes "slow" and "fast" amplitudes. Consider the general differential equation $ay'' + by = \cos(\omega t)$ that governs undamped motion. Assume that $\sqrt{\frac{b}{a}} \neq \omega.$

138. Find the general solution to this equation (*Hint:* call $\omega_0 = \sqrt{b/a}$).

139. Assuming the system starts from rest, show that the particular solution can be written as $y = \frac{2}{a\left(\omega_0{}^2 - \omega^2\right)}\sin\left(\frac{\omega_0 - \omega t}{2}\right)\sin\left(\frac{\omega_0 + \omega t}{2}\right).$

140. **[T]** Using your solutions derived earlier, plot the solution to the system $2y'' + 9y = \cos(2t)$ over the interval $t = [-50, 50].$ Find, analytically, the period of the fast and slow amplitudes.

For the following problem, set up and solve the differential equations.

141. An opera singer is attempting to shatter a glass by singing a particular note. The vibrations of the glass can be modeled by $y'' + ay = \cos(bt),$ where $y'' + ay = 0$ represents the natural frequency of the glass and the singer is forcing the vibrations at $\cos(bt).$ For what value b would the singer be able to break that glass? (*Note*: in order for the glass to break, the oscillations would need to get higher and higher.)

APPENDIX A | TABLE OF INTEGRALS

Basic Integrals

1. $\int u^n\,du = \frac{u^{n+1}}{n+1} + C,\ n \neq -1$

2. $\int \frac{du}{u} = \ln|u| + C$

3. $\int e^u\,du = e^u + C$

4. $\int a^u\,du = \frac{a^u}{\ln a} + C$

5. $\int \sin u\,du = -\cos u + C$

6. $\int \cos u\,du = \sin u + C$

7. $\int \sec^2 u\,du = \tan u + C$

8. $\int \csc^2 u\,du = -\cot u + C$

9. $\int \sec u \tan u\,du = \sec u + C$

10. $\int \csc u \cot u\,du = -\csc u + C$

11. $\int \tan u\,du = \ln|\sec u| + C$

12. $\int \cot u\,du = \ln|\sin u| + C$

13. $\int \sec u\,du = \ln|\sec u + \tan u| + C$

14. $\int \csc u\,du = \ln|\csc u - \cot u| + C$

15. $\int \frac{du}{\sqrt{a^2 - u^2}} = \sin^{-1}\frac{u}{a} + C$

16. $\int \frac{du}{a^2 + u^2} = \frac{1}{a}\tan^{-1}\frac{u}{a} + C$

17. $\int \frac{du}{u\sqrt{u^2 - a^2}} = \frac{1}{a}\sec^{-1}\frac{u}{a} + C$

Trigonometric Integrals

18. $\int \sin^2 u\,du = \frac{1}{2}u - \frac{1}{4}\sin 2u + C$

19. $\int \cos^2 u\,du = \frac{1}{2}u + \frac{1}{4}\sin 2u + C$

20. $\int \tan^2 u\,du = \tan u - u + C$

21. $\int \cot^2 u\,du = -\cot u - u + C$

22. $\int \sin^3 u\,du = -\frac{1}{3}\left(2 + \sin^2 u\right)\cos u + C$

23. $\int \cos^3 u\,du = \frac{1}{3}\left(2 + \cos^2 u\right)\sin u + C$

24. $\int \tan^3 u\,du = \frac{1}{2}\tan^2 u + \ln|\cos u| + C$

25. $\int \cot^3 u\,du = -\frac{1}{2}\cot^2 u - \ln|\sin u| + C$

26. $\int \sec^3 u\,du = \frac{1}{2}\sec u \tan u + \frac{1}{2}\ln|\sec u + \tan u| + C$

27. $\int \csc^3 u\,du = -\frac{1}{2}\csc u \cot u + \frac{1}{2}\ln|\csc u - \cot u| + C$

28. $\int \sin^n u\,du = -\frac{1}{n}\sin^{n-1} u \cos u + \frac{n-1}{n}\int \sin^{n-2} u\,du$

29. $\int \cos^n u\,du = \frac{1}{n}\cos^{n-1} u \sin u + \frac{n-1}{n}\int \cos^{n-2} u\,du$

30. $\int \tan^n u\,du = \frac{1}{n-1}\tan^{n-1} u - \int \tan^{n-2} u\,du$

31. $\int \cot^n u\,du = \frac{-1}{n-1}\cot^{n-1} u - \int \cot^{n-2} u\,du$

32. $\int \sec^n u\,du = \frac{1}{n-1}\tan u \sec^{n-2} u + \frac{n-2}{n-1}\int \sec^{n-2} u\,du$

33. $\int \csc^n u\,du = \frac{-1}{n-1}\cot u \csc^{n-2} u + \frac{n-2}{n-1}\int \csc^{n-2} u\,du$

34. $\int \sin au \sin bu\,du = \frac{\sin(a-b)u}{2(a-b)} - \frac{\sin(a+b)u}{2(a+b)} + C$

35. $\int \cos au \cos bu\,du = \frac{\sin(a-b)u}{2(a-b)} + \frac{\sin(a+b)u}{2(a+b)} + C$

36. $\int \sin au \cos bu\,du = -\frac{\cos(a-b)u}{2(a-b)} - \frac{\cos(a+b)u}{2(a+b)} + C$

37. $\int u \sin u\,du = \sin u - u \cos u + C$

38. $\int u \cos u\,du = \cos u + u \sin u + C$

39. $\int u^n \sin u\,du = -u^n \cos u + n\int u^{n-1} \cos u\,du$

40. $\int u^n \cos u\,du = u^n \sin u - n\int u^{n-1} \sin u\,du$

41. $$\begin{aligned}\int \sin^n u \cos^m u\,du &= -\frac{\sin^{n-1} u \cos^{m+1} u}{n+m} + \frac{n-1}{n+m}\int \sin^{n-2} u \cos^m u\,du \\ &= \frac{\sin^{n+1} u \cos^{m-1} u}{n+m} + \frac{m-1}{n+m}\int \sin^n u \cos^{m-2} u\,du\end{aligned}$$

Exponential and Logarithmic Integrals

42. $\int ue^{au}\, du = \frac{1}{a^2}(au - 1)e^{au} + C$

43. $\int u^n e^{au}\, du = \frac{1}{a}u^n e^{au} - \frac{n}{a}\int u^{n-1} e^{au}\, du$

44. $\int e^{au} \sin bu\, du = \frac{e^{au}}{a^2 + b^2}(a \sin bu - b \cos bu) + C$

45. $\int e^{au} \cos bu\, du = \frac{e^{au}}{a^2 + b^2}(a \cos bu + b \sin bu) + C$

46. $\int \ln u\, du = u \ln u - u + C$

47. $\int u^n \ln u\, du = \frac{u^{n+1}}{(n+1)^2}[(n+1)\ln u - 1] + C$

48. $\int \frac{1}{u \ln u}\, du = \ln|\ln u| + C$

Hyperbolic Integrals

49. $\int \sinh u\, du = \cosh u + C$

50. $\int \cosh u\, du = \sinh u + C$

51. $\int \tanh u\, du = \ln \cosh u + C$

52. $\int \coth u\, du = \ln|\sinh u| + C$

53. $\int \operatorname{sech} u\, du = \tan^{-1}|\sinh u| + C$

54. $\int \operatorname{csch} u\, du = \ln\left|\tanh \frac{1}{2}u\right| + C$

55. $\int \operatorname{sech}^2 u\, du = \tanh u + C$

56. $\int \operatorname{csch}^2 u\, du = -\coth u + C$

57. $\int \operatorname{sech} u \tanh u\, du = -\operatorname{sech} u + C$

58. $\int \operatorname{csch} u \coth u\, du = -\operatorname{csch} u + C$

Inverse Trigonometric Integrals

59. $\int \sin^{-1} u\, du = u \sin^{-1} u + \sqrt{1 - u^2} + C$

60. $\int \cos^{-1} u\, du = u \cos^{-1} u - \sqrt{1 - u^2} + C$

61. $\int \tan^{-1} u\, du = u \tan^{-1} u - \frac{1}{2}\ln\left(1 + u^2\right) + C$

62. $\int u \sin^{-1} u\, du = \frac{2u^2 - 1}{4}\sin^{-1} u + \frac{u\sqrt{1 - u^2}}{4} + C$

63. $\int u\cos^{-1}u\,du = \frac{2u^2-1}{4}\cos^{-1}u - \frac{u\sqrt{1-u^2}}{4} + C$

64. $\int u\tan^{-1}u\,du = \frac{u^2+1}{2}\tan^{-1}u - \frac{u}{2} + C$

65. $\int u^n\sin^{-1}u\,du = \frac{1}{n+1}\left[u^{n+1}\sin^{-1}u - \int\frac{u^{n+1}\,du}{\sqrt{1-u^2}}\right],\ n \neq -1$

66. $\int u^n\cos^{-1}u\,du = \frac{1}{n+1}\left[u^{n+1}\cos^{-1}u + \int\frac{u^{n+1}\,du}{\sqrt{1-u^2}}\right],\ n \neq -1$

67. $\int u^n\tan^{-1}u\,du = \frac{1}{n+1}\left[u^{n+1}\tan^{-1}u - \int\frac{u^{n+1}\,du}{1+u^2}\right],\ n \neq -1$

Integrals Involving $a^2 + u^2$, $a > 0$

68. $\int\sqrt{a^2+u^2}\,du = \frac{u}{2}\sqrt{a^2+u^2} + \frac{a^2}{2}\ln\left(u+\sqrt{a^2+u^2}\right) + C$

69. $\int u^2\sqrt{a^2+u^2}\,du = \frac{u}{8}\left(a^2+2u^2\right)\sqrt{a^2+u^2} - \frac{a^4}{8}\ln\left(u+\sqrt{a^2+u^2}\right) + C$

70. $\int\frac{\sqrt{a^2+u^2}}{u}\,du = \sqrt{a^2+u^2} - a\ln\left|\frac{a+\sqrt{a^2+u^2}}{u}\right| + C$

71. $\int\frac{\sqrt{a^2+u^2}}{u^2}\,du = -\frac{\sqrt{a^2+u^2}}{u} + \ln\left(u+\sqrt{a^2+u^2}\right) + C$

72. $\int\frac{du}{\sqrt{a^2+u^2}} = \ln\left(u+\sqrt{a^2+u^2}\right) + C$

73. $\int\frac{u^2\,du}{\sqrt{a^2+u^2}} = \frac{u}{2}\left(\sqrt{a^2+u^2}\right) - \frac{a^2}{2}\ln\left(u+\sqrt{a^2+u^2}\right) + C$

74. $\int\frac{du}{u\sqrt{a^2+u^2}} = -\frac{1}{a}\ln\left|\frac{\sqrt{a^2+u^2}+a}{u}\right| + C$

75. $\int\frac{du}{u^2\sqrt{a^2+u^2}} = -\frac{\sqrt{a^2+u^2}}{a^2u} + C$

76. $\int\frac{du}{\left(a^2+u^2\right)^{3/2}} = \frac{u}{a^2\sqrt{a^2+u^2}} + C$

Integrals Involving $u^2 - a^2$, $a > 0$

77. $\int\sqrt{u^2-a^2}\,du = \frac{u}{2}\sqrt{u^2-a^2} - \frac{a^2}{2}\ln\left|u+\sqrt{u^2-a^2}\right| + C$

78. $\int u^2\sqrt{u^2-a^2}\,du = \frac{u}{8}\left(2u^2-a^2\right)\sqrt{u^2-a^2} - \frac{a^4}{8}\ln\left|u+\sqrt{u^2-a^2}\right| + C$

79. $\int\frac{\sqrt{u^2-a^2}}{u}\,du = \sqrt{u^2-a^2} - a\cos^{-1}\frac{a}{|u|} + C$

80. $\int\frac{\sqrt{u^2-a^2}}{u^2}\,du = -\frac{\sqrt{u^2-a^2}}{u} + \ln\left|u+\sqrt{u^2-a^2}\right| + C$

81. $\int \frac{du}{\sqrt{u^2 - a^2}} = \ln\left|u + \sqrt{u^2 - a^2}\right| + C$

82. $\int \frac{u^2\, du}{\sqrt{u^2 - a^2}} = \frac{u}{2}\sqrt{u^2 - a^2} + \frac{a^2}{2}\ln\left|u + \sqrt{u^2 - a^2}\right| + C$

83. $\int \frac{du}{u^2\sqrt{u^2 - a^2}} = \frac{\sqrt{u^2 - a^2}}{a^2 u} + C$

84. $\int \frac{du}{\left(u^2 - a^2\right)^{3/2}} = -\frac{u}{a^2\sqrt{u^2 - a^2}} + C$

Integrals Involving $a^2 - u^2$, $a > 0$

85. $\int \sqrt{a^2 - u^2}\, du = \frac{u}{2}\sqrt{a^2 - u^2} + \frac{a^2}{2}\sin^{-1}\frac{u}{a} + C$

86. $\int u^2\sqrt{a^2 - u^2}\, du = \frac{u}{8}\left(2u^2 - a^2\right)\sqrt{a^2 - u^2} + \frac{a^4}{8}\sin^{-1}\frac{u}{a} + C$

87. $\int \frac{\sqrt{a^2 - u^2}}{u}\, du = \sqrt{a^2 - u^2} - a\ln\left|\frac{a + \sqrt{a^2 - u^2}}{u}\right| + C$

88. $\int \frac{\sqrt{a^2 - u^2}}{u^2}\, du = -\frac{1}{u}\sqrt{a^2 - u^2} - \sin^{-1}\frac{u}{a} + C$

89. $\int \frac{u^2\, du}{\sqrt{a^2 - u^2}} = -\frac{u}{u}\sqrt{a^2 - u^2} + \frac{a^2}{2}\sin^{-1}\frac{u}{a} + C$

90. $\int \frac{du}{u\sqrt{a^2 - u^2}} = -\frac{1}{a}\ln\left|\frac{a + \sqrt{a^2 - u^2}}{u}\right| + C$

91. $\int \frac{du}{u^2\sqrt{a^2 - u^2}} = -\frac{1}{a^2 u}\sqrt{a^2 - u^2} + C$

92. $\int \left(a^2 - u^2\right)^{3/2}\, du = -\frac{u}{8}\left(2u^2 - 5a^2\right)\sqrt{a^2 - u^2} + \frac{3a^4}{8}\sin^{-1}\frac{u}{a} + C$

93. $\int \frac{du}{\left(a^2 - u^2\right)^{3/2}} = -\frac{u}{a^2\sqrt{a^2 - u^2}} + C$

Integrals Involving $2au - u^2$, $a > 0$

94. $\int \sqrt{2au - u^2}\, du = \frac{u - a}{2}\sqrt{2au - u^2} + \frac{a^2}{2}\cos^{-1}\left(\frac{a - u}{a}\right) + C$

95. $\int \frac{du}{\sqrt{2au - u^2}} = \cos^{-1}\left(\frac{a - u}{a}\right) + C$

96. $\int u\sqrt{2au - u^2}\, du = \frac{2u^2 - au - 3a^2}{6}\sqrt{2au - u^2} + \frac{a^3}{2}\cos^{-1}\left(\frac{a - u}{a}\right) + C$

97. $\int \frac{du}{u\sqrt{2au - u^2}} = -\frac{\sqrt{2au - u^2}}{au} + C$

Integrals Involving *a* + *bu*, *a* ≠ 0

98. $\int \frac{u\,du}{a+bu} = \frac{1}{b^2}(a + bu - a\ln|a + bu|) + C$

99. $\int \frac{u^2\,du}{a+bu} = \frac{1}{2b^3}\left[(a + bu)^2 - 4a(a + bu) + 2a^2\ln|a + bu|\right] + C$

100. $\int \frac{du}{u(a+bu)} = \frac{1}{a}\ln\left|\frac{u}{a+bu}\right| + C$

101. $\int \frac{du}{u^2(a+bu)} = -\frac{1}{au} + \frac{b}{a^2}\ln\left|\frac{a+bu}{u}\right| + C$

102. $\int \frac{u\,du}{(a+bu)^2} = \frac{a}{b^2(a+bu)} + \frac{1}{b^2}\ln|a + bu| + C$

103. $\int \frac{u\,du}{u(a+bu)^2} = \frac{1}{a(a+bu)} - \frac{1}{a^2}\ln\left|\frac{a+bu}{u}\right| + C$

104. $\int \frac{u^2\,du}{(a+bu)^2} = \frac{1}{b^3}\left(a + bu - \frac{a^2}{a+bu} - 2a\ln|a + bu|\right) + C$

105. $\int u\sqrt{a+bu}\,du = \frac{2}{15b^2}(3bu - 2a)(a + bu)^{3/2} + C$

106. $\int \frac{u\,du}{\sqrt{a+bu}} = \frac{2}{3b^2}(bu - 2a)\sqrt{a+bu} + C$

107. $\int \frac{u^2\,du}{\sqrt{a+bu}} = \frac{2}{15b^3}\left(8a^2 + 3b^2u^2 - 4abu\right)\sqrt{a+bu} + C$

108. $$\begin{aligned}\int \frac{du}{u\sqrt{a+bu}} &= \frac{1}{\sqrt{a}}\ln\left|\frac{\sqrt{a+bu} - \sqrt{a}}{\sqrt{a+bu} + \sqrt{a}}\right| + C, \quad \text{if } a > 0 \\ &= \frac{2}{\sqrt{-a}}\tan - 1\sqrt{\frac{a+bu}{-a}} + C, \quad \text{if } a < 0\end{aligned}$$

109. $\int \frac{\sqrt{a+bu}}{u}\,du = 2\sqrt{a+bu} + a\int \frac{du}{u\sqrt{a+bu}}$

110. $\int \frac{\sqrt{a+bu}}{u^2}\,du = -\frac{\sqrt{a+bu}}{u} + \frac{b}{2}\int \frac{du}{u\sqrt{a+bu}}$

111. $\int u^n\sqrt{a+bu}\,du = \frac{2}{b(2n+3)}\left[u^n(a + bu)^{3/2} - na\int u^{n-1}\sqrt{a+bu}\,du\right]$

112. $\int \frac{u^n\,du}{\sqrt{a+bu}} = \frac{2u^n\sqrt{a+bu}}{b(2n+1)} - \frac{2na}{b(2n+1)}\int \frac{u^{n-1}\,du}{\sqrt{a+bu}}$

113. $\int \frac{du}{u^n\sqrt{a+bu}} = -\frac{\sqrt{a+bu}}{a(n-1)u^{n-1}} - \frac{b(2n-3)}{2a(n-1)}\int \frac{du}{u^{n-1}\sqrt{a+bu}}$

APPENDIX B | TABLE OF DERIVATIVES

General Formulas

1. $\frac{d}{dx}(c) = 0$

2. $\frac{d}{dx}(f(x) + g(x)) = f'(x) + g'(x)$

3. $\frac{d}{dx}(f(x)g(x)) = f'(x)g(x) + f(x)g'(x)$

4. $\frac{d}{dx}(x^n) = nx^{n-1}$, for real numbers n

5. $\frac{d}{dx}(cf(x)) = cf'(x)$

6. $\frac{d}{dx}(f(x) - g(x)) = f'(x) - g'(x)$

7. $\frac{d}{dx}\left(\frac{f(x)}{g(x)}\right) = \frac{g(x)f'(x) - f(x)g'(x)}{(g(x))^2}$

8. $\frac{d}{dx}[f(g(x))] = f'(g(x)) \cdot g'(x)$

Trigonometric Functions

9. $\frac{d}{dx}(\sin x) = \cos x$

10. $\frac{d}{dx}(\tan x) = \sec^2 x$

11. $\frac{d}{dx}(\sec x) = \sec x \tan x$

12. $\frac{d}{dx}(\cos x) = -\sin x$

13. $\frac{d}{dx}(\cot x) = -\csc^2 x$

14. $\frac{d}{dx}(\csc x) = -\csc x \cot x$

Inverse Trigonometric Functions

15. $\frac{d}{dx}\left(\sin^{-1} x\right) = \frac{1}{\sqrt{1 - x^2}}$

16. $\frac{d}{dx}\left(\tan^{-1} x\right) = \frac{1}{1 + x^2}$

17. $\frac{d}{dx}\left(\sec^{-1} x\right) = \frac{1}{|x|\sqrt{x^2 - 1}}$

18. $\frac{d}{dx}\left(\cos^{-1} x\right) = -\frac{1}{\sqrt{1 - x^2}}$

19. $\frac{d}{dx}\left(\cot^{-1} x\right) = -\frac{1}{1 + x^2}$

20. $\frac{d}{dx}\left(\csc^{-1} x\right) = -\frac{1}{|x|\sqrt{x^2 - 1}}$

Exponential and Logarithmic Functions

21. $\frac{d}{dx}(e^x) = e^x$

22. $\frac{d}{dx}(\ln|x|) = \frac{1}{x}$

23. $\frac{d}{dx}(b^x) = b^x \ln b$

24. $\frac{d}{dx}(\log_b x) = \frac{1}{x \ln b}$

Hyperbolic Functions

25. $\frac{d}{dx}(\sinh x) = \cosh x$

26. $\frac{d}{dx}(\tanh x) = \operatorname{sech}^2 x$

27. $\frac{d}{dx}(\operatorname{sech} x) = -\operatorname{sech} x \tanh x$

28. $\frac{d}{dx}(\cosh x) = \sinh x$

29. $\frac{d}{dx}(\coth x) = -\operatorname{csch}^2 x$

30. $\frac{d}{dx}(\operatorname{csch} x) = -\operatorname{csch} x \coth x$

Inverse Hyperbolic Functions

31. $\frac{d}{dx}\left(\sinh^{-1} x\right) = \frac{1}{\sqrt{x^2 + 1}}$

32. $\frac{d}{dx}\left(\tanh^{-1} x\right) = \frac{1}{1 - x^2}(|x| < 1)$

33. $\frac{d}{dx}\left(\operatorname{sech}^{-1} x\right) = -\frac{1}{x\sqrt{1 - x^2}} \quad (0 < x < 1)$

34. $\frac{d}{dx}\left(\cosh^{-1} x\right) = \frac{1}{\sqrt{x^2 - 1}} \quad (x > 1)$

35. $\frac{d}{dx}\left(\coth^{-1} x\right) = \frac{1}{1 - x^2} \quad (|x| > 1)$

36. $\frac{d}{dx}\left(\operatorname{csch}^{-1} x\right) = -\frac{1}{|x|\sqrt{1 + x^2}} (x \neq 0)$

APPENDIX C | REVIEW OF PRE-CALCULUS

Formulas from Geometry

$A = \text{area}, \quad V = \text{Volume}, \text{ and } \quad S = \text{lateral surface area}$

Parallelogram

$A = bh$

Triangle

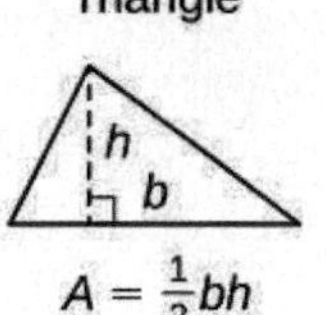

$A = \frac{1}{2}bh$

Trapezoid

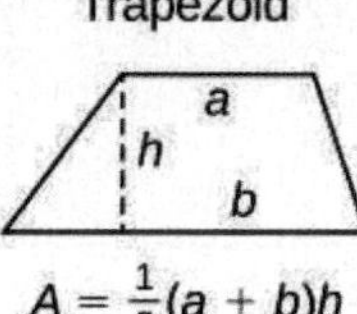

$A = \frac{1}{2}(a + b)h$

Circle

$A = \pi r^2$
$C = 2\pi r$

Sector

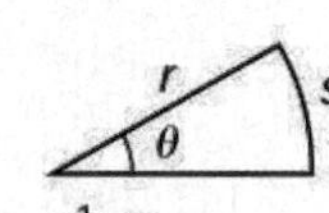

$A = \frac{1}{2}r^2\theta$

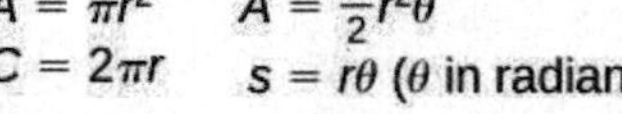

$s = r\theta$ (θ in radians)

Cylinder

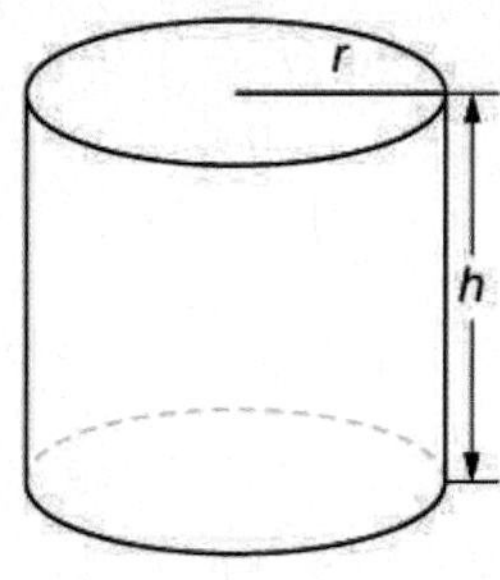

$V = \pi r^2 h$
$S = 2\pi rh$

Cone

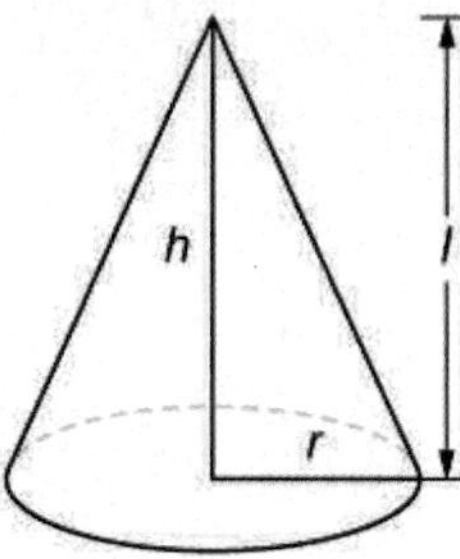

$V = \frac{1}{3}\pi r^2 h$
$S = \pi rl$

Sphere

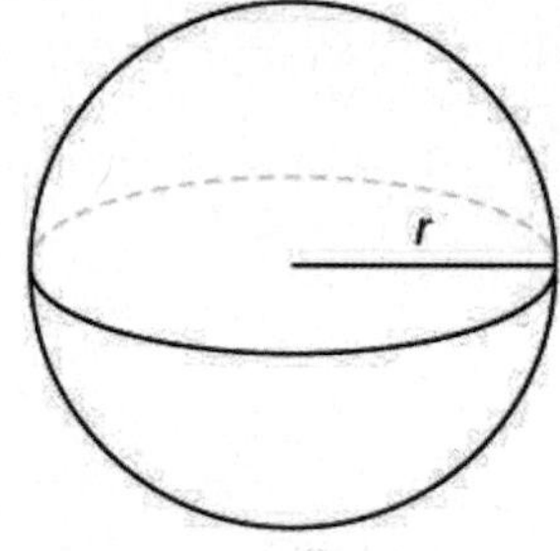

$V = \frac{4}{3}\pi r^3$
$S = 4\pi r^2$

Formulas from Algebra

Laws of Exponents

$$x^m x^n = x^{m+n} \qquad \frac{x^m}{x^n} = x^{m-n} \qquad (x^m)^n = x^{mn}$$

$$x^{-n} = \frac{1}{x^n} \qquad (xy)^n = x^n y^n \qquad \left(\frac{x}{y}\right)^n = \frac{x^n}{y^n}$$

$$x^{1/n} = \sqrt[n]{x} \qquad \sqrt[n]{xy} = \sqrt[n]{x}\sqrt[n]{y} \qquad \sqrt[n]{\frac{x}{y}} = \frac{\sqrt[n]{x}}{\sqrt[n]{y}}$$

$$x^{m/n} = \sqrt[n]{x^m} = (\sqrt[n]{x})^m$$

Special Factorizations

$$x^2 - y^2 = (x + y)(x - y)$$
$$x^3 + y^3 = (x + y)\left(x^2 - xy + y^2\right)$$
$$x^3 - y^3 = (x - y)\left(x^2 + xy + y^2\right)$$

Quadratic Formula

If $ax^2 + bx + c = 0$, then $x = \dfrac{-b \pm \sqrt{b^2 - 4ca}}{2a}$.

Binomial Theorem

$$(a+b)^n = a^n + \binom{n}{1}a^{n-1}b + \binom{n}{2}a^{n-2}b^2 + \cdots + \binom{n}{n-1}ab^{n-1} + b^n,$$

where $\binom{n}{k} = \dfrac{n(n-1)(n-2)\cdots(n-k+1)}{k(k-1)(k-2)\cdots 3\cdot 2\cdot 1} = \dfrac{n!}{k!(n-k)!}$

Formulas from Trigonometry

Right-Angle Trigonometry

$\sin\theta = \dfrac{\text{opp}}{\text{hyp}}$ $\csc\theta = \dfrac{\text{hyp}}{\text{opp}}$

$\cos\theta = \dfrac{\text{adj}}{\text{hyp}}$ $\sec\theta = \dfrac{\text{hyp}}{\text{adj}}$

$\tan\theta = \dfrac{\text{opp}}{\text{adj}}$ $\cot\theta = \dfrac{\text{adj}}{\text{opp}}$

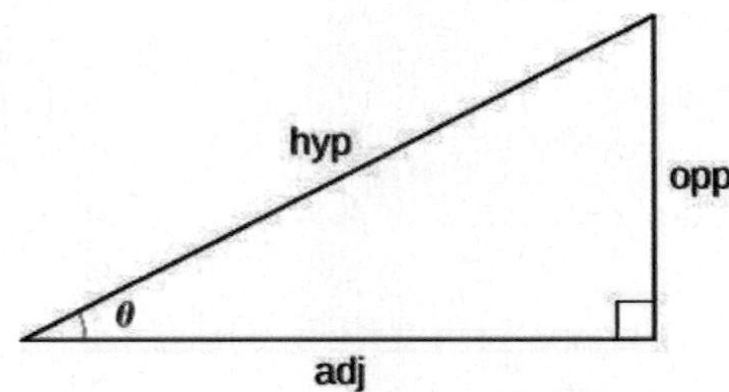

Trigonometric Functions of Important Angles

θ	Radians	$\sin\theta$	$\cos\theta$	$\tan\theta$
0°	0	0	1	0
30°	$\pi/6$	1/2	$\sqrt{3}/2$	$\sqrt{3}/3$
45°	$\pi/4$	$\sqrt{2}/2$	$\sqrt{2}/2$	1
60°	$\pi/3$	$\sqrt{3}/2$	1/2	$\sqrt{3}$
90°	$\pi/2$	1	0	—

Fundamental Identities

$$\begin{aligned} \sin^2\theta + \cos^2\theta &= 1 & \sin(-\theta) &= -\sin\theta \\ 1 + \tan^2\theta &= \sec^2\theta & \cos(-\theta) &= \cos\theta \\ 1 + \cot^2\theta &= \csc^2\theta & \tan(-\theta) &= -\tan\theta \\ \sin\left(\frac{\pi}{2} - \theta\right) &= \cos\theta & \sin(\theta + 2\pi) &= \sin\theta \\ \cos\left(\frac{\pi}{2} - \theta\right) &= \sin\theta & \cos(\theta + 2\pi) &= \cos\theta \\ \tan\left(\frac{\pi}{2} - \theta\right) &= \cot\theta & \tan(\theta + \pi) &= \tan\theta \end{aligned}$$

Law of Sines

$$\frac{\sin A}{a} = \frac{\sin B}{b} = \frac{\sin C}{c}$$

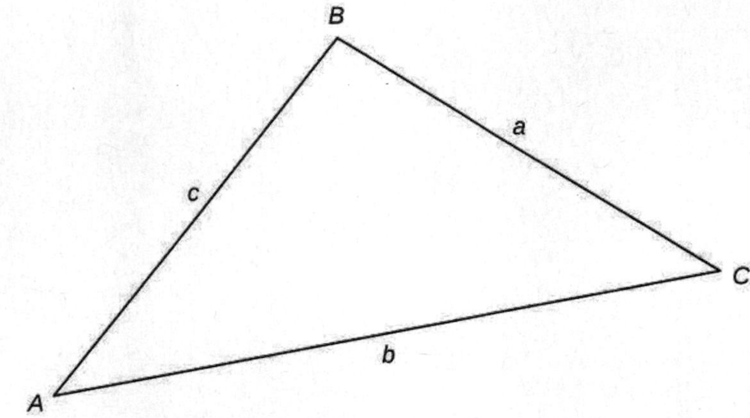

Law of Cosines

$$\begin{aligned} a^2 &= b^2 + c^2 - 2bc\cos A \\ b^2 &= a^2 + c^2 - 2ac\cos B \\ c^2 &= a^2 + b^2 - 2ab\cos C \end{aligned}$$

Addition and Subtraction Formulas

$$\begin{aligned} \sin(x + y) &= \sin x\cos y + \cos x\sin y \\ \sin(x - y) &= \sin x\cos y - \cos x\sin y \\ \cos(x + y) &= \cos x\cos y - \sin x\sin y \\ \cos(x - y) &= \cos x\cos y + \sin x\sin y \\ \tan(x + y) &= \frac{\tan x + \tan y}{1 - \tan x\tan y} \\ \tan(x - y) &= \frac{\tan x - \tan y}{1 + \tan x\tan y} \end{aligned}$$

Double-Angle Formulas

$$\begin{aligned} \sin 2x &= 2\sin x\cos x \\ \cos 2x &= \cos^2 x - \sin^2 x = 2\cos^2 x - 1 = 1 - 2\sin^2 x \\ \tan 2x &= \frac{2\tan x}{1 - \tan^2 x} \end{aligned}$$

Half-Angle Formulas

$$\sin^2 x = \frac{1 - \cos 2x}{2}$$
$$\cos^2 x = \frac{1 + \cos 2x}{2}$$

ANSWER KEY

Chapter 1

Checkpoint

1.1.

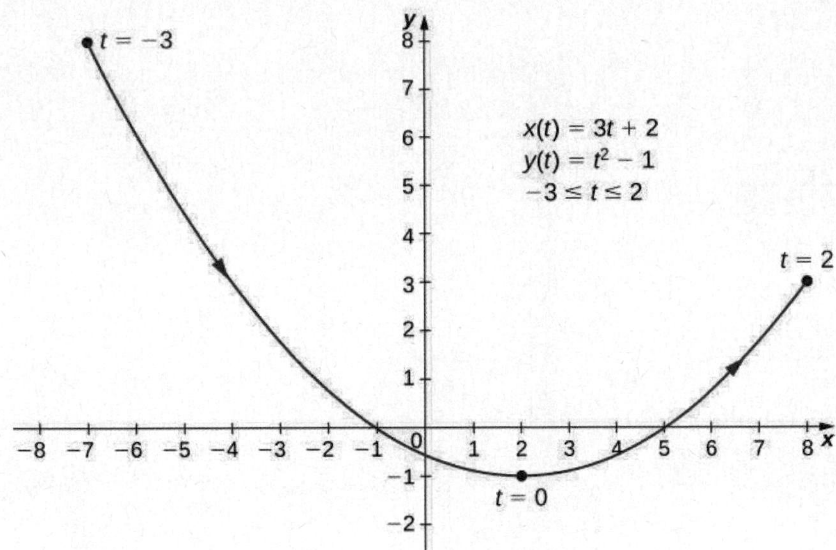

1.2. $x = 2 + \frac{3}{y+1}$, or $y = -1 + \frac{3}{x-2}$. This equation describes a portion of a rectangular hyperbola centered at $(2, -1)$.

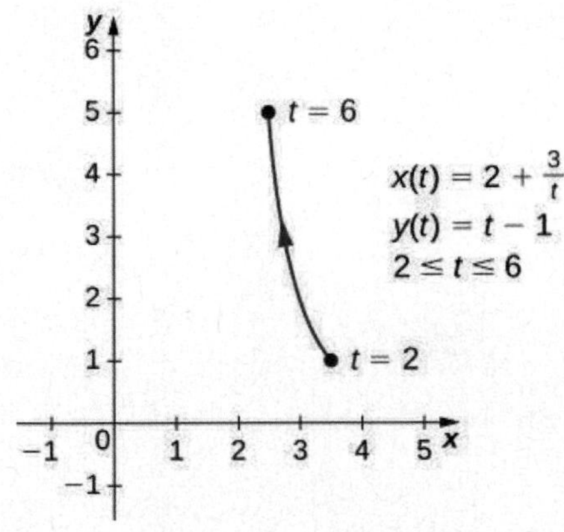

1.3. One possibility is $x(t) = t, \quad y(t) = t^2 + 2t$. Another possibility is $x(t) = 2t - 3, \quad y(t) = (2t-3)^2 + 2(2t-3) = 4t^2 - 8t + 3$. There are, in fact, an infinite number of possibilities.

1.4. $x'(t) = 2t - 4$ and $y'(t) = 6t^2 - 6$, so $\frac{dy}{dx} = \frac{6t^2 - 6}{2t - 4} = \frac{3t^2 - 3}{t - 2}$.

This expression is undefined when $t = 2$ and equal to zero when $t = \pm 1$.

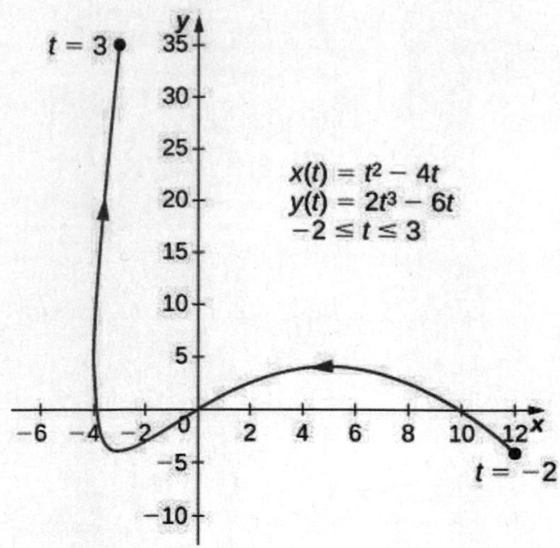

1.5. The equation of the tangent line is $y = 24x + 100.$

1.6. $\frac{d^2y}{dx^2} = \frac{3t^2 - 12t + 3}{2(t-2)^3}$. Critical points $(5, 4), (-3, -4),$ and $(-4, 6).$

1.7. $A = 3\pi$ (Note that the integral formula actually yields a negative answer. This is due to the fact that $x(t)$ is a decreasing function over the interval $[0, 2\pi];$ that is, the curve is traced from right to left.)

1.8. $s = 2\left(10^{3/2} - 2^{3/2}\right) \approx 57.589$

1.9. $A = \frac{\pi\left(494\sqrt{13} + 128\right)}{1215}$

1.10. $\left(8\sqrt{2}, \frac{5\pi}{4}\right)$ and $\left(-2, 2\sqrt{3}\right)$

1.11.

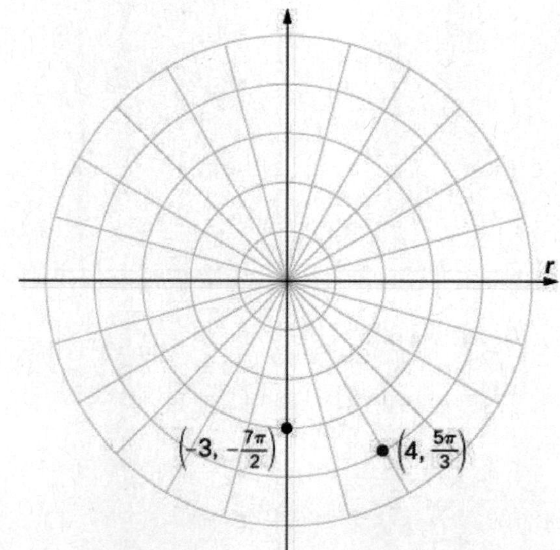

1.12.

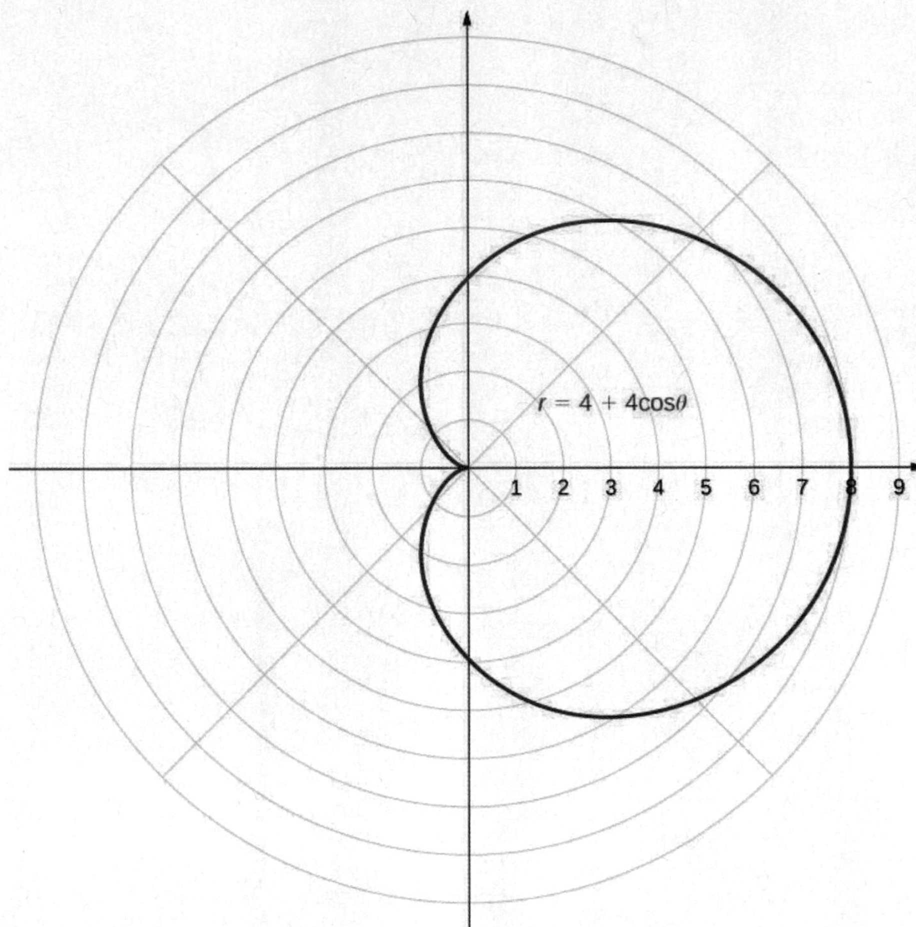

The name of this shape is a cardioid, which we will study further later in this section.

1.13. $y = x^2$, which is the equation of a parabola opening upward.

1.14. Symmetric with respect to the polar axis.

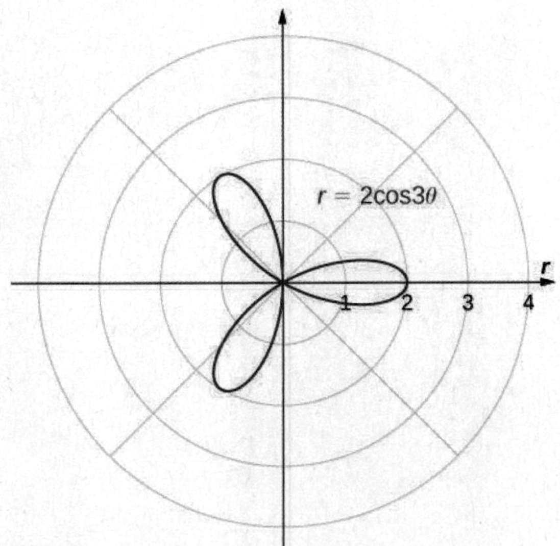

1.15. $A = 3\pi/2$

1.16. $A = \frac{4\pi}{3} + 4\sqrt{3}$

1.17. $s = 3\pi$

1.18. $x = 2(y+3)^2 - 2$

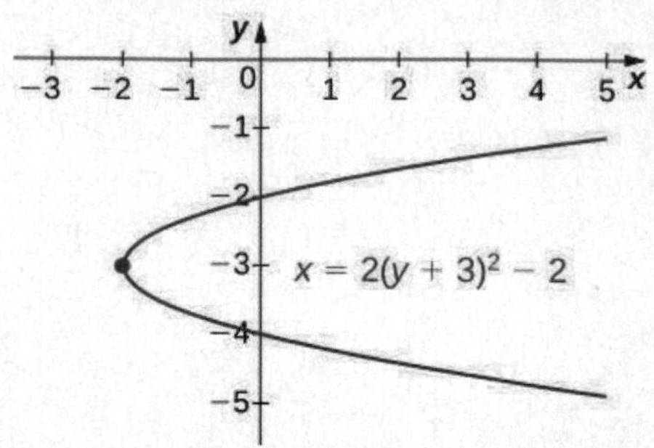

1.19. $\frac{(x+1)^2}{16} + \frac{(y-2)^2}{9} = 1$

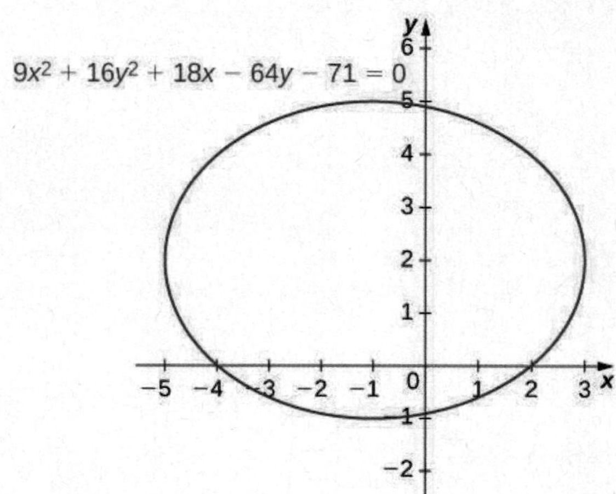

1.20. $\frac{(y+2)^2}{9} - \frac{(x-1)^2}{4} = 1$. This is a vertical hyperbola. Asymptotes $y = -2 \pm \frac{3}{2}(x-1)$.

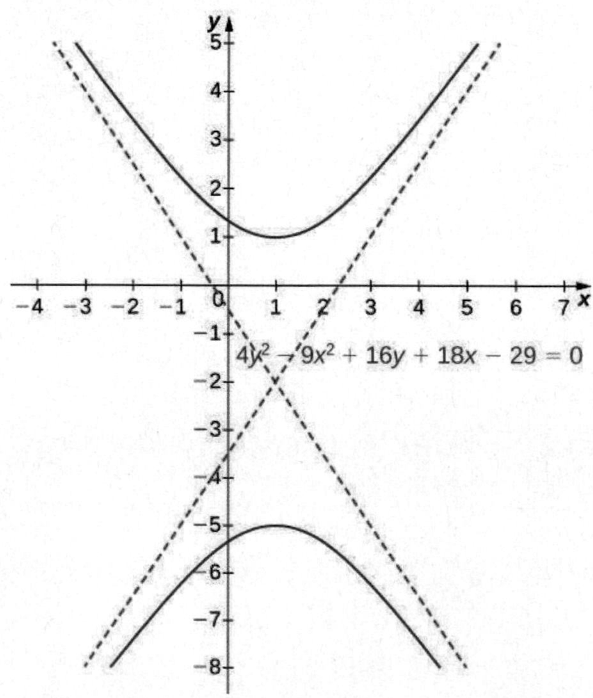

1.21. $e = \frac{c}{a} = \frac{\sqrt{74}}{7} \approx 1.229$

1.22. Here $e = 0.8$ and $p = 5$. This conic section is an ellipse.

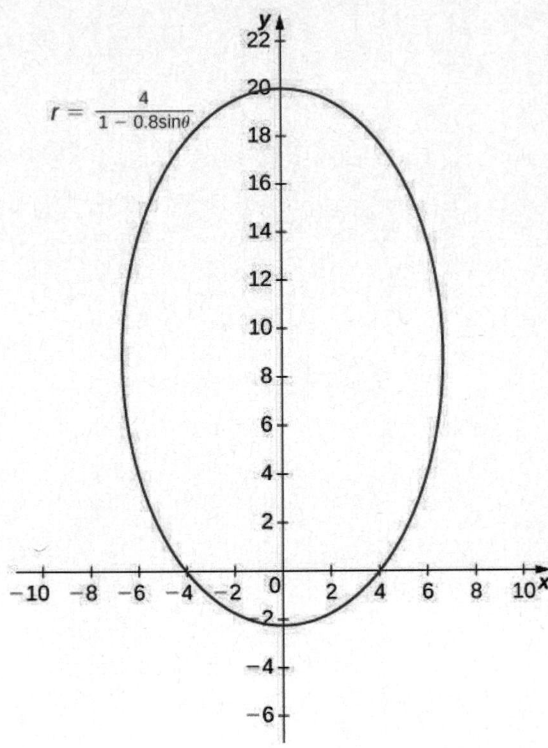

1.23. The conic is a hyperbola and the angle of rotation of the axes is $\theta = 22.5°$.

Section Exercises

1.

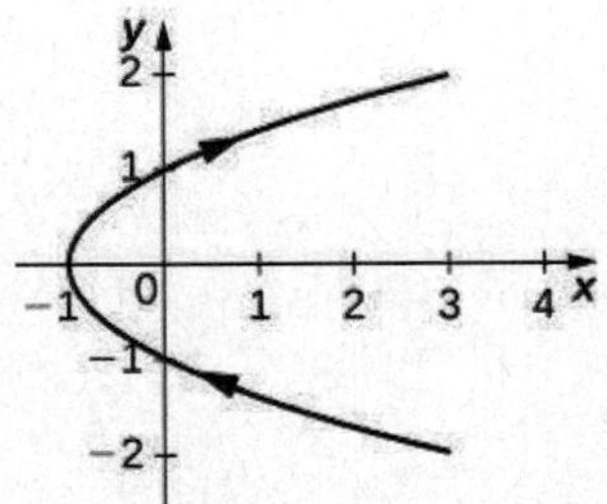

orientation: bottom to top

3.

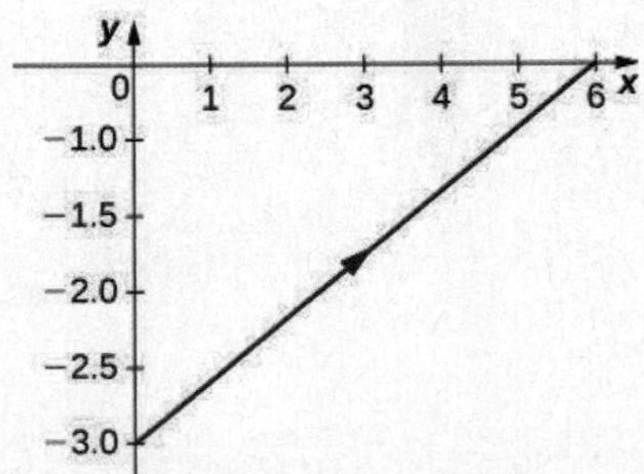

orientation: left to right

5. $y = \frac{x^2}{4} + 1$

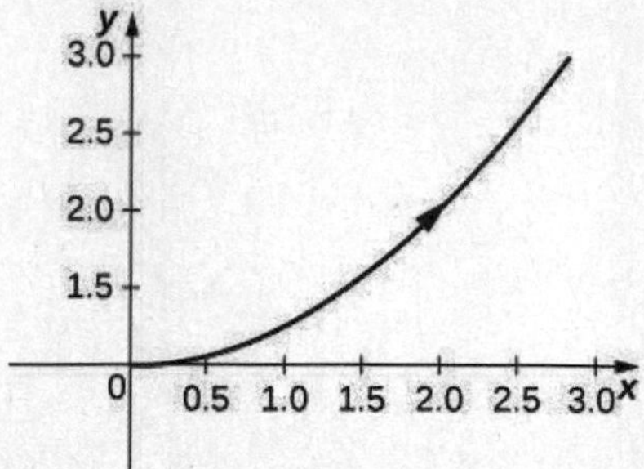

7.

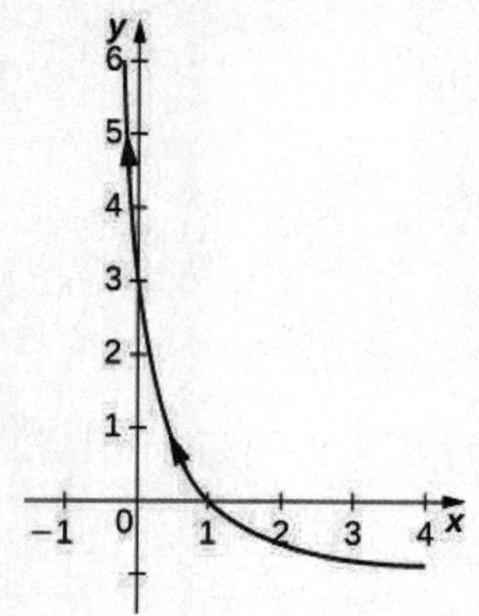

9.

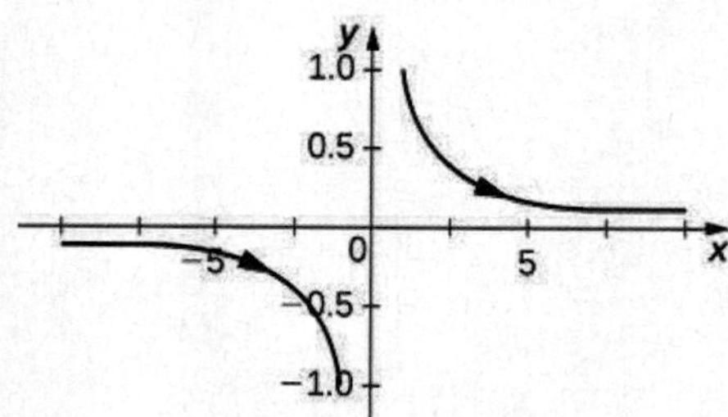

11.

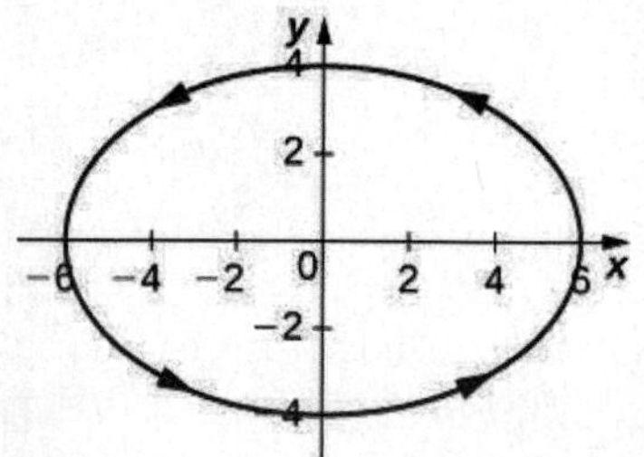

13.

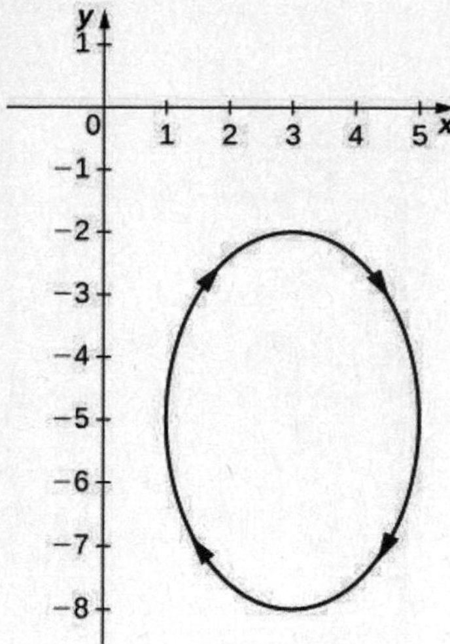

15.

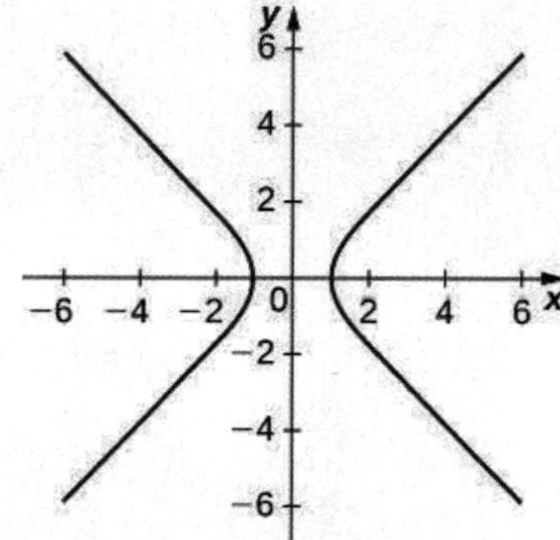

Asymptotes are $y = x$ and $y = -x$

17.

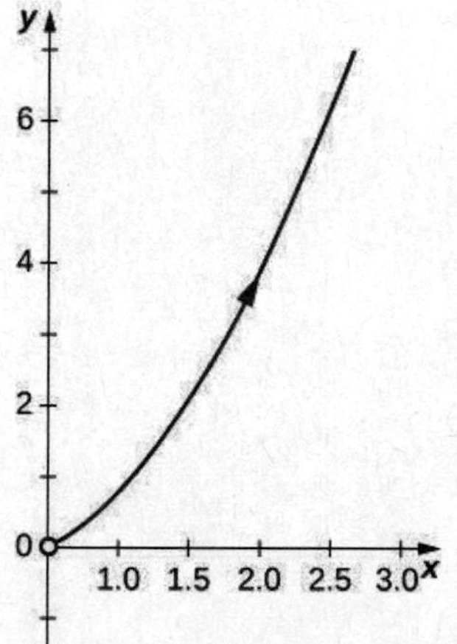

19.

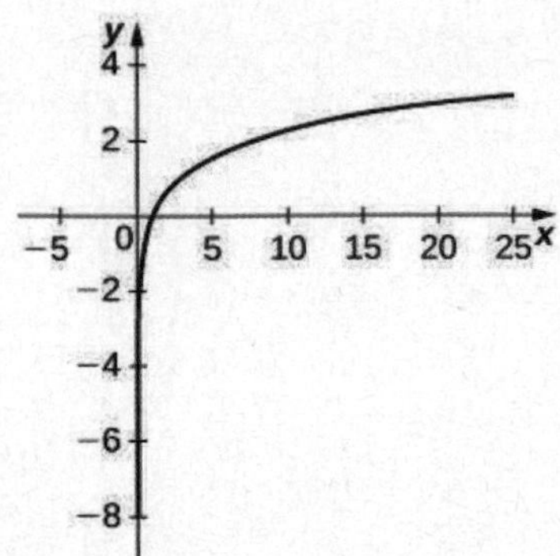

21. $x = 4y^2 - 1;$ domain: $x \in [1, \infty)$.

23. $\frac{x^2}{16} + \frac{y^2}{9} = 1;$ domain $x \in [-4, 4]$.

25. $y = 3x + 2;$ domain: all real numbers.

27. $(x - 1)^2 + (y - 3)^2 = 1;$ domain: $x \in [0, 2]$.

29. $y = \sqrt{x^2 - 1};$ domain: $x \in [-1, 1]$.

31. $y^2 = \frac{1 - x}{2};$ domain: $x \in [2, \infty) \cup (-\infty, -2]$.

33. $y = \ln x;$ domain: $x \in (0, \infty)$.

35. $y = \ln x;$ domain: $x \in (0, \infty)$.

37. $x^2 + y^2 = 4;$ domain: $x \in [-2, 2]$.

39. line
41. parabola
43. circle
45. ellipse
47. hyperbola
51. The equations represent a cycloid.

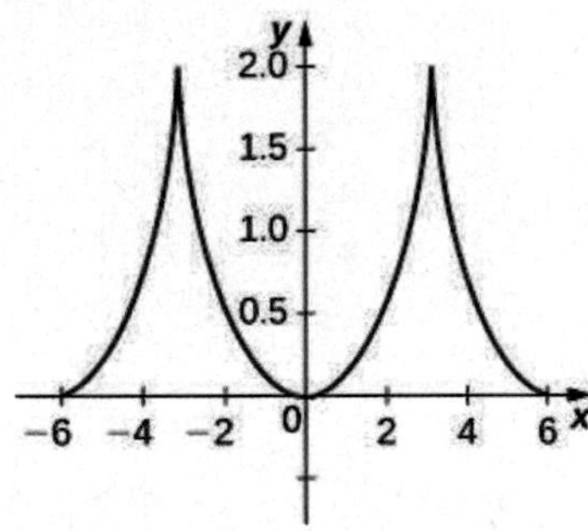

53.

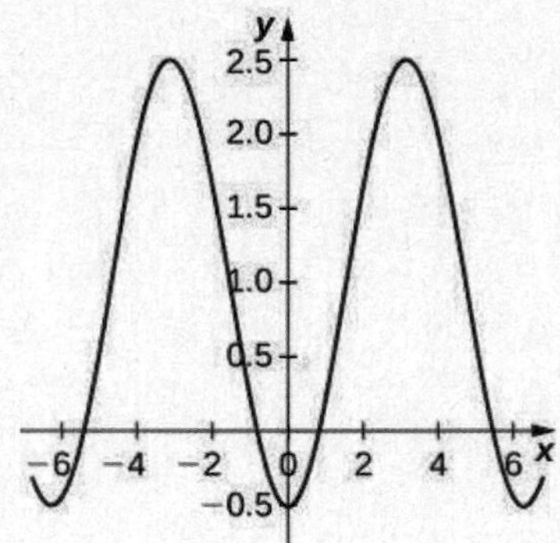

55. 22,092 meters at approximately 51 seconds.

57.

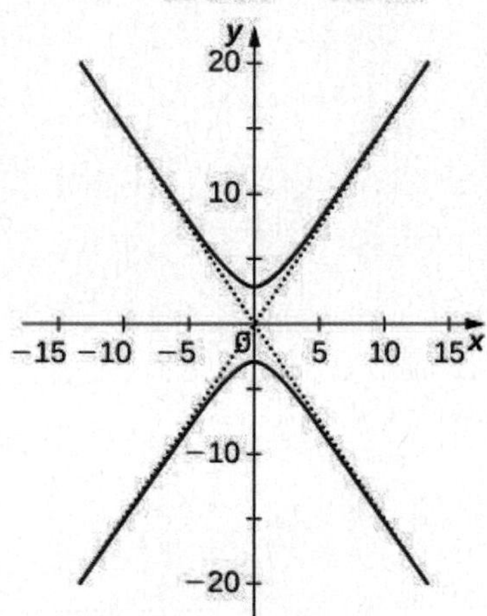

59.

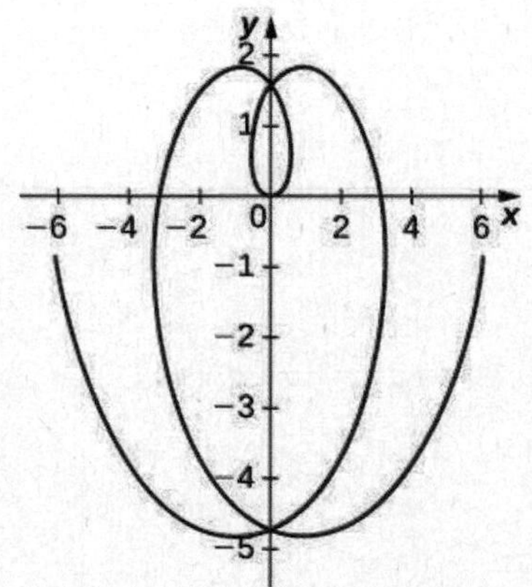

61.

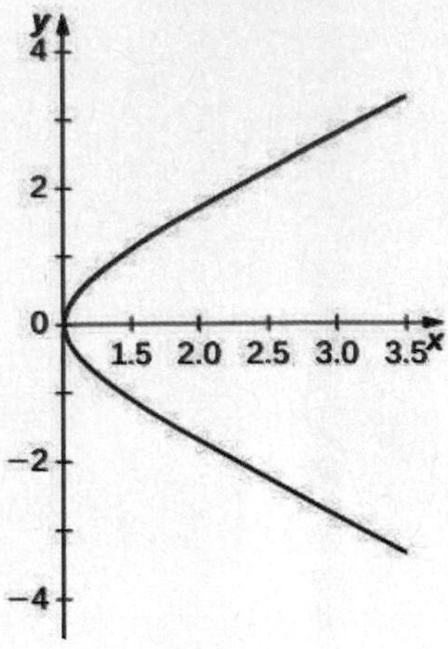

63. 0

65. $\frac{-3}{5}$

67. Slope = 0; $y = 8$.

69. Slope is undefined; $x = 2$.

71. $t = \arctan(-2)$; $\left(\frac{4}{\sqrt{5}}, \frac{-8}{\sqrt{5}}\right)$.

73. No points possible; undefined expression.

75. $y = -\left(\frac{2}{e}\right)x + 3$

77. $y = 2x - 7$

79. $\frac{\pi}{4}, \frac{5\pi}{4}, \frac{3\pi}{4}, \frac{7\pi}{4}$

81. $\frac{dy}{dx} = -\tan(t)$

83. $\frac{dy}{dx} = \frac{3}{4}$ and $\frac{d^2y}{dx^2} = 0,$ so the curve is neither concave up nor concave down at $t = 3$. Therefore the graph is linear and has a constant slope but no concavity.

85. $\frac{dy}{dx} = 4, \frac{d^2y}{dx^2} = -6\sqrt{3};$ the curve is concave down at $\theta = \frac{\pi}{6}$.

87. No horizontal tangents. Vertical tangents at $(1, 0), (-1, 0)$.

89. $-\sec^3(\pi t)$

91. Horizontal $(0, -9)$; vertical $(\pm 2, -6)$.

93. 1

95. 0

97. 4

99. Concave up on $t > 0$.

101. 1

103. $\frac{3\pi}{2}$

105. $6\pi a^2$

107. $2\pi ab$

109. $\frac{1}{3}(2\sqrt{2} - 1)$

111. 7.075

113. $6a$

115. $6\sqrt{2}$

119. $\frac{2\pi\left(247\sqrt{13}+64\right)}{1215}$

121. 59.101

123. $\frac{8\pi}{3}(17\sqrt{17}-1)$

125.

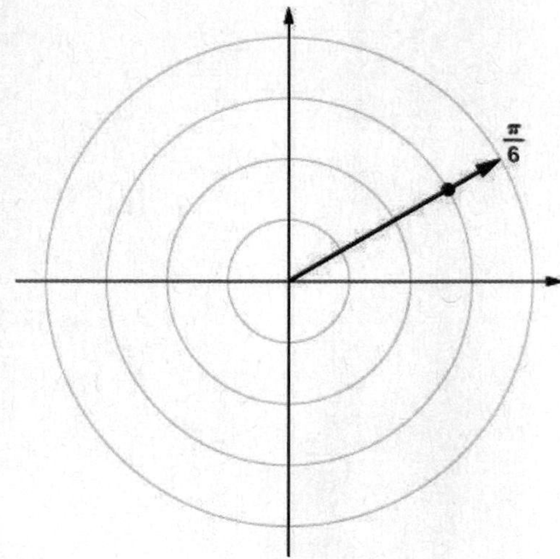

127.

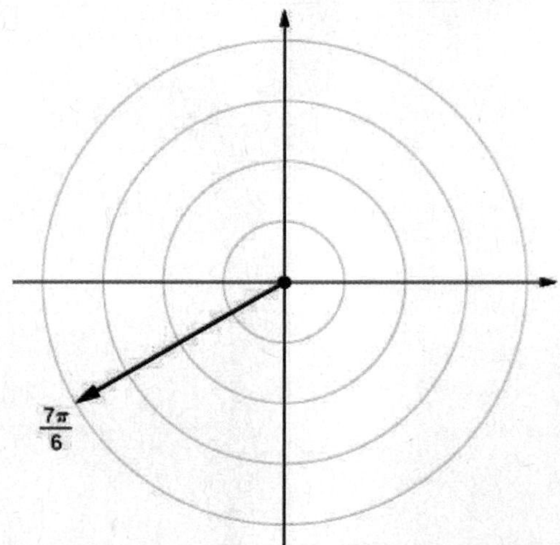

129.

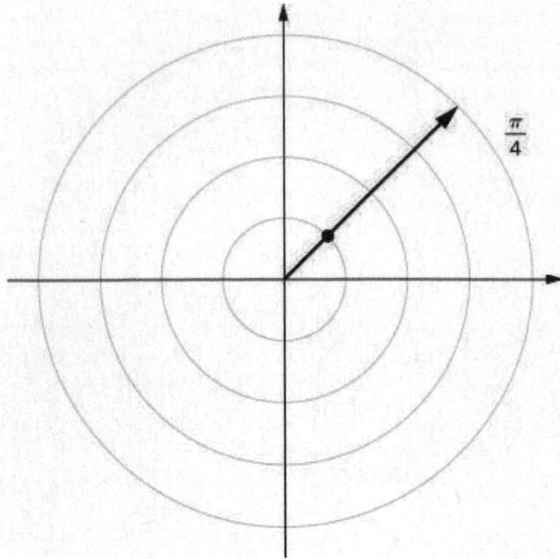

131.

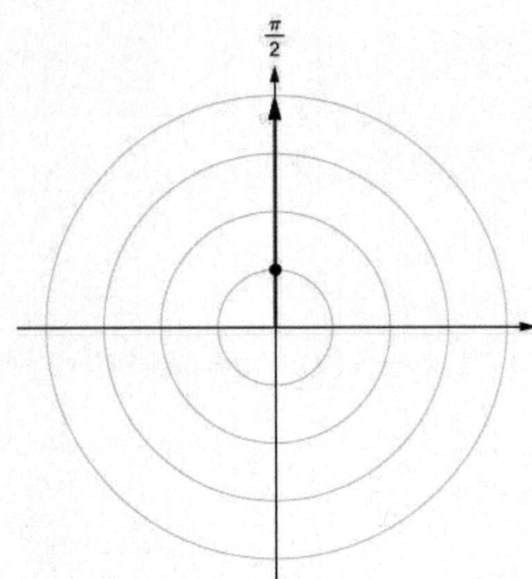

133. $B\left(3, \frac{-\pi}{3}\right)\ B\left(-3, \frac{2\pi}{3}\right)$

135. $D\left(5, \frac{7\pi}{6}\right) D\left(-5, \frac{\pi}{6}\right)$

137. $(5, -0.927)\ (-5, -0.927 + \pi)$

139. $(10, -0.927)(-10, -0.927 + \pi)$

141. $\left(2\sqrt{3}, -0.524\right)\left(-2\sqrt{3}, -0.524 + \pi\right)$

143. $\left(-\sqrt{3}, \ -1\right)$

145. $\left(-\frac{\sqrt{3}}{2}, \ \frac{-1}{2}\right)$

147. $(0, \ 0)$

149. Symmetry with respect to the *x*-axis, *y*-axis, and origin.
151. Symmetric with respect to *x*-axis only.
153. Symmetry with respect to *x*-axis only.
155. Line $y = x$

157. $y = 1$

159. Hyperbola; polar form $r^2 \cos(2\theta) = 16$ or $r^2 = 16 \sec \theta$.

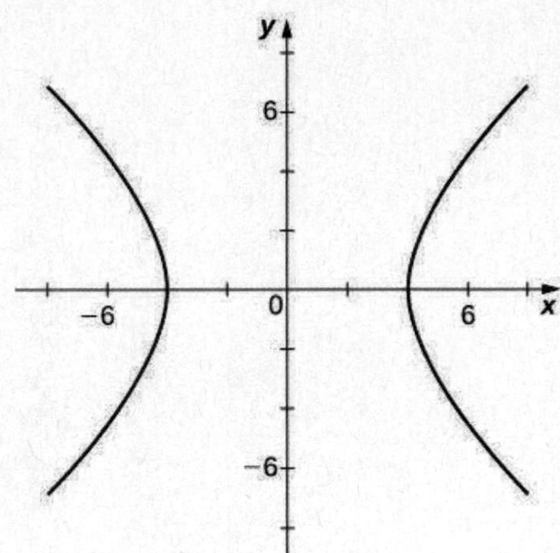

161. $r = \dfrac{2}{3\cos\theta - \sin\theta}$

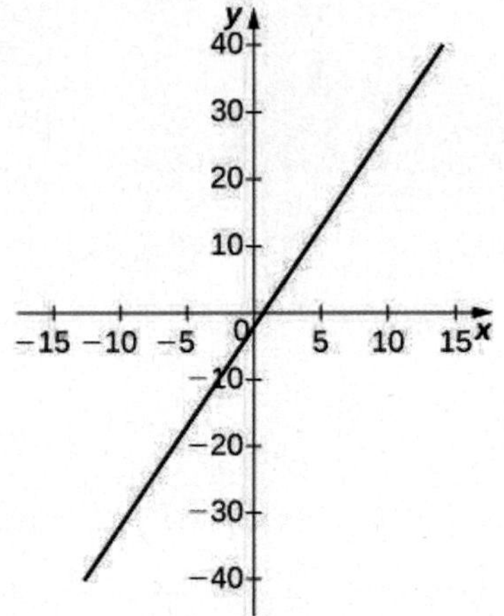

163. $x^2 + y^2 = 4y$

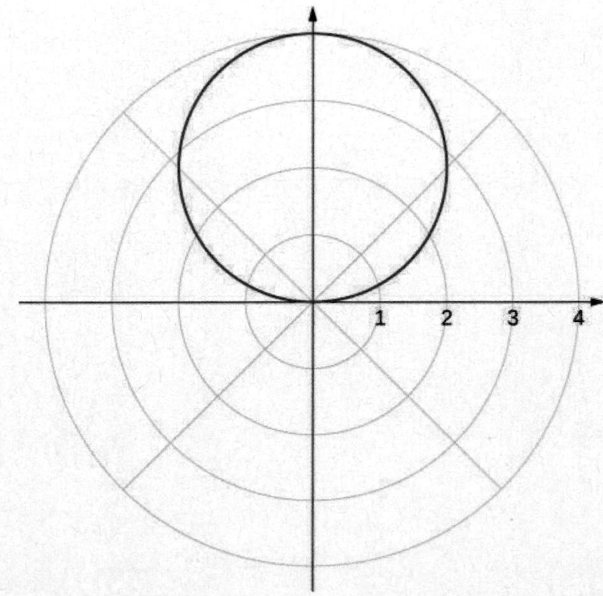

165. $x \tan\sqrt{x^2 + y^2} = y$

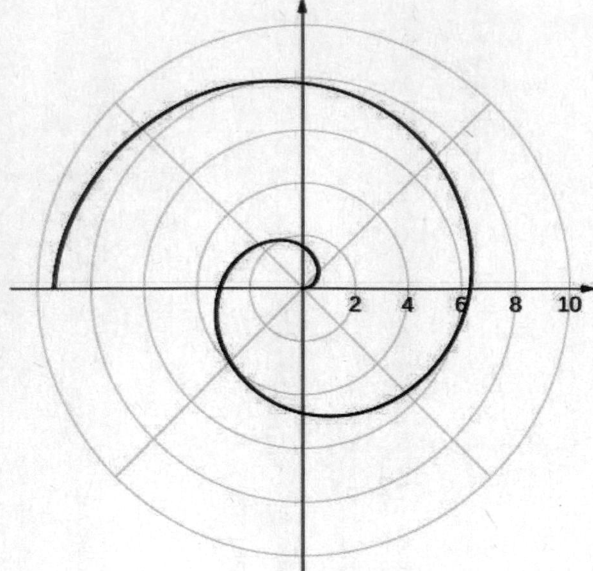

167.

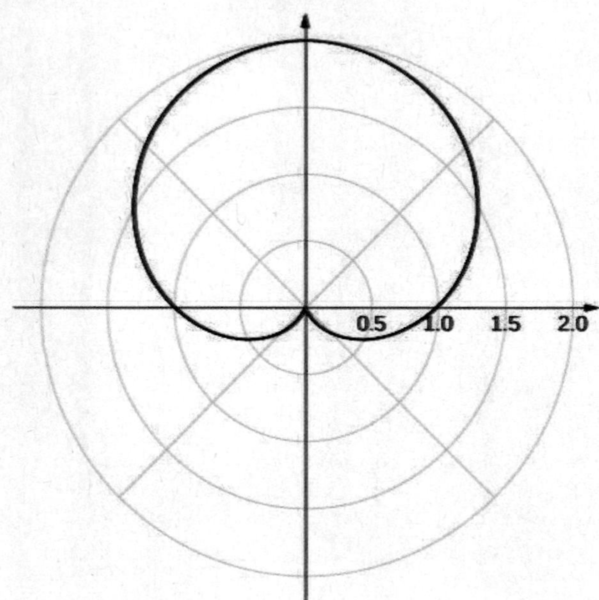

y-axis symmetry

169.

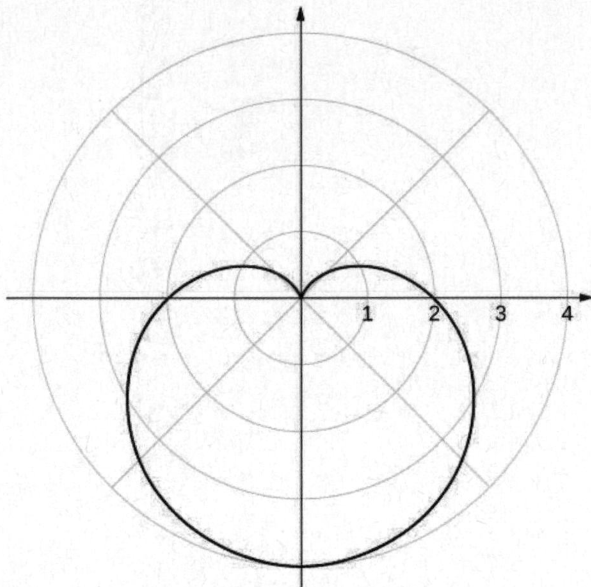

y-axis symmetry

171.

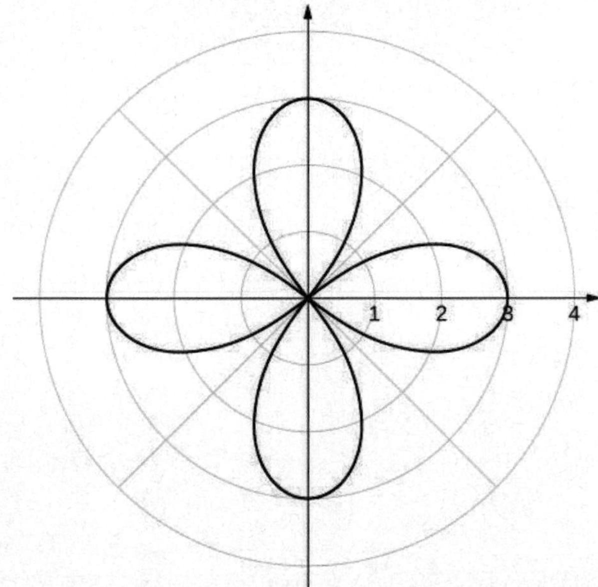

x- and *y*-axis symmetry and symmetry about the pole

173.

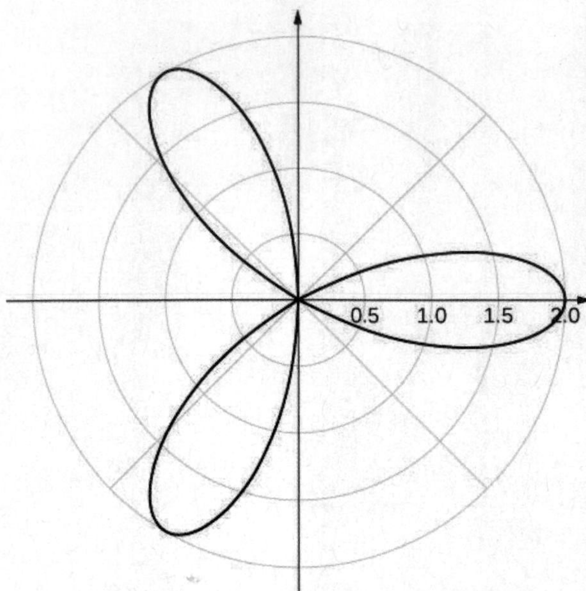

x-axis symmetry

175.

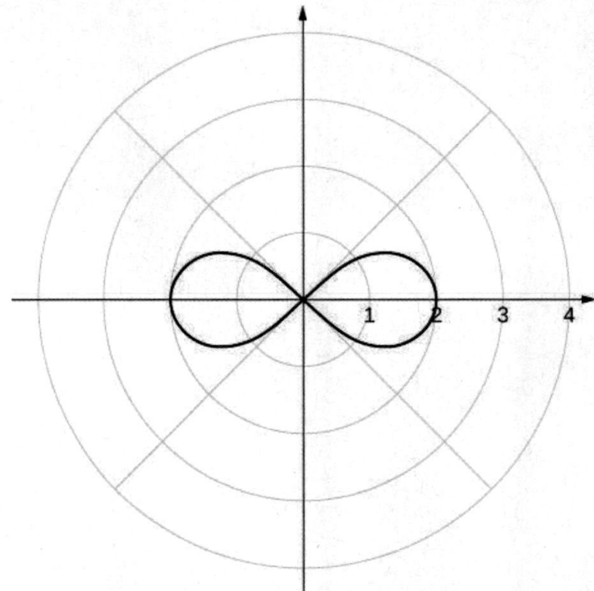

x- and *y*-axis symmetry and symmetry about the pole

177.

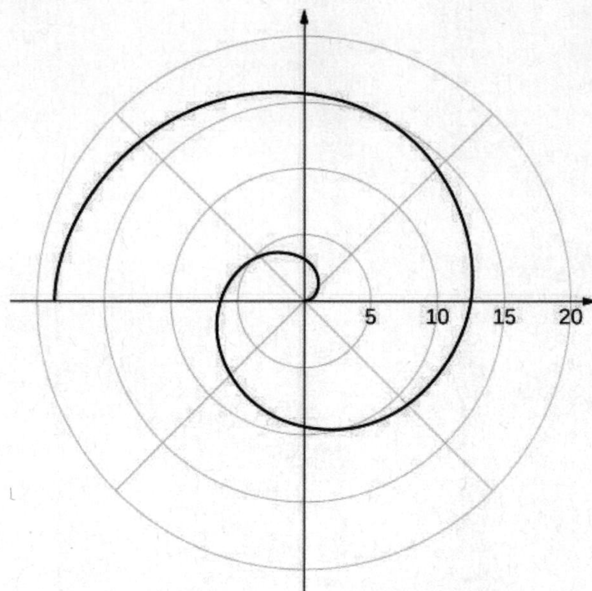

no symmetry

179.

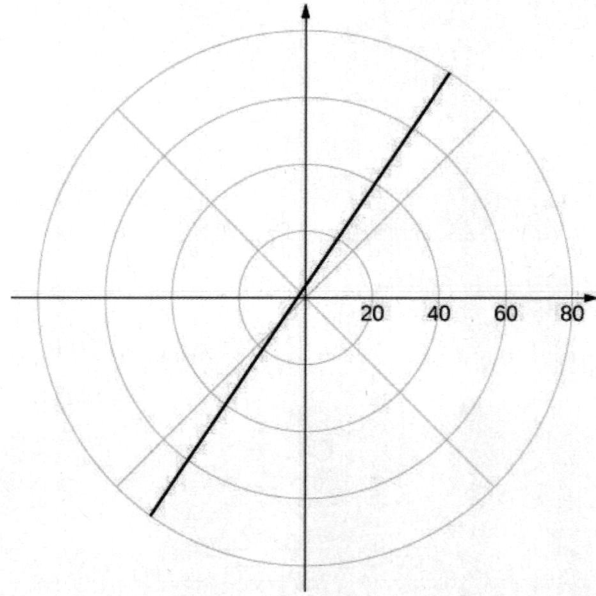

a line

181.

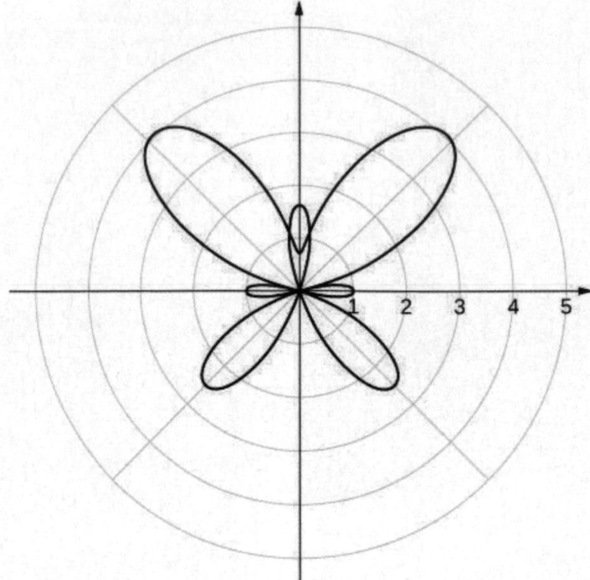

183.

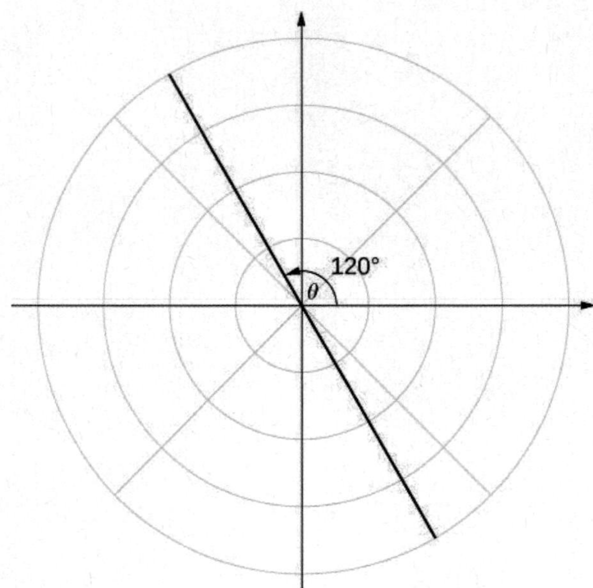

185.

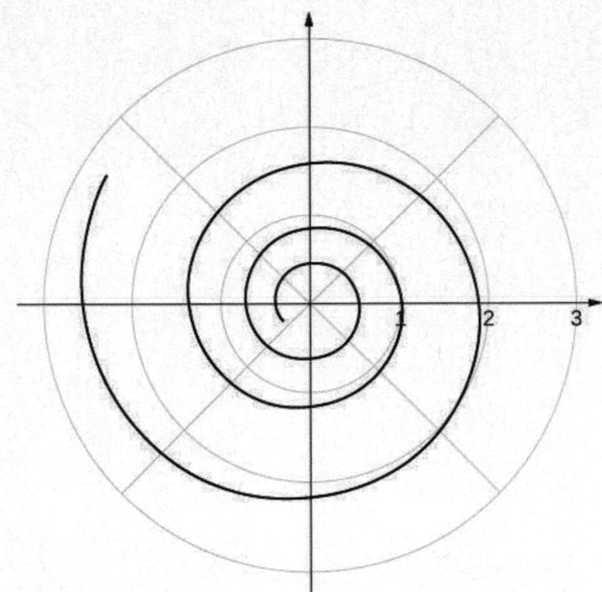

187. Answers vary. One possibility is the spiral lines become closer together and the total number of spirals increases.

189. $\frac{9}{2}\int_0^{\pi} \sin^2\theta \, d\theta$

191. $32\int_0^{\pi/2} \sin^2(2\theta)d\theta$

193. $\frac{1}{2}\int_{\pi}^{2\pi} (1 - \sin\theta)^2 \, d\theta$

195. $\int_{\sin^{-1}(2/3)}^{\pi/2} (2 - 3\sin\theta)^2 d\theta$

197. $\int_0^{\pi} (1 - 2\cos\theta)^2 \, d\theta - \int_0^{\pi/3} (1 - 2\cos\theta)^2 d\theta$

199. $4\int_0^{\pi/3} d\theta + 16\int_{\pi/3}^{\pi/2} \left(\cos^2\theta\right) d\theta$

201. 9π

203. $\frac{9\pi}{4}$

205. $\frac{9\pi}{8}$

207. $\frac{18\pi - 27\sqrt{3}}{2}$

209. $\frac{4}{3}\left(4\pi - 3\sqrt{3}\right)$

211. $\frac{3}{2}\left(4\pi - 3\sqrt{3}\right)$

213. $2\pi - 4$

215. $\int_0^{2\pi} \sqrt{(1 + \sin\theta)^2 + \cos^2\theta} d\theta$

217. $\sqrt{2}\int_0^1 e^{\theta} \, d\theta$

219. $\frac{\sqrt{10}}{3}\left(e^6 - 1\right)$

221. 32

223. 6.238

225. 2

227. 4.39

229. $A = \pi\left(\frac{\sqrt{2}}{2}\right)^2 = \frac{\pi}{2}$ and $\frac{1}{2}\int_0^{\pi}(1 + 2\sin\theta\cos\theta)d\theta = \frac{\pi}{2}$

231. $C = 2\pi\left(\frac{3}{2}\right) = 3\pi$ and $\int_0^{\pi} 3d\theta = 3\pi$

233. $C = 2\pi(5) = 10\pi$ and $\int_0^{\pi} 10\,d\theta = 10\pi$

235. $\frac{dy}{dx} = \frac{f'(\theta)\sin\theta + f(\theta)\cos\theta}{f'(\theta)\cos\theta - f(\theta)\sin\theta}$

237. The slope is $\frac{1}{\sqrt{3}}$.

239. The slope is 0.

241. At $(4, 0)$, the slope is undefined. At $\left(-4, \frac{\pi}{2}\right)$, the slope is 0.

243. The slope is undefined at $\theta = \frac{\pi}{4}$.

245. Slope = −1.

247. Slope is $\frac{-2}{\pi}$.

249. Calculator answer: −0.836.

251. Horizontal tangent at $\left(\pm\sqrt{2}, \frac{\pi}{6}\right)$, $\left(\pm\sqrt{2}, -\frac{\pi}{6}\right)$.

253. Horizontal tangents at $\frac{\pi}{2}, \frac{7\pi}{6}, \frac{11\pi}{6}$. Vertical tangents at $\frac{\pi}{6}, \frac{5\pi}{6}$ and also at the pole $(0, 0)$.

255. $y^2 = 16x$

257. $x^2 = 2y$

259. $x^2 = -4(y - 3)$

261. $(x + 3)^2 = 8(y - 3)$

263. $\frac{x^2}{16} + \frac{y^2}{12} = 1$

265. $\frac{x^2}{13} + \frac{y^2}{4} = 1$

267. $\frac{(y - 1)^2}{16} + \frac{(x + 3)^2}{12} = 1$

269. $\frac{x^2}{16} + \frac{y^2}{12} = 1$

271. $\frac{x^2}{25} - \frac{y^2}{11} = 1$

273. $\frac{x^2}{7} - \frac{y^2}{9} = 1$

275. $\frac{(y + 2)^2}{4} - \frac{(x + 2)^2}{32} = 1$

277. $\frac{x^2}{4} - \frac{y^2}{32} = 1$

279. $e = 1$, parabola

281. $e = \frac{1}{2}$, ellipse

283. $e = 3$, hyperbola

285. $r = \dfrac{4}{5 + \cos\theta}$

287. $r = \dfrac{4}{1 + 2\sin\theta}$

289.

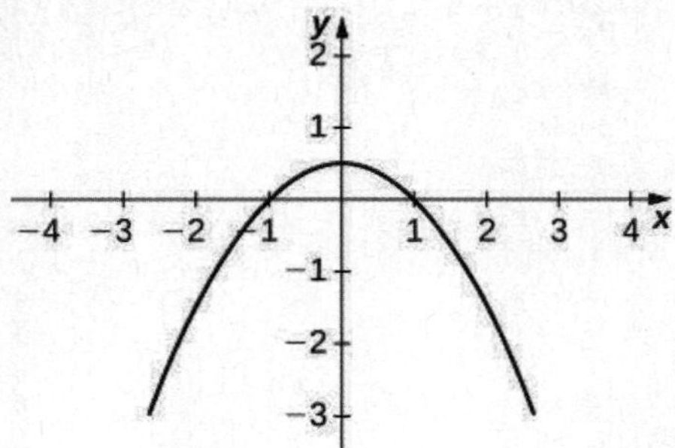

291.

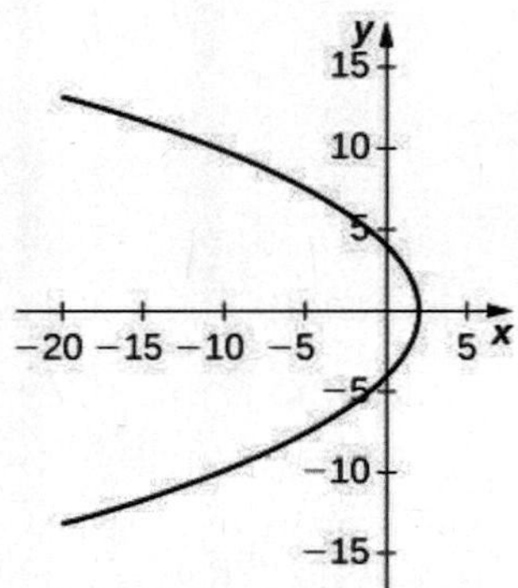

293.

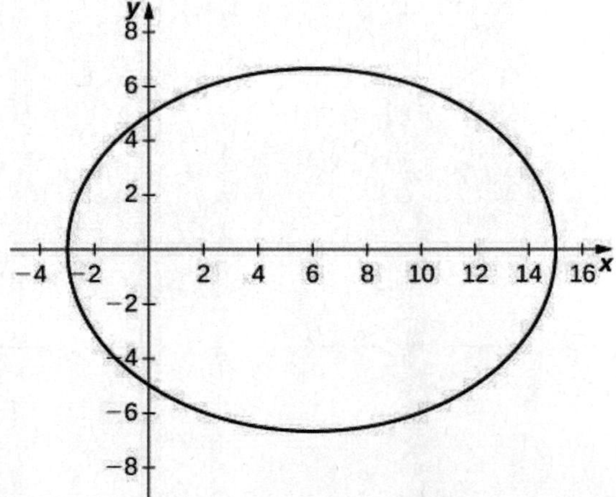

295.

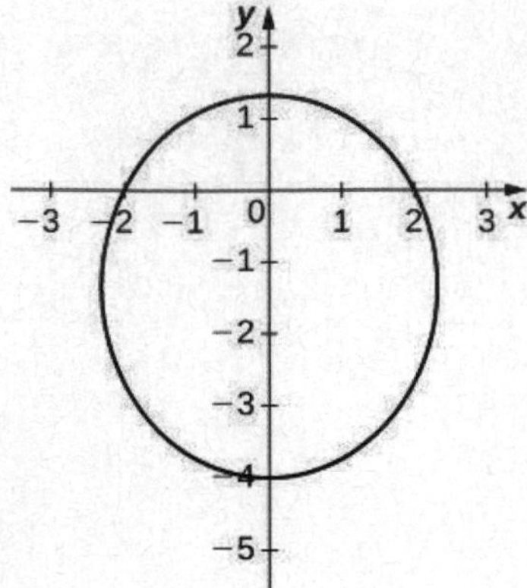
y
x
2
1
−1
−2
−3
−4
−5
−3
−2
−1
0
1
2
3

297.

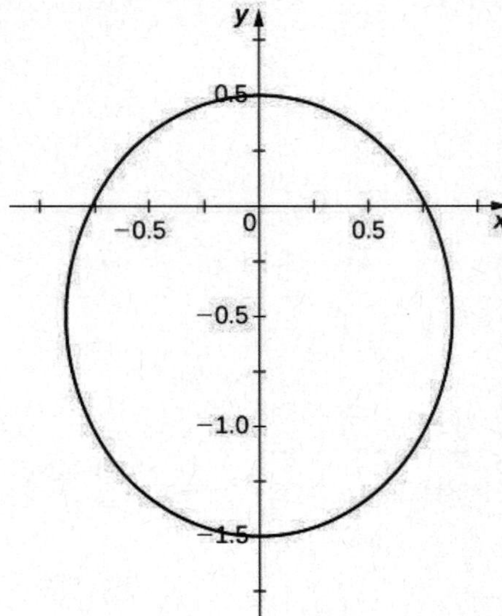
y
x
0.5
−0.5
−1.0
−1.5
−0.5
0
0.5

299.

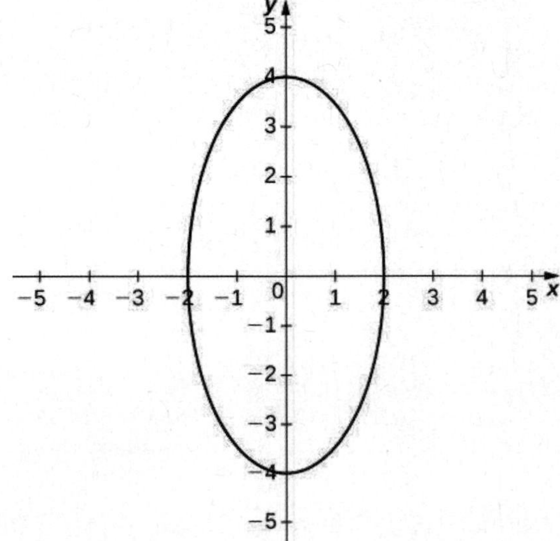
y
x
5
4
3
2
1
−1
−2
−3
−4
−5
−5
−4
−3
−2
−1
0
1
2
3
4
5

301.

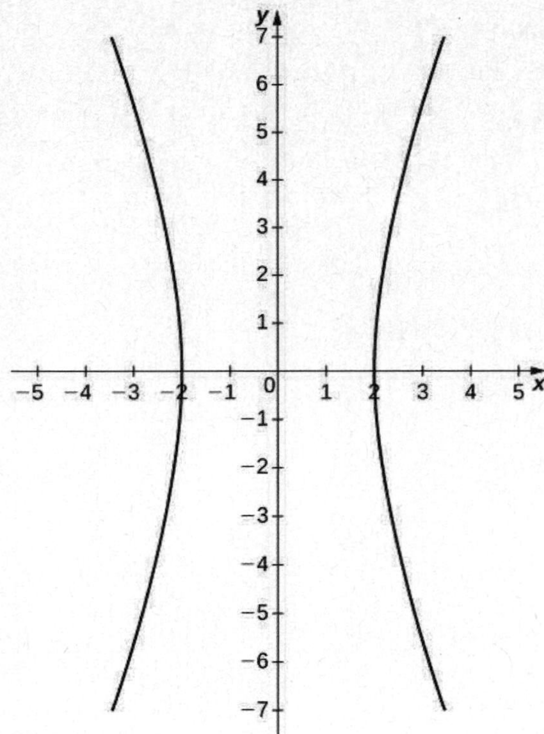

303.

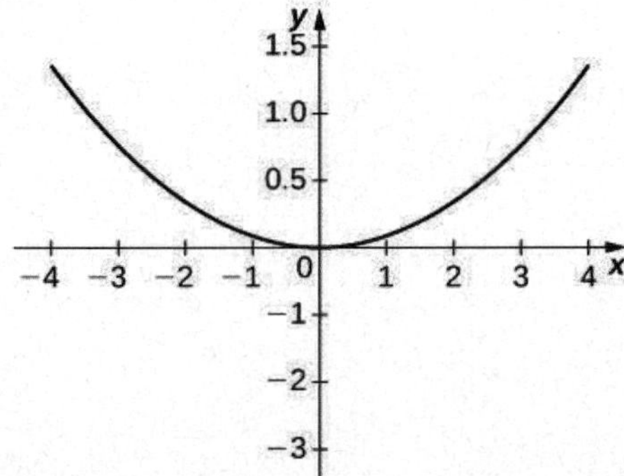

305.

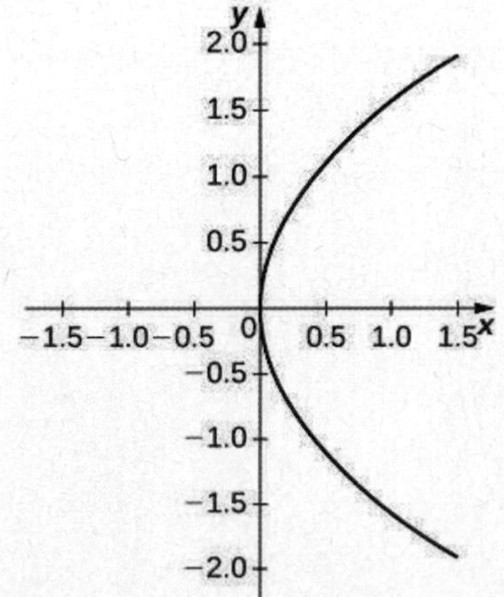

307. Hyperbola
309. Ellipse

311. Ellipse
313. At the point 2.25 feet above the vertex.
315. 0.5625 feet
317. Length is 96 feet and height is approximately 26.53 feet.
319. $r = \frac{2.616}{1 + 0.995 \cos \theta}$
321. $r = \frac{5.192}{1 + 0.0484 \cos \theta}$

Review Exercises

323. True.
325. False. Imagine $y = t + 1, \quad x = -t + 1.$
327.

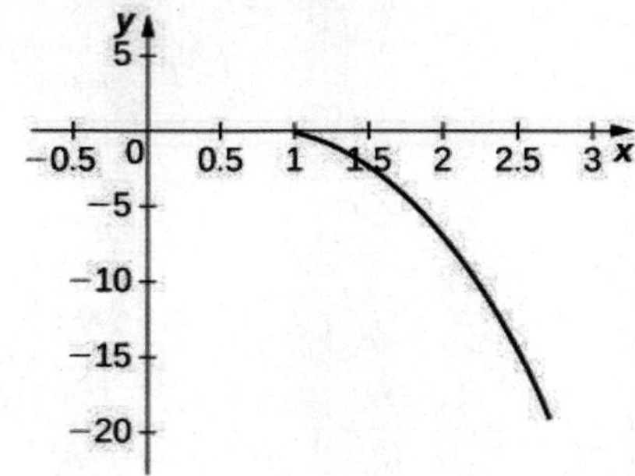

$y = 1 - x^3$

329.

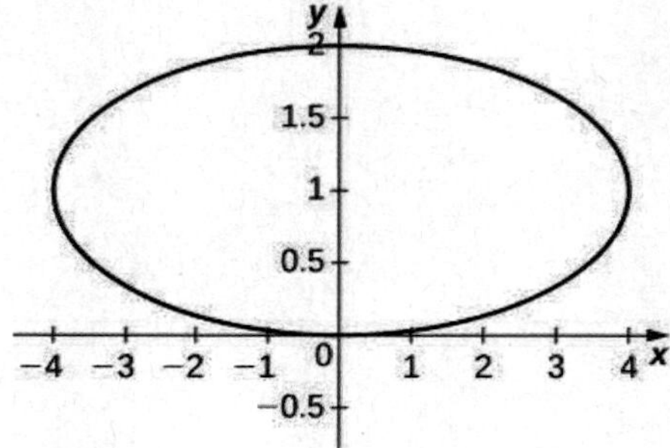

$\frac{x^2}{16} + (y - 1)^2 = 1$

331.

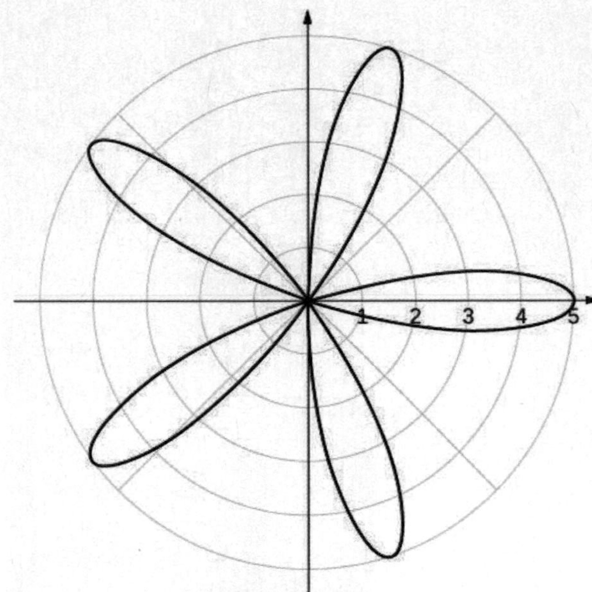

Symmetric about polar axis

333. $r^2 = \dfrac{4}{\sin^2\theta - \cos^2\theta}$

335.

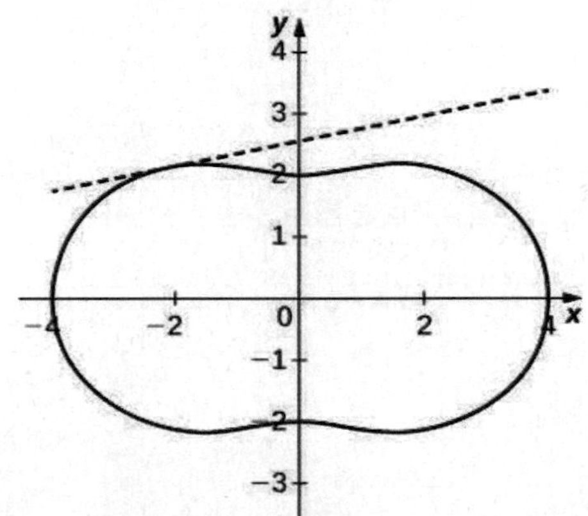

$y = \frac{3\sqrt{2}}{2} + \frac{1}{5}\left(x + \frac{3\sqrt{2}}{2}\right)$

337. $\frac{e^2}{2}$

339. $9\sqrt{10}$

341. $(y+5)^2 = -8x + 32$

343. $\dfrac{(y+1)^2}{16} - \dfrac{(x+2)^2}{9} = 1$

345. $e = \frac{2}{3}$, ellipse

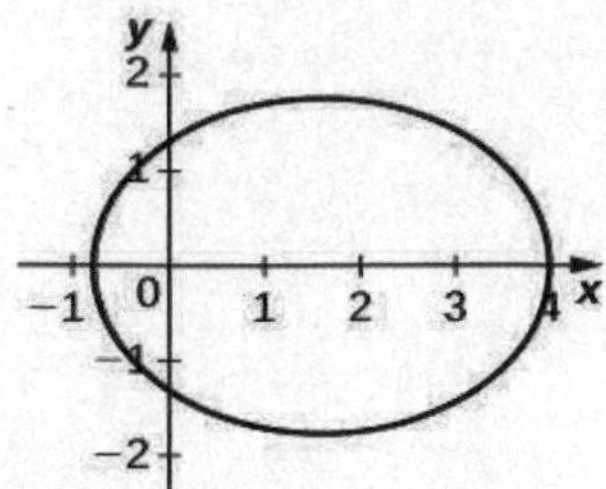

347. $\frac{y^2}{19.03^2} + \frac{x^2}{19.63^2} = 1, \quad e = 0.2447$

Chapter 2

Checkpoint

2.1.

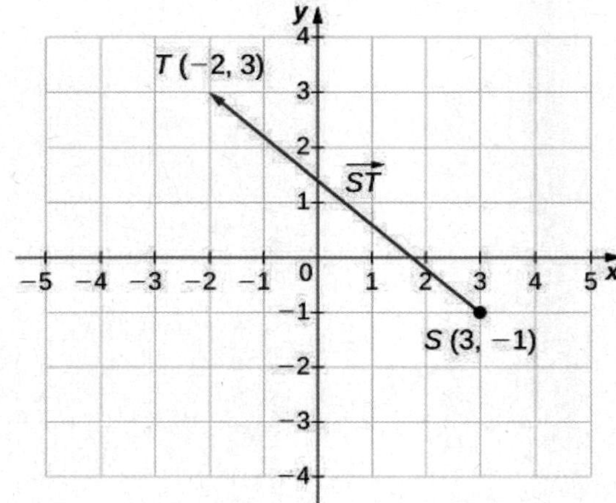

2.2.

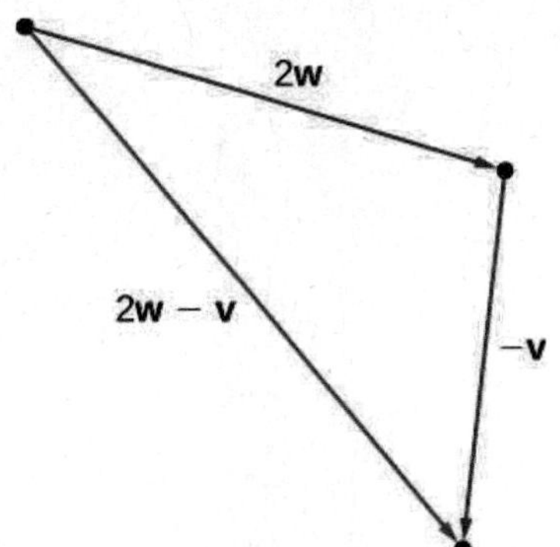

2.3. Vectors $\mathbf{a}$, $\mathbf{b}$, and $\mathbf{e}$ are equivalent.

2.4. $\langle 3, 7 \rangle$

2.5. a. $\| \mathbf{a} \| = 5\sqrt{2}$, b. $\mathbf{b} = \langle -4, -3 \rangle$, c. $3\mathbf{a} - 4\mathbf{b} = \langle 37, 15 \rangle$

2.7. $\mathbf{v} = \langle -5, 5\sqrt{3} \rangle$

2.8. $\langle -\frac{45}{\sqrt{85}}, -\frac{10}{\sqrt{85}} \rangle$

2.9. $\mathbf{a} = 16\mathbf{i} - 11\mathbf{j}, \quad \mathbf{b} = -\frac{\sqrt{2}}{2}\mathbf{i} - \frac{\sqrt{2}}{2}\mathbf{j}$

2.10. Approximately 516 mph

2.11.

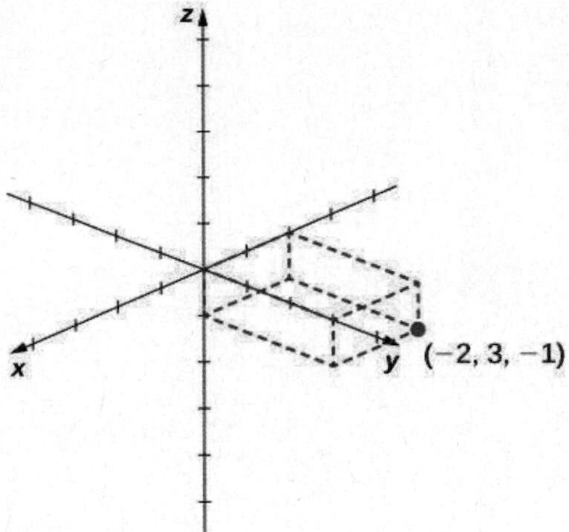

2.12. $5\sqrt{2}$

2.13. $z = -4$

2.14. $(x+2)^2 + (y-4)^2 + (z+5)^2 = 52$

2.15. $x^2 + (y-2)^2 + (z+2)^2 = 14$

2.16. The set of points forms the two planes $y = -2$ and $z = 3$.

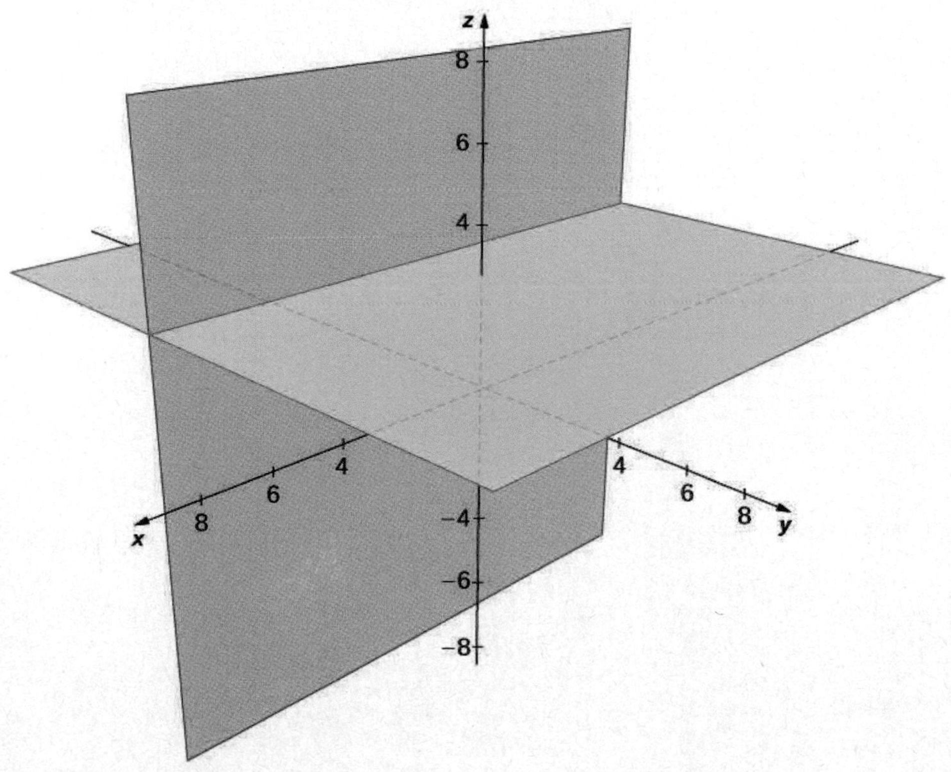

2.17. A cylinder of radius 4 centered on the line with $x = 0$ and $z = 2$.

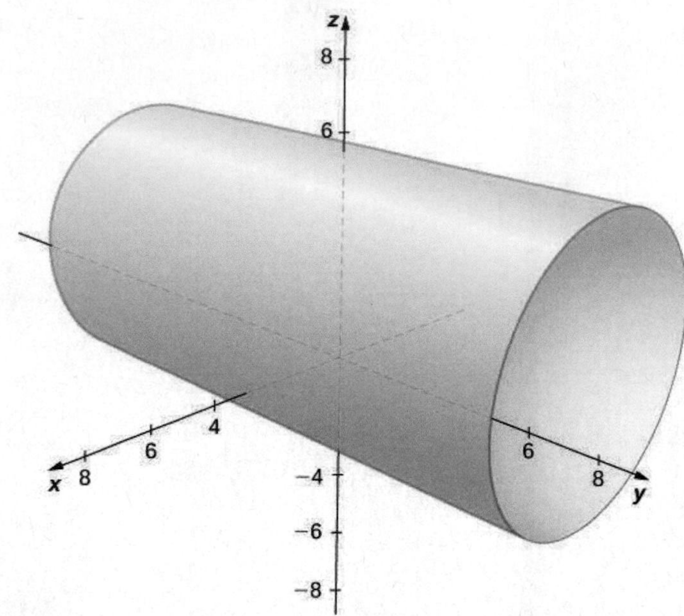

2.18. $\overrightarrow{ST} = \langle -1, -9, 1 \rangle = -\mathbf{i} - 9\mathbf{j} + \mathbf{k}$

2.19. $\langle \frac{1}{3\sqrt{10}}, -\frac{5}{3\sqrt{10}}, \frac{8}{3\sqrt{10}} \rangle$

2.20. $\mathbf{v} = \langle 16\sqrt{2}, 12\sqrt{2}, 20\sqrt{2} \rangle$

2.21. 7

2.22. a. $(\mathbf{r} \cdot \mathbf{p})\mathbf{q} = \langle 12, -12, 12 \rangle$; b. $\| \mathbf{p} \|^2 = 53$

2.23. $\theta \approx 0.22$ rad

2.24. $x = 5$

2.25. a. $\alpha \approx 1.04$ rad; b. $\beta \approx 2.58$ rad; c. $\gamma \approx 1.40$ rad

2.26. Sales = $15,685.50; profit = $14,073.15

2.27. $\mathbf{v} = \mathbf{p} + \mathbf{q}$, where $\mathbf{p} = \frac{18}{5}\mathbf{i} + \frac{9}{5}\mathbf{j}$ and $\mathbf{q} = \frac{7}{5}\mathbf{i} - \frac{14}{5}\mathbf{j}$

2.28. 21 knots

2.29. 150 ft-lb

2.30. $\mathbf{i} - 9\mathbf{j} + 2\mathbf{k}$

2.31. Up (the positive *z*-direction)

2.32. $-\mathbf{i}$

2.33. $-\mathbf{k}$

2.34. 16

2.35. 40

2.36. $8\mathbf{i} - 35\mathbf{j} + 2\mathbf{k}$

2.37. $\langle \frac{-3}{\sqrt{194}}, \frac{-13}{\sqrt{194}}, \frac{4}{\sqrt{194}} \rangle$

2.38. $6\sqrt{13}$

2.39. 17

2.40. 8 units^3

2.41. No, the triple scalar product is $-4 \neq 0$, so the three vectors form the adjacent edges of a parallelepiped. They are not coplanar.

2.42. 20 N

2.43. Possible set of parametric equations: $x = 1 + 4t, y = -3 + t, z = 2 + 6t$; related set of symmetric equations: $\frac{x-1}{4} = y + 3 = \frac{z-2}{6}$

2.44. $x = -1 - 7t,\ y = 3 - t,\ z = 6 - 2t,\ 0 \le t \le 1$

2.45. $\sqrt{\frac{10}{7}}$

2.46. These lines are skew because their direction vectors are not parallel and there is no point $(x,\ y,\ z)$ that lies on both lines.

2.47. $-2(x - 1) + (y + 1) + 3(z - 1) = 0$ or $-2x + y + 3z = 0$

2.48. $\frac{15}{\sqrt{21}}$

2.49. $x = t,\ y = 7 - 3t,\ z = 4 - 2t$

2.50. 1.44 rad

2.51. $\frac{9}{\sqrt{30}}$

2.52.

2.53. The traces parallel to the *xy*-plane are ellipses and the traces parallel to the *xz*- and *yz*-planes are hyperbolas. Specifically, the trace in the *xy*-plane is ellipse $\frac{x^2}{3^2} + \frac{y^2}{2^2} = 1,$ the trace in the *xz*-plane is hyperbola $\frac{x^2}{3^2} - \frac{z^2}{5^2} = 1,$ and the trace in the *yz*-plane is hyperbola $\frac{y^2}{2^2} - \frac{z^2}{5^2} = 1$ (see the following figure).

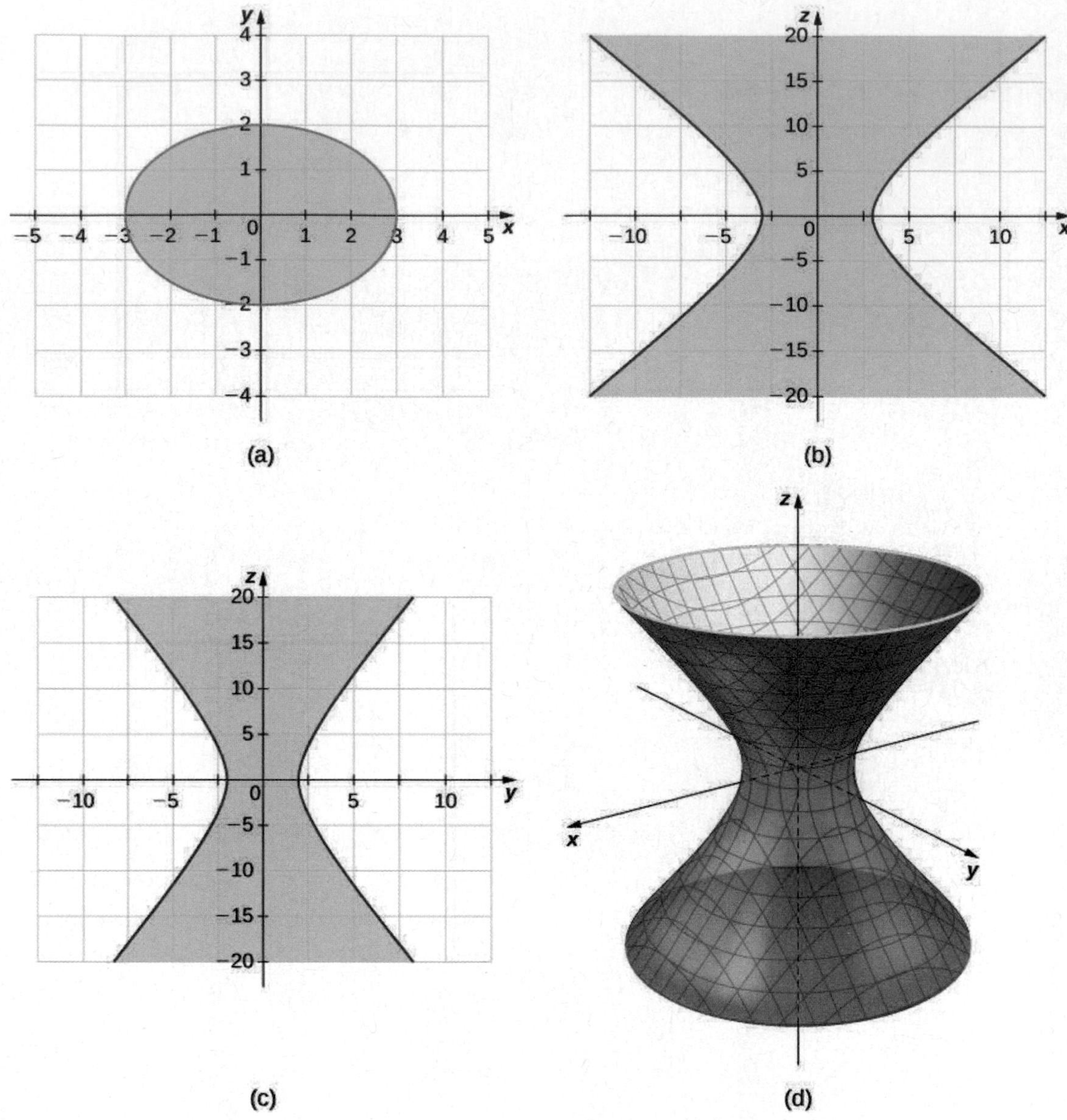

2.54. Hyperboloid of one sheet, centered at $(0, 0, 1)$

2.55. The rectangular coordinates of the point are $\left(\frac{5\sqrt{3}}{2}, \frac{5}{2}, 4\right)$.

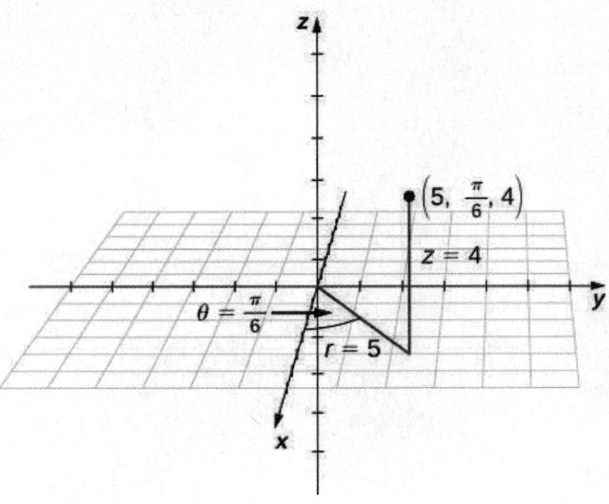

2.56. $\left(8\sqrt{2}, \frac{3\pi}{4}, -7\right)$

2.57. This surface is a cylinder with radius 6.

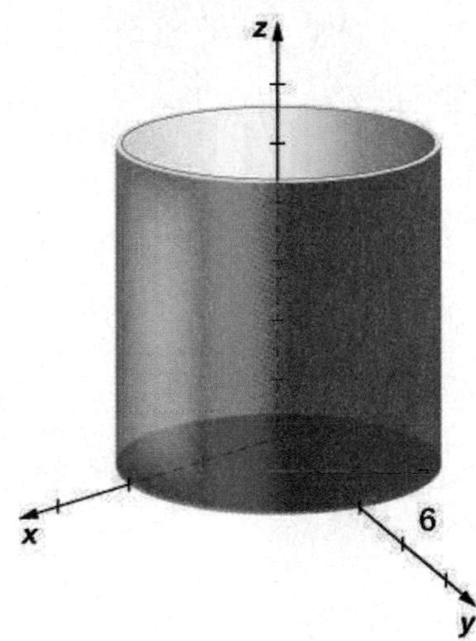

2.58.

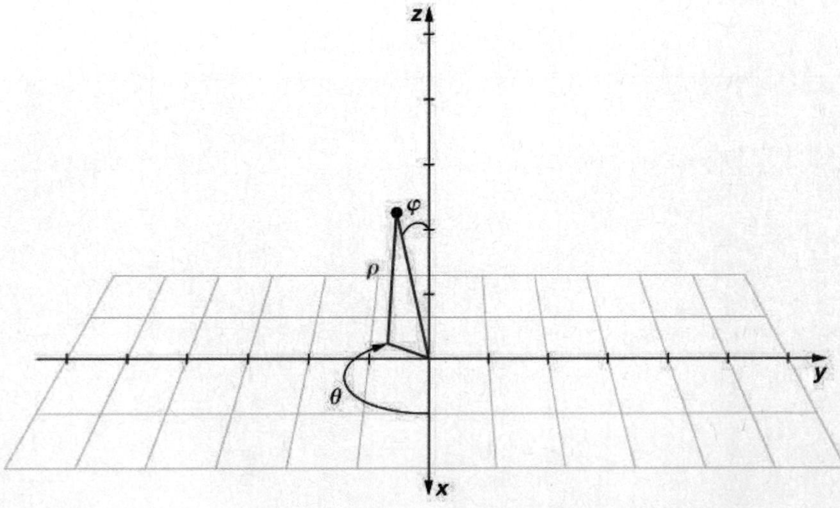

Cartesian: $\left(-\frac{\sqrt{3}}{2}, -\frac{1}{2}, \sqrt{3}\right)$, cylindrical: $\left(1, -\frac{5\pi}{6}, \sqrt{3}\right)$

2.59. a. This is the set of all points 13 units from the origin. This set forms a sphere with radius 13. b. This set of points forms a half plane. The angle between the half plane and the positive *x*-axis is $\theta = \frac{2\pi}{3}$. c. Let P be a point on this surface. The position vector of this point forms an angle of $\varphi = \frac{\pi}{4}$ with the positive *z*-axis, which means that points closer to the origin are closer to the axis. These points form a half-cone.

2.60. $(4000, 151°, 124°)$

2.61. Spherical coordinates with the origin located at the center of the earth, the *z*-axis aligned with the North Pole, and the *x*-axis aligned with the prime meridian

Section Exercises

1. a. $\overrightarrow{PQ} = \langle 2, 2 \rangle$; b. $\overrightarrow{PQ} = 2\mathbf{i} + 2\mathbf{j}$

3. a. $\overrightarrow{QP} = \langle -2, -2 \rangle$; b. $\overrightarrow{QP} = -2\mathbf{i} - 2\mathbf{j}$

5. a. $\overrightarrow{PQ} + \overrightarrow{PR} = \langle 0, 6 \rangle$; b. $\overrightarrow{PQ} + \overrightarrow{PR} = 6\mathbf{j}$

7. a. $2\overrightarrow{PQ} - 2\overrightarrow{PR} = \langle 8, -4 \rangle$; b. $2\overrightarrow{PQ} - 2\overrightarrow{PR} = 8\mathbf{i} - 4\mathbf{j}$

9. a. $\langle \frac{1}{\sqrt{2}}, \frac{1}{\sqrt{2}} \rangle$; b. $\frac{1}{\sqrt{2}}\mathbf{i} + \frac{1}{\sqrt{2}}\mathbf{j}$

11. $\langle \frac{3}{5}, \frac{4}{5} \rangle$

13. $Q(0, 2)$

15. a. $\mathbf{a} + \mathbf{b} = 3\mathbf{i} + 4\mathbf{j}$, $\mathbf{a} + \mathbf{b} = \langle 3, 4 \rangle$; b. $\mathbf{a} - \mathbf{b} = \mathbf{i} - 2\mathbf{j}$, $\mathbf{a} - \mathbf{b} = \langle 1, -2 \rangle$; c. Answers will vary; d. $2\mathbf{a} = 4\mathbf{i} + 2\mathbf{j}$, $2\mathbf{a} = \langle 4, 2 \rangle$, $-\mathbf{b} = -\mathbf{i} - 3\mathbf{j}$, $-\mathbf{b} = \langle -1, -3 \rangle$, $2\mathbf{a} - \mathbf{b} = 3\mathbf{i} - \mathbf{j}$, $2\mathbf{a} - \mathbf{b} = \langle 3, -1 \rangle$

17. 15

19. $\lambda = -3$

21. a. $\mathbf{a}(0) = \langle 1, 0 \rangle$, $\mathbf{a}(\pi) = \langle -1, 0 \rangle$; b. Answers may vary; c. Answers may vary

23. Answers may vary

25. $\mathbf{v} = \langle \frac{21}{5}, \frac{28}{5} \rangle$

27. $\mathbf{v} = \langle \frac{21\sqrt{34}}{34}, -\frac{35\sqrt{34}}{34} \rangle$

29. $\mathbf{u} = \langle \sqrt{3}, 1 \rangle$

31. $\mathbf{u} = \langle 0, 5 \rangle$

33. $\mathbf{u} = \langle -5\sqrt{3}, 5 \rangle$

35. $\theta = \frac{7\pi}{4}$

37. Answers may vary

39. a. $z_0 = f(x_0) + f'(x_0)$; b. $\mathbf{u} = \frac{1}{\sqrt{1 + [f'(x_0)]^2}} \langle 1, f'(x_0) \rangle$

43. $D(6, 1)$

45. $\langle 60.62, 35 \rangle$

47. The horizontal and vertical components are 750 ft/sec and 1299.04 ft/sec, respectively.

49. The magnitude of resultant force is 94.71 lb; the direction angle is 13.42°.

51. The magnitude of the third vector is 60.03 N; the direction angle is 259.38°.

53. The new ground speed of the airplane is 572.19 mph; the new direction is N41.82E.

55. $\|\mathbf{T}_1\| = 30.13$ lb, $\|\mathbf{T}_2\| = 38.35$ lb

57. $\|\mathbf{v}_1\| = 750$ lb, $\|\mathbf{v}_2\| = 1299$ lb

59. The two horizontal and vertical components of the force of tension are 28 lb and 42 lb, respectively.

61. a. $(2, 0, 5), (2, 0, 0), (2, 3, 0), (0, 3, 0), (0, 3, 5), (0, 0, 5)$; b. $\sqrt{38}$

63. A union of two planes: $y = 5$ (a plane parallel to the *xz*-plane) and $z = 6$ (a plane parallel to the *xy*-plane)

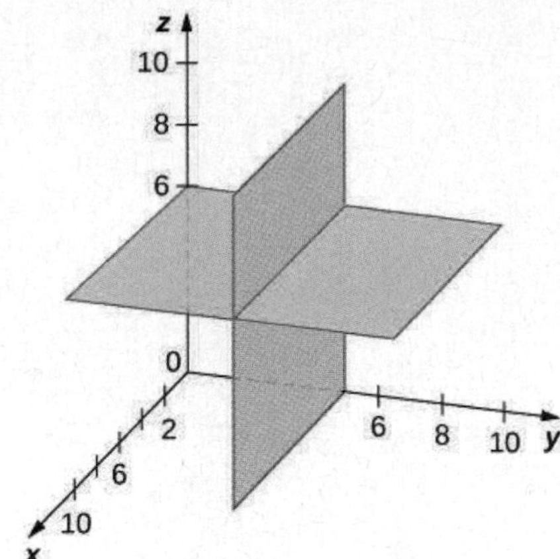

65. A cylinder of radius 1 centered on the line $y = 1, z = 1$

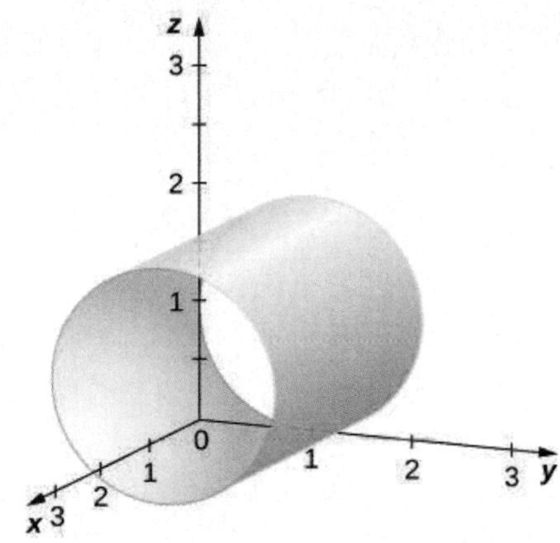

67. $z = 1$

69. $z = -2$

71. $(x + 1)^2 + (y - 7)^2 + (z - 4)^2 = 16$

73. $(x + 3)^2 + (y - 3.5)^2 + (z - 8)^2 = \frac{29}{4}$

75. Center $C(0, 0, 2)$ and radius 1

77. a. $\overrightarrow{PQ} = \langle -4, -1, 2 \rangle$; b. $\overrightarrow{PQ} = -4\mathbf{i} - \mathbf{j} + 2\mathbf{k}$

79. a. $\overrightarrow{PQ} = \langle 6, -24, 24 \rangle$; b. $\overrightarrow{PQ} = 6\mathbf{i} - 24\mathbf{j} + 24\mathbf{k}$

81. $Q(5, 2, 8)$

83. $\mathbf{a} + \mathbf{b} = \langle -6, 4, -3 \rangle$, $4\mathbf{a} = \langle -4, -8, 16 \rangle$, $-5\mathbf{a} + 3\mathbf{b} = \langle -10, 28, -41 \rangle$

85. $\mathbf{a} + \mathbf{b} = \langle -1, 0, -1 \rangle$, $4\mathbf{a} = \langle 0, 0, -4 \rangle$, $-5\mathbf{a} + 3\mathbf{b} = \langle -3, 0, 5 \rangle$

87. $\| \mathbf{u} - \mathbf{v} \| = \sqrt{38}$, $\| -2\mathbf{u} \| = 2\sqrt{29}$

89. $\| \mathbf{u} - \mathbf{v} \| = 2$, $\| -2\mathbf{u} \| = 2\sqrt{13}$

91. $\mathbf{a} = \frac{3}{5}\mathbf{i} - \frac{4}{5}\mathbf{j}$

93. $\left\langle \frac{2}{\sqrt{62}}, -\frac{7}{\sqrt{62}}, \frac{3}{\sqrt{62}} \right\rangle$

95. $\left\langle -\frac{2}{\sqrt{6}}, \frac{1}{\sqrt{6}}, \frac{1}{\sqrt{6}} \right\rangle$

97. Equivalent vectors

99. $\mathbf{u} = \langle \frac{70}{\sqrt{59}}, -\frac{10}{\sqrt{59}}, \frac{30}{\sqrt{59}} \rangle$

101. $\mathbf{u} = \langle -\frac{4}{\sqrt{5}}\sin t, -\frac{4}{\sqrt{5}}\cos t, -\frac{2}{\sqrt{5}} \rangle$

103. $\langle \frac{5}{\sqrt{154}}, \frac{15}{\sqrt{154}}, -\frac{60}{\sqrt{154}} \rangle$

105. $\alpha = -\sqrt{7}, \quad \beta = -\sqrt{15}$

111. a. $\mathbf{F} = \langle 30, 40, 0 \rangle$; b. 53°

113. $\mathbf{D} = 10\mathbf{k}$

115. $\mathbf{F}_4 = \langle -20, -7, -3 \rangle$

117. a. $\mathbf{F} = -19.6\mathbf{k}, \quad \|\mathbf{F}\| = 19.6$ N; b. $\mathbf{T} = 19.6\mathbf{k}, \quad \|\mathbf{T}\| = 19.6$ N

119. a. $\mathbf{F} = -294\mathbf{k}$ N; b. $\mathbf{F}_1 = \langle -\frac{49\sqrt{3}}{3}, 49, -98 \rangle$, $\mathbf{F}_2 = \langle -\frac{49\sqrt{3}}{3}, -49, -98 \rangle$, and $\mathbf{F}_3 = \langle \frac{98\sqrt{3}}{3}, 0, -98 \rangle$ (each component is expressed in newtons)

121. a. $\mathbf{v}(1) = \langle -0.84, 0.54, 2 \rangle$ (each component is expressed in centimeters per second); $\|\mathbf{v}(1)\| = 2.24$ (expressed in centimeters per second); $\mathbf{a}(1) = \langle -0.54, -0.84, 0 \rangle$ (each component expressed in centimeters per second squared); b.

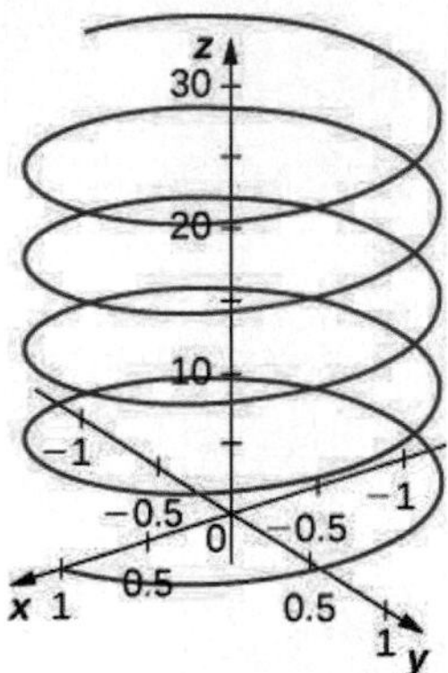

123. 6

125. 0

127. $(\mathbf{a} \cdot \mathbf{b})\mathbf{c} = \langle -11, -11, 11 \rangle$; $(\mathbf{a} \cdot \mathbf{c})\mathbf{b} = \langle -20, -35, 5 \rangle$

129. $(\mathbf{a} \cdot \mathbf{b})\mathbf{c} = \langle 1, 0, -2 \rangle$; $(\mathbf{a} \cdot \mathbf{c})\mathbf{b} = \langle 1, 0, -1 \rangle$

131. a. $\theta = 2.82$ rad; b. θ is not acute.

133. a. $\theta = \frac{\pi}{4}$ rad; b. θ is acute.

135. $\theta = \frac{\pi}{2}$

137. $\theta = \frac{\pi}{3}$

139. $\theta = 2$ rad

141. Orthogonal

143. Not orthogonal

145. $\mathbf{a} = \langle -\frac{4\alpha}{3}, \alpha \rangle$, where $\alpha \neq 0$ is a real number

147. $\mathbf{u} = -\alpha\mathbf{i} + \alpha\mathbf{j} + \beta\mathbf{k}$, where α and β are real numbers such that $\alpha^2 + \beta^2 \neq 0$

149. $\alpha = -6$

151. a. $\vec{OP} = 4\mathbf{i} + 5\mathbf{j}, \quad \vec{OQ} = 5\mathbf{i} - 7\mathbf{j}$; b. 105.8°

153. 68.33°

155. **u** and **v** are orthogonal; **v** and **w** are orthogonal.

161. a. $\cos\alpha = \frac{2}{3}, \cos\beta = \frac{2}{3}$, and $\cos\gamma = \frac{1}{3}$; b. $\alpha = 48°, \quad \beta = 48°$, and $\gamma = 71°$

163. a. $\cos\alpha = -\frac{1}{\sqrt{30}}$, $\cos\beta = \frac{5}{\sqrt{30}}$, and $\cos\gamma = \frac{2}{\sqrt{30}}$; b. $\alpha = 101°$, $\beta = 24°$, and $\gamma = 69°$

167. a. $\mathbf{w} = \langle \frac{80}{29}, \frac{32}{29} \rangle$; b. $\text{comp}_{\mathbf{u}}\mathbf{v} = \frac{16}{\sqrt{29}}$

169. a. $\mathbf{w} = \langle \frac{24}{13}, 0, \frac{16}{13} \rangle$; b. $\text{comp}_{\mathbf{u}}\mathbf{v} = \frac{8}{\sqrt{13}}$

171. a. $\mathbf{w} = \langle \frac{24}{25}, -\frac{18}{25} \rangle$; b. $\mathbf{q} = \langle \frac{51}{25}, \frac{68}{25} \rangle$, $\mathbf{v} = \mathbf{w} + \mathbf{q} = \langle \frac{24}{25}, -\frac{18}{25} \rangle + \langle \frac{51}{25}, \frac{68}{25} \rangle$

173. a. $2\sqrt{2}$; b. $109.47°$

175. $17\text{N}\cdot\text{m}$

177. $1175\ \text{ft}\cdot\text{lb}$

179. 4330.13 ft-lb

181. a. $\| \mathbf{F}_1 + \mathbf{F}_2 \| = 52.9$ lb; b. The direction angles are $\alpha = 74.5°$, $\beta = 36.7°$, and $\gamma = 57.7°$.

183. a. $\mathbf{u} \times \mathbf{v} = \langle 0, 0, 4 \rangle$;

b.

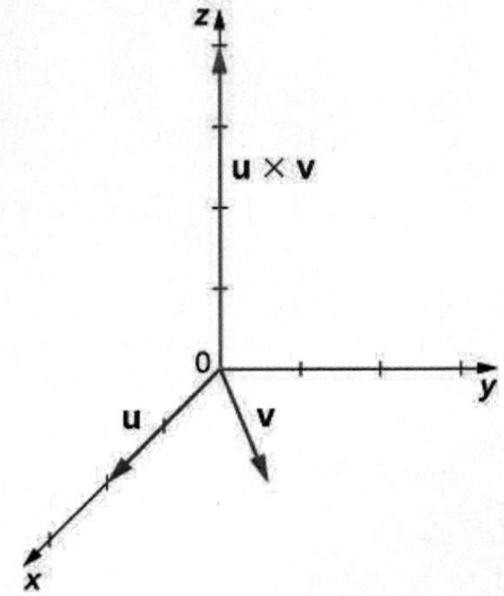

185. a. $\mathbf{u} \times \mathbf{v} = \langle 6, -4, 2 \rangle$;

b.

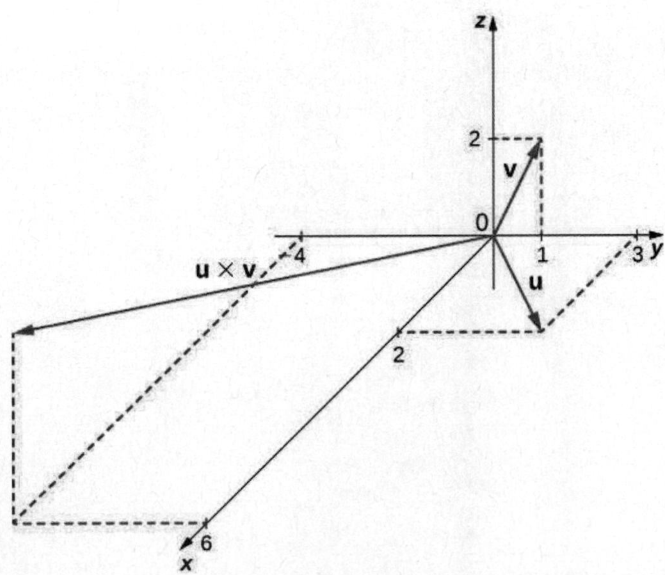

187. $-2\mathbf{j} - 4\mathbf{k}$

189. $\mathbf{w} = -\frac{1}{3\sqrt{6}}\mathbf{i} - \frac{7}{3\sqrt{6}}\mathbf{j} - \frac{2}{3\sqrt{6}}\mathbf{k}$

191. $\mathbf{w} = -\frac{4}{\sqrt{21}}\mathbf{i} - \frac{2}{\sqrt{21}}\mathbf{j} - \frac{1}{\sqrt{21}}\mathbf{k}$

193. $\alpha = 10$

197. $-3\mathbf{i} + 11\mathbf{j} + 2\mathbf{k}$

199. $\mathbf{w} = \langle -1, e^t, -e^{-t} \rangle$

201. $-26\mathbf{i} + 17\mathbf{j} + 9\mathbf{k}$

203. $72°$

209. 7

211. a. $5\sqrt{6}$; b. $\frac{5\sqrt{6}}{2}$; c. $\frac{5\sqrt{6}}{\sqrt{59}}$

213. a. 2; b. 2

215. $\mathbf{v} \cdot (\mathbf{u} \times \mathrm{w}) = -1, \quad \mathbf{w} \cdot (\mathbf{u} \times \mathbf{v}) = 1$

217. $\mathbf{a} = \langle 1, 2, 3 \rangle, \quad \mathbf{b} = \langle 0, 2, 5 \rangle, \quad \mathbf{c} = \langle 8, 9, 2 \rangle; \ \mathbf{a} \cdot (\mathrm{b} \times \mathrm{c}) = -9$

219. a. $\alpha = 1$; b. $h = 1$,

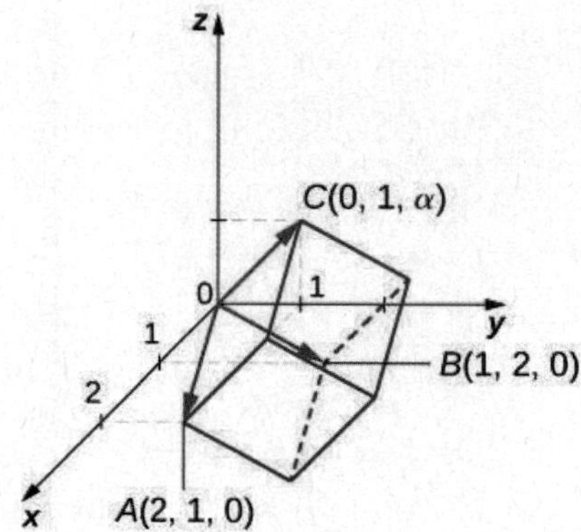

225. Yes, $\overrightarrow{AD} = \alpha\overrightarrow{AB} + \beta\overrightarrow{AC}$, where $\alpha = -1$ and $\beta = 1$.

227. $-\mathbf{k}$

229. $\langle 0, \pm 4\sqrt{5}, 2\sqrt{5} \rangle$

233. $\mathbf{w} = \langle w_3 - 1, w_3 + 1, w_3 \rangle$, where w_3 is any real number

235. 8.66 ft-lb

237. 250 N

239. $\mathbf{F} = 4.8 \times 10^{-15}\,\mathbf{k}\,\mathbf{N}$

241. a. $\mathbf{B}(t) = \langle \frac{2\sin t}{\sqrt{5}}, -\frac{2\cos t}{\sqrt{5}}, \frac{1}{\sqrt{5}} \rangle$;

b.

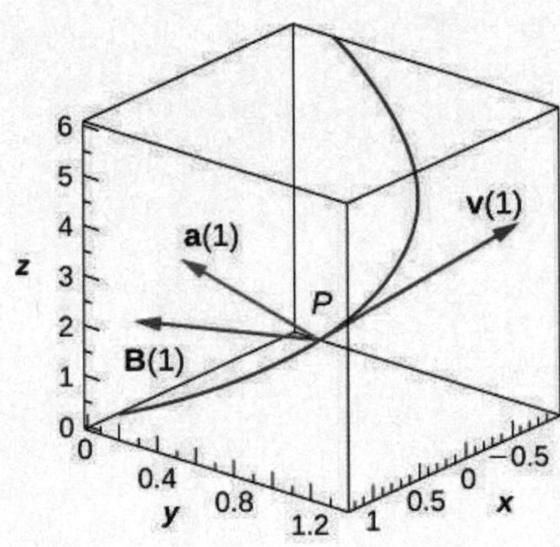

243. a. $\mathbf{r} = \langle -3, 5, 9 \rangle + t\langle 7, -12, -7 \rangle, \quad t \in \mathbb{R}$; b. $x = -3 + 7t, y = 5 - 12t, z = 9 - 7t, \quad t \in \mathbb{R}$; c. $\frac{x+3}{7} = \frac{y-5}{-12} = \frac{z-9}{-7}$; d. $x = -3 + 7t, y = 5 - 12t, z = 9 - 7t, \quad t \in [0, 1]$

245. a. $\mathbf{r} = \langle -1, 0, 5 \rangle + t\langle 5, 0, -2 \rangle, \quad t \in \mathbb{R}$; b. $x = -1 + 5t, y = 0, z = 5 - 2t, \quad t \in \mathbb{R}$; c. $\frac{x+1}{5} = \frac{z-5}{-2}, y = 0$; d. $x = -1 + 5t, y = 0, z = 5 - 2t, \quad t \in [0, 1]$

247. a. $x = 1 + t, y = -2 + 2t, z = 3 + 3t, \quad t \in \mathbb{R}$; b. $\frac{x-1}{1} = \frac{y+2}{2} = \frac{z-3}{3}$; c. $(0, -4, 0)$

249. a. $x = 3 + t, y = 1, z = 5, \quad t \in \mathbb{R}$; b. $y = 1, z = 5$; c. The line does not intersect the *xy*-plane.

251. a. $P(1, 3, 5), \quad v = \langle 1, 1, 4 \rangle$; b. $\sqrt{3}$

253. $\frac{2\sqrt{2}}{\sqrt{3}}$

255. a. Parallel; b. $\frac{\sqrt{2}}{\sqrt{3}}$

259. $(-12, 6, -4)$

261. The lines are skew.

263. The lines are equal.

265. a. $x = 1 + t, y = 1 - t, z = 1 + 2t, \quad t \in \mathbb{R}$; b. For instance, the line passing through A with direction vector $\mathbf{j} : x = 1, z = 1$; c. For instance, the line passing through A and point $(2, 0, 0)$ that belongs to L is a line that intersects; $L : \frac{x-1}{-1} = y - 1 = z - 1$

267. a. $3x - 2y + 4z = 0$; b. $3x - 2y + 4z = 0$

269. a. $(x - 1) + 2(y - 2) + 3(z - 3) = 0$; b. $x + 2y + 3z - 14 = 0$

271. a. $\mathbf{n} = 4\mathbf{i} + 5\mathbf{j} + 10\mathbf{k}$; b. $(5, 0, 0), \quad (0, 4, 0),$ and $(0, 0, 2)$;

c.

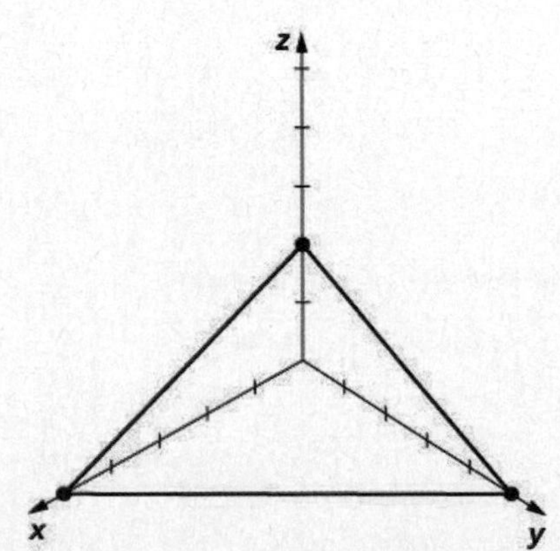

273. a. $\mathbf{n} = 3\mathbf{i} - 2\mathbf{j} + 4\mathbf{k}$; b. $(0, 0, 0)$;
c.

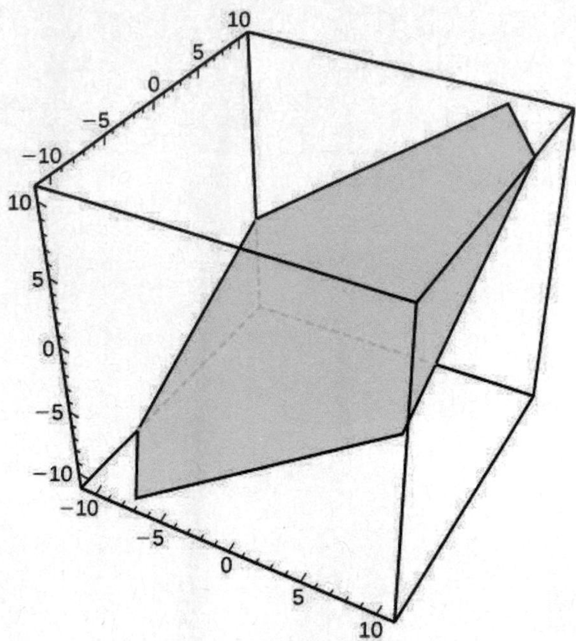

275. $(3, 0, 0)$

277. $x = -2 + 2t,\ y = 1 - 3t,\ z = 3 + t, \quad t \in \mathbb{R}$

281. a. $-2y + 3z - 1 = 0$; b. $\langle 0, -2, 3 \rangle \cdot \langle x - 1, y - 1, z - 1 \rangle = 0$; c. $x = 0,\ y = -2t,\ z = 3t, \quad t \in \mathbb{R}$

283. a. Answers may vary; b. $\frac{x-1}{1} = \frac{z-6}{-1},\ y = 4$

285. $2x - 5y - 3z + 15 = 0$

287. The line intersects the plane at point $P(-3, 4, 0)$.

289. $\frac{16}{\sqrt{14}}$

291. a. The planes are neither parallel nor orthogonal; b. $62°$

293. a. The planes are parallel.

295. $\frac{1}{\sqrt{6}}$

297. a. $\frac{18}{\sqrt{29}}$; b. $P\left(-\frac{51}{29}, \frac{130}{29}, \frac{62}{29}\right)$

299. $4x - 3y = 0$

301. a. $\mathbf{v}(1) = \langle \cos 1, -\sin 1, 2 \rangle$; b. $(\cos 1)(x - \sin 1) - (\sin 1)(y - \cos 1) + 2(z - 2) = 0$;
c.

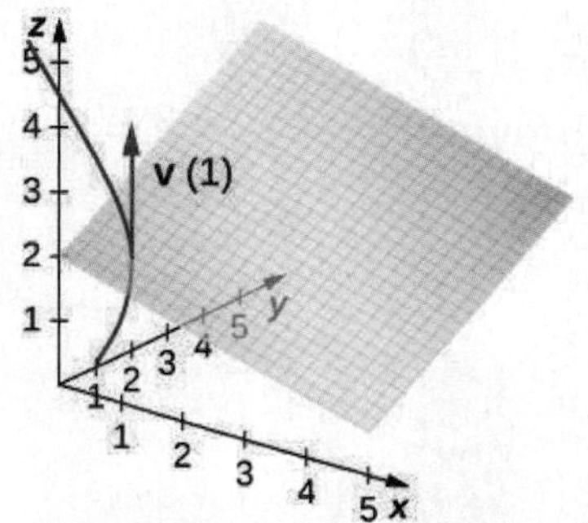

303. The surface is a cylinder with the rulings parallel to the y-axis.

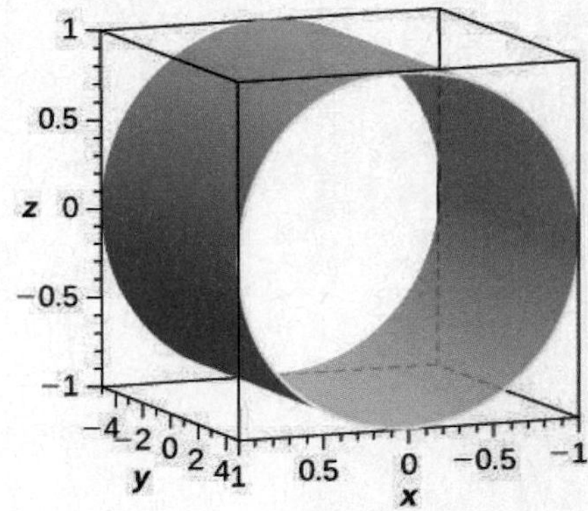

305. The surface is a cylinder with rulings parallel to the y-axis.

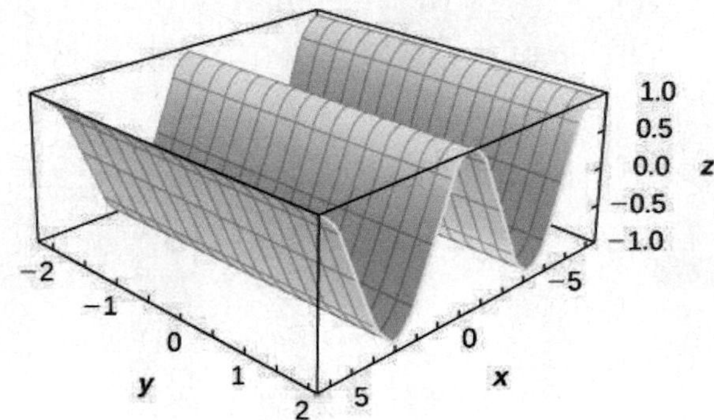

307. The surface is a cylinder with rulings parallel to the x-axis.

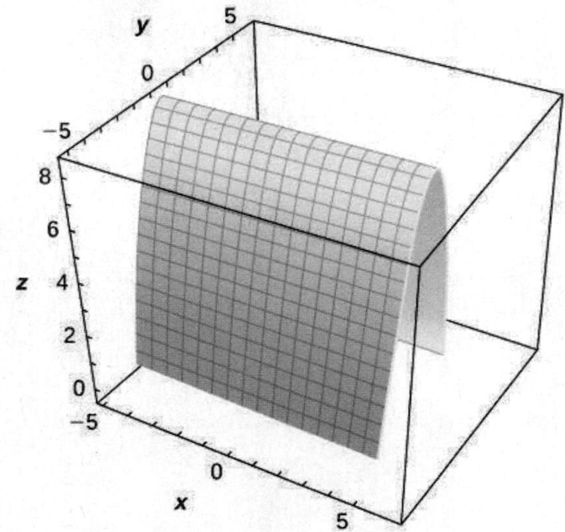

309. a. Cylinder; b. The x-axis
311. a. Hyperboloid of two sheets; b. The x-axis
313. b.
315. d.
317. a.

319. $-\frac{x^2}{9}+\frac{y^2}{\frac{1}{4}}+\frac{z^2}{\frac{1}{4}}=1,$ hyperboloid of one sheet with the x-axis as its axis of symmetry

321. $-\frac{x^2}{\frac{10}{3}}+\frac{y^2}{2}-\frac{z^2}{10}=1,$ hyperboloid of two sheets with the y-axis as its axis of symmetry

323. $y = -\frac{z^2}{5} + \frac{x^2}{5},$ hyperbolic paraboloid with the y-axis as its axis of symmetry

325. $\frac{x^2}{15} + \frac{y^2}{3} + \frac{z^2}{5} = 1,$ ellipsoid

327. $\frac{x^2}{40} + \frac{y^2}{8} - \frac{z^2}{5} = 0,$ elliptic cone with the z-axis as its axis of symmetry

329. $x = \frac{y^2}{2} + \frac{z^2}{3},$ elliptic paraboloid with the x-axis as its axis of symmetry

331. Parabola $y = -\frac{x^2}{4},$

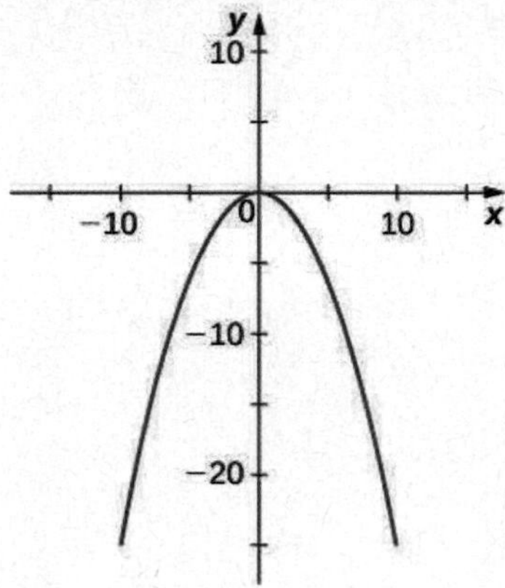

333. Ellipse $\frac{y^2}{4} + \frac{z^2}{100} = 1,$

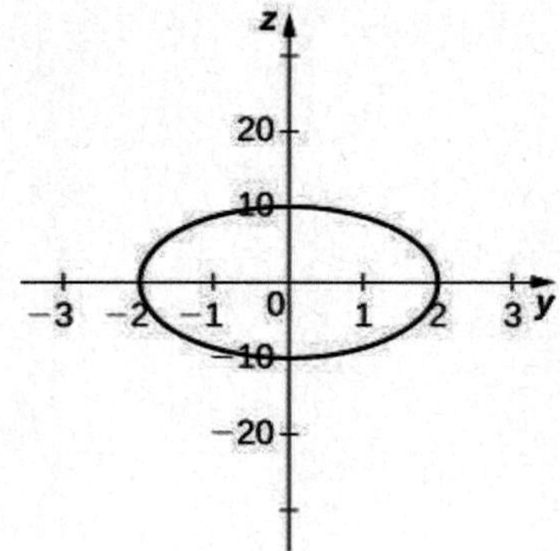

335. Ellipse $\frac{y^2}{4} + \frac{z^2}{100} = 1,$

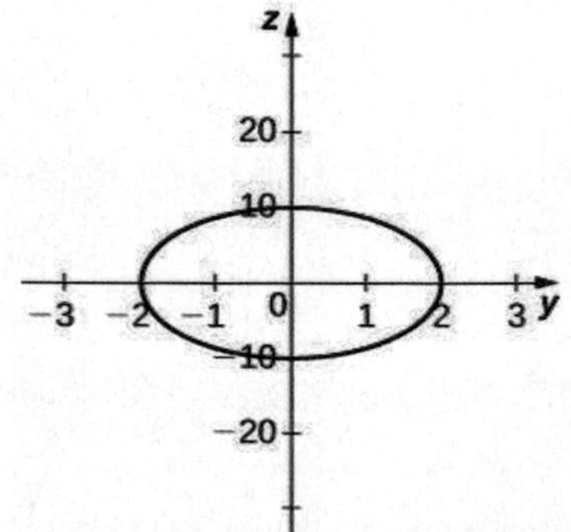

337. a. Ellipsoid; b. The third equation; c. $\frac{x^2}{100} + \frac{y^2}{400} + \frac{z^2}{225} = 1$

339. a. $\frac{(x+3)^2}{16} + \frac{(z-2)^2}{8} = 1$; b. Cylinder centered at $(-3, 2)$ with rulings parallel to the *y*-axis

341. a. $\frac{(x-3)^2}{4} + (y-2)^2 - (z+2)^2 = 1$; b. Hyperboloid of one sheet centered at $(3, 2, -2)$, with the *z*-axis as its axis of symmetry

343. a. $(x+3)^2 + \frac{y^2}{4} - \frac{z^2}{3} = 0$; b. Elliptic cone centered at $(-3, 0, 0)$, with the *z*-axis as its axis of symmetry

345. $\frac{x^2}{4} + \frac{y^2}{16} + z^2 = 1$

347. $(1, -1, 0)$ and $\left(\frac{13}{3}, 4, \frac{5}{3}\right)$

349. $x^2 + z^2 + 4y = 0$, elliptic paraboloid

351. $(0, 0, 100)$

355. a. $x = 2 - \frac{z^2}{2}$, $y = \pm\frac{z}{2}\sqrt{4 - z^2}$, where $z \in [-2, 2]$;

b.

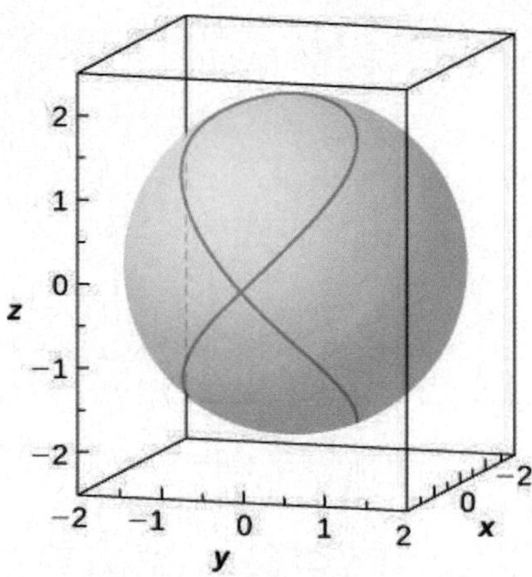

357.

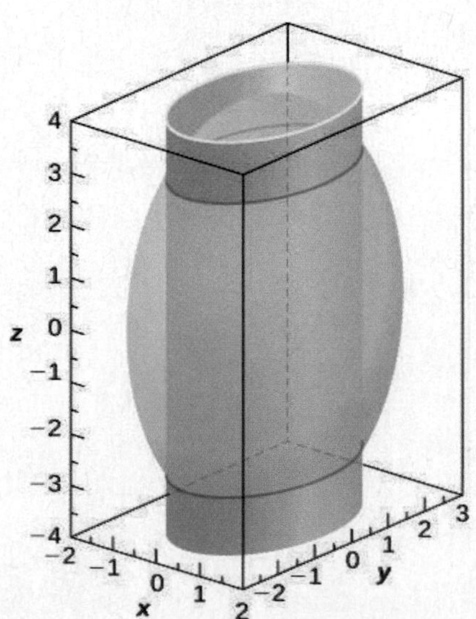

two ellipses of equations $\frac{x^2}{2} + \frac{y^2}{\frac{9}{2}} = 1$ in planes $z = \pm 2\sqrt{2}$

359. a. $\frac{x^2}{3963^2} + \frac{y^2}{3963^2} + \frac{z^2}{3950^2} = 1$;

b.

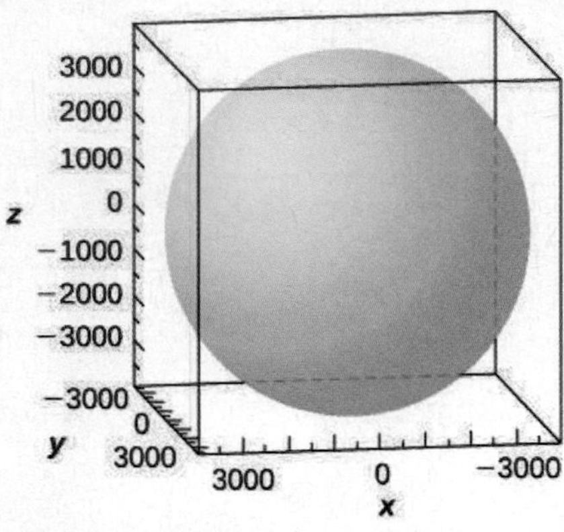

;

c. The intersection curve is the ellipse of equation $\frac{x^2}{3963^2} + \frac{y^2}{3963^2} = \frac{(2950)(4950)}{3950^2}$, and the intersection is an ellipse.; d. The intersection curve is the ellipse of equation $\frac{2y^2}{3963^2} + \frac{z^2}{3950^2} = 1$.

361. a.

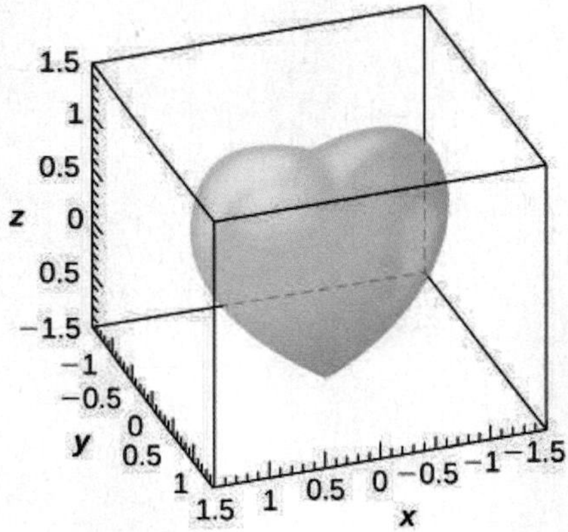

b. The intersection curve is $\left(x^2 + z^2 - 1\right)^3 - x^2 z^3 = 0$.

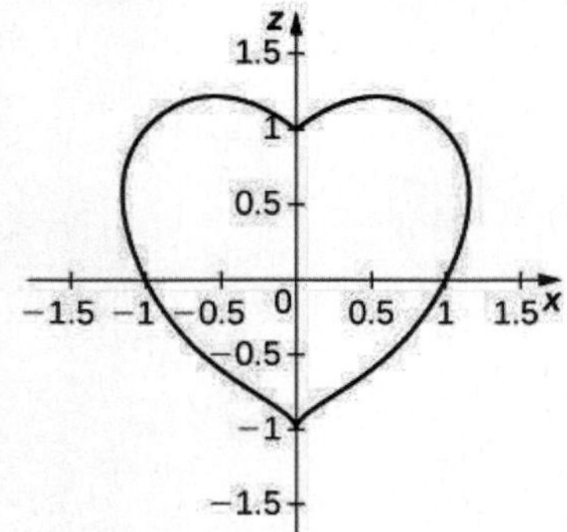

363. $\left(2\sqrt{3}, 2, 3\right)$

365. $\left(-2\sqrt{3}, -2, 3\right)$

367. $\left(2, \frac{\pi}{3}, 2\right)$

369. $\left(3\sqrt{2}, -\frac{\pi}{4}, 7\right)$

371. A cylinder of equation $x^2 + y^2 = 16,$ with its center at the origin and rulings parallel to the z-axis,

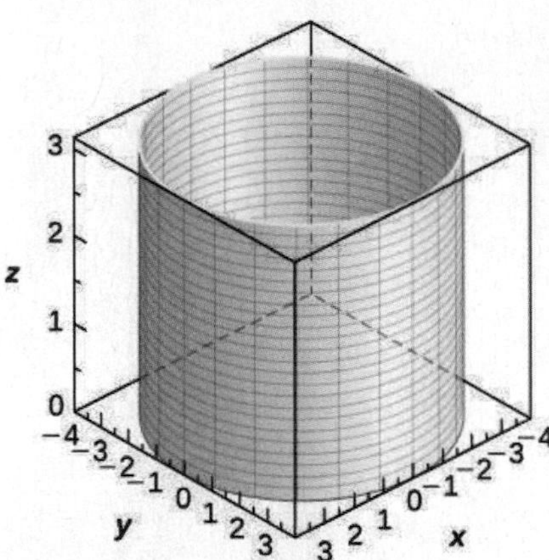

373. Hyperboloid of two sheets of equation $-x^2 + y^2 - z^2 = 1,$ with the y-axis as the axis of symmetry,

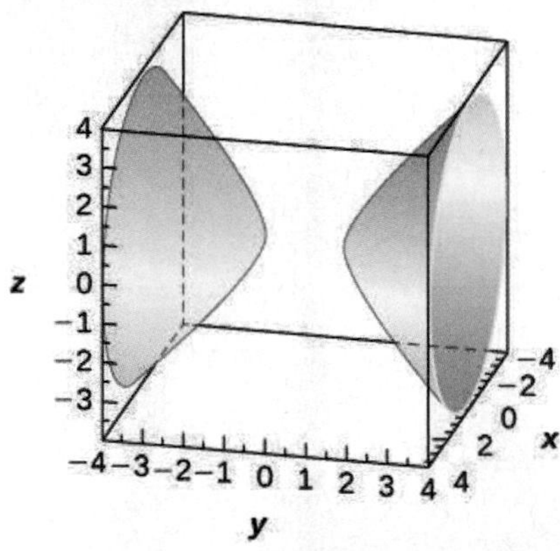

375. Cylinder of equation $x^2 - 2x + y^2 = 0,$ with a center at $(1, 0, 0)$ and radius $1,$ with rulings parallel to the z-axis,

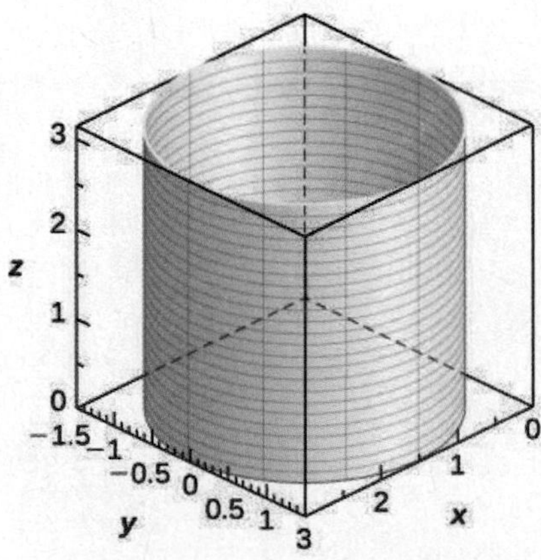

377. Plane of equation $x = 2,$

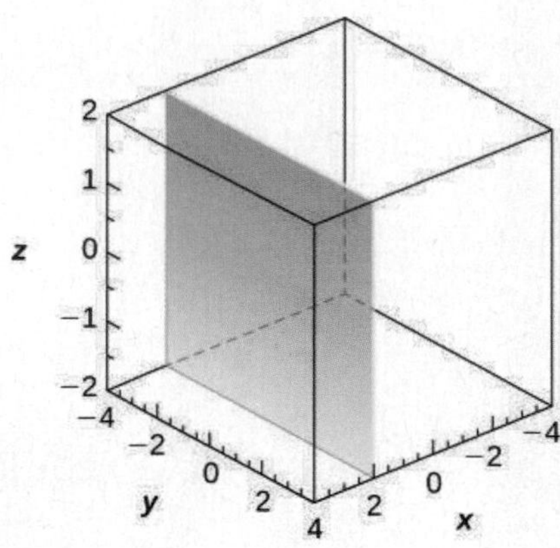

379. $z = 3$

381. $r^2 + z^2 = 9$

383. $r = 16 \cos \theta,\ r = 0$

385. $(0,\ 0,\ -3)$

387. $\left(6,\ -6,\ \sqrt{2}\right)$

389. $(4,\ 0,\ 90°)$

391. $(3,\ 90°,\ 90°)$

393. Sphere of equation $x^2 + y^2 + z^2 = 9$ centered at the origin with radius 3,

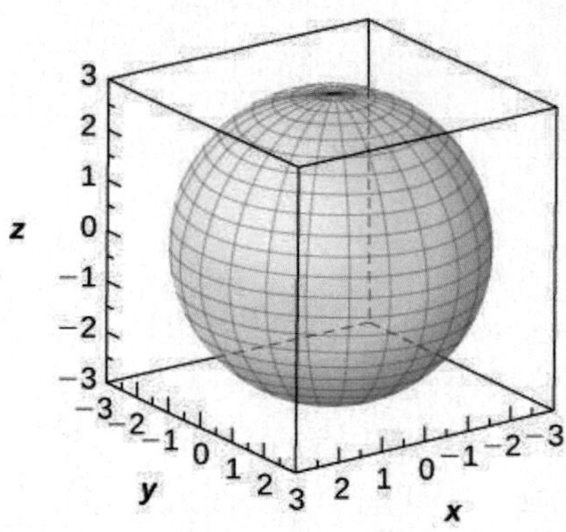

395. Sphere of equation $x^2 + y^2 + (z - 1)^2 = 1$ centered at $(0,\ 0,\ 1)$ with radius 1,

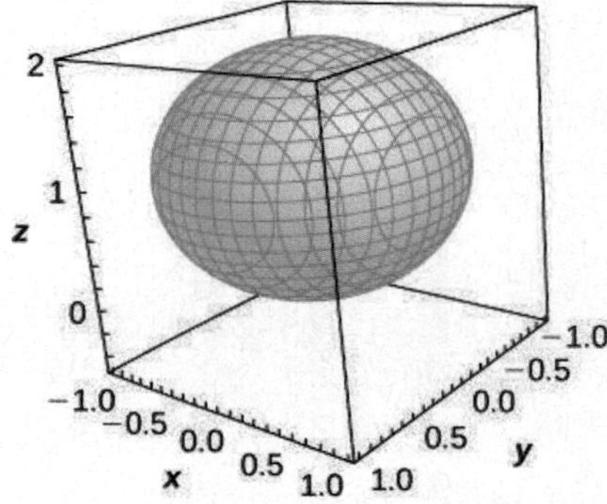

397. The *xy*-plane of equation $z = 0$,

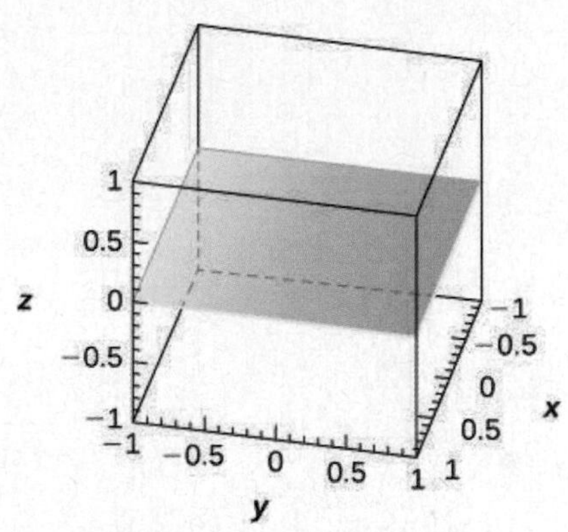

399. $\varphi = \frac{\pi}{3}$ or $\varphi = \frac{2\pi}{3}$; Elliptic cone

401. $\rho \cos \varphi = 6$; Plane at $z = 6$

403. $\left(\sqrt{10}, \frac{\pi}{4}, 0.3218\right)$

405. $\left(3\sqrt{2}, \frac{\pi}{2}, \frac{\pi}{4}\right)$

407. $\left(2, -\frac{\pi}{4}, 0\right)$

409. $\left(8, \frac{\pi}{3}, 0\right)$

411. Cartesian system, $\{(x, y, z) | 0 \le x \le a, 0 \le y \le a, 0 \le z \le a\}$

413. Cylindrical system, $\left\{(r, \theta, z) \middle| r^2 + z^2 \le 9, r \ge 3 \cos \theta, 0 \le \theta \le 2\pi\right\}$

415. The region is described by the set of points $\left\{(r, \theta, z) \middle| 0 \le r \le 1, 0 \le \theta \le 2\pi, r^2 \le z \le r\right\}$.

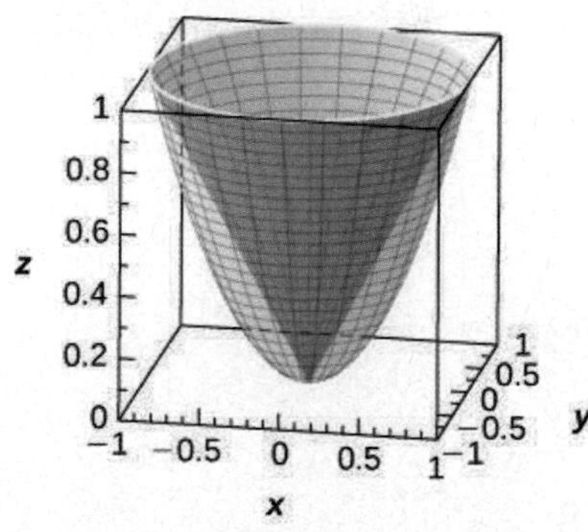

417. (4000, −77°, 51°)

419. 43.17°W, 22.91°S

421. a. $\rho = 0$, $\rho + R^2 - r^2 - 2R \sin \varphi = 0$;

c.

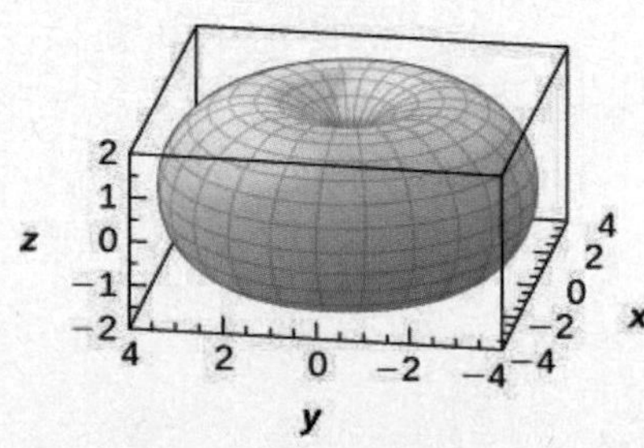

Review Exercises

423. True
425. False
427. a. $\langle 24, -5 \rangle$; b. $\sqrt{85}$; c. Can't dot a vector with a scalar; d. -29

429. $a = \pm 2$

431. $\langle \frac{1}{\sqrt{14}}, -\frac{2}{\sqrt{14}}, -\frac{3}{\sqrt{14}} \rangle$

433. 27

435. $x = 1 - 3t,\ y = 3 + 3t,\ z = 5 - 8t,\ \mathbf{r}(t) = (1 - 3t)\mathbf{i} + 3(1 + t)\mathbf{j} + (5 - 8t)\mathbf{k}$

437. $-x + 3y + 8z = 43$

439. $x = k$ trace: $k^2 = y^2 + z^2$ is a circle, $y = k$ trace: $x^2 - z^2 = k^2$ is a hyperbola (or a pair of lines if $k = 0$), $z = k$ trace: $x^2 - y^2 = k^2$ is a hyperbola (or a pair of lines if $k = 0$). The surface is a cone.

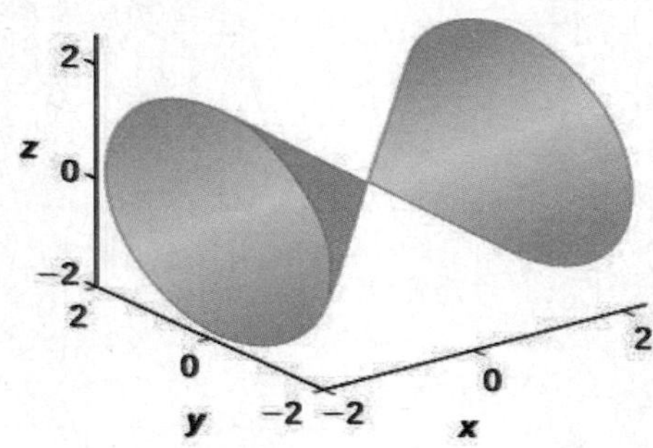

441. Cylindrical: $z = r^2 - 1$, spherical: $\cos\varphi = \rho\sin^2\varphi - \frac{1}{\rho}$

443. $x^2 - 2x + y^2 + z^2 = 1$, sphere

445. 331 N, and 244 N
447. 15 J
449. More, 59.09 J

Chapter 3

Checkpoint

3.1. $\mathbf{r}(0) = \mathbf{j},\ \mathbf{r}(1) = -2\mathbf{i} + 5\mathbf{j},\ \mathbf{r}(-4) = 28\mathbf{i} - 15\mathbf{j}$ The domain of $\mathbf{r}(t) = (t^2 - 3t)\mathbf{i} + (4t + 1)\mathbf{j}$ is all real numbers.

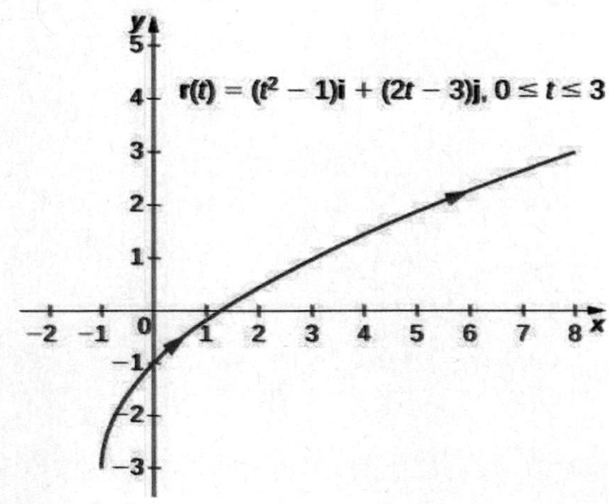

3.2.

3.3. $\lim_{t \to -2} \mathbf{r}(t) = 3\mathbf{i} - 5\mathbf{j} - \mathbf{k}$

3.4. $\mathbf{r}'(t) = 4t\mathbf{i} + 5\mathbf{j}$

3.5. $\mathbf{r}'(t) = (1 + \ln t)\mathbf{i} + 5e^t\,\mathbf{j} - (\sin t + \cos t)\mathbf{k}$

3.6. $\frac{d}{dt}[\mathbf{r}(t) \cdot \mathbf{r}'(t)] = 8e^{4t}$ $\frac{d}{dt}[\mathbf{u}(t) \times \mathbf{r}(t)] = -\left(e^{2t}(\cos t + 2\sin t) + \cos 2t\right)\mathbf{i} + \left(e^{2t}(2t+1) - \sin 2t\right)\mathbf{j} + (t\cos t + \sin t - \cos 2t)\mathbf{k}$

3.7. $\mathbf{T}(t) = \frac{2t}{\sqrt{4t^2+5}}\mathbf{i} + \frac{2}{\sqrt{4t^2+5}}\mathbf{j} + \frac{1}{\sqrt{4t^2+5}}\mathbf{k}$

3.8. $\int_1^3 \left[(2t+4)\mathbf{i} + \left(3t^2 - 4t\right)\mathbf{j}\right]dt = 16\mathbf{i} + 10\mathbf{j}$

3.9. $\mathbf{r}'(t) = \langle 4t, 4t, 3t^2 \rangle$, so $s = \frac{1}{27}\left(113^{3/2} - 32^{3/2}\right) \approx 37.785$

3.10. $s = 5t$, or $t = s/5$. Substituting this into $\mathbf{r}(t) = \langle 3\cos t, 3\sin t, 4t \rangle$ gives $\mathbf{r}(s) = \langle 3\cos\left(\frac{s}{5}\right), 3\sin\left(\frac{s}{5}\right), \frac{4s}{5} \rangle,\ s \geq 0.$

3.11. $\kappa = \frac{6}{101^{3/2}} \approx 0.0059$

3.12. $\mathbf{N}(2) = \frac{\sqrt{2}}{2}(\mathbf{i} - \mathbf{j})$

3.13. $\kappa = \frac{4}{\left[1 + (4x-4)^2\right]^{3/2}}$ At the point $x = 1$, the curvature is equal to 4. Therefore, the radius of the osculating circle is $\frac{1}{4}$. A graph of this function appears next:

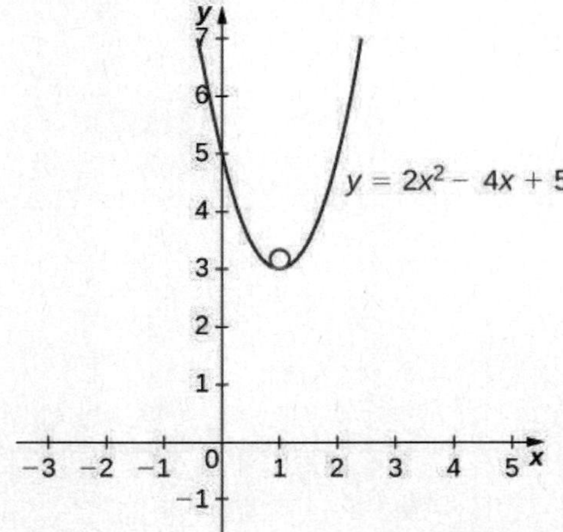

The vertex of this parabola is located at the point $(1, 3)$. Furthermore, the center of the osculating circle is directly above the vertex. Therefore, the coordinates of the center are $\left(1, \frac{13}{4}\right)$. The equation of the osculating circle is $(x-1)^2 + \left(y - \frac{13}{4}\right)^2 = \frac{1}{16}$.

3.14.

$$\begin{aligned}\mathbf{v}(t) &= \mathbf{r}'(t) = (2t-3)\mathbf{i} + 2\mathbf{j} + \mathbf{k} \\ \mathbf{a}(t) &= \mathbf{v}'(t) = 2\mathbf{i} \\ v(t) &= \|\mathbf{r}'(t)\| = \sqrt{(2t-3)^2 + 2^2 + 1^2} = \sqrt{4t^2 - 12t + 14}\end{aligned}$$

The units for velocity and speed are feet per second, and the units for acceleration are feet per second squared.

3.15.

a.

$$\begin{aligned}\mathbf{v}(t) &= \mathbf{r}'(t) = 4\mathbf{i} + 2t\,\mathbf{j} \\ \mathbf{a}(t) &= \mathbf{v}'(t) = 2\mathbf{j} \\ a_{\mathbf{T}} &= \frac{2t}{\sqrt{t^2+4}},\ a_{\mathbf{N}} = \frac{2}{\sqrt{t^2+4}}\end{aligned}$$

b. $a_{\mathbf{T}}(-3) = -\frac{6\sqrt{13}}{13}, a_{\mathbf{N}}(-3) = \frac{2\sqrt{13}}{13}$

3.16. 967.15 m

3.17. $a = 1.224 \times 10^9 \text{ m} \approx 1{,}224{,}000 \text{ km}$

Section Exercises

1. $f(t) = 3\sec t, \ g(t) = 2\tan t$

3.

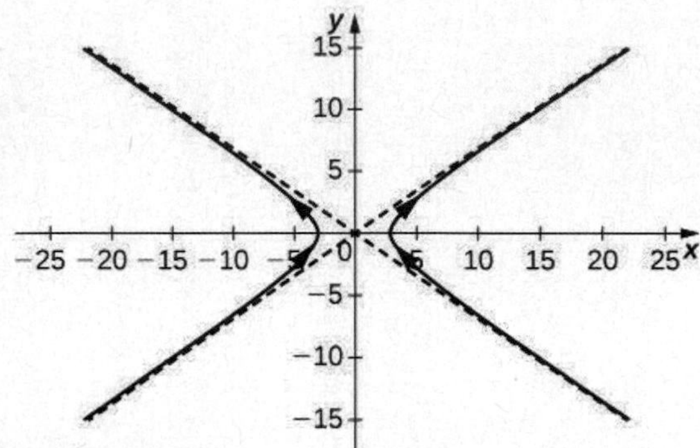

5. a. $\langle \frac{\sqrt{2}}{2}, \frac{\sqrt{2}}{2} \rangle$, b. $\langle \frac{1}{2}, \frac{\sqrt{3}}{2} \rangle$, c. Yes, the limit as t approaches $\pi/3$ is equal to $\mathbf{r}(\pi/3)$, d.

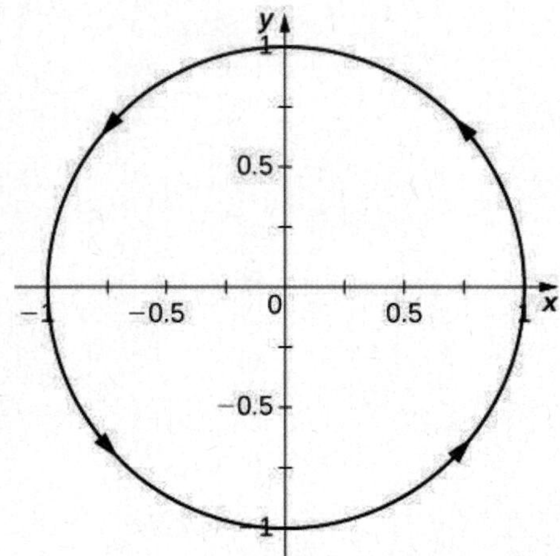

7. a. $\langle e^{\pi/4}, \frac{\sqrt{2}}{2}, \ln\left(\frac{\pi}{4}\right) \rangle$; b. $\langle e^{\pi/4}, \frac{\sqrt{2}}{2}, \ln\left(\frac{\pi}{4}\right) \rangle$; c. Yes

9. $\langle e^{\pi/2}, 1, \ln\left(\frac{\pi}{2}\right) \rangle$

11. $2e^2\,\mathbf{i} + \frac{2}{e^4}\mathbf{j} + 2\mathbf{k}$

13. The limit does not exist because the limit of $\ln(t-1)$ as t approaches infinity does not exist.

15. $t > 0, t \neq (2k+1)\frac{\pi}{2}$, where k is an integer

17. $t > 3, t \neq n\pi$, where n is an integer

19.

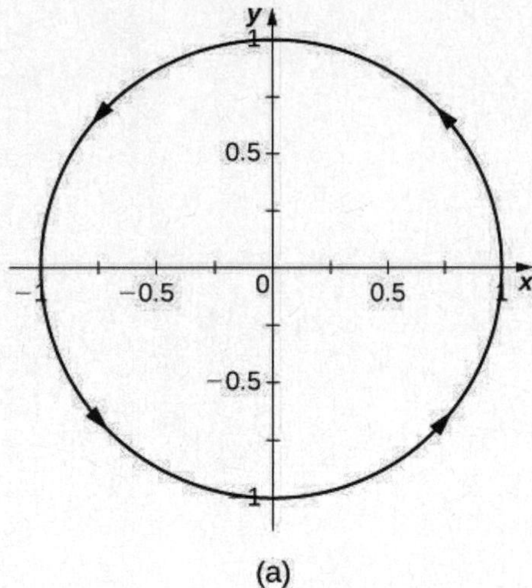

(a)

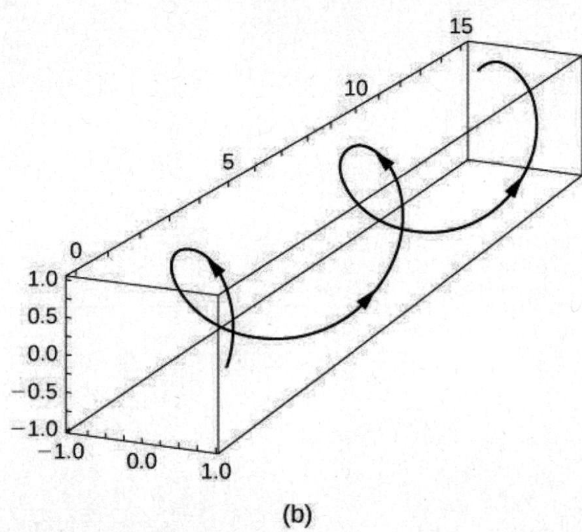

(b)

21. All t such that $t \in (1, \infty)$

23. $y = 2\sqrt[3]{x}$, a variation of the cube-root function

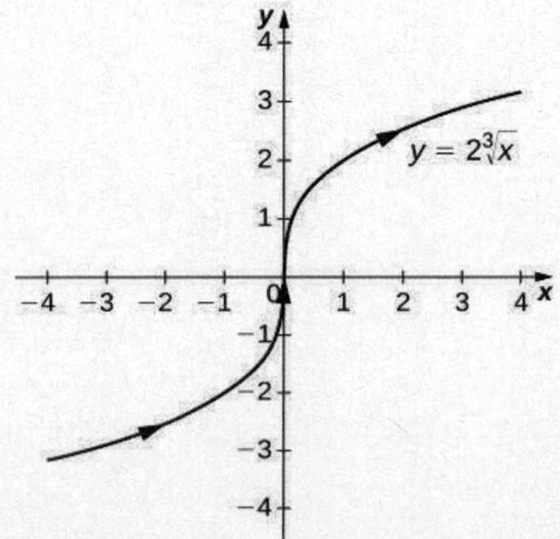

25. $x^2 + y^2 = 9,$ a circle centered at $(0, 0)$ with radius 3, and a counterclockwise orientation

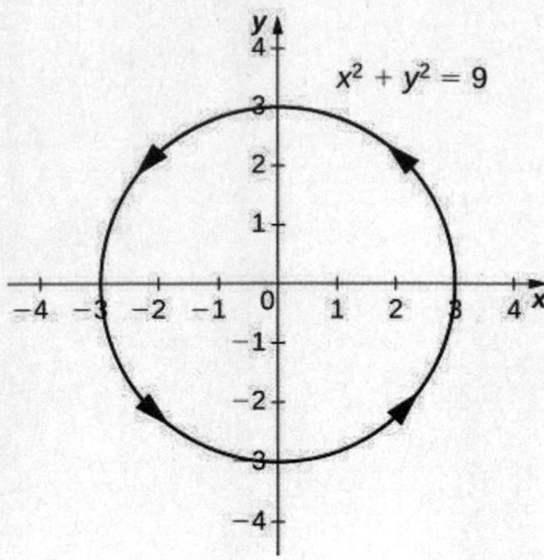

27.

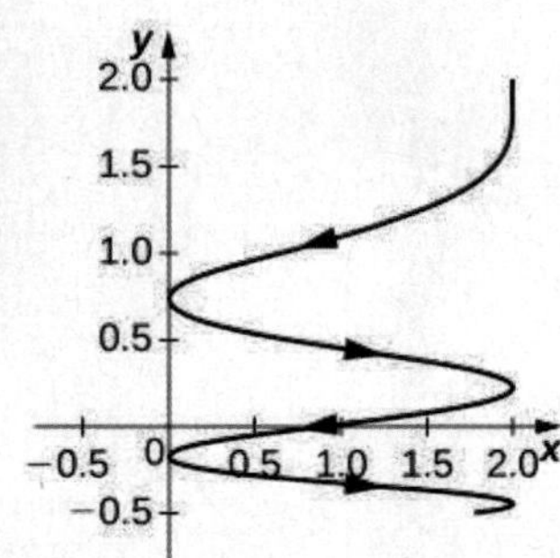

29.

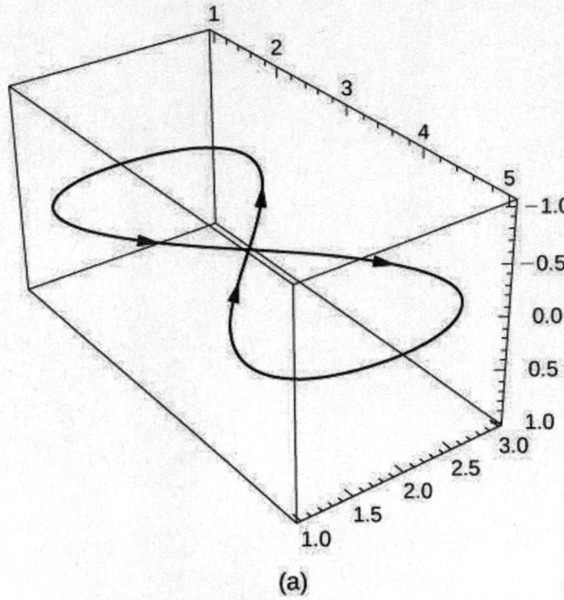

(a)

View in the *yt*-plane

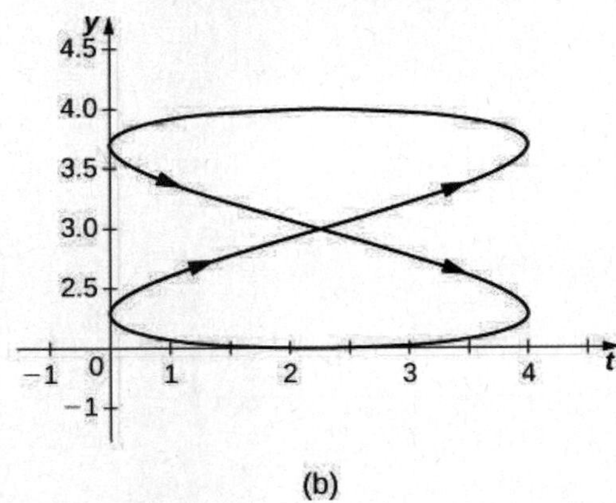

(b)

Find a vector-valued function that traces out the given curve in the indicated direction.

31. For left to right, $y = x^2$, where t increases

33. (50, 0, 0)

35.

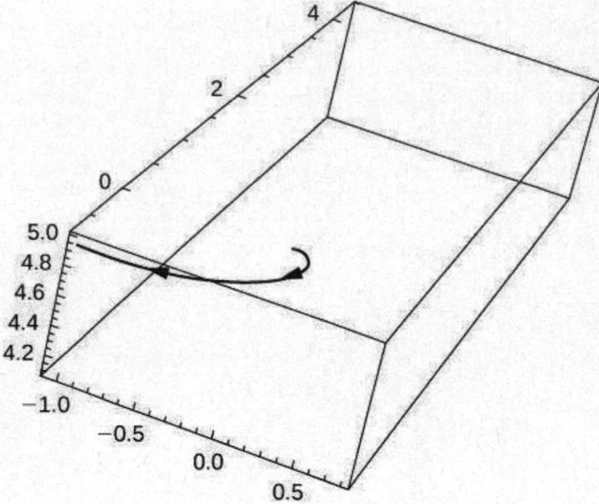

37.

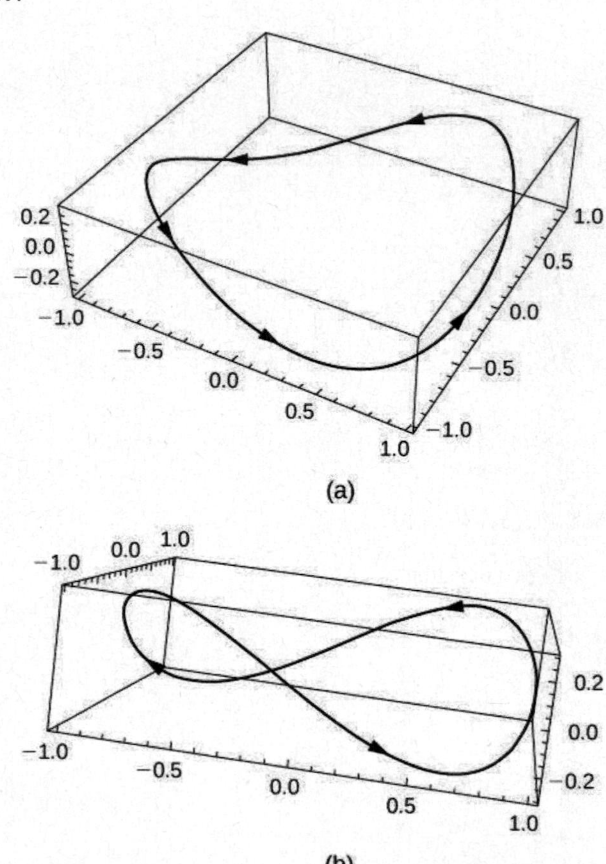

39. One possibility is $r(t) = \cos t\mathbf{i} + \sin t\mathbf{j} + \sin(4t)\mathbf{k}$. By increasing the coefficient of t in the third component, the number of turning points will increase.

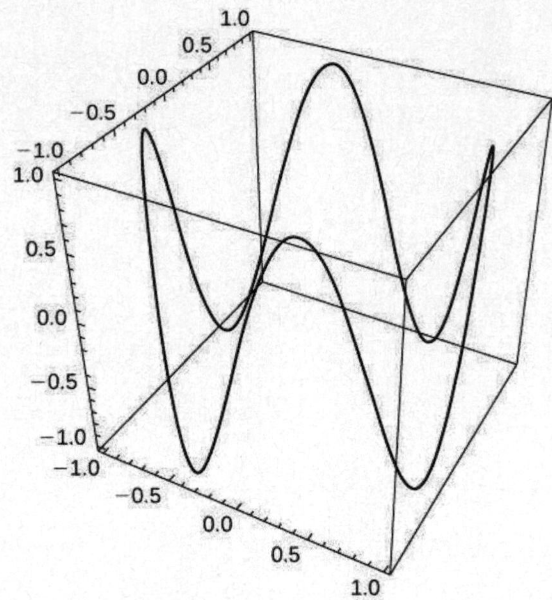

41. $\langle\, 3t^2,\ 6t,\ \frac{1}{2}t^2 \,\rangle$

43. $\langle\, -e^{-t},\ 3\cos(3t),\ \frac{5}{\sqrt{t}} \,\rangle$

45. $\langle\, 0,\ 0,\ 0 \,\rangle$

47. $\langle\, \frac{-1}{(t+1)^2},\ \frac{1}{1+t^2},\ \frac{3}{t} \,\rangle$

49. $\langle\, 0,\ 12\cos(3t),\ \cos t - t\sin t \,\rangle$

51. $\frac{1}{\sqrt{2}}\langle\, 1,\ -1,\ 0 \,\rangle$

53. $\frac{1}{\sqrt{1060.5625}}\langle\, 6,\ -\frac{3}{4},\ 32 \,\rangle$

55. $\frac{1}{\sqrt{9\sin^2(3t)+144\cos^2(4t)}}\langle\, 0,\ -3\sin(3t),\ 12\cos(4t) \,\rangle$

57. $\mathbf{T}(t) = \frac{-12}{13}\sin(4t)\,\mathbf{i} + \frac{12}{13}\cos(4t)\,\mathbf{j} + \frac{5}{13}\mathbf{k}$

59. $\langle\, 2t,\ 4t^3,\ -8t^7 \,\rangle$

61. $\sin(t) + 2te^t - 4t^3\cos(t) + t\cos(t) + t^2e^t + t^4\sin(t)$

63. $900t^7 + 16t$

65.

a.

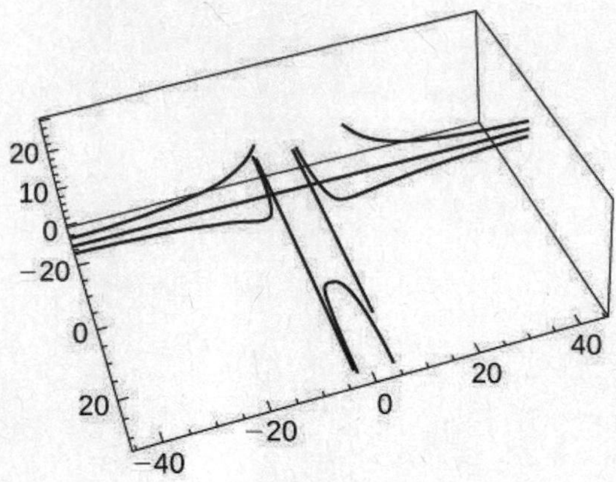

b. Undefined or infinite

67. $\mathbf{r}'(t) = -b\omega\sin(\omega t)\mathbf{i} + b\omega\cos(\omega t)\mathbf{j}$. To show orthogonality, note that $\mathbf{r}'(t) \cdot \mathbf{r}(t) = 0$.

69. $0\mathbf{i} + 2\mathbf{j} + 4t\mathbf{j}$

71. $\frac{1}{3}\left(10^{3/2} - 1\right)$

73.

$$\begin{aligned} \|\mathbf{v}(t)\| &= k \\ \mathbf{v}(t) \cdot \mathbf{v}(t) &= k \\ \frac{d}{dt}(\mathbf{v}(t) \cdot \mathbf{v}(t)) &= \frac{d}{dt}k = 0 \\ \mathbf{v}(t) \cdot \mathbf{v}'(t) + \mathbf{v}'(t) \cdot \mathbf{v}(t) &= 0 \\ 2\mathbf{v}(t) \cdot \mathbf{v}'(t) &= 0 \\ \mathbf{v}(t) \cdot \mathbf{v}'(t) &= 0. \end{aligned}$$

The last statement implies that the velocity and acceleration are perpendicular or orthogonal.

75. $\mathbf{v}(t) = \langle 1 - \sin t,\ 1 - \cos t \rangle$, $\text{speed} = -\mathbf{v}(t)\| = \sqrt{4 - 2(\sin t + \cos t)}$

77. $x - 1 = t,\ y - 1 = -t,\ z - 0 = 0$

79. $\mathbf{r}(t) = \langle 18, 9 \rangle$ at $t = 3$

81. $\sqrt{593}$

83. $\mathbf{v}(t) = \langle -\sin t, \cos t, 1 \rangle$

85. $\mathbf{a}(t) = -\cos t\mathbf{i} - \sin t\mathbf{j} + 0\mathbf{j}$

87. $\mathbf{v}(t) = \langle -\sin t, 2\cos t, 0 \rangle$

89. $\mathbf{a}(t) = \langle -\frac{\sqrt{2}}{2}, -\sqrt{2}, 0 \rangle$

91. $\|\mathbf{v}(t)\| = \sqrt{\sec^4 t + \sec^2 t \tan^2 t} = \sqrt{\sec^2 t(\sec^2 t + \tan^2 t)}$

93. 2

95. $\langle 0, 2\sin t\left(t - \frac{1}{t}\right) - 2\cos t\left(1 + \frac{1}{t^2}\right), 2\sin t\left(1 + \frac{1}{t^2}\right) + 2\cos t\left(t - \frac{2}{t}\right) \rangle$

97. $\mathbf{T}(t) = \langle \frac{t^2}{\sqrt{t^4 + 1}}, \frac{-1}{\sqrt{t^4 + 1}} \rangle$

99. $\mathbf{T}(t) = \frac{1}{3}\langle 1, 2, 2 \rangle$

101. $\frac{3}{4}\mathbf{i} + \ln(2)\mathbf{j} + \left(1 - \frac{1}{e}\right)\mathbf{j}$

103. $8\sqrt{5}$

105. $\frac{1}{54}\left(37^{3/2} - 1\right)$

107. Length $= 2\pi$

109. 6π

111. $e - \frac{1}{e}$

113. $\mathbf{T}(0) = \mathbf{j}, \quad \mathbf{N}(0) = -\mathbf{i}$

115. $\mathbf{T}(t) = \langle\ 2e^t,\ e^t \cos t - e^t \sin t,\ e^t \cos t + e^t \sin t\ \rangle$

117. $\mathbf{N}(0) = \langle\ \frac{\sqrt{2}}{2},\ 0,\ \frac{\sqrt{2}}{2}\ \rangle$

119. $\mathbf{T}(t) = \frac{1}{\sqrt{4t^2+2}} < 1,\ 2t,\ 1 >$

121. $\mathbf{T}(t) = \frac{1}{\sqrt{100t^2+13}}(3\mathbf{i} + 10t\mathbf{j} + 2\mathbf{k})$

123. $\mathbf{T}(t) = \frac{1}{\sqrt{9t^4+76t^2+16}}\left(\left[3t^2-4\right]\mathbf{i} + 10t\mathbf{j}\right)$

125. $\mathbf{N}(t) = \langle\ -\sin t,\ 0,\ -\cos t\ \rangle$

127. Arc-length function: $s(t) = 5t$; r as a parameter of s: $\mathbf{r}(s) = \left(3 - \frac{3s}{5}\right)\mathbf{i} + \frac{4s}{5}\mathbf{j}$

129. $\mathbf{r}(s) = \left(1 + \frac{s}{\sqrt{2}}\right)\sin\left(\ln(1 + \frac{s}{\sqrt{2}})\right)\mathbf{i} + \left(1 + \frac{s}{\sqrt{2}}\right)\cos\left[\ln\left(1 + \frac{s}{\sqrt{2}}\right)\right]\mathbf{j}$

131. The maximum value of the curvature occurs at $x = \sqrt[4]{5}$.

133. $\frac{1}{2}$

135. $\kappa \approx \frac{49.477}{\left(17 + 144t^2\right)^{3/2}}$

137. $\frac{1}{2\sqrt{2}}$

139. The curvature approaches zero.

141. $y = 6x + \pi$ and $x + 6 = 6\pi$

143. $x + 2z = \frac{\pi}{2}$

145. $\frac{a^4 b^4}{\left(b^4 x^2 + a^4 y^2\right)^{3/2}}$

147. $\frac{10\sqrt{10}}{3}$

149. $\frac{38}{3}$

151. The curvature is decreasing over this interval.

153. $\kappa = \frac{6}{x^{2/5}\left(25 + 4x^{6/5}\right)}$

155. $\mathbf{v}(t) = (6t)\mathbf{i} + (2 - \cos(t))\mathbf{j}$

157. $\mathbf{v}(t) = \langle\ -3\sin t,\ 3\cos t,\ 2t\ \rangle, \quad \mathbf{a}(t) = \langle\ -3\cos t,\ -3\sin t,\ 2\ \rangle, \quad \text{speed} = \sqrt{9 + 4t^2}$

159. $\mathbf{v}(t) = -2\sin t\,\mathbf{j} + 3\cos t\,\mathbf{k}, \quad \mathbf{a}(t) = -2\cos t\,\mathbf{j} - 3\sin t\,\mathbf{k}, \quad \text{speed} = \sqrt{4\sin^2(t) + 9^{\cos}(t)}$

161. $\mathbf{v}(t) = e^t\mathbf{i} - e^{-t}\mathbf{j}, \quad \mathbf{a}(t) = e^t\mathbf{i} + e^{-t}\mathbf{j}, \quad \|\ \mathbf{v}(t)\ \|\ \sqrt{e^{2t} + e^{-2t}}$

163. $t = 4$

165. $\mathbf{v}(t) = (\omega - \omega\cos(\omega t))\mathbf{i} + (\omega\sin(\omega t))\mathbf{j}$,

$\mathbf{a}(t) = \left(\omega^2\sin(\omega t)\right)\mathbf{i} + \left(\omega^2\cos(\omega t)\right)\mathbf{j}$,

$\text{speed} = \sqrt{\omega^2 - 2\omega^2\cos(\omega t) + \omega^2\cos^2(\omega t) + \omega^2\sin^2(\omega t)} = \sqrt{2\omega^2(1 - \cos(\omega t))}$

167. $\|\ \mathbf{v}(t)\ \| = \sqrt{9 + 4t^2}$

169. $\mathbf{v}(t) = \langle e^{-5t}(\cos t - 5\sin t), -e^{-5t}(\sin t + 5\cos t), -20e^{-5t} \rangle$

171. $\mathbf{a}(t) = \langle e^{-5t}(-\sin t - 5\cos t) - 5e^{-5t}(\cos t - 5\sin t),$ $-e^{-5t}(\cos t - 5\sin t) + 5e^{-5t}(\sin t + 5\cos t), 100e^{-5t} \rangle$

173. 44.185 sec

175. $t = 88.37$ sec

177. 88.37 sec

179. The range is approximately 886.29 m.

181. $\mathbf{v} = 42.16$ m/sec

183. $\mathbf{r}(t) = 0\mathbf{i} + \left(\frac{1}{6}t^3 + 4.5t - \frac{14}{3}\right)\mathbf{j} + \left(\frac{t^3}{6} - \frac{1}{2}t + \frac{1}{3}\right)\mathbf{k}$

185. $a_T = 0, \quad a_N = a\omega^2$

187. $a_T = \sqrt{3}e^t, \quad a_N = \sqrt{2}e^t$

189. $a_T = 2t, \quad a_N = 4 + 2t^2$

191. $a_T \frac{6t + 12t^3}{\sqrt{1 + t^4 + t^2}}, \quad a_N = 6\sqrt{\frac{1 + 4t^2 + t^4}{1 + t^2 + t^4}}$

193. $a_T = 0, \quad a_N = 2\sqrt{3}\pi$

195. $\mathbf{r}(t) = \left(\frac{-1}{m}\cos t + c + \frac{1}{m}\right)\mathbf{i} + \left(\frac{-\sin t}{m} + \left(v_0 + \frac{1}{m}\right)t\right)\mathbf{j}$

197. 10.94 km/sec

201. $a_T = 0.43 \text{ m/sec}^2,$

$a_N = 2.46 \text{ m/sec}^2$

Review Exercises

203. False, $\frac{d}{dt}[\mathbf{u}(t) \times \mathbf{u}(t)] = 0$

205. False, it is $|\mathbf{r}'(t)|$

207. $t < 4, \quad t \neq \frac{n\pi}{2}$

209.

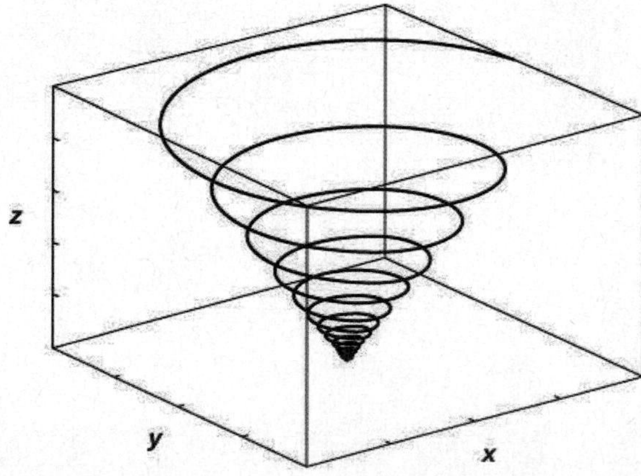

211. $\mathbf{r}(t) = \langle t, 2 - \frac{t^2}{8}, -2 - \frac{t^2}{8} \rangle$

213. $\mathbf{u}'(t) = \langle 2t, 2, 20t^4 \rangle, \quad \mathbf{u}''(t) = \langle 2, 0, 80t^3 \rangle, \quad \frac{d}{dt}[\mathbf{u}'(t) \times \mathbf{u}(t)] = \langle -480t^3 - 160t^4, 24 + 75t^2, 12 + 4t \rangle,$ $\frac{d}{dt}[\mathbf{u}(t) \times \mathbf{u}'(t)] = \langle 480t^3 + 160t^4, -24 - 75t^2, -12 - 4t \rangle, \quad \frac{d}{dt}[\mathbf{u}(t) \cdot \mathbf{u}'(t)] = 720t^8 - 9600t^3 + 6t^2 + 4,$ unit tangent vector: $\mathbf{T}(t) = \frac{2t}{\sqrt{400t^8 + 4t^2 + 4}}\mathbf{i} + \frac{2}{\sqrt{400t^8 + 4t^2 + 4}}\mathbf{j} + \frac{20t^4}{\sqrt{400t^8 + 4t^2 + 4}}\mathbf{k}$

215. $\frac{\ln(4)^2}{2}\mathbf{i} + 2\mathbf{j} + \frac{2(2 + \sqrt{2})}{\pi}\mathbf{k}$

217. $\frac{\sqrt{37}}{2} + \frac{1}{12}\sinh^{-1}(6)$

219. $\mathbf{r}(t(s)) = \cos\left(\frac{2s}{\sqrt{65}}\right)\mathbf{i} + \frac{8s}{\sqrt{65}}\mathbf{j} - \sin\left(\frac{2s}{\sqrt{65}}\right)\mathbf{k}$

221. $\frac{e^{2t}}{\left(e^{2t} + 1\right)^2}$

223. $a_T = \frac{e^{2t}}{\sqrt{1 + e^{2t}}}, \quad a_N = \frac{\sqrt{2e^{2t} + 4e^{2t}\sin t\cos t + 1}}{\sqrt{1 + e^{2t}}}$

225. $\mathbf{v}(t) = \langle 2t, \frac{1}{t}, \cos(\pi t) \rangle$ m/sec, $\mathbf{a}(t) = \langle 2, -\frac{1}{t^2}, -\sin(\pi t) \rangle$ m/sec^2, speed $= \sqrt{4t^2 + \frac{1}{t^2} + \cos^2(\pi t)}$ m/sec; at $t = 1$, $\mathbf{r}(1) = \langle 1, 0, 0 \rangle$ m, $\mathbf{v}(1) = \langle 2, -1, 1 \rangle$ m/sec, $\mathbf{a}(1) = \langle 2, -1, 0 \rangle$ m/sec^2, and speed $= \sqrt{6}$ m/sec

227. $\mathbf{r}(t) = \mathbf{v}_0 t - \frac{g}{2}t^2\,\mathbf{j}, \quad \mathbf{r}(t) = \langle \mathbf{v}_0(\cos\theta)t, \mathbf{v}_0(\sin\theta)t, -\frac{g}{2}t^2 \rangle$

Chapter 4

Checkpoint

4.1. The domain is the shaded circle defined by the inequality $9x^2 + 9y^2 \leq 36,$ which has a circle of radius 2 as its boundary. The range is $[0, 6]$.

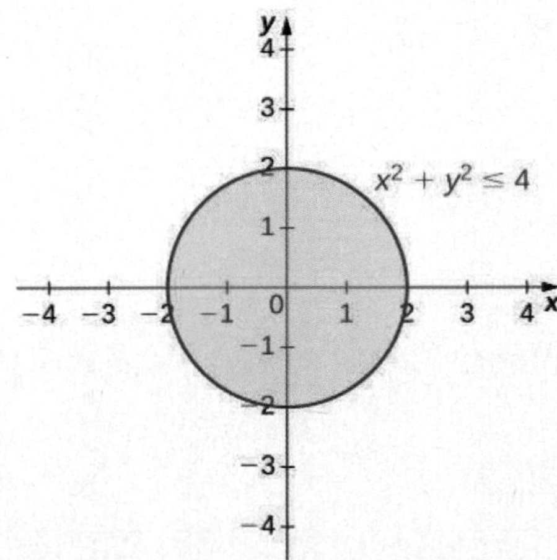

4.2. The equation of the level curve can be written as $(x - 3)^2 + (y + 1)^2 = 25,$ which is a circle with radius 5 centered at $(3, -1)$.

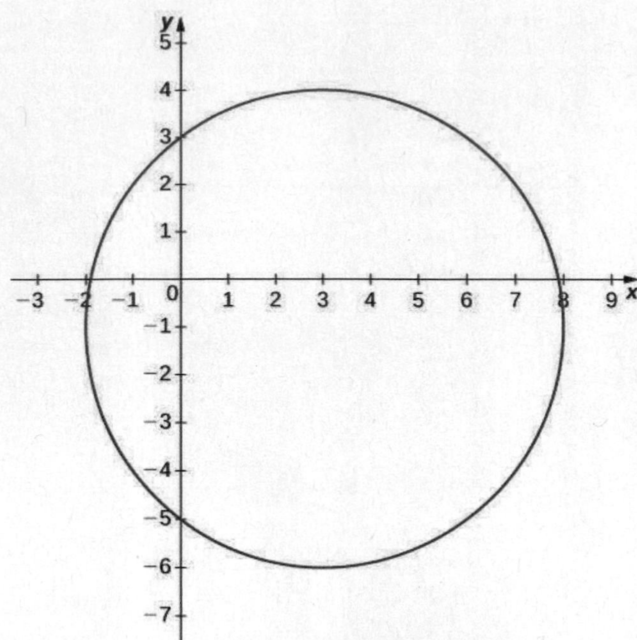

4.3. $z = 3 - (x - 1)^2$. This function describes a parabola opening downward in the plane $y = 3$.

4.4. $\text{domain}(h) = \{(x, y, t) \in \mathbb{R}^3 | y \geq 4x^2 - 4\}$

4.5. $(x - 1)^2 + (y + 2)^2 + (z - 3)^2 = 16$ describes a sphere of radius 4 centered at the point $(1, -2, 3)$.

4.6. $\lim_{(x, y) \to (5, -2)} \sqrt[3]{\frac{x^2 - y}{y^2 + x - 1}} = \frac{3}{2}$

4.7. If $y = k(x - 2) + 1$, then $\lim_{(x, y) \to (2, 1)} \frac{(x - 2)(y - 1)}{(x - 2)^2 + (y - 1)^2} = \frac{k}{1 + k^2}$. Since the answer depends on k, the limit fails to exist.

4.8. $\lim_{(x, y) \to (5, -2)} \sqrt{29 - x^2 - y^2}$

4.9.

1. The domain of f contains the ordered pair $(2, -3)$ because $f(a, b) = f(2, -3) = \sqrt{16 - 2(2)^2 - (-3)^2} = 3$
2. $\lim_{(x, y) \to (a, b)} f(x, y) = 3$
3. $\lim_{(x, y) \to (a, b)} f(x, y) = f(a, b) = 3$

4.10. The polynomials $g(x) = 2x^2$ and $h(y) = y^3$ are continuous at every real number; therefore, by the product of continuous functions theorem, $f(x, y) = 2x^2 y^3$ is continuous at every point (x, y) in the xy-plane. Furthermore, any constant function is continuous everywhere, so $g(x, y) = 3$ is continuous at every point (x, y) in the xy-plane. Therefore, $f(x, y) = 2x^2 y^3 + 3$ is continuous at every point (x, y) in the xy-plane. Last, $h(x) = x^4$ is continuous at every real number x, so by the continuity of composite functions theorem $g(x, y) = \left(2x^2 y^3 + 3\right)^4$ is continuous at every point (x, y) in the xy-plane.

4.11. $\lim_{(x, y, z) \to (4, -1, 3)} \sqrt{13 - x^2 - 2y^2 + z^2} = 2$

4.12. $\frac{\partial f}{\partial x} = 8x + 2y + 3, \quad \frac{\partial f}{\partial y} = 2x - 2y - 2$

4.13.
$$\frac{\partial f}{\partial x} = \left(3x^2 - 6xy^2\right)\sec^2\left(x^3 - 3x^2y^2 + 2y^4\right)$$
$$\frac{\partial f}{\partial y} = \left(-6x^2y + 8y^3\right)\sec^2\left(x^3 - 3x^2y^2 + 2y^4\right)$$

4.14. Using the curves corresponding to $c = -2$ and $c = -3$, we obtain $\left.\frac{\partial f}{\partial y}\right|_{(x,\, y) = (0,\, \sqrt{2})} \approx \frac{f(0, \sqrt{3}) - f(0, \sqrt{2})}{\sqrt{3} - \sqrt{2}} = \frac{-3 - (-2)}{\sqrt{3} - \sqrt{2}} \cdot \frac{\sqrt{3} + \sqrt{2}}{\sqrt{3} + \sqrt{2}} = -\sqrt{3} - \sqrt{2} \approx -3.146.$ The exact answer is $\left.\frac{\partial f}{\partial y}\right|_{(x,\, y) = (0,\, \sqrt{2})} = (-2y|_{(x,\, y) = (0,\, \sqrt{2})} = -2\sqrt{2} \approx -2.828.$

4.15. $\frac{\partial f}{\partial x} = 4x - 8xy + 5z^2 - 6, \quad \frac{\partial f}{\partial y} = -4x^2 + 4y, \quad \frac{\partial f}{\partial z} = 10xz + 3$

4.16.
$$\frac{\partial f}{\partial x} = 2xy\sec\left(x^2y\right)\tan\left(x^2y\right) - 3x^2yz^2\sec^2\left(x^3yz^2\right)$$
$$\frac{\partial f}{\partial y} = x^2\sec\left(x^2y\right)\tan\left(x^2y\right) - x^3z^2\sec^2\left(x^3yz^2\right)$$
$$\frac{\partial f}{\partial z} = -2x^3yz\sec^2\left(x^3yz^2\right)$$

4.17.
$$\frac{\partial^2 f}{\partial x^2} = -9\sin(3x - 2y) - \cos(x + 4y)$$
$$\frac{\partial^2 f}{\partial x \partial y} = 6\sin(3x - 2y) - 4\cos(x + 4y)$$
$$\frac{\partial^2 f}{\partial y \partial x} = 6\sin(3x - 2y) - 4\cos(x + 4y)$$
$$\frac{\partial^2 f}{\partial y^2} = -4\sin(3x - 2y) - 16\cos(x + 4y)$$

4.19. $z = 7x + 8y - 3$

4.20. $L(x, y) = 6 - 2x + 3y,$ so $L(4.1, 0.9) = 6 - 2(4.1) + 3(0.9) = 0.5$ $f(4.1, 0.9) = e^{5 - 2(4.1) + 3(0.9)} = e^{-0.5} \approx 0.6065.$

4.21. $f(-1, 2) = -19, \quad f_x(-1, 2) = 3, \ f_y(-1, 2) = -16, \ E(x, y) = -4(y - 2)^2.$

$$\begin{aligned}
\lim_{(x,\, y) \to (x_0,\, y_0)} \frac{E(x, y)}{\sqrt{(x - x_0)^2 + (y - y_0)^2}} &= \lim_{(x,\, y) \to (-1,\, 2)} \frac{-4(y - 2)^2}{\sqrt{(x + 1)^2 + (y - 2)^2}} \\
&\leq \lim_{(x,\, y) \to (-1,\, 2)} \frac{-4\left((x + 1)^2 + (y - 2)^2\right)}{\sqrt{(x + 1)^2 + (y - 2)^2}} \\
&= \lim_{(x,\, y) \to (2,\, -3)} -4\sqrt{(x + 1)^2 + (y - 2)^2} \\
&= 0.
\end{aligned}$$

4.22.
$$\begin{aligned}
dz &= 0.18 \\
\Delta z &= f(1.03, -1.02) - f(1, -1) = 0.180682
\end{aligned}$$

4.23.
$$\begin{aligned}
\frac{dz}{dt} &= \frac{\partial f}{\partial x}\frac{dx}{dt} + \frac{\partial f}{\partial y}\frac{dy}{dt} \\
&= (2x - 3y)(6\cos 2t) + (-3x + 4y)(-8\sin 2t) \\
&= -92\sin 2t\cos 2t - 72\left(\cos^2 2t - \sin^2 2t\right) \\
&= -46\sin 4t - 72\cos 4t.
\end{aligned}$$

4.24. $\frac{\partial z}{\partial u} = 0, \quad \frac{\partial z}{\partial v} = \frac{-21}{(3\sin 3v + \cos 3v)^2}$

4.25. $\dfrac{\partial w}{\partial u} = 0$

$\dfrac{\partial w}{\partial v} = \dfrac{15 - 33\sin 3v + 6\cos 3v}{(3 + 2\cos 3v - \sin 3v)^2}$

4.26. $\dfrac{\partial w}{\partial t} = \dfrac{\partial w}{\partial x}\dfrac{\partial x}{\partial t} + \dfrac{\partial w}{\partial y}\dfrac{\partial y}{\partial t}$

$\dfrac{\partial w}{\partial u} = \dfrac{\partial w}{\partial x}\dfrac{\partial x}{\partial u} + \dfrac{\partial w}{\partial y}\dfrac{\partial y}{\partial u}$

$\dfrac{\partial w}{\partial v} = \dfrac{\partial w}{\partial x}\dfrac{\partial x}{\partial v} + \dfrac{\partial w}{\partial y}\dfrac{\partial y}{\partial v}$

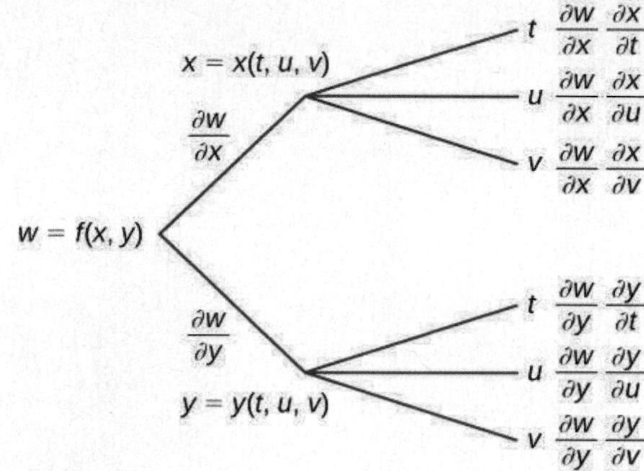

4.27. $\dfrac{dy}{dx} = \dfrac{2x + y + 7}{2y - x + 3}\Big|_{(3,\,-2)} = \dfrac{2(3) + (-2) + 7}{2(-2) - (3) + 3} = -\dfrac{11}{4}$

Equation of the tangent line: $y = -\dfrac{11}{4}x + \dfrac{25}{4}$

4.28.

$D_{\mathbf{u}} f(x, y) = \dfrac{(6xy - 4y^3 - 4)(1)}{2} + \dfrac{(3x^2 - 12xy^2 + 6y)\sqrt{3}}{2}$

$D_{\mathbf{u}} f(3, 4) = \dfrac{72 - 256 - 4}{2} + \dfrac{(27 - 576 + 24)\sqrt{3}}{2} = -94 - \dfrac{525\sqrt{3}}{2}$

4.29. $\nabla f(x, y) = \dfrac{2x^2 + 2xy + 6y^2}{(2x + y)^2}\mathbf{i} - \dfrac{x^2 + 12xy + 3y^2}{(2x + y)^2}\mathbf{j}$

4.30. The gradient of g at $(-2, 3)$ is $\nabla g(-2, 3) = \mathbf{i} + 14\mathbf{j}$. The unit vector that points in the same direction as $\nabla g(-2, 3)$ is $\dfrac{\nabla g(-2, 3)}{\|\nabla g(-2, 3)\|} = \dfrac{1}{\sqrt{197}}\mathbf{i} + \dfrac{14}{\sqrt{197}}\mathbf{j} = \dfrac{\sqrt{197}}{197}\mathbf{i} + \dfrac{14\sqrt{197}}{197}\mathbf{j}$, which gives an angle of $\theta = \arcsin\left((14\sqrt{197})/197\right) \approx 1.499$ rad. The maximum value of the directional derivative is $\|\nabla g(-2, 3)\| = \sqrt{197}$.

4.31. $\nabla f(x, y) = (2x - 2y + 3)\mathbf{i} + (-2x + 10y - 2)\mathbf{j}$

$\nabla f(1, 1) = 3\mathbf{i} + 6\mathbf{j}$

Tangent vector: $6\mathbf{i} - 3\mathbf{j}$ or $-6\mathbf{i} + 3\mathbf{j}$

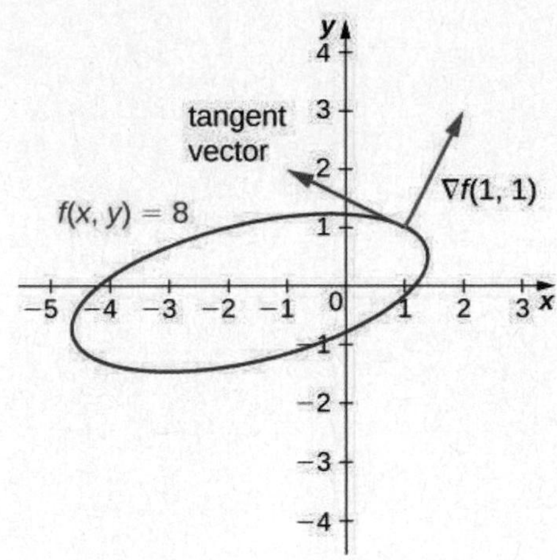

4.32.
$$\nabla f(x, y, z) = \frac{2x^2 + 2xy + 6y^2 - 8xz - 2z^2}{(2x + y - 4z)^2}\mathbf{i} - \frac{x^2 + 12xy + 3y^2 - 24yz + z^2}{(2x + y - 4z)^2}\mathbf{j} + \frac{4x^2 - 12y^2 - 4z^2 + 4xz + 2yz}{(2x + y - 4z)^2}\mathbf{k}.$$

4.33.
$$D_{\mathbf{u}} f(x, y, z) = -\frac{3}{13}(6x + y + 2z) + \frac{12}{13}(x - 4y + 4z) - \frac{4}{13}(2x + 4y - 2z)$$
$$D_{\mathbf{u}} f(0, -2, 5) = \frac{384}{13}$$

4.34. $(2, -5)$

4.35. $\left(\frac{4}{3}, \frac{1}{3}\right)$ is a saddle point, $\left(-\frac{3}{2}, -\frac{3}{8}\right)$ is a local maximum.

4.36. The absolute minimum occurs at $(1, 0)$: $f(1, 0) = -1$. The absolute maximum occurs at $(0, 3)$: $f(0, 3) = 63$.

4.37. f has a maximum value of 976 at the point $(8, 2)$.

4.38. A maximum production level of 13890 occurs with 5625 labor hours and $\$5500$ of total capital input.

4.39.
$$f\left(\frac{\sqrt{3}}{3}, \frac{\sqrt{3}}{3}, \frac{\sqrt{3}}{3}\right) = \frac{\sqrt{3}}{3} + \frac{\sqrt{3}}{3} + \frac{\sqrt{3}}{3} = \sqrt{3}$$
$$f\left(-\frac{\sqrt{3}}{3}, -\frac{\sqrt{3}}{3}, -\frac{\sqrt{3}}{3}\right) = -\frac{\sqrt{3}}{3} - \frac{\sqrt{3}}{3} - \frac{\sqrt{3}}{3} = -\sqrt{3}.$$

4.40. $f(2, 1, 2) = 9$ is a minimum.

Section Exercises

1. 17, 72

3. 20π. This is the volume when the radius is 2 and the height is 5.

5. All points in the xy-plane

7. $x < y^2$

9. All real ordered pairs in the xy-plane of the form (a, b)

11. $\{z | 0 \leq z \leq 4\}$

13. The set $\mathbb{R}$

15. $y^2 - x^2 = 4$, a hyperbola

17. $4 = x + y$, a line; $x + y = 0$, line through the origin

19. $2x - y = 0$, $2x - y = -2$, $2x - y = 2$; three lines

21. $\frac{x}{x + y} = -1$, $\frac{x}{x + y} = 0$, $\frac{x}{x + y} = 2$

23. $e^{xy} = \frac{1}{2}$, $e^{xy} = 3$

25. $xy - x = -2, \quad xy - x = 0, \; xy - x = 2$

27. $e^{-2}x^2 = y, \;\; y = x^2, \; y = e^2x^2$

29. The level curves are parabolas of the form $y = cx^2 - 2.$

31. $z = 3 + y^3,$ a curve in the zy-plane with rulings parallel to the x-axis

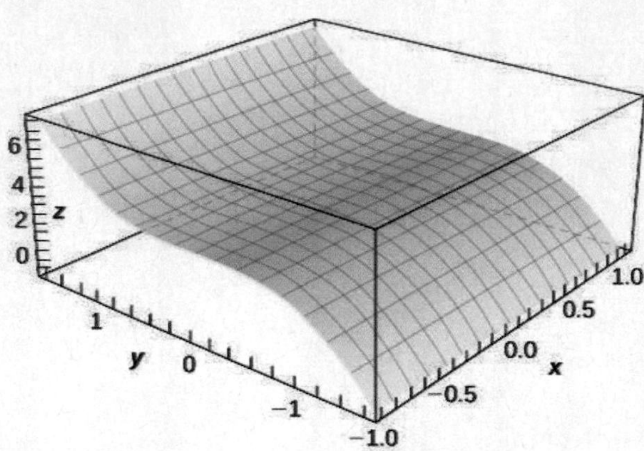

33. $\frac{x^2}{25} + \frac{y^2}{4} \le 1$

35. $\frac{x^2}{9} + \frac{y^2}{4} + \frac{z^2}{36} < 1$

37. All points in xyz-space

39.

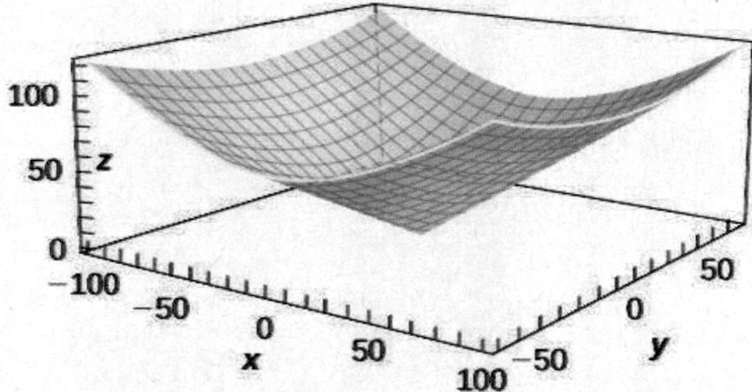

41.

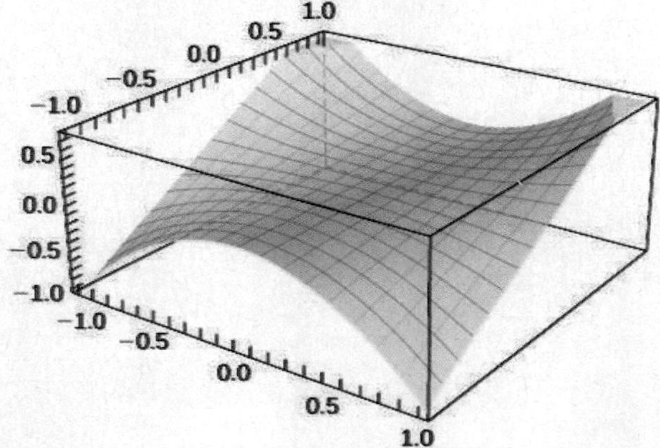

43.

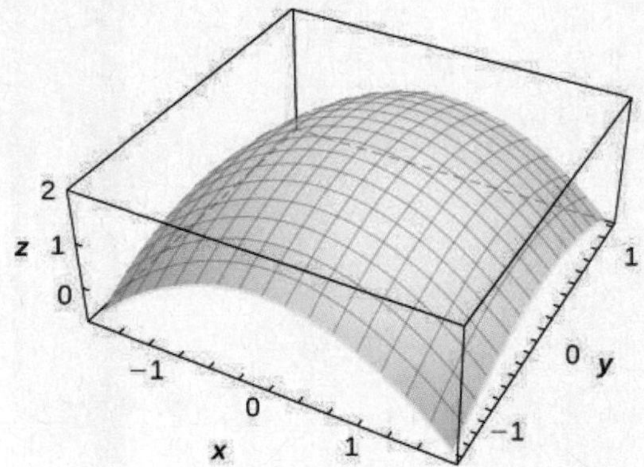

45.

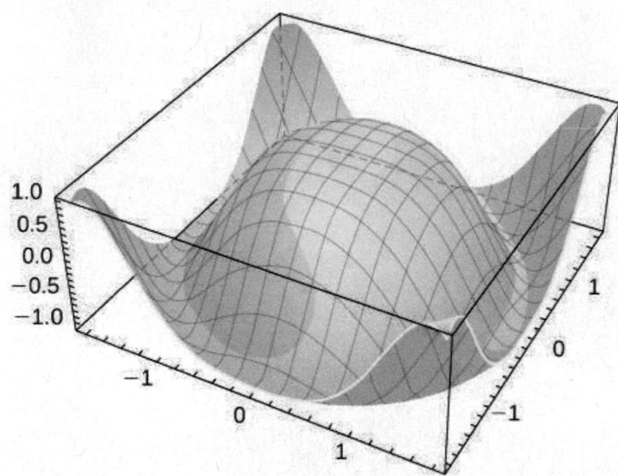

47. The contour lines are circles.

49. $x^2 + y^2 + z^2 = 9,$ a sphere of radius 3

51. $x^2 + y^2 - z^2 = 4,$ a hyperboloid of one sheet

53. $4x^2 + y^2 = 1,$

55. $1 = e^{xy}(x^2 + y^2)$

57. $T(x, y) = \dfrac{k}{x^2 + y^2}$

59. $x^2 + y^2 = \frac{k}{40},$ $x^2 + y^2 = \frac{k}{100}.$ The level curves represent circles of radii $\sqrt{10k}/20$ and $\sqrt{k}/10$

61. 2.0

63. $\frac{2}{3}$

65. 1

67. $\frac{1}{2}$

69. $-\frac{1}{2}$

71. e^{-32}

73. 11.0

75. 1.0

77. The limit does not exist because when x and y both approach zero, the function approaches $\ln 0,$ which is undefined (approaches negative infinity).

79. every open disk centered at (x_0, y_0) contains points inside R and outside R

81. 0.0

83. 0.00

85. The limit does not exist.

87. The limit does not exist. The function approaches two different values along different paths.

89. The limit does not exist because the function approaches two different values along the paths.

91. The function f is continuous in the region $y > -x$.

93. The function f is continuous at all points in the xy-plane except at $(0, 0)$.

95. The function is continuous at $(0, 0)$ since the limit of the function at $(0, 0)$ is $0,$ the same value of $f(0, 0)$.

97. The function is discontinuous at $(0, 0)$. The limit at $(0, 0)$ fails to exist and $g(0, 0)$ does not exist.

99. Since the function $\arctan x$ is continuous over $(-\infty, \infty)$, $g(x, y) = \arctan\left(\frac{xy^2}{x+y}\right)$ is continuous where $z = \frac{xy^2}{x+y}$ is continuous. The inner function z is continuous on all points of the xy-plane except where $y = -x$. Thus, $g(x, y) = \arctan\left(\frac{xy^2}{x+y}\right)$ is continuous on all points of the coordinate plane *except* at points at which $y = -x$.

101. All points $P(x, y, z)$ in space

103. The graph increases without bound as x and y both approach zero.

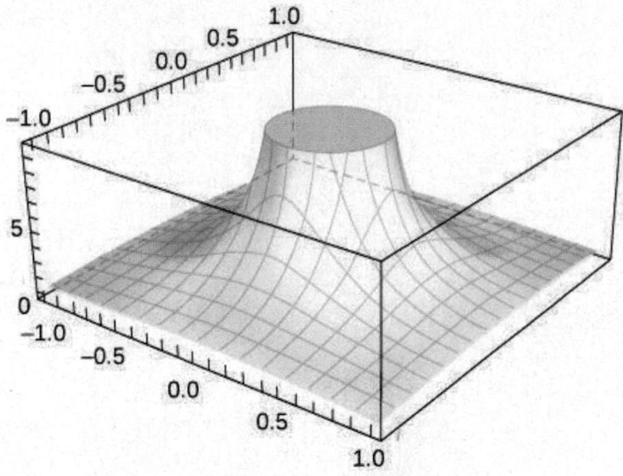

105. a.

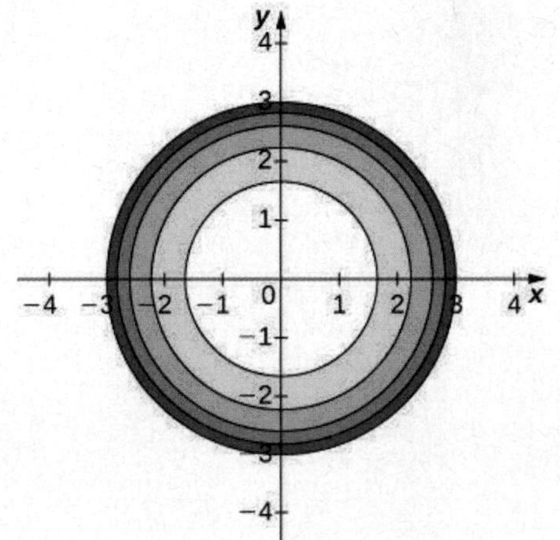

b. The level curves are circles centered at $(0, 0)$ with radius $9 - c$. c. $x^2 + y^2 = 9 - c$ d. $z = 3$ e. $\{(x, y) \in \mathbb{R}^2 | x^2 + y^2 \le 9\}$ f. $\{z | 0 \le z \le 3\}$

107. 1.0

109. $f(g(x, y))$ is continuous at all points (x, y) that are not on the line $2x - 5y = 0$.

111. 2.0

113. $\frac{\partial z}{\partial y} = -3x + 2y$

115. The sign is negative.

117. The partial derivative is zero at the origin.

119. $\frac{\partial z}{\partial y} = -3\sin(3x)\sin(3y)$

121. $\frac{\partial z}{\partial x} = \frac{6x^5}{x^6 + y^4}; \frac{\partial z}{\partial y} = \frac{4y^3}{x^6 + y^4}$

123. $\frac{\partial z}{\partial x} = ye^{xy}; \frac{\partial z}{\partial y} = xe^{xy}$

125. $\frac{\partial z}{\partial x} = 2\sec^2(2x - y), \frac{\partial z}{\partial y} = -\sec^2(2x - y)$

127. $f_x(2, -2) = \frac{1}{4} = f_y(2, -2)$

129. $\frac{\partial z}{\partial x} = -\cos(1)$

131. $f_x = 0, \quad f_y = 0, \quad f_z = 0$

133. a. $V(r, h) = \pi r^2 h$ b. $\frac{\partial V}{\partial r} = 2\pi rh$ c. $\frac{\partial V}{\partial h} = \pi r^2$

135. $f_{xy} = \frac{1}{(x - y)^2}$

137. $\frac{\partial^2 z}{\partial x^2} = 2, \frac{\partial^2 z}{\partial y^2} = 4$

139. $f_{xyy} = f_{yxy} = f_{yyx} = 0$

141.
$$\begin{aligned} \frac{d^2 z}{dx^2} &= -\tfrac{1}{2}\left(e^y - e^{-y}\right)\sin x \\ \frac{d^2 z}{dy^2} &= \tfrac{1}{2}\left(e^y - e^{-y}\right)\sin x \\ \frac{d^2 z}{dx^2} + \frac{d^2 z}{dy^2} &= 0 \end{aligned}$$

143. $f_{xyz} = 6y^2 x - 18yz^2$

145. $\left(\frac{1}{4}, \frac{1}{2}\right), (1, 1)$

147. $(0, 0), (0, 2), (\sqrt{3}, -1), \left(-\sqrt{3}, -1\right)$

149. $\frac{\partial^2 z}{\partial x^2} + \frac{\partial^2 z}{\partial y^2} = e^x \sin(y) - e^x \sin y = 0$

151. $c^2 \frac{\partial^2 z}{\partial x^2} = e^{-t}\cos\left(\frac{x}{c}\right)$

153. $\frac{\partial f}{\partial y} = -2x + 7$

155. $\frac{\partial f}{\partial x} = y\cos xy$

159. $\frac{\partial F}{\partial \theta} = 6, \frac{\partial F}{\partial x} = 4 - 3\sqrt{3}$

161. $\frac{\delta f}{\delta x}$ at $(500, 1000) = 172.36$, $\frac{\delta f}{\delta y}$ at $(500, 1000) = 36.93$

163. $\left(\frac{\sqrt{145}}{145}\right)(12\mathbf{i} - \mathbf{k})$

165. Normal vector: $\mathbf{i}+\mathbf{j}$, tangent vector: $\mathbf{i}-\mathbf{j}$

167. Normal vector: $7\mathbf{i}-17\mathbf{j}$, tangent vector: $17\mathbf{i}+7\mathbf{j}$

169. $-1.094\mathbf{i}-0.18238\mathbf{j}$

171. $-36x-6y-z=-39$

173. $z=0$

175. $5x+4y+3z-22=0$

177. $4x-5y+4z=0$

179. $2x+2y-z=0$

181. $-2(x-1)+2(y-2)-(z-1)=0$

183. $x=20t+2,\ y=-4t+1,\ z=-t+18$

185. $x=0,\ y=0,\ z=t$

187. $x-1=2t;\ y-2=-2t;\ z-1=t$

189. The differential of the function $z(x, y)=dz=f_x dx+f_y dy$

191. Using the definition of differentiability, we have $e^{xy}x \approx x+y$.

193. $\Delta z=2x\Delta x+3\Delta y+(\Delta x)^2$. $(\Delta x)^2 \to 0$ for small Δx and z satisfies the definition of differentiability.

195. $\Delta z \approx 1.185422$ and $dz \approx 1.108$. They are relatively close.

197. $16\ \text{cm}^3$

199. $\Delta z=$ exact change $=0.6449$, approximate change is $dz=0.65$. The two values are close.

201. 13% or 0.13

203. 0.025

205. 0.3%

207. $2x+\frac{1}{4}y-1$

209. $\frac{1}{2}x+y+\frac{1}{4}\pi-\frac{1}{2}$

211. $\frac{3}{7}x+\frac{2}{7}y+\frac{6}{7}z$

213. $z=0$

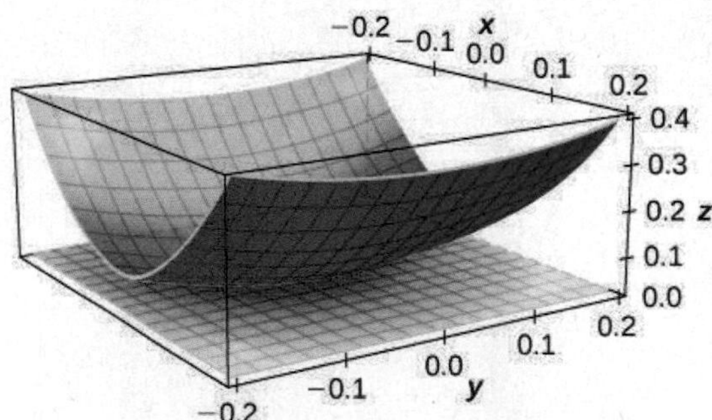

215. $\frac{dw}{dt}=y\cos z+x\cos z(2t)-\frac{xy\sin z}{\sqrt{1-t^2}}$

217. $\frac{\partial w}{\partial s}=-30x+4y,\quad \frac{\partial w}{\partial t}=10x-16y$

219. $\frac{\partial f}{\partial r}=r\sin(2\theta)$

221. $\frac{df}{dt}=2t+4t^3$

223. $\frac{df}{dt}=-1$

225. $\frac{df}{dt} = 1$

227. $\frac{dw}{dt} = 2e^{2t}$ in both cases

229. $2\sqrt{2}t + \sqrt{2}\pi = \frac{du}{dt}$

231. $\frac{dy}{dx} = -\frac{3x^2 + y^2}{2xy}$

233. $\frac{dy}{dx} = \frac{y - x}{-x + 2y^3}$

235. $\frac{dy}{dx} = -\sqrt[3]{\frac{y}{x}}$

237. $\frac{dy}{dx} = -\frac{ye^{xy}}{xe^{xy} + e^y(1 + y)}$

239. $\frac{dz}{dt} = 42t^{13}$

241. $\frac{dz}{dt} = -\frac{10}{3}t^{7/3} \times e^{1 - t^{10/3}}$

243. $\frac{\partial z}{\partial u} = \frac{-2 \sin u}{3 \sin v}$ and $\frac{\partial z}{\partial v} = \frac{-2 \cos u \cos v}{3 \sin^2 v}$

245. $\frac{\partial z}{\partial r} = \sqrt{3}e^{\sqrt{3}}, \quad \frac{\partial z}{\partial \theta} = \left(2 - 4\sqrt{3}\right)e^{\sqrt{3}}$

247. $\frac{\partial w}{\partial t} = \cos(xyz) \times yz \times (-3) - \cos(xyz)xze^{1 - t} + \cos(xyz)xy \times 4$

249. $f(tx,\, ty) = \sqrt{t^2 x^2 + t^2 y^2} = t^1 f(x,\, y), \quad \frac{\partial f}{\partial y} = x\frac{1}{2}\left(x^2 + y^2\right)^{-1/2} \times 2x + y\frac{1}{2}\left(x^2 + y^2\right)^{-1/2} \times 2y = 1f(x,\, y)$

251. $\frac{34\pi}{3}$

253. $\frac{dV}{dt} = \frac{1066\pi}{3}\text{cm}^3/\text{min}$

255. $\frac{dA}{dt} = 12\ \text{in.}^2/\text{min}$

257. 2°C/sec

259. $$\begin{aligned}\frac{\partial u}{\partial r} &= \frac{\partial u}{\partial x}\left(\frac{\partial x}{\partial w}\frac{\partial w}{\partial r} + \frac{\partial x}{\partial t}\frac{\partial t}{\partial r}\right) + \frac{\partial u}{\partial y}\left(\frac{\partial y}{\partial w}\frac{\partial w}{\partial r} + \frac{\partial y}{\partial t}\frac{\partial t}{\partial r}\right)\\ &+ \frac{\partial u}{\partial z}\left(\frac{\partial z}{\partial w}\frac{\partial w}{\partial r} + \frac{\partial z}{\partial t}\frac{\partial t}{\partial r}\right)\end{aligned}$$

261. $-3\sqrt{3}$

263. -1

265. $\frac{2}{\sqrt{6}}$

267. $\sqrt{3}$

269. -1.0

271. $\frac{22}{25}$

273. $\frac{2}{3}$

275. $\frac{-\sqrt{2}(x + y)}{2(x + 2y)^2}$

277. $\frac{e^x\left(y + \sqrt{3}\right)}{2}$

279. $\frac{1+2\sqrt{3}}{2(x+2y)}$

281. $\langle 5, 4, 3 \rangle$

283. -320

285. $\frac{3}{\sqrt{11}}$

287. $\frac{31}{255}$

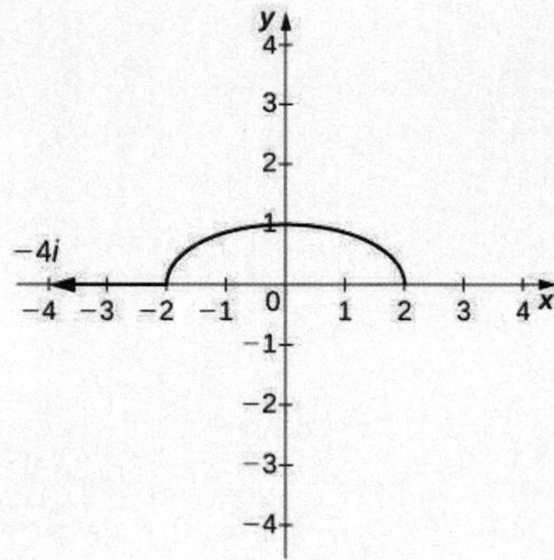

289.

291. $\frac{4}{3}\mathbf{i} - 3\mathbf{j}$

293. $\sqrt{2}\mathbf{i} + \sqrt{2}\mathbf{j} + \sqrt{2}\mathbf{k}$

295. $1.6(10^{19})$

297. $\frac{5\sqrt{2}}{99}$

299. $\sqrt{5},\ \langle 1, 2 \rangle$

301. $\sqrt{\frac{13}{2}},\ \langle -3, -2 \rangle$

303. a. $x+y+z=3$, b. $x-1=y-1=z-1$

305. a. $x+y-z=1$, b. $x-1=y=-z$

307. a. $\frac{32}{\sqrt{3}}$, b. $\langle 38, 6, 12 \rangle$, c. $2\sqrt{406}$

309. $\langle u, v \rangle = \langle \pi\cos(\pi x)\sin(2\pi y), 2\pi\sin(\pi x)\cos(2\pi y) \rangle$

311. $\left(\frac{2}{3}, 4\right)$

313. $(0, 0)$ $\left(\frac{1}{15}, \frac{1}{15}\right)$

315. Maximum at $(4, -1, 8)$

317. Relative minimum at $(0, 0, 1)$

319. The second derivative test fails. Since $x^2y^2 > 0$ for all *x* and *y* different from zero, and $x^2y^2 = 0$ when either *x* or *y* equals zero (or both), then the absolute minimum occurs at $(0, 0)$.

321. $f\left(-2, -\frac{3}{2}\right) = -6$ is a saddle point.

323. $f(0, 0) = 0$; $(0, 0, 0)$ is a saddle point.

325. $f(0, 0) = 9$ is a local maximum.

327. Relative minimum located at $(2, 6)$.

329. $(1, -2)$ is a saddle point.

331. $(2, 1)$ and $(-2, 1)$ are saddle points; $(0, 0)$ is a relative minimum.

333. $(-1, 0)$ is a relative maximum.

335. $(0, 0)$ is a saddle point.

337. The relative maximum is at $(40, 40)$.

339. $\left(\frac{1}{4}, \frac{1}{2}\right)$ is a saddle point and $(1, 1)$ is the relative minimum.

341. A saddle point is located at $(0, 0)$.

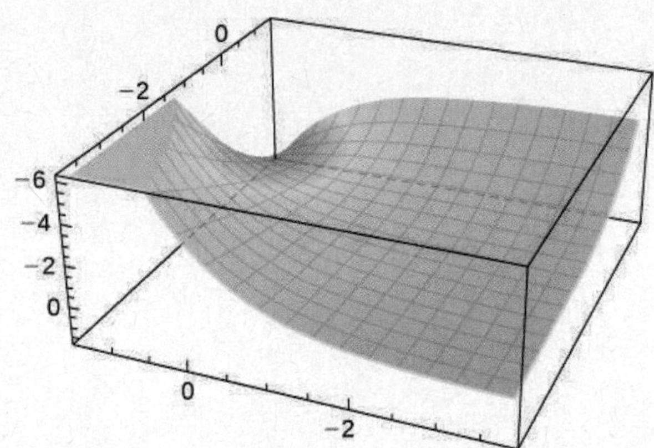

343. There is a saddle point at (π, π), local maxima at $\left(\frac{\pi}{2}, \frac{\pi}{2}\right)$ and $\left(\frac{3\pi}{2}, \frac{3\pi}{2}\right)$, and local minima at $\left(\frac{\pi}{2}, \frac{3\pi}{2}\right)$ and $\left(\frac{3\pi}{2}, \frac{\pi}{2}\right)$.

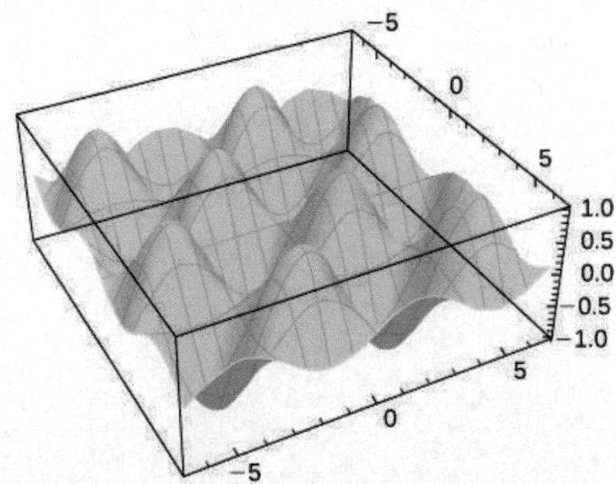

345. $(0, 1, 0)$ is the absolute minimum and $(0, -2, 9)$ is the absolute maximum.

347. There is an absolute minimum at $(0, 1, -1)$ and an absolute maximum at $(0, -1, 1)$.

349. $(\sqrt{5}, 0, 0), (-\sqrt{5}, 0, 0)$

351. 18 by 36 by 18 in.

353. $\left(\frac{47}{24}, \frac{47}{12}, \frac{235}{24}\right)$

355. $x = 3$ and $y = 6$

357. $V = \frac{64{,}000}{\pi} \approx 20,\ 372\ \text{cm}^3$

359. maximum: $2\frac{\sqrt{3}}{3}$, minimum: $\frac{-2\sqrt{3}}{3}$

361. maximum: $\left(\frac{\sqrt{2}}{2}, 0, \sqrt{2}\right)$, minimum: $\left(\frac{-\sqrt{2}}{2}, 0, -\sqrt{2}\right)$

363. maximum: $\frac{3}{2}$, minimum $= 1$

365. maxima: $f\left(\frac{3\sqrt{2}}{2}, 2\sqrt{2}\right) = 24, \quad f\left(-\frac{3\sqrt{2}}{2}, -2\sqrt{2}\right) = 24$; minima: $f\left(-\frac{3\sqrt{2}}{2}, 2\sqrt{2}\right) = -24, \quad f\left(\frac{3\sqrt{2}}{2}, -2\sqrt{2}\right) = -24$

367. maximum: $2\sqrt{11}$ at $f\left(\frac{2}{\sqrt{11}}, \frac{6}{\sqrt{11}}, \frac{-2}{\sqrt{11}}\right)$; minimum: $-2\sqrt{11}$ at $f\left(\frac{-2}{\sqrt{11}}, \frac{-6}{\sqrt{11}}, \frac{2}{\sqrt{11}}\right)$

369. 2.0

371. $19\sqrt{2}$

373. $\left(\frac{1}{\sqrt[3]{2}}, \frac{-1}{\sqrt[3]{2}}\right)$

375. $f(1, 2) = 5$

377. $f\left(\frac{1}{3}, \frac{1}{3}, \frac{1}{3}\right) = \frac{1}{3}$

379. minimum: $f(2, 3, 4) = 29$

381. The maximum volume is 4 ft^3. The dimensions are $1 \times 2 \times 2$ ft.

383. $\left(1, \frac{1}{2}, -3\right)$

385. 1.0

387. $\sqrt{3}$

389. $\left(\frac{2}{5}, \frac{19}{5}\right)$

391. $\frac{1}{2}$

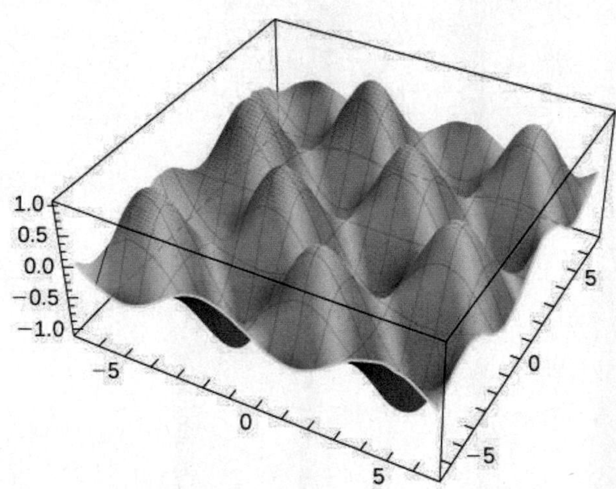

393. Roughly 3365 watches at the critical point $(80, 60)$

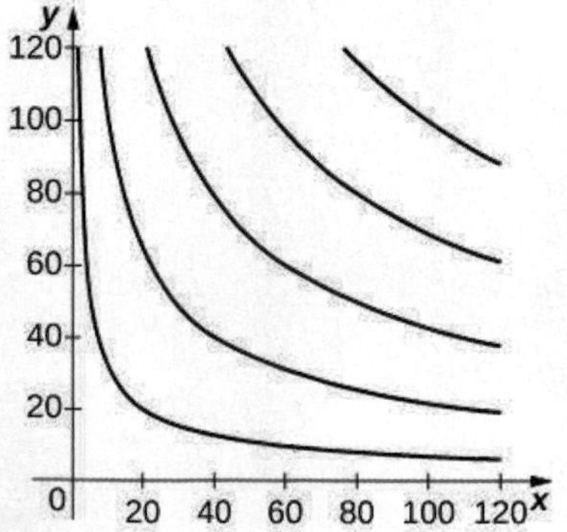

Review Exercises

395. True, by Clairaut's theorem

397. False
399. Answers may vary
401. Does not exist
403. Continuous at all points on the x, y-plane, except where $x^2 + y^2 > 4.$

405. $\frac{\partial u}{\partial x} = 4x^3 - 3y,\ \frac{\partial u}{\partial y} = -3x,\ \frac{\partial u}{\partial t} = 2,\ \frac{\partial u}{\partial t} = 3t^2,\ \frac{\partial u}{\partial t} = 8x^3 - 6y - 9xt^2$

407. $h_{xx}(x, y, z) = \frac{6xe^{2y}}{z},\quad h_{xy}(x, y, z) = \frac{6x^2 e^{2y}}{z},\quad h_{xz}(x, y, z) = -\frac{3x^2 e^{2y}}{z^2},\quad h_{yx}(x, y, z) = \frac{6x^2 e^{2y}}{z},$

$h_{yy}(x, y, z) = \frac{4x^3 e^{2y}}{z},\quad h_{yz}(x, y, z) = -\frac{2x^3 e^{2y}}{z^2},\quad h_{zx}(x, y, z) = -\frac{3x^2 e^{2y}}{z^2},\quad h_{zy}(x, y, z) = -\frac{2x^3 e^{2y}}{z^2},$

$h_{zz}(x, y, z) = \frac{2x^3 e^{2y}}{z^3}$

409. $z = \frac{1}{9}x - \frac{2}{9}y + \frac{29}{9}$

411. $dz = 4dx - dy,\quad dz(0.1, 0.01) = 0.39,\quad \Delta z = 0.432$

413. $3\sqrt{85},\ \langle 27, 6 \rangle$

415. $\nabla f(x, y) = -\frac{\sqrt{x} + 2y^2}{2x^2 y}\mathbf{i} + \left(\frac{1}{x} - \frac{1}{\sqrt{x}y^2}\right)\mathbf{j}$

417. maximum: $\frac{16}{3\sqrt{3}}$, minimum: $-\frac{16}{3\sqrt{3}}$

419. $2.3228\ \text{cm}^3$

Chapter 5

Checkpoint

5.1. $V = \sum_{i=1}^{2} \sum_{j=1}^{2} f(x_{ij}^*, y_{ij}^*)\Delta A = 0$

5.2. a. 26 b. Answers may vary.

5.3. $-\frac{1340}{3}$

5.4. $\frac{4 - \ln 5}{\ln 5}$

5.5. $\frac{\pi}{2}$

5.6. Answers to both parts a. and b. may vary.

5.7. Type I and Type II are expressed as $\{(x, y) | 0 \le x \le 2, x^2 \le y \le 2x\}$ and $\left\{(x, y) | 0 \le y \le 4, \frac{1}{2}y \le x \le \sqrt{y}\right\}$, respectively.

5.8. $\pi/4$

5.9. $\{(x, y) | 0 \le y \le 1, 1 \le x \le e^y\} \cup \{(x, y) | 1 \le y \le e, 1 \le x \le 2\} \cup \{(x, y) | e \le y \le e^2, \ln y \le x \le 2\}$

5.10. Same as in the example shown.

5.11. $\frac{216}{35}$

5.12. $\frac{e^2}{4} + 10e - \frac{49}{4}$ cubic units

5.13. $\frac{81}{4}$ square units

5.14. $\frac{3}{4}$

5.15. $\frac{\pi}{4}$

5.16. $\frac{55}{72} \approx 0.7638$

5.17. $\frac{14}{3}$

5.18. 8π

5.19. $\pi/8$

5.20. $V = \int_0^{2\pi}\int_0^{2\sqrt{2}}\left(16 - 2r^2\right)r\,dr\,d\theta = 64\pi$ cubic units

5.21. $A = 2\int_{-\pi/2}^{\pi/6}\int_{1+\sin\theta}^{3-3\sin\theta} r\,dr\,d\theta = 8\pi + 9\sqrt{3}$

5.22. $\frac{\pi}{4}$

5.23. $\iiint_B z\sin x\cos y\,dV = 8$

5.24. $\iiint_E 1dV = 8\int_{x=-3}^{x=3}\int_{y=-\sqrt{9-x^2}}^{y=\sqrt{9-x^2}}\int_{z=-\sqrt{9-x^2-y^2}}^{z=\sqrt{9-x^2-y^2}} 1dz\,dy\,dx = 36\pi.$

5.25. (i) $\int_{z=0}^{z=4}\int_{x=0}^{x=\sqrt{4-z}}\int_{y=x^2}^{y=4-z} f(x, y, z)dy\,dx\,dz,$ (ii) $\int_{y=0}^{y=4}\int_{z=0}^{z=4-y}\int_{x=0}^{x=\sqrt{y}} f(x, y, z)dx\,dz\,dy,$ (iii) $\int_{y=0}^{y=4}\int_{x=0}^{x=\sqrt{y}}\int_{z=0}^{z=4-y} f(x, y, z)dz\,dx\,dy,$ (iv) $\int_{x=0}^{x=2}\int_{y=x^2}^{y=4}\int_{z=0}^{z=4-y} f(x, y, z)dz\,dy\,dx,$ (v) $\int_{x=0}^{x=2}\int_{z=0}^{z=4-x^2}\int_{y=x^2}^{y=4-z} f(x, y, z)dy\,dz\,dx$

5.26. $f_{\text{ave}} = 8$

5.27. 8

5.28. $\iiint_E f(r, \theta, z)r\,dz\,dr\,d\theta = \int_{\theta=0}^{\theta=\pi}\int_{r=0}^{r=2\sin\theta}\int_{z=0}^{z=4-r\sin\theta} f(r, \theta, z)r\,dz\,dr\,d\theta.$

5.29. $E = \left\{(r, \theta, z)|0 \le \theta \le 2\pi,\ 0 \le z \le 1,\ z \le r \le 2 - z^2\right\}$ and $V = \int_{r=0}^{r=1}\int_{z=r}^{z=2-r^2}\int_{\theta=0}^{\theta=2\pi} r\,d\theta\,dz\,dr.$

5.30. $E_2 = \left\{(r, \theta, z)|0 \le \theta \le 2\pi,\ 0 \le r \le 1,\ r \le z \le \sqrt{4-r^2}\right\}$ and $V = \int_{r=0}^{r=1}\int_{z=r}^{z=\sqrt{4-r^2}}\int_{\theta=0}^{\theta=2\pi} r\,d\theta\,dz\,dr.$

5.31. $V(E) = \int_{\theta=0}^{\theta=2\pi}\int_{\phi=0}^{\varphi=\pi/3}\int_{\rho=0}^{\rho=2} \rho^2\sin\varphi\,d\rho\,d\varphi\,d\theta$

5.32. Rectangular: $\int_{x=-2}^{x=2}\int_{y=-\sqrt{4-x^2}}^{y=\sqrt{4-x^2}}\int_{z=-\sqrt{4-x^2-y^2}}^{z=\sqrt{4-x^2-y^2}} dz\,dy\,dx - \int_{x=-1}^{x=1}\int_{y=-\sqrt{1-x^2}}^{y=\sqrt{1-x^2}}\int_{z=-\sqrt{4-x^2-y^2}}^{z=\sqrt{4-x^2-y^2}} dz\,dy\,dx.$

Cylindrical: $\int_{\theta=0}^{\theta=2\pi}\int_{r=1}^{r=2}\int_{z=-\sqrt{4-r^2}}^{z=\sqrt{4-r^2}} r\,dz\,dr\,d\theta.$

Spherical: $\int_{\varphi=\pi/6}^{\varphi=5\pi/6}\int_{\theta=0}^{\theta=2\pi}\int_{\rho=\csc\varphi}^{\rho=2} \rho^2\sin\varphi\,d\rho\,d\theta\,d\varphi.$

5.33. $\frac{9\pi}{8}$ kg

5.34. $M_x = \frac{81\pi}{64}$ and $M_y = \frac{81\pi}{64}$

5.35. $\bar{x} = \frac{M_y}{m} = \frac{81\pi/64}{9\pi/8} = \frac{9}{8}$ and $\bar{y} = \frac{M_x}{m} = \frac{81\pi/64}{9\pi/8} = \frac{9}{8}.$

5.36. $\bar{x} = \frac{M_y}{m} = \frac{1/20}{1/12} = \frac{3}{5}$ and $\bar{y} = \frac{M_x}{m} = \frac{1/24}{1/12} = \frac{1}{2}$

5.37. $x_c = \frac{M_y}{m} = \frac{1/15}{1/6} = \frac{2}{5}$ and $y_c = \frac{M_x}{m} = \frac{1/12}{1/6} = \frac{1}{2}$

5.38. $I_x = \int_{x=0}^{x=2}\int_{y=0}^{y=x} y^2\sqrt{xy}\,dy\,dx = \frac{64}{35}$ and $I_y = \int_{x=0}^{x=2}\int_{y=0}^{y=x} x^2\sqrt{xy}\,dy\,dx = \frac{64}{35}.$ Also, $I_0 = \int_{x=0}^{x=2}\int_{y=0}^{y=x} \left(x^2 + y^2\right)\sqrt{xy}\,dy\,dx = \frac{128}{21}.$

5.39. $R_x = \frac{6\sqrt{35}}{35}$, $R_y = \frac{6\sqrt{15}}{15}$, and $R_0 = \frac{4\sqrt{42}}{7}.$

5.40. $\frac{54}{35} = 1.543$

5.41. $\left(\frac{3}{2}, \frac{9}{8}, \frac{1}{2}\right)$

5.42. The moments of inertia of the tetrahedron Q about the yz-plane, the xz-plane, and the xy-plane are $99/35$, $36/7$, and $243/35$, respectively.

5.43. $T^{-1}(x, y) = (u, v)$ where $u = \frac{3x - y}{3}$ and $v = \frac{y}{3}$

5.44. $J(u, v) = \frac{\partial(x, y)}{\partial(u, v)} = \begin{vmatrix} \frac{\partial x}{\partial u} & \frac{\partial x}{\partial v} \\ \frac{\partial y}{\partial u} & \frac{\partial y}{\partial v} \end{vmatrix} = \begin{vmatrix} 1 & 1 \\ 0 & 2 \end{vmatrix} = 2$

5.45. $\int_0^{\pi/2}\int_0^1 r^3\,dr\,d\theta$

5.46. $x = \frac{1}{2}(v + u)$ and $y = \frac{1}{2}(v - u)$ and $\int_{-4}^{4}\int_{-2}^{2} \frac{4}{u^2}\left(\frac{1}{2}\right)du\,dv.$

5.47. $\frac{1}{2}(\sin 2 - 2)$

5.48. $\int_0^3\int_0^2\int_1^2 \left(\frac{v}{3} + \frac{vw}{3u}\right)du\,dv\,dw = 2 + \ln 8$

Section Exercises

1. 27.

3. 0.

5. 21.3.

7. a. 28 ft^3 b. 1.75 ft.

9. a. 0.112 b. $f_{\text{ave}} \simeq 0.175$; here $f(0.4, 0.2) \simeq 0.1$, $f(0.2, 0.6) \simeq -0.2$, $f(0.8, 0.2) \simeq 0.6$, and $f(0.8, 0.6) \simeq 0.2.$

11. $2\pi.$

13. 40.

15. $\frac{81}{2} + 39\sqrt[3]{2}.$

17. $e - 1.$

19. $15 - \frac{10\sqrt{2}}{9}.$

21. 0.

23. $(e-1)(1+\sin 1-\cos 1)$.

25. $\frac{3}{4}\ln\left(\frac{5}{3}\right)+2\ln^2 2-\ln 2$.

27. $\frac{1}{8}\left[(2\sqrt{3}-3)\pi+6\ln 2\right]$.

29. $\frac{1}{4}e^4\left(e^4-1\right)$.

31. $4(e-1)(2-\sqrt{e})$.

33. $-\frac{\pi}{4}+\ln\left(\frac{5}{4}\right)-\frac{1}{2}\ln 2+\arctan 2$.

35. $\frac{1}{2}$.

37. $\frac{1}{2}(2\cosh 1+\cosh 2-3)$.

49. a. $f(x,\, y)=\frac{1}{2}xy\left(x^2+y^2\right)$ b. $V=\int_0^1\int_0^1 f(x,\, y)dx\,dy=\frac{1}{8}$ c. $f_{\text{ave}}=\frac{1}{8}$;

d.

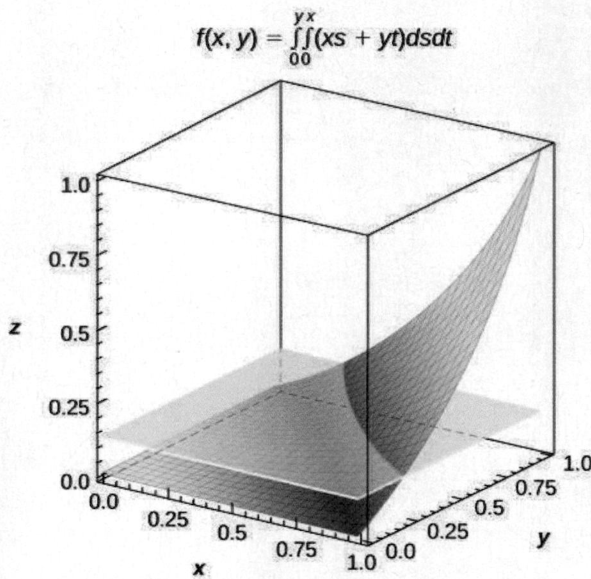

53. a. For $m=n=2$, $I=4e^{-0.5}\approx 2.43$ b. $f_{\text{ave}}=e^{-0.5}\simeq 0.61$;

c.

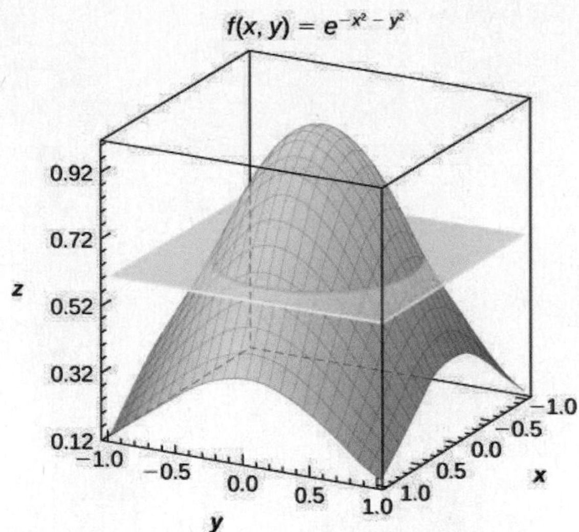

55. a. $\frac{2}{n+1} + \frac{1}{4}$ b. $\frac{1}{4}$

59. 56.5° F; here $f(x_1^*, y_1^*) = 71,\quad f(x_2^*, y_1^*) = 72,\quad f(x_2^*, y_1^*) = 40,\quad f(x_2^*, y_2^*) = 43,$ where x_i^* and y_j^* are the midpoints of the subintervals of the partitions of $[a, b]$ and $[c, d],$ respectively.

61. $\frac{27}{20}$

63. Type I but not Type II

65. $\frac{\pi}{2}$

67. $\frac{1}{6}(8 + 3\pi)$

69. $\frac{1000}{3}$

71. Type I and Type II

73. The region D is not of Type I: it does not lie between two vertical lines and the graphs of two continuous functions $g_1(x)$ and $g_2(x).$ The region D is not of Type II: it does not lie between two horizontal lines and the graphs of two continuous functions $h_1(y)$ and $h_2(y).$

75. $\frac{\pi}{2}$

77. 0

79. $\frac{2}{3}$

81. $\frac{41}{20}$

83. -63

85. π

87. a. Answers may vary; b. $\frac{2}{3}$

89. a. Answers may vary; b. $\frac{8}{12}$

91. $\frac{8\pi}{3}$

93. $e - \frac{3}{2}$

95. $\frac{2}{3}$

97. $\int_0^1 \int_{x-1}^{1-x} x\,dy\,dx = \int_{-1}^0 \int_0^{y+1} x\,dx\,dy + \int_0^1 \int_0^{1-y} x\,dxdy = \frac{1}{3}$

99. $\int_{-1/2}^{1/2} \int_{-\sqrt{y^2+1}}^{\sqrt{y^2+1}} y\,dx\,dy = \int_1^2 \int_{-\sqrt{x^2-1}}^{\sqrt{x^2-1}} y\,dy\,dx = 0$

101. $\iint_D (x^2 - y^2) dA = \int_{-1}^1 \int_{y^4-1}^{1-y^4} (x^2 - y^2) dx\,dy = \frac{464}{4095}$

103. $\frac{4}{5}$

105. $\frac{5\pi}{32}$

109. 1

111. 2

113. a. $\frac{1}{3}$; b. $\frac{1}{6}$; c. $\frac{1}{6}$

115. a. $\frac{4}{3}$; b. 2π; c. $\frac{6\pi - 4}{3}$

117. 0 and 0.865474; $A(D) = 0.621135$

119. $P[X + Y \le 6] = 1 + \frac{3}{2e^2} - \frac{5}{e^{6/5}} \approx 0.45$; there is a 45% chance that a customer will spend 6 minutes in the drive-thru line.

123. $D = \left\{(r, \theta) | 4 \le r \le 5, \frac{\pi}{2} \le \theta \le \pi\right\}$

125. $D = \{(r, \theta) | 0 \le r \le \sqrt{2}, 0 \le \theta \le \pi\}$

127. $D = \{(r, \theta) | 0 \le r \le 4 \sin \theta, 0 \le \theta \le \pi\}$

129. $D = \left\{(r, \theta) | 3 \le r \le 5, \frac{\pi}{4} \le \theta \le \frac{\pi}{2}\right\}$

131. $D = \left\{(r, \theta) | 3 \le r \le 5, \frac{3\pi}{4} \le \theta \le \frac{5\pi}{4}\right\}$

133. $D = \left\{(r, \theta) | 0 \le r \le \tan \theta \sec \theta, 0 \le \theta \le \frac{\pi}{4}\right\}$

135. 0

137. $\frac{63\pi}{16}$

139. $\frac{3367\pi}{18}$

141. $\frac{35\pi^2}{576}$

143. $\frac{7}{576}\pi^2 \left(21 - e + e^4\right)$

145. $\frac{5}{4}\ln\left(3 + 2\sqrt{2}\right)$

147. $\frac{1}{6}(2 - \sqrt{2})$

149. $\int_0^\pi \int_0^2 r^5\,dr\,d\theta = \frac{32\pi}{3}$

151. $\int_{-\pi/2}^{\pi/2} \int_0^4 r \sin\left(r^2\right) dr\,d\theta = \pi \sin^2 8$

153. $\frac{3\pi}{4}$

155. $\frac{\pi}{2}$

157. $\frac{1}{3}\left(4\pi - 3\sqrt{3}\right)$

159. $\frac{16}{3\pi}$

161. $\frac{\pi}{18}$

163. a. $\frac{2\pi}{3}$; b. $\frac{\pi}{2}$; c. $\frac{\pi}{6}$

165. $\frac{256\pi}{3}\ \text{cm}^3$

167. $\frac{3\pi}{32}$

169. 4π

171. $\frac{\pi}{4}$

173. $\frac{1}{2}\pi e(e-1)$

175. $\sqrt{3} - \frac{\pi}{4}$

177. $\frac{133\pi^3}{864}$

181. 192

183. 0

185. $\int_1^2 \int_2^3 \int_0^1 \left(x^2 + \ln y + z\right) dz\, dx\, dy = \frac{35}{6} + 2\ln 2$

187. $\int_1^3 \int_0^4 \int_{-1}^2 \left(x^2 z + \frac{1}{y}\right) dz\, dx\, dy = 64 + 12\ln 3$

191. $\frac{77}{12}$

193. 2

195. $\frac{439}{120}$

197. 0

199. $-\frac{64}{105}$

201. $\frac{11}{26}$

203. $\frac{113}{450}$

205. $\frac{1}{160}\left(6\sqrt{3} - 41\right)$

207. $\frac{3\pi}{2}$

209. 1250

211. $\int_0^5 \int_{-3}^3 \int_0^{\sqrt{9-y^2}} z\, dz\, dy\, dx = 90$

213. $V = 5.33$

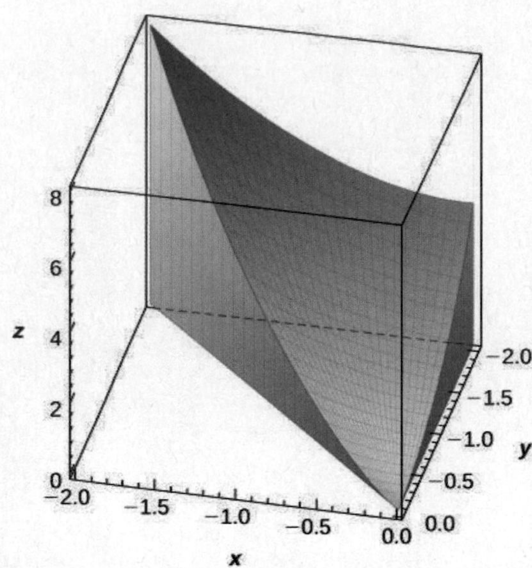

215. $\int_0^1 \int_1^3 \int_2^4 \left(y^2 z^2 + 1\right) dz\, dx\, dy;\ \int_0^1 \int_1^3 \int_2^4 \left(x^2 y^2 + 1\right) dy\, dz\, dx$

219. $V = \int_{-a}^{a} \int_{-\sqrt{a^2 - z^2}}^{\sqrt{a^2 - z^2}} \int_{\sqrt{x^2 + z^2}}^{a^2} dy\, dx\, dz$

221. $\frac{9}{2}$

223. $\frac{156}{5}$

225. a. Answers may vary; b. $\frac{128}{3}$

227. a. $\int_0^4 \int_0^{\sqrt{r^2 - x^2}} \int_0^{\sqrt{r^2 - x^2 - y^2}} dz\, dy\, dx;$ b. $\int_0^2 \int_0^{\sqrt{r^2 - y^2}} \int_0^{\sqrt{r^2 - x^2 - y^2}} dz\, dx\, dy,\ \int_0^r \int_0^{\sqrt{r^2 - z^2}} \int_0^{\sqrt{r^2 - x^2 - z^2}} dy\, dx\, dz,$

$\int_0^r \int_0^{\sqrt{r^2 - x^2}} \int_0^{\sqrt{r^2 - x^2 - z^2}} dy\, dz\, dx,\ \int_0^r \int_0^{\sqrt{r^2 - z^2}} \int_0^{\sqrt{r^2 - y^2 - z^2}} dx\, dy\, dz,\ \int_0^r \int_0^{\sqrt{r^2 - y^2}} \int_0^{\sqrt{r^2 - y^2 - z^2}} dx\, dz\, dy$

229. 3

231. $\frac{250}{3}$

233. $\frac{5}{16} \approx 0.313$

235. $\frac{35}{2}$

241. $\frac{9\pi}{8}$

243. $\frac{1}{8}$

245. $\frac{\pi e^2}{6}$

249. a. $E = \left\{(r, \theta, z) \middle| 0 \le \theta \le \pi, 0 \le r \le 4 \sin \theta, 0 \le z \le \sqrt{16 - r^2}\right\};$ b. $\int_0^{\pi} \int_0^{4 \sin \theta} \int_0^{\sqrt{16 - r^2}} f(r, \theta, z) r\, dz\, dr\, d\theta$

251. a. $E = \left\{(r, \theta, z) \middle| 0 \le \theta \le \frac{\pi}{2}, 0 \le r \le \sqrt{3}, 9 - r^2 \le z \le 10 - r(\cos\theta + \sin\theta)\right\}$; b. $\int_0^{\pi/2}\int_0^{\sqrt{3}}\int_{9-r^2}^{10-r(\cos\theta+\sin\theta)} f(r, \theta, z) r\, dz\, dr\, d\theta$

253. a. $E = \left\{(r, \theta, z) \middle| 0 \le r \le 3, 0 \le \theta \le \frac{\pi}{2}, 0 \le z \le r\cos\theta + 3\right\}$, $f(r, \theta, z) = \frac{1}{r\cos\theta + 3}$; b. $\int_0^3\int_0^{\pi/2}\int_0^{r\cos\theta+3} \frac{r}{r\cos\theta + 3} dz\, d\theta\, dr = \frac{9\pi}{4}$

255. a. $y = r\cos\theta, z = r\sin\theta, x = z$, $E = \left\{(r, \theta, z) \middle| 1 \le r \le 3, 0 \le \theta \le 2\pi, 0 \le z \le 1 - r^2\right\}$, $f(r, \theta, z) = z$; b. $\int_1^3\int_0^{2\pi}\int_0^{1-r^2} zr\, dz\, d\theta\, dr = \frac{356\pi}{3}$

257. π

259. $\frac{\pi}{3}$

261. π

263. $\frac{4\pi}{3}$

265. $V = \frac{\pi}{12} \approx 0.2618$

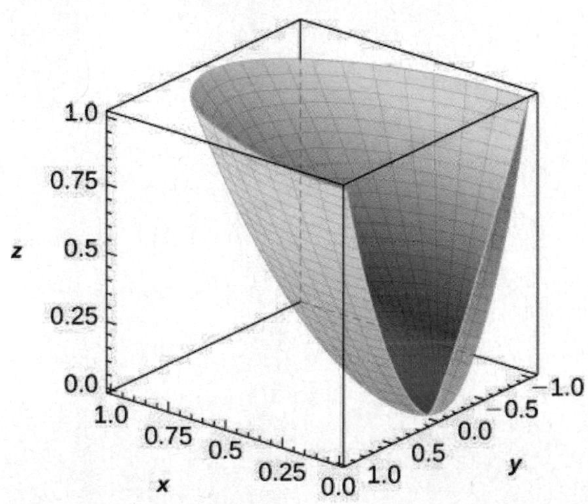

267. $\int_0^1\int_0^{\pi}\int_{r^2}^{r} zr^2\cos\theta\, dz\, d\theta\, dr$

269. $180\pi\sqrt{10}$

271. $\frac{81\pi(\pi - 2)}{16}$

277. a. $f(\rho, \theta, \varphi) = \rho\sin\varphi(\cos\theta + \sin\theta)$, $E = \left\{(\rho, \theta, \varphi) \middle| 1 \le \rho \le 2, 0 \le \theta \le \pi, 0 \le \varphi \le \frac{\pi}{2}\right\}$; b. $\int_0^{\pi}\int_0^{\pi/2}\int_1^2 \rho^3\cos\varphi\sin\varphi\, d\rho\, d\varphi\, d\theta = \frac{15\pi}{8}$

279. a. $f(\rho, \theta, \varphi) = \rho\cos\varphi$; $E = \left\{(\rho, \theta, \varphi) \middle| 0 \le \rho \le 2\cos\varphi, 0 \le \theta \le \frac{\pi}{2}, 0 \le \varphi \le \frac{\pi}{4}\right\}$; b. $\int_0^{\pi/2}\int_0^{\pi/4}\int_0^{2\cos\varphi} \rho^3\sin\varphi\cos\varphi\, d\rho\, d\varphi\, d\theta = \frac{7\pi}{24}$

281. $\frac{\pi}{4}$

283. $9\pi(\sqrt{2} - 1)$

285. $\int_0^{\pi/2} \int_0^{\pi/2} \int_0^4 \rho^6 \sin\varphi \, d\rho \, d\varphi \, d\theta$

287. $V = \frac{4\pi\sqrt{3}}{3} \approx 7.255$

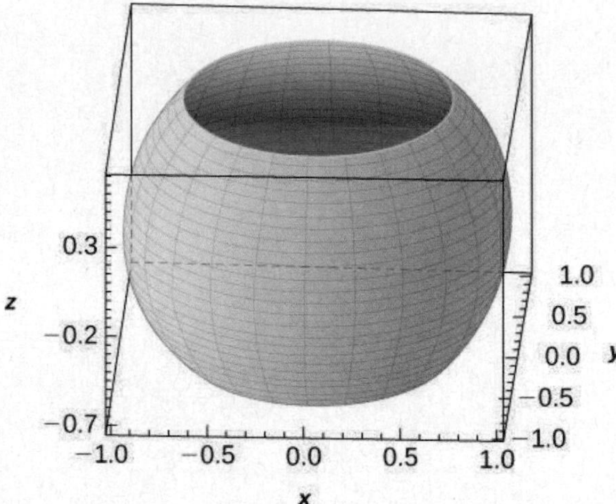

289. $\frac{343\pi}{32}$

291. $\int_0^{2\pi} \int_2^4 \int_{-\sqrt{16-r^2}}^{\sqrt{16-r^2}} r \, dz \, dr \, d\theta$; $\int_{\pi/6}^{5\pi/6} \int_0^{2\pi} \int_{2\csc\varphi}^{4} \rho^2 \sin\rho \, d\rho \, d\theta \, d\varphi$

293. $P = \frac{32P_0\pi}{3}$ watts

295. $Q = kr^4 \pi\mu C$

297. $\frac{27}{2}$

299. $24\sqrt{2}$

301. 76

303. 8π

305. $\frac{\pi}{2}$

307. 2

309. a. $M_x = \frac{81}{5}$, $M_y = \frac{162}{5}$; b. $\bar{x} = \frac{12}{5}$, $\bar{y} = \frac{6}{5}$;

c.

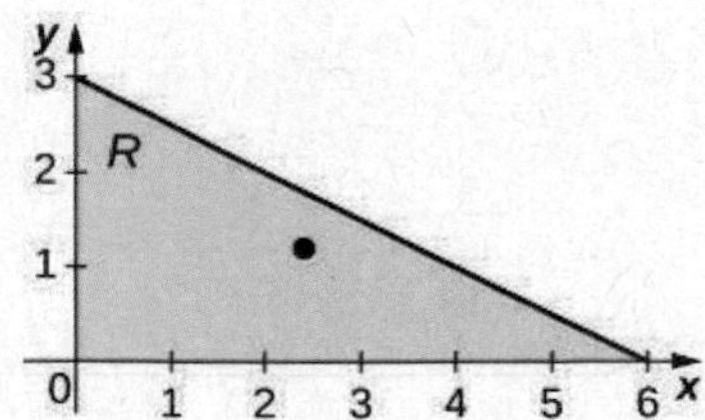

311. a. $M_x = \frac{216\sqrt{2}}{5}$, $M_y = \frac{432\sqrt{2}}{5}$; b. $\bar{x} = \frac{18}{5}$, $\bar{y} = \frac{9}{5}$;

c.

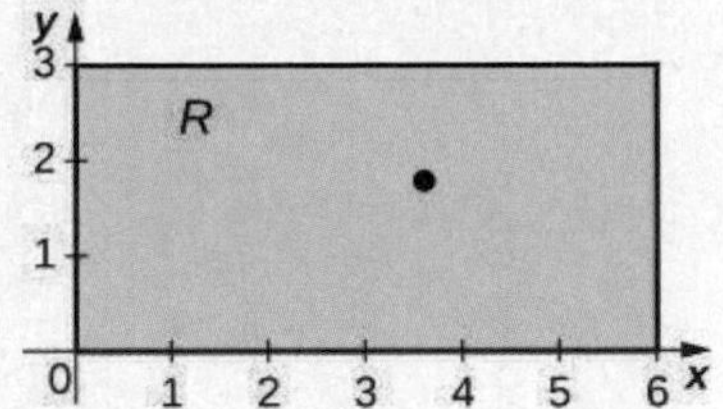

313. a. $M_x = \frac{368}{5}$, $M_y = \frac{1552}{5}$; b. $\bar{x} = \frac{92}{95}$, $\bar{y} = \frac{388}{95}$;

c.

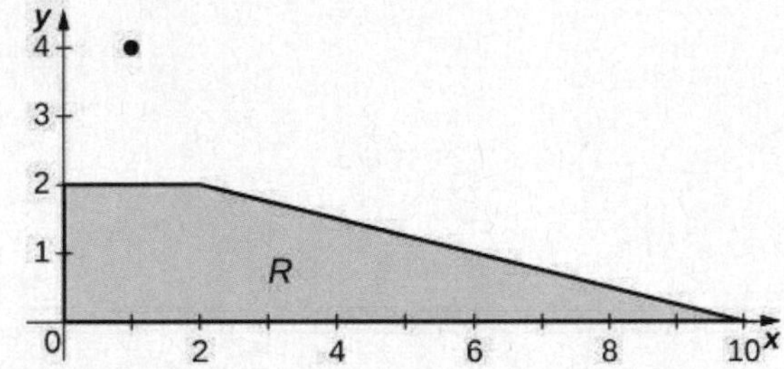

315. a. $M_x = 16\pi$, $M_y = 8\pi$; b. $\bar{x} = 1$, $\bar{y} = 2$;

c.

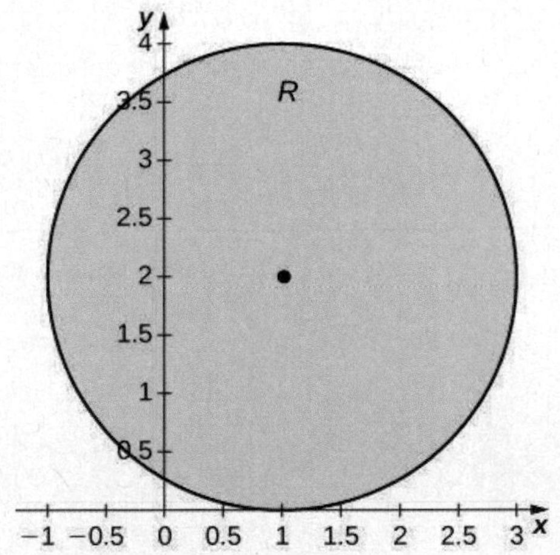

317. a. $M_x = 0$, $M_y = 0$; b. $\bar{x} = 0$, $\bar{y} = 0$;

c.

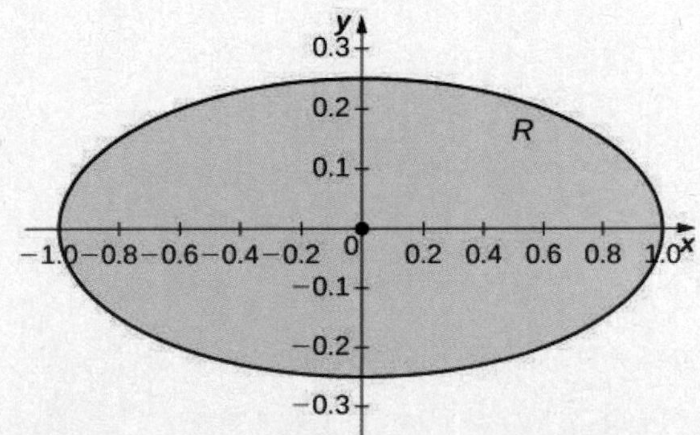

319. a. $M_x = 2$, $M_y = 0$; b. $\bar{x} = 0$, $\bar{y} = 1$;

c.

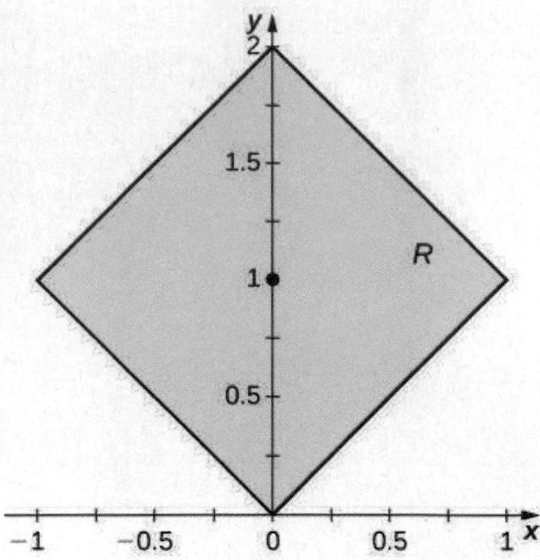

321. a. $I_x = \frac{243}{10}$, $I_y = \frac{486}{5}$, and $I_0 = \frac{243}{2}$; b. $R_x = \frac{3\sqrt{5}}{5}$, $R_y = \frac{6\sqrt{5}}{5}$, and $R_0 = 3$

323. a. $I_x = \frac{2592\sqrt{2}}{7}$, $I_y = \frac{648\sqrt{2}}{7}$, and $I_0 = \frac{3240\sqrt{2}}{7}$; b. $R_x = \frac{6\sqrt{21}}{7}$, $R_y = \frac{3\sqrt{21}}{7}$, and $R_0 = \frac{3\sqrt{105}}{7}$

325. a. $I_x = 88$, $I_y = 1560$, and $I_0 = 1648$; b. $R_x = \frac{\sqrt{418}}{19}$, $R_y = \frac{\sqrt{7410}}{19}$, and $R_0 = \frac{2\sqrt{1957}}{19}$

327. a. $I_x = \frac{128\pi}{3}$, $I_y = \frac{56\pi}{3}$, and $I_0 = \frac{184\pi}{3}$; b. $R_x = \frac{4\sqrt{3}}{3}$, $R_y = \frac{\sqrt{21}}{3}$, and $R_0 = \frac{\sqrt{69}}{3}$

329. a. $I_x = \frac{\pi}{32}$, $I_y = \frac{\pi}{8}$, and $I_0 = \frac{5\pi}{32}$; b. $R_x = \frac{1}{4}$, $R_y = \frac{1}{2}$, and $R_0 = \frac{\sqrt{5}}{4}$

331. a. $I_x = \frac{7}{3}$, $I_y = \frac{1}{3}$, and $I_0 = \frac{8}{3}$; b. $R_x = \frac{\sqrt{42}}{6}$, $R_y = \frac{\sqrt{6}}{6}$, and $R_0 = \frac{2\sqrt{3}}{3}$

333. $m = \frac{1}{3}$

337. a. $m = \frac{9\pi}{4}$; b. $M_{xy} = \frac{3\pi}{2}$, $M_{xz} = \frac{81}{8}$, $M_{yz} = \frac{81}{8}$; c. $\bar{x} = \frac{9}{2\pi}$, $\bar{y} = \frac{9}{2\pi}$, $\bar{z} = \frac{2}{3}$; d. the solid Q and its center of mass are shown in the following figure.

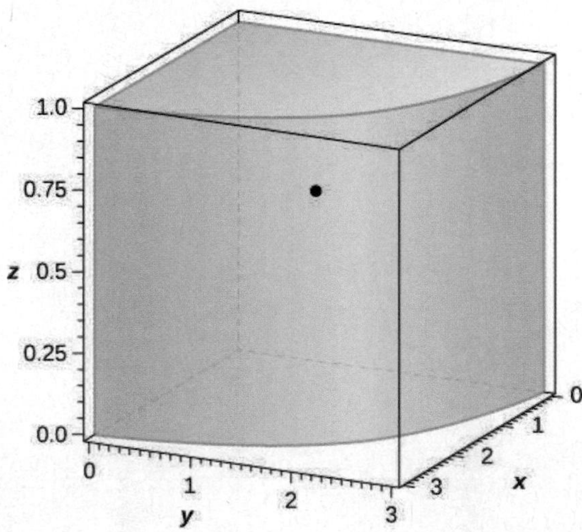

339. a. $\bar{x} = \frac{3\sqrt{2}}{2\pi}$, $\bar{y} = \frac{3(2-\sqrt{2})}{2\pi}$, $\bar{z} = 0$; b. the solid Q and its center of mass are shown in the following figure.

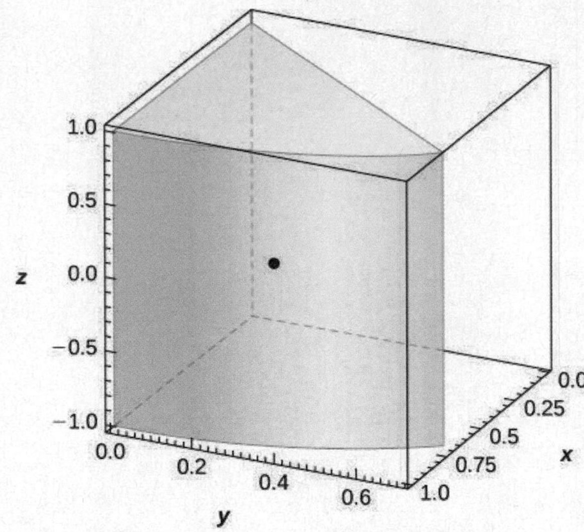

343. $n = -2$

349. a. $\rho(x, y, z) = x^2 + y^2$; b. $\frac{16\pi}{7}$

351. $M_{xy} = \pi(f(0) - f(a) + af'(a))$

355. $I_x = I_y = I_z \simeq 0.84$

357. a. $T(u, v) = (g(u, v), h(u, v))$, $x = g(u, v) = \frac{u}{2}$ and $y = h(u, v) = \frac{v}{3}$. The functions g and h are continuous and differentiable, and the partial derivatives $g_u(u, v) = \frac{1}{2}$, $g_v(u, v) = 0$, $h_u(u, v) = 0$ and $h_v(u, v) = \frac{1}{3}$ are continuous on S; b. $T(0, 0) = (0, 0)$, $T(1, 0) = \left(\frac{1}{2}, 0\right)$, $T(0, 1) = \left(0, \frac{1}{3}\right)$, and $T(1, 1) = \left(\frac{1}{2}, \frac{1}{3}\right)$; c. R is the rectangle of vertices $(0, 0)$, $\left(\frac{1}{2}, 0\right)$, $\left(\frac{1}{2}, \frac{1}{3}\right)$, and $\left(0, \frac{1}{3}\right)$ in the xy-plane; the following figure.

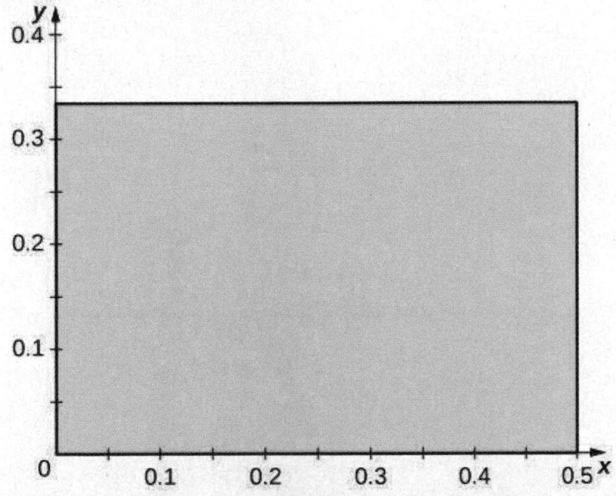

359. a. $T(u, v) = (g(u, v), h(u, v))$, $x = g(u, v) = 2u - v$, and $y = h(u, v) = u + 2v$. The functions g and h are continuous and differentiable, and the partial derivatives $g_u(u, v) = 2$, $g_v(u, v) = -1$, $h_u(u, v) = 1$, and $h_v(u, v) = 2$ are continuous on S; b. $T(0, 0) = (0, 0)$, $T(1, 0) = (2, 1)$, $T(0, 1) = (-1, 2)$, and $T(1, 1) = (1, 3)$; c. R is the parallelogram of vertices $(0, 0)$, $(2, 1)$, $(1, 3)$, and $(-1, 2)$ in the xy-plane; see the following figure.

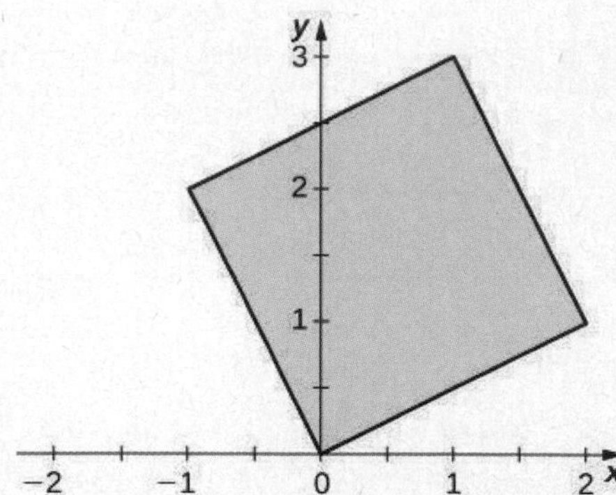

361. a. $T(u, v) = (g(u, v), h(u, v))$, $x = g(u, v) = u^3$, and $y = h(u, v) = v^3$. The functions g and h are continuous and differentiable, and the partial derivatives $g_u(u, v) = 3u^2$, $g_v(u, v) = 0$, $h_u(u, v) = 0$, and $h_v(u, v) = 3v^2$ are continuous on S; b. $T(0, 0) = (0, 0)$, $T(1, 0) = (1, 0)$, $T(0, 1) = (0, 1)$, and $T(1, 1) = (1, 1)$; c. R is the unit square in the xy-plane; see the figure in the answer to the previous exercise.

363. T is not one-to-one: two points of S have the same image. Indeed, $T(-2, 0) = T(2, 0) = (16, 4)$.

365. T is one-to-one: We argue by contradiction. $T(u_1, v_1) = T(u_2, v_2)$ implies $2u_1 - v_1 = 2u_2 - v_2$ and $u_1 = u_2$. Thus, $u_1 = u_2$ and $v_1 = v_2$.

367. T is not one-to-one: $T(1, v, w) = (-1, v, w)$

369. $u = \frac{x - 2y}{3}, v = \frac{x + y}{3}$

371. $u = e^x, v = e^{-x + y}$

373. $u = \frac{x - y + z}{2}, v = \frac{x + y - z}{2}, w = \frac{-x + y + z}{2}$

375. $S = \{(u, v) | u^2 + v^2 \le 1\}$

377. $R = \{(u, v, w) | u^2 - v^2 - w^2 \le 1, w > 0\}$

379. $\frac{3}{2}$

381. -1

383. $2uv$

385. $\frac{v}{u^2}$

387. 2

389. a. $T(u, v) = (2u + v, 3v)$; b. The area of R is

$$A(R) = \int_0^3 \int_{y/3}^{(6-y)/3} dx\,dy = \int_0^1 \int_0^{1-u} \left|\frac{\partial(x, y)}{\partial(u, v)}\right| dv\,du = \int_0^1 \int_0^{1-u} 6dv\,du = 3.$$

391. $-\frac{1}{4}$

393. $-1 + \cos 2$

395. $\frac{\pi}{15}$

397. $\frac{31}{5}$

399. $T(r, \theta, z) = (r\cos\theta, r\sin\theta, z)$; $S = [0, 3] \times \left[0, \frac{\pi}{2}\right] \times [0, 1]$ in the $r\theta z$-space

403. The area of R is $10 - 4\sqrt{6}$; the boundary curves of R are graphed in the following figure.

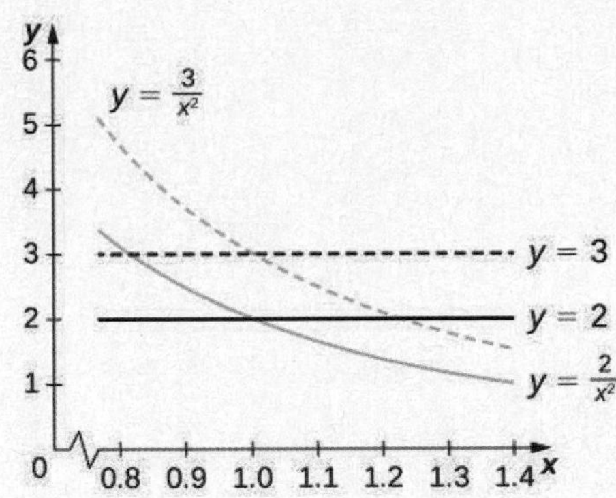

405. 8

409. a. $R = \{(x, y) | y^2 + x^2 - 2y - 4x + 1 \le 0\}$; b. R is graphed in the following figure;

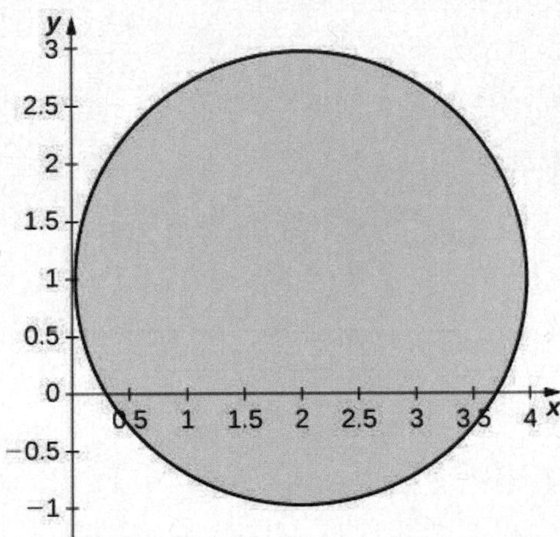

c. 3.16

411. a. $T_{0,2} \circ T_{3,0}(u, v) = (u + 3v, 2u + 7v)$; b. The image S is the quadrilateral of vertices $(0, 0)$, $(3, 7)$, $(2, 4)$, and $(4, 9)$; c. S is graphed in the following figure;

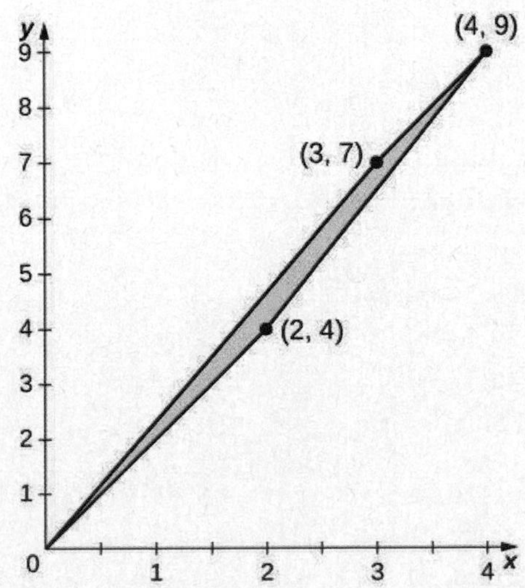

d. $\frac{3}{2}$

413. $\frac{2662}{3\pi} \simeq 282.45 \text{ in}^3$

415. $A(R) \simeq 83{,}999.2$

Review Exercises

417. True.

419. False.

421. 0

423. $\frac{1}{4}$

425. 1.475

427. $\frac{52}{3}\pi$

429. $\frac{\pi}{16}$

431. 93.291

433. $\left(\frac{8}{15}, \frac{8}{15}\right)$

435. $\left(0, 0, \frac{8}{5}\right)$

437. $1.452\pi \times 10^{15}$ ft-lb

439. $y = -1.238 \times 10^{-7}x^3 + 0.001196x^2 - 3.666x + 7208;$ average temperature approximately $2800°C$

441. $\frac{\pi}{3}$

Chapter 6

Checkpoint

6.1. $12\mathbf{i} - \mathbf{j}$

6.2.

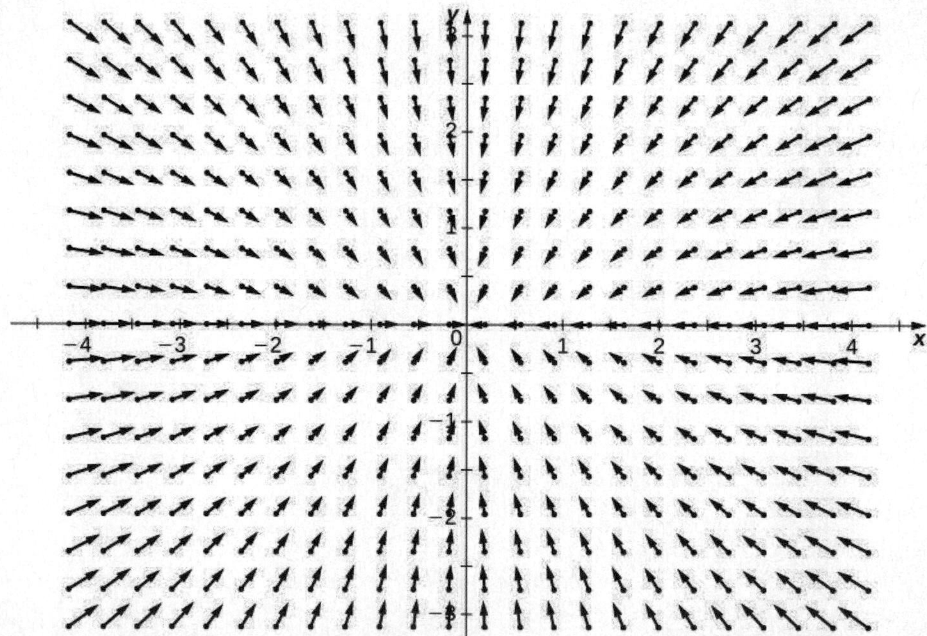

6.3. Rotational

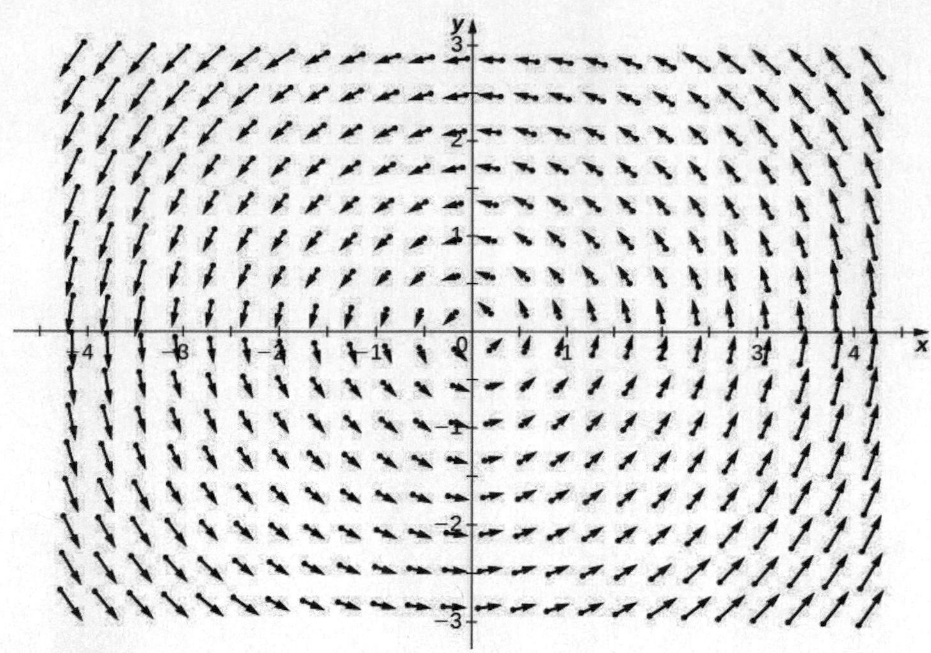

6.4. $\sqrt{65}$ m/sec

6.5. No.

6.6.

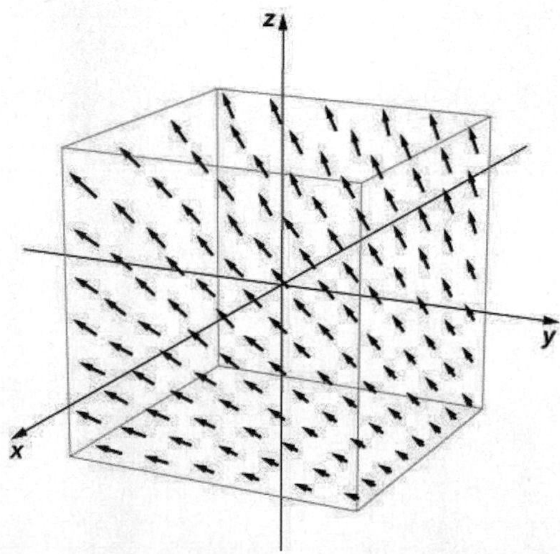

6.7. 1.49063×10^{-18}, 4.96876×10^{-19}, 9.93752×10^{-19} N

6.8.

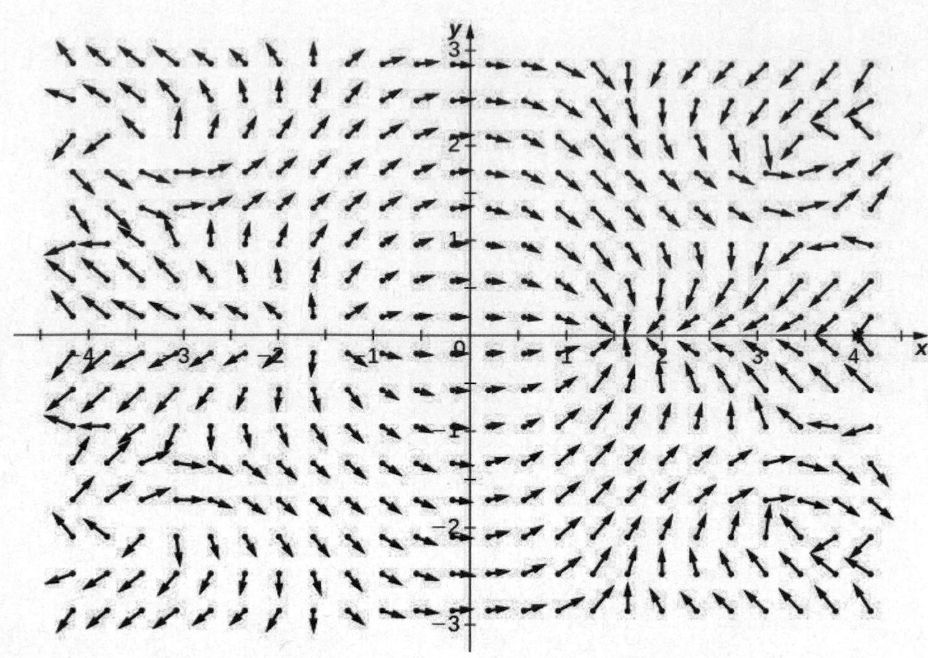

6.9. No

6.10. $\nabla f = \mathbf{v}$

6.11. $P_y = x \neq Q_x = -2xy$

6.12. No

6.13. $\sqrt{2}$

6.14. $\frac{1}{3} + \frac{\sqrt{2}}{6} + \frac{3\pi}{4}$

6.15. Both line integrals equal $-\frac{1000\sqrt{30}}{3}$.

6.16. $4\sqrt{17}$

6.17. $\int_C \mathbf{F} \cdot \mathbf{T} ds$

6.18. -26

6.19. 0

6.20. $18\sqrt{2}\pi^2$ kg

6.21. 3/2

6.22. 2π

6.23. 0

6.24. Yes

6.25. The region in the figure is connected. The region in the figure is not simply connected.

6.26. 2

6.27. If C_1 and C_2 represent the two curves, then $\int_{C_1} \mathbf{F} \bullet d\mathbf{r} \neq \int_{C_2} \mathbf{F} \bullet d\mathbf{r}$.

6.28. $f(x, y) = e^x y^3 + xy$

6.29. $f(x, y, z) = 4x^3 + \sin y \cos z + z$

6.30. $f(x, y, z) = \frac{G}{\sqrt{x^2 + y^2 + z^2}}$

6.31. It is conservative.

6.32. -10π

6.33. Negative

6.34. $\frac{45}{2}$

6.35. $\frac{4}{3}$

6.36. $\frac{3\pi}{2}$

6.37. $g(x, y) = -x \cos y$

6.38. No

6.39. 105π

6.40. $y - z^2$

6.41. Yes

6.42. All points on line $y = 1$.

6.43. $-\mathbf{i}$

6.44. $\text{curl } \mathbf{v} = \mathbf{0}$

6.45. No

6.46. Yes

6.47. Cylinder $x^2 + y^2 = 4$

6.48. Cone $x^2 + y^2 = z^2$

6.49. $\mathbf{r}(u, v) = \langle u \cos v, u \sin v, u \rangle, \quad 0 < u < \infty, 0 \leq v < \frac{\pi}{2}$

6.50. Yes

6.51. ≈ 43.02

6.52. With the standard parameterization of a cylinder, **Equation 6.201** shows that the surface area is $2\pi rh$.

6.53. $2\pi\left(\sqrt{2} + \sinh^{-1}(1)\right)$

6.54. 24

6.55. 0

6.56. $38.401\pi \approx 120.640$

6.57. $\mathbf{N}(x, y) = \left\langle \frac{-y}{\sqrt{1 + x^2 + y^2}}, \frac{-x}{\sqrt{1 + x^2 + y^2}}, \frac{1}{\sqrt{1 + x^2 + y^2}} \right\rangle$

6.58. 0

6.59. 400 kg/sec/m

6.60. $-\frac{440\pi}{3}$

6.61. Both integrals give $-\frac{136}{45}$.

6.62. $-\pi$

6.63. $\frac{3}{2}$

6.64. $\text{curl } \mathbf{E} = \langle x, y, -2z \rangle$

6.65. Both integrals equal 6π.

6.66. 30

6.67. $9 \ln(16)$

6.68. $\approx 6.777 \times 10^9$

Section Exercises

1. Vectors

3. False

5.

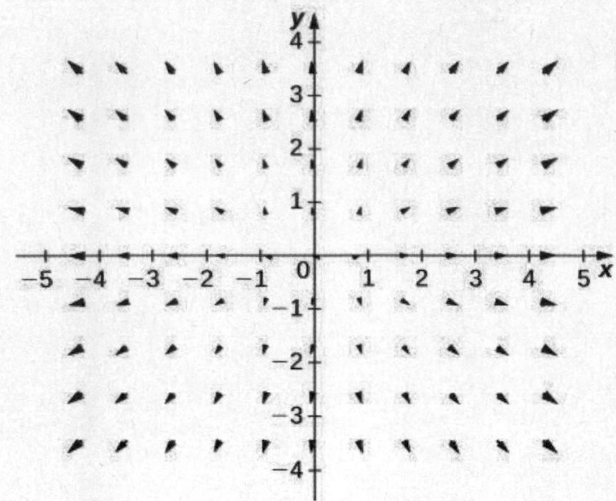
y
4
3
2
1
0
−1
−2
−3
−4
−5 −4 −3 −2 −1 1 2 3 4 5 x

7.

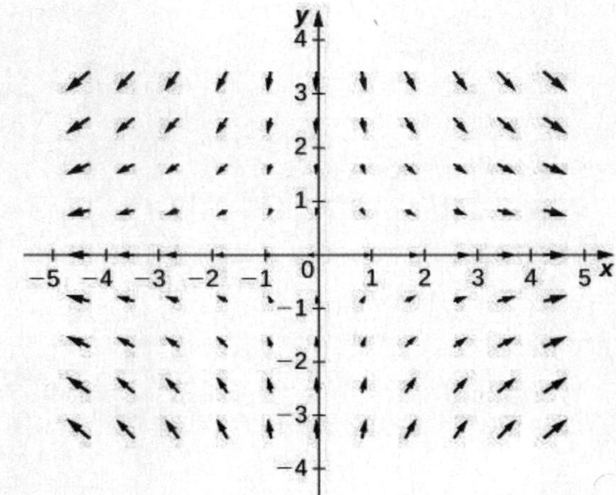
y
4
3
2
1
0
−1
−2
−3
−4
−5 −4 −3 −2 −1 1 2 3 4 5 x

9.

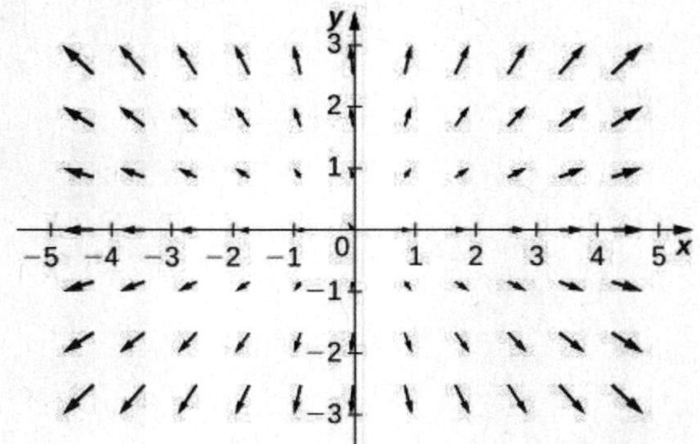
y
3
2
1
0
−1
−2
−3
−5 −4 −3 −2 −1 1 2 3 4 5 x

11.

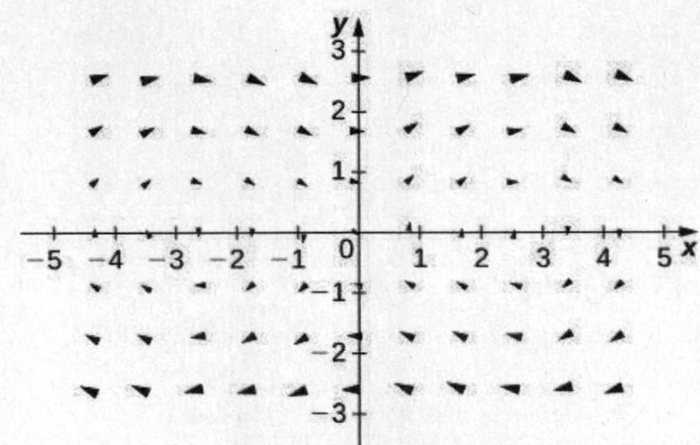

13.

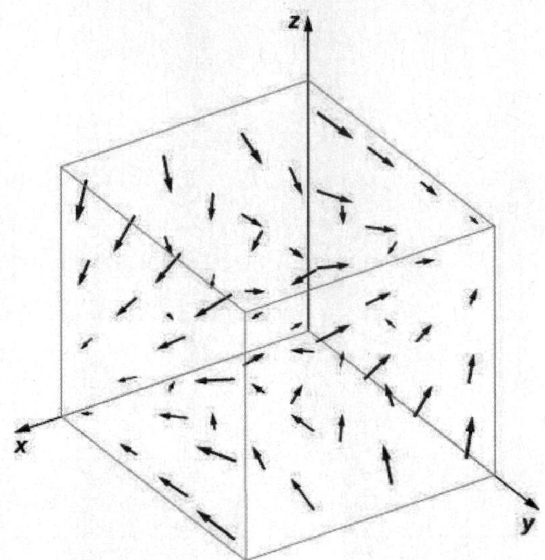

15. $\mathbf{F}(x, y) = \sin(y)\mathbf{i} + (x \cos y - \sin y)\mathbf{j}$

17. $\mathbf{F}(x, y, z) = (2xy + y)\mathbf{i} + (x^2 + x + 2yz)\mathbf{j} + y^2\mathbf{k}$

19. $\mathbf{F}(x, y) = \left(\frac{2x}{1 + x^2 + 2y^2}\right)\mathbf{i} + \left(\frac{4y}{1 + x^2 + 2y^2}\right)\mathbf{j}$

21. $\mathbf{F}(x, y) = \frac{(1 - x)\mathbf{i} - y\mathbf{j}}{\sqrt{(1 - x)^2 + y^2}}$

23. $\mathbf{F}(x, y) = \frac{(y\mathbf{i} - x\mathbf{j})}{\sqrt{x^2 + y^2}}$

25. $\mathbf{F}(x, y) = y\mathbf{i} - x\mathbf{j}$

27. $\mathbf{F}(x, y) = \frac{-10}{\left(x^2 + y^2\right)^{3/2}}(x\mathbf{i} + y\mathbf{j})$

29. $E = \frac{c}{|r|^2} r = \frac{c}{|r|} \frac{r}{|r|}$

31. $\mathbf{c}'(t) = \left(\cos t,\ -\sin t,\ e^{-t}\right) = \mathbf{F}(\mathbf{c}(t))$

33. **H**

35. d. $-\mathbf{F} + \mathbf{G}$

37. a. $\mathbf{F} + \mathbf{G}$

39. True

41. False

43. False

45. $\int_C (x-y)ds = 10$

47. $\int_C xy^4\, ds = \frac{8192}{5}$

49. $W = 8$

51. $W = \frac{3\pi}{4}$

53. $W = \pi$

55. $\int_C \mathbf{F} \cdot d\mathbf{r} = 4$

57. $\int_C yzdx + xzdy + xydz = -1$

59. $\int_C \left(y^2\right)dx + (x)dy = \frac{245}{6}$

61. $\int_C xydx + ydy = \frac{190}{3}$

63. $\int_C \frac{y}{2x^2 - y^2} ds = \sqrt{2} \ln 5$

65. $W = -66$

67. $W = -10\pi^2$

69. $W = 2$

71. a. $W = 11$; b. $W = 11$; c. Yes

73. $W = 2\pi$

75. $\int_C \mathbf{F} \cdot d\mathbf{r} = \frac{25\sqrt{5} + 1}{120}$

77. $\int_C y^2\, dx + \left(xy - x^2\right)dy = 6.15$

79. $\int_\gamma xe^y\, ds \approx 7.157$

81. $\int_\gamma \left(y^2 - xy\right)dx \approx -1.379$

83. $\int_C \mathbf{F} \cdot d\mathbf{r} \approx -1.133$

85. $\int_C \mathbf{F} \cdot d\mathbf{r} \approx 22.857$

87. $\text{flux} = -\frac{1}{3}$

89. $\text{flux} = -20$

91. $\text{flux} = 0$

93. $m = 4\pi\rho\sqrt{5}$

95. $W = 0$

97. $W = \frac{k}{2}$

99. True

101. True

103. $\int_C \mathbf{F} \cdot d\mathbf{r} = 24$

105. $\int_C \mathbf{F} \cdot d\mathbf{r} = e - \frac{3\pi}{2}$

107. Not conservative

109. Conservative, $f(x, y) = 3x^2 + 5xy + 2y^2$

111. Conservative, $f(x, y) = ye^x + x\sin(y)$

113. $\oint_C (2ydx + 2xdy) = 32$

115. $\mathbf{F}(x, y) = (10x + 3y)\mathbf{i} + (3x + 10y)\mathbf{j}$

117. **F** is not conservative.

119. **F** is conservative and a potential function is $f(x, y, z) = xye^z$.

121. **F** is conservative and a potential function is $f(x, y, z) = z$.

123. **F** is conservative and a potential function is $f(x, y, z) = x^2y + y^2z$.

125. **F** is conservative and a potential function is $f(x, y) = e^{x^2 y}$

127. $\int_C \mathbf{F} \cdot dr = e^2 + 1$

129. $\int_C \mathbf{F} \cdot dr = 41$

131. $\oint_{C_1} \mathbf{G} \cdot d\mathbf{r} = -8\pi$

133. $\oint_{C_2} \mathbf{F} \cdot d\mathbf{r} = 7$

135. $\int_C \mathbf{F} \cdot d\mathbf{r} = 150$

137. $\int_C \mathbf{F} \cdot d\mathbf{r} = -1$

139. 4×10^{31} erg

141. $\int_C \mathbf{F} \cdot d\mathbf{s} = 0.4687$

143. circulation $= \pi a^2$ and flux $= 0$

147. $\int_C 2xydx + (x + y)dy = \frac{32}{3}$

149. $\int_C \sin x \cos ydx + (xy + \cos x \sin y)dy = \frac{1}{12}$

151. $\oint_C (-ydx + xdy) = \pi$

153. $\int_C xe^{-2x}\,dx + \left(x^4 + 2x^2y^2\right)dy = 0$

155. $\oint_C y^3\,dx - x^3\,dy = -24\pi$

157. $\oint_C -x^2ydx + xy^2\,dy = 8\pi$

159. $\oint_C \left(x^2 + y^2\right)dx + 2xydy = 0$

161. $A = 19\pi$

163. $A = \frac{3}{8\pi}$

165. $\int_{C+} \left(y^2 + x^3\right)dx + x^4\,dy = 0$

167. $A = \frac{9\pi}{8}$

169. $A = \frac{8\sqrt{3}}{5}$

171. $\int_C \left(x^2y - 2xy + y^2\right)ds = 3$

173. $\int_C \frac{xdx + ydy}{x^2 + y^2} = 2\pi$

175. $W = \frac{225}{2}$

177. $W = 12\pi$

179. $W = 2\pi$

181. $\oint_C y^2 dx + x^2 dy = \frac{1}{3}$

183. $\int_C \sqrt{1 + x^3} dx + 2xydy = 3$

185. $\int_C \left(3y - e^{\sin x}\right) dx + \left(7x + \sqrt{y^4 + 1}\right) dy = 36\pi$

187. $\oint_C \mathbf{F} \cdot d\mathbf{r} = 2$

189. $\oint_C (y + x)dx + (x + \sin y)dy = 0$

191. $\oint_C xydx + x^3 y^3 dy = \frac{22}{21}$

193. $\oint_C \mathbf{F} \cdot d\mathbf{r} = \frac{15\pi}{4}$

195. $\int_C \sin(x + y)dx + \cos(x + y)dy = 4$

197. $\int_C \mathbf{F} \cdot d\mathbf{r} = \pi$

199. $\oint_C \mathbf{F} \cdot \hat{\mathbf{n}} ds = 4$

201. $\oint_C \mathbf{F} \cdot \mathbf{n} ds = 32\pi$

203. $\int_C \left[-y^3 + \sin(xy) + xy\cos(xy)\right] dx + \left[x^3 + x^2 \cos(xy)\right] dy = 4.7124$

205. $\oint_C \left(y + e^{\sqrt{x}}\right) dx + \left(2x + \cos\left(y^2\right)\right) dy = \frac{1}{3}$

207. False

209. True

211. True

213. $\text{curl}\,\mathbf{F} = \mathbf{i} + x^2 \mathbf{j} + y^2 \mathbf{k}$

215. $\text{curl}\,\mathbf{F} = \left(xz^2 - xy^2\right)\mathbf{i} + \left(x^2 y - yz^2\right)\mathbf{j} + \left(y^2 z - x^2 z\right)\mathbf{k}$

217. $\text{curl}\,\mathbf{F} = \mathbf{i} + \mathbf{j} + \mathbf{k}$

219. $\text{curl}\,\mathbf{F} = -y\mathbf{i} - z\mathbf{j} - x\mathbf{k}$

221. $\text{curl}\,\mathbf{F} = 0$

223. $\text{div}\,\mathbf{F} = 3yz^2 + 2y\sin z + 2xe^{2z}$

225. $\text{div}\,\mathbf{F} = 2(x + y + z)$

227. $\text{div}\,\mathbf{F} = \frac{1}{\sqrt{x^2 + y^2}}$

229. $\text{div}\,\mathbf{F} = a + b$

231. $\text{div}\,\mathbf{F} = x + y + z$

233. Harmonic

235. $\text{div}\,(\mathbf{F} \times \mathbf{G}) = 2z + 3x$

237. $\text{div}\,\mathbf{F} = 2r^2$

239. $\text{curl}\,\mathbf{r} = 0$

241. $\text{curl}\,\frac{\mathbf{r}}{r^3} = 0$

243. $\text{curl}\,\mathbf{F} = \frac{2x}{x^2 + y^2}\mathbf{k}$

245. $\text{div}\,\mathbf{F} = 0$

247. $\text{div}\,\mathbf{F} = 2 - 2e^{-6}$

249. $\text{div}\,\mathbf{F} = 0$

251. $\text{curl}\,\mathbf{F} = \mathbf{j} - 3\mathbf{k}$

253. $\text{curl}\,\mathbf{F} = 2\mathbf{j} - \mathbf{k}$

255. $a = 3$

257. **F** is conservative.

259. $\text{div}\,\mathbf{F} = \cosh x + \sinh y - xy$

261. $(bz - cy)\mathbf{i}(cx - az)\mathbf{j} + (ay - bx)\mathbf{k}$

263. $\text{curl}\,\mathbf{F} = 2\omega$

265. $\mathbf{F} \times \mathbf{G}$ does not have zero divergence.

267. $\nabla \cdot \mathbf{F} = -200k\left[1 + 2\left(x^2 + y^2 + z^2\right)\right]e^{-x^2 + y^2 + z^2}$

269. True

271. True

273. $\mathbf{r}(u, v) = \langle u, v, 2 - 3u + 2v \rangle$ for $-\infty \le u < \infty$ and $-\infty \le v < \infty$.

275. $\mathbf{r}(u, v) = \langle u, v, \frac{1}{3}(16 - 2u + 4v) \rangle$ for $|u| < \infty$ and $|v| < \infty$.

277. $\mathbf{r}(u, v) = \langle 3\cos u, 3\sin u, v \rangle$ for $0 \le u \le \frac{\pi}{2}, 0 \le v \le 3$

279. $A = 87.9646$

281. $\iint_S z\,dS = 8\pi$

283. $\iint_S \left(x^2 + y^2\right)z\,dS = 16\pi$

285. $\iint_S \mathbf{F} \cdot \mathbf{N}\,dS = \frac{4\pi}{3}$

287. $m \approx 13.0639$

289. $m \approx 228.5313$

291. $\iint_S g\,dS = 3\sqrt{4}$

293. $\iint_S \left(x^2 + y - z\right)d\mathbf{S} \approx 0.9617$

295. $\iint_S \left(x^2 + y^2\right)d\mathbf{S} = \frac{4\pi}{3}$

297. $\iint_S x^2 z\,d\text{S} = \frac{1023\sqrt{2\pi}}{5}$

299. $\iint_S (z + y)\,d\text{S} \approx 10.1$

301. $m = \pi a^3$

303. $\iint_S \mathbf{F} \cdot \mathbf{N}\,dS = \frac{13}{24}$

305. $\iint_S \mathbf{F} \cdot \mathbf{N}\,dS = \frac{3}{4}$

307. $\int_0^8 \int_0^6 \left(4 - 3y + \frac{1}{16}y^2 + z\right)\left(\frac{1}{4}\sqrt{17}\right)dz\,dy$

309. $\int_0^2 \int_0^6 \left[x^2 - 2(8 - 4x) + z\right]\sqrt{17}\,dz\,dx$

311. $\iint_S (x^2 z + y^2 z) dS = \frac{\pi a^5}{2}$

313. $\iint_S x^2 yz dS = 171\sqrt{14}$

315. $\iint_S yz dS = \frac{\sqrt{2}\pi}{4}$

317. $\iint_S (x\mathbf{i} + y\mathbf{j}) \cdot d\mathbf{S} = 16\pi$

319. $m = \frac{\pi a^7}{192}$

321. $F \approx 4.57$ lb.

323. $8\pi a$

325. The net flux is zero.

327. $\iint_S (\text{curl } \mathbf{F} \cdot \mathbf{N}) dS = \pi a^2$

329. $\iint_S (\text{curl } \mathbf{F} \cdot \mathbf{N}) dS = 18\pi$

331. $\iint_S (\text{curl } \mathbf{F} \cdot \mathbf{N}) dS = -8\pi$

333. $\iint_S (\text{curl } \mathbf{F} \cdot \mathbf{N}) dS = 0$

335. $\int_C \mathbf{F} \cdot d\mathbf{S} = 0$

337. $\int_C \mathbf{F} \cdot d\mathbf{S} = -9.4248$

339. $\iint_S \text{curl } \mathbf{F} \cdot d\mathbf{S} = 0$

341. $\iint_S \text{curl } \mathbf{F} \cdot d\mathbf{S} = 2.6667$

343. $\iint_S (\text{curl } \mathbf{F} \cdot \mathbf{N}) dS = -\frac{1}{6}$

345. $\int_C \left(\frac{1}{2} y^2 dx + z dy + x dz\right) = -\frac{\pi}{4}$

347. $\iint_S (\text{curl } \mathbf{F} \cdot \mathbf{N}) dS = -3\pi$

349. $\int_C (c\mathbf{k} \times \mathbf{R}) \cdot d\mathbf{S} = 2\pi c$

351. $\iint_S \text{curl } \mathbf{F} \cdot d\mathbf{S} = 0$

353. $\oint \mathbf{F} \cdot d\mathbf{S} = -4$

355. $\iint_S \text{curl } \mathbf{F} \cdot d\mathbf{S} = 0$

357. $\iint_S \text{curl } \mathbf{F} \cdot d\mathbf{S} = -36\pi$

359. $\iint_S \text{curl } \mathbf{F} \cdot \mathbf{N} = 0$

361. $\oint_C \mathbf{F} \cdot d\mathbf{r} = 0$

363. $\iint_S \text{curl}(\mathbf{F}) \cdot d\mathbf{S} = 84.8230$

365. $A = \iint_S (\nabla \times \mathbf{F}) \cdot \mathbf{n} dS = 0$

367. $\iint_S (\nabla \times \mathbf{F}) \cdot \mathbf{n} dS = 2\pi$

369. $C = \pi(\cos\varphi - \sin\varphi)$

371. $\oint_C \mathbf{F} \cdot d\mathbf{r} = 48\pi$

373. $\iint_S (\nabla \times \mathbf{F}) \cdot \mathbf{n} = 0$

375. 0

377. $\int_S \mathbf{F} \cdot \mathbf{n} ds = 75.3982$

379. $\int_S \mathbf{F} \cdot \mathbf{n} ds = 127.2345$

381. $\int_S \mathbf{F} \cdot \mathbf{n} ds = 37.6991$

383. $\int_S \mathbf{F} \cdot \mathbf{n} ds = \frac{9\pi a^4}{2}$

385. $\iint_S \mathbf{F} \cdot d\mathbf{S} = \frac{\pi}{3}$

387. $\iint_S \mathbf{F} \cdot d\mathbf{S} = 0$

389. $\iint_S \mathbf{F} \cdot d\mathbf{S} = 241.2743$

391. $\iint_D \mathbf{F} \cdot d\mathbf{S} = -\pi$

393. $\iint_S \mathbf{F} \cdot d\mathbf{S} = \frac{2\pi}{3}$

395. $16\sqrt{6}\pi$

397. $-\frac{128}{3}\pi$

399. -703.7168

401. 20

403. $\iint_S \mathbf{F} \cdot d\mathbf{S} = 8$

405. $\iint_S \mathbf{F} \cdot \mathbf{N} dS = \frac{1}{8}$

407. $\iint_S \| \mathbf{R} \| \mathbf{R} \cdot n ds = 4\pi a^4$

409. $\iiint_R z^2 dV = \frac{4\pi}{15}$

411. $\iint_S \mathbf{F} \cdot d\mathbf{S} = 6.5759$

413. $\iint_S \mathbf{F} \cdot d\mathbf{S} = 21$

415. $\iint_S \mathbf{F} \cdot d\mathbf{S} = 72$

417. $\iint_S \mathbf{F} \cdot d\mathbf{S} = -33.5103$

419. $\iint_S \mathbf{F} \cdot d\mathbf{S} = \pi a^4 b^2$

421. $\iint_S \mathbf{F} \cdot d\mathbf{S} = \frac{5}{2}\pi$

423. $\iint_S \mathbf{F} \cdot d\mathbf{S} = \frac{21\pi}{2}$

425. $-\left(1 - e^{-1}\right)$

Review Exercises

427. False

429. False

431.

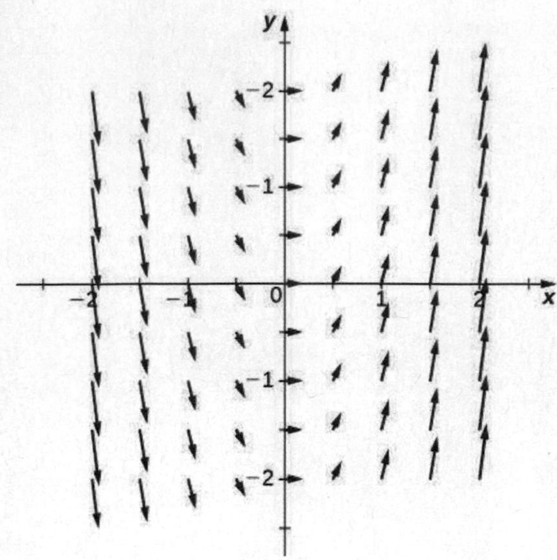

433. Conservative, $f(x, y) = xy - 2e^y$

435. Conservative, $f(x, y, z) = x^2 y + y^2 z + z^2 x$

437. $-\frac{16}{3}$

439. $\frac{32\sqrt{2}}{9}\left(3\sqrt{3} - 1\right)$

441. Divergence: $e^x + xe^{xy} + xye^{xyz}$, curl: $xze^{xyz}\mathbf{i} - yze^{xyz}\mathbf{j} + ye^{xy}\mathbf{k}$

443. -2π

445. $-\pi$

447. $31\pi/2$

449. $\sqrt{2}(2 + \pi)$

451. $2\pi/3$

Chapter 7

Checkpoint

7.1.

a. Nonlinear
b. Linear, nonhomogeneous

7.4. Linearly independent

7.5. $y(x) = c_1 e^{3x} + c_2 xe^{3x}$

7.6.

a. $y(x) = e^x(c_1 \cos 3x + c_2 \sin 3x)$
b. $y(x) = c_1 e^{-7x} + c_2 xe^{-7x}$

7.7. $y(x) = -e^{-2x} + e^{5x}$

7.8. $y(x) = e^x(2\cos 3x - \sin 3x)$

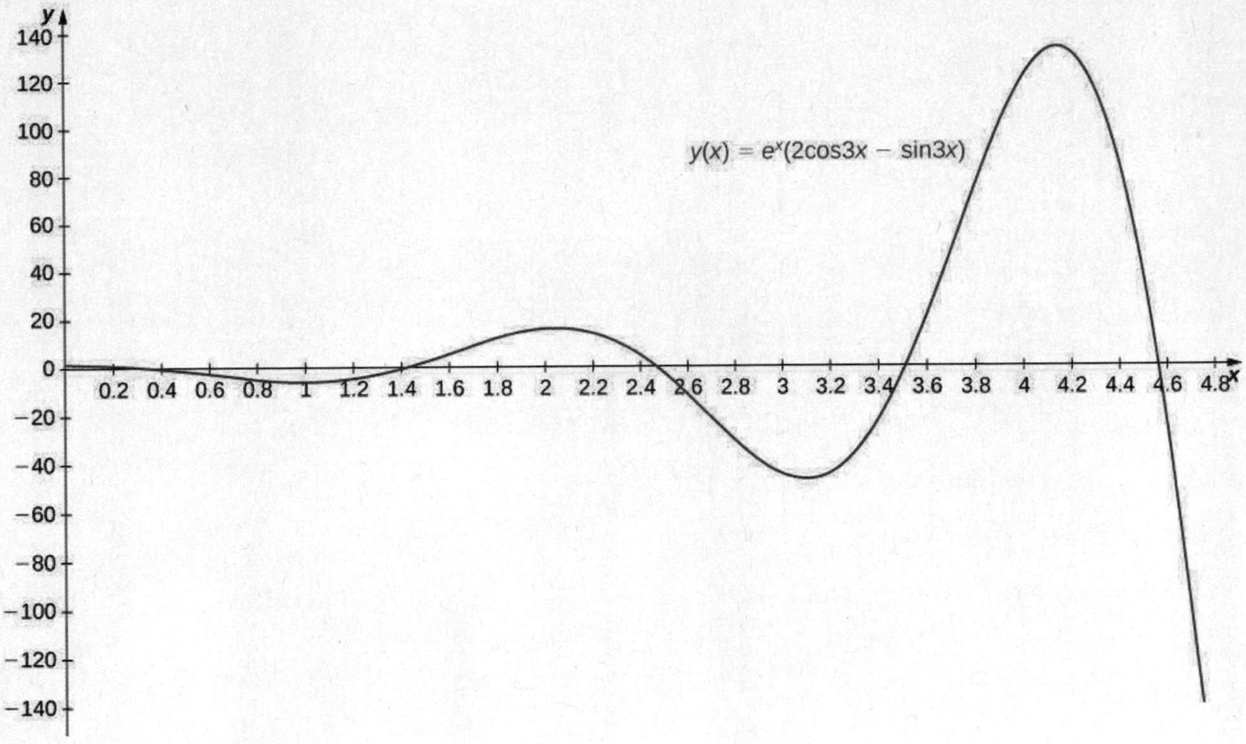

7.9. $y(t) = te^{-7t}$

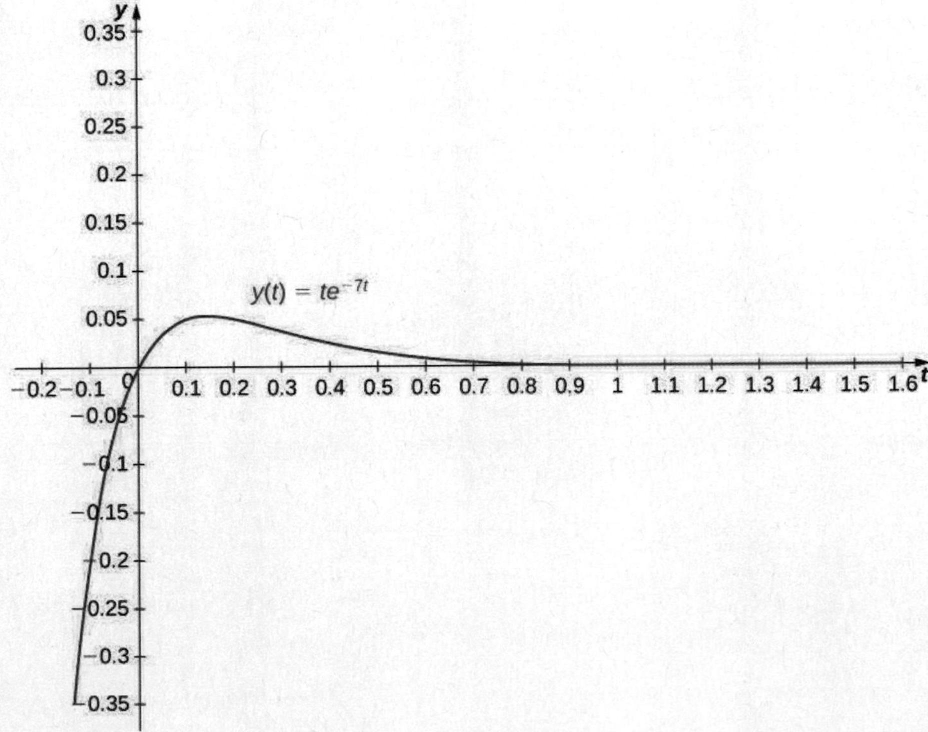

At time $t = 0.3$, $y(0.3) = 0.3e^{(-7*0.3)} = 0.3e^{-2.1} \approx 0.0367$. The mass is 0.0367 ft below equilibrium. At time $t = 0.1$, $y'(0.1) = 0.3e^{-0.7} \approx 0.1490$. The mass is moving downward at a speed of 0.1490 ft/sec.

7.10. $y(x) = c_1 e^{-x} + c_2 e^{4x} - 2$

7.11. $y(t) = c_1 e^{2t} + c_2 te^{2t} + \sin t + \cos t$

7.12.

a. $y(x) = c_1 e^{4x} + c_2 e^x - xe^x$

b. $y(t) = c_1 e^{-3t} + c_2 e^{2t} - 5\cos 2t + \sin 2t$

7.13. $z_1 = \frac{3x+3}{11x^2}, \quad z_2 = \frac{2x+2}{11x}$

7.14.

a. $y(x) = c_1 \cos x + c_2 \sin x + \cos x \ln|\cos x| + x \sin x$

b. $x(t) = c_1 e^t + c_2 te^t + te^t \ln|t|$

7.15. $x(t) = 0.1\cos(14t)$ (in meters); frequency is $\frac{14}{2\pi}$ Hz.

7.16. $x(t) = \sqrt{17}\sin(4t + 0.245), \quad \text{frequency} = \frac{4}{2\pi} \approx 0.637, \quad A = \sqrt{17}$

7.17. $x(t) = 0.6e^{-2t} - 0.2e^{-6t}$

7.18. $x(t) = \frac{1}{2}e^{-8t} + 4te^{-8t}$

7.19. $x(t) = -0.24e^{-2t}\cos(4t) - 0.12e^{-2t}\sin(4t)$

7.20. $x(t) = -\frac{1}{2}\cos(4t) + \frac{9}{4}\sin(4t) + \frac{1}{2}e^{-2t}\cos(4t) - 2e^{-2t}\sin(4t)$

Transient solution: $\frac{1}{2}e^{-2t}\cos(4t) - 2e^{-2t}\sin(4t)$

Steady-state solution: $-\frac{1}{2}\cos(4t) + \frac{9}{4}\sin(4t)$

7.21. $q(t) = -25e^{-t}\cos(3t) - 7e^{-t}\sin(3t) + 25$

7.22.

a. $y(x) = a_0 \sum_{n=0}^{\infty} \frac{(-1)^n}{n!} x^{2n} = a_0 e^{-x^2}$

b. $y(x) = a_0(x+1)^3$

Section Exercises

1. linear, homogenous

3. nonlinear

5. linear, homogeneous

11. $y = c_1 e^{5x} + c_2 e^{-2x}$

13. $y = c_1 e^{-2x} + c_2 xe^{-2x}$

15. $y = c_1 e^{5x/2} + c_2 e^{-x}$

17. $y = e^{-x/2}\left(c_1 \cos\frac{\sqrt{3}x}{2} + c_2 \sin\frac{\sqrt{3}x}{2}\right)$

19. $y = c_1 e^{-11x} + c_2 e^{11x}$

21. $y = c_1 \cos 9x + c_2 \sin 9x$

23. $y = c_1 + c_2 x$

25. $y = c_1 e^{((1+\sqrt{22})/3)x} + c_2 e^{((1-\sqrt{22})/3)x}$

27. $y = c_1 e^{-x/6} + c_2 xe^{-x/6}$

29. $y = c_1 + c_2 e^{9x}$

31. $y = -2e^{-2x} + 2e^{-3x}$

33. $y = 3\cos(2x) + 5\sin(2x)$

35. $y=-e^{6x}+2e^{-5x}$

37. $y=2e^{-x/5}+\frac{7}{5}xe^{-x/5}$

39. $y=\left(\frac{2}{e^{6}-e^{-7}}\right)e^{6x}-\left(\frac{2}{e^{6}-e^{-7}}\right)e^{-7x}$

41. No solutions exist.

43. $y=2e^{2x}-\frac{2e^{2}+1}{e^{2}}xe^{2x}$

45. $y=4\cos 3x+c_2\sin 3x,$ infinitely many solutions

47. $5y''+19y'-4y=0$

49. a. $y=3\cos(8x)+2\sin(8x)$

b.

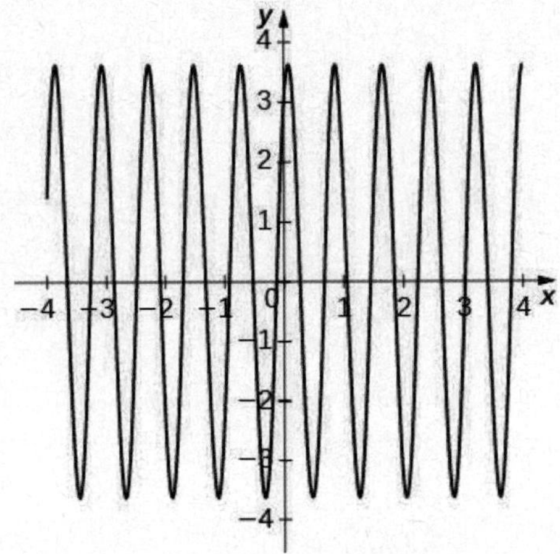

51. a. $y=e^{(-5/2)x}\left[-2\cos\left(\frac{\sqrt{35}}{2}x\right)+\frac{4\sqrt{35}}{35}\sin\left(\frac{\sqrt{35}}{2}x\right)\right]$

b.

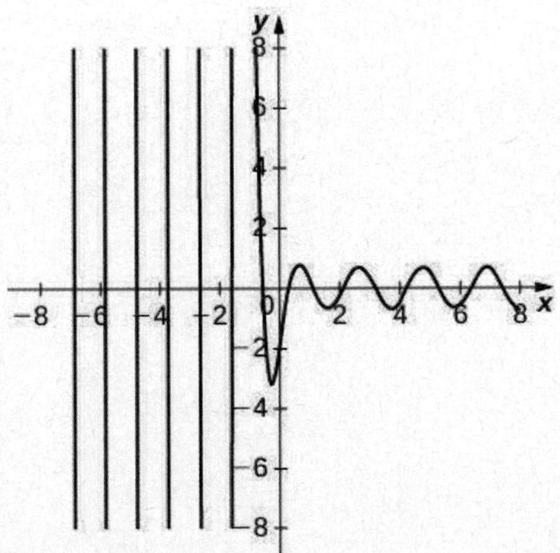

55. $y=c_1e^{-4x/3}+c_2e^{x}-2$

57. $y=c_1\cos 4x+c_2\sin 4x+\frac{1}{20}e^{-2x}$

59. $y=c_1e^{2x}+c_2xe^{2x}+2x^2+5x$

61. $y=c_1e^{-x}+c_2xe^{-x}+\frac{1}{2}\sin x-\frac{1}{2}\cos x$

63. $y = c_1 \cos x + c_2 \sin x - \frac{1}{3} x \cos 2x - \frac{5}{9} \sin 2x$

65. $y = c_1 e^{-5x} + c_2 x e^{-5x} + \frac{1}{6} x^3 e^{-5x} + \frac{4}{25}$

67. a. $y_p(x) = Ax^2 + Bx + C$

b. $y_p(x) = -\frac{1}{3}x^2 + \frac{4}{3}x - \frac{35}{9}$

69. a. $y_p(x) = \left(Ax^2 + Bx + C\right)e^{-x}$

b. $y_p(x) = \left(\frac{1}{4}x^2 - \frac{5}{8}x - \frac{33}{32}\right)e^{-x}$

71. a. $y_p(x) = \left(Ax^2 + Bx + C\right)e^x \cos x \ + \left(Dx^2 + Ex + F\right)e^x \sin x$

b. $y_p(x) = \left(-\frac{1}{10}x^2 - \frac{11}{25}x - \frac{27}{250}\right)e^x \cos x \ + \left(-\frac{3}{10}x^2 + \frac{2}{25}x + \frac{39}{250}\right)e^x \sin x$

73. $y = c_1 + c_2 e^{-2x} + \frac{1}{15} e^{3x}$

75. $y = c_1 e^{2x} + c_2 e^{-4x} + x e^{2x}$

77. $y = c_1 e^{3x} + c_2 e^{-3x} - \frac{8x}{9}$

79. $y = c_1 \cos 2x + c_2 \sin 2x - \frac{3}{2} x \cos 2x + \frac{3}{4} \sin 2x \ln(\sin 2x)$

81. $y = -\frac{347}{343} + \frac{4}{343} e^{7x} + \frac{2}{7} x^2 e^{7x} - \frac{4}{49} x e^{7x}$

83. $y = -\frac{57}{25} + \frac{3}{25} e^{5x} + \frac{1}{5} x e^{5x} + \frac{4}{25} e^{-5x}$

85. $y_p = \frac{1}{2} + \frac{10}{3} x^2 \ln x$

87. $x'' + 16x = 0, \quad x(t) = \frac{1}{6}\cos(4t) - 2\sin(4t),$ period $= \frac{\pi}{2}$ sec, frequency $= \frac{2}{\pi}$ Hz

89. $x'' + 196x = 0, \quad x(t) = 0.15\cos(14t),$ period $= \frac{\pi}{7}$ sec, frequency $= \frac{7}{\pi}$ Hz

91. a. $x(t) = 5\sin(2t)$

b. period $= \pi$ sec, frequency $= \frac{1}{\pi}$ Hz

c.

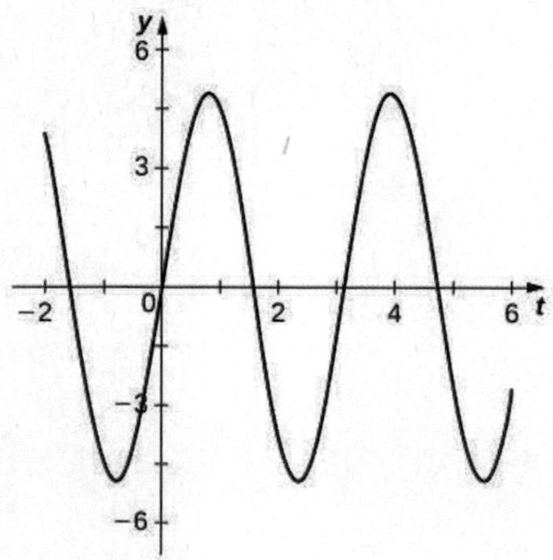

d. $t = \frac{\pi}{2}$ sec

93. a. $x(t) = e^{-t/5}(20\cos(3t) + 15\sin(3t))$

b. underdamped

95. a. $x(t) = 5e^{-4t} + 10te^{-4t}$

b. critically damped

97. $x(\pi) = \frac{7e^{-\pi/4}}{6}$ ft below

99. $x(t) = \frac{32}{9}\sin(4t) + \cos(\sqrt{128}t) - \frac{16}{9\sqrt{2}}\sin(\sqrt{128}t)$

101. $q(t) = e^{-6t}(0.051\cos(8t) + 0.03825\sin(8t)) - \frac{1}{20}\cos(10t)$

103. $q(t) = e^{-10t}(-32t - 5) + 5, \quad I(t) = 2e^{-10t}(160t + 9)$

105. $y = c_0 + 5c_1 \sum_{n=1}^{\infty} \frac{(-x/5)^n}{n!} = c_0 + 5c_1 e^{-x/5}$

107. $y = c_0 \sum_{n=0}^{\infty} \frac{(x)^{2n}}{(2n)!} + c_1 \sum_{n=0}^{\infty} \frac{(x)^{2n+1}}{(2n+1)!}$

109. $y = c_0 \sum_{n=0}^{\infty} \frac{x^{2n}}{n!} = c_0 e^{x^2}$

111. $y = c_0 \sum_{n=0}^{\infty} \frac{x^{2n}}{2^n n!} + c_1 \sum_{n=0}^{\infty} \frac{x^{2n+1}}{1 \cdot 3 \cdot 5 \cdot 7 \cdots (2n+1)}$

113. $y = c_1 x^3 + \frac{c_2}{x}$

115. $y = 1 - 3x + \frac{2x^3}{3!} - \frac{12x^4}{4!} + \frac{16x^6}{6!} - \frac{120x^7}{7!} + \cdots$

Review Exercises

117. True

119. False

121. second order, linear, homogeneous, $\lambda^2 - 2 = 0$

123. first order, nonlinear, nonhomogeneous

125. $y = c_1\sin(3x) + c_2\cos(3x)$

127. $y = c_1 e^x\sin(3x) + c_2 e^x\cos(3x) + \frac{2}{5}x + \frac{2}{25}$

129. $y = c_1 e^{-x} + c_2 e^{-4x} + \frac{x}{4} + \frac{e^{2x}}{18} - \frac{5}{16}$

131. $y = c_1 e^{(-3/2)x} + c_2 xe^{(-3/2)x} + \frac{4}{9}x^2 + \frac{4}{27}x - \frac{16}{27}$

133. $y = e^{-2x}\sin(\sqrt{2}x)$

135. $y = \frac{e^{1-x}}{e^4 - 1}(e^{4x} - 1)$

137. $\theta(t) = \theta_0\cos\left(\sqrt{\frac{g}{l}}t\right)$

141. $b = \sqrt{a}$

INDEX

Symbols

A

B

C

D

E

F

G

H